THE SUPREME COURT IN CONFERENCE (1940–1985)

A critical page from Justice Harold Burton's conference notes on the landmark school desegregation case, *Brown v. Board of Education* (1954). Reproduced from the collection of the Manuscript Division of the Library of Congress, Washington. D.C.

THE
SUPREME
COURT
IN
CONFERENCE

(*1940–1985*)

The Private Discussions Behind
Nearly 300 Supreme Court Decisions

EDITED BY
DEL DICKSON

OXFORD
UNIVERSITY PRESS

2001

OXFORD

UNIVERSITY PRESS

Oxford   New York
Athens   Auckland   Bangkok   Bogotá   Buenos Aires   Cape Town
Chennai   Dar es Salaam   Delhi   Florence   Hong Kong   Istanbul   Karachi
Kolkata   Kuala Lumpur   Madrid   Melbourne   Mexico City   Mumbai   Nairobi
Paris   São Paulo   Shanghai   Singapore   Taipei   Tokyo   Toronto   Warsaw
and associated companies in
Berlin   Ibadan

Copyright © 2001 by Oxford University Press

Published by Oxford University Press, Inc.
198 Madison Avenue, New York, New York 10016

www.oup.com

Oxford is a registered trademark of Oxford University Press

Library of Congress Cataloging-in-Publication Data
The Supreme Court in conference, 1940-1985: The private discussions behind
nearly 300 Supreme Court decisions / edited by Del Dickson.
p. cm.
Includes bibliographical references and index.
ISBN 0-19-512632-7
1. United States. Supreme Court—Records and correspondence.   2. United States.
Supreme Court—History—Sources.   3. Constitutional history—United States—Sources.   4.
Judicial process—United States—History—Sources.   I. Dickson, Del.
KF8742 .S917 2000
347.73'26'0264—dc21   00-057492

1   3   5   7   9   8   6   4   2
Printed in the United States of America
on acid-free paper

For my parents, Bill and Margaret Dickson

CONTENTS

PART III
Civil Rights and Liberties

EDITOR'S NOTE

LAWYERS HAVE A VENERABLE AND OCCASIONALLY ANNOYING HABIT OF arguing over the meaning of every stray comma and preposition in legal documents. While the conference discussions reproduced here are faithful to the Justices' original conference notes, these notes have been treated as shorthand notations rather than as sacred text. Instead of simply publishing the Justices' notes verbatim, they were carefully edited in the spirit of what they are—abbreviated versions of what was actually said in conference.

The editing process was not unlike using a stenographer's notes to reconstruct courtroom proceedings. William O. Douglas, William Brennan, Harold Burton, Tom Clark, and the other Justices whose conference notes are represented here often left out punctuation and "nonessential" vocabulary in reporting what transpired at conference. Whenever possible, these elements have been restored to give the notes a more natural, conversational tone. Sentence fragments have been completed and abbreviations made whole, so that the notes read more as they were originally spoken in conference. No new sentences or thoughts were added. The notes transcribed here contain only what the Justices themselves reported. If it was not reasonably clear what a Justice meant by a particular comment or sentence fragment, then the passage was either omitted or left verbatim.

A more controversial editing decision was to combine different Justices' conference notes when multiple sets were available for a given case. By combining several versions of the same discussion, the reader will have a more complete picture of what transpired in conference. If the multiple sources complemented each other, then the most complete set of notes was used as the foundation and the additional notes were incorporated to provide a more complete account of the conference. Occasionally, however, the Justices' notes varied significantly or even contradicted each other. Major discrepancies, as well as some more subtle differences, are highlighted in footnotes. The sources for all conference notes are clearly marked for each case. Where multiple sources were used, the Justices' names are listed in rank order, like the ingredient list on a cereal box.

Some of William Brennan's reported conference comments were adapted from his talking papers. These were memoranda that Brennan and his clerks began to write in 1980 to serve as detailed outlines for Brennan's conference remarks. The decision to use Brennan's talking papers was an easy one, as the only alternative was to lose his conference contributions entirely. Like most Justices, Brennan never included his own remarks in his conference notes, and his talking papers provide the best available evidence of what he said in conference. These materials, when used, are clearly identified.

Each editing decision carries a risk of error. Many of the notes were difficult to transcribe with complete confidence, and some were nearly illegible. The difficulty of transcribing these notes accurately has caused considerable problems in the past (for one such incident, see the frontispiece and the conference notes for *Brown v. Board of Education*).

In transcribing these notes it is to be hoped that the editor's eye has been vigilant, and his hand reasonably light and conservative. My intent was to respect both the letter and the spirit of the original sources while making the notes more useful and complete. For any mistakes, I accept full responsibility.

I would like to thank the following people who made this book possible. First, my thanks to the wonderful people at the Library of Congress's Manuscript Reading Room, particularly Jeff Flannery, Fred Bauman, Mary Wolfskill, and Mike Klein. Mike Widener at the Tarlton Law Library, School of Law, University of Texas at Austin, gave invaluable help and advice in using Tom Clark's papers. Franz Jantzen, curator of the Photograph Collection, Office of the Curator, United States Supreme Court, was extraordinarily helpful in providing photographs and information about the conference room and the history of the Court.

I am especially grateful to Cathleen Douglas Stone for her kind and enthusiastic permission to make extensive use of William O. Douglas's papers and conference notes; to William Brennan and his estate for their permission to use his papers and conference notes; to William E. Jackson and Mrs. G. Bowdoin Craighill for their generous permission to use Robert Jackson's papers and conference notes; and to Hugo Black Jr. for his help and most courteous permission to use his father's conference notes for *Ex parte Quirin*. Harold Burton, Felix Frankfurter, and Earl Warren deserve special credit for placing all or part of their collections in the public domain at the Library of Congress.

A special thanks to Christopher Collins, Nancy Hoagland, Matthew Giarratano, and Will Moore at Oxford University Press for all their help, and to Cynthia Crippen, of AEIOU, Inc., for the index.

My two main sounding boards and all-around sources of information, ideas, insight, and support were Michael Klarman of the University of Virginia and John Schmidhauser, professor emeritus of the University of Southern California. They provided an unmatched knowledge of constitutional law and history and caught too many potentially embarrassing errors. Francene Engel of the University of Southern California did a terrific job checking my transcriptions and provided thoughtful comments on my rough drafts.

Thanks to Robert Burt of Yale University and Neil Cogan of the Quinnipiac School of Law for their helpful comments regarding my original proposal to the Oxford University Press. Thanks to Noelle Norton and Joe Colombo of the University of San Diego, who provided comments and encouragement on my rough draft; to Beth Bowles of the John Glenn Institute at Ohio State, for her help; and to Doug Raidt, who helped to create the graphs.

I am deeply indebted to Dean Patrick Drinan and the University of San Diego for their generous support. Without their assistance, this project never could have been contemplated, let alone completed.

My warmest thoughts and thanks go to my wife, Ann Woods Dickson. Aside from the countless hours she spent patiently proofreading and editing, she was a constant source of ideas, encouragement, support, inspiration, understanding, and tolerance. Finally, thanks to Argus and Sid, who stood guard at my office door and barked when necessary.

INTRODUCTION

Pay no attention to that man behind the curtain. —The Wizard of Oz

THOSE WHO BELIEVE THAT SUPREME COURT DECISIONS ARE DETERMINED PRImarily by lawyers' arguments and precedent tend to emphasize the importance of oral argument and published opinions in explaining how the Supreme Court works. These scholars focus on the *public* Court. They accept Lewis Powell's argument that the Supreme Court is the most transparent of government institutions because its decisions are all publicly announced and explained. This means that in order to understand the Supreme Court, all one needs to do is to study the public record.

In contrast, those who believe that law is primarily a political process tend to look to the *private* Court for clues as to how and why Justices decide cases as they do. They suspect that the drama of oral argument is more spectacle than substance and that written opinions often obscure more than they illuminate. In order to understand how the Supreme Court really works, we must peek behind the red-velvet curtain that hangs behind the Justices in the courtroom and separates the Court's public realm from the private hallways and chambers where cases are really decided. To paraphrase former Attorney General John Mitchell, one needs to watch what the Justices do, not what they say. This involves exploring the secret life of the Court—examining the Justices' backgrounds and personal lives, including conference discussions, private memoranda, and eyewitness accounts of what goes on inside the marble temple.

Felix Frankfurter called the conference the workshop of the living Constitution. One of the most intriguing aspects of the conference discussions published here is that they provide new information about *both* public and private aspects of Supreme Court decision making. They help to fill out the public record and shed new light on the Justices' intentions in deciding some three hundred landmark cases. But they also allow us to look directly inside the sanctum sanctorum of Supreme Court decision making, providing new insights on the Justices' personal thoughts, the internal dynamics of the Court, and the private life of the law.

Unfortunately, there is little reliable, firsthand evidence about the internal workings of the Supreme Court. The Court has always been a secretive place, and the Justices have done little to encourage public scrutiny. The institution that is the last line of constitutional defense for free speech and a free press is itself obsessed with secrecy, and controls its press corps like a Third World dictatorship. Reporters and academics who try to peek behind the velvet curtain are either repelled or carefully controlled. For the most part, those who study the private Court must rely on an unsatisfactory mixture of rumors, leaks, gossip, and inferences to find out what goes on behind the scenes at the Supreme Court.

There are three main sources of inside information about the Court. The first consists of the Justices' public records: published opinions, books, articles, memoirs, interviews, oral histories, and speeches. These can on occasion be insightful, but more often they are self-serving and of modest candor. In dealing with the public Court, it is often impossible to tell where the truth ends and mythology begins.

Although case opinions purport to explain and justify all Supreme Court decisions, the Justices do not make public every significant decision of the Court, nor do they necessarily explain their decisions fully or candidly. It is not simply that the Justices purposefully dissemble in their written opinions, although they may do so on occasion. The real problem is that written opinions do not reveal what the Justices really thought about a case; at best, they provide *clues* as to their thoughts and preferences. Case opinions are not written reason, nor do they provide a complete explanation of how the Justices reached their decisions. Too often they offer rationalizations rather than reasons, shadow rather than substance.

One reason why Supreme Court opinions often mystify rather than educate is that many Justices do not write well. Stanley Reed, a notoriously slow and laborious writer, once said wistfully, "Wouldn't it be nice if we could write the way we think?"[1] Another problem is that Supreme Court opinions in some respects are as stylized as Kabuki theater. Justices are expected to recite the facts and the relevant law and to provide conventional legal reasons for their decisions. This is often done in a stiff, formal, and ritualistic way.

There are a variety of factors that influence case outcomes that are rarely, if ever, reflected in published opinions. Contrary to the Justices' claims, it does *not* all come out in the writing. In order to gain a full understanding of the Supreme Court, we need to look beyond the Justices' public explanations and justifications.

The second source of inside information about the Court is the staff, notably the Justices' clerks. Justices strongly discourage their clerks from talking to outsiders, and this policy is enforced through confidentiality agreements and a strong institutional culture of secrecy. Inside information from these sources tends to be less guarded and more interesting than the Justices' own public commentary. Clerks, however, may be limited in their ability to provide reliable information about what goes on inside the conference

---

1. O'Brien, *Storm Center,* 128.

room. Most clerks are young, inexperienced, and somewhat naive about the Court and its role in our political system. Moreover, they do not attend conferences and are not privy to many of the most confidential aspects of Court business. In short, in spite of their inestimable value as sources of inside information, clerks may not know as much about the inner workings of the conference as some might think.[2]

The final source of inside information about the Court comes from the Justices' private papers, including their conference notes. These records are compiled during the daily course of business and are not intended for public consumption. As a result, they are often less filtered and more blunt than other inside information about the Court. Because conference discussions are conducted in strict privacy, the Justices tend to be more candid in speaking to each other than they are in their public statements. More importantly, unless the rumors about government surveillance of the conference room are true, the Justices' conference notes are the *only* contemporary, firsthand record of what goes on inside the conference room.

Conference notes have their own problems and limitations. First, they do not provide a full or objective account of how or why the Justices decided cases as they did. What the Justices *say* about a case in conference does not necessarily prove what actually motivated them to act. Their conference remarks are influenced by a variety of extraneous considerations, both conscious and subconscious. Just because the Justices may be more inclined to speak their minds in private than in their published opinions or public pronouncements, it does not necessarily follow that they tell each other everything. If conference discussions are not windows to the Justices' souls, they still provide invaluable clues about the Justices' behavior and are often more insightful than information culled from other sources.

The second problem with conference notes is that they necessarily reflect one Justice's subjective view of what transpired in conference. They are neither complete nor objective transcripts but are a partial record of what interested the note-taker at the time. Moreover, the quality and completeness of these notes vary wildly. On some occasions the Justices reported what transpired in conference in fascinating detail, but at other times their notes are frustratingly incomplete and impressionistic.

The third problem is that each Justice has absolute control over which of his or

---

2. Some clerks, like Gerald Gunther and E. Barrett Prettyman Jr., had extensive prior legal and political experience before becoming clerks and came to the job with a sophisticated idea of how the Court operated. Other clerks, like William Norris (who worked for William O. Douglas before becoming a distinguished federal judge for the Ninth Circuit Court of Appeals) candidly admit that they were too young and too busy to understand the subtleties of conference politics. Still others may think that they know more about the conference than they really do. In his memoirs of his year and a half stint as one of Justice Jackson's clerks, William Rehnquist described the typical clerk—including himself—as hypercritical, arrogant, scornful, and, above all, naive in their understanding of judicial behavior. As Byron White put it, clerks are "rarely in doubt, but often in error." Telephone interview with William A. Norris, July 1992; Rehnquist, *The Supreme Court*, 37; Worthen, "Shirt-Tales," 350.

her records are made public. In the end, we see only what each Justice wanted us to see. While most Justices take conference notes, they usually destroy or withhold at least part of them when they donate their papers to the Library of Congress or other repository. Only a handful of Justices have systematically preserved their conference notes, which means that in most cases our view of the conference is limited to just one or two perspectives.

Despite these problems, conference notes remain one of the most interesting and useful sources of inside information about Supreme Court decision making. No aspect of Supreme Court life is more closely guarded from public scrutiny than the conference, and these notes provide a unique opportunity to peek inside the conference room and see what the Justices said to each other at the decisive moment in hundreds of landmark cases.

Fortunately, the integrity of the surviving conference notes is quite good. There is no indication that any of the Justices relied on here ever attempted to go back and edit or revise their work. Their notes are all purely contemporaneous records, made during the daily course of Court business. They are raw history, and as such they have many advantages for scholars and students over the Justices' carefully polished memoirs, opinions, and other materials intended for public consumption.

Presented here are edited and annotated versions of conference notes preserved among the private papers of eight Justices who served on the Court between 1940 and 1985: Felix Frankfurter, William O. Douglas, Frank Murphy, Robert Jackson, Harold Burton, Tom Clark, Earl Warren, and William Brennan. The best notes, in terms of providing a relatively complete and comprehensive conference record, come from Douglas and Burton. Douglas clearly intended for his conference notes to be used by legal scholars. His notes are systematic and virtually complete, covering most of the important cases decided during his thirty-six years on the Court. Never much of a team player and always skeptical of government secrecy, Douglas was one of the few Justices to leave behind a detailed account of the Supreme Court in conference. His conference notes make a surprisingly restrained and objective record, with a minimum of personal commentary aimed at making himself look better or his opponents look worse than they were.

Harold Burton also preserved a large body of conference notes during the relatively short time that he was on the Court. Burton's motivations are less clear than Douglas's. He was a compulsive writer who kept a diary, took extensive notes on oral arguments, and relied heavily on his clerk's written case summaries. It seems likely that Burton was not making any particular philosophical statement by making his notes available to the public. He was simply a careful recordkeeper who saw no particular reason to destroy what he had worked so hard to preserve throughout his career.

Frank Murphy and William Brennan are also well represented here. Murphy was a perpetually distracted and often unhappy Justice. He took conference notes sporadically, and they are of inconsistent quality; at times they are cursory and even incomprehensible, but at other times his observations are quite interesting and entertaining.

Brennan took notes systematically during conferences and left behind a relatively complete set over his thirty-four years on the Court. But his notes are often brief and impressionistic, and lack the fullness and detail that Douglas and Burton provided. Though ideologically close to Douglas, Brennan was more respectful of the Court's tradition of secrecy, and it is somewhat surprising that he included his conference notes among his papers. He thought that the need to preserve the secrets of the conference room was compelling and self-evident, and he consistently defended the practice until his death. In the end, perhaps his desire to leave a complete historical record overcame his instincts to protect the secrets of the conference.

The other four Justices whose conference notes are cited here—Frankfurter, Clark, Jackson, and Warren—preserved only a small percentage of their notes. Their general preference for secrecy, however, did not prevent them from preserving their conference notes on several of the most important cases, notably *Brown v. Board of Education*. No fewer than six Justices preserved their conference notes on *Brown*, including several who left behind little or no other record of conference discussions. They all knew that *Brown* was going to be one of the most important cases in Supreme Court history, and they apparently wanted to leave behind a record of their participation in this case.

Those who enjoy salacious gossip about the Court may be somewhat disappointed by what they read here. The Justices rarely allude to personal antagonisms or conference infighting in their notes, which for the most part reflect the business of Supreme Court decision making. Occasionally, however, the notes reveal some of the more contentious personal conflicts that took place inside the conference room.

Those who believe that the Justices rely solely on law and precedent in deciding cases may be in for a shock. Those who believe the opposite—that Supreme Court decisions are simply the product of Justices' personal preferences—might be equally surprised. The conference discussions presented here reflect a more complex truth: Supreme Court decisions are an intricate and shifting composite of law, politics, policy, principle, efficiency, expedience, pragmatism, dogmatism, reason, passion, detachment, individual personality, group psychology, institutional forces, and external pressures.

In order to understand the role of the conference in Supreme Court decision making, we must first explore the historical forces that have shaped the conference and the Court. Over the next three chapters, we will see how the Court's evolving structures, procedures, and personalities have affected the life of the conference and the development of the law over the past two hundred years.

PART I

THE CONFERENCE

CHAPTER 1

INSIDE THE CONFERENCE ROOM

*"Acts are foredoomed to failure when undertaken undiscussed." To decide
cases with inadequate discussion is to disregard the conception of a Court. If
we just decide as individuals then we ought to have, as the English have,
opinions seriatim by the individual judges. And so, for me it has always been a
postulate of the work of this Court that we should have full and candid
collective discussion.*

—Felix Frankfurter[1]

SUPREME COURT CASES ARE ARGUED IN OPEN COURT, BUT THEY ARE
decided in the privacy of the conference room. Unlike the public spectacle of oral argument, the conference is conducted in quiet seclusion. Only the nine Justices may attend.
There are no clerks, secretaries, reporters, stenographers, lawyers, family, friends, or
observers present. Even when the conference room is not in use, it is kept off-limits to
the public and few ordinary Americans have been allowed so much as a glimpse inside.[2]

The conference room is located near the Chief Justice's chambers, directly behind
the courtroom. It is a large, rectangular room with a high ceiling that gives a sense of
spaciousness. The walls are lined with elegantly carved American oak. Fluted wood pi-
lasters frame the tall windows overlooking Second Street to the east. Built-in bookshelves
contain hundreds of volumes of case law and treatises. Along the walltops, a Doric frieze
runs in a repetitive pattern of triglyphs and metopes. The room still has its original red
volute carpeting from when the building first opened in 1935.

The middle of the room is sparsely, and oddly, furnished. A large conference table
used to dominate the room; but when Warren Burger became Chief Justice in 1969, one
of his first decisions was to move all of the original furniture off to one side so that he
could use the room as his private lunchroom and ceremonial chambers. The only furniture remaining in the center of the room is a small desk that Burger brought in for his

---

1. Felix Frankfurter, Memorandum to the Conference, October 22, 1942, Douglas Papers, OT 1942,
box 78. The opening sentence is from Pericles' *Funeral Oration.*

2. Details about the conference room come from a combination of personal observations from a brief
visit in 1994, as well as from photographs and information provided by Franz Jantzen, Office of the Curator of the Court.

personal use. It was one of nine desks originally built for the Justices' chambers in the 1930s, but now it looks lost and out of place beneath the room's grand crystal chandelier. Its sole official function is to hold a book for important guests to sign when they visit the Court.

Aside from a few stuffed easy chairs scattered around the perimeter, most of the room's original furniture is crowded into the north end of the chamber. A neatly furled American flag stands in the northwest corner, next to a door leading to one of two adjoining offices reserved for the exclusive use of the Chief Justice. Built into the center of the north wall is a large, black marble fireplace with a matching mantle clock. The fireplace is still used to warm the room during the cold winter months. Above the mantle hangs a fine portrait of John Marshall, painted from life by John Martin in 1830. To the left, and hung significantly lower, is a portrait of Stephen Field, painted circa 1895 by Albert Rosenthal. Beneath Field's picture is a small kidney-shaped desk that was built in the late nineteenth century and formerly belonged to the Clerk of the Court. An old-fashioned lamp and two telephones sit on the desktop. One phone is for regular calls, the other for emergencies. Otherwise the desk is no longer used, except to store the Court's emergency supply of paper, pencils, and cough drops.

Directly in front of the fireplace sits a massive twelve-foot-long mahogany table surrounded by nine high-backed, green-leather and mahogany chairs. Like the rest of the building's furniture, they were handmade by the Court's own team of skilled carpenters. This is where the Supreme Court meets in conference.

The Chief Justice sits at the east end of the table with his back to the window, facing the senior Associate Justice seated opposite. To the Chief's right, the next three most senior Associate Justices sit with their backs to the fireplace. To the Chief's left are the four most junior Justices. The Chief Justice and the senior Associate Justice have plenty of room at the table ends, and the three Justices nearest the fireplace are quite comfortable. The remaining four Justices have little elbow room and must regret that the Court's craftsmen did not make the table a foot or two longer. Seating is by seniority, and the Justices change places at the table whenever a more senior Justice retires or dies. Occasionally, however, a Justice will refuse to move when a new Justice is appointed.

Throughout most of each term, the Justices meet in conference twice weekly—on Wednesdays and Fridays. A buzzer is supposed to sound in each of the chambers to call the Justices to conference, but the system is unreliable and new Justices quickly learn to watch the clock or risk arriving late. The Justices do not wear their robes to conference. There to do business, they wear business attire.

When the Justices have gathered beneath John Marshall's portrait, they close the door on the world behind them and shake hands all around. Chief Justice Melville Fuller began this ritual more than a century ago to remind the Justices that their disagreements are professional rather than personal. As William Brennan put it, "It is a symbol that harmony of aims, if not of views, is the Court's guiding principle."[3] But the practice always reminded Jimmy Byrnes of nine boxers preparing to go to their corners and come out fighting.[4]

Six Justices constitute a quorum. Attendance is not a condition of participating in a case, and when Justices miss a conference they often vote by proxy and then borrow another Justice's conference notes to see what they missed.

Except for the Justices, no one is allowed to enter the room while the conference is in progress. A member of the Supreme Court police force stands guard outside the door to make sure that the Justices are not disturbed. Inside the conference room, the most junior Justice sits closest to the door and serves as the Court's messenger, delivering outgoing messages to the young pages who wait outside in the hallway. These messages might include requests for books or case records, or word that the Justices wish to be served lunch. Tom Clark, who served as the junior Justice for nearly six years during the 1950s, glumly referred to himself as "the highest paid doorkeeper in the world."[5]

Incoming messages are announced with a polite knock on the door. The junior Justice answers the door, takes the note, and delivers it directly to the Chief. Because the Justices dislike the idea of allowing the outside world to intrude on their conferences, incoming messages are rare and invariably carry news that the Justices consider vitally important. What they think important, however, can range from the first word of President Kennedy's assassination in Dallas to the latest World Series score.

The junior Justice performs a number of other menial conference duties. When Chief Justice Burger proved incapable of keeping an accurate count of conference votes, he gave up and assigned the task to the junior Justice. Keeping track of these votes is routine but crucial work, because they decide the cases and determine who will control the opinion assignments. The junior Justice also stays behind after the conference adjourns on Friday to dictate the text of orders that will appear on the Court's order list, which is published each Monday. Junior Justices usually suffer these little indignities quietly, hoping that it will not be too long before a new Associate Justice is appointed.

When Sandra Day O'Connor was appointed to the Court in 1981, the other Justices considered exempting her from these traditional duties. They were worried that it would not look good to have the first female Justice wait on the rest of the conference like a nursemaid. When the brethren ultimately decided to treat O'Connor as they would any other junior Justice, no one was happier than John Paul Stevens. After enduring six long years as the junior Justice, he was finally able to move up a seat at the conference table

3. Westin, *Autobiography of the Supreme Court*, 301.
4. Byrnes, *All in a Year*, 137.
5. O'Brien, *Storm Center*, 185.

and safely away from the door. Any thoughts of treating the new junior Justice differently quickly disappeared—it was O'Connor whom Burger first assigned to tally the conference votes.

While the outside world is barred from the conference room, the Justices themselves are free to come and go as they please. James McReynolds, the most obnoxious man ever to serve on the Court, often left the room when Louis Brandeis spoke. McReynolds, a virulent anti-Semite, stood just outside the door until the first Jewish Justice finished speaking and then returned to his seat.

For his part, Brandeis grew irritated whenever conferences dragged on past the Justices' customary 5:30 P.M. quitting time. One day when his patience ran out, he stood and told Chief Justice Charles Evans Hughes, "Your jurisdiction is at an end. You know how I am going to vote in this case." Then he packed his briefcase and left.[6]

Toward the end of his career, Thurgood Marshall developed chronic health problems and could not sit for more than twenty minutes without having to go to the bathroom. Every time he left the conference room he looked at the young interns and messengers waiting expectantly outside the conference door and grumbled, "When you gotta go, you gotta go." Then he shook his head and chuckled to himself as he began another long, slow walk down the hall to the men's room.[7]

At the end of each conference, a second buzzer sounds to warn the staff that the Justices are leaving the conference room. Clerks casually peek out of their offices to catch a glimpse of the Justices walking down the hall, looking for signs of what transpired in conference and hoping that the Justices will be in the mood to gossip when they return to chambers.

The Court's routine varies somewhat between the Wednesday and Friday conferences. Wednesday conferences begin in the afternoon immediately following the day's oral arguments and deal with the four cases argued the previous Monday. These conferences are relatively brief, often lasting just an hour or two.[8] Friday conferences are much longer, and the agenda is more varied and difficult. The Justices first discuss administrative and procedural matters—certiorari petitions, appeals by right, and jurisdictional problems. They also decide which cases are finished and ready to be announced the coming week. Then the Justices turn to the main business of the conference, to discuss and decide the eight cases that were argued on Tuesday and Wednesday. Friday conferences usually begin at 9:30 A.M. and end around 5:00 P.M., with a half-hour lunch break.

During weeks when no oral arguments are scheduled and the Court is in recess, the Justices meet in conference only once, on Thursdays. These recess conferences begin at

---

6. Pusey, 2 *Charles Evans Hughes*, 673.
7. Interview with Francene Engel, July 1, 1998.
8. White, "The Work of the Supreme Court," 383. Oral arguments are normally heard on Mondays, Tuesdays, and Wednesdays, with four cases argued each day.

10:00 A.M. and usually end by 4:30 P.M., with a forty-five-minute lunch break.[9] The Justices can afford a more relaxed schedule because there are no new argued cases and usually only a few cert petitions to consider.[10]

In addition to the regularly scheduled conferences, *special conferences* are called throughout the term as necessary to allow the Justices to keep up with their work. Special conferences tend to be concentrated in the first days and weeks after the Justices return from summer and Christmas recess. Because cert petitions are filed in the Clerk's office year-round, whether the Court is in session or not, the Justices have to meet every day for a week or more at the beginning of each term and for several days after the Christmas break to catch up with the cert petitions that accumulated while they were away. Since 1975, the Justices have met in special conference every day during the last week of September, before the official opening of the fall term in October, to get a head start on the summer backlog of cert petitions.

THE WORK OF THE CONFERENCE

The work of the conference can be divided into three basic categories: administrative matters, procedural issues, and deciding cases.

Administrative matters involve the Court's internal operations. While most routine administrative decisions concerning the Court's budget, staff, and physical plant are left to the Chief Justice, many important issues—and more than a few trivial ones—are discussed and decided in conference. The Justices discuss a wide range of administrative matters in conference, from deciding whether to lobby Congress for new appropriations to planning the Court's annual Christmas party.

The second task of the conference is to decide procedural issues of case selection and management. This aspect of the conference, called *cert conferences* or *screening conferences*, involves deciding whether to grant petitions for certiorari, how to deal with appeals by right, resolving jurisdictional questions, and ruling on the large number of miscellaneous petitions filed by litigants and third parties. Cert conferences are where the Justices decide what to decide, selecting the cases they will consider on the merits and determining how best to proceed to judgment.

To streamline cert discussions, the Chief Justice's chambers vets all certiorari petitions every week and posts each case to one of two lists: the *discuss list* or the *dead list.* The discuss list contains forty to fifty cases each week that the Chief Justice believes might merit conference discussion. The dead list includes another seventy to eighty cases (70 percent of all cert petitions) that the Chief Justice believes to be unworthy of further consideration.

---

9. O'Brien, *Storm Center*, 184.
10. Rehnquist, *The Supreme Court*, 287.

Both lists are circulated to all chambers several days before each conference, and any Justice may transfer a case from the dead list to the discuss list simply by asking. All of the petitions for certiorari that remain on the dead list are summarily denied without any conference discussion. About 70 percent of the cases on the discuss list are also summarily denied with little or no conference discussion.[11]

In conference, the Chief Justice mentions each case on the discuss list and explains briefly why it might deserve a hearing on the merits. If an Associate Justice placed the case on the discuss list, he or she begins the discussion. Discussion and voting are in descending order of seniority. According to the customary *rule of four*, if four Justices agree then the Court will accept the case and consider it on the merits.

The third and most important task of the conference is to discuss and decide cases on the merits. This is called the *argued cases conference* or the *conference on the merits*. These cases have already been accepted, briefed, and argued in open court. The Justices try to decide each argued case in conference the same week as they hear the oral arguments. As Potter Stewart observed, the Justices never know more about the case than they do at that moment, when they have the lawyers' arguments fresh in their minds and their attention is focused by the competitive atmosphere of the conference.[12]

The Justices also use argued cases conferences to decide some cases summarily, without requiring oral argument. More rarely, they vote in conference to dismiss an argued case without ruling on the merits. It only takes a simple majority to dismiss a case at any time before the Court's judgment is officially announced. This is usually done by dismissing the writ of certiorari as improvidently granted (DIG). This is most likely to happen when the majority discovers—or manufactures—a procedural or factual flaw to justify dismissing a case, even after it has been fully briefed and argued. It is the Court's way of saying "oops." Unlike denials of cert, DIGged cases have been *considered* on the merits, even if they are not *decided* on the merits.

The Court spends approximately 156 hours in conference each term. Most of that time is devoted to argued cases. As a rule, cert conference discussions are not as thorough or detailed as for argued cases. Each cert petition on the discuss list receives an average of six minutes of discussion, while each argued case is allotted twenty to thirty minutes or more.[13] Most cert petitions are disposed of with little or no discussion, while some difficult or controversial argued cases may be discussed at several conferences spread over a number of weeks, months, or even years.

---

11. O'Brien, *Storm Center*, 186.

12. Powell, "What Really Goes on at the Supreme Court," 722.

13. O'Brien, *Storm Center*, 230–31.

THE RULES OF ENGAGEMENT

The argued cases conference marks the point in the Court's decision-making process when individual contemplation ends and collective deliberation begins.[14] This is the Justices' first, best, and often only opportunity to discuss the issues with each other face to face. Justices rarely discuss cases with one another before the conference, and afterward they communicate almost exclusively by written memoranda or indirectly through their clerks.

Justices have three main priorities at these conferences: to share their views, to decide cases, and to determine who will write. The Chief Justice presides and speaks first on each case, summarizing, framing the issues, and usually indicating how he will vote. If the Chief is absent or recuses himself, then the senior Associate Justice presides. The other Justices speak in descending order of seniority. They may defer their comments if they have trouble making up their minds or if they want to hear from a junior Justice who has special expertise in the area. During the conference discussion of *Wyman v. James*, for example, Potter Stewart passed to allow Byron White to interpret a precedent he had written.[15] After White spoke, Stewart took his turn.

Senior Justices tend to speak at far greater length than junior Justices, because as the discussion moves down the line there is inevitably less to talk about. There are nine Justices, but only rarely nine distinct perspectives on a case. Senior Justices often come to conference armed with *talking papers*, usually written by their clerks, which serve as detailed outlines for their conference remarks. Junior Justices seldom bother with talking papers because they know that all the good arguments will almost certainly have been made by the time it is their turn to speak.

Newly appointed Justices are often surprised to discover how little impact they have on conference deliberations.[16] As a young Associate Justice, William Rehnquist quickly

---

14. Rehnquist, *The Supreme Court*, 287.

15. *Wyman v. James*, 400 U.S. 309 (1971). This case is discussed in chapter 13.

16. One possible exception is when a new Justice is appointed to a closely divided Court. On May 12, 1970, the same day that Harry Blackmun was confirmed as Abe Fortas's replacement, Chief Justice Burger mailed two large sacks of mail to Blackmun's home in Minnesota—weeks before Blackmun was due in Washington to begin work. These sacks contained more than two hundred petitions for certiorari that had been held for "Justice X" since Fortas resigned from the Court a year earlier. In many of these cases, Blackmun was the potential fourth vote needed to grant cert. Also waiting for Blackmun in Washington were a number of argued cases where the other Justices had split 4–4, leaving Blackmun as the deciding vote. This meant that even as the newest Justice, Harry Blackmun briefly held the future course of American law in his hands. Even under these "ideal" circumstances, however, none of the other Justices really cared what Blackmun had to say about the cases—all they wanted to know was how he was going to vote. They had already talked themselves hoarse arguing the issues before Blackmun arrived, and there was nothing new left to say. While Blackmun was the pivotal vote, he had no chance to persuade anyone to change their views. Woodward and Armstrong, *The Brethren*, 99–103.

became frustrated with his lack of influence in the conference and lobbied for years to change the traditional seriatim discussion format to a more free-wheeling roundtable debate.[17] He continued to push for conference reform until he became Chief Justice in 1986 and came to appreciate the wisdom of tradition and the seniority system. As Chief Justice, Rehnquist has not instituted any significant reforms in conference procedures and has not asked the Court's carpenters to build a round conference table.

Occasionally, a junior Justice will find a way to overcome the obstacles of the seniority system and learn to punch above their weight in conference discussions. While William Brennan and Thurgood Marshall served on the Court together, they were in such close agreement in most cases that their clerks referred to them behind their backs as Justice Brennanmarshall. Marshall was the junior Justice, and for twenty-four years had to sit in silence while Brennan spoke first and laid out their common views of each case. Marshall learned to leave the legal arguments to Brennan and used his turn to discuss the real world consequences of the cases that interested him.[18] This gave Marshall a chance to educate and persuade the rest of the conference, a role that he greatly enjoyed. Later in his career, unfortunately, he began to lose his hearing and was less effective in this role. In the end, Marshall was reduced to leaning over to ask Harry Blackmun, "Harry, how did Brennan vote?" and he rarely spoke more than a few words in conference.[19]

VOTING

After the Justices have all had their say, the conference votes to decide the case. The Justices vote in descending order of seniority, beginning with the Chief Justice.

There are several good reasons to postpone the vote until the end of the discussion. The most important benefit is that it facilitates compromise and consensus. Social science research into small-group behavior confirms that separating discussion from voting encourages flexibility and accommodation on the part of group members. An atmosphere of negotiation and compromise tends to persist until a formal vote is taken, at which point positions begin to harden and compromise becomes more difficult.[20]

Prior to 1941, when consensus building was more important than it is today, the Justices were more careful to discuss each case fully before voting. The hope was that the conference discussion would lead to consensus and that the formal vote at the end would help to lock all nine Justices into place.

---

17. Rehnquist, *The Supreme Court*, 290–91.

18. Tushnet, *Making Constitutional Law*, 57.

19. Ibid., 63.

20. For example, juries that discuss the case fully before voting tend to reach a common agreement more readily than juries that begin their deliberations by taking a preliminary vote. The former tend to be more evidence driven and cooperative, while the latter tend to be verdict driven and combative. Kassin and Wrightsman, *The American Jury on Trial*, 203–4.

Because Justices today are less interested in consensus building, the line between discussion and voting has gradually blurred. Justices now routinely indicate how they will vote during their initial comments, rather than reserving their votes until the end of the discussion. In especially difficult or controversial cases, however, the first round of discussion is often followed by a general debate, and in the resulting confusion the Justices still find a formal vote useful to clarify the final division.

While Justices now are generally content with majority verdicts, they still must negotiate to mass the five votes required to decide each case. Postponing the final vote until the end of the discussion helps to promote compromise, if not consensus. As a result, the Justices' conference views are often expressed in tentative terms, and they routinely communicate a willingness to compromise in order to make a court. Whether building a majority of five or a consensus of nine, it remains easier to compromise before a formal vote is taken.

Even on the modern Court, consensus remains important in politically sensitive cases. Under these circumstances, conference votes take on renewed importance. In *Brown v. Board of Education*, the Justices initially were divided over the issue of school desegregation.[21] Both Chief Justice Fred Vinson and his successor, Earl Warren, thought it essential to reach a unanimous decision, and they avoided taking a formal conference vote in the hope that the Justices would not allow their views to harden by committing to a particular position too quickly.[22] Warren, in particular, feared that a premature vote might make it impossible to make the concessions and compromises necessary to forge a consensus. It was only after the Justices all informally agreed on what to do that Warren called for a vote, knowing in advance that he had secured a unanimous mandate to end state-sponsored racial segregation in public schools.

There remains some controversy as to how conference votes are conducted. Today, voting proceeds in the same order as discussion, in descending order of seniority. For most of the Court's history, however, voting was in reverse order of seniority, with the most junior Justice voting first and the Chief Justice voting last. This unique system of *juniority voting* was consistently followed until 1946 and employed at least occasionally until the 1960s.

The conventional justification for juniority voting is that by voting first, junior Justices would not be unduly influenced or intimidated by more senior Justices.[23] Earl Warren argued that it also relieved junior Justices of the responsibility of having to break tie votes.[24] Both are plausible explanations, but neither is true.

---

21. *Brown v. Board of Education*, 347 U.S. 483 (1954).

22. Fred Vinson was Chief Justice when *Brown v. Board of Education* first came before the Court during the 1952 term. Apparently following Robert Jackson's suggestion, Vinson did not poll the conference on the merits of the case—a tactic that Earl Warren continued after becoming Chief Justice in 1953.

23. Clark, "Inside the Supreme Court," in Westin, *Autobiography of the Supreme Court*, 48.

24. Warren, *Memoirs*, 282–83.

Far from giving junior Justices an advantage by allowing them to vote first, juniority voting was intended to give the Chief Justice the advantage of voting last. Conference votes determine who will write the lead majority and dissenting opinions. By tradition, the Chief Justice assigns the opinion on whichever side he votes, while the senior Associate Justice voting on the other side controls that assignment. By speaking first and voting last, the Chief Justice could see how the vote was going and cast his lot with the majority in order to control the opinion.

Charles Evans Hughes was a master of this tactic, and took full advantage of his prerogative to vote last as a means of guiding the Court.[25] Thirty years later Warren Burger tried to duplicate Hughes's mastery of conference voting, with notably less success.

By the time Burger became Chief Justice, the practice of juniority voting had long since disappeared. As late as the 1975 term, however, Burger continued to argue in conference that formal conference procedures required juniority voting. When the other Justices refused to allow this prerogative to be restored, Burger sought to control opinion assignments by passing or reserving his vote or by casting an ambiguous vote and then later claiming the right to assign the majority opinion after the other votes were recorded.[26] Burger's defenders maintain that the Chief Justice was within his rights to defer his votes, while others acknowledge that Burger was notoriously inept at keeping track of conference votes and admit that he might occasionally have assigned opinions when he had no real right to do so. Whether Burger's behavior was due to Machiavellian calculation or administrative incompetence, it caused considerable resentment inside the conference room. His successor, William Rehnquist, has scrupulously avoided criticism on this count by casting unambiguous votes, clearly announcing the conference vote in each case and allowing the other Justices to challenge his tally on the spot.

SECRECY

The intimacies of the conference room—the workshop of the living Constitution—are illuminations denied to the historian.—Felix Frankfurter[27]

Sunlight is said to be the best of disinfectants.—Louis Brandeis[28]

In the days of John Marshall (1801–35) and Roger Brooke Taney (1836–64), the Justices were somewhat less obsessive about conference secrecy than they are today. During much of this period, all of the Justices lived together in the same boardinghouses when the Court

---

25. Charles Evans Hughes, *The Supreme Court*, 58.
26. Woodward and Armstrong, *The Brethren*, 495–96.
27. Frankfurter, *The Commerce Clause Under Marshall, Taney, and Waite*, 11.
28. Quoted in Howard, "Comment on Secrecy and the Supreme Court," 837.

was in session. They often discussed cases informally over dinner at a common table in the company of as many as thirty other men. After dinner, however, the Justices withdrew, usually with a bottle or two of madeira, to talk more formally in private.

Marshall institutionalized the Court conference and began its tradition of secrecy. There were two main reasons for this: to protect the Court from political attacks by the other two branches of government and to help maintain the appearance of unanimity in Court decisions.[29]

For most of Marshall's tenure as Chief Justice, the popular branches of government were controlled by his political enemies, including Thomas Jefferson, James Madison, and Andrew Jackson. Surrounded by more powerful foes, Marshall sought to frustrate his adversaries and reinforce the Court's authority by imposing a sense of collective responsibility among the Justices and by presenting a united front to an often hostile world. Marshall used the privacy of the conference to encourage the Justices to negotiate a common position and establish a consensus in each case. Whenever possible, the Justices delivered unanimous judgments, rather than separate individual judgments (seriatim opinions), as was customarily done before Marshall became Chief Justice. If the Justices could not agree, they usually stifled any public dissent and announced their decision *as if* the case had been decided unanimously. As far as Marshall was concerned, the more united the Court appeared, and the less anyone knew about the Justices' individual views, the better.

This sense of collective decision making and consensus, achieved through secret negotiations and compromise in conference, helped the Justices to claim that they were an apolitical institution that merely "found" the law and applied it in an objective manner. This in turn allowed the Justices to pretend that they were above the vicious partisan politics of the day. With sharks circling menacingly all around them, the Justices tried their best to convince the world that they could walk on water.

Judicial suspicion of the other branches of government persists today, which helps to explain the Court's continued obsession with conference secrecy. There has been periodic concern among the Justices that the conference room has been the target of government or private surveillance. When Charles Evans Hughes was Chief Justice (1930–41), a District of Columbia policeman allegedly paid two Court employees to plant a microphone in the conference room. Hughes directed the marshal to fire the two employees, and a listening device was apparently found and removed. It was never clear who else was involved or why the device was planted.[30]

During the Johnson and Nixon administrations, several Justices suspected that the government had bugged the conference room. At William O. Douglas's insistence, Earl

---

29. Miller and Sastri, "Secrecy and the Supreme Court," 808.
30. Douglas, *The Court Years*, 256.

Warren had the room swept for listening devices in 1966. Because the Court could not afford the $5,000 expense, Warren asked the FBI to do the job. This made no sense to Douglas, who thought that asking the FBI to investigate government surveillance was like asking Al Capone to investigate bootlegging. No bugs were found, but Douglas remained convinced that the government was listening in on the Justices' conferences and that the FBI was probably behind it.[31]

In 1969, a Justice Department official by the name of Jack Landau carried a disturbing message to Earl Warren from the Nixon administration, threatening that "something terrible would happen to the Court" unless it changed its ruling in *Alderman v. United States*.[32] In that case the Court imposed new restrictions on government surveillance and penalized government agents who engaged in illegal practices. Warren called a special conference to discuss the matter. In conference, Douglas asked the Chief whether he had asked Landau

> about the bug which I am sure exists in our conference room. He said no, but he had asked whether his office (the Chief Justice's) was bugged, and Landau, expressing great surprise and astonishment, held up his hands and said, "Certainly not."[33]

Douglas did not believe Landau. In 1973, Douglas made the front page of the *New York Times* when he wrote in a dissenting opinion that he was "morally certain that the conference room has been 'bugged.'"[34]

Some of the Justices have managed to have fun with the surveillance rumors. Lewis Powell once gave a droll description of the uncertain privacy of the conference room: "There are no law clerks, no secretaries, and no tape recorders—at least none of which we have knowledge."[35] Harry Blackmun discovered by accident one day that his hearing aid emitted a high-pitched electronic squeal if he brushed his hand across his hair a certain way. He noticed that when he did this in the conference room, Sandra Day O'Connor looked around the room with a puzzled look on her face. Suspecting that O'Connor thought that the room was bugged, Blackmun set off his hearing aid on purpose just to worry her.[36]

A second justification commonly offered to justify the secrecy of the conference is to protect the integrity of the Court's decisions. Earl Warren warned that it would be a disaster for national markets if word ever leaked out prematurely about the Court's deci-

---

31. Ibid., 256–57.

32. *Alderman v. United States*, 394 U.S. 165 (1969).

33. Urofsky, *The Douglas Letters*, 208–9; Douglas, *The Court Years*, 260.

34. *Heutsche v. United States*, 414 U.S. 898, 898 (1973); *New York Times*, October 16, 1973, 1.

35. Powell, "What Really Goes on at the Supreme Court," 722. The Justices routinely share at least some of what happens at conference with their clerks. One of Justice Robert Jackson's better-known former clerks, for example, reported that after the May 1952 conference on *Youngstown Sheet & Tube Co. v. Sawyer*, President Truman's landmark steel seizure case, Jackson came back to his chambers and told his two clerks, "Well, boys, the President got licked." Rehnquist, *The Supreme Court*, 91–92.

36. Cooper, *Battles on the Bench*, 165.

sions in economic cases.[37] This justification is taken more seriously today than it used to be. For much of the Court's history, servants were allowed to remain in the conference room to wait on the Justices and to serve drinks.[38] This practice ended in 1910, when two attendants allegedly leaked the vote in an important economic case and caused a panic on Wall Street. The two men were summarily fired, although as it turned out, they were both innocent. A lawyer who had listened to the oral arguments had correctly guessed which way the Justices were going to vote and sold a large block of company stock, which caused the company's stock price to collapse. Since that time, however, no outsider has been allowed to set foot inside the conference room during the Justices' deliberations.[39]

Felix Frankfurter offered a third justification for conference secrecy. Invading the privacy of the conference room, he argued, would have a chilling effect on the frank exchange of views among the Justices. Years later, Lewis Powell added that secrecy allowed the Justices to be more flexible in deciding cases than if their conference votes were immediately made public. By taking secret votes, Justices remained free to review their initial judgments and to change their minds without public consequences.[40] On a more personal level, Justice O'Connor has said that the Justices simply do not want to read what they said in conference on Friday in the *New York Times* on Saturday. William Rehnquist added another intriguing justification: that limiting the conference to the Justices alone serves to remind the Justices to do their own work.[41] Rehnquist maintains that the closed and competitive nature of the conference helps to motivate the Justices to stay on top of their cases.[42] Finally, like many Justices, William Brennan thought that the need for secrecy was so obvious that he never even bothered to justify it.[43]

Except for Brennan's "self-evident" nonjustification, these are all legitimate arguments. Taken together, they provide a compelling justification to permit the Justices to discuss and decide cases privately, out of the public eye. But none of these arguments, considered alone or collectively, justifies the permanent shroud of secrecy that hangs over the conference room.

For the most part, the various justifications for conference secrecy lose their force at the moment that the results of each case are announced in open court. With few excep-

---

37. Warren, *Memoirs*, 284–85.

38. Douglas, *The Court Years*, 34.

39. Westin, *The Supreme Court: Views From the Inside*, 46.

40. Powell, "What Really Goes On," 722.

41. When Louis Brandeis was asked the difference between the Supreme Court and the other branches of government, he replied, "Here we do our own work." Stewart, "Reflections on the Supreme Court," 9.

42. Rehnquist, *The Supreme Court*, 288–89.

43. Brennan wrote that the conference demanded "absolute secrecy" for "obvious reasons." Brennan, "Working at Justice," in Westin, *Autobiography of the Supreme Court*, 301. However, Brennan left his conference notes among his papers at the Library of Congress, where, subject to some restrictions, they are readily accessible to scholars.

tions, Supreme Court decisions are not like military or diplomatic secrets, which by their nature might justify long-term confidentiality.[44]

Even Frankfurter's "chilling effect" argument is hardly a compelling justification for perpetual secrecy. First, the need for confidentiality in the judicial branch is no greater than in the legislative or executive branches, where constitutional and statutory norms have long required far greater transparency. Second, Frankfurter's argument ignores the fact that virtually all of the Justices are experienced lawyers and politicians and are inured to the ways of public life. They are unlikely to be intimidated or dissuaded from speaking their minds by the mere prospect that their remarks might someday be made public. Third, even if some Justices feel pressure to censor their conference remarks because of the prospect of public disclosure, this is not entirely undesirable. It would encourage the Justices to stay on top of their cases and to consider what they say carefully before speaking.

Whatever pressure might result from public disclosure of conference discussions pales in comparison to the competitive pressures of the conference itself. Justices are motivated to prepare carefully for conferences in part by the knowledge that everything they say will be subject to instant dissection and criticism by their peers. Charles Evans Hughes used the competitive nature of the conference to ensure that the other Justices did their homework. His thorough preparation for conferences was legendary, and the other Justices knew that their arguments had to be sound and well presented or Hughes would eviscerate them. Now *that* was a chilling effect, and it goes to prove that not all chills are unhealthy.

It is possible that some Justices might be so unnerved by the prospect of public disclosure of their conference comments that they would lose their spontaneity and candor. At worst, their conference remarks would be as formalistic and bland as their written opinions. This is a serious argument, but one that, for obvious reasons, the Justices themselves are unlikely to make.

There is good reason, however, to believe that this worst-case scenario will not happen. Or perhaps it is more accurate to say that if it was ever going to happen, it already happened long ago. Most of the Justices take conference notes, and they routinely gossip about what goes on in conferences with their clerks. The Justices have always known that anything said in conference might eventually become part of the public record. The risk of public disclosure has always existed and will continue to exist, at least until all of the Justices' conference notes are systematically gathered up and destroyed.

During the 1970s, Warren Burger sought to do just that, by proposing a new Court rule that would have required all Justices to destroy their conference notes upon their

---

44. Ironically, most military and intelligence records are subject to eventual disclosure under the Freedom of Information Act. These laws have never been applied to Supreme Court Justices' papers or records, which have been treated as personal property to be disposed of as each Justice alone sees fit.

deaths. Burger's plan would have allowed Justices to use their conference notes to write their memoirs, while ensuring that no independent record of the Court's conferences survived them. The Chief Justice established an advisory committee for the sole purpose of recommending this course of action, and he was deeply disappointed when the conference did not agree with his recommendations.[45] But Burger's actions had their intended effect. Even Thurgood Marshall, who had no sympathy for the Chief Justice, felt compelled to return a $250,000 advance for his autobiography because, he said, "I can just see the headlines in the *Washington Post*: 'The First Negro on the Supreme Court Opens up the Conference Room and Discloses the Confidences of the Justices.'"[46]

While there is no rule governing the disposal of the Justices' conference notes, most former Justices have secreted, vetted, limited access to, lost, or destroyed their conference notes. The most tragic example of this behavior involved Hugo Black. Black spent his entire judicial career building a complete set of conference notes—a priceless historical record of his thirty-four years on the Court. On his deathbed, Black changed his mind and insisted that his wife and son burn all of his conference records. After trying unsuccessfully to dissuade the dying Justice, they reluctantly complied with his wishes, knowing that Black would gain nothing from their actions and history would lose much.

Apart from the frailties of age, two events drove Black to take such self-destructive measures. First, Black was heartbroken when he read Alpheus Mason's excellent biography of Harlan Fiske Stone (which relied heavily on conference notes and other primary sources) and discovered that Stone—whom Black had always considered a close friend—had never liked him. Second, Black was furious when political scientist Sidney Ulmer, using Harold Burton's conference notes in *Brown v. Board of Education*, claimed that Black had initially been willing to reaffirm *Plessy v. Ferguson* and uphold racial segregation in public schools. Black vehemently denied that he had done any such thing. As it turns out, Black had good reason to be upset; Ulmer misinterpreted Burton's conference notes and falsely accused Black of inconstancy in his commitment to desegregation.[47]

Other Justices have, unfortunately, tended to follow Hugo Black's example and destroyed their conference notes. This distressing trend was reinforced several years ago when the Library of Congress made public Thurgood Marshall's papers within a few months after his death. Most of the sitting Justices were livid that the general public had unrestricted access to Marshall's judicial papers and could read internal Court memoranda about cases that had been decided as little as a year previously. Even though the episode caused no perceptible damage to the Court (the Marshall papers painted a flat-

---

45. White Burkett Miller Center of Public Affairs, *The Office of Chief Justice*, 185–86.

46. Marshall's autobiography was to be written with Carl Rowan. Tushnet, *Making Constitutional Law*, 195.

47. See Harold Burton's conference notes on *Brown v. Board of Education*, in chapter 13.

tering portrait of life on the Court and contained no hint of scandal or dishonorable behavior), several Justices reacted by withdrawing all or part of their planned donations to the Library of Congress. At least one Justice personally went through files already in storage at the Library of Congress and "stripped them . . . [of] everything that anyone might find useful. They are not getting much from me." The affair also apparently convinced Byron White to destroy his conference notes.

Many—perhaps most—of the Justices do not want to see the veil of secrecy lifted from the conference, ever. This is largely because they see nothing to gain from disclosure. To a greater extent than any other department of government, Supreme Court Justices control their own history. They assert complete control over the public record, as reflected in their published opinions, and they remain free to dispose of their public and private papers however they wish. No laws compel disclosure of the Court's deliberations or any internal Court documents or decisions. Nor is there any reliable source of independent inside information about the Court. Even the Supreme Court press corps is completely housebroken and has rarely challenged the Justices' claimed right to control all information emanating from the marble temple.

The Justices may not be able to control what the public *thinks* of the Court, but they have nearly absolute control of what we *know* about the Court. Under these circumstances, the value of leaving a full and accurate historical record is simply not compelling to most Justices. They see little reason to allow public access to their candid and unvarnished conference discussions when we already have their carefully polished published opinions to read. As a result, we have ample tangible evidence of the *results* of their decisions (the published opinions), but we have little reliable inside information about the *process* of Supreme Court decision making. Court observers who try to find out what goes on behind the velvet curtain are in some respects like Cold War scholars who tried to divine what went on behind the Iron Curtain—except that they had more interesting photographs to work with.

The Justices take the metaphor of the marble temple seriously. They continue to present themselves as oracles of the law, deny that the Court is a political institution, and quietly perpetuate the myth that legal decisions spring from their heads like Athena— fully clothed and immaculate. Mysticism has always benefited oracles, and the Justices are no exception.

The reason why the Justices continue to guard the secrets of the conference so zealously is evident in the conference notes published here. The notes clearly demonstrate the tentativeness and negotiated nature of most Court decisions and illuminate the close relationship that exists between law and politics. Even in this day and age, many—perhaps most—Justices would profess to be shocked, *shocked* to hear that there is politics going on inside the marble temple. Given the choice, they would rather remain silent and be thought a political institution than to speak and remove all doubt. The conference notes remove all doubt.

Fortunately, there are some notable exceptions when it comes to perpetuating the cult of the robe.[48] While Felix Frankfurter originally thought that the intimacies of the conference should be kept forever secret, he later modified his views somewhat:

> That the Supreme Court should not be amenable to the forces of publicity to which the Executive and the Congress are subjected is essential to the effective functioning of the Court. But the passage of time may enervate the reasons for this restriction, particularly if disclosure rests not on tittle-tattle or self-serving declarations.[49]

It is difficult to understand how timely public disclosure of the Court's conference discussions would cause any erosion of the quality of justice or public confidence in the Court. It seems rather more likely that the opposite would occur. The Justices' conference discussions are for the most part frank and thoughtful conversations among the country's leading jurists. This is precisely what makes them so interesting.

Those who favor the perpetual secrecy of the conference tend to ignore the fact that it is secrecy, not openness, that encourages public distrust and dissatisfaction. This is especially true in a free society accustomed to open government. Secrecy by its nature provokes suspicion when, in the absence of solid information, rumors about the Court inevitably leak into the public domain.

It is hard to give credence to the Justices' complaints that the media publish inaccurate or incomplete accounts of what goes on inside the Court, when it is the Justices themselves who are primarily responsible for this situation. Secrecy inhibits responsible research, but encourages the sort of speculative and sensational exposés about the Court that we see published with increasing frequency. There is a legal maxim that if the documentary evidence is ambiguous or doubtful, then any doubts should be resolved against the party responsible for the uncertainty. If the Justices choose to complain that the public misunderstands and misinterprets what they do, then they should release more information, not less.

The need to protect the secrets of the conference is compelling only until the case is decided, and perhaps for a brief time afterward if the case is remanded and the same

---

48. Frank, *Courts on Trial*, 254. Judge Jerome Frank argued that judicial mysticism and secrecy are dangerous for democratic government because they help judges to maintain an illusion of infallibility, inhibit public understanding about what judges really do, and hinder reform:

"It is the essence of democracy that the citizens are entitled to know what all their public servants, judges included, are doing, and how well they are doing it. The best way to bring about the elimination of those shortcomings of our judicial system which are capable of being eliminated is to have all our citizens informed as to how that system now functions. It is a mistake, therefore, to try to establish and maintain, through ignorance, public esteem for our courts." Frank, *Courts on Trial*, 2–3.

49. Frankfurter, "Mr. Justice Roberts," 313–14.

issues will be immediately relitigated. Otherwise, once a case has been decided the Justices' residual interest in secrecy should promptly way to the more compelling interests of open government, public accountability, and public understanding of government decision making.

FIGHTING IN THE CONFERENCE ROOM?

Lewis Powell and other Justices have long claimed that the conventional media portrayal of the Supreme Court as a geriatric soap opera of feuds, passions, and bitter rivalries is a myth powered by equal parts of imagination, ignorance, and calculation. While admitting that some personal animosities exist, Powell suggested that the media greatly exaggerated and romanticized these problems in order to sell newspapers. On a personal level, Powell said, relations among the Justices were always cordial while he was on the Court.[50]

From the conference discussions reproduced here, it would appear that conference discussions are almost invariably civil. Even in the most controversial cases, there is remarkably little interplay or debate among the Justices, let alone fighting.[51]

This is not entirely surprising for small-group behavior. The Justices belong to a small and relatively stable social group. With life tenure, they have little choice but to learn to live with each other. It simply does not pay to allow doctrinal or personal disagreements to escalate into blood feuds if it can be helped. Earl Warren likened the situation to a marriage. To be productive, he said, "you can't be in a brawl every day and still get any satisfaction out of life."[52] William Brennan also talked about the importance of getting along in conference:

> It's absolutely essential in a small body of nine people who have to work as closely as
> we do [to get along with each other]. You simply can't afford to let your convictions
> affect your personal relationships. . . . I have sat now with about a fifth of all the
> Supreme Court justices there have been, and I have never had a cross word with one
> of them.[53]

Brennan acknowledged that the Frankfurter-Douglas feud was an epic exception to the rule. "They were more than distant," he admitted. "They were almost snarling at one another."[54] Even so, there is considerable institutional pressure to keep such problems

---

50. Powell, "What Really Goes On," 722–23.
51. Rehnquist, *The Supreme Court*, 290.
52. O'Brien, *Storm Center*, 121.
53. Henthoff, "Justice Brennan," 58.
54. Ibid., 58.

within the family. In public, both Frankfurter and Douglas resolutely denied that there was ever any real animosity between them. In his autobiography, Douglas improbably claimed that he and Frankfurter had never been enemies, and as if to prove the point he listed Frankfurter as one of the top seven Justices with whom he had served.[55]

---

55. Douglas, *The Court Years*, 42. Frankfurter was less reticent than Douglas to discuss their personal enmity, although for the most part he was content to attack Douglas in his diary, his private correspondence, and by proxy through his small army of protégés and acolytes. Douglas, of course, did much the same thing on a smaller scale.

CHAPTER 2

A BRIEF HISTORY OF THE CONFERENCE: JOHN JAY THROUGH MORRISON WAITE (1789–1888)

JOHN JAY, JOHN RUTLEDGE, AND OLIVER ELLSWORTH: THE UNSETTLED YEARS (1789–1801)

For the first twelve years of the Supreme Court's existence, few could have disagreed with Alexander Hamilton's opinion that the federal judiciary was the least dangerous branch of government. Between 1789 and 1801 the Court struggled, for the most part unsuccessfully, to establish its authority and build institutional respect and prestige within the new federal system. The Court barely managed to function, let alone take its designated place as a co-equal department.

The Court met for the first time on February 1, 1790, in the Royal Exchange in New York. Only three of the six Justices appeared, and lacking a quorum, they quickly adjourned until the next day. The following year the Justices followed the legislature to Philadelphia, convening either in Independence Hall or Old City Hall for the next ten years. The Justices met for two brief sessions annually, once in February and again in August. There was little to do. Most litigation took place in state courts, and while the federal circuit courts were relatively busy, the few cases that made it to the Supreme Court were almost all routine, private law cases.

Under the first three Chief Justices—John Jay, John Rutledge, and Oliver Ellsworth—the Court decided just a small handful of important public law cases dealing with questions of separation of powers and federalism.

Among the first separation of powers cases was *Hayburn's Case*. With this case, the Justices began to separate the duties of the judicial department from the other two branches of government and came tantalizingly close to establishing the principle of judicial review more than a decade before *Marbury v. Madison*.[1] *Hayburn's Case* was not a formal Supreme Court decision but a collection of three separate circuit court cases, where five of the six Supreme Court Justices sat individually as circuit judges. (Justices at that time served as appellate judges on the various circuit courts of appeals, along with their regu-

---

1. *Hayburn's Case*, 2 U.S. (2 Dall.) 409 (1792).

lar Supreme Court duties.) These cases all concerned a 1792 law that authorized federal judges to decide claims against the government brought by disabled Revolutionary War veterans.

All five Justices separately criticized the law and questioned its constitutionality.[2] They complained that the act violated constitutional principles of separation of powers and infringed on judicial independence by (a) requiring judges to perform nonjudicial duties; (b) subjecting judicial decisions to review and revision by the executive branch (all judicial determinations were subject to veto by the secretary of war); and (c) requiring judges to deliver what were essentially advisory opinions to the executive branch.

Had the Supreme Court decided *Hayburn's Case,* the Justices almost certainly would have struck down the law as unconstitutional. After the case was briefed and argued, however, the Justices postponed their decision until the following term. In the interim, Congress mooted the case by amending the law to abolish the secretary's veto and excising all of the other objectionable provisions.[3]

In a series of other cases, Chief Justice John Jay declined President Washington's repeated requests to issue advisory opinions on several questions of international law. Jay's refusals confirmed one of the central tenets of *Hayburn's Case*—that the Court's jurisdiction was limited to real cases and controversies and did not permit advisory opinions.

The earliest federalism cases included *Chisholm v. Georgia,* in which the Court held that states could be sued in federal courts by citizens of other states.[4] The decision was controversial and was reversed by the Eleventh Amendment, which took away federal jurisdiction in such cases. Another landmark case, *Ware v. Hylton* established the supremacy of treaties over state law.[5] These two decisions set the tone for the future, as the Court played a crucial role in nationalizing political power and presided over the accretive transfer of most important governmental responsibilities from the states to the federal government.

The Federalists were slow to appreciate the political usefulness of the federal courts. After years of virtually ignoring the judiciary, Federalist leaders changed their minds when they saw the crucial role that Federalist judges played in enforcing the party's controversial Alien and Sedition Acts. Federalist judges enforced these unpopular laws

---

2. The three separate appellate cases that constituted *Hayburn's Case* were decided by federal circuit courts in Pennsylvania (Wilson, Blair), New York (Jay, Cushing), and North Carolina (Iredell).

3. When it became apparent that the case was moot and that there would be no Supreme Court opinion, the Court reporter, Alexander J. Dallas, edited and published the five separate circuit court opinions and a letter about the cases that the Justices sent to President Washington. *Hayburn's Case,* 2 U.S. (2 Dall.) 409 (1792).

4. *Chisholm v. Georgia,* 2 U.S. (2 Dall.) 419 (1793).

5. *Ware v. Hylton,* 3 U.S. (3 Dall.) 198 (1796).

with partisan zeal, helping to limit political dissent and stifle criticism of Federalist officials. Federalist efforts to consolidate their control of the judicial branch gained a new sense of urgency after the election of 1800, when Thomas Jefferson was elected president and the Federalists were run from power everywhere except for the federal judiciary.

In the four-month window between Jefferson's November election and his inauguration on March 4, 1801, the last Federalist Congress hurriedly passed the Judiciary Act of 1801. This act created a large number of new judgeships and greatly expanded federal court jurisdiction in a last-ditch effort to make the courts a fortress of Federalism against Jefferson's insurgent Democratic-Republicans, who would control the White House and have overwhelming majorities in both houses of Congress. In a transparently political ploy, the last Federalist Congress also sought to deprive Jefferson of a Supreme Court appointment by reducing the size of the Court from six to five Justices, beginning with the next resignation.

At the same time, the six Federalist Justices were contemplating expanding their own jurisdiction.[6] They debated establishing a federal common law, which would have expanded the federal judicial power by giving federal judges general jurisdiction over a wide range of criminal and civil cases, even in the absence of congressional legislation. Predictably, the Federalists favored the idea while the Jeffersonians were vehemently opposed. Jefferson feared that the creation of a federal common law would allow the courts—and Congress—to circumvent established constitutional limits on their powers. He argued that the common law was the exclusive domain of the states and that the jurisdiction of federal courts was strictly limited to cases properly established by Congress acting within its constitutional authority. Surprisingly, the Justices eventually accepted Jefferson's position and rejected the idea of federal common law in *United States v. Hudson and Goodwin*.[7]

While the Justices' Supreme Court duties were not very demanding, they were also obliged to serve as federal circuit judges. They spent the better part of each year riding assigned circuits, presiding over local trials as they moved from town to town. This was an arduous and time-consuming task, made more difficult by the country's primitive transportation system and rough accommodations. Justice James Iredell contemptuously described circuit riding as living "the life of a postboy."[8] Circuit duties consumed most

---

6. Thomas Jefferson, in a letter to William C. Jarvis, criticized the Federalist judiciary, saying that their guiding maxim was "boni judicis est ampliare jurisdictionem"—the task of any good judge is to expand his jurisdiction. Murphy and Pritchett, *Courts, Judges, and Politics*, 305.

7. *United States v. Hudson and Goodwin*, 11 U.S. (7 Cranch) 32 (1812).

8. Letter from James Iredell to Arthur Iredell, February 1, 1791, quoted in Gerber, *Seriatim*, 215.

of the Justices' efforts and were far more onerous than their modest Supreme Court responsibilities.[9]

The pay was also poor. From 1789 to 1819, Chief Justices were paid just $4,000 and Associate Justices $3,500 annually. Top lawyers like Daniel Webster made over $20,000 per year. In order to make ends meet, some of the Justices continued to pursue private employment and business interests while on the Court, and some even continued to give legal advice. The difficult conditions, low pay, and low prestige all contributed to a high turnover rate on the Court. Many of the most eminent potential candidates, such as Patrick Henry, refused to serve at all.[10]

With most of their time and energy invested elsewhere, the Justices' Supreme Court duties were not always their highest priority. The Court barely existed as an institution. The Justices rarely saw each other. They met for a mere four to six weeks each year, and there was little time to establish any personal or institutional loyalties. In most respects, the Court was little more than an occasional gathering of itinerant circuit judges.

The Justices' isolation and autonomy were further reinforced when the first Chief Justice, John Jay, adopted the English practice of issuing seriatim opinions. Rather than delivering a collective decision of the Court, each Justice delivered an individual judgment explaining his personal views of each case. There was no need for the Justices to meet in conference to discuss and decide cases because there were no common opinions. The verdict was merely the sum of the individual judgments; it was left to the lawyers to count votes and look for common threads among the various opinions to determine what, if anything, had been decided.

Seriatim opinions were popular among judges, lawyers, and politicians. Judges preferred them because most of them had been trained in English law and were used to the peculiar rhythms of English justice. This was especially true of the first Federalist judges, including John Jay, John Blair, William Cushing, and William Paterson. They naturally preferred their old and familiar habits learned as colonial lawyers and judges, and they brought these practices with them to the new Supreme Court. William Cushing even continued to wear his traditional English horsehair judge's wig and the scarlet and ermine robes of the King's Court. The use of seriatim opinions also reflected the relative absence of partisan political competition and the virtually unchallenged political monopoly of the Federalists during the republic's first decade.[11]

---

9. As circuit judges, the Justices individually presided over trials involving serious crimes, copyright, patent, piracy, slave and Indian cases, civil lawsuits worth more than $500, and diversity cases. They also had limited appellate jurisdiction from the local district courts, often sitting with a local judge. White, *The Marshall Court and Cultural Change*, 161.

10. Ibid., 163.

11. Schmidhauser, *The Supreme Court*, 108. The English practice of issuing seriatim opinions is not as freewheeling as it sounds. The English judiciary has historically been drawn from a narrow and homoge-

Thomas Jefferson, the leader of the emerging opposition, favored the use of seriatim opinions as the style of judicial decision making best suited to democratic government. He thought that individual, independent judgments discouraged secret cabals, conspiracies, and the use of coercion to force judges to submit to the dominant will of the Court. That each Justice presented his own reasons and authorities in each case, Jefferson wrote, rightly required every judge to "throw himself in every case on God and his country; both will excuse him for error and value him for his honesty."[12]

Chief Justice Jay quickly grew discouraged with life on the Court, and he abruptly resigned in 1795. He found circuit riding intolerable and complained bitterly about the difficult travel, poor accommodations, bad food, and loneliness.

His successor, John Rutledge, had earlier served as an Associate Justice from 1790 to 1791 but resigned to become chief justice of South Carolina's Court of Common Pleas. After Jay's departure, President Washington summoned Rutledge to Philadelphia during the summer of 1795 and named him Chief Justice as a recess appointment.

Although Rutledge was appointed to the Supreme Court on two different occasions, he never managed to attend a single meeting of the full Court. When he was an Associate Justice, an attack of gout and a lack of court business kept Rutledge away from both sessions in 1790, and he resigned early the following year. After becoming Chief Justice in 1795, he sat for the Court's August Term, but there were so few cases that the full Court never met. When Congress reconvened in the fall, the Senate rejected Rutledge's appointment by a 14–10 vote, and he lost his seat. The Senate vote stemmed in part from Rutledge's opposition to the Jay Treaty, but it also reflected a growing suspicion among lawmakers that Rutledge was emotionally unstable. When Rutledge heard that his nomination had been rejected, he threw himself into Charleston Bay and tried to drown himself.[13] He

---

neous segment of society, which has allowed English judges to maintain a high degree of cohesion and uniformity despite the use of independent individual judgments. Greater social and intellectual diversity among American judges has resulted in relatively high rates of dissent in the United States, despite the use of institutional procedures—such as the conference—designed to encourage greater collaboration and consensus.

12. Schmidhauser, *The Supreme Court*, 107, citing a letter from Thomas Jefferson to William Johnson, March 4, 1823, Paul Leicester Ford, ed., 7 *Jefferson's Works*, 276. As Professor Michael Klarman rightly observes, however, there is no documentary evidence that Jefferson actively supported the use of seriatim opinions until after 1800. This might indicate that Jefferson's attachment to seriatim opinions had less to do with longstanding principle than with his personal enmity toward Marshall. Letter from Michael Klarman to the author, January 12, 1999.

13. Rutledge had previously tried to drown himself while returning home from Georgia in November after completing his circuit riding duties. At that time, his family placed him under observation, but they were not able to prevent his second suicide attempt. Professor James Haw claims that Rutledge likely had not yet heard about his rejection when he threw himself into Charleston Bay for a second time, on December 26 or 27. The Senate vote took place on December 15, 1795, while Rutledge mailed a letter resigning his seat on December 28, after his suicide attempt. Haw plausibly argues that Rutledge would not have bothered to submit his resignation had he known of the Senate vote. Gerber, *Seriatim*, 88.

was saved by two passing slaves, but to little effect. Rutledge died miserably in 1800, deeply in debt and alone, without leaving any positive imprint on the Court.[14]

Rutledge's successor was Oliver Ellsworth. He was best known as the architect of the Connecticut Compromise at the constitutional convention, which established the bicameral Congress. Like Jay, Ellsworth was a dedicated acolyte of the English common law. Continuing the tradition of rapid turnover and instability, Ellsworth served only four years as Chief Justice, 1796–1800. He was ill and spent most of his time abroad, participating in fewer than a dozen insignificant cases.[15]

Consistent with his harmonizing role at the Constitutional Convention, Ellsworth earned a reputation during his brief time on the Court as a skillful mediator and consensus builder. The Court became more deeply involved in political controversies, especially in the Justices' often blatantly partisan enforcement of the Alien and Sedition Acts. Several of the Justices tried to browbeat juries with their personal views during sedition trials while sitting as circuit judges. The Justices also became more determined in their efforts to establish a federal common law.[16]

The Justices continued to deliver seriatim opinions. Ellsworth personally favored collective per curiam opinions, which he thought better reflected the general will of the Court.[17] But while the Court issued a few per curiam opinions during Ellsworth's tenure, seriatim opinions continued to be the rule, so there was still no need for formal consultations among the Justices.

JOHN MARSHALL AND THE RISE OF THE CONFERENCE
(1801–1835)

When Oliver Ellsworth retired in 1800, John Adams again turned to his close friend John Jay, nominating him to serve a second term as Chief Justice. The Senate quickly and overwhelmingly confirmed him. The only problem was that no one had bothered to consult Jay about the appointment. He refused to serve, noting that all of his previous efforts "to place the Judicial Department on a proper footing have proved fruitless." The Supreme Court, he complained, was "so defective" that it could not possibly hope "to

---

14. Other Justices had personal problems that further bruised the young Court's tender reputation. James Wilson was an unsuccessful land speculator who died broke in a seedy North Carolina boarding-house, while Samuel Chase was habitually near bankruptcy due to a series of ill-advised land speculation schemes.

15. Cushman, *The Supreme Court Justices*, 49.

16. Schmidhauser, *The Supreme Court*, 108. Federalist judges, including Supreme Court Justices, often used jury instructions as a bully pulpit to "educate" the public on Federalist political principles and to justify the Alien and Sedition Acts. Haskins and Johnson, *Foundations of Power*, 140.

17. There is some evidence that *Brown v. Barry*, 3 U.S. (3 Dall.) 365 (1797), was not delivered seriatim but as "the opinion of the Court." Miller and Sastri, "Secrecy and the Supreme Court," 808.

acquire the public confidence and respect."[18] Adams was forced to turn to his second choice, his forty-five-year-old secretary of state, John Marshall.[19]

Marshall had no prior judicial experience, but he was a seasoned politician who understood the nature of political power. Once confirmed, he moved quickly and decisively to end the use of seriatim opinions, limit the autonomy of Associate Justices, and concentrate new powers in the office of the Chief Justice. Marshall in effect established a new Supreme Court. Rather than speaking with six individual voices seriatim, the new Court spoke with one voice—Marshall's.

Marshall announced the Court's decision in every case during his first five years on the bench, except for a few instances where he recused himself due to conflicts of interest.[20] Over the next seven years, Marshall announced the Court's decision in 130 cases, while the other Justices combined announced just thirty decisions.[21] The other Justices participated more in Marshall's later years; overall, Marshall delivered 519 of 1,215 total judgments.[22]

Most of the great constitutional cases of the Marshall era dealt either with federalism or separation of powers. In the former category of cases, the Court was strongly nationalistic and helped to centralize power in the hands of the national government. In the latter category, the Court sought to allocate political power among the three branches of government and to define the Supreme Court's role in the emerging federal system. These cases were especially perilous, because they invariably brought the Court into potential conflict with the other two branches of government.

As a rule, Marshall sought to expand the Court's authority without risking unnecessary confrontations with the president or Congress. In his battles with the Jeffersonians,

---

18. Cushman, *The Supreme Court Justices*, 4.

19. Marshall served simultaneously as secretary of state and Chief Justice for one month, from February 3 to March 3, 1800.

20. In one of the cases in which Marshall recused himself, *Martin v. Hunter's Lessee*, 14 U.S. (1 Wheat.) 304 (1816), the Chief Justice quietly intervened behind the scenes to make sure that the case made it to the Supreme Court. Marshall, who had a direct financial stake in the outcome of the case, participated secretly as a legal adviser for petitioner Denny Martin. White, *The Marshall Court and Cultural Change*, 168–74.

21. Haines, *The Role of the Supreme Court*, 226, 630. Most of the cases Marshall did not deliver were issued per curiam; only 9 percent of the Court's decisions were delivered by other Justices. Haskins and Johnson, *Foundations of Power*, 380.

22. Roper, "Judicial Unanimity and the Marshall Court," 119. Of the cases Marshall announced, it is impossible to know what percentage he actually wrote. While modern practice is that the Justice who writes the opinion also announces it, different procedures were followed in Marshall's day. For one thing, opinion writing was a collaborative process rather than an individual effort. Second, while Justices signed concurring and dissenting opinions, the majority opinion went unsigned because it was considered to be the opinion of the Court rather than of a particular Justice. During Marshall's first decade on the Court, the senior presiding Justice almost invariably announced the Court's decision in each case; but there is no reason to think that he was also expected to write each opinion. After 1814, seniority ceased to be the best predictor of who delivered the Court's opinions, and the prerogatives of authorship might have grown more important. Haskins and Johnson, *Foundations of Power*, 386–87.

Marshall proved to be a clever political strategist, often absorbing tactical losses in order to secure long-term advantages for the Court. The most famous of these maneuvers was *Marbury v. Madison*.[23]

William Marbury was one of the "midnight judges" appointed to newly created judicial posts created by the lame duck Federalist Congress following Jefferson's election in 1800. As secretary of state under outgoing President John Adams, Marshall himself was responsible for delivering the new judicial commissions before Jefferson took office. He delegated the task to his brother James, who carelessly failed to deliver Marbury's commission before Jefferson's innauguration on May 4, 1801. President Jefferson immediately ordered his new secretary of state, James Madison, to withhold Marbury's commission. Marbury responded by filing a lawsuit directly with the Supreme Court. He was permitted to do this under the Judiciary Act of 1801, which expanded the Court's original jurisdiction to hear such cases as a court of first resort.

The case placed Marshall in a politically untenable position. He not only refused to recuse himself from a case in which he had an obvious conflict of interest, but he also knew that if he ordered the administration to deliver Marbury's commission, Jefferson would almost certainly refuse and the Court would risk becoming a laughingstock. As Warren Burger later observed, the young Supreme Court might have been able to withstand hard blows, but not ridicule.[24] Marshall decided to accept defeat in this case but managed to turn the situation to the Court's advantage in the long term. Jefferson won the case and Marbury never received his commission. Technically, the Justices dismissed the case for want of jurisdiction and did not decide Marbury's claim on the merits. The case had to be dismissed, Marshall explained, because Congress had acted unconstitutionally in expanding the Court's original jurisdiction beyond the specific cases enumerated in Article 3.

Marshall conceded the day to Jefferson but claimed for the Court a more precious prize—the right to review the constitutional propriety of legislative and executive actions. He also managed to pillory Jefferson in print for "illegally" refusing to deliver Marbury's commission, while avoiding the folly of actually ordering Jefferson to do anything about it.

Marshall proved more judicious and circumspect than his enemies expected. Having claimed the right to review federal legislation, the Marshall Court never exercised the power again. More than fifty years passed before the Supreme Court, under Roger Brooke Taney, exercised the power of judicial review for the second time—disastrously—in *Dred Scott v. Sandford*.[25]

---

23. *Marbury v. Madison*, 5 U.S. (1 Cr.) 137 (1803).
24. Burger, "The Doctrine of Judicial Review," in Cannon and O'Brien, *Views from the Bench*, 14.
25. *Dred Scott v. Sandford*, 60 U.S. (19 How.) 393 (1857).

The Supreme Court did not escape from *Marbury v. Madison* unscathed. The Jeffersonians moved quickly to repeal the Judiciary Act of 1801, which had greatly expanded the size and power of the federal judiciary. The Justices were divided as to how to respond to what they saw as an offensive and punitive political attack. Most importantly, the act had promised to end the hated practice of circuit riding. Sixteen new circuit judges had already been appointed to relieve the Justices of this burdensome task. When the act was repealed, the newly appointed circuit judges were sacked and the Justices' circuit riding duties restored.[26]

A secret caucus of Federalist leaders met with the Justices and encouraged them to refuse to perform their circuit riding duties. Samuel Chase agreed and pushed for a boycott. He thought that requiring Supreme Court Justices to ride circuit was insulting, if not unconstitutional, and he believed that Jefferson's dismissal of the newly appointed circuit judges was clearly unconstitutional. But Bushrod Washington vigorously disagreed and argued that the Justices' circuit duties were well established and should be continued. Marshall polled the conference by mail, and when a majority of the Justices backed Washington, Marshall convinced Chase to concede the point. The Justices continued to ride circuit until Congress ended the practice in 1891.

In contrast to the Marshall Court's delicate treatment of federal judicial review, the Justices routinely reviewed *state* laws to determine whether they were constitutional. In a landmark series of cases, the Court confidently asserted federal and judicial supremacy over state governments, firmly and repeatedly establishing the principle that the national government had supervisory power over the states and would have the last word in disputes involving two states, a state and the federal government, or a state and a foreign government.[27]

States' rights advocates, led by Spencer Roane of Virginia, claimed that the principle of state sovereignty meant that federal courts had no right to be the final arbiter of the constitutional limits of either state or federal laws, and above all could not have the final say in determining or delimiting state constitutional powers. Marshall personally led the opposition to Roane's advocacy of state sovereignty and states' rights.

The Marshall Court vigorously rejected Roane's theory of dual sovereignty—the idea that the national government and state governments were each supreme within their own

---

26. In 1802, Congress reorganized the federal judiciary and established six circuits, with a Justice assigned to each circuit. As westward expansion added more national territory, new circuits were created and new Supreme Court Justices were initially added at the same rate. Haskin and Johnson, *Foundations of Power*, 376.

27. *United States v. Peters*, 9 U.S. (5 Cr.) 115 (1809); *Fletcher v. Peck*, 10 U.S. (6 Cr.) 87 (1810); *Martin v. Hunter's Lessee*, 14 U.S. (1 Wheat.) 304 (1816); *McCulloch v. Maryland*, 17 U.S. (4 Wheat.) 315 (1819); *Cohens v. Virginia*, 19 U.S. (6 Wheat.) 264 (1821); *Osborn v. Bank of the United States*, 22 U.S. (9 Wheat.) 738 (1824); *Gibbons v. Ogden*, 22 U.S. (9 Wheat.) 1 (1824).

separate and exclusive spheres of responsibility—and established that national supremacy was limited only by the terms of the Constitution. Because the Constitution was created by an act of a sovereign people rather than by sovereign states, the national government held sovereign power in trust under the rules and limits established by the Constitution.

McCulloch v. Maryland helped to expand federal power by recognizing a broad grant of congressional authority under the doctrine of implied powers and the necessary and proper clause. Congress, Marshall wrote, was not limited to the powers specifically enumerated in the Constitution but was free to draw on a broad range of implied powers as needed to exercise its constitutional responsibilities. Marshall's theory of implied powers relied on what amounted to "penumbras and emanations" from Congress's enumerated powers.[28]

The scope and breadth of Marshall's doctrinal innovations were matched only by his revolutionary impact on the private life of the Supreme Court. Marshall inherited a feeble and ineffective institution, and from such unpromising beginnings shaped a respected, authoritative, and truly co-equal branch of government. His first priority for the Court, aside from concentrating authority in the office of Chief Justice, was to create a new sense of cooperation among the Justices.

Marshall arranged for all six men (seven after 1807) to live together in the same boardinghouse or inn whenever the Court was in session. By living, dining, socializing, and working together, Marshall nurtured group loyalties among the Justices. Their communal lifestyle was reminiscent of the old English Inns of Court, where barristers lived and dined together near London's law and chancery courts. It was from this intensive social and professional interaction that the Supreme Court conference was born.

In 1801, Marshall arranged for the Justices to live together at Conrad and McMunn's boardinghouse on Capitol Hill. Rooms cost $15 per week, including firewood, candles, and liquor. In subsequent years, the Justices roomed together at a number of other Washington boardinghouses and residential hotels.[29] No wives, children, or other family distractions intruded on the Justices' collective lifestyle. The Justices took their meals together, sitting at a single table with the other boarders, discussing cases, and gossiping. Joseph Story was struck by this new camaraderie:

> The Judges here live with perfect harmony, and as agreeably as absence from friends
> and from families could make our residence. Our intercourse is perfectly familiar and

---

28. Marshall's theory later served as a model for William O. Douglas's equally creative and expansive theory of privacy, articulated in *Griswold v. Connecticut* more than 145 years later. *Griswold v. Connecticut*, 381 U.S. 479 (1965).

29. Beveridge, 3 *The Life of John Marshall*, 7. Another nearby boardinghouse, the Indian Queen, charged $1.50 per day, including brandy and whiskey.

unconstrained, and our social hours when undisturbed with the labors of law, are passed in gay and frank conversation, which at once enlivens and instructs.

Marshall feared that if the Justices were allowed to scatter and resume their independent lives, they would quickly return to writing seriatim opinions, and he was determined to prevent that.[30]

The social habits created by living together, combined with the Justices' isolation from families, friends, and Washington society, helped to forge a cohesive group identity. The Justices became a family of sorts, with Marshall as the patriarch. They were driven together not only by their common lives and work, but by their common suffering in the grim conditions of the nation's capital—a town that Daniel Webster scornfully dismissed as "this dismal place."[31]

In jettisoning seriatim opinions in favor of a single collective judgment of the Court, Marshall followed a uniquely American legal tradition of adopting radical English reforms that were first proposed in, and emphatically rejected by, that country.[32] As Jefferson reported, Lord Mansfield first sought to introduce to the English bench the habit of caucusing opinions in conference:

> The judges met at their chambers, or elsewhere, secluded from the presence of the public, and made up what was to be delivered as the opinion of the court. On the retirement of Mansfield, Lord Kenyon put an end to the practice, and the judges returned to that of seriatim opinions, and practice it habitually to this day.[33]

According to Jefferson, Judge Pendleton, the head of the Virginia Court of Appeals, admired Lord Mansfield and introduced to America "the practice of making up opinions in secret and delivering them as the Oracles of the court, in mass." Pendleton's fellow Virginian, John Marshall, carried these ideas to Washington.[34]

Marshall sought to create a Supreme Court that reached its decisions neither by seriatim voting nor by majority rule but by consensus. He knew that only resolute unity would allow the Court to remain an effective instrument of moderate Federalism and

---

30. Schmidhauser, *The Supreme Court*, 112, quoting a letter from John Marshall to Joseph Story, May 3, 1831. Marshall had some help in arranging the Justices' living arrangements. In 1814, Marshall passed responsibility for finding accommodations to Bushrod Washington. Letter from John Marshall to Bushrod Washington, December 29, 1814, *The Papers of John Marshall*, 63.
31. Beveridge, 4 *The Life of John Marshall*, 86.
32. In *Marbury v. Madison*, 5 U.S. (1 Cr.) 137 (1803), Marshall adopted Coke's theory of judicial review, which Coke had advocated in *Dr. Bonham's Case*, 77 Eng. Rep. 638, 652 (C.P. 1610). England emphatically rejected Coke's doctrine of judicial review, but Hamilton, Madison, Marshall, and other American legal elites embraced Coke. Another example of this phenomenon is William Blackstone, whose *Commentaries* have always been far more warmly received in the United States than in England.
33. Schmidhauser, *The Supreme Court*, 107, quoting Jefferson.
34. Ibid.

enable the Justices to withstand the anticipated Jeffersonian onslaught. Marshall used his position as Chief Justice to institutionalize his preferences:

> The opinion, which is to be delivered as the opinion of the court, is previously submitted to the consideration of all the judges; and, if any part of the reasoning be disapproved, it must be so modified as to receive the approbation of all, before it can be delivered as the opinion of all.[35]

The Justices met in almost continual conference when the Court was in session. They discussed cases informally over meals and afterward held formal consultations in private boardinghouse rooms six days a week, and perhaps met occasionally in the Capitol as well.[36]

The Court convened in various rooms inside the Capitol from 1801 until the modern Supreme Court building opened in 1935. It is not clear whether the Justices had a separate conference room in the Capitol building during the Marshall era. Joseph Story referred to a conference room in his 1835 eulogy of John Marshall, and Albert Beveridge claimed that the Marshall Court had a consultation room and a regularly scheduled consultation day. But there is little specific evidence as to whether the Justices' consultation room was in the Capitol or "uptown" where the Justices lived.

There are several reasons to doubt whether the Justices had a conference room in the Capitol building. Congress controlled all of the facilities in the Capitol building, and for the most part treated the Supreme Court rather shabbily. The Justices had no staff, offices, judicial chambers, or library inside the Capitol building, so there is no reason to assume that they had a consultation room there.[37]

Even if Congress did provide a consultation room in the Capitol, it is doubtful that the Justices would have used it on a regular basis. What little space Congress provided for the Court amounted to a few dismal rooms on the first floor, and later in the basement. The rooms changed from year to year, but they were invariably dark, damp, stuffy, hot in summer, and cold in winter. The Justices would have had little reason to leave their boardinghouses to work in such unpleasant conditions, except as necessary to hear oral arguments and announce their decisions. It is likely that most, if not all, of their consultations were held at or near where the Justices lived.[38]

---

35. O'Brien, *Storm Center*, 108.

36. In turning down a dining invitation from John Randolph, Marshall wrote, "I cannot absent myself from our daily consultation without interrupting the course of the business and arresting its progress." He explained that Sunday was the only day of the week that the Justices did not meet in conference. Letter from John Marshall to John Randolph, March 4, 1816, *The Papers of John Marshall*, 127.

37. The Court did not obtain library space in the Capitol building until 1843. Swisher, *Taney*, 11.

38. White, *The Marshall Court and Cultural Change*, 160. The Marshall Court initially met on the first floor of the Capitol building and was later relegated to a series of rooms in the basement. Although the rooms were subject to change, gloominess was a constant. Their quarters were described by contemporaries as an "artificial cave" and "a grim catacomb." Swisher, *Taney*, 11. Inclement weather drove the Justices

Having the Justices live together made it more difficult for individual Justices to disrupt the harmony of the group or oppose the general will. This *boardinghouse mentality* encouraged consensus, or at least discouraged public dissent. Marshall hated open disagreements, and he took advantage of every opportunity to encourage cooperation and compromise. Concurring and dissenting opinions were actively discouraged, and this new group identity was reinforced by the use of collective, anonymous decisions delivered by the Chief Justice, acting in his capacity as the senior judge.

Marshall was aided in his efforts by the broad ideological agreement among the Justices, which lasted throughout most of his tenure. With the Jeffersonians in control of the every department of government except the judiciary, the Federalist Justices circled the wagons, and the formerly rapid turnover rate that had characterized the Court until 1800 slowed dramatically. Jefferson did not get his first appointment until 1804, when he nominated William Johnson to replace Alfred Moore.

Until 1812, the presiding Justice almost invariably announced the opinion of the Court, whether or not he wrote the opinion. Other Justices had the option to announce their own views, but for the most part they declined to make their private disagreements public. With only one opinion announced as the judgment of the Court, there was no way to tell whether the absence of *announced* concurring or dissenting opinions meant that the Justices were in complete agreement, or whether disagreements were registered in conference but not publicly recorded.

There was general agreement among the Justices that public dissents were to be avoided if at all possible. In 1818, Joseph Story wrote a letter to Henry Wheaton explaining that "the habit of delivering dissenting opinions on ordinary cases weakens the authority of the Court, and is of no public benefit." There were occasions, Story revealed in a second letter to Wheaton, that the majority of the Court disagreed with at least part of Marshall's opinions but did not record their dissents because their disagreements were not crucial to the case.[39]

The culture that Marshall built was one where consensus ruled whenever possible, and all public divisions, doubts, and disagreements were suppressed whenever neces-

---

out of their quarters during the February 1809 term, and the Court convened in Long's Tavern. In 1810, the Court moved into its new "permanent" home in the basement, directly underneath the Senate's original chamber. After the British sacked the Capitol in August 1814, the Court met at the home of Clerk of Court Elias B. Caldwell, 1814–17. This building later became the Bell Tavern. In 1817, a temporary courtroom was installed in an especially dark and unpleasant room in the undamaged north wing of the Capitol. In 1819, the Court was again assigned "permanent" rooms in the basement, although the arrangements changed somewhat from year to year until the Court finally moved upstairs into the Senate's original chamber in 1860.

39. White, *The Marshall Court and Cultural Change*, 187.

sary. If the Justices could not all agree in the privacy of the conference room, then they settled for the appearance of unanimity in the courtroom. Justices routinely swallowed their desire to dissent and acquiesced to decisions with which they personally disagreed. Marshall himself often compromised his own views to accommodate others. On several occasions he wrote and delivered decisions with which he did not fully agree, or which were either significantly narrower or broader than he wanted.[40] During his thirty-four years on the Court, Marshall dissented only eight times, and just once in a constitutional case.

In one of his rare dissents, *Bank of the United States v. Dandridge*, Marshall wrote that whenever he had the "misfortune" to differ from the Court, his usual practice was to acquiesce silently to the Court's opinion. He felt compelled to dissent in this case, he explained, only because the lower court's decision "gave general surprise to the profession, and was generally condemned."[41]

The Justices' boardinghouse mentality proved unusually seductive and durable. After waiting four years for his first Supreme Court appointment, Jefferson selected one of his most trusted lieutenants, William Johnson, to disrupt the cozy Federalist collective that haunted Jefferson's dreams. A former state judge from South Carolina, Johnson was used to writing seriatim opinions and was a staunch Jeffersonian. He was used to speaking his mind from the bench, and his views clashed with Marshall's in several important respects. Jefferson was flabbergasted when Johnson took his place on the Supreme Court and virtually disappeared. Johnson dissented at about the same rate as everyone else—hardly ever. A distressed Jefferson wrote Johnson to ask why he remained silent. Johnson replied:

> [After my appointment] some case soon occurred in which I disagreed from my brethren and I thought it a thing of course to deliver my opinion. But, during the rest of the session I heard nothing but lectures on the indecency of judges cutting at each other, and the loss of reputation which the Virginia appellate court had sustained by pursuing such a course, etc. At length I found that I must either submit . . . or become a cypher in our consultations as to effect no good at all. I therefore bent to the current.[42]

Much the same thing happened with Jefferson's next two appointees. H. Brockholst Livingston and Thomas Todd were appointed with the hope that they would assert their

---

40. Smith, *John Marshall*, 378–79; Roper, "Judicial Unanimity and the Marshall Court," 127–30.

41. *Bank of the United States v. Dandridge*, 25 U.S. (12 Wheat.) 64, 90 (1827).

42. Letter from William Johnson to Thomas Jefferson, December 10, 1822, quoted in White, *The Marshall Court and Cultural Change*, 189.

independence of Marshall's leadership. Instead, they were quickly socialized and assimilated.[43]

Nothing much changed when James Madison succeeded Jefferson as president. When Chase and Cushing died within months of each other, they were replaced in 1811 by two Madison appointees, Gabriel Duvall and Joseph Story. For the first time, the Jeffersonians controlled a majority of seats on the Court, with the number of Federalists on the Court reduced to just two of seven. Yet Marshall continued to preside over the Court much the same as before, as though nothing had changed.

There are no known records of Marshall's conferences. Few significant historical records about conferences during this period survive, aside from a handful of recollections and memoirs written by some of the parties involved. Cases were discussed informally and decided orally, without any exchange of memoranda or draft opinions, meaning that there is little documentary evidence of the Justices' deliberations. From contemporary accounts, it appears that conferences commenced every evening after dinner and ended around 8:00 P.M., although at least occasionally these discussions continued past midnight.[44]

The Justices' consultations were lubricated by the Court's private stock of vintage madeira. Marshall had several cases of wine shipped to Washington each term in special bottles labeled "The Supreme Court."[45] Marshall's closest ally on the Court, Joseph Story, wrote to his wife about the Justices' drinking habits in conference:

> We are great ascetics, and even deny ourselves wine except in wet weather, but it does sometimes happen that the Chief Justice will say to me, when the cloth is removed, "Brother Story, step up to the window and see if it does not look like rain." And if I tell him that the sun is shining brightly, Judge Marshall will sometimes reply, "Our jurisdiction extends over so large a territory that the doctrine of chances makes it certain that it must be raining somewhere."[46]

In a letter to Samuel P. Fay on January 24, 1812, Story called the Court's conference discussions freewheeling and a "pleasant and animated interchange of legal acumen."[47]

---

43. In his sixteen years on the Court, Livingston delivered just four dissenting opinions, and in nineteen years Todd delivered only one dissenting opinion. Todd's sole dissent was his first opinion as a Justice—a brief, five-line dissent in an unimportant land title case. Roper, "Judicial Unanimity and the Marshall Court," 122.

44. Smith, *John Marshall*, 642. As evidence, Smith cites a letter from a contemporary portrait artist who scheduled a sitting with Marshall after the Court's consultations ended at 8:00 P.M. As Smith readily admits, such scant evidence is hardly definitive. From other accounts, it appears likely that the conference often adjourned later than 8:00 P.M.

45. Warren, *A History of the Supreme Court*, 791.

46. Beveridge, 4 *The Life of John Marshall*, 87–88.

47. Newmeyer, *Supreme Court Justice Joseph Story*, 78.

I find myself considerably more at ease than I expected. My brethren are very interesting men, with whom I live in the most frank and unaffected intimacy. Indeed we are all united as one, with a mutual esteem which makes even the labors of jurisprudence light. . . . We moot every question as we proceed, and by familiar conferences at our lodgings often come to a very quick, and I trust, a very accurate opinion, in a few hours.[48]

In 1835, Story had this to say about Marshall's conference leadership:

[H]e excelled in the statement of a case; so much so, that it was almost of itself an argument. If it did not at once lead the hearer to the proper conclusion, it prepared him to assent to it, as soon as it was announced. Nay, more; it persuaded him, that it must be right, however repugnant it might be to his preconceived notions. . . . He would by the most subtle analysis resolve every argument into its ultimate principles, and then with a marvelous facility apply them to the decision of the cause.[49]

The pace of decision making was rapid by modern standards. Even major cases were usually announced within a few days of oral arguments; *McCulloch v. Maryland*, for example, was announced just three days after the end of oral arguments.

This was partly because of the Court's habit of conducting running conferences. Cases were discussed at the Justices' boardinghouses even as they were being argued. The Justices likely did not disagree with each other less than they do today, but they put much more effort into the process of reaching a common judgment, and this meant continuous discussions and negotiations even as the cases progressed.

Oral arguments had no time limits then, and advocates often argued for several days. These presentations tended to be oratorical rather than Socratic, and Justices used part of the time to contemplate their decisions.[50] As John Marshall explained, "The acme of judicial distinction means the ability to look a lawyer straight in the eyes for two hours and not hear a damned word he says."[51]

Marshall was not what one might expect from a conventional "great" leader. He was reserved and businesslike, with an even temper. He was a relentless compromiser, quiet and awkward with strangers but talkative and animated among friends. He was good natured and unpretentious, and he enjoyed jokes and stories. His laugh, Story said, was much too hearty for an intriguer.[52] Marshall disliked open conflict and sought to remain on cordial terms with his political opponents, save for Jefferson. For his part, Jefferson dismissed all offered proofs of Marshall's good character as "profound hypocrisy."[53]

48. Warren, *A History of the Supreme Court*, 423–24.
49. Westin, *Autobiography of the Supreme Court*, 183.
50. White, *The Marshall Court and Cultural Change*, 181–82.
51. Beveridge, 4 *The Life of John Marshall*, 83.
52. Newmeyer, *Justice Joseph Story*, 76.
53. Smith, *John Marshall*, 394; Beveridge, 3 *The Life of John Marshall*, 60–62.

Marshall was not the most intelligent, clever, or learned man on the Court. He had no real academic training and lacked the intellectual reputation enjoyed by other Justices, especially the brilliant and scholarly Joseph Story. Yet the conference united under Marshall's leadership and became a far more cohesive and effective political force than it had ever been under Jay, Rutledge, or Ellsworth.

Marshall succeeded as Chief Justice by being modest, amiable, informal, and unassuming. He had simple tastes and he strongly preferred a casual style of dress. His clothes were described by a friend as "gotten from some antiquated slop-shop of second-hand raiment . . . the coat and breeches cut for nobody in particular."[54] He looked so ordinary that on a courtesy visit to a relative's house, his relative's wife mistook Marshall for a butcher and ordered her servant to take the Chief Justice to the stables to begin slaughtering their animals.[55]

On the bench, Marshall insisted that the Justices wear simple black robes. He rejected William Cushing's pleas to wear his horsehair wig and ermine robe. Marshall preferred a republican aesthetic, and Cushing complied with his wishes.[56]

Marshall had—and has—his critics. Several notable scholars have called Marshall's leadership style "dictatorial" and "antidemocratic."[57] Albert Beveridge remarked that while Marshall was generally amiable, he could be "hard and unpleasant" to anyone who opposed him.[58]

Among Marshall's contemporaries, Thomas Jefferson was his most famous and most formidable adversary. "How dexterously he can reconcile law to his personal biases," Jefferson observed. "The law is nothing more than an ambiguous text, to be explained by his sophistry into any meaning that may subserve his personal malice."[59] Marshall certainly invited controversy with his highly partisan behavior during Aaron Burr's trial and his interested participation in *Marbury v. Madison.*

Jefferson rightly blamed Marshall for forcing the Court to abandon the use of seriatim opinions, and perhaps less rightly viewed the Justices' conferences as the worst sort of corrupt, back-room politics.[60] Jefferson complained that under Marshall the Justices conspired to decide cases while "huddled up in conclave, perhaps by a majority of one, delivered as if unanimous, and with the silent acquiescence of lazy or timid associates, by a crafty chief judge, who sophisticates the law to his mind by the turn of his own rea-

---

54. Beveridge, 4 *The Life of John Marshall,* 91.
55. Beveridge, 3 *The Life of John Marshall,* 60–62.
56. Smith, *John Marshall,* 285–86.
57. Haines, Charles, *The Role of the Supreme Court,* 628, 630.
58. O'Brien, *Storm Center,* 108.
59. Warren, *History of the Supreme Court,* 401.
60. Schmidhauser, *The Supreme Court,* 106–7, citing an 1822 letter from Jefferson to Justice William Johnson.

soning."[61] The unanimity of the Marshall Court, in Jefferson's eyes, had to be coerced, illusory, dishonest, and undemocratic. At best, for the Justices to issue a single, "unanimous" judgment of the Court encouraged judicial irresponsibility and sloth, and allowed the judges to hide from public accountability for their actions.[62]

As more Democratic-Republicans were appointed to the high court, Jefferson was at a loss to understand how Marshall could continue to command the Court as though nothing had changed, unless he was doing it dishonestly. William Johnson initially echoed Jefferson's view that Marshall dominated the other Justices:

> Cushing was incompetent, Chase could not be got to think or write—Patterson [*sic*] was a slow man and willingly declined the trouble, and the other two judges [Marshall and Washington] you know are commonly estimated as one judge.[63]

However, John Schmidhauser's careful analysis of Marshall's correspondence with the other Justices demonstrated that the fundamental changes Marshall enacted were not imposed through intimidation or intrigue, or aided by the other Justices' laziness or incompetence. These reforms were adopted with the voluntary and knowing consent of the other Justices.

Whatever his flaws, Marshall was not the backroom bully that Jefferson made him out to be. He could not possibly have succeeded as Chief Justice for so long had he been so. The Marshall Court was at heart a cooperative, collaborative, and collegial institution. New procedures were adopted by consensus and put into effect for a common purpose—to build the reputation of the Court as *the* source of reliable, predictable, and definitive final judgments in legal and constitutional matters.[64]

William Johnson, though a great disappointment to Jefferson, successfully challenged Marshall's leadership in one respect. He helped to break Marshall's monopoly in delivering opinions. At Johnson's insistence, the Chief Justice began to appoint other Justices to deliver a growing number of majority opinions. Moreover, Marshall agreed that each Justice would be free to record concurring or dissenting opinions at their sole discretion. This great procedural compromise between the Jeffersonians' attachment to seriatim opinions and Marshall's preference that the Court speak with one voice marked the beginning of the modern Supreme Court.

Marshall pushed hard for unanimity in every case. There were strong individual and group pressures to compromise and to submit to the general will. But there was already

61. Hughes, *The Supreme Court*, 64–65, quoting a letter from Jefferson to Thomas Ritchie, December 25, 1820, in Ford, 7 *Works of Thomas Jefferson*, 191.
62. Smith, *John Marshall*, 456.
63. Schmidhauser, *The Supreme Court*, 110.
64. Schmidhauser, *The Supreme Court*, 110–111; see also Haskins and Johnson, *Foundations of Power*, 85.

a natural consensus among the Justices on most of the important constitutional issues. They were all strong nationalists who agreed on the crucial issues of federalism and the need for a strong judiciary. They also accepted the need for an integrated national economy and favored a broad reading of the commerce clause.

The Justices were equally united in their defense of property rights. They sought to encourage trade and economic growth by limiting government power and by placing vested private property and economic rights beyond the reach of government. This was accomplished through a broad reading of the contracts clause that limited state governments' powers to regulate private corporations.[65] However, the Marshall Court recognized the primary authority of state governments to establish, define, and protect their citizens' civil rights. This led the Court to rule, for example, that the Bill of Rights applied only to the federal government and did not bind the states.[66]

While many consider William Johnson to be the first great dissenter on the Court, he was in close agreement with the other Justices on virtually all of the major constitutional issues of the day. The only Justice to challenge the Marshall Court's broad constitutional consensus was John McLean, a later Jackson appointee.[67] Even when the Justices disagreed among themselves, however, they all agreed that dissents threatened to undermine their authority and were disinclined to dissent without a compelling reason.[68]

The cohesiveness of the Marshall Court is striking by modern standards. Between 1800 and 1807, the Court decided sixty-seven cases with only one dissenting opinion—a case dissent rate of just 1.5 percent. During the last five years of Marshall's tenure, all of his fellow Federalists were either dead or retired, and the Court was dominated by judges appointed by Jefferson, Madison, and Jackson. Yet while the dissent rate jumped significantly, Marshall held the Court together to a remarkable degree, considering the profound political transformation taking place around him. Between 1830 and 1835 there were twenty-six dissenting opinions scattered among 276 cases, for a case dissent rate of 9.4 percent—high compared to Marshall's prime years on the Court but quite modest by later standards. For Marshall's career, from 1800 to 1835, the Court had an overall case dissent rate of 6.5 percent.[69]

The growing strength of Democratic-Republicans and Jacksonian Democrats on the Court after 1811 was not the only reason for the sudden spike in the dissent rate after 1830.

---

65. *Dartmouth College v. Woodward*, 17 U.S. (4 Wheat.) 517 (1819).

66. *Barron v. Baltimore*, 32 U.S. (7 Pet.) 243 (1833).

67. Haines, *The Role of the Supreme Court*, 630.

68. The area of greatest disagreement on the Court was in admiralty and maritime cases. Marshall and the Federalists favored limiting American admiralty powers to coastal waters except in wartime prize cases, while the Jeffersonians favored sweeping national power to enforce American trade laws and interests on the high seas. Haskins and Johnson, *Foundations of Power*, 387.

69. Data compiled from Epstein, *The Supreme Court Compendium*, 195.

In 1830, Marshall was compelled to attend Virginia's state constitutional convention, and he could not travel to Washington before the start of the term as he usually did to arrange the Justices' housing. It was inauspicious timing. There were two new Justices on the Court that year, John McLean and Henry Baldwin, and Marshall was not available to socialize them about the habits and expectations of the Court. When Marshall finally arrived in Washington on January 20, he found to his dismay that the other Justices had already scattered across town. It was the first time in twenty-nine years that the Justices did not all live together. Even worse, in Marshall's eyes, some of the Justices brought their wives and families. With their monastic life disrupted, Marshall complained in a letter to his wife, Polly, "We cannot carry on our business as fast as usual."[70] Dissents were up sharply that year, with each Justice dissenting at least once and Johnson filing dissenting opinions in three cases.

The following year the Justices were together again at Brown's Indian Queen Hotel, but they were not all happy. Henry Baldwin complained about the expense and began to grow hostile toward the other Justices. No one knew it at the time, but he was suffering from the early stages of mental illness. Baldwin had a nervous breakdown in 1833 and missed the entire term. Marshall worried that the brethren would begin to live apart permanently, and "if the Judges scatter *ad libium*, the docket I fear will remain quite compact, losing [resolving] very few causes; and the few it may lose, will probably be carried off by seriatim opinions."[71]

In 1832, five of the seven Justices, including Henry Baldwin, moved into the home of Tench Ringold, the marshal of the District of Columbia. McLean chose to live apart with his family, and William Johnson also planned to live elsewhere but fell ill and missed the entire term. Matters improved temporarily in 1834, when all of the Justices lived together. Lawyer Charles Sumner described the life of the conference that year:

> All the Judges board together, having rooms in the same house and taking their meals from the same table, except Judge McLean, whose wife is with him, and who consequently has a separate table, though in the same house. . . . Judge Duvall is 82 years old and is so deaf as to be unable to participate in conversation.[72]

By degrees, Marshall lost control of the Court as new appointments replaced his old friends and allies and as Marshall himself grew older and less vigorous. In 1834, the Court had to postpone several important cases when Marshall could not build a consensus.[73]

In 1835, Andrew Jackson nominated Roger Brooke Taney to replace Associate Justice Duvall. The Senate voted to postpone consideration of Taney's nomination, effec-

70. Smith, *John Marshall*, 507.
71. Ibid., 510–11.
72. Warren, *A History of the Supreme Court*, 792.
73. Haines, *The Role of the Supreme Court*, 610.

tively killing his appointment. But then John Marshall suddenly died on July 6, 1835, and Jackson resubmitted Taney's name to replace Marshall as Chief Justice. After a bitter debate, the Senate confirmed Taney's second nomination by a vote of 29–15.

ROGER BROOKE TANEY: MESS-STYLE JUSTICE (1835–1864)

Taney continued Marshall's legacy of defending the American trinity of individual liberty: private property, laissez-faire economics, and the sanctity of contracts. The Court's main task, as Taney understood it, was to interpret and enforce private contracts and property rights, but otherwise to interfere as little as possible in private business relationships. Under Taney, however, the Justices began to see the states, rather than the federal government, as the main engine of economic innovation and growth.

While the Marshall Court almost invariably sided with the national government in state-federal disputes, Taney sought to reposition the Court as a "disinterested arbiter" of state-federal relations—the umpire of federalism. The Taney Court recognized state autonomy in some areas while reinforcing federal supremacy in others. The notion of dual federalism became fashionable, and the Justices accepted that there were significant areas where states had exclusive authority. Taney himself believed that the task of separating the respective responsibilities of the two sovereigns was uniquely suited to the judicial branch. His approach to federalism was reflected most clearly in the doctrine of state police powers, which gave state governments primary—if not exclusive—authority to protect the health, safety, and morals of citizens.[74]

States became more active in establishing banks and corporations, using powers of eminent domain to condemn property for public purposes, and investing resources to build transportation systems and other infrastructure to spur economic development. This marked the beginning of a prolonged boom in state public works projects, with new roads, rivers, canals, and railroads being built at an unprecedented pace.

In tilting toward the states as the preferred mechanism of economic development, the Taney Court narrowed the scope of the commerce clause and warmed to the idea of concurrent commerce powers, which allowed states to regulate interstate commerce in the absence of clear federal intentions to the contrary. While *Cooley v. Pennsylvania Board of Wardens* (1851) ultimately limited this idea to the relatively narrow doctrine of "selective exclusiveness," the Taney Court recognized concurrent state powers to regulate commerce and strongly implied that the federal commerce power was neither exclusive nor unlimited.[75]

---

74. For an early case dealing with state police powers, see *Charles River Bridge v. Warren Bridge*, 36 U.S. (11 Pet.) 419 (1837).
75. *Cooley v. Pennsylvania Board of Wardens*, 53 U.S. (12 How.) 299 (1851).

The Court also tilted toward states' rights when it came to slavery. Vigorously enforcing the fugitive slave laws, the Taney Court—which was dominated by Southern Justices and sympathizers—ruled that slaves were not ordinary articles of commerce and were not subject to federal regulation under the commerce clause. The most ominous consequence of this approach was that it encouraged slaveowners to view their peculiar institution as a matter that the Constitution left exclusively to the states, beyond federal control or regulation.

While reallocating government authority in favor of the states in many areas, the Taney Court continued to centralize federal *judicial* authority and used its growing political muscle to check both state and federal governments. The Court claimed new federal equitable powers and established a limited federal common law in commercial cases based on the Court's diversity jurisdiction.[76] This meant that in commercial cases, at least, federal courts would not be bound by state laws, or even congressional statutes, but could build an independent body of federal judge-made law.

The Supreme Court's internal organization and procedures were little changed during the early years of the Taney era. For the most part, the practices and procedures that proved so useful to Marshall and the Federalists were equally serviceable for Taney and the Democratic-Republicans. In particular, Taney continued Marshall's legacy of collegiality and consensus within the conference.

There was one significant change in how the Court announced its decisions. Where Marshall delivered the opinion of the Court in virtually all significant cases, Taney often assigned even crucial constitutional cases to Associate Justices. This change benefited Taney at least as much as it did the Associate Justices, as the power to assign cases quickly became an important source of patronage for the Chief Justice.

The Justices continued to live together while the Court was in session. Although this communal "mess-style" living began to show signs of strain after 1830, most of the Justices continued to live together for another twenty years. They often boarded at Morrison's on 4½ Street, Dawson's on Capitol Hill, or along Pennsylvania Avenue at Miss Polk's, Mrs. Turner's, or Elliot's. The typical room charge was $16 per week, or $40 with a wife. The price difference was enough to discourage most Justices from bringing their spouses to Washington.[77]

Taney reported that living conditions in the capital varied from tolerable to "abominably filthy." The city was horribly polluted. Of all the streets that crisscrossed the sprawling boomtown, only Pennsylvania Avenue was paved. The rest were choked with dust in

---

76. *Swift v. Tyson*, 41 U.S. (16 Pet.) 1 (1842).

77. Swisher, *Roger B. Taney*, 353; Pearson and Allen, *The Nine Old Men*, 37. At the time, Washington was considered an unfit place for ladies to live, and from the punitive pricing schemes it is clear that women were not welcome at boardinghouses.

dry weather and became swampy quagmires during the rainy season. Pigs, fowl, and other livestock were allowed to roam freely on neighborhood streets. There were no sewers. Wastewater ran down the streets into ditches and streams that emptied directly into the Potomac. At high tide, the effluent flowed upstream with the tidal surge back into the city. Drinking water, pumped from streetcorner wells, was badly contaminated after decades of unsanitary practices.[78]

In 1841, the Justices' mess-style living arrangements began to fall apart. That year only five Justices boarded at Mrs. Turner's (Taney, Story, McLean, Thompson, and Barbour). The following year only Story and McLean roomed together, although three other Justices lived nearby.[79] In 1845, Taney and three other Justices lived in one boardinghouse, three others lived in a nearby hotel, and the remaining two lived in private homes. By 1850, the Justices abandoned the communal lifestyle completely. The era of mess-style living was over, although as late as 1862 five judges boarded together at Morrison's.[80]

With the breakdown in the Justices' traditional living arrangements came increased internal strains on their working relationships. Regional, ideological, and doctrinal disagreements grew more pronounced as the Justices became more directly involved in partisan politics. Taney, a loyal Democratic party activist, routinely gave advice to Presidents Jackson, Polk, and Buchanan while on the bench.[81] John Catron, another Democratic activist, was especially close to Polk. Several other Justices harbored political ambitions of their own. John McLean pursued the presidency relentlessly and with a spectacular lack of success with five different political parties (Democratic, Anti-Mason, Free Soil, Whig, and Republican). Levi Woodbury and Samuel Nelson were contenders for the Democratic presidential nomination in 1848 and 1860, respectively.

The Court's caseload soared with the beginning of industrialization, ending any thoughts of returning to seriatim opinions. To save time and to protect the conference, the Justices cut back on oral arguments and for the first time imposed time limits on advocates. In 1844, Congress scaled back the Justices' circuit duties to one sitting per year and rolled back the beginning of the Court's annual term from the second Monday in January to the second Monday in December.[82] Beginning in 1845, the Court sat from December through March, adjourned in April to allow the Justices to perform their circuit duties, and then reconvened briefly in May to finish their work before retiring for the summer.

Although circuit duties were reduced to one sitting per year, circuit riding responsibilities were more onerous than ever. With westward expansion the country was grow-

---

78. Swisher, *Roger B. Taney*, 353, 471–72.
79. Newmeyer, *Justice Joseph Story*, 438.
80. Swisher, *Roger B. Taney*, 352; Warren, *A History of the Supreme Court*, 792.
81. Newmeyer, *Justice Joseph Story*, 438.
82. Act of June 17, 1844.

ing rapidly, but the transportation network was still rudimentary and travel was difficult. On average, each Justice had to travel two thousand miles annually riding circuit.
Beginning in 1837, John Catron and John McKinley were assigned the two new western
circuits, one of which required 3,852 miles of travel and the other ten thousand miles each
year.[83]

The Supreme Court itself was still relegated to the Capitol basement. Justice Catron
described the courtroom in blunt and unflattering terms:

> [I was] grievously annoyed by the dampness, darkness, and want of ventilation of the
> old basement room; into which, I have always supposed, the Supreme Court was
> thrust in a spirit of hostility to it, by the Political Department.[84]

Lawyer Reverdy Johnson reported in 1848 that during weeks when the Court heard
oral arguments, the Court still sat in conference almost every day. During most of the
Taney era, Congress appropriated money annually for a conference room and library
located "uptown," at Morrison's boardinghouse.[85] The Court also had a conference room
in the Capitol, but it seems to have been rarely used. The Justices did most of their work
at home, and returning to the Capitol after dinner would have been pointless. Moreover, their uptown facilities were more convenient and pleasant than their dismal rooms
in the Capitol. As Justice David Davis wrote to his wife, "The society of judges is a good
deal, and the Library [at Morrison's] is everything."[86] Conferences began after dinner at
7:00 P.M., and typically lasted for anywhere between two and five hours, although they
occasionally carried on past midnight.[87]

In 1860, the Court was finally promoted from the Capitol basement into the Old
Senate Chamber, where it remained until the Supreme Court building opened in 1935.
The vice president's old office was turned into a conference room, while the Justices' old
conference room was converted into a study. The old courtroom, which was almost directly beneath the Old Senate Chamber, became the new Supreme Court library. Congress then stopped paying for the uptown conference room and library in 1862 and the
Justices began to hold their conferences at the Capitol.[88]

Benjamin R. Curtis described Taney's performance in the conference room in glow-
ing, and perhaps somewhat idealized, terms:

---

83. Swisher, *Roger B. Taney*, 354–55.

84. Letter from J. Catron to William Thomas Carroll, September 29, 1860, quoted in Swisher, *The Taney
Period*, 717.

85. Congress appropriated an average of $250 per month for the uptown conference room and library.
Ibid., 716–17.

86. Fairman, 1 *Reconstruction and Reunion*, 67.

87. Schmidhauser, *The Supreme Court*, 116.

88. Fairman, 1 *Reconstruction and Reunion*, 67.

There, his dignity, his love of order, his gentleness, his caution, his accuracy, his discrimination, were of incalculable importance. The real intrinsic character of the tribunal was greatly influenced by them, and always for the better.[89]

The most detailed information on conferences during Taney's tenure came from John Archibald Campbell. In his address to the Supreme Court bar on the death of Benjamin Curtis, Campbell described the Justices' consultations:

> The duties of the Justices of the Supreme Court consist in the hearing of cases; the preparations for the consultations; the consultations in the conference of the judges; the decision of the cause there, and the preparation of the opinion and the judgment of the court. Their most arduous and responsible duty is in the conference.
>
> . . . The Chief Justice presided, the deliberations were usually frank and candid. It was a rare incident in the whole of this period the slightest disturbance from irritation, excitement, passion, or impatience. There was habitually courtesy, good breeding, self-control, [and] mutual deference. . . . There was nothing of cabal, combination, or exorbitant desire to carry questions or cases. Their aims were honorable and all the arts employed to attain them were manly arts. The venerable age of the Chief Justice, his gentleness, refinement, and feminine sense of propriety, were felt and realized in the privacy and confidence of these consultations. . . .
>
> In these conferences, the Chief Justice usually called the case. He stated the pleadings and facts that they presented, the arguments and his conclusions in regard to them, and invited discussion. The discussion was free and open among the Justices till all were satisfied.
>
> The question was put, whether the judgment or decree should be reversed, and each Justice, according to his precedence, commencing with the junior judge, was required to give his judgment and his reasons for his conclusion. The concurring opinions of the majority decided the cause and signified the matter of the opinion to be given. The Chief Justice designated the judge to prepare it.[90]

Justice John McLean described the life of the conference under Taney in this way:

> The case after being argued at the Bar is thoroughly discussed in consultation. Night after night, this is done, in a case of difficulty, until the mind of every judge is satisfied, and then each judge gives his views of the whole case, embracing every point of it. In this way the opinion of the judges is expressed, and then the Chief Justice requests a particular judge to write, not his opinion, but the opinion of the Court. And after the opinion is read, it is read to all of the judges, and if it does not embrace the views of the judges, it is modified and corrected.[91]

---

89. Westin, *Autobiography of the Supreme Court*, 187. Curtis's opinion of Taney changed in the aftermath of the *Dred Scott* decision (discussed below).

90. Campbell, "Benjamin Robbins Curtis," x.

91. O'Brien, *Storm Center*, 109.

Like Marshall, Taney fought incessantly to discourage dissenting opinions. Despite the stresses and strains of industrialization, slavery, and partisan politics, the Court struggled to operate much as it had in Marshall's day. Increasing the size of the Court to nine in 1837 slowed the Court's efficiency and made collegiality and consensus more difficult. As Joseph Story wrote to Charles Sumner in 1838,

> "Many men of many minds" require a great deal of discussion to compel them to come to definite results; and we found ourselves often involved in long and very tedious debates. I verily believe, if there were twelve judges, we should do no business at all, or at least very little.[92]

Despite the difficulties, cohesiveness remained high for most of Taney's tenure. Between 1836 and 1863, the Taney Court had a case dissent rate of 12 percent.[93] This figure seems quite low by modern standards, but it seemed high at the time, especially compared to the unity of the Marshall Court. By the 1850s, deep public disagreements among the Justices emerged in cases involving the commerce clause and slavery. The Taney Court's biggest test—and greatest disaster—was *Dred Scott*.[94]

Dred Scott was a slave who traveled with his owner, Dr. Emerson, from the slave state of Missouri to the free state of Illinois and into the free territory beyond (which eventually became Iowa and Minnesota). When the group returned to Missouri several years later, Dr. Emerson died. Scott, his wife Harriet, and their two daughters automatically became part of Dr. Emerson's estate. Scott sued for his freedom in a Missouri court, claiming that because he and his family had not been considered slaves during their travels through Illinois and the upper Louisiana territory, they could not lose their freedom by returning to Missouri. Scott won at the trial level, but Dr. Emerson's widow appealed to the state supreme court. The high court reversed, holding that the laws of Illinois and the free territories were irrelevant and that under Missouri law Scott and his family remained slaves. Mrs. Emerson then married and left the Scott family in the custody of her brother, John Sanford of New York (a court clerk incorrectly spelled the name "Sandford" on the official case record).

Scott then filed a second lawsuit in federal court, charging that Sanford had committed trespass against Scott and his family. Scott argued that because he was a citizen of Missouri and Sanford was a citizen of New York, the case belonged in federal court on diversity grounds as a dispute between citizens of different states. In response, Sanford challenged the federal court's diversity jurisdiction, claiming that Scott could not be a citizen of Missouri because he was black and a slave. Sanford also disputed the case on

---

92. Schmidhauser, *The Supreme Court*, 117.
93. Data compiled from Epstein, *The Supreme Court Compendium*, 195–96.
94. *Dred Scott v. Sandford*, 60 U.S. (19 How.) 393 (1857).

the merits, claiming that he had the legal right to hold Scott and his family as his private property. Scott countered that he had been emancipated by his residence in free territory, which gave him the rights of all free citizens, including the right to sue in federal court. Also potentially at issue was whether Congress, in passing the Missouri Compromise, had the power to prohibit slavery in the free territories of the Louisiana Purchase.

The Missouri Compromise was originally intended to resolve the bitter dispute over whether slavery would be allowed in the Louisiana Purchase territories.[95] When Missouri sought admission to the Union as a slave state in 1819, antislavery Federalists in the House passed legislation that would have required Missouri to phase out slavery after a period of years. The Senate, however, rejected the House plan and proposed a compromise under which Missouri would be admitted as a slave state and Maine would be admitted as a free state. The compromise also provided that slavery would be prohibited in the Louisiana Territories north of 36 degrees 30 minutes latitude—a line corresponding to Missouri's southern border. Many Southerners opposed the compromise, arguing that placing such conditions on statehood violated the principle that new states would be admitted on an equal footing with all other states. Opponents also argued that it was unconstitutional for the federal government to prohibit slavery in any state or territory or to restrict the rights of slaveholders to take their slaves wherever they wished.

The Missouri Compromise offended Southern sensibilities by implicitly recognizing that the federal government had the power to restrict, or even abolish, slavery in federal territories and states. Northern abolitionists argued that the federal government had the right to regulate or prohibit slavery in the federal territories and had the right to impose such conditions on statehood.

In the final analysis, the Missouri Compromise resolved nothing and the dispute over slavery continued to fester. A second attempt to reconcile the irreconcilable resulted in the Compromise of 1850. This was a series of federal legislation mostly dealing with slavery in the Southwest and West, although Congress tried to include something for just about everyone. In a bow to the abolitionists, California was admitted as a free state and the slave trade in the District of Columbia was abolished. For the South, a new fugitive slave law was passed and the Wilmot Proviso (which promised that slavery would not be allowed in any territory gained in the recent war with Mexico) was abrogated. The question of slavery in the New Mexico and Utah territories was left to the territorial residents to determine for themselves.

The third round of conflict and compromise over slavery came in 1854 with the Kansas-Nebraska Act. This act effectively repealed the Missouri Compromise and allowed the residents of all federal territories to decide for themselves whether to be slave or free.

---

95. This account borrows heavily from Kelly, Harbison, and Belz, 1 *The American Constitution*, 254–62.

Two major issues remained unresolved. First, there was disagreement over when the decision regarding the status of slavery in each territory was to be made. Southerners claimed that territories could not legally decide the slavery issue until they formally applied for statehood and wrote their state constitutions. Northerners argued that territories could decide to abolish slavery at any time. Second, Southerners argued that slaveowners retained the right to pass freely through all federal territories and states with their slaves without endangering the legal status of their "property." With these crucial issues left open, the overall impact of these compromises was that the South won significant concessions and realized that the mere threat of secession gave the region considerable political leverage over national policy.

Compromise did not bring peace or reconciliation. Rival pro- and antislavery territorial governments were established in Kansas and other federal territories, and violence followed.[96] These clashes created a highly charged political atmosphere into which two sparks jumped: the founding of the Republican party in 1854 and the *Dred Scott* decision.

The Republican party was established in reaction to what partisans saw as Democratic appeasement of Southern interests. The Republicans rejected the Democrats' announced policy of federal "neutrality" on slavery and sought to nationalize the issue of abolition.

After the Kansas-Nebraska Act of 1854, Congress quit trying to mediate a national solution to the issue of slavery. The Taney Court, in contrast, grew more assertive in deciding constitutional doctrine, including questions about slavery. The Court's debut as the new constitutional arbiter-in-chief came with *Dred Scott*.

Even before the decision was announced, anxiety ran high among abolitionists, who despaired of the Court's pronounced Southern sympathies. Horace Greeley growled that it would make more sense to trust a dog with one's dinner than to trust the Supreme Court with the question of slavery.[97]

When the Justices first met in conference to discuss the case on February 15, 1857, a 7–2 majority agreed to decide the case narrowly—as a matter of Missouri state law—and avoid the broader constitutional questions.[98] While the Southern position would win, no real precedent would be set. The Court would dispose of the case quickly and quietly, without addressing the thorny issues of slavery, citizenship, or the Missouri Compromise. Because it was not intended to be a landmark case, Taney assigned the opinion to Samuel Nelson of New York.

---

96. Antislavery "Jayhawkers" from Kansas engaged in a bloody series of border raids with proslavery Missouri "Bushwhackers." As one Kansan described the carnage, "The Devil came to the border, liked it, and decided to stay awhile." Miller, *Plain Speaking*, 74.

97. Swisher, *The Taney Period*, 592.

98. In *Strader v. Graham*, 51 U.S. (10 How.) 82 (1850), the Court unanimously rejected the argument that a slave was automatically freed if he resided in a free state and left the decision to state courts.

But then John McLean (who at the time was a candidate for the Republican presidential nomination) and Benjamin Curtis informed the conference that they would argue in dissent that the Missouri Compromise was constitutional and that Congress had the power to prohibit slavery in the federal territories. This caused an uproar in the conference room, and the majority quickly caucused to reconsider their options. Taney withdrew Nelson's assignment, took the lead opinion himself, and wrote a broad and inflammatory opinion invalidating the Missouri Compromise on constitutional grounds.[99]

Taney's majority threatened to fall apart when Robert C. Grier of Pennsylvania balked at this change in tactics. Grier's vote was crucial, because he was the only credible Northern Justice voting with the majority. Although Samuel Nelson was from New York, he came from a slaveholding family and was closely identified with the proslavery wing of the Democratic party. Nelson's education at Middlebury College had been partly financed by his father's sale of a slave girl. He was widely, and rightly, regarded as a "Northern man with Southern principles." The other five Justices in the majority were Southern men with Southern principles.

John Catron of Tennessee desperately wanted to keep Grier in the fold and avoid a transparently sectional division. On February 19, 1857, Catron wrote to President-elect James Buchanan and asked him to talk to Grier, a close friend and fellow Pennsylvanian, and tell him that settling the constitutional question would be good for the country. Catron did not tell Buchanan which way the Court had voted, but revealed that the final conference vote was 7–2. Buchanan promptly wrote to Grier, and Grier replied on February 23, telling Buchanan in confidence the details of the Court's vote.[100] Buchanan incorporated this intelligence into his inaugural speech, telling the country that the question of slavery in the territories would be "speedily and finally settled" and disingenuously promised that he would "cheerfully submit" to the Court's decision "whatever this may be."[101]

---

99. Despite the hostility directed toward McLean and Curtis, at least two of the Justices in the majority had planned from the beginning to discuss the constitutional issues in concurring opinions. Kelly, Harbison, and Belz, 1 *The American Constitution*, 269. The Missouri Compromise was a moot issue anyway, as it had already effectively been repealed by the Compromise of 1850 and the Kansas and Nebraska Acts in 1854.

100. Warren, 2 *A History of the Supreme Court*, 294–97. Some scholars have argued that Catron also leaked the vote to Buchanan.

101. The press also had a good idea of how the case was going to be decided, possibly due to leaks from one or more Justices. On March 5, 1857, the day after Buchanan's address, the *New York Tribune* mocked his speech, saying that it was not surprising that Buchanan would "cheerfully submit to whatever the five slaveholders and two or three doughfaces on the bench of the Supreme Court may be ready to utter on the subject." Swisher, *The Taney Period*, 621.

While nominally a 7–2 decision rejecting Dred Scott's claims and striking down the Missouri Compromise, the Court divided nine ways, with each Justice writing separately. It was, for all practical purposes, a seriatim opinion. For all of Taney's emphasis on consensus building, the Court fell to pieces deciding the case of the century.

Taney's lead opinion was the most controversial. Even members of the majority complained afterward that the opinion Taney read in Court differed significantly from what had been approved in conference.[102] In the most provocative passage, Taney used the doctrine of original intent to interpret the Constitution and noted that at the time that the basic law was adopted, blacks were

> regarded as beings of an inferior order; and altogether unfit to associate with the white race, either in social or political relations; and so far inferior, that they had no rights which the white man was bound to respect.[103]

Taney's opinion posed a direct challenge to the new Republican party, whose original party platform in 1856 declared that slavery was illegal in the federal territories because it denied slaves their liberty without due process of law. Taney turned this idea on its head, arguing that the due process clause protected *slaveholders'* vested property rights and prevented Congress from interfering with those rights in any state or territory.[104]

After *Dred Scott*, the Court was more bitterly divided than at any other time in its history. Even reading the case today, the decision is so convoluted and fragmentary that it is difficult to determine precisely what was decided. Inside the conference room, the unity of the conference was shattered. Taney was certain that either Curtis or McLean had leaked the result of the case to the *New York Tribune*, and he accused Curtis of treachery after Curtis gave an advance copy of his dissent to a Boston newspaper. The fallout from the case poisoned the Justices' already strained personal and professional relationships.[105] Curtis resigned over the incident, and he and Taney stopped speaking to each other.

Buchanan was wrong in his inaugural speech. *Dred Scott* resolved nothing. It offered no honorable compromise and provided no practical solutions for the problems of race and slavery. It was the only Supreme Court decision ever overturned by a war, at a cost of 620,000 American lives or nearly 2 percent of the population. As for Dred Scott, he was set free in Missouri within three months after the Court's decision. He died just a year later in 1858, and his wife, Harriet, died soon after.[106]

---

102. O'Brien, *Storm Center*, 110.

103. *Dred Scott v. Sandford*, 60 U.S. (19 How.) 393, 407 (1857).

104. Schmidhauser, *Constitutional Law in American Politics*, 190–91.

105. McLean, a close friend of *Tribune* reporter William E. Harvey, was the most likely source of the leak. Swisher, *The Taney Period*, 606.

106. Warren, 2 *A History of the Supreme Court*, 302. After Scott was freed, the *New York Tribune* noted sarcastically that "we suppose that now he has rights which white men are bound to respect." Swisher, *The Taney Period*, 652.

Dred Scott was a self-inflicted wound from which the Supreme Court did not fully recover for nearly a century. The Taney Court came down squarely on the wrong side of history in racial issues, a mistake that the Court compounded with the *Civil Rights Cases* (1883) and *Plessy v. Ferguson* (1896) and only began to set right with *Brown v. Board of Education* in 1954.

SALMON CHASE AND MORRISON WAITE: THE POSTBELLUM YEARS (1864–1888)

After Taney's death in 1864, Salmon Chase inherited a deeply troubled Court. The Justices had squandered much of the Court's reputation and moral authority with *Dred Scott*, and in the shadow of the Civil War the Court was confronted by a new set of challenges.

The Civil War concentrated new powers into the hands of the federal government, particularly the executive branch. Significant restrictions on civil liberties, such as President Lincoln's unilateral suspension of the writ of habeas corpus, posed a challenge to the idea of limited government and the rule of law. Yet there was also reason to remain optimistic. Throughout the course of the most vicious war ever fought on American soil, the civilian government and courts continued to function, and elections took place on schedule.

The consolidation of federal power continued after the war. Instead of political power continuing to flow to the executive branch, as it had during the war, Congress grew more powerful and assertive following Lincoln's assassination and the succession of the weak and unpopular Andrew Johnson. The Radical Republicans launched an ambitious and punitive program of Southern Reconstruction, and it remained to be seen whether the Supreme Court would dare to limit congressional zeal.

The war marked the end of serious debate about the idea of state sovereignty. Before Fort Sumter, the issue of state sovereignty had been left open and allowed to drift with the ebb and flow of national politics. After the war, sovereign authority settled permanently on the federal government.

In some ways, the Supreme Court's efforts to rehabilitate and reassert itself proceeded smoothly. After the war, the Justices became an established part of the Washington scene. They began to bring their wives and families to Washington as a matter of course, and with higher pay and social status they were welcomed into the highest circles of Washington life.[107] The Justices went from living in close association with each other but in

---

107. The Justices' Salaries

	1789	1819	1855	1871	1873	1903
Chief Justice	$4,000	$5,000	$6,500	$8,500	$10,500	$13,000
Associate Justices	$3,500	$4,500	$6,000	$8,000	$10,000	$12,500

Source: Fairman, 1 *Reconstruction and Reunion*, 68.

relative isolation from Washington society, to being more intimate with the Washington establishment but more distant from one another.

It proved impossible to restore the Justices' once-close working relationships. The days of communal living were over, but the days of a common workplace had not yet arrived. The Justices did not have chambers, office space, or staff in the Capitol building, and they had to work alone in their own homes.[108] The resulting isolation reinforced the growing sense of estrangement. While some close friendships continued to develop, aside from conferences and oral arguments most of the Justices rarely saw each other.

Between 1864 and 1888, the Justices had a separate consultation room in the Capitol basement. They might also have met in the library, which was somewhat larger and more comfortable, though still dark and unpleasant. Instead of holding daily conferences as they had done when the Justices lived together, they now met just once a week, on Saturdays. Because Congress by tradition convened at noon on weekdays, the Justices also began their Saturday conferences at noon. Conferences were relatively brief, usually lasting until four or five in the afternoon. Cases were discussed, decided, and assigned on the same day. Opinions were usually written within two to three weeks, and the drafts were read at conference for further discussion and final approval.[109]

The Court's internal procedures slowly began to move away from consensual decision making toward majority rule, with new protections for the minority built into the Court's procedures. The rule of four was created toward the end of the nineteenth century to ensure that a minority could determine which discretionary cases would be accepted and decided. It has been claimed that the rule was meant to reassure the public that the Court's cert decisions were not arbitrary or capricious, but the rule's existence was kept secret for several decades and was not disclosed to the public until 1924, when it was revealed during congressional hearings on proposed legislation that would become the Judiciary Act of 1925.[110]

Maintaining consensus in hard cases became increasingly difficult. The Justices found themselves deeply divided on a broad range of war-related issues, including emancipation, the draft, paper money, and Reconstruction. Perhaps wisely, the Chase Court kept a low profile in dealing with these issues. For the most part, the Court stayed discretely on the sidelines, treating Reconstruction cases as posing nonjusticiable political rather than legal questions, and avoiding a series of potential confrontations with Congress over

---

108. In 1866, Justice Robert C. Grier asked to be allowed to live in the Capitol building and was politely but firmly rebuffed. Fairman, 1 *Reconstruction and Reunion*, 83.

109. Fairman claims that the conferences began at 11:00 A.M. Ibid., 66, 69–70, 83–84.

110. The Judiciary Act of 1925 gave the Court control over its own docket by establishing discretionary writs of certiorari as the primary means of appeal to the Supreme Court.

Reconstruction policies in Mississippi, Georgia, and Texas.[111] The Chase Court was perhaps more notable for the decisions it avoided than for the decisions it made.

In general, the Court implicitly supported Reconstruction, and Congress in turn depended on the federal courts (though not necessarily the Supreme Court) to help legitimize and enforce its Southern policy. Congress increased federal court jurisdiction with the Habeas Corpus Act of 1863, which allowed for the removal to federal courts of any case involving acts ordered by federal officials. The Habeas Corpus Act of 1867 expanded the federal habeas corpus power to cover all persons held in possible violation of the Constitution, treaties, or laws of the United States (under the previous Judiciary Act of 1789, federal habeas corpus was available only to those held by federal authorities and did not include state prisoners). Finally, the Jurisdiction and Removal Act of 1875 extended federal court jurisdiction to all cases arising under the Constitution, laws, and treaties of the United States and broadened federal jurisdiction in diversity cases to include lawsuits between citizens and foreigners and in cases where the United States was a plaintiff.

Chase favored a quick end to military rule in the South and pushed for rapid normalization and reintegration of Southern states into the Union. The Court at one point seemed willing to confront at least some of the excesses of Reconstruction. The Justices accepted jurisdiction in a habeas appeal filed by William McCardle, a Southern newspaper editor convicted by a military tribunal for publishing allegedly seditious and libelous articles. The federal circuit court in Mississippi denied McCardle's habeas petition, but most observers expected him to receive a sympathetic hearing at the Supreme Court. Congress, however, did not want to risk a constitutional challenge to Reconstruction and repealed the Supreme Court's appellate jurisdiction to hear cases arising under the Habeas Corpus Act of 1867.[112] Rather than confront Congress, the Court quietly backed down in the face of this direct congressional challenge to its authority. The Justices unanimously dismissed the case, ruling that Congress had been within its rights to withdraw the Court's appellate jurisdiction in habeas corpus cases.[113]

In cases dealing with the Civil War amendments (the Thirteenth, Fourteenth, and Fifteenth Amendments), the Chase Court at first appeared inclined to use these amend-

---

111. *Mississippi v. Johnson*, 71 U.S. (4 Wall.) 475 (1866); *Georgia v. Stanton*, 73 U.S. (6 Wall.) 50 (1867); *Texas v. White*, 74 U.S. (7 Wall.) 700 (1868).

112. Congress's partial repeal of the Habeas Corpus Act applied only to the Supreme Court. It eliminated the high court's jurisdiction to review habeas decisions made by inferior federal judges but left untouched the broad habeas jurisdiction of the lower federal courts. Congress considered federal district court judges to be reliable allies in enforcing its Reconstruction policies, but did not want to risk Supreme Court interference in congressional efforts to punish Southern troublemakers and to protect federal officials from harassment.

113. *Ex parte McCardle*, 74 U.S. (7 Wall.) 506 (1869).

ments to nationalize a broad range of civil rights.[114] But as the country's passion for Reconstruction, reform, and renewal cooled, the Court began to back away from such ideas, and old notions of states' rights made something of a comeback. Beginning in 1873, the Chase Court began to place new restrictions on the scope of the Civil War amendments.

The *Slaughterhouse Cases* (1873) eviscerated the privileges and immunities clause of the Fourteenth Amendment. The majority distinguished the privileges of state citizenship from federal citizenship and then attributed most meaningful benefits of citizenship to the states. This case ended any lingering optimism that the Supreme Court might give a broad reading to the Civil War amendments or promote a national standard of civil rights. In other cases, the Justices used a crabbed reading of the Fourteenth Amendment to bar women from claiming a constitutional right to practice law, and limited the scope of the Fifteenth Amendment by ruling that the right to vote was a state right rather than a privilege of national citizenship.[115]

Even for a Chief Justice, Salmon Chase was an extraordinarily ambitious and opportunistic politician. He sought the Republican nomination for president before the Civil War and the Democratic nomination afterward. During the war, Chase was a member of Lincoln's cabinet. He was often shockingly disloyal to President Lincoln, whom Chase viewed as little more than a second-rate political rival. As the administration's resident gadfly, Chase vocally criticized administration policy during the war, protected by his strong abolitionist credentials and the support of Charles Sumner and other leading congressional Republicans.[116]

Chase was widely criticized for continuing to pursue his political ambitions even after he became Chief Justice. Upon hearing of Chase's death on May 7, 1873, Rutherford B. Hayes wrote in his diary:

> [His] contempt for the great office he held and his willingness to degrade it, should have made lawyers, at least, chary of praise. I have heard him speak of himself and his associates on the bench as old women, and he always preferred the title of Governor to that of Chief Justice. He often expressed preference for the place of Senator to that of

---

114. In the case of *In re Turner*, Chief Justice Chase, sitting as a circuit judge, relied on the Civil Rights Act to void an apprenticeship contract between a young black girl and her former master. The contract did not provide the financial and educational benefits white apprentices were entitled to under Maryland indenture statutes. Chase voided the contract because it failed to give the girl the "full and equal benefit of all laws and proceedings for the security of persons and property as is enjoyed by white citizens." *In re Turner*, 24 F. Cas. 337, 339 (C.C.D. Md. 1867). Similarly, Noah Swayne upheld the Civil Rights Act in *United States v. Rhodes*, 27 F. Cas. 785 (C.C.D. Ky. 1867) (1868).

115. *Bradwell v. Illinois*, 83 U.S. (16 Wall) 130 (1873); *Minor v. Happersett*, 88 U.S. (21 Wall.) 162 (1875).

116. Chase was convinced that he would have been a far better president than Lincoln. Harry Truman later joked that Chase caused Lincoln "more trouble than all the generals put together, and that was not an easy thing to do." Lincoln, for his part, said that Chase was never happy unless he was unhappy and complained that "he has every attribute of a dog, except loyalty." Miller, *Plain Speaking*, 209–210.

Chief Justice. Political intrigue, love of power, and a selfish and boundless ambition were the striking features of his life and character.[117]

Although Chase lacked prior judicial experience and was more interested in politics than in law, he did a creditable job of restoring a degree of collegiality and normalcy to the conference. Chase maneuvered deftly to avoid a series of potentially divisive and damaging confrontations with Congress over Reconstruction, and he presided skillfully over Andrew Johnson's impeachment trial.

Chase also sought to distance the Court from *Dred Scott*. He repeatedly wrote to Presidents Lincoln and Johnson recommending that blacks be guaranteed full suffrage and other civil rights. He toured the South after the war and spoke to both black and white audiences about universal suffrage. He made no promises, however, telling the crowds that "having nothing to do with politics, I am not prepared to say what will be the action of the government."

The Chase Court's well-earned reputation for caution was reflected not only in the issues the Justices avoided but in the cases they decided. Perhaps the most controversial and significant case of the Chase era was *Ex parte Milligan*, in which the Court decided, safely after the fact, that the Bill of Rights remained in effect during wartime.[118]

Despite Chase's best efforts to restore a sense of normalcy to the Court, he was not able to recoup all of the Court's former reputation and authority.[119] Despite continuing divisions on the Court, Chase was more successful in reestablishing a sense of common purpose and consensus. Overall, the Chase Court managed a respectable case dissent rate of 10 percent.[120]

After Chase died in 1873, Ulysses S. Grant nominated Morrison Waite of Ohio to become the new Chief Justice.[121] Waite was the third Chief Justice out of four who lacked any prior judicial experience. Yet he proved to be an adept conference leader. Waite presided over a Court that was troubled by vicious personal animosities and rivalries, including at least two Justices—Stephen Field and Joseph Bradley—who were bitterly disappointed that they had not been promoted to the center chair.

Waite made a nice contrast to Chase. He was neither politically ambitious nor particularly partisan. A moderate Democrat, he was by nature conciliatory, friendly, kind hearted, and humble—at least for a Supreme Court Justice.[122]

---

117. Fairman, 1 *Reconstruction and Reunion*, 1475.

118. *Ex parte Milligan*, 71 U.S. (4 Wall.) 2 (1866).

119. Fairman, 1 *Reconstruction and Reunion*, 85–88.

120. Data compiled from Epstein, *The Supreme Court Compendium*, 196.

121. President Grant had considerable difficulty replacing Salmon Chase. Waite was Grant's sixth choice and was selected only after five previous candidates—all Grant cronies—were rejected or withdrew because they were corrupt, incompetent, or both. To many, Waite's most important qualification was that he was not a member of Grant's inner circle.

122. Cushman, *The Supreme Court Justices*, 213.

Under Waite's leadership, the Justices gradually grew more confident and assertive in reclaiming the Court's self-appointed role as the main national arbiter of constitutional values. Three types of cases dominated the Waite Court's docket: industrialization, corporations, and railroads. Waite's appointment marked the beginning of a profoundly conservative trend of judicial decision making that would dominate judicial politics for more than sixty years. The Court became a champion of private economic interests and increasingly began to take a close and skeptical look at government attempts to regulate business.

The Waite Court was particularly sympathetic to railroads and blocked most state attempts to regulate shipping rates. State price regulations were usually passed to keep rates low, at the insistence of local agricultural interests. The Court used the due process clause of the Fourteenth Amendment to look beyond whether state legislatures followed fair *procedures* in establishing rail rates and began to question whether the *object* of the laws were reasonable and proper. This approach became known as substantive due process.

The Court struck down an Illinois rate scheme in *Wabash, St. Louis and Pacific Ry. Co. v. Illinois* (1866).[123] While the same Court later upheld the same state's new rate regulations in *Munn v. Illinois* (1877), Waite's majority opinion made it clear that the Justices took a dim view of such laws, and he warned that the Court would impose strict limits on states' abilities to regulate private enterprise.[124]

In 1886, the Court ruled that corporations were "persons" for most constitutional purposes, creating legal advantages for corporations that continue to the present.[125] These cases were crucial steps in the evolution of the Court's emerging philosophy that business should not be unnecessarily burdened by either state or federal governments.

Decades of consecutive Republican presidents during the mid-nineteenth and early twentieth centuries led to a Court dominated by a relatively homogeneous group of economic liberals, most of whom were politically active and whose prior legal experience was in corporate or railroad law. Not surprisingly, this had a profound impact on how the Court viewed economic cases. As Justice Samuel F. Miller observed,

> It is vain to contend with judges who have been at the bar the advocates for forty years of railroad companies, and all the forms of associated capital, when they are called upon to decide cases where such interests are in contest. All their training, all their feelings are from the start in favor of those who need no such influence.[126]

While the Waite Court was openly friendly to big business, corporate interests as of yet had no firm expectations of winning due process cases, and the Court remained sym-

---

123. *Wabash, St. Louis and Pacific Ry. Co. v. Illinois*, 118 U.S. 557 (1866).
124. *Munn v. Illinois*, 94 U.S. 113 (1877).
125. Naturally, it was a railroad case. *Santa Clara County v. Southern Pacific Ry. Co.*, 118 U.S. 394 (1886).
126. Fairman, *Mr. Justice Miller and the Supreme Court*, 374.

pathetic to at least some state regulation through their police powers.[127] In close cases, the Court still usually sided with government.

The Waite Court showed little interest in protecting civil rights under the Civil War amendments. In *United States v. Cruikshank* (1874) and *United States v. Harris* (1883), the Justices continued to restrict the scope of the Fourteenth Amendment, ruling that it could only be used to remedy state-sponsored discrimination and could not be used to punish private wrongs—what Waite called "the rights of one citizen as against another." In the *Civil Rights Cases* (1883), the Court invalidated the Civil Rights Act of 1875, the most comprehensive civil rights statute in history, on the ground that it impermissibly regulated private discrimination and exceeded Congress's Fourteenth Amendment powers. While the Thirteenth and Fifteenth Amendments could reach private discrimination, Waite noted, these amendments were only applicable under narrowly defined circumstances and could not be used to justify this act.

One Justice, however, had a profound change of heart when it came to racial discrimination. John Marshall Harlan had initially opposed ratification of the Civil War amendments, but while serving on the Waite Court he reversed himself and with the zeal of a convert began to interpret these amendments broadly, allowing Congress far more discretion to enforce their terms than the majority was willing to recognize. "The man whose mind has never undergone change since 1855," Harlan later explained, "was either a knave or a fool."[128] Harlan was often alone in his opposition to racial discrimination and his support of an expansive reading of the Civil War amendments. Yet despite the Waite Court's restrictive views of these amendments, the Court recognized that the Fourteenth and Fifteenth Amendments prohibited state-sponsored racial discrimination in voting and jury service.[129]

Nationalization of the Bill of Rights continued to be a topic of interest and debate. With the privileges and immunities clause effectively read out of the Fourteenth Amendment, the next best hope of those who advocated nationalizing the Bill of Rights was the equal protection clause. Such ideas, however, had no hope of success with Morrison Waite, who strongly believed that the states, not the federal government, were primarily responsible for defining and protecting individual rights.

During Morrison Waite's fourteen-year tenure, the Court had a low case dissent rate of 6 percent.[130]

---

127. For example, *Munn v. Illinois*, 94 U.S. 113 (1877). The Court also upheld the use of state police powers to regulate liquor in *Mugler v. Kansas*, 123 U.S. 623 (1887).

128. Fairman, 2 *Reconstruction and Reunion*, 567–68.

129. *Strauder v. West Virginia*, 100 U.S. 303 (1880).

130. Data compiled from Epstein, *The Supreme Court Compendium*, 196.

CHAPTER 3

A BRIEF HISTORY OF THE CONFERENCE: MELVILLE FULLER TO WILLIAM REHNQUIST (1888–PRESENT)

MELVILLE FULLER: OIL ON TROUBLED WATERS (1888–1910)

Melville Weston Fuller did not look much like a Chief Justice. He was so short that the Court's carpenters had to raise his chair several inches so that he could see over the bench; he looked more like the Court's mascot than its leader when he stood next to his brethren for photographs.[1] But his diminutive height did not prevent Fuller from asserting effective leadership of the Court. Surrounded by big men with inflated egos, Melville Fuller became one of the most admired and respected Chief Justices in the history of the Court.

No less than Oliver Wendell Holmes called Fuller the greatest Chief Justice he ever knew. Holmes served under seven chief justices—four in Massachusetts and three in Washington—and said that "there never was a better presiding officer, or rather, and more important in some ways, a better moderator inside the council chamber, than this quiet gentleman from Illinois."[2] At conferences, Holmes said, Fuller was well prepared, prompt, decisive, and "perfectly courageous." He presided with "the least possible friction, with inestimable good humor that relieved any tension with a laugh."[3] "I suspect," Holmes concluded, "that it would be easier to get a man who wrote as well as Marshall than to get one who would run the Court as well as Fuller."[4]

Fuller worked incessantly to prevent the Justices' intramural feuds from disrupting the life of the Court or damaging its public reputation. The Court was in the midst of a great generational change, as the Civil War Justices began to give way to a core of dour, conservative Grover Cleveland and Benjamin Harrison Republicans. It was no small feat that Fuller, a lifelong and dedicated Democrat, managed to unite a Court dominated by bickering Republicans.

---

1. Most collective portraits of the Fuller Court show the Justices seated, with the Chief Justice using a strategically placed footstool to make himself appear taller than he really was. Fuller usually stretched one foot to the floor and rested the other on the stool, creating the illusion that both feet could have reached the floor had the footstool not been in the way.

2. Frankfurter, "Chief Justices I Have Known," 889.

3. White Burkett Miller Center of Public Affairs, *The Office of Chief Justice*, 25.

4. Holmes to Baroness Moncheur, July 14, 1910, in Fiss, *Troubled Beginnings of the Modern State*, 27.

Fuller succeeded by being extraordinarily friendly and solicitous and by remaining scrupulously nonpartisan in his management of the conference. The Fuller Court rarely voted along party lines, either in deciding cases or in dealing with internal matters.[5]

Fuller hated the Court's assigned consultation room beneath the Old Senate Chamber. It was poorly ventilated, and when filled with nine argumentative Justices the room quickly grew hot and close. In 1888, Fuller moved the conference into his own home, where the Justices met each Saturday evening until Fuller retired in 1910. Fuller's home had originally been one of the boardinghouses for the Marshall Court from 1831 to 1833, and while the Justices did not return to the days of mess-style living, meeting in Fuller's home added a welcome touch of informality, comfort, hominess, and fresh air.

Horace Gray observed that even when conference discussions grew heated, Fuller remained "a calm moderator, of pleasant manners."[6] Faced with constant internal frictions, Fuller introduced the practice of shaking hands in the conference room in an attempt to calm passions and remind the Justices that their disagreements were professional rather than personal.

David Brewer vividly described the life of the conference under Fuller:

> When they all get settled, the tug of war commences. They are all strong men, and do
> not waste a word. They lock horns and the fight is stubborn; arguments are hurled
> against each other, the discussion grows animated and continues for hours. But we
> always think that justice is triumphant—except the dissenters.[7]

The Chief Justice developed a reputation for being scrupulously fair and generous in assigning cases. He routinely assigned the bigger and more interesting cases to other Justices and resisted the temptation to punish colleagues by withholding case assignments when they misbehaved. There is evidence that Fuller occasionally assigned cases even when he did not vote with the majority in conference, but no one ever accused him of abusing his powers.[8] Fuller also controlled which circuits the Justices rode, and he made these assignments fairly and without favor. All of this created considerable goodwill for the Chief Justice and enabled him to maintain good personal relations with the other members of the Court.[9]

Fuller was obsessed with promoting the Court's political and social prestige. Unlike many of his predecessors, Fuller enjoyed Washington society and nightlife, and he used his social position as Chief Justice to the Court's advantage. He saw to it, for example,

---

5. Ely, *Melville Fuller*, 30.
6. Quoted in ibid., 34.
7. Quoted in ibid., 34.
8. Fiss, *Troubled Beginnings of the Modern State*, 23.
9. Ely, *Melville Fuller*, 36, 48.

that as a matter of official Washington protocol Supreme Court Justices were promoted to the top of the rank list.[10]

As Felix Frankfurter observed, it would have been difficult to predict Fuller's success as a Chief Justice by reading his opinions. Fuller's writing, Frankfurter cautioned, "will give you nothing of his charming qualities. He's rather diffuse. He quotes too many cases. And generally he's not an opinion writer whom you read for literary enjoyment."[11] Fuller wrote only one major opinion in his last fifteen years on the Court and authored just one significant dissent in his entire career—the *Insular Cases*.[12] Yet there was no doubt that it was Fuller's Court, and the Chief Justice set the tone of the place. Attorney General Richard Olney called Fuller's Court "the most agreeable tribunal in the country to appear before." As a young lawyer, Frankfurter argued several cases before the Fuller Court and was struck by Fuller's "great, gentle firmness."[13]

Fuller had to be a skilled mediator to control a Court so full of difficult personalities. Stephen J. Field was a strong-willed and ill-tempered man who was never so completely convinced of anything as he was that he should have been named Chief Justice instead of Fuller. When Fuller took his place on the Court, the other Justices expected Field to "eat Fuller in one bite." Instead, Fuller skillfully courted Field, and through an artful combination of deference, tact, and flattery he cultivated a lifelong friendship with the combative Californian. As Field grew older, he became senile and his work deteriorated. After the 1895 Term, the Chief Justice stopped assigning him any more cases. But Fuller took this drastic step with enough tact that Field forgave him.[14]

Joseph P. Bradley also thought that Field should have been named Chief Justice instead of Fuller and was equally prepared to make life difficult for the new Chief. But Fuller won him over in the same way that he gained Field's confidence, seeking Bradley out for advice, flattering him, and deferring to his opinions and suggestions whenever he could.

Samuel F. Miller was yet another difficult and complex person. Although Miller rarely said a kind word about anyone, in a moment of weakness he called Fuller "a most lovable, congenial man" and told friends that while he had worked under Taney, Chase, and Waite, Fuller was the best presiding judge of them all.[15]

Horace Gray was the Court's self-appointed scholar and something of a martinet. Fuller clashed with Gray more than he did with the other Justices, but in the end Gray came to respect Fuller's skillful management of the conference. Fuller won Gray over by

---

10. Mason, *William Howard Taft*, 193.
11. Westin, *An Autobiography of the Supreme Court*, 216.
12. The *Insular Cases*, 182 U.S. 1 (1901).
13. Ely, *Melville Fuller*, 33.
14. Ibid., 48.
15. Ibid., 25–27.

appealing to his vanity, constantly complimenting Gray's academic skills and pointedly seeking his help in complex and difficult cases.[16]

Fuller did the best that he could with poor Joseph McKenna, whom Fuller thought incompetent and unfit to sit on the Court. Fuller assigned McKenna the easiest cases but otherwise wasted little time on him. Fortunately, McKenna did not have a disruptive personality and accepted his lot without complaint. A quiet and deferential man by nature, McKenna rarely spoke in conference. He favored decisions by consensus and often passed his vote until he could see which way the case was going to go and then joined the majority.[17]

Fuller might have expected to have the most difficulty with John Marshall Harlan. When Fuller was a practicing Chicago lawyer, he had led the local opposition to Harlan's appointment to the Supreme Court. Harlan was a native Kentuckian and a former slave owner, and Fuller disliked the idea of having such a man riding circuit in Illinois. After Harlan's nomination was confirmed, the two men got to know each other and became intimate friends. Several years before Fuller was appointed to the Court, he hired Harlan's son to work in his law firm. (Of course, it rarely hurts one's law practice to be on good terms with a Supreme Court Justice.) The two men remained close friends for the rest of their lives.

Fuller also unexpectedly developed a warm friendship with the reserved and distant Holmes. While Holmes was something of an outsider on the Court, he and Fuller developed a unique personal and professional rapport. The Chief Justice often visited Holmes's home on Sundays to talk shop and to seek Holmes's help in running the conference and assigning cases.

Fuller's friendships with Holmes and Harlan were fortuitous. Harlan and Holmes had much in common, including the fact that they hated each other. Both men had fought in the Union Army during the Civil War. Harlan was a colonel in the 10th Kentucky Volunteer Infantry until 1863, when he resigned to return to his law practice after his father died. Holmes was a captain with the Massachusetts Volunteers. In battle he sustained serious neck, chest, and leg wounds and still had three Confederate bullets lodged in his body when he died in 1935. His injuries caused him to miss the Battle of Gettysburg, where ten of the regiment's thirteen officers and half of the enlisted men were slaughtered.

Harlan could not tolerate Holmes, and for his part Holmes enjoyed baiting Harlan in conference, mockingly calling him "my lion-hearted friend." The two men often lost their tempers and fought in conference, but Fuller was usually able to keep them from crushing innocents underfoot. Holmes freely admitted that both he and Harlan were quick tempered and that they both came to Fuller's house every Saturday prepared for

---

16. Ibid., 27.

17. Pusey, *Charles Evans Hughes*, 284. Holmes said that McKenna "had little to say in conference—was hesitant to express a definite view, often saying that he would prefer not to vote until he could see the opinion." Bickel and Schmidt, *The Judiciary and Responsible Government*, 69.

war. Holmes, as Frankfurter later put it, carried a rapier, while Harlan wielded a battle-axe. Holmes had a "pithy" style of speaking, while Harlan was more "oratorical" and often spoke at great length in conference, which irritated Holmes.

It was left to Fuller to referee this difficult and occasionally violent relationship. Holmes enjoyed telling a story about Fuller's control of the conference. One Saturday evening, Harlan carried on in conference even longer than usual, and Holmes lost his temper. He interrupted Harlan—a serious breach of the discipline and decorum of the conference room—growling, "That won't wash. That won't wash." Harlan exploded with rage. He clenched his fists and began to shout. At the head of the table, Fuller made hand motions as if using a washboard and quietly interjected, "Well, I'm scrubbing away. I'm scrubbing away." The other Justices laughed, breaking the tension before there were any casualties.[18]

Like John Marshall, Fuller worked hard to socialize each new Justice as he came to the Court. He broke in eleven new Justices in his twenty-two years on the bench, using each opportunity to train the new Justice about institutional traditions and expectations. This personal attention and careful housetraining helped Fuller maintain a collegial Court.

There were several significant procedural reforms during Fuller's tenure as Chief Justice that affected the life of the conference. The Judiciary Act of 1891 set up the modern three-tier appellate system (district courts, circuit courts of appeals, and the Supreme Court) and ended the Justices' circuit riding duties. This eased their workload temporarily, although any savings were soon offset by an explosion of economic cases resulting from industrialization. By the turn of the century, the Court's workload approached modern levels, with approximately 4,500 new cases filed each year and the Court deciding an average of 150 cases per year.[19] Fuller successfully lobbied Congress for more discretion to reject cases and greater control of the Court's docket, taking the first significant steps toward the Court's modern certiorari jurisdiction.

The Fuller Court had an overall case dissent rate of 12 percent. This was considered a shockingly high dissent rate at the time and elicited a great deal of public commentary. In retrospect, however, the figure seems surprisingly low, considering the nature of the cases and the difficult personalities Fuller had to deal with.[20] Like his predecessors, Fuller vigorously encouraged compromise and consensus and actively discouraged dissents. Fuller himself dissented in 112 cases over twenty-two years, for an overall dissent rate of 2.3 percent. The Fuller Court as a whole never had a dissent rate over 20 percent in any given year, although the Justices found themselves divided on many of the big constitutional issues—*Pollock v. Farmer's Loan and Trust Co.*, *Lochner v. New York*, *Champion v. Ames*, and the *Insular Cases*.

---

18. Frankfurter, "Chief Justices I Have Known," 888–89.
19. White, "The Work of the Supreme Court," 347.
20. Data complied from Epstein, *Supreme Court Compendium*, 196–97.

John Marshall Harlan was the Court's leading dissenter. He wrote seventy-nine dissents and dissented without opinion in another 208 cases. Oliver Wendell Holmes is often called "The Great Dissenter," but he rarely dissented under Fuller. This was largely because Fuller had socialized Holmes with particular care. In 1904 Holmes said, "I think it useless and undesirable, as a rule, to express dissent." It was not until Fuller died that Holmes changed his mind and went on to earn his nickname in a series of memorable dissents.[21]

The law and politics of the Fuller era were largely defined by four types of cases: immigration, industrialization, urbanization, and imperialism. It was a time of great ideological clashes and political instability, with conservatism, progressivism, laissez-faire capitalism, unionism, socialism, communism, and anarchism all competing as significant political and social movements. The country was transfixed by the Robber Barons, Eugene Debs, the Pullman and Homestead Strikes, the Haymarket Riot, the Spanish-American War, and the nation's colonial adventures in Cuba, Puerto Rico, Panama, the Philippines, and Hawaii.[22] It was, in short, one of the most dynamic and tumultuous times in American history.

The Fuller Court's docket was often dominated by commercial cases involving business trusts and railroads. Virtually all of the Justices came from corporate and railroad backgrounds, and they were deeply suspicious of any government attempt to regulate private industry. The Fuller Court's business was business. There has never been a Supreme Court more sympathetic to corporate interests. The Justices defended entrepreneurial capitalism with equal zeal from both government and organized labor. It was an era of class conflict, and there was no doubt about whose side the Supreme Court was on.[23]

The idea of substantive due process came to full flower under Fuller's leadership. Rather than being content to examine the adequacy and fairness of government hearings and regulatory *procedures*, the Court focused on the *ends* of government. Although the formal test was reasonableness, the real test was whether the Justices agreed with what the law was trying to accomplish. The Justices boldly second-guessed the motives of both state and federal legislatures, and they rarely hesitated to strike down economic regulations that they thought unwise. Republican principles of individualism and liberty were freely adapted to protect corporate rights.

---

21. Ely, *Melville Fuller*, 39.

22. Fiss, *Troubled Beginnings of the Modern State*, 37.

23. Owen Fiss, however, argued that the Fuller Court was not an instrument of corporations and monied interests, but that the Justices were sincerely interested in individual liberty. Fiss, *Troubled Beginnings of the Modern State*, 18.

The Fuller Court limited corporate liability for injuries to workers and consumers and struck down repeated attempts by both the federal and state governments to regulate railroads. The Justices limited the scope of state police powers and simultaneously narrowed the reach of the commerce clause, creating a twilight zone of privacy for big business that lay beyond the reach of both state and federal governments.

Chicago, Milwaukee, and St. Paul Ry. Co. v. Minnesota (1890)—known as the *Minnesota Rate Case*—was the first of a series of cases where the Court reviewed state-imposed railroad rate and regulatory schemes. The Court approached the issues like a mini-legislature, declaring that its duty was to review state economic regulations to determine whether they were reasonable. The Justices abandoned even the qualified presumption in favor of state regulatory schemes announced previously in *Munn v. Illinois*. The Court later expanded its discretion to review similar legislation in *Smythe v. Ames* (1898)[24] and restricted the power of the federal Interstate Commerce Commission to set railroad rates in *ICC v. Cincinnati, New Orleans, and Texas Pacific Ry. Co.* (1897).[25]

Just as the Court shielded business from government, there was an equal willingness to protect capital from organized labor. Labor movements at this time were widespread and often radical, and the Court steadfastly opposed union efforts to disrupt the normal flow of business. The Fuller Court read the Sherman Antitrust Act of 1890 so narrowly as to make it virtually worthless to restrain corporate trusts[26] but read the same act quite broadly to enjoin union activities and punish union leaders.[27] Lower federal courts also exercised broad statutory and equitable powers to enjoin strikes and work actions. Deciding labor dispute cases in equity had the added benefit of denying labor organizers jury trials, where they might have received a more favorable hearing than from judges, many of whom were former corporate counsel for railroads or other large companies.

The Fuller Court vigorously opposed a broad spectrum of progressive reforms. In a series of controversial cases, the Court invalidated the federal income tax and attacked the progressive redistributive politics on which the tax was based.[28] As a result, the Court became a target of Democrat William Jennings Bryan's 1896 presidential campaign, which called for a progressive federal income tax and an end to "government by injunction."

In *Lochner v. New York* (1905), the Court invalidated a state law imposing a sixty-hour maximum work week on the ground that it violated employees' constitutional freedom to contract for however many hours they wished to work. The majority decided that the law was not a wise exercise of New York's police powers. In one of the most fa-

24. *Smythe v. Ames*, 169 U.S. 466 (1898).
25. *ICC v. Cincinnati, New Orleans, and Texas Pacific Ry. Co.*, 167 U.S. 479 (1897).
26. *United States v. E. C. Knight Co.*, 156 U.S. 1 (1895).
27. *In re Debs*, 158 U.S. 564 (1895); Loewe v. Lawlor, 208 U.S. 274 (1908).
28. *Pollock v. Farmer's Loan and Trust Co.*, 157 U.S. 429 (1895).

mous and influential dissents of all time, Oliver Wendell Holmes attacked the doctrine of substantive due process and reminded the majority that "the Fourteenth Amendment does not enact Mr. Herbert Spencer's *Social Statistics*" or any other socioeconomic orthodoxy. But Holmes dissented alone, and for most of the Fuller era he remained isolated and had little influence inside the conference room.[29]

There were a few partial victories for the working classes scattered among the Fuller Court's long list of probusiness decisions. In *Muller v. Oregon* (1908), the Court upheld a state law mandating a ten-hour per day maximum workload for women. But the result was not all that it appeared to be. Rather than vindicating the rights of government or unions to protect workers' interests, the Court acted on the paternal belief that women needed greater protection in the workplace than men. Men—whether in labor or in management—could presumably make contracts freely as equals, so there was no need for government interference in employer-employee negotiations. Women, however, were a weak and vulnerable class in need of "especial care." The majority placed supposedly benign limits on women's freedom of contract in order to protect them from the perils of the marketplace.[30] The upshot was that state governments could act out of paternal concern to limit working hours for women and children, but not for men.

In *United States v. E. C. Knight Co.* (1895), the Court interpreted both the Sherman Antitrust Act and the commerce clause narrowly to strike down federal attempts to regulate the American Sugar Refining Company, a giant trust that controlled 98 percent of the country's refined sugar. The majority distinguished commerce from production and ruled that the E. C. Knight Company was involved only in sugar *production*, which was a local activity and beyond the reach of the commerce clause.

While the Fuller Court thought that the power to regulate corporate trusts was largely beyond the reach of Congress, the Justices initially implied that states could use their police powers to regulate and control corporate activities. The Tenth Amendment, the majority said in *E. C. Knight*, meant that the intrastate production of commodities could only be regulated by the states. In practice, however, states like New Jersey and Delaware courted corporations in the hope of raising state tax revenues and increasing local employment. Subject to few regulations and favorable state laws, these giant trusts continued to operate with impunity.

The federal government, however, had not abandoned its efforts to regulate big business. During President Theodore Roosevelt's famous trust-busting campaign, the federal government won several notable court victories. As time passed, the Fuller Court gradually warmed to Roosevelt's efforts. But Roosevelt preferred to regulate corporations through administratively enacted rules and regulations and sought to wrangle "gentle-

---

29. *Lochner v. New York*, 198 U.S. 45, 75 (1905). Compare with *Adair v. United States*, 208 U.S. 161 (1908).
30. *Muller v. Oregon*, 208 U.S. 412 (1908).

men's agreements" from trusts rather than attacking them through the courts.[31] While offering some support to Roosevelt's trust-busting efforts, the Justices remained strongly probusiness and Fuller's antiregulatory views continued to dominate Supreme Court thinking for nearly three decades after his death in 1910.

Outside of the Court a growing tide of populism and progressive politics was reflected in the elected branches of government. Politicians began to favor greater federal regulation of large corporations, especially through a more expansive use of Congress's commerce clause and taxing powers.

If the Fuller Court was hostile to labor and government regulation, it was even less sympathetic to racial civil rights cases and equal protection claims. In 1896, the Court endorsed the "separate but equal" doctrine in *Plessy v. Ferguson*, which legitimized state-sanctioned racial segregation throughout the South. The racial situation might have been even worse than it was during the period just prior to the Civil War because this time, in contrast to *Dred Scott*, virtually all of the Northern Justices joined the majority in *Plessy*. Henry Brown, a New England Brahmin from Massachusetts (Brown came from a long line of Puritan stock in which, he bragged, "there has been no admixture of alien blood for two hundred and fifty years"), wrote the majority opinion for an 8–1 Court. Only Harlan of Kentucky dissented. The Court also approved the use of literacy tests, poll taxes, and other devices states commonly employed to disenfranchise blacks.[32]

The Court's public reputation declined dramatically during Fuller's last years on the Court. Teddy Roosevelt complained in a letter to his friend Horace H. Lurton that

> the condition of the Supreme Court is pitiable. . . . Really the Chief Justice is almost senile; Harlan does no work; Brewer is so deaf that he cannot hear and has got beyond the point of the commonest accuracy in writing his opinions; Brewer and Harlan sleep almost through all the arguments. I don't know what can be done. It is most discouraging to the active men on the Bench.[33]

EDWARD WHITE: "GOD HELP US!" (1910–1921)

When Melville Fuller died of a heart attack in 1910, John Marshall Harlan and Edward Douglass White were both determined to succeed him. Oliver Wendell Holmes and William Day also briefly entertained the idea of becoming Chief Justice but quickly fell out of the running.

---

31. See, for example, *Northern Securities Co. v. United States*, 193 U.S. 197 (1903); *Swift and Co. v. United States*, 196 U.S. 375 (1905).

32. See, for example, *Williams v. Mississippi*, 170 U.S. 213 (1898). After Fuller died, the Court later struck down the use of most grandfather clauses in *Guinn v. United States*, 238 U.S. 347 (1915).

33. Bickel and Schmidt, *The Judiciary and Responsible Government*, 7.

Harlan was a Southern Republican of the old school—Holmes called him "the last of the tobacco-spitting judges"—while White was a Southern Catholic Democrat and the only Louisiana native ever appointed to the Court.[34] He had been a Confederate drummer boy and aide-de-camp during the Civil War and was captured and held as a prisoner of war until Union soldiers allowed him to return home for the remainder of the war.[35]

President William Howard Taft considered several other candidates, most seriously Charles Evans Hughes. Taft had earlier promised to appoint Hughes as Chief Justice when Fuller left the Court, but the timing of Fuller's death was awkward. Hughes had just recently been confirmed as an Associate Justice to replace David Brewer, and the other Justices would have resented such a quick promotion. Taft apparently intended to nominate Hughes anyway, but at the last moment he changed his mind and chose White instead.[36] Taft's change of heart was based on a simple political calculation: he wanted to appeal to Southern Democrats and Catholics at the next general election.

Taft submitted White's name to the Senate on December 12, 1910, and he was confirmed by voice vote later the same day. He was the first Chief Justice to be promoted from inside the Court.

White was delighted to be Chief Justice and was a gracious winner. He was a polite and proper man, whom friends described as "early Victorian in his courtesies."[37] Seeking to project a more dignified image as Chief Justice, White gave up his favorite habit of tearing five-cent cigars into bits and chewing the pieces during conference.[38] Always quiet and introverted as an Associate Justice, White worked to become more outgoing and solicitous and eventually came to enjoy the social aspects of his new job. According to Charles Evans Hughes, the new Chief Justice

> assumed his new duties with manifest pleasure and with a most earnest desire to discharge them well. He was no longer distant or difficult. On the contrary, he was considerate and gracious in his dealings with every member of the Court, plainly anxious to create an atmosphere of friendliness and to promote agreement in the disposition of cases. . . . [W]e became a reasonably happy family.[39]

White was personable, had a good sense of humor, and took an interest in looking after the other Justices' welfare. He tried to improve his health by walking and often invited other Justices to walk with him. He learned Fuller's art of appealing to his colleagues' egos to encourage their cooperation. White often dropped by Charles Evans

34. Pusey, *Charles Evans Hughes*, 277.
35. Bickel and Schmidt, *The Judiciary and Responsible Government*, 34–35.
36. Taft also considered Elihu Root and Secretary of State Philander C. Knox. Ibid., 37.
37. Ibid., 39.
38. Pusey, *Charles Evans Hughes*, 282.
39. Quoted in Bickel and Schmidt, *The Judiciary and Responsible Government*, 79–80.

Hughes's house for a visit and invariably asked Hughes's secretary whether "the Great Man" was in. White would say that he was in trouble again and desperately needed the Great Man's advice.[40]

With Fuller's house no longer available for conferences, the Justices reluctantly moved back into their old consultation room in the Capitol basement. According to Hughes, during conferences the room quickly "became overheated and the air foul . . . and not conducive to good humor."[41] It hardly helped that White's conferences tended to be rather dull. The unhappy combination of heat and boredom caused Holmes to grow irritable. When conference discussions did not move quickly enough to suit him, Holmes would sit at the table with his face buried in his hands. When he could not take any more, he would lift his head, roll his eyes, and moan, "Christ!" and then let his face fall back into his hands. If the speaker continued, Holmes would raise his head again and groan, "God!" and if things did not wrap up quickly after that, he would let loose a string of obscenities.[42]

Despite White's efforts, camaraderie remained difficult to cultivate. The Justices still did not have chambers or a common working or dining area in the Capitol building, and they continued to work alone at home.[43]

Naturally cautious, White sought to avoid controversial cases or to delay difficult decisions for as long as possible. This earned him the nickname "The Great Procrastinator."[44]

Overall, White had mixed success as a conference leader. He nurtured a generally positive and cooperative attitude among the Justices, but he was an indifferent task leader and was ineffective in guiding conference discussions. White was not especially skilled at presenting case summaries. He was neither clear nor concise in setting out the facts or the law, and he let the other Justices wander off point and only rarely managed to bring them back around again. Conference discussions became increasingly long-winded and inefficient, and the Court fell behind in its work.

The issues before the Court continued to grow more contentious and difficult, and the Court's divisions deepened. White was a deeply religious man, and in especially troublesome cases where the conference was divided, he had the disconcerting habit of throwing up his hands in despair and crying, "God help us!"[45] It was, Hughes said, "as

---

40. Each Justice received a $2,000 furniture allowance, plus a small amount annually for routine maintenance and repairs. Congress appropriated enough funds each year to maintain a common library at the Capitol and for small personal libraries in each Justice's home. Pusey, *Charles Evans Hughes*, 282.

41. Bickel and Schmidt, *The Judiciary and Responsible Government*, 81.

42. Pearson and Allen, *The Nine Old Men*, 39.

43. Pusey, *Charles Evans Hughes*, 275.

44. Mason, *William Howard Taft*, 194.

45. Pusey, *Charles Evans Hughes*, 283. White was the second Catholic on the Court; Roger Brooke Taney was the first.

though he counted on God to decide a case."[46] Hughes personally liked White and thought him a "very dear man" but believed that the Chief Justice "completely lacked executive ability" and was "very unsatisfactory at Conferences, as he would talk for an hour, yet not be well prepared, and not take a position on most of the cases."

There was still tremendous institutional pressure on the Justices to edit their opinions in order to maintain consensus in conference and avoid dissents. Holmes, who was fond of sweeping language and vivid imagery in his opinions, was a frequent target of this pressure. He often complained to his friends that "The boys generally cut one of the genitals out of [my opinions]."[47]

Holmes was not disposed to dissent alone, and if no one else joined him he usually sat on his hands, "mute and sorrowful." Holmes gradually became less reluctant to dissent alone, though he preferred to have company.[48] Still, the tensions in the conference room affected him. During a break in one conference, Holmes wrote to Felix Frankfurter: "I stepped out of a cloud of biting mosquitoes for a word of freedom with you. Now I go back to the swamp."[49]

The White Court, however, might have been a bit *too* collegial for John Marshall Harlan. He complained to Charles Evans Hughes that there was too little disagreement on the Court to suit him.[50]

Hughes was perhaps the most reluctant dissenter on the White Court. Throughout his career, he clung to his belief that dissents were a last resort, to be used with "utmost restraint."[51] While dissents were important—Hughes famously called them "an appeal to the brooding spirit of the law, to the intelligence of a future day"—he thought that such appeals were best made rarely, and only for the most compelling reasons. Hughes resigned in 1916 and entered private practice. When he returned to the Court in 1930 as Chief Justice, his main goal was to avoid repeating Edward White's mistakes.

Under White, the Supreme Court was less hostile to the idea of government economic regulation than it had been under Melville Fuller, and a majority often sided with

---

46. Lash, *From the Diaries of Felix Frankfurter*, 313–14 (Friday, April 25, 1947).

47. Pusey, *Charles Evans Hughes*, 286. Holmes often groused about this sort of treatment in letters to friends. In 1919, Holmes wrote to Felix Frankfurter complaining that the conference had eliminated some "innocuous enfantiallages" and "exuberances" in one of his draft opinions and had substituted "some pap that would not hurt an infant's stomach." In 1920, he wrote again to Frankfurter to say that another of his draft opinions "had a tiny pair of testicles . . . as originally written" but that "the scruples of my Brethren have caused their removal and it speaks in a very soft voice now." Letter from Oliver Wendell Holmes to Felix Frankfurter (October 24, 1920), and letter from Oliver Wendell Holmes to Felix Frankfurter (November 30, 1919), quoted in White, "Holmes and American Jurisprudence," 112.

48. Pusey, *Charles Evans Hughes*, 286–87.

49. White, *Justice Oliver Wendell Holmes*, 314.

50. Pusey, *Charles Evans Hughes*, 283.

51. Ibid., 293.

the government. World War I (1917–19) triggered another round of rapid growth in the size of the federal government, especially of executive agencies. As the federal government grew and assumed new regulatory responsibilities, Congress became more active in managing the national economy. Unprecedented federal controls were placed on manufacturing, transportation, and commodity prices. While the Court struck down some price-control legislation as vague and lacking specific administrative standards, the Court rarely interfered in the government's wartime economic policies.

Congress used its commerce clause and taxing powers to claim new federal police powers aimed at protecting health, safety, welfare, and morals on a national scale.[52] This idea gradually gained acceptance with a series of laws intended to protect farmers, workers (especially women and children), and consumers. The Court approved a new federal scheme to set railroad prices through the Interstate Commerce Commission, which claimed the authority to regulate both interstate and intrastate rates.[53] There were also new federal laws promoting national moral standards, including statutes regulating or prohibiting alcohol, narcotics, and prostitution.[54]

The Court's tolerance of ambitious federal economic programs came to an abrupt end with *Hammer v. Dagenhart* (1918), which struck down the Child Labor Act on the grounds that it usurped state police powers in violation of the Tenth Amendment and exceeded Congress's commerce clause powers. Chief Justice White ruled that the act was an impermissible *prohibition* rather than a *regulation* of commerce. The goods produced by child labor in themselves were not dangerous and could not reasonably be prohibited from the national stream of commerce on that basis. The Court confirmed this abrupt shift in doctrine when it subsequently struck down Congress's second effort to regulate child labor using its tax and spend powers.[55]

Yet, the White Court was more sympathetic to the federal government's antitrust efforts than the Fuller Court had been. Congress was permitted to determine for itself what was "reasonable" in terms of antitrust regulations, in sharp contrast to the Fuller Court's tendency to second-guess the wisdom and desirability of federal economic legislation.

In civil rights cases, World War I precipitated a significant erosion of individual civil liberties, and the White Court did little to staunch the flow. The federal government

---

52. *Shreveport Rate Case (Houston, East and West Texas Ry. Co. v. United States)*, 234 U.S. 342 (1914).

53. *Shreveport Rate Case*, 234 U.S. 342 (1914).

54. The leading example is the Mann Act (1910), also known as the "White Slave Traffic Act," which prohibited the transportation of women across state lines for the purposes of "prostitution or debauchery, or for any other immoral practice." The White Court upheld the statute in *Hoke v. United States*, 227 U.S. 308 (1913).

55. *Bailey v. Drexel Furniture Co.*, 259 U.S. 20 (1922). By this time, William Howard Taft had replaced Edward White as Chief Justice.

passed new legislation restricting free speech and free press, including the Espionage Act of 1917, the Trading with the Enemy Act of 1917, and the Sedition Act of 1918. The Supreme Court deferentially approved these and other wartime restrictions on individual rights.[56] Many state governments followed with their own antisyndicalism acts to suppress allegedly dangerous and subversive political movements such as communists, socialists, and anarchists.

WILLIAM HOWARD TAFT:
THE PERSONAL EQUATION (1921–1930)

History is full of Supreme Court Justices who wanted to be president. William Howard Taft was the president who wanted to be a Supreme Court justice. He was never happier than when he left the White House and became Chief Justice. Taft thrived on the collegiality and shared responsibilities of the Court, where the deliberate and collective decision making better suited his ideas of how government should work than the solitary authority of presidents.[57]

Long before he became Chief Justice, President Taft took a deep personal interest in the Supreme Court and actively promoted its independence and prestige. As Chief Justice, he was arguably the most effective judicial lobbyist ever, using his considerable political influence to secure unprecedented resources for the Court.

More than a century after the Supreme Court moved to Washington from Philadelphia, the Justices still had no chambers or office space in the Capitol building, and they continued to do virtually all their work at home. This arrangement suited most of the Justices, but for Taft the slight was intolerable. He was convinced that the only way for the Court to receive the respect it deserved was to have a suitably impressive home of its own. As president, Taft began a one-man crusade to build a new Supreme Court building and allow the Court to step out of the shadow of Congress.

As president, and later as Chief Justice, Taft lobbied both Congress and the conference with single-minded determination. Ironically, his most difficult task was convincing the other Justices to leave the Old Senate Chamber. Two Chief Justices, Melville Fuller and Edward White, both strongly opposed Taft's proposal for a new building. They were convinced that the Court's prestige would suffer if it moved out of the Capitol and away from the reflected authority of Congress. Not one of the other Justices shared Taft's enthusiasm for his idea.[58]

---

56. *Schenck v. United States*, 249 U.S. 47 (1919), upholding the Espionage Act of 1917 as amended and expanded by the Sedition Act of 1918.

57. Mason, *William Howard Taft*, 233.

58. Pusey, *Charles Evans Hughes*, 275.

After he became Chief Justice, Taft moved cautiously. He refused to bring the issue before the conference until he was sure of the outcome. After considerable wrangling and back-room maneuvering, he finally submitted the question to the conference. Despite his best efforts, the best he could manage was a deeply ambivalent 5–4 vote in favor of the new building. Taft immediately claimed a mandate and never brought the matter before the conference again. Congress duly authorized funds for the new building in 1925. Taft proudly attended the groundbreaking ceremonies and actively supervised the initial planning and construction, but he died in 1930, five years before the Court's new home could be finished.

Taft had three priorities as Chief Justice: harmony, efficiency, and unanimity. As for harmony, Taft was a genial and self-deprecating man. He was by nature highly social and sought to inspire camaraderie on the Court. This was easier said than done, as the great personal and ideological divisions on the Court that had emerged under Fuller and White continued unabated. There was a growing public perception that deep personal antagonisms were tearing the Court apart. While the level of infighting seems unexceptional by modern standards, at the time it seemed as though the Court might fall to pieces. Of course such infighting was hardly new. What was unprecedented was the degree to which the Court's internal politics were being publicized by journalists and legal scholars.

When Taft first came to the Court, most people expected him to use his famous powers of charm, tact, humor, and diplomacy to bind the Court's wounds and end the internal divisions that had troubled the previous two Chief Justices. Of course that did not happen. Felix Frankfurter found it humorous that even serious journalists were so naive as to believe that just because Taft was now Chief Justice "that Van Devanter would say, 'For ten years I've been disagreeing with Holmes, but now that you've smiled at both of us, why we just love each other.'" As Frankfurter wryly noted, the dissent rates and number of 5–4 decisions remained about the same, and the conference room was "just as lively a place."[59]

If Taft did not succeed in solving all of the Court's problems, the other Justices considered him to be an excellent conference leader. Holmes said that "with the present CJ things go as smoothly as possible." Conferences "were perhaps pleasanter than I have ever known them—thanks largely to the CJ." Before Taft became Chief Justice, Holmes observed, the Justices treated each difference of opinion expressed in conference "as an invitation to a cockfight." Taft was more inclined than either Fuller or White to step in "to stop the other side when the matter seems clear." "Never before," Holmes concluded, "have we gotten along with so little jangling and dissension."[60]

59. Frankfurter, "Chief Justices I Have Known," 900.
60. Schwartz, *History of the Supreme Court*, 213–14.

Taft paid close attention to the social relations of the Court, which he called "the personal equation."[61] He performed countless small favors for the other Justices and their families, sending salmon to Van Devanter, giving Holmes and Brandeis rides home after Saturday conferences, and mailing a constant stream of holiday cards and condolence cards to Justices and their families. He quietly did big favors as well, such as making sure that Holmes's wife, Fanny, received an executive waiver to be buried at Arlington National Cemetery.[62]

Taft was the first Chief Justice to concentrate on the task of making the Court an efficient institution. *The Christian Science Monitor* reported that while other men sought riches, Taft sought a clear docket.

When Taft became Chief Justice, the Court was nearly three years behind in its work. Taft and his righthand man, Willis Van Devanter, lobbied Congress in 1925 to pass a law that would severely limit the use of mandatory appeals and emphasize discretionary writs of certiorari. With the Judiciary Act of 1925, the Court ceased to be a Court of Error, where 80 percent of the Court's business consisted of mandatory appeals. For the first time in the Court's history, the Justices assumed nearly complete control over their own docket and could hear or reject most cases at will. The Chief Justice also tried, with less success, to cut the Court's recess from seventeen weeks to twelve. The other Justices objected and pressed Taft to cut down the number of weeks allotted to oral argument instead.

Taft excelled at administrative routine, which further increased the Court's efficiency. He believed in collective responsibility and shared the workload in important administrative and procedural matters. Taft thought that teamwork and a sense of common purpose were essential to maintain efficiency and to enhance the Court's authority. By increasing the efficiency of Court operations, Taft drastically cut the Court's printing costs and was able to reduce the costs to litigants significantly. Under his leadership the Court returned a small budget surplus each year.[63] This transformation of the Court's way of doing business enabled the Justices to catch up with the backlog of cases. During the 1922 term, the Court disposed of a record number of cases, and the average time to have a case heard fell from fifteen months to less than twelve.[64]

More than a clear docket, Taft wanted unanimous decisions. He used every trick to encourage consensus and discourage dissent. He used his case assignment powers to great advantage, assigning cases according to each Justice's particular interests and expertise. He used his considerable political skills—persuasion, courtesy, charm, deference, flattery, and old-fashioned arm twisting—to discourage dissents and to restore a coopera-

61. Mason, *William Howard Taft*, 195.
62. Ibid., 205.
63. Ibid., 192–94.
64. Ibid., 194–95.

tive spirit to opinion writing. Taft insisted that the Justices negotiate, compromise, and seek consensus rather than settle for a bare majority. He referred to this process as "massing the Court," and he believed that it was the most important role that a Chief Justice could play to promote the authority and prestige of the Court. Taft passionately believed that Justices should not dissent unless their consciences demanded it.[65]

Taft himself was perfectly willing to make major concessions in his own opinions in order to mass the Court, and the others tended to follow his lead. Brandeis later admitted that with Taft's active encouragement, in the interest of unity he regularly endorsed opinions with which he did not agree.[66] Even independent-minded Harlan Fiske Stone became a self-proclaimed "team player." Stone acknowledged that he cooperated in part because Taft was extraordinarily generous in assigning cases, regularly keeping the routine cases for himself and assigning the more interesting cases to others.[67] It was only after Taft died that Stone began to dissent regularly.

In contrast with Edward White, Taft was not one to avoid deciding hard cases; he preferred to face difficult issues head-on and get them out of the way. In conference, he refused to hold cases over, insisting that each case be decided the same week that it was argued—even if it meant holding five- or six-hour conferences. Even octogenarian Holmes agreed that the results were worth the extra effort, although the constant struggle to keep up was a strain. Some of the other Justices grumbled, particularly McReynolds, but Taft dismissed him as a lazy judge who was "always trying to escape work."[68]

Some commentators have tried to minimize Taft's role in moderating conflicts inside the conference room, arguing that he benefited from a new breed of Justice—those who were more professional and less likely to take disagreements personally.[69] This argument is not entirely persuasive, given that James McReynolds was still on the Court.

Holmes called McReynolds "a savage," which only showed Holmes's occasional talent for understatement. McReynolds was the most foul-tempered and bigoted man ever to serve on the Court. He was the Ty Cobb of the Supreme Court, only far less talented at his chosen profession. McReynolds particularly hated Louis Brandeis and refused to associate either personally or professionally with the first Jewish Justice.[70] McReynolds declined all social invitations where Brandeis might be present, saying, "I don't dine with the Orient." McReynolds even balked at sitting with Brandeis for Court photographs, causing so many problems that in 1924 there was no group picture. McReynolds once

65. Ibid., 200–1, 234.
66. Bickel, *The Unpublished Opinions of Mr. Justice Brandeis*, 203–6; Mason, *William Howard Taft*, 201.
67. Mason, *William Howard Taft*, 203–4.
68. Ibid., 194.
69. Ibid., 199.
70. O'Brien, *Storm Center*, 236.

refused to travel with the Court to Philadelphia for a ceremonial occasion, writing Taft a brief note to say, "As you know, I am not always to be found when there is a Hebrew abroad. Therefore my 'inability' to attend must not surprise you."[71]

Brandeis was hardly the only Justice whom McReynolds hated. He despised the second Jewish Justice, Benjamin Cardozo, nearly as much as he detested Brandeis. McReynolds refused to sign John Clarke's retirement letter, and of course he refused to sign Brandeis's as well.[72] But Taft managed to maintain good personal relations with McReynolds and for the most part kept him on a short leash.

There were other personnel problems that Taft handled with special care. He continued his predecessors' practice of giving Joseph McKenna only the easiest assignments. McKenna's work was so unsatisfactory, however, that the Chief Justice finally decided that "nothing is too easy for him." When Taft had to miss a conference, by convention McKenna presided as the senior Associate Justice. McKenna was so hopeless that Taft usually had to conduct the same conference all over again when he returned.[73] Toward the end of his career, McKenna's voting behavior grew increasingly erratic. Taft wrote that McKenna "makes up his mind now on the impressionistic principle. He is a Cubist on the bench, and Cubists are not safe on the bench."[74]

Perhaps Taft's greatest challenge in solving the personal equation was the Chief Justice's own longstanding enmity with Louis Brandeis. Taft had opposed Brandeis's appointment to the Court in 1916, and he had signed a mean-spirited petition by several former presidents of the American Bar Association urging the Senate to reject Brandeis. Soon after he became Chief Justice, Taft sought Brandeis out to clear the air and the two reconciled—at least publicly. Brandeis later reported that he eventually came to respect and appreciate Taft's leadership abilities. Things went "happily in the conference room," he said. "The Judges go home less tired emotionally and less weary physically than in White's day. When we differ, we agree to differ without any ill feeling. It's all very friendly."[75] Holmes agreed that the Court was "very happy" under Taft. The Chief Justice, Holmes noted, was good humored, laughed readily, and above all kept things moving in conference.

The Court continued its longstanding tradition of economic conservatism.[76] Significantly, however, the Justices took the first tentative steps toward nationalizing the Bill of Rights in striking down a state law prohibiting the teaching of foreign languages to ele-

---

71. Mason, *William Howard Taft*, 216–17.

72. Ibid. Clarke hated the conforming pressures of the conference and quickly wearied of Court life. He was often depressed and was a notorious hypochondriac. He abruptly and unexpectedly resigned in 1922. Bickel and Schmidt, *The Judiciary and Responsible Government*, 413.

73. Mason, *William Howard Taft*, 213.

74. Ibid., 214.

75. Mason, *William Howard Taft*, 200.

76. See, for example, *Truax v. Corrigan*, 257 U.S. 312 (1921); *Adkins v. Children's Hospital*, 261 U.S. 525 (1923); *Wolff Packing Co. v. Court of Industrial Relations*, 262 U.S. 522 (1923).

mentary school children in *Meyer v. Nebraska*.[77] The Justices ruled that part of the Fourteenth Amendment's liberty rights included the right of parents to raise children as they saw fit. Two years later the Court struck down another state law requiring children between eight and sixteen to attend public school in *Pierce v. Society of Sisters*.[78]

Toward the end of Taft's tenure, conference feuds and dissents grew sharper and more frequent, due to Taft's declining health and the growing willingness of the liberal wing of the Court to go its own way. Beginning in 1925, a core of three progressive justices— Holmes, Brandeis, and Stone—began to dissent on a regular basis.

Taft called this group "the Knockers," or "the Three Dissenters." He blamed them for undermining the efficiency and teamwork that Taft cherished. Taft considered Stone the most dangerous, privately calling him a Bolshevik. The Chief Justice continued to do his best to discourage dissents, but in the end he had to settle for trying to marginalize the Knockers as best he could and minimize the damage to the Court's unity and morale.

Taft's health worsened after 1924, and the Chief Justice was forced to rely more heavily on Van Devanter to run the conference. By 1927, Van Devanter's health began to fail and Taft lost control of the conference. By modern standards, Taft did an extraordinary job of holding the Court together until the very end. During Taft's tenure as Chief Justice, the Court's dissent rate was 9 percent.[79]

CHARLES EVANS HUGHES:
NEW TREASURES AND LOST PLEASURES (1930–1941)

When Taft discovered that he was dying, he pleaded with Herbert Hoover to appoint Charles Evans Hughes as his successor. Taft feared that Hoover wanted to promote Harlan Fiske Stone instead and thought that it would be a terrible mistake. "Stone is not a leader," Taft said, "and would have a great deal of trouble *in massing the Court*."[80] Hoover granted Taft's dying wish and nominated Hughes to become Chief Justice.[81] Hughes was confirmed by the Senate on February 24, 1930, and Taft died just twelve days later.

---

77. *Meyer v. Nebraska*, 262 U.S. 390 (1923).

78. *Pierce v. Society of Sisters*, 268 U.S. 510 (1925).

79. Data complied from Epstein, *Supreme Court Compendium*, 197.

80. Pusey, 2 *Charles Evans Hughes*, 650.

81. There is a story about Hughes's appointment that deserves to be true but is probably apocryphal. Hoover was reluctant to appoint Hughes Chief Justice but felt obliged to honor his promise to Taft. One of Hoover's advisers reassured the president that the offer would surely be declined, because Hughes's son was the solicitor general and would have to resign if his father became Chief Justice. Encouraged, Hoover called Hughes on the spot and offered him the job. After a brief conversation, Hoover hung up the phone and angrily said, "The son of a bitch doesn't give a damn about his son's career." Rauh, "Historical Perspectives," 69 *N.C.L. Rev.* 213, 214–15 (1990).

Hughes certainly *looked* like a Chief Justice. He was tall and fit, with thinning hair but a memorable, intelligent face. He had sharp, penetrating eyes framed by expressive, scholarly eyebrows, and a majestic white beard and moustache that gave him a distinctive and recognizable face. He once received a letter with no address on it except for a penciled caricature.[82] Felix Frankfurter called him "Bushy" behind his back.

Hughes had a personality that was well suited to being Chief Justice. He possessed a healthy ego and a keen intellect, leavened by an engaging, friendly, self-deprecating, and dignified demeanor. Merlo Pusey characterized Hughes's personality as "meekness with power."[83]

Conferences under the compulsively punctual Hughes began precisely at noon on Saturdays and usually finished by 4:30 or 5:00 P.M. Hughes prided himself on being prepared for conference. His comments were lucid and concise, setting the tone for the discussions, which he expected to be similarly focused, disciplined, and restrained.[84] William O. Douglas thought that Hughes was "brilliant" in conference. "He knew how to conduct a judicial conference," Douglas said. "He had perfect command of the cases."[85]

Hughes's critics, particularly Harlan Fiske Stone, thought that he was too domineering and schoolmasterish. These complaints were probably exaggerated; it would have been impossible to control this group of independent, confident, and opinionated judges by playing teacher or drill sergeant. Cardozo's backhanded compliment was perhaps more accurate and cutting when he characterized Hughes as a "brilliant and efficient Chief Justice, but one without wisdom."[86]

Hughes dominated the conference, but he did so subtly. Taking his cue from Taft, he concentrated most of his efforts in two areas: efficiency and collegiality.[87] In terms of efficiency, Hughes was perhaps even better at managing the Court's workload than Taft.[88] Hughes also worked to maintain harmonious personal and professional relationships on the Court. According to Drew Pearson, "There is no god before whom the Chief Justice prostrates himself more abjectly than before the goddess of harmony. He is the great harmonizer of the Supreme Court."[89] But there were factors beyond Hughes's control that ultimately thwarted his dream of restoring the more closely knit and harmonious Court of the Marshall era.

---

82. Pearson and Allen, *The Nine Old Men*, 92. Hughes was so tickled by the letter that he carried it in his coat pocket, showing it to anyone he thought might be interested.
83. Pusey, 2 *Charles Evans Hughes*, 791.
84. Rehnquist, *The Supreme Court*, 292.
85. Simon, *Independent Journey*, 11.
86. Rauh, "Historical Perspectives," 69 *N.C.L. Rev.* 213, 215 (1990).
87. Pusey, 2 *Charles Evans Hughes*, 676.
88. Pearson and Allen, *The Nine Old Men*, 35.
89. Pearson and Allen, *The Nine Old Men*, 40.

After seventy-five years in the Old Senate Chamber, the Court finally emerged from the shadow of Congress in 1935 and moved across the street into the new Supreme Court building. The Justices, however, were ambivalent about the change of address. For the most part they would have preferred to remain in the Capitol building. Only George Sutherland and Owen Roberts took chambers in the new building. The rest, including the Chief Justice, continued to work at home. Hughes considered the new building nothing more than "a place to hang my hat." Stone growled about the preposterous scale of the building, which he said made the Justices look like nine black beetles scurrying about in Karnak's temple.[90] Stone hated the place and continued to work at home even after he became Chief Justice in 1941.

Life sometimes imitates architecture, and once inside the massive new temple the Court quickly grew bigger, more imposing, more complex, more impersonal, and more bureaucratic. The building reinforced the Justices' sense of isolation and mutual estrangement. Except for the Saturday conferences and oral arguments, the Justices rarely saw each other. Even though they now had a common workplace, they continued to work alone.[91]

Before he was appointed to the Supreme Court, Benjamin Cardozo served on the New York Court of Appeals. He thoroughly enjoyed the close and cordial relations he had with his fellow judges in Albany, and when President Hoover appointed him to the Supreme Court in 1932, Cardozo looked forward to establishing similar relationships with his new brethren. He was sorely disappointed by the sense of estrangement and isolation he found in Washington.[92] Before the Court moved into the new building, Cardozo discovered that the only place in the Capitol where the Justices could socialize and gossip was in the men's room outside the Old Senate Chamber. Moving into the new building ended even that modest interaction. Cardozo complained that "now that we have moved into the new building with its private washrooms, there is no pleasure even in urination any more."[93]

Despite the Justices' misgivings, the new building was a complete success as far as the public was concerned. Its classical architecture and impressive size helped to cement the Court's reputation as an independent and co-equal branch of government. The Su-

---

90. O'Brien, *Storm Center*, 115.

91. The Justices had clerks, or secretaries, as they were originally called. In 1882, Horace Gray started the practice of hiring recent law school graduates every year to serve as his secretaries. In the beginning, Gray often paid for his clerks out of his own pocket. Holmes continued the practice when he replaced Gray on the Court, and then Brandeis, Stone, and the rest followed. O'Brien, *Storm Center*, 124.

92. It did not take Cardozo long to realize that the Supreme Court was not as cordial as his old court. He knew that he was not in Albany any more when, during his swearing-in ceremony, he looked up to see James McReynolds reading his morning newspaper on the bench. Cushman, *The Supreme Court Justices*, 373.

93. Pearson and Allen, *The Nine Old Men*, 38.

preme Court was no longer the poor relative of the Congress consigned to the bowels of the Capitol building; it was a powerful and important institution in its own right.

In 1937, Hugo Black became the first new Justice to accept chambers in the new building, and every subsequent appointee followed him. Because of continued resistance among the older Justices, the transition into the new building took more than ten years. The first time all nine Justices had chambers in the new building was under Fred Vinson in 1946.

The Court's new home had some obvious advantages for the conference. While Hughes continued to work at home, the conference met each Saturday in the new and luxurious conference room. The Justices customarily dined together on conference days, and Hughes tried to make these common meals purely social events—periods of "complete relaxation."[94]

As a conference leader, Hughes ranks among the best. The Justices who knew him best agreed that he radiated authority. Frankfurter compared Hughes to Arturo Toscanini as a maestro of the business of judging. Frankfurter tried to reduce Hughes's conference performance to a single word: *taut*. He immediately conceded, however, that *dynamic* and *effective* were probably also necessary to give a more complete picture of Hughes's leadership. Frankfurter consciously chose the word *effective* rather than *efficient*, because he wanted to avoid any implication that Hughes was overly regimented.[95]

Despite the Chief Justice's best efforts, the Court continued to suffer from the same infighting that had plagued his predecessors. The situation led Holmes memorably to describe the Court as "the quiet of a storm center." The Court initially divided into two relatively stable but contentious blocs. On the right, Willis Van Devanter, Pierce Butler, James McReynolds, and George Sutherland were known as the Four Horsemen. They resisted the New Deal at every step and decried the Court's growing inclination to favor civil rights over corporate and economic rights. The Horsemen usually relied on either Hughes or Owen Roberts to provide a fifth conservative vote.[96] On the left were Holmes (replaced by Cardozo in 1932), Brandeis, and Stone.

The Four Horsemen made up a formidable group. They held regular strategy sessions as they rode together by car to and from the Supreme Court building each day. In response, the liberal bloc began to meet at Brandeis's home on Friday evenings to discuss the next day's conference.[97]

These deep and abiding ideological divisions were the subject of countless newspaper articles and editorials, but they also provoked lighter commentary and satire. Dur-

94. Pusey, 2 *Charles Evans Hughes*, 664.

95. Frankfurter, "Chief Justices I Have Known," 902.

96. Roberts later became famous for changing sides in 1937 and voting with the liberal bloc to uphold Roosevelt's minimum wage legislation in *West Coast Hotel v. Parrish*, 300 U.S. 379 (1937).

97. Rauh, "Historical Perspectives," 69 *N.C.L. Rev.* 213, 214 (1990).

ing a public dinner that Hughes and several other Justices attended, the Chace Dancing School did a modern interpretive dance about the Court. The three liberal Justices danced by themselves on left side of the stage, the Four Horsemen and Owen Roberts danced together on the right side, with Hughes "hovering uncertainly between."[98]

The rift became the center of national attention when the Court, in a series of controversial decisions, struck down New Deal legislation intended to bring the country through the Great Depression. The resulting commotion inspired Wilmott Lewis of the *London Times* to observe that "legislation in the United States is a digestive process by Congress with frequent regurgitations by the Supreme Court."[99]

Despite their often bitter legal, ideological, and policy disagreements, the Justices' personal relationships remained surprisingly good. Owen Roberts recalled that at the beginning of conferences, Holmes would often seek out one of his main antagonists, George Sutherland, and cheerfully plead, "Sutherland, J., tell us a story."[100]

The most intractable personal problem on the Court remained the largely one-sided McReynolds-Brandeis feud. Hughes held two social dinners per year, and he had to take care to segregate McReynolds and Brandeis so that they never met. Despite their mutual enmity, McReynolds and Brandeis both remained on good terms with Hughes. McReynolds's only positive contribution to the well-being of the Court was that he refused to allow the other Justices to smoke in the conference room, angrily telling anyone who tried, "Tobacco smoke is personally objectionable to me." Few dared to test his resolve on the matter, and no one ever got away with it.[101]

Pierce Butler was another strong personality who occasionally challenged Hughes's resolve to maintain a collegial Court. Butler was a former railroad lawyer, a true believer in social and economic Darwinism and the sworn enemy of all progressive politics and politicians. As a lawyer, Butler was notorious for his brutal courtroom demeanor and his ruthless bullying of anyone who crossed his path. As a Supreme Court Justice he remained aggressive and stubborn, although unlike McReynolds, he could also be charming and genial. Like everyone else, Butler remained on good terms with Hughes.[102] Of the other Justices, Stone was the most outspoken and sarcastic and was perhaps the only member of the Court who actively (though secretly) disliked Hughes. The rest of the Justices were calm, if not amiable, in their professional dealings with one another.

Hughes had the advantage of being an exceptionally friendly and forgiving man. Hugo Black expected the worst when he was appointed to the Court in 1937. As the junior senator

---

98. Pearson and Allen, *The Nine Old Men*, 89.
99. Pearson and Allen, *The Nine Old Men*, 44.
100. Cushman, *The Supreme Court Justices*, 349.
101. Douglas, *The Court Years*, 13.
102. Cushman, *The Supreme Court Justices*, 353–55.

from Alabama, Black had voted against Hughes's appointment as Chief Justice in 1930 because he believed that Hughes had sold out to corporate interests when he returned to private practice after resigning from the Court for the first time in 1916. Black also led the Democratic attack on the Hughes Court in 1937, when FDR presented his Court-packing plan to Congress. To make matters worse, news of Black's former membership in the Ku Klux Klan was made public just before Black took his seat on the Court. Black knew that Hughes had good cause and plenty of ammunition to make his life miserable. But when Black arrived for his first day at the Court, Hughes greeted him as warmly, Black said, as if he had been the most distinguished jurist in the land. Hughes never retaliated against Black, not even in the privacy of the conference room, even though Black often criticized the Chief's views and broke with tradition by filing numerous lone dissents (including eight solo dissents in his first year on the Court). What could have been a bitter rivalry never materialized, and Black came to consider Hughes one of his best friends.[103]

Hughes was equally supportive and accommodating of the other Justices. Felix Frankfurter recorded in his diary that just after he was appointed to the Court, he showed up at his first conference wearing an alpaca coat that he often wore at Harvard. When Frankfurter walked into the conference room he discovered, to his embarrassment, that all of the other Justices were wearing suits. Aghast, he ran home at lunch and changed into a business suit, only to find on his return that Hughes had also gone home and changed into an alpaca coat to make Frankfurter feel at ease.[104]

Hughes often said that all he tried to do at conference was to avoid repeating Edward White's mistakes. Hughes hated White's indecisive case summaries and his inability to control conference debates, and he tried to limit his case summaries and commentary to four minutes per case. He also sought to confine conference debates to the salient issues, in order to minimize frictions and improve the Court's morale and efficiency.[105]

As a rule, Hughes refused to discuss cases with the other Justices outside of the conference room. While he did not object when the other Justices caucused among themselves informally, he thought it counterproductive for a Chief Justice to be seen behaving that way. According to Owen Roberts, no one knew Hughes's views on a case until he announced them at conference.[106]

In 1948, Roberts gave these insightful observations about the Saturday conferences under Hughes:

> The conferences of the Court took place on Saturdays at noon. If the Saturday in
> question fell in an argument week, the agenda . . . might contain a half dozen jurisdic-

---

103. Pusey, 2 *Charles Evans Hughes,* 773.
104. Lash, *From the Diaries of Felix Frankfurter,* 66.
105. Pusey, 2 *Charles Evans Hughes,* 672.
106. Ibid., 676.

tional statements on appeal, twenty to thirty petitions for certiorari, a few miscellaneous motions, and ten or fifteen cases which had been argued that week.

In the Supreme Court, the Chief Justice opens the discussion of all questions. Chief Justice Hughes would dispose of administrative matters with the greatest promptness. He would then take up the jurisdictional statements and petitions for certiorari. . . . He had a marvelous power of condensing the facts without omitting any that were important, and, on the basis of this statement, he would announce his views as to the action the Court should take. So complete were his summaries, that in many cases nothing needed to be added by any of his associates. . . .

Then came consideration of the argued cases. Again the Chief Justice spoke from lead pencil notes at which he occasionally glanced. His presentation of the facts of a case was full and impartial. His summary of the legal questions arising out of the facts was equally complete, dealing with the opposing contentions so as to make them stand out clearly. When this had been done, he would usually look up with a quizzical smile and say, "Now I will state where I come out," and would then outline what he thought the decision of the Court should be. Again, in many cases his treatment was so complete that little, if anything, further could be added by any of the Justices. In close and difficult cases, where there were opposing views, the discussion would go around the table from the senior to the junior, each stating his views and the reasons for his concurrence or his difference with those outlined by the Chief. After the Chief Justice had finished his statement of the case and others took up the discussion, I have never known him to interrupt or get into an argument with the Justice who was speaking. He would wait until the discussion had closed and then briefly and succinctly call attention to the matters developed in the discussion as to which he agreed or disagreed, giving his reasons. These conference sessions lasted from twelve o'clock sometimes to six, sometimes until six-thirty in the evening, and sometimes the session had to be adjourned until Monday afternoon to finish the business on hand. It is not hard to understand that, at the close of such a conference, most of the Justices were weary. The sustained intellectual effort demanded was great. The way the Chief Justice came through these difficult conferences was always a matter of wonder and admiration to me. After the conference was concluded, he sent for a clerk and assigned the cases. A slip of paper bearing the numbers of the cases assigned to each Justice was sent to his home within an hour and a half after the close of the conference. . . .

He neither leaned on anyone else for advice nor did he proffer advice or assistance to any of us, but left us each to form his own conclusions to be laid on the table at conference in free and open discussion. . . . Many of the associates between argument and conference would discuss the questions involved in the case and would exchange views with their brethren. Certainly there was nothing wrong with this practice, but it seems to me the Chief Justice held a far better position with his Court by not indulging in any such practice, but by beating out his conclusions himself, for announcement to the whole body of the Court in open conference. I am sure that this calculated course greatly strengthened his position and authority with his brethren. . . .

. . . Strong views were often expressed around the conference table, but never in eleven years did I see the Chief Justice lose his temper. Never did I hear him pass a personal remark. Never did I know him to raise his voice. Never did I witness his interrupting a Justice or getting into a controversy with him. . . . The result was a feeling of personal cordiality and comradeship that I think was unique in a Court so seriously divided in its views on great matters of constitutional policy and law. Men whose views were as sharply opposed as those of Van Devanter and Brandeis, or those of Sutherland and Cardozo, were at one in their admiration and affectionate regard for their presiding officer.[107]

Before each conference, Hughes spent hours vetting the cert petitions. He typically eliminated 60 percent of the cases, putting them on the "black list" (later called the "dead list"), which meant that cert would be summarily denied without a formal conference discussion or vote. Any Justice could remove any case from the black list, but Hughes was so good at analyzing cert petitions that this happened only six times in eleven years.[108]

With Hughes's painstaking conference preparations, cert decisions on even the most difficult cases were made quickly, leaving more time for the argued cases. The rule of four was applied loosely in those days; if three or even two Justices felt strongly about accepting a case, the rule was waived and the case was accepted for oral argument.[109] After Hughes retired and the Court's workload increased, the rule began to be more strictly enforced. Today, if fewer than four Justices vote to accept cert, the best that the minority can hope for is that the case will be held over for a time ("relisted") while they try to muster four votes.

Like Taft, Hughes insisted on staying current with the Court's business and required that each case be argued and decided in conference the same week. The other Justices occasionally complained, but Hughes never relented. Even Brandeis, who was often irritated by Hughes's stubbornness and occasionally just packed up and left when a conference ran late, freely acknowledged that Hughes was the greatest executive genius he had ever met.[110]

The other Justices quickly learned to do their homework and have their facts straight before challenging the Chief Justice about a case at conference.[111] Hughes prided himself on his careful conference preparation. He had an amazing memory and he could be intimidating, although for the most part he was a gentle bully. Hughes kept conference discussions brief and to the point. Speaking out of turn was not tolerated, and Hughes

---

107. Westin, *Autobiography of the Supreme Court,* 207–10, citing Justice Roberts's Memorial Address to the New York Bar, December 12, 1948.

108. Pusey, 2 *Charles Evans Hughes,* 672. Prior to Hughes, every case that came before the Court was discussed in conference, at least in theory. Hughes changed this practice by creating the black (dead) list. The initial presumption was that every case not placed on the dead list would be discussed in conference. As the Court's workload increased, this tradition changed and the critical list became the discuss list. The modern presumption is that a case will *not* be discussed in conference unless at least one Justice requests it.

109. Ibid., 673.

110. Ibid.

111. Ibid., 672.

quickly stepped in whenever the discussion threatened to degenerate into bickering. Owen
Roberts observed that

> if discussion among the other members of the Court deteriorated into wrangling,
> Hughes would promptly cut it off. Every Justice had complete freedom to speak his
> mind, and rebuttals and general discussion were permissible. But as soon as heat
> began to supplant analysis and reason, the Chief would say, "Brethren, the only way to
> settle this is to vote."[112]

Hughes interrupted not to get in the last word but to move the conference back to the
business at hand. The typical Hughes conference lasted four hours, but little time
was wasted. By all accounts, Hughes's conferences were extraordinarily efficient and
productive.

Despite Hughes's best efforts to control the conference, discussions grew heated on
occasion, and Hughes himself was prone to lose his temper. In one particularly contentious debate over the Agricultural Adjustment Act (AAA),[113] the Justices began yelling
at each other, and their voices could be heard clearly in the corridor outside the conference room. Above the din, Court employees heard Hughes shout, "*Gentlemen! You are
not only ruining this country, you are ruining this Court!*"[114] He had his priorities.

After each case was discussed, the Justices voted in reverse order of seniority, with
Hughes voting last. After voting, Hughes again quickly summed up the case and then
tried to determine how to find the consensus and avoid dissents.[115]

After the conference, Hughes took it upon himself to smooth any ruffled feathers.
He constantly reminded the other Justices that the passions of the conference room should
be left behind when the conference adjourned. On the rare occasion when the Court
rejected Hughes's proposed resolution of a case, he always made it a point to seek out
his main antagonist afterward and chat with him publicly during their postconference
meal, to show everyone that there were no hard feelings.[116]

Felix Frankfurter said that "no Chief Justice . . . equaled Chief Justice Hughes in
the skill and the wisdom and the disinterestedness with which he made his assign-

---

112. Ibid., 676.

113. *United States v. Butler,* 297 U.S. 1 (1936). The Court struck down the Agricultural Adjustment Act,
an important piece of New Deal legislation, on a 6–3 vote. For a time, this case revitalized the Tenth Amendment and reestablished the idea of dual federalism.

114. Pearson and Allen, *The Nine Old Men,* 43. Hughes initially voted with the minority liberal bloc in
this case, which would have yielded a narrow 5–4 decision to strike down the New Deal legislation. In part
motivated by his desire to avoid a close decision on such an important case, Hughes changed his mind
after conference and voted with the majority to deliver a more decisive 6–3 verdict. Harlan Fiske Stone,
who had assumed that Hughes was busy writing the lead dissent, was stunned by the last-minute switch
and hastily had to scribble his own dissenting opinion.

115. Pusey, 2 *Charles Evans Hughes,* 677.

116. Ibid.

ments."[117] Each Saturday evening, long after the conference was over and the other Justices had gone home, Hughes stayed behind and huddled with his clerk to chart the votes and assign cases. Later that evening, the clerk delivered the completed assignment slips to each Justice's home. There were two exceptions to this routine. After Benjamin Cardozo suffered a heart attack, Hughes postponed delivering his assignments until Sunday or Monday, because he wanted to make sure that Cardozo had an evening or two of rest. Because Van Devanter lived in the same building as Cardozo, Hughes delivered his assignment slips late so that Cardozo would not catch on to his little ruse.[118]

Hughes hated dissents. He tried his best in every case to harmonize the views of the conference and avoid public disagreements. Hughes himself rarely broke ranks, averaging just four dissents per year.[119] He occasionally changed his own vote to support an opinion with which he personally disagreed, as in *United States v. Butler*. These maneuvers gave the Court the appearance of having a greater unity of views than it actually possessed and masked the Court's internal divisions without resolving the underlying problems. Hughes's behavior, however, also gave him an important tactical advantage; by voting with the majority he could control opinion assignments and influence the results in ways he could not have done in dissent.[120]

In contrast to Hughes, the liberal bloc of Brandeis, Stone, and Cardozo routinely dissented at least ten to twenty times each year. Ironically, it was the emerging majority bloc of New Deal Justices who unexpectedly ended once and for all Hughes's dream of a unified Court. With a solid majority of progressive judges after 1938, Hughes hoped that some measure of consensus could finally be restored inside the conference room. He soon discovered, however, that the Roosevelt appointees were just as likely to fight with each other as with the dwindling number of conservatives on the Court.

Not everyone approved of Hughes's leadership. Harlan Fiske Stone hated what he called Hughes's "machine-gun" delivery in conference and thought that Hughes dominated the conference like a drill sergeant, always barking out orders. Stone dreamed of having more dynamic and interactive conference discussions, but he never openly challenged Hughes's leadership, and Hughes died unaware of Stone's dissatisfaction.

Stone sublimated his desire for more freewheeling conference debates by holding "rump conferences" on Fridays before each scheduled Saturday conference. He enjoyed presiding over these bull sessions, which were regularly attended by Frankfurter, Roberts, Douglas, and occasionally Murphy. They continued until Stone became Chief Justice in 1942.

117. Frankfurter, "Chief Justices I Have Known," 905.
118. Douglas, *The Court Years*, 22.
119. Pearson and Allen, *The Nine Old Men*, 40–42.
120. White Burkett Miller Center of Public Affairs, *The Office of Chief Justice*, 28.

Among outside observers, muckraking journalist Drew Pearson was one of Hughes's most relentless critics. In *The Nine Old Men*, Pearson reported that "despite his stately bearing, Charles Evans Hughes . . . is the most pathetic figure on the Supreme Court." Pearson characterized Hughes as "a weak-kneed oscillator between the two wings of the Court, until he fell, discredited and exhausted, in the middle." He accused the Chief Justice of being guided by one principle: what was best for Charles Evans Hughes. Hughes was, in Pearson's judgment, "a tragic failure as chief justice of the United States. . . . probably the most tragic in contemporary history."[121] But even Pearson acknowledged that Hughes grew into his role as Chief Justice as he learned the art of "unbending." Hughes was, Pearson admitted, good natured, charming, sociable, and had a "delightful" sense of humor.[122]

The Hughes Court initially was openly hostile to the New Deal and actively impeded the Roosevelt administration's efforts to cope with the Great Depression. After unanimously striking down three pillars of the New Deal on Black Monday, May 27, 1935, the Court subsequently issued a series of controversial decisions holding that other important New Deal programs were also unconstitutional.[123] As the Depression deepened, however, the Court gradually grew more divided and tentative in its opposition to the New Deal. But the Justices did not move in the right direction as quickly as President Roosevelt wished.

In 1937, a frustrated Roosevelt sought to break the backs of the Four Horsemen by restructuring the Supreme Court. His plan encouraged Justices to retire at age seventy and gave the president the right to appoint a new Justice for every Justice over seventy who refused to retire. The plan would have given Roosevelt an instant majority and could have increased the size of the Court from nine to fifteen Justices.

Although Roosevelt's court-packing plan was ultimately defeated in Congress, it had an impact inside the conference room. Chief Justice Hughes and Owen Roberts, who until recently had voted against most New Deal legislation, began voting consistently to affirm similar laws beginning in 1937, and the Court began to defer to the president and

---

121. Pearson and Allen, *The Nine Old Men*, 76, 96–97.

122. Ibid., 89.

123. The "Black Monday" cases were *Schechter Poultry Corp. v. United States*, 295 U.S. 495 (1935), invalidating the National Industrial Recovery Act; *Louisville Joint Stock Land Bank v. Radford*, 295 U.S. 555 (1935), invalidating the Frazier-Lemke Act; and *Humphrey's Executor v. United States*, 295 U.S. 602 (1935), rejecting the president's dismissal of the federal trade commissioner. Other key decisions striking down New Deal legislation included *Panama Refining Co. v. Ryan*, 293 U.S. 388 (1935); *United States v. Butler*, 297 U.S. 1 (1936); *Carter v. Carter Coal Co.*, 298 U.S. 238 (1936); *Morehead v. New York ex rel. Tipaldo*, 298 U.S. 587 (1936). The last case was not aimed directly at the New Deal, but it invalidated New York's effort to create a minimum wage law for women as a violation of liberty of contract and due process. President Roosevelt used the case to resurrect his charge that the Supreme Court was intent on creating a "no-man's land" where business was free to operate beyond the reach of either state or federal governments.

Congress on economic policy.[124] This change in Court voting patterns became known as "the switch in time that saved nine," although it has never been proved that there was any direct connection between Roosevelt's threats and the Justices' changes of heart. In retrospect, it hardly mattered. In less than two years, Justices Van Devanter, Sutherland, and Brandeis resigned, and Cardozo and Butler died, giving FDR his majority. In 1941, McReynolds and Hughes resigned, leaving Roosevelt's appointees in control of the Court.

While the Hughes Court initially called into question the federal government's domestic economic powers, from the beginning it strongly and unequivocally supported the federal government's efforts in foreign affairs. The Hughes Court affirmed that the president had broad inherent powers to conduct foreign affairs, including the right to make executive agreements that had the same legal status as treaties.[125]

In questions involving state-federal relations, the Hughes Court was strongly nationalist, with one notable exception. Just before he retired in 1938, Louis Brandeis left an enduring legacy to states' rights with *Erie Railroad v. Tompkins.* That case overturned *Swift v. Tyson* and established that there was no federal common law after all, not even in commercial cases. Federal courts were required to follow both state statutory and common law in the absence of supervening federal statutes and regulations.[126]

Perhaps the most important legacy of the Hughes Court was that for the first time the Supreme Court leavened its longstanding preoccupation with economic and property rights with a growing concern for noneconomic human rights. Hughes took in forma pauperis petitions far more seriously than his predecessors. He assumed full responsibility for vetting hundreds of these cases every term, and spent many hours each week reviewing the often crudely written petitions from prisoners and poor petitioners who could not afford lawyers.

The Hughes Court also took several significant steps toward nationalizing the Bill of Rights. In *Powell v. Alabama* (1932), the Justices extended the Sixth Amendment's right to counsel to cover state trials, finding that the right was a fundamental part of due process guaranteed by the Fourteenth Amendment. This case marked the beginning of a new trend toward nationalizing selected procedural safeguards in criminal trials, which allowed the federal courts to place a check on regional justice.

In 1935, the Court reversed Alabama's conviction of another black defendant. Clarence Norris was convicted of rape by an all-white jury in Jackson County, where no black had served as a juror in living memory. At Hughes's urging, the Court changed the long-

---

124. *West Coast Hotel v. Parrish,* 300 U.S. 379 (1937); *NLRB v. Jones and Laughlin Steel Corp.,* 301 U.S. 1 (1937); *United States v. Darby Lumber Co.,* 312 U.S. 100 (1941).

125. For example, *United States v. Curtiss-Wright Export Corp.,* 299 U.S. 304 (1936); *United States v. Belmont,* 301 U.S. 324 (1937).

126. *Erie R.R. v. Tompkins,* 304 U.S. 64 (1938), overruling *Swift v. Tyson,* 41 U.S. (16 Pet.) 1 (1842).

established rule in such cases, which required defendants to prove racial discrimination in each specific case. Instead, evidence of "long-continued, unvarying and wholesale exclusion of Negroes from jury service" would be sufficient to establish a constitutional violation.[127]

Those who anticipated that the entire Bill of Rights would quickly be incorporated and applied to the states via the Fourteenth Amendment were to be disappointed. In *Palko v. Connecticut* (1937), the Court rejected the argument that the Fourteenth Amendment included constitutional protections against double jeopardy in state criminal trials. While total incorporation appeared to be dead—at least for the moment—Cardozo's opinion explicitly endorsed the idea of partial incorporation. Cardozo believed that some, though not all, of the protections offered by the Bill of Rights were fundamental to ordered liberty and could be applied to the states via the due process clause. The only real question was which rights were fundamental and which could be left to the states to decide for themselves.

Hugo Black rejected Cardozo's theory of *preferred rights*. He argued that *all* of the rights listed in the first eight amendments were equally important and should be fully incorporated through the Fourteenth Amendment.[128] But Black's theory of total incorporation never commanded a majority. Black himself eventually settled for a variation of Cardozo's partial incorporation theory, hoping that in the long run the results would be the same—that the Bill of Rights would be fully incorporated in small bites, rather than swallowed whole.

A year after *Palko*, the Court quietly announced a revolutionary change in how it would deal with economic and human rights cases. In the fourth footnote of a minor economic case, *United States v. Carolene Products Co.* (1938), Harlan Fiske Stone gave notice that the Court was abandoning its longstanding judicial activism in reviewing government economic regulations but would adopt a more activist stance in reviewing legislation affecting noneconomic rights. Stone's footnote marked the death of substantive due process in economic cases; but even as he gave the eulogy, Stone implicitly promised to resurrect the idea to protect selected individual rights and liberties. The Supreme Court, Stone said, would use "more exacting scrutiny" to evaluate laws that infringed on individual rights and civil liberties, particularly those that touched on the "preferred freedoms" enumerated in the Bill of Rights or other specific constitutional provisions. The Court would also use heightened scrutiny to evaluate laws that discriminated on the basis

---

127. *Norris v. Alabama*, 294 U.S. 587, 597 (1935).

128. Black, however, accepted the idea of preferred rights as far as the First Amendment was concerned, arguing that free speech rights, in particular, were absolute and always trumped other conflicting constitutional values. Urofsky, *Division and Discord*, 37.

of race, religion, or nationality or that prejudiced the rights of discrete and insular minorities.[129]

History has been kind to Hughes. The five influential New Deal appointees who served under Hughes—Black, Frankfurter, Reed, Douglas, and Murphy—all respected him and later remembered him with great fondness and nostalgia. Most modern scholars recognize that Hughes was uniquely effective as both the social and task leader of the Court and consider him to be among the most successful Chief Justices in history. Despite presiding over one of the most ideologically divided benches in Court history, Hughes managed to keep the case dissent rate under 15 percent.[130]

Over time, Hughes has become the archetype of the modern Chicf Justice. While Harlan Fiske Stone, and to a lesser degree Fred Vinson, conspicuously rejected Hughes's example and looked elsewhere for inspiration, Earl Warren, Warren Burger, and William Rehnquist all consciously sought to emulate Hughes in leading the conference.

HARLAN FISKE STONE: PILLAR OF THE LAW,
PILL OF THE CONFERENCE (1941–1946)

Just as Charles Evans Hughes tried to avoid repeating Edward White's failures as Chief Justice, Harlan Fiske Stone vowed not to run the conference like Hughes. As an Associate Justice, Stone had chafed under the strict discipline that Hughes imposed. He rebelled against Hughes's efforts at consensus building, and relished his status as a dissenter. As Chief Justice, Stone encouraged more open and freewheeling conference discussions and did not care in the least about building consensus.[131]

The nature of the conference changed dramatically in a very short time. The tradition of "massing the Court" to decide cases by consensus was abandoned, and conferences became a contest to gather five votes. The Stone era marked the end of the idea of the "Court as community" and the apotheosis of judicial individualism. There was little pressure to conform to the collective norms of the Court. The stigma of dissent disappeared, and the Justices began to vote their individual consciences as a matter of course. Consensus was supplanted by "the rule of five," where any coalition of five Justices could do pretty much anything they wanted.

---

129. *United States v. Carolene Products Co.*, 304 U.S. 144 (1938). Stone's law clerk, Louis Lusky, and Charles Evans Hughes helped Stone to draft what is often simply referred to as "Footnote Four."

130. Data complied from Epstein, *Supreme Court Compendium*, 197–98.

131. Stone, "The Chief Justice," 407. Stone's antipathy for Hughes recalls the story of Aristides the Just. After Aristides led Greek forces to victory at Marathon and later became a respected democratic politician, the Athenians unexpectedly voted to ostracize him (they voted with oyster shells). Plutarch claimed that when asked whether Aristides had ever done anything to harm Athens, one voter said, "No, but it vexes me to hear him everywhere called 'The Just.'"

The Court's dissent rates skyrocketed. The Stone Court had an overall dissent rate of 50 percent.[132] The openly hostile and personal tone of many of the dissents was also unprecedented. The Justices not only disagreed, they were often quite disagreeable about it.[133] It was a tumultuous and not especially happy time in the Court's history.

Most of Stone's contemporaries, even his closest allies, judged him a failure as Chief Justice. William O. Douglas claimed that when Stone assumed the center chair he reverted to his old professorial mode. In contrast to Hughes's concise case summaries, Stone often talked in conference at great length, and he constantly interrupted the other Justices to argue. Stone enjoyed himself, but the other Justices often found his conferences inefficient, frustrating, and unsatisfying. Douglas thought that Stone "was not good as Chief Justice. We were always in conference. He couldn't move the cases along."[134]

Frank Murphy criticized Stone for failing to control the conference and for giving the Justices too much rein. Instead of trying to mediate disagreements in conference, Stone usually jumped into the fray. Stone had been combative and sarcastic as an Associate Justice, and he refused to change just because he was now Chief Justice. If anything, Stone's behavior during conferences was even less restrained than before, because he was finally in charge and felt little need to defer to anyone.

Stone's fiercely competitive nature, which had served him well as an Associate Justice, became a liability in his new role as Chief Justice. Without a referee in conference, there was little discipline or focus to discussions. Speaking out of turn became commonplace. For his part, Stone groused about the burdens of his job and complained that he had "much difficulty herding my collection of fleas."[135]

Saturday conferences routinely lasted eight hours or more, with only a short break for lunch. The other Justices agreed that lunch was usually the high point of the day.[136] They ate lunch together in a room on the second floor, with each Justice served by messengers who brought in food from the public dining room or from nearby restaurants. Stone, who considered himself a gourmet and a wine expert, regularly had a collection of cheeses brought in. Jimmy Byrnes remembered luncheon conversations as being "stimulating and entertaining, with only one subject barred—the work of the Court."[137]

In order to finish at a reasonable hour, conference starting times were moved back from noon to 11:00 A.M. and then moved back again to 10:00 A.M. But the Justices found

---

132. Data complied from Epstein, *Supreme Court Compendium*, 198.

133. Fine, *Frank Murphy*, 244.

134. Yarbrough, *John Marshall Harlan*, 11.

135. Mason, *Harlan Fiske Stone*, 605.

136. In 1942, Felix Frankfurter suggested that conferences be limited to four hours. His proposal was interpreted as an attack on the conference, and he was forced to abandon the idea. Felix Frankfurter, Memorandum to the Conference, October 22, 1942, William O. Douglas Papers, OT 1942, box 77.

137. Byrnes, *All in One Lifetime*, 136.

that they still could not finish their work by 6:00 P.M., and cases routinely had to be held over into the following week. To keep up, the Court often met in special conference on Mondays from 10:00 A.M. until five minutes before noon, adjourned to hear oral arguments for four hours, and then reconvened at 4:00 P.M. for another couple of hours. Occasionally they met on Tuesdays at 4:00 P.M., and on Wednesdays from 10:00 to 12:00 and 4:00 to 6:00 P.M. It was, in Douglas's view, "almost a continuous conference."[138]

Stone continued Melville Fuller's practice of having the Justices shake hands before each conference. Like many new Justices, Jimmy Byrnes initially thought it a silly custom but later confessed that he learned to enjoy the ceremony as a reminder of the need for courtesy and mutual respect. The Justices apparently continued to vote on cases in reverse order of seniority.[139]

Some Justices flourished under Stone's freewheeling leadership. Hughes was undoubtedly more disciplined and efficient, but he was also more authoritarian, and his conference discussions were in some respects more superficial and less vigorous than the competitive debates Stone encouraged.

Frankfurter called Stone an "easy Boss." While he hardly meant it as a compliment, Stone's style suited Frankfurter perfectly. Certainly Frankfurter abused the latitude that Stone gave the conference as much as anyone—except perhaps for Stone himself. Frankfurter and Stone both loved to speak at length to captive audiences. Frankfurter often literally lectured to the conference. If a case interested him, he often talked for fifty minutes—the same length of time as a Harvard law class.[140]

Frankfurter's relationship with Stone was complex and interesting. Both Justices shared many of the same personality traits—extraordinary intelligence, pathological insecurities, and cutting, sarcastic wit. In one conference exchange, Frankfurter attacked Stone's willingness to interpret the Constitution to suit his own purposes:

> FRANKFURTER: I suppose you know more than those who drafted the Constitution.
>
> STONE: I know some things better than those who drafted the Constitution.
>
> FRANKFURTER: Yes, on wine and cheese (laughter).[141]

138. Douglas, *The Court Years*, 223. Douglas wrote to a friend, "We have [conferences] all the time these days and they seem eternally long—and often dull." Douglas to Fred Rodell, October 25, 1943, quoted in Urofsky, *Division and Discord*, 40.

139. Byrnes, *All in One Lifetime*, 137–38. Frank Murphy's conference notes confirm this practice.

140. Schwartz, *Inside the Warren Court*, 24.

141. Frank Murphy Papers, (No. 13 O.T. 1944, roll 131). *State of Georgia v. Pennsylvania Railroad*, 324 U.S. 439 (1945).

Yet Frankfurter was harshly critical of Stone, while he remembered Hughes fondly. In contrast to Hughes's buttoned-down discipline, Frankfurter complained that there was a lot of "wasteful . . . repetitious . . . and foolish talk" under Stone.[142] It also rankled Frankfurter that Stone always had to have the last word.[143] Frankfurter recorded in his diary that Stone carried on a

> running debate with any justice who expresses views different from his. The result is not only the usual undesirable atmosphere created by contentious debate, but lack of that austerity of atmosphere which I thought so admirable in a scrupulous observance of each man's saying his say in turn without an interruption, as Hughes conducted the Conference, but also an inevitable dragging out of the discussion.[144]

Elsewhere, Frankfurter described Stone in blunt terms:

> He was fundamentally a petty character, self-aggrandizing and ungenerous. . . . Hardly anybody was any good, hardly any lawyer was any good, hardly any argument was adequate, hardly anybody ever saw the real point of a case, etc., etc.[145]

In other words, Stone was very much like Frankfurter himself. But where Associate Justice Frankfurter could get away with such behavior, Chief Justice Stone could not.

Stanley Reed agreed that Stone "delighted to take on all comers around the conference table." As William O. Douglas put it, Stone believed in free speech for everyone, but especially for himself.[146] Stone had the temperament of a precocious child, and he never lost his boyish enthusiasm or combativeness. He even had every boy's fantasy in his home—a hinged bookcase with a secret passageway.[147]

In matters of law, as in the conference room, the Supreme Court under Stone revolutionized and reinvented itself. In economic cases, the Court abandoned the doctrine of substantive due process and adopted an abjectly deferential view toward federal economic regulation. With *Wickard v. Filburn* (1942) the Justices defined Congress's interstate commerce powers so broadly as to allow Congress effectively to determine for itself the limits of its commerce clause powers.[148] In 1946, Frank Murphy summed up this new feeling of judicial deference in economic cases by saying that the commerce clause "was as broad as the economic needs of the nation."[149] The Stone Court approved every piece

---

142. Frankfurter, "Chief Justices I Have Known," 902–3.
143. Schwartz, *History of the Supreme Court*, 247.
144. Lash, *From the Diaries of Felix Frankfurter*, 152 (Saturday, January 9, 1943).
145. Urofsky, *Felix Frankfurter*, 199.
146. Douglas, *The Court Years*, 223.
147. Pearson and Allen, *The Nine Old Men*, 106. The passageway led from his office into the dining room.
148. *Wickard v. Filburn*, 317 U.S. 111 (1942).
149. *American Power and Light Co. v. S.E.C.*, 328 U.S. 90, 141 (1946).

of federal economic legislation brought before it during World War II, including some highly controversial price and rent control legislation.[150]

While the "new" Supreme Court was more tolerant of federal economic regulation than it had ever been before, even the most progressive of Roosevelt's appointees remained fundamentally probusiness. Despite their reformist and populist credentials, the New Deal Justices never seriously questioned the Court's earlier decisions granting corporations legal status as persons or countless other special benefits and privileges. The Court's new progressives were simply "not seriously inclined to attack the more fundamental special privileges that American corporations had gained and expanded since early in the nineteenth century."[151]

In contrast, Stone had a deep and abiding interest in civil rights and liberties, and the Court became increasingly interested in cases involving noneconomic rights. Under other circumstances, Stone's legacy in this area might have been revolutionary; but Stone was Chief Justice during World War II, and the war caused significant anomalies and distortions when it came to civil rights and liberties.

As a consequence, the Stone Court's record on civil rights was mixed. The Justices quickly reversed a 1940 Hughes Court decision upholding a state law requiring schoolchildren to salute the American flag each morning.[152] In *West Virginia State Board of Education v. Barnette* (1943), the Stone Court held that the government could not compel students to say the Pledge of Allegiance.[153]

Perhaps the most significant civil rights cases of the era were the Japanese curfew, exclusion, and internment cases, *Hirabayashi*, *Korematsu*, and *Ex parte Endo*.[154] *Hirabayashi* gave Supreme Court approval to wartime curfews and travel restrictions on all persons of Japanese ancestry, both foreign nationals and American citizens. *Korematsu* allowed for the assembly and exclusion of Japanese Americans from the West Coast without any prior government effort to determine individual loyalties. *Endo*, which was announced the same day as *Korematsu*, limited the government's relocation powers somewhat, ruling that American citizens whose loyalty was admitted by the government could not be held against their will in internment camps.

In civil rights cases not directly connected to the war, the Court held in *Smith v. Allwright* (1944) that political parties holding racially exclusive primary elections were

---

150. Urofsky, *Division and Discord*, 49–50. Price control cases included *Yakus v. United States*, 321 U.S. 414 (1944), and *Stewart and Co. v. Bowles*, 322 U.S. 398 (1944). The leading rent control case was *Bowles v. Willingham*, 321 U.S. 503 (1944).

151. Schmidhauser, *Constitutional Law in American Politics*, 400–1.

152. *Minersville School District v. Gobitis*, 310 U.S. 586 (1940).

153. *West Virginia State Board of Education v. Barnette*, 319 U.S. 624 (1943).

154. *Hirabayashi v. United States*, 320 U.S. 81 (1943); *Korematsu v. United States*, 323 U.S. 214 (1944); *Ex parte Endo*, 323 U.S. 283 (1944).

agents of the state and that white primaries violated the Fifteenth Amendment's protections against denying or abridging the right to vote on the basis of race or color.[155] In *Screws v. United States* (1945), the Court expanded federal power to prosecute state officials accused of violating an individual's civil rights under color of law.[156]

For better or worse, Stone was Chief Justice for only five years. He had little time to develop as a conference leader. Although his personality was markedly different from Hughes, Stone had some qualities that might have allowed him to grow into the job, if given more time. He was at heart amiable, humorous, and likable, which could have been useful had he chosen to assert himself as the Court's social leader. He was fiercely intelligent and could have been the Court's task leader with relatively little effort. But Stone eschewed either role and saw his promotion as his opportunity to mix it up with the boys in the conference room, as Hughes had never allowed him to do.

Stone's supporters argue that he encouraged free discussion in the conference room, while Hughes throttled it. Frankfurter, however, thought it ridiculous to say that Hughes or anyone else could intimidate eight Supreme Court Justices into submission. Frankfurter also denied that Hughes ever inhibited a free and full airing of views in conference. The crucial difference between Hughes and Stone, he said, was that Hughes carefully and thoroughly prepared for each conference and took pains to give a complete, accurate, and concise statement of each case; Stone did not.[157]

Frankfurter's relationship with Hugo Black, William Douglas, and Frank Murphy also deteriorated while Stone was Chief Justice, although Stone himself was hardly to blame. The differences between Frankfurter and his fellow New Deal Justices were both doctrinal and personal. Frankfurter felt betrayed when Black, Douglas, and Murphy deserted him and joined Stone in voting to overturn Frankfurter's beloved *Gobitis* flag-salute decision in *West Virginia State Board of Education v. Barnette*.[158] Frankfurter passionately believed that the need for national unity and patriotism permitted state officials to compel children to recite the Pledge of Allegiance at school. After initially accepting Frankfurter's leadership on the issue in *Gobitis*, Black, Douglas, and Murphy soon after changed their minds about the case, and Frankfurter took it personally. The aftermath of these two cases helped to sour the personal relationships on the Court for more than

---

155. *Smith v. Allwright*, 321 U.S. 649 (1944).

156. *Screws v. United States*, 325 U.S. 1 (1945). While some scholars applauded the Court's decision as a landmark of civil rights, others thought that Douglas's majority opinion unintentionally created new barriers to winning civil rights cases. Thurgood Marshall, who at the time was the head of the NAACP Legal Defense Fund, said that as much as he admired Douglas, he could never forgive him for *Screws*. Urofsky, *Division and Discord*, 104.

157. Lash, *From the Diaries of Felix Frankfurter*, 315 (Friday, April 25, 1947).

158. *Minersville School District v. Gobitis*, 310 U.S. 586 (1940); *West Virginia State Board of Education v. Barnette*, 316 U.S. 624 (1943).

two decades. Douglas grimly noted that the fallout from *Barnette* did not add much tension on the Court, except for Mondays through Saturdays.[159]

Frankfurter complained that every conference with Hugo Black turned into "a championship by Black of justice and right and decency and everything, and those who take the other view are impliedly always made out to be the oppressors of the people and the supporters of some exploiting interest." He thought that Black was "the cheapest soapbox orator," with Douglas and Murphy serving as his Greek chorus, chanting "I agree with Justice Black" and "me-tooing Black."[160] Frankfurter dismissed Murphy as a lightweight career bureaucrat who enjoyed the company of showgirls more than he liked his judicial duties.[161] Frankfurter saved his most intense, visceral hatred for William O. Douglas. While Frankfurter and Black reconciled toward the end of Frankfurter's life, his rivalry with Douglas grew even more acrimonious over time.

After *Barnette*, Frankfurter began to refer to Black, Douglas, and Murphy as "the Axis." When Stone and Jackson joined Frankfurter in the surreptitious name-calling, these three Justices implicitly became "the Allies." The three allies, however, did not get along with each other any better than Roosevelt, De Gaulle, and Stalin.[162]

Personal relationships on the Court deteriorated so badly that the Justices could not even agree on the wording of a simple retirement letter for Owen Roberts. Black and Douglas squared off against Frankfurter and Jackson over whether the letter should say that the Justices "regretted" Robert's retirement or that Roberts had made "fidelity to principle" his guide in deciding cases. Black and Douglas refused to sign any letter containing either phrase, and Frankfurter and Jackson refused to sign any letter that did not include them. In the end, Roberts did not receive a card or any other acknowledgment from the brethren on his retirement.[163]

One of the quarrels that later helped to define the Vinson Court actually began under Stone. In 1944, the Court decided a routine case involving the Fair Labor Standards Act of 1938.[164] At issue was whether coal miners were to be paid from the moment they entered the mine until the moment they reemerged into the sunlight (portal-to-portal), or whether they were on the clock only when they were actually working the coal. Because many coal mines were deep and it often took workers as much as an hour to get from the

159. Simon, *Independent Journey*, 11.

160. Lash, *From the Diaries of Felix Frankfurter*, 174 (Saturday, January 30, 1943).

161. Stone shared Frankfurter's opinion of Murphy. He rarely assigned Murphy important or interesting cases because he believed that Murphy was lazy and depended too much on his clerks in writing his opinions.

162. Frankfurter occasionally seemed to take these labels literally. He commonly referred to Black, Douglas, and Murphy as "the enemy," and once he screamed at a clerk (who did not take Frankfurter's rivalry with the Axis seriously enough) that "this is a *war* we are fighting!" Urofsky, *Division and Discord*, 40.

163. Ibid., 45–46.

164. *Jewell Ridge Coal Corp. v. Local 6167 United Mine Workers*, 325 U.S. 161 (1945).

mine entrance to the worksite and back, the issue became a major sticking point in labor contract negotiations.

While important at the time, the case would have been forgotten long ago, except: (1) the Fair Labor Standards Act was also known as the Black-Connery Act and was one of Hugo Black's last legislative acts before joining the Court; (2) the lawyer arguing the case on behalf of the coal miners was Crampton Harris, Black's former law partner and his own personal lawyer; and (3) Black stubbornly refused to recuse himself from the case.

Black favored the coal miners but initially wound up on the losing side of a 5–4 conference vote. Stone assigned the case to Robert Jackson, and nothing more would have happened except that Stanley Reed unexpectedly changed his vote and gave Black's side the majority. Black immediately reassigned the case to Frank Murphy, who wrote a decision recognizing the miners' right to be paid portal-to-portal. The coal company immediately petitioned for a rehearing, arguing that Black should have recused himself.

Even at this point, nothing untoward had happened. Stone thought that the company's petition should be dismissed summarily, because recusal decisions were by tradition left solely to the discretion of each individual Justice. Many previous Justices, including Holmes, Brandeis, and even Stone himself had heard cases argued by former law partners. Stone favored publishing a brief per curiam opinion explaining the Court's recusal policies. Black angrily argued that no explanation was necessary and warned that if anyone published an opinion on the subject of recusal, it "would mean a declaration of war."[165]

Robert Jackson believed that silence would wrongly imply that everyone on the Court agreed with Black's decision to participate in the case. Goaded by Frankfurter, Jackson published a brief concurring opinion implicitly criticizing Black's failure to recuse himself and hinting that his failure to withdraw from the case had been improper.[166] Black was furious, and the incident caused a small public scandal. Jackson felt vindicated when Congress amended the Fair Labor Standards Act to match what he had argued in dissent in the *Jewell Ridge* case. Even at this point, the matter might have ended with no worse than bruised feelings. As things turned out, however, the *Jewell Ridge* case was over but not forgotten.

After the 1944 Term, Jackson seriously considered retiring from the Court. He hated the conference room intrigue and had lost all respect for Black, whom he blamed for creating a partisan political atmosphere on the Court. "With few exceptions," Jackson grumbled, "we all knew which side of a case Black would vote on when he read the names of the parties." In Jackson's view, Black was not a real judge but a senator still fighting for his old constituents.[167]

---

165. Urofsky, *Division and Discord*, 138–39.
166. *Jewell Ridge Coal Corp. v. Local 6167 United Mine Workers*, 325 U.S. 161, 170 (1945).
167. Hutchinson, "The Black-Jackson Feud," 229–30.

Rather than resigning, Jackson accepted President Truman's invitation in April 1945 to lead the American team prosecuting Nazi war criminals before the International Military Tribunal at Nuremberg. Jackson took an unannounced leave of absence from the Court without even informing the Chief Justice of his plans. He planned to be in Germany a relatively short time but ended up staying for the better part of two years. Things did not go well for Jackson in Washington or in Germany. In Nuremberg, his performance was lackluster and it was generally conceded that Nazi general Hermann Goering got the better of him during the most important cross-examination of the trials. Things would go even worse for Jackson back home.

FRED VINSON: TRUMAN'S PAL (1946–1953)

On April 22, 1946, Stone suffered a cerebral hemorrhage while delivering a dissenting opinion in a naturalization case, and he died later that afternoon. Jackson, who was still in Nuremberg, believed that he would become the next Chief Justice. In 1941, Roosevelt had all but promised him the job, and Jackson expected President Truman to honor FDR's wink-and-nod commitment.[168]

Then Jackson began to hear stories that Truman had cooled to the idea. Trapped in Europe and far removed from events in Washington, Jackson felt helpless and out of touch. His frustration turned to rage when Francis Shea (a former subordinate at the Justice Department) wrote to Jackson claiming—falsely—that Hugo Black had paid a personal visit to Truman and torpedoed Jackson's nomination.[169] At the same time, there was a new round of news stories revisiting the old *Jewell Ridge* feud between Black and Jackson. Virtually all of these accounts favored Black's side of the story, and many of them were so detailed that Jackson knew that the information had to have come from inside the conference room. In Jackson's mind, the only possible answer was that Black was sabotaging his chances to become Chief Justice. Jackson's fears were realized when Truman nominated Fred Vinson to become the new Chief Justice on June 6, 1946. Jackson was left with a simple choice: accept defeat gracefully or seek revenge.

On June 10, Jackson cabled the Senate and House judiciary committees, publicly denouncing Hugo Black for his participation in the *Jewell Ridge* case. He accused Black of pressuring the other Justices to decide the case quickly to benefit organized labor. (The miners were on strike when case was decided, and Jackson claimed that Black wanted to give the union leverage to extract a favorable settlement from mine owners.) Jackson

---

168. Ibid., 203–5.

169. Ibid. Hutchinson argues convincingly that Shea wrote the fateful letter. Others, however, maintain that it was Frankfurter who spread the news to Nuremberg, although their evidence is circumstantial. Allen and Shannon, *The Truman Merry-Go-Round*, 366–67.

decried Black's repeated participation in cases where he had conflicts of interest, said that he "wanted the practice stopped," and promised that if it happened again he would write an opinion that would make his *Jewell Ridge* concurrence "look like a letter of recommendation by comparison." Jackson also falsely accused Black of meddling in Truman's choice of a Chief Justice.[170] Jackson's letter caused a media firestorm, with some commentators suggesting that both Jackson and Black should resign. Hugo Black never publicly responded to Jackson's charges, and when the dust settled the incident damaged Jackson's reputation without doing any lasting harm to Black.

Predictably, the atmosphere inside the conference room grew more toxic. In the brief interlude after Stone's death but before Vinson took his seat, a leaderless and bitterly divided Court decided one of the most difficult and important political cases of the century, *Colegrove v. Green.*[171]

Kenneth Colegrove, a Northwestern University law professor, asked the Court to enjoin the upcoming Illinois congressional elections, because the state's voting districts had not been reapportioned for forty-five years and district populations were grossly disproportionate. Because of the state's rapid urbanization, some rural congressional districts had as few as 100,000 voters while some urban districts had more than 900,000 voters. Such gross disparities gave rural voters far greater influence in congressional elections than city dwellers. Professor Colegrove also asked the Court to order the state to reapportion its voting districts more equitably.

A seven-judge Supreme Court rejected Colegrove's plea (the Court was shorthanded because Stone had died a month after oral arguments, and Jackson was still in Nuremberg). Felix Frankfurter wrote the lead opinion for a plurality of three Justices. The case, he said, presented a nonjusticiable political question. Reapportionment cases were a dangerous "political thicket" into which the Court should not venture. The opinion was a classic restatement of Frankfurter's theory of judicial restraint. He argued that redress in such cases must come from the popularly elected branches of government, not from the courts. Only Stanley Reed and Harold Burton agreed with him. Wiley Rutledge concurred in the judgment to give Frankfurter his fourth vote, but Rutledge disagreed with most of what Frankfurter said. Rutledge agreed with the dissenters that reapportionment cases were justiciable, but he thought that the Court should decline jurisdiction in this instance because there was too little time to craft an appropriate judicial remedy before the next election.

---

170. Hutchinson argues that the likely source of the press leaks and the person who lobbied against Jackson with President Truman was William O. Douglas. Hutchinson, "The Black-Jackson Feud," 216–17. Jackson himself later blamed Douglas for most of his problems, although in truth most of Jackson's wounds were self-inflicted.

171. *Colegrove v. Green*, 328 U.S. 549 (1946).

The three dissenters, Black, Douglas, and Murphy, argued that Illinois's failure to redistrict represented a failure of the democratic process and that the courts were specifically designed to redress such injustices. The constitutional violations were clear, and the popular branches of government could not be relied on to correct the situation because they were responsible for creating and perpetuating the problem in the first place. The courts, on the other hand, were uniquely suited to resist the pressures of electoral politics and ensure a fair system of apportionment.

Colegrove captured the essence of the fundamental differences in temperament and legal philosophy between the Frankfurter and Black factions. These tensions would divide the Court for the next twenty years.

In his brief tenure as Chief Justice, Fred Vinson proved even less able to lead the conference than Stone. Vinson lacked the intellect, legal reputation, administrative competence, political skills, or personality necessary to hold the Court together. He came to the job amid whispers that he was a legal lightweight and a hack politician whose primary qualification to become Chief Justice was that he was a crony of Harry Truman's. Vinson did little to change anyone's mind. According to William K. Bachelder, who was Sherman Minton's clerk during the 1952 Term, some of the Justices "would discuss in [Vinson's] presence the view that the Chief's job should rotate annually and . . . made no bones about regarding him—correctly—as their intellectual inferior."[172]

In Frankfurter's estimation, Vinson conducted the conference "with ease and good humor," but only by "disposing of each case rather briefly by choosing . . . to float merely on the surface of the problems raised by the cases."[173] The other Justices agreed that Vinson was shallow and disorganized. He stressed the obvious points of a case in his conference summaries, while avoiding the subtle issues and complex problems. Everyone liked him—Vinson was at heart a friendly and sociable man—but they did not respect him.[174] Vinson assigned himself relatively few cases and soon developed a reputation for being, in Robert Jackson's words, "just plain lazy."[175]

Frankfurter was a constant source of irritation. He baited and taunted Vinson in conference until the Chief Justice finally lost his temper one day and screamed at Frankfurter, "No son of a bitch can ever say that to Fred Vinson!" Shay Minton and Tom Clark quickly interceded and convinced Vinson to apologize.[176] But Frankfurter lost few opportunities to demean the Chief behind his back.

Perhaps unfairly, all four of Harry Truman's Supreme Court appointees are remembered—to the extent that they are remembered at all—as a mediocre group of political

172. Kluger, *Simple Justice*, 585 (1976).
173. Lash, *From the Diaries of Felix Frankfurter*, 283 (Saturday, October 27, 1946).
174. Urofsky, *Division and Discord*, 149.
175. Ibid., 151.
176. Cooper, *Battles on the Court*, 94.

insiders and presidential cronies. Harold Hitz Burton, Truman's first appointment, was a modest, moderate Republican who often got lost on a Court dominated by more colorful personalities. Yet Burton was an extraordinarily fair-minded judge, and he showed considerable foresight in the Court's race cases, particularly *Louisiana ex rel. Francis v. Resweber* (1947)[177] and *Brown v. Board of Education* (1954).[178]

Tom Clark was a Truman friend and former attorney general. He was also sympathetic to the civil rights movement, although as an elder of the Texas political establishment he had a distinctly southern perspective on American race relations. As attorney general, Clark had led early Cold War prosecutions of Communist leaders, and as a Justice he remained indifferent to their First Amendment claims. Clark's thinking changed over time, and he gradually began to vote more often with the Court's liberal wing. Douglas claimed that unlike Truman's other appointees, Clark had a "capacity to develop, so that with the passage of time he grew in stature and expanded his dimensions."[179] Then again, Clark had more of a chance to adapt, as he served on the Court nine years longer than any of Truman's other appointees.

Sherman Minton, the last Truman appointee, had little long-term impact on the Court. With Harold Burton, he gave strong and crucial early support to desegregation in *Brown v. Board of Education*. But Minton lacked the stomach for political infighting and was in poor health for most of his seven years on the Court. On his retirement in 1956, Minton sadly observed that the country was much more interested in who would succeed him than in what he had accomplished on the bench.

Despite their personal disagreements, Vinson tended to gravitate toward Frankfurter's view of the Constitution and his theory of judicial restraint. A government man at heart, Vinson favored the federal government over the states, and both federal and state governments over individual rights.

In economic cases, the Vinson Court was a friend of government and business, in that order. Most of the Justices were avidly nationalistic; there was little talk of states' rights in economic cases, and the federal government enjoyed virtually unlimited power to regulate the national economy.[180] The Court tended to favor both government and business interests over the rights of labor unions and individuals. The Justices restricted unions' rights to conduct job actions at federally operated busi-

---

177. *Louisiana ex rel. Francis v. Resweber,* 329 U.S. 459 (1947). Louisiana sought to electrocute a black defendant a second time, after the state's first attempt to kill him failed.

178. *Brown v. Board of Education,* 347 U.S. 483 (1954).

179. Urofsky, *Division and Discord,* 155.

180. Frank, "Vinson and the Chief Justiceship," 237–38. For example, the Court favored national control of offshore natural resources in *United States v. California,* 332 U.S. 19 (1947), and *United States v. Texas,* 339 U.S. 707 (1950). Vinson also opposed any state burdens on commerce, and for the most part the rest of the Court went along with his preferences.

nesses,[181] refused to extend free speech protections to picketing,[182] and upheld provisions of the Taft-Hartley Act that required union leaders to swear an oath that they were neither affiliated nor had any sympathy with the Communist party or any other subversive organization.[183]

The most famous labor case of the Vinson era was also a landmark separation of powers case. In *Youngstown Sheet and Tube Co. v. Sawyer* (1952), President Truman seized control of the nation's steel industry in order to avert a threatened steelworkers' strike and to protect steel production during the Korean War. With Vinson, Reed, and Minton dissenting, the Court ruled 6–3 that Truman's actions were unconstitutional, whether there was a national emergency or not.[184]

Despite the Justices' New Deal and Fair Deal credentials, none of the Justices—not even Hugo Black—was especially sympathetic to workers' rights. If the Court was no longer implacably hostile to organized labor as it was during Fuller's and Taft's day, the Justices still sided with management most of the time.

In civil rights cases, the Vinson Court retreated from the nascent trend toward growing judicial concern for noneconomic civil rights and liberties.[185] The Court's views in this area were defined by the Cold War, and as a group the Justices tolerated a significant erosion of free speech rights in the name of national self-defense against Communists and other alleged subversives. The Cold War reinforced the majority's conservative instincts and their skepticism about free speech, especially when made by Communists.

The Court's declining tolerance for unpopular speech was confirmed in *Terminiello v. Chicago* (1949), *Feiner v. New York* (1951), and *Beauharnais v. Illinois* (1952).[186] In *Terminiello*, the Court reversed a breach of peace conviction on the ground that the Chicago city ordinance had been unconstitutionally used to punish a provocative speech that had merely *invited* dispute. Just two years later, however, the Court reversed course and upheld a similar breach of peace conviction in *Feiner v. New York*. When Feiner delivered a racially provocative speech on a Syracuse street corner, several listeners took offense and threatened violence. Police made no attempt to control the crowd and in-

---

181. *United States v. United Mine Workers of America*, 330 U.S. 258 (1947). Here, the government assumed operation of the country's bituminous coal industry in response to a national strike by mineworkers. The Court ruled that the Norris-LaGuardia Act, which limited federal courts' powers to enjoin strikes and to punish unions and their leaders for contempt of court, did not apply to the federal government or federally operated business.

182. *Giboney v. Empire Storage and Ice Co.*, 336 U.S. 490 (1949). For a cogent account of the Vinson Court's treatment of labor unions, see Urofsky, *Division and Discord*, 184–206.

183. *American Communications Ass'n v. Douds*, 339 U.S. 382 (1950).

184. *Youngstown Sheet and Tube Co. v. Sawyer*, 343 U.S. 579 (1952).

185. Frank, "Vinson and the Chief Justiceship," 246.

186. *Terminiello v. Chicago*, 337 U.S. 1 (1949); *Feiner v. New York*, 340 U.S. 315 (1951); *Beauharnais v. Illinois*, 343 U.S. 250 (1952).

stead arrested Feiner. In affirming Feiner's conviction, the Court wrote that when a "clear and present danger of riot, disorder, interference with traffic upon the public street, or other immediate threat to public safety, peace, or order appears, the power of the State to prevent or punish is obvious." In *Beauharnais*, the Court upheld a state statute prohibiting anyone from making derogatory comments about any racial or religious group.[187]

On the national level, the Truman administration initiated a new federal loyalty program for civilian employees of all federal agencies and established a Loyalty Review Board to investigate all current and prospective federal employees. Before he was appointed to the Supreme Court, Attorney General Tom Clark created the first official list of subversive organizations for the Loyalty Review Board to use in its investigations. The Vinson Court approved the use of this list in *Joint Anti-Fascist Refugee Committee v. McGrath* (1949). The Court, however, also ruled that the attorney general had wrongly included the Joint Anti-Fascist Refugee Committee on his list of subversive organizations and ordered it removed along with the names of two other groups.[188] The 5–3 majority carefully avoided the First Amendment speech and association issues presented by the case.

With the Court's approval, loyalty oaths, background investigations, and blacklists were put in place from Washington to Hollywood. Government agencies, public universities, and private industries all began to require employees to sign loyalty oaths as a condition of employment.[189]

The Truman administration dusted off the Smith Act (passed in 1940 to curb Communists and other radical groups, but rarely invoked during the war) and used it to prosecute Communists and others suspected of conspiracy or advocacy to overthrow the government. In *Dennis v. United States* (1951), the Court upheld the Smith Act and relaxed the clear and present danger test to allow the government greater discretion to limit speech in the interest of national self-defense. Vinson wrote that the threat posed by Communists and other subversives was so clear and dangerous that it no longer had to be present before the government could act to defend itself.[190]

The Court was closely divided in most of these cases. The Vinson-Frankfurter faction favored continued use of the clear and present danger test, which required the Court

---

187. *Beauharnais v. Illinois*, 343 U.S. 250 (1952). The dissenters in this case eventually got their way; *Beauharnais* was severely limited by *New York Times, Inc. v. Sullivan*, 346 U.S. 254 (1964).

188. *Joint Anti-Fascist Refugee Committee v. McGrath*, 341 U.S. 123 (1951).

189. For loyalty oath cases, see, for example, *Garner v. Los Angeles*, 341 U.S. 716 (1951); *Adler v. Board of Education*, 342 U.S. 485 (1952). As a regent of the University of California, Earl Warren consistently voted against requiring faculty to sign loyalty oaths. As governor, however, Warren called a special session of the legislature in 1950 to enact legislation requiring all state employees, including public university faculty, to sign loyalty oaths. Years later, as Chief Justice, Warren voted to strike down faculty loyalty oaths as violation of academic freedom under the First Amendment. *Keyishian v. Board of Regents*, 385 U.S. 589 (1967).

190. *Dennis v. United States*, 341 U.S. 494 (1951).

to balance free speech rights against the government's right of self-defense. The Black-Douglas faction, however, began to question the clear and present danger test and moved toward an absolutist position in free speech cases. They saw Vinson's balancing scheme as little more than an elaborate rationalization for prior restraints, censorship, and mind control in the name of national security.

The Vinson-Frankfurter faction remained in control for most of the early 1950s. In the few free speech cases where the liberal faction "won" (*Joint Anti-Fascist, Terminiello*), the Court usually avoided the underlying constitutional issues and based its decisions on narrow procedural grounds. When the conservatives "won" (*Feiner, Beauharnais, Dennis*), the cases were often decided on much broader constitutional grounds.

In the Ethel and Julius Rosenberg spy case, the customary battle lines blurred. Frankfurter and Black found themselves allied in their sympathy with the Rosenbergs. The episode further aggravated Frankfurter's hatred of William Douglas, whose wild vacillations in the case reinforced Frankfurter's belief that Douglas was an unprincipled, venal, politically ambitious, and shameless grandstander who was obsessed with his public image as the champion of fashionable rights.

The Court was also deeply divided on religious issues. Again, the voting patterns were not always predictable. During the Vinson era there were three cases of special note: *Everson v. Board of Education* (1947), *Illinois ex rel. McCollum v. Board of Education* (1948), and *Zorach v. Clausen* (1952).[191] In *Everson*, Hugo Black and the majority adopted an accommodationist stance in this establishment clause case, ruling that New Jersey school boards could reimburse parents for the costs of sending their children to school—including parochial schools—on public transportation. The program was permissible, Black wrote, because it was designed to benefit children rather than provide aid directly to religious schools. Wiley Rutledge and Felix Frankfurter led the dissenters, arguing that the New Jersey program directly benefited parochial schools and was unconstitutional.

In *McCollum*, the Court appeared to move significantly in Rutledge's direction. Black again wrote the majority opinion. This time an 8–1 Court struck down an Illinois program in which religion teachers gave religious instruction to voluntary participants during school hours in public school rooms. The Justices could not agree on the details, however, and there were four separate concurrences.

In *Zorach v. Clausen*, the Court narrowly approved New York City's released-time religious instruction program. Under this voluntary program, participating students left school grounds during the day to receive religious instruction elsewhere. This time Douglas wrote the majority opinion. Black, Frankfurter, and Jackson were in dissent, argu-

191. *Everson v. Board of Education*, 330 U.S. 1 (1947); *Illinois ex rel. McCollum v. Board of Education*, 333 U.S. 203 (1948); *Zorach v. Clausen*, 343 U.S. 306 (1952).

ing that the program was inherently coercive and directly aided religion in violation of the First Amendment.

In part because of the Vinson Court's mixed record in free speech and religion cases, it rarely gets the credit it deserves for beginning to roll back laws supporting racial discrimination and segregation. Among the landmark race cases decided during the Vinson years were *Oyama v. California* (1948), invalidating a state law prohibiting Japanese nationals from owning property in California,[192] and *Shelley v. Kraemer*, which held racially restrictive covenants unenforceable under the Fourteenth Amendment and the courts' equitable powers.[193] In education, *Sipuel v. Board of Regents of Oklahoma* (1948) and *McLaurin v. Oklahoma State Regents* (1950) helped to desegregate Oklahoma's graduate law and education programs,[194] while *Sweatt v. Painter* (1950) desegregated the law school at the University of Texas.[195] The Vinson Court also wrestled with *Brown v. Board of Education* but could come to a decision before Vinson suddenly died of a heart attack in 1953 and it fell to Earl Warren to finish the job.

Unsurprisingly, the Vinson Court had unprecedented dissent rates. During Vinson's tenure, only 19 percent of the Court's cases were decided unanimously—a record low. The Vinson Court's cumulative case dissent rate was 57 percent.[196]

EARL WARREN: THE *LEADER* LEADER (1953–1969)

Earl Warren was able to moderate some of the antagonisms that had divided the conference under Vinson. The personal rivalries remained, but they were softened by Warren's efforts to restore a sense of group identity and common purpose to the Court. In politically sensitive cases—such as the school desegregation cases—the Justices coalesced around Warren as they never had for Vinson or Stone.

Felix Frankfurter was again the main thorn in the Chief Justice's side, attempting to dominate the Court both inside and outside the conference room and becoming unhappy and petulant when he failed. For the most part, the other Justices responded to Warren's warm and charismatic leadership, even if most of them suspected that they were better jurists than the ex-governor from Bakersfield. However highly the other Justices thought of themselves—and that would be difficult to exaggerate—they all recognized that ultimately Earl Warren was in charge. Others might have considered themselves to be the

---

192. *Oyama v. California*, 332 U.S. 633 (1948).
193. *Shelley v. Kraemer*, 334 U.S. 1 (1948).
194. *Sipuel v. Board of Regents of the University of Oklahoma*, 332 U.S. 631 (1948); *McLaurin v. Oklahoma State Regents for Higher Education*, 339 U.S. 637 (1950).
195. *Sweatt v. Painter*, 339 U.S. 629 (1950).
196. Data compiled from Epstein, *Supreme Court Compendium*, 198.

intellectual, social, or moral leaders of the Court, but as Potter Stewart said, everyone knew that Warren was the *leader* leader.[197]

On his first day as Chief Justice, Warren's first call was to Hugo Black's chambers, where he asked the senior Associate Justice to explain the mysteries of the conference room to him. Warren asked Black to manage the conference until he felt more comfortable leading the discussion; and according to Warren, Black graciously agreed to act as interim conference leader. Black then escorted Warren to the other chambers and introduced him to the other Justices.[198] Afterward, Warren took his constitutional oath privately in the conference room, with only the other Justices present. He later took his judicial oath publicly in the courtroom.[199]

During Warren's first week on the Court, the Justices met every day to dispose of hundreds of cert petitions that had piled up over the summer. Warren played no part in these discussions, as he had not had the opportunity to study any of the cases.[200]

Like Taft, Warren had the social instincts of a great politician. He looked after the Justices' welfare like a ward captain. He sent notes, flowers, and gifts to the other Justices and their families, and visited them in times of great happiness, sickness, or need. Not even the lowliest sparrow died around the Court without Warren finding out about it and sending a card.

When Potter Stewart was first appointed to the Court, he arrived by train at Union Station at 6:45 A.M. to find Earl Warren waiting alone on the platform to meet him. Stewart was flattered and thought that Warren's countless small but thoughtful gestures demonstrated the Chief Justice's "instinctive qualities of leadership and humanity and friendliness."[201]

Beginning with the 1955 Term, Warren changed the way that the Court scheduled oral arguments. Instead of hearing oral arguments Mondays through Fridays, Warren worked out a four-day schedule, where the Court heard oral arguments Monday through Thursday. He did this by adding an additional week of arguments in the fall and two more weeks in the spring. The main reason for these changes was that Warren wanted to move the Court's conferences from Saturdays to Fridays.[202]

Cynical Beltway reporters snickered that Warren wanted his Saturdays free to watch college football. Warren denied it, saying that the only college football game he ever attended was the annual Army-Navy game. He claimed that he needed Saturdays to catch

---

197. Schwartz, *History of the Supreme Court*, 268.

198. Warren, *Memoirs*, 277–78.

199. Ibid., 278–79.

200. Ibid., 280.

201. Stewart, "Reflections on the Supreme Court," 13.

202. O'Brien credits Warren Burger with moving the conferences back to Fridays. O'Brien, *Storm Center*, 110.

up with his administrative work in relative quiet and without interruption. Warren considered Saturdays to be his most productive work day, because he could concentrate on his work without the usual stream of telephone calls and visitors.[203] The Chief, however, could be found occasionally on Saturdays taking in a college football game or attending a Senators home game during baseball season.

Just as Marshall relied on Joseph Story and Taft depended on Willis Van Devanter, Earl Warren chose William Brennan to serve as his trusted lieutenant and aide-de-camp. Soon after Brennan was appointed in 1956, the two men began to meet quietly every Thursday in Brennan's chambers to review the cases to be discussed at conference the following day. While these strategy sessions were done discreetly, they were an open secret on the Court and they caused some grumbling among the other Justices. But the meetings continued and they were undoubtedly useful, as Warren and Brennan were usually able to guide the conference toward the positions they favored.[204]

During the weeks that the Court was in session, conferences began on Fridays at 10:00 or 11:00 A.M. and lasted until 5:00 or 6:00 P.M., with a half-hour lunch break. Occasionally the conference met again on Saturday or early the following week to catch up with the docket. There were approximately twenty-six conferences per term. Unlike the rigidly punctual Charles Evans Hughes, Earl Warren was easily diverted and rarely on time for anything, including conferences.

The first order of business was to consider cert petitions, appeals by right, and in forma pauperis cases. Warren allotted approximately five minutes for each case on the discuss list, about thirty seconds per Justice. Most cases were resolved with little or no discussion at all.

Argued cases were considered last. There was no time limit on these discussions. Warren made sure that each Justice spoke in order of seniority and that there were no interruptions.[205] In at least some controversial cases as late as 1963, the Court continued to vote in reverse order of seniority, beginning with the most junior Justice and Warren voting last.[206] One of Warren's strengths was his ability to frame the issues in simple and

---

203. Warren, *Memoirs*, 348.

204. Even after Earl Warren retired and the Court grew more conservative, Brennan remained the Court's most effective negotiator and coalition builder and quietly continued to guide crucial decisions his way. In 1987, Brennan's clerks celebrated his thirtieth anniversary on the Court by papering the hallway from the conference room to Brennan's chambers with placards announcing Brennan's many landmark decisions. They watched Brennan stop at each placard and read the name aloud as he returned to chambers from conference. Brennan did not realize that Antonin Scalia was following behind him also reading each card. Brennan had just finished reading the last placard and stepped into his chambers when Scalia burst through the door and said, "My Lord, Bill, have you got a lot to answer for!" Rosenkranz, "Remembering and Advancing the Constitutional Vision of Justice William J. Brennan," 3.

205. Clark, "Inside the Court," in Westin, *Autobiography of the Supreme Court* 46–47.

206. Harlan, "A Glimpse of the Supreme Court," 6.

straightforward language, stripped of legal jargon and pettifogging. This helped to make him, at least in Potter Stewart's eyes, an ideal Chief Justice.[207]

Warren claimed that in most respects, running the conference was not especially difficult:

> The procedure was very simple. In each case, the Chief Justice would, in a few sentences, state how the case appeared to him, and how he was inclined to decide it. Then, beginning with Justice Black, the senior Justice, each would speak his mind in a similar manner. He might only say, "I look at it the same way the Chief does and come to the same conclusion," or he might say, "I view the case differently. It seems to me this is the real issue, etc.," defining it. Or, "I believe it is controlled by the case of So-and-So v. So-and-So (citing precedent), and that brings me out the other way." Then we proceeded down the line until everyone had spoken briefly in this informal manner. During all of this, nobody was interrupted and there was no debate. If we were all of one mind and no one desired to say anything more, the case was ready for assignment. . . . If, after the first canvassing of the Court, as I have described it, there was a difference of opinion, the case was open for debate. We did not observe Robert's Rules of Order or any other definite procedure. It was a self-disciplined affair, each Justice deferring to the speaker until he was finished. The discussion proceeded in an orderly manner until all had spoken as much as they desired. If they were ready to vote, we did so at that time. In voting, we reversed the process and first called upon the junior member, going up the ladder with the Chief Justice voting last. I have tried diligently to learn when and why this procedure was first adopted, but without success. It is one of those things that grew up in the dim past and has been carried on without question. The reason assigned by some is that by voting first the junior member is relieved of casting the deciding vote when the other eight members are in a four-to-four deadlock. I suppose that is as good as any other reason. We then moved from case to case in this manner until all had been decided. The conference started at ten o'clock, and, with the exception of a half hour for lunch, which had been ordered beforehand and was always on the table in our dining room directly above the Conference Room, we continued throughout the day until we had discussed all our cases. Usually we adjourned shortly after five, but often not until after six. On rare occasions we recessed until Monday morning to complete our work.
>
> During these conferences, no one was in the room except the Justices—not a secretary, a law clerk, or even a messenger. If it were necessary for anyone to contact us, it was done by written message and a knock on the door. When there was a knock, the junior member of the Court answered it unless he was speaking at the time, in which case some other Justice would respond. We had a telephone in the room, but I have no recollection of its ever having been used during a conference while I was on the Court.[208]

---

207. Schwartz, *The Ascent of Pragmatism*, 12.
208. Warren, *Memoirs*, 282–83.

Not surprisingly, the Frankfurter-Douglas rivalry posed the greatest single threat to collegiality during the Warren years. Both men were eccentric and extremely difficult to get along with. Douglas treated his colleagues, clerks (who he referred to as "the lowest form of life"), and staff brusquely, if not harshly. Frankfurter was a pretentious and insecure man who was more inclined than Douglas to be personable to those around him, but only so long as they deferred to his superior intellect and judgment. Part of the problem was that Douglas refused to defer to Frankfurter on anything.

Douglas complained that Frankfurter constantly engaged in histrionics during conferences, bringing in piles of books, reading at length from them, and pounding on the table for emphasis. Frankfurter, Douglas said, always sought to proselytize and sow doubt in the minds of the other Justices and would often interrupt and make derisive comments in a stage whisper while others were speaking.[209] Frankfurter in turn complained constantly about Douglas, telling his clerks that Douglas was an "opportunist" and a "malingerer" who was more concerned with his public image than his work. "He just decides who he wants to win and then votes—a lazy, contemptible mind."[210]

In 1954, Douglas and Frankfurter got into a row over two unimportant ICC cases, *Secretary of Agriculture v. United States* and *Florida Citrus Commission v. United States*.[211] Immediately after the conference was adjourned, Douglas sent Frankfurter a peckish note, saying:

> Today at Conference I asked you a question concerning your memorandum opinion. . . . The question was not answered. An answer was refused, rather insolently. This was so far as I recall the first time one member of the Conference refused to answer another member on a matter of Court business. We all know what a great burden your long discourses are. So I am not complaining. But I do register a protest at your degradation of the Conference and its deliberations.[212]

In 1960, Douglas threatened to quit attending conferences so long as Frankfurter remained on the Court. He wrote a memorandum to the Chief absurdly threatening to resign from the conference:

> The continuous violent outbursts against me in Conference by my Brother Frankfurter give me great concern. They do not bother me. . . . But he's an ill man; and these violent outbursts create a fear in my heart that one of them may be his end. . . . In the interest of his health and long life, I have reluctantly concluded to participate in

---

209. Douglas, *The Court Years*, 22.

210. Goodwin, *Remembering America*, 28–29 (1988). Richard Goodwin clerked for Felix Frankfurter during the 1958 Term.

211. *Secretary of Agriculture v. United States*, 347 U.S. 645 (1954) (decided with *Florida Citrus Commission v. United States*).

212. Urofsky, *William O. Douglas Letters*, 85.

no more conferences while he is on the court. For cert lists I will leave my vote. On argued cases I will leave a short summary of my views.[213]

As usual, Earl Warren was able to calm Douglas down and talk him into shelving his memorandum.[214]

Douglas occasionally left the conference table while Frankfurter was speaking, sat down in an easy chair in another part of the room and read or wrote personal letters. Douglas enjoyed antagonizing Frankfurter by saying something at the conclusion of Frankfurter's remarks like, "When I came into this conference I agreed with the conclusion that Felix has just announced. But he's just talked me out of it." Potter Stewart reported that no matter how many times Douglas pulled the same stunt, it never failed to make Frankfurter angry.[215] William Brennan was slightly more sympathetic toward Frankfurter, noting that the other Justices "would have been inclined to agree with Felix more often in conference if he had cited Holmes less frequently."[216]

Douglas claimed that despite Frankfurter's seniority, he often volunteered in conference to pass messages to the pages who waited outside the door. Douglas alleged that Frankfurter would not simply hand the note to the messenger but would drop it on the floor and make the page pick it up. Douglas said that he was puzzled why Frankfurter would go through this bizarre exercise in "compelled obeisance" but guessed that it was due to Frankfurter's insecurities and a Napoleon complex.[217]

When Earl Warren first came to the Court, Frankfurter sought to become the Chief Justice's mentor. Warren rebuffed Frankfurter's efforts, and their relationship quickly chilled. In an otherwise routine conference on *Machibroda v. United States*, Earl Warren finally blew up at Frankfurter. In his 1962 conference notes, Douglas described the scene as the Chief Justice attempted to clear up a procedural issue for Potter Stewart:

> While the CJ was answering [Potter Stewart's question on a procedural matter], FF was snickering and passing notes to John Marshall Harlan as is his custom. The CJ stopped and said, "I am goddamn tired of having you snicker while I am talking. You do it even in the courtroom and people notice it." FF denied he was snickering. There followed a long harangue in which the CJ said he had reached the limits of his tolerance for FF.[218]

Despite his deserved reputation as a skillful mediator, Warren presided over a badly divided Court. With the notable exception of the school desegregation cases, the very

213. Ibid., 90.
214. Cooper, *Battles on the Bench*, 110, citing Memorandum to the Conference, November 23, 1960, William O. Douglas Papers, box 1258.
215. Cooper, *Battles on the Bench*, 110.
216. Urofsky, *Felix Frankfurter*, 205.
217. Douglas, *The Court Years*, 23.
218. Douglas's conference notes on *Machibroda v. United States*, 368 U.S. 487 (1962).

idea of the Supreme Court deciding difficult cases by consensus was dead. The Warren Court had an overall case dissent rate of 60 percent.[219]

The range of landmark civil rights cases that the Warren Court decided was unprecedented and established the Warren Court's reputation as an activist, progressive Court. Ironically, it was President Eisenhower who nominated both Earl Warren and William Brennan to the Court, and these two appointments tilted the balance of power decisively toward the progressives. The Warren Court became the most activist Court in history, in terms of its willingness to interpret the Bill of Rights broadly and apply it against both the federal and state governments. The Court fought to end de jure school desegregation and to end most other forms of legally mandated racial segregation.[220] It also waded into the political thicket of reapportionment,[221] expanded the rights of the accused (including groundbreaking decisions dealing with confessions, access to counsel, search and seizure protections, and new procedural rights for children accused of crime),[222] extended free speech and free press rights,[223] erected new barriers between church and state,[224] and issued the first landmark cases dealing with the emerging right of privacy.[225]

WARREN BURGER: COUNTING TO FIVE (1969–1986)

Warren Burger was a well-intentioned but unexceptional Chief Justice. An admirer of Charles Evans Hughes, Burger's priorities were to promote the Court's public image and prestige and to discourage private discord inside the conference room. He was at best only partially successful in his efforts, and he often proved to be his own worst enemy.

Although Burger modeled himself after Hughes, even his closest judicial ally, William Rehnquist, diplomatically suggested that Burger fell at best half-way between Hughes and Harlan Fiske Stone in managing the conference. Burger got off on the wrong foot during his first month as Chief Justice, when he unilaterally tried to commandeer the

---

219. Data complied from Epstein, *Supreme Court Compendium*, 198.

220. *Brown v. Board of Education*, 349 U.S. 294 (1954); *Bolling v. Sharpe*, 347 U.S. 497 (1954).

221. *Baker v. Carr*, 369 U.S. 186 (1962).

222. *Mapp v. Ohio*, 367 U.S. 643 (1961); *Gideon v. Wainwright*, 372 U.S. 335 (1963); *Miranda v. Arizona*, 384 U.S. 436 (1966); *In re Gault*, 387 U.S. 1 (1967). The Warren Court flirted with resurrecting the old doctrine of substantive due process and recasting it to protect individual rights, especially in dealing with the rights of the accused. Felix Frankfurter and John Marshall Harlan used similar notions to very different effect in their due process–based analysis of criminal and civil rights cases. The two used a "shock the conscience" test to determine whether a government practice was constitutional or not. *Rochin v. California*, 342 U.S. 165 (1952); *Breithaupt v. Abram*, 352 U.S. 432 (1957).

223. *Memoirs of a Woman of Pleasure v. Massachusetts*, 383 U.S. 413 (1966); *New York Times v. Sullivan*, 376 U.S. 254 (1964).

224. *Engel v. Vitale*, 370 U.S. 421 (1962).

225. *Griswold v. Connecticut*, 381 U.S. 479 (1965).

conference room as his own personal dining room and ceremonial office.[226] Things did not improve significantly afterward.

Burger looked more like a Chief Justice than anyone except for Hughes, but in Burger's case it was mostly a facade. He did not have a reputation as a leading legal scholar or judge, and behind his back the other Justices mocked his modest education, mediocre legal abilities, poor grasp of federal law, and pompous manner. Even his friends acknowledged that Burger did not rank among the best or brightest. He was a vain, arrogant, self-aggrandizing, and insecure man. While Burger was politically active for most of his adult life, he did not have the innate political skills that Taft, Hughes, and Warren employed so effectively in guiding the Court.

Under Burger, the Court reduced the time allotted for oral arguments from two hours per case to one, and the conference began to meet twice weekly, on Wednesdays and Fridays. Burger was not particularly skilled at leading conference discussions. During his own comments he tried to emphasize the most important aspects of the case and left the remaining issues for others to raise as the discussion moved around the table. But Burger was rarely focused or concise in his case summaries, and he relied too heavily on case memoranda prepared by his clerks. One Justice called him "the least prepared member of the Court."[227] Other Justices criticized his lack of conference preparation, his poor organizational skills, and his tendency to editorialize, whether or not his comments were relevant to the case.[228] Brennan complained that Burger gave "the same law-and-order speech in every damn criminal case."[229]

Not only were Burger's case summaries meandering and disjointed, he often ended his comments by either passing or giving an ambiguous vote. His indecisive behavior heightened suspicions, especially among the liberals, that he was manipulating the conference in order to vote last and control opinion assignments. Douglas repeatedly accused Burger of purposefully delaying or misreporting his votes and of trying to assign majority opinions when he had no right to do so. Douglas attributed Burger's alleged misbehavior to a combination of Machiavellian ambition and administrative incompetence.[230]

---

226. Douglas, *The Court Years*, 231.

227. O'Brien, "Institutional Norms and Supreme Court Opinions," in Clayton and Gillman, *Supreme Court Decision-Making*, 109.

228. O'Brien, *Storm Center*, 189.

229. Cooper, *Battles on the Bench*, 95.

230. Douglas, *The Court Years*, 232–33. At conference during the 1975 Term, Potter Stewart passed to William Rehnquist a fanciful sketch of Burger's tombstone, with the epitaph "I'll Pass for the Moment." Stewart's second sketch was of Blackmun's tombstone, which said, "I Hope the Opinion Can Be Narrowly Written." Rehnquist laughed out loud. Woodward and Armstrong, *The Brethren*, 490.

The Chief Justice, however, was by nature a rambling and tentative judge, and it is not clear to what extent Douglas's charges were true. Burger's conference behavior was basically the same whether the case was important or minor and whether or not the vote was close. He routinely miscounted conference votes and constantly had to be corrected by the other Justices. The situation finally got so bad that he gave up trying to tally the votes and assigned the task to Sandra Day O'Connor.[231]

In contrast to Hughes, who issued case assignments the same day as the conference, Burger often delayed several weeks before distributing opinion assignments. These delays added to suspicions that he was using the extra time to lobby and manipulate the assignments. Burger also developed an unfortunate reputation for punishing those who disagreed with him by withholding desirable case assignments.[232]

Burger had his admirers on the Court. John Marshall Harlan thought that Burger ran a fairer conference than Earl Warren. Harlan never forgave Warren for his preconference caucuses with Brennan, which Harlan considered brazen attempts to organize conference votes in advance. Harlan was relieved when Burger put a stop to such backroom behavior.[233]

Like Hughes, Burger often sought to join the majority even when the decision did not reflect his own personal views. He then did his best to influence the final result by using his privileged position as Chief Justice to assign the case to himself or to the Justice whose views most closely matched his own. While personally conservative, Burger's positions on many important issues—such as abortion, church and state, and the environment—were often quite flexible. Burger rarely worried about taking a consistent position one way or the other on most issues, and he often joined the majority whichever way the vote went. This made him either a pragmatic realist or an unprincipled opportunist, depending on one's perspective.

Law and order cases were different. Burger's sympathies in these cases were invariably with prosecutors and police. He was openly dismissive of what he saw as the Warren Court's attempts to coddle criminals and protect the rights of rapists and murderers, while decent citizens no longer felt safe in their homes or on the streets. In these cases, Burger rarely compromised his personal views in order to lead the Court. Then again, he rarely had to. The Burger Court was already inclined to be conservative when it came to law and order issues. The Justices limited *Miranda* protections, gave police more leeway in

---

231. Woodward and Armstrong, *The Brethren*, 204.

232. When Lewis Powell resisted Burger's efforts to lobby his vote on a criminal case, Powell confided to another Justice that he was "resigned to writing nothing but Indian affairs cases for the rest of my life." Harry Blackmun agreed that "if one's in the doghouse with the Chief, he gets the crud." Schwartz, *The Ascent of Pragmatism*, 4.

233. Yarbrough, *John Marshall Harlan*, 321.

search and seizure cases (e.g., allowing warrantless airplane surveillance in *California v. Ciraolo* [1986]), and scaled back the exclusionary rule (e.g., the "inevitable discovery" exception, *Nix v. Williams* [1984], and the good faith exception to the exclusionary rule, *United States v. Leon* [1984]).[234]

Perhaps the most important battles Burger faced in criminal cases involved the death penalty. It began inauspiciously for the Chief Justice, who strongly favored capital punishment. In the end, however, Burger largely got his way. After several years of sharp but inconclusive skirmishes over capital punishment, a liberal 5–4 majority struck down all existing state capital punishment statutes in *Furman v. Georgia* (1972).[235] Virtually everyone on the Court, including the Chief Justice, thought that they had witnessed the last legal execution in the United States. Burger's dissent in *Furman*, however, encouraged states to restructure and reenact their death penalty statutes. Most of these states used Burger's opinion as their template. When the revised death statutes came back before the Court less than four years later, a 7–2 majority upheld the new laws in *Gregg v. Georgia* (1976).[236]

The initial expectation among legal scholars was that the Burger Court would repeal many of the legal landmarks established by the Warren Court in civil rights and liberties cases. It was a counterrevolution that never happened. For the most part, the Burger Court limited, but did not overrule, the most important Warren Court precedents. Some Warren-era decisions involving privacy and desegregation were even extended. The Court remained badly divided throughout most of Burger's tenure, with a handful of Justices in the middle—usually Potter Stewart, Lewis Powell, and Sandra Day O'Connor—controlling the balance of power in closely contested cases. In many cases, this meant doctrinal instability.

Among the most crucial decisions that the Burger Court faced in the area of state-federal relations was *National League of Cities v. Usery* (1974). William Rehnquist used this case to resurrect the idea that the Tenth Amendment offered state governments substantive protection from the federal government by recognizing an area of traditional state responsibilities that lay beyond the reach of the federal government.[237] Soon after the case was announced, Harry Blackmun had second thoughts about the case and decided that Rehnquist's plan was unworkable. Because Blackmun was the fifth vote in a 5–4 decision, it was only a matter of time before Rehnquist's opinion was challenged. In 1985, a 5–4 Court overruled *National League of Cities* in *Garcia v. San Antonio Metropolitan Transit Authority*, with Blackmun writing the majority opinion. Rehnquist was furi-

234. *California v. Ciraolo*, 467 U.S. 207 (1986); *Nix v. Williams*, 467 U.S. 431 (1984); *United States v. Leon*, 468 U.S. 897 (1984).
235. *Furman v. Georgia*, 408 U.S. 238 (1972).
236. *Gregg v. Georgia*, 428 U.S. 153 (1976).
237. *National League of Cities v. Usery*, 426 U.S. 833 (1976).

ous and publicly vowed to overturn *Garcia* the moment that he found five votes.[238] Fifteen years later, *Garcia* remains on the books, but Rehnquist has forged a new majority and undercut the case so severely that it is no longer a reliable precedent. He might now have the five votes he needs to overrule *Garcia* outright.

In separation of powers cases, three Burger Court decisions deserve particular attention. First, *Gravel v. United States* (1972) established the limits of congressional immunity from prosecution under the speech and debate clause.[239] Second, *United States v. Nixon* (1974) established executive privilege as a constitutional prerogative of the president yet held that President Nixon's general and unsupported claim of privilege had to yield to a particularized need for necessary and specific evidence in a criminal case.[240] Third, *Immigration and Naturalization Service v. Chadha* (1983) struck down the one-house legislative veto as a violation of separation of powers.[241]

In free speech cases, the Burger Court made it easier for states to prosecute obscenity cases, updating the old *Roth* test in *Miller v. California* (1973).[242] The Court also struck down significant portions of Congress's 1974 Campaign Finance Reform Act, limiting campaign expenditures on free speech grounds in *Buckley v. Valeo* (1976).[243]

The Burger Court had a mixed record on free press cases, protecting the right of the press and public to cover trials but limiting the ability of reporters to protect confidential sources.[244] The Court also extended new First Amendment protections to the press in defamation cases involving public officials and public figures.[245]

In freedom of religion cases, Burger was an accommodationist who favored allowing greater interaction between church and state. While Burger himself promulgated a rigorous test separating church and state in *Lemon v. Kurtzman*, in subsequent cases he sought to distance himself from his own test by suggesting that he had meant it to be merely a starting point for discussion rather than a rigid formula. On the whole, the Burger Court was quite permissive when it came to religious participation in state affairs and encouraged state accommodation of religious practices. A majority, including the Chief Justice, voted to permit states to use public money to hire official legislative chaplains[246] and approved the use of public funds to create and maintain government-sponsored Christmas displays.[247]

---

238. *Garcia v. San Antonio Metropolitan Transit Authority* (1985).
239. *Gravel v. United States*, 408 U.S. 606 (1972).
240. *United States v. Nixon*, 418 U.S. 683 (1974).
241. *Immigration and Naturalization Service v. Chadha*, 462 U.S. 919 (1983).
242. *Roth v. United States*, 354 U.S. 476 (1957); *Miller v. California*, 413 U.S. 15 (1973).
243. *Buckley v. Valeo*, 424 U.S. 1 (1976).
244. *Nebraska Press Assn. v. Stuart*, 427 U.S. 539 (1976); *Branzburg v. Hayes*, 408 U.S. 665 (1972).
245. *Gertz v. Robert Welch, Inc.*, 418 U.S. 323 (1974).
246. *Marsh v. Chambers*, 463 U.S. 783 (1983).
247. *Lynch v. Donnelly*, 465 U.S. 668 (1984).

The Burger Court's treatment of school desegregation and race cases was mixed and somewhat inconsistent. In *Swann v. Charlotte-Mecklenburg Board of Education* (1971), the Court granted federal judges broad discretion to deal with de jure segregation, including the right to order busing or other creative remedies. But the Justices limited the scope and nature of remedies in school districts where segregation was caused by private housing choices (de facto segregation).[248] The Court decided several landmark affirmative action cases, including *Regents of the University of California v. Bakke* (1978), which held that race could be considered as one factor among many in admitting students to public professional schools. *Fullilove v. Klutznick* (1980) allowed Congress considerable latitude to establish minority hiring targets in the awarding of federal construction contracts.[249]

Gender cases were another flashpoint during the Burger era. Laws categorizing persons on the basis of sex initially received the lowest level of judicial scrutiny. Under the *rational basis test*, laws are presumed to be constitutional and the Court is strongly predisposed to defer to legislative judgments so long as they are not irrational. The party challenging the law's validity has the burden of proof to demonstrate that there is no reasonable relationship between any legitimate end of government and the means adopted to achieve that end. Those attacking gender-based discrimination encouraged the Court to use the more demanding *strict scrutiny* test to evaluate these laws. The strict scrutiny test places the burden on the government to prove that discrimination is necessary to achieve a compelling state interest and that there is no less intrusive way to achieve the same result.

The Burger Court gave equal rights advocates a partial victory in *Reed v. Reed* (1971), ruling that laws discriminating on the basis of sex would be subject to some unspecified "higher" form of scrutiny than the minimalist rational basis test.[250] The Court briefly flirted with the idea that laws discriminating on the basis of sex were inherently suspect and should receive strict scrutiny,[251] before settling uncomfortably in the middle and creating a third test, which the majority labeled "*intermediate scrutiny.*"[252]

The Burger Court charted new territory in privacy cases. The most famous of these decisions was *Roe v. Wade* (1973), which established women's constitutional right to abortion.[253] The Burger Court subsequently placed limitations on abortion rights, and there were numerous legislative attempts to limit or reverse *Roe*. The Burger Court limited

---

248. *Swann v. Charlotte-Mecklenburg Bd. of Ed.*, 402 U.S. 1 (1971); *Milliken v. Bradley*, 418 U.S. 717 (1974).
249. *Regents of the University of California v. Bakke*, 438 U.S. 265 (1978); *Fullilove v. Klutznick*, 448 U.S. 448 (1980). After Rehnquist became Chief Justice, the latter case was reexamined and ultimately overruled. *Adarand Constructors, Inc. v. Pena*, 515 U.S. 200 (1995).
250. *Reed v. Reed*, 404 U.S. 71 (1971).
251. *Frontiero v. Richardson*, 411 U.S. 677 (1973).
252. *Craig v. Boren*, 429 U.S. 190 (1976).
253. *Roe v. Wade*, 410 U.S. 113 (1973).

privacy rights in other cases, ruling that the right of privacy did not extend to prison-ers[254] and did not cover consensual sodomy in one's own home.[255]

The nature of the conference continued to evolve under Burger's leadership. The Justices became less interested in using the conference to exchange ideas, debate, or per-suade others. Instead, they began to view the conference merely as an opportunity to declare their individual positions and count votes.[256] In a sense, this marked a return to the seriatim style of the earliest days of the Court, where each Justice explained (albeit only to each other) their individual judgments and reasoning without attempting to work out a common opinion.

There was considerable dissatisfaction inside the conference room. Several Justices complained about a decline in conference discipline, saying that Burger tolerated too many interruptions and too much cross-talk.[257] Most of the other Justices—including some of Burger's closest allies—found Burger's conference behavior frustrating. When William Rehnquist first came to the Court, he was dismayed by the lack of interplay among the Justices in conference. Other junior Justices were struck by how "extraordinarily impersonal" the Supreme Court was compared to smaller and more intimate state and federal courts.[258]

The conference drifted apart for a variety of reasons. Technological advances such as photocopying and computerization made independent research and writing more feasible. The growing bureaucratization of the Court, with expanded judicial responsi-bilities and an increasingly large staff, drove the Justices deeper into their own chambers and away from other members of the conference. More than ever, the Court operated like nine independent law firms.[259] Personal interchanges among the Justices continued to decline, and what few channels of communications remained were almost exclusively by written memoranda or through the back door via the clerks' network.

Conference discussions were also more constrained because of the emerging sense of judicial restraint among the Justices—especially the four Nixon appointees—in civil rights cases. The Nixon appointees were judicial activists in many respects, but the Burger Court marked an end to the zeal and the sense of institutional mission that had characterized the Warren Court on such lightning-rod issues as race, poverty, and the rights of the accused.

---

254. *Hudson v. Palmer*, 468 U.S. 517 (1984).

255. *Bowers v. Hardwick*, 478 U.S. 186 (1986).

256. Schwartz, *History of the Supreme Court*, 311.

257. Stewart, "Reflections on the Supreme Court," 12.

258. Ibid.

259. The characterization of the Court as nine independent law firms is often attributed to Lewis Powell, who used the metaphor in his "Address to the American Bar Association Annual Meeting," 62 *ABA J.* 1454 (1976). Potter Stewart, however, attributed the phrase to the second John Marshall Harlan, who often said that the Court operated "like nine independent law firms, sometimes practicing against each other." Stewart, "Reflections on the Supreme Court," 12.

Burger was at his best as the Court's chief lobbyist. He worked tirelessly to publicize the Court and to make the judicial process more efficient. His administrative and ceremonial duties often required him to be away from Washington on Court business. Whenever Burger was absent, William O. Douglas ran the conference, until he retired in 1975.

Douglas had no more success as a conference leader than the Chief Justice. Douglas's conferences typically wrapped up several hours earlier than Burger's, which Douglas and his staff attributed to Douglas's plain speaking, incisive analysis, and efficiency. Most of the other Justices disagreed with this assessment. One Justice complained that "Bill didn't discuss anything. He would just say, 'This is a case involving such and such a statute. The issue is such and such. I vote to affirm.' No wonder we were out of there so early."[260] Lewis Powell added that "Bill was impatient at Conference. . . . Instead of really encouraging people to discuss a case, all he was interested in was how they were going to vote."[261]

In 1975, a series of strokes left Douglas virtually incapacitated. He began to sleep through conferences, and at other times he suffered severe pain and had to leave early. To protect the Court's image and the integrity of their decisions, the other Justices informally agreed among themselves to ignore Douglas's votes when he voted with the majority in 5–4 cases, treating these cases as if they were tied 4–4 and holding them for reargument the next term. The Justices also refused to allow Douglas to cast the decisive fourth vote at cert conferences to accept new cases. His votes were not counted unless at least four other Justices also voted to grant cert. In cases where conference votes gave Douglas the right as senior Justice to assign cases, Burger and Brennan cooperated to assign the opinions instead.[262]

Douglas resigned his seat on November 12, 1975; but to everyone's embarrassment, he still claimed to be a voting member of the Court and presented himself to the conference as the tenth Justice. He even sought to publish an opinion in the landmark campaign financing case, *Buckley v. Valeo* (1976).[263] Burger finally had to order the Court staff to ignore Douglas's demands. It was a sad end to a long and distinguished career.[264]

Warren Burger presided over what was perhaps the most divided Court in history. Overall, the Burger Court had a case dissent rate of 64 percent.[265]

260. Simon, *An Independent Journey*, 431.

261. Urofsky, "Getting the Job Done: William O. Douglas and Collegiality on the Supreme Court," in Wasby, *He Shall Not Pass This Way Again*, 35.

262. Woodward and Armstrong, *The Brethren*, 435, 466. Several Justices complained bitterly about Douglas's continued presence at conference for various reasons, from inefficiency to incontinence. Ibid., 464.

263. *Buckley v. Valeo*, 424 U.S. 1 (1976)

264. Simon, *An Independent Journey*, 451. Burger was sympathetic and kind to Douglas during his incapacity, writing to Douglas and sending him homemade bread and peach jam fortified with brandy. Woodward and Armstrong, *The Brethren*, 456.

265. Data compiled from Epstein, *Supreme Court Compendium*, 198–99.

WILLIAM REHNQUIST: EVERYBODY GETS
ONE BITE OF THE APPLE (1986–)

Like other Chief Justices promoted from within, one of William Rehnquist's immediate priorities was to avoid repeating the mistakes of his predecessor. As a junior Associate Justice, Rehnquist was frustrated during conferences when senior Justices began debating issues among themselves before he had a chance to speak. As Chief Justice, Rehnquist tries to make sure that each Justice gets "one bite of the apple" before allowing any general discussion or debate. He keeps his opening presentations concise and moves conferences along by discouraging interruptions and cross-talk, but he admits that there is little he can do if the other Justices persist in talking out of turn.[266]

Rehnquist considers lengthy conference discussions to be a waste of time and is far more concerned with deciding cases efficiently and getting the votes recorded accurately.[267] He quickly distanced himself from Burger's tendency to manipulate conference votes. At the end of each case, he immediately announces his tally and allows the other Justices to challenge his count on the spot.[268] Once the cases are assigned, he expects the other Justices to circulate their opinions promptly and assigns cases based in part on each Justice's track record for circulating opinions on time.

Rehnquist's leadership style has worked to his personal disadvantage in some respects. He rarely seeks out the politically advantageous middle ground, as Hughes and Burger so often did, in order to control assignments and influence majority opinions. He has generally refused to compromise his views in order to join and shape majorities with which he does not agree. Even after Brennan, Marshall, and Blackmun retired and the ideological center of the Court shifted significantly to the right, Rehnquist still has not consistently been able to rally the Court around him. He is closely identified with the right wing of a conservative Court, and that is where he is content to remain. As a consequence, in many doctrinal matters, Justices O'Connor and Kennedy command the center and have often been more influential than the Chief Justice in determining how close cases are decided.

In other respects, Rehnquist's leadership style has served him well. Even his staunchest ideological opponents freely admit that he is an honest, able, and amiable conference leader. He is widely regarded as well organized, efficient, and fair, with an excellent sense of humor and little inclination to carry a grudge. As a student of Supreme Court history, Rehnquist learned early to attend to Taft's "personal equation." He enjoys good personal and working relationships with all the other Justices, despite the often sharp political and personal differences that divide the Court. Conferences are significantly more efficient

---

266. Rehnquist, *The Supreme Court*, 293.
267. Tushnet, *Making Constitutional Law*, 56.
268. Rehnquist, *The Supreme Court*, 293.

and pleasant under Rehnquist than they were under Warren Burger, and on the whole the Court is a quieter and a happier place to work.

Thurgood Marshall predicted early on that Chief Justice Rehnquist "is going to be, if he isn't already, a damn good Chief Justice."[269] Marshall thought that Rehnquist was a significant improvement over Burger. Rehnquist "has no problems, wishy-washy, back and forth. He knows exactly what he wants to do, and that's very important as a Chief Justice."[270] Marshall, however, had no illusions about which direction the Court was headed, and he left standing instructions with his clerks that if he died at his desk they were to "prop [him] up and keep voting."[271]

Good individual relationships with the Chief have not necessarily translated into close or collegial working relationships among the other Justices. The conference remains highly factionalized and uncommunicative. Whether out of animosity or indifference, many of the Justices have all but given up talking to each other, let alone trying to persuade others in conference or attempting to forge a consensus. Gathering five votes is all most of the Justices are interested in at this point, and the conference is in danger of becoming little more than a vote-counting exercise.[272] Antonin Scalia, perhaps the most combative Justice on the Court and one who would relish more spirited conference exchanges, described conference discussions under Rehnquist with a touch of disappointment:

> Not much conferencing goes on [at the conference]. In fact, to call our discussion of a case a conference is really something of a misnomer; it's much more a statement of the views of each of the nine Justices, after which the totals are added and the case is assigned.[273]

Edward Lazarus, one of Harry Blackmun's former clerks, describes it in more bleak terms:

> [The Court has] broken into unyielding factions that have largely given up on a meaningful exchange of their respective views or, for that matter, a meaningful explication or defense of their own views.[274]

According to Lazarus, outside of the conference the only communications between the Court's factions are accusations of bad faith or stupidity.[275]

The Justices physically work more closely to one another today than they did in Melville Fuller's day, when they all worked alone at home. Psychologically, however, the

---

269. Tushnet, *Making Constitutional Law*, 47.

270. Schwartz, *The Ascent of Pragmatism*, 12.

271. Lazarus, *Closed Chambers*, 279.

272. There are a few noteworthy exceptions, such as the Court's unanimous decision to deny President Clinton's claim of legal immunity in the Paula Jones civil case. *Clinton v. Jones*, 520 U.S. 681 (1997).

273. Justice Scalia, *New York Times*, February 22, 1988, A16, cited in Schwartz, *The Ascent of Pragmatism*, 398–99.

274. Lazarus, *Closed Chambers*, 6.

275. Ibid., 286.

Justices are farther apart than ever. In most respects, they might as well be working in different parts of the country. Some of the Justices have begun to do just that. Beginning in the late 1980s, John Paul Stevens began to fly to his condominium in Florida for extended stays during the winter. He now reportedly leaves so often and for so long that he is referred to around the Court as the FedEx Justice.[276] Stevens uses overnight mail and e-mail to stay in close, daily contact with his chambers while he is in Florida.

E-mail and other similar technologies hold promise for allowing the Justices to regain some sense of at least a virtual community. It permits quick and interactive communications, whether the Justices are separated by a single marble wall or by several states. Many of the clerks use e-mail incessantly to communicate with each other during the day. The Justices themselves, however, are not yet prepared to supplement their weekly conferences with daily e-conferences.

There have been relatively few revolutionary doctrinal developments from the Rehnquist Court. Two dominant themes have emerged, though sometimes observed only in the breach: judicial restraint and states' rights. While the Rehnquist Court has been relatively restrained in establishing new and innovative constitutional doctrines, the Justices have been quite active in revisiting and limiting many of the most important landmark decisions of the Warren and Burger Courts. The Rehnquist Court has continued the Burger Court's practice of stealth activism—limiting established judicial doctrines and precedents without explicitly overruling them.

Federalism is one of the areas where the Rehnquist Court has been most active. Rehnquist has tried to position the Court to play a role similar to that which Roger Brooke Taney staked out more than 150 years ago: to serve as an impartial umpire in federal-state relations. To that end, Rehnquist has resurrected the idea of dual federalism to promote states' rights, contain federal authority, and establish a new equilibrium in state-federal relations.

Rehnquist's conception of states' rights, however, is perhaps less a full-blown theory of dual federalism (think of a house with a line painted down the middle, with the states in control of one half of the house and the federal government responsible for the other half) than a vision of island federalism (think of small, scattered areas of state responsibility in a sea of federal power). His preoccupation with protecting these islands of traditional state responsibilities can be seen in both the Court's economic and civil rights decisions.[277] The Rehnquist Court has interpreted the doctrine of adequate and independent state grounds more expansively than previous Courts, and as a consequence state

---

276. Ibid., 279.

277. Antonin Scalia's theory of federalism is more ambitious. In his opinion in *Planned Parenthood v. Casey*, 505 U.S. 833, 979–980 (1992), he argued that if reasonable minds disagree about liberty issues like abortion, bigamy, or the right to die, then unless the claims involve *specifically protected constitutional liberties* or perhaps well-founded national traditions, states should be free to choose whatever policies they want, subject only to minimal judicial scrutiny using the rational basis test.

constitutional law has recently become a more active and more interesting field of litigation and research.

Conventional legal wisdom has long held that the Tenth Amendment offers no substantive protection for states against the federal government. Instead, states are thought to be protected by their overwhelming representation in Congress and by other provisions of the Constitution that specifically define and limit the powers of the central government. But William Rehnquist has long dreamed of reviving the Tenth Amendment and using it to carve out a sovereign and unassailable realm for state governments. His first major attempt to use the Tenth Amendment to define and protect "traditional state functions" was announced in *National League of Cities v. Usery* (1976). Nine years later, Rehnquist's approach was abandoned as arbitrary and unworkable, and *National League of Cities* was overruled by *Garcia v. San Antonio Metropolitan Transit Authority* (1985). Rehnquist considers *Garcia* to be a temporary setback and has vowed to overturn it as soon as he can find four additional votes. While he has not yet found enough support to bring the issue back before the conference, it is clear that the Chief Justice has already launched an indirect assault on *Garcia*.

In 1995, the Court struck down the federal Gun Free School Zones Act, which outlawed the possession of firearms near schools.[278] This was the first time in more than fifty years that the Court struck down a federal law because it exceeded Congress's commerce clause powers. The decision put Congress on notice that there might be substantive limits to its commerce clause power. According to *United States v. Lopez* (1995), the subject of commerce clause legislation must have a "substantial relationship" to interstate commerce. The majority noted that the act did not require that guns confiscated inside school zones have any demonstrable effect on or connection to interstate commerce and ruled that there had to be some tangible link to interstate commerce before Congress could act.

Despite the widespread media attention given to *Lopez*, it imposed little more than a symbolic limitation on Congress's commerce powers. Standing alone, the case represents only a small step back from *Wickard v. Filburn*, which established that Congress's commerce powers were plenary and virtually self-defining. The real importance of the case is that it may represent the first step toward imposing new limits on federal efforts to regulate essentially local activities. This would leave the door open for the Court to reposition the Tenth Amendment as the constitutional source of those limits.[279]

In criminal cases, the Rehnquist Court significantly limited the scope of the *Miranda* rule, but later reaffirmed that *Miranda* warnings were constitutionally required and could

---

278. *United States v. Lopez*, 514 U.S. 549 (1995).

279. For more recent cases reinforcing this view, see *Alden v. Maine*, 527 U.S. 706 (1999); *College Savings Bank v. Florida Prepaidpostsecondary Education Expense Board*, 527 U.S. 666 (1999); *Regents of the University of California v. Genentech, Inc.*, 527 U.S. 1031 (1999).

not be overturned by federal legislation. The latter decision was by an unexpectedly lopsided 7–2 vote, with the Chief Justice writing the majority opinion.[280] The Court also gave
police increased discretion in search and seizure cases and placed new limits on the exclusionary rule.[281]

The Rehnquist Court has vigorously supported state death penalty statutes, stream-
lining the appeals process in capital cases and quickening the pace of executions by limiting federal habeas corpus rights, restricting forum shopping, and curtailing collateral
attacks on state convictions. Some states, particularly Texas and Florida, have executed
large numbers of inmates in recent years, clearing backlogs on death row where some
prisoners have been awaiting execution for more than twenty-five years.

Rehnquist believes that opponents of the death penalty "mak[e] a mockery of our
criminal justice system" by delaying executions through appeals and dilatory tactics.
Rehnquist calls such stalling "pulling a Rosenberg." The phrase comes from his days as
Robert Jackson's clerk, when Ethel and Julius Rosenberg delayed their executions through
a continuous stream of petitions and appeals.[282] Rehnquist believes that states can be
trusted to review capital cases and that state courts will enforce defendants' due process
rights at least as effectively as federal courts. Accordingly, he has sought to downplay the
supervisory role of federal courts in capital cases and has voted to affirm every death
penalty case that has come before the Court on appeal.

In religion cases, the Rehnquist Court changed established rules governing the free
exercise clause in *Employment Division v. Smith* (1990). The Court permitted Oregon to
fire two state employees and withhold their state unemployment benefits after they in-
gested peyote as part of a religious ritual. State drug laws banned all use of peyote and
other hallucinogenic drugs. The Court abandoned the traditional requirement that laws
infringing on the free exercise of religion must serve a compelling state interest and ruled
that Oregon could proscribe the use of peyote in religious ceremonies and refuse un-

---

280. In *New York v. Harris*, 495 U.S. 14 (1990), for example, the Court permitted the use of Harris's
second confession even though his first confession had been illegally obtained and had to be excluded. The
Court reaffirmed *Miranda* in *Dickerson v. United States*, 120 S. Ct. 2326 (2000).

281. In *United States v. Alvarez-Machain*, 504 U.S. 655 (1992), the Court permitted federal agents to
kidnap a criminal suspect in Mexico and bring him to the United States for trial. Under a new rule announced in *Wyoming v. Houghton*, 119 S. Ct. 1297 (1999), if police have probable cause to suspect an automobile driver of wrongdoing, they may search not only the driver and his belongings, but any packages
and containers belonging to passengers that could contain the object of the search. According to Scalia's
majority opinion, automobile passengers, like drivers, have a lower expectation of privacy regarding property stored in automobiles than for property kept elsewhere.

282. When Rehnquist clerked for Justice Jackson, he wrote a memo to his boss saying that it was
unfortunate that the Rosenbergs were only going to be electrocuted when they deserved to be drawn and
quartered. Rehnquist was baffled by the Court's preoccupation with the Rosenbergs and wondered aloud
why the "highest court of the nation must act like a bunch of old women" whenever it dealt with capital
cases. Savage, *Turning Right*, 34; Lazarus, *Closed Chambers*, 140.

employment payments to anyone fired for such misconduct, so long as the state's laws were (a) equally applicable to everyone and (b) not directed at religious practices or beliefs.[283] Congress acted quickly to overturn the Court's decision with the Religious Freedom Restoration Act of 1993.[284] In 1997, however, the Court struck down the RFRA on constitutional grounds, as a violation of the establishment clause.[285]

Also in 1997, the Court rejected an attempt by the city of Hialeah, Florida, to prohibit animal sacrifices in Santeria religious ceremonies. The majority ruled that the ordinance was neither neutral nor generally applicable, because the city permitted other animals to be hunted and slaughtered within the city limits for food, pest control, and other reasons.[286]

In establishment clause cases, the Rehnquist Court loosened rules prohibiting state aid to sectarian schools by sustaining a federal law permitting equal access to public high schools for noncurricular religious organizations. Support for religious activities on school grounds was permissible, the Justices said, so long as the program benefited a broad class of citizens without reference to religion.[287] But in another case, the Court ruled 6–3 that the state of New York violated the establishment clause when it established a special, exclusive public school district to accommodate the needs of a small group of disabled students, all of whom belonged to the same Satmar Hasidic sect.[288] The Court also declared unconstitutional a Texas school policy permitting student-led prayers to be broadcast over loudspeakers at football games.[289]

In race and affirmative action cases, the Rehnquist Court has been especially keen to limit or overturn precedents established under Warren and Burger. After the Burger Court narrowly approved a congressional job set-aside program for minority-owned business in *Fullilove v. Klutznick*, the Rehnquist Court placed that decision in doubt in

---

283. *Employment Division v. Smith*, 494 U.S. 872 (1990).

284. The RFRA prohibited the government from "substantially burdening" a person's exercise of religion, even if the burden resulted from a rule of general applicability, unless the government proved that the burden (1) furthered a compelling governmental interest and (2) was the least restrictive means of furthering that interest.

285. *Boerne v. Flores*, 521 U.S. 507 (1997).

286. *Church of the Lukumi Babalu Aye, Inc. v. City of Hialeah*, 508 U.S. 520 (1993).

287. *Zobrest v. Catalina Foothills School Dist.*, 509 U.S. 1 (1993), allowing a state-employed interpreter to serve as a translator for a deaf child enrolled in a Catholic school; *Westside Community Bd. of Ed. v. Mergens*, 496 U.S. 226 (1990), affirming the constitutionality of the Equal Access Act, which guaranteed student religious groups the same access to public school facilities as secular, noncurricular groups.

288. *Board of Education of Kiryas Joel Village School Dist. v. Grumet*, 512 U.S. 687 (1994). Virtually all of the other Satmar children attended private religious schools, but the community wanted to use state and federal public funds to cover the high costs of educating their disabled children while insulating them from corrupting gentile influences.

289. *Doe v. Santa Fe Independent School District*, 120 S.Ct. 2464 (2000).

City of Richmond v. J. A. Croson Co. (1989).[290] In a 6–3 decision by Sandra Day O'Connor, the Court ruled that all legal classifications based on race, whether benign or invidious, were subject to strict scrutiny. O'Connor distinguished *Fullilove*, presumably because the earlier case involved a congressional statute, while *Croson* involved a city ordinance. Even after *Croson*, most commentators believed that Congress retained greater discretion to act in this area than states because of Congress's unique commerce clause powers.

Those thoughts were laid to rest in *Adarand Constructors, Inc.* v. *Pena* (1995). With O'Connor again writing for the majority, the Court explicitly overruled *Fullilove* and announced that state and federal affirmative action programs would receive the same level of strict scrutiny.[291] In subjecting all forms of de jure racial discrimination to strict scrutiny, the Court placed new limits on the government's ability to enact race-conscious affirmative action programs, whether at the state or federal level.

For now, most debate inside the Court has been limited to whether *any* affirmative action plan might pass strict scrutiny analysis under any circumstances. O'Connor insisted in her *Adarand* opinion that affirmative action programs might be permissible under some circumstances. Antonin Scalia, however, argued that the strict scrutiny test is "strict in theory but fatal in fact." In Scalia's judgment, laws creating racial categories are inherently invidious, and no affirmative action plan could ever pass the strict scrutiny test if it is honestly applied. The three Justices who dissented in *Adarand*—Marshall, Brennan, and Blackmun—argued that so-called benign affirmative action programs should be subjected to intermediate scrutiny. All three resigned from the Court soon afterward, and support for affirmative action on the Court has withered.

The Rehnquist Court also acted to limit established privacy rights, restrict constitutional abortion rights, and give states and the federal government more discretion to define and delimit individual privacy. After nearly overruling *Roe v. Wade* in a 1986 case, *Webster v. Reproductive Health Services*, six years later the Court unexpectedly reversed course and reaffirmed what the majority called the "essential holding" of *Roe* in *Planned Parenthood v. Casey*.[292] *Roe* was recast, however, so that states may impose additional restrictions on access to abortions. The majority abandoned *Roe's* use of strict scrutiny to evaluate state laws restricting access to legal abortions during the first trimester and

---

290. *Richmond v. J. A. Croson Co.*, 488 U.S. 469 (1989).

291. *Adarand Constructors, Inc. v. Pena*, 515 U.S. 200 (1995).

292. *Webster v. Reproductive Health Services*, 492 U.S. 490 (1986); *Planned Parenthood of Southeastern Pennsylvania v. Casey*, 505 U.S. 833 (1992). Despite a caution that Pennsylvania's conditions came close to imposing an impermissible undue burden on women's constitutional right to seek an abortion, the Court upheld the state's mandatory twenty-four-hour waiting period, "informed consent" requirements, and a parental notification scheme for minors that required either prior parental notification or judicial permission before a minor could obtain an abortion.

permitted states to place "reasonable" burdens on women who seek to abort a nonviable fetus. States, however, cannot impose an "undue burden" or place "substantial obstacles" on a woman's right to seek an abortion during the first trimester.

In a line of privacy cases, the Rehnquist Court upheld a series of government programs requiring federal employees to submit to drug tests. In *Skinner v. Railway Labor Executives Ass'n* (1989), the Court approved mandatory blood and urine tests for railroad employees after train accidents. In *National Treasury Employees Union v. Von Raab* (1989) a 5–4 Court approved mandatory urine tests for Customs Service employees in hiring, transfers, or promotions to positions involving drug interdictions or jobs where employees are permitted to carry firearms.[293] The Court also refused to extend constitutional privacy rights to cover terminally ill patients who wanted to hasten their own deaths voluntarily. These and other privacy issues have been left largely to the states to decide.[294]

From 1986 through 1994, the Rehnquist Court's case dissent rate was 59 percent.[295]

---

293. *Skinner v. Railway Labor Executives Ass'n*, 489 U.S. 602 (1989); *National Treasury Employees Union v. Von Raab*, 489 U.S. 656 (1989). See also, *Consolidated Rail Corp. v. Railway Labor Executives*, 491 U.S. 299 (1989), allowing the Conrail Corporation to test employees for drug use periodically, including urine tests administered upon return from leave or vacation. In all three cases, the Court ruled that these requirements did not violate employees' privacy rights or Fourth Amendment protections against unreasonable searches and seizures.

294. *Cruzan v. Director, Missouri Dept. of Health*, 497 U.S. 261 (1990).

295. Data compiled from Epstein, *Supreme Court Compendium*, 199.

PART II

SEPARATION OF POWERS
AND FEDERALISM

CHAPTER 4

THE SUPREME COURT

ARTICLE 3

Northern Pipeline Construction Company v. Marathon Pipeline Company,
458 U.S. 50 (1982)
(Brennan)

The Bankruptcy Act of 1978 established a new system of federal bankruptcy courts.[1] Under the law, bankruptcy judges did not enjoy the same privileges and protections as ordinary federal judges but served as adjuncts to the federal district courts.[2] Unlike other federal judges, bankruptcy judges were appointed to fourteen-year terms; their salaries could be reduced while they were in office; and they could be removed by local circuit judicial councils for incompetence, misconduct, neglect of duty, or disability.

Marathon Pipeline Company claimed that the Bankruptcy Act was unconstitutional because it conferred Article 3 powers on bankruptcy judges without providing them with Article 3 protections for tenure and salary. Northern Pipeline Construction Company argued that Congress properly established the bankruptcy courts using its Article 1 powers, which authorizes Congress to establish specialized legislative courts to carry out essentially legislative duties.[3] A three-judge district court agreed with Northern Pipeline that the new courts were Article 1 legislative courts rather than Article 3 judicial courts and ruled that the Bankruptcy Act of 1978 was constitutional.

---

1. 28 U.S.C. §1471.

2. Ordinary federal judges include district court, circuit court, and supreme court judges. They are referred to as "Article 3 judges" because Article 3 of the Constitution provides them with special protections: they cannot have their salaries reduced while in office (the "non-diminution" clause); and they serve on good behavior and cannot be removed from office involuntarily except upon impeachment by the House and conviction by two-thirds of the Senate (the "lifetime tenure" clause).

3. Congress may establish Article 1 courts in "specialized areas having particularized needs and warranting distinctive treatment." Examples include the Tax Court, military courts, and some federal courts for the District of Columbia. These courts are considered legislative courts rather than constitutional courts, and their judges may not have the powers or protections granted to Article 3 judges. The jurisdiction of military courts, for example, is limited to members of the armed services. *Solorio v. United States,* 483 U.S. 435 (1987). For the special rules that apply to District of Columbia courts, see *Palmore v. United States,* 411 U.S. 389 (1973).

The Court of Claims and the Court of Customs and Patent Appeals were initially created as Article 1 courts, but Congress later declared them to be Article 3 courts. Despite some misgivings, the Supreme Court deferred to Congress's judgment in changing their status. *Glidden Co. v. Zdanok,* 370 U.S. 530 (1962). These two courts have retained characteristics of both Article 1 and Article 3 courts, which has caused some constitutional problems.

BURGER: We still have some territorial courts around exercising complete Article 3 jurisdiction. The Court of Military Appeals exercises unreviewable life and death jurisdiction.

BRENNAN:[4] The question presented is whether the exercise by bankruptcy judges of the jurisdiction defined in 28 U.S.C. §1471 violates Article 3 of the Constitution. In answering this question, I cannot ignore the fact that Congress has vested in the bankruptcy courts not only the jurisdiction to resolve and adjudicate bankruptcies and reorganizations, but also jurisdiction to resolve numerous other disputes that involve bankrupts (e.g., divorces, contract disputes). For the Congress to grant such broad jurisdiction to a federally created court, it is my view that the court must be an Article 3 creation. Yet the bankruptcy judges lack the characteristics of Article 3 judges (e.g., they are appointed for fourteen-year terms rather than on good behavior).

I do not think that our prior precedents demonstrate the constitutionality of the judicial scheme under attack. While the Court has held constitutional the creation of non-Article 3 courts in the District of Columbia (*United States v. Palmore*) [*sic*] and in the territories, I view this line of cases as isolated to specialized *geographic* problems, which are not present in the instant case.[5]

Nor does the existence of the administrative agencies require this Court to uphold the bankruptcy scheme. Many of the administrative agencies offering judicial forums subject to "substantial evidence" review in the federal courts of appeals carry out tasks that prior to the existence of the agencies were resolved without any recourse to the courts and were unreviewable under the doctrine of sovereign immunity. Other agencies resolve public-law disputes, and I do not view bankruptcy as a public-law issue. And in almost all instances in which legislative courts have been established in the agencies, the "courts" have not been granted the far-ranging powers of final-dispute-resolution given to the bankruptcy courts.

If the Court chooses to decide the question of whether a holding of unconstitutionality should be retroactively applied, an issue I would prefer to avoid, I would follow *Chicot County Drainage District* and conclude that the Court's holding is not retroactive.[6]

I would affirm the judgment of the District Court for the District of Minnesota.

Congress also has the power under Article 4 to establish territorial courts in American possessions, including the Virgin Islands and the Northern Mariana Islands. See, for example, *American Ins. Co. v. 356 Bales of Cotton*, 26 U.S. (1 Pet.) 511 (1828); *Ex parte Bakelite Corp.*, 279 U.S. 438 (1929).

Finally, Congress has constitutional authority to establish judicial adjuncts for federal judges, including federal court commissioners and magistrates, who do not have Article 3 powers or protections. See, for example, *Gomez v. United States*, 490 U.S. 858 (1989).

4. Adapted from Brennan's talking papers, Brennan Papers, OT 1981, box 597.

5. *Palmore v. United States*, 411 U.S. 389 (1973). Palmore was convicted of a felony by the Superior Court of the District of Columbia. The Supreme Court rejected his claim that he was entitled to be tried by an Article 3 judge with lifetime tenure and salary protections, saying that Congress had plenary power under Article 1 to establish a separate court system in the District of Columbia.

6. *Chicot County Drainage District v. Baxter State Bank*, 308 U.S. 371 (1940). In a bond refinancing case, bondholders filed a federal lawsuit after a bond district defaulted. None of the parties questioned the constitutionality of the federal act that the plaintiffs relied on to bring their suit. When the statute was subse-

WHITE: I feel strongly that this is a constitutional structure. This is certainly an appropriate area for specialized judges.

MARSHALL: I agree with Bill Brennan.

BLACKMUN: Article 3 protects all federal judges and implies that the exercise of the judicial power of the United States should be by Article 3 judges. His argument that you can do this with state judges has been rejected. I would affirm.

POWELL: I agree with Byron. The bankruptcy power is a specific subject of congressional authority. Administrative agencies act on a national basis and adjudicate important rights.

REHNQUIST: I am torn between deference to Congress and the obvious practical problems that point to reversal. But my analysis points toward affirmance. The duties of these judges go way beyond those of referees. Where would this stop if we sustained this? I will pass for now.

STEVENS: I started with a presumption of validity, but now I have come to view this as the most important case we have had since I came here. The rationale that if you can do it with state judges then you can also do this can't possibly prevail—it would be the end of Article 3. We have to stop Congress from establishing any number of these courts.

O'CONNOR: I am tentative to affirm. If Congress could ignore Article 3, we would give very broad authority to Congress. The Framers did not mean to do that. I would treat this as a non-Article 3 court.

Result: Worried that Congress might use its Article 1 powers to "supplant completely our system of adjudication in independent Article 3 tribunals and replace it with a system of 'specialized' legislative courts," the Court struck down the Bankruptcy Act of 1978. William Brennan, in a plurality opinion, wrote that the act impermissibly sought to confer Article 3 judicial powers on an Article 1 structure. The powers and discretion conferred on bankruptcy judges were simply too great to allow bankruptcy courts to be established under Article 1; if bankruptcy judges were to exercise such broad judicial powers, they must also have Article 3 tenure and salary protections. To rule otherwise, Brennan wrote, would invite Congress "to replace the independent Article 3 Judiciary through a 'wholesale assignment of federal judicial business to legislative courts.'" Only three other Justices joined Brennan's opinion. Rehnquist and O'Connor joined only in the result. The decision triggered a strong reaction from Byron White, who criticized Brennan's approach as heavy-handed and arbitrary.

Ironically, Congress had originally tried to establish bankruptcy courts as Article 3 courts, but federal judges successfully lobbied to kill the bill because they did not want bankruptcy judges to be accorded the same status and prestige as "real" federal judges.

---

quently found to be unconstitutional in another, unrelated matter, the bond district tried to reopen the case. The Supreme Court ruled that the matter was res judicata and that the parties were estopped from raising the issue retroactively. Where the lower court had apparent authority to decide the case on the merits, its decision was subject to direct appeal but could not be collaterally attacked.

STANDING

Flast v. Cohen, 392 U.S. 83 (1968)
(Douglas)

Florence Flast and others brought a taxpayers' suit against Wilbur Cohen, the secretary of Health, Education, and Welfare, challenging the use of federal funds to support religious schools. A three-judge district court ruled that all plaintiffs lacked standing under the rules for taxpayer suits established in Frothingham v. Mellon.[7] *There was also a question of whether the three-judge district court had been properly convened.*

Conference of March 15, 1968

WARREN: I reverse. Standing is not an absolute; it varies with the position of the parties. There is little opportunity for persons in cases of this kind to have constitutional questions decided. There are hundreds of different situations where this can apply in the allocation of federal funds to education and other benefits. I hope that a decision can be written so as not to open a Pandora's box. A three-judge district court is proper to hear this type of complaint.

BRENNAN: They have no problem in administering this kind of rule in New Jersey. It is used there not only to challenge appropriations but also contracts.[8]

BLACK: I reverse. I agree with the Chief Justice.

DOUGLAS: I reverse. I agree with the Chief Justice.

HARLAN: I agree with the Chief Justice on the three-judge court issue. *Frothingham* reached a good result. I will stand by it, at least to prevent an opening of the floodgates. The First Amendment does not stand differently than other provisions of the Constitution. I affirm.

BRENNAN: I reverse. The three-judge court was proper. The problem is not peculiar to the First Amendment—unless in peculiar nature of this problem a taxpayer can raise the question, no one can. I would not overrule *Frothingham*. [DOUGLAS: Warren agrees.] The New Jersey rule would not be a good national rule.

STEWART: I reverse. I would confine our decision to the claim that it violates the establishment clause of the First Amendment. Congress's spending power is qualified by the establishment clause.

---

7. *Frothingham* limited the ability of taxpayers to challenge congressional appropriations in federal courts. In order to have standing, plaintiffs must prove a particularized and direct injury. Most taxpayer suits, the Court said, involve only indirect and abstract injuries suffered in common with other people generally. The majority ruled that this was not enough of a personal stake in the litigation to allow standing under the "case or controversy" requirement of Article 3. *Frothingham v. Mellon,* 262 U.S. 447 (1923).

8. Brennan was originally from New Jersey, where he practiced corporate law for nearly twenty years before being named to the state court of appeals (1950–52) and the state supreme court (1952–56) prior to his appointment to the U.S. Supreme Court in 1956.

WHITE: I would reverse narrowly and save as much of *Frothingham* as possible.

FORTAS: I am greatly troubled. I would be on the side of *Frothingham* if a broad opinion were written. I will reverse if the decision is restricted to the expenditure of public money. When Congress is implementing the general welfare, then *Frothingham* applies in full vigor. It reflects on separation of powers. The courts should not interfere in mere policy questions.

MARSHALL: I reverse.

Result: On an 8–1 vote, the Court ruled that taxpayers had standing to sue when the suit was brought under the tax or spend clause and where it was alleged that tax dollars were being spent in violation of a specific constitutional protection against an abuse of legislative power—in this case, the establishment clause. Frothingham *was distinguished but not overruled, and it soon made a comeback.*

Sierra Club v. Morton, 405 U.S. 727 (1972)
(Douglas)

In 1960, the U.S. Forest Service approved the Walt Disney Corporation's plan to build a new ski resort in the Mineral King area of California's Sequoia National Forest. The Sierra Club sued to block implementation of the plan on the ground that development would damage the aesthetic and environmental quality of the wilderness. The club claimed no particular or individualized injury to the organization or its members. The district court granted a temporary injunction against the project, but the court of appeals reversed on the ground that the Sierra Club lacked standing because it failed to show irreparable injury to the club or any of its members.

Conference of November 19, 1971

BURGER: I am strongly tempted to be liberal on standing. The fundamental question goes way beyond this case. How much judicial surveillance of executive actions should there be? The issue of standing in *Overton Park* was easier than this.[9] I want to decide this case very narrowly. I do not want to trust the government all the time. Have Sierra Club members used the area themselves? I would not want to let it go into everything, for government would be immobilized. *Flast* surprised me when it came down.[10]

DOUGLAS: I pass.

BRENNAN: This case did not require the Sierra Club to present the issue as broadly as it did. No injury in fact is pleaded. That relates to the use of the Mineral King area by Sierra Club members. That kind of evidence could be brought in under allegations on the petition. That supports the ruling of the district court and brings it under *Data Process-*

---

9. *Citizens to Preserve Overton Park v. Volpe*, 401 U.S. 402 (1971). A collection of private citizens and environmental groups sued Secretary of Transportation John Volpe to stop construction of a six-lane highway through a public park in Memphis, Tennessee. The lower courts granted summary judgment in favor of the government. In a decision by Thurgood Marshall, the Supreme Court found that the petitioners had standing.

10. *Flast v. Cohen*, 392 U.S. 83 (1968).

ing.[11] Is standing a function of the case or controversy requirement? It is a real case or controversy, as my separate opinion in *Data Processing* shows. The latter allows aesthetic as well as economic factors to be taken into account.

WHITE: I would not decide that issue here.

BRENNAN: I do not know whether it is on the district court record.

WHITE: It is not.

BRENNAN: I would not decide the broad question if we need not. I would reverse and remand.

STEWART: I cannot agree with the district court; I agree with court of appeals. I would be willing to decide the broad question and remand this, but I would prefer to affirm.

WHITE: The Sierra Club can't sue to enjoin an unaesthetic building in New York City.

BURGER: The United States has the right to be wrong in allowing Disney to develop the Mineral King area.

WHITE: Unless the Sierra Club had proved its standing. I affirm.

MARSHALL: I affirm.

BLACKMUN: I am about where Brennan is—I may be reaching for a position I emotionally desire enough here in the interest of Sierra Club members to sustain their standing.

Result: The Court held 4–3 that the Sierra Club lacked standing to sue. The majority ruled that parties had to allege a direct personal injury and have a sufficient personal stake in the issues to meet Article 3's real case or controversy requirement. Stewart wrote the majority opinion. Black, Douglas, and Blackmun dissented. Lewis Powell and William Rehnquist were appointed to the Court after the case was discussed in conference and did not participate in the decision. While the Sierra Club lost the legal battle, it won the political war. The case galvanized public and congressional opposition to the proposed development. In 1978, Congress attached the Mineral King area to Sequoia National Park, which forced Disney to abandon the project.

United States v. Richardson, 418 U.S. 166 (1974)
(Brennan)

William Richardson filed a taxpayer suit claiming that the Central Intelligence Agency Act, which established the CIA, was unconstitutional. Richardson claimed that the agency's secret, or "black," budget violated Article 1 §9 cl.7, which requires a regular accounting of public funds. The district court

---

11. *Data Processing Service v. Camp,* 397 U.S. 150 (1970). A data processing company and several individual data processors sued the federal Comptroller of the Currency to block a federal proposal to allow banks to provide data processing services to other banks and their customers. The district court dismissed the case on the ground that the petitioners lacked standing, but the Supreme Court reversed, holding that the petitioners stood to suffer real economic injuries and met Article 3's case or controversy requirement.

ruled that Richardson lacked standing to sue, citing Flast v. Cohen.[12] *The court of appeals reversed, saying that Richardson met the* Flast *test because: (1) his constitutional challenge was ultimately based on the taxing and spending clause of Article 1 §8; and (2) there was a nexus between his status as a taxpayer and a specific constitutional limitation on the tax and spend power.*

BURGER: Does this taxpayer satisfy the *Flast* criteria? Isn't there a complex of political question, standing, and case or controversy problems present with this? Was *Flast* limited to the religion clauses in giving standing? I would hold that there is no standing and am inclining to vacate and reinstate the district court's judgment, including the holding of no political question.

STEWART: If *Flast* is only a narrow exception to *Frothingham*, then Judge Adams was right that this is still a *Frothingham* situation.[13] But the respondent also sued as a citizen, and if the Constitution has anything besides the accounts and journal clause for benefit of citizenry generally, I can't find it. Because of this affirmative duty, the citizen has standing and I don't reach the justiciability questions. I am not wholly firm, however.

WHITE: This is a citizen and not a taxpayer case. Yet one of the strands of standing is that litigants ought to have some special stake and not just be citizens as such. If there is a textual commitment to Congress, then there is no standing.

MARSHALL: In essence, this is issuing a writ of mandamus against Congress. The fact that one is a citizen does not give him standing.

BLACKMUN: The Framers' use of "time to time" reflects their belief that what Congress has provided satisfies the clause. Congress has the textual commitment. This could mean challenges by any citizen to any government expenditure.

POWELL: Standing has two aspects: (1) case or controversy; and (2) prudential, that is, judicial self-restraint on exercising judicial power. *Flast* does not control this case. I would emphasize the judicial restraint aspect. It is hard for me to conceive of anything more legislative in nature than this.

Result: On a 5–4 vote, the Court ruled that Richardson did not have standing to sue. Under Frothingham, *a generalized grievance about governmental conduct or the allocation of government power was not sufficient to justify standing. Moreover, Richardson's case was not a tax and spend suit but an attack on CIA accounting and reporting procedures. There was no nexus between Richardson and any constitutional limitation of the taxing and spending clause—Congress had simply chosen not to require the sort of detailed financial reports from the CIA that Richardson wanted. This case left the interpretation of the statement and account clause to Congress, which decided that publication of the country's intelligence budget—even in the aggregate—was too great a risk to national security.*[14]

---

12. *Flast v. Cohen*, 392 U.S. 83 (1968).

13. *Frothingham v. Mellon*, 262 U.S. 447 (1923). Circuit Judge Arlin Adams wrote the dissenting opinion for the court of appeals.

14. Fisher, "Constitutional Interpretation by Members of Congress."

Alexander v. Americans United, 416 U.S. 752 (1974)
(Brennan)

The IRS sought to revoke the tax-exempt status of Americans United for Separation of Church and State. The government alleged that the group had engaged in political lobbying to influence legislation, which was prohibited by §§170 and 501 of the Internal Revenue Code. Americans United and two of its benefactors (who wanted to ensure that any future contributions would be tax deductible) claimed that the IRS action was unconstitutional and sought an injunction to have the organization's tax-exempt status restored. The district court dismissed the suit, ruling that the Anti-Injunction Act prohibited lawsuits to restrain the assessment or collection of any tax.[15] The court of appeals ruled that the act barred the two benefactors from joining the suit but did not preclude Americans United from seeking relief.

In conference, Blackmun and Powell wrestled with their personal feelings about the IRS. Donald C. Alexander was the commissioner of Internal Revenue.

BURGER: The IRS's revocation of Americans United's §501(c)(3) exemption, by taking it off the list (not statutory but regulatory), costs it dearly.[16] This meant that Americans United lost the tax-deduction to donors and it also subjected Americans United to withholding taxes. As for the *Williams Packing* rule, Americans United is entitled to it only "if under no circumstances the government can prevail."[17]

STEWART: The statute admits on its face of no exceptions, and maybe *Enochs* was wrong.

WHITE: The whole object of the lawsuit was to keep the IRS from taxing donors, and §7421 bars it. This is probably true even if a refund for employment taxes is not available.

BLACKMUN: I have to watch my biases here because of the frustrating experiences I have had with the IRS. But §7421 is so flat in its terms to prevent disruption of revenues. Procedurally, this is better set-up than *Bob Jones.*[18] But I am persuaded that this is not a suit

---

15. Section 7421(a) of the Internal Revenue Code. The purpose of this act was to withdraw state and federal jurisdiction over suits seeking to enjoin the collection of federal taxes. It permits the federal government to assess and collect taxes without judicial intervention and requires taxpayers who wish to challenge their assessments to file a case in Tax Court or to pay their taxes and then file suit for a refund.

16. Section 501(c)(3) of the Internal Revenue Code defines tax-exempt organizations (EOs), including "corporations . . . organized and operated exclusively for religious, charitable, scientific . . . or educational purposes."

17. *Enochs v. Williams Packing and Navigation Co.,* 370 U.S. 1 (1962). This case carved out an exception to §7421(a), saying that an injunction might be granted to prevent the government from collecting disputed taxes if: (1) the taxpayer could prove irreparable harm or that their remedy at law was otherwise inadequate (such as evidence that the taxpayer's business would be ruined); and (2) it was clear that under no circumstances could the government ultimately prevail, even given the most favorable view of the law and the facts.

18. *Bob Jones University v. Simon,* 416 U.S. 725 (1974). The IRS announced its intention to revoke the university's tax-exempt status and warned potential donors that their donations might no longer be tax-deductible. The university sued to enjoin the IRS from revoking its tax-exempt status and from assessing any new taxes or seeking to collect back taxes.

The Court ruled that the university did not fall within the *Enochs* exception and that the Anti-Injunction Act deprived both federal and state courts of jurisdiction to enjoin the assessment or collection of taxes.

within §7421. The tax consequences are unilateral only. I think that *Enochs* looks that way in finding a way to avoid the statute. I am not sure that §170 equates with the declaratory judgment statute's definite language.[19] Historically one could argue identity with §7421. My sympathies lead me to lean to affirm.

POWELL: I could end up with Harry if I could get around these statutes. The life and death power of the IRS is a frightening business. Yet the statutory wording and *Enochs* almost compel me to reverse.

REHNQUIST: Our decision in *Standard Nut Margarine* led to *Enochs*.[20]

Result: The Court ruled that both Americans United and the two benefactors were barred from seeking injunctive relief under the Anti-Injunction Act, regardless of whether their claims were based on the Constitution or the tax code. If the organization wanted to litigate the issue, Lewis Powell wrote, it would have to file an ordinary common law suit to recover the unemployment taxes that Americans United was required to pay when it lost its tax-exempt status.

If the university wanted to contest the matter, it could either file a claim in the Tax Court or pay any assessed taxes and then sue for a refund. Bob Jones University chose the latter course, and the results of that case are reported elsewhere in this volume.

19. Section 170 of the Internal Revenue Code permits taxpayers to deduct charitable gifts and contributions from their federal income taxes.

The federal declaratory judgment statute (28 U.S.C. §2201) states: "In a case of actual controversy within its jurisdiction . . . any court in the United States . . . may declare the rights and other legal relations of any interested party seeking such declaration. . . . Any such declaration shall have the force and effect of a final judgment or decree and shall be reviewable as such."

20. *Miller v. Standard Nut Margarine Co.*, 284 U.S. 498 (1932). After the government assessed a special tax on oleomargarine, the Standard Nut Margarine Company obtained several court decisions that the Oleomargarine Tax Act did not cover its product because its margarine contained no animal fats and did not compete directly with butter. The IRS also assured the company that it would not be taxed under the act. Sometime later, however, the IRS changed its mind and sought to assess a tax of ten cents per pound on the company's products. The company went to court and obtained a permanent injunction enjoining the IRS from collecting the tax. The lower courts accepted the company's arguments that: (1) its products were not oleomargarine and were not covered by the act; (2) the assessment was not a tax but a punitive assessment calculated to protect the butter industry; and (3) the assessment, if collected, would drive the Standard Nut Company out of business.

The Supreme Court ruled that the tax was not a penalty and could not be disputed on that ground. However, the Court then ruled that the company's products were not covered by the Oleomargarine Tax Act. Moreover, while under federal law courts could not as a rule enjoin the assessment or collection of taxes, an injunction was permissible if the plaintiff proved that: (1) the assessment was illegal; and (2) there were "special and extraordinary circumstances" that would bring the case within the court's equitable powers.

In this case, the IRS decision to tax the company was judged to have been clearly erroneous, arbitrary, and capricious. The Court also accepted the trial court's findings that enforcement of the ten cents per pound tax would have destroyed the petitioner's business, ruined it financially, and inflicted a loss for which it would have no remedy at law. Having met the required conditions for equity, the Supreme Court allowed the injunction to remain in effect.

Valley Forge Christian College v. Americans United, 454 U.S. 464 (1982)
(Brennan)

Under the authority granted him by Congress, Secretary of Health, Education, and Welfare Caspar Weinberger transferred seventy-seven acres of federal land to Valley Forge Christian College, a private religious institution. The property had an appraised value of over $500,000, but the secretary applied a 100 percent "public benefit" allowance, which meant that the college got the land and buildings for free. Americans United, an interest group dedicated to maintaining a separation between church and state, sued to block the transfer, claiming that it violated the establishment clause and that the group's members would be deprived of the "fair and constitutional use" of their tax dollars. The district court dismissed the lawsuit on the ground that Americans United did not have standing under Flast v. Cohen.[21] *The court of appeals reversed, saying that while American United lacked standing as taxpayers under* Flast, *they had standing as citizens claiming real injury.*

BURGER: The establishment clause injury found here was the main justification for finding a personal stake and standing by the Third Circuit. The injury, therefore, was not rested on the taxpayer claim. *Richardson* and *Reservists* said only that generalized interests as citizens was not enough to establish standing.[22] In *Flast,* the plaintiff claimed a money loss. This case is an effort to extend *Flast.* But the question presented here does not rely on the fact that the respondents are taxpayers, so how can *Flast* control?

BRENNAN:[23] This case is not distinguishable from *Flast v. Cohen.* The establishment clause imposes as definite a limitation on the power of Congress to dispose of property under the property clause as it does on the spending power, and thus petitioners have standing as taxpayers. It might be remembered exactly what *Flast* does allow taxpayers to challenge—only expenditure programs. It does not allow challenges under the establishment clause to federal statutes and laws generally, or to incidental expenditures involved in the enforcement of federal laws and programs. Non-giveaway programs can be challenged only by persons affected by the laws and enforcement programs. (Of course, this handles the Chief's AWACS case, as well, since all the government did was authorize those sales, not actually sell the planes.)[24] Thus, the *Flast* doctrine operates only within narrow limits.

---

21. *Flast v. Cohen,* 392 U.S. 83 (1968).

22. *United States v. Richardson,* 418 U.S. 166 (1974); *Schlesinger v. Reservists' Committee to Stop the War,* 418 U.S. 208 (1974). In the latter case, members of the armed forces reserves indirectly challenged the legality of the war in Vietnam. The Supreme Court ruled that the plaintiffs did not have standing as taxpayers because they had not demonstrated a nexus between their taxpayer status and their constitutional claims and because they had not suffered any particularized or direct injuries.

23. Adapted from Brennan's talking papers, OT 1981, box 582.

24. In 1980, the Reagan administration authorized an $8.5 billion sale of Boeing AWACS (Airborne Warning and Control Systems) and other planes to Saudi Arabia. Congress retained a veto power over foreign arms sales (Congress had delegated considerable power to the president in the mid-1970s to negotiate arms sales but retained a two-house veto over any deals). The House voted against authorizing the sale in 1981, but the Senate narrowly approved the plan. The key vote was cast by William Cohen (R-ME), who later became secretary of defense under President Clinton. The first AWACS plane was delivered to Saudi Arabia in 1986, and by 1999 Saudi Arabia had five AWACS aircraft in operation.

The solicitor general is exactly wrong when he suggests that decisions involving the establishment clause are committed to the political branches.[25] If the establishment clause was intended to do anything, it was intended to halt the majoritarian impulse to establish the religion of the majority as the religion of the nation. The nature of the limitation itself—it does not affect the government's interaction with individuals (controlled by the free exercise clause), but rather imposes a much more abstract obligation on the government to keep from endorsing any religion—it controls the nature of the interest needed to assert it. I affirm.

WHITE: Maybe you can't distinguish cash from property on a principled basis, but affirmance here would not prevent any taxpayers from relying on some other constitutional provision. I would not extend *Flast*—indeed, I would overrule it. There is no sufficient personal stake on the part of these plaintiffs.

MARSHALL: I can't get over *Flast*.

BLACKMUN: The respondent has a bona fide interest, and has a stake in this. So I would affirm, though it should be limited to establishment clause cases.

POWELL: I agree with the Chief and with Byron. *Flast* is out of step and ought to be overruled. But even if not, we can view this as an extension. There is no distinction here between a generalized interest of taxpayer and a generalized interest of a citizen.

REHNQUIST: I agree with Lewis. *Flast* ought to be confined or even overruled, and I would do that. We can't say that we have citizen standing for one but not for other constitutional provisions.

STEVENS: Taxpayer standing isn't enough. But *Flast* said a plus-establishment clause gave it standing. The source of adversary interest in *Flast* was the "something different" in that. Here, the establishment clause question is raised by an organization with a great reason to litigate. Talking about the establishment clause and nothing else would not open the floodgates.

O'CONNOR: We are at a *Flast* crossroads. Either abandon it, or if we stick to it I would reverse and limit it to the spending and tax clause.

Result: By a 5–4 vote, the Court ruled that Americans United lacked standing either as taxpayers or as citizens claiming real injuries. The group was not really protesting Congress's actions, William Rehnquist wrote, but was challenging the decision of the secretary of Health, Education, and Welfare. This meant that the lawsuit was not brought under the taxing and spending clause but under the property clause. This difference helped the majority to use the Flast *"double nexus test" to deny standing. Rehnquist ruled that a mere claim of a constitutional violation was not sufficient to establish standing, nor was standing granted according to the intensity of one's beliefs. Standing could be established only by showing a real injury to the group or its individual members, and there was no evidence of any such injury in this case. This case limited the scope of* Flast *and further restricted the use of taxpayer or citizen suits.*

---

25. The solicitor general was Rex Lee.

STATUTORY INTERPRETATION

Mortensen v. United States, 322 U.S. 369 (1944)
(Murphy) (Douglas)

Hans and Lorraine Mortensen owned and operated the Nifty Rooms, a bordello in Grand Island, Nebraska. In 1940, the couple took two female employees on a vacation to Yellowstone National Park and to visit Mrs. Mortensen's parents in Salt Lake City.[26] After enjoying an innocent vacation, the group returned to Grand Island and the women went back to their "nifty" rooms. The Mortensens were arrested and charged under the Mann Act. Prosecutors claimed that although the outbound trip was innocent, the group's return to Nebraska constituted transportation of women across state lines for prostitution, debauchery, and other immoral purposes.

STONE: This was a circular tour with whores—Grand Island, Nebraska to Salt Lake City and return. The next day after their return one lady (?) returned to her job, and four days later the other did. The evidence shows no immoral practices while they were away. There were no acts of prostitution en route. The case was submitted to the jury with proper charges on purpose and intent. The main issues were (1) Did their journey start in Nebraska and end there—and thereby violate the statute? Or did the character of the journey take it out of the Mann Act? [MURPHY: He reads §2 of statute and defines the term "interstate commerce."] Transportation as defined does not say where the journey shall start or end. (2) On the question of purpose, it was submitted to the jury. Was the evidence of purpose adequate for the jury? There was evidence to support the verdict. (3) There was transportation, and I see no ground for disturbing the indictment. Has the character of the journey taken it out of the provision that takes it outside statute? There was evidence here. I would affirm. The indictment connects several acts. They could have charged each of the acts in separate counts and gotten convictions in all or some. Government took an added burden by putting them all together. But that did not vitiate the indictment.

ROBERTS: I can't hold that there was a question of purpose. This was not crossing interstate lines for an "immoral purpose" in the meaning of the act. Unless the purpose is there, it is not. I would reverse. I would affirm on the bill of exceptions point.

JACKSON: I think that we ought to dismiss this as improvidently granted. This takes "purpose" out of the act and adds to *Caminetti* dictum.

Result: On a 5–4 vote, the Court reversed the Mortensens' convictions. Frank Murphy wrote that the Mortensens' "innocent vacation trip" did not fall within the letter or the intent of the Mann Act. In dissent, Harlan Fiske Stone argued that while the outbound trip was innocent, the return trip was admittedly for the purpose of going back to work and was punishable.

---

26. At least one of the women offered to pay for her share of the gasoline and oil. The Mortensens refused to take any money, saying that they were going to have to use the same amount of fuel whether the women came along or not.

On his way home to Goose Prairie that summer, Bill Douglas drove well out of his way to visit Grand Island. He wanted to find the Nifty Rooms, steal some stationery, and forge a thank-you note from the Mortensens to Murphy. But the Nifty Rooms were gone, and Douglas settled for sending Murphy a phony letter on Grand Island Chamber of Commerce stationery thanking him for protecting the town's "local industry."[27]

Cleveland v. United States, 329 U.S. 14 (1946)

(Burton)

When Heber Kimball Cleveland and other male members of the polygamous Mormon Fundamentalist sect crossed state lines with their multiple wives, the patriarch was charged with violating the Mann Act (also called the White Slave Traffic Act of 1910), which prohibited the transportation of women across state lines for prostitution, debauchery, or other immoral purposes.

Conference of October 17, 1945

STONE: This is a Mann Act case. It boils down to the phrase, "for an immoral purpose." Is this case within the purpose of the act? Here, there is no element of prostitution, and the game is how close must the "immorality" come to it. The history at time of the act— the focus of the Senate Committee and the work preceding it—is that it must be akin to prostitution.

But, in additional legislative history, "for immoral purposes" had appeared in alien importation statutes. In the *Bitty* case, a concubine was urged by the defendant not to be the same thing as prostitution (instead, it was said to be simple fornication).[28] We held the act to include other types of sexual immorality besides prostitution. And then this language was added to the Mann Act, and the congressional committee reported that they chose the words to extend the act to the facts of the case in *Bitty*.

The *Caminetti* case: This involved a special sexual spree, and we were urged again to hold it down.[29] The Court disagreed, and held that the Mann Act applied. [BURTON: Stone says that there were no dissents, but there were three.] We so held clearly, and Congress has not amended the act in twenty-five years. And so this was an immoral act—where a married man crossed state lines and took a juvenile girl with him. And this *Court has* applied this standard in similar circumstances. We should affirm here.

---

27. Douglas, *The Court Years*, 25.

28. *United States v. Bitty*, 208 U.S. 393 (1908). John Bitty was convicted under the Immigration Act of 1907 of importing an English woman to live with him as a paramour. The Immigration Act prohibited importing "any alien woman or girl for the purpose of prostitution or for any other immoral purpose." The trial judge held that the words "other immoral purpose" applied only to activities associated with prostitution and that concubines and mistresses were not covered by the act. The Supreme Court reversed, with the first John Marshall Harlan ruling that Congress intended a broad exclusion of women of "loose moral character."

29. *Caminetti v. United States*, 242 U.S. 470 (1917). F. Drew Caminetti, the son of Woodrow Wilson's commissioner of immigration, and Maury I. Diggs, the former state architect of California, were prosecuted under the Mann Act for transporting two high school girls from California to Reno, Nevada. The Supreme Court sustained Caminetti's conviction. Professor Powell of Harvard argued unsuccessfully that the Mann Act applied only to commercialized vice and did not cover "nonpecuniary interstate fornication."

The *Kidnapping Act*: The question of "holding" after the taking—no one has empha-sized that—[BURTON: But the Chief Justice did, in open court.] It was not raised on the record or at oral argument. With an adult, one could not say "held," but one possibly could say that they "held" a child, although there were no physical restraints used. We should remand.

BLACK: I would reverse *on both*. I think that this kind of transportation was not intended to be covered under the Mann Act. I think that the decision below extended the *Caminetti* case, and I disagree with the *Caminetti* case. I think that they both ignored the legislative history, and that the act should *not* be extended at all—such as is done here. I regard it as beyond the facts of the *Caminetti* case. I do not think that it was within the Mann Act in the *Caminetti* case, and that this case a fortiori was not meant to be covered by the act.

The case was not tried on a proper theory, and the Mann Act does not cover this kind of case. It does not cover an illegal marriage and "holding."

REED: I would affirm on the Mann Act. This was within the principles of the *Caminetti* case. I favor affirmance of the Mann Act conviction. There was no guilt of kidnapping, however. It should be sent back for trial of the case.

FRANKFURTER: I reverse on the kidnapping question. I have reviewed the *Bitty* case. I believe that Congress codified the *Bitty* case in passing the Mann Act. I would not re-verse the *Caminetti* case and *would not extend it*. Do these facts extend it? I think that this case is within the terms of the act (crossing state lines with an additional wife). There are questions about the types of *motive*. It has their positive sanction of religious belief.

STONE: Is "immoral purpose" an objective or subjective standard?

FRANKFURTER: It is not a relative differentiation.

REED: How about the *Reynolds* case?[30]

FRANKFURTER: It renders the practice of polygamy as criminal.

REED: *Caminetti* says that "carnal knowledge" across state lines is illegal. Can you do it with religious authorization?

FRANKFURTER: It is a real question whether you are extending adultery in your argu-ment. Their religious motives are sincere; their religious tenets do not, however, protect a man.

DOUGLAS: I reverse on kidnapping. I would probably join in overruling *Caminetti*.

---

30. *Reynolds v. United States*, 98 U.S. 145 (1879) upheld federal criminal punishment of polygamy against a free exercise challenge by George Reynolds, the Mormon defendant. Under the law, polygamy could be punished by a fine of $500 and a maximum of five years in prison at hard labor. Morrison Waite wrote the opinion for a unanimous Court.

MURPHY: I do not believe that Congress did not mean what *Caminetti* says. I would vote to overrule the *Caminetti* case, and I certainly would not extend it. In all of our actions we legislate to a degree as we go into the legislative history. I would reverse both cases.

RUTLEDGE: I will not extend kidnapping as a Mann Act case. I believe that the *Caminetti* case was wrongly decided, and I favor limiting the scope of this act.

BURTON: I affirm.

Conference of October 19, 1946
(*Vinson had replaced Stone as Chief Justice*)

VINSON: Affirm.

BLACK: Reverse.

REED: Affirm (*Caminetti*).

FRANKFURTER: Affirm.

DOUGLAS: I affirm. Last term, I thought that we should overrule *Caminetti*. Here, however, we don't have to rely on *Caminetti*—a crude practice of holding polygamous households to be illegal on something more permanent than *Caminetti*. It is fair to say it was included in "other immoral purposes," whatever you say on *Caminetti*.

MURPHY: Reverse.

JACKSON: Reverse. This involves an extension of *Caminetti* to a new field, and we do not need to.

RUTLEDGE: Reverse.

BURTON: Affirm.

Result: This case was a classic example of the fluidity of judicial choice. At the October 1945 conference, the Court was evenly divided and a final decision was postponed until the following term. In 1946, Vinson succeeded Stone as Chief Justice, but voted as Stone had done to affirm Cleveland's conviction. The 4–4 deadlock was finally broken when Robert Jackson returned from Nuremburg, temporarily giving a 5–4 majority to reverse. But when Jackson refused to join the rest of the majority to overrule Caminetti, *both Douglas and Rutledge changed their votes, transforming a 5–4 decision to reverse to a 6–3 majority to affirm. As often happens in close cases, the most reluctant member of the majority—in this instance, Douglas—was assigned to write the majority opinion.[31] The other reluctant member of the majority, Wiley Rutledge, pointedly stated in his concurring opinion that* Caminetti *should be overruled, but that until it was he felt compelled to follow it.*

---

31. This is known as the "least persuaded" theory, and reflects the hope that the most reluctant member of the majority will be more likely to stay persuaded if they write the opinion.

BUSINESS, SPORTS, AND THE COURT

Toolson v. New York Yankees, 346 U.S. 356 (1953)
Kowalski v. Chandler
Corbett v. Chandler[32]
(Douglas) (Burton)

George Earl Toolson was a minor league pitcher for the Red Sox's AAA team in Newark, New Jersey. He was traded to the Yankees in 1948 and immediately demoted to their A team in Binghamton. Toolson refused to report, and the Yankees suspended him. Toolson sought to play elsewhere, but because of baseball's reserve clause no other team would sign him as long as he remained under contract with the Yankees.[33] *He sued under the Sherman Act, asking for $375,000 in damages.*

There was no shortage of baseball fans on the Supreme Court. Sherman Minton had played college and semipro ball, and Earl Warren was passionate about the sport. The two Justices regularly attended Washington Senators games. (As everyone knows, the Senators were "first in war, first in peace, and last in the American League.")

Conference of October 17, 1953

BLACK: I do not agree with the former decision, and would have voted against *Federal Baseball* at that time.[34] It was not qualified by reason or facts. We could distinguish those facts from the present ones on the ground that times have changed, but that is not realistic. Congress has confirmed that organized baseball is not covered under the Sherman Act. There is no constitutional question—this is merely statutory construction. The lower court could have done better with the facts, and that could be a reason to remand. I am inclined to favor a per curiam affirming our old decision. I can vote either way; I am willing to affirm and cite the old case.

REED: If this case is affirmed, it should be per curiam, based on the old case. But the old case was more than statutory construction, and was decided on the Constitution. I don't believe the *Federal Baseball* case determined it came under the antitrust act. Holmes made

---

32. Jack Corbett owned the El Paso team in the Texas League. He sued when the major leagues prevented him from signing players who were suspended for playing in the Mexican League. Walter Kowalski was a Dodger farmhand who was also challenging the reserve clause. Both men were represented by Frederic Johnson. Albert B. Chandler was the commissioner of baseball.

33. Established in 1879, the reserve clause effectively tied players to their teams for their entire careers. In modern times, the reserve clause has been weakened by free agency but remains in effect.

34. *Federal Baseball Club of Baltimore, Inc., v. National League,* 259 U.S. 200 (1922). The Federal Baseball League was formed in 1913 to challenge the National and American Leagues. The new league lured star players with the promise of bigger salaries, long-term contracts, and no reserve clause. There was exciting competition, but mostly in court. The Federal League folded in 1915, with the National and American Leagues agreeing to pay $50,000 to each Federal League club owner, assuming some of the owners' debts, and allowing two Federal League owners to buy new franchises. The owner of the Baltimore Terrapins refused the offered settlement and sued, asking for treble damages under the Sherman Act. He won in district court, but the court of appeals reversed. The Supreme Court, in an opinion by Oliver Wendell Holmes, rejected the Terrapins' suit on the ground that baseball was a sport, not interstate commerce, and was exempt from antitrust laws and other statutes governing interstate commerce.

a constitutional decision. He said that it is a game, not a trade or interstate commerce. Therefore, we have to look at all of the changes. Holmes spoke of production. The reserve clause violates the anti-trust laws. The sport of baseball is a trade under the act. I would vote to send it back for hearings. I reverse.

FRANKFURTER: Stanley gilts the lines greatly. I did not suppose that anyone so interpreted Holmes. Holmes interpreted the statute—it was not decided on the constitutional question. He meant that baseball was not a trade or commerce under that statute.[35] The old case turned on the statute, not the Constitution. I affirm on that decision. I agree with Hugo. The Department of Justice has not disputed that the reserve clause is reasonable. We should allow it to be at rest. I would affirm per curiam and cite *Federal Baseball.*

DOUGLAS: I affirm per curiam on the old decision.

JACKSON: I am willing to affirm per curiam on the old case. But I would spell out the reasons for sticking by the old case. We should say that this invites us to reexamine the case and that we decline to reexamine the merits. This is a flagrant and continual violation. I would affirm and cite the old case.

BURTON: I am unable to say that baseball is not trade. This is an unfair practice. I vote to reverse.

CLARK: I affirm on the old case. The "farms" were not in the old case. But I am willing to stand by the old one.

MINTON: I affirm on *Federal Baseball.*[36]

WARREN: Do we have to forever give sanctity to the name of baseball that it cannot be in violation of federal anti-trust laws? We can't say that baseball is immune to federal anti-trust laws no matter what they do. There are very substantial differences in the game now. Baseball is hooked up with Mexico, with radio, with television, with the farm system—all of these things change the entire character of the game. We need not reverse the old case to hold that the present method of handling the game is different. If the decision is to affirm on *Federal Baseball* and if we go per curiam—in short form—I will go along. But I will not agree on the merits.

---

35. Frankfurter's argument was spirited but probably wrong. Holmes clearly based his decision in *Federal Baseball* on his reading of the commerce clause. In his brief opinion, Holmes argued that baseball was a sport involving "personal effort, not related to production, [and] is not a subject of commerce." Any interstate aspects, such as the transportation of men and equipment across state lines, he said, was "a mere incident, not an essential thing." Holmes compared baseball to a law firm sending a lawyer to another state to argue a case, or a lecture bureau sending an expert to give a lecture out of state. Such matters, he concluded, were not interstate commerce but were "purely state affairs." *Federal Baseball Club of Baltimore, Inc. v. National League,* 259 U.S. 200 (1922).

36. Minton, the former ballplayer, thought that all sports should be exempt from the Sherman Act. He never understood how an athlete who traveled from one state to another carrying only his own equipment in a "ditty bag" had anything to do with interstate commerce. Gugin and St. Clair, *Sherman Minton,* 259; compare with *United States v. International Boxing Club,* 348 U.S. 236 (1955) (Minton dissenting).

Result: The Court refused to reexamine the underlying issues and in a one-paragraph per curiam opinion reaffirmed that antitrust laws did not apply to baseball, citing Federal Baseball. *The seven-member majority refused, however, to reaffirm that baseball did not affect interstate commerce and quietly recast Holmes's decision as a matter of statutory rather than constitutional interpretation, holding that "the business of providing public baseball games . . . was not within the scope of the federal antitrust laws." The Court implicitly criticized the exemption but left it to Congress to decide what—if anything—to do about it: "We think that if there are evils in this field which now warrant application to it of the antitrust law it should be done by legislation."*

In dissent, Burton and Reed discussed the interstate economic impact of professional baseball and noted that Congress had never explicitly exempted baseball from the nation's antitrust statutes. The problem, Burton argued, was initially caused by Holmes's opinion in Federal Baseball, *and Burton concluded that the Court should assume responsibility for setting the matter right.*

While the lawsuit was pending, the Yankees released Ernie Toolson. He played for one more season in the Pacific Coast League before retiring in 1950. He never got a chance to play in the major leagues.

Flood v. Kuhn, 407 U.S. 258 (1972)
(Douglas) (Brennan)

When the St. Louis Cardinals traded Curt Flood to the Philadelphia Phillies without his consent, Flood filed an antitrust suit against Bowie Kuhn, the commissioner of Major League Baseball, challenging baseball's reserve clause. The reserve clause tied baseball players to a single major league team by preventing players from becoming free agents or seeking independent contracts with other major league teams. The district court upheld baseball's longstanding antitrust exemption and the court of appeals affirmed.

Conference of March 20, 1972

BURGER: *Toolson* is probably wrong.[37]

DOUGLAS: I vote to reverse and remand for a trial. Baseball, football, and basketball should be treated alike. *Toolson* is out of our "stream of commerce" decisions. So it is under antitrust laws.

BRENNAN: I dissented in *Radovich*, but would overrule *Toolson*.[38] The issue of labor exemption was not treated in *Toolson*, and I would pass that by and remand for a trial. That means that there is no room for state anti-trust laws here. The reserve clause may have certain advantages, but I would not reach that issue.

STEWART: I affirm. This is tantamount to an explicit congressional exemption of baseball from antitrust laws. We have now the equivalent of an explicit congressional excep-

37. *Toolson v. New York Yankees, Inc.,* 346 U.S. 356 (1953); *Federal Baseball Club of Baltimore v. National League,* 259 U.S. 200 (1922).

38. *Radovich v. National Football League,* 352 U.S. 445 (1957), holding that federal antitrust laws applied to professional football.

tion—an implied exemption from state laws on antitrust. Congress knew about this and did nothing. The omission is not inadvertent. There is an implied preemption of state laws. I would leave it to Congress to decide.

WHITE: I agree with Potter and affirm.

MARSHALL: I agree with Potter and affirm.[39]

BLACKMUN: Baseball was a sport, not a business. Today it is a business. This seems more like a labor dispute than an antitrust problem. It is intolerable to apply state laws—there should be a federal preemption. I tentatively affirm.

POWELL: I will take no part in this decision. I own stock in Anheuser-Busch, which owns the St. Louis Cardinals.[40] I will state my views tentatively. I would reverse. It makes no sense any longer to have an exception applicable to baseball that is not applicable to football, etc. Congressional inaction only means that they won't act unless we force them to by reversing. Congress is apt to be mute as long as we have solved the problem for them.

REHNQUIST: I agree with Potter. *Toolson* crossed the bridge. Congress has had the chance to act and has not. I think that state antitrust laws might apply, and would remand for further proceedings on that. I affirm on *Toolson*, although I might remand on the state law point.

BURGER: I reverse.

Result: After the conference, Marshall and Burger changed their minds in opposite directions, while Powell—in spite of pressure from other Justices and his clerks to stay in the case—decided to recuse himself.[41] The Court again refused to overturn baseball's historic exemption from federal antitrust laws and reaffirmed that any change would have to go through Congress. Blackmun, the most tentative vote to affirm in conference, wrote the majority opinion.

NCAA v. Board of Regents, University of Oklahoma, 468 U.S. 85 (1984)
(Brennan)

In 1981, the NCAA promulgated a new policy for televising college football games. The organization limited the number of televised college games and restricted the number of times each school could appear on television. Several major football schools subsequently made their own separate deal with NBC. When the NCAA threatened to sanction any university that honored the NBC contract, the University of Oklahoma and the University of Georgia brought suit in federal court. The district court ruled that the NCAA had violated §1 of the Sherman Antitrust Act (which prohibited price-fixing) by

---

39. Marshall was fond of telling a story about a young boy who once approached him and asked for an autograph. When Marshall agreed, the youngster handed the Justice eight cards. Marshall asked him why he had to sign eight cards, and the kid responded, "For eight of yours I can trade for one Willie Mays."

40. August Busch Jr., the principal owner of Anheuser-Busch, Inc., also owned the Cardinals.

41. Although the published opinion stated that Powell did not participate in the consideration or decision in this case, he obviously participated in the conference discussion.

reducing output and raising prices in an anticompetitive manner. The court of appeals affirmed, cit-
ing two different theories: (1) that the situation amounted to per se price fixing; and (2) that under
the totality of the circumstances, the anticompetitive nature of the deal was not sufficiently offset by
any procompetitive justifications. In conference, the Justices referred to the first theory as per se price
fixing and the second theory as the "rule of reason."

BURGER: Is this a price fixing case? Certainly this has enormous protection of market power. The NCAA could not show different. . . .

BRENNAN:[42] I would treat this case as any other price-fixing case, and hold the NCAA's Television Plan illegal per se. Although, as the solicitor general points out, there is some amount of cooperation among universities that is beneficial—and indeed, necessary—I do not believe that cooperation in setting prices falls within the range of beneficial cooperation.

I would be willing, however, to affirm on the rule of reason, as well. In doing so, I would rely on the two-court rule in finding that the NCAA has market power. My only concern here is that we avoid explicitly announcing the mid-tier rule of reason that the solicitor general proposes. That approach is inherent in the rule of reason as it currently stands, and we could only confuse matters by attempting to formalize it. I affirm.

WHITE: It is easy to say that this is a per se price fix, but I am going to try to reverse. We should avoid challenges to the NCAA's other regulations—eligibility rules and so forth, which are designed to assure fair competition and avoid dominance of schools like Oklahoma.

MARSHALL: There is no question but that the NCAA has done a great job in spreading around the goodies. But this is a price fix.

BLACKMUN: I feel caught in a current to affirm, but like Byron I am going to try to reverse. I hate to see the Oklahomas, Notre Dames, etc., have a monopoly—they are professional teams.

POWELL: I can't see how we can reverse. I will affirm, but not on per se price fixing—only on the rule of reason.

REHNQUIST: I think that it is ludicrous to analyze this as if non-profit corporations were in the business of maximizing profits. The NCAA has other legitimate motives. This is simply not an antitrust case for me.

STEVENS: I agree with Bill Brennan. It is much like *Broadcast Music*, where an individual song writer could sue his own show.[43] But individual schools here can't have even regional broadcasts of their games. Colleges may be non-profit, but not in the football business. I would not impose the per se rule here—I am not sure that it is proper. Under the district court's findings, there is a violation of the rule of reason.

---

42. Adapted from Brennan's talking papers, OT 1983.

43. *Broadcast Music, Inc. v. Columbia Broadcasting System, Inc.*, 441 U.S. 1 (1979). CBS sued the two major music publishers, the American Society of Composers, Authors and Publishers (ASCAP) and Broad-

O'Connor: We probably have to affirm. Was there market power? Two courts found so, and I can't find that their conclusions were clearly erroneous. I would not go on the per se rule, however.

Result: Using the rule of reason, the Court found that the NCAA plan violated the Sherman Act. While horizontal price-fixing would ordinarily be illegal per se, the majority ruled that some horizontal restraints on competition were inherent to organized college athletics, making the per se rule inappropriate. In this case, however, the NCAA failed to prove sufficient procompetitive aspects of their plan to override its fundamentally anticompetitive nature. Byron White, the former college football hero, dissented along with William Rehnquist, whose college athletic achievements are less well documented.

---

cast Music, Inc. (BMI), alleging that sales of blanket licenses to use copyrighted music was illegal price fixing. Blanket licenses gave licensees the right to use any compositions owned by the members of these organizations. Fees were negotiated according to a percentage of total revenues or on a flat rate, rather than being based on what music was actually used. The Supreme Court rejected CBS's claim, finding that the sale of blanket music licenses was not per se price fixing but remanded the case to determine whether the sale of blanket licenses violated the rule of reason. Byron White wrote the majority for an 8–1 Court. In dissent, Stevens agreed that the use of blanket licenses was not per se price fixing but argued that the Court should also have ruled that the sale of blanket licenses did not violate the rule of reason, rather than remanding the issue to the court of appeals for further proceedings.

CHAPTER 5

CONGRESS AND THE COURTS

CONGRESSIONAL POWER

Tennessee Valley Authority v. Hill, 437 U.S. 153 (1978)
(Brennan)

The Endangered Species Act of 1973 (ESA) allowed the secretary of interior to list any threatened species as endangered. Section 7 of the ESA required the federal government to take all necessary action to avoid jeopardizing the existence of listed species, including avoiding the destruction or modification of essential habitat.

The snail darter was a listed species of fish that lived exclusively along a stretch of the Little Tennessee River scheduled to be submerged behind the federally funded Tellico Dam. Hiram Hill began a class action suit to stop construction of the dam, claiming that it would destroy the small perch's only known habitat. By the time the case worked its way through the courts, however, the dam was nearly completed.

The main problem was conflicting evidence of congressional intent. While the ESA indicated that Congress wanted to protect endangered species like the snail darter regardless of cost, Congress continued to appropriate millions of dollars each year to build the dam. The district court dismissed Hill's complaint on the grounds that the annual appropriations to fund the dam showed Congress's overriding intent and that it would be unreasonable to stop construction so near completion. The court of appeals reversed and issued a permanent injunction against any further work on the dam until (1) Congress exempted the project from compliance with the ESA; (2) the snail darter was taken off the endangered species list; or (3) the fish's critical habitat was redefined to exclude the area behind the Tellico Dam.

This case is an interesting example of the Justices debating and ultimately deferring to a congressional judgment that many of them thought foolish.

BURGER: The Department of Interior did not list the fish until nine years after the dam project was begun. Yet we have to assume that the fish will become extinct if the project goes ahead. My approach is to treat this case as one for an equitable injunction against the federal government. That requires a weighing of equities. I would hold that the department's classification of a fish nine years after the project began can't stop the United States from completing it. Maybe I could go with a unanimous Court to affirm.

STEWART: Section 7 unambiguously imposes an absolute obligation. That duty followed several predecessor statutes that allowed balancing or weighing.

MARSHALL: Congress has a right to be a jackass.

BLACKMUN: This is the fable of the snail darter and the Tellico Dam. Common sense is with the attorney general here. After all, NEPA cases are some guide.[1] As to completed or almost completed projects, no hold is required. I give more weight to appropriations bills than Brennan does, so I will reverse.

POWELL: If Congress's interest were clear here, I would give it full effect—but I find it murky. Of course appropriations acts don't of themselves repeal substantive acts. But Congress's appropriations committees didn't address this very conflict, and I would reverse.

REHNQUIST: I wouldn't rule out going along with Lewis. But it seems to me that the best choice is to give weight to appropriations committee reports or vote, and since it is a suit for an injunction, I would apply ordinary criteria and turn this on the Appropriations Act. I would do that even though I agree that it can be assumed that there is a violation of §7 of the ESA.

STEVENS: None of the three theories favoring reversal is persuasive. The Appropriations Act law ought not be changed—it is too important in other areas. The real question here is who makes the policy decisions here. Certainly, the Department of Interior can and maybe should delist this fish. If it doesn't, then Congress's judgment, however stupid, must prevail—we can't arrogate that function to judiciary.

Result: After passing in conference, Warren Burger took the case himself to write a 6–3 decision that Congress's overriding intent in enacting the ESA was to protect endangered species irrespective of cost. While the annual appropriations for the Tellico Dam were not irrelevant, Burger noted, they only reflected the judgments of appropriations committees, while general legislation like the ESA represented the considered intent of Congress as a whole.

INS v. Chadha, 462 U.S. 919 (1983)
(Brennan)

The Immigration and Nationality Act granted the attorney general and the INS discretion to allow otherwise deportable aliens to remain in the United States. Their decisions, however, were subject to veto by either house of Congress. Jagdish Rai Chadha, an ethnic East Indian from Kenya who held a British Commonwealth passport, was admitted to the United States on a student visa to attend Bowling Green University in Ohio. He remained in the country illegally after his visa expired. At a deportation hearing, an immigration judge used his discretion to suspend deportation proceedings against Chadha.[2]

---

1. NEPA is the National Environmental Policy Act of 1969. Some of the key cases interpreting this act are *Environmental Defense Fund v. TVA,* 339 F. Supp. 806 (E.D. Tenn.), aff'd, 468 F. 2d 1164 (CA6 1972); *Environmental Defense Fund v. TVA,* 371 F. Supp. 1004 (E.D. Tenn.), aff'd, 492 F. 2d 466 (CA6 1974).

2. Although Chadha was born and raised in Kenya, he had declined an offer of Kenyan citizenship, and Kenya would not take him back. It was also difficult for Asian and African holders of Commonwealth passports to gain resident status in Great Britain. These were the main factors that influenced the immigration judge to grant a "compassionate suspension" of deportation proceedings under §244 of the Immigration and Nationality Act. It was also true, however, that Chadha wanted to stay in the United States and that he had not worked very hard to find anyplace else to live.

As required, the attorney general sent a report on the case to Congress. A year and a half later, the House of Representatives passed a one-house resolution vetoing the judge's decision and ordering deportation efforts against Chadha to resume. The immigration judge reopened the deportation hearing and ordered Chadha expelled from the country.

Chadha pursued administrative and judicial relief, claiming that the one-house veto was unconstitutional because it violated principles of separation of powers. He argued that all acts of Congress had to be passed by both houses and presented to the president for signature or veto. The Ninth Circuit Court of Appeals agreed and invalidated the one-house veto in an opinion by Anthony Kennedy. Although the INS agreed with Chadha that the one-house veto was unconstitutional, the courts ruled that the agency had sufficient interest in the case to be named as an "adversarial" party.

The Supreme Court wrestled with two major issues at conference. The first was whether the one-house veto was constitutional. Assuming that the legislative veto was unconstitutional, the second issue was whether the Justices should try to salvage the rest of the act or strike down the entire statute.

First Conference

BURGER: There are no serious jurisdiction problems here. Nor need we reach the question of severability unless we hold the one-house veto to be unconstitutional. Congress and the president have found it to be a useful tool for over fifty years. There is no lack of justiciable controversy just because the INS and Chadha take the same view.[3] This is no political question case, either. Can Congress exercise its legislative function using this tool, or does it take whole scheme—both houses and presentment to the president? Provisions for one Senate action suggests that is all.

BRENNAN:[4] The possibility that Chadha *might* be entitled to stay here because he is married, or the possibility that he *might* have a Refugee Act remedy cannot substitute for the fact that if we affirm, Chadha will immediately gain citizenship. It would not be "prudent" to allow him to suffer continuing disabilities because he *might* have some alternative route to residence.

On the merits, I am fully in accord with the views expressed by the solicitor general.[5] If this be the passage of a law, then there must be presentment and bicameral approval; if this be something else, then it is beyond the power of Congress. For example, if Congress was merely delegating to itself the powers of an administrative agency to apply the law, where is the judicial review? Indeed, if the matter would be subject to revision by Congress, how could we review the determinations of the attorney general when he acts under §244? In any event, I believe that whatever Congress might assign to an executive branch official, it cannot assign the functions of the executive branch to *itself*. Because the bicameral and presentment clauses were designed to hold in check and "overweening" legislative branch, this attempt to extend Congress's power is justiciable, and unconsti-

---

3. Both the Senate and the House intervened in the case to argue that the one-house veto was constitutional. In addition, the INS had concluded that it had no authority to question the constitutionality of the House's order to resume deportation proceedings against Chadha and had begun to implement that order in good faith until proceedings were stopped by the court of appeals decision.

4. Adapted from Brennan's talking papers, Brennan Papers, OT 1982, box 611.

5. The solicitor general was Rex Lee.

tutional. It may be possible to declare it so in a narrow opinion; the issue might be a bit closer with respect to congressional review of agency rulemaking, since that would appear to be a quasi-legislative delegation of power.

With respect to severability, I again agree with the solicitor general. It is impossible to discern legislative intent in any objective sense, and we must therefore rely on presumptions. The presumption to be applied here is that we save as much as we can, unless given a persuasive reason to the contrary. I frankly think that it would be too disruptive to the workings of the federal government if we declared this act unconstitutional without strongly indicating that severance is the preferred route. To hold otherwise might cripple the ability of the president, and thus the government, pursuant to any number of other acts containing similar veto provisions. If Congress really believes that these delegations to the executive should not be allowed to stand without a veto provision, Congress can act to revoke the delegations. I affirm.

WHITE: I am not wholly at rest, but am inclined to reverse. I am not sure that presentment to Congress or that its action in this context is legislative. There was no invasion of any constitutionally assigned powers of the president. I don't see much to the separation of powers argument—the same three parties have to agree, just as in the case of private bills.

MARSHALL: Congress gave itself the power to adjudicate, and that they cannot do.

BLACKMUN: The preliminary questions are without merit. On the merits, the exceptions listed in the Constitution are exclusive. I do not prefer a separation of powers decision. I would rather rely on procedural provisions for the enactment of legislation. There is an invasion here of judicial as well as executive prerogatives.

POWELL: We can reach the issue, and I am inclined to agree with Thurgood that Congress delegated a judicial-type function to the attorney general—and then without a hearing of any kind, reversed his decision. I would write an opinion not going all the way with the solicitor general, but leaving open the CADC case.[6] Congress can't delegate to the executive branch a quasi-judicial function and then take it back, as it did here.

REHNQUIST: There are some two hundred statutes where this was worked out as a compromise. I don't favor tumbling down the whole structure in some abstract way. I would say that §241 is not severable. I see no interference with judicial prerogatives. I want very

---

6. The Court of Appeals for the District of Columbia. Powell was presumably referring to two pending District of Columbia cases dealing with legislative vetoes. The first of these cases was *Consumer Energy Council of America v. Federal Regulatory Commission*, 673 F.2d 425 (D.C. Cir. 1982). The court of appeals struck down a one-house legislative veto provision in the Natural Gas Policy Act of 1978, which Congress had used to overturn new natural gas pricing regulations. In the second case, *Consumers Union of the United States v. Federal Trade Commission*, 691 F.2d 575 (D.C. Cir. 1982), the court of appeals struck down a two-house legislative veto written into the Federal Trade Commission Improvements Act of 1980. Congress had exercised its veto power to kill the FTC's "used car rules," which required increased warranty coverage and required additional disclosure of information by auto dealers in the sale of used cars.

Both cases were subsequently affirmed summarily in *Process Gas Consumers Group v. Consumer Energy Council*, 463 U.S. 1216 (1983). The Court announced its decision on July 6, 1983, two weeks after *Chadha* was decided. Byron White wrote a dissenting opinion.

much to find a way to avoid deciding this case on the merits. On the merits, the solicitor general seems to offer the clearest route, but for now I pass.

STEVENS: We should reach the severability issue first. If we hold that it isn't severable, we would therefore hold that there is no case or controversy. Congress had many reasons for getting out of private bills, and that helps to make this severable. If the veto is an exercise of executive power, *Myers* makes it unconstitutional.[7] It really is a legislative power that has been delegated partly to the executive and partly back to itself. The latter is on a standardless basis, and the only proper standard is full legislative powers.

O'CONNOR: The preliminary hurdles are not difficult. It is severable, and I will likely affirm. But we should do it very narrowly.

Second Conference

BURGER: Chadha suffered a serious injury by being selected out. Whether it is an executive or a judicial function in the INS, it doesn't matter. Perhaps a bit of both, and Congress cannot recall or set aside a particular decision just because they don't like it. If the veto is an exercise of legislative power, it is an action that alters the rights of an individual—they can't do that without presentment powers. There is no severability clause—the whole statute falls as I see it.

BRENNAN:[8] I vote to affirm the decision of the Ninth Circuit. I find no merit in any of the threshold arguments presented by the House and Senate, including the challenge to our appellate jurisdiction under §1252.

On the merits, I agree with the Ninth Circuit that the legislative veto provision is unconstitutional. Assuming that the veto amounts to a legislative action, it is unconstitutional because it fails to comply with the bicameralism and presentment requirements of the Constitution. The mere fact that the Constitution gives Congress plenary power over immigration and naturalization does not justify an unconstitutional exercise of that power.

Assuming that the veto is something other than a legislative action, it violates the separation of powers doctrine by intruding on the functions of the executive and judicial branches. Congress enacted a statute giving the executive the power to make certain determinations regarding the status of aliens; in effect, to enforce and to execute the law. It violates the separation of powers doctrine for Congress to attempt to share that func-

7. *Myers v. United States*, 272 U.S. 52 (1926). With the advice and consent of the Senate, President Wilson appointed Frank Myers postmaster first class, an office that under federal law had a term of four years. Wilson then sought to remove Myers before the end of his first term without the consent of the Senate. The Court, in an opinion by former President William Howard Taft, ruled that the office of postmaster was inherently executive in nature, and as the president had ultimate constitutional authority and responsibility to execute the laws he must have virtually unlimited powers to remove subordinate executive officers. Separation of powers meant that the Senate could not reserve for itself the power to give its advice and consent regarding the *removal* of executive officers. The removal power was "incident to the power of appointment, not to the power of advising and consenting to appointment."

8. Adapted from Brennan's talking papers, Brennan Papers, OT 1982, box 611.

tion through the use of a legislative veto. In essence, Congress is assigning to itself the powers of the executive branch. This is precisely the sort of concentrated power with which the Framers were concerned. There also is force to the argument that the one-house veto impermissibly intrudes on the functions of the judiciary. Through the veto provision, Congress has undertaken to interpret the law it has passed and to decide particular controversies. These are the traditional functions of the judiciary.

Finally, I think the veto provision is severable. There is a severability clause in the statute. It also is clear that Congress enacted the statute to relieve itself of the burden of enacting private bills in the immigration area. Even assuming that the provision is not severable, I do not think that this affects Chadha's standing. There is ample precedent for reaching the merits of a case even if the party before the Court may not be entitled to relief because of the non-severability of the statutory provision at issue.

WHITE: Congress would never have passed (a) if (c) was unconstitutional.[9] So I don't think that the statute is severable. And if (c) is unconstitutional, so is (a) and Chadha loses. That is a way of avoiding the constitutional issue. But if we reach it, I would say that the legislative veto is constitutional. This is only reverse legislation; there is no unilateral invasion of the rights of the president.

MARSHALL: I agree with Bill Brennan and the Chief Justice.

BLACKMUN: It is severable, and for reasons of last term I would affirm.

POWELL: The bottom line here is that I might agree with Byron if he can persuade me. I would hate to see us invalidate this useful practice. But presentment and separation of powers arguments all point toward affirmance. I had assumed that it was not severable.

REHNQUIST: This particular proviso is not severable, and if this is a constitutional adjudication, it won't help Chadha if we don't reach the constitutional question. Besides, the executive has unclean hands here, since it urged this statute on Congress. I would presume that this was not meant to be severable. Congress would not have given the executive branch this authority unless it could veto their decisions.

STEVENS: First, I think that it is clearly severable. Second, this is an abominable device. On the merits, it is just unconstitutional.

O'CONNOR: It was not a proper INS appeal, and we should take the House and Senate applications.[10] I would affirm on separation of powers. I would not decide the case on the presentment argument. The best argument is the contingent legislation theory. Because this is an adjudicative-type function, it violates separation of powers. The severability issue is hard for me, but I tend to think that it is severable.

---

9. Section 244(a) of the act allowed the INS to suspend deportation proceedings and allowed the attorney general to permit a particular deportable alien to remain in the United States. Section 244(c) of the act allowed either House of Congress to override any decision by the attorney general to allow a deportable alien to remain in the United States.

10. Along with *INS v. Chadha*, the other two cases before the Court were No. 80-2170, *United States Senate v. INS*; and No. 80-2171, *United States House of Representatives v. INS*.

Result: The Court struck down the one-house legislative veto but ruled that the act was severable and saved the rest of the statute. Warren Burger, writing for the majority, focused on separation of powers issues. The one-house legislative veto violated the Constitution because it allowed Congress to avoid two constitutionally required steps for legislation: (1) having both houses approve all legislation; and (2) presenting legislation to the president for executive approval or veto. Lewis Powell (who concurred in the judgment) and William Rehnquist (who dissented) both wanted to resolve the case on grounds other than the legislative veto. Only Byron White dissented on the veto question.

White wrote a powerful dissent, emphasizing the longstanding tradition and utility of the one-house legislative veto.[11] Without the legislative veto, he wrote, Congress faced a Hobson's choice of trying to perform all legislative tasks itself without delegating any responsibilities to other agencies or abdicating its legislative responsibilities entirely to the executive and judicial branches. White also worried about the scope of Burger's opinion, which effectively invalidated at least part of more than two hundred acts of Congress—invalidating more federal laws than all previous Supreme Court decisions combined. The result, he argued, was unnecessarily harsh and destructive of congressional power.

Despite the majority's expectations and White's dire prediction, the legislative veto has not disappeared; it remains alive and well in various forms. Congress has proven to be persistent, clever, and quietly subversive in its attempts to get around Chadha.[12]

Chadha *became an American citizen, married, and settled with his wife and children in a small town near San Francisco.*

Bowsher v. Synar, 478 U.S. 714 (1986)
(Brennan)

In an attempt to control a ballooning federal budget deficit, the Gramm-Rudman-Hollings Act of 1985 required the directors of the Office of Management and Budget (OMB) and the Congressional Budget Office (CBO) to report their deficit and budget reduction estimates to the comptroller general. The comptroller general then delivered a report to the president, who in turn was required to order spending cuts as the comptroller suggested. The spending cuts were to take effect automatically unless Congress legislated its own deficit reduction plan. The comptroller general was removable only by Congress, either by a joint resolution or by impeachment.

Congressman Mike Synar (D-OK) and the National Treasury Employees Union sued Comptroller General Charles A. Bowsher, challenging the act on separation of powers grounds. A three-judge district court (which included Antonin Scalia) found that although the comptroller general was under congressional control, he functioned in an executive capacity in violation of separation of powers principles.

---

11. Between 1930 and 1980, more than two hundred statutes incorporated some form of legislative veto.

12. See Fisher, "The Legislative Veto: Invalidated, It Survives," outlining Congress's noncompliance with *Chadha*. Initially, Congress seemed content to ignore *Chadha*, attaching legislative vetoes to more than two hundred new laws in the ten years after *Chadha* was decided. The use of legislative vetoes continues today, largely behind closed doors. Rather than voting in open session, legislative vetoes nowadays are quietly exercised in appropriations committees, in continuing resolutions, in congressional requirements that agencies obtain prior congressional approval for their actions, and in informal meetings between congressional leaders and federal agencies.

BURGER: Comptrollers have always thought they were congressional aides and not in-dependent actors.[13] Standing is clear, since the union is a party. The 1985 act pointedly refused to give the president the powers vested here in the comptroller general. He is required to decide and to issue reports to the president that bind the latter. The imple-menting responsibility is the comptroller general's. Is that constitutional? *Myers* said that the power of removal was crucial to the presidency.[14] But that power, as to the comptroller general, rests with Congress—without any meaningful review anywhere. *Humphrey's* was a limitation of presidential power.[15] *Humphrey's* did not overrule *Myers.*

BRENNAN:[16] I would affirm. My view is that the statute does not violate the delegation doctrine as developed in the case law. Although it seems to me abundantly clear that the law was passed because Congress knew that it would be incapable of balancing the bud-get unless it created a mechanism which in effect forced it to do so, it also seems to me that this is not enough to give rise to an excessive delegation claim.

First of all, Congress has made the hard choices here. It has, after all, made the deci-sion that cuts shall be imposed across the board, i.e., equally with respect to defense and non-defense programs. Second, although much was made at argument of the discretion that vests in the OMB, CBO and comptroller general, the fact is that the Federal Reserve exercises just as much discretion on a daily basis as it seeks to regulate the supply of money. We were told that Congress could not choose between smaller budgets and more bomb-ers and more social welfare programs, and so they shunted the problem over to the comp-troller. Well, when Congress is torn between clean air and a healthy automobile indus-try, it turns to an agency to determine the appropriate balance. This is the reality of the administrative state. Third, there are standards to guide the comptroller general. He is instructed, for example, as to many of the economic assumptions that must underlie his calculations. I have no trouble saying that the statute does not violate the delegation doctrine.

Turning to the separation of powers issue, I agree with the district court that the act is unconstitutional, but for slightly different reasons. Basically, "separation of powers" refers to the separation of the power to legislate from the power to execute from the power to adjudicate. This separation reflected the Framers' wise acceptance of Montesquieu's maxim. A separate concern, generally included under the heading "separation of powers," is the Framers' decision to have a unitary executive.

This case raises only the concern with keeping basic governmental powers distinctly separate. That is, what is problematic about Gramm-Rudman is that it involves a blend-ing of legislative and executive functions.

---

13. One of the main reasons for this basic lack of independence was that while comptrollers general were nominated by the president and confirmed by the Senate, they were removable "at any time" by a joint resolution of Congress for any number of listed reasons, including inefficiency, neglect of duty, and malfeasance.

14. *Myers v. United States*, 272 U.S. 52 (1926).

15. *Humphrey's Executor v. United States*, 295 U.S. 602 (1935).

16. Adapted from Brennan's talking papers, Brennan Papers, OT 1985, box 717.

I do not believe that there is any such thing as "inherently executive" activity. The executive function is only that which Congress leaves to be done to enforce the laws it passes. If Congress establishes standards for clean air in its enactment, establishing such standards is legislative; if Congress delegates the establishment of standards to an agency, this same task becomes executive. This is why the Framers feared Congress so much more than they feared the other branches of government—because the legislative branch has the power to define the duties and functions that will be left to the other branches. In my view, "execution"—properly understood—begins where the bill passed by Congress leaves off. And, except as expressly limited by the Constitution, Congress may choose how specific to get, how much to include in its law and how much to leave to administrators.

However, having made its choice in drafting legislation, Congress's participation must end. Having chosen to leave tasks for administrators, Congress cannot also control the administration and execution of its enactment. This, of course, is the real import of *Chadha*. Congress cannot keep the power directly to supervise the officer it leaves with the task of administering and executing a law. If Congress controls that officer, it controls executive as well as legislative power. And such a blending of those powers violates the fundamental principle of separation of powers.

That brings me to the removal power. As I have explained, I do not believe that the power to remove is somehow "inherently executive." But the power to remove is the power to *control*. The Constitution does not permit Congress to do that. The law in *Myers* was unconstitutional for just this reason—Congress required the president to obtain approval from the Senate before allowing removal. Since only Congress has the power to remove the comptroller, it is Congress which has the power to control what the comptroller does.[17] This, in turn, gives Congress the power to control the administration and execution of Gramm-Rudman.

There are several other factors which give Congress power to control the comptroller. Specifically, there is Congress's participation in the appointment process and the fact that, historically, the comptroller has been considered "Congress's boy." However, I do not think it necessary or wise to rely on these additional factors. The power to remove suffices to create the constitutional objection.

Lloyd Cutler raised the possibility of saving Gramm-Rudman by striking down Congress's removal power. For a number of reasons, I do not think we can take that course. First, as the solicitor general argued, the comptroller has numerous functions, most unrelated to Gramm-Rudman. I would not reconstitute an office which has existed for sixty-five years under such circumstances. Second, we cannot conclude that Congress would prefer to sacrifice its power to control the comptroller. Gramm-Rudman is only a small part of the comptroller's duties. It is very important to Congress to be able to remove the comptroller if he is negligent or inefficient. Third, the legislative history of the 1921 act convinces me that Congress wanted to have removal power to the extend that it could do so constitutionally. At least some of the comptroller's functions *are* consistent with removability by Congress. Fourth, Congress was not unaware of the problem raised by its power to remove, and it included the fallback provision in the event we

---

17. *Myers v. United States*, 272 U.S. 52 (1926).

were to find the act unconstitutional. We should rely on that provision. Finally, as Bill Rehnquist noted at the argument, striking down Congress's removal power might lead to the conclusion that the president *has* some removal authority. That result is *clearly* contrary to Congress's intent. Therefore the act must fail.

One final point. Having separated the issue of Congress's participation in the removal process from the issue of limiting the president's removal power (which was the issue in *Humphrey's*), I would make very clear that *Humphrey's* is still good law.[18] The notion that Congress can limit the president's power to remove as long as Congress does not itself participate in the removal precess is no longer open to question. It is important to reaffirm *Humphrey's*, because the district court opinion includes a lot of dicta which questions the continuing validity of that case. This is wrong and unwarranted, and we should make this very clear.

WHITE: There is no excessive delegation. I disagree with the solicitor general that the president must have sole removal power. Even if the removal power is crucial, it is enough to say it is a retention by Congress. Why not limit it to these particular functions?

MARSHALL: I agree with Bill Brennan.

BLACKMUN: *Glidden* comes close to this.[19] I don't think that we have to remove the comptroller general. I am inclined to reverse.

POWELL: The appointing power and the duty to execute are presidential. But the delegation here was to execute a substantial portion of law, and Congress reserved the power to remove. You can make a strong argument for reversal, but I would affirm.

---

18. *Humphrey's Executor v. United States*, 295 U.S. 602 (1935).

19. *Glidden Co. v. Zdanok*, 370 U.S. 530 (1962). The Supreme Court initially ruled that the Court of Claims and the Court of Customs and Patent Appeals were Article 1 (legislative) courts rather than Article 3 courts. *Ex parte Bakelite Corp.*, 279 U.S. 438 (1929); *Williams v. United States*, 289 U.S. 553 (1933). In 1953 and 1958, however, Congress sought to overrule the Court's decisions and declared that both courts were Article 3 courts. It was widely thought that the Supreme Court still viewed these courts as Article 1 courts, and a legal challenge was inevitable.

Glidden was a consolidation of two cases, one involving the Court of Claims and the other involving the Court of Customs and Patent Appeals. In the first case, the Glidden Company lost a federal diversity suit for breach of a collective bargaining agreement. The majority opinion at the court of appeals was written by Judge J. Warren Madden, a Court of Claims judge sitting by special designation of the Chief Justice of the United States. The company appealed, claiming that as an Article 1 judge, Judge Madden had no business sitting on an Article 3 court. The second case was a federal criminal appeal, where the trial judge was a retired judge of the Court of Customs and Patent Appeals, also sitting by designation of the Chief Justice. In both cases, the petitioners claimed that these judges were Article 1 judges, as they had only *statutory* protections of tenure and salary, not the *constitutional* protections offered under Article 3.

The Court refused to follow its earlier decisions and ruled that both the Court of Claims and the Court of Customs and Patent Appeals were Article 3 courts after all. The judges were said to enjoy full Article 3 protections and were subject to designation and assignment by the Chief Justice.

There remain some concerns that the Court sacrificed important separation of powers principles in deferring to Congress in this case. Both the Court of Claims and the Court of Customs and Patent Appeals display an odd combination of Article 1 and Article 3 attributes.

REHNQUIST: I would reject the invitation to invalidate the 1921 act. The delegation argument is not very strong. It gets down to removal—can the comptroller general participate in the execution of a law? The removal issue does not seem too important to me. It is the lack of presidential control, rather than the congressional power of removal, that is the flaw. The district court was substantially right.

STEVENS: Our cases on removal counsel a very narrow opinion. We should assume the constitutionality of the 1921 statute and base our decision on the *Chadha* principle that Congress must delegate the execution power to someone other than itself.[20] I would rely not solely on the removal power—that recognizes that the comptroller general is an agent or arm of Congress. Executive decision-making by a legislative person is the flaw for me.

O'CONNOR: The act violates basic separation of powers concerns. Executive branch powers are given to the *legislature*, and you can't do that—the comptroller general is a *legislative* person.

Result: The Court struck down the statute as a violation of separation of powers. Congress, Warren Burger wrote for a 5–2–2 majority, could not play a direct role in the execution of federal laws. Under the Gramm-Rudman-Hollings Act, Congress had assigned the comptroller duties that were executive by nature; but in retaining the right to remove the comptroller general by a joint resolution of Congress, the legislature had retained improper control over the office. By making the comptroller subservient to congressional will, Congress had impermissibly injected itself into the executive branch and infringed on the prerogatives of the president.

Stevens and Marshall concurred in the judgment, while White and Blackmun dissented. White pointed out that the comptroller's budget duties were really legislative in nature, not presidential. Because the task of appropriating funds was committed to Congress under Article 1 §9, the retention of legislative control over the comptroller did not improperly interfere with presidential powers. Blackmun added that Congress should have considerable discretion in establishing procedures for removing the comptroller general.

This was Warren Burger's final case; it was announced on July 7, 1986, his last day as an active Chief Justice.

ELIGIBILITY

Powell v. McCormack, 395 U.S. 486 (1969)
(Douglas) (Brennan)

Adam Clayton Powell (D-NY) was duly elected to the 90th Congress. Following allegations that he had misappropriated public funds and abused the legal process, the House of Representatives passed a resolution barring Powell from taking his seat the House. Powell sued the Speaker of the House, John McCormack (D-MA), asking for a writ of mandamus ordering McCormack to administer the oath of office. Powell argued that the resolution violated Article 1 §2, which he claimed set out the exclusive list of qualifications to serve in Congress. All parties admitted that Powell met all three requirements listed in Article 1 with respect to his age, citizenship, and residency.

---

20. *INS v. Chadha,* 462 U.S. 919 (1983).

The district court dismissed the case for lack of jurisdiction. The court of appeals reversed on jurisdiction but in an opinion written by Warren Burger ruled that the matter was nonjusticiable. While the case was pending before the Supreme Court, Powell was reelected to the 91st Congress with 80 percent of the vote. This time he was allowed to take his seat. To prevent the case from becoming moot, Powell pressed his demand for back pay.

Among the issues the Court had to decide were (1) whether the case was moot; and (2) whether Powell had been expelled *from the 90th Congress (Article 1 §5 allows expulsions only upon a two-thirds vote of the House) or whether he had been* excluded *(which would shift the debate to Article 1 §2 qualifications).*

Conference of April 25, 1969

WARREN: I would reverse. I would render a declaratory judgment that Congress must seat any elected congressman who meets the three qualifications specified in the Constitution. The Constitution was designed to avoid some of the things done by the Parliament in England. [DOUGLAS: He refers to James Madison in *The Federalist Papers.*] Congress is limited to the three qualifications in the Constitution when it comes to excluding him. They can, of course, oust a man on a two-thirds vote, but this is not a constitutional expulsion merely because two-thirds of the members voted not to seat him. But the two (expulsion and exclusion) are different. The question of salary remains, so the case is not moot. I see nothing to overturn the argument in light of his salary claims. I also think that Congress has no power to impose a fine on admission or exclusion, although they could do so on expulsion. But that issue is not here.

BLACK: I agree with the Chief Justice.

DOUGLAS: I agree with the Chief Justice.

HARLAN: I reverse. We should certainly send him back to the court of claims on back salary, where the petitioner can have offsets for this thievery. Bromley's basic argument is simply untenable.[21] Congress can be confined within the limits set by the Constitution. It is not necessary to get into the problem of the fine. Salary becomes important, however, for it saves the case from being moot.

BRENNAN: I reverse.

STEWART: The speech and debate clause would give me trouble, except I think that the case is moot under our *Philippine* case.[22] I would vacate this case as moot and dismiss on that ground.

---

21. Bruce Bromley argued the case for the respondents, a collection of congressmen and congressional employees. Bromley was a colorful litigator, best known as the self-proclaimed master of filing "endless (and endlessly profitable) anti-trust cases."

22. *Alejandrino v. Quezon*, 271 U.S. 528 (1926). After the governor general appointed Jose Alejandrino to the Philippine Senate, that body voted to suspend him and deprive him of all benefits and privileges for a year. The Philippine Supreme Court refused to intervene, and by the time the case got to the U.S. Supreme Court, Alejandrino's suspension was over and he had taken his Senate seat. The Supreme Court dismissed the case as moot. Having done that, however, the Justices briefly considered whether the issue of back pay was sufficient to allow the Court to retain jurisdiction. They decided that Alejandrino had not

WHITE: I reverse and agree with the Chief Justice.

FORTAS: The issue is justiciable. I had worked out a theory that this was an expulsion, but I will go along. I reverse and go with the Chief Justice.

MARSHALL: I reverse.

Result: The Court ruled that it had jurisdiction and that the question was justiciable. While the speech or debate clause immunized individual members of Congress, Powell could still sue the legislative employees responsible for preventing him from taking his seat. The Court treated the matter as an exclusion rather than an expulsion. The majority found that the qualifications listed in Article 1 were exclusive, and because Powell met all three conditions he had been wrongfully excluded from the 90th Congress. Thurgood Marshall initially voted with Stewart to deny certiorari in this case but later joined the majority to back Powell's claim in the Court's published opinion.

IMMUNITY

Gravel v. United States, 408 U.S. 606 (1972)
(Douglas)

Senator Mike Gravel (D-AK) read portions of top-secret documents on American policy during the Vietnam War (The Pentagon Papers) *before the Senate Public Works subcommittee. He then placed forty-seven volumes of classified papers into the public record. He also planned to publish the volumes privately with Beacon Press. When a grand jury subpoenaed Gravel's aide, Leonard Rodberg, and his publisher to testify about the matter, Gravel intervened and sought to quash the subpoenas, claiming immunity for himself, his aide, and his publisher based on the speech or debate clause. The district court denied Gravel's motion but limited the permissible scope of questioning. The court of appeals for the First Circuit upheld the subpoenas but granted Rodberg extensive immunity from questions regarding "legislative acts" and extended to Rodberg a common law privilege protecting government officials from libel suits.*

Conference of April 21, 1972

BURGER: I am not prepared to vote. The staff of senators have no privilege. Aides and staff were not unknown at the time of the Constitution. The printing does not come under the vote and debate clause.

DOUGLAS: One cannot get at the senator through his secretary; otherwise, the privilege becomes emasculated.

---

sufficiently argued the issue in his brief and that the Court did not have enough information to allow it to retain jurisdiction. Calling the issue of back pay a "mere incident" to Alejandrino's equity suit, the Court dismissed the case.

In deciding *Powell v. McCormack,* the majority carefully noted that the Court in *Alejandrino* had not considered the issue of back pay to be a trivial matter; that case was dismissed only because the issue had not been adequately raised or argued.

BRENNAN: The purpose is not to protect the senator, but the public. You can't ask the aide what you can't ask the senator. Bailey said that they could be examined except as to the "motives and purposes" of Gravel—I am not sure that is correct.[23] What you can't ask the senator, you can't ask his aide.

MARSHALL: You can't ask any member of the senator's staff what you can't ask the Senator.

BLACK: I can't agree with Irvin [sic] that it is up to Congress to define the privilege— it is a judicial matter.[24] This clause was more for the protection of the member than for the public. Our opinions indicate that aides were not included under any legislative privilege.

STEWART: The law ought to cover some aides. There must be some so close to the senator that they have benefit of the privilege. Not all aides are included. On publication, any Congressman can print anything in the *Congressional Record*, but going to an outside publisher shocks me very much.

REHNQUIST: Negative on the republication—I am not sure on the other aspects.

Conference of May 4, 1972

BURGER: Does the speech and debate provision extend to aides? The grand jury inquiry is very broad. It is a judicial inquiry—courts can protect witnesses against harassment. The Fifth Amendment is applicable. The protection of the clause, however, does not protect the aide. If there is protection, it is wholly derivative. A senator has no immunity if there is a bank robbery. A senator who engages in (a) legislative activities; or (b) legitimate political activities would be immune. A senator campaigning would have no immunity. *Johnson* indicates that going to the FCC for a constituent is in the legitimate political realm, but not within the speech or debate clause.[25] It is not important at what time Gravel held the hearing. If an employee overheard what the senator said, it would be protected. Senators must be able to rely on their assistants. [DOUGLAS: He refers to the *Dodd* case against Drew Pearson.[26]] Senators should be able to stop an aide from giv-

---

23. Bailey Aldrich was the Chief Judge of the First Circuit Court of Appeals. He wrote the majority opinion appealed here. *United States v. Doe*, 455 F.2d 753 (CA 1st 1972). The grand jury originally subpoenaed Rodberg—the "Doe" in this case—and Senator Gravel's publisher, but not the senator himself.

24. Sam Ervin Jr. (D-NC) argued the case as amicus curiae on behalf of the Senate.

25. *United States v. Johnson*, 383 U.S. 169 (1966). Thomas Johnson was one of several former members of Congress charged with conflict of interest and defrauding the federal government. He had allegedly conspired to persuade the Justice Department not to prosecute several savings and loan companies for fraud and other crimes. Among other things, the savings and loan industry had apparently bribed Johnson to read a speech in Congress favorable to the industry. The Supreme Court ruled that the speech or debate clause precluded federal courts from inquiring as to the content of, or motives for, Johnson's speeches. Nor could his speeches be made the basis of a criminal action. Johnson could still be criminally prosecuted, but the case had to be limited to evidence outside the broad immunity granted by the speech or debate clause.

26. *Pearson v. Dodd*, 410 F.2d 701 (D.C. Cir), cert. denied 395 U.S. 947 (1969). Several former employees and current aides of Senator Thomas Dodd (D-CT) entered his office without permission and duplicated some incriminating documents. Journalists Drew Pearson and Jack Anderson published the documents in an article accusing Dodd of corruption. Dodd eventually resigned from the Senate but sued for conversion and invasion of privacy. The court of appeals rejected both of his claims.

ing out a secret. When the United States printed up the paper, that was no publication. Beacon Press was doing what normally the United States would do. There was no committee authority in the Beacon Press publication. Beacon Press has no standing.

DOUGLAS: I would affirm the judgment of the court of appeals except as to Beacon Press, and I would refuse to let it be questioned under the First Amendment.

BRENNAN: I would decide this case narrowly. What is the focus of the grand jury? It is how the information came into Gravel's possession. That inquiry makes the grand jury proceeding proper. May it question the aide about how the senator got them? No. This is not inconsistent with what we said in *Kilbourne*[27] and *Powell*,[28] for the men in those cases were not *aides*. Moreover, in *Dombrowski*, the charge was invasion of privacy of a third party—no speech and debate issue was present.[29] Nothing that was done here related to a third party's report. This was a legislative act by Gravel, and the aide was being examined about that act. The district court did a better job than Aldrich. I would not except "motive or purpose." Beacon Press is in the circle also. I would affirm Bailey with a slight change as to motive and purpose. I vote to affirm the U.S. case.

STEWART: I agree with Bailey Aldrich and vote to affirm in both cases.

WHITE: An aide need not testify about communications with a senator about a legislative act. But the senator or aide can be called if they stole the paper, or for receiving stolen property. On the face of the record, a crime was committed somewhere. He can't be punished for publishing the paper while performing a legislative act, but the privilege does not cover republication.

The first paragraph of the court of appeals order is too narrow and is meaningless. Paragraph 2 is much too broad, for it covers "course of employment." Many of the things that aides do are not legislative acts. Stealing papers is not a legislative act. Receiving stolen goods by a senator can be punished. I would affirm *Gravel* insofar as it concerns republication. I disagree with the U.S. to the extent that it says that there is no privilege. For me, there would be no question asked of an aide that would be privileged under speech and debate clause.

MARSHALL: Beacon Press is not protected. If it has a First Amendment right, it should fight it out on its own. The questions that you can ask a senator, or cannot ask, are the same ones you can or can't ask the aide. It is premature to decide what questions can be asked. I would set aside the court of appeals order.

---

27. *Kilbourne v. Thomson*, 103 U.S. 168 (1881).

28. *Powell v. McCormack*, 395 U.S. 486 (1969).

29. *Dombrowski v. Eastland*, 387 U.S. 82 (1967). Dombrowski, the executive director of a Louisiana civil rights organization (the Southern Conference Education Fund, Inc.), contended in a civil action that Senate subcommittee chairman Senator James O. Eastland (D-MS) and the subcommittee's chief counsel had conspired with Louisiana state officials to deprive him of his property in violation of the Fourth Amendment. The Court ruled that members of Congress had broad legislative immunity and that Senator Eastland was not subject to civil suit. However, the Court ruled that the scope of staff immunity was less inclusive than for members of Congress and that Dombrowski could continue to pursue his civil suit against the subcommittee's chief counsel.

BLACKMUN: I agree with Byron. I agree with the district court and disagree with paragraph 2 of the court of appeals opinion. I agree also on Beacon Press.

POWELL: I agree with the status of aides. The speech and debate clause does not cover private publication. Aldrich wrote a fine opinion, but I disagree with him on the common law privilege. I can't approve the protective order. Paragraph 1 is too restrictive. Paragraph 2 is incredible—I agree with Byron.

WHITE: I would adopt the district court's order, or quite close to it. Paragraph 1 is better than the court of appeals, and paragraph 2 is still too broad.

REHNQUIST: I remain partly at sea. Aides have some insulation. Is a senator from Alaska a compellable witness in California? The aide's immunity is here coterminous with the senator's. The power to compel testimony applies to committees, not to a single senator. I disagree with Brennan's distinction of the *Dombrowski* case. Putting a burden on an assistant is improper. *Dombrowski* was wrongly decided. The aide there was the same as the aide here.

WHITE: *Dombrowski* was not a testimonial case.

REHNQUIST: I would put this case on narrow ground. The court of appeals and the district court both acted too much in an adversarial role. I am up in the air, although I agree generally with Byron.

BURGER: I agree with Byron, Harry, Lewis, and Bill Rehnquist.

Result: The Court held that the court of appeals protective order was overly broad. Leonard Rodberg had immunity regarding conduct connected to the legislative process, but his immunity did not extend to questions regarding the private publication of The Pentagon Papers. *So long as no legislative act was implicated by the questions, Rodberg could be questioned as to the source of* The Pentagon Papers. *Stewart dissented in part, while Douglas, Brennan, and Marshall dissented outright. Brennan argued that the majority's decision "so restricts the privilege of speech or debate as to endanger the continued performance of legislative tasks that are vital to the workings of our democratic system."*

Hutchinson v. Proxmire, 443 U.S. 111 (1979)
(Brennan)

Senator William (D-WI) Proxmire presented a Golden Fleece Award each month to a federally funded project he considered to be a waste of taxpayers' money. His first Golden Fleece Award went to Ronald Hutchinson, a behavioral scientist at Kalamazoo State Hospital in Michigan. Hutchinson spent a half-million dollars in federal funds attempting to establish an objective measure of human aggression by measuring jaw clenching and tooth grinding among primates. Proxmire mocked the project in a press release and a newsletter, both of which were widely publicized.[30] Hutchinson filed a defamation suit in federal court, but the district court ruled in a summary judgment that the speech or debate clause

---

30. Proxmire said, among other things, that Hutchinson had "made a fortune from his monkeys and in the process made a monkey out of the American taxpayer."

gave Proxmire absolute immunity. The trial judge also ruled that, had Proxmire not been immune, Hutchinson was a public figure and would have had to prove actual malice to recover.[31] *The court of appeals affirmed.*

BURGER: Does the speech and debate clause protect newsletters and press releases? Not as to all. Is Hutchinson a public figure? If so, should there have been summary judgment?

STEWART: I agree that we must decide the speech and debate issue first. Then, if it does not apply, we must decide whether the publications were defamatory. And if they were defamatory, the third, we must decide whether the *New York Times* rule applies to this plaintiff. I think that there is no speech and debate immunity in publishing newsletters and so forth, but there is for calls to agencies, etc. I would stop there and remand for the lower court to consider whether non-immune statements were defamatory, and if so whether Hutchinson was a public figure, and if so, whether since he is not a member of the media he has the burden of meeting the *New York Times* test.

WHITE: I agree with Potter, except perhaps on the calls to agencies.

MARSHALL: I would apply *Brewster* and deny speech and debate immunity to anything said except what is said on the floor.[32] On other issues, I go along with Potter.

BLACKMUN: Television interviews and follow-up telephone calls have been held under the Seventh Amendment to be outside the speech and debate clause, and we have here only newsletters. *Brewster* holds that they are not protected. So I come out with Potter and Byron. I don't think that the plaintiff is either a public official or a public figure, but we need not decide that question.

POWELL: I agree that the speech and debate clause does not cover press releases or newsletters. I thought that we should reach the public figure issue.

REHNQUIST: I could agree with Potter, except for the issue in *Wolston*—that summary judgment is especially appropriate in libel cases—but I will go along with Potter on all issues.[33]

---

31. *New York Times Co. v. Sullivan*, 376 U.S. 254 (1964).

32. *United States v. Brewster*, 408 U.S. 501 (1972). Senator Daniel Brewster (D-MD) was charged with soliciting and accepting bribes. The district court dismissed the indictment on the ground that the speech or debate clause protected Brewster from any prosecution for bribery to perform a legislative act. The Supreme Court reversed, saying that the clause did not fully protect congressmembers from all conduct related to the legislative process. Because the indictment and evidence in this case did not require the courts to look into legislative acts or motives, Brewster was not immune and could be prosecuted. Thurgood Marshall joined Burger's majority opinion.

33. *Wolston v. Reader's Digest Assn., Inc.*, 443 U.S. 157 (1979). Several Reader's Digest publications falsely listed Wolston as a Soviet agent operating in the United States. The Supreme Court, in an opinion by Justice Rehnquist, ruled that Wolston (who had once been held in contempt of court for failing to testify before a grand jury in an espionage case involving his uncle and aunt) had not sought to thrust himself into the public spotlight, and the mere fact that he had a prior criminal conviction and had suffered brief public notoriety was not enough to make him a public figure. As a private person, he did not have to meet the "actual malice" standard of *New York Times v. Sullivan*.

STEVENS: It is outrageous to say that press releases and newsletters have speech and debate clause protection.

BRENNAN:[34] I think that we must reconsider *Davis v. Passman* if we are going to follow Potter's order. Indeed, on the merits, I think that Passman may have speech and debate protection.[35] (Potter agrees with this.)

Result: In an 8–1 decision, the Court ruled that the speech or debate clause did not protect information published by members of Congress in press releases or newsletters. The Court also ruled that Hutchinson was not a "limited purpose" public figure either prior to or after the publication of the Golden Fleece Award and that he did not have to meet the more difficult New York Times v. Sullivan standard of proving actual malice.

In 1980, Proxmire and Hutchinson settled the case for $10,000. The Senate, however, had to pay more than $124,000 to cover Proxmire's legal expenses. This caused so much public controversy that Proxmire agreed to repay part of his debt by assigning to the Senate a portion of his book royalties.

---

34. Brennan penciled these comments in a box immediately below Stevens's comments. While it is not entirely clear, these two sentences probably reflect Brennan's thoughts rather than Stevens's.

35. *Davis v. Passman*, 442 U.S. 228 (1979). Shirley Davis sued Congressman Otto Passman (D-LA) for sexual discrimination, claiming that she had been improperly fired from her job as his deputy administrative assistant in violation of the equal protection component of the due process clause of the Fifth Amendment. In his letter to Davis terminating her employment, Passman wrote that while she was able, energetic, and a hard worker, he had come to the conclusion that "it was essential that the understudy to my administrative assistant be a man."

The district court held that Davis had no private cause of action, and the court of appeals added that neither was there an implied cause of action under the Fifth Amendment. The Supreme Court reversed. William Brennan wrote the majority opinion in a 5–4 decision, recognizing a cause of action and a damages remedy for violations of the due process clause of the Fifth Amendment. Potter Stewart was among the dissenters.

CHAPTER 6

THE PRESIDENT AND THE COURTS

Youngstown Sheet and Tube Co. v. Sawyer, 343 U.S. 579 (1952)
(Burton) (Clark) (Douglas) (Jackson)

When North Korea invaded South Korea in June 1950, the United States responded with military force under the auspices of the United Nations and fought a bloody, undeclared war against North Korea and China. In late 1951, the American steel industry fell into crisis when labor and management failed to negotiate a new collective bargaining agreement. In December, the United Steelworkers Union gave notice of their intent to strike when the current labor agreement expired at the end of the year. Worried about the possible impact of a strike on the war effort, President Harry S. Truman intervened. After the Federal Mediation and Conciliation Service failed to facilitate a new agreement, Truman referred the matter to the federal Wage Stabilization Board (WSB) on December 21. The union agreed to postpone its strike, but when the WSB also failed to broker an agreement, the union again gave notice on April 4, 1952, that it would call a national strike on April 9.

On April 8, just a few hours before the strike deadline, President Truman issued an executive order commanding Secretary of Commerce Charles Sawyer to seize and operate the nation's steel mills. Truman notified Congress of his actions the following day and again a month later, but Congress took no action.

Sawyer notified steel plant managers that they should carry on as before but that they would be subject to his orders. The steel companies complied but filed suit in federal court to stop the takeover. Truman did not claim any specific statutory authority for his actions, saying that he was empowered to act by the inherent constitutional powers of the president. On April 29, District Court Judge David A. Pine issued a preliminary injunction against the government and ordered the steel mills returned to their private owners. The court of appeals immediately stayed Judge Pine's order (averting another threatened labor walkout) but commanded Secretary Sawyer not to grant the steelworkers a promised pay increase pending a final resolution of the case. The government, seeking a quick resolution of the issue, sought to bypass the court of appeals and made an extraordinary direct appeal to the U.S. Supreme Court. At the Supreme Court, the Justices first had to decide whether to allow the government to bypass the court of appeals before they could turn their attention to the merits of the case.

Certiorari Conference of May 3, 1952

VINSON: The question is whether the court of appeals should be bypassed. Ordinarily, I would want to wait on the court of appeals and not bypass it. I have not been able to figure out the possibilities that would result from our not taking the case—the practical questions. On balance, this situation is in line with the *Lewis* case, and has such possibilities that I would bypass.[1] If we grant cert, what should be our schedule? Should we set

---

1. *United States v. United Mine Workers*, 330 U.S. 258 (1947). In 1946, President Truman issued an executive order seizing control of most of the country's bituminous coal mining operations. He acted under

the case down at the earliest date we feel would give parties sufficient time and opportunity to prepare and present their views?

This is an interesting, though not a new, problem as to the powers of the president. Judge Pine dealt with the merits when considering his preliminary injunction.

During World War II, I had these problems and we had lots of discussions then as to the power of the president.[2] [BURTON: Very interesting and sound statements.] Prior to World War II, there were some precedents. *In re Neagle*,[3] and *In re Debs*.[4] Both discuss the powers of the president. Lincoln waged war for several months without Congress. It is hard to feel that Congress can really ratify this, although it would be welcome. Ratification by Congress, however, can't breathe life into a corpse (i.e., *the president must have constitutional power*).

The president here sent a message to Congress immediately *after* the seizure, asking for action either way. Robert Jackson has written on it as attorney general.

---

his authority as commander in chief and the authority delegated to him by the Smith-Connally War Labor Disputes Act of 1943. When the union leadership threatened a national strike, the government obtained a restraining order against the union and its leadership, prohibiting any calls for a strike during the wartime emergency. When union president John L. Lewis and others violated the restraining order, a district court judge found Lewis and the union to be in criminal and civil contempt. While their appeal was pending before the Court of Appeals for the District of Columbia, the Supreme Court granted certiorari under §240(a) of the Judicial Code, bypassing the court of appeals. A badly divided Court affirmed the district court's judgment, with a few minor modifications. Vinson wrote the majority opinion; Jackson and Frankfurter concurred, while Black and Douglas concurred in part and dissented in part. Murphy and Rutledge dissented.

2. Vinson was the director of the Office of Economic Stabilization from 1943 to 1945. He was responsible for controlling inflation during the war and managed a complex and often controversial system of wartime wage and price controls. He later briefly served as the chief administrator of the Federal Loan Agency before becoming the director of the Office of War Mobilization and Reconversion.

3. *In re Neagle*, 135 U.S. 1 (1890). After Supreme Court Justice Stephen J. Field received death threats from the losing party to a lawsuit, the attorney general assigned Federal Marshal David Neagle to protect Justice Field. When the disgruntled litigant later approached Justice Field, allegedly in a threatening manner, Neagle shot and killed him. Neagle was arrested and charged with murder in a California state court. He was released on a writ of habeas corpus issued by a federal court. California appealed, arguing that there was no federal law authorizing the executive to assign bodyguards to protect federal officeholders and that Neagle's actions were legally unauthorized. The Supreme Court, in a 6–2 vote (Field did not participate), ruled that the president had inherent powers under Article 2 to "take care that the laws be faithfully executed" and to keep the "peace of the United States." Both the attorney general and Neagle, the Court decided, had acted within their lawful authority. Two dissenters, Fuller and Lamar, argued that the president and other executive officers had no power to go beyond the explicit provisions of the Constitution and federal law. They maintained that only Congress, through the "necessary and proper" clause, had the advantage of implied powers. Article 2, which established executive authority, has no equivalent clause.

4. *In re Debs*, 158 U.S. 564 (1895). In response to the Pullman railroad strike of 1894, President Grover Cleveland deployed federal troops and obtained an injunction ordering striking railroad workers to go back to work. When the strike continued, Eugene Debs—the union president and a leading socialist politician—was arrested and cited for contempt. Debs argued that the president did not have constitutional or statutory authority to intervene.

The Supreme Court reiterated and broadened its holding in *Neagle*, ruling that the president had the inherent authority to do what was necessary to "command obedience" to the law and to keep the peace, so long as his actions were not expressly prohibited by the Constitution or by federal law.

In the *Montgomery Ward* case, the district court—on a weak ground—said that the seizure was invalid. The Seventh Circuit Court of Appeals *reversed*, and no cert here.[5]

Regarding the Smith-Connally Act of 1943, a special committee reported twelve seizures between Pearl Harbor and passage of the Smith-Connally Act, and a total of eighteen to date. There are a number of statutes on the books now, and they are appropriate and productive and democratic. (Lawless company—not a clean slate.) I believe that we should grant cert and enter a stay.[6]

BLACK: I would take them. I would set the cases for next week, if possible on Monday, and dispose of the matter then. I don't know whether we have to grant certiorari.

REED: I would grant cert and set the cases down for argument as soon as we can. We should grant cert without argument, and also grant a stay to avoid any change of wages. The idea suggested by Black—that we might set these cases for argument to consider both cert and the merits at one time—is no good. I would grant cert and pass on the stay today.

FRANKFURTER: I don't have that feeling of certainty. Let's start with a consideration of the effects and the value of a court of appeals decision. My guiding consideration is: *what will settle this business?* The answer is a collective agreement. What we may do may make this *more* difficult. My disposition runs against an eagerness to settle this. Look at the *Dred Scott* case.[7] The minimum wage case.[8] *Myers*[9] and *Humphrey's Case.*[10] There is a

---

5. *United States v. Montgomery Ward & Co.*, 150 F. 2d 369 (CA 7th 1945). President Franklin Roosevelt ordered the seizure of several Montgomery Ward properties in seven states to avert a potentially disruptive strike during World War II. Prior to the seizures, the War Labor Board had ruled against the company in a wartime labor dispute, and the company had refused to comply with the board's findings. Roosevelt claimed that the seizures were permissible under the president's implied powers as commander in chief or, alternatively, that the seizures were authorized under the Smith-Connally War Labor Disputes Act of 1943. District Court Judge Sullivan ruled that the seizures were unauthorized and illegal (58 F. Supp. 408 [N.D. Ill. 1945]). The court of appeals reversed, finding that the War Labor Disputes Act had authorized Roosevelt's course of action. The appeals court implied that the president also might have had the inherent power as commander in chief to seize the properties but did not explicitly decide the issue.

6. According to Robert J. Donovan, President Truman privately sought the advice of Chief Justice Fred Vinson before issuing Executive Order 10340 authorizing the seizure of the steel mills. Vinson reportedly told the president to go ahead. Robert J. Donovan, *The Tumultuous Years*, 386.

7. *Dred Scott v. Sandford*, 60 U.S. 393 (1857). Frankfurter used this list of cases to illustrate his argument that some of the Court's most serious blunders were the product of haste.

8. The two most likely candidates are *Adkins v. Children's Hospital*, 261 U.S. 525 (1923), and *West Coast Hotel Co. v. Parrish*, 300 U.S. 379 (1937). In *Adkins*, the Court struck down on a 5–3 vote minimum wage legislation for women and children in the District of Columbia. George Sutherland wrote the majority opinion, and Taft, Holmes, and Sanford were in dissent. Frankfurter was lead counsel for the losing side and predictably thought that the decision was a disaster. He had submitted a long and intricate sociological brief, which Sutherland summarily dismissed as "interesting but only mildly persuasive."

West Coast Hotel overruled *Adkins* on a 5–4 vote. Four members of the old *Adkins* majority—Sutherland, Van Devanter, McReynolds, and Butler—were now in dissent. While Frankfurter agreed with the outcome, he knew that the Court's timing was poor. The case was decided only two months after President Roosevelt

heaviness of heart and history about rushing in. I would not take the case now. There is a stay out already, and the men will have to stay on the job.

On ratification, we can talk of lack of due process in the seizure of property. Judge Pine had no business to go constitutionally. I am with the government on that issue. The only issue is, was it frivolous? It was Judge Pine's job to decide the case in equity. If it were up to me alone, I would send the case back to Pine on the temporary injunction problem, and tell him to pass on the injunction and to forget about the big questions until the case is tried on the merits. Stay off the large issues—these people should just sit and talk. My deepest concern runs against the eagerness of this Court to seize a big, abstract issue. The arguments below were too hurried. The government's argument in the district court was terrible.[11] It was differently handled in the court of appeals. Ratification is important, and it dates back to inception.

DOUGLAS: Grant.

JACKSON: Pass.

BURTON: I would deny both. Intermediate consideration is helpful.

CLARK: Grant.

MINTON: We have to grant.

---

had announced his court-packing plan, and it looked to many observers like the Court had buckled under to political pressure.

Frankfurter also might have been referring to *Morehead v. New York ex rel. Tipaldo*, 298 U.S. 587 (1936). Decided the year before *West Coast Hotel*, the Court narrowly upheld a New York minimum wage law for women and children by a 5–4 majority. Frankfurter might have been arguing that under the circumstances this case should have been postponed until there was a clear majority one way or the other—rather than reaffirming *Adkins* in haste by the narrowest of margins, only to reverse course and overrule the same case less than a year later.

9. *Myers v. United States*, 272 U.S. 52 (1926).

10. *Humphrey's Executor v. United States*, 295 U.S. 602 (1935). This case limited the president's power to remove *nonexecutive* officials from office, in contrast with the president's virtually unlimited power of removal of executive officials, recognized in *Myers v. United States*, 272 U.S. 52 (1926). William E. Humphrey had just been appointed to a second term on the Federal Trade Commission (FTC) by outgoing President Herbert Hoover. Incoming President Roosevelt summarily fired Humphrey, and he sued for back wages. Humphrey died before the matter could be decided, and his executor continued the action on behalf of his estate.

The Supreme Court ruled in Humphrey's favor, finding that the FTC post was quasi-judicial and quasi-legislative, rather than executive in nature. Congress had established the office with a set term in order to keep it free of partisan politics and independent of the political branches of government. The government argued, unsuccessfully, that permitting the establishment of such "independent" bureaucracies would allow Congress to undermine important executive prerogatives in violation of Article 2 and separation of powers principles. In rejecting Roosevelt's argument, the Court said that it would be easy for the courts to determine which offices were executive in nature and which were quasi-judicial or quasi-legislative.

11. Assistant Attorney General Holmes Baldridge argued before Judge Pine that while the Constitution and Bill of Rights limited congressional and judicial powers, they placed no limitations on executive power. The president, Baldridge argued, was accountable only "to the country." This extreme position caused an uproar and was subsequently abandoned, but not before it did a great deal of public damage to the president's case.

Stay: Should the stay below be modified?

VINSON: Stay.

BLACK: The status quo should be preserved or no stay granted. Both sides are entitled to have the status quo maintained. I would grant both stays, *that is, to stay Pine's judgment but prevent any wages from being increased.*

REED: Maintain the status quo—including steel. I don't know to what effect that may be.

FRANKFURTER: Maintain the status quo and make it clear as to collective bargaining.

DOUGLAS: Status quo.

JACKSON: Out.

BURTON: Status quo.

CLARK: Status quo.

MINTON: Status quo.

Conference of May 16, 1952

VINSON: To take either extreme position—that the president has either unlimited power or no power—is untenable. It runs in the face of the history of our government. At the one end, it is said that the president's power is unlimited. But unlimited power is not urged here, and it could not be. On the other end, it is urged that the executive has no power of his own and that he must rely on an act of Congress. I don't agree with that. Arguments of prior seizures are not pertinent here. In many instances seizures have been pursuant to an act, but others have not been pursuant to an act. *Here*, we have a seizure ordered at 10:30 P.M., on the eve of the 12:01 strike deadline. The sending of a message by the chief executive to the Congress the next morning, pointing out the seriousness of the situation, showed good faith and reveals the nature of the crisis. Here is the chief executive saying to Congress, "This strike is going to be called, stopping production. I tried to work it out. I may be wrong, but I am taking the only step known to me. If I am wrong, tell me and provide a method for meeting this emergency, and I will abide." There could be no criticism of this.[12]

It is said the president was so wrong in using the Wage Stabilization Board Act that he got off the main line (the Taft-Hartley Act) and had no power to seize.[13] I can't see how

---

12. Burton's notes read: "Ordinarily nobody could quarrel with that (we are in an unusual situation)."

13. Two statutes were crucial to this case. The first was the Wage Stabilization Act, which was originally passed in 1943. The Wage Stabilization Board that Truman used in his attempt to mediate a settlement was established in 1950 when the law was reenacted under a new name, the Defense Production Act. The second statute was the Taft-Hartley Act, officially known as the Labor Management Relations Act of 1947. This piece of Republican legislation, intended to weaken the power of trade unions, was passed over Truman's emphatic veto. Truman stubbornly refused to implement the act's provisions to settle labor disputes. Even when threatened with a national steel strike, Truman declined to use the Taft-Hartley Act to call for an additional eighty-day cooling-off period. Truman argued that the Taft-Hartley Act was intended

the Taft-Hartley Act is exclusive. John Davis admitted that the president was not compelled to go the Taft-Hartley route.[14] I don't take to the idea that you can amend the statute by action in substantial compliance with it, or by doing what the statute might have authorized. Here, it was pretty close.

The Taft-Hartley Act was passed in 1946–47. The Wage Stabilization Board Act was passed in 1950, and was extended by Congress in 1951. Lots had happened in the interim, since 1947. In essence, Congress looked the world situation in the face and reluctantly called on the president to furnish arms, men, and matériel, and to see to it that our armed forces should be greatly augmented. These are commitments which placed serious responsibility on the president. Only two members of the Senate voted against our participation in the world's attempt to stop aggression abroad (NATO, U.N.) and to rescue Korea. Appropriations have been in the billions.

There is no doubt but that there is a war on, and that the United States is preparing against it. That was the situation prior to World War II when Roosevelt seized the plants. Here the circumstances are clearer than in World War II. The present situation has more heavy and definite commitments than the ones at that time. Here, Congress has placed many responsibilities on the president, and he is doing no more than carrying out his obligations to execute the laws. Hence it was the duty of president, in seeing that the laws are enforced, to seize mills. He must carry on that program. The United States has a right to defend itself and prepare itself for war.

Congress enacted law after law directing the president to prepare us. You also have Congress entering the inflation fight. The Wage Stabilization Board is like the old War Labor Board of World War II to fight inflation. Congress gave it labor dispute functions. *When the bill came up for extension in 1951, they sought to take away this function, and that failed.*

In my opinion, the president had a choice, in his discretion, to go either route. It was not compulsory to go the Taft-Hartley route, because of the alternative WSB route. The Taft-Hartley route is not an invariable rule. Since it was not compulsory to go the Taft-Hartley route, and since the Wage Stabilization Board dealt with inflation as well as labor disputes, the president chose the WSB. He should have gone to the WSB, and he did. There were no questions raised at that time. Then the WSB broke down and the president seized the steel mills. The steel companies were interested in a price increase only as a quid pro quo for a wage increase. The steel companies were not concerned with the wage increase if they could get a price increase. The price increase is the real issue here.

The president was called upon to seize. If he had not seized, the howls would have been greater than the howls we hear now. It was his duty, and he would have been derelict if he had not seized. And *he would have been derelict in his duty to choose Taft-Hartley route* and pass by the wage stabilization program, since the Wage Stabilization Act had inflationary functions.

---

solely to cover peacetime labor disputes and that the Wage Stabilization (or Defense Production) Act was meant to resolve wartime labor crises. When the Wage Stabilization Board failed to avert a strike, Truman claimed that he had no alternative at that point but to seize the steel mills to ensure uninterrupted war production. Subsequently, Truman followed the advice of Attorney General Tom Clark, and perhaps Chief Justice Vinson, and argued that he had used his inherent constitutional powers to order the seizure.

14. John W. Davis argued the case for the Youngstown Sheet and Tube Company.

There is no question that steel is central to the economy. The stoppage of steel production would paralyze the war effort. It is funny to me (*if it was not so serious*) that in the past you had small plants seized without any law, but now that we are confronted with a threatened stoppage in big steel plants, there is hesitation.

Under the opinions of this Court—and they are legion—the history of presidential power of seizure has been exercised, and *it has been upheld again and again*. The *Montgomery Ward* case—that involved the obedience of industry to orders of the War Labor Board.

The National Defense Production Act—Congress in that act stated that its policy was to speed up and stabilize production, and to cut out wage controversies that interrupted production. It provided effective procedures to settle disputes in labor emergencies. [BURTON: But it did not provide for *seizure*.] Reports show it was intended to meet this sort of situation.

Look at *Neagle* and *Debs* on executive power. *Debs* went into courts, and still the power was exercised—this is compared as to a grain of sand.

I don't think that you can divorce world conditions from the problem, or divorce congressional authorization and appropriations under the WSB from the president's actions. In December, the president took the WSB road. He did not have to take the other course. This is not a defiance of Congress. His letter to Congress was written in a spirit of humility, and in a desire to solve the problem. He did not say that he did not have the power to seize. He did not say, "I am seizing alone." He wrote to Congress, "I have done it; maybe it's wrong. If I was not right, let Congress choose the method." Congress has done nothing. I affirm.

BLACK: I agree with what Vinson said at the beginning—that all of us have considered this and we didn't take any chances this morning. I don't think that anyone's mind will be changed by what is said here. My view is that most of what Vinson said is irrelevant to my decision.

The president had a right to follow either statute, but under only one statute was he authorized to seize steel plants. Under Taft-Hartley, he was authorized to seize by getting an injunction if Congress had declared war. The other law has no such power. The question is, do these statutes authorize the president to seize? *I think not*. If Congress had *declared war*, then the president could do *everything* to produce war materials. But here, the president could not invoke all laws necessary for the prosecution of the war. The question is, do these acts give congressional authority to seize? There is no relevance here in any congressional authority to seize. The question is, whether the president had the power to seize without a statute. The Taft-Hartley Act has ideas as to when property should be seized, but *Taft-Hartley is wholly immaterial to me*.

My views on this are old. I opposed the NRA, because I thought it delegated legislative power and authorized someone other than Congress to make laws.[15] There are times when people think *we* make laws here. There are times when the Court—in admiralty

15. The National Recovery Administration (NRA) was the centerpiece of Roosevelt's plan to end the Great Depression by assuming executive responsibility to limit economic production, stabilize prices, raise wages, and regulate destructive business practices.

rulings or in announcing new Rules of Court—does some lawmaking, in effect. However, we try *to avoid* that.

The issue is whether the president can make laws. Here we have a labor dispute and lawmaking concerning it. That power, under the Constitution, is in the Congress. If FDR seized without statutory authority in order to settle disputes, I would have said that FDR acted without authority.

When anyone devises a system for taking over property it is a *law*, and that is not an executive power. Controlling labor disputes, as here, is making law. My feeling as to the different branches of government is abhorrent to this. The president has two powers on legislation: (1) he can recommend; and (2) he can veto (and execute). *There are no others.* This is legislation. Perhaps this is doctrinaire, but it is not to me.

I regret that it came up this way and at this time. *The howls make no difference.* I thought that the Brotherhood lawyer hit the nail on head that we do not, even in war, turn over legislative power to the president.[16] We depend on the legislative branch as supreme in declaring the relations of citizens to property, and so forth.

This Court has decided cases in last two years that encroach more on liberty than the president's actions here, but that makes no excuse for more encroachment. Talk about the president, that just because he must see that the laws are enforced also gives him right to make the laws, is *tommyrot*.

I don't subscribe to the idea that this is the most dangerous decision. There have been others within two years more serious. This, however, *is* lawmaking. Only Congress can draft and seize and fix wages.

Should we reach the merits and should we enjoin? I think we have to. I think that there would be irreparable damage by the federal government taking over control of private management. Taking over a plant and giving it to strangers certainly is irreparable. Taking over private contracts is enough. If the Court holds that what Truman did was beyond the constitutional power of the president, *then it should write what should be done.* I trust Congress more than any executive, without meaning any personalities.

Regarding an injunction, it is a serious thing for this Court, with no army and only prestige, to tell the president what to do. I felt somewhat that if the Court holds that this was beyond the president's power, that we should not issue a writ. It would probably be best to handle this as we do in a mandamus to a judge. It is not to be supposed that any order will be disobeyed, and we can assume that the agent of the president will obey the views of the Court.

I am afraid of any use of an "emergency" system. This is not a case of the president tearing down the house in order to stop a fire. The conditions are not that serious. We are not far enough yet in governing the affairs of the nation. This will take power from Congress. I affirm.

REED: I am starting where Hugo concluded. I would hope that we *don't* reach the constitutional issue. Perhaps it can't be avoided. The elections are coming at a bad time.[17]

---

16. Arthur Goldberg argued the case for the United Steelworkers, as amicus curiae by special permission of the Court.

17. There was a presidential election in 1952. General Dwight D. Eisenhower later won in a landslide over Democrat Adlai Stevenson.

Damages are here, and they are irreparable. *On the type of order:* I think if we sent it back (with power in the president to increase wages, but with no change in working conditions) for a hearing in the lower court, that would be a better course. But the issue is here on a *temporary injunction* (although the issue is such that we could not change our minds). If we sent this back—leaving the president in possession pending final order—and let it be heard in the lower courts. I would like to avoid this.

I agree as to separation of powers. The question is *where to draw the line.* The lines between the powers of the three branches of government are not clear. We would do well to hold something back while Congress and the president worked it out. We should keep the president in control of the plants to see what Congress may do. But we can't rely on Congress. If we can't do that, we have serious issues.

If we must act on the merits: (1) I don't agree that the president's seizure power is limited to acts of Congress. History does not support such a conclusion. It is the practice of presidents and the assent of the people that shape constitutional law. *Milligan* is not authority, because war has changed.[18] Perhaps the war power was properly used here. It was also decided after the Civil War was over—the dispute was in 1867 [*sic*] to decide it then. Perhaps we should *go to the war power,* as of today, and say that the president has the power to seize as commander-in-chief. Couldn't the president seize a railroad in order to move troops?

(2) FDR's bank closing is apropos—there is no difference. He used a crisis to act to protect our currency, and Congress passed an act to expressly affirm the bank closings. It may be that would happen here, but it was probably not necessary.

(3) The president does not have unlimited power—*only in an emergency.* When is it a sufficient "emergency"? That is the issue. It is the kind of emergency that calls for special knowledge—where the evidence is that there is an emergency, and decisions are made by people who know what is going on.

(4) Can this Court say that an emergency must be imminent? You probably can't have a determination by the Court that this situation permits him to seize. No, the president must have leeway—and this is within the leeway. There plainly is an emergency here. Steel is very important. *Newspapers or clothing, etc., not so—they are different. These are rules of necessity. Here, atomic energy is involved. I would leave the President in control.* My preference is to put off the decision. [BURTON: Reed probably would have used Taft-Hartley.] I hope that the issue can be avoided and the case remanded for a hearing on a permanent injunction.

FRANKFURTER: I hope that nine opinions will be written. It is highly desirable that everyone writes. I am the most doctrinaire fellow at this table. I miss the vivid impact as to this emergency, since I have no sons.

I agree with Vinson that there is no unlimited power of the president, or of Congress. The doctrine of separation of powers is wound into this case. [BURTON: Frankfurter refers to a long piece on separation of powers he wrote twenty-five years ago.] I agree with Black on this.

---

18. *Ex parte Milligan*, 71 U.S. (4 Wall.) 2 (1866). The Supreme Court struck down a presidential order authorizing the trial of civilians by military tribunals but waited until after the Civil War was safely over to do it.

I begin where Hugo left off. *Assuming that the case is to be affirmed, what are we to do?* There is always Rule 34—automatically holds up twenty-five days—but I would be opposed. I prefer a more affirmative attitude than merely holding up the mandate.[19] I disagree with Stanley, for we might as well say that we won't decide the case because it is political. If the president is reversed, a new situation is created. We have the power to affirm, reverse, etc. And this Court, by the terms of its power—and the president's power—instructions should be held so as to give time for the president and Congress to act. We must give the parties time to work out the details—Congress, or the president, or both.

I strive like a beaver not to reach constitutional questions. The less this Court pronounces constitutional doctrine the better. But we cannot escape it here.

There is equity here. The emergency was obvious on April 8—probably even on March 20—and probably earlier than that. Any fair likelihood of an agreement was dashed at that time. On equity grounds, Judge Pine might have denied the injunction. I worked hard to find a reason for saying Pine had no cause to act, but p. 21 of Arthur Goldberg's Union brief—that the government's proposed settlement was *not* satisfactory to the union—precluded that. Goldberg's brief shows that this is equity. It is clear that no settlement imposed by the government can be final.

Hence we must reach the separation of powers issue. President Truman cannot lump all of his powers together and thereby get authority: (a) He cannot go to his war powers, for *no war was declared.* Only Congress can take that step. Speeches made by the president and secretary of state are "not war." (b) Quasi-war powers? *No such thing.* (c) The Wage Stabilization Board. The president was not required to go Taft-Hartley. I hope that we won't say whether the president was right or wrong on policy—the wisdom of his actions is no business of this Court. There is no significance in Truman's decision to go to the Wage Stabilization Board, for the president needs no act of Congress to set up voluntary mediation procedures. Woodrow Wilson appointed such a commission. In choosing it, Truman thought that might settle it.

I differ a little from Black. *If there had been no statutes on books, in my opinion the president could have seized the steel mills, at least temporarily, in order to bring the matter to the attention of the Congress*—a holding operation. For example, look at the *Midwest* case.[20] But that is not here. This was not a holding operation. Precedents are most to be avoided when carried out for good purposes.

---

19. Supreme Court Rule 34 provided for certain periods of time before Supreme Court decisions—such as a decision to deny certiorari—would take effect. This time was intended to allow the losing party to file a petition for rehearing.

20. *United States v. Midwest Oil Co.*, 236 U.S. 459 (1915). The Court upheld a longstanding presidential prerogative to exempt public lands from being made available for private purchase in the public interest. In 1908, Congress set aside a large tract of federal property for private purchase by oil companies. In 1910, President Taft submitted to Congress a report listing properties that he had exempted from the sale "in the public interest." The Court decided that Taft had the implied power to exempt the specified tracts from public purchase, noting that Congress had long acquiesced to this custom.

[Burton: Frankfurter reads from Reuben Clark's 1,100 page book—a compilation of all emergency legislation before 1917, beginning with the Colonies.][21] With the exception of an identified statute on Lincoln's seizure of the railroads in 1862, there is no act of Congress between 1862 and 1916 dealing with seizure. For the period from 1916 to 1951, there have been at least sixteen statutes conferring seizure powers on the president. Those acts were meticulous in their detail and very particular as respects compensation. They empowered the president grudgingly and reluctantly—for limited periods, under limited conditions, and limited by special appropriations, such as war, ship expenditures, filing orders, finding of emergency, failure of voluntary negotiations, etc. The laws required detailed conditions and formal findings. Parties have rights—act of safe agency was a condition. Question of compensation—remedy at large (administrative officer). These are *grants, not recognition* of the power.

Legislative history is cloudy—it shoots both ways. Here, there is no history to sustain that this was an inherent power, and there is no such experience. The use of seizures is a government strike-breaking technique, says Jim Carey.[22]

It is not that the president has to take the Taft-Hartley route or he is gone. *If the situation arises, the president should go to Congress before seizure.* In the *Midwest* case, *Taft made the statement* that the president should come before Congress.[23] The power exercised here is not inherent in the office; I do not think that this power is inherent in the president by virtue of his duty to enforce the laws. As Holmes said, the duty of the president does not go beyond the laws of Congress, and it does not require him to do more than Congress requires.

As for earlier seizures by Franklin Roosevelt: we cannot determine the power of the president by what he occasionally does. (1) Roosevelt's seizures from 1941 to 1945. There were 68 seizures (60 aimed at labor, 8 at management). Three were before Pearl Harbor was attacked, and all were agreed upon: (a) *North American* (the CIO agreed);[24]

---

21. J. Reuben Clark Jr., *Emergency Legislation Passed Prior to December 1917, Dealing With the Control and Taking of Private Property for the Public Use, Benefit or Welfare: Presidential Proclamations and Executive Orders of Analogous Legislation Since 1775* (1918).

22. James B. Carey was the secretary of the CIO. He testified on this point before Congress when he opposed passage of the War Labor Disputes Act. Frankfurter cited his testimony in his concurring opinion in this case, 343 U.S. 579, 602 (1952).

23. *United States v. Midwest Oil Co.*, 236 U.S. 459 (1915).

24. *United States v. North American Transportation and Trading Co.*, 253 U.S. 330 (1920). This case involved General Randall's summary seizure of a placer mining claim near Nome, Alaska, to build barracks for his army troops. After a long delay, the mining company sought compensation for the seizure. Louis Brandeis, writing for the majority, ruled that because General Randall's initial seizure was executed solely on his own authority and was not authorized, the government was not liable to pay compensation. However, the seizure was later ratified by the secretary of war, the president, and Congress—who subsequently authorized money to build a barracks on the property and delegated authority to the secretary of war to determine the details. These ratifying actions gave the company a private right of action against the government for compensation.

(b) *Federal Ships and Dry Docks* (the shipyard asked for seizure);[25] and (c) *Bendix* (a New Jersey company).[26] Between Pearl Harbor and the Smith-Connally Labor Disputes Act of 1943, there were eight seizures. There were nine seizures after VJ Day, but before the presidential proclamation of December 31 and the formal termination of the president's seizure right. Six seizures continued after the date of the proclamation.

On the emergency of steel, there is also great reliance on steel for civilian use.

Holmes—I share his conclusion that nobility in the law is a panacea. I believe in Montesquieu. The general condition is what runs the law—not a single act. [BURTON: Frankfurter makes sapient remarks on separation of powers, discussing Louis Brandeis's dissenting opinion in *Myers*.[27]] The 1787 Constitution was not meant for efficiency, but to preclude arbitrary power.

I would quote §2106 of the Judicial Code and Rule 34, giving time for a mandate. *Rule 34 provides that twenty-five days will expire* before the mandate issues. I affirm.

DOUGLAS: Much has been said, but I am inclined to agree with Hugo. This is a legislative function in the nature of a condemnation for a short term. In *Causby*, for example, a statute authorized the flying.[28] Like *Peewee Coal*, the power *must* be in the legislature, as it alone can appropriate funds.[29] It is something like seizing to hold for Congress, but the President was not authorized to do that. There should be no temporary seizure pending Congressional action—I would not agree with Felix on that. If Congress were to act, it would make the case moot. As of now, I affirm.

---

25. *Sloan Shipyards Corp. v. United States Emergency Fleet Corp.*, 258 U.S. 549 (1922). A Holmes opinion. United States Emergency Fleet was a federally owned and operated corporation. In the course of a shipbuilding contract with the Sloan Shipyards during World War I, the Fleet Corporation seized the Sloan Shipyards in December 1917 and changed the original contracts to terms more favorable to the federal government. Sloan Shipyards sued in a federal district court, but Fleet claimed sovereign immunity as a government agency and argued that any claims would have to be pursued in the court of claims. The Court ruled that sovereign immunity did not extend to a federally owned corporation merely because it was an agent of the government. Such entities were more closely akin to private enterprises, Holmes said, and could be sued at law unless barred by a constitutional or legislative grant of immunity.

26. *Matter of Bendix Aviation Corp.*, 58 F. Supp. 953 (1945). In 1940, the Department of Justice seized over 100,000 pages of business records in a criminal antitrust case. In 1942, the grand jury investigating the matter was dismissed without delivering any indictments. Later that year, however, the government filed a civil antitrust action. The Bendix Company asked for its records back, saying that it needed them for its defense. By the end of 1944, the government returned about half of the company's records but refused to return the rest. The district court ruled that the seized records remained the company's exclusive property and had to be returned as soon as proper use and examination were completed. Once the grand jury was dissolved, the judge ruled, the government had no authority to impound the records and was obliged to return them promptly.

27. *Myers v. United States*, 272 U.S. 52 (1926).

28. *United States v. Causby*, 328 U.S. 256 (1946). The federal government signed a six-month lease with an airport to allow low-level military flights. The flights disturbed production at a nearby chicken farm, causing the Causby's frightened chickens to crash into walls and injure or kill themselves. The Causbys successfully argued that the disruption, though temporary, was a taking that required government compensation.

29. *United States v. Peewee Coal Co.*, 341 U.S. 114 (1951). The government seized a coal mine to avert a national miners' strike.

JACKSON: I cannot add much. It is a great deal easier to criticize others than to make a statute yourself. This Court should not review whether there is an emergency! Stanley Reed might involve us in that. If the president declares an emergency, *I will take the president's judgment. The question of how the president deals with an emergency is different.* How can he deal with it? Here, the Department of Justice has been demoralized. The crowd that wants to claim everything has taken over. The president is in an untenable situation. (1) *The government does claim* inherent powers here! (2) The president can throw the Constitution overboard—but we can't. We can't sustain Perlman's argument without going beyond the Constitution.[30] (3) The claim that there were *statutes authorizing* this seizure: (a) contract orders, (b) Taft-Hartley. (4) Whatever emergency is claimed does not support such drastic action. (5) He could have placed obligatory orders. Whatever justification, this Court can't approve it here. I would affirm. On the issue of delay, my offhand impression is for it to go out in regular course. There should be no exceptions. Wisdom in the use of the power, in the past, has been in keeping it out of the courts. I would affirm, doing as little damage as possible.[31]

BURTON: The remedy at law is not adequate. The validity of the seizure should be passed on, and there is no reason to postpone a decision on the merits. This is a decision that requires policy-making, and therefore it is for Congress to decide. Congress has the power to provide a remedy. *Do not face the proposition of a failure of Congress to provide a remedy.* Here we have the Taft-Hartley Act. It was passed for this very purpose. Congress has almost said that there shall be no seizure. The legislative history indicates that Congress would provide for seizure after the Taft-Hartley remedy was exhausted. The president, having used the wage statute, is in no better position than if he had used the Taft-Hartley remedy. He has no power to seize apart from the statute. The Wage Stabilization Board is a general, special procedure. If it doesn't work out, then an emergency may be present. It does not meet the Taft-Hartley Act's paralysis emergency section. You don't have any orders here. The president has done an *unauthorized act—it was unlawful.* We should hold the mandate for the regular twenty-five days. That is appropriate. Everyone would have this waiting period. I affirm.

CLARK: In any event, we should limit our decision to this case. I am unwilling to say that the President has no power to act. It is a useful power. Here, we have a situation that could have been averted by two statutory methods not involving seizure. The wage stabilization program does not carry great power to be delegated to the president. Congress has been careful as to the power it gave, and as to the limitations. The president might have the power to prevent the stoppage of work on atomic bombs. Martial law would be

---

30. Solicitor General Phillip Perlman replaced the controversial Holmes Baldridge as the government's advocate on appeal.

31. When Robert Jackson was Franklin Roosevelt's attorney general, he vigorously supported the president's right to seize the North American Aviation plant and use the airplanes in the war effort. When Shay Minton confronted Jackson about this apparent inconsistency, Jackson shrugged his shoulders and replied, "But I was Attorney General then, and I'm a Justice now." Gugin and St. Clair, *Sherman Minton*, 219.

the way there. We will not pass on whether there is an emergency. I can't put this on a commander-in-chief basis, and it is not claimed to be. The commander-in-chief power has been declared with Japan, but this is not a declared war in Korea. Possibly the president could act under the Military Training Act or the Selective Service Act—the president could seize on specific orders.

MINTON: I am not as easy about this. I don't want a strike. The president did everything he could to avoid a strike. I cannot believe that this government was constructed without a power of self-defense. There are no dark spots, or power vacuums, where no one can act when the nation's safety is imperiled.

The power of self-defense resides in Congress, and in the president, and in everyone in public life. We have an acute emergency hanging over the world. The president seized the mills in self-defense of the nation. Was it for a mere show of power? He exercised only the power of self-defense. To help the nation in its extremity, he acted in his extremity. If not, why is Eisenhower in Europe? We should care if there is a strike. Truman seized the plants because the defense of the country required it. *That is not a legislative power—it is a defensive seizure.* The president had to act. [DOUGLAS: Minton is very excited about this and pounds on the table.] There is an emergency, and we do care, and we cannot forecast the damage to the nation. Nothing would be more tragic than our boys in Korea needing bullets and having none available because of this strike. The president can seize any property in an emergency. If Congress has not prohibited it and the Constitution has not, then the president need not stand by. He has the implied power to act in an emergency to defend the United States. His implied power goes back to (a) his commander-in-chief status; and (b) his power to execute the laws.

It is said that he must use statutory authority. The president followed the last word of Congress. He was granted wide jurisdiction in the *Wage Stabilization Act*—stabilization, etc. There is no exclusive grant of power to Congress here. Congress has only inherent powers here, not specific powers. Government either grows or it dies. Woodrow Wilson said that government is not a machine, but a living thing. We have a living Constitution. The Taft-Hartley Act is not mandatory—it was not the only route. Truman was right to follow the WSB. The president gets his inherent power from the power to defend the nation in a day of peril. I reverse.

Result: The Court ruled 5–1–3 that President Truman was not authorized either by the Constitution or by Congress to seize the steel mills. There were seven opinions in all, six by members of the majority and one dissenting opinion. Hugo Black, writing for the Court, ruled that Truman lacked any inherent constitutional authority to act, whether his claim was based on Article 2 or any other part of the Constitution, and that Congress had neither explicitly nor implicitly authorized him to act. In passing the Taft-Hartley Act, Congress had specifically considered and rejected an amendment that would have conferred upon the president the authority to order such a seizure. The authority Truman claimed was essentially a lawmaking power, which was vested solely in Congress—whether in good times or in crisis.

This was one of the rare instances where a concurring opinion—Robert Jackson's—in time became the authoritative opinion of the case. Jackson created an elegant and useful tripartite model of executive power, establishing that the limits of presidential authority depend to a great degree on

Congress: (1) executive power is maximized when the president acts with explicit or implied congressional authorization, in effect massing the combined powers of both branches of government; (2) where the president acts without either congressional authorization or opposition, presidential authority is in a "zone of twilight" where pragmatic considerations govern the limits of executive authority; and (3) where the president acts against the explicit or implied will of Congress, executive authority is at its weakest, because the president can rely "only upon his own constitutional powers minus any constitutional powers of Congress over the matter."

Tom Clark, who as attorney general had advised Truman to use his "inherent" powers to seize the mills, concurred in the judgment.[32] chief Justice Vinson wrote the lone dissent, joined by Reed and Minton.

A week after the decision was announced, the Justices tried to make it up to President Truman by throwing him a private stag party at Hugo Black's home in Alexandria. As Douglas remembered it, "We all went and poured a lot of bourbon down Harry Truman. He didn't change his mind, but he felt better, at least for a few hours." Truman was a good sport, although Douglas thought he was a bit testy. The president teased Black and the other members of the majority and insisted to anyone who would listen that his friend Fred Vinson had written a "masterful dissent."[33]

United States v. Nixon, 418 U.S. 683 (1974)
Nixon v. United States
(Brennan)

Seven members of the Nixon administration, including several White House staff and reelection committee members, were indicted on a variety of charges. After it became public knowledge that Nixon had used a sophisticated tape-recording system to monitor most Oval Office conversations, Special Prosecutor Leon Jaworski subpoenaed sixty-four tape recordings and other materials relating to conversations held inside the White House. President Nixon sought to quash the subpoena on three grounds: (1) the case was non-justiciable, because separation of powers precluded judicial interference in an internal dispute within the executive branch of government; (2) there was a general right of confidentiality of White House communications; and (3) the doctrine of executive privilege gave the president an absolute right to refuse to comply with the subpoena. The district court presumed the existence of executive privilege but found that the special prosecutor overcame the presumption by demonstrating a specific need for the evidence for use in a criminal trial. District Judge John Sirica ordered the president to submit the tapes and other materials for a private, in camera examination but stayed the order to allow all parties to appeal. President Nixon's lawyer, James St. Clair, appealed to the court of appeals, but Special Prosecutor Jaworski sought to skip the court of appeals and applied directly to the Supreme Court for a "writ of certiorari before judgment." This procedure had only been used six times in American history, and not since the Youngstown *steel-seizure case twenty-two years earlier.*

---

32. Harry Truman was infuriated by Tom Clark's "betrayal" and never forgave his old friend. Nearly twenty years later, Truman insisted that appointing Clark to the Court was the biggest mistake he made as president. Truman told author Merle Miller that Clark "was no damn good as Attorney General, and on the Supreme Court . . . it doesn't seem possible, but he has been even worse. He hasn't made one right decision that I can think of. . . . It isn't so much that he's a *bad* man. It's just that he's such a dumb son of a bitch. He's about the dumbest man I think I've ever run across." Miller, *Plain Speaking*, 225–26.

33. Douglas, *The Court Years*, 244–45; Ball, *Hugo L. Black*, 179.

The first conference centered on whether the Court should allow the special prosecutor to skip the court of appeals, while the second conference focused on the merits of the case.

First Conference

BURGER: I see three different categories of executive privilege: (1) congressional committees; (2) grand jury; and (3) criminal prosecution. In the first category, I think that the executive branch has a very broad privilege. In the second category, the privilege remains broad but is narrower. Number three is the tough one—it is the *Burr* situation.[34]

---

34. *United States v. Burr*, 25 F. Cas. 30 (No. 14,692d) (CC Va. 1807); *United States v. Burr*, 25 F. Cas. 187 (No. 14,694) (CC Va. 1807). After Aaron Burr was arrested and accused of treason in a successionist conspiracy, he sought to subpoena President Jefferson to produce letters and documents that Burr claimed were essential to his defense. In the first *Burr* decision, John Marshall, who was sitting as a circuit court judge, had to decide whether the president could be subpoenaed to appear personally and whether he could be ordered to bring papers and records with him (a subpoena duces tecum).

Marshall found no exceptions in federal law or the Constitution that allowed a president general immunity from a defendant's right of compulsory process in criminal cases. He acknowledged that there was an exception in common law for the British king but distinguished that office from the presidency. Unlike the president, the king "can do no wrong"; no one could legally accuse the king of bad motives or name him in debate. The crown was also hereditary and the monarch could not legally be removed from office. The American president, however, was elected, served for a limited term, and could be removed from office for misbehavior. The president's legal status, Marshall argued, was more like that of state governors, who admittedly were subject to the courts' subpoena powers. Marshall recognized that presidents might make a specific claim of exemption based on the president's need to use his time "for national objects." Such a defense might excuse the president from *obeying* a subpoena but would not prevent the courts from *issuing* a subpoena.

The government also argued that even if the court could order the president to appear personally, he was immune from a subpoena duces tecum. Marshall saw no legal difference between the two types of subpoena. Again, if the president claimed that the material subpoenaed contained confidential information that should not be made public, that claim would be judged upon the return of the subpoena, not its issuance.

The second *Burr* case dealt with President Jefferson's response to the subpoena duces tecum. After the first case was decided, Jefferson gave all of the subpoenaed records to his attorney and instructed him to use his own discretion in deciding what to produce and what to withhold. Jefferson's attorney censored some of the documents, claiming the need to protect the president's confidences.

Marshall sought to balance the defendant's need for evidence with the president's need for confidentiality. In Marshall's view, there could be no set or general rule. The president would have to submit his reasons for not producing certain materials for the court to consider. In this case, Jefferson himself offered no reasons at all for withholding any information, having left the decision to his lawyer. To Marshall, this was unsatisfactory in two respects: (1) Jefferson claimed sole discretion to decide which documents to produce, leaving himself to be the sole judge of his own case; and (2) the courts needed to know what was on *president's* mind, not what was on the mind of his lawyer, in seeking to withhold requested information. Marshall claimed that the president's claims of confidentiality would be taken most seriously and promised that the courts would take special steps to protect the president's confidences from public disclosure. Noting, however, that Jefferson himself never sought to explain his reasons for withholding information, Marshall ordered that the subpoenas be obeyed in full.

Afterward, Marshall himself presided over Colonel Burr's trial. On Marshall's patently sympathetic charge to the jury, Burr was acquitted. *United States v. Burr*, 25 F. Cas. 55 (No. 14,693) (C.C.D. Va. 1807).

DOUGLAS: *Nixon v. Sirica* seems to cover this, and that may be a good reason to let it stay in the court of appeals.[35] I see no merits in the question raised. It would be shocking to withhold exculpatory materials that would free a man. I would prefer not to bypass, but will acquiesce if the Court grants cert.

STEWART: I agree that the court of appeals has canvassed the executive privilege issue. On the issue of "requiring immediate settlement in this Court," I don't see that this qualifies. The criminal trial can be put off without real damage. Other issues that the court of appeals hasn't yet confronted: exculpatory evidence, and whether this is an intra-branch fight. Is identification of material here as good as last fall's? If we deny, I hope that we would have a per curiam opinion saying, "We'll stand by." I'm with Bill Douglas.

WHITE: I am reluctant to bypass. The government's application does not really demonstrate an immediate need for review. It is just a transparent effort to have an impact on the impeachment proceedings. I don't think we should let ourselves be used that way. In addition to Potter's points as to other issues, there is the question of appealability and whether we can take mandamus out of the court of appeals. And I don't want, before the court of appeals, to examine the secret material. I would prefer to deny.

MARSHALL: I don't see that the impeachment proceeding is a relevant consideration here. I also don't see why we should go to the court of appeals when the president didn't appeal *Nixon v. Sirica.*

BLACKMUN: There has been no past expedited case except when the executive was on one side and a private party on the other side. A six-month delay in a criminal case is no irreparable injury. If the court of appeals has crossed the bridge already, their decision of this must be prompt. The politics of the thing are that impeachment is the real issue. It may be an unpopular decision, and I would deny.

POWELL: I agree with Douglas, Marshall, Stewart and White. On the merits, I am inclined to say that the president can't claim privilege to keep material from the defense. I would expedite any appeal from court of appeals, but not under Rule 20.

[BRENNAN: From 6–2, votes changed: Powell and Stewart, on the ground that every other institution has delayed, and we have a duty to our institution and to the public not to be one of them—so the case will be set for July 8.[36]]

---

35. *Nixon v. Sirica*, 487 F. 2d 700 (1973). After the grand jury investigating the Watergate scandal issued a subpoena duces tecum ordering President Nixon to produce the Watergate tapes and other materials, the president refused to obey. Special Prosecutor Archibald Cox sought a federal court order requiring Nixon to comply. After several hearings, Judge John Sirica ordered the president to submit the requested materials to him for an in camera inspection so that he could determine whether any part of the requested records should be exempted from disclosure. Nixon appealed, claiming that the judge's order was illegal and that the president alone had the right to determine what, if anything, to submit. The court of appeals disagreed and refused to modify Judge Sirica's order.

36. Blackmun and White were the only two Justices who voted to deny cert. It is unfortunate in this case that Brennan did not account for his own comments in conference, as he was apparently a major influence in convincing the rest of the conference to allow Leon Jaworski to bypass the court of appeals. In conference, Brennan reportedly stressed the history of the Court at critical moments in American history,

Second Conference

BURGER: No claim of internal security, state secrets, or military secrets. It is essentially a confidentiality claim. Jurisdiction: this was an appealable order, and I do not reach mandamus or the All Writs Act question. Justiciability: on whether this is an intra-branch dispute, the president has diluted his own discretion to control this case. What about Rule 17(c) on the admissibility of the president's and Colson's statements? He is an unindicted co-conspirator, so I doubt it is necessary. Can we dismiss as improvidently granted the cross-petition? On executive privilege, I think that this is different from a presidential privilege. When communication is required for a criminal trial, there is still a presidential privilege. It is a qualified privilege, limited to official duties. Who decides when it is becomes crucial. Conduct outside of Article 2 is not covered.

DOUGLAS: On the unindicted co-conspirator issue, I say that constitutionally a president can be named as an unindicted co-conspirator, and under the Constitution we can't go back of grand jury's action.[37] I would DIG the cross-petition: (1) because it is not relevant to the issue of discovery; and (2) because insofar as it is relevant to Watergate, it is a political question.

WHITE: I would prefer mandamus, but will go along.

BLACKMUN: I prefer mandamus but will go along.

[From Brennan's Conference Notes]:

	Jurisdiction	Intra-Branch	Rule 17c	Unindicted co-conspirator	Exec. Priv.
CJ	Affirm	Affirm	Affirm	DIG	Affirm
Douglas	Affirm	Affirm	Affirm	DIG	Affirm
Brennan	Affirm	Affirm	Affirm	DIG	Affirm
Stewart	Affirm	Affirm	Affirm (pass)	DIG	Affirm
White	Affirm	Affirm	Affirm	DIG	Affirm
Marshall	Affirm	Affirm	Affirm	DIG	Affirm
Blackmun	Affirm	Affirm	Affirm	DIG	Affirm
Powell	Affirm	Affirm	Affirm	DIG	Affirm

[Other questions:]

a) don't apply the Fifth Amendment waiver rules to presidential privilege.

b) no political question in either pending impeachment or otherwise. Also no reason for staying our hand.

c) specific waiver by release of twenty transcripts.

---

such as when it headed off Truman's seizure of American steel mills and when it stepped into the breach during the struggle to integrate the schools in Little Rock. To hand the decision off to the lower court under these circumstances, Brennan argued, would be an act of cowardice. After Brennan's remarks, Douglas changed his vote to bypass and was prepared to assign the opinion to Brennan, but then Warren Burger also switched his vote and assigned himself the opinion. Eisler, *A Justice for All*, 251–52.

Ironically, Brennan was involved in his own tape-recording scandal during World War II. He had routinely taped office telephone conversations while working at the War Department. Unlike the *Nixon* case, Brennan's tapes saved him from being ensnared in a profiteering and bribery scandal. They convinced

Result: A unanimous Court ruled that the special prosecutor had proved his need to subpoena the tapes. William Rehnquist did not participate in the decision.[38] In what was arguably the most significant portion of the opinion, Chief Justice Burger explicitly recognized that executive privilege was an implied constitutional right, but he then ruled that President Nixon's general, unlimited, and unexplained claim of executive privilege did not justify quashing the subpoena in this case. The Court ordered the president to deliver the disputed tapes to Judge Sirica. Despite President Nixon's public threat to defy any court order to deliver the tapes, in the end he complied. He resigned when the tapes revealed that he had actively participated in the Watergate cover-up.[39]

Nixon v. Administrator of General Services, 433 U.S. 425 (1977)
(Brennan)

Former President Nixon contracted with Arthur F. Sampson, head of the General Services Administration (GSA), to store and care for his presidential materials, including the so-called White House tapes. Under the terms of the contract, there was no right of public access to the tapes. The GSA administrator was required to destroy any tapes Nixon requested after a five-year period, and the administrator was obligated to destroy all remaining tapes after ten years or upon Nixon's death, whichever came first. Ten days after the deal was announced, Congress introduced new legislation designed to abrogate the deal. Congress quickly passed the Presidential Recordings and Materials Preservation Act, which President Ford signed into law ten days later.[40] The new law ordered the GSA to preserve all materials with historical value indefinitely and instructed the GSA to enact new rules for public access to the Nixon materials. Nixon sued, claiming that the act (1) violated separation of powers; (2) infringed on executive privilege; (3) was an unreasonable seizure of his property in violation of his and other persons' rights of privacy and association; and (4) was a bill of attainder. A three-judge district court dismissed the suit, and Nixon appealed directly to the Supreme Court.

---

a special Senate investigating committee that Brennan was just being "a good soldier" and following orders with which he did not personally agree. Clark, *Justice Brennan,* 42; Eisler, *A Justice for All,* 49–50.

37. The fact that the grand jury had found Nixon to be an unindicted co-conspirator was kept secret until the case reached the Supreme Court. Special Prosecutor Leon Jaworski hoped that a well-timed revelation that the subpoenaed tapes would show that the president was personally implicated in Watergate crimes would undercut Nixon's strategy of seizing the moral high ground and claiming that he had merely been defending the office of the presidency.

The prosecution also sought another psychological advantage. President Nixon's appeal to the circuit court was entitled *Nixon v. Sirica.* By appealing directly to the Supreme Court, prosecutors succeeded in renaming the case *United States v. Nixon,* making it clear that they were representing the entire country rather than just a lowly district court judge. Lacovara, "*United States v. Nixon,*" 1065.

38. Rehnquist had been an assistant attorney general in the Nixon administration. After Rehnquist recused himself, Warren Burger put him in charge of allocating tickets to government officials, dignitaries, reporters, and spectators who wanted to hear the oral arguments.

39. President Harry Truman claimed that Richard Nixon was "one of the few in the history of this country to run for high office talking out of both sides of his mouth at the same time and lying out of both sides." Asked whether he thought that President Nixon had ever read the Constitution, Truman replied, "If he has, he doesn't understand it." Miller, *Plain Speaking,* 179, 335.

40. For a detailed discussion of the legislative history, see *Nixon v. Richey,* 513 F.2d 430, 439–445 (D.C. Cir. 1975).

BURGER: I would not say that Congress had no power to legislate in this area. The separation of powers principle does not terminate with the end of incumbency. This statute poses a grave threat of a chilling effect on free communication between presidents and their aides. No government official has any business looking at my private papers for the purpose of sifting them from non-private papers or anything else. This statute significantly impairs executive privilege of all presidents—it violates principles of separation of powers. It is a bill of attainder in the sense of being a congressionally imposed deprivation of access to his own property.

STEWART: There are three attacks facially: (1) separation of powers; (2) bill of attainder; and (3) violation of the First and Fourth Amendments. I do not think that it is a bill of attainder, notwithstanding *Brown*[41] and *Lovett*[42] language. The First and Fourth Amendment issues are and will be very difficult for me as events arise in the future. Seven criteria in §104(a) are designed to protect these when regulations are promulgated. Claims under separation of powers are different, because they involve his presidential actions. This could be made into a statute applicable to all future presidents. Neither Ford nor Carter sees any merit on this claim. I have concluded that as to a former president, it is not unconstitutional.

WHITE: I don't think that there is a bill of attainder that destroys the whole statute. Nor on its face does it violate separation of powers—the United States can take custody of official papers. In the sense of crippling the presidency, this may arise down the road under the regulations as applied. It is not for Congress, but for the courts to decide this. Nor does a seizure of private effects with official materials affect a facial challenge to the statute. But as applied, any private materials ought to go back.

MARSHALL: The government can seize everything for purposes of finding out what's in it.

---

41. *United States v. Brown*, 381 U.S. 437 (1965). A federal act made it a crime for Communist party members to serve as labor union officers or employees. On a 5–4 vote, the Supreme Court struck down the provision as an unconstitutional bill of attainder. The Court tied its decision to separation of powers concerns and said that the clause should be "liberally interpreted." Congress, the majority said, could not use general legislation to punish designated individuals or groups, whether its aim was to punish past acts or to discourage future conduct.

42. *United States v. Lovett*, 328 U.S. 303 (1946). Congress passed legislation firing three named individuals from government jobs in the executive branch and permanently excluding them from any future government employment for which they would be paid, including jury duty. The Court ruled that the act of permanently barring the three from any future public employment violated the bill of attainder clause. The Court ruled that any congressional act that applied either to named individuals or to easily identified members of groups and inflicted punishment without judicial trial was unconstitutional.

Justice Black, writing for the Court, said that "those who wrote our Constitution well knew the danger inherent in special legislative acts which take away the life, liberty, or property of particular named persons because the legislature thinks them guilty of conduct which deserves punishment." The three also claimed that they had been improperly fired, but those claims were pending before the court of claims and were not considered here.

BLACKMUN: Because of my NHPC membership, I am not sure whether I should stay in.[43] I come out with Byron in emphasizing the facial challenge and not seeing any merit in the bill of attainder claim. I think that Carl McGowan made a satisfactory effort to decide what is here now.[44] I will affirm for now, but I may not stick to it.

POWELL: If Ford had vetoed this law, the case would be easy. This is a wholesale intrusion by the legislature into the executive branch, with skimpy protections.[45] But it became law with the concurrence of the legislative and executive branches, even though the statute can hold up a president to ridicule and infamy. Since the president and Congress agree, I don't see how the judicial branch can say that it is facially unconstitutional at a suit of a former president. It is not Nixon, but the private lives of others. I would write a most narrow opinion that nevertheless exposed problems down the road. They should have a substantial deferment in time to publication written into the regulations.

REHNQUIST:[46] I would reject the ex post-facto and bill of attainder claims. Neither *Brown* nor *Lovett* were rightly decided. I am not sure of my ground on the First or Fourth Amendment claims. I am concerned that separation of powers principles require invalidation of this statute. Ford and Carter's views are entitled to respect, but that's all. *Myers'* set-aside in appointment was concurred in by the president—so incumbents' agreement does not determine the issue.[47] But does Nixon have standing? Yes, since Eugene McCarthy was allowed to join as a party in *Buckley v. Valeo*.[48]

STEVENS: The threat of regulations emphasizes disclosure and not deferral for 30 years. But Nixon does not have standing to assert the privacy interests of people whose privacy Nixon himself invaded. On the separation of powers issue, for the most part, custody remains in the executive branch and I have trouble seeing how that invades the executive sphere, even though regulations would require congressional approval. The only problem I have is the bill of attainder claim. If a serious detriment to a named individual is the test, and we presume that Nixon is innocent, this looks like attainder—it is worse than *Lovett*.

Result: The Court rejected all of Nixon's constitutional claims and upheld the act. White, Powell, and Blackmun concurred in the judgment but joined only parts of Brennan's opinion.

---

43. Blackmun was one of fifteen commissioners of the National Historical Publications and Records Commission, which is affiliated with the National Archives and charged with preserving, promoting, and disseminating important historical documents.

44. Federal Circuit Judge McGowan wrote the opinion below.

45. Not only had President Ford signed the bill into law, but his successor, President Jimmy Carter, ordered Solicitor General Wade McCree to defend the law before the Supreme Court.

46. Although Rehnquist recused himself in *United States v. Nixon*, he chose to participate in this case.

47. *Myers v. United States*, 272 U.S. 52 (1926).

48. The Court allowed failed independent presidential candidate Eugene McCarthy to participate as a plaintiff in the landmark campaign financing case, *Buckley v. Valeo*, 424 U.S. 1 (1976).

Kissinger v. Halperin, 452 U.S. 713 (1981)
(Brennan)

Morton Halperin was Secretary of State Henry Kissinger's chief aide on the National Security Council from 1969 until 1970. He resigned in 1970 to protest President Nixon's decision to bomb Cambodia. Kissinger subsequently authorized a wiretap on Halperin's home phone. The tap remained operational for at least twenty-one months, with the results reported to Kissinger and to H. R. Haldeman, Nixon's chief aide. Several years later, when Halperin found out about the tap, he sued various Nixon adminis-tration officials for damages, including Nixon, Kissinger, Haldeman, and Attorney General John Mitchell.[49] Halperin claimed that the wiretap violated Title 3 of the Omnibus Crime Control and Safe Streets Act of 1968 and violated his and his family's Fourth Amendment rights.[50]

The Circuit Court for the District of Columbia ruled that Kissinger, Mitchell, and Haldeman had limited immunity if they reasonably believed that their actions were legal and if they had acted without malice or bad faith. The court ruled that Nixon also had only limited civil immunity, citing the American tradition of equal justice under law.

BURGER: Do the president and his closest advisors have absolute immunity from most damage claims? If not, are they entitled to qualified immunity, and does that mean gra-dients? Does our holding in *Keith* bear on this? In that case, §2511 was held to require a warrant.[51]

Judges and U.S. attorneys deserve absolute civil immunity, stemming from the spe-cial nature of their duties. Since the president delegated the duties to the U.S. attorney, his immunity must be as broad. The attorney general stands between the president and the U.S. attorney. Kissinger was a direct arm of the president. *Keith* allowed wiretaps, but required warrants.

STEWART: A constitutional violation was established as to the Halperins. But we don't reach that issue if the defendants had absolute civil immunity. It is strong medicine, but I am inclined to think that the president has absolute civil immunity for everything he does as president. I also think that derivative immunity is absolute to those who carry out a service that the president personally initiated.

---

49. Halperin found out that his phone had been tapped during an unrelated criminal prosecution of Daniel Ellsberg. *United States v. Russon & Ellsberg,* Crim. No. 9373 (C.D. Cal. May 11, 1973).

50. One time while Halperin was on the phone talking to a friend, his wife accidentally picked up the extension phone. She apologized for interrupting and laughingly added, "Be careful what you say to Mort. The phone is probably bugged." The FBI agent who was transcribing the conversation duly reported to his superiors: "Mrs. Halperin is paranoid. She believes her phone is tapped." Lionel Van Deerlin, *San Diego Union Tribune,* November 30, 1993, B-5. Kissinger also ordered phone taps on other NSC staff he suspected of being soft on the Nixon administration's Vietnam policy, including Anthony Lake.

51. *United States v. U.S. District Court,* 407 U.S. 297 (1972). Often referred to as the *Keith* case, the Court ruled that the Fourth Amendment prohibited warrantless wiretaps in cases involving domestic threats to national security. Prior to this case, the question of whether Kissinger needed a warrant to tap Halperin's phone had not been clearly established.

The tap on Halperin's phone lasted from May 1969 until February 1971. Unless *Keith* were applied retroactively, Kissinger and the other defendants could claim immunity by arguing that they had reason-ably believed that they had the authority to order warrantless wiretaps in domestic national security cases, whether they actually had that authority or not.

WHITE: Both courts held that at a point in time, the tap ceased being a national security tap—and remanded the case to decide whether from the outset it was a national security tap. Liability under the statute suggested at the point when the tap ceased to be tied to national security. The United States did not bring the remand here, and isn't that a tacit conclusion that a statutory violation would not be immune from damages?

If we get over this, the president has some absolute immunity, but it can't be in every situation. But investigation of a possible crime doesn't have absolute immunity. Is this like that? I can't put it on separation of powers, as Potter Stewart does. All have qualified civil immunity as a matter of law.

MARSHALL: I agree with Bill Brennan. I would not DIG.

BLACKMUN: I can't see any difference between absolute immunity with exceptions and qualified immunity as a matter of law. Basically, I agree with Byron, but I would not DIG.

POWELL: The president has absolute immunity from liability in national security cases. These taps were originally ordered to find leaks. I mean immunity from civil liability, not criminal.

We don't need to say that is true of everything he does under Article 2 of the Constitution. We can limit this to national security cases, and resolve any conflict over whether it was purely political surveillance in favor that it wasn't. As to Haldeman, et al., after Halperin left, did he know? I would accept the finding of district court and say that the court of appeals misread the record. I disagree with the holding that *Keith* is retroactive. I would give aides derivative immunity.

REHNQUIST: Out.[52]

STEVENS: I come out close to Lewis. The distinction between absolute and qualified immunity is that the former requires no inquiry into motives. It is very important that presidents have absolute immunity in many areas—not for speeding, etc., and other things where he is not acting as president.

The president has a duty to obey statutes—here, the wiretap statute. In this case, I would say that he was absolutely immune, since he authorized the tap in first place. I would not give absolute immunity to others, however—they would get only qualified immunity.

Result: On a 4–4 tie vote, by default the Court affirmed the court of appeals' decision. Halperin's case was remanded and finally settled in 1991, when Kissinger issued a formal written apology to Halperin and his family. Halperin later returned to the NSC staff under President Bill Clinton, as did Anthony Lake, the target of another of Kissinger's phone taps.

The following year, Nixon v. Fitzgerald *examined whether the president and his aides had absolute immunity from civil liability in cases relating to their official acts and duties.*

---

52. Rehnquist recused himself because he was a former member of Richard Nixon's Justice Department and because one of the named defendants was his former boss, John Mitchell. Rehnquist, however, did not recuse himself in the next case, *Nixon v. Fitzgerald.*

Nixon v. Fitzgerald, 457 U.S. 731 (1982)
(Brennan)

In 1968, Defense Department employee A. Ernest Fitzgerald testified before Congress about cost overruns and production problems associated with the C-5A transport plane. Two years later, he was fired. Fitzgerald filed a grievance with the Civil Service Commission, claiming that he had been fired in retaliation for his testimony. The commission ruled that Fitzgerald had been fired for purely personal reasons and ordered him reinstated with back pay. Fitzgerald then sued a number of White House and Defense Department officials, alleging that they had been responsible for his firing. The list of defendants was gradually whittled down to three: President Nixon and two White House aides, Alexander Butterfield and Bryce Harlow.

The federal district court ruled that Fitzgerald had a valid cause of action and that President Nixon could not claim absolute immunity. Nixon filed a collateral appeal with the court of appeals, which dismissed the appeal summarily for lack of jurisdiction. After Nixon appealed to the Supreme Court, all sides in the litigation agreed that the three named defendants would pay Fitzgerald liquidated damages of $28,000 if the Supreme Court ruled that the president was not entitled to absolute immunity and that Fitzgerald would drop the suit if the Court upheld Nixon's claim of immunity.

BURGER: On *Nixon*, $28,000 turns on what we decide, so for me there is a live case. So I won't DIG or moot the case. There is no cause of action under any statutes. I agree with Lewis that there is no *Bivens* action here—Fitzgerald can pursue only administrative remedies.[53] The president has absolute immunity, and I prefer deciding this case on that ground rather than on the ground that there is no *Bivens* action available. I think that our decision in *Gravel* compels a finding of absolute immunity for both Harlow and Butterfield.[54]

BRENNAN:[55] As to the issue of whether implied causes of action exist in this case, I would choose not to reach it on the merits. The rulings of the district court, that respondent Fitzgerald does have implied rights of action under the Constitution, 5 U.S.C. §7211 and 18 U.S.C. §1505, were not appealable as collateral orders, and those rulings were not certified for interlocutory appeal. The issue was thus not before the court of appeals, as respondents Harlow and Butterfield conceded. Of course we could reach this issue if we wanted to, but we need not. I would choose not to do so.

If we did reach the merits, I would agree with the district court that respondent does have implied causes of action under the Constitution, 5 U.S.C. §7211, and 18 U.S.C. §1505. The respondent is entitled to sue under the First Amendment by virtue of our holding in

---

53. *Bivens v. Six Unknown Federal Narcotics Agents*, 403 U.S. 388 (1971). *Bivens* recognized a judicial cause of action against federal officers who, acting under color of law, caused injury resulting from an illegal search conducted in violation of the Fourth Amendment. Fitzgerald's case was based on a similar theory, known as a "*Bivens* action," claiming that the defendants, acting under color of law, had violated his First Amendment rights.

54. *Gravel v. United States*, 408 U.S. 606 (1972).

55. Adapted from Brennan's talking papers, Brennan Papers, OT 1981, box 581.

Bivens, as recently explained in *Carlson v. Green*.[56] I find no "special factors counseling hesitation" in this case, nor do I find that "Congress has provided an alternative remedy which it explicitly declared to be a *substitute* for recovery directly under the Constitution and viewed as equally effective." Respondent is also entitled to sue under the cited statutes. The flat prohibitions of those statutes, and their obvious intention to benefit federal employees who testified before Congress, lead me to this view. That respondent obtained partial relief from the Civil Service Commission is of no consequence, for that relief is not, and could not be considered, a "*substitute*" for, or "equally [as] effective" as, respondent's present suit.

As to the issue of whether Nixon should enjoy absolute immunity, I feel strongly that we should DIG, primarily because of Nixon's settlement agreement with respondent. This agreement reduces the controversy before us to a mere wager. It is not true, as Nixon suggests, that this agreement is basically the same as any other liability-limiting agreement, because the numbers are all wrong: the great bulk of the payments has already been made, and only a tiny percentage of the overall settlement amount depends on future events. Clearly, this agreement is, from Nixon's standpoint, simply a device to extract a favorable ruling from this Court in the present case—which he would then be able to use in the remanded *Halperin* case—without risking trial in this case, as well.[57]

The way that this issue has been handled by the parties has been deceptive and manipulative from the start. First, the parties didn't even inform us of the agreement for almost a month, and by their own admission they were only prompted to do so by news stories about it. Second, when they did inform us, they were positively misleading. In the "Joint Statement" on this subject they suggested, without actually saying so, that no money had been paid and that money would not be paid until after "subsequent proceedings in the district court." This was untrue: most of the money had been paid already, and most of the rest was to be paid within a few weeks. Moreover, the parties had agreed *not* to go to trial, so that no "subsequent proceedings in the district court" were or are ever going to the place. Finally, the parties didn't actually produce the text of their agreement until August 1981, over a year after it was signed, and then only in response to the Halperins' motion to intervene and the attendant news reports. In short, we have been misled and manipulated from the start on this issue. I just don't think that we should give tacit approval to such conduct by ignoring it.

Even in the absence of this agreement's objectionable overtones, we should DIG. The issue before us is a difficult one under the best of circumstances, and it should be decided on a complete record, including district and circuit court opinions. For all practical purposes, we have *neither* in this case. That's why so much of the briefs, and the oral arguments, addressed the *facts*: both sides are still trying to persuade us that they are in

---

56. *Carlson v. Green*, 446 U.S. 14 (1980). This case allowed a federal cause of action for violations of the Eighth Amendment. Here, a federal prisoner in Indiana died as a result of maltreatment, and his mother was permitted to sue prison officials for violating her son's Eighth Amendment rights. What Brennan proposed here was that as *Carlson* extended the logic of *Bivens* from the Fourth to the Eighth Amendments, the Court should now find a similar cause of action for First Amendment violations. Brennan wrote the majority opinion in both *Carlson* and *Bivens*.

57. *Kissinger v. Halperin*, 452 U.S. 713 (1981).

the right on the underlying issue of liability, apart from the immunity question. More-over, Nixon and Fitzgerald have already agreed not to go to trial. Nixon will never need to interpose any immunity defense against Fitzgerald. So we are being asked to decide an important issue in a case in which our holding will not affect any subsequent proceed-ings (because there won't be any subsequent proceedings), and in which the record be-fore us is remarkably incomplete and sketchy.

Finally, it seems to me that if, at the time we considered Nixon's cert petition, we knew about this settlement agreement, then clearly we would have denied cert. Why, then, should we not DIG now that we do know all the facts?

If we were to reach the merits on this issue, I would vote to affirm for the reasons stated by Justice White in his memorandum in the *Halperin* case.

As to the issue of whether Harlow and Butterfield should enjoy absolute immunity, I think that we should affirm. The case of a president's aides seems to me to be completely controlled by our holdings in *Scheuer v. Rhodes* and *Butz v. Economou*.[58] This conclusion is reinforced by our disposition of Haldeman's case in *Halperin*. Even those who joined with Justice Powell in favoring absolute immunity for the president agreed that Haldeman, who "did not have any recognized or official national-security responsibilities . . . should be treated like other executive officials, who possess only qualified immunity."[59] In this case, there is no claim that Harlow and Butterfield were exercising any national security responsibilities with respect to respondent, so I should think that affirmance is plainly called for on this point.

I could also agree to a DIG on this issue, though. Much of the argument advanced by Harlow and Butterfield is that they should have absolute immunity "derivative" from Nixon's. If we decline to reach the immunity issue with respect to Nixon, there is no reason to reach it respecting them. A DIG would also be consistent with our actual disposition of Haldeman in *Halperin*.

> My votes: 1. I would not reach the issue of implied causes of action.
> 2. I would DIG with respect to Nixon, or alternatively affirm.
> 3. I would affirm with respect to Harlow and Butterfield, or alternatively DIG.

---

58. *Scheuer v. Rhodes*, 416 U.S. 232 (1974). The Court recognized only a limited, qualified immunity for state governors. This case grew out of a lawsuit against the governor of Ohio and other state officials following the May 4, 1970, killing of four Kent State University students during an antiwar demonstration. The court of appeals ruled that the common-law doctrine of executive immunity was absolute and barred any legal action against the named state officials. The Supreme Court reversed, defining executive immu-nity on a sliding scale based on a range of variables, including the official's responsibilities, the scope of their discretion, and the overall circumstances at the time.

In *Butz v. Economou*, 438 U.S. 478 (1978), the Court rejected the government's claim that federal offi-cers were absolutely immune from civil lawsuits alleging that they violated citizens' constitutional rights, even if the violations were knowing and deliberate. The majority reasoned that "if [federal officers] are accountable when they stray beyond the plain limits of their statutory authority, it would be incongruous to hold that they may nevertheless willfully or knowingly violate constitutional rights without fear of li-ability." Instead, federal executive officials were entitled only to qualified immunity, except for "excep-tional situations" where absolute immunity was "essential for the conduct of public business."

59. Citing Justice Powell's draft opinion of May 19, 1981, p. 42.

WHITE: I don't agree with Brennan. There is a controversy. On the cause of action, we can undertake it even if it was not appealed. I think that civil service remedies may caution courts not to imply either a *Bivens* or a statutory cause of action. I would go off on that ground and reverse. If we reach the immunity issue, I think the same thing.

MARSHALL: I would DIG. There is no absolute immunity for the president.

BLACKMUN: This case stinks after the agreement. This is a feigned, lawyer lawsuit, and lawyers misled the Court. Why is the issue of absolute immunity presented now, when it will never go to trial? I would DIG both cases. I would let the lower courts rule on any implied cause of action, and on the president's immunity. I agree with Byron—there is only qualified immunity.

POWELL: The case ought not to be DIGged. We have to reach the cause of action question, and I would. I would hold that there is no basis for implying either against the president. I would say, therefore, that there is no reason to get to the immunity questions. I think that *Bivens* is a threshold question, and we can reach it if we want to—it disposes of both of these cases.

REHNQUIST: I would imply that there is no *Bivens* or statutory cause of action here. I think that the president is absolutely immune. I could join four others in saying that there is no cause of action here. I have problems with the settlement agreement. I would reverse with Powell last year, or on a *Bell v. Hood* analysis that the cause of action issue is jurisdiction enough to reach.[60] Can we decide a case where the case got to the court of appeals under the collateral order doctrine?

STEVENS: On the merits, maybe we should expedite *Bush v. Lucas*—there is not a cause of action in the employment area.[61] We should never imply a cause of action against the

---

60. *Bell v. Hood*, 327 U.S. 678 (1946). Plaintiffs sued individual FBI agents for damages sustained during a search that allegedly violated the Fourth and Fifth Amendments. The lower courts summarily dismissed the suit for want of federal jurisdiction, on the ground that the Fourth and Fifth Amendments did not give private individuals a cause of action for cash damages. The Supreme Court reversed on the jurisdictional question, saying that the federal courts had jurisdiction to consider all cases arising under the Constitution and the laws of the United States. The possibility that the plaintiffs' complaint did not state a valid cause of action did not foreclose federal jurisdiction. The district court should have accepted jurisdiction first and *then* decided whether the complaint stated a valid cause of action. The Supreme Court limited itself to the jurisdictional question and did not decide whether the plaintiffs had a valid cause of action.

61. *Bush v. Lucas*, 462 U.S. 367 (1983). The Court unanimously decided that federal employees did not have a cause of action against their superiors for First Amendment violations. In this case, a NASA engineer was demoted after he made several public comments critical of his employer. Justice Stevens, writing for the Court, ruled that there was no need to authorize a new, nonstatutory cause of action in this case, because the employee already had a comprehensive system of grievance procedures and substantive remedies provided under Civil Service Commission regulations. In this case, the Civil Service Commission's Appeals Review Board recommended that Bush be restored to his former position and awarded back pay, and NASA complied with the recommendation.

Stevens was careful to add that the federal courts' jurisdiction to decide federal questions included the power to authorize nonstatutory causes of action to award damages for constitutional violations, even if Congress has not expressly authorized such a remedy.

president, who anyway is absolutely immune. But I would not allow derivative immunity to the President's aides.

O'CONNOR: I don't see how we can reach the implied cause of action issue. If we could, I would say that there was none. On immunity, the president is absolutely immune. I am troubled by the settlement, in that there is nothing left for the district court to decide.

Result: In an opinion by Lewis Powell, the Court ruled 5–4 that President Nixon had absolute immunity against civil suits for damages caused in the course of his official acts. The four dissenters, White, Brennan, Marshall, and Blackmun, claimed that the president was entitled only to a limited grant of immunity. In a related case, Harlow v. Fitzgerald, *the Court decided 8–1 that the president's aides had only qualified immunity, rather than derivative absolute immunity.*[62]

---

62. *Harlow v. Fitzgerald,* 457 U.S. 800 (1982). The Court decided on an 8–1 vote that presidential aides were immune unless their actions violated clearly established law. Because the events in *Halperin* took place before *Keith* clearly made warrantless taps illegal, Kissinger, Mitchell, and Haldeman argued that they were immune, unless *Keith* was retroactive. Powell, writing for the Court, also indicated that White House aides might be entitled to absolute immunity if they could prove that their actions "embraced a function so sensitive as to require a total shield from liability." Only Chief Justice Burger dissented, arguing that presidential aides should have derivative absolute immunity.

CHAPTER 7

FOREIGN AFFAIRS

Schneiderman v. United States, 320 U.S. 118 (1943)
(Murphy)

William Schneiderman was born in Rumanov, Russia, in 1905 and emigrated with his parents to the United States in 1908. He grew up in Los Angeles and filed to become a citizen in 1924. On his citizenship application he swore that he was not an anarchist (anarchists were the only political group specifically excluded from becoming naturalized citizens). Schneiderman submitted his naturalization petition in 1927, stating under oath that he was attached to the principles of the Constitution. He became a citizen later the same year.

In 1939, the Immigration and Naturalization Service (INS) sought to revoke Schneiderman's citizenship on the ground that he had obtained citizenship by fraud. The INS alleged that he gave a false oath of allegiance and was not sincerely attached to the principles of the Constitution. Schneiderman was a member of the Communist Workers Party of America, the Young Workers League, and other Communist organizations, and according to the INS, these groups were inherently hostile to the Constitution and "the American way." Schneiderman claimed that his membership in these associations was consistent with his support of the Constitution and that he had never sought, advocated, or taught the overthrow of the United States. A federal district court in California ruled that Schneiderman had obtained citizenship fraudulently and ordered his citizenship revoked. The court of appeals affirmed.

The conference discussion contains an interesting exchange about Solicitor General Charles Fahy and defense lawyer Wendell Willkie. Fahy had repeatedly urged the Court to delay its decision, and several Justices suspected that he was seeking a delay for purely political reasons. Willkie, the unsuccessful Republican candidate for president in 1940, represented Schneiderman. Fahy was solicitor general under Roosevelt and Truman. In 1949, Fahy became a judge on the U.S. Court of Appeals for the D.C. Circuit, where he served until his death in 1979.

Certiorari Conference of April 22, 1943

STONE: Schneiderman brought the case here in fall, and the government has been stalling it off ever since because of our Soviet allies. I take no stand in this, because we ought not to have to appease our allies. [MURPHY: Fahy wrote to the Chief Justice, who reads the letter, referring to Willkie's letter encouraging delay—February 25, 1942.] I feel embarrassed by that kind of request (Fahy's, for non-judicial considerations), and if we yield to it we might be criticized as determining policy here as an adjunct to diplomatic policy, and we ought not to do that.

The onus ought not to be placed on us. It ought to be placed on the State Department. The only thing that keeps this Court alive and gives it influence is that we are not influenced by things extrinsic to our job.

ROBERTS: I think that we ought to take it.

BLACK: The charge would be that the New Deal Court delayed the case, and I would prefer to try it. But our foreign policy is such, and this nation is in such desperate danger, that we ought to follow it. This is not a run of the mine case.

STONE: I can't recall a case where we have shaped our course by anything other than the law and the record.

BLACK: We have a responsibility that we cannot escape.

REED: We are not separate and apart from rest of government. I would allow the government's request for a postponement.

FRANKFURTER: I don't see the constitutional issues thrown up in this discussion. This proposition is that the time of hearing a case should be heard by extra-legal considerations. When this Court decides it shall not hand down a decision until another case is decided, or when an opinion is announced by a southerner rather than a northerner in certain cases, these are extra-legal and appropriate considerations.[1] What Willkie says, in effect, is that there is no foreign issue involved—I will take this policy from the State Department, not Willkie.

Schneiderman may be disadvantaged, because this is a desirable time to win his case. So the client is not to suffer by delay. Imagine the consequences of seeing Willkie saying that the government is taking this position when Russia is saving our lives.

DOUGLAS: I would hear it.

MURPHY: I would hear it.

BYRNES: I think it ought to be heard, but I would just have the Chief Justice call in Fahy and Willkie.

[MURPHY: After a prolonged and heated discussion, the Chief Justice decides, and all agree, to ask Solicitor General to move in open court for a continuance—to file a formal motion and let Willkie reply. Finis.]

Second Conference

STONE: The government canceled Schneiderman's citizenship papers on the ground that they were procured by fraud and were unlawfully procured. I will begin by first examining the statute which contains the naturalization provisions on which government relies. I disregard §8 for my purposes. The section was directed at anarchists. It is the government's contention here that he is communist. That is a form of government. Section 381 provides that the applicant shall declare and renounce, etc. The government relies

---

1. Frankfurter was prescient. Seven months later, in November 1943, Harlan Fiske Stone assigned Frankfurter to write the majority opinion in *Smith v. Allwright*, invalidating Texas's white primary system. After Robert Jackson warned Stone that it would be a mistake to have a Jewish northerner take the lead in such a case, the Chief Justice withdrew the assignment and reassigned it to Stanley Reed of Kentucky. For more details, see *Smith v. Allwright* in chapter 15.

on the fact that he did not bear true faith and allegiance to the Constitution of the United States, but that is not separable from an attachment to the principles of the United States. So I give this no importance. Section 130 is the important one.

The evidence overwhelmingly supports the trial judge's finding of facts. Schneiderman was associated with the Communist party. It promotes his interests. The trier of fact could find that he knew what their propaganda was. He was willing to have those ideas preached, and if they indicated a want of attachment, the trier of fact could find a lack of attachment. What do the documents say? What do they show? They show that they taught systematic disobedience of the law. They advised all sorts of things to upset military discipline and to make the army ineffective. The means was first to undermine the legal functioning of the government. If one advised future citizens that the thing for them to do is to tear down systematically and lawlessly the government, one is not attached to the Constitution.

Two courts below found by the evidence that this man believed and advocated the overthrow of the government. They did not mean anything like moral ideas—simply bullets and guns.

Exhibit 8: *State and Revolution*, by Vladimir Illyich Lenin. Revolution is not by force of moral ideas, but by bullets and guns. This was to be a proletarian revolution achieved by force. They wanted to do away with representative government, destroy private property, and set up a dictatorial form of government. It was not for the protection of the minority—it was for strictly a minority rule. There would be no Bill of Rights. It would be an abolition of all existing forms of government. Inasmuch as it was achieved by force, the right to amendment is by one way. If we do not uphold the trier of fact when he is right, we disregard the Congress. *Part of the program is the freedom to disclaim everything.* It is within the meaning of the statute that this naturalization was unlawfully acquired, for by his conduct he showed that he was not attached to the Constitution of the United States. He did not disclaim anything, and the triers of fact could have found as they did. Congress can keep men out of this country who are not attached to the government of the United States.

ROBERTS: If this showing had been made at the time of Schneiderman's application, it would have been good grounds for a refusal to grant citizenship.

BLACK: I oppose. He testified that he did not and never has been dedicated to or believed in force and violence. What right did they have to say he believed in those things when his conduct was exemplary? He never did an act of violence. And I don't agree with you politically. The doctrine of imputed guilt is offensive to me. The judgment of the district court should be reversed. It is the punishment of a man today because of his beliefs, and nothing else. There is nothing to support the findings as I see them.

Reconsidering for ten years after he became a citizen—that is something. But then you have two types of citizens, apparently—one born and the other naturalized. I would not try it on rights of patent. Without fraud or deception he was given citizenship, and now to draw a fine distinction between behavior and belief is not realistic. He is being tried because he was a Communist.

STONE: Congress never intended to exclude a man because of belief or his opinions. [MURPHY: ?????]. The clear and present danger test has nothing to do with it.

REED: Congress has plenary power in an absolute sense. They can make a man's skin the subject of the citizenship test. Has he behaved as a man—as a man should who is attached to the Constitution? We should not construe him as unattached to the Constitution just because he taught communism. I do not think there was enough for the trier of fact. If I felt otherwise, I would not go along.

FRANKFURTER: I have never registered in the primary in any party. I have voted in all of them. I am a Mugwump.[2] Debs, LaFollette, and others I have voted for. If you are going to do this about the Communists, what are you going to do with keeping this country as a powerful example as the last great hope of mankind, as Lincoln said. This is as near to religion as I know it; I have no formal religion. I am for affirming.

RUTLEDGE: My present inclination is to reverse.

STONE: There is, under this statute, a probability that he could be canceled forty years after his admission to citizenship.

Result: The Court ruled 5–3 that Schneiderman's citizenship could not be revoked absent "clear, unequivocal and convincing" evidence of fraud in procuring his citizenship. Frank Murphy, writing for the majority, noted that while Congress had plenary discretion to establish the conditions of naturalized citizenship, there were other rights at stake here and special burdens of proof were required when the government sought to revoke—rather than to deny—a person's citizenship. While Murphy did not explicitly decide the case on the basis of Schneiderman's First Amendment rights, these concerns were implicitly central to Murphy's analysis, which focused largely on Schneiderman's rights of speech, thought, freedom, toleration, and the free play of ideas.

Douglas and Rutledge concurred, noting that Congress could have barred Communists from being naturalized (as it had barred anarchists) but that it had never done so and certainly could not do so retroactively. Rutledge worried that if Schneiderman's citizenship could be stripped away more than a decade after it was granted, then naturalized citizens could never be secure in their rights and would literally be reduced to second-class citizenship.

In dissent, Stone, Roberts, and Frankfurter argued that there was ample evidence that Schneiderman had lied to obtain his citizenship and that the revocation was amply justified on that basis. Jackson did not participate in the case because he had been attorney general during the early stages of government proceedings against Schneiderman.

Bridges v. Wixon, 326 U.S. 135 (1945)
(Murphy)

Harry Renton Bridges, an Australian seaman, emigrated to the United States in 1920 and became a leader of the Marine Workers Industrial Union in San Francisco. In 1938, the federal government tried to deport him because of his alleged affiliation with the Communist party. Harvard Law School dean James Landis conducted the hearing. After hearing testimony from witnesses on both sides, Landis

2. The Mugwumps were a progressive Republican faction in the late nineteenth century who stressed the virtues of community and civil society. The term came from an Algonquian Indian word meaning "great men."

found that Bridges was not currently a member or affiliate of the party (under the statute in effect at the time, current membership or affiliation was required to justify deportation) and ruled that Bridges should be allowed to remain in the country.[3] In 1940, the House of Representatives passed a private bill to deport Bridges, but Attorney General Robert Jackson lobbied against the bill and it died in the Senate. That same year, however, another bill aimed at deporting Bridges passed both houses of Congress. The new law, which became §23 of the Smith Act, allowed the government to deport resident aliens if, at the time of entering the United States or at any time afterward, they had belonged to or were ever affiliated with any organization that believed in, advocated, advised, or taught the overthrow of the American government by force or violence.

Judge Charles Sears presided over Bridges's second deportation hearing.[4] Largely on the unsworn testimony of two government witnesses (Harry Lundeberg and James D. O'Neil), Judge Sears found that Bridges had formerly belonged to the Communist party. Combined with Bridges's union activities, it was enough for Sears to recommend that Bridges be deported. On appeal, however, the Board of Immigration Appeals unanimously reversed Sears's findings and voted to allow Bridges to remain in the United States. But then Attorney General Francis Biddle overruled the board's decision and restored Sears's deportation order. Bridges surrendered to federal authorities and immediately filed for a writ of habeas corpus. The writ was denied by both the district court and the court of appeals, and Bridges appealed to the Supreme Court. I. F. Wixon was the district director of the Immigration and Naturalization Service.

STONE: I will begin by stating the facts. Harry Bridges is an alien and subject to the power of Congress. Some years, the statute was that one affiliated with any political party that taught subversive things was held to be deportable. Such a proceeding was under way when this Court held that it was at time proceedings were brought. Dean Landis's hearing came first. And then Congress amended the statute, and a new proceeding was instituted. Judge Sears was appointed specially to hear the *wholly administrative* proceeding, without review, except by habeas corpus. It was held that Bridges was a member of the party, and it went to the administrative review board, who reversed Judge Sears. And then the attorney general reversed the board and the case comes to us on habeas corpus.

The first principle here is that the power to exclude at will, as with the power to admit and naturalize, resides in Congress. It is a plenary power. While in this country he is, although an alien, entitled to Fifth and Fourth Amendment protections.

It is a different question as to whether Congress can expel a man for any reason, or no reason. Picture Czechoslovakia under a constitution such as ours, and their problems with Sudeten Germans.

Proof and procedure come next. Where Congress sets up standards, he is entitled to trial. There must be notice and a hearing. But it must be administrative. The situation is the same as a review of a Labor Board decision, although those reviews are direct.

---

3. Prior to the first Bridges hearing, Dean Landis was widely rumored to be on the inside track for the next Supreme Court seat. After ruling in Bridges's favor, however, he was no longer welcome on Capitol Hill or in the White House. After resigning from Harvard and going to work for Joe Kennedy, Landis was convicted of tax evasion in 1961. Within a year after he served a brief jail term, Landis apparently drowned in his swimming pool. Larrowe, *Harry Bridges*, 220–21.

4. Sears was formerly a judge on the New York Court of Appeals.

The narrow question is this: Congress has set up this narrow standard. Was Bridges a member of the organization so described? Were there rules not observed, so as not amounting to due process? What evidence is before us? Whether he was a member comes down to testimonies: (1) Lundeberg, who was an unfriendly witness, gave his testimony.[5] He claimed that Bridges said that he was a member of the party. Bridges denied this. *The other witnesses were not called.* It has some significance. It is a conflict of testimony, and it is for the trier of fact to determine who is to be believed. (2) O'Neil's testimony.[6] Bridges denied all.

All of it was evidence to be considered by the trier of fact. He determines the weight and the probity of the evidence. A question is raised whether it was properly reserved under the rules. He is supposed to make a record of it. Another rule plainly contemplates that those who heard the statement may give testimony. Judge Sears and the attorney general held that it was not a rule of exclusion. It was for the trier of fact.

Kelly and Barlow's testimony was then discussed. This again is for the trier of fact. On affiliation, there was a great deal of testimony for Judge Sears and the attorney general. The attorney general has filed a communication in which he points out that he did receive it, and it was entitled to a consideration on the *merits*.

Our function here is a narrow one. Did this man come within the relevant act, and was there evidence to support it? If so, our duty ends. Exportation because of affiliation with the Communist party is said to infringe on the Constitution. But can it be if Congress has plenary power to exclude? Holmes said that a man has no constitutional right to be a policeman. There is no limit on the right of Congress to expel a man. His presence here is contrary to the will of Congress.

BLACK: Suppose it said a member of Democratic or Republican party.

ROBERTS: This is a trying case. But I have the attorney general acting in a capacity under which he is authorized to act, and he is acting in good faith. Congress has made it letter clear, and I come out where you do with the greatest reluctance.

BLACK: I would reverse it. If you once concede they have constitutional rights, I am not willing to say he can be deported when not liable for deportation at the time that he did it. And you have a finding on the evidence. I doubt that the Court would let this stand for a conviction of any crime—and this is not a crime. Its consequences are the same. I don't see how Sears could do it. I don't understand the mental operations of how a man could do it. You have a board—where there is more than one mind and you have views contrary. And then the attorney general supported Sears. When you come to talk of other government charges, it is weak and nebulous. The proofs required in *Schneiderman* ought to be appreciated here. There is guilt here applied retroactively.

---

5. Harry Lundeberg was the president of a rival union, the Maritime Federation of the Pacific. He testified that Bridges admitted to him in 1935 that he was a Communist.

6. At one point in the investigation, James D. O'Neil gave incriminating testimony against Bridges, but he was not under oath at the time and he recanted soon afterward.

STONE: No, there isn't.

BLACK: I won't sustain it. I can't understand a man accepting such evidence as O'Neil's, and whether one of them would have sustained this conviction but for O'Neil's testimony, which is like accepting hearsay evidence. He is deported because he is a labor union leader. *If an alien leader has constitutional rights, I am not going to say that he can be deported for his labor leadership.*

REED: I lay aside the questions of assembly and free speech. I hope that I lay aside the fact that he is a labor leader, because Congress has the power to do what it did. When I come to the evidence, I say that I must depend on what the administrative agency does. And it must have substantial evidence. We have no right to say that Sears did not have evidence before him that justified his actions. Congress has the power, so we come to one thing—and that is whether we should sustain the conviction. My feeling is that he has not had a fair hearing when you sum it all up. It offends my sense of how we shall approach a deportation.

FRANKFURTER: I am not persuaded by Reed. But as a lad brought over here to become an American citizen, I have a special appreciation of this, having come in as an alien. I speak from a depth of conviction about this country and its future. If you reverse this, don't write a law on the books that will embarrass the future of the Congress and this country. I consider the action of the attorney general as unwise and foolish. But don't reach a judgment that will seriously hamper the freedom of action of this country. It will be a great injustice to immigrants to this shore. They wanted a freer country. You will be doing a great injustice to the future, because members of Congress will say that we will let no one come in. Lincoln spoke of pernicious abstractions.[7] Aliens are protected under due process because they are persons. We are here concerned with the power of Congress to deal with aliens. He spoke of the fellowship of "American fellowship."

Congress may do it by a general act or by administrative machinery. Is the mode of administration justifiable? I think that Biddle is a *damn fool* in this action.

BLACK: It was an organized industry, as the court that started it tapped wires and gathered all of the evidence.

FRANKFURTER: But it was Biddle who reversed what the board did. If there are any attacks on constitutional grounds, I could not sustain without saying that this Court's practice has been wrong for 150 years. I don't want to shut the doors on Congress. I haven't reached the point that it is an outrage. I beg of your conscience not to write into law something born out of a special situation.

---

7. Abraham Lincoln used this phrase to avoid taking sides in a debate that raged during the closing days of the Civil War—whether Southern states would have to be readmitted to the Union or whether retained their place in an indivisible Union with their rights, privileges, and most importantly, their congressional representation intact. Lincoln wanted to avoid the "pernicious abstractions" and struggled to find a pragmatic solution that all sides could accept.

DOUGLAS: If this provision was in the statute at the time that he was admitted, I would have to view it differently. I can't agree with the broad dicta this Court gave to ex post facto law. See, for example, *Ex parte Garland*.[8]

STONE: It was a rotten thing that Congress did, but I would be slow to subject others to greater injustices in an effort to save Bridges.

DOUGLAS: I can't see where it is anything but an ex post facto law.

Result: The Court ruled 5–3, in a decision written by William O. Douglas, that resident aliens have First Amendment rights and that Bridges's political and union activities were constitutionally protected. To Douglas, the fact that Bridges was a militant trade unionist was not sufficient under any applicable statutes to justify deportation. The case turned on the majority's definition of "affiliation," which Douglas narrowly defined as a working alliance to bring to fruition the overthrow of the federal government. The definition of affiliation urged by Sears and Biddle, Douglas said, was "too loose." Douglas also ruled that O'Neill's testimony should have been excluded from evidence entirely and that Lundeberg's testimony was not credible. Frank Murphy wrote a concurring opinion that was even more harshly critical of the government's efforts to deport Bridges.[9]

Stone, Roberts, and Frankfurter dissented. Robert Jackson did not participate in the decision because of his prior participation in the case as attorney general.

The case caused considerable hard feelings inside the Court when Owen Roberts and Felix Frankfurter accused Black, Douglas, and Murphy of leaking the conference vote to syndicated columnist Drew Pearson. Pearson published an article predicting the vote the day before the decision was scheduled to come down. Stone called a special conference to discuss how to respond, and the Justices decided to delay the decision for several weeks so that Pearson's story would not be entirely accurate. At the special conference, Frankfurter accused Black, Douglas, and Murphy of leaking the vote. Even though all

---

8. *Ex Parte Garland*, 71 U.S. (4 Wall.) 333 (1867). In 1860, A. H. Garland was admitted to the Supreme Court bar. In 1861, he joined the Confederacy and was elected to the Confederate Congress. After the war, he received a full presidential pardon. In 1865, a new federal law prohibited lawyers from practicing in federal courts without swearing an oath, on penalty of perjury, that they had remained loyal citizens and had not participated in any hostilities against the Union. The Court ruled that the oath requirement was unconstitutional because it violated both the ex post facto and bill of attainder clauses. The oath amounted to an ex post facto law, the Court said, because it criminalized actions that were legal when committed and inflicted new penalties on actions that were previously criminal, but for which Garland had been pardoned. The Court considered the permanent exclusion from practicing one's profession for past behavior, or any exclusion from "the ordinary avocations of life," to be a severe enough punishment to trigger the ex post facto clause. The Court also noted that Garland had been admitted to federal practice prior to the change in the oath. His pardon helped, as the Court ruled that Congress could not impose additional conditions on presidential pardons. Finally, the Court distinguished this oath from a nearly identical oath that Congress required of most public officials. Such oaths could be required as a condition of public office, but lawyers, though officers of the court, were not officers of the United States.

9. Murphy wrote, in part: "The record in this case will stand forever as a monument to man's intolerance of man. Seldom if ever in the history of this nation has there been such a concentrated and relentless crusade to deport an individual because he dared to exercise the freedom . . . guaranteed to him by the Constitution. . . . For more than a decade powerful economic and social forces have combined with public and private agencies to seek the deportation of Harry Bridges."

three denied it, Owen Roberts severed his formerly close friendship with Black and from that day on refused to shake hands with Black, Douglas, or Murphy.[10]

Harry Bridges later became an American citizen and lived in San Francisco until his death in 1990.

Banco Nacional de Cuba v. Sabbatino, 376 U.S. 398 (1964)
(Douglas)

An American commodities broker, Farr, Whitlock and Company, contracted to buy Cuban sugar from C.A.V., an American-owned Cuban corporation.[11] *Before the contract could be executed, the Cuban government seized all of C.A.V.'s Cuban property. In order to secure its sugar shipment, Farr, Whitlock made a second contract with the new Cuban entity that replaced C.A.V. The new contract assigned the bills of lading to the Banco Nacional de Cuba (BNC).*[12] *BNC had its agent in New York deliver the bills of lading to Farr, Whitlock, which accepted the paper and used it to secure payment from their customers. The American company then refused to pay BNC for the sugar, claiming that any payments rightfully belonged to C.A.V. The Supreme Court of King's County, New York, ordered Farr, Whitlock to deliver payment in full for the sugar to C.A.V., which it promptly did. BNC then filed suit in federal court, claiming that the money was rightfully theirs.*

The federal district court acknowledged that the act of state doctrine ordinarily would preclude judicial review of any act by a recognized sovereign government within its own territory. However, the district court issued a summary judgment against BNC on the ground that the act of state doctrine did not apply when the state's actions violated international law.

The court of appeals affirmed, ruling that the matter was justiciable under the so-called Bernstein *exception to the act of state doctrine, which allows judicial review of foreign governments' actions if the executive branch explicitly says that it does not oppose judicial review in a particular case.*[13] *The court of appeals ruled that the executive branch did not oppose judicial review, citing as evidence two*

---

10. Douglas, *The Court Years*, 32–33. According to Douglas, Drew Peason later revealed to him who had leaked the vote, but Douglas did not say who it was.

11. Compania Azucarera Vertientes-Camaguey de Cuba. Peter Sabbatino was a temporary receiver appointed to represent the stockholders of the original Cuban sugar corporation in the United States after Fidel Castro's government seized the company's Cuban assets.

12. A bill of lading is a combination of a receipt, title document, and transportation contract. It is issued by the party in charge of transporting the goods to acknowledge possession of the goods to be shipped. It identifies the goods, the parties, and the terms of the contract and contains an agreement to deliver the goods at a particular time and place.

13. The *Bernstein* exception was established in two cases decided in the Second Circuit Court of Appeals between 1947 and 1949. The first case was written by Learned Hand, and the second by his cousin, Augustus Hand. In *Bernstein v. Van Heyghen Freres Societe Anonyme,* 163 F.2d 246 (2d Cir.), cert. denied, 332 U.S. 772 (1947), Arnold Bernstein was the sole stockholder in a German corporation, the Arnold Bernstein Line, which owned a ship called the *Gandia.* During World War II, the Nazis imprisoned Bernstein and forced him to transfer ownership of the company to a German citizen, Marius Boeger, who transferred the shares to the Belgian corporation named in the lawsuit. After the war, Bernstein sued to recover damages for lost use of the vessel and for insurance payments collected when the ship was sunk during the war. Learned Hand ruled that the only relevant consideration for the court was "how far our Executive has indicated any positive intent to relax the doctrine that our courts shall not entertain actions of the kind at bar."

U.S. State Department letters stating that the American government did not wish to comment on the Sabbatino *case while it was being litigated.*

Both the certiorari conference, where the Justices discussed whether or not to hear the case, and the conference after oral argument are included here. The certiorari conference provides an interesting look at how several Justices sought to avoid the case entirely—not because they thought it lacked merit, but out of concern for what Tom Clark called "judicial statesmanship."

Certiorari Conference

WARREN: I want to ask the solicitor general for his views before we act on it.

BLACK and DOUGLAS: Both vote to grant. Douglas says that it is wrong.

CLARK: I think that the decision below is right and would deny cert.

HARLAN: It is out of line with prior cases, but it may be right since the petitioner is a branch of the Cuban government.

BRENNAN: I vote to grant cert. We might want to ask the solicitor general to argue on the merits.

STEWART: I would ask for the solicitor general's views now.

WHITE: I would deny cert, although I think that our decision was wrong and that we should reverse.

GOLDBERG: This is an act of state case, and I would ask for the solicitor general's response.

CLARK: The Court will reverse this case, so I want to avoid the results of the decision reversing the lower court. Judicial statesmanship requires ducking.

HARLAN: This is a case where the petitioner is an arm of a hostile government, and the federal courts need not open its doors to it.

Conference of October 25, 1963

WARREN: I reverse. I agree in large part with the United States government's position. The act of state doctrine is positive law, but I would not go so far as to say that when the executive says we should not interfere we should not. We have the power, but of course we should give great weight if the executive says it would be embarrassed if we intervened.

Because the executive branch had remained silent, Hand applied the act of state doctrine and dismissed Bernstein's complaint.

In 1949, Augustus Hand initially dismissed Bernstein's claims in a similar action against a Dutch corporation. *Bernstein v. N.V. Nederlandsche-Amerikaansche Stoomvaart-Maatschappij,* 173 F.2d 71, 75–76 (2d Cir. 1949), modified, 210 F.2d 375 (2d Cir. 1954). Shortly after that decision, however, the State Department issued a letter stating that the government did not object to a judicial determination of Bernstein's case. Based on this "*Bernstein* letter," Judge Hand modified his initial order and permitted Bernstein's lawsuit to proceed.

BLACK: I reverse. The act of state doctrine is the proper law. We should follow it. We need not follow what the executive says, though we should adhere to our government's policy.

WARREN: If we have no word from the executive, we still should follow the act of state doctrine. It would be within the discretion of the Court, whatever representations the executive makes.

DOUGLAS: I reverse.

CLARK: I would vacate with directions to dismiss. I would prefer that, but I will reverse.

HARLAN: I would reverse. The act of state doctrine is hoary and sound. It is still good and it is substantive federal law. Hand's substitute in *Bernstein* need not be reached here. This is federal law, not state law. This is not a constitutional rule, but is federal common law—*Clearfield*, interstate water apportionment, etc.—that is binding on the states.[14] It borders on a separation of powers problem. We should not swallow a hegemonic international law argument.

BRENNAN: I agree with what has been said. The act of state doctrine is judge-made federal law—I would reverse.

STEWART: I agree with the Chief Justice and vote to reverses. I also agree with Harlan on the act of state doctrine—not abstention doctrine.

WHITE: I reverse. I am not entirely clear as to the scope of the act of state doctrine. It should be a rule of federal law. *Erie R.R.* does not cover this, but on that I am not so sure. However, since this way or it is a violation of international law, perhaps we should not defer to the executive. The guarantor could have been impleaded, and if it had happened the district court would have no jurisdiction, as there would be an alien on both sides. I would deny the motion.

GOLDBERG: I would reverse.

Result: The Court reversed in an 8–1 decision. Under the act of state doctrine, Harlan wrote, the case was not justiciable. The State Department letters meant merely that the State Department did not wish to comment on pending litigation, and such vague, noncommittal statements were not sufficient to trigger the

---

14. *Clearfield Trust Co. v. United States*, 318 U.S. 363 (1943). The Court decided that the Constitution did not require federal courts to apply state common law where the federal government's constitutional prerogatives were at stake. The decision seemed to contradict *Erie v. Tompkins*, which had previously held that there was no such thing as federal general common law.

The case involved a forged check, drawn on the federal treasury, which the J.C. Penney Co. cashed in good faith. The company's collection agent, Clearfield Trust, endorsed the check with "Prior Endorsements Guaranteed" and collected on the check from the federal government, also in good faith. When the fraud was discovered, the government sought reimbursement from Clearfield Trust, saying that it had guaranteed all prior endorsements. Clearfield claimed that local Pennsylvania law barred the federal claim because the government had waited for more than a year before giving the company notice of the forgery. The Supreme Court, however, refused to follow local law. Justice Douglas wrote that federal law governed the rights and duties of the United States on commercial paper and that in the "absence of an applicable Act of Congress, it is for the federal courts to fashion the governing rule of law according to their own standards."

Bernstein *exception. The Court broadly defined the act of state doctrine and narrowed the potential scope of the* Bernstein *exception by arguing that the executive branch was better situated than the courts to review and respond to foreign expropriations, and that as a rule judges had no business reviewing such matters. The majority pointedly did not rule on the validity of the* Bernstein *exception. Byron White, the sole dissenter, argued that the courts could review the legality of Cuba's actions under international law, absent a specific objection by the State Department or other responsible executive authority.*

Alfred Dunhill of London, Inc. v. Cuba, 425 U.S. 682 (1976)
(Brennan)

In 1960, Cuba nationalized five large cigar manufacturing companies. Several import companies then mistakenly paid the Cuban government for cigars shipped by the privately owned companies before they were nationalized. The original factory owners sued to recover these payments, and they also sought restitution for the purchase price of cigars shipped after nationalization.

The district court ruled that the act of state doctrine meant that the Cuban government's decision to nationalize property owned by Cuban nationals was not reviewable in American courts and that Cuba had the right to all post-nationalization payments as the new owner of the plants. The court also ruled, however, that the former factory owners could recover the pre-nationalization payments mistakenly paid to the Cuban government. The court of appeals reversed on this point, ruling that because the debt situs of the pre-nationalization payments was Cuba, the act of state doctrine applied to these payments as well.

Antonin Scalia argued on behalf of the United States as amicus curiae seeking reversal of the court of appeals judgment.

BURGER: There are two claimants against a single debtor—the owners and the investors. Dunhill paid Cuba and was sued by the owners for the same money. Cuba hasn't proved that its decree appropriated these accounts. The district court held that Castro had been paid for pre-seizure and so could the owners. The court of appeals said that they could not have judgment against Castro and mistakenly paid him. Thus I could DIG, but if not I would affirm.

DOUGLAS: I would reverse for Byron's reasons.

WHITE: This reduces down to Cuba suing A and B, and claiming $10 from each. And A says Cuba owes me $5, and B says Cuba owes me $15. When Cuba can get only $5 from A, why shouldn't B get Cuba's $5 that it's getting from A?

BLACKMUN: No statement of the lawyer is an act of state—it is the retention of payments mistakenly made by Dunhill to Cuba that is the act of state. Dunhill has to share the hardships of everybody else where properties were appropriated by Cuba.

POWELL: I did not vote with the majority on *Banco*.[15] There has been an act of state by Cuba, but our courts are not bound by this if our State Department doesn't say we shouldn't.

REHNQUIST: Judge Mansfield did as much as possible with our disparate opinions in *Banco*.

---

15. *Banco Nacional de Cuba v. Sabbatino*, 376 U.S. 398 (1964).

Conference Following Reargument

BURGER: It was not the lawyer's words, but Cuba's refusal to honor the claim that is enough to be an act of state. But when a foreign country uses our courts, it takes our procedures lock, stock, and barrel. If the debt situs was in the United States, maybe we can ignore the 1960 decree. If I were to overrule the act of state doctrine, it couldn't be because of what the secretary of state tells us. We granted cert to reconsider *Sabbatino*.

WHITE: The court of appeals said that the act of state was not the original decree, but the course of conduct that repudiated the original debt. I don't think that repudiation was an act of state, but I could come out with an affirmative judgment in any event, based on *Citibank*.[16] Or I would buy the attorney general's new dichotomy between political and commercial transactions. But now nobody supports the court of appeals holding as to the act of state it found. I would reverse and say that an affirmative judgment is warranted.

BLACKMUN: I agreed with Thurgood last time, and I haven't been pushed off that ground.

POWELL: I would have voted with Byron in *Sabbatino*, and while the Court should consider the fact of foreign involvement, it should not be conclusive as the act of state doctrine holds.

REHNQUIST: I agree with Byron.

STEVENS: I don't thoroughly understand your positions to affirm—whether this was an act of state—no matter how I analyze this case.

Result: The Supreme Court ruled that the importers' mistaken payments to the Cuban government were not covered by the act of state doctrine and that Cuba could be ordered to pay restitution to the original factory owners. Byron White's plurality opinion restricted the act of state doctrine and limited sovereign immunity. The act of state doctrine, he wrote, was limited to acts that were both public *and* governmental *in nature. White distinguished Cuba's sovereign activities from its commercial activities. The Cuban government was not immune because Cuba's debt was purely commercial—regardless of its original reasons for expropriating the cigar manufacturers' property. Cuba did not exercise "powers peculiar to sovereigns" but "only those powers that can also be exercised by private citizens."*[17]

---

16. *First National City Bank v. Banco Nacional de Cuba*, 406 U.S. 759 (1972).

17. While most of White's opinion attracted only four votes, his views commanded a clear majority in Congress. Faced with growing problems caused by commercial enterprises run by foreign governments, Congress passed the Foreign Sovereign Immunities Act (FSIA) of 1976, which limited foreign sovereign immunity claims to "public, governmental acts." The act vested jurisdiction in the federal courts to decide cases involving foreign states engaged in commercial activity directly affecting the United States, and "nonjury civil actions against foreign states in which an exception to sovereign immunity is applicable." The FSIA left the issue of sovereign immunity for the courts to decide, rather than the State Department, on the theory that judges were more likely to decide cases "on purely legal grounds rather than on an ad hoc, diplomatic basis." *Sanchez v. Banco Central de Nicaragua*, 770 F.2d 1385, 1390 (5th Cir. 1985). Most federal judges, however, have been cautious about limiting sovereign immunity or extending the "commercial activities" exception and have allowed foreign governments to assert the act of state doctrine as a complete defense to civil lawsuits.

First National City Bank v. Banco Para El Comercio Exterior de Cuba,
462 U.S. 611 (1983)
(Brennan)

In 1960, Cuba established the Banco Para El Comercio Exterior de Cuba (Bancec) as an "autonomous credit institution." Bancec sued the First National City Bank (Citibank) to recover money owed on a contract executed prior to the Cuban revolution to deliver Cuban sugar to an American buyer. When the Cuban government confiscated Citibank's Cuban assets, Citibank sought to set off the value of its seized assets against any judgment. Bancec claimed that as an autonomous credit institution, it could not legally be held responsible for the acts of the Cuban government. The Cuban government later dissolved Bancec and divided its assets between Banco Nacional de Cuba and the Cuban Ministry of Foreign Trade. The district court ruled that Bancec was never independent of the Cuban government and allowed the set-off. The court of appeals reversed, ruling that Bancec was a legally autonomous institution and not merely an alter ego of the Cuban government.

In conference, the Justices attempted to balance domestic law, international law, American foreign policy, and their individual perceptions of national interest.

BURGER: That bank was Cuba from the beginning. The court of appeals treated the bank as separate and apart from Cuba.

BRENNAN:[18] I don't agree with either the district court or the Second Circuit in this case. On balance, however, I would affirm.

There is a sort of threshold problem in this case, namely why Bancec is still supposedly litigating at all when it hasn't been in existence for twenty years. It would have made much more sense to find out who the Cuban claim belongs to now, and what the chain of title was, and litigate it on that basis. But it appears that the parties didn't litigate the case that way, so I suppose we are stuck with the assumption that Bancec is still the plaintiff; and so we have to decide whether Bancec is identical to the Cuban government. On the other hand, if someone makes a persuasive argument that we should remand to ascertain who the present owner of the claim is, I would not object to doing so.

On the identity question, it seems to me that the heart of the district court's holding was its finding that Bancec was conducting a "governmental function"—indeed, a function that would be governmental even in a noncommunist society. That might be a sensible place to draw the line; it includes entities like Bancec without reaching a boot factory in Moscow. However, I am inclined to think that "governmental function" alone is not enough. There is some legitimate social and international utility in having these separate government corporations to deal in commercial or banking matters, and we should not lightly breach their separate existence. What it comes down to is this: would we be willing to allow a foreign citizen to assert a counterclaim against the Export-Import Bank or the Federal Reserve Bank, based on an alleged tort of the CIA or the army? I would say not; these special, separate corporations should be allowed their independent status even though they are concededly part of the government.

---

18. Adapted from Brennan's talking papers, Brennan Papers, OT 1982, box 618.

On the other hand, the Second Circuit's test might be too restrictive. It would pierce the corporate veil only when the corporation is itself involved in the government's wrongful act. That exception is no exception at all; in any case the corporation would probably be liable in its own right as a joint tortfeasor. I can conceive of other situations where we would want to permit counterclaims of this type—for example, where the foreign corporation is itself the confiscated property, or where the foreigner's claim is closely factually related to the counterclaim. But that is not the case here. Here, there is really nothing more than the fact that Bancec is a government entity, which in my view is not enough.

WHITE: The act of state doctrine is not in this case at all if Bancec was doing a commercial function, even if it was governmental. If the district court was right, we hold that Bancec was performing functions which exposed it to the counterclaim. The court of appeals' test is wrong—a crime would be more like what is necessary to pierce the corporate veil.

MARSHALL: This bank is an alter ego, and Citibank's counterclaim lies.

BLACKMUN: Bancec is the holder for our purposes. Does Citibank get 100 percent, or must it share with everyone else? So I would not pierce the veil, but would take Bancec on its own terms and affirm.

POWELL: Given the fact that we have no relations with Cuba and that it does not recognize international law, Bancec should be treated as an alter ego engaged in commercial business—as such, department can file a counterclaim under federal law. The Second Circuit decision is contrary to our law and national interest.

REHNQUIST: I don't agree that there is a presumption of alter ego, rather of juridical independence.

STEVENS: There is a presumption of judicial autonomy. We can't have different rules of law. The fight here is really between this bank and other American concerns whose property was seized by Cuba. I agree with Harry. I agree with Brennan that Bancec may not own their claim. I would affirm, but would remand to trace ownership of the claim.

O'CONNOR: I would remand to see what entity succeeded to Bancec's claim. That does not seem to command a Court. I would start with a presumption of judicial autonomy according to international law.

Result: In a 6–3 decision, Sandra Day O'Connor ruled that Citibank had the right to set off the value of its confiscated property. She began by noting that while the FSIA did not control the outcome of the case, it established a presumption of separateness between a foreign state and state-owned enterprises. This presumption would be respected unless (1) equity mandated otherwise or (2) the foreign state so dominated the subsidiary that it became an alter ego or agent of the government. In this case, equitable principles of both "federal common law" and international law mandated Citibank's right to a set-off.

Although Bancec was established as a separate juridical entity, the Cuban government had dissolved it and had transferred its assets to governmental entities. This meant that the real beneficiary of any decision to respect Bancec's separate juridical status would have been the Cuban government. O'Connor refused to allow Cuba to gain a windfall in American courts that it could not have obtained for itself without waiving its sovereign immunity and answering for its illegal seizure of Citibank's assets. Nor could Cuba escape from Citibank's counterclaims by retransferring assets to other separate juridical entities. To permit this, O'Connor concluded, would allow governments to flout international law simply by creating new juridical entities whenever the need arose.

Zemel v. Rusk, 381 U.S. 1 (1965)
(Douglas) (Brennan)

After the State Department banned American travel to Cuba, Louis Zemel, a private citizen, sought to visit the island to gather information and satisfy his intellectual curiosity. When Secretary of State Dean Rusk refused to validate Zemel's passport, he sued, claiming that the travel restrictions violated his First Amendment free speech and association rights and his Fifth Amendment liberty and due process rights.

The federal government claimed that the executive branch could impose foreign travel restrictions in either of two ways—as authorized by the Passport Act of 1926 and the Immigration and Nationality (McCarran-Walter) Act of 1952 or by using the inherent authority of the president under Article 2.

Conference of March 5, 1965

WARREN: I would affirm. This is a Fifth Amendment case, and there would be no violence to *Kent* or *Aptheker* to affirm.[19] While Americans have a right to travel abroad, it must be in keeping with national policy. The president does not have the power to regulate travel as he sees fit—the *Steel* case—he must have congressional authorization. But here, the Constitution's pervasive foreign affairs power allows Congress to paint with a broad brush.[20] It has done this under the 1926 act. Here, there was an appropriate dele-

19. *Kent v. Dulles*, 357 U.S. 116 (1958). The Court, in a 5–4 decision, reversed Secretary of State John Foster Dulles's refusal to issue passports to Rockwell Kent and others who refused to file affidavits with the government denying that they belonged to the Communist party. Douglas wrote the majority opinion, which held that the Passport Act of 1926 did not authorize the secretary of state to deny passports based on applicants' beliefs or associations. Douglas thought that the right to travel—both domestically and internationally—was an important aspect of liberty protected under the Fifth Amendment. "Outside areas of plainly harmful conduct," Justice Douglas wrote, "every American is left to shape his own life as he thinks best, do what he pleases, go where he pleases." Any regulation of this liberty must be pursuant to the proper law-making functions of Congress, and any attempted congressional delegation of that authority must have adequate standards and will be narrowly construed. Douglas suggested, however, that not even Congress could refuse to issue passports based solely on an applicant's political beliefs or associations.

In *Aptheker v. Secretary of State*, 378 U.S. 500 (1964), Herbert Aptheker and other American Communist party officials sued the secretary of state after they were refused passports on the ground that they were "political subversives." The Court, in a 5–4 decision by Arthur Goldberg, sided with Aptheker and struck down the sections of the Subversive Activities Control Act (also called the McCarran Act or the Internal Security Act) which authorized the secretary of state to deny passports to "subversives" on the ground that these provisions too broadly and indiscriminately restricted freedom of travel. Goldberg tied the right to travel to constitutional rights of liberty, speech, and association under the First and Fifth Amendments.

20. *Youngstown Sheet and Tube Co. v. Sawyer*, 343 U.S. 579 (1952).

gation of congressional power, and the president acted permissibly under his executive order of 1956. His power was like that under the Taft-Hartley law in the *Steelworkers* case. The emergency still exists. Area restrictions have been exercised since the Civil War. If we did not have area restrictions, U.S. citizens would or might get us into war by storming Cuba and killing Castro. I would affirm on the 1926 act and the executive order of the president.[21] We do not have to reach the 1952 act. The three-judge court is O.K.[22]

BLACK: The three-judge court is O.K. I agree that there is a right to regulate travel. The right rests not with the president, but with Congress. Congress alone can do it, at least in peacetime. The existence of war would make a difference, but we are not at war and I don't reach the war powers question. There is ample reason to regulate travel, but the 1926 act does not give the president this type of power. The president has no power to do this without an act; that gets into lawmaking. Therefore, this is within the *Steel Seizure* case for me. We should require that the delegation be explicit. Congress can't delegate the power to the secretary of state. I don't agree with *Curtiss-Wright*.[23]

DOUGLAS: It was not a proper three-judge court. On the merits, I would agree with Hugo. I don't think that the 1926 act is sufficient, although I think that Congress may constitutionally do so. But the target is a regulation and not a statute, and therefore the three-judge court is wrong. I would remand for an appeal to the court of appeals.

CLARK: It was a proper three-judge court. I agree with the Chief, but I think that we might have to reach the 1952 act as well to define his powers.[24] We need not reach the "inherent" power of the president, for the 1926 and 1952 acts are sufficient authority.

---

21. The Passport Act of 1926 authorized the president and secretary of state to withhold passports on national security and foreign policy grounds and allowed the executive branch broad discretion to establish rules governing foreign travel and passports.

22. There was some question as to whether the three-judge district court was properly empaneled to decide Zemel's constitutional challenges. Zemel made both constitutional and nonconstitutional claims. He questioned the constitutionality of the 1926 and 1952 acts, but he also claimed that the secretary of state had exceeded his statutory authority under these laws in refusing to validate Zemel's passport.

The government argued that Zemel's case was really an attack on administrative policy and did not raise any serious constitutional issues and that a three-judge district court should not have been convened. The Court ultimately decided that the three-judge court was proper. Zemel's case raised substantial constitutional questions, and Zemel should not be forced to give up his nonconstitutional claims in order to have his case heard by a three-judge court.

23. *United States v. Curtiss-Wright Export Corp.*, 299 U.S. 304 (1936). *Curtiss-Wright* recognized that the executive and legislative branches had broad authority to conduct foreign policy and that their authority over foreign affairs was much greater that their authority to regulate domestic politics. Because of the delicacy of external relations and the extraordinary authority of the president to conduct foreign policy, Congress could delegate to the president a degree of discretion and authority that would not be admissible in domestic affairs. The Court specifically noted that the executive branch had broad inherent authority to respond to international emergencies, even in the absence of congressional approval or authorization.

24. The Immigration and Nationality Act (also known as the McCarran-Walter Act) of 1952 made it unlawful to travel abroad without a passport. Congress left untouched, however, the broad discretion that had been exercised by the executive branch in this area since the original Passport Act was passed in 1926. Many scholars argued that congressional silence implicitly ratified these long-established administrative practices.

BLACK: I am not sure on the three-judge court question.

HARLAN: I agree with Bill Douglas that it was not a proper three-judge court. On the merits, I agree with the Chief and with what Tom has said subject to the 1956 act. We need not reach the president's "inherent" power.

BRENNAN: On the three-judge court, it is an attack on the statute. On the merits, Congress has the power and it does not turn on an emergency. The president has no "inherent" power. The 1926 act is adequate. The 1952 act does not support it, as it is a criminal statute. The secretary of state may impose area restrictions, but it does not mean that there can be criminal penalties. Whether there is would be dependent on other acts, for example the 1952 act. I affirm.

STEWART: I affirm. The three-judge court was proper.

WHITE: I affirm.

GOLDBERG: I affirm. I agree with the Chief. I do not reach the 1952 act. The 1926 act allows area restrictions to be applied.

Result: Writing for a 6–3 Court, Earl Warren held that Congress could deny American citizens the right to travel to other countries, even in peacetime. The Passport Act of 1926 was a valid delegation of congressional power to the executive branch, and the secretary of state acted within his delegated authority in imposing restrictions on American travel to Cuba. Zemel's Fifth Amendment liberty rights were not absolute and were subject to reasonable limitation, while his rights of free speech and association did not include an unlimited right to travel to a foreign country to gather information. "The right to speak and publish," Warren concluded, "does not carry with it the unrestrained right to gather information."

In dissent, Hugo Black argued that the Passport Act unconstitutionally delegated legislative powers to the executive branch. William O. Douglas added that any restrictions on the right of travel during peacetime must be highly particularized, so that First Amendment rights would not be abridged in the absence of a clear, countervailing national interest. Arthur Goldberg argued that the executive branch had no inherent power to restrict peacetime travel, and that Congress had not delegated any authority to impose travel restrictions in either the 1926 or 1952 acts. Regional travel restrictions have proved extremely difficult to enforce and for the most part have been abandoned, although some travel restrictions to Cuba remain in force.[25]

---

25. *United States v. Laub*, 385 U.S. 475 (1967); *Travis v. United States*, 385 U.S. 491 (1967). These cases held that while government-imposed area travel restrictions were permissible civil regulations, violations by persons holding valid passports were not criminally punishable under §215(b) of the Immigration and Nationality Act. In 1999, the Clinton administration began to relax travel restrictions to Cuba for journalists, academics, students, and those with relatives on the island.

Haig v. Agee, 453 U.S. 280 (1981)
(Brennan)

Philip Agee, a former CIA employee living abroad, renounced his oath of confidentiality and began exposing CIA officials working in other countries.[26] In 1979, he suggested that Iran release the American hostages in exchange for CIA documents, which Agee would help to analyze. Using the Passport Act of 1926, Secretary of State Edmund Muskie revoked Agee's passport. The State Department informed Agee that he had the right to an administrative hearing and offered to hold such a hearing in West Germany (where Agee was living) within five days. Agee immediately sued, claiming that the secretary of state was not authorized by Congress to revoke passports and that the State Department's actions violated Agee's right of freedom of travel and his right to criticize government policy. Agee also alleged that the summary process by which his passport was revoked violated his due process rights under the Fifth Amendment. The district court ordered Agee's passport restored, ruling that Muskie had exceeded his authority under the Passport Act. The D.C. Circuit Court of Appeals affirmed. By the time the Supreme Court decided the case, Alexander Haig had replaced Edmund Muskie as secretary of state.

BURGER: Agee's acts were in violation of his own agreements, and he will continue as his speech shows—and that has no First Amendment protection. I would reverse on the narrow ground that he openly violated his contract with the government.

STEWART: *Kent v. Dulles* seemed to say that Congress had to authorize regulations as to passports.[27] That creates tension with *Curtiss-Wright*.[28] I am not concerned that the administrative practice test is the proper standard.

WHITE: The statute does not authorize any cancellation of passports, but it is conceded that passports may be revoked for the same reasons that they may be denied. If that is so, whenever a reason comes up it is the first time, and administrative practice is not a controlling requirement.

MARSHALL: I agree with Judge Robb, reading him as resting on the Constitution.[29]

BLACKMUN: I agree with Judge MacKinnon, and would also decide the constitutional questions raised and find them to be without merit.[30]

POWELL: Section 211(a) has been on the books a long time and there has never been an attempt to limit its broad authority to the president. The regulation is perfectly clear on its face, and the statute authorizes it. The only shadow over it are *Kent* and *Zemel,* and they can be easily distinguished.[31] I would also reach the constitutional issue. The First Amendment can't protect fingering American agents.

---

26. Agee reportedly exposed up to a thousand agents and operatives worldwide. Several American agents were brutally murdered after Agee identified them, including Richard Welch, the CIA chief of station in Athens.

27. *Kent v. Dulles,* 357 U.S. 116 (1958).

28. *United States v. Curtiss-Wright Export Corp.,* 299 U.S. 304 (1936).

29. Circuit Judge Roger Robb wrote the majority opinion below. *Agee v. Muskie,* 629 F.2d 80 (1980).

30. Circuit Judge MacKinnon wrote the dissent in the case below. *Agee v. Muskie,* 629 F.2d 80 (1980).

31. *Zemel v. Rusk,* 381 U.S. 1 (1965).

REHNQUIST: I would reverse, but may write separately to emphasize my view that the First Amendment argument fails for the same reason that revelation of troop ship sailing dates failed in *Near v. Minnesota*.[32] As to the right of travel abroad, it may be regulated or canceled by Congress. I also doubt that Congress can restrict the president's right to regulate passports—*Zemel* and *Kent* are wrong.

STEVENS: I agree with Byron, assuming that *Kent* and *Zemel* are correct and that this is for Congress. I would say that §211 is a delegation to the president of a broad, indeed, a complete discretion, including the power to revoke. Even though Robb was right on the history, Byron is correct that it is always a first time. There is no substance to either constitutional claim.

Result: The Supreme Court ruled 7–2 that the revocation of Agee's passport was both congressionally authorized and constitutionally proper. Warren Burger, writing for the majority, noted that under the Passport Act the secretary of state had the explicit power to deny passports. While the act never explicitly conferred upon the secretary of state the power to revoke passports, Congress had implicitly consented to this administrative construction through a long succession of Passport Acts. Burger concluded that the power to revoke was indistinguishable from the power to deny.

The Court also confirmed that there was no fundamental right to international travel and no violation of due process in the summary manner that Agee's passport was revoked. Finally, the majority rejected Agee's First Amendment argument, ruling that it was his conduct and not his beliefs that were being regulated. The Court found a high likelihood of serious damage to national security by Agee's conduct, which justified the government's decision to revoke his passport.

William Brennan's dissent focused on the "staggering" discretion given to the executive branch in this case, with its potential to be used against citizens who merely disagreed with the government's foreign policy.

---

32. *Near v. Minnesota ex rel. Olson*, 283 U.S. 697 (1931). Chief Justice Charles Evans Hughes wrote that restrictions on a free press, including prior restraints, could only be imposed in the most exceptional circumstances, such as during wartime. Hughes began by quoting Holmes's opinion in *Schenck v. United States*, 249 U.S. 47 (1919), and then he added the famous illustration to which Rehnquist refers: "'When a nation is at war many things that might be said in time of peace are such a hindrance to its effort that their utterance will not be endured so long as men fight and that no Court could regard them as protected by any constitutional right.' No one would question but that a government might prevent actual obstruction to its recruiting service or the publication of the sailing dates of transports or the number and location of troops."

CHAPTER 8

FEDERALISM

THE LIMITS OF CONGRESSIONAL POWER

United States v. Darby Lumber Company, 312 U.S. 100 (1941)
(Douglas) (Murphy)

The Fair Labor Standards Act of 1938 (FLSA) set minimum wages and maximum working hours for employees engaged in the production of goods for interstate commerce and prohibited the interstate shipment of goods made by child labor.[1] The act also required employers to keep adequate records of their employees' wages and hours worked.

Fred W. Darby, the owner of Darby Lumber Company in Georgia, was indicted for violating the FLSA wage and hour limits and for failing to keep adequate employee records. Darby claimed that all of his lumber manufacturing was done intrastate and was beyond the constitutional authority of Congress. The district court agreed and quashed the indictment. District Judge Barrett ruled that Congress did not have the authority to regulate or prohibit the intrastate manufacture of lumber and could not penalize employers for failing to conform with federal wage and hour provisions, regardless of whether the lumber would eventually be shipped in interstate commerce. To allow Congress such broad powers over intrastate production, he wrote, would infringe on sovereign state powers and undermine our federal system of "an indestructible union composed of indestructible states." The federal government appealed from the district court directly to the Supreme Court.

In conference, Hughes had an unintended effect on James McReynolds and Harlan Fiske Stone.

Conference of January 4, 1940

HUGHES: States the case and all the issues. Sections 6 and 7 are involved here, also §15.[2] Section 3, dealing with definitions, should be noted first.[3] "Commerce," "goods," and "produced means" are defined, but there is no definition of the word "for" in "Production *for* commerce." The district court said that if the scope of the statute is limited to production directly connected with interstate commerce, the act was valid. But even an

---

1. 29 U.S.C. §201 et seq.

2. Section 6 established minimum wage guidelines, initially set at 25 cents per hour. Section 7 established a standard work week of forty-four hours. Section 15 prohibited the shipment of any goods made in violation of §6 or 7 and required employers to keep adequate records of employees' wages and hours worked.

3. Section 3 defined commerce as "trade, commerce, transportation, transmission, or communication among the several states or from any state to anyplace outside thereof."

intent to use products later in commerce was not sufficient. Note what the indictment charges. Paragraph 4 of the first count: that a "large proportion" was pursuant to outside orders. Paragraph 19: the absence of charges was noted by the district court. In construing the indictment, the district court noted Darby's intention to sell his goods in commerce. The indictment also charges that production was complete. Are we bound by the district court's interpretation of the indictment? Does the same rule apply to constitutional issues as to cases involving the statute?

1. Congress's interstate commerce power knows no limitation except as in the Constitution itself. This we have always held, since *Gibbons v. Ogden*.[4] How about *Dagenhart*[5] and the *Kentucky Whip and Collar* case?[6] The latter involved pure intrastate production, but Congress was held to have the power to regulate its shipment. Where there is no action in support of state action, can Congress act? Yes. Transportation is an act in commerce, and unless due process is involved, Congress can do as it wants. Congress must not impinge on the constitutional qualifications of its power, and this qualification is in the due process provision. Unless the Fifth Amendment intervenes, Congress can use its power for any purpose it sees fit. Questions of ulterior motives are not

---

4. *Gibbons v. Ogden*, 22 U.S. (9 Wheat.) 1 (1824). This landmark case involved rival government licenses to operate ferryboat service between New York and New Jersey. Aaron Ogden purchased a New York state license giving him the exclusive right to operate his boats in New York waters. In 1793 his main competitor, Thomas Gibbons, obtained a federal license from Congress to operate a ferry line between the two states. The Supreme Court ruled that Ogden's state license violated the commerce clause and was void. John Marshall's opinion recognized that Congress had broad power to regulate interstate commerce, including the right to regulate activities within individual states if they threatened to affect the flow of commerce. Marshall defined commerce broadly to include all forms of commercial intercourse that concerned, extended to, or affected more than one state. Congress also had the right to make the rules for carrying out such intercourse, including the power to regulate navigation. Marshall implied, however, that states retained some concurrent powers to regulate interstate commerce, as long as their actions were compatible with federal policy. In his concurring opinion, William Johnson argued that Congress's commerce clause powers were exclusive and that individual states had no power to regulate interstate commerce even in the absence of federal law or policy. Aaron Ogden soon went bankrupt, and Thomas Gibbons became a very wealthy man.

5. *Hammer v. Dagenhart*, 247 U.S. 251 (1918). Congress barred from interstate commerce goods produced by children under the age of fourteen (under the age of sixteen in some cases). Roland Dagenhart sued U.S. Attorney W. C. Hammer on behalf of his two minor children, asking the courts to invalidate the law and allow his two children to continue working in a North Carolina cotton mill. The Court ruled 5–4 that the law exceeded Congress's commerce clause powers and invaded state police powers over local manufacturing, production, and trade. William Rufus Day wrote that *excluding* goods from interstate commerce was not the same as *regulating* commerce, especially when the goods themselves were not inherently harmful. Justice Day also ruled that the Tenth Amendment "expressly" limited the scope of the commerce clause and granted the states broad police powers. Finally, the Court temporarily revived the idea that the manufacture and production of goods was distinct from commerce and was exclusively a state concern.

6. *Kentucky Whip and Collar Co. v. Illinois Central Ry. Co.*, 299 U.S. 334 (1937). The plaintiff company sought to compel the railroad to ship goods made by prison labor. Congress had passed a law prohibiting the shipment in interstate commerce of most convict-made goods and had required that exempted goods be clearly labeled if made by prison inmates. In upholding the statute, the Court distinguished *Hammer v. Dagenhart*, ruling that Congress's interstate commerce powers were plenary and unlimited, except by the terms of the Constitution itself.

material. Here the amount paid was $500 (circa) a year. There was no deprivation of property in a due process sense.

The transportation counts are O.K. The transportation counts stand on a different policy from the production counts. The latter are not a part of interstate commerce and are deficient. The present act is unique in that it reaches into the field of production. A mere intent to engage in commerce does not make it a part of commerce. But there is another principle. Where an act is not part of commerce, it still may be regulated by Congress if there is a substantial relation to commerce—that is, if there is an injury, close and immediate, to interstate commerce. That is an express constitutional power. Local acts may be within the reach of Congress. While a transaction may be local and intrastate, it may still be within reach of Congress if it has a close and substantial relation to interstate commerce. In all labor board cases, the board has considered the facts and have applied them to interstate commerce, and we have, too.

But a single qualification should be noted. If these principles are extended to remote relationships, our dual system would be at an end. Production is not in itself commerce. But the "close and substantial relationship" test cuts in. Usually, Congress has provided machinery for determining that question. Here, however, it provides no machinery for determining whether a relationship of production to interstate commerce exists in a particular case. Rep. No. 2182—House Labor Committee report—production in the act covers every act, no matter how trivial, which has a relationship to commerce. The serious question is whether the act could be upheld where there is no way provided for an employer of finding a way out if he was under a net of the act.

The first question is: is the statute too indefinite to permit criminal prosecution, and is that because of a lack of a proper definition of "*for* production" in the phrase "production for commerce?" How could an employer be advised? Would an employer know he was subjected to the act?

The second question is: if we undertake to construe the act to give it content as to the meaning of the phrase "production *for* commerce," does it mean any production where later there may be a shipment of goods outside the state? Are we to decide production *for* commerce in the sense that goods are ordered for interstate commerce? If the act would be valid if applied to production of goods ordered in commerce, then it might be restricted. If a statute is of doubtful constitutionality if construed one way but valid another way, we should take the latter.

The third question is: what is the construction of this indictment? Does "said" relate to whatever has been ordered? If the act is construed as debarring the defendant from showing the relationship of his business to commerce, then it is bad.

So with this I pass to case #330.[7] Here there is a minimum wage order providing a minimum wage in excess of the statutory minimum. We go to §6 of the act. It defines the industry committees. Paragraph 6: the industry committee may recommend highest wage for classification, and in determining this they shall consider, etc. But there was no

---

7. The companion case was *Opp Cotton Mills v. Administrator of the Wage and Hour Division of the Department of Labor*, 312 U.S. 126 (1941). After a series of hearings, an industry committee appointed by the administrator recommended that a uniform minimum wage of 32.5 cents per hour be established for the textile industry. After the administrator adopted the committee's recommendations, Opp Cotton Mills

classification in this case. The idea is that first, an industry committee is to make a general investigation, but not in the technical sense of holding hearings for findings. The committee divided on sectional lines. Who is to fix the standards for the committee? That is important in a conviction with what the committee did.

The administrator then made his findings and issued his orders. The committee, he finds, reached its findings in accordance with the law. But that, I sense, is only in conviction with the propriety of the procedure. On page 309 the administrator observes, "I find there will be no substantial employment, etc." On page 318, his conclusion: "I hereby find, etc." It is clear to me that that is all that he did find.

[MURPHY: *McReynolds is sound asleep, mouth open—and Stone is dozing away.*]

The court of appeals (3–0) has little to say on the subject. There is nothing here in the administrative findings, such as we have had in labor cases, as to the connections of the business and whether there is a close and substantial relation to interstate commerce. The finding of the administrator was consciously and solely directed on its connections with *employment.* It is an unusual statute in its application. I think of the first case as to validity of statute, and in the second of this extraordinary report of the administrator.

Then the final, final point: Is this act within the power of Congress? This is the most important case we have had by far in connection with the commerce power. I pass.[8]

McREYNOLDS: I pass.

STONE: On the first point, I think that the transportation charge is valid. It is a regulation of Congress, without or with its motions. On the other branch of the case, which has to do with it affecting commerce, acts affecting commerce could be brought into a constitutional scheme. Congress has the constitutional power to regulate, as it did in the *Shreveport* case.[9] Here we are dealing with a new situation. It may be found in the act's introductory language that a sub-standard wage in any state does have a profound effect on commerce. No textile manufacturer would say that substandard wages did not affect commerce in general and his commerce in particular. I think that this act should be sustained. This act means that wages paid in the manufacture of goods is so related to commerce that Congress could stop the evil at its source. If at the time of manufacture the goods were intended for interstate commerce, then it could be sustained.

---

and other textile manufacturers sued to have the administrator's orders set aside and asked the Supreme Court to declare the FLSA unconstitutional.

The Court, speaking through Harlan Fiske Stone, held that the FLSA was within the commerce power of Congress and did not violate either the Fifth or Tenth Amendments. Because of the complexities of the country's economic situation, Stone wrote, Congress of necessity had to delegate some of its authority to administrative agencies. Congress could reasonably rely on the agency's factfinding as long as the process conformed to established legislative standards and definitions. In this case, there were adequate standards and definitions to guide the industry committee and the administrator, and the administrator's rulings were consistent with the act's declared intent to raise the minimum wage to 40 cents per hour "as rapidly as economically feasible without substantially curtailing employment."

8. Murphy's conference notes show that in the formal conference vote at the end of discussion, the Justices voted in reverse order of seniority, with Hughes and McReynolds both passing.

9. *Shreveport Rate Case,* 234 U.S. 342 (1914).

Once you cross the bridge that substandard wages operate to disrupt commerce, then you do not need a finding in a particular case. I am rather inclined to think that this is one of the few cases where you can say, without a finding, that substandard wages affect commerce. Does the wage paid in the manufacture of goods always count for commerce? No, if it covers goods which may or may not go into commerce. I would interpret those words to mean "goods intended or destined for commerce."

The question of the indictment remains. I would interpret the indictment as meaning just that—we could interpret the indictment differently from the trial court. This is an extraordinary case. But I would go with the majority on that point.

HUGHES: The first question is in regard to the indictment. We have always said that the construction of the indictment is a matter for the trial court.

ROBERTS: With respect to transportation and comity, I agree with you. With respect to control of goods, I think that we have to give credence to what Congress said, and stop discrimination between states. I think that we have to uphold it as an effort to reach something which has a direct effect on commerce. The committee report says that production in the act covers every act, no matter how trivial, which has a relationship to commerce. On the indictment, I think that we could take the trial court's construction and go right to the statute. To reach an evil, maybe you have to affect something else. I would reverse in the first case [*Darby*] and affirm in the other [*Opps*].

BLACK: I agree with Stone and Roberts on commerce. It is not essential that they be intending this at the time.[10]

REED: It was fully within the power of Congress to determine this issue for itself.

FRANKFURTER: The suggestion of the Chief Justice is that if Congress passed an act complementary to the state, we could not escape this case. The root of this case is the reach of the commerce clause. These products have to go into the stream of commerce. I hope that the Court will adhere to the procedures worked out—narrowly. All questions of criminal procedure should be left where they belong. I think that there is enough in the indictment.

Result: A unanimous Court upheld the Fair Labor Standards Act and overruled Hammer v. Dagenhart. *This case was the death knell for idea of dual federalism—the theory that the Tenth Amendment set a specific limitation on the power of the federal government—and blurred the distinction between local and national commerce.*

Harlan Fiske Stone wrote that the Tenth Amendment was "but a truism that all is retained which has not been surrendered." It was, he said, a mere declaration of the relationship that existed between the state and the federal government as established by the Constitution before the amendment was passed. Its intent was merely to "allay fears that the new national government might seek to exercise powers not granted, and that the states might not be able to exercise fully their reserved powers." The

---

10. Black helped to steer this legislation through the Senate in one of his last legislative acts before taking his seat on the Court. In effect, Black voted for the legislation twice—once as a senator and the second time as an Associate Justice.

amendment did not deprive the federal government from resorting "to all means for the exercise of a granted power which are appropriate and plainly adapted to the permitted end." The power of Congress over interstate commerce was extended to intrastate activities that so affected interstate commerce—or affected Congress's ability to regulate interstate commerce—as to make the regulations an appropriate means to the attainment of a legitimate government end. With this ruling, the Supreme Court left the scope and reach of the interstate commerce to the sole discretion of Congress in all but the most extreme cases. Behind the scenes, however, Hughes was deeply unhappy with the decision and only grudgingly joined Stone's opinion. McReynolds, who had also passed at the conference, retired from the Court before the decision was announced.[11]

Progressives cheered the decision, which removed the last legal doubts about the constitutionality of New Deal legislation. Critics, especially in the south where attachment to state's rights ran strongest, complained that states' rights were now "as dead as the gallant boys from North Carolina who fell on the scarred slopes of Gettysburg" and that "now the states, like the Negro in the Dred Scott *decision, have no real rights which the Federal Government is bound to respect."[12]*

Wickard v. Filburn, 317 U.S. 111 (1942)
(Douglas) (Murphy)

The Agricultural Adjustment Act of 1938 was intended to limit wheat production and stabilize prices. Under the act, chicken farmer Roscoe Filburn accepted an allotment of 11.1 acres and a maximum yield of 239 bushels of wheat for his 1941 wheat crop. Instead, he planted 23 acres and exceeded his production quota by 223 bushels. After he was caught, Filburn claimed that the surplus was to feed his family and farm animals. He was fined for exceeding his production quota and sued, claiming that Congress did not have the right to control wheat production intended for private, personal use. After an initial round of oral arguments in May 1942, five Justices asked that the case be reargued the following term.

Conference of May 7, 1942

STONE: The respondent planted grain when provisions of the act respecting quotas were different. Before he planted his wheat, he had notice of his quota allotment. At the same time, the secretary of agriculture made a speech failing to mention that there was an amendment of the law. Prior to this, there had been a penalty on marketing in interstate commerce. The farmer could ship it if he paid a penalty or fed it to his stock, etc. The amendment provided for an increase in the penalty to 49 cents, and he could turn the wheat over to the secretary, or store it, or borrow on it. Respondent says that the law is bad: (a) as a regulation of production; and (b) it is being applied retroactive as to him in such an offensive way as to violate the Fifth Amendment. As to the latter, we can assume there was no act at all when the crop was planted. If the act forbade shipment in interstate commerce, it would still be okay as a regulation of commerce under

---

11. Cushman, "A Stream of Legal Consciousness: The Current of Commerce Doctrine from *Swift* to *Jones & Laughlin.*"

12. Mason, *Harlan Fiske Stone,* 555, citing "Constitutional Change," *Asheville* (N.C.) *Citizen,* Feb. 4, 1941.

Mulford.[13] The retroactivity issue drops out if it is an exercise of commerce power. If the government can regulate by regulating goods planted before the act came in, then it can do this, provided that this is a regulation of Congress's commerce power. The government says that this is a regulation of commerce, because to fix the amount that moves in commerce is the very purpose of regulation. This is a regulation of commerce, and it is no more retroactive than the regulation in the *Mulford* case.

The act is applicable to goods which may be used only intrastate. Here, we only know that some of his crop was used on his farm. The government says that it is regulating commerce, since the purpose is to regulate a crop which moves in commerce. They have to take control of the whole crop—if he can feed this to his stock, then it affects commerce. I find it difficult to say as a matter of logic and economics that this is not a means of regulating commerce—perhaps even an indispensable means. This raises the question of where the permissible regulation of commerce ends. Congress can regulate intrastate commerce where it has fair relation to interstate commerce. We said that in the milk case. This case is closely parallel. Also the *Darby* case. I do not care for the result.

ROBERTS: I pass. I am in doubt on both features of this case.

BLACK: I agree with the Chief Justice.

REED: I take no part. I have money invested in a farm.

FRANKFURTER: I agree with the Chief Justice.

DOUGLAS: I agree

MURPHY: I agree.

BYRNES: I agree.

JACKSON: I agree.

Conference of October 17, 1942

STONE: On the two main issues: (1) On the retroactive increase of the penalty for overproduction, I am guided by the *Mulford* case. (2) On the constitutional scope of the commerce power, previous regulation of amounts for shipment without including farm consumption was ineffective. This is an appropriate regulation of something which *affects* commerce.

ROBERTS: I am for reversal.

Result: A unanimous Court ruled that Congress had the right to control wheat production, even when it was intended for private, personal use and only indirectly affected interstate commerce. Filburn could be fined for exceeding his wheat quota even if the harvest never entered interstate commerce or even if the wheat never left his farm. Homegrown wheat, Robert Jackson wrote, "overhangs the market," com-

---

13. *Mulford v. Smith*, 307 U.S. 38 (1939). The Court upheld the Agricultural Adjustment Act, including a provision requiring farmers who exceeded their allotments to pay their penalties at the warehouses, the point at which their crops entered the stream of commerce.

peting with marketed wheat in the sense that "it supplies a need of the man who grew it which would otherwise be reflected by purchases in the open market." If there was any doubt about the scope of the commerce clause after Darby Lumber, *this case made it clear that the Court would not question Congress's authority to regulate intrastate economic activities that had even a tenuous impact on interstate commerce. Roberts changed his mind and joined the majority, and Reed also participated in the decision after initially recusing himself.*

Southern Pacific R.R. Co. v. Arizona, 325 U.S. 761 (1945)
(Douglas) (Murphy)

The Arizona Train Limit Law required that trains traveling through the state have no more than fourteen passenger cars or seventy freight cars. In 1940, Arizona sued the Southern Pacific Railroad Company to recover fines and penalties for the railroad company's alleged failure to obey the state limitations on two occasions. Arizona claimed that it had concurrent powers to regulate commerce to protect the health and safety of its citizens. The railroad company attacked the constitutionality of the state law, citing the strong national interest in uniform and efficient interstate transportation. Using its commerce clause powers, Congress temporarily suspended the state's Train Limit Law during World War II but otherwise did not address the problem. The trial court found in favor of the railroad, but the Arizona Supreme Court reversed and directed judgment for the state.

Conference of March 31, 1945

STONE: The Interstate Commerce Commission suspended operations of the Arizona statute under war conditions. The issue here is the liability of the railroad company for fines which accrued prior to the action of the ICC. Can Arizona enforce that law because of its impact on the commerce clause? Arizona said it was a safety measure. Big train operation was commerce. It produced an efficient operation. The state statute is said to interfere with the operative aspect of commerce, as distinguished from being a mere burden on the doing of it. The principal safety argument is based on slack between the cars.

It was reversed below on the narrow ground that the state had plenary power on safety measures. *On these undisturbed findings, is the authority of state so plenary that it can disregard interstate commerce regulations?*

The lower court's reliance on *Barnwell* was not sound.[14] There we had peculiarly a state problem. We started with a place where it was the duty of the state to regulate in the interest of safety. There is scope for state regulations affecting safety—but there is a limitation on it, as for example, where it operates to restrict transportation. The length of trains is peculiarly one of national concern. If you control interstate trains in each state, you seriously load down the nation's commerce operation. You also have a mandate under

---

14. *South Carolina Highway Department v. Barnwell Bros.,* 303 U.S. 177 (1938). The Court upheld South Carolina's attempt to limit the weight and width of vehicles allowed to travel its highways. States, the Court reasoned, traditionally had more control over highway traffic than railroad traffic—in part because states built, owned, and maintained most internal highways (this was before construction of the national interstate highway system began in the 1950s). The Court also ruled that the state limits did not cause any significant inconvenience to interstate commerce.

the Interstate Commerce Act for economy and efficiency in train operations. You cannot escape a balancing of convenience and conflicting interests. So we have said that there is some scope for local interest and does not affect whole transportation field or cannot act. Here you have conflicting interests which a state alone may not control. Here, state regulation is not merely incidental to commerce—it controls the movement of interstate commerce. The fact that there is a safety element is not sufficient. In this case, the whole business of safety washes itself out. It is inconclusive whether the danger is greater in one case than another, and I don't think that the state can break down what Congress has done. A state does not have sufficient interest to break down this interstate operation. The *Kelly* case allows inspection and certain kinds of equipment, but not the structure, etc.[15] Arizona has not made out a case. I would reverse.

ROBERTS: I agree, and I reverse.

BLACK: I cannot quite understand the position you take. I do not see how this Court has the power to declare this act unconstitutional. Under *Marbury v. Madison*, we can hold statutes unconstitutional. I could understand it if the Court thought that national uniformity was necessary. If Congress had said something, I could understand it. Or if the Court thought that Congress had acted. But I do not see how a state which has power to legislate cannot make its policy determination. This Court makes a question of state policy a justiciable issue. I think that the question is for the legislature, not the courts. This is an effort to make courts above the legislative body in government. Admitting that the state has jurisdiction, you try it out as a question of fact, and then you hear evidence on the propriety of the policy. What is the burden of proof? On whom does it rest? What is the measure of the burden, and what is it that they have to prove?

STONE: My point is, does the national government have a right to regulate commerce? Yes, it is in Congress. Now the state has a right to regulate safety. There is a conflict. So is it an encroachment on the powers of Congress? That is a justiciable question. And we have to act. The state cannot take away a power reserved to Congress.

BLACK: If it is necessary to save dollars and railroads and human beings, I am for saving human lives. I won't retry the facts, because you are transferring to the courts a legislative function.

REED: It is a close case. Whether the facts indicate regulation or otherwise, I don't know. We have always said uniformity was essential. This case falls between the *Kelly* case and the *Terminal* case. I incline toward the view of the Chief Justice and I reverse.

FRANKFURTER: I come out where you do. I think this is a practical obstruction to commerce. The Arizona act passed in 1912. For years, Arizona made it impossible to get the

---

15. *Kelly v. Washington*, 302 U.S. 1 (1937). The Court permitted states to inspect boats for seaworthiness in the absence of congressional policy, mostly because the Justices did not think that uniformity was necessary. States could not, however, impose particular standards of structure, design, equipment, or operation unless they were plainly essential to safety or seaworthiness. States ran the risk of being caught in a catch-22, because if the standards were necessary for safety or seaworthiness, Congress would then be called on to impose uniform requirements.

case into court. It refused to give its consent to suit, and there was no threat of enforcement. No one can say that Congress has not the power to make commerce regulations. There is a problem here where Congress has not acted and the state has gone beyond state lines in its enactments. It took the finding of a single judge to upset what the state has done. That is why there is the Supreme Court, to see that such is not done. This legislation has been vetoed by thirty-odd states. This is a practical obstruction which exists under this legislation.

Result: By a vote of 6–1–2, the Court held that the Arizona law violated the commerce clause. Even without a clear expression of congressional intent, Harlan Fiske Stone wrote, the law was inimical to national commerce. When Congress failed to act, he said, the Supreme Court—not the state legislatures—became the final arbiter of the commerce clause and would balance competing state and national interests. In the view of the majority, the state law plainly obstructed interstate train operations and adversely affected the efficiency of train transportation far beyond what was necessary to promote rail safety. There was no evidence that the law lessened the danger of accident, which meant that the state's interest in safety was easily outweighed by the national interest in ensuring an efficient and uniform system of rail transportation. Stone noted that there had been 164 bills to impose train limits in state legislatures over the previous twenty years, and if each state were permitted to set its own limits on train length, the national train network would quickly be reduced to chaos. Although only two states had actually enacted laws limiting train length (Arizona and Oklahoma), the operating costs of railroad companies in those states had jumped by nearly 30 percent. Wiley Rutledge concurred in the judgment.

Hugo Black's dissent accused the Court of acting like a "super-legislature," striking down a state law merely because a majority thought it unwise. The question was one of public policy and should be left to the states and Congress to work out among themselves. William O. Douglas also dissented, arguing that the Court should have intervened only if the state legislation was "out of harmony" with congressional intent. Both Congress and the ICC appeared content to let states make local safety regulations, and in Douglas's judgment the railroads had not overcome the presumption of validity to which the train limit law was entitled.

Tee-Hit-Ton Indians v. United States, 348 U.S. 272 (1955)
(Clark)

In 1947, a Joint Resolution of Congress authorized the sale of timber on Alaskan land occupied by the Tee-Hit-Ton Indians, near the Tongass National Forest. The Indians claimed some 350,000 acres of land and 150 square miles of water, and they demanded just compensation under the Fifth Amendment.

The immediate problem for the Court was to determine the nature of Indian title to the land in question—if any. Under established precedents, the Court did not ordinarily acknowledge aboriginal property claims, absent explicit congressional recognition of tribal ownership. The Tee-Hit-Ton Indians claimed to have taken title of the land either during the period of Russian ownership of Alaska or by implicit congressional recognition in the Organic Act for Alaska (1884) or the Alaska Act of 1900 (which provided for civil government in Alaska). The court of claims ruled that the Indians had no title except for a right of possession at the pleasure of Congress, meaning that the legislature's decision to sell timber on federal government lands was not a compensable taking of tribal property under the Fifth Amendment.

WARREN: I don't believe that they have any title. Only the czar had it during the Russian era. No title was recognized under this treaty. But I disagree with the government on other rights. They do have rights of possession. The act of Congress guarantees them basic rights of possession. This record does not show these rights. The trial court would have to find them. I would send the case back to the court of claims to determine what possessory rights they have. It is compensable and vested. I would reverse on this ground.

BLACK: The thing that you say is not here. I could not say that the statute gave a vested right—the treaties don't. Giving a right of possession does not mean in perpetuity. Congress could give it to them if it wished. You don't salve consciences or salve the Indians in this way. If they had fishing rights, maybe they could cut a fishing pole. They only claim the timber. Congress can take away these rights. Nothing to it except the Indians. If Congress grants permanent possession, perhaps vested—that is tantamount to title. The Organic Act gave no title, merely possession. There are 500,000 acres of land. Under the *Lynch* case, they would own the land if Congress gave them title.[16]

REED: I start with the proposition that the burden is on the Indians to prove ownership. They are in the same position as Indians in the United States. The czar gave them nothing (except private individual property). There is no such thing as aboriginal title. Section 27 of the Act of 1884 said that Indians shall not be disturbed in any lands, nor in their possession, nor in their use during their occupation. They had no title—only what the act gave them. I would affirm. I think that the government could sell any part of the land that it wishes. The only *obligation* on the part of the government is to care for them as an act of grace. The Chief says that the Indians were driven from California and were mostly killed off. The government negotiated treaties, but never ratified them.

FRANKFURTER: My extended observations may not be welcome. Sorry, but this case raises very important questions of construction and *opinions in footnotes.* I can't decide on

---

16. *Franklin v. Lynch*, 233 U.S. 269 (1914). Emmer Sisney was a white woman who married a Choctaw. When her husband died, she sued to become a member of the tribe by right of marriage. Having no money to press her claim, she conveyed to her lawyers, Franklin and Apple, any future interest in any land—other than homestead property—that she might receive as a member of "the Five Civilized Tribes." She was made a tribal member and received her allotment of land, which she promptly sold to a third party, Lynch and Simmons.

When Franklin and Apple sued, the Court ruled that Mrs. Sisney had not been legally entitled to sell a future allotment of property to her original lawyers. As a rule, the Court said, Indians had no transferrable interest in tribal property, absent a treaty or federal statute recognizing and defining tribal property rights. Even where Congress had recognized *tribal* ownership rights, there was no *individual* ownership in tribal lands, and no individual claims or transfers of tribal property were permitted absent an enabling law or treaty. In this case, a federal law recognized tribal ownership of property belonging to the Five Civilized Tribes and permitted the tribes to divide and sell tribal lands to individuals. But the law also provided that tribal lands could not be sold or transferred until the patents were actually issued.

Sisney claimed that she was not subject to these restrictions, because as a white woman she had the legal capacity to convey a future expectancy. The Supreme Court disagreed, ruling that she could not have it both ways by claiming to be an Indian for purposes of receiving property but a white person for the purposes of selling it. The federal laws that governed the sale of Choctaw property prevented Sisney from transferring her property allotment before she had actually received it.

questions of dollars and cents, costs, etc. The dearest friend of my life was the Indian commissioner, and I was his counsel.[17] That's the source of my interest. The use of big words like "title" create *obfuscation*. We can't use such terms in these cases. Totem poles were used here to denote ownership.

Paragraph 5 of the complaint is fee. Paragraph 6 is *in the alternative: the right is one of possession and use.* No one has decided that what was given in *1884* survived the *1947* act. The former recognized possessory rights—the 1900 act confirmed them. The state of Utah's brief is illuminating on this point.[18]

There was a misuse of *footnotes*. The court of claims says that *footnote 28* in *Hynes* has settled this case.[19] It was dictum, but was taken as law of the case by the court of claims. Their opinion is forty-one pages long. I would decide it irregardless of footnote 28.

DOUGLAS: This tribe had what was known as Indian title, and this was recognized by the United States in 1867. The *Miller* case said it was not recognized.[20] The present act has a provision to the effect that present claims are not affected. What the rights may be, however, I don't know. Some in the West recognized the right of Indians to stand on rocks and fish. The case should be remanded.

BURTON: I affirm—me and Minton.

Result: The Court, in a 6–3 opinion, ruled that because the Tee-Hit-Ton tribe was nomadic and had only possessive rights to the land, it was not entitled to compensation under the Fifth Amendment. In

---

17. One of Frankfurter's closest friends was Benjamin Cohen, Frankfurter's former roommate and one of the principal architects of FDR's wartime Lend-Lease program. Frankfurter also developed a close professional and personal friendship with Cohen's son (and Frankfurter's namesake), Felix S. Cohen. The younger Cohen served as associate solicitor of Indian affairs and wrote *The Handbook of Federal Indian Law* (1942). This was not Frankfurter's only connection with the Bureau of Indian Affairs. When Frankfurter worked in the War Department during the Taft administration, he lived in a house on 19th Street owned by Robert G. Valentine, then the commissioner of Indian affairs.

18. Utah attorney general E. R. Callister wrote the brief as an amicus curiae.

19. *Hynes v. Grimes Packing Co.*, 337 U.S. 86, 106 (1949). Footnote 28 of Justice Reed's majority opinion cited a federal statute that explicitly recognized the property claims of Alaska's Metlakahtla tribe. As a rule, Reed wrote, only explicit congressional recognition of tribal ownership of tribal lands was sufficient to establish compensable property rights. He noted that even the president's power to create temporary reservations for Indian immigrants was quite limited. Reed discredited dicta in *Miller v. United States*, 159 F.2d 997, 1001 (CA 9th 1947), which implied that government termination of tribal occupation rights *might* be compensable under some circumstances, even absent prior federal recognition of tribal ownership. Reed bluntly stated that the judges in that case were mistaken and had wrongly relied on *United States v. Alcea Band of Tillamooks*, 329 U.S. 40 (1946)—which, Reed maintained, recognized no such exception. Indian occupancy rights were *not* compensable absent explicit and specific congressional recognition of tribal ownership.

20. *Miller v. United States*, 159 F. 2d 997 (CA 9th 1947). The court of appeals, citing a series of Supreme Court precedents, ruled that the Tlingit Indians did not have a compensable interest in tidelands condemned by the federal government to build a wharfage in Juneau, Alaska. The court decided that as a rule, aboriginal claims amounted only to occupation rights. These could be terminated at will by the federal government, absent a treaty or other prior federal recognition of Indian ownership. The judges, however, seemed to imply that there might be an exception to the general rule that aboriginal title did not create compensable property rights. This was precisely what Stanley Reed objected to in *Hynes v. Grimes Packing Co.*

the first place, Stanley Reed argued, aboriginal claims were not recognized as property for Fifth Amendment purposes unless the claims were explicitly recognized by a congressional act or federal treaty. Second, the prior occupation of Alaska by the Russians did not change anything, because the Russian government did not recognize any Indian property rights beyond those acknowledged by other European and American governments. Third, Congress consistently refused to recognize Indian title in Alaskan land, and neither the Organic Act nor the Alaska Act recognized any permanent rights of Alaskan Indians to the lands that they occupied. This policy of nonrecognition culminated in Congress's 1949 Joint Resolution selling the timber on the land occupied by the tribe without compensation. Because the tribe held only permissive occupancy rights, Congress was free to change or terminate these rights at will.

The three dissenters, Douglas, Warren, and Frankfurter, argued that the 1884 Organic Act implicitly recognized Tee-Hit-Ton property claims, even though the act contained no specifics regarding what lands or rights were involved.

National League of Cities v. Usery, 426 U.S. 833 (1976)
California v. Usery
(Brennan)

In 1938, Congress used its commerce powers to pass the Fair Labor Standards Act (FLSA), which set minimum wages and maximum work hours in private industry. The law originally exempted state public employees. Beginning in 1961, however, Congress gradually extended the FLSA to cover state employees. In 1974, Congress amended the FLSA to cover virtually all state workers. The National League of Cities, along with twenty states, five cities, and the National Governors' Conference, filed separate lawsuits against William J. Usery, the secretary of labor, to stop the law from going into effect. A three-judge district court dismissed all of their claims, and they appealed to the Supreme Court.

STEWART: Bill Douglas's *Wirtz* dissent, which I joined, put sovereignty of states in the role of a brake on commerce clause, and until *Wirtz* is overruled I have to affirm.[21]

BLACKMUN: *Fry* is more troublesome than *Wirtz*, but it was control down and not an imposition up.[22]

POWELL: I would draw on an equal protection analogy to say that the implications of federalism require strict scrutiny of federal legislation that is a direct infringement on state personnel practices. It is a traditional principle of necessity. *Fry* is an illustration of its application.

---

21. *Maryland v. Wirtz,* 392 U.S. 183 (1968) upheld two congressional amendments extending the FLSA to cover state workers. In 1961, Congress extended the act to cover all state enterprises producing goods for commerce. In 1966, Congress extended the act again to include state employees at public hospitals, institutions, and schools. Harlan wrote the majority for a 6–2 Court, with Douglas and Stewart in dissent. Marshall did not participate.

22. *Fry v. United States,* 421 U.S. 542 (1975) approved the Economic Stabilization Act of 1970, which temporarily froze the wages of all state and local public employees. The Court reaffirmed one of the central ideas of *Wickard v. Filburn*—that Congress could regulate intrastate commerce if its cumulative effects affected interstate or international commerce.

REHNQUIST: I am not sure that *Wirtz*, as applied to hospitals competing with private hospitals, should be overruled.

STEVENS: In terms of personal philosophy, the whole FLSA premise is unsatisfactory. But there is a commerce issue, and though *Wirtz* is distinguishable, it is an affirmative authority in commerce terms. Then I come to the federalism argument. The non-discriminatory argument of the solicitor general was not persuasive. Yet Congress always does things that impose on state sovereignty. I don't think that a requirement of minimum wages is that intrusive on state sovereignty. It is not a political question, yet how does one explain state representatives going along with this? I can't think of a judicially enforceable standard distinguishing this from *Wirtz* and *California*.[23]

[BRENNAN: After the vote was taken, 5–4 to affirm, Rehnquist, Powell, and Blackmun—who thought *Wirtz* need only be partly overruled—agreed when Stewart said that he could only totally overrule it and changed to say that they would totally overrule *Wirtz*. The Chief Justice said that he, too, could do that. Reverse and overrule *Wirtz*: Burger, Stewart, Blackmun, Powell, Rehnquist. Affirm: Brennan, White, Marshall, Stevens.]

Result: Writing for a tenuous 5–4 majority, William Rehnquist overruled Wirtz *and ruled that Congress had exceeded its authority under the commerce clause in passing the 1974 version of the FLSA. The act unconstitutionally infringed on states' ability to establish employment policies in areas of traditional state functions (among the examples Rehnquist cited were fire, police, sanitation, public health, parks, and recreation). Congress could not directly compel states to follow congressional preferences in making essential decisions regarding integral government functions. Rehnquist interpreted* Fry *loosely to justify the proposition that the Tenth Amendment was not a mere truism but protected states from undue federal government interference that would undermine states' ability to function effectively within a federal system. Rehnquist's majority was precarious; the fifth vote, Harry Blackmun, wrote an odd concurring opinion that said, in effect, that the majority position was not quite as poorly reasoned as the dissenters claimed.*

In dissent, Brennan, White, and Marshall argued that Congress's commerce power was plenary and that the proper check on this power was not the Tenth Amendment but the states' overwhelming representation in the federal government. The dissenters argued that this dispute was a problem that should be worked out within the political process, not in the courts. Stevens chided the majority for establishing the dubious constitutional principle that the federal government could not interfere with a state's "right" to pay its employees substandard wages.

Garcia v. San Antonio Metropolitan Transit Authority, 469 U.S. 528 (1985)
(Brennan)

The San Antonio Metropolitan Transit Authority (SAMTA) was a municipal public authority partly subsidized by federal funds. After the U.S. Department of Labor ruled that SAMTA was subject to federal minimum wage and overtime requirements under the Fair Labor Standards Act (FLSA), SAMTA sought a declaratory judgment that municipal mass transportation was a "traditional state

---

23. *United States v. California*, 297 U.S. 175 (1936), the primary precedent for *Wirtz*.

function" and that it was exempt from federal wage and overtime mandates under National League of Cities v. Usery.[24] *Joe Garcia and other SAMTA employees filed suit for overtime pay they claimed they were entitled to under federal law. Because the facts were virtually identical to* National League of Cities, *the district court ruled that SAMTA performed a traditional state function and was exempt from FLSA requirements.*

Harry Blackmun was in the hot seat. His reluctant concurrence in National League of Cities *had provided the crucial fifth vote protecting state governments from FLSA requirements. By 1985, however, he was becoming increasingly uncomfortable with the unwieldy "traditional government functions" test.*

BURGER: *National League of Cities* is at a crossroads in this case. Private mass transit has faded out and large cities have gone public. Federal funds subsidize 75 percent of the cost and only 25 percent of operating costs come from revenue. Still, transit systems are essentially local. This is like water in that respect and is here to stay. The federal government can attach conditions. I don't think that *Long Island* controls this case.[25]

BRENNAN:[26] The question presented in this case is whether the operation of a publicly owned and operated mass transit system is a "traditional state function" for purposes of the 10th Amendment. In my view, it is not.

In *United Transportation Union v. Long Island Railroad*, we held that the determination whether a federal regulation affects a traditional state function, rests on whether that regulation "affects basic state prerogatives in such a way as would be likely to hamper the state government's ability to fulfill its role in the Union and endanger its separate and independent existence." Although we also stated in *Long Island Railroad* that the traditional state function inquiry does not impose a "static historical view of state functions," there can be no question that history plays a vital role in this inquiry. In *Long Island Railroad* itself, we relied heavily on history. For example, we stated that "It is certainly true that some passenger railroads have come under state control in recent years . . . but that does not alter the historical reality that operation of the railroads is not among the functions traditionally performed by state and local governments." Indeed, if the states have not traditionally performed a particular function, they have, of course, survived as independent entities without performing that function at all. It is, therefore, difficult to see how federal regulation of that function can threaten the states' independent existence.

In this case, there is no question that the states have not traditionally operated mass transit systems. Until recently, these systems were largely privately operated. Thus, the

24. *National League of Cities v. Usery*, 426 U.S. 833 (1976).

25. *United Transportation Union v. Long Island R. Co.*, 455 U.S. 678 (1982). Union workers called for a strike at a state-owned railroad in New York. The union claimed that the strike was permitted by the federal Railway Labor Act, while the railroad managers claimed that state law prohibited strikes by public employees and argued that using the Railway Labor Act to preempt the applicable state law would violate *National League of Cities v. Usery*. The Supreme Court ruled in favor of the union. Congress, Burger wrote, historically has enjoyed extensive regulatory authority over railroads, and the Railway Labor Act did not impair the state's "integral operations in areas of traditional governmental functions."

26. Adapted from Brennan's talking papers, Brennan Papers, OT 1983, box 656.

history of private operation of mass transit strongly suggests that operation of mass transit systems is not a traditional state function.

The recent large scale entry of the states into the mass transit field does not alter this conclusion. This development occurred when massive amounts of federal funds were made available to the states to operate mass transit systems. Additionally, the various conditions on grants under the Urban Mass Transit Act have undoubtedly played a vital role in determining the nature of the mass transit services that the states provide. Thus, the states' large scale involvement in mass transit has been a joint venture with the federal government, rather than a matter of purely local concern. Because the federal government has been so involved in mass transit during the period in which the states acquired mass transit facilities, it is difficult to conceive of mass transit as the kind of state function that must be free of federal regulation to preserve the independent existence of the states. To my knowledge, none of the other functions which we have previously identified as traditional state functions is characterized by an absence of historical state involvement *and* the presence of federal funding in the states' development of that function. Finally, it is worth noting that over 80 percent of the publicly owned mass transit systems became public after 1966, when the Fair Labor Standards Act was amended to apply to publicly owned mass transit. As in *Long Island Railroad*, these states acquired their mass transit operations knowing that the operations would be subject to federal regulation.

For these reasons, I believe that the operation of a mass transit system is not a traditional state function. As a result, the Tenth Amendment is not violated when the Fair Labor Standards Act is applied to state operated mass transit systems. I reverse.

WHITE: I agree with Brennan.

MARSHALL: I agree with Brennan.

BLACKMUN: This is a tough case for me after my concurrence in *National League*. Municipal mass transit reeks of localism, like police, fire, and so forth. I agree that a good opinion can be written either way. I come down on the side that this is local, and I will vote to affirm.

POWELL: One can write a principled decision either way, and I agree with Harry. We are talking here of driving people to and from their work—a service that is essential to provide.

REHNQUIST: I agree with Harry and Lewis.

STEVENS: How much should be entrusted to the democratic process is a guide for me. It is anomalous to think that municipalities, with their political powers, should be protected against Congress. It is too much for me.

O'CONNOR: The third *National League* test is my focus. I don't think that history freezes traditional public service—the test is whether Congress goes too far.

After Reargument

BURGER: Mass transit should not be subject to federal control.

BRENNAN:[27] I was fully ready to join in Harry's opinion last term, and I continue to stand ready to do so. It is a splendid piece of scholarship, and it properly emphasizes that the federalism restraints on Congress commerce clause power lie *primarily* in the political process—*not* the judicial process.

I would only add that, if there is sentiment for *expressly* overruling *National League of Cities*, I would join in such a disposition without hesitation. Such an outcome may, in fact, be required by Harry's analysis. Of course, there would continue to be restraints on Congress's commerce power. As we emphasized in *Maryland v. Wirtz* and *United States v. California*, the courts must ensure that challenged legislation is a valid regulation of interstate commerce.[28] Beyond that, I believe that further judicial inquiry is not required by the Constitution—indeed, it is prohibited. Reverse.

WHITE: I would reconsider *National League* and reverse.

MARSHALL: I am still with Harry and would overrule *National League*.

BLACKMUN: It was a disappointing argument from all concerned.[29] The traditional government function test doesn't approach.

POWELL: I would treat the traditional function test as whether it is essentially a matter of local or national concern. I don't think that the federal interest here is that great.

REHNQUIST: I am still to affirm.

STEVENS: There is no doubt what Congress meant here. Any balancing here is for Congress to do, as Brennan says. Indeed, this is a classic case where it is wrong for the judiciary to intervene.

O'CONNOR: This is a watershed case. The Framers encouraged a system of state and federal sovereignty, and pay of state employees is for the states to determine.

Result: The initial conference vote was 5–4 to affirm National League of Cities, *but Blackmun's vote was shaky. Chief Justice Burger assigned the opinion to Blackmun in the hope that on the "least persuaded" theory he could keep Blackmun on board.[30] In this instance, however, the tactic backfired. While researching and writing the opinion, Blackmun changed his mind about the case and the nine-year-old* National League of Cities *majority collapsed. Saying that he could find no principled way to affirm, Blackmun switched sides and wrote the majority opinion in a 5–4 decision overruling* National League of Cities. *The "traditional and historic" government functions test, Blackmun concluded, was arbitrary, contradictory, and unworkable. The case was reargued on the question of whether the Court*

---

27. Adapted from Brennan's talking papers, Brennan Papers, OT 1984, box 673.

28. *Maryland v. Wirtz*, 392 U.S. 183 (1968); *United States v. California*, 297 U.S. 175 (1936).

29. Presenting oral arguments were (1) Solicitor General Rex Lee and Assistant Attorney General Theodore B. Olson for the U.S. Department of Labor; (2) Laurence Gold, special counsel to the AFL-CIO on behalf of Joe Garcia; and (3) William T. Coleman Jr. for SAMTA.

30. Under the "least persuaded" theory, the most tentative member of the majority is assigned the opinion in the hope that their vote can be made more secure by giving them primary responsibility for shaping the outcome.

should reconsider National League of Cities, *but the new arguments changed nothing. The Tenth Amendment was once again "but a truism that all is retained that has not been surrendered."*[31] *Or, as Lewis Powell complained in his dissent, the Tenth Amendment was "meaningless rhetoric when Congress acts pursuant to the commerce clause."*

Rehnquist wrote a blistering dissent, blasting the majority for overruling a recent precedent and ironically vowing to overrule Garcia *and restore* National League of Cities *as soon as he could find a fifth vote. While the Court has never overruled* Garcia *directly, Rehnquist has orchestrated an effective indirect attack on the case and has probably succeeded in overruling it implicitly. A direct attack on* Garcia *may follow.*[32]

COMITY

Screws v. United States, 325 U.S. 91 (1945)
(Murphy) (Douglas) (Jackson)

Sheriff Claude Screws of Baker County, Georgia, and two deputies arrested Robert Hall late one night on suspicion of stealing a tire.[33] *Prior to the arrest, the three officers had been drinking in a bar and talking about Hall, a thirty-year-old black man whom all three officials knew personally. The bartender overheard their discussion and pleaded with them not to arrest Hall that night. Screws allegedly held a longstanding grudge against Hall and had vowed to get him.*

After arresting Hall without incident, the four men arrived by car at the courthouse square. Sheriff Screws claimed that Hall insulted him and tried to reach for a gun. The three officers beat the handcuffed suspect for between fifteen and thirty minutes with their fists and an eight-inch, solid-bar blackjack. Then they dragged the unconscious man feet first into the jail and left him in a heap on a cell floor, where he died within the hour.

When no state charges were filed, federal prosecutors charged Sheriff Screws in federal court with violating §20 of the Criminal Code. This law was part of the Civil Rights Act of 1866, which made it a crime to willfully deprive a person of any right, privilege, or immunity secured by the Constitution or laws of the United States.[34] *Prosecutors alleged that Screws had violated Hall's Fourteenth Amendment due process rights to life and liberty. A federal jury convicted Screws, and the Fifth Circuit Court of Appeals affirmed.*

There were two key issues on appeal. The first was whether Screws's conduct could be prosecuted in federal courts or if Georgia had exclusive authority to decide whether or not to prosecute. The second issue was whether §20 was unconstitutionally vague. Screws claimed that the law did not provide an ascertainable standard of guilt. He argued that the Fourteenth Amendment was so broad, imprecise, and fluid in scope that there was no way to specifically define which actions violated the

---

31. *United States v. Darby Lumber Co.,* 312 U.S. 100 (1941).

32. Recent cases indicate that *Garcia* may no longer be viable. See *Alden v. Maine,* 527 U.S. 706 (1999); *Printz v. United States,* 521 U.S. 898 (1997); *Seminole Tribe of Florida v. Florida,* 517 U.S. 44 (1996); *New York v. United States,* 505 U.S. 144 (1992).

33. The two men with Sheriff Screws were Frank Edward Jones and Jim Bob Kelly.

34. 18 U.S.C. §242.

law. In other words, in attempting to criminalize any violation of due process, potential defendants had no fair prospective warning as to what actions might be illegal and subject to punishment.

Conference of October 23, 1944

STONE: The petitioners were indicted under §20 of the Criminal Code. This law goes back to postbellum civil rights times. The petitioners—a local sheriff, a police officer and a citizen summoned to his aid, acting under a warrant, beat him to death. The prisoner was armed. The case was submitted to the jury on a narrow case of whether they used unnecessary force. The jury found that the sheriff exceeded lawful force—that the sheriff acted under color of his office, exceeded his authority, and acted wilfully.

There are two questions here: (1) Does a state officer proceeding under state law who exceeds his authority violate §20? The sheriff is a state officer—is his action state action? (2) Is §20 constitutional? Is the section within the power of Congress to pass such a law as an aid to others? Is the statute too vague?

(1) The general rule is that a principal may be bound, though an agent acts beyond their authority. When the Fourteenth Amendment was passed, people were aware that in cases of relations of private persons, there was responsibility even though he exceeded the instruction of his principals. As in the case of chauffeurs who are forbidden to speed but do—you are responsible. The question is whether a state is similarly held responsible under the Fourteenth Amendment. Did they adopt the Fourteenth Amendment to place, or was it intended to place, that responsibility on the states? It was early contended that the Fourteenth Amendment covered state action, and except in the *Barney* case, it has been held so consistently.[35]

Look at the Amendment. There is interesting confirmation in it. The first clause speaks of law. "Law" in §2 of the Fourteenth Amendment included all "law," both judicial and legislative—and the due process of law clause speaks of deprivations by a state. Then it goes on to say not by legislation, but *any means whatsoever.* That means the officers. If you don't say that, you do not have a Fourteenth Amendment. Judicial action isn't ratification within their authority.

Judge Sibley said that this was state action.[36] It was done under color of state law, and came within section and was within power of Congress to act (the government has just filed its brief).

---

35. *Barney v. City of New York*, 193 U.S. 430 (1904). Barney was a New York City property owner who filed a federal lawsuit charging city transit officials with building a subway tunnel in violation of state law and claiming that their actions had violated his Fourteenth Amendment rights. A unanimous Court dismissed the case on the ground that if state officials were acting in *violation* of state law, as Barney alleged, then they were not acting under *color* of law. By narrowly defining the meaning of state action to exclude actions by state officials that violated state law, federal courts had no jurisdiction and any remedy would have to be provided by state courts. The *Barney* doctrine has never been overruled, but it has been widely discredited and is now rarely, if ever, followed.

36. Circuit Judge John A. Sibley dissented from the Fifth Circuit Court of Appeals judgment affirming Screws's conviction. Sibley acknowledged that the officers had acted under color of law but thought that they did not have specific intent to violate Hall's Fourteenth Amendment rights. Accordingly, he thought that §20 of the federal criminal code was inapplicable and that the officers could only be tried under state law.

We cannot go back to *Barney* and use it to emasculate the Fourteenth Amendment. Subsequent cases and prior decisions look the other way. It is not clear what the Court was thinking of in *Barney*. Anyway, the distinction is not this case.

There is no statute saying that an officer should not do what he did here. He is authorized to use force. When he went beyond taking and keeping his prisoner—if he intentionally goes beyond that—he exceeds his authority and it is state action. So far as state action is concerned, I am not prepared, despite *Barney*, to go back on what Edward White said in *Los Angeles*[37] or what Louis Brandeis said in *Bennett*.[38] These acts are not to be tolerated when doing excessive things in states, the same as individuals.

(2) In respect to indefiniteness, this is not the *Cohen Grocery Store* case.[39] It is more like the *Nash* case.[40] It is not as vague as the Sherman Act cases. If a man intentionally does an act, under color of his office, under authority of his office, and he denies another their rights and privileges of the Fourteenth Amendment, he need not intend to produce that result if he acts willfully. I would affirm.

ROBERTS: I do not believe that the Fourteenth Amendment or §20 were meant to justify this sort of an action under federal jurisdiction, whatever might have been state remedy. The Fourteenth Amendment was never intended to reach this. I pass. I would reverse, but I can't state my reasons—I am not sure how to work it out.

STONE: I would not want to cut the Fourteenth Amendment to mean only where state legislation, etc., directs.

REED: This was action by a state officer. Next, the statute protects all interference by state law of privileges and immunities arising from federal law. This comes under due process

---

37. *Home Telephone and Telegraph Co. v. Los Angeles,* 227 U.S. 278 (1913). This case distanced itself from the *Barney* doctrine and expanded the definitions of "color of law" and state action. Edward White's majority opinion allowed a federal action under the Fourteenth Amendment as long as the state officer was "clothed" with state authority. In this case, city officials *claimed* to act under state authority in fixing new rates for telephone service. The telephone company sued, claiming that the rates were so low that they were confiscatory in violation of their Fourteenth Amendment due process rights.

38. *Iowa-Des Moines National Bank v. Bennett,* 284 U.S. 239 (1931). This was an action by two banks to force Iowa state tax collectors to issue refunds. The banks claimed that the state taxed shares of a national bank at a higher rate than it taxed local corporations. The Supreme Court agreed that Iowa's discriminatory tax scheme violated the Fourteenth Amendment. Because the state's behavior was intentional and systematic, and because the state retained the ill-gained tax funds through a lengthy series of appeals to the highest state court, Louis Brandeis distinguished *Barney* and ruled in favor of the banks. The quote to which Stone referred in conference was: "The prohibition of the Fourteenth Amendment, it is true, has reference exclusively to action by the State, as distinguished from action by private individuals. But acts done by virtue of a public position under a state government and in the name and for the state, are not to be treated as if they were the acts of private individuals, although in doing them the official acted contrary to an express command of the state law."

39. *United States v. Cohen Grocery Co.,* 255 U.S. 81 (1921), held that laws must be precisely written, and that a defendant cannot be placed on trial for an undefined offense that gives no specific warning of what behaviors are proscribed.

40. *Nash v. United States,* 229 U.S. 373, 377 (1913). Holmes, writing for an 8–1 Court, rejected a vagueness challenge to the Sherman Antitrust Act. Several defendants had been charged under the act for conspiracy to restrict and monopolize trade. Mahlon Pitney dissented without opinion.

and that alone. It is difficult for me to define this as a denial of due process. I would reverse, although I am not sure how.

FRANKFURTER: If you can indict, you can also bring a civil suit. There would be pressure on state officials—indictments and civil actions hanging over every state official. The *Barney* case was not overruled by *Des Moines*. The point is the effect upon the whole administration of law within the state government. I would reverse on the ground that the statute does not apply to this case.

STONE: Here you have a command of Congress. It says to take jurisdiction. It does not say to do it when a state fails to act.

BLACK: Suppose this statute does cover it. Why doesn't self-defense justify their actions? They tried it on the theory that self-defense justified it. We would have to set standards. Why should he be convicted if he did an act in self-defense?

STONE: I think that they passed this law in carpetbagger times, and they meant to hell with state courts.

BLACK: If I thought *Barney* was wrong, I would overrule it. I don't think that there is any reason to tread around it.

STONE: Hasn't it already been undermined?

BLACK: Before you reach the constitutional question, was the act intended to correct this? If the act means something, you can't set it aside because of the consequences. Every officer in the union could be indicted for search and seizure, and for assaults on prisoners. You are deciding guilt of murder, but we are talking here about the right to try every state offense in federal courts.

STONE: But here he is doing it under color of his office.

BLACK: If Congress had passed a law saying "any state officer," then I would have a different question. I can't believe that the enactment of that law was intended to embrace the indictment of every state officer in denying due process. I believe that the *Cohen* doctrine is here too, because a man must have some vague idea of what he is up against. I am impressed by the *Cohen Grocery* doctrine.

Every officer—every agent—may run afoul of the law if he acts even privately. Unless we define due process finer than we have, a guy would be in trouble. If you are going to overrule the *Barney* case, I would limit it.[41]

STONE: It may be that the key to this is its vagueness when applied to the Fourteenth Amendment. We should consider it very carefully. The concept of agency in private law has not been adopted here. The application of doctrine to a criminal statute cannot be too vague.

DOUGLAS: I agree with you on *Barney*. I would construe §20 as a discrimination statute, but we are past this. I would follow Black and put this on narrow grounds.

---

41. According to Jackson's notes, Black said: "Would overrule *Barney* if touch it at all."

STONE: Leave some of the specific things under the Fourteenth Amendment.

MURPHY: I take the view expounded by the Chief Justice. I think that §20 is constitutional. Those in authority can be lawless. I would affirm.

JACKSON: I don't find a good analogy to a chauffeur here. I don't think we can transfer into federal action things that are not intended to be. You can't run these things from Washington. Problems of local justice must be left to their communities. If we sustain this, every time a Negro is beaten you are going to have the President and others jumping on the state for action. And then your local officer will lay down on the job, and so will the local judge. They will say, "Let Washington do it." I feel as Black does.

STONE: But when Congress passed this, they didn't want to limit it.

JACKSON: I consider that period one of the most shameful of our times. Scholars and Charles Sumner were not giving it this interpretation.[42] This interpretation belongs to Frank.[43] It was never used, up until that time. We are going to be misunderstood as favoring a beating. They did not contemplate the Fourteenth Amendment doing anything as is claimed here.

STONE: I don't believe that they contemplated the use of the statute to punish every act in excess of authority. They had in mind what was happening then—the deprivation of the Negro's suffrage.

RUTLEDGE: If the question were open, I would agree on discrimination. But that was closed. Congress intended to reach carpetbagging. Due process was large then. It is different now. I think that the act is void for vagueness for charging a man with "violation of constitutional rights."

Conference of November 4, 1944

STONE: There is a different problem here where you are dealing with interpreting the generalities of the Fourteenth Amendment, rather than when you have specific guarantees. If a specific guarantee was involved, then I could sustain conviction. But when the state law says what it does here, the standard comes close to incorporating the law library into the statute. So far as applied to the Fourteenth Amendment, you have a statute which has all the vices of the *Cohen Grocery* case. I would be prepared to say that it violated the due process requirements of the criminal statute. The fact that this statute has been on the books for so many years without any prosecutions shows that they never thought that this statute would work. If you couldn't prosecute in *Cohen*—you are going much further here. I would not go into the state action quagmire.

ROBERTS: I am certain that the Fourteenth Amendment was not meant to punish every petty offender.

---

42. Senator Charles Sumner of Massachusetts was a leader of the Radical Republican congressional faction during the Civil War and Reconstruction periods.

43. It is not clear to whom Jackson was referring—perhaps Attorney General Francis Biddle? See note 44 below.

STONE: Here the amendment (or statute) says due process.

ROBERTS: I want to keep away from state action. I admit that it is difficult to handle.

BLACK: Look at Francis Biddle's speech on civil liberties.[44] He says that for many years the Civil Rights Act of 1894 prevented the use of this approach, but it was restored in the *Classic* case.[45] And now, anybody who violates due process can be prosecuted criminally. This is no different from an anti-lynching law. Biddle says further that it will include police officials and judges. Certainly we don't agree ourselves on due process.

JACKSON: This is an anti-lynching bill, if the government is sustained.

BLACK: We, if we uphold this, are doing what Congress has not intended to do.

REED: I shudder from declaring this statute unconstitutional. When we go into the legislative history, it will go badly for us. I am for reversal, but I am not sure why.

BLACK: This statute violates due process. This man is now to be tried under a statute that should definitely inform him.

REED: Do we have to say that this is under color of statute?

ROBERTS: You couldn't indict him without a statute.

REED: I can't say that he committed murder under state action.

---

44. Francis Biddle was a key Roosevelt administration insider with a longstanding interest in civil rights. He served in several capacities under President Roosevelt, including wartime service as attorney general. In 1943 and 1944 he gave two noteworthy speeches on civil rights: an address on November 11, 1943, before the Jewish Theological Seminary of America on "Democracy and Racial Minorities"; and the Edward L. Bernays Lecture in 1944, "Civil Rights and the Federal Law in Safeguarding Liberty Today." In both speeches, Biddle spoke about the *Screws* case and applauded the lower federal courts for convicting Screws and the others for their "acts of horrible brutality." Biddle maintained that the use of criminal sanctions to protect civil rights would be restricted for the most part to cases involving official misuse of power or cases involving individual rights directly guaranteed by federal laws or the Constitution. He noted that the use of criminal laws to punish civil rights abuses helped to vindicate democratic values in America's fight against fascism and concluded that "race intolerance is no longer a matter merely of domestic concern. For it undermines our moral authority as a nation, which apparently can profess but cannot practice democracy." See Troutt, "Screws, Koon, and Routine Aberrations," 53.

45. After the Civil War, Congress passed a series of civil rights laws, including the Enforcement Act of 1870, intended to enforce the terms of the Fifteenth Amendment by prohibiting any abridgement of the right to vote on account of race, color, or previous condition of servitude; the Force Act of 1871, which prohibited the use of force and violence in connection with voter registration and provided for federal supervision of polling places; and the Ku Klux Klan Act of 1871, which prohibited conspiracies aimed at depriving individuals of, or hindering them in exercising, their right to vote. The Election Law Repeal Act of 1894 revoked most of these protective measures. Some of these were subsequently restored in later legislation, including the Corrupt Practices Act of 1925. The Supreme Court helped this process by turning back constitutional challenges to this sort of legislation in cases such as *United States v. Classic*, 313 U.S. 299 (1941). Gardner, "Consent, Legitimacy and Elections," 237–38.

FRANKFURTER:[46] I am clear on two grounds. Suppose an injunction had been entered. We would say that it was not a court of equity. We could give certainty out of uncertainty. *Wilson* granted—the situation was not necessary to most penal laws.[47] *United States v. Lee*—regarding Arlington—and *Virginia v. Rives*.[48] First, there isn't a law—an appropriate law. I would reverse on both grounds.

DOUGLAS: I would favor a construction of the statute to exclude the cloudy grounds.

JACKSON: I would like to see it reversed if we could put it on grounds that we could stomach.

STONE: I don't believe that the people who drafted the Fourteenth Amendment intended any such thing.

RUTLEDGE: If the question were new, I would seize on the language that you took out of the statute and make this strictly discrimination. If we don't do it on that, I prefer to whittle the act down to a narrow basis.

BLACK: They did not try him for due process—they charged him.

STONE: Whoever writes this, I hope that they will keep us out of state action.

Result: Six months of internal discussion and debate left the Court badly divided. In a plurality decision, William O. Douglas expressed sympathy for Screws's argument that the statute was dangerously vague.[49] Douglas acknowledged that the law could have potentially broad and uncertain application, given the changing nature of case law interpreting the Fourteenth Amendment. But Douglas concluded that reading the statute narrowly and focusing on the requirement that the violation be "willful" limited the scope of the statute enough to save it. In order to be punishable, Screws must have had specific intent to violate a known constitutional right. While this statute has subsequently been used on occa-

---

46. Murphy's record of Frankfurter's remarks was largely illegible or nonsensical, and Jackson's notes were almost as cryptic. Frankfurter's comments should be read with particular caution—or perhaps with particular haste.

47. *Lane v. Wilson*, 307 U.S. 268 (1939). In this case, election officials discriminated illegally against blacks by not allowing them to register to vote. Their actions, however, were not in defiance of a state law but were carried out under the state's authority. Frankfurter wrote the majority opinion for a 6–2 Court. McReynolds and Butler dissented, while Douglas did not participate.

48. *United States v. Lee*, 106 U.S. 196 (1882); *Virginia v. Rives*, 100 U.S. 313 (1879). The *Lee* case involved the Arlington estate of General Robert E. Lee's wife, Mary. The U.S. government purchased the property at a tax sale and the secretary of war ordered the land set aside for a national cemetery. When the family challenged the seizure, the attorney general argued that the doctrine of executive immunity meant that the courts lacked jurisdiction. In rejecting this argument, Justice Samuel Miller wrote, "No man in this country is so high that he is above the law. No officer of the law may set that law at defiance with impunity. All the officers of the government, from the highest to the lowest, are creatures of the law and are bound to obey it." While this case dealt with federal officials, the Court referred interchangeably to decisions in suits against federal officials and suits against state officials brought in federal court. Fallon, *The Federal Courts and the Federal System*, 1016.

49. Joining Douglas were Stone, Black, and Reed.

sion to punish police brutality, Douglas's restrictive interpretation limited the number of successful prosecutions.[50]

There were two very different dissents. Frank Murphy argued that the convictions should have been affirmed. Owen Roberts, joined by Frankfurter and Jackson, argued that the statute was unconstitutionally vague and that the indictments should have been dismissed. In Roberts's opinion, the act was being misused; it was intended to cover voting cases, not homicides. Moreover, the law had only rarely been used in any context—Roberts called it a "dead letter" statute. Finally, citing Barney, Roberts maintained that the phrase "under color of law" was not intended to apply to state officers acting in violation of state law. This was a patently local crime, he concluded, and it should be left to the states to decide what to do.

Perhaps the most intriguing opinion was Rutledge's concurrence. Rutledge made it clear that his heart and mind were with Murphy, but his vote was with Douglas. He characterized what happened to Hall as a willful, brutal, and premeditated murder, but he felt compelled to join Douglas because he wanted the Court to send a clear judgment on remand. He could not tolerate allowing an even split between those who wanted to remand the case for a new trial and those who wanted to remand with an order to dismiss the indictments. With a brief apology, Rutledge made what he considered to be the only practical decision.

On remand, a new jury was instructed to decide whether Sheriff Screws and his deputies had willfully deprived Robert Hall of his constitutional rights. All three defendants were acquitted. Soon after the end of the trial, Sheriff Screws was elected to the Georgia state senate.

Williams v. Georgia, 349 U.S. 375 (1955)
(Burton) (Clark) (Douglas)

To select juries in Georgia, county jury commissioners put the names of white prospective jurors on white cards and the names of prospective jurors of other races on yellow cards and then put all of the cards into a jury box. Local judges or commissioners then drew cards as needed to create jury panels. Any yellow cards that were drawn were invariably placed on criminal panels, where prosecutors could systematically use their peremptory challenges to excuse all non-whites from jury service. In 1953, the Supreme Court condemned this system of jury selection in Avery v. Georgia.[51] *Six months later, how-*

---

50. One recent federal prosecution under the Civil Rights Act of 1866 was against four Los Angeles police officers charged with the brutal beating of Rodney King in 1991. After being acquitted of criminal charges in state court, the four were indicted in 1992 by a federal grand jury and charged with willfully violating King's constitutional rights. The Constitution's double jeopardy clause did not protect the officers, because state and federal governments are considered to be separate sovereign entities when it comes to criminal prosecutions. Laurence Powell, Timothy Wind, and Theodore Briseno were charged with depriving King of his Fourth Amendment rights to be secure and free from the intentional use of unreasonable force. Stacy Koon, the officer in charge, was charged with violating King's Fourteenth Amendment right to due process, including the "right to be free from harm while in official custody." Powell and Koon were convicted, while Wind and Briseno were acquitted. For Judge John Davies's sentencing memorandum, see *United States v. Koon,* 833 F. Supp. 769 (Cent. Dist. Cal. 1993).

51. *Avery v. Georgia,* 345 U.S. 559 (1953), involved a rape case against a black defendant. Not one of the sixty people on the jury array was black, which was both statistically improbable and quite common in Georgia. The Supreme Court ruled that Avery had made out a prima facie case of racial discrimination in state jury selection procedures and remanded the case for a new trial. On remand, James Avery was allowed to plead guilty and was sentenced to twenty years in prison.

ever, Georgia was still using the same color-coded system to empanel all-white juries. One such all-white jury convicted a black defendant by the name of Aubry Williams of the murder of a liquor store clerk. Williams's lawyer did not object to the racist jury selection procedures at trial but later filed an extraordinary motion for a new trial, claiming that he had not known about Avery. The state courts refused to grant Williams a new trial, claiming that the state had an absolute rule that defendants must challenge the jury when it was "put on" the defendant or accept the consequences. Williams argued that the rule was discretionary and could be waived in extraordinary circumstances. In light of the unconstitutionality and gross unfairness of Georgia's jury selection procedures in a capital case, Williams argued that to refuse a new trial in this case was a denial of due process. There were also concerns about the incompetence of Williams's trial lawyer, Carter Goode.

WARREN: I am troubled on some of the points raised in Harlan's memo.[52] I agree with Harlan, but I believe further that Williams really had no representation of counsel at the trial or on appeal. He might as well have had no lawyer at all.[53] Eugene Gressman asked for the record from Georgia, and they denied letting the record go out of the state. I asked to have the record written up. Carter Goode did nothing with the case and practically abandoned it, and when he made out his affidavit he probably told the truth—he did not know about the *Avery* case and he did not care.[54] The worst thing in this case is the failure of the Georgia courts to act. They did nothing, even after Georgia Supreme Court condemned the practice in *Avery*, and said that it would be unconstitutional discrimination.[55] A year later, the trial judge still drew different colored cards, knowing that the practice had been condemned. I can't let this man die as a result of that procedure. I could not have this man's life on my conscience. To let him die without a fair trial would be a discrimination. His constitutional rights were violated, and they want to hide behind this lawyer. The Georgia courts can't hide behind the procedural dodge. The trial judge himself violated the Constitution. I agree with Harlan, up to his conclusion to send it back to the Georgia Supreme Court for reconsideration. I would instead reverse and grant a new trial. If we just send it back, the court would *fix it up burglary proof.* I would reverse, citing *Avery*.

BLACK: I agree with the Chief Justice. I also agree with Harlan's memo that the local judge and the state supreme court had discretion to set the verdict aside—the facts show that.

52. John Harlan was deeply concerned by this case and immediately after oral argument asked his clerk, E. Barrett Prettyman Jr., to look for a way to "vindicate the constitutional rights of the petitioner, so far admittedly thwarted." Prettyman's investigation revealed that the Georgia waiver rule was not absolute, as the Georgia courts had insisted, but allowed for exceptions in extraordinary cases. Harlan circulated a memorandum to the conference suggesting that in the interest of comity the Court should merely remand the case and give the state courts a second chance to put matters right.

53. Less than two weeks before oral argument, defense counsel Carter Goode wrote a letter to the Supreme Court declining to appear on Williams's behalf. Goode said that he was scheduled to appear in a divorce suit in Georgia the same week and that traveling to Washington might cost him a paying client. Warren then turned to Eugene Gressman, a young but highly respected Washington lawyer, and invited him to submit a brief and argue Williams's case.

54. *Avery v. Georgia*, 345 U.S. 559 (1953).

55. *Avery v. State*, 70 S.E.2d 716 (Ga. 1952).

That discretion should have been exercised. I, too, am afraid that if we send it back it would just be patched up. The *Scottsboro* defendants had better representation.[56] The state's extraordinary motion procedure is discretionary. Reverse and cite *Avery*, as the Chief Justice says.

REED: In view of the attitudes of the Chief Justice and Black, I hesitate about my conclusions. Georgia procedure was not followed. Exception was not taken to the panel. If you don't challenge the jury at that point, it is too late. In *Avery*, Georgia upheld the defendant's conviction. The local judge here looked on his situation as being the same as in *Avery*. But there is a time to challenge the array—before selection. *Brown v. Allen* was the same as this, but we have to have this procedure.[57] I am here: the Georgia court had discretion and exercised it as they saw fit. I would affirm on the procedural point.

FRANKFURTER: The implications of this case are highly important in the relation of federal power to the states. This is not just a case. There are difficulties:

(1) I have *very strong views* of the duty of this Court to be alert against taking over the administration of criminal law from the states. We *should not run* counter to local enforcement bodies; if we run counter to state law bodies, they will in practice not be respectful of what we do. We must not weaken the state courts. The question is, what is the due process requirement? We must be alert against harsh cases. When life is at stake, close scrutiny is necessary. While our standards are woeful, we should not let a harsh case bring us into violence with the states' administration of justice.

(2) *On the other side*, we must enforce standards in federal courts, which is our charge. In the federal system we are supervisors—that is different.

(3) If Georgia wants to devise explicit lines in appellate review in criminal cases, they can do so and we should respect it. *If the state* gives discretion, then it is a different matter, for that does violate due process. If the state has a definite time set, then it must be complied with.

On the other hand, if the state's failure to use discretion in an appropriate case is shocking, it violates due process. Harlan's memo is a fair statement of Georgia law. It shows that there is relief in exceptional cases. There is no hard and fast rule regarding the time granted to challenge the jury array. We should substitute our views for Georgia's—otherwise due process is violated. The situation here is special. If there is discretion, this is a convincing case for it. I would go beyond Harlan's memo. We should—when we do upset state decisions—we should enlist the understanding of the local courts.

Here, there are compelling circumstances against the finality of the state order. I would remand in a nice way, in a considerate opinion not telling them what Georgia law is. I

---

56. *Powell v. Alabama*, 287 U.S. 45 (1932).

57. *Brown v. Allen*, 344 U.S. 443 (1953) combined five separate cases involving claims of racial discrimination in the selection of North Carolina juries. The Court ruled that where a state court's decision is based on adequate and independent state grounds, no further examination of the case was required by federal courts unless no state remedy for the violation of a claimed federal constitutional right *ever existed*. The Court denied relief in one case because the state had a sixty-day limit to perfect appeals, and the defendant perfected his appeal on the sixty-first day. The Court ruled that the defendant's failure to use the available state remedy precluded him from filing a federal habeas corpus claim.

assume that Georgia will yield to its available remedy. I would imply that failure to grant the motion would violate due process. I would do that only on my conviction that failure to make a qualification would be a lack of due process. I would not remand on the basis that it is for Georgia to settle this point and put it so that they could frustrate us. I would not leave much room for Georgia to stand pat. If we remand and leave open a contingency that the Georgia Supreme Court might deny—if they did, I would reverse it when it came back.

I would *not* agree with the Chief Justice that, in effect, Williams was without counsel—that he had "no" lawyer. We must be careful in finding that counsel was ineffective. This option holds dangerous possibilities. I can't reverse on *Avery*. I might go along, however, if the case is brought under *Powell*.[58]

DOUGLAS: I would not reverse on counsel ground—he was just slow. I would assume the impartiality of state judges. I would reverse on *Avery*. I would not send it back for Georgia to take another crack. I reverse, because in this refusal to exercise discretion is due process of law. I would not let it be washed out. I would reverse.

BURTON: I would remand with Harlan to the Georgia Supreme Court for the exercise of their discretion.

CLARK: I would affirm. Eugene Gressman thinks that the jury selection procedure used in *Avery* is conclusively illegal. *Avery* is not a conclusive rule. It does not necessarily violate due process to use colored slips. *Georgia* said that use of these sheets was prima facie discrimination—all we did was to apply it. *Here*, the prima facie rule is to some extent rebutted. There were four colored men on this jury.[59] We can't condemn the judge on that. There was nothing in *Avery* that made it an absolute rule. I can't say that the system used was misapplied here. The Georgia cases do not allow new trial on late challenges to the panel. Under Harlan's memo, those cases only related to petit juries, not to panel questions. *Cornelious* holds that a defendant's failure to challenge the panel is a waiver.[60] *Cumming* was also a waiver case.[61] So there was no *discretion* in this case—it was too late. The most that we could do would be to send it back to find out if a judge could use his discretion.

---

58. *Powell v. Alabama*, 287 U.S. 45 (1932).

59. Clark was wrong; there were four blacks on the jury *panel*. The trial judge excused three of them for cause, and the prosecutor used his first peremptory challenge to eliminate the fourth.

60. *Cornelious v. State*, 17 S.E.2d 156 (Ga. 1941). In this murder case, the defendant waited until his appeal to claim that the state's jury selection procedures violated the Fourteenth Amendment by systematically excluding blacks and women. The state supreme court ruled that because Cornelious had not raised these issues before his trial commenced, he had waived his right to appeal the issue. The state court appeared to recognize an exception to this waiver rule—in habeas corpus proceedings where the indictment was invalid on its face—but the court noted that this possible exception was not applicable to Cornelious's case.

61. *Cumming v. State*, 117 S.E. 378 (Ga. 1923). Where the defendant participated in selecting the jury for his murder trial without making any specific objections or challenging the jury array, the state supreme court held that the defendant had waived his rights and could not challenge the array on appeal. The defendant, the court said, "took his chances" with the array and could not complain after he was convicted.

MINTON: I agree with Clark. We are not dealing with Georgia practice. Georgia has a rule that the array must be challenged at the threshold (due process). I would affirm.

HARLAN: I would remand to the Georgia Supreme Court. The Georgia Supreme Court's opinion is muddy. There is no statutory time limit. Is there a judge-imposed limit? The Georgia Supreme Court says: (1) the challenge was untimely; and (2) the affidavits must be adequate.[62] I am reluctant to say that we can now reverse without a remand, but we can indicate what we think and tell them that we are sending back to give them a chance. Also, remanding the case gives the Georgia courts an opportunity to act, after the concession that the court knew of the *Avery* violation. I think that Georgia law had discretion to grant or deny—but there is sufficient doubt about it—so I vote to remand.

Result: The Court remanded the case and advised—but did not order—the state of Georgia to grant Aubry Williams a new trial. In a blistering response, the Georgia Supreme Court angrily refused to grant Williams a new trial, in effect telling the Supreme Court to go to hell.[63] Perhaps the most extraordinary aspect of Chief Justice Duckworth's opinion was his ruling that the U.S. Supreme Court lacked jurisdiction to hear the case and that the state supreme court was not bound by anything that the federal Supreme Court had to say. After his contemptuous show of defiance, Duckworth fully expected to be dragged before the Supreme Court in chains and held in contempt. Instead, worried about growing southern resistance in the wake of Brown v. Board of Education, the Warren Court backed down. The Justices voted 9–0 to deny cert when the case again came before the Court in early 1956.[64] Aubry Williams was executed a month later.[65]

Rizzo v. Goode, 423 U.S. 362 (1976)
(Brennan)

Gerald Goode filed a federal class action suit accusing Philadelphia mayor Frank Rizzo, the city's managing director, police commissioner, and other municipal officials of engaging in a pervasive pattern of unconstitutional police treatment of Philadelphia residents, especially racial minorities and the poor.[66] District Court judge John P. Fullam found a pattern of police abuse—though not on the part of any of the named city officials—and directed that new city guidelines and police procedures be established under the court's supervision to deal with citizen complaints. The court of appeals affirmed.

In conference, the Justices worried about asserting federal control over local police departments.

BURGER: Judge Fullam treated the police department like *Penn Central.*[67] I don't want to take over receivership of the police department and write guidelines for them.

---

62. The state courts ruled that the affidavits submitted by Carter Goode and his partner were "mere opinion" and were not supported by sufficient evidence.

63. *Williams v. State,* 88 S.E.2d 376 (Ga. 1955). E. Barrett Prettyman first used this phrase to describe the Georgia court's reaction. Prettyman, *Death and the Supreme Court,* 290.

64. *Williams v. Georgia,* 350 U.S. 950 (1956).

65. For a full discussion of the legal and political importance of this case, see Dickson, "State Court Defiance and The Limits of Supreme Court Authority: *Williams v. Georgia* Revisited."

66. 42 U.S.C. §1983.

67. Judge Fullam supervised the reorganization of the Penn Central Railroad. *In re Penn Central Transportation Co.,* 458 F. Supp. 1346 (E.D. Pa. 1978).

STEWART: If there had been a finding of impermissible police department policy from the chief or the director of public safety, then the remedy imposed here would be O.K. But here there wasn't such a finding, and therefore no permissible remedy.

WHITE: I don't think that anyone can maintain a federal lawsuit based on a violation of other people's rights. The only proper members of the class can be those whose own rights were violated. The certification of this class of Philadelphia citizens was therefore improper. There is no equity for this remedy in this case. At most, they could relegate individuals to damages under §1983.

MARSHALL: The failure of city officials to prevent these things from happening is the gravamen of this cause of action. Judge Fullam said, "You set up these rules, and I'll lift the injunction."

BLACKMUN: Judge Fullam found a violation in the city's failure to take steps to prevent these things, and then carefully fashioned a remedy that was self-corrective and not punitive. It is startling to have the federal courts intrude in such matters, however.

POWELL: I agree with Byron. The people who were injured should pursue their own remedies. The federal courts should not be running city police departments. The assertion of judicial power over state operations is thus contrary to our very fundamental premises of self-government.

Result: The Court avoided most of the substantive issues, ruling 5–3 that the case was not justiciable for want of a real case or controversy. Writing for the majority, William Rehnquist maintained that none of the named defendants was responsible for any real or immediate injuries and that any damages that Gerald Goode and the others might have suffered were so speculative that they did not have a sufficient personal stake in the outcome of the case. Moreover, Rehnquist added, the district court's judgment amounted to an unwarranted federal judicial intrusion into state business.

Monell v. Department of Social Services of the City of New York,
436 U.S. 658 (1978)
(Brennan)

The New York Department of Social Services and other city departments required pregnant employees to take unpaid leaves of absence before they were medically required to stop working. Jane Monell and others sued under 42 U.S.C. §1983, which allowed civil suits against persons who deprived them of their civil rights under color of law. The district court found that the city's mandatory leave policy violated the women's civil rights but ruled that the Supreme Court's decision in Monroe v. Pape *gave city departments immunity against such suits.[68] The court of appeals affirmed.*

---

68. *Monroe v. Pape,* 365 U.S. 167 (1961). The Court held that under §1983, individual state law enforcement officials could be sued in federal court for police brutality and for depriving persons of their civil rights under color of law. The Court broadly defined "color of law" to include acts where officials did not have authority to act. On the issue of exhaustion of state remedies, the Court declared that the federal remedy was supplementary to existing state remedies and that state remedies did not have to be exhausted before the federal remedy was invoked.

After a routine first conference, the second conference saw two issues come quickly to the fore: whether Monroe v. Pape *should be overruled and whether city departments could be considered "persons" under §1983.*

Conference of March 6, 1978

BURGER: I see no basis for overruling *Monroe* and would affirm.

BRENNAN: I would reverse.

STEWART: I would reverse.

WHITE: I would reverse.

MARSHALL: I would reverse.

BLACKMUN: I would reverse and not decide immunity at this time.

POWELL: I reverse. They should have immunity unless constitutional doctrine has been settled, as it was not here.

REHNQUIST: I would affirm.

STEVENS: I would reverse. We should not discuss immunity, even to the extent that Lewis wants to. We must overrule *Monroe* squarely, along with other cases. The city allowed police carte blanche to do as they please. I would save vicarious liability. Error was much more than the 60–40 in *Monroe*. Reliance interests there were not as heavy here. Our decision should not be influenced by how *Bivens* applies to the Fourteenth Amendment.[69]

STEWART: Originally, I thought that a municipality could be held as "person" for its own deliberate actions with a *Wood v. Strickland* defense. I would decide it and not leave the issue undecided.[70]

Second Conference

BURGER: Either corporate entities or city officials must be "persons" if a case may be maintained. I would say that they are not, under *Monroe v. Pape.*

STEWART: Can city officials be included in damages? This question is not reached if the school board itself is a "person" and can be sued. I think that *Monroe v. Pape* bars a suit against city on *respondeat superior*—a reflection of the Sherman Amendment, which shows

---

69. *Bivens v. Six Unknown Federal Narcotics Agents*, 403 U.S. 388 (1971).

70. *Wood v. Strickland*, 420 U.S. 308 (1975). After an Arkansas high school expelled several students for violating school rules prohibiting alcohol at school events, Peggy Strickland and other parents sued in federal court, alleging that school officials, including John Wood, had violated their children's due process rights. The parents claimed the right to sue for damages under 42 U.S.C. §1983. School officials claimed that absent malice, they were immune from such suits. The Court ruled 5–4 that school officials were not immune from liability under §1983 if they knew or should have known that their disciplinary actions would violate students' constitutional rights or if they acted with malicious intent. Compensation was limited to cases where school officials had acted with malice or in bad faith. Powell, Burger, Blackmun, and Rehnquist dissented, arguing that school officials should have broad qualified immunity.

that they can't be sued within boundaries on a theory of absolute liability. But our school desegregation cases make it clear that a school board can be sued for direct violations by the board, as here. But even the city ought be held to its own direct acts. There may be a *Wood v. Strickland* defense here. I will pass.

WHITE: I would not extend *Monroe v. Pape* to the school board. Whether I agree how far it should be cut back is irrelevant. When agents do precisely what they are authorized to do, the body should be considered a "person" for purposes of liability.

MARSHALL: I would like to be as gentle as possible with *Monroe v. Pape*—leave it there, and not extend it here.

BLACKMUN: I am at sea in this case. *Monroe v. Pape* has bothered me. I think that Bill Douglas was wrong on his history. The issue of "person" was not raised in the school cases, and *Monroe* suggests that we must affirm. If we want to pull back from it, we have the problem that Congress has not backed away from it. I have to affirm because I think that I am bound by it.

POWELL: Frankfurter was right in *Monroe v. Pape*. It never made sense to me to say those cops acted under "color of state action." I would go with the idea that when a policy of the body violates the Constitution, that is a violation of §1983 by a "person." So I lean toward Potter's views. I have difficulties getting around the language of *Kenosha*, and so I have to be tentative.[71]

REHNQUIST: The §1983 "person" issue was never raised in the school cases. It was the officials, clearly, under §1983 who were enjoined under Gurfein's analogy to *Ex parte Young*.[72] If stare decisis means anything, our rejection of Felix Frankfurter's better position means that we would have to open up both the Sherman Act and the color of state law points. I can't draw a line between policy making officials and subordinate officials.

STEVENS: On the "person," question, I agree with Bill Brennan. The Court would look ridiculous to say that a school board is not a person. I have doubts about *Monroe v. Pape*,

---

71. *City of Kenosha v. Bruno*, 412 U.S. 507 (1973). Bar owners in two Wisconsin towns had their liquor license renewal applications denied because they offered nude entertainment. Bruno and the other bar owners sued the municipalities of Racine and Kenosha in federal court, alleging that both city governments had violated the bar owners' due process and other federal rights. The owners attacked the cities' licensing schemes and argued that they had a right to full adversarial hearings before their licenses could be revoked. The lawsuits were filed under 42 U.S.C. §1983 and 28 U.S.C. §1343, which allowed federal lawsuits against any "person" who, under color of law, deprived another of their civil rights. In an 8–1 decision, the Supreme Court ruled that cities were not "persons" under §1983 or 1343. Because Bruno and the other owners had only sued the municipalities, there was no federal jurisdiction. The Court remanded the case to the district court to decide whether there were other adequate grounds to support the bar owners' lawsuit. Douglas dissented in part, complaining that the Court should not have limited lawsuits against city governments under §1983 without requiring the issues to be fully briefed and orally argued.

72. Circuit Judge Murray Gurfein wrote the majority opinion below in *Monell v. Department of Social Services*, 532 F. 2d 259 (1976). *Ex Parte Young*, 209 U.S. 123 (1908).

but it and *Moor v. Alameda County* were about police officials.[73] This board is engaged in a wholly different kind of activity. I would thus limit *Monroe* to cases where police officials are involved.

Result: The Court voted 7–2 to overrule Monroe v. Pape. *William Brennan, writing for the majority, held that local governments, departments, and officials were not necessarily immune from suits brought under §1983. Stevens joined most of Brennan's opinion and also wrote a concurring opinion. Burger and Rehnquist dissented.*

INTERSTATE DISPUTES AND STATE REGULATION OF INDIAN AFFAIRS

United States v. California, 332 U.S. 19 (1947)
(Douglas)

After oil was discovered off the California coast in 1894, the state sold lease rights to private oil companies beginning in 1921. In 1945, the federal government sued to stop the leases and claimed exclusive ownership rights of "lands, minerals, and other things of value" from the low-tide mark to the three-mile limit then claimed as American territorial waters. California claimed title to the marginal sea and seabed out to the three-mile limit based on the "equal footing" doctrine.[74] The state argued that the thirteen original states held common law title to their marginal seas and seabeds and that California was admitted to the Union on an equal basis.[75] The federal government argued that it had exclusive claim to all territorial seas and seabeds. Justice Jackson did not participate because he had been involved in the controversy as attorney general.

---

73. *Moor v. Alameda County*, 411 U.S. 693 (1973). David Moor brought a civil rights action under 42 U.S.C. §§1983 and 1988 against county sheriff's officers and the county itself, alleging both federal and state claims. Moor claimed that the federal courts had diversity jurisdiction and sought to have both his state and federal claims heard in federal court. The county claimed that because the municipality was not a "person," it could not be sued under §1983 (citing *Monroe v. Pape*, 365 U.S. 167). On an 8–1 vote, the Supreme Court dismissed the §§1983 and 1988 charges against the county. Thurgood Marshall, writing for the majority, also ruled that the district court had been within its discretion to refuse to decide the state claims. However, the Court decided that the county was a citizen for diversity jurisdiction purposes. Douglas dissented, arguing that while the county was not a "person" under §1983 in a suit for damages, it *was* a person in cases where plaintiffs asked for equitable relief.

74. The equal footing clause originally appeared in the Northwest Ordinance, which provided for the admission of new states after the Revolutionary War. Article 5 of the ordinance said that new states "shall be admitted . . . into the Congress of the United States on an equal footing with the original states, in all respects whatsoever." This language has appeared in every enabling statute admitting states into the Union, except for Texas. Fitzgerald, "The Tidelands Controversy Revisited," 215.

75. *Pollard's Lessee v. Hagan*, 44 U.S. (8 How.) 212 (1845). This case used the equal footing doctrine to vindicate state ownership of lands under navigable intrastate waterways. The decision followed *Martin v. Lessee of Waddell*, 41 U.S. (16 Pet.) 367 (1842), which held that after the Revolutionary War the original states succeeded to the English crown's sovereign control over internal navigable waterways—and the lands under them—for the common use of the people.

In this case, the question was whether the state or the federal government owned the land under Alabama's navigable waterways when it became a state in 1819. Pollard and others claimed private owner-

Conference of March 17, 1947

VINSON: This is a difficult case. I am not ready to state my views. The United States makes a strong case respecting their ownership. I am not certain what weight should be given to the interim actions of the state. States are entitled to the "same footing" on admissions. They have title to land under navigable waters within the state. The *Abby Dodge* case has strong language in support of the state's view.[76] It is necessary for us to decide this case free from the oil question.

BLACK: Precedents do not foreclose us. Complete power of control of water over land is what the law will protect. The *Mobile* case would be better if it had said that the U.S. government had left regulation with the states.[77] The United States can control the three-mile strip. Look at the *Commodore Park* case.[78] Ownership of land under navigable waters is with the state, but it is a "technical" ownership. I am not willing to extend the doctrine of ownership of navigable streambeds to the ocean floor. The federal government has complete power over the waters, the fish, sponges, oil, and all else that is there.

REED: Everything points in one direction. We are dealing here not with power, ownership, or sovereignty, but the relationship between states and the nation. The width of our maritime belt depends on our ability to defend it. The states took over all navigable waterways. It is not so much ownership as a trusteeship for its people. The federal power is one of commerce only. It could not prevent the drilling of an oil well from shore at an angle. The only case that makes me hesitate is the air case—*Causby*—but that is not applicable to navigable waters.[79] The three-mile limit was pretty well accepted when our federation was made.

FRANKFURTER: I agree substantially with Reed. If you want the United States to run it, the United States will run it. This case tests your understanding of what role the judge will perform. To give the United States what it wants is to discard one hundred years of

---

ship of land that used to lie under the Mobile River and the tidelands of Mobile Bay, based on an 1836 Act of Congress which confirmed an 1809 Spanish Land Grant. The Court ruled that because the original states held title to their submerged lands prior to the establishment of the Union, the equal footing doctrine required that Alabama enjoy the same ownership rights as other states and that Congress had no authority to grant title in these lands to private parties. Alabama held sovereign jurisdiction over all territory within its limits, subject only to the common law. The Court avoided the problem of Spanish cession by saying that Spain had never held clear, uncontested title to the territory (the area had also been claimed by Georgia) and could not have passed clear title either to the United States or to any private parties.

76. *The Abby Dodge*, 223 U.S. 166 (1912). The American government claimed that the ship illegally took sponges from the Gulf of Mexico in violation of federal law. The Court, however, held that the statute applied only outside Florida's "territorial limits." Any broader reading of the federal statute, the Court said, would have exceeded Congress's constitutional authority.

77. *Pollard's Lessee v. Hagan*, 44 U.S. (8 How.) 212 (1845).

78. *United States v. Commodore Park*, 324 U.S. 386 (1945). The Supreme Court permitted the federal government to dredge a bay in order to improve navigation without compensating the owner of riparian property for damages caused when the deposited sediment blocked his access to the waterway.

79. *United States v. Causby*, 328 U.S. 256 (1946). The Court required the federal government to compensate a chicken farmer after low-flying military aircraft frightened his poultry and hurt his business.

history. There is no intellectually honest answer to Shaw in the early Massachusetts case.[80] I was surprised at the body of authority. The state has the same proprietary interest in the oil as Massachusetts would have in pearls.[81] The *Port of Seattle* case talks of ownership.[82] Title or proprietary interest. It is not a question of national vs. state power. If the United States wants this land, it can purchase it or condemn it. If it belonged to the United States, then officials can't change that. But government practice is entitled to weight as casting light on what the ambiguities mean.

REED: Once I was told that this is an extension of property rules previously laid down, I now am compelled to sustain the federal claim. The state constitution is not a grant of federal right in these lands. I incline toward Douglas's position that more than common law concepts are involved here. These are vast defense regions. There is rational room to distinguish on a title basis between the original thirteen states and later ones. I can't say that the United States did not get title to the marginal sea any more than it did not get western lands. It is a different thing than the lands under navigable rivers. It stands on a footing closer to air.

MURPHY: I vote tentatively for the United States.

BURTON: I am intrigued by this case. I approached the problem with the view that the state was right, and came out the other way. I was not decided before. On the original interpretation of the Constitution, whatever California got they got on admission. Then they claimed sovereignty. The United States had what it got from Mexico. It was involved in title beyond the tidelands. We must consider it as if it involved land four or more miles out. A piece of land broken up—you can't treat it as uplands. The United States would claim an island by right of discovery. But the three mile continental shelf is pretty much the same thing. The only difference is that internationally, others will not intrude by agreement. When Mexico made its treaty with the United States, it gave title to everything except where Mexicans had settled. Until California can show that the United States has turned over the marginal sea, it does not get it. With sovereignty and equal footing come certain things. Tidelands, navigable waters, and the like—all that goes. It has been settled. That also explains what happens in the Great Lakes. I don't think that the thirteen original states got the marginal sea, either, but it is not necessary to pass on them. Neither the crown nor the states had ownership in the three-mile belt at the time of fed-

---

80. *Dunham v. Lamphere*, 69 Mass. (3 Gray) 268 (1855). Chief Justice Shaw argued that the right to regulate resources along coasts and tidewaters was left to the states, subject only to Congress's powers to regulate interstate and international commerce.

81. There was a series of cases dealing with state ownership of oyster beds. *McReady v. Virginia*, 94 U.S. 391 (1876), held that Virginia could prevent citizens of other states (in this case, Maryland) from planting oysters in the Ware River and could keep the tidal beds for the exclusive use of Virginia citizens. *Smith v. Maryland*, 59 U.S. 71 (1855), allowed Maryland's seizure of a ship that was caught dredging oysters in state-owned oyster beds on Chesapeake Bay.

82. *Port of Seattle v. Oregon and Washington R.R. Co.*, 255 U.S. 56 (1921). The Court ruled that when Washington became a state, it retained full and absolute proprietary ownership over all of the state's tidelands and navigable waters, including the lands under them. The state's ownership rights were subject only to federal regulations necessary to protect and promote commercial navigation. Louis Brandeis wrote the majority opinion.

eration. No one had reason to claim title out there, and no claim was made. Congress can do with this public land what it does with others. Is this result so inconsistent on policy as to cast a poor reflection on our legal reasoning? In 1945, the president laid claim to the continental shelf. If we are going to claim that, where do we come out if the states can run to that line? If logic compels us to give it to states, it is hard to see why we should stop at three miles.

Conference of March 29, 1947

VINSON: I gave this case further consideration. I am of the opinion that California's strongest position is that of equal footing with the original states. The Treaty of Guadalupe went to the Pacific Ocean. The boundary of the 1783 Treaty with Great Britain is the Atlantic Ocean. In 1793, Jefferson wrote his note about the three-mile limit. The claims of the original states to three-mile limits started in 1858 or 1859. Four or five states followed with statutes. About five of the states have not taken any action at all. It was variable in ancient law. Roman law recognized open seas. Britain called the seas its dominion. There wasn't any law on this at the time of Union—it is hard to see how the United States got title. The federal government certainly had authority over it, but so did the states. It may not require an ordinary concept of property title. I don't see how the states got it if the United States did not have it. If it became attached as a matter of title or ownership, then it came after formation of the Union. I am inclined to think that the United States wins. It is hard to say how the United States has title, but it is a question of power. Power comes from the federal government. With the exception of *Abby Dodge*, all you have is waters within the states. *Abby Dodge* is closer than any other precedent—but it did not deal with jurisdiction over soil, but with a criminal offense. *Skiriotes* tightens that case.[83] I come out on the side of the United States.

FRANKFURTER: If the thirteen original states got ownership of the three-mile belt, then equal footing would give the same to California.

VINSON: Some twenty wells were drilled without leave from California. The state moved in in 1921. The Treaty of Paris refers to the Atlantic Ocean. The Treaty of Guadalupe refers to the east line on the ocean plus three miles, but in the west the line goes merely to the ocean.

Result: The Court, in a 6–2 decision, backed the federal government's claims to the marginal sea and seabed to the three-mile limit. For the majority, Hugo Black held that the federal government's rights transcended mere property ownership and touched on two aspects of federal sovereignty: (1) the right and responsibility of the federal government to do whatever was necessary to protect the country from danger; and (2) its inherent right as a member of "the family of nations" to assert absolute, unencumbered control over the marginal sea and seabed.

Black, probably incorrectly, claimed that there was no historical support for the argument that the thirteen original states had ever asserted ownership of the marginal seabed. He argued that it was only after the founding of the Union that the idea of asserting such claims developed to protect Ameri-

---

83. *Skiriotes v. Florida*, 313 U.S. 69 (1941). Charles Evans Hughes recognized Florida's interest in regulating the harvesting of sponges in state territorial waters "in the absence of conflicting federal legislation."

can neutrality, to guard American shores from enemies and smugglers, and to engage in commerce as a maritime nation. While states often exercised police powers within littoral waters, it was by leave of the federal government and did not diminish the federal government's sovereign rights to control the resources of the continental shelf within the three-mile zone.

Black distinguished The Abby Dodge case, which involved sponge harvesting in Florida waters. The California case did not involve renewable resources of small consequence—it concerned the use and depletion of nonrenewable resources of the highest national and international importance. Moreover, Black observed, The Abby Dodge did not decide the question of ownership of lands under the marginal sea.

Reed and Frankfurter dissented, arguing that the thirteen original states retained ownership of the seabeds adjacent to their coasts and that equal footing doctrine meant that California had equal rights to its coastal resources.

United States v. Texas, 339 U.S. 707 (1950)
(Douglas)

Like California, Texas claimed ownership of its marginal seabed. Texas sought to distinguish its claim from California's by asserting its unique prior status as an independent republic. Unlike the original thirteen colonies or any other state, Texas had briefly been a fully sovereign state, and it claimed to have retained both dominium (proprietary ownership) and imperium (the right to assert governmental regulation and control) of the coastal seabed when it joined the Union.

Conference of April 1, 1950

VINSON: I believe that Texas is different. I am not certain of my position. Texas was a republic. It was a state of annexation. The equal footing doctrine deals merely with political standing. The U.S. argument about unappropriated or waste lands is inconsistent with its argument in California. There is nothing to the provision regarding ports, harbors, etc. I rely heavily on the boundary clause.

BLACK: Texas and California are the same on this issue.

REED: I would hate to see a difference between California and the rest of the states on one hand, and Texas on the other. I don't understand the California case. I hope that we will be able to make Texas and California the same.

FRANKFURTER: There is no reason why there should be uniformity among the states. The California case did not deal with property, but with national sovereignty.

BURTON: When lands come in, we must determine what came in. Texas's line was three miles out as a republic. Nations claimed that far out as their sovereignty, but not as their property. Even if Texas had this land as a republic, it lost it when it came in.

MINTON: You can't shrink the boundary line of Texas without violating the provision of the Constitution saying that the claims of a state shall not be denied. Texas had a boundary line—how was it lost? I can't see how.

Result: The Justices ruled 4–1–2 that while Texas had a stronger claim to its offshore lands than other states, the equal footing doctrine required that any sovereign rights Texas might have had in its off-

shore resources were surrendered to the United States upon the republic's admission to the Union. Douglas wrote the majority opinion. Reed and Minton dissented, arguing that Texas had sovereign possession of the marginal seabed as an independent republic and that there was no evidence that Texas had ever surrendered its rights under the terms of annexation and union. Frankfurter did not expressly dissent but complained in a separate opinion that it remained a mystery to him how the state's sovereign control of the marginal seabed could have passed to the federal government. Jackson and Clark did not participate.

United States v. California, 381 U.S. 139 (1964)
(Douglas)

Convinced that the Supreme Court's decisions were wrong, coastal states furiously lobbied Congress to pass legislation giving coastal states clear title to offshore lands. President Truman vetoed two such bills on the ground that the laws would have given coastal states special rights to resources that Truman believed belonged to the nation as a whole. Dwight Eisenhower favored state ownership of coastal lands and made the issue a main theme of his 1952 presidential campaign. With Eisenhower's encouragement, Congress passed the Submerged Lands Act of 1953, which returned to the states the ownership of oil and other resources to the three-mile limit. There were two forms of grants: (1) an unconditional grant of ownership of the marginal seabed for three miles from the "seaward limit of the state's inland waterways"; and (2) a possible second grant conditioned on each state's particular history. Gulf Coast states, for example, claimed rights to more extensive territorial boundaries that they claimed at the time they were admitted to the Union. These special claims, however, were limited to a maximum of three leagues (approximately nine miles). The practical effect of the SLA was that California regained control of most—though not all—of its offshore oil fields.

New problems arose because no one had precisely defined where the state's "inland waterways" ended and the new three-mile claims began. California claimed that "inland waters" should be defined as of the date that California joined the Union. The state argued that its harbors and bays should be counted as inland waterways, as well as the waters that lay between the mainland and California's offshore islands. This would have given California ownership of the seabed more than fifty miles from the mainland in some areas. The United States claimed that the end of the state's inland waterways (and the beginning of the state's new three-mile claims) should be defined according to international law and the Court's 1947 ruling in United States v. California.

After the first California *and* Texas *decisions, the Court appointed a special master to determine the precise border between state and federal property, especially in contentious areas such as the states' larger bays and harbors.*

Conference of December 11, 1964

WARREN: Not sitting.

BLACK: We should not accept the findings of the master, as they preceded the act which will have an effect on this discussion. All we have here is a question of boundaries. There is no rule of inland waters that we can follow. This issue was not decided by *United States v. California.* Perhaps the boundary should be that found in the California constitution when California was admitted to the Union.

DOUGLAS: I would decide it now. The Submerged Lands Act has nothing to do with it. I would not appoint a new master. I would take as the boundaries the description found in the California constitution at the time of admission.

HARLAN: The Submerged Lands Act does give to the states some rights. How does it define "coastline"? Congress intended the inland waters concept to be what the United States says. The Submerged Lands Act does not freeze the situation as of the date of its passage. It means that the prevailing federal policy that existed at time of the dispute prevails. We are parties to the Geneva Convention that establishes a 24-mile headland. The mean of the low low tide should be the boundary. I would not remand to the case to a special master.

BRENNAN: I agree substantially with Harlan. I think, however, that the Submerged Lands Act is the cutoff date.

STEWART: I agree with Brennan. The Submerged Lands Act does not define inland waters. Along the shore, the coastline should be the lowest of the low tide. "Inland waters" acquires meaning from international law and U.S. policy. The coastline is the issue, not the boundary. As to bays, it means "headlands," as defined by international law. The United States can give more to California.

WHITE: I agree with Brennan and Stewart.

GOLDBERG: On inland waters, I agree with Harlan. You measure it by the Geneva Convention.

Result: In a 5–2 decision, the Court rejected California's claims.[84] *Writing for the majority, John Marshall Harlan ruled that the SLA had left it to the courts to define inland waters, and the majority defined it according to established international law—specifically the 1958 Convention on the Territorial Sea and the Contiguous Zone, which the United States ratified in 1961.*

Black and Douglas dissented. In their view, the Court had no business defining the limits of the states' inland waterways. If nothing else, they argued, the problem should have been returned to the Congress for an expression of its will.

Arizona v. California, 373 U.S. 546 (1963)

(Douglas)

As Mark Twain once said, whiskey is for drinking and water is for fighting over. The history of the western United States is the story of the struggle to secure adequate supplies of fresh water in a region that is largely desert, and no body of fresh water has been more important than the Colorado River. Even today it remains the only reliable water supply for more than 25 million people—nearly 10 percent of the country's population. The seven states of the Colorado River basin have fought for

---

84. Earl Warren did not participate in the case because of his involvement in the issue as governor of California. Tom Clark did not participate because of his involvement on the other side of the issue when he was attorney general during the Truman administration.

more than a century for control of the river and its tributaries. The dispute is longstanding and often bitter, with all of the players jealously claiming their share of the stuff that dreams are really made of.[85]

In the early twentieth century, the greatest fear of other basin states was that California, which had developed earlier and more rapidly than the rest of the region, would use the established western water law doctrines of prior appropriation ("first in time, first in right") and equitable apportionment to lay permanent claim to most of the river's waterflow. Through complex interstate negotiations and with congressional assistance, six of the seven basin states ratified the Colorado River Compact in 1922. The compact promised an equitable apportionment of the river and its tributaries. It divided the river into two separate water basins, with the line drawn at Lee's Ferry, Arizona. The upper basin states were Colorado, New Mexico, Utah, and Wyoming. The lower basin states were Arizona, California, and Nevada. The upper and lower river basins were treated as two separate water sources, with each basin allotted 7.5 million acre feet of water per year.[86]

The compact left unresolved many of the more difficult issues. The first unanswered question was how the states within each basin would divide their respective allocations. Arizona and Nevada were worried that California might still claim most of the lower basin's allotment under established Western water law. Second, Arizona was the only basin state that refused to sign the compact, because the agreement included all tributary waters in calculating each state's water allotment. Arizona wanted to retain exclusive rights to its only tributary, the Gila River, without having it counted against Arizona's share of Colorado River water. Arizona finally signed the compact in 1944 but continued to claim exclusive rights to the Gila. Third, Arizona and Nevada bordered the river in both the upper and lower basins, and the other states worried that they would try to claim separate water rights in both basins. Finally, it was unclear how the compact would affect the water rights of several Indian tribes living along the river. The states tried but failed to negotiate additional compacts to decide these and other issues.

In 1928, Congress passed the Boulder Canyon Project Act, apportioning the water to be stored in Lake Mead among Arizona (2.8 million acre feet), California (4.4 million acre feet), and Nevada (300,000 acre feet) each year. Arizona and California were to share equally any surpluses.[87] The act also empowered the secretary of the interior to contract for water usage among individual water users within each state.

In 1952, Arizona sued California over this division of river water. The Supreme Court exercised its original jurisdiction and appointed a special master to hear testimony and issue findings and recommendations.[88] At the end of the trial, Simon Rifkind sent his report and a proposed decree to the Court.

---

85. Colorado River water irrigates more than one million acres of farmland in the seven basin states of Arizona, California, Colorado, Nevada, New Mexico, Utah, and Wyoming.

86. The suggestion to divide the river into two separate basins is generally attributed to Secretary of Commerce Herbert Hoover, a specially designated federal representative at the compact negotiations.

87. Among the upper basin states, Colorado was entitled to 3.9 million acre feet of water, Utah 1.725 million acre feet, Wyoming 1.05 million acre feet, and New Mexico 825 thousand acre feet. One acre foot is the amount of water it would take to cover a level acre of land to a depth of one foot.

88. To help sort through the complex facts in this case, the Court appointed a special master, George I. Haight. Haight died soon after his appointment and was replaced by well-known lawyer Simon H. Rifkind. Rifkind conducted hearings for two years, from June 14, 1956, through August 28, 1958. He took testimony from 340 witnesses, generated some 25,000 pages of trial transcripts, and produced a 433-page volume of findings, conclusions, and recommendations, which he submitted to the Court on January 16, 1961. The

He found that in the absence of state compacts, the contracts created by the secretary of the interior authoritatively apportioned the water of the "mainstream" (water stored in reservoirs along the river, such as Lake Mead) and that Congress had not intended to include tributary river water in allocating Colorado river water among the basin states. Finally, Rifkind recommended that in the event of a water shortage, each state would be burdened in proportion to its share of the allotment.

California protested the master's findings and claimed that under the doctrines of prior appropriation and equitable apportionment, California was legally entitled to a greater share of any surplus water than the other states. California also argued that the same two doctrines limited the secretary's discretion to apportion water among the lower basin states in times of drought. California also contested the master's decision to recognize Arizona's exclusive claim to the Gila River, arguing that all tributaries should be counted in determining each state's apportionment of Colorado river water.[89]

Conference of 1961

BLACK: There are only two or three basic issues. I sat through the debates.[90]

(1) The controversy went on for many, many years. The river has been used for irrigation for 2,000 years. The law of prior appropriation developed from the idea that the first user was entitled to water before later users. California was aggressive and up and coming from the beginning, and the other states were afraid. They couldn't get there the "fastest," and they wanted to be protected against the day that they would have money enough to do what California had been able to do first.

The upper basin states carried the ball at first. The idea of a settlement through state compacts was uppermost on their minds. Negotiations finally produced the compact. But I think that this dealt not so much with what went on intra-state or intra-basin, but basin-to-basin. I think that the compact created a clear division between the two basins and left the other problems to other settlements. The lower basin states never could get together on a compact as was hoped. Finally, when they went to build the Boulder Dam, there were still high hopes that a compact would be worked out. The Boulder Canyon Project Act, with its provisions for a compact between the three Lower Basin states, had this in view. But Arizona wanted the Gila River above everything else—it was being worked to the point of preemption of prior rights.

So the act gave the states the power to settle it themselves, if they would. But the Congress got tired of it, and wrote a statute with two aspects: (a) what the law would be if there was a compact; and (b) what the law was if they did not. It forced California to a limitation as part of this. Until they did make a compact, Congress gave the secretary of interior the power to contract, subject to compact. Congress also divided the water among the three states—careful, however, to protect the owners of rights. These are the "present

---

Court then heard oral arguments on the case for more than twenty-two hours in 1961 and 1962. Rifkind had been a classmate of William O. Douglas at Columbia and represented Douglas during his impeachment proceedings. In his autobiography, Douglas called Rifkind the "most outstanding advocate of all." Douglas, *The Court Years*, 188.

89. This was hardly a disinterested argument. Among the seven basin states, only California does not provide a single tributary to the Colorado River.

90. Black was in the Senate (D-AL) when the Boulder Canyon Project Act was debated in 1928.

perfect rights" as of 1929. They also divided the "mainstream," but I don't agree with the master's finding that a state may take from above Lake Mead to Lee's Ferry without giving credit.[91] The provision for 75 million acre feet over 10 years meant that much over the dam.

I can't agree with Bill Douglas that there is an applicable doctrine of equitable apportionment, because Congress has spoken. It has said, "we will settle this; we will make the apportionment if they don't agree." Key Pittman was very influential on this.[92] The final annual division of water among the three lower basin states was 4,400,000 acre feet for California, 2,800,000 acre feet for Arizona, and 300,000 acre feet for Nevada. This was the picky thing that they got behind them.

(2) I don't think that we should necessarily reach the next question. If we did, I might differ from Bill and Felix. When the federal government wants to, it may take over a navigable stream and its tributaries—even the non-navigable ones. I can't say, in the light of the Boulder Canyon Act, that references to the compact, and the compact itself, are irrelevant. But the §4(a) one was written in the framework of a compact which never came about. Tom Clark's case in *Ivanhoe*,[93] Bill Douglas's in *Atkinson*[94] and David Brewer's in *Rio Grande*[95] spell out congressional power. Why should we decide the question of

---

91. This issue concerned Arizona and Nevada, which bordered the river both above and below Lee's Ferry. The other basin states were concerned that those two states might "double-dip" by claiming the right to take two water allotments, one from the upper basin and another from the lower basin.

92. Senator Key Pittman (D-NV).

93. *Ivanhoe Irrigation District v. McCracken*, 357 U.S. 275 (1958). In 1902, Congress passed the Reclamation Act, which provided federal funds for western water projects. The project's main intent was to help small farms and homesteaders—only land parcels of less that 160 acres were permitted to purchase federally subsidized water. The law provided that nothing in the act was intended to disturb state water rights or state policies concerning "the control, appropriation, distribution, or use" of water.

As it turned out, the federal program conflicted with California law in at least two respects: it disrupted the state's own water distribution scheme; and California emphatically rejected the federal law's 160-acre limit for small farms and homesteads. The Court ignored the deferential language in the federal statute and ruled that nothing in the 1902 act required the federal government to deliver project water under conditions imposed by individual states. The decision effectively exempted the federal government from having to comply with state water distribution policies. Tom Clark wrote the majority opinion.

Clark's decision was later overruled in part by *California v. United States*, 438 U.S. 645 (1978), which allowed states to place conditions on the control, appropriation, distribution, and use of federal project water, as long as they were not inconsistent with congressional directives authorizing the project in question.

94. *Oklahoma v. Guy F. Atkinson Co.*, 313 U.S. 508 (1941). Douglas wrote the majority opinion, finding that Congress could use its interstate commerce powers to construct a comprehensive flood control program for the Mississippi River. The federal project included damming the Red River in Oklahoma, even though much of that river was no longer used for commerce and parts of it were not navigable at all. The Court ruled that Congress had complete discretion to control unused and nonnavigable waterways in order to preserve and promote commerce on navigable waterways.

95. *United States v. Rio Grande Dam and Irrigation Co.*, 174 U.S. 690 (1899). David Brewer wrote the majority opinion permitting the federal government to block construction of a state dam across a non-navigable portion of the Rio Grande River, which had been intended for irrigation purposes. The Court ruled that the federal government's right to maintain the nation's navigable waterways was superior to New Mexico's power to control its internal, nonnavigable waterways. The federal government claimed that the dam would interfere with commercial navigation on the river further downstream.

interstate priorities now? There is no actual case or controversy now over whether the secretary's contracts have to call state law into question. If I had to reach this, I must say that I am of the impression that the secretary can contract as he pleases, subject only to rights existing at the time.

(3) So far as the Indian reservations are concerned, I think that the *Winters* case decides this.[96] I am with the master generally on this.

I agree with the master that this is about the mainstream, but the states can't take from above Lake Mead to Lee's Ferry without credit. I don't think that is inconsistent with allowing Arizona exclusive rights to the Gila River. Equitable apportionment should not govern the apportionment of the mainstream. I agree with the master's proration, if that contingency ever does arise.

So I largely support the master's proposed decree, except as to rights above Lake Mead to Lee's Ferry. We don't have to pass on what is a "perfected right." As to the Nevada contract, I don't think that we have to pass on that, since there is no fight about it. We would have to give a partial declaration, and I think that we can't do better until there's a squabble over it. I would oppose the appointment of a water master.

FRANKFURTER: *Wyoming v. Colorado* is the most illuminating opinion on equitable apportionment.[97] Van Devanter was truly an authority in this field. His decree at the end of the opinion reflects his extraordinary ability as a draftsman. David Brewer, too, knew that territory well (*Kansas v. Colorado*, regarding the shared use of the Arkansas River, was his opinion).[98] He provisioned the detention rate that is so important in these interstate water controversies. Compacts, not courts, are the best modes of resolving these problems.

---

96. *Winters v. United States*, 207 U.S. 564 (1908). The Court allowed the federal government to block construction of a series of dams on the Milk River, a nonnavigable waterway in Montana, which would have limited the amount of water flowing to the Fort Belknap Indian Reservation. The decision rested in part on the federal government's treaty obligations with the Indian tribe, incurred before Montana became a state. The Court ruled that the federal government had the right to reserve waters flowing through federal territories and to exempt them from appropriation when the territory became a state.

97. *Wyoming v. Colorado*, 259 U.S. 419 (1922). This case stemmed from Colorado's proposed diversion of the Laramie River. Wyoming claimed that by the western rule of prior appropriation, it had prior claim to most of the flow of the Laramie River and that Colorado's planned diversion would irreparably damage those rights—particularly in dry years. Colorado claimed that as the home of the river's headwaters, it had the right to control and use all water within its territory however it chose. Alternatively, Colorado maintained that the state's planned diversion project involved no more than its equitable share of river water.

The Court ruled that the upper state on an interstate stream did not have an unencumbered right to divert the water however it wished. The division of water must be equitable, although it did not necessarily have to be equal, and both states had the duty to exercise their appropriation rights "reasonably and in a manner calculated to conserve the common supply." In a complex and impressively detailed opinion, Van Devanter—a long-time resident of Wyoming—ruled that Wyoming was entitled by right of prior appropriation to 95 percent of the available water flow. He allowed Colorado to divert the remaining water, only a small fraction of what Colorado had originally planned to take.

98. *Kansas v. Colorado*, 206 U.S. 46 (1907). Kansas sued Colorado, claiming that it had diverted so much of the Arkansas River that the river bed was virtually dry when it reached the Kansas border. While

Here, I think that nothing that must not be taken up should not be. I see absolutely no constitutional problem at all, and so none to be avoided through a narrow interpretation of the statute. When Congress exercises its power under the commerce clause, it can go whole hog as to rights, interests, and everything else. But Douglas goes off the rails completely in seeing this as a problem of statutory construction, independently of the backdrop of history. Not only Pittman, but even Hiram Johnson of California made a case for the master's conclusions.[99] I agree with Hugo and the master on the "mainstream," and that he can't cut it off at Lake Mead but must also credit any water taken above Lake Mead to Lee's Ferry. We must decide the Indian problem, and I agree with the master on this issue. We must, of course, avoid any waste of water, and in applying the master's case we must suppose that the Department of Interior will lease so that it won't go to waste. On questions of priorities, I think that we should take Hugo's line that it is not before us. If I had to reach the questions of proration and priority, I would be against the master. It is premature to make any decision as to the appointment of a water master.

CLARK: I am opposed to the appointment of a river master. I think that the secretary of the interior is actually the overseer of the river. I am in full agreement with Hugo and Felix, which puts pressure on California to try out the compact route—which was Congress's original idea. I pass on the questions of the mainstream, the Gila River, on taking water above Lake Mead, and on the Indians. I think that is as far as we should go: (1) mainstream, and (2) Indians.

HARLAN: I am worried about how we can limit the case. I agree that the master is right in excluding the tributaries from the California limitation. I agree that the master was wrong in excluding the Lake Mead-Lee's Ferry sector. But can we stop there? I can't see a "controversy" where it is over a prospective water shortage—for no one has said that however the water is apportioned—federally, or, e.g., apportionment—that there is any problem, except under the contingency of a shortage. So I have trouble avoiding a decision about whether the federal scheme of arbitration or traditional western water law applies. As to that, I agree with Bill Douglas. The most valuable thing in the case are the two appendices of legislative history. I can't escape the conclusion that there was no purpose to set aside established western water law rules.

I don't think that "present perfected rights" in §6 of Project Act qualifies western water law, and I would go with California on that question. The Gila River question has to be reached, but not the other tributaries. I would reach both "mainstream" and "priority issues," and I agree with the former.

Kansas admitted that Colorado had prior appropriation rights, it argued that Colorado had no right to destroy the rights of downstream users to their accustomed flow of river water.

The Court used this case to establish the principle that both states had the right to an equitable share of river water. Justice Brewer ruled that Colorado's use of the water had worked a great benefit in reclaiming arid land in that state and that the diminution of flow was not so great as to make Colorado's impoundment of the Arkansas River inequitable. The Court left the door open for Kansas to renew its suit at any time that Colorado's appropriation of Arkansas River water worked an inequitable hardship on the state.

99. Senator Hiram Johnson (D-CA).

WHITTAKER: The master has done a generally good and a correct job, except as to water rights on the river from Lake Mead to Lee's Ferry. By present perfected rights, I think that the master was right that there are such, as exerted when the Project Act became effective. On the question of whether there is a federal power under the secretary's contracts to apportion water between the states, I think that there is such a power. As to the Indians, I think that the master was correct.

STEWART: This is only a statutory construction case. I think that there is a justiciable controversy, although I am not so sure, except on the basis of a shortage of water. I did not think that we could avoid deciding this. On the first basic question of California's limitation, I agree that it covers the mainstream from Lee's Ferry to the Mexican border, excluding tributaries. The second big issue is: how is this water to be allocated? I thought that we had to reach this in the eventuality of a shortage. On this, I would begin by assuming that western water law applies, unless and until it is clearly changed by federal statute or compact. On "present perfected rights," I would think that the master was right, but it is not before us since the master set the time for this. On the Nevada contract, I would think that it was all right. On the question of the Indian reservations and enclaves, I have trouble as to the post-statehood federal power. But I can't think of a better answer than the master's.

Conference of 1962

BLACK: What is here that we *must* decide? Because I would decide as little as possible. Too many new situations are bound to arise. I can't but be led irresistibly to the conclusion that California's part was fixed at 4,400,000 acre feet, and that any reason for an equitable apportionment disappeared. I also think that §8(b) fortifies the conclusion that the *secretary of the interior* was to contract unless the states compacted, and they never did. Thus when the secretary apportioned water among the three states, he was carrying out what Congress planned should be done in the absence of a compact. I have no doubt Congress can do this.

Neither *Wyoming*,[100] *First Iowa*,[101] or *Ivanhoe* is controlling here because they were under the Reclamation Act. Equitable apportionment is nothing but what this Court orders done by fiat. It is much better to let Congress decide what amount of water should go to each state. Unless Congress says that state law shall distribute the water, I would not say that state law can govern the apportionment of water from a navigable stream. If I have to, I would say so as to any situation where the master says that state law applies.

---

100. *Wyoming v. Colorado*, 259 U.S. 419 (1922). See also *Nebraska v. Wyoming*, 295 U.S. 40 (1935), which divided the water of the North Platte among Colorado, Wyoming, and Nebraska. Michael J. Doherty was the special master in the latter case.

101. *First Iowa Hydro-Electric Cooperative v. Federal Power Commission*, 328 U.S. 152 (1946). The petitioner applied to the Federal Power Commission (FPC) to build a dam across the Cedar River, a navigable river near Moscow, Iowa. Iowa sought to block the project, arguing that the company had not obtained a required state permit. The Supreme Court ruled that under the terms of the Federal Power Act, the company had no duty to apply for a state permit. Congress and the FPC, as the responsible federal agency, had sole discretion to determine how to regulate the nation's navigable waterways.

I would not be willing to say that anything but *actually* perfected rights are saved. I am not sure whether we have to reach the issue of how to resolve a water shortage, but I would agree with the master if we do.

I would think that the upper basin cases should be heard before the issue of water shortages is dealt with. I would conserve past perfected rights in case of shortage—that would be 4,400,000 acre feet for California, and Arizona's and Nevada's have not been settled.

I don't think that §18 of the Project Act affects this. I don't think that any of the states had any rights superior to the rights of the federal government—it was a *navigable* stream.

California's "presently perfected rights" are 3,600,000 acre feet. That is a floor in case of shortage; over that amount, California gets 44/75ths of the balance.

DOUGLAS: I would include the Gila River and all waters, and would apply state irrigation laws. I would go with the government on the Indians' rights.

CLARK: Where Congress determines this, Congress can take away rights—except perhaps that stopping perfected rights would require compensation. Perhaps the literal language supports California on the limitation point. But looking at the whole picture, the Gila River is out in computing the state's sources—in other words, the mainstream is stored water.

On justiciability of the limitation issue, it is here since the secretary has told Congress that the Central Arizona project is feasible. But I think that we can stop right there. But if we must reach it, I would say that the West has its own water law. We should adhere to it unless Congress overrides it—and Congress has—but the secretary may do so by proration, or by state law, or as he will—it's all within the authority that Congress has given him. He has tipped his hand only as to *intrastate* distribution, but not as to interstate.

BRENNAN: (1) Congress took this up—they may do so. What did it do?
   (a) It allocated the mainstream.
   (b) It divided shortages.
   (c) It left the secretary free within distributions to exercise discretion to apply state law intrastate.
   (d) It determined Indian rights.

WHITE: I come out against California on the limitation issue. But I don't see that Congress has dealt with a shortage. It is easier to find that Congress has given the secretary powers to deal with one. But I don't find that the secretary has ever acted on such a power. He has so far followed state law. In general, I feel with Bill Douglas that there is no expressed purpose of Congress to ignore state laws. I would rather see Congress decide this issue in light of modern conditions. I would follow Tom Clark and leave it to Congress or the secretary to exercise their discretion. Although if I have to, I would say that Congress didn't give him the power.

GOLDBERG: I am against California on the limitation issue. I think that Congress has apportioned 44 for California, 28 for Arizona, and 3 for Nevada. It has also determined what happens in the event of a shortage. Johnson's "prior apportion" deletion. Perfected rights.

I think that this was a final settlement and was intended to be such. Even equitable proportion could not come out with a different result. I would protect the Indians.

*Result: In a 5–3 decision, the Court ruled that Congress had properly used its powers to regulate navi-
gable rivers to enact the Boulder Canyon Project and impose its own apportionment scheme on the
three lower basin states. Hugo Black, writing for the majority, said that the Boulder Canyon Project
Act left each state in control of its own tributaries. This meant that Arizona could claim exclusive control
of the Gila River water without having it count against its Colorado River apportionment. The Court
also rejected California's claim that the doctrines of equitable apportionment or prior appropriation
should be used to apportion water rights. However, the Court decided that Nevada and Arizona could
not claim water rights in both the upper and lower basins. Any water that Nevada or Arizona took
from above Lake Mead would count against that state's apportioned share of lower basin water.*

*The majority decided that Congress had properly delegated authority to the secretary of the inte-
rior to make exclusive contracts for water delivery to users in all three states and that the secretary
could use any reasonable means to apportion water during times of shortage. Finally, the Court supported the master's findings that the Indian tribes bordering the river had "present perfected rights" at
the time that the act was passed and could continue to use the river water as they always had for irrigation and other needs.*

*In dissent, William O. Douglas attacked Black with unusual vehemence from the bench when the
decision was announced. Literally spitting out his words, Douglas called the majority opinion "the
baldest attempt by judges in modern times to spin their own philosophy into the fabric of the law in
derogation of the will of the legislature."[102]*

*More than thirty years later, the current river master, Interior Secretary Bruce Babbitt of Ari-
zona, continued the struggle to resolve ongoing water disputes, especially among the three lower basin
states. Among other reforms, Babbitt proposed allowing lower basin states to purchase surplus water
from upper basin states and allowing Arizona and Nevada to store their unused shares of water in
underground aquifers for later use. This would end California's longstanding practice of supplement-
ing its own water allocation by claiming other states' unused water shares each year. Indian rights to
Colorado River water are also still being litigated, generally on terms favorable to the tribes.[103]*

Puyallup Tribe v. Department of Game of Washington, 391 U.S. 392 (1968)
Kautz v. Department of Game of Washington
(Douglas) (Brennan)

*Members of the Puyallup and Nisqually Indian tribes used gill nets on the Puyallup and Nisqually
Rivers to snare steelhead and four species of salmon for personal, tribal, and commercial purposes.[104]
State fish and game officials claimed that by the 1960s local runs of anadromous fish had dropped
precipitously, and that the entire fishery was in danger of collapse.[105] Losses were so serious that by the*

---

102. Black and Black, *Mr. Justice and Mrs. Black,* 156.

103. *Arizona v. California,* 530 U.S. 392 (2000).

104. By treaty, only Indians could use gill nets to catch salmon and steelhead. Tribal members used
the nets on tribal lands and near river mouths, which were far from reservation lands.

105. In Washington, the Department of Game was responsible for the steelhead trout, while salmon
were within the jurisdiction of the Department of Fisheries.

time the fish runs reached the reservation there were just enough fish left to renew the species. In the name of conservation, state officials sought to enjoin both tribes from using gill nets and required them to use less efficient hook and line.

The tribes sought a declaratory judgment that they were not subject to state conservation measures. They claimed that the 1854 Treaty of Medicine Creek gave the tribes exclusive use of reservation lands, including an unrestricted right to take fish. The treaty also recognized that tribes had the right to fish "in common with all citizens . . . at all usual and accustomed grounds and stations." The tribes argued that this language allowed them to use gill nets anywhere along the two rivers.

The state trial court issued an injunction prohibiting the tribes from using gill nets. The trial court also ruled that the Puyallups were not a recognized Indian tribe and had no legally recognized reservation. The state supreme court affirmed the injunction but reversed the trial court's other findings for want of jurisdiction. The tribes then argued that a Ninth Circuit Court of Appeals case, Maison v. Confederated Tribes of Umatilla Reservation, *required that any state restrictions on Indian fishing practices must be "indispensable" to preserve the fishery.[106] The high court, however, remanded the case with instructions that the injunction had to be limited to regulations "reasonable and necessary" to preserve fish stocks. The lower court reaffirmed its ban on gill net fishing.*

Conference of March 29, 1968

WARREN: This is a very involved case, and I am not too clear on how we should come out. Indians have some rights under this treaty, as the United States has recognized by taking census counts, tribe enrollments, and so forth. A one-hundred-year-old treaty gives them rights. These are federal rights, and a state's conservation powers can't be used to wipe these rights out. On the merits, what the state did is in the interest of conservation. [DOUGLAS: Warren refers to his actions as governor in eliminating net fishing in San Francisco Bay rivers.] These regulations operate against the Indians. Congress can amend the treaty. The time is long past when they should have done it, but Congress has not acted. Until Congress acts, we should hold that the Indians have federal rights under this treaty. While states have conservation rights, I don't think that its regulations can wipe out these rights without paying some compensation for it. If the state takes away the rights, the state must pay. We can't very well adjudicate in this case what those rights are here, although I do think that they must have a definition from some federal authority. I would rule to some extent for the Indians.

BLACK: I am inclined to affirm. I want Bill Douglas's views, but here Washington has saved only the issue of its power to regulate Indian fishing with nets. The government has not been helpful with its notion of "let the Indians do what's reasonable." I think that Washington has that power.

DOUGLAS: I affirm. This Indian practice is devastating to the resource. Their nets catch everything that swims. But this treaty deals only with "all accustomed grounds," secured "in common at those places." Therefore, I think that this is inviting permissible state action so long as the state bars everyone from using nets. This is outside the reservation, and not within one.

---

106. *Maison v. Confederated Tribes of Umatilla Reservation,* 314 F.2d 169 (1963).

HARLAN: I affirm. I agree with Bill Douglas.

BRENNAN: The Chief thinks that everything taken away must be paid for. I do not interpret the treaty as narrowly as does Douglas. I would reverse or modify. "In common with" does not mean that what can be done to others can be done to the Indians.

STEWART: The treaty gave them two things as respects off-reservation fishing: (1) the right to fish at accustomed grounds without a license; and (2) the right to fish "in common" with all citizens. That is a guarantee of equal protection. I agree with Bill Douglas. There can be no discrimination against the Indians. The Indians really got nothing as to off-reservation fishing, except an equal protection clause, beyond excusal from licenses. The issue of licenses is covered by *Tribe*. As to seasons, no issue is here. I affirm.

WHITE: I affirm.

FORTAS: I would take the Ninth Circuit formula and reverse here, instructing the court that it is "necessary" to adopt this. Conservation means that the state can operate when and as necessary in the interest of conservation. I would reverse or vacate on that ground. I would send the case back for a determination that this conservation measure *was necessary* for conservation. Take the Ninth Circuit formula. That really means that we are only vacating, because on this record the Ninth Circuit test could be satisfied.[107] The treaty right covers the right to take fish at this place. I would try to escape the "in common with all" argument by pointing to the allowance of net fishing in salt water, and saying that they are barred from using nets only in the river. The Indians' right to fish is in the river. I would say that the state does have the police power to supervise this treaty right, and it can supersede Indian rights if they pay for it. The Indians have a cause of action versus the state if the state does not stay within the "necessary" regime of conservation.

Result: William O. Douglas, writing for a unanimous Court, ruled that while the Indian tribes had treaty rights to fish virtually anywhere along the river, the specific manner and purpose of fishing were not established by treaty and could be regulated. The Court construed the treaty's recognition of Indian fishing rights "in common with all citizens of the Territory" to mean that fishing by both Indians and non-Indians was subject to state conservation efforts. The state could regulate the manner and size of the take, and impose restrictions on commercial fishing, as long as the regulations did not discriminate against Indians. The Justices remanded the case to determine whether state regulations prohibiting the use of gill nets were reasonably required for conservation, whether these restrictions gave due consideration to the tribes' treaty rights, and whether the regulations improperly discriminated against the tribes.

This case caught Douglas in a dilemma, conflicted between two of his most cherished values. Douglas saw himself as a staunch defender of Indian rights, but he was also an ardent environmentalist. While he felt a great deal of sympathy for the Indians, he felt an even greater empathy with the endangered wild steelhead and salmon of the Puyallup and Nisqually Rivers.

---

107. Brennan's notes have "*would* be satisfied."

Department of Game of Washington v. Puyallup Tribe, 414 U.S. 44 (1973)
Puyallup Tribe v. Department of Game of Washington
(Douglas) (Brennan)

On remand, the case degenerated into a three-way battle among state officials, the Puyallup tribe, and the state's sportsfishing industry. The Department of Fisheries decided to allow the tribes to renew net fishing for salmon along much of the Puyallup River, except for the spawning grounds, and this ruling ended that portion of the dispute. The Department of Game, however, extended its ban on net fishing for steelhead by prohibiting all net fishing off the reservation and severely restricting the use of nets on reservation lands. Only if sufficient numbers of steelhead made it past the sportsfishermen would tribal members be permitted to use nets on reservation land, and then only to catch surplus fish beyond the number necessary to preserve the steelhead run. The tribe protested that the rules unfairly discriminated against Indians and violated treaty rights that gave the tribe exclusive and unlimited rights to fish on reservation lands. The tribe also complained that these regulations sacrificed their rights in favor of sportsfishermen and claimed that sportsfishing should be limited to ensure that the tribe got its fair share of steelhead upriver. Sportsfishermen argued that the state's preference for sportsfishing was fair, because between 50 percent and 80 percent of the steelhead run consisted of stocked fish, which were paid for almost entirely by sportsfishermen (the fish were purchased with money from fishing licenses, which Indians did not buy).

The state supreme court held that the ban was valid for 1970 but that new regulations would be required annually and would have to be supported by data showing that the rules were necessary for fish conservation. Both the tribe and the state's Department of Game appealed.

Conference of October 12, 1973

BURGER: The Indians' treaty rights are subject to reasonable conservation measures. I am not sure that the state has given Indians the rights it gives to the sportsmen. I have doubts whether the state regulations comport with the treaty.

DOUGLAS: I would affirm in #481, reverse in #746.[108] The priority given to sports fishermen denies priority that the treaty meant for the Indians to have. The government could condemn the historical way that Indians fish, even though that's not in conservation terms the best way. I think that we should decide before-hand how much must be set aside for conservation.

BRENNAN: I agree with Bill Douglas.

STEWART: In #746, the court assumes that no fishing by Indians would be allowed until whites got their full quota. That is not correct—it is not giving enough weight to the treaty. Sportsmen, however, support the whole program of stocking the river. I affirm in #481.

WHITE: I affirm in #481 and reverse in #746. I am reluctant to give Indians priority. The treaty allows them to fish commercially. If Indians have treaty rights communally to fish, they can't be denied in favor of game fishing. The natural run is one thing, the run of

---

108. *Department of Game v. Puyallup Tribe* (#72-481) and its companion case, *Puyallup Tribe v. Department of Game* (#72-746).

stocked fish may be a different matter. Can the state answer if it did not study how many could be fished by Indians? Why should the Indians have any priority in stocked fish?

MARSHALL: I affirm in #481 and reverse in #746.

BLACKMUN: I would affirm in #481 and reverse in #746. We must keep the species going, but the Indians have rights. Yet they are subject to conservation measures.

POWELL: I am doubtful on what follows, but I follow Bill Douglas.

REHNQUIST: I would affirm in each case.

BURGER: Guidelines are needed in #746—I will vote to reverse. I affirm in #481.

Result: With Douglas again writing for a unanimous Court, the Justices struck down the ban on net fishing as discriminatory. The steelhead run, the Court ruled, must be fairly apportioned between the tribe and the sportsfishermen. Douglas was careful to point out, however, that the state retained the power to ensure the survival of the steelhead, including the right to impose a complete ban on fishing. "The police power of the State is adequate to prevent the steelhead from following the fate of the passenger pigeon; and the Treaty does not give the Indians a federal right to pursue the last living steelhead until it enters their nets."

Puyallup Tribe v. Department of Game of Washington, 433 U.S. 165 (1977)
(Brennan)

This time on remand, the state trial court ruled that the state of Washington had the authority to limit the tribe's steelhead catch both on and off the Puyallup reservation. The trial judge interpreted the Treaty of Medicine Creek to award the tribe 45 percent of the harvestable native run of steelhead, but none of the hatchery-bred steelhead run. He also limited the number of steelhead the tribe could catch with nets, directed the tribe to submit an annual list of qualified tribal fishermen, and required the tribe to file a weekly report on their catch. The state supreme court affirmed.

On appeal, the tribe claimed sovereign immunity from state court jurisdiction and asserted that by treaty the tribe had unlimited fishing rights both on and off reservation lands. In any case, the tribe argued, the judicially imposed limits were not necessary for steelhead conservation. Amazingly, the issues of whether the Puyallup tribe was a recognized tribe, or whether they had a legally cognizable reservation, were still open questions.

BURGER: I can't say that the tribe enjoys immunity. On res judicata, AS is not before us and so that does not come into play.[109] Is there a reservation, and should that be litigated? Ought we remand on that after we denied cert in *United States v. Washington*?[110]

---

109. It is not clear what Burger is referring to here, although this might be a reference to "artificial source" runs (hatchery-bred fish), which previous cases had decided were not included under the terms of the Treaty of Medicine Creek.

110. *United States v. Washington*, 496 F. 2d 620 (1974), cert. denied, 419 U.S. 1032 (1974). The court of appeals held that the Puyallup tribe and reservation lands were officially recognized and legally cognizable.

STEWART: I would dismiss as improvidently granted, and wait for Judge Boldt's case.[111] There is only a very narrow question here that is not of particular importance. The Washington supreme court simply tried to do what our mandate told them to. Is this a reservation? I don't know. Only §3 and not §2 is involved.[112] Anyway, very little was imposed on this tribe.

WHITE: The Washington State Supreme Court claims the power to regulate on reservation fishing, and has no interest in the artificial run. In holding that it had the power to regulate, the state court only held what we said they might do as to the natural run. If I can get around the sovereign immunity question, I would affirm.

MARSHALL: I go with Brennan.

BLACKMUN: I come out where Potter does, except for his DIG. On sovereign immunity, the tribe has been here from the beginning—so I would affirm.

POWELL: Unless I am unhorsed on immunity, I would affirm.

REHNQUIST: My main obstacle to affirmance is sovereign immunity. *Edelman v. Jordan* said that immunity of the states under the Eleventh Amendment can be raised for first time in this Court.[113] But this case has been here twice before without anyone raising it, so I would say that it is too late and I would do an *Ex parte Young* on the chairperson.[114]

STEVENS: I don't think that there is a reservation here and I would affirm, unless we send it back on *Rosebud*.[115] I am not too troubled about sovereign immunity. In *Fidelity*, it was asserted against a money judgment and not, as here, merely equitable.[116]

Result: In an opinion by John Paul Stevens, the Court rejected the tribe's claim to unlimited fishing rights both on and off the reservation. The tribe did not have exclusive rights to the fish passing through

---

111. District Judge Boldt was the presiding judge in *United States v. Washington*, 384 F. Supp. 312 (WD Wash. 1974), which involved Indian fishing rights in Puget Sound. The case was still being litigated in 1977.

112. The state courts used §3 of the treaty to justify its allocation of steelhead. Section 2 was the part of the treaty that the tribe argued gave them exclusive fishing rights on reservation lands.

113. *Edelman v. Jordan*, 415 U.S. 651 (1974). The Court ruled here that the Eleventh Amendment barred lawsuits against states seeking retroactive damages to be paid out of public funds where the state did not waive its right of sovereign immunity. Justice Rehnquist wrote the majority opinion.

114. *Ex parte Young*, 209 U.S. 123 (1908). This case established the principle that private parties could seek declaratory and injunctive relief against individual state officers, even though states themselves enjoyed sovereign immunity and could not be sued without their consent. Moreover, while federal judges might instruct individual state *officers* what to do (and hold them individually liable if they disobeyed), they generally cannot instruct state *governments or institutions* what to do.

115. *Rosebud Sioux Tribe v. Kneip*, 430 U.S. 584 (1977). The Rosebud Sioux Tribe sought a declaratory judgment that their original 1889 treaty establishing the tribe's reservation boundaries had not been diminished by later acts of Congress, which had opened unallotted Sioux lands to settlement. The Supreme Court ruled that congressional intent had been to disestablish most of the reservation.

116. *United States v. U.S. Fidelity and Guaranty Co.*, 309 U.S. 506 (1940). The Court held that Indian tribes retained the right to claim sovereign immunity—in the tutelage of the federal government—to protect the tribes' scarce financial resources. The Court did not extend the claim of immunity to individual tribal members.

the reservation, because the tribe's "sovereign" territory did not include the river itself. Moreover, the tribe's fishing rights off the reservation were held in common with all other citizens and were equally subject to reasonable state regulation. The state could take any reasonable and necessary steps to protect the steelhead run, whether on or off the reservation. To rule otherwise, Stevens wrote, would undermine any apportionment between Indians and other fishermen, as the tribe would be able to interdict or even destroy the river's steelhead.

While state courts ordinarily had no jurisdiction over the tribe, Stevens continued, they could assert jurisdiction over individual tribal members. And while the tribe's sovereign immunity meant that the state could not compel the tribe to disclose the status of individual tribal members or the size of its catch on reservation land, the Court encouraged the tribe to report its take voluntarily "to minimize the risk of an erroneous enforcement effort."

Brennan and Marshall dissented in part, agreeing with the majority on the issue of tribal immunity but disagreeing with Steven's analysis of the treaty regarding the tribe's fishing rights. Brennan argued that the treaty explicitly gave the tribe exclusive fishing rights on reservation lands and that these rights could be restricted only by proof that the proposed regulations were necessary for the survival of the steelhead.

On remand, there were still more problems . . .

Washington v. Washington State Commercial Passenger Fishing Vessel Ass'n.,
443 U.S. 658 (1979)
Washington v. Puget Sound Gillnetters Ass'n.
Washington v. United States
Puget Sound Gillnetters Ass'n. v. United States District Court, Western District of Washington
(Brennan)

Because of continued deterioration of the salmon and steelhead runs, the Puyallup Indians and six other tribes pressured the federal government to bring an action against the state of Washington. The Indians maintained that state regulations violated their sovereign rights and alleged that the state violated their treaty rights by allowing commercial and sportsfishermen to take virtually all of the harvestable fish before they reached reservation lands. The tribes also complained about non-Indian commercial fishing, poor state hatchery practices, and a loss of fish habitat due to logging, energy development, and pollution.

At the district court, Judge George Boldt ruled that the "in common" clause meant that Washington Indian tribes were entitled to one-half of all "harvestable" salmon and steelhead (i.e., surplus fish beyond the spawning escapement) at traditional off-reservation sites. Judge Boldt also exempted fish caught on reservation lands from counting against the Indians' share of the fish run and allowed the tribes to take extra fish for subsistence and ceremonial purposes.[117] Judge Boldt ruled that any state regulations of tribal fishing had to be necessary for species conservation and could not discriminate against the Indians. Because of the ongoing problems, Judge Boldt retained jurisdiction to examine all future state regulation of Indian fishing.

---

117. *United States v. Washington*, 384 F. Supp. 312 (WD Wash. 1974).

STEWART: I started out with Brennan's finality approach, but the more I thought about it, the more I concluded that we ought not say that the state court acted improperly. So, reviewing treaties, I think that Judge Boldt gave an improper construction to the treaty. *Winans* said that they had an easement to get to the usual places and that you can't require licenses there.[118] But "in common" implies that this is not an exclusive right, and Boldt was dead wrong on his 50-50 formula. It is only a right to take fish—meaning that neither the feds nor the state can so regulate as to result in no fish. On enforcement, all of the problems of *Walker v. Birmingham* are there, even if Boldt is reversed.[119]

WHITE: I am closer to Potter than to Brennan. *Winans* confirmed that the treaty assured the Indians that there would be fish to catch. So someone has to say how many. Boldt went too far in saying 50 percent.

MARSHALL: If I have to reach merits, I would agree with Boldt.

BLACKMUN: On the state case, I can either reverse or send it back. I am close to Brennan, but I would prefer a definitive decision on the merits, rather than to go on a finality approach. Water rights cases are the best analogy—*Puyallup III*. On enforcement, isn't the fishery management issue moot, since Boldt has been superseded by regulations of the feds?

POWELL: I would reach the merits, since it is open to us to do so. In doing so, I can't construe Article 3 to give the Indians 50 percent. I would rather find some "equal opportunity" notion. So I would remand to let Washington come up with something.

REHNQUIST: The finality argument has no merit for me. Basically, I agree with Potter, Byron, and Lewis.

STEVENS: Don't duck on finality. On the merits, the state says 1/3 and *Puyallup II* said 45 percent, so I would give them 50 percent, counting against it something not now deducted.

---

118. *United States v. Winans*, 198 U.S. 371 (1905). This case involved disputed Yakima tribal fishing rights on the Columbia River. The Court ruled that the right to take fish "at all the usual and accustomed places" and the right to erect temporary buildings to cure fish were not a grant of rights to the Indians but a *reservation of rights* by the Indians that they already possessed and retained. These reserved rights continued to be enforceable against the United States and its grantees, as well as against the state and its grantees. This was known as the "reserved rights doctrine."

In the *Puyallup* litigation, Washington argued that since hatchery fish were neither in existence nor contemplated by the parties at the time of the treaty negotiations, the Indians could not have any reserved rights to these fish. Federal district court Judge Orrick, however, ruled that *Winans* meant that Indian treaty rights survived changing conditions and that the tribe had reserved the right to a share of *all* fish, whether native or hatchery bred. *United States v. Washington* (Phase II), 506 F. Supp. 187 (WD 1980).

119. *Walker v. Birmingham*, 388 U.S. 307 (1967). In *Walker*, the Court ruled that protest marches and demonstrations could not continue in the face of a judicial injunction. So long as the federal courts had personal and subject matter jurisdiction, a party who disregarded the court's orders could be held in contempt even though the order might later be found to be invalid. In the present case, Stewart was likely concerned that the Washington Department of Game had defied a series of state and federal court decrees ordering the agency not to promulgate or enforce fishing regulations against the Indian tribes. This was what led Judge Boldt to retain jurisdiction over the matter indefinitely and to threaten to take direct control of the state's fisheries.

Result: *John Paul Stevens wrote on behalf of a 6–3 majority that the treaties did not merely guarantee access to the river and an equal opportunity to fish, they also guaranteed an equitable share of each anadromous fish run. The majority agreed with Judge Boldt that the basic equitable formula would be to divide each harvestable fish run evenly between treaty and nontreaty interests. While affirming Judge Boldt's 50 percent apportionment, Stevens made several significant changes to Boldt's calculations. First, Stevens ruled that the Indians' treaty share could be reduced if tribal needs could be met by a lesser amount (if, for example, the number of tribe members "dwindled to a few members"). More significantly, the Court ruled that the district court judge had erred in excluding fish caught on reservation lands and fish used for subsistence and ceremonial purposes from counting against the Indians' share. Instead, the Court ruled that the 50-50 division included all anadromous fish, wherever caught and for whatever purpose. The Court affirmed Judge Boldt's authority to retain jurisdiction and to assume direct supervision of the state fishery if circumstances required.*

Powell, Stewart, and Rehnquist dissented, arguing that the treaties did not guarantee a set percentage of the fish catch but gave Indians the right of access to the river to continue to fish at their usual and accustomed fishing grounds, gave them the exclusive right to fish on reservation lands, guaranteed enough fish to satisfy their subsistence and ceremonial needs, and exempted them from state fisheries regulations except as necessary for conservation and for the good of all fishermen.

PART III

CIVIL RIGHTS
AND LIBERTIES

CHAPTER 9

FREE SPEECH

DANGEROUS SPEECH AND ASSOCIATIONS

Nazis and Communists

Haupt v. United States, 330 U.S. 631 (1947)
(Murphy) (Douglas) (Burton)

During World War II, a Nazi submarine secretly landed eight German saboteurs, including Herbert Haupt, on the East Coast of the United States. After coming ashore in Long Island, Haupt went immediately to the home of his father, Hans Max Haupt, who lived in New York.[1] What the Haupts did not know was that one of the other saboteurs had a change of heart and had already notified the FBI about the German operation.

Federal authorities put the Haupts under surveillance. Two FBI agents saw Hans Haupt provide shelter for his son in the family home, and other witnesses later testified that the elder Haupt helped his son buy a car and obtain a job at the manufacturing plant where Nordon bomb sights were manufactured. But no one overheard them planning to do anything illegal or saw them break any laws.

The younger Haupt was arrested, convicted of espionage, and executed.[2] His father was convicted of treason and initially sentenced to die. His first conviction was reversed, and after a second trial he was again convicted and sentenced to life in prison. Haupt claimed that his conviction was improper because the Constitution required two witnesses to an overtly treasonous act, yet no one had testified that he had done anything beyond what any father would do to help his son find shelter, transportation, and a job.

Conference of December 14, 1946

VINSON: I was impressed with the government's argument. I pass and will wait to listen to the discussion. I have questions especially as to direct evidence of treason.

BLACK: I don't think that the *Cramer* case covers this.[3] [BURTON: Black refers to Douglas's dissent in the *Cramer* case.]

---

1. Like the other saboteurs, Herbert Haupt had spent much of his life in the United States and spoke fluent English. Raised in New York, he returned to Germany before the beginning of World War II to escape a pregnant girlfriend. See *Ex Parte Quirin,* 317 U.S. 1 (1942), discussed in chapter 12.

2. *Ex Parte Quirin,* 317 U.S. 1 (1942).

3. *Cramer v. United States,* 325 U.S. 1 (1945). Two witnesses saw Anthony Cramer talk to enemy agents but could not hear what was said. The Court overturned Cramer's conviction because there was insuffi-

REED: I would reverse on the judge's instruction, which permitted a finding of guilt if Haupt performed *any* of these overt acts. I would reverse on Instruction 50.[4]

FRANKFURTER: In view of that instruction, the record would have to establish that every overt act was proved by two witnesses. As it was, it was left to the jury—and for a general verdict to be satisfied by any one count would not do. I am not prepared to say that every overt act satisfies the test. If they are not all good, then I reverse.

DOUGLAS: I pass. I was in dissent in *Cramer*. My offhand opinion, if I understand *Cramer*, is that the overt act of admitting to one's own house one's own son was less impressive as an overt act than the conversation in the *Cramer* case. I reserve judgment.

MURPHY: *Cramer* covers it and we should reverse.

JACKSON: I don't think that this is the *Cramer* case at all. These acts, if they were performed, were acts of aid and comfort. If all were perceived by two witnesses, it is clear sailing. If any one of the alleged acts is not proved, then I see no escape from reversal. I think that they were all perceived by two witnesses. I want to go through the record carefully on this point. At this moment, I vote to affirm.

RUTLEDGE: I am inclined to think that these are sufficient overt acts within the *Cramer* case. I am a little doubtful about taking his son into his home. But the confession troubles me, and I may reverse on that.[5] I think that the confession is only good if made in open court.

---

cient evidence that he had given aid and comfort to the enemy and because there was no overt act of treason witnessed by at least two people.

4. With jury instruction #50, the trial judge told the jury that they were to find Haupt guilty if they found that he performed *any one* of the twelve allegedly treasonable acts submitted to the jury, as long as the act was perceived by two witnesses and as long as all of the other elements of treason were proved. Because the jury gave a general verdict, Haupt argued that under *Cramer* it was necessary to support *each* of the twelve acts to sustain his conviction. Footnote 45 in the *Cramer* case stated that a general verdict on treason must be set aside "if any of the separable acts submitted was insufficient." *Cramer v. United States*, 325 U.S. 1, 36 (1945).

5. There were two issues involving confessions, one at Haupt's first trial and the other at his second trial. At the first trial, the government introduced into evidence four different statements Haupt signed while he was in custody. Haupt challenged these confessions on the ground that they were illegally obtained, citing *McNabb v. United States*, 318 U.S. 332 (1943). Haupt was held incommunicado and interrogated intermittently for five days and was not presented to a federal magistrate until several weeks after his arrest and after Haupt had signed all four confessions. The FBI claimed that Haupt had signed a written waiver of his right to be taken promptly before a federal committing officer, although no such waiver was produced at trial. The federal circuit court reversed Haupt's conviction and ordered that the confessions be excluded from the evidence.

At the second trial, prosecutors claimed that Haupt had voluntarily confessed to FBI agents in August 1942 and that he had made other incriminating statements to friends, co-workers, and other prisoners. The Constitution provides that "No Person shall be convicted of Treason unless on the Testimony of two Witnesses to the same overt Act, or on Confession in open Court." On appeal, Haupt argued that because these confessions were not made in open court, they were inadmissible.

Rutledge was clearly referring to the second issue, as the first had already been resolved. The majority, including Rutledge, ultimately decided that if Haupt's admissions had been the only evidence against

BURTON: I was impressed by the *Cramer* rule that you have to prove all overt acts. I think that they are all good, however, and I vote tentatively to affirm.

VINSON: I was hesitant about what evidence was direct evidence. Here, the evidence could prove an overt act—it was of such a nature that it was sufficient to prove an overt act. The father's expressed attitude was that he was harboring and sheltering regardless of any father and son relationship.

JACKSON: The defense attorneys failed to show a clear absence of proof. The strength of the father and son relationship—it makes no difference. If any one act is not proved, however, we would have to reverse.

REED: Suppose that they find that each act is adequately proven. How do you know which ones the jury thought were adequate?

JACKSON: They should charge that each act is a count—that would be better. As it is, if all of the acts were sufficiently proved, we don't have to know which *ones* or *any one* were sufficiently proved.

FRANKFURTER: There was no charge to find a particular act. The question is whether this is a question for a general verdict.

RUTLEDGE: I am inclined to think that they all are sufficient overt acts under the *Cramer* rule. I have a doubt as to the one Douglas mentioned. Confessions not given in open court are also doubtful. I am tending to reverse.

BLACK: *If one falls out then the verdict fails.* I vote tentatively to affirm—but I will be open to questions on any one that falls out—the same as Jackson.

VINSON: [BURTON: Apparently the same as Jackson.] The father and son, the automobile—it looks innocent, but it can be tied in. I vote tentatively to affirm.

BLACK: I vote tentatively to affirm.

Result: The Court voted 7–1–1 to affirm Haupt's conviction. Robert Jackson wrote for the majority, finding that the constitutional requirement of two witnesses to the same overt act was satisfied. Jackson distinguished Cramer, *saying that it was up to the jury to determine whether Haupt's actions were motivated out of parental concern or loyalty to a hostile country during wartime. Douglas concurred in the judgment.*

In dissent, Murphy argued that Cramer *was on point and that Haupt's conviction was unconstitutional. Like Anthony Cramer, Haupt did not commit any overt acts of treason witnessed by two people. His actions were in themselves innocent, and the incriminating evidence was not provided by two witnesses but by inference and circumstantial evidence that fell far short of the constitutional requirements for proving treason.*

---

him, this would have been a crucial issue. Because all of the substantive evidence was based on the testimony of two witnesses, however, there was nothing in the Constitution to preclude the use of out-of-court admissions to corroborate eyewitness testimony.

Dennis v. United States, 339 U.S. 162 (1949)
(Burton)

Eugene Dennis was convicted in federal court for not responding to a subpoena issued by the House Un-American Activities Committee (HUAC). On appeal, he claimed that his conviction was improper because seven of twelve trial jurors were government employees, all of whom had been vetted by the government's loyalty program designed to eliminate "subversives" from public employment. As a result, Dennis alleged, these jurors were hopelessly prejudiced against him.[6]

At conference, the Justices discussed the fairness of having government employees constitute a majority of the jury in such a politically charged case.

Conference of November 12, 1949

VINSON: Here seven of the twelve jurors were federal government employees. We are told that we should not look to the issues presented. That may be technically correct, but here he asked to testify and was refused. Only the jury issue is here, however. Dennis made no proof with regard to opposing the government's loyalty program (it depends on whether we can determine that the loyalty program has the effect of biasing the jury). The petitioner questioned all of the venire as to whether the loyalty program would prevent them from rendering an unbiased verdict if they were otherwise qualified to serve as jurors. Unless you want to say that government employees can't sit on any criminal trial, I think that under *Wood*[7] or *Frazier*[8] that federal employees could be excluded because of that. I would affirm.

BLACK: In this kind of a case, federal employees should not sit. I would reverse.

REED: The indictment was for contempt, and the communist issue was not included in it. But we can't stand on that ground, because the indictment charges that it is a communist trial. The *Wood* case does reach this—that is an ordinary criminal case. It was a sound result there. *Frazier* does not apply. I think that the judge denied petitioners the *opportunity* to make a showing of bias. We must say either that you can or you can't make a principal challenge of government employees per se (and no grounds for rejecting them, etc.). I would say "*no, you cannot* challenge government employees *as a group.*" The defense can move to change venire and so forth—as in England, they allowed the king's servant to serve on a jury. You never can challenge in principle—that is, you never can challenge the class. I would affirm.

---

6. Besides being required to take loyalty oaths, federal employees were subject to loyalty investigations by their supervisors and could be fired if there were any problems. Membership in any group named on the attorney general's official list of subversive organizations could lead to dismissal.

7. *United States v. Wood,* 299 U.S. 123 (1936). The Court refused to impose a blanket ban on government employees sitting on criminal cases prosecuted by the federal government but ruled that the relationship between the employees' jobs and the matter involved could establish actual bias to justify removal for cause.

8. *Frazier v. United States,* 335 U.S. 497 (1948). This was a federal narcotics case where the jury was composed entirely of federal employees. In a 5–4 decision, the Court affirmed Frazier's conviction and ruled that a jury of federal employees did not violate the Sixth Amendment's fair trial guarantees. Rutledge wrote the majority opinion, while Jackson, Frankfurter, Douglas, and Murphy dissented.

FRANKFURTER: I would reverse. [BURTON: Frankfurter discusses the *Burr* case and gives a Marshall quotation as to the exclusion of relatives.[9]] The law suspects a bias, not that he *is* biased. We must recognize, in fact, the undisputed influences of the loyalty investigations—ten new cases, etc. I would differentiate the *Frazier* case. The impact in the D.C. area is greater than in Virginia. In the metropolitan area it would be the same.

JACKSON: (1) Lambastes the rule in *Frazier* and is ready to overrule it. (2) Lambastes anybody that accepts that remedy for a Communist.

BURTON: I would affirm. There is no bias in fact. There was no showing of bias for a principal challenge, and no judicial knowledge or atmosphere that can supply that lack of evidence.

CLARK: I felt at first like Stanley, that there never would be a challenge in principle. But it is very involved, and the loyalty program is in this case, and I was so close to it, and I advised the president. I am out of the case.[10]

MINTON: I would affirm.

Result: The Court, in a 4–1–2 opinion by Sherman Minton, affirmed Dennis's conviction. Government employees were by law eligible for jury duty, and the existence of a government loyalty program was not enough by itself to demonstrate actual bias on the part of individual jurors. Reed joined the majority opinion but added in a separate concurrence that government employees could be excluded on account of implied bias in appropriate cases. Jackson concurred in the judgment. He adhered to his dissent in Frazier *and said that while a criminal jury was not impartial when entirely composed of government employees, as long as* Frazier *was not overruled Jackson was not going to make an exception for communists. Black and Frankfurter dissented, while Douglas and Clark did not participate in the decision (although Clark obviously participated in the conference discussion).*

Dennis v. United States, 341 U.S. 494 (1951)
(Douglas)

Dennis and ten other Communist party organizers were prosecuted for violating the Smith Act, which made it illegal to advocate the overthrow or destruction of the U.S. government by force or violence or to organize, assist, or conspire to organize such a group.[11] Dennis had committed no overtly revolutionary acts; he was accused of conspiring to establish a political party that would teach and advocate the overthrow of the American government. The defendants admitted teaching from books written by Marx, Engels, Lenin, and Stalin but claimed that these activities were protected by the First Amendment. Trial judge Harold Medina instructed the jury to find the defendants guilty if they found that the defendants intended to overthrow the American government when the opportunity arose.

---

9. 2 *Burr's Trial* (D. Robertson ed. 1875).

10. Clark recused himself because he was attorney general when federal charges were first filed against Dennis.

11. The Smith Act was also known as the Alien Registration Act of 1940. Like the original Alien and Sedition Acts of 1798, the law had little to do with aliens and much to do with sedition, real or imagined.

Dennis and the others were convicted, and the court of appeals affirmed in an opinion by Learned Hand. Hand recast the clear and present danger test, stating that courts "must ask whether the gravity of the 'evil,' discounted by its improbability, justifies such invasion of free speech as to avoid the danger." This time, the main issues before the Court were the clear and present danger test and the right of government to defend itself against allegedly dangerous groups.[12] Unfortunately, as Douglas notes, the conference discussion was fairly superficial.

Conference of December 9, 1950

VINSON: Affirms. [DOUGLAS: Practically no discussion.]

BLACK: The clear and present danger test was not satisfied. I reverse.[13]

REED: I affirm.

FRANKFURTER: (1) The status of the clear and present danger since *Gitlow*.[14] (2) How imminent must the substantive evils be? (3) Should the clear and present danger test be submitted to the jury? In Holmes' and Brandeis' opinions, that is a question of

---

12. *Schenck v. United States*, 249 U.S. 47 (1919). Holmes's original formulation of the clear and present danger test was whether words were used in such circumstances or were of such a nature that there was "a clear and present danger that they will bring about the substantive evils that Congress has a right to prevent."

13. Gerald Dunne argues that Hugo Black's sympathy for Dennis and other accused communists was rooted in Black's memory of what had happened to him when his Klan membership was publicly exposed and he was subjected to ex post facto condemnation for behavior that had not seemed very sinister to him at the time. Dunne, *Hugo Black and the Judicial Revolution*, 282. Others have argued, however, that Black was simply sincere in his belief in the right of free expression for everyone, including communists.

14. *Gitlow v. New York*, 268 U.S. 652 (1925), incorporated the First Amendment and applied it to the states. The Court, however, affirmed Benjamin Gitlow's conviction under the state syndicalism act for his membership in a revolutionary faction of the Socialist party. Edward Sanford's test was whether Gitlow's utterances tended to bring about a specific evil that government had a right to prevent. This was a variation of the "bad tendency" test, the predecessor and less restrictive alternative to Holmes's clear and present danger test. Under the bad tendency test, prosecutors did not have to prove that Gitlow's speech posed a clear an present danger of inciting the violent overthrow of government—only that it *tended* to have that effect. Holmes and Brandeis dissented, arguing that the clear and present danger test should be applied to state as well as federal prosecutions. In their view, Gitlow's publication, *Left Wing Manifesto*, was a voice in the wilderness and posed no present danger to civil government.

Black and Douglas accepted Harlan Fiske Stone's argument that the First Amendment articulated "preferred rights" which trumped other competing rights. They believed that *Gitlow* represented Holmes's first step *away* from his original formulation of the clear and present danger test and toward more vigorous protection of First Amendment rights. Frankfurter, who emphatically rejected the idea that some constitutional rights were inherently more important than others, liked Holmes's clear and present danger test because it allowed judges to analyze and balance different interests in a way that fit Frankfurter's perception of the judicial role.

For his part, Black contemptuously called Frankfurter and his supporters "the balancers" and argued that Frankfurter's approach left fundamental constitutional rights in constant jeopardy—forever subject to the fickle whims of unelected judges. Douglas also blasted Frankfurter for refusing to recognize that there was a fundamental difference between the free speech clause and the commerce clause. Urofsky, *Felix Frankfurter*, 115–16.

fact. (4) Can we take judicial notice of the existence of the evil and danger? I would affirm.

DOUGLAS: I agree with Black and will reverse.

JACKSON: The United States can protect itself against this sort of activity. It can stop some things because they are inherently dangerous, without reference to clear and present danger. I have not made up my mind. I pass, but will probably affirm.

BURTON: The danger here was clear and probable, rather than clear and present, which is the test. I still affirm. We can take judicial knowledge of the danger.

MINTON: I affirm.[15]

[DOUGLAS: The amazing thing about this conference on this important case was the brief nature of the discussion. Those wanting to affirm had their minds closed to argument or persuasion. The conference discussion was largely pro forma. It was the more amazing because of the drastic revision of the "clear and present danger" test which affirmance requires.]

Result: In a 6–2 vote, the Court upheld the Smith Act and confirmed Dennis's conviction. Chief Justice Fred Vinson's plurality opinion closely tracked Judge Hand's "gravity of evil" test. Vinson believed that the danger in this case was so clear that it did not have to be present, at least not in the sense of posing an immediate threat to the government. America, the Chief Justice wrote, did not have to wait for the putsch to begin before defending itself from Communist conspiracies. Frankfurter switched sides from the first Dennis case and voted with the majority to affirm Dennis's conviction. He refused to join Vinson's opinion, however, and instead emphasized in his concurring opinion that the courts should defer to the reasonable legislative judgment that the communist conspiracy was a substantial threat to national order and security.

In dissent, Black and Douglas showed little respect for the majority, and privately they teased Vinson without mercy. In his response to one of Vinson's draft opinions, Black wrote that the Communist party was nothing but a "ghost conspiracy" and mockingly warned the Chief Justice that "the goblins are going to get you."[16] Black argued that the defendants were unconstitutionally convicted for "pure speech" and "mere advocacy." In Black's view, there were no punishable acts in what Dennis and the others had done. At the very least, he argued, the defendant's capacity for criminal action had to be proved to a jury, rather than assumed by the Court. Douglas also rejected Vinson's imagery of communists locked in a life-and-death struggle with the American way of life and described party members as "miserable merchants of unwanted ideas" who posed no real threat to the republic. But where Black announced an absolute protection for speech, Douglas still accepted the clear and present danger test—not Learned Hand's version, but the test as he believed Holmes and Brandeis intended it to be applied.

---

15. Shay Minton had already voted for the Smith Act once, in 1940 as a Democratic senator from Indiana.

16. Ball, *Hugo L. Black,* 194–95.

Yates v. United States, 354 U.S. 298 (1957)
Schneiderman v. United States
Richmond and Connelly v. United States
(Douglas) (Burton)

Fourteen defendants, including Oleta O'Connor Yates, William Schneiderman, Al Richmond, and Philip Connelly were indicted in 1951 for violating the Smith Act. The defendants were allegedly founders of the Communist party in the United States. They were charged with conspiracy to organize the party in the United States to overthrow the American government by force and violence and with conspiracy to teach and advocate the overthrow of the American government by force and violence.

The defendants argued that "organizing" meant to establish, found, or bring into existence. They claimed that because the party was fully operational by 1945 at the latest, and because the indictments were not issued until 1951, the Smith Act's three-year statute of limitations had expired on the organizing charges.[17] The government argued that organizing the party was an ongoing, continuous process and that Smith Act prosecutions could be brought at any time. The defendants also claimed that the trial judge, in his jury instructions, failed to distinguish properly between advocacy of abstract doctrine, *which was constitutionally protected, and advocacy intended to promote unlawful action, which they conceded was punishable under the Smith Act.*

Conference of October 12, 1956

WARREN: I have only tentative views. It is a pretty involved case.

(1) The government has not made a very clear case of proof concerning the violent purpose of the party. They proved only that some classic books were introduced. Can we infer that individual members adhere to the dogma of the party? Ordinarily no, not in case of the usual party. In any party, individuals are not bound by all. A university group, for example, might join without regard to some of its purposes. The proof must be made clearly. *Dennis* was a *limited* grant of certiorari.[18] We made no decision that a particular corpus of evidence proved a history of advocating a violent overthrow on the part of the Communist party. We have not passed on the question of the quantum of proof required for such a finding, and that needs to be shown here. The evidence here is weak and not substantiated. As respects the editor of the paper, there is not a word showing that the paper advocated the overthrow of the government or promoted it.

It is important that it be proved beyond reasonable doubt. Proof of intent is required, as stated in *Dennis.* And it was not established here. In connecting these people up with the conspiracy, the government has fallen short in most of them, to wit, Connelly, Richmond, and Yates. We can't permit that to be done. As to every one of these defendants, nothing in the way of criminal motives has been shown except a bare connection to the party. For Connelly and Richmond, for example, the government did not show that they were for revolution by force and violence. If we must connect them fully with the Com-

---

17. The Communist party in the United States was originally established in 1919. In 1944, the party was dissolved and replaced by the Communist Political Association, which was in turn replaced in 1945 by a reconstituted Communist party.

18. *Dennis v. United States,* 341 U.S. 494 (1951).

munist party and if *intent* is necessary, none of that was shown. The evidence was weak on the Communist party, and weak on their connections. The same as to Mrs. Yates, who did not advocate violence. She was for doing it by ballot.

(2) The government has proved only membership in the Communist party. There has been no evidence of unlawful conduct. The only two overt acts were attendances at the public meetings for the Lenin Memorial. These were public meetings, and there was nothing said there relative to the doctrine of force and violence. Although it does not have to be criminal, it has to connect into a conspiracy more than this does. *De Jonge* allows the right of assembly, and that is very much what we have here.[19] The government has not demonstrated the required overt acts. Neither membership nor office-holding is enough under the act. The United States does not answer that. The United States says that these meetings are the way of getting people in, but that is far-fetched. It rests only on inferences from the lay membership.

(3) As to incitement, the judge's instructions to the jury were not adequate. The trial court refused to give the instructions that they gave in *Dennis*. What the district court gave on advocacy was not the equivalent of incitement. Not all of them are engaged in incitement.

(4) On the organizing charges, the organization was not complete at the start. I don't know about the "organization." I doubt whether all of these people "organized." Some who go about organizing are organizers—but the publisher of a paper is not an organizer.

(5) On the trial atmosphere, we find the congressional committee releasing the FBI report at a crucial time in midst of the trial, and there was a series of lurid articles. In *Mesarosh*, the committee held a meeting in the town of the trial during the trial.[20] I do not think that is a fair procedure. It is not coincidental that these things are happening.

(6) I was not much impressed by Schneiderman's claims of res judicata or estoppel.

---

19. *De Jonge v. Oregon*, 299 U.S. 353 (1937). The Court reversed the conviction of a labor organizer prosecuted under Oregon's criminal syndicalism act. The majority ruled that the state law was unconstitutional as applied and said that inflicting criminal punishment for participating in a public meeting that was otherwise lawful—merely because the meeting was sponsored by an organization that taught or advocated the use of violence or other unlawful acts or methods—violated De Jonge's rights of free speech and assembly. The case incorporated the right of peaceable assembly as a fundamental right and applied it to the states via the Fourteenth Amendment.

20. *Mesarosh v. United States*, 352 U.S. 1, 14 (1956). In another Smith Act prosecution, Stephen Mesarosh and five others were convicted in a Pittsburgh federal court of conspiring to overthrow the government. There was something of a circus atmosphere surrounding the trial. The movie *I Was a Communist for the FBI* premiered with a splash in Pittsburgh during the trial. It claimed to depict the life story of Matt Cvetic, one of the government's star witnesses. Another of the government's key witnesses, Joseph Mazzei, testified at trial, while at the same time he testified against various Communist party members at several congressional committee and subcommittee hearings, at least one of which was held in Pittsburgh while Mesarosh's trial was under way. On appeal, Solicitor General J. Lee Rankin "confessed error" after learning that Mazzei had given untruthful testimony and asked the Court to remand the case to allow the district court judge to decide whether a new trial was necessary. In a 5–3 per curiam opinion, the Court denied Rankin's motion, reversed the convictions outright, and ordered a new trial for all six defendants. Frankfurter, Burton, and Harlan dissented; Brennan did not participate.

(7) On freedom of the press, there may be a real issue. Nothing these men have published has been attacked.

In the aggregate this was a weak record, and in a sense there was no evidence at all. I vote to reverse.

BLACK: I would reverse. The Smith Act provides for political trials, and this is a political trial—which the First Amendment was supposed to prevent. As to sufficiency of the evidence, it depends on what you have to prove. In my opinion, the evidence is not sufficient. The proof here is sufficient if Marx and Lenin were on trial. If membership was enough, and if Marx and Lenin incited the overthrow of the government, and if they had knowledge of the conspiracy and stayed in, then the government has proved its case.

With the actual defendants, if the government need only show ideas, they proved that. If they need only "act," they did so. You can't convict here unless you want to convict. It was a far stronger case in *Dennis* than here. The government has *not* met the *Dennis* standard. We can't say what the party intends, and there is no evidence tying these people in.

Schneiderman—we *must* give him a new trial. Under *Sealfon v. United States* [BURTON: Black reads a *Lawyer's Edition* note], he is protected by collateral estoppel.[21] The government can't relitigate an issue previously adjudicated. Civil adjudication of an issue is binding in a criminal case.

(2) There were no organizers here. Merely adding new members is not organizing, although establishing new units, of course, is. Reorganization might be organization, but merely belonging to an organization is not organizing. The judge did not instruct the jury properly on "organize," and the government did not prove what is required. Merely soliciting membership here would meet the test stated, and that is not enough.

(3) The judge's failure to give a charge on incitement was error. He should have given the Medina charge.[22]

---

21. *Sealfon v. United States*, 332 U.S. 575 (1948). The government alleged that Sealfon and a co-conspirator sought to evade sugar rationing limits by presenting false invoices of sales to organizations that were exempt from rationing and that they made false representations to the sugar ration board. Sealfon and his alleged partner were initially charged with conspiracy to defraud the government, but Sealfon was acquitted. The government then tried to prosecute Sealfon a second time using the same evidence, this time charging him with the substantive offense of defrauding the government. He was convicted, but the Supreme Court reversed. Because the false invoices were all prepared and turned in by Sealfon's partner, the Court ruled that Sealfon was liable only as an accessory and that his acquittal on conspiracy charges was res judicata as to the issue of complicity. Douglas wrote the opinion for a unanimous Court. The note to which Black referred said, "Res judicata may be a defense to one acquitted of conspiring with others to commit an offense, in a prosecution for committing it, or vice versa. . . . The doctrine of res judicata applies to criminal as well as civil proceedings, and operates to conclude those matters in issue which the verdict determined, though the offenses be different."

22. Judge Harold R. Medina was the trial judge in *United States v. Foster*. On appeal, the case was renamed and became *Dennis v. United States*, 341 U.S. 494 (1951). In the group trial of eleven defendants, Judge Medina reduced the government's complex case to a single charge of conspiracy to overthrow the government by force and violence. He gave a lengthy, detailed, and evenhanded charge to the jury, telling jurors, among other things, that mere membership in the party was not sufficient to justify conviction. Medina's jury instructions were published in *United States v. Foster*, 9 F.R.D. 367, 373–394 (District Court for the Southern District of New York, 1949).

(4) Criminal statutes should be narrowly construed. It is a *criminal statute*, and you cannot expand it. Giving the statute its broadest meaning possible, the government's evidence is not sufficient. I reverse.

REED: I recognize the weakness of the evidence as compared with *Dennis.* There is little evidence hooking up the defendants to force and violence. But we must test the indictments. The indictments are for conspiracy to organize and acts to bring about overthrow of the U.S. government by force and violence. This does not require that the overt acts *themselves* be unlawful. The Communist party by now is established as advocating force and violence for a century. It is plain that they so urge. Congress wanted to eliminate the Communist party. Today it is too late to say that the teaching of Marxist-Leninist classics is not teaching the overthrow of the government. "Organizing" is more generic than Black says, and it covers these party activities. Organizing means growth or expansion, as well as initiation. Seeking new members is organizing. The judge's instruction on incitement was adequate. As to Schneiderman, there is no equitable estoppel here—did it—we don't have a decided issue. I would affirm.

FRANKFURTER: I am not prepared to vote on all of the issues today. I cannot now decide what questions *have* to be passed on. The contested substantive issues don't have to be reached. I have some questions as to the judge's charge.

I am gratified by the Chief Justice's remarks as to the unfair trial due to the poisoning of the atmosphere at this trial. It is too bad that the court of appeals accepted this. Look at the *Delaney* case in the First Circuit.[23] I also agree with Black on collateral estoppel in the case of Schneiderman. It is clear that it is enough if the same issue was *contested*—it does not have to be adjudicated. Look at *United States v. Oppenheimer.*[24]

---

23. *Delaney v. United States*, 199 F.2d 107 (1st Cir. 1952). Denis Delaney, the collector of Internal Revenue for Massachusetts, was charged with accepting bribes and issuing false certificates of discharge of tax liens. It was a high-profile prosecution and there was pervasive publicity. The House Subcommittee on Administration of the Internal Revenue Laws—also known as the King Committee—decided to conduct its own highly publicized investigation of Delaney's activities, in spite of requests by both Delaney's defense attorney and the Department of Justice not to hold public hearings immediately before or during the trial.

Delaney was convicted. The circuit court of appeals, however, vacated the conviction and remanded the case on the ground that the trial judge should have granted Delaney a continuance until the effects of the adverse publicity "had so far worn off that the trial could proceed free of the enveloping hostile atmosphere and public preconception of guilt prevalent . . . when appellant was brought to trial." The court of appeals noted that the district judge sought to minimize the prejudicial effects of the adverse publicity by giving cautionary remarks in his charge to the jury. This might have been a step in the right direction, but it was not enough. The appellate court quoted Robert Jackson's opinion in *Krulewitch v. United States*, 336 U.S. 440, 453 (1949): "The naive assumption that prejudicial effects can be overcome by instructions to the jury . . . all practicing lawyers know to be unmitigated fiction."

24. *United States v. Oppenheimer*, 242 U.S. 85 (1916). The Supreme Court quashed an indictment because a previous indictment for the same offense was barred by the statute of limitations. The government claimed—unsuccessfully—that the doctrine of res judicata no longer existed in criminal cases, except in modified form in the Fifth Amendment's double jeopardy clause. The Court ruled that the Fifth Amendment was not intended to supplant the common law doctrine of res judicata in criminal cases. Holmes wrote the opinion for a unanimous Court.

[BURTON: The United States says collateral estoppel does not apply in criminal cases—except as to double jeopardy?]

I would start with *Dennis.* The first question is what the Smith Act required. The judge's charge including this is essential, and there are questions about the clarity of the instructions. On incitement, I think it doubtful whether the district court gave the proper instruction. I have concluded that on the essential part of Smith Act, the charge is inadequate as to the essential points of advocacy and incitement. At best, it is not clear enough for the jury to act upon. I also think that the district court's conception of and instruction on "organizing" is wrong. A new trial is required. Beyond those points I have not reached a decision on the merits of the case.[25]

DOUGLAS: I agree with Frankfurter and Burton on estoppel, and with Warren as to the trial. An overt act is very difficult to see here. These two meetings are thin. I would reverse.

BURTON: I agree with Reed, with a reservation on Schneiderman. What about the sufficiency of evidence as to Richmond? Connelly? Kennedy? I would affirm, subject to Schneiderman and the strength of the evidence.

CLARK: I agree with Reed. There was sufficient evidence on Schneiderman and Richmond. They wrote one of the books. The proof is sufficient against the party—it is the same evidence as in *Dennis.* I think that is enough. Solicitation of funds at the Lenin meetings was enough of an overt act. The charge of incitement is O.K. I think that there is probably sufficient evidence against all of them. There are more formidable charges than in *Dennis.* I affirm.

MINTON: I have read enough to reach a conclusion. I am inclined to the view that the judgment should be affirmed. I can't agree that the Smith Act is for political trials. It is to wipe out a conspiracy dedicated to and financed by a foreign government. We can take judicial notice of it. We have gone a long way from *De Jonge* and the first *Schneiderman* case.[26] The Communist party does advocate the overthrow of the United States by force and violence. Its members conducted classes teaching it in indoctrination schools, with the recruitment of members, money, papers—all in the interest of the Communist party. All the activities of the party supported its aim to overthrow the American government. The *Schneiderman* case is not barred by collateral estoppel. It was a different issue there. Equitable estoppel did not come up. The court did not pass on it, only as to citizenship. Richmond and Connelly went to headquarters of the Communist party and related institutions. The "organizing" test was satisfied. "Organization" is more than K of P; it includes all members. Affirm.

---

25. District Judge William C. Mathes defined organizing broadly to include "the recruiting of new members and the forming of new units, and the regrouping or expansion of existing clubs, classes and other units of any society, party, group or other organization." *United States v. Schneiderman,* 106 F. Supp. 906, 935–936 (CD Cal., 1952).
26. *Schneiderman v. United States,* 320 U.S. 118 (1943).

HARLAN: I am not ready to vote. The overriding question is the sufficiency of the evidence. We must make a close analysis of the evidence. I am not at all sure that these cases are successfully reached. Sufficiency of the evidence depends on what *must* be found. There may be other questions that could dispose of these cases. I have no present view on that. On incitement, I think that the judge's charge is inadequate. I would reverse on that ground. The charges on recruitment were also inadequate. As to "organize," I think that *Dennis* was right and that organizing does not include recruiting.

Conference of November 2, 1956: Yates

FRANKFURTER: I think that the charge is inadequate and defective. We must have an active incitement. The judge's charge was confusing and not guiding. On clear and present danger, we do not have to use that test here. The trial judge should have given Medina's charge. Reverse and cite Medina. I am also against the judge's charge on "organize." Organizing does not mean expanding your membership. There must be an overt act to *further* the conspiracy. I have not reached a conclusion as to the sufficiency of the evidence.

BLACK: I reverse. This was a political trial. I do not know what the crime is. Teaching is not a crime. I will wait and see what is written.

REED. I affirm. On the judge's charge, there is very little difference between this and Medina's charge. Here, "urge" is enough. The organizing test was satisfied here. As far as proof, we don't have to go to extremes. There was enough to go to the jury.

DOUGLAS: I reverse.

BURTON: I affirm on all points.

CLARK: I affirm. I start by finding any differences between the two charges. The judge's instruction follows *Dennis*. This follows Vinson closer than it did Medina. "Inquiry" is enough. There was sufficient evidence. Each case is the same. I know that the party is the same.

As to the individuals, there are seventeen cases. Anybody who was a Communist party official, and ten against the newspaper, *Peoples' World*. The evidence is adequate. It is the same evidence as in the *Dennis* case. And every one of our precedents has approved this type of case.

HARLAN: I am not through all of the evidence yet. The evidence should be reviewed. The charge is inadequate because it is "muddy" and the jury can misconstrue the law. They are entitled to something undebatable, and the charges here were not clear enough. On "organizing," the charges are also defective. *Dennis* was right. The judge here used the wrong legal theory—the clear and present danger test is not sufficient here; it is no good. The evidence and the instructions will determine whether he is acquitted or should be granted a new trial (perhaps we should *not* acquit). I reverse on the two grounds mentioned, and reserve my decision on the evidence.

WARREN: I agree that the charge was defective. The jury was not properly instructed on incitement, on organizing, or on intent. The press release and hearing also disturb me—they should be considered in the opinion.

Conference of November 2, 1956: Richmond and Connelly

WARREN: There is nothing in the evidence but their membership in the party. There is no proof of anything except that those men ran a newspaper and went up to the Communist party headquarters. "Intent" is absent under the *Dennis* rule. I reverse on insufficiency of evidence.

BLACK: I have not looked at the evidence. Party membership is the basis for conviction in all of the cases. Prior history, not action in the Communist party. I reverse.

REED: We must give wide scope to the evidence that is introduced. This is competent evidence. There is enough evidence. I affirm.

FRANKFURTER: I would reverse on the charge, citing *Yates*. I have not yet re-examined the evidence. I probably would have to direct an acquittal.

DOUGLAS: I reverse on the evidence.

BURTON: Those tied up with a newspaper of this kind are close enough. Membership is enough. I affirm.

CLARK: I affirm. I found enough evidence. Membership and going to meetings, producing articles every day, being praised by the party. Richmond was elected by the Communist party to run the paper. He was a mere spokesman for the party. The paper was an instrument of the party.

HARLAN: I reverse on the charge, not yet on the evidence. I have not yet examined the evidence. If there is not enough evidence, he still must be retried in discretion.

Conference of November 2, 1956: Schneiderman

WARREN: Reversal as to Yates means reversal here, also. But there is the additional question of estoppel. Schneiderman is entitled to rely on equitable estoppel. I reverse on res judicata here, also.

BLACK: I reverse. This is res judicata.

REED: I affirm. These are different crimes and different cases. There was no determination in the first case that he did not belong to a party of that character. The question as to the nature of the party was put aside in the deportation case.

FRANKFURTER: If you carve out what was put into evidence in the deportation case, there is very little left here.

DOUGLAS: I reverse.

BURTON: I affirm. There is a different standard of test here.

CLARK: I am amazed that estoppel in a 1929 case could influence this trial. The program of the party was not decided in the earlier case. I affirm.

HARLAN: There is no collateral estoppel. The opinion in *Schneiderman* did not consider it. Questioning it might affect the only real issue—that he committed no overt act. The question is what was *necessarily* decided, not what was an element in this case. The degree of proof must be as great. I affirm.[27]

Result: The Court voted 6–1 that the federal statute of limitations had expired on the organizing charges and that the trial judge had erred in instructing the jury on advocacy. All of the convictions were reversed, with the organizing charges dismissed outright. As for the advocacy charges, some of the defendants were ordered acquitted due to insufficient evidence and new trials were ordered for the rest.

John Marshall Harlan, writing for the majority, discarded Fred Vinson's open-ended version of the clear and present danger test that the Court had adopted in Dennis. *The trial judge, in Harlan's view, mistakenly believed "that* Dennis *obliterated the traditional dividing line between advocacy of abstract doctrine and advocacy of action." Harlan admitted that it was difficult to distinguish between advocating or teaching abstract communism with evil intent and advocacy directed to stirring people to action. The main difficulty was that, as Oliver Wendell Holmes said, "every idea is an incitement." This meant that trial judges had to be especially clear in their jury instructions.*

The main effects of this decision were to (1) limit Dennis; *(2) end prosecutions for organizing the Communist party; and (3) require a more strict standard of proof in subsequent Smith Act prosecutions. The decision limited the Smith Act's usefulness in prosecuting Communist party members and gave significantly greater First Amendment protection to groups and individuals opposed to the American system of government.*

Black and Douglas concurred in part and dissented in part. They thought that all of the charges should have been dismissed outright because they violated the defendants' First Amendment speech, press, and assembly rights.

Tom Clark, dissenting from the other direction, thought that all of the convictions should have been affirmed under Dennis. *In Clark's view, while the defendants here were lower in the party hierarchy than those on trial in* Dennis, *they were all "in the same army and were engaged in the same mission." Brennan and Whittaker did not participate.*

Communist Party of the United States v. Subversive Activities Control Board,

351 U.S. 115 (1956)

(Douglas)

Under the Internal Security Act of 1950, Congress declared communism to be a clear and present danger to the United States and established the Subversive Activities Control Board (SACB) to enforce the act.[28] After conducting hearings, the SACB ordered the Communist Party of the United States of

---

27. Douglas's notes list Harlan as voting to reverse.

28. The Internal Security Act was also known as the McCarran Act, or the Subversive Activities Control Act. It was passed over President Truman's veto, who called it the greatest danger to American freedom since the Sedition Act of 1798. All communist and communist-front organizations and all other organizations deemed subversive by the Subversive Activities Control Board had thirty days to comply with the law's registration requirements. Violators, including all officers and members, were subject to severe criminal penalties, including fines of up to $10,000 and a maximum of five years in prison for each violation. Each *day* that violators failed to register counted as a separate offense.

America (CPUSA) to register with the attorney general as a "communist-action" organization.[29] *The CPUSA appealed to the federal Court of Appeals for the District of Columbia and filed a motion to allow additional evidence to be considered—namely, that three of the attorney general's witnesses who testified against the CPUSA had committed perjury.*[30] *The government did not deny these allegations but maintained that there was enough untainted testimony to justify the SACB's decision. The court of appeals affirmed the board's decision, with Judge Bazelon dissenting.*

This case came before the Supreme Court twice: in 1956 and again in 1961. In both instances, the published opinions studiously avoided most of the substantive issues raised by the case. The Justices, however, discussed their personal views at length in conference, and the conference notes are far more enlightening than the written opinions. Note Earl Warren's defense of jury trials as the ultimate guarantee of our civil rights.

Conference of November 18, 1955

WARREN: My views are somewhat tentative. Does the act control peaceful activities of the Communist party? Yes. The act draws no line between the legal and the illegal. It strikes at the right of political action and at First Amendment rights. Are the sanctions serious, so serious as to smother the party? Yes. This is not a registration statute, it is a death penalty statute. The sanctions are very heavy. The question of membership is not here, but if the sanctions are to exist there will be no members, for they can't withstand the pressures of not traveling and of not being able to get a job. If a member goes to work in a plant certified by the attorney general and fails to advise them when he goes to work that he is a member of the party, he can go to jail. If he merely asks for a passport, he goes to jail.

A board, not a jury, determines guilt. If you can't make up an administrative procedure to outlaw cattle rustlers, you can't do it here. A jury trial is necessary. There are very serious First Amendment rights at stake here. On the Fifth Amendment question, you have about the same problems as under the First Amendment. I am troubled by the trial by jury question, and leaving to the jury only the question of whether the member actively belonged to the party. If a board can take away one right a man has and not let a jury pass on it, it is a dangerous step. Self incrimination is a serious question. Does the party have standing to raise the question? Yes. It is here and properly so. It can't be raised in the criminal trial. Is this a bill of attainder? It is an important question. I have very grave doubts as to the constitutionality of this act.

BLACK: This act violates almost all of the Bill of Rights, except for the quartering of troops. Party registration can be required to show where the propaganda comes from. I do not, however, think that this is a registration law. It is like *Ex parte Young*, where there was a law which, if enforced, would have made it impossible for a company to have any officers.[31]

---

29. Section 7(a) of the act required all Communist-action organizations (1) to register with the attorney general; (2) to submit the names, aliases, and addresses of officers and members; and (3) to provide a list of all printing presses under the control of the organization or members.

30. The three admitted perjurers were Paul Crouch, Manning Johnson, and Harvey Matusow.

31. *Ex parte Young*, 209 U.S. 123 (1908). Minnesota unilaterally slashed state railroad passenger rates by one-third (from three cents per mile to two) and imposed severe penalties on any railroad officer or

Under this act, the penalties are so severe for registration that they are gone before they start. The finding of the board is a finding of the critical point in the case. Members are heavily penalized, by being disqualified for civil posts, and so forth. They can't personally test the act by individual lawsuits. This act apes totalitarian methods. Today I would not sustain a sentence of this act, feeling as I do.

REED: This is not much different from our decision in *Joint Anti-Fascist.*[32] The act is a legitimate exercise of governmental power. This is not a criminal prosecution, though it will have a very deleterious effect. There is no right to a jury trial involved here. The act does not keep communists from making any speeches they want. I am not prepared to answer the question on self-incrimination. With the one reservation on the issue of self-incrimination, I think that the registration requirement is a proper exercise of governmental power and can be required.

FRANKFURTER: I am not ready on this case. I pass.

DOUGLAS: This act is bad on two grounds: (1) this is not a proper registration act; and (2) this act violates the self-incrimination provision of the Fifth Amendment.

BURTON: I have tried to hold this up as a registration act, but I am having difficulty with that. It really is not a registration act. We must look at it as a whole. Some of these things are inconsistent with our Constitution. I am inclined to hold it unconstitutional.

CLARK: On separability, I agree with Judge Prettyman and I think that we can salvage part of the act.[33] Congress can interdict the party and set up a regulatory scheme. The party is controlled by a foreign government, and its object is to advance the world communist movement. There is no difference from requiring this party to register than in requiring the Ku Klux Klan to register.[34] This Court sustained the KKK law. The KKK law does not have the sanctions of this law.[35] We would have to carve out some of the sanctions. The self-incrimination point comes too early—see, for example, the *White*

---

employee who caused, counseled, advised, or assisted a railroad company to violate the law. While the state's sovereign immunity prevented Young from suing Minnesota to enjoin enforcement of the statute, the Supreme Court permitted him to sue individual state officials—in this instance the state attorney general—in equity to enjoin the statute's enforcement. This became known as the *Ex parte Young* exception to state sovereign immunity.

32. *Joint Anti-Fascist Refugee Committee v. McGrath*, 341 U.S. 123 (1951).

33. Judge E. Barrett Prettyman wrote the majority decision for the court of appeals.

34. *Bryant v. Zimmerman*, 278 U.S. 63 (1928). The Court sustained a New York state law requiring the Ku Klux Klan to file its local membership lists with state officials. No Fifth Amendment claims were raised in this case. The Court ruled that New York could require secretive, oath-bound organizations to file copies of their constitutions, by-laws, rules, regulations, oaths of membership, and membership rosters without violating free association rights or the Fourteenth Amendment's privileges and immunities, liberty, or equal protection clauses. Willis Van Devanter wrote the opinion for an 8–1 Court, with James McReynolds alone in dissent. The case lost most of its legal authority after *Brandenburg v. Ohio*, 395 U.S. 444 (1969), but it has never been formally overruled.

35. It was a misdemeanor criminal offense to violate New York's registration statute.

case.[36] We can carve out some portions of the act and uphold it as a registration act. The sanctions in the act on party members' civil activities are not really new. They are in force now for those who want to work in the defense plant or in the government. [DOUGLAS: But the act also makes it a crime for a member even to apply for a passport.] We can carve out the sanctions as to members. There is nothing in the act that says that the board's order is final or binding on the members. I would invoke the separability clause and would save the center of the act.

MINTON: The party's purpose is to destroy us. The greatest enemy of liberty is the Communist party. Their primary purpose is the overthrow of the government. I think that we have only the registration provisions of the act before us, and we can act solely on that basis. The government's right to register them is clear. It is no different from requiring the registration of the Ku Klux Klan. I would reserve the question on the sanctions, but I would not be sorry if the whole party was destroyed, and the members too.

HARLAN: I have no firm views on the act. We should try to limit the case to registration, but I am not at all sure that we can. If this is only a registration act, why all the collateral elements? I think that the solicitor general did not meet the question in oral argument. We should explore the question of separability and see if a part of the act can be saved. I am not sure that it can be. As of now, I find it difficult to treat the registration provisions separately.

FRANKFURTER: Perhaps the government's power to outlaw the Communist party is present. The Mormon church was dissolved by Congress, and in *Mormon Church v. United States* that act was sustained.[37]

Conference of March 8, 1956

WARREN: (1) The act in its entirety is before us. (2) The action of the board in requiring registration put all of the machinery of the act into operation. We must consider not only the rights of the party, but also the rights of its members. In the *Frozen Food* case,

---

36. *United States v. White*, 322 U.S. 694 (1944). Citing his Fifth Amendment right against self-incrimination, a labor union official refused to obey a subpoena duces tecum requiring him to produce union records in his possession for a grand jury criminal investigation. The Court held that the Fifth Amendment was designed to protect only "natural individuals," not labor, business, or corporate interests. White could not claim the privilege in his official capacity or on behalf of third parties, whether natural or corporate. The papers were not his private property, nor did he hold them in a purely personal capacity. Finally, White had not personally been ordered to testify, nor had he been accused of personally authorizing or participating in any illegal actions.

37. *Mormon Church v. United States*, 136 U.S. 1 (1890). The "state" of Deseret incorporated the Church of Jesus Christ of Latter Day Saints (Mormons) in 1851. This act, which also legitimized polygamous marriages, was quickly affirmed by the Utah Territorial Legislature. In 1862, Congress criminalized polygamy. Then in 1887, Congress repealed the Mormon church's act of incorporation, abrogated its charter, and began proceedings to seize church property. The Supreme Court ruled that Congress's power over federal territories was plenary and that its actions were constitutional.

the United States argued that the Interstate Commerce Commission's order adequately affected 200 shippers to give it justiciability.[38] We should do so here.

We must consider the overall purpose of Congress. Was it a registration act, or did it contemplate outlawing the Communist party? If it was merely a registration law, we can save it. If it is outlawing the party by legislative fiat, we can't save it. If registration pulls down sanctions on the individual, it is outlawing—there is no middle ground.

In enacting this law, Congress wanted to go as far as it could toward outlawing the party and the members. If we sustain the act and these sanctions, we will have more sanctions, and a few more would outlaw the party as well as the members. If trade unions can't employ a leaf raker, it would be written into the law that no commie could belong to a labor union. If that is good, then the residential zone next to defense plants can be restricted. The act constitutes outlawing. It will either drive the party underground or expose its members to punishment. *Electric Bond and Share* is not applicable.[39] The *Mormon Church* case is not applicable. Congress there dealt only with corporations of its own creation.

I do not think that Congress can outlaw the Communist party. I would apply *De Jonge v. Oregon*[40] and *Thomas v. Collins*.[41] I would strike the act down if it is considered as a whole. I would be inclined to hold the act valid if the registration provision alone is considered. The mail provision and tax exemption provisions are not objectionable in light of our cases. They could be required to register as foreign agents.

---

38. *Frozen Food Express v. United States*, 351 U.S. 40 (1956). Under federal law, motor vehicles carrying "agricultural commodities" were exempt from obtaining permits and certificates required of other carriers. The Interstate Commerce Commission issued an order delisting many items that it had formerly listed as agricultural commodities. Frozen Food Express, a motor carrier that hauled goods that would no longer be exempted, sued to enjoin enforcement of the new regulations. The government claimed that the ICC's actions were not binding and that the agency was simply reporting on the outcome of its investigation into agricultural commodities. Accordingly, the government maintained (contrary to Earl Warren's argument in conference) that there was no real case or controversy and that the case was not justiciable.

The Supreme Court ruled that the case was justiciable and that Frozen Food Express had standing to sue. William O. Douglas, writing for the majority, held that the regulations were enforceable in court and would have an immediate and practical impact on carriers who transported delisted goods.

39. *Electric Bond and Share Co. v. Securities Exchange Commission*, 303 U.S. 419 (1938). The Electric Bond and Share Company was a large, multistate system of interconnected electric and gas holding companies. The company refused to register with the government or provide requested information on the company's organization, finances, and activities as required by the Public Utility Holding Company Act of 1935. The SEC obtained an injunction against the company prohibiting it from using the mails or other facilities of interstate commerce until it complied, and the Supreme Court affirmed.

40. *De Jonge v. Oregon*, 299 U.S. 353 (1937).

41. *Thomas v. Collins*, 323 U.S. 516 (1945). Texas law required all labor organizers to register with state officials and to obtain an organizer's card before soliciting union memberships. R. J. Thomas ignored a state court's order enjoining him from violating the statute and made a public speech where he urged audience members to unionize. Thomas was cited for contempt, fined, and jailed. The Supreme Court reversed, ruling that the state law was an unconstitutional prior restraint on free speech and assembly. The state could not require individuals to register with the state before making a public speech soliciting support for a lawful cause, absent a clear and present danger to public welfare.

BLACK: If Congress has the power to outlaw the Communist party and its members, we should say so. I can't treat this as a registration act, since it provides a penalty. It is like requiring a holding company to register, and then making membership in the holding company a crime. Here the party is found guilty of a crime—or is rather guilty of that which is a crime. It is like the bills of pain and other similar penalties in Greece and Rome, or bills of attainder in England. This is an advanced type of a bill of attainder. This is an indirect way of establishing who has violated the Smith Act. This violates the First, Fifth, and Sixth Amendments, including the specific provisions against bills of attainder. I can sustain no part of this act.

REED: The purpose of disclosure is to put the Communists where they can be watched. The aim is to stop sedition before it gets dangerous. I think that the registration portion of the act can be isolated from the rest of the act. I would write very narrowly, and sustain the registration provisions.

FRANKFURTER: I differ violently with Hugo. I do not look to history to determine the meaning of the Constitution. It is the business of Congress to make the judgments of history and to appraise the risks. We should be slow to upset Congress. Look at Hitler and Eastern Europe. No risk is excluded to the nation. The Smith Act and the *Dennis* prosecution were foolish. Our security policy is foolish. But that does not make it unconstitutional.

I would respect the principle of separability. I was opposed to *Chenery*.[42] Maybe Congress intended to tie the whole thing together, but they made the act separable. I will separate the registration provisions.

When people engage in violence, they can be stopped from non-violent conduct. If this statute had nothing but sanctions against the party, it would still be constitutional. Requiring the registration of this party alone is not fatal, for Congress was reaching the problem of the use of force and violence. I can see no objection to any of the penalty provisions of the act. They automatically come into operation, so we must consider all

---

42. *Securities Exchange Commission v. Chenery Corp.*, 332 U.S. 194 (1947). In a corporate reorganization proceeding, the SEC used judicial equity principles to rule that company managers who had purchased company stock during the reorganization would not be permitted to convert that stock into shares of the new company but had to surrender them at cost plus interest. On appeal, the Supreme Court decided that the SEC should not have based its decision on judicially derived principles of equity and remanded the case for further review. Frankfurter wrote the original majority in a 5–3 decision. Black, Reed, and Murphy dissented, while Douglas did not participate. *SEC v. Chenery Corp.*, 318 U.S. 80 (1943).

On remand, the SEC reached the same decision, but on a different ground—that to allow company managers to keep their profits would violate the Public Utility Holding Company Act of 1935. This time the Court approved the SEC's findings. The new majority pointedly said that it had been compelled to remand the case the first time, knowing that the agency could exercise its discretion to reach the same result for a different reason. The majority acknowledged that "the choice between rulemaking and adjudication lies in the first instance within the Board's discretion" and that judicial review ended when it became evident that the commission's action was based on substantial evidence and was consistent with the authority granted to it by Congress. On a 4–1–2 vote, the Court deferred to the SEC's judgment because of the agency's administrative experience and expertise. Murphy wrote the majority opinion, Burton concurred in the result, and Frankfurter and Jackson dissented. Neither Vinson nor Douglas participated.

of them. I conclude that §§5(a-d), 6, 8, and 10 relating to the individuals automatically came into operation. I think that we must face that. The individuals are not the ones who are hurt.

I have serious misgivings about some of these sanctions, because they violate due process. I think that the passport provision is invalid, and perhaps others. But I would separate them out. The individual sanctions are infused into the entire act. But if anything can be saved, it should be. All of these provisions are not invalid. Some must be excised in this case. If this were a criminal case, I could not affirm as to the three perjurers—that is very bothersome. The problem is that it taints the record, which should be purged.

DOUGLAS: I would reverse. This is executive and legislative outlawry, and it is prohibited by the Constitution.

BURTON: The determination step is O.K. The registration step is also O.K. There are all sorts of intermediate steps that could be taken, and so we can take only a part of the act. I would look beyond registration, and cut off a few penalties and sustain most. I think that the passport provision is bad. I think that the employment provision is bad because it is automatic. I would modify the affirmance.

CLARK: I read the whole transcript. There were twenty-two witnesses.[43] There was ample evidence. The passport issue is not here. So far as we know, none of them will apply for a passport. The governmental end covered by the passport provision is to prevent them from getting a passport to give to someone else. I would strike down the application of the passport provisions, but it is premature to consider it. Other sanctions against holding jobs are not at issue. It will be soon enough to raise the problem when an employee is cut out of a job.

WARREN: The mere application for a job is a criminal offense under this act.

CLARK: There is no final order here. The case is premature. The registration provisions are O.K. The Ku Kluxers were required to register. Taft's opinion went even further.[44] We should consider only the issue of registration and the possible sanctions against the party. We should avoid considering sanctions against the individuals. If individuals are considered, I will be willing to excise the "application" provisions regarding jobs and passports. I affirm with modifications.

MINTON: There are mere questions of policy involved here. The congressional policy is constitutional—they can stop these people who are out to destroy us. Only the registration provision is here. To excise this and that is to amend the act. We should meet these issues only when they come here in separate cases. I affirm.

---

43. The witnesses' statements were quite lengthy; some were more than one hundred pages long.

44. Clark might have meant Willis Van Devanter, who wrote the majority opinion in the Ku Klux Klan registration case, *Bryant v. Zimmerman*, 278 U.S. 63 (1928).

HARLAN: I think that this act is unwise, but it is not our job to pass on its wisdom. If this was a declaratory judgment, everything would be before us. Nothing is here but the determination question. If registration is here, then everything is here. I am prepared to go along and treat the act as a whole. Everything is here except for the tax exemptions. I reserve my decision about whether the record should be sent back in view of the incompetent evidence. I agree with Frankfurter, and I would affirm.

WARREN: I have decided to reverse on Matusow's evidence. On the act, I would sustain the registration provisions and strike down all of the personal sanctions against party officers and members. I would reserve the Fifth Amendment question.

BLACK: I reverse.

REED: I affirm.

FRANKFURTER: I am with the Chief Justice.

CLARK: I am willing to excise the application provisions for jobs and passports. If we pass on the constitutionality of the board, etc., I would be willing to reverse because of Matusow's testimony.

MINTON: I will not excise anything.

HARLAN: I reach all of the questions except for the tax exemptions. I would excise the provision punishing applications for jobs. I vote to reverse on Matusow's testimony.

WARREN: I think that all of the personal disabilities are here, and I would strike them all down. It loses character as a registration statute when fewer are punished.

Result: In a 6–3 decision, the Court ruled that the court of appeals should have remanded the case to the SACB for further consideration of the perjured testimony. The Court avoided the substantive constitutional issues. Frankfurter wrote the majority opinion, with Clark, Reed, and Minton in dissent. The board subsequently reconsidered its findings, after excluding the testimony of the three tainted witnesses, and reaffirmed its initial decision requiring the CPUSA to register as a Communist-action organization. The CPUSA again appealed to the Supreme Court, arguing that the registration requirements violated their First Amendment free speech rights and their Fifth Amendment due process rights and privileges against self-incrimination. The organization also complained that Congress's actions amounted to an unconstitutional bill of attainder.

Communist Party of the United States v. Subversive Activities Control Board, 367 U.S. 1 (1961)
(Brennan) (Clark)

WARREN: There are a number of grounds on which this decision can be reversed: (1) Budenz's testimony;[45] (2) the sufficiency of the evidence under a high standard of

---

45. Lewis F. Budenz was formerly the managing editor of the *Daily Worker* and a former Communist party member. He testified against the party and numerous alleged Communists, including folk singer Pete Seeger.

proof; and (3) the fact that this case was pending for nine years. Reversal on one of those grounds is possible. But the major constitutional questions are here and should be reached. The act violates the First Amendment on association and the Fifth Amendment on self-incrimination. Now that some of our other cases are reading into the statute certain elements, I cannot escape the fact that the act requiring individuals to register is violative of the Fifth Amendment. Since membership is prosecutable, revelation of this fact invalidates the statute under the Fifth Amendment's self-incrimination clause. I also think that it is out under the First Amendment and due process clauses. The sanctions are also bad, since they affect the party as well as its members. I don't take to the idea of cutting off sanctions (severability) one by one and thus eliminating our objections.

BLACK: This act violates due process. It is also a bill of attainder—like the one in Ireland—despite its legal formula and sophisticated statements. This act is intended to hurt people by legislative fiat.

FRANKFURTER: It is the duty of this Court to deal with this statute not at large, but on specifics. This case makes every man face his conception of judicial review and his relationship as a member of this Court to the Congress. I am in the group in favor of avoiding declaring legislation unconstitutional. I spent half of my life being critical of the Court for striking down statutes on perceived formulas, such as happened in the *Lochner* case.[46] This is a duplicate argument of *Electric Bond and Share*.[47] That case controls the separability issue. There, congressional integration of all parts was its clear desire. But look what this Court did—it decided no more than was before the Court. Who are here? No individual is here. Assuming that Congress may deal with the party as such and make it register, does the fact of individual sanctions of doubtful validity prevent this? I vote to affirm the judgment below, restricted to filing by the party, so that no individual has to do a thing— and when he must, he can then claim constitutional protections.

DOUGLAS: There is a finding here that this party is the agent of a foreign power. I would have no hesitancy in saying such a requirement would be valid. But this simple solution is not available here, in view of our result in *Scales*.[48] Filing of a paper produces an ingredient of a crime. If §4(f) had eliminated the Smith Act's membership clause I could affirm registration, but not otherwise.[49]

CLARK: I think all that is needed is that the party should register, and we can read out any requirements for signatures.

HARLAN: I recognize the force of *Electric Bond and Share*, if there is no distinction between property and individual rights. I cannot distinguish *Electric Bond*, but I think that

46. *Lochner v. New York*, 198 U.S. 45 (1905).

47. *Electric Bond and Share Co. v. Securities Exchange Commission*, 303 U.S. 419 (1938). This case was potentially useful for avoiding some of the thornier issues here. Since the only action that the SACB actually took against the party was to order it to register with the attorney general, the registration requirement was the only constitutional question before the Court. This allowed Frankfurter to argue that the broader constitutional issues did not have to be considered.

48. *Scales v. United States*, 367 U.S. 203 (1961).

49. For further discussion of this issue, see *Scales v. United States*, 367 U.S. 203 (1961), discussed below.

we should reach the sanctions that flow from registration, including the effects on individuals. This is not merely an information-gathering registration, it is a registration with consequences. There are considerations of judicial administration which argue for treating the sanctions and everything else. Do it now, rather than to do this thing piecemeal. As to self incrimination, I don't think that we should excise the attorney general's regulation. The *White* case disposes of self-incrimination as to officers.[50] But we would not reach this privilege as to other people until it is asserted. The individual sanctions apply only during your membership. You can qualify for passports and jobs, etc., by getting out. Two sanctions are no good: (1) Preventing members from applying for passports, which prevents travel anywhere and is too broad. We can sever that provision or modify it. (2) The qualification for holding office in labor organization is also bad, because it goes to something that is not regulable by Congress.

BRENNAN: There were three main trial errors. Budenz's evidence should be stricken, which would leave no proof of the purpose of the Communist party. The finding under §13-7 (secrecy and purpose), *Chenery* requires reversal.[51] I doubt the constitutionality of §7(a). They must have officers sign, and this would incriminate them.

WHITTAKER: Can the Communist party be required to register? (Put aside individuals, etc.) While the statute says "any forms supplied by Attorney General," Congress impliedly requires them to be *valid* regulations. I would construe §7(a) to eliminate any illegal requirements.

STEWART: I have trouble with (1) the *Gitlow* memorandum holding, denying him stuff for technical reasons.[52] The petitioner should have a *Gitlow* memorandum. (2) Section 3 defines the control component and the objectives component. I doubt whether these were properly construed by either the court of appeals or the board, and I doubt whether, if they did construe them properly, that the evidence sufficed. But if we apply the rule that our review is limited to saying whether any contrary conclusions of the court of appeals are irrational, maybe we must affirm. Also, I think that the evidence is insufficient.

On the constitutional questions: (1) Congress can compel registration; (2) I would defer the self-incrimination issue until someone claims it; and (3) as to organizational sanctions, the tax exemption is O.K., the labeling requirement is O.K., the contributions provisions are O.K. I don't reach individual sanctions until an individual wants a job, etc.

---

50. *United States v. White*, 322 U.S. 694 (1944).

51. *SEC v. Chenery Corp.*, 332 U.S. 194 (1947).

52. In 1940, Benjamin Gitlow, a former high-ranking official of the Communist party, presented the FBI with a large number of party documents and papers and dictated a series of memoranda explaining and interpreting these materials. At the original hearing in the government's subsequent proceedings against the CPUSA, Gitlow testified for the prosecution, and many of his documents were admitted into evidence. The party asked the board to compel the attorney general to produce Gitlow's memoranda for their inspection, but the board refused. The CPUSA did not push the issue at oral arguments in 1955 or in 1960, but after the Court ordered reargument in 1960 the party again raised the issue. The board again refused to compel prosecutors to produce Gitlow's memoranda. For Gitlow's initial experience before the Supreme Court, see *Gitlow v. New York*, 268 U.S. 652 (1925).

Result: In a 5–4 vote, the Supreme Court affirmed the board's decision to require the CPUSA to register with the attorney general. Frankfurter again wrote the majority opinion, with Warren, Black, Douglas, and Brennan in dissent. Frankfurter upheld the act's registration requirements on the ground that they were "regulatory" and not "prohibitory," but he avoided any real discussion of the thornier issues: whether the Subversive Activities Control Act was a bill of attainder, or whether the registration requirements violated the defendants' free speech or due process rights. The Court also reserved the question of whether requiring party officers to file registration statements violated their Fifth Amendment protections against self-incrimination.[53]

Watkins v. United States, 354 U.S. 178 (1957)
(Douglas)

John T. Watkins, a United Auto Workers organizer, was summoned by the House Un-American Activities Committee (HUAC) and questioned about his alleged ties to several subversive organizations. Watkins freely discussed his own actions and associations but refused to answer questions about other people. He claimed that such questions were outside of the scope of the committee's responsibilities. Watkins was held in contempt of Congress.

Conference of March 8, 1957

WARREN: I would reverse. He was an honest witness. There is no claim of dishonesty. He explained his history with the Communists. There is no claim of illegal associations. He went to jail because he would not be an informer. While Congress has the right to investigate this matter and has great latitude in determining what legislation is necessary, this is a good case to state the limits of that power. It is one thing for Congress to punish a man itself—it is another thing to require the courts to punish a man without any standards of pertinence or fairness. The least we could require in this type of case is that the committee show the relevance of the questions. Then the courts can pass on the relevance. But we should not allow shotgun questions making him state his beliefs, associations, and politics, and then pick up one question and put him in jail for that refusal. Congress can't combine prosecutions and a judicial function. That is not the American way. He could not be punished for these things in a court proceeding. The witness must be apprised of the relevancy of the question if they are going to put him in jail for not answering.

---

53. Frankfurter also stated that the party had waived any right it might have had to subpoena Gitlow's memoranda. Even assuming that the board had erred in refusing to order the attorney general to produce the materials, Frankfurter noted that the error should have been raised on appeal in 1955. Had it been raised then, the Supreme Court could have cured any mistake at the time that the case was first remanded to the board. To rule otherwise, Frankfurter wrote, "would be promoting the 'sporting theory' of justice, at the potential cost of substantial expenditures of agency time. . . . To allow counsel to withhold in this Court and save for a later stage procedural error would tend to foist upon the Court constitutional decisions which could have been avoided had those errors been invoked in a timely manner."

BLACK: I reverse. Contempt before the Congress is one thing, and contempt of court is a different thing. [DOUGLAS: Black refers to his dissent in *Rogers*.[54]] This man was not informed of relevancy. The presumption of relevance is not as strong as the presumption of innocence. When a man is tried by judicial procedure, relevancy must be shown. The committee knew the names of all these people—why force this man to disclose his associations? Look at Owen Roberts's case on littering the streets,[55] or my dissent in *Fleischman*.[56]

WARREN: On the issue of exposure, the solicitor general admitted there was no right to expose for exposure's sake.[57] Exposing governmental corruption, etc. is one thing. No idea of exposing individuals for private conduct. That was not the original idea. There is no purpose to expose people for their private conduct just to build up public opinion for legislation.

FRANKFURTER: We should not talk big in this field. You can't distinguish between informing and legislating. Congress can't investigate merely "to show up" A, B, or C. Committees should have the broadest investigating power. I was critical of *Kilbourn* for its

---

54. *Rogers v. United States*, 340 U.S. 367 (1951). Rogers was held in contempt of court for refusing to answer several grand jury questions about the activities of the Communist party in Denver, Colorado. Rogers freely admitted her own activities, including the fact that she had been the party treasurer for a time. She refused, however, to identify the person to whom she had turned over the party's books and records. The majority ruled that: (1) Rogers had no Fifth Amendment protection against self-incrimination, because the question did not ask her to incriminate herself but to incriminate a third party; and (2) Rogers had waived her right against self-incrimination by answering other questions about her party activities.

In dissent, Black gave a spirited defense of the Fifth Amendment. He argued that the right against self-incrimination deserved broad construction to protect individuals from suffering under the tyranny of coercive, inquisitorial, and despotic state investigations and that the rules governing waiver of Fifth Amendment rights should be read narrowly for the same reasons. Black argued that Rogers was within her rights to refuse to answer questions about her successor, because the information could have been used against her at a subsequent trial. Moreover, Black argued, Rogers could not waive her Fifth Amendment rights unintentionally; to be valid, a waiver had to be specific and knowing.

55. *Schneider v. State*, 308 U.S. 147 (1939). Owen Roberts, writing for the Court, ruled that a city's desire to keep its streets clean did not justify banning citizens in public places from handing leaflets to those willing to receive them.

56. *United States v. Fleischman*, 339 U.S. 349 (1950). Fleischman was convicted for willfully failing to comply with a subpoena issued by the House Committee on Un-American Activities. She and other directors of the Joint Anti-Fascist Refugee Committee had been ordered to produce the association's records, but all the directors individually denied that they had possession or control of the subpoenaed records. The majority upheld Fleischman's conviction, holding that the directors were all jointly and severally responsible for the organization's records.

In dissent, Hugo Black and Felix Frankfurter argued that Mrs. Fleischman did not have personal possession or control of the records and had no power to obtain or produce them and that this was a complete defense to the charge of willfully failing to comply with the subpoena duces tecum. Even in a contempt case, Black argued, a defendant could only be punished when she failed to comply with an order specifying precisely what she must do and when she had the power to do what was ordered.

57. The solicitor general was J. Lee Rankin. Rankin was perhaps best known for his arguments on behalf of the Eisenhower administration during the school desegregation cases, where he developed a reputation for candor when he frankly admitted several weaknesses in the government's position.

broad language.[58] Landis's article on investigations[59] turned the trick in the *Daugherty* case in this Court and led it to uphold the powers of Congress.[60] Not until 1857 could the courts punish for legislative contempt. The only case where the Supreme Court held that congressional inquiries were beyond the range of the congressional power of inquiry was *Kilbourn*. In procedures before the Congress, a witness should be apprised of relevancy. When Congress tells the court to put a man in jail, then the court has a duty to determine relevancy. Watkin's refusal to be an informer was honorable. If the committee had a purpose to pursue it, they should have shown relevancy. I reverse.

DOUGLAS: I reverse.

BURTON: Not in the case.

CLARK: I would affirm. It would throw these people into the fire to refer them to the Congress for trial. In that sort of trial, the witness has no lawyer and no appeal. Velde told the witness of the committee's function—that is enough.[61] The witness had plenty of time to talk to the chairman and to find out the relevancy of the questions. The pertinency of the questions seems obvious to me.

HARLAN: I agree with Frankfurter on relevancy.

BRENNAN: I would reverse.

---

58. *Kilbourn v. Thompson*, 103 U.S. 168 (1881). Hallet Kilbourn was subpoenaed by a House committee to testify about a bankruptcy. Kilbourn testified about himself but refused to answer questions about the activities of five other people. He also refused to produce certain records that the committee requested. Kilbourn was held in contempt and imprisoned for forty-five days on the authority of John Thompson, the sergeant-at-arms of the House. He sued Thompson and several congressmen for false imprisonment.

The Court ruled that neither house of Congress had a general power to investigate the private affairs of its citizens or to punish nonmembers for contempt. As a rule, separation of powers principles meant that these powers must rest in the judicial branch alone. Noting that the matter under investigation was already the subject of judicial inquiry, the Court ruled that the House had exceeded its authority, that the House lacked the authority to imprison Kilbourn, and that Thompson had no immunity against a suit for false imprisonment. The speech or debate clause, however, meant that the congress members named in Kilbourn's suit were immune as long as they had not directly participated in Kilbourn's assault, arrest, and imprisonment.

59. James Landis, "Constitutional Limitations on the Congressional Power of Investigation." Landis was Frankfurter's colleague and co-author; he later became dean of the Harvard Law School.

60. *McGrain v. Daugherty*, 273 U.S. 135 (1927). Mally Daugherty was arrested in Ohio and brought to Washington, D.C., as a "contumacious witness" on a warrant issued by the president of the Senate. This was in connection with a Senate investigation of the Justice Department's alleged failure to prosecute monopolies and other restraints of trade under the Sherman Antitrust and Clayton Acts. The Senate investigation was connected to the Teapot Dome scandal, which broke under President Warren G. Harding. Daugherty was the brother of former Attorney General Harry Daugherty and the president of the Midland National Bank of Ohio. Daugherty sought a writ of habeas corpus against John McGrain, the deputy sergeant-of-arms of the Senate.

The Court limited the scope of *Kilbourn*, ruling that each House had broad investigative powers, including the power to enforce subpoenas and compel witnesses to appear. This case helped to spark a dramatic expansion of the nature and scope of congressional investigations.

61. Representative Harold Velde (R-IL) was the chair of the House Committee on Un-American Activities.

*Result: On Red Monday, June 17, 1957, the Court reversed Watkins's conviction on narrow due pro-
cess grounds.[62] Earl Warren, writing for a 6–1 majority, ruled that the conviction violated due process
because the committee failed to explain the relevance of its inquiries and because Watkins had no
opportunity to determine whether he had the right to refuse to answer the committee's questions.
Warren wrote much as he spoke in conference. Congress's investigative powers were broad, but not
unlimited. Congressional committees had to justify their actions when they sought to expose the private affairs of individuals, and they could not expose for the sake of exposure. Questions had to be
related to a legitimate legislative purpose, and Congress was required to establish committee jurisdiction and responsibilities with sufficient specificity to ensure that the power of compulsory process would
not be abused. Clark was alone in dissent, while Burton and Whittaker did not participate.[63]*

Scales v. United States, 367 U.S. 203 (1961)
Lightfoot v. United States
(Douglas) (Brennan)

*In 1956, Junius Irving Scales was convicted of violating the membership clause of the Smith Act, which
made it a crime to belong to any organization advocating the violent overthrow of the United States
government. Scales operated a "Communist Party Training School" in Virginia, where instructors
allegedly taught students some jujitsu that they "might use on picket lines" and showed students how
to kill a person by driving a pencil through the heart.*

*The trial judge instructed the jury not to convict Scales unless the government proved that the
Communist party advocated taking action to overthrow the government as soon as circumstances allowed; that Scales was an active member of the party; and that Scales had knowledge of the party's
illegal advocacy and its intent to overthrow the government with violence as soon as circumstances
would permit. The evidence against Scales included testimony that the party sought to incite rebellion
among southern blacks by publishing pamphlets graphically describing alleged American atrocities
during the Korean War and drawing parallels between North Korea's struggle and conditions in "The
Negro Nation of the Black Belt." The court of appeals affirmed Scales's conviction.*

*Scales followed a dizzying procedural path to the Supreme Court. A short-handed Court of seven
Justices first heard oral arguments on the case during the 1956 Term. At Frankfurter's suggestion, the
case was scheduled for reargument the following term, but the Solicitor General voluntarily agreed to
grant Scales a new trial after the Court's intervening decisions in* Jencks *and* Yates.[64] *On retrial, Scales
was again convicted and the court of appeals again affirmed. The Supreme Court granted certiorari
and heard oral arguments during the 1958 Term but then ordered the case to be reargued the following
term. The reappearance of* Communist Party v. SACB *led the Justices to postpone* Scales *yet again,
so that both cases could be decided together during the 1960 Term. In the meantime, Potter Stewart*

---

62. Announced on the same day were *Sweezy v. New Hampshire,* 354 U.S. 234 (1957); *Yates v. United States,* 354 U.S. 298 (1957); and *Service v. Dulles,* 354 U.S. 363 (1957). Together, these cases took most of the wind out of the Smith Act's sails. Prosecutions fell off dramatically afterward and soon stopped altogether. The Smith Act had its last hurrah with the prosecution of Junius Scales.

63. Warren's suggestion that the Court would closely scrutinize congressional investigations was largely abandoned in *Barenblatt v. United States,* 360 U.S. 109 (1959).

64. The government told the Court that FBI reports concerning two witnesses had been withheld by the prosecution in violation of *Jencks.* See also *Yates v. United States,* 354 U.S. 298 (1957).

was appointed to the Court and took his seat knowing that he would cast the deciding vote. Stewart's struggle to decide the case is the highlight of the later conferences.

Conference of October 12, 1956

WARREN: I would dispose of this on the indictment without reaching the Constitution. The federal government has here a boot strap operation. They add a new element to the crime by adding "intent" to overthrow the government. The indictment must stand or fall on membership. The addition of intent is fatal. Congress made its choice whether it would have registration or knowing membership as an offense—Congress could not have both. That was recognized by §4(f).[65] The legislative intent is clear. By "any other criminal statute," Congress meant the Smith Act. "Per se" does not save it, for that would apply the registration provisions to those without knowledge—in other words, it would apply to the more innocent members of the Communist party. In statutory interpretation, the specific provisions of a statute prevail over the general.

BLACK: I agree with the Chief Justice. I would, if necessary, say that membership cannot be made a crime.

REED: "Intent" is in the section. It should be read into it. Intent is used in the first section, but not in the others. Intent must be in that first section if you are to have a fair method of proof. If you leave "intent" out here, it overrules *Dennis*.[66] I disagree with the Chief Justice on §4(f); "per se" means that membership without knowledge or intent is not sufficient. I affirm.

FRANKFURTER: The addition of "intent" would not vitiate the indictment, as it merely adds to the burden of proof of the government. The government added it to the case of §4(f). I am inclined toward the Chief Justice's view. I am not yet prepared to vote definitively on it. My forecast is that the legislative history is not conclusive. Section 4(f) is not meaningful unless it undercuts the Smith Act. It does not negate something that existed, for membership was not an offense prior to that.

DOUGLAS: I would reverse on §4(f).

BURTON: I reverse on §4(f). We need not reach the other questions.

CLARK: I agree with Reed. The government must prove "intent." If you don't have to, then you overrule *Dennis*. If this §4(f) repeals the Smith Act's membership clause, it also repeals (a) and (c) in §10 of the Security Act.

MINTON: I agree with Reed and Clark. I affirm.

HARLAN: I am on the fence. Section 4(f) is the threshold question. I am inclined to think that it is a repealer. I very tentatively vote to reverse. The other arguments have to be considered, but it is hard to see what the clause means unless it gives immunity here.

---

65. Section 4(f) of the Internal Security Act of 1950 stated that membership in the Communist party was not per se a violation of the Smith Act. One of the key issues was whether this amendment repealed the membership clause of the Smith Act.

66. *Dennis v. United States*, 341 U.S. 494 (1951).

CLARK: Intent was added to the indictment here because of our decision in *Screws.*[67]

HARLAN: I am troubled by the judge's charge. The government says that intent plus active membership is necessary, but the judge said nothing about the character of the membership of these petitioners. That looks like a defect in the charge. If I reach the evidence, I would consider it adequate in the case of *Scales,* and inadequate in case #32, *Lightfoot.*[68]

Conference of November 2, 1956

WARREN: The indictment fails to state an offense. The membership clause of the Smith Act has been repealed. There is no public crime here. If I have to reach the membership clause, I would declare it unconstitutional on its face. I reverse.

BLACK: I reverse. There is no public crime.

REED: I would affirm.

FRANKFURTER: Section 4(f) has not supplanted the Smith Act's membership clause. I have not examined the evidence. The FBI statements raised here raise different question than in *Jencks.*[69] In *Jencks,* there was a foundation laid for the statements. There was no foundation here. I am not prepared to lay down a rule requiring production from all government agents, and I can't make an exception in favor of FBI I reach the constitutional questions, and I think that a government like ours can pass a statute outlawing those who don't want to use constitutional means for change. Force and violence are unconstitutional means. I think the law is unwise, but it is not unconstitutional. If you can reach the organization, you can reach the members. I affirm.

DOUGLAS: I reverse.

BURTON: Section 4(f) does not repeal the membership clause. The statute is constitutional. I affirm.

CLARK: I affirm. The evidence is adequate. I agree with Burton and Frankfurter on §4(f), and that the membership clause is constitutional. As to the FBI reports, there must be same predicate laid. The procedure followed here was proper.

HARLAN: On §4(f), I agree with Burton and Frankfurter. If specific intent and active membership are read into the act, it is constitutional. But I have trouble reading active membership into the act. I come out for reversal on that, and on the charge.

Conference of March 22, 1957

WARREN: I reverse on the §4(f) issue. That was put in to protect us.

BLACK: I reverse.

67. *Screws v. United States,* 325 U.S. 91 (1945).
68. *Lightfoot v. United States* was the companion case to *Scales.*
69. *Jencks v. United States,* 353 U.S. 657 (1957).

FRANKFURTER: Section 4(f) does not repeal the Smith Act. I would reach the constitutionality of the act. The FBI reports are involved. Affiliation is involved, as is the adequacy of evidence under the charge. In *Lightfoot*, the government's burden of evidence is not satisfied. On the statute, I find the act valid under the Constitution. I reverse.

DOUGLAS: I reverse.

BURTON: Section 4(f) is not adequate. The FBI reports were declared. "Membership" included both knowledge and intent. I vote to affirm in *Scales* and will vote to reverse in *Lightfoot*.

CLARK: I affirm both *Scales* and *Lightfoot*. There is plenty of evidence. I agree with Frankfurter's analysis of §4(f). The record shows that Scales taught communism and believes in it. Lightfoot was high in the party.

HARLAN: I agree with Frankfurter—§4(f) is not a repealer. There is a gap in the evidence on intent.

Conference of May 1, 1959

WARREN: I would reverse. I do not reach the Constitution. The evidence is insufficient under *Yates*, on the ground that he did not have intent to overthrow the government by force and violence. There is also error in the admission of evidence on the Communist party's aims. The Korean documents were irrelevant.[70] Section 4(f) of the Security Control Law supplanted the Smith Act's membership clause.

BLACK: I reverse.

FRANKFURTER: I pass on the evidence question. I have to see how the record sustains their conviction. I am clear on §4(f): it did not repeal the membership clause of the Smith Act.

DOUGLAS: I reverse. I thought that §4(f) repealed the membership clause of the Smith Act.

CLARK: Section 4(f) did not effect a repeal of the membership clause. The evidence on the party is sufficient—we so held before. As to Scales's conviction, I thought that they had a pretty strong case. There was evidence to show that Scales's job was not only to be chairman, but also to carry out instructions to overthrow the government. I affirm.

HARLAN: If I had to reach the constitutional question, I would hold that the statute is constitutional. In my opinion, §4(f) does not affect the situation. I must read the record to decide the *Yates* point. I think there is enough evidence to override *Yates*.

---

70. Among the materials admitted into evidence was a pamphlet entitled *I Saw the Truth in Korea*, which the prosecution alleged was part of a Communist conspiracy to provoke southern blacks to rebel. The booklet contained graphic descriptions of alleged American atrocities during the Korean War and claimed that the war was being used by American capitalists to oppress American blacks. Black soldiers, the pamphlet claimed, were being sent abroad to fight Koreans who were seeking the same rights that black Americans were fighting for in the United States. In his majority opinion, Harlan conceded that the trial judge had been wrong to admit this evidence but argued that it was not prejudicial and did not justify reversal.

BRENNAN: On §4(f), I have concluded that there is no repeal of the membership clause. Either as a matter of construction it applies only to the big shots, or if it reaches the camp followers it is unconstitutional because of remoteness, since he can't do much to bring it about. The connection of Scales is too tenuous to support conviction. I tentatively reverse.

WHITTAKER: The §4(f) point is not good. I don't think that it repeals the membership clause. I think that there is abundant evidence as to the purpose of the party and that the petitioner knew of it. I am not sure that there is adequate evidence to show Scales's intent to carry out the party's objectives as soon as possible. On the whole, it is enough. I affirm.

STEWART: I am still doubtful on §4(f). On the evidence, there is a lot more than there was in *Yates*. But I must read the evidence—I doubt whether it is sufficient. I expect to find insufficient evidence under *Yates* and I expect to reverse.

Conference of June 5, 1959

FRANKFURTER: On §4(f), it is clear that the Smith Act has not been displaced. If this were a narcotics case, there would be evidence enough for the jury to convict. The weight of the evidence is tied up with *Yates*. I pass to Harlan.

CLARK: The evidence shows that Scales advocated personally the overthrow of the federal government. On the Communist party, the evidence in this case is stronger than in *Yates*. There are four schools in the county.

HARLAN: Section 4(f) does not affect the case. The statute is constitutional. On the evidence, this case is wholly different from *Yates*. In *Yates*, there was no perceived participation. Here, there is evidence that connects Scales with the planned *overthrow* of the government, and that he had knowledge about the Communist party. If this is not enough evidence, no prosecution could ever be had under the Smith Act.

STEWART: I think that the evidence Harlan refers to is merely a prediction of things to come, and that is not enough. Anything like handing out rifle is not a mere prediction. Also, showing people how to kill a man with a pencil is action. I had difficulty following *Yates*. There is probably enough here to affirm, but there is a lot here that is mere prophecy. The teaching of gunnery techniques to paralyze a city is also some evidence, perhaps enough to affirm. But there is a lot of talk, like the Republicans make about getting the support of the Negroes, etc. The theory that alienating people from our current leaders amounts to an overthrow is nonsense—that is what every political party does.

HARLAN: *Yates* holds that advocacy of action at some point along the line is necessary. "As soon as circumstances permit" is enough. Clontz's testimony is that ultimate overthrow can only come by force.[71]

STEWART: I still have many doubts, but I am inclined to affirm under *Yates*.

---

71. Ralph C. Clontz Jr. was one of three eyewitnesses called to testify against Scales. Clontz was a student at Duke University's law school when he became an FBI informant on alleged Communist party

Conference of October 14, 1960

WARREN: I reverse on non-constitutional grounds. The act is, however, unconstitutional on its face for not requiring intent and activity. If those elements are added, the membership clause is identical to the advocacy clause. If so, it becomes hard to see why Congress put §4(f) into the act. It could only apply to the Smith Act, and it would extend to its membership clause. Section 4(f) negates the membership clause. There are narrower grounds that I could go on, but I think it best to go on §4(f). The indictment was insufficient because it does not charge the elements that the government now is trying to read into it—intent and activity. The indictment is therefore defective. If we read intent and activity into the indictment, the evidence is insufficient. There is a prejudicial error of evidence showing party aims, of which petitioner was not shown to have any knowledge. The Korean document was also irrelevant.

BLACK: I reverse. I think that §4(f) covers it. I don't think that in order to save it constitutionally that we should read in what the government wants us to do. I find it difficult to say that Congress enacted §4(f) to save the Smith Act's membership clause. Even if we read in intent and knowledge, I couldn't find this constitutional. "Activities" means more than membership—it also means overt acts, as in the membership clause. Prosecuting membership alone is precluded by the Constitution. The mere fact you can convict a party member of a crime does not mean that you can proscribe a party—and that was the basic congressional place of this series of acts. Congress cannot proscribe political parties, and this party can't function as a political party under the statutes that have been discussed this week. If we had the same Constitution as France does, it would be judicial usurpation to reverse this outlawry of the Communist party.

FRANKFURTER: We should dispose of §4(f). I still think that §4(f) does not repeal the membership clause or bar membership clause prosecutions. Unless Congress is to be charged with repeal by absentmindedness, we couldn't reach that conclusion. The whole history of this body of enactments is to punish, punish, punish in this way. Thus we get to: (1) construction of the clause; (2) what to read in that isn't there in words; and (3) its constitutionality. Applying the postulate that statutes must be saved, it is easier here to read into this statute what the government wants to do than to do what was done in *Screws*.

DOUGLAS: I still feel as I did in my 1959 memorandum. Section 4(f) says that membership shall not "constitute per se," and not "membership per se shall not constitute." Therefore, §4(f) bars membership prosecutions. I also think that I could reverse on any of the Chief Justice's grounds. I reverse.

CLARK: I can't agree that this is a political party or that the congressional acts involved here are designed to outlaw, punish, etc. First, the Communist party not a party. Second, the act requiring registration is not a penal one, it is merely a disclosure statute. I

---

activities in North Carolina. When he wrote to Scales expressing an interest in Communism, Scales responded by sending Clontz a box of Communist literature to read. Clontz testified that Scales told him that a violent revolution was necessary in the United States and explained to him that the "basic strategy" for the planned revolution was to organize the proletariat and southern blacks into a revolutionary force with funding and moral support from the Soviet Union.

agree with Frankfurter that §4(f) does not bar this prosecution. The membership clause is constitutionally valid, and I believe that the evidence was sufficient. There is no question but that the evidence in *Scales*—and maybe *Noto*, too—meets the test of *Yates*.[72]

HARLAN: I agree with Frankfurter on §4(f). I still think that it was not a repealer. New elements of knowledge, intent, and activities—which I embrace—support the constitutionality of this act. I have no difficulty with the issue of constitutionality. Conduct that is constitutionally punishable must be something more than mere moral support or encouragement. Beliefs are not punishable—conduct must do more than encourage an illegal enterprise. If only "knowledge and intent" were elements, we would be in a doubtful area that approaches the borderline of constitutionality. Membership of that kind is merely assent to a cause, doing nothing to further it—if you merely pay dues and never go to a meeting and so forth. That is not enough—or may not be enough. I have no difficulty reading "intent" into the act. "Activity" is a construction of congressional intent, as well as an introduction to save its constitutionality. The evidence here is sufficient and satisfies the *Yates* case. The testimony of Clontz differentiates the case. It is direct evidence of Scales's *advocacy of action*, as distinguished from the advocacy of ideas. I affirm.

BRENNAN: Section 4(f) settles these cases. The government puts a conspiracy element back into the Act without the protection which a conspiracy indictment would give. The membership clause is not available here. Congress wanted to save all it could, but it ended up giving a barrier to prosecution.

WHITTAKER: I can't say that Congress intended to repeal the membership clause or to bar prosecutions for membership. Section 4(f) is no barrier to this prosecution. I would construe that section as if it read "membership per se." This would only eliminate prosecutions of membership per se; it would not prohibit prosecutions of the kind of membership involved with knowledge of the party's purpose and with intent to accomplish its goals. Is it necessary to introduce "activity" for constitutional purposes? If activity is necessary, it is no more of a stretch to include it than to include intent. If we could add "intent" in *Dennis*, surely we can add activity here if it is needed. I affirm.

STEWART: I would reach the §4(f) issue. I do not think that §4(f) is a repealer or a barrier to these prosecutions. The Smith Act requires *knowledge*. I think that we should read into the statute personal intent and activity factors. Reading them in saves the membership clause's constitutionality. There is no outlawry of the party. Highwaymen, by call-

---

72. *Noto v. United States*, 367 U.S. 290 (1961). This was a companion case to *Scales*. The Court unanimously reversed the membership clause conviction of John F. Noto on the ground of insufficient evidence, citing *Yates*. Harlan wrote the opinion, saying that "the mere abstract teaching of Communist theory, including the teaching of the moral propriety or even moral necessity for a resort to force and violence, is not the same as preparing a group for violent action and steeling it to such action." The evidence, Harlan said, must prove that Noto presently advocated the forcible overthrow of the government, using language reasonably and ordinarily calculated to incite persons to action, whether immediately or in the future. Noto's actions consisted mostly of reading communist literature and encouraging others to read it. He also made several offhand remarks that certain individuals who were hostile to the party would one day have to be shot, but Harlan considered these comments to be innocuous.

ing themselves a party, could not get beyond the reach of the law. As to the evidence, I am not sure that I understand *Yates*. *Yates* was a conspiracy case, this is a membership case. There is not enough evidence to satisfy the *Yates* standard as to party advocacy. I pass for this conference, although I am inclined to reverse on the evidence. I am concerned as to the evidence used here—some of it is apparently prejudicial.

FRANKFURTER: We must save an act if we can. I affirm—the evidence is adequate.

Conference of October 21, 1960

STEWART: I have changed my mind. Section 4(f) is no barrier to prosecution under the membership clause. I was concerned about the sufficiency of the evidence under the *Yates* standard. I cannot come to rest on that, but I am inclined to affirm.

FRANKFURTER: Predicting, as distinguished from promoting, came out of the Laski libel trial. That is not this case. The statute is constitutional. I am opposed to the Smith Act personally. But I totally reject the view that the Communist party is just another party. You cannot say that the threat of the Communist party is too remote. [DOUGLAS: Frankfurter reads from *Dennis*, and refers to the billions of dollars appropriated by Congress to fight communism.]

[DOUGLAS: After JMH finished talking, Black passed me the following note: "His analysis goes back to the philosophy of hope for the distant future that the clear and present danger test was precisely designed to make non-punishable." . . .]

Result: On a 5–4 vote, the Court affirmed Scales's conviction. John Marshall Harlan wrote that §4(f) did not repeal the membership clause of the Smith Act and that the membership clause did not violate the First or Fifth Amendments. It did not punish speech or impute guilt by association or sympathy but required concrete personal involvement in criminal conduct. Harlan narrowly construed the membership clause, bringing it into line with Yates. *Unlike that case, Harlan found ample evidence of Scales's activities beyond mere party membership. Scales was aware of the Communist party's illegal aims and had a "specific intent" to accomplish those goals.[73]*

The dissenters argued that Scales was being punished merely for his party membership and for exercising his right of free speech. Douglas quoted Mark Twain:

it is by the goodness of God that in our country we have those three unspeakably precious things: freedom of speech, freedom of conscience, and the prudence never to practice either of them.

In confirming Scales's conviction, while narrowing the scope of the membership clause, the Supreme Court avoided a direct confrontation with Congress over the Smith Act, while making future prosecutions virtually impossible. Scales served fifteen months of a six-year prison term before President Kennedy commuted his sentence.

---

73. Harlan cited the jujitsu and pencil of death lessons at the school as evidence of Scales's specific intent and activities. *Scales v. United States,* 367 U.S. 203, at 250.

THE SOUTH GOES AFTER THE NAACP

Shelton v. Tucker, 364 U.S. 479 (1958)
(Brennan)

An Arkansas law (Act #10 of 1958) required public schoolteachers to submit affidavits disclosing every organization to which they belonged or made donations during the previous five years. The law was specifically aimed at ferreting out National Association of Colored People (NAACP) members. Another state law (Act #115 of 1959) prohibited NAACP members from holding any state job, including teaching. Arkansas teachers did not have tenure or civil service protection but were all hired on year-to-year contracts. Three teachers refused to submit the required affidavits and were fired. B. T. Shelton, a twenty-five-year teacher and a member of the NAACP, sued in federal court. The defendant, Everett Tucker Jr., was the president of the Little Rock school board. At the same time, Max Carr, an associate professor at the University of Arkansas, and Ernest T. Gephardt, who taught high school, sued over the same issues in state court. The federal court struck down the law prohibiting NAACP members from holding state jobs, but both the federal district court and the state supreme court upheld the membership disclosure law.

WARREN: The language of this statute is just too broad. The rights of association of the school teachers are invaded. They have no tenure and no right to a hearing. School officials have a right to inquire into teachers' membership in organizations bearing on fitness, such as professional organizations. But requiring information on membership and contributions to church, political party, and social organizations goes too far. On that narrow ground, and laying aside creative or racial considerations, I would reverse. There is no provision in the act, moreover, making the information confidential.

BLACK: This is peculiarly a case where breadth and scope have to be considered. Otherwise, the only way his constitutional rights could be raised not to give names would be by giving the names of the organizations to which he belonged. Even if the information were to be kept confidential, I would still come out the same way.

FRANKFURTER: The state may certainly search the thought processes of teachers. It is relevant to ask about the organizations to which teachers belong, including what church, because it is relevant to know the associations teachers have if we are to know how to appraise their fitness. If this complaint had set forth that discriminatory or coercive use of information would be made, then it would be like *Yick Wo.*[74] These cases do not con-

---

74. *Yick Wo v. Hopkins,* 118 U.S. 356 (1886). Yick Wo was jailed for violating a San Francisco ordinance prohibiting commercial laundries from operating in anything other than a brick or stone building, except by permission of the board of supervisors. Of 320 laundries in San Francisco, all but 10 operated out of wooden buildings, and 240 of them were owned and operated by Chinese nationals. Virtually all applications to the board of supervisors for licenses to operate out of wooden structures submitted by Chinese laundry owners were refused, while license applications submitted by non-Chinese were routinely granted. Moreover, only Chinese laundry owners were ever charged under the ordinance. The 80-odd laundry companies not in compliance with the ordinance but owned by members of other races and nationalities were left largely unmolested.

tain such allegations, and therefore the litigation is premature. I would read the Arkansas state supreme court opinion to say that the information is confidential. I won't take judicial notice that the state statute will be misused.

CLARK: The teacher is not in the same category as others. He has certain obligations, as Justice Burton said in *Beilan*, to cooperate in giving information as to his associations.[75] Even though the Arkansas Supreme Court may not have plainly said that the information was confidential, the record in this case is that so far it has been kept confidential.

HARLAN: I don't believe that *Alabama v. NAACP* touches this.[76] The essence of that case was given the situation and because there was no state interest of *any* kind there, let alone a superior one. Here, the question is whether in the field of education a state may inquire into one's associations. There is no practical way to draw a line, so the state can go whole hog. If a state fires or refuses to hire for a reason having no rational relation to teaching fitness, then as applied the courts may strike it down. Abuse—not to weigh qualifications but to harass by publication of personal information—can't be assumed.

WHITTAKER: Since Act #115 was struck down, the Court has, in effect, said that the state can't abuse teachers with this information.

STEWART: This case is not nearly so clear and easy as *NAACP v. Alabama* or *Little Rock*, since in those cases there were no relevant connections between the asserted purpose for disclosure and the disclosure.[77] Here there is a state interest, obviously. In those other cases, too, there was affirmative evidence of reprisal and discouragement of association.

The Supreme Court ruled that Chinese subjects legally residing in the United States were entitled to equal protection under the laws, and unanimously declared that the law was unconstitutional as applied. Even though the law was fair on its face and impartial in appearance, it had been applied by the city "with an evil eye and an unequal hand." Equal protection meant that there could not be arbitrary and unjust discrimination based on racial differences among people otherwise similarly situated.

75. *Beilan v. Board of Public Education, School District of Philadelphia,* 357 U.S. 399 (1958). Beilan was a schoolteacher who refused to tell his district superintendent whether he had ever been a member of the Communist party. The district declared Beilan incompetent and summarily fired him. The Court held 5–4 that Beilan's failure to answer the superintendent's question provided sufficient evidence of incompetency and unreliability to justify his dismissal.

76. *NAACP v. Alabama,* 357 U.S. 449 (1958), prevented the state from compelling the disclosure of NAACP membership lists where there was evidence that previous disclosures had resulted in economic reprisals, firings, and violence against NAACP members.

77. *Bates v. Little Rock,* 361 U.S. 516 (1960), was a unanimous decision striking down two city ordinances in Arkansas requiring the NAACP to disclose its membership lists. The ordinances required the payment of occupational license taxes by any person, firm, or corporation engaged in any "trade, business, profession, vocation or calling" within the city limits. With the NAACP in mind, both ordinances were amended in 1957 to require organizations to submit upon request a list of their members, detailed financial records, and other information to the city clerk for public display. The NAACP submitted all requested information except for its membership lists. The Supreme Court ruled that the ordinances violated NAACP members' rights of free association and noted that there was no correlation between the asserted government interest in collecting occupational license taxes and the compelled disclosure and publication of the NAACP's membership lists.

Yet I think that on the ground of being too broad, this law is bad. The state can inquire broadly, but not demand specifics.

Result: In a 5–4 decision written by Potter Stewart, the Court struck down the membership disclosure law as a violation of the teachers' associational rights. While the state had an important interest in investigating the fitness and competence of its teachers, the unlimited and indiscriminate inquiry conducted here went beyond the state's legitimate needs and unnecessarily stifled the teachers' fundamental liberties.

In dissent, Felix Frankfurter acknowledged that the law was a "crude state intrusion" into teachers' lives and objectionable on policy grounds. But he argued that this did not mean that the law was unconstitutional. John Marshall Harlan noted that there had been no evidence of racial prejudice either on the face of the statute or in its application. Because the state's actions had substantial relevance to the state's legitimate purpose of investigating teacher fitness and competence, Harlan could see not see any legitimate constitutional grounds for striking down the law.

NAACP v. Alabama ex rel. Patterson, 357 U.S. 449 (1958)
(Douglas)

The NAACP, a nonprofit New York corporation, maintained a network of chartered, independent, and unincorporated affiliate associations in other states. When the organization opened a state office and a network of local associations in Alabama, it failed to comply with a state law requiring foreign corporations to file a copy of their corporate charter and designate an agent and place of business for service of process. In 1956, state attorney general John Patterson sought to enjoin all NAACP activities in Alabama and oust the organization from the state. Trial judge Walter Jones, an ardent segregationist, imposed a temporary restraining order (TRO) prohibiting the NAACP from either registering or conducting any activities within the state until the case could be heard on the merits. Judge Jones also ordered the NAACP to produce its corporate records and membership lists.[78] The NAACP agreed to produce all requested records except for its membership lists. Judge Jones held the organization in contempt and fined it $100,000.[79] The Alabama Supreme Court twice declined to hear

---

78. Southern states, including Arkansas, Florida, Louisiana, Mississippi, and Virginia, required the NAACP to disclose its membership lists in the hope that public pressure and intimidation would scare away all but the most brave and foolish members. Ironically, these states justified their actions by citing a 1928 Supreme Court case that allowed New York to compel the Ku Klux Klan to disclose its membership lists. *Bryant v. Zimmerman*, 278 U.S. 63 (1928). Southern states also sought to use laws originally designed to combat communist organizations to investigate and punish the NAACP. Another reason that the NAACP refused to disclose its membership lists in such cases was that several southern states, such as South Carolina, prohibited NAACP members from holding government jobs. Some states, notably Arkansas, Mississippi, and South Carolina, tried to determine who belonged to the NAACP by requiring employees (especially teachers and other professionals) to file annual affidavits with state officials declaring their membership in or contributions to any political, religious, economic, and social organizations.

79. Thurgood Marshall unsuccessfully urged the NAACP to comply fully with Judge Jones's order and voluntarily disclose its membership lists. Marshall rightly thought that Alabama would use any noncompliance as an excuse to shut down all NAACP activities in the state indefinitely. Tushnet, *Making Civil Rights Law*, 284–85.

the NAACP's appeals, and Judge Jones refused to schedule a trial on the merits, leaving the TRO in effect indefinitely.

Conference of January 17, 1958

WARREN: The state has cut into the constitutional rights of NAACP members and put an end to them. It is not necessary for the petitioners to use mandamus or lose their rights. The difference between mandamus and certiorari is not clearly defined.[80] I reverse.

BLACK: I reverse. The Alabama high court's decisions are a plain invitation to bring the cases up that way. The *Dixon* [*sic*] case is on one side, *Hart* is on the other.[81] Where it was raised by mandamus, I hope that we do not attribute to Alabama an aim to keep these people from having their cases decided. The state, however, should not be allowed to defeat the federal courts. The petitioners were not given a fair trial. The statute merely required a $10 fine, and the state has turned it into a different suit. They inflict penalties before giving a trial. The real vice of the matter is that it is a procedure which imposes penalties without giving them a chance to defend themselves on the merits.

FRANKFURTER: I would reverse. The state procedure is so doubtful that this is, in effect, retroactive. The state procedure is so uncertain that the NAACP's federal right is being lost. They are fined $100,000 contempt for what? The names of their officers could be required. There is such a disparity between state interests in disclosure and the rights of the individuals involved as to make this an unconstitutional assertion of state power. Can a corporation assert these rights? Yes.

DOUGLAS: I would reverse. This case involves First Amendment rights.

BURTON: I agree with Frankfurter.

CLARK: Reverse.

HARLAN: Reverse.

BRENNAN: Reverse.

WHITTAKER: Reverse.

Result: After the conference, two major internal conflicts prevented the Court from reaching its customary consensus on race cases. First, Hugo Black and William O. Douglas sharply disagreed with Felix Frankfurter on the proper grounds for reversal. Black and Douglas favored deciding the case on

---

80. When the NAACP first appealed to the state supreme court, the state high court rejected the appeal on the ground that the NAACP should have asked for a writ of certiorari. When the NAACP filed for a writ of certiorari the state supreme court again rejected the petition, this time claiming that the NAACP should have filed for a writ of mandamus. Earl Warren called such runaround tactics "the procedural dodge."

81. *Ex parte Dickens,* 50 So. 218 (Ala. 1910), and most other Alabama state precedents indicated that the proper remedy in this case was to seek a writ of certiorari, which was what the NAACP had done. *Ex parte Hart,* 200 So. 783 (Ala. 1941), suggested that a production order "may be reviewed on petition for mandamus." The Alabama Supreme Court relied on *Hart* and ignored most of its own precedents in refusing to grant the NAACP's petition for a writ of certiorari.

First Amendment grounds, while Frankfurter wanted to decide the case on due process grounds, without mentioning the Bill of Rights. Warren assigned the case to John Harlan, who struggled to placate both sides. In the end, Harlan came down closer to Frankfurter's position. Harlan's second problem was that Tom Clark initially broke ranks and threatened to dissent on the ground that the state's interests had not adequately been presented. Frankfurter and others lobbied Clark and finally convinced him to abandon his position.

In the end, the Court unanimously ruled that the NAACP could not be compelled to disclose its membership lists. Compulsory disclosure of membership lists, Harlan wrote, would violate the NAACP's fundamental liberty rights, including privacy and free association. The state had not demonstrated a sufficiently important interest to override these rights. Harlan distinguished Bryant v. Zimmerman, which required a New York chapter of the Ku Klux Klan to divulge its membership, on the ground that the Klan's activities involved unlawful intimidation and violence. The Court refused to set aside the TRO, however, stating that the state courts had not yet decided the case on the merits and that the issue was not properly before the Court.

On remand, the Alabama Supreme Court defied the U.S. Supreme Court, reaffirming the trial judge's contempt order and reinstating the $100,000 fine. The state court claimed that the U.S. Supreme Court had acted on a "mistaken premise" and that its ruling was clearly erroneous. The state court ruled that the U.S. Supreme Court was mistaken in saying that the NAACP had complied with Judge Jones's orders, except for its failure to disclose its membership.

The U.S. Supreme Court, in a per curiam decision by Harlan, again reversed and emphatically reaffirmed its original ruling.[82] Harlan noted that the state had never contested the NAACP's claim that, apart from the membership issue, the organization was in full compliance with Judge Jones's orders, and it was too late to argue the point now. The Justices, however, again refused to consider the legality of the TRO until the state had a reasonable opportunity to decide the case on the merits. Once again, the Justices assumed that Alabama would conduct a prompt trial on the merits of the case, and once again they were mistaken. In the meantime, without ever going to trial, Alabama had shut down NAACP operations in the state for more than five years. The case had to come back before the Court one more time.

John Patterson, an ardent segregationist, defeated George Wallace to become governor of Alabama in 1959 and later became a judge on the Alabama Court of Criminal Appeals until he retired in 1997.

NAACP v. Alabama ex rel. Flowers, 377 U.S. 288 (1964)
(Douglas)

Following the second remand in NAACP v. Alabama ex rel. Patterson (1959), Alabama's judicial system went into a four-corner stall. Judge Walter Jones refused to schedule a trial on the merits and the state appellate courts sat mute, effectively making Judge Jones's "temporary" restraining order permanent.

In 1960, the NAACP sued in federal court to force the issue. The following year, the U.S. Supreme Court ruled that if Alabama did not try the case by January 2, 1962, the local federal district court would assume jurisdiction and try the case itself. Judge Jones at last scheduled a hearing, and on De-

---

82. *NAACP v. Alabama ex rel. Patterson*, 360 U.S. 240 (1959).

*cember 29, 1961, just four days before the federal trial was scheduled to begin, he ruled against the
NAACP and issued a permanent injunction prohibiting the organization from ever doing business in
the state again.*[83] *The Alabama Supreme Court refused to hear the NAACP's appeal for almost a year
and then refused to review the case on the merits, instead affirming the trial court's decision on the
ground that the NAACP had not followed state procedures.*[84] *Richmond Flowers was the attorney
general of Alabama.*

Conference of March 27, 1964

WARREN: I would reach the merits and reverse. The state ground is not adequate. Alabama does not adhere to its own rule. On the merits, they have not allowed the petitioner to register. The only penalty under state law is a fine. To disallow them even to register is to discriminate against them. I would reverse on the merits.[85]

BLACK: The fact that the petitioner is a corporation raises a background problem similar to the *Berea College* case.[86] The claimed state ground has been in existence for a long time. This rule is a trap for the unwary. I won a case once on that rule. The state supreme court remembers and forgets the rule at the "right time." Those rules are O.K. in private litigation, but they can't be used to block this Court's right to protect a constitutional right. I reverse on the merits.

DOUGLAS: I reverse on the merits.

CLARK: I would reverse on the merits and formulate a decree so that Alabama could not interfere here any more.

---

83. One of Judge Jones's justifications for issuing the permanent injunction was his belief that the NAACP had conspired to prevent the University of Alabama football team from playing in the Liberty Bowl. *NAACP v. Alabama ex rel. Flowers*, at 303.

84. The state supreme court claimed that the NAACP's appellate brief did not sufficiently separate specific "assignments of error." While the NAACP brief enumerated twenty-three separate errors, it compressed these errors into five sections. The state court claimed that this was a violation of state procedural rules, because each section discussed more than one claimed error. If even one error in a section was found to be nonmeritorious, the court said, the entire section would be disregarded. The state court claimed that at least one claim of error in each section was nonmeritorious and so refused to consider the brief any further on the merits.

85. The chief justice of the Alabama Supreme Court, J. Ed Livingston, boasted that he stood far to the right of George Wallace when it came to segregation. He bragged that Wallace had merely stood in front of the schoolhouse door to block the integration of the University of Alabama, while where Livingston was from they burned the schools down. Letter from Elizabeth Black to Ethel and John M. Harlan, Aug. 22, 1968, cited in Yarbrough, *John Marshall Harlan*, 167.

86. *Berea College v. Kentucky*, 211 U.S. 45 (1908). Kentucky law required racial segregation at both public and private schools. The majority ducked the constitutional question of whether states could mandate the segregation of private institutions and ruled that the law was an internal matter between Kentucky and a domestic corporation. In effect, the state law was treated as amending the college's corporate charter and placing limits on corporate rights and privileges that might not be constitutional if they had been applied to individuals. Justices Harlan and Day dissented, criticizing the majority for hiding behind the law of corporations and for failing to consider the individual rights that were at stake. The dissenters argued that the statute was unconstitutional as applied and that Kentucky could not prohibit the "voluntary meeting" of the different races for innocent purposes.

HARLAN: I would reverse on the merits. Alabama plays ducks and drakes with us. The Alabama rule is a discretionary one. A state ground can't be used to defeat a federal right. I doubt whether we should try to do what Tom Clark says respecting a decree.

BRENNAN: I would reverse and would fashion a specific decree.

HARLAN: We could put into the opinion our permission for NAACP to apply for a writ of mandamus to us.

STEWART: I favor direct, firm action by us.

WHITE: We must reach the corporation question mentioned by Hugo. Can it keep corporations out forever? I would reverse. Even if the state ground is good, one of the points is sufficiency of the evidence, and that is here because Alabama passed on it.

GOLDBERG: I reverse.

Result: The Supreme Court, again speaking through John Marshall Harlan, reluctantly asserted its right to decide the case on the merits. The Court found that the NAACP had substantially complied with state procedural rules and that the state's failure to try the case on the merits was unwarranted. Even so, the Court once again remanded the case, this time ordering the state courts to enter a decree vacating the permanent injunction and allowing the NAACP to resume operations in Alabama. The state supreme court capitulated and dissolved the injunction. Eight years after the temporary injunction was first imposed, the NAACP was back in business in the state of Alabama.

Richmond Flowers, a segregationist during the 1950s, became a born-again moderate in Alabama's racial politics during the 1960s. As attorney general he aggressively prosecuted Ku Klux Klan members and publicly attacked George Wallace's segregationist views. His political life was cut short by two fatal mistakes: in reaching out to black voters he lost virtually all of his white political support, and he was convicted on federal bribery and extortion charges in 1968 and spent eighteen months in federal prison. He was later pardoned by President Jimmy Carter.

Harrison v. NAACP, 360 U.S. 167 (1959)
(Douglas)

In 1956, Virginia sought to limit NAACP involvement in school desegregation cases by enacting five new statutes expanding state prohibitions against barratry, champerty, and maintenance.[87] The new laws prohibited the solicitation of legal business, employment, or compensation by any business or organization that was not a party to or had no pecuniary interest in the case, and they prohibited persons or organizations from soliciting business for an attorney.[88] Virginia also placed strict new limits

---

87. *Barratry* is the practice of stirring up litigation. *Champerty* involves a third party assuming the risks and costs of litigation in return for a share of a prospective award. *Maintenance* is the support or promotion of another person's litigation.

88. Other southern states joined the attack on NAACP litigation. State legislatures in Georgia, Mississippi, and South Carolina expanded traditional ethical restrictions on fundraising to support litigation, soliciting legal business, and supporting clients—all done specifically to stop the NAACP. While most of this was pure harassment, the NAACP was not always blameless. Texas attorney general Ben Shepperd won

on "racial litigation" and required all organizations participating in such cases to register with the state and disclose their membership lists.

Before the state courts could interpret these statutes, the NAACP filed a federal lawsuit seeking a declaratory judgment that the state laws were unconstitutional. A three-judge district court declared three of the statutes unconstitutional and enjoined their enforcement. The district court retained jurisdiction over the remaining two statutes, pending state court construction and interpretation. The state of Virginia argued that the federal courts should have abstained from taking action until state courts had authoritatively interpreted all five laws.

The conference notes indicate that the Justices were torn between their commitment to comity with state governments and their determination to reach the final outcome they all desired. Albertis S. Harrison was attorney general of Virginia.

Conference of March 27, 1959

WARREN: I would affirm. These laws were intended to put the respondent out of business. Publishing their membership lists would put them out of business. It is not a question of motives, but of avowed legislative purpose. There is no reason to refer this back to the state courts. These laws deny equal protection, for they allow legal aid societies to represent the poor but not the respondent.

BLACK: I affirm and adhere to my original position. I want to hear other views.

FRANKFURTER: I agree with Hugo.

DOUGLAS: I affirm.

CLARK: I would send the case back to the state court. Maybe legal aid societies are included under the act. There is no chance of reprisals against the respondent in the interim.

HARLAN: I agree with Tom Clark and would send the case back to the state court. I find the same ambiguity in chapter 35 as in the others that went to state court. The main vice in chapters 31 and 32 is the disclosure of the NAACP's membership lists. If the statute is limited by construction to barratry and cases of officers, it would be O.K. It is difficult to distinguish the *Windsor* case from this one.[89] The easy thing to do is to affirm. I might go along with affirmance.

---

a permanent injunction against the NAACP in 1957, largely because local counsel for the NAACP paid Heman Sweatt $3,500 per month during his litigation—a serious violation of ethical norms. Tushnet, *Making Civil Rights Law*, 272–73.

89. *Government Civic Employees Organizing Committee v. Windsor*, 353 U.S. 364 (1957). Under Alabama law, any public employee who joined a labor union forfeited the "rights, benefits, or privileges" of public employment. Public employees sued, claiming that the law violated their constitutional rights of free expression, free association, due process, privileges and immunities, and equal protection. A three-judge district court deferred its decision to allow Alabama to interpret the statute. The state courts ruled that the law applied to the plaintiffs but did not clarify any of the constitutional issues. The three-judge court then dismissed the employees' case with prejudice, saying that it was unlikely that Alabama would ever interpret the statute in such a way as to make it unconstitutional. The U.S. Supreme Court reversed. Because the state courts had failed to address the constitutional issues, the Justices ordered the district court to retain jurisdiction until all efforts to obtain a full state adjudication of the plaintiffs' constitutional claims were exhausted.

BRENNAN: We should give this case the same treatment as any other. The Civil Rights Act encouraged the district court exercising authority to enjoin a state statute. They have a duty to do so. Hutcheson is quite wrong in his dissent as to equitable considerations.[90] Chapter 35 has discrimination right on its face, especially in light of the evidence in case, with reference to legal aid societies. I affirm.

WHITTAKER: These chapters are all unconstitutional. If this was not a segregation case, we would remand it to the state court under *Windsor*. We should have a unanimous court. I would affirm, but I would prefer to send it back to the state court.

STEWART: I agree with Harlan and vote to send it back to the state court. But I would require an affirmance.

FRANKFURTER: I can't distinguish this because the case comes under the Civil Rights Act. I can't answer Harlan.

BLACK: I still think that I will affirm. If the Court will not affirm unanimously, it would be bad. I am inclined to go with the majority if it decides to remand the case to the state court. We all seem to agree that there should be an injunction to protect the respondent while litigating in state court.

Result: The majority ruled that the district court should have abstained from ruling on any of the five laws on the merits to give the Virginia courts a reasonable time to construe them. John Marshall Harlan went out of his way in the majority opinion to warn Virginia against taking any further action against the NAACP until these issues were resolved. Black and Frankfurter, apparently concerned by the prospects of a divided Court to affirm, switched sides after the conference to give Harlan his majority.

In dissent, Douglas, Warren, and Brennan attacked the majority's use of the abstention doctrine as an ill-advised delaying tactic, a tactic they thought unjustified in the wake of Virginia's defiant stand against the constitutional rights of its black citizens. Ironically, Brennan had earlier provided the fourth vote to hear the case on the merits. Had he voted to affirm summarily, the judgment of the three-judge court below would have been affirmed without raising the abstention issue.

Albertis Harrison was governor of Virginia from 1962 to 1966. He led the state's last stand against integration and later served on the state supreme court from 1966 to 1981. In 1999, Brunswick County dedicated the new Albertis S. Harrison Courthouse.

NAACP v. Button, 371 U.S. 415 (1963)
(Brennan) (Douglas)

When the NAACP's case returned to the Virginia courts, the state trial court struck down three of the laws but upheld the antibarratry statute and the law prohibiting advocating lawsuits against the state. On appeal, the state supreme court struck down the anti-advocacy law, leaving the antibarratry statute as the only one of the five original laws still in effect.

At conference, a majority of Justices thought that this case would decide the fate of the NAACP in Virginia. John Marshall Harlan saw things differently. He predicted that the case would seal the fate

---

90. Chief Judge Hutcheson dissented in the decision below, arguing for complete abstention. *NAACP v. Patty*, 159 F. Supp. 503 (E.D. Va. 1958).

of Brown v. Board of Education *in the state, and his perspective led him to a very different conclusion. Frankfurter's comments echo the remarks of one of Frankfurter's heroes, Justice Joseph Bradley, who wrote in the* Civil Rights Cases *that blacks should no longer expect to be treated as "special favorites of the law."*[91]

Robert Y. Button, another leading segregationist and a loyal member of Harry F. Byrd's Democratic political machice, was attorney general of Virginia. He later defended the state's antimiscegenation laws in Loving v. Virginia.[92]

Conference of November 10, 1961

WARREN: I reverse. The statute is discriminatory and irrational because it says that in order to do these things, one has to have a "pecuniary" interest in the case. This turns history around, since barratry statutes originally were aimed at the commercialization of litigation. The purpose of the statute is obviously to circumvent *Brown.*

BLACK: I reverse. This law was one of a group of laws designed as a package to thwart our segregation decision in *Brown.* This is part of a scheme to defeat the Court's order, and I would go on that ground. Sooner or later, we will have to grapple with these problems in those terms. The NAACP is finished if this law stands. I will try to go along if the Court reverses it on a narrow ground. The state cannot handicap and hobble those who are trying to enforce constitutional rights by contributing their time or money as this was done. This associated support is necessary if these Negro rights are to be enforced.

FRANKFURTER: I affirm. I can't imagine a worse disservice than to continue being the guardians of the Negroes.[93] I got no light from Carter on the argument that this law is discriminatory.[94] If the John Birch Society does this, is the law still unconstitutional? Here, there is control of the litigation in the NAACP, and that is the end at which the statute is aimed. This act does not deal with more than fomenting litigation. There is nothing in the record to show that this statute is aimed at Negroes as such!!!!!![95] Compare this to the *American Sugar Refining* case, where the act was aimed only at one possible person or group.[96] Colored people are now people of substance. Colored people now have re-

---

91. *Civil Rights Cases,* 109 U.S. 3 (1883).

92. *Loving v. Virginia,* 388 U.S. 1 (1967).

93. Frankfurter later claimed that he had also criticized the executive branch in his conference remarks. In Frankfurter's estimation, the White House under President Kennedy had become a "mere adjunct of the NAACP." Frankfurter to Alexander Bickel, note on *Bailey v. Patterson,* Dec. 18, 1961, quoted in Tushnet, *Making Civil Rights Law,* 277.

94. Robert L. Carter argued the case for the NAACP.

95. The exclamation marks are Brennan's.

96. *McFarland v. American Sugar Refining Co.,* 241 U.S. 79 (1916). Another of Frankfurter's countless references to Oliver Wendell Holmes. Led by Holmes, the Court struck down a Louisiana law aimed specifically at the American Sugar Refining Company, which was the only sugar refining company in the state. The statute made it a presumptive violation of the state's antitrust laws if "any sugar refinery in Louisiana" systematically paid less for sugar in Louisiana than what the company paid in any other state. The law, Holmes said, violated the company's equal protection and due process rights by irrationally equating price differentials with antitrust violations. Holmes also implied that the state legislature had improperly singled out the company for punishment, saying that it was impermissible for a legislature to declare that a person was guilty or presumptively guilty of a crime.

sponsible positions. The NAACP assumes state functions since Virginia, it says, is not protecting their interests.

DOUGLAS: I reverse. I agree with the Chief Justice.

CLARK: I would affirm. This practice would have been in violation of Virginia law prior to the 1956 act. There are several Virginia decisions to that effect cited in the briefs. Or look at the *Automobile Club* cases.[97] To strike this law down, we would have to discriminate in favor of Negroes.

HARLAN: I affirm. Virginia applies in its statute the proper standards for law practice. This law was aimed at the NAACP and the school problem, but a state has that right.

BRENNAN: I would reverse. I agree with the Chief Justice and with Hugo.

WHITTAKER: The NAACP can pay legal fees for indigents. That is not this case. This law, if applied to the white supremacy group, would be constitutional. We should be color blind on this law. I affirm.

STEWART: A three-judge court has never construed this act. This act, as construed, requires affirmance. The act governs only fomenting litigation and channeling it to its own lawyers.

Result: After the conference vote, Frankfurter cobbled together a 5–4 majority to uphold Virginia's antibarratry statute. He wrote a lengthy majority opinion, but before the decision could be announced, Charles Whittaker retired. With the Court now deadlocked 4–4, the Justices scheduled the case for reargument the following term. Then Frankfurter suffered a massive stroke and was forced to resign. President Kennedy appointed Byron White to replace Whittaker and Arthur Goldberg to replace Frankfurter. When the Justices met in October to discuss the case a second time, the Court had a markedly different outlook.

Conference of October 12, 1962

WARREN: I reverse. The NAACP has a right to be in business. These people have a right to organize to protect their constitutional rights. If this suit goes against the NAACP, it is out of business. Virginia not only broadens their laws of barratry, but they deny equal protection of the law in the requirement for proof of no pecuniary interest. This was not originally barratry—there is no commercial reason here for the NAACP. The act discriminates against those who organize to protect civil rights in favor of those who have a "pe-

---

97. *In re Maclub of America, Inc*, 3 N.E. 2d 272 (Mass. 1936); *People ex rel. Chicago Bar Association v. Chicago Motor Club*, 199 N.E. 1 (Ill. 1935). The Massachusetts Supreme Court held that the Maclub automobile club had illegally engaged in the practice of law because it reimbursed members' legal fees for matters related to automobile ownership and operation. In the Illinois case, the Chicago Motor Club hired staff lawyers to offer club members legal advice. The Chicago Bar Association initially endorsed the practice but later withdrew its support and sued. The club claimed that it should be exempt from the law because it was a voluntary, nonprofit, public interest organization. The state high court ruled that the club was illegally engaged in the practice of law.

cuniary" interest. There is nothing that the NAACP has done that is immoral. If this does not violate equal protection, it falls for vagueness and indefiniteness. I will go on *Yick Wo,* or I am willing to do so.[98]

BLACK: I reverse. For many reasons, this violates equal protection as it operates. It would come within *Yick Wo* before they apply it. This isn't barratry as it has been understood, or if it is, it is clear on the face of it that it is nothing but a legal contraption aimed at putting the NAACP out of business. It is aimed at that group, and it must fall.

DOUGLAS: I would reverse, either on equal protection ground or on the ground that this law is aimed at driving this group out of business.

CLARK: I thought that the record showed the solicitation of a law suit. That would violate Texas law. But there was an admission that there was an NAACP list of approved lawyers. If that is all there is, then it takes the sting out of the law. The test, counsel said, was whether the NAACP controlled the litigation. I would affirm, but I would point up these admissions and indicate that these actions were valid activities. I don't think that the amendment of the "capper" or "runner" act is constitutional. But the admissions by counsel this time disturbed me. I thought that they solicited law suits and powers of attorney.

HARLAN: This act is plainly constitutional. Virginia's decision does not reverse the law of champerty. Solicitation was impermissible for a lawyer or for a group acting as this group acted. Financing this sort of activity violates traditional standards. Controlling litigation is the crux of the situation, as determined by the Virginia courts. Virginia has left open things that can be done, and the NAACP can preach about the importance of suing in courts. They can act as a legal aid society. There is no reason why the NAACP is immune from regular rules of champerty. The Anti-Saloon League would be subject to this law; the NAACP should be, too, and can be. *Brown v. Board of Education* will never work out if it is left in the federal domain.[99] The states must do it. We have no reason to reverse Virginia on this law.

BRENNAN: The statute is so vague on soliciting as to violate due process. The NAACP may assemble, it may provide a lawyer, it may recommend the suits, it may finance them. The NAACP may not control them. Virginia concedes that much. These concessions can't be found in the opinion of the Supreme Court of Virginia. Equal protection is in the act on its face. The law can't be applicable to insurance companies, etc. It would be applicable only to agencies enforcing civil rights.

STEWART: I am not sure, but I am inclined to reverse on the narrow ground that constitutional rights are not treated like "pecuniary" rights under state law.

---

98. *Yick Wo v. Hopkins,* 118 U.S. 356 (1886).
99. *Brown v. Board of Education,* 347 U.S. 483 (1954).

WHITE: Can Virginia constitutionally prevent the NAACP from recommending lawyers? We need not decide that issue, because Virginia says that is not what is involved. I do not know where I stand. "Control" of litigation is apparently crucial. The Virginia act does not mention control. The Virginia Supreme Court discusses control, but apparently only in relation to ethics. The NAACP can't rely on Virginia's admissions before our Court. Virginia can constitutionally prevent the NAACP from controlling litigation, but not from urging litigation to be brought. Everyone recommends lawyers. I would hold the act vague. I don't think that Virginia can constitutionally prevent representation by members of the NAACP's legal staff when the case has been solicited by the NAACP. Virginia can't prevent the recommendation of a lawyer.

GOLDBERG: Virginia made many admissions. The NAACP can urge litigation, and recommend the lawyer, and pay the lawyer. There is no evidence here of control of litigation once it has started. I would reverse on the posture presented here. I think, moreover, that equal protection was violated. It is not a valid classification to distinguish constitutional rights from other rights, in this case, "pecuniary" rights. There is a substantial equal protection point here and I could reverse on that.

Conference of October 16, 1962

STEWART: I am now doubtful of the position that I originally took in this case.

Result: The loss of Frankfurter and Whittaker shifted the Court from what would have been a 5–4 vote to uphold Virginia's antibarratry statute to a 5–1–3 decision to reverse.[100] *William Brennan, writing for the Court, ruled that the NAACP's litigation tactics were a form of political expression protected under the First and Fourteenth Amendments. Traditional state interests in preventing barratry, champerty, and maintenance were not sufficient to justify the state's efforts to prohibit the NAACP from pursuing its legal strategy to desegregate state schools. Brennan found a crucial difference between litigating to vindicate constitutional rights and the oppressive, malicious, or avaricious use of the legal process for private gain. The decision potentially gave broad constitutional protection to public interest law organizations. Byron White concurred in part and dissented in part, but voted to reverse with the majority.*

John Marshall Harlan argued in dissent that there was no racial discrimination in this case. The NAACP was merely one of hundreds of organizations expected to comply with state laws prohibiting lawsuit solicitation and the unauthorized practice of law. For Harlan, this was a case of speech combined with action, and states had more leeway to deal with "speech plus" than with cases involving pure speech.

---

100. Frankfurter was dismayed that he and Whittaker were replaced by "wholly inexperienced men as Goldberg and White, without familiarity with . . . the jurisprudence of the Court either as practitioners, or scholars, or judges." Frankfurter to Alexander Bickel, Mar. 18, 1963, quoted in Tushnet, *Making Civil Rights Law,* 279.

Louisiana ex rel. Gremillion v. NAACP, 366 U.S. 293 (1961)
(Douglas)

Louisiana sought to prevent the NAACP from doing business in the state, alleging that the organiza-
tion had violated two state statutes: one requiring the NAACP to register the names of its officers and
members, and the other requiring an annual affidavit that none of its officers were affiliated with
communist or other subversive organizations. The federal district court temporarily enjoined the state
from enforcing these two laws against the NAACP. Jack Gremillion was the state attorney general.[101]

Conference of April 28, 1961

WARREN: The second act is almost conceded to be bad. Officers can't know what other officers are associated with what. The second act is governed by *Shelton.*[102] I affirm.

BLACK: I affirm.

FRANKFURTER: I affirm. If this act is applied not against the NAACP alone but to hundreds of other organizations, that could be shown on the permanent injunction. This applies to all organizations.

DOUGLAS: I affirm.

CLARK: I affirm. On a final hearing they could introduce any evidence.

HARLAN: There is no reason why *Alabama v. NAACP* is not applicable.[103] The state has shown no justification. The act *as applied* is bad. It is one thing to apply it to the NAACP, and another to apply it to a garden club or the Communist party.

BRENNAN: I agree with Harlan, and I agree with the early per curiam decision by Potter Stewart.[104] I affirm.

WHITTAKER: I affirm, but I think that the injunction is too broad. The state could require the NAACP to give the names of its officers to state officials.

HARLAN: The state has shown no need to get anything from the NAACP.

STEWART: I affirm. I think that officers should be excluded.

HARLAN: I think that officers should be excluded.

FRANKFURTER: The decree only goes to the duty of officers filing a membership list.

Result: The Court unanimously upheld the district court's injunction.

---

101. Gremillion was a colorful and controversial figure in Louisiana law and politics. As attorney general his political instincts were unmatched, but his legal skills were suspect. Governor Earl Long once said that the best way to hide something from Jack Gremillion was to put it in a lawbook. In 1971, Gremillion was convicted of lying to a federal grand jury about using his office to help a loan company, and he spent fifteen months in prison.

102. *Shelton v. Tucker,* 364 U.S. 479 (1960).

103. *NAACP v. Alabama,* 357 U.S. 449 (1958).

104. Brennan was probably referring to the per curiam opinion Stewart wrote in *NAACP v. Patterson,* 360 U.S. 240 (1959).

TIME, PLACE, AND MANNER RESTRICTIONS

Edwards v. South Carolina, 372 U.S. 229 (1963)
(Douglas)

Two hundred black students protested racial discrimination in South Carolina by assembling in a public area outside the State House in Columbia. Although the demonstrators were quiet and orderly, police ordered them to disperse. The protestors ignored the police and continued to make speeches and sing patriotic and religious songs. Police acknowledged that there was never any threat of violence or disorder, but they arrested Edwards and several others for breach of the peace. They were all convicted, and the state supreme court affirmed.

Conference of December 14, 1962

WARREN: I would reverse. There was no breach of the peace. There was no mass demonstration. There was no blockage of traffic.

BLACK: I am also inclined to that view, although it must be based on "no evidence." The state might have made a charge, but there was no evidence to support the thing charged here.

DOUGLAS: I reverse. These people were exercising their constitutional rights to speech and assembly.

CLARK: I would affirm. There was ample evidence of breach of the peace. This was a patently dangerous situation.

HARLAN: I affirm. The *Cantwell* point is not valid.[105] The *Thompson* case should be carefully confined.[106] This is not a "no evidence" case. The police need not disperse the whites rather than the blacks. This is not a racial discrimination case.

BRENNAN: I reverse.

STEWART: I fear to reopen the *Thompson* case, but it can rest on *Garner.*[107] There is an exercise of First Amendment rights here, and there is police interference with that right.

---

105. *Cantwell v. Connecticut,* 310 U.S. 296 (1940). Cantwell distributed religious literature and solicited funds for religious purposes in a public area. He briefly played an anti-Catholic record that offended some listeners and was arrested and convicted of breaching the peace. The Supreme Court reversed on First Amendment grounds.

106. *Thompson v. Louisville,* 362 U.S. 199 (1960). Although no one in the Louisville café objected to "Shuffling Sam" Thompson's habit of quietly dancing by himself to jukebox music, two police officers arrested him and charged him with loitering and disorderly conduct. Thompson, who had been arrested fifty-three times on similar charges, claimed that the arrest was part of a police scheme to harass him. The Supreme Court threw out his conviction on the ground that the charges were completely devoid of evidence. This case provided a tempting precedent for the Court in race cases, because it allowed the Justices to reverse summarily on evidentiary grounds without having to address the underlying racial issues.

107. *Garner v. Louisiana,* 368 U.S. 157 (1961). Garner and five others were involved in a peaceful lunchcounter protest, where a group of black students quietly sat in seats ordinarily reserved for whites. The Court threw out their breach of the peace convictions for lack of evidence. Their convictions, Warren wrote

WHITE: I vote to reverse, at least tentatively. The evidence does not fit the charge of violence.

GOLDBERG: I reverse, and could go on either a narrow or broad ground. The latter is a petition for redress of grievances. This constitutional right is not restricted to conditions of tranquillity.

Result: The Court reversed Edwards's conviction in an 8–1 decision. John Marshall Harlan switched sides after conference, leaving Tom Clark alone in dissent.

Cox v. Louisiana, 379 U.S. 536 and 379 U.S. 559 (1965)
(Douglas) (Brennan)

Elton Cox led a group of two thousand black students to protest the earlier arrest of other students who had picketed against segregation in Baton Rouge, Louisiana.[108] *Sheriff Kling asked Cox to disband the group, but he refused and led the protestors in an orderly manner to the courthouse where the students arrested the previous day were jailed. Police Chief Wingate White told Cox to keep his group across the street from the courthouse, and Cox complied. Standing opposite the jail on the other side of St. Louis Street, the demonstrators waved signs, sang songs, and listened to speakers. Some of the jailed students heard the commotion and responded vocally from their cells. Cox then said, "It's lunch time. Let's go eat." Knowing that Cox planned to lead the group into town to picket segregated lunch counters, Sheriff Kling again ordered the crowd to disperse. Cox told the crowd to stay where they were, and police then used tear gas to break up the demonstration. Cox was arrested the next day and charged with disturbing the peace, obstructing public passages, and picketing a courthouse. He was convicted on all three counts, and the Louisiana Supreme Court affirmed.*

Cox's case came to the Supreme Court as two separate cases: #24 included the first two charges, disturbing the peace and obstructing public passages, while #49 involved the third count of picketing a courthouse.

Conference of October 23, 1964

WARREN: My views are tentative, as I have not read the record. The parade was in no sense illegal, and the police having undertaken to direct it meant that the mere congregation of the crowd opposite the courthouse was no offense. The conduct on the way there—the singing and walking and speechmaking—were not offenses. The police acquiesced up to making a speech. If there were offenses, they were controlled from that time on. This was confirmed by the chief, when he said "all right" up to there. So any crime has to develop out of what followed. A crowd of two thousand people that is there with police approval—

for the majority, were so totally devoid of evidentiary support that they violated the due process clause of the Fourteenth Amendment. Stewart thought that this case was more easily defensible than the Court's decision in *Thompson.* Louisiana defined disturbing the peace as the commission of any act in such a manner as to unreasonably disturb or alarm the public. Not only was this law significantly more vague and uncertain than the ordinance involved in *Thompson,* it was also clear that the students had done nothing to unreasonably disturb or alarm the public, no matter how broadly that phrase was defined.

108. Reverend Cox was the field secretary for the Congress of Racial Equality (CORE).

they have a responsibility to proceed in an orderly manner. When the police told them to end it all and go, and Cox resisted and said "don't move," it is pretty close to *Feinberg* [*sic*].[109] In the context of the situation, with Cox's order to go to the restaurants, the chance of riot was really imminent. The tear gas was bad, but perhaps was justified. On the breach of the peace charge, I am inclined to affirm, but what happened afterwards added nothing to what went on before in obstruction. In #49, I am inclined to reverse. Congregating there was not an attempt to obstruct justice. Any wrong took place when Cox refused to obey the dispersal order. I am not so sure about the sidewalk issue, as they had permission to be on them. I reverse that in #24; I might go either way on the sidewalk issue.

BLACK: I have trouble with the charges of obstructing the sidewalk and with breach of the peace. There was ample evidence to convict them under both laws if the laws are valid, but I doubt their validity as written or as applied. You can't treat the sidewalk issues in isolation from the breach of peace statute—there is no statute against "obstructing" sidewalks as such. The statute seems to leave it up to the policeman alone.

Regulations of conduct tied up with freedom of speech are usually O.K., but here the law excepts labor unions. That picks out certain kind of speech and permits it, but does not permit speech on segregation or something we don't like. It eliminates discrimination of certain kinds of information, e.g., labor disputes. Consider that in connection with the fact that there is no prohibition against parading. They do not even require a license. Whether you call it lack of notice or vagueness, there is too much uncertainty about the act to sustain a conviction. The state can protect the use of its streets. But there is nothing to say that they didn't have a right to be there. If labor can be there why can't these people?

On breach of the peace, the construction of this act runs into *Terminiello*[110] and *Edwards*.[111] If you merely stir people up, it is an offense and they can arrest you. That

---

109. *Feiner v. New York*, 340 U.S. 315 (1951). Irving Feiner gave a provocative speech on a street corner in Syracuse. He spoke for thirty minutes about race and politics, criticizing President Truman and other white political leaders and urging blacks to arm themselves and fight for their rights. During Feiner's speech the crowd became agitated, and there was at least one threat of violence. Police asked Feiner to stop speaking three times, and when he refused they arrested him for breach of the peace. The Supreme Court upheld Feiner's conviction on the grounds that he had not been prosecuted for the content of his speech, but for the potentially violent actions which the speech provoked; and that while police cannot suppress unpopular views, when a speaker goes beyond attempts to persuade and seeks to incite a riot, police may take action to prevent a breach of the peace.

110. *Terminiello v. Chicago*, 337 U.S. 1 (1949). Arthur Terminiello gave a controversial speech on race and politics inside a Chicago auditorium. The speech attracted a large number of protesters, and after breaking up several violent confrontations police arrested Terminiello for breach of the peace. The Court reversed on a 5–4 vote. William O. Douglas, writing for the majority, ruled that while Terminiello's speech was provocative and "invited public dispute," it was still protected speech. Public inconvenience, annoyance, or unrest were not sufficient reasons to carve out a new exception to First Amendment protections. The state law was unconstitutional as applied, rather than on its face, because the state courts had correctly ruled that the only speech that could be punished under the statute was "fighting words." The Court quashed Terminiello's conviction because the trial judge's instructions to the jury failed to limit the scope of the statute to fighting words and because the jury returned a general verdict it was impossible to say whether Terminiello had been properly convicted.

111. *Edwards v. South Carolina*, 372 U.S. 229 (1963).

makes this act bad. Moreover, a policeman, without standards, is allowed to tell people to move on—that is surrender and the means of a police state. Licensing acts without standards are bad. This is in the same category. This act is a perfect trap for a person who wants to say something in the street, but who insults a policeman. The trigger can be pulled automatically when he says something that the police don't want him to say. The mere fact that the crowd was dangerous does not give the police a right to arrest this petitioner. The rule that the statute must be narrow and precise applies here. I would reverse both convictions in #24.

In #49—maybe they intended to obstruct justice. But with the phrase of "influencing the administration of justice," the courthouse statute covers this case like a blanket. The only ambiguity is in the phrase "on or near"—it may be too imprecise. The counterpart of this statute is a federal statute, and the Court approved it prior to its passage. It is a good law. We are settling by law what used to be settled by combat. Congregating outside a courthouse can generate fear, and destroy a court. If this Louisiana mob can scare that court, a John Birch crowd can surround this courthouse. There is a limit to where they can go. Here, they passed the limit. I affirm in #49. As a result of what they did, they influenced the court, for the prosecutions were dropped and the cases dismissed.

DOUGLAS: Baton Rouge has no licensing system. This is not a case where they went without permission. Therefore, this was a lawful assembly and it must be for something they did after they got there. I would reverse all three cases for reasons like those in my dissent in *Feinberg* [*sic*]. The word "sit-in" triggered all of these convictions.

CLARK: I agree with Hugo in #49 and I would affirm. In #24, I follow Black in reversing on the construction of the statute in this breach of peace case. As to the obstruction charge, I have difficulty. Here, the police gave them authority to be on the sidewalk. The hollering from the jail would not aid or affect it in any way. We should not convict them after the police had said it was O.K. for them to be there. As to police approval to be at the particular place in #49, I think that the subsequent disturbances constituted a violation of the Courthouse Act.

HARLAN: In #49, a common demonstration is that what went on before Cox told the crowd, "Don't move." I would sustain any conviction. I disagree with the state's argument that the police could not waive the statute. I think that the police had the authority to waive the statute. If all they did was to go down to the courthouse, this conviction could not stand. But from the time that the police felt that the demonstration was getting out of hand and told them to go, there was a violation of the law when they refused to leave when told to do so. I would affirm.

In #24, the other two convictions should stand or fall on how the acts were applied. We can't invalidate them just because they except labor unions. On vagueness in the breach of peace statutes, there is much in what Hugo says. But the police gave an order that the crowd disobeyed, and that is the common law definition of breach of peace. I would affirm the breach of the peace conviction. When the cops told them to move, it became a common law breach of the peace, and the statute should be read that way— plus the warning. The police need not depend on Cox to keep his Negroes into custody. It was the Negroes, not the whites, that caused the trouble. As to the sidewalk conviction, I affirm.

BRENNAN: I have no trouble with #24—I agree with Hugo. His emphasis is on the fact that the acts are not narrowly drawn and are violated or not violated at the whim of the police. I also reverse in #49. They declared their reasons for their assembly to the police and were allowed to do so.

GOLDBERG: They did not get police assent, but after the assembly the police tried to placate a bad situation.

BRENNAN: I pass on my vote in #49. For me to vote to reverse depends on whether there was police approval. If the police acquiesced, I would reverse. I am not sure about *Feiner*—I am with Bill Douglas. In #49, I have trouble saying that "near" is not vague. I pass on #49.

STEWART: I am not at rest in anything. I think that the breach of the peace issue is pretty much covered by *Edwards v. South Carolina*. I reverse on disturbing the peace. On the sidewalk ordinance, I have trouble with the concept of estoppel against the police. We can't entrap the police—they must have large discretion. I think that after they were told to move on and they refused, that is enough to show a violation. The statute is specific, and I am inclined to affirm that conviction. In #49, the courthouse law is perfectly good. But I have trouble seeing any intent to obstruct justice—it was to protest their arrest. Also, they weren't being noisy. I can't make that law applicable to this conduct. Refers to *Bridges*,[112] *Terminiello, Wood v. Georgia*, and others.[113] This ordinance should, by those cases, be narrowly drawn to survive. I would reverse.

WHITE: I would reverse in #24. I agree with Potter. In #49, I agree with Hugo. I would affirm in the sidewalk phase of #24.

GOLDBERG: I would reverse #24 and affirm #49. The meeting was to protest the arrest of the pickets. The police did not approve; they acquiesced after trying to stop the movement. The meeting was broken up when Cox announced the proposal to invade white restaurants. Police then ordered the meeting ended, but Cox stood mute. As to the side-

---

112. *Bridges v. California*, 314 U.S. 252 (1941). During legal proceedings involving a labor dispute, the *Los Angeles Times* published a series of editorials criticizing the trial judge for being too lenient on union "gorillas." On the other side of the dispute, labor leader Harry Bridges published a telegram that he sent to the secretary of labor criticizing the judge as antiunion and warning that the judge's decree, if enforced, would result in a strike. The trial judge was not amused, and Bridges and the publisher and editor of the *Times* were all held in contempt of court. The state claimed that it had the right to punish people if what they published had a tendency to interfere with the fair and orderly administration of justice or caused disrespect for judges or the judicial system. The trial court ruled that the public interest in the defendants' First Amendment rights had to yield to the greater public interest in judicial impartiality and decorum.

The Supreme Court reversed all three convictions on the grounds that they violated the defendants' free speech, free press, and petition rights. Hugo Black, writing for the majority, said that the clear and present danger test meant that in order to justify an infringement of First Amendment rights, the substantive evil that government had the right to prevent had to be both extremely serious and imminent. It was doubtful whether these convictions met either prong of that test. California could not punish a mere "tendency" to interfere with the administration of justice or cause disrespect for judges or the legal process.

113. *Terminiello v. Chicago*, 337 U.S. 1 (1949); *Wood v. Georgia*, 370 U.S. 375 (1962).

walk ordinance, I would apply *Schneider* and the absence of standards for police.[114] In #49, there is a narrowly drawn act.

WARREN: I am now willing to reverse on both statutes in #24.

Result: After the conference, Stewart changed his mind on the obstruction charge and joined the majority to reverse Cox's conviction. Perhaps more significantly, Arthur Goldberg changed his vote on the more contentious courthouse charge to turn the original 5–3–1 vote to uphold Cox's conviction to a 5–4 majority to reverse. Goldberg wrote the majority opinion for both cases. He found that Chief White had given the protesters permission to demonstrate across the street from the courthouse and ruled that to affirm their convictions would violate due process by sanctioning "an indefensible sort of entrapment by the state—convicting a citizen for exercising a privilege which the State had clearly told him was available to him." The protesters had the right to ignore Sheriff Kling's subsequent order to disperse because there was no valid reason for the order. The group had not disturbed the peace, and Cox "had a right to stay where he was for the few additional minutes required to conclude the meeting." Black and Clark joined the majority in #24 but dissented in #49, arguing that Cox had "brazenly" defied the law by picketing at the courthouse and that state officials had no authority to give the protesters permission to break the law. Clark wrote:

> *I never knew until today that a law enforcement official—city, state, or national—could forgive a breach of the criminal laws. I missed that in my law school, in my practice, and for the two years while I was head of the Criminal Division of the Department of Justice.*

White and Harlan concurred in reversing the breach of peace conviction but voted to affirm Cox's convictions for obstructing public passageways and picketing the courthouse.

Walker v. City of Birmingham, 388 U.S. 307 (1967)
(Douglas) (Brennan)

In 1963, Martin Luther King Jr., Ralph Abernathy, Wyatt Tee Walker, and other civil rights leaders organized a grass-roots effort to desegregate Birmingham, Alabama, through a series of public marches and demonstrations. The city required a permit from the city commission for any parade or demonstration. Commissioners had broad discretion to deny applications in the name of public welfare, peace, safety, health, decency, good order, morals, or convenience. The group tried to obtain a permit from

---

114. *Schneider v. State*, 308 U.S. 147 (1939). Four local ordinances prohibited the distribution of handbills and other unsolicited literature on public streets and sidewalks. In reversing Schneider's conviction, the Court ruled that while government had a duty to keep streets open and available for public use, state regulations could not abridge the constitutional liberties of persons who sought to use public thoroughfares to impart information through speech or the distribution of literature. Within limits, cities could impose reasonable regulations against: (1) obstructing traffic; (2) interfering with the passage of pedestrians to compel acceptance of literature or other solicitations; or (3) littering or other similar conduct. A city's reasonable desire for clean and neat streets, however, was not sufficient to justify laws that prohibited persons from reasonably using public thoroughfares to hand out literature to those willing to accept it. There were other, less restrictive ways to prevent littering the Court pointed out, such as punishing those who actually threw rubbish onto the streets.

police commissioner Eugene "Bull" Connor, who summarily refused their application. They marched to City Hall anyway and were arrested for parading without a permit. The city obtained an ex parte temporary injunction from a state court prohibiting the group from planning or executing any public protests without a permit. The group ignored the injunction and marched to City Hall twice more, on Good Friday and on Easter Sunday. Several marchers were arrested, including Walker. This time the state trial court held the group in contempt for defying the court's injunction and sentenced each defendant to five days and fifty dollars. The Alabama Supreme Court affirmed.

WARREN: This is a close case. The underlying ordinance is void on its face and as applied, because it gives unfettered discretion to regulate First Amendment rights without standards. There was an application here to one commissioner, and they changed the deal on the petition by saying that the application had to be made to all of the commissioners. The conduct here was conduct on the sidewalk. We should at least remand for a determination of whether the ordinance applies to walking on the sidewalk. The injunction was simply a copy of ordinance, and I don't think that they can bootstrap it by putting it in the form of an injunction. I would prefer to reverse outright.

BLACK: I affirm.

DOUGLAS: I reverse. This is not a narrowly drawn ordinance—it is in the *Cantwell* tradition.[115]

CLARK: I affirm. The *United Mine Workers* case governs this.[116] They never tried to comply with the ordinance. It takes more than one commissioner to turn down an application. This was an outright violation of an injunction. They took the law into their own hands. If they didn't like the ordinance, they should get it repealed.

HARLAN: I reverse. I do not agree with the Chief Justice, but they should have had an opportunity to prove that there was a discriminatory application of the ordinance. If they could prove it, there would be a reversal of the contempt conviction. The allegations are clear, and proof may be difficult. I would vacate for a rehearing.

BRENNAN: I would reverse for a broader hearing, including Harlan's idea. An injunction of this kind under Alabama law does not preclude an attack on the underlying ordinance or its discriminatory application. *NAACP v. Alabama* covers this.[117] Alabama can't make up a new law merely to fit this case.

STEWART: The state need not follow *Mine Workers*, but it has done so. That is the only rule we can live under. I would affirm.

---

115. *Cantwell v. Connecticut*, 310 U.S. 296 (1940).

116. *United States v. United Mine Workers*, 330 U.S. 258 (1948). Union leaders defied a federal anti-strike injunction and were held contempt of court. The union challenged the validity of the injunction, claiming that it had been based on an unconstitutional statute. The Supreme Court ruled that the validity of an injunction or statute could not be challenged in a contempt proceeding. An injunction issued by a court with apparent jurisdiction had to be obeyed until reversed through orderly and proper judicial proceedings, even if the statute on which the order was based was unconstitutional.

117. *NAACP v. Alabama*, 357 U.S. 449 (1958).

WHITE: I affirm.

FORTAS: I vote to reverse. I would vacate the judgment and remand the case for a hearing. They would have to obey the order while they got a hearing. If the ordinance is void, you can violate the injunction with impunity, at your peril—that is Alabama law.

HARLAN: This injunction says that the petitioners cannot violate the law. It does not enjoin parades, only parades without a permit. That is quite different from *Mine Workers*.

Conference of March 24, 1967

WARREN: I would reverse. An unconstitutional ordinance was turned into a prior restraint.

HARLAN: I am changing my vote. I had thought that I would remand for proof of discrimination. I now think that the state has the right to insist on obedience to temporary restraining order, as the ordinance is valid on its face.

BLACK: I will assign the case to Potter Stewart for wording.

Result: In a 5–4 decision, the Court affirmed the defendants' convictions. Potter Stewart, writing for the majority, found a difference between defying a statute and ignoring a court injunction. While anyone who violates an unconstitutional statute or ordinance has committed no crime, no one may defy an injunction with impunity—even if the injunction later proves to be invalid. As long as the injunction was duly issued by a court with apparent jurisdiction, upon a proper plea and with proper service on the parties, it must be obeyed no matter how improper the court's action may be. Based on the need to enforce respect for the rule of law and the judicial process, any violation of a standing court order— even one that is void—is punishable as contempt of court.

The four dissenters argued that both the ordinance and the injunction were facially and obviously invalid and that the defendants had the right to exercise their First Amendment freedoms without fear of penalty or punishment. Warren noted the majority's double standard in allowing defendants to take their chances disobeying a legislative enactment but imposing an absolute duty to obey an invalid judicial order. He thought it odd that the Court was less concerned about enforcing respect for the legislative process than for the judicial process.

Adderley v. Florida, 385 U.S. 39 (1966)
(Douglas)

Harriett Louise Adderley was one of 250 black students from Florida A&M who demonstrated in front of the Leon County jail to protest the earlier arrest of other students who tried to integrate Tallahassee movie theaters. Adderley's group marched peacefully, obeying a deputy sheriff's request to stay toward the middle of the jail's driveway. The students sang, chanted, and danced. Although some prisoners shouted down to the students, there was no evidence that jailhouse operations were disrupted in any way. When the sheriff arrived, he gave the crowd ten minutes to disperse and then arrested more than one hundred students, including Adderley. Of those arrested, thirty-two were charged with trespassing with malicious and mischievous intent. They were tried as a group and convicted.

Conference of October 21, 1966

WARREN: I reverse. This is controlled by *Cox*[118] and *Edwards*.[119] Conviction is not under a tightly drawn act. The parties were lawfully on public property, and they could not be converted into trespassers by the order of the sheriff. This was a mass arrest at the option of a sheriff who does not like the gathering.

BLACK: I affirm. They were on the grounds of the jail and tried to get in. The sheriff is the custodian of the jail and the jail grounds under Florida law.

DOUGLAS: I reverse.

CLARK: I affirm.

HARLAN: I would either affirm or dismiss as improvidently granted. We do not know where the people were. If they were where people normally park, they would not be trespassers. We don't know the facts, so I would dismiss.

BRENNAN: Reverse.

STEWART: I would dismiss as improvidently granted, as we don't know the facts.

WHITE: I will vote to dismiss or affirm.

STEWART: If the case is not dismissed, I might reverse on *Edwards* and *Cox*.

WHITE: Many were blocking the driveway, but only one of the petitioners was in that group.

FORTAS: I would reverse on *Cox*. It is the mass trial that bothers me—the thirty-two chosen were put on trial and convicted on evidence not specifically directed to them.

BLACK: I am willing to dismiss if the case is written out and the statute is upheld, or I would reverse for a new trial.

HARLAN: I would dismiss, giving reasons.

Result: In a 5–4 decision, Hugo Black wrote that the trespass statute was constitutionally sound and properly applied. Security concerns at the jail, and the fact that the driveway was not an area traditionally open to the public, meant that the law regulated a specific category of conduct and was not prone to the same abuses as the common law breach of peace statutes struck down in Edwards v. South Carolina and Cox v. Louisiana.

In dissent, Douglas, Warren, Brennan, and Fortas argued that the law violated the defendants' free speech and their right to petition the government. Douglas wrote:

The jailhouse, like an executive mansion, a legislative chamber, a courthouse, or the statehouse itself is one of the seats of government, whether it be the Tower of London, the Bastille, or a small county jail.[120]

---

118. *Cox v. Louisiana*, 379 U.S. 536 (1965).
119. *Edwards v. South Carolina*, 372 U.S. 229 (1963).
120. *Adderley v. Florida*, 385 U.S. 39, 49 (1966).

Lloyd Corp. v. Tanner, 407 U.S. 551 (1972)
(Douglas)

Donald Tanner, Betsy Wheeler, and Susan Roberts sought to protest the Vietnam War and the draft by distributing handbills in a Portland, Oregon, mall owned by the Lloyd Corporation. Security guards asked the three to leave or face arrest. They left but then sued, claiming that the mall's actions deprived them of their First Amendment rights. The district court, following the Court's decision in Amalgamated Food Employees Union v. Logan Valley Plaza, *held that the group had a constitutional right to distribute handbills inside the shopping center because the mall was open to the general public and was the functional equivalent of a public business district.*[121] *The court of appeals affirmed.*

Conference of April 21, 1972

BURGER: This case has only a superficial resemblance to *Logan Valley.* In every sense it is a public shopping center. The First Amendment does not protect this sort of activity. Police status has no relevance. The fact that the land was once city-owned is irrelevant. The size of the mall has nothing to do with the case. I reverse.

DOUGLAS: I affirm. This is a mixture of private and public functions.

BRENNAN: I affirm.

STEWART: This is *Logan Valley.* This is a big complex, and this also comes under *Marsh v. Alabama.*[122] The subject matter of the demonstration is irrelevant. There can be valid time and place regulations—littering, obstruction, etc. I affirm.

WHITE: I would not extend *Logan Valley.* I reverse. This is an unrelated use of the property.

MARSHALL: I affirm. This is, a fortiori, from *Logan Valley.*

BLACKMUN: Leaflets are protected. Thurgood left this open in footnote nine in *Logan Valley.*[123] No littering. I agree with Potter that this is like the *Marsh* case. I am not at rest, but am inclined to affirm.

POWELL: *Marsh* is not applicable here. This is a shopping center in a big city. The area involved is an enclosed area. There are no streets, only sidewalks in the particular area. This type of activity has not been allowed except once every four years. The other groups are legitimate charities—there has been no political activity here at all. I would not extend *Logan Valley* to cover this sort of enclosed area. This political activity had no relation to the activities of the stores. I reverse.

---

121. *Amalgamated Food Employees Union v. Logan Valley Plaza,* 391 U.S. 308 (1968). The Court recognized the right of union members to picket a particular store inside of a mall that was involved in a labor dispute.

122. *Marsh v. Alabama,* 326 U.S. 501 (1946). This case involved a privately owned "company town." The Court treated the privately owned town as the functional equivalent of a municipality for First Amendment purposes.

123. In footnote 9 of *Logan Valley,* Marshall left open the question of whether private property rights could justify a ban on picketing not directly related to the intended use of the property.

REHNQUIST: I reverse. *Marsh v. Alabama* was wrongly decided. A shopping center is not the government.

BURGER: I lean toward reversing, but I want to re-read *Marsh*.

Result: In a Lewis Powell opinion, the Court ruled 5–4 that the Lloyd Corporation was not constitutionally required to dedicate its private property for public activities unrelated to the shopping center's operations. Powell distinguished both Marsh *and* Logan Valley. *Unlike a shopping mall, the company town in* Marsh *had "all the attributes" of a municipality. In* Logan Valley, *the union's activities were directly related to the operation of one of the mall's stores, and the pickets had no other adequate means of communicating their message to store patrons. In this case, however, the protesters had no relation to the operation of the shopping center, and they had numerous alternative means of communicating with the public, including distributing leaflets from the public sidewalks adjacent to the mall.*

This was one of the cases where Warren Burger allegedly played fast and loose with the opinion assignments. After the conference vote, Douglas assumed that he was the senior member of the majority and assigned the opinion to Marshall. Three days later, Burger issued the assignment to Powell. Douglas responded by sending the Chief Justice a defiant note:

> *You led the Conference battle against affirmance, and that is your privilege. But it is also the privilege of the majority, absent the Chief Justice, to make the assignment. Hence,* Lloyd *was assigned and is assigned. . . . If the Conference wants to authorize you to assign all opinions, that will be a new procedure. Though opposed to it, I will acquiesce. But unless we make a frank reversal in our policy, any group in the majority should and must make the assignment. . . .* Lloyd *stays assigned to Thurgood.*[124]

Harry Blackmun, however, changed his mind about the case after the conference and joined Powell as the fifth vote to reverse. Lloyd *stayed assigned to Powell.*

Pruneyard Shopping Center v. Robins, 447 U.S. 74 (1980)
(Brennan)

Michael Robins and a group of students went to a shopping center to solicit signatures opposing a UN resolution equating Zionism with racism. A security guard asked the group to leave because the mall's rules prohibited activities not directly related to commercial purposes. Robins sued, claiming that the mall had violated his free speech and petition rights. The trial court ruled in favor of Pruneyard, but the California Supreme Court reversed on the ground that California's state constitution protected reasonable speech and petition activities in shopping centers. The state supreme court also found that Robins's activities did not violate the mall's constitutional rights.

Pruneyard appealed, claiming that (1) California law exceeded the state's constitutional police powers; (2) the mall's First Amendment rights would be violated if it were compelled to allow public speeches on their private property; and (3) the state supreme court's decision amounted to a taking of mall property without compensation, in violation of the Fifth and Fourteenth Amendments. The key

---

124. Memorandum from Douglas to Burger, May 1, 1972. Douglas Papers, box 1485.

difference between this case and Lloyd v. Tanner *is that the lower court based its decision on the state rather than the federal constitution. The issue was the extent to which states could balance free speech and private property rights according to state law and independently of the federal Constitution.*

BURGER: This shopping center is essentially like the one in *Lloyd v. Tanner.*[125] But here it is a state law that forces a balance between the constitutional right of speech and a property owner's right to use his property for his own purposes. The district court's [*sic*] finding of an abundance of alternate places of communication is relevant.[126]

STEWART: This case is properly here on appeal from a state law upheld against a claim that it offends the Constitution. State law obligates this shopping center to permit the distribution of leaflets. That sort of state infringement on fee simple private property is permissible under *Penn Central.*[127]

WHITE: To the extent property rights must give way, and to the extent that speech rights must be accommodated, I agree. There is, however, the other claim of interference with the shop owners' own speech right—I can't say that the California Supreme Court necessarily decided it. So I would affirm only on the property interest issue.

MARSHALL: There is no Fifth or Fourteenth Amendment violation here. I would reach and reject the owners' own First Amendment claim.

BLACKMUN: Is this a proper appeal? I am not sure. I am about where Brennan is, as per my dissent in the *Skokie* case.[128] I can agree that the owners' free speech right issue is not

---

125. *Lloyd v. Tanner,* 407 U.S. 551 (1972).
126. California's main trial court is the superior court, not the district court.
127. *Penn Central Transportation Co. v. New York City,* 438 U.S. 104 (1978). New York's Landmarks Preservation Law protected historic landmarks and neighborhoods from action that would destroy or fundamentally alter their character. The Landmarks Preservation Commission designated Grand Central Station as a historic landmark and rejected on aesthetic grounds plans proposed by Penn Central (which owned the station) to construct a fifty-story office building over the terminal. Penn Central sued, claiming that the city had "taken" its property without due process, in violation of the Fourteenth Amendment. The Supreme Court ruled 6–3 that the commission's actions did not amount to a taking. First, the commission's ruling did not transfer control of the property to the city but merely restricted Penn Central's use of its property in what amounted to a conventional zoning restriction. Second, due process demands were satisfied because: (1) Penn Central had adequate opportunities to oppose the station's designation as a landmark and could have proposed alternative uses of the property; (2) Penn Central remained free to use the terminal as it always had; (3) Penn Central had not proved that they could not otherwise earn a reasonable return on their investment; (4) Penn Central was not foreclosed from proposing other uses of the space above the terminal; and (5), under the state's transferable development rights program, Penn Central could gain development rights elsewhere in exchange for surrendering its rights to change the area around the station.
128. *Collin v. Smith,* 578 F.2d 1197 (7th Cir. 1978), cert. denied, 439 U.S. 916 (1978). Frank Collin and the Nazi Party of America wanted to march through the largely Jewish neighborhood of Skokie, Illinois. The court of appeals voted to allow the march to take place, and the Supreme Court denied certiorari. Blackmun, joined by White, dissented from the decision to deny cert. Blackmun argued that the Court should accept the case because the issue was so important and because the Seventh Circuit's decision seemed to conflict with the Court's precedent established in *Beauharnais v. Illinois,* 343 U.S. 250 (1952). *Beauharnais* upheld a state law that made it a crime to exhibit in any public place any publication that portrayed "de-

here. Then it is fairly easy to decide as a land use regulations case, although it might be different if private homes were involved.

POWELL: I haven't considered the owners' free speech issue. The right of the state to regulate property is the issue here—not the First Amendment. How do you rationalize the California Supreme Court's decision? Does it reach ma-and-pa shops, hotel lobbies, etc? Can we reach a decision that this shopping center is the functional equivalent of downtown area?

REHNQUIST: I go along with Byron. We have to say that there is no effort to effect a taking here. So I would reject the owner's Fifth Amendment claim. The AFL-CIO brief was particularly good on this.[129] I am not fully at rest on the tying of First Amendment rights to property rights.

STEVENS: There is no merit to the owners' property argument, and none to their First Amendment *Maynard* argument, either.[130]

Result: The Court unanimously ruled that the state supreme court's decision was within the scope of state police powers and that the decision did not amount to a taking under the Fifth and Fourteenth Amendments. The Court rejected the mall owners' claim that the state supreme court had violated their First Amendment rights. William Rehnquist, writing for the majority, noted that the mall owners could easily disassociate themselves from any messages expressed on mall property. White, Marshall, Powell, and Blackmun all concurred in the judgment.

Perry Education Association v. Perry Local Educators' Association,
460 U.S. 37 (1983)
(Brennan)

Under a collective bargaining agreement, the Perry Education Association (PEA) became the sole bargaining representative for teachers in Perry Township in Indianapolis, Indiana. The agreement gave the union exclusive access to the district's internal mailing system and teachers' mailboxes. A rival union, the Perry Local Educators' Association (PLEA) sued, claiming that this favoritism violated PLEA's free speech and equal protection rights. The district court issued a summary judgment in PEA's favor, but the court of appeals reversed. The case came to the Supreme Court on appeal rather than by writ of certiorari, which briefly caused the Justices a procedural headache.

BURGER: This is not a proper appeal. I am for treating this case as a cert. On the merits, I am troubled. The school's communications and mail apparatus is not a public forum.

---

pravity, criminality, unchastity, or lack of virtue of a class of citizens, of any race, color, creed or religion" and exposed them "to contempt, derision, or obloquy." Blackmun thought that the case presented an opportunity to consider the proper limits—if any—on the exercise of free speech where a proposed demonstration was "overwhelmingly offensive" to local residents. "It just might," he wrote, "fall into the same category as one's 'right' to cry 'fire' in a crowded theater."

129. The AFL-CIO filed an amicus curiae brief urging the Court to affirm the judgment of the California Supreme Court.

130. *Wooley v. Maynard*, 430 U.S. 705 (1977).

This case is troublesome, because access by a rival union may disturb labor peace. Do we have to reach this, or can't we dismiss this case as improvidently granted?

BRENNAN:[131] I vote to affirm the decision of the Seventh Circuit. The jurisdictional question appears to have been resolved by our disposition of *Lockwood v. Jefferson Area Teachers Association*, No. 81-2236.[132] That case involved an appeal from a state court decision rejecting a federal constitutional challenge to an "agency shop" provision in a collective bargaining agreement covering teachers. I put *Lockwood* on the discuss list and suggested that we might want to hold it for this case. We disposed of that case, however, by dismissing it for want of jurisdiction and denying cert. If the collective bargaining provision in *Lockwood* was not a state statute, then the collective bargaining provision here is not a state statute and we lack appellate jurisdiction.

I am inclined to treat the case as involving a petition for cert and to vote to grant the petition. I think the case is sufficiently important to warrant review.

As I indicated, I would affirm on the merits. I think that the opinion below, with the exception of footnote 41,[133] is well-reasoned and is faithful to the *Mosley* line of decisions in this Court.[134] It is not a public forum case. It is an equal access and viewpoint discrimination case. Judge Wisdom's opinion makes this clear.[135] He states at one point that even if the school board excluded all private messages but the incumbent union's, and limited the incumbent union to messages directly related to its special duties, the exclusive access policy still would be unconstitutional, "for it might be difficult—both in practice and in principle—effectively to separate 'necessary' communications from propaganda." Wisdom went on to state that, "more fundamentally . . . an exclusive access policy would be invalid even aside from questions of fit because it furthers no discernible state interest." It seems clear to me that the exclusive access policy involves viewpoint discrimination, and that the incumbent union failed to establish that it furthered a substantial state interest. I affirm.

---

131. Adapted from Brennan's talking papers, Brennan Papers, OT 1982, box 617.

132. *Lockwood v. Jefferson Area Teachers Association*, 433 N.E.2d 604 (Ohio, 1982), appeal dismissed and cert. denied, 459 U.S. 804 (1982).

133. Footnote 41 suggested that PLEA's claims might deserve strict judicial scrutiny. With the state legislature, the schoolboard, and the dominant union all aligned against it, the court noted that PLEA had no adequate way to protect itself in the political arena. Because PLEA suffered from de jure discrimination and was without hope of political recourse, the court theorized that its situation was comparable to a "discrete and insular minority" and might deserve "particular judicial solicitude." *Perry Local Educators' Assoc. v. Hohlt*, 625 F.2d 1286 (7th Cir. 1981).

134. *Police Dept. of Chicago v. Mosley*, 408 U.S. 92 (1972). This case dealt with a city ordinance prohibiting picketing within 150 feet of a school, except for peaceful picketing of schools involved in labor disputes. The Court found that the ordinance violated the equal protection clause by drawing an unfounded distinction between peaceful labor picketing and other forms of peaceful picketing. "Above all else," Thurgood Marshall wrote for the majority, "the First Amendment means that government has no power to restrict expression because of its message [or] its ideas."

135. Judge John Minor Wisdom, who wrote the majority opinion at the appellate level, was a Senior Circuit Judge for the Fifth Circuit sitting by designation. *Perry Local Educators' Assoc. v. Hohlt*, 625 F.2d 1286 (7th Cir. 1981). Judge Wisdom was perhaps best known for his early and enthusiastic support for *Brown v. Board of Education* and judicially sanctioned affirmative action programs.

WHITE: I could dismiss the appeal, but I would reverse. There is enough of a state interest to do this. Lots of collective bargaining agreements, both private and public, contain such clauses. Maintenance of labor peace is sufficient justification. Otherwise, you will be in constant turmoil.

MARSHALL: You can't give one side this much of a head start.

BLACKMUN: This is an improper appeal. This is not a public forum. Reasonableness and content neutrality is the proper test. I think that the standard is satisfied here and I would reverse.

POWELL: This is not a proper appeal. On the merits, there is no public forum in any full sense of that term, but here a public agency is furthering a speech opportunity to one union and denying it to another. I don't see the justification of labor peace being used to deny equal access to what a public entity has opened up.

REHNQUIST: This is not a proper appeal. On the merits, I agree with Byron and Harry, and would reverse. If we strike this down, we will strike down a common provision in federal labor contracts.

STEVENS: I agree with Bill Brennan and Lewis, and I would affirm. It is not a public forum, but we have such a strong bias in opinions that there just isn't any defense that we should recognize here. This is an outrageous violation of the neutrality principle.

O'CONNOR: On the merits I would reverse, agreeing with Byron and Harry.

Result: The Court finessed the procedural problem by dismissing the appeal and then immediately voting to grant certiorari. On the merits, the majority found no constitutional violation in PEA's privileged access to Perry teachers. The school's mail system was neither by tradition nor by government designation used for public communications. This meant that the state could regulate the use of the teachers' mailboxes so long as the restrictions were reasonable and were not part of an effort to suppress free expression on the basis of content. The Court found that the state law was reasonable because PEA was the sole representative of the teachers. By law, PLEA still had equal access and speech rights during union representation elections. Because there were no other fundamental rights at stake, the Court used the rational basis test to evaluate PLEA's equal protection claim and found that the state law was rationally related to the state's legitimate interest in maintaining labor peace. PEA remains the official union of Perry Township teachers.

JUVENILES AND FREE SPEECH

Tinker v. Des Moines School District, 393 U.S. 503 (1969)
(Brennan) (Douglas)

In 1965, five public school students, including four members of the Tinker family, planned to wear black armbands to school to protest American policy in Vietnam and to show their support for that year's Christmas truce.[136] *Although school officials tolerated students wearing other political symbols (includ-*

---

136. The students were Christopher Eckhardt (sixteen), John Tinker (fifteen), Mary Beth Tinker (thirteen), Hope Tinker (eleven), and Paul Tinker (eight).

ing the German Iron Cross), when administrators found out about the armband scheme they quickly enacted a new policy banning armbands. The policy provided that students who wore armbands to school and refused to remove them when asked would be suspended. Several students wore black armbands to school as planned. Three of the students refused to remove them when asked and were suspended. They sued the school district through their fathers, asking for damages and an injunction to overturn the suspensions. The district court dismissed the suit and the court of appeals affirmed by an equally divided court.

Conference of November 15, 1968

WARREN: I would reverse this on the narrow ground of equal protection. Here, the board singled out a particular kind of conduct or ideas. Schools can abolish all badges, etc. I would not say that schools could not abolish all discussions of this kind. But here there was discrimination—they allowed the wearing of fascist crosses and so forth. Would go a long way to support, air thoughts.

BLACK: I affirm on a broad ground—as broad as possible.

DOUGLAS: I reverse, and will go on equal protection. I could go on a narrow ground, but I could go as broadly as *Dombrowski* if need be.

HARLAN: I affirm.

BRENNAN: I reverse; I agree with the Chief Justice.

STEWART: I reverse; I agree with the Chief Justice. School authorities have the power to discipline students, and I would not want to see anything written that questions that power. Even in the district court's own test, there is no evidence of disruption.

WHITE: I am inclined to reverse. I am not sure of the equal protection ground. If school authorities are empowered to maintain order and protect discipline, the school must be allowed to classify what disrupts communication among students—to ban labels that arouse violence, etc. The armband communicates in competition with the teacher. But they did not ban this badge only from the classroom, but from the entire school. The state does not defend the armband prohibition on that ground but on a physically disruptive ground, of which there is no evidence. They can ban some communication, but not others.

FORTAS: I would reverse. I am closer to Byron than to the Chief. School authorities can and must control the schools, but they must show some shred of a justification in the sense of the prohibition being necessary to carrying on school functions. The justification must be in terms of school functions, not equality. But here, there was no justification shown.

MARSHALL: I go with Byron and Abe. I reverse.

WARREN: I would go along with Byron.

DOUGLAS: Could the students be required to take off their Klan hoods?

STEWART: I could go with Byron.

MARSHALL: They could ban all political buttons if some buttons cause problems. They should be required to make a showing.

BLACK: The schools are in great trouble. Children need discipline. The country is going to ruin because of it. This is no First Amendment problem—the question is whether the rule is reasonable.

WARREN: Byron's ground is the narrowest.

Result: In reversing the decision below and reinstating the students' lawsuit, Abe Fortas emphasized that the protest was quiet, did not disrupt school discipline, and did not infringe on anyone else's rights. Fortas thought that the armbands were more closely akin to pure speech than conduct and deserved First Amendment protection. He noted that the school district had selectively singled out symbolic speech against the Vietnam War and had improperly censored student speech on the basis of its political content. The Court also ruled, however, that school officials could prohibit expressions of student opinions when necessary for school discipline or to protect other people's rights.

Hugo Black dissented, joined by John Marshall Harlan. Black argued that the case involved conduct rather than speech and could be freely regulated or even prohibited by school officials. Even if the armbands were considered pure speech or nondisruptive symbolic speech, Black wrote, school officials could still use reasonable time, place, and manner restrictions to ban them during school hours. The majority, he said, was ushering in "a new revolutionary era of permissiveness," where responsibility for school discipline would be taken away from school administrators and exercised by judges—and the students themselves. This would encourage students who "are already running loose, conducting break-ins, sit-ins, lie-ins and smash-ins," to misbehave, leaving public schools "to the whims and caprices of their loudest-mouthed, but maybe not their brightest students."

COMPELLED SPEECH

Wooley v. Maynard, 430 U.S. 705 (1977)
(Brennan)

New Hampshire required automobile owners to display license plates embossed with the motto "Live Free or Die." George and Maxine Maynard were Jehovah's Witnesses who claimed that the slogan was an affront to their religious and political beliefs. They cut out the offending mottos and were convicted on three separate occasions of mutilating license plates. The Maynards refused to pay the fines and eventually spent fifteen days in jail. They sought declaratory relief and an injunction against further state enforcement of the law against them. A three-judge district court found the statute unconstitutional as applied to the Maynards and enjoined the state from prosecuting the couple.

BURGER: His sincerity is certainly established. He did not go through the state courts, but we let him come anyway. The three-judge court says that it is symbolic speech. The state can't compel me to convey its message on a picket sign. I don't think that his claim under the religion clause is a specious one. I could turn an affirmance on this.

STEWART: *Huffman v. Pursue* and collateral estoppel are here, but I reach the merits.[137]

---

137. *Huffman v. Pursue, Ltd.,* 420 U.S. 592 (1975). The owner of an adult theater was found to be operating a public nuisance under Ohio law, and after a hearing state officials confiscated his theater and

BLACKMUN: The merits are before us. I can't attribute this motto to them, but I think that the *O'Brien* tests are satisfied here—the least restrictive alternative.[138]

POWELL: I think that the merits are here, and I will affirm.

REHNQUIST: On the non-merits issue the case is not frivolous, but they are after prospective relief only. On the merits, I agree with Harry—symbolic speech is not applicable.

Result: The Court ruled 7–2 that the First Amendment prohibited states from requiring individuals to advocate an official ideology or disseminate an ideological message by compelling them to display the message on private property. The Court decided the case on free speech grounds rather than on free exercise grounds, ruling that there was no compelling state interest at stake here to justify either a compromise or a balancing of two competing rights.

Byron White dissented in part. He would not have allowed the district court to issue an injunction because he did not see a compelling need. There were no state charges pending or threatened, and a declaratory judgment presumably would have been sufficient to stay any further state action.

COMMERCIAL SPEECH

Virginia State Board of Pharmacy v. Virginia Citizens Consumer Council, Inc.,
425 U.S. 748 (1976)
(Brennan)

A group representing prescription drug consumers challenged the validity of a Virginia law prohibiting pharmacists from advertising drug prices. The state claimed that the advertising ban helped to maintain the professional standards of licensed pharmacists and protected both pharmacists and the public from freewheeling price competition. A three-judge district court struck down the law as a violation of the First Amendment.

---

personal property. Rather than appeal through the state courts, the theater owner sued in federal district court claiming that the state law was unconstitutional. The district court struck down the state law, but the Supreme Court reversed on the ground that federal courts should not interfere with an ongoing state civil proceeding unless it is being conducted with an intent to harass or in bad faith or if the challenged state law is flagrantly and patently unconstitutional. This case basically extended the *Younger v. Harris* doctrine to cover state civil proceedings. *Younger v. Harris*, 401 U.S. 37 (1971).

138. *United States v. O'Brien*, 391 U.S. 367 (1968). After O'Brien burned his draft card to protest the war in Vietnam, he was arrested and prosecuted under a federal law prohibiting the mutilation or destruction of draft documents. O'Brien appealed on the ground that the law violated his First Amendment free speech rights and served no legislative purpose. The Supreme Court upheld his conviction, ruling that governmental regulations were justified if (1) the subject matter was within the constitutional power of the government; (2) it furthered an important or substantial governmental interest unrelated to the suppression of free expression; and (3) the incidental restriction on First Amendment freedoms was no greater than necessary. The Court ruled that the government had the right to act under Congress's Article 1 war powers, that there was a substantial reason for the law unrelated to the suppression of free expression (the orderly administration of the military draft), and that the law had only an incidental and negligible effect on O'Brien's free speech rights.

BURGER: Does the advertising of prices reach interests that the state would protect? I tentatively would affirm.

STEWART: There is no such thing as a constitutional "right to know." The Constitution only derivatively secures the opportunity to receive speech or writing. *Lamont* and *Mandel* held that potential receivers or readers have standing to vindicate pharmacists' right to speak or write.[139] But I have difficulty seeing how commercial price advertising is protected by the First Amendment. If it is a law to prohibit false, misleading or unfair advertising now regulated by federal and state laws, it is only traditional economic regulation.

WHITE: I would affirm. I had thought that because something was under the First Amendment, it is absolutely immune from regulation. Since Virginia says that price undercutting is legal, I can't see how Virginia can prohibit the advertising of prices.

BLACKMUN: *Bigelow* is the only case really on point,[140] and it did restrict and confine *Chrestensen* to hold that some First Amendment protection applies to commercial ad-

---

139. *Lamont v. Postmaster General*, 381 U.S. 301 (1965) upheld the First Amendment right of citizens to receive political publications from abroad. The Court, in an opinion by William O. Douglas, struck down a federal law that required Dr. Corliss Lamont to submit a request to the post office in writing before he could take delivery of mail from abroad containing Communist propaganda (a copy of *Peking Review*). Douglas ruled that the law was unconstitutional because it imposed an affirmative obligation on the addressee that unconstitutionally limited his First Amendment right to receive the information.

Kleindienst v. Mandel, 408 U.S. 753 (1972), recognized that First Amendment speech rights included the corollary right to receive information and ideas. The Court nonetheless allowed the Nixon administration to withhold a visa from Ernest Mandel, a Belgian Marxist who had planned a lecture tour of American colleges. Mandel, along with a group of American professors who had invited him, asked the courts to order Attorney General Richard Kleindienst to issue the visa. In a 6–3 decision, Harry Blackmun ruled that Congress had delegated plenary power to the executive branch to exclude undesirable aliens and that the attorney general had permissibly denied to issue a visa for a "legitimate and bona fide reason." Although the government had the right to exclude such aliens, Blackmun noted that this did not preclude the professors from asserting their own First Amendment rights to receive information from Mandel. Blackmun recognized that even though the professors had access to Mandel's ideas through his writings, tape recordings, telephone hookups, and the like, there was also recognized First Amendment value in sustained face-to-face discussion and debate. This interest precluded any holding that the existence of other alternative forms of communication might extinguish rights to more intimate, face-to-face discussion. Douglas, Brennan, and Marshall dissented.

140. *Bigelow v. Virginia*, 421 U.S. 809 (1975). Virginia law made it a misdemeanor to sell or distribute any publication that encouraged abortion. John C. Bigelow, a local newspaper editor, was convicted under the law after he printed an ad from a New York City firm offering low cost, legal abortions. The Virginia Supreme Court ruled that commercial speech was not protected by the First Amendment and that states could use their police powers to regulate or prohibit commercial speech dealing with the health, safety, and morals of its citizens. The U.S. Supreme Court reversed, holding that this was a case of "pure speech" and that merely because the message was in the form of an advertisement did not mean that it fell outside of the First Amendment. Harry Blackmun's majority opinion noted that the speech in this case was not purely commercial but contained factual material of public interest. This case extended constitutional protections to commercial speech and limited the use of state police powers to suppress the dissemination of truthful, nonmisleading, and noncoercive information about legal activities.

vertising.[141] The real emphasis is upon the free flow of information. The state justifications here seem rather impotent. The monitoring idea is frivolous. I am inclined to affirm, but preserve areas.

POWELL: Potter's point has substance, and if there were any doubt in my mind affecting FTC power to regulate deceptive advertising I would take a second look. But presently I see no basis for state's interests claimed here.

REHNQUIST: If the right to hear is derivative from the right to speak, then these pharmacists must have a First Amendment right to protection of the very core of commerce—price. Because I don't think there is a First Amendment right here, but only a Fourteenth Amendment equal protection right, I would reverse.

Result: On behalf of a 7–1 majority, Harry Blackmun struck down the Virginia law by blurring the distinction between "pure" commercial speech and commercial speech that conveyed important information of public interest. Professional pharmacists, Blackmun wrote, had a First Amendment right to disseminate price information, as did any potential recipients of such information. Openly questioning Chrestensen without overruling it, the Court extended the First Amendment to cover even purely commercial advertisements in recognition of the strong public interest in a free flow of commercial information.

Virginia's ban on price advertisements could not be justified by the state's claimed interest in protecting the professional standards of pharmacists. There were better ways to promote professionalism and protect licensed pharmacists from competition than keeping the public ignorant of the prices that other pharmacists were charging (Blackmun suggested subsidies as one possible alternative). Because the state's advertising ban was absolute, Blackmun claimed that it exceeded any reasonable time, place, or manner restrictions the state might have been able to impose. Finally, there was no claim that the information involved was false, misleading, or illegal—the advertising was truthful and involved a lawful activity.

In dissent, William Rehnquist questioned the wisdom of extending First Amendment protections to pure commercial speech. Elevating commercial speech to the same constitutional plane as political speech, he warned, would open the door to a host of new problems and litigation that the Court had so far wisely avoided. This decision, he predicted, would lead to more aggressive litigation by drug, liquor, and cigarette manufacturers to advertise products that society had traditionally sought to discourage. John Paul Stevens did not participate in the decision.

Bates v. State Bar of Arizona, 433 U.S. 350 (1977)
(Brennan)

John Bates and Van O'Steen, two recent Arizona State law school graduates, placed a newspaper advertisement offering their legal services for "reasonable fees." The state bar ruled that the advertisement violated a state supreme court disciplinary rule prohibiting lawyers from advertising. Bates and

---

141. *Valentine v. Chrestensen*, 316 U.S. 52 (1942), held that "pure" commercial advertising was not protected by the First Amendment. The Court upheld a New York law banning the distribution of handbills, circulars, and other advertising materials on city streets. The Court ruled that the handbills were purely commercial speech, even though one side contained a political statement criticizing the antihandbill ordi-

O'Steen argued that the ban violated the Sherman Antitrust Act by restricting competition and violated their First Amendment free speech rights. The Arizona Supreme Court ruled that the state could prohibit lawyer advertising.

BURGER: The *Parker Brown* state action exception applied to reach the First Amendment.[142] Lawyers for me are a special breed of officers, of course, whose First Amendment rights are inhibited. If *we* are ready to extend *Virginia Pharmacy* to professional services, *I'm* not. Maybe it is overbroad to say that they can give only name and address. Here you don't have true legal aid organization, but only a couple of guys soliciting clients. I could go either way, however—*Virginia Pharmacy* is no help to me.[143]

STEWART: On *Parker Brown*, I agree that the state is compelled to immunize them from anti-trust laws. Is any advertising deceptive, as the ABA seems to think? I basically agree with the ABA brief.

WHITE: I am close to Bill Brennan. The rule on its face may not be an absolute, but the exceptions are so narrow as to be too restrictive. This particular ad would have to be held O.K., unless we strike down the state rule on overbreadth grounds.

MARSHALL: This ad is all right. I would await other concrete regulations and not decide too much.

BLACKMUN: *Bigelow* and *Virginia Pharmacy* go far to sustain the 1st Amendment attack here. I am not sure that I would go too far. Maybe we ought to stop with saying that this ad is O.K. States are entitled to time, place, and manner regulability. I would prefer not to go on an overbreadth theory, but go right to the First Amendment and say that this ad is O.K.

POWELL: The only problem here is the First Amendment issue. I would not sustain an absolute ban on lawyer advertising. But anything beyond *Martindale* is likely to be inherently deceptive and misleading. When you let this genie out of the bottle, there will be hell to pay. A state is constitutionally free to decide that an ad like this is inherently deceptive. I lean that way, although I am clear that a flat ban would violate the First Amendment. I agree that whatever we do, we should write narrowly.[144]

REHNQUIST: The learned professions problem was reserved in *Virginia Pharmacy*.[145] If overbreadth is going to apply in the area of commercial speech, it will open a Pandora's

---

nance. This case has repeatedly been questioned, criticized, and limited, and after *Virginia Pharmacy* it is widely considered to be overruled in spirit if not in fact.

142. The *Parker Brown* doctrine states that a state law or regulation can serve as the basis for antitrust immunity if the state (1) articulates a clear policy to allow anticompetitive conduct and (2) provides active supervision of such conduct. *Parker v. Brown*, 317 U.S. 341 (1943).

143. *Virginia State Board of Pharmacy v. Virginia Citizens Consumer Council*, 425 U.S. 748 (1976).

144. Before joining the Court, Lewis Powell had been president of the ABA. Potter Stewart and Warren Burger were also deeply involved in ABA activities.

145. Blackmun's majority opinion in *Virginia Pharmacy* left open the question of whether the "learned" professions of law and medicine could be treated differently than pharmacy and other just-a-bit-less-learned professions. Blackmun noted that lawyer-client relations (including client solicitation and advertisements)

box in the area of laws on deceptive advertising. I would urge that we don't apply the overbreadth doctrine here. This brings me to this particular ad. It is hard to say that on its face or from the record that these fellows were deceptive. Therefore if, say, you treat this ad as if it were deceptive, you allow the state to legislate against that danger. I would let the state bars assume that as to price advertising, which this is.

STEVENS: I can't read the Arizona opinion as resting on a deception concept. I would not use the overbreadth doctrine in the area of commercial advertising. We don't really have an absolute ban today—*Martindale* and other information, including pricing, are not un-familiar. I would base our decision on the First Amendment and sustain this particular ad.

Result: The Court rejected the Sherman Act argument but reversed on free speech grounds. Even purely commercial speech, Harry Blackmun wrote for a 5–4 majority, served significant social interests in that it "may often carry information of import to significant issues of the day." Permitting limited lawyer advertising also served the best interests of potential clients, whose "concern for the free flow of commercial speech . . . may be far keener than his concern for urgent political dialogue." Because of the unique nature of the profession, Blackmun cautioned, lawyers could still be subject to restrictions and limitations that might not apply to other professions. States, however, could no longer impose a blanket ban on lawyer advertising.

Capital Cities Cable, Inc. v. Crisp, 467 U.S. 691 (1984)
(Brennan)

Oklahoma law prohibited the advertising of alcoholic beverages on television. In 1980, the state attorney general extended the law to prohibit cable companies from rebroadcasting out-of-state liquor advertisements. Richard A. Crisp, director of the Oklahoma Alcoholic Beverage Control Board, threatened criminal prosecutions if any cable companies failed to comply. Capital Cities Cable filed suit in federal court asking for declaratory and injunctive relief, claiming that the state law violated the First Amendment and that the state law was preempted by federal regulations and the supremacy clause. The district court ruled that the state law violated the First Amendment, but the court of appeals reversed.

BURGER: The Twenty-first Amendment is a tough barrier in a confrontation with federal statutes.[146] Advertising is a big chunk of distillers' costs, and I don't see how you can separate it from "importation and transportation." Do values of commercial speech outrank the Twenty-first Amendment? I lean toward saying no.

---

historically have been more closely regulated than client relations in other businesses and professions for two reasons. First, lawyers play a unique and essential role in the administration of justice, and their privileged role as officers of the court makes it possible for them to manipulate the system of justice for their own purposes. Second, unlike pharmacists, the products and services offered by lawyers are not standardized but are of an almost infinite nature and variety, which creates a greater possibility of client confusion and deception. Because legal training is so exclusive, and because lawyers are potentially so powerful, clients cannot be expected to bargain with lawyers on equal terms. As a consequence, lawyers must accept both higher ethical standards and greater regulation of their conduct than other professions. 425 U.S. 748, 773.

146. The Twenty-first Amendment gives states the power to regulate the time, place, and manner under which liquor may be imported and sold.

BRENNAN:[147] Although preemption is a constitutional issue, it is the kind of question that we generally consider before turning to other constitutional claims. I find the commercial speech question in this case far closer and more complex than the preemption question and would therefore decide the preemption question first.

Oklahoma concedes, as I think it must, that its ban on cable television liquor commercials would clearly be preempted by the Copyright Act and the FCC regulations if it were not for the Twenty-first Amendment—no one disputes that there is a direct conflict between the cable operators' obligations under state and federal law. I think it is also clear, and important to note, that a state statute with the effect of eliminating or substantially reducing the availability of cable television would be preempted. The reason for this is that, in the FCC regulations as well as in the Copyright Act itself, the federal government has expressed a very strong interest in promoting this medium of information and entertainment, especially in the rural parts of the country that would otherwise be without television service.

That interest, as reaffirmed by the 1976 Congress, led directly to the compulsory licensing scheme under which cable companies may not delete advertisements. Congress obviously wanted to protect the holders of copyrights in television programming, but if it had no other purpose the compulsory licensing scheme would have been unnecessary: it could merely have deemed broadcast retransmission without consent an infringement and left the matter to the marketplace. But Congress explicitly noted an additional and equally important purpose—promotion of cable television. And because of its express finding that individual negotiations would result in relatively little broadcast retransmission, it granted the cable companies a compulsory license. Given these express congressional findings, a state statute that requires cable companies to delete certain commercials quite clearly threatens both purposes advanced by the federal scheme: (1) protection and compensation for the copyright holder; and (2) promotion of cable TV.

When the Twenty-first Amendment comes into play, the preemption analysis is, of course, altered by virtue of our decision in *California Retail Liquor Dealers Ass'n v. Midcal Aluminum, Inc.*[148] Under that decision, we must: (1) evaluate the interests underlying both the state and federal statutes and the relationship between those interests and the means employed; (2) consider the nexus between those interests and the constitutional powers conferred on each sovereign; and (3) balance the two. Oklahoma's interest is obviously to discourage the consumption of liquor and, unlike some of the economists cited in the briefs, I have no doubt that an advertising ban serves that interest to some extent, although we do have a district court finding suggesting that extent is limited. On the other

---

147. Adapted from Brennan's talking papers, Brennan Papers, OT 1983, box 656.

148. *California Retail Liquor Dealers Ass'n v. Midcal Aluminum, Inc.*, 445 U.S. 97 (1980). The Court struck down a California law requiring wine producers, wholesalers, and rectifiers to file fair trade contracts or price schedules with the state. The law had the effect of fixing prices, allegedly to protect small retailers. The Court ruled that while the Twenty-first Amendment gave states broad authority to control the importation and distribution of liquor, that power was not absolute and could be balanced against conflicting federal laws passed under Congress's commerce clause authority. In this case, the Sherman Act's intent to protect free competition outweighed California's claimed interest in protecting small liquor retailers.

hand, Oklahoma's advertising ban, by excluding out-of-state newspapers and magazines, seems somewhat selective. The federal interests, as I have noted, are quite strong and clearly and directly served by the scheme Congress settled upon. Under *Midcal*, it is relevant to note that Oklahoma's advertising ban is at least one step removed from its "core" Twenty-first Amendment power, prohibition of sale or importation, whereas the FCC regulations and the Copyright Act assert interests—protection of authors of creative works and promotion of the wider dissemination of information—plainly within the "core" of federal power under the copyright and commerce clauses. For these reasons, therefore, I believe the balancing required by *Midcal* tips here, as in that case, decisively in favor of the federal statute.

WHITE: I agree with Bill Brennan. This is an attempt to get into another industry—advertising. The Twenty-first Amendment does not reach that far.

BLACKMUN: This law is a flat ban on truthful commercial speech about legal products. Unless the state has no other alternatives, the Twenty-first Amendment does not protect this state law. I agree with Brennan and Byron.

POWELL: I agree with Brennan. The preemption argument in the solicitor general's brief is persuasive.[149] So we can go on preemption and not address the commercial speech issue.

REHNQUIST: I will try to come out in favor of the state on the balance.

STEVENS: Clearly there was preemption, and the Twenty-first Amendment does not apply to advertising. Our policy of avoiding unnecessary constitutional questions justifies reversal on the preemption ground.

O'CONNOR: It is not enough to do the balancing on the preemption ground. I thought that we should remand and tell them to address the preemption question, and do a *Midcal* balancing analysis. I would not reach the commercial speech question.

Result: William Brennan, writing for a unanimous Court, ruled that Oklahoma's attempt to ban the rebroadcast of alcohol advertisements was preempted by federal FCC regulations and the Communications Act of 1934. The FCC, Brennan wrote, had clearly and explicitly prohibited this sort of state regulation of cable television. The state law also conflicted with FCC "must carry" rules, which required cable operators to carry certain local broadcasts made within a thirty-five-mile radius—which often compelled cable companies located near state borders to carry programming from neighboring states. In this instance, federal regulations required Oklahoma cable companies to carry broadcasts from Missouri and Kansas.

The Twenty-first Amendment did not protect Oklahoma because the federal government had overriding interests in establishing uniform national regulations for cable operators to ensure availability and diversity of cable services nationwide. These "important and substantial" interests outweighed Oklahoma's narrow and selectively applied interest in discouraging the consumption of alcohol. Moreover, Brennan noted, the Twenty-first Amendment was at best only indirectly relevant:

---

149. The solicitor general was Rex Lee.

Oklahoma's ban on out-of-state advertising of alcoholic beverages had little or no direct effect on Oklahoma's right to regulate the importation and distribution of alcohol within the state. The Court largely avoided the First Amendment issues embedded in this case.

Posadas de Puerto Rico Associates v. Tourism Company of Puerto Rico,
478 U.S. 328 (1986)

(Brennan)

In 1984, Puerto Rico legalized casino gambling in a bid to promote tourism. The commonwealth, however, banned casino advertising and discouraged Puerto Rican residents from gambling in local casinos. These rules were later amended to allow casinos to advertise, but only outside of Puerto Rico. Posadas de Puerto Rico (Posadas) advertised in several Puerto Rican media and was fined for violating the advertising ban. Posadas sued, claiming that the ban violated its First Amendment rights. The local superior court judge strained to save the law, ruling that local advertising was permissible under the statute as long as it was aimed exclusively at non–Puerto Ricans.

BURGER: The casino is legal. This is a facial challenge that was denied after the trial judge narrowed the reach of the statute. We have jurisdiction here under §1253.[150] The challenge is on federal grounds. The government's violation of the First Amendment seems clear. The statute has nothing to do with deceptive ads.

BRENNAN:[151] First, we properly have jurisdiction to decide the constitutional issues presented in this case. Although the record of the proceedings below is somewhat muddled, appellant clearly raised a facial challenge to the gaming statute before both the superior court and the Supreme Court of Puerto Rico, both of which passed on the merits of that claim. While the superior court substantially narrowed the scope of the law, appellant claims that the statute as construed is still repugnant to the federal constitution. We have jurisdiction to decide this issue.

Second, casino advertising clearly constitutes commercial speech entitled to First Amendment protection, although our decisions have extended less protection to commercial speech vis a vis non-commercial speech. We have recognized that commercial speech which is not false or deceptive and which concerns lawful activities may be regulated only through means that directly advance a substantial government interest. Under this standard, I do not believe that Puerto Rico has justified a ban on casino advertising to residents.

While Puerto Rico may certainly decide to ban casinos altogether, it has chosen not to do so, and allows residents to patronize these establishments. Thus, it is clear that the advertisements prohibited by the statute concern entirely lawful activity. Nevertheless, Puerto Rico argues that it may constitutionally restrict casino advertising in order to discourage residents from patronizing casinos and ultimately to control the harmful ef-

---

150. Burger probably meant 28 U.S.C. §1258, which gave the Supreme Court jurisdiction in cases from Puerto Rican courts when Puerto Rican judges upheld the validity of local laws against the federal Constitution. Section 1253 provided for direct appeals to the U.S. Supreme Court from three-judge district courts.

151. Adapted from Brennan's talking papers, Brennan Papers, OT 1985, box 712.

fects that casinos would have on Puerto Rican society. I reject the contention that Puerto Rico has a legitimate and substantial interest in discouraging its residents from gambling, since the commonwealth places no restrictions on advertising to residents for other gambling activities. Moreover, while the commonwealth may have a substantial interest in regulating the "secondary effects" that accompany casinos, a ban on advertising to residents does not directly advance that interest. There are a whole range of less restrictive mechanisms available to the commonwealth.

WHITE: I agree. I affirm.

MARSHALL: I agree.

BLACKMUN: My separate concurrence in *Central* answers for me.[152]

POWELL: This is almost a non-statute before us, after the judge stuffed it. It is a perfect absurdity. There is a public interest in regulating gambling by state law. What of cigarette ads? But the state interest here is possibly de minimis. I will pass.

REHNQUIST: I would affirm. I think that the state can regulate, however foolishly, to protect residents against themselves.

STEVENS: I would reverse, but narrowly. If a state allows gambling, it must treat everyone the same way. The First Amendment prohibits cutting up the ads' audience into pieces, as is done here.

O'CONNOR: The state interest in controlling gambling is very great. So the idea that the First Amendment says that you can't target its advertising about something bannable troubles me. So I will affirm.

Result: The Chief Justice switched sides after the conference, and by a 5–4 vote the Court upheld the Puerto Rican law as interpreted by the superior court. The majority, in an opinion by William Rehnquist, used a four-prong test for commercial speech: (1) it must advertise a lawful activity and must not be misleading or fraudulent; (2) to restrict commercial speech, there must be a substantial government interest (e.g., protecting the health, safety and welfare of Puerto Rican residents); (3) restrictions must "directly advance" the government interest and must not be underinclusive (e.g., all gambling advertisements must be equally restricted); and (4) restrictions can be no more restrictive than necessary to advance the government interest (e.g., casinos could use local advertising to target tourists). Brennan, Marshall, Blackmun, and Stevens dissented.

---

152. *Central Hudson Gas and Electric Corp. v. Public Service Commission,* 447 U.S. 557 (1980). The Court ruled that a state public service commission's regulation banning all promotional advertising by electric utilities violated the First Amendment. The majority established that even truthful commercial speech about legal activities could still be suppressed if it would directly advance a substantial government interest and if the regulation was not more extensive than necessary to advance that interest.

In his concurring opinion, Blackmun argued that the majority's test was satisfactory only in cases where commercial speech was at least potentially misleading or coercive. He concluded that truthful, nonmisleading, and noncoercive commercial speech should be given the same constitutional protection as noncommercial speech—subject only to reasonable time, place, and manner restrictions and the clear and present danger test.

FLAG DESECRATION

Street v. New York, 394 U.S. 576 (1969)
(Brennan) (Douglas)

In 1966, James Meredith, the man who broke the color barrier at the University of Mississippi, was shot by a sniper during a civil rights march. When Brooklyn bus driver and war hero Sidney Street heard the initial reports of the shooting—which mistakenly said that Meredith had been killed—he retrieved an American flag from his home and set it on fire in front of his house, screaming, "We don't need no damn flag. . . . If they did that to Meredith, we don't need an American flag." Street was arrested for violating a state law that made it a crime to mutilate, deface, defile, defy, trample, or cast contempt upon an American flag by words or acts.

Street claimed that his actions were expressive communication protected by the First Amendment. He also argued that the state law was facially invalid because it punished desecration by words. Finally, he maintained that the statute was unconstitutionally vague because it did not clearly define what behaviors were prohibited and it was impossible to say what "defying the flag" or "casting contempt upon the flag" meant. The New York Court of Appeals upheld Street's conviction, finding that his ideas had been conveyed by actions rather than by speech.

Conference of October 25, 1968

WARREN: I would affirm in light of Judge Fuld's opinion.[153] The uncertainties that trouble the appellant are not in this case. The only question is whether New York can punish the public burning of an American flag. I think that the state can do so to prevent riots and so forth. It is conduct, and not pure speech or symbolic speech.

BLACK: I would be bothered if I thought that the New York statute punished anyone for burning the flag and for the speech.

HARLAN: I would not deal with the statute on its face. I think that Fuld's opinion is ambiguous and that he can't prevent us from looking at the record, and that put the speech element of this incident into the case. I can't say that Street's conviction did not rest on verbal expression. Reverse and remand.

WHITE: This was a conviction with a speech element.

FORTAS: The speech element plays a substantial part.

MARSHALL: I agree with Harlan.

HARLAN: I can't tell if the conviction was based on speech or flag burning.

FORTAS: He can be convicted for flag burning alone.

BRENNAN: I doubt that.

---

153. Chief Judge Stanley H. Fuld of the New York Court of Appeals wrote for a unanimous court confirming Street's conviction.

WARREN: The flag burning issue is here and we should decide it. We should decide that it can be punished.

HARLAN: This case does not present that issue.

WARREN: When Judge Fuld below said it was done "in protest," he was not relying on free speech.

Result: To preserve a precarious 5–4 majority, Harlan wrote a narrow decision that avoided the main constitutional issues. The Court ruled that the law was overbroad and that the jury might have wrongly convicted Street on the basis of his verbal expression, rather than for his conduct.

Earl Warren led the dissenters, arguing that Street had clearly been convicted for his conduct and not for his speech. Warren strongly believed that flag burning was not entitled to constitutional protection. Hugo Black expressed his admiration for Judge Fuld's "excellent" opinion affirming Street's conviction, while Byron White chided Harlan for avoiding the real issues. Abe Fortas, who initially voted with the majority, changed his mind and argued that Street had been rightly convicted for his actions and not for speaking his mind. In a memo to the conference, Fortas apologized to Harlan for his "inconstancy" and admitted that he was "losing [his] enthusiasm for symbolic speech."[154]

Radich v. New York, 401 U.S. 531 (1971)
(Douglas)

Stephen Radich owned an art gallery on Madison Avenue in New York City. In 1966, he opened an installation that featured thirteen works made with American flags. He claimed that the exhibit was a protest against the war in Vietnam. On display were a flag in the form of an erect penis hanging from a cross, a flag shaped as a human figure hanging from a noose, and a flag in the shape of an octopus. Radich was convicted for violating New York's flag desecration law and the state court of appeals affirmed.

Conference of February 26, 1971

BURGER: This is a flag preservation case. On the basis of *Street,* I would like to ask John Harlan to speak first. *Street* was written to avoid the present issue.

HARLAN: This is an emotional field. If Congress or the states want to pass an act that the American flag can't be used for a protest meeting, that is one thing—but here there is no such law. There is only a judicial rule that the flag can't be used in a protest against government action. I would reverse.

BURGER: Making a male penis out of a flag is desecration. I affirm. If any act on flag desecration can be supported, this one is it. I follow Earl Warren's dissent in the *Street* case.

BLACK: I have had two bouts with my clerks about this issue. The government can create a symbol and protect it. One can speak against the flag, but he can't use the flag to desecrate it. That is true here. I affirm.

---

154. Laura Kalmen, *Abe Fortas,* 286.

HARLAN: I reverse.

BRENNAN: This is not the sculptor, but an exhibitor. There is an exception in the act, and to apply it to him is a denial of equal protection.

STEWART: There is only conduct here in the exhibition. However, the conduct here is "First Amendment conduct"—it is no different from talking. Radich did not destroy or burn the flag. I would reverse on *Street*.

WHITE: The essence of the crime was casting contempt on the flag. Under Potter's view, the sculptor would be guilty. The act of exhibition is as execrable as creating the work of art. I affirm.

MARSHALL: The man who runs the art gallery is the vehicle for people's ideas. I have doubts as to the sculptor. I reverse.

BLACKMUN: I lean to vote for affirmance. This is a pesky case. This is a commercial case. I am inclined to support Hugo's view.

WHITE: I would like to ask for the case to be held over, as I am not firm on it.

DOUGLAS: Is out of the case.[155]

Result: After the conference, the Justices found themselves hopelessly deadlocked. By default, the judgment below was affirmed by a 4–4 Court, with Douglas not voting. Three years later, a federal district court judge quashed Radich's conviction on a writ of habeas corpus.[156]

OFFENSIVE SPEECH

Cohen v. California, 403 U.S. 15 (1971)
(Douglas) (Brennan)

Paul Cohen wore a jacket into a Los Angeles courthouse with the words "Fuck the Draft" scrawled on the back. Although Cohen took the coat off before entering the courtroom, a bailiff confronted him and later filed charges. Cohen was tried and convicted under California Penal Code §415, which prohibited malicious and willful disturbance of the peace or quiet of any neighborhood or individual by offensive conduct. The state court of appeal affirmed Cohen's conviction, and the state supreme court denied review. John Marshall Harlan initially voted to dismiss cert, calling the case a "peewee." But after four other Justices voted to accept the case, he found that he had trouble making up his mind how it should be decided.

---

155. Douglas recused himself because the law firm defending Radich had represented Douglas during his impeachment hearings. Woodward and Armstrong, *The Brethren,* 147.

156. *United States ex rel. Radich v. Criminal Court,* 385 F.Supp. 165 (SDNY 1974).

Conference of February 26, 1971

BURGER: This is not a speech case—this is conduct. He used an offensive word in public. The sense in which it was received, rather than its intent to disparage, should be the test. This disturbs the peace by offensive conduct, and California has the right to make criminal the use of offensive words. I affirm.

BLACK: I affirm.

DOUGLAS: I would reverse. This was pretty rough speech, but it is constitutionally protected. You can't punish rough talk.

HARLAN: I affirm. This is a close case. States can regulate vulgarity.

BRENNAN: I reverse.

STEWART: I reverse. If this isn't speech, I don't know what it is.

WHITE: It is like the flag cases, for it has no First Amendment value. People can be restrained from public utterances of this kind. California can prevent people from tapping a woman on the shoulder and saying "fuck you." I affirm.

MARSHALL: I reverse. I do not know what "offensive" conduct is. I doubt whether this was offensive to anyone.

BLACKMUN: I would affirm. It is conduct, not speech.

[DOUGLAS: After an initial conference vote to affirm Cohen's conviction, Harlan began to have second thoughts and asked the case to be held over to the next conference.]

Conference of March 5, 1971

HARLAN: I am changing my vote and will reverse. I would put the decision on the California law's lack of specificity.

Result: As the "least persuaded," Harlan wrote the majority opinion reversing Cohen's conviction on a 5–4 vote. He ruled that the state needed either to come up with a more particularized statute or a more compelling reason to make the mere public display of a four-letter word a crime. Harlan summed up the case with perhaps his most famous phrase: "one man's vulgarity is another man's lyric."[157]

Erznoznik v. Jacksonville, 422 U.S. 205 (1975)
(Brennan)

The University Drive-In Theatre in Jacksonville, Florida, showed an R-rated movie (The Class of '44) containing several nude scenes. A city ordinance prohibited any display of nudity on a drive-in

---

157. According to Woodward and Armstrong, the phrase was coined by one of Harlan's clerks. *The Brethren,* 132.

screen visible from any public street or place. Because the drive-in screen was visible from two streets and a church parking lot, the city cited Richard Erznoznik, the theater's manager, for operating a public nuisance. The state stayed its prosecution to allow Erznoznik to test the ordinance's constitutionality. After Florida state courts ruled that the law was constitutional, Erznoznik appealed to the U.S. Supreme Court.

BURGER: This is not a First Amendment case for me.

DOUGLAS: Out.

STEWART: I would have no trouble with an ordinance that prohibited any movie from any public street or public place. What bothers me here is the censorship of content.

WHITE: Once you can say that you can sustain an ordinance against nudity in public places, you can say that they can't show movies in public places showing nudity. The traffic thing is not very persuasive, and these laws don't seem to protect people who don't want to see these movies.

MARSHALL: The city could have an ordinance against showing such movies to children, but this ordinance is not to protect children. I would like the opinion to say so.

BLACKMUN: This was a poorly drawn ordinance. They could put one together. But this is directed at only public places, not private homes. This ordinance is overbroad, in reaching non-obscene material and in not protecting groups that could be protected.

POWELL: I came in here prepared to affirm as a valid government purpose of preventing the distraction of motorists. This discussion has shaken me. Must the city have its ordinance written so as fully to protect groups that could be protected?

Result: After the conference, Lewis Powell changed his mind and voted to strike down the ordinance both on its face and as applied. Writing for a 6–3 Court, Powell noted that the law went well beyond permissible obscenity criteria in banning all public displays of nudity and that the ban was not supported by a sufficiently important state interest. There was a minimal privacy interest, as people on the street who did not wish to see the movie could easily avert their eyes. The law could not be justified as a law intended to protect children, as it prohibited all nudity—even displays that were innocent or educational—rather than being more narrowly aimed at sexually explicit conduct. Nor could the law be justified on traffic safety grounds, because it was underinclusive—the ordinance singled out nudity among all other potential driving distractions. Potter Stewart initially voted to affirm but later changed his mind and joined the majority. William O. Douglas, who missed the conference because he had suffered a stroke, argued in his concurring opinion that government could never regulate movies by their content.

Warren Burger and William Rehnquist dissented on three grounds: (1) that the law did not suppress ideas but was analogous to laws prohibiting indecent exposure; (2) that the law was a reasonable time, place, and manner restriction; and (3) that the law promoted the state's interest in traffic safety. Byron White dissented on the ground that the state had the right to regulate drive-in movies to protect the privacy of innocent passers-by.

OBSCENITY AND PORNOGRAPHY

Roth v. United States & Alberts v. California, 354 U.S. 476 (1957)
Kingsley Books, Inc. v. Brown, 354 U.S. 436 (1957)
(Clark) (Douglas) (Burton)

These three obscenity cases included one federal and one state criminal prosecution, plus a state civil action to suppress an adult comic book. In Roth, *a federal criminal statute prohibited the mailing of "obscene, lewd, lascivious or filthy" material or other publications of "indecent character."[158] In* Alberts, *California made it a crime to sell or advertise "obscene or indecent" materials. Both Samuel Roth and David Alberts were convicted, and their convictions were sustained on appeal. In* Kingsley Books, *a New York civil statute prohibited the publication of material of "indecent character," which was defined as "obscene, lewd, lascivious, filthy, indecent or disgusting . . . or immoral." A state trial judge sitting without a jury found one issue of the* Nights of Horror *comic book series to be obscene, enjoined its distribution, and ordered the sheriff to confiscate and destroy all available copies.[159]*

At conference, Stewart cut straight to the heart of the question that still troubles the Court more than four decades later.

Conference of April 26, 1956

WARREN: We should sustain *Alberts* and *Roth*, and reverse *Kingsley Books v. Brown*. On the first two cases there is no First Amendment problem. Both the state and federal governments have the right to protect society against this kind of depravity. I take no stock in the mail connection. I would limit the power of the state to punishing abuse. The New York statute, however, is censorship and is a prior restraint. You can't say to the press, on a censorship ground, that the Board knows best. I would limit the statute's reach to punishment after publishing. On vagueness, the law is not too vague. The words "obscenity" or "filth" are sufficient, and cannot be further distilled. We cannot write a definition. For me they a have common meaning. These statutes are not vague; the words employed here are as certain as many we have sustained.

BLACK: I agree with the Chief in the New York case, but I would reverse the California and federal cases. I was impressed with Jerome Frank's last opinion.[160] These statutes can't

---

158. Samuel Roth was an Austrian immigrant and a Columbia University graduate. He owned the Poetry Bookstore in Greenwich Village and published *Two Worlds Monthly* magazine. He had been prosecuted repeatedly for publishing indecent literature, including James Joyce's *Ulysses*, D. H. Lawrence's *Lady Chatterley's Lover*, and Ben Franklin's *To a Young Man on How to Choose a Mistress*. This time he was convicted for publishing a magazine called *American Aphrodite*. Eisler, *A Justice For All*, 141.
    Roth made a fortune pirating literary works such as *Ulysses* without paying the authors any royalties. James Joyce sued Roth for unfair competition, asking for $500,000 in damages, but the attention only drove Roth's operations underground. Spoo, "The Case of James Joyce's *Ulysses* in America."
    159. In judging *Nights of Horror* obscene, trial judge Matthew Levy focused more on the series' violence than on the books' relatively tame—though often suggestively sadistic—sexual content. *Burke v. Kingsley Books*, 142 N.Y.S.2d 735 (N.Y. Sup. Ct. 1955).
    160. Judge Jerome Frank of the Second Circuit Court of Appeals wrote a concurring opinion sustaining Roth's conviction as a matter of law, but adding that he thought the conviction unjust. Frank argued

stand in the form in which they are written. There might be a narrow ground, and I might change. I would reverse all three convictions.

FRANKFURTER: *I would sustain all three.* The idea that these laws are no good because you can't frame a definition of "obscene" to meet all notions of people's varying tastes, etc., is nonsense. Obscenity is an adequate phrase. The Fourteenth Amendment is similarly vague and that is O.K. I don't propose to define it, and I don't rest on any formula. The clear and present danger test is not an escape. The mystery arose because of Coburn's [*sic*] opinion.[161] Three opinions—*Kennerly,*[162] *Ulysses,*[163] and *Levine*—[164] these three cases

---

that obscenity was constitutionally protected speech but that "filthy" materials could be regulated by adapting the clear and present danger test and using breach of the peace statutes to limit its availability. He noted that many of the founding fathers enjoyed (and, in Ben Franklin's case, wrote) books that would have violated the obscenity laws challenged here. *United States v. Roth,* 237 F.2d 796 (2nd Cir. 1956).

161. Lord Cockburn laid down the first "modern" test of obscenity in *Regina v. Hicklin,* 3 L.R.—Q.B. 360, 371 (1868): "Whether the tendency of the matter charged as obscenity is to deprave and corrupt those whose minds are open to such immoral influences and into whose hands a publication of this sort may fall."

162. *United States v. Kennerly,* 209 F. 119 (1913). While Learned Hand felt constrained to follow *Regina v. Hicklin,* he sharply criticized Lord Cockburn's test: "The rule as laid down, however consonant it may be with mid-Victorian morals, does not seem to me to answer to the understanding and morality of the present time, as conveyed by the words, 'obscene, lewd, or lascivious.' I question whether in the end men will regard that as obscene which is honestly relevant to the adequate expression of innocent ideas, and whether they will not believe that truth and beauty are too precious to society at large to be mutilated in the interests of those most likely to pervert them to base uses. Indeed, it seems hardly likely that we are even to-day so lukewarm in our interest in letters or serious discussion as to be content to reduce our treatment of sex to the standard of a child's library in the supposed interest of a salacious few, or that shame will for long prevent us from adequate portrayal of some of the most serious and beautiful sides of human nature." Hand endorsed using juries to decide whether a work was obscene: "If there be no abstract definition, such as I have suggested, should not the word 'obscene' be allowed to indicate the present critical point in the compromise between candor and shame at which the community may have arrived here and now? If letters must, like other kinds of conduct, be subject to the social sense of what is right, it would seem that a jury should in each case establish the standard much as they do in cases of negligence. To put thought in leash to the average conscience of the time is perhaps tolerable, but to fetter it by the necessities of the lowest and least capable seems a fatal policy."

163. *United States v. One Book Entitled* Ulysses *by James Joyce,* 72 F.2d 705 (1934). In a prearranged test case, American customs agents seized a shipment of James Joyce's *Ulysses* on the ground that the book violated §305(a) of the Tariff Act of 1930, which prohibited the importation into the United States of any obscene material. Random House, the American publisher, denied that the book was obscene. The trial judge, John Woolsey, repudiated *Regina v. Hicklin* and found that the book, taken as a whole, "did not tend to excite sexual impulses or lustful thoughts but that its net effect was only that of a somewhat tragic and very powerful commentary on the inner lives of men and women." He dismissed the government's libel for forfeiture.

On appeal, Judge Augustus Hand tipped his judgment in framing the question: "The question before us is whether such a book of artistic merit and scientific insight should be regarded as 'obscene.'" While Hand acknowledged that some passages, considered in isolation, might be judged obscene "in the administration of statutes aimed at the suppression of immoral books, standard works of literature have not been barred merely because they contained some obscene passages, and that confiscation for such a reason would destroy much that is precious in order to benefit a few." In Hand's judgment, the proper test was to judge the dominant effect of the book, balancing its established critical reputation against its tendency to promote lust.

164. *United States v. Levine,* 83 F.2d 156 (1936). A New York jury convicted Levine of circulating an obscene advertisement promoting five books, including *Secret Museum of Anthropology, Crossways of Sex,*

have all the wisdom on obscenity. On the clear and present danger test, Brandeis says that it is a rule of reason—it can be applied correctly only on common sense. Pornography can't be protected. If free speech is absolute, you can't protect even children. As to *Kingsley*, there is no censorship. In New York, if the state finds only four pages bad and condemns all, it might be different. This is not like the *Near* case—it is more like a descendent of the common law.[165] The New York statute only says that after a determination of obscenity, a judge can enjoin the instruments of the crime. Pending a determination of the issue of obscenity, the book must be held up.

DOUGLAS: I have three questions: (1) Is the definition of *obscene* adequate, and what does it mean? Is there an adequate standard? (2) How is it applied? The correct standard is to judge the book as a whole. (3) How do you charge the jury? California said that the standard was excitation of lustful thoughts or sexual impulses according to the common conscience of community. In New York, the difficulty is with the definition. We should put tight reins on the judges' instructions. I have read hundreds of cases in this field. The standard of these cases is dangerous, and is not consistent with the First Amendment. It should be closer to the border of excitement. I would reverse both criminal convictions. I am not ready on the New York case. There is a lot in what Felix says—the material is concededly obscene. Can New York collect these books and condemn them? Intolerance is at a new peak. Druggists have adopted a formal resolution condemning books, following the lists provided by the National Organization for Decent Literature.[166]

BURTON: I would affirm all three decisions. We have here the hard core of obscenity. I am in favor of the confiscation of condemned books.

CLARK: I would affirm *California* and *Roth*, and also *Kingsley*.[167]

HARLAN: In *Kingsley*, there was no prior restraint. That was the mere taking of property shown to be obscene. On *Alberts* and *Roth*, I am close to Bill Douglas's position. The states

---

and *Black Lust*. The first included "nude female savages of different parts of the world"; the second claimed to be a scientific treatise on sexual pathology; and the third was an erotic novel about the adventures of an English girl captured by the Dervishes after the fall of Khartoum. Learned Hand thought that the scientific pretensions of the first two books were "extremely tenuous," although they could not reasonably be considered obscene. He found the third book to be "of considerable merit" but acknowledged that it was "patently erotic . . . and would arouse libidinous feelings in almost any reader." In reversing, Hand criticized the trial judge for following *Regina v. Hicklin* in charging the jury and established that the test involved the dominant effect that the material had on the average person in the community.

165. *Near v. Minnesota*, 283 U.S. 697 (1931).

166. The National Organization for Decent Literature (NODL) was a Catholic group that sought to ban books they considered inappropriate for decent people to read—including works by Faulkner, Hemingway, Zola, and others. The group often objected to books based solely on the cover art, proving that some people can judge a book by its cover. NODL published lists of disapproved books, inspected bookstores, and asked booksellers to remove listed books. If the store was pronounced "clean," the owner was allowed to display a NODL-approved certificate in the shop window.

167. Prior to oral arguments, the Justice Department shipped to the Court several boxes of pornography unrelated to the case, as evidence of what might happen if the Court overturned these convictions. Clark and Douglas took some of the material into the courtroom and passed it around on the bench during oral argument, but no one in the gallery noticed. Eisler, *A Justice for All*, 142.

have a wider field in defining obscenity than the federal government. The problem is a local one. I would give the states broad leeway. As to the federal government, the United States has a control with a wider impact than one state. I would hold the federal government to stricter standard. I am inclined to sustain the California law.

In the federal case, Roth could have been tried under the federal purveyor statute, making it a crime to hold one's self out as a purveyor (Roth's use of the mails was not mentioned). The stuff is very thin in *Roth*. It's cheap—there is nothing approaching the hard core of obscenity. I agree with Bill Douglas that the charge was bad in this case. I am troubled by the conventional charge to the jury, and I would reverse on the federal case on the basis of the judge's charge. The advertisements furnish the easiest basis for conviction, but they were not the basis of the jury charge.

BRENNAN: Obscenity is outside the protection of the First Amendment. None of these statutes are too vague. Obscenity should be reached only by criminal laws. The test should be the "dominant note" test. The place for judges is before it goes to the jury, as to whether the "dominant note" is sufficient for a jury question. If there is a jury question, then let the jury decide. I would reverse the New York civil case decision. As far as the jury questions are concerned, I can't quarrel with the judge's charge. In the New York case, the procedure is bad because it eliminates the essential step a jury determination in the trial of first instance. I do not like it to be left to a judge. There should be a jury, but even if a jury is afforded, the law is still bad. I would allow a criminal action only, with a jury.[168]

WHITTAKER: Smut is not protected by the First Amendment. Both the states and the federal government must have the right to control this. As to the question of vagueness, the term "obscene" is sufficiently concrete; there is no definition that is exact. We should resolve it by the common sense of community. *I would affirm* all three. In the New York case, the only question is prior restraint—all that happens is pendente lite. I would affirm that decision, if possible.

STEWART: This was a most amazing discussion. Those who affirm in *Alberts* and *Roth* never mentioned once what the standard for obscenity is, or what standard would (and what would not) be compatible with the First Amendment. It was merely stated that smut could be suppressed, but the definition of smut was not attempted. I was the only one who advanced a suggestion on a definition. I said that it was not constitutional to ban literature merely because it produced lustful thoughts. That the words had to be close to action, and that some measurement in terms of conduct had to be made.

WHITTAKER: I affirm all three. No expert. It is fundamental that the state and federal governments must have the power. Obscenity is not protected by the First Amendment. The laws are not *too* vague.

---

168. When Brennan's father was director of public safety in Newark, New Jersey, he tried to prevent the showing of a government-approved sex-education film, *The Naked Truth*, in a local theater. William Brennan Sr. was overruled by the city council, and the episode became a legal case that Bill Brennan Jr. later studied—much to his amusement—at Harvard. Eisler, *A Justice for All*, 26–29.

BRENNAN: I affirm in California and the federal case and *reverse* in New York.

HARLAN: I affirm in California and the federal case [*sic*], and *reverse* in the federal case.[169]

CLARK: I affirm all three.

BURTON: I affirm all three.

DOUGLAS: I reverse on two, and *pass* on New York?[170]

FRANKFURTER: I affirm all three.

BLACK: I reverse all three.

WARREN: I *affirm* in California and the federal case, and *reverse* in New York

Result: In upholding all three statutes, the Court ruled that obscenity was not speech and was not protected by the First Amendment. William Brennan, writing for the majority, defined obscenity as: (1) whether to the average person applying contemporary community standards, (2) the dominant theme of the material, (3) taken as a whole, (4) appealed to the prurient interest. The wording of both the federal and California statutes were deemed close enough to satisfy the test. As for Nights of Horror, *the Court held that the trial judge's ruling was not a prior restraint because the comic had been published before it was seized and destroyed.*

John Marshall Harlan agreed with the state convictions because he thought that state governments should be permitted considerable latitude to regulate or outlaw pornography. He dissented and voted to overturn Roth's *federal conviction because he thought that the federal government had no such broad police powers. For Harlan, the thought that residents of some states would not be allowed to read certain books and magazines was acceptable, but the idea "that no person in the United States should be allowed to do so seems . . . intolerable." Black and Douglas dissented in all three cases on the ground that the First Amendment protected* all *speech, even—perhaps especially—speech that a majority of Supreme Court Justices found to be objectionable. Samuel Roth went to prison at Lewisburg, Pennsylvania, where he died five years later at age sixty-seven.*

Jacobellis v. Ohio, 378 U.S. 184 (1964)
(Douglas)

Nico Jacobellis, the manager of a movie theater in Cleveland Heights, was convicted under Ohio's obscenity statute for exhibiting an art-house French film, Les Amants (The Lovers). *The state supreme court affirmed.*

---

169. Clark was mistaken with regard to Harlan's vote. Harlan voted to affirm in the two state cases and voted to reverse in the federal case.

170. Clark listed Douglas as passing on *Kingsley* in conference, but Douglas listed himself as voting to reverse.

Conference of April 3, 1964

WARREN: In the county where I was raised, only the "Douglas Test" was used.[171] As respects *Roth*, I stand by it as we don't know how to do better by any other test.[172] When a court applies *Roth* I would sustain the result unless there was no evidence. It is impossible to have a national standard that will produce an even result on any one book. I think that it is terrible to peddle this stuff to school children. I affirm.

BLACK: This country was raised on the idea that sex is taboo. I do not think that these things can be stopped. I have seen these kinds of things since I was six years old. Sex will not destroy the nation. Training youngsters how not to have children is important. *Roth* would ban *For Whom the Bell Tolls*. I reverse.[173]

DOUGLAS: I would reverse on *Roth*.

CLARK: I affirm on *Roth*, like the Chief.

HARLAN: I affirm. If a test has to be verbalized, *Roth* is as good as any. But it is impossible to verbalize it. This is the type of thing that has as a test only the offense to one's taste or mind. *Roth* goes for "community" standards, not national standards. I can't allow a book to be condemned in one state and cleared in another, both claiming to follow *Roth*. There should either be a national standard or separate state standards. In the federal field, I would go almost as far as Hugo and Bill Douglas. In the state field, I would give the states great flexibility. This picture, compared with *Lady Chatterley's Lover*, is insipid. States should be given great leeway in the field.

BRENNAN: What John says is powerful, if the First Amendment means something different for states than for the federal government. I once thought that *Roth* could be rewritten, but now I think otherwise. The "no evidence" case is one exception. The judge's charge to jury included the very words of *Roth*—the judge gave a trial without fault. Yet I must reverse, for this is a weak case. I could not let *Tropic of Cancer* be held good in California and bad in New York. We must choose which is correct. If #449 had been a criminal prosecution, I would affirm.[174] If *Tropic of Cancer* had resulted in a conviction,

---

171. The meaning of this comment is not entirely clear. Warren grew up in the rough-and-tumble town of Bakersfield, in Kern County, California. As the railroad and agricultural center of the southern Central Valley, Bakersfield had more than its share of bordellos and adult entertainment, and the town generally took a libertarian approach to such matters. Warren might have been joking that Bakersfield anticipated William O. Douglas's laissez-faire views about sex and obscenity.

172. *Roth v. United States* and *Alberts v. California*, 354 U.S. 476 (1957).

173. Unlike many of his brethren, Hugo Black held himself to a stricter standard of propriety than he sought to impose on the rest of the country. He was something of a prude and once refused to see the Liz Taylor–Richard Burton movie *Who's Afraid of Virginia Woolf* because "he heard it was filthy." Hugo and Elizabeth Black, *Mr. Justice and Mrs. Black*, 148.

174. *A Quantity of Copies of Books v. Kansas*, 378 U.S. 205 (1964). More than 1,300 copies of allegedly obscene books were seized without a prior adversarial hearing. Following the seizure there was a hearing, at the conclusion of which the judge ruled that the materials were obscene and ordered them destroyed. The state supreme court affirmed but the U.S. Supreme Court reversed, ruling that the absence of a pre-seizure adversarial hearing amounted to an unconstitutional prior restraint.

I would reverse. I go on a "constitutional hunch" in these cases, and I do not fear to act as a censor at the level of this Court. I reverse.

STEWART: I have about concluded that in the area of the First and Fourteenth Amendments, all a person could be convicted of is hard core pornography. This is not that. I reverse.

WHITE: I would reverse on the merits, based on *Roth*. This is not hard core pornography. I would reach the Chief's result by denying cert in these cases.

GOLDBERG: The First and Fourteenth Amendments do not protect obscenity. I would draw the line at hard core pornography. I would apply a national standard. This movie cannot be condemned by that standard. I saw it, and it is innocuous. If material is purveyed as pornography, I will not vote to reverse the book or movie. But if it has literary merit, as does *Tropic of Cancer*, I would reverse.

Result: The Supreme Court voted 6–3 to overturn Jacobellis's conviction, but the majority was deeply divided as to their reasons and standards. There were five different opinions by members of the majority, and no opinion garnered more than two votes. In his famous concurrence, Potter Stewart argued that only hard-core pornography could be prohibited. He bluntly admitted that he could not define obscenity, "But I know it when I see it, and the motion picture involved in this case is not that." Warren dissented, arguing that the Court should stick with the Roth *test, at least until a better definition could be devised.*

Stanley v. Georgia, 394 U.S. 557 (1969)
(Douglas) (Brennan)

Police served a search warrant at Robert Stanley's home to look for gambling materials. Instead, they found three reels of pornographic movies. After watching the movies for several hours in Stanley's home, police decided that the films were obscene and arrested him for knowingly possessing obscene matter. The Georgia Supreme Court affirmed.

Conference of January 17, 1969

WARREN: I would reverse on the lack of evidence to prove scienter. There is no evidence that the petitioner even knew what was in the films.

BLACK: Possession can't be made a crime in this field. I would reverse.

DOUGLAS: Reverses.

HARLAN: I would reverse on possession. States can't enact this kind of law. A state can't make a crime out of what an individual draws or paints in the privacy of his own room.

BRENNAN: I would reverse on scienter. I would be willing to go on possession, although I have trouble bringing possession into the First Amendment.

STEWART: There is a Fourth Amendment violation at the threshold of this case that can support a reversal. This was not contraband that they took. The seizure was unlawful—they can't go open locked cases in the desk drawer. I reverse. I have difficulty on possession or scienter. I think that there was circumstantial evidence sufficient to prove scienter. Assuming that this is hard-core pornography, I would go on the Fourth Amendment.

WHITE: I would reverse on both Fourth Amendment and scienter grounds.

FORTAS: I reverse. The possession issue is here. My favorite ground is that a man can possess anything not lethal, at least without proof that he is going to distribute or commercialize it.

MARSHALL: I reverse.

Result: After concentrating on the issue of scienter in conference, the Court decided follow John Marshall Harlan's tentative idea and ruled that the First and Fourteenth Amendments prohibited the proscription of mere private possession of obscene materials in one's own home. This case was one of Thurgood Marshall's most famous opinions and one of his proudest moments on the Court. Black, Brennan, Stewart, and White all concurred in the result but did not join Marshall's opinion.

Kaplan v. California, 413 U.S. 115 (1973)
(Douglas)

Murray Kaplan owned the Peek-A-Boo adult bookstore in Los Angeles. When he saw a man thumbing through the magazines, Kaplan reminded him that the shop "was not a lending library." The man asked Kaplan for a "good, sexy book." Kaplan offered a book not on public display, Suite 69, *a plain-cover book that contained explicit descriptions of sex but had no pictures. The customer was an undercover police officer, who arrested Kaplan for selling obscene materials.*

Conference of October 24, 1972

BURGER: These cases cannot be resolved until the one yet to be reargued is also heard.[175] I am not prepared to vote. I believe, however, that a state has as much control over obscene publications as it has over the environment, garbage, and so forth.

DOUGLAS: I reverse. You must pass a constitutional amendment on obscenity, as there is no power to regulate it under the First Amendment.

BRENNAN: I agree with Bill Douglas that the English Commission's report is not relevant here, because we have a First Amendment.[176] *Roth* established that all erotic expressions have complete First Amendment protection unless it is "obscene."[177] *Redrup*—which was unanimous—makes it necessary for this Court to make judgments on particularized applications.[178] While the Court had a majority in *Roth,* never since then has the Court agreed on a set of fact in applying *Roth. Redrup* was a compromise. We reversed thirty-one judgments with *Redrup.* I think that *Redrup* was unwise. I did not join *Stanley,* be-

---

175. *Miller v. California,* 413 U.S. 15 (1973).

176. Brennan was probably referring to the Select Committee of the House of Commons on the Obscene Publications Bill of 1958, whose report led to the Obscene Publications Act of 1959. This act modestly liberalized British obscenity laws, although the government retained broad powers to regulate pornographic and indecent materials far beyond what *Roth* allowed in the United States.

177. *Roth v. United States,* 354 U.S. 476 (1957).

178. *Redrup v. New York,* 386 U.S. 767 (1967).

cause I thought *Roth* covered the suppression of all obscenity.[179] I am now prepared to accept *Stanley* and to apply it to incoming cases. I now think that a consenting adult's right to read anything he wants wisely limits the power of government to act. The government can protect distribution to minors. Any notice requirement must be explicit to include pictures of nudes if it unites action and all hard-core pornography, fellatio, cunnilingus, etc. Marketing methods would have to be restricted. The aim is to protect nonconsenting adults and juveniles. I would let this state fix the age of juveniles. I would not bar the government from prohibiting live shows even for consenting adults—that is conduct, which Bill Douglas says the federal government could control in his *Roth* dissent. I am thinking of hard core live shows, which could be seen in movies, but not in the flesh. Juveniles have 1st Amendment rights. Yet in the sexual area, *Ginzburg* recognizes that they do not have the power to make considered judgments in check.[180] What John Harlan said in *Jacobellis* is O.K. with me.[181]

STEWART: I think that live shows are protected by the First Amendment. But that problem is not involved here. The First Amendment was made applicable against state action. I do not agree with the Harlan view that the First Amendment as applied to the states is not the same as when applied to the federal government. Only if we reversed a long line of cases could we go with the Chief Justice on putting obscenity in the same category as garbage and the like. *Prince v. Massachusetts* holds that the state has special power to control juveniles.[182] Juveniles are not able to make free choices. The *Pollak* case recognizes that the state has the power to protect captive audiences.[183] *Roth* was an abstract definition. I end up about where Bill Brennan does, but by a slightly different route. I am not quite ready to vote.

---

179. *Stanley v. Georgia*, 394 U.S. 557 (1969).

180. *Ginzburg v. United States*, 383 U.S. 463 (1966).

181. Harlan argued in favor of allowing states greater latitude to deal with obscenity than the federal government, holding the federal government with a "tight rein" while allowing states "wide, but not federally unrestricted" latitude in dealing with obscene materials. Harlan subsequently favored applying the *Roth* standard to the federal government and using a rational basis/reasonableness test to judge state obscenity laws. He thought that this dual standard would allow state and federal governments—and the courts— latitude to strike a sensible balance between censorship and free expression. *Jacobellis v. Ohio*, 378 U.S. 184 (1964).

182. *Prince v. Massachusetts*, 321 U.S. 158 (1944). The Court upheld Sarah Prince's conviction after she allowed her nine-year-old niece to distribute Jehovah's Witnesses religious literature door to door in violation of state child labor laws. The Court said that government had a duty to protect children from some activities that adults may freely choose to do.

183. *Public Utilities Commission v. Pollak*, 343 U.S. 451 (1952). Franklin Pollak sued to stop Washington, D.C., from broadcasting government-approved radio programs on public buses. Pollak claimed that the First Amendment protected captive audiences from such intrusions. The Court rejected Pollak's argument but acknowledged that forcing captive audiences to listen to unwanted messages raised constitutional concerns, particularly if the messages involved political propaganda. Douglas dissented, arguing that the First Amendment prevented the government from broadcasting *any* form of officially sanctioned programming to captive audiences.

WHITE: Obscenity does not deserve the attention we or the country give it. If I were a legislator, I would do away with obscenity laws. As a judge, I see no more than a marginal First Amendment interest in what is published. So I would let the states have their own way. There is a national standard in our review. But I would let juries apply their own standards. I would prefer to stick with the *Roth* idea. But I am not much concerned with which way we go on the problem.

MARSHALL: I will go along with Bill Brennan. A city can reach a theater in various ways, including revoking its license. States can handle juveniles. They can control live shows. If those shows continue at a particular place, the place can be closed down as a nuisance.

WHITE: I would not overrule *Roth*. I would keep it, and add Brennan's new formula on distribution to consenting adults.

BLACKMUN: The First Amendment is not absolute. I can't say that the standard is national. As a practical matter, the local standard applies. Local standards, and some evidence of redeeming social values, are relevant. Consenting adults can consume all the erotic literature they desire. *Suite 69* does not deserve easy access by anyone. I would allow states to go to age 21 in defining juveniles. I am intrigued by the idea of privacy. We can live with *Roth*. I am not at rest. I would like to see more unity on this issue.

POWELL: Obscenity cases are brand new to me. What I read and see shocks me in this field. I will not go with Bill Brennan. That view would practically eliminate state or federal control of obscenity. I am closer to the Chief Justice's formulation of the solution. I am bothered by the vagueness problem. Perhaps an administrative procedure could be devised in advance of a criminal prosecution. I am not at rest, and will not vote today.

REHNQUIST: I could go along with the Chief Justice. In *Gitlow*, Holmes said that the First Amendment did not apply with full force to the states.[184] States were supposed to have very substantial authority over morals. [DOUGLAS: He apparently overlooks the force of the Fourteenth Amendment.] I would reaffirm *Roth*. The kind of people who are now

---

184. *Gitlow v. New York*, 268 U.S. 652 (1925). The Court upheld Benjamin Gitlow's conviction for violating New York's criminal syndicalism act. Holmes argued in dissent that the law violated the First Amendment: "The general principle of free speech, it seems to me, must be taken to be included in the Fourteenth Amendment, in view of the scope that has been given to the word 'liberty' as there used, although perhaps it may be accepted with a somewhat larger latitude of interpretation than is allowed to Congress by the sweeping language that governs or ought to govern the laws of the United States." Holmes gave a broad reading to the First Amendment and sought to limit the scope of his own clear and present danger test: "If what I think the correct test is applied, it is manifest that there was no present danger of an attempt to overthrow the government by force on the part of the admittedly small minority who shared the defendant's views. It is said that this manifesto was more than a theory, that it was an incitement. Every idea is an incitement. It offers itself for belief and if believed it is acted on unless some other belief outweighs it or some failure of energy stifles the movement at its birth. The only difference between the expression of an opinion and an incitement in the narrower sense is the speaker's enthusiasm for the result. Eloquence may set fire to reason. But whatever may be thought of the redundant discourse before us it had no chance of starting a present conflagration. If in the long run the beliefs expressed in proletarian dictatorship are destined to be accepted by the dominant forces of the community, the only meaning of free speech is that they should be given their chance and have their way."

on the margin were not entitled to the protection of the First Amendment. I would not apply the same standard to the states as to federal prosecutions.

BURGER: The core definition of pornography would be my cutoff point.

BRENNAN: The new Oregon definition of obscenity goes too far.[185]

WHITE: I would not distinguish between adults and juveniles.

BURGER: Once a definition is made, then it can be eliminated as conduct. There is no difference between a movie and a live act. I will stay with most of *Roth*, except for the "redeeming value" theme.

Result: Chief Justice Burger, writing for a 5–4 majority, held that Kaplan could be prosecuted under state obscenity statutes. Acknowledging that after Roth *had been decided there had been only one case finding a book to be obscene, Burger said that books could still be judged obscene on the basis of text alone, even without pictures or other graphics.[186] The case was remanded to the state courts to determine whether the jury's verdict was consistent with the Court's new standard for obscenity announced in* Miller. *In dissent, Douglas voted to dismiss the criminal proceeding, while Brennan, Stewart, and Marshall were content to refer to their dissents in* Paris Adult Movie Theater I[187] *and* Miller.

Miller v. California, 413 U.S. 15 (1973)
(Douglas)

One sunny day in Newport Beach, California, a restaurant manager and his mother opened their mail together and saw an unsolicited, sexually explicit advertisement for a movie, Marital Intercourse, *and four books:* Intercourse, Man-Woman, Sex Orgies Illustrated, *and* An Illustrated History of Pornography. *The ads contained sexually explicit pictures with genitalia prominently displayed. They filed a complaint with state authorities. Marvin Miller—the man who distributed the advertisements—was arrested and convicted of violating California's obscenity law, which was modeled on Brennan's plurality opinion in* Memoirs of a Woman of Pleasure v. Massachusetts.[188]

---

185. Oregon's obscenity laws were fairly broad, prohibiting, for example, any public display of nudity or sexual content for advertising purposes. After *Miller*, the state legislature passed a more narrowly drawn statute to match the Supreme Court's newly announced standard. The Oregon Supreme Court promptly struck the new law down as a violation of free expression under the state constitution. *Oregon v. Henry*, 732 P.2d 9 (1987).

186. The case was *Mishkin v. New York*, 383 U.S. 502 (1966), a Brennan opinion that affirmed an obscenity conviction involving illustrated books.

187. *Paris Adult Movie Theater I v. Slaton*, 413 U.S. 49 (1973).

188. *A Book Named* John Cleland's Memoirs of a Woman of Pleasure *v. Massachusetts*, 383 U.S. 413 (1966). This case established a narrow definition of obscenity, where the state had to prove independently each of three elements before a book could be found obscene: (1) the dominant theme of the material taken as a whole appealed to a prurient interest in sex; (2) the material was patently offensive because it affronted contemporary community standards relating to the description or representation of sexual matters; and (3) the material was utterly without redeeming social value. The last qualification proved to be an almost impossible burden for state prosecutors to meet, as it allowed otherwise obscene movies to escape prosecution by including, for example, bits of Shakespeare scattered among the action.

The Court had been wrestling with the definition of obscenity since Roth *in 1957.*[189] *With* Redrup v. New York, *the Justices basically agreed to disagree and began deciding pornography cases on a case-by-case basis, with each Justice using his own personal definition of obscenity.*[190] Miller *represented a new opportunity for the Chief Justice to forge a new, authoritative definition of obscenity. Among the issues discussed in conference were whether the definition of obscenity should be decided according to local tastes or whether there should be a uniform national standard.*

Conference of January 21, 1972

BURGER: Miller was convicted in a jury trial. The material is obscene. The jury was instructed under *Roth* and *Memoirs.* There was no objection to the state standard. No evidence was presented on national standards. The jury is the keeper of the community's conscience. This is a hard-core pornography case. There cannot be a national standard. I affirm. We should leave it to the states. I would affirm that this must be treated like a nuisance.

DOUGLAS: I reverse. The statute is vague for vagueness [*sic*].

BRENNAN: *Roth* dealt with vagueness. *Redrup* was the main precedent for other cases; it was where a civil case was first decided. The government is the case—I was interested in the idea of requiring a civil decision prior to a criminal case. On national standards, I am for it—as in *Jacobellis.*[191] Here, the state standards were not objected to. Here, there are advertisements showing hard core pornography. This is obscene under national standards, so it is harmless error not to give an instruction on that score. I affirm.

STEWART: I pass. I did not hear the oral argument.

WHITE: I affirm. The national versus local standards is a straw man. When we come to our own decisions on obscenity, we decide on the basis of what the juries find. There is not much dispute over what is obscene.

MARSHALL: This is obscene no matter what standard is used. I affirm.

BLACKMUN: I affirm. On the merits, I am against national standards. Moreover, it assumes incorporation of the First Amendment in the Fourteenth Amendment.

POWELL: I affirm. This field is mysterious to me, and I am not sure where in time I will end up. *Roth* governs here.

REHNQUIST: The issue of national standards was not raised, but I affirm.

Conference of November 10, 1972

DOUGLAS: These and the other obscenity cases on today's list were not discussed, as Brennan is writing on this whole group of obscenity cases.

---

189. *Roth v. New York and Alberts v. California,* 354 U.S. 476 (1957).
190. *Redrup v. New York,* 386 U.S. 767 (1967).
191. *Jacobellis v. Ohio,* 378 U.S. 184 (1964).

Result: In a 5–4 decision, the Court resurrected the Roth *definition of obscenity, with some subtle modifications. Burger's majority opinion rejected the more lenient* Memoirs *standard (requiring that a work be utterly without redeeming social value before it could be banned) and allowed juries to define prurient appeal and patent offensiveness by the standards of the "forum community."* Miller *established a three-pronged test: (1) whether the average person, applying contemporary community standards, would find that the work, taken as a whole, appealed to the prurient interest; (2) whether the work depicted or described, in a patently offensive way, sexual conduct specifically defined by state law; and (3) whether the work, taken as a whole, lacked serious literary, artistic, political, or scientific value.*

Ironically, the decision to restore an updated version of Roth *came over the original author's objection. Brennan dissented and publicly renounced his old definition as untenable. In a later interview he said, "I put sixteen years into that damn obscenity thing. . . . I tried and I tried, and I waffled back and forth, and I finally gave up. If you can't define it, you can't prosecute people for it."*[192] *But Brennan was now in the minority.*

Young v. American Mini-Theatres, 427 U.S. 50 (1976)
(Brennan)

Two Detroit zoning ordinances were amended in 1972 to prohibit adult theaters from being located within one thousand feet of any two other regulated uses, or within five hundred feet of a residential area.[193] *The owners of a small chain of mini-theaters (theaters with fewer than fifty seats) claimed that the ordinances' definition of adult movies and the procedures required to seek a zoning waiver were unconstitutionally vague.*[194] *The district court upheld the ordinances, but the court of appeals reversed, finding that the laws were an invalid prior restraint on constitutionally protected expression and that classifying theaters on the basis of film content violated the equal protection clause of the Fourteenth Amendment.*

BURGER: This is a time, place, and manner regulation.

STEWART: This ordinance depends, finally, on prohibiting content—and this only arguendo.

WHITE: Accepting *Erznoznik* I may have to affirm, but I am going to fight hard to reverse.[195]

BLACKMUN: I don't think that this is a time, place, or manner case. It is a vagueness 1st Amendment case.

POWELL: I am about where Byron is. I view this as simply a zoning case—inverse zoning, creating restricted uses. I can't say that the 1972 amendment was anything but an

---

192. Hentoff, "The Constitutionalist," *New Yorker*, Mar. 12, 1990, 56.

193. Under the ordinance, "regulated uses" included ten listed types of businesses, including adult bookstores, bars, cabarets, and hotels.

194. The ordinance banned showing proscribed "sexual activities" or "specified anatomical areas" and included specific examples of banned activities and anatomical areas.

195. *Erznoznik v. City of Jacksonville*, 422 U.S. 205 (1975).

enlargement of land use regulations. Only theaters are involved here. The state interest is compelling, because few problems are more serious than urban decay. This is a "place" regulation, I think.

REHNQUIST: This is a regulation based on content, but government can regulate where there is a clear and present danger of something that the state can prohibit.

STEVENS: I don't think that there is any suppression of ideas, so the city can do this. Vagueness and overbreadth are inapplicable here, except as to the parties before the Court. I don't think that there is any kind of expression here—not having a criminal statute here—for overbreadth analysis.

Result: The Court ruled 5–4 that the ordinances were constitutional. John Paul Stevens, writing for the majority, characterized the ordinances as nothing more than standard, routine components of city planning and zoning.

New York v. Ferber, 458 U.S. 747 (1982)
(Brennan)

A New York law prohibited the distribution of any materials depicting a sexual performance by a child under the age of sixteen. The statute contained a list of examples of proscribed sexual performances and conduct, including: real or simulated intercourse, masturbation, and the lewd exhibition of genitals. Paul Ferber, a bookstore owner, was convicted for selling films of young boys engaged in sexual performances. The New York Court of Appeals reversed his conviction on the ground that the state statute was both underinclusive and overbroad. Among other things, the court said, the statute did not contain an adequate definition or standard of obscenity, and the law's language was so sweeping that it could be used to suppress material clearly protected by the First Amendment.

BURGER: Traditional obscenity statutes do not apply to children. The state here is trying to prevent children from being used as performers, and that injury flowing from a minor's appearance risking identification later in life. Holding that only obscenity can be reached is wrong. The First Amendment claim here is frivolous. The statute is not overbroad.

BRENNAN:[196] I find this to be a most difficult case. I do agree with the premise of the petitioners: that they may regulate, beyond the boundaries of obscenity, in order to protect *children* as *participants* in the production of sexual materials. I also agree that this regulation need not necessarily be limited to prohibition of the actual use of a child as a sexual performer, where the legislature has found that such prohibitions are ineffectual to stop the clandestine production of movies involving children. But surely in this sensitive area, where the state is clearly regulating non-obscene and therefore protected expression, precision of regulation is the key.

---

196. Adapted from Brennan's talking papers, Brennan Papers, OT 1981, box 597.

We are bound by the state court's construction of this statute, and under that construction, I find the statute to be substantially overbroad. According to the state court, the statute would prohibit the sale, showing, or distribution of medical or education materials containing photographs of a child "portraying a defined sexual act, real or simulated, in a non-obscene manner." The production of such materials, depending upon how they were gathered, may or may not have been harmful to the children depicted. Moreover, according to the New York Court, the statute would cover a filmed report of New Guinea fertility rites, a performance clearly not harmful to the children depicted. This is in my view, a sufficient amount of protected expression, for which the state lacks any compelling justification in suppression, to render the statute invalid on this facial attack. My vote is to affirm the New York Court of Appeals.

WHITE: The state's definition of "sexual performance" limits the statute to "lewd" exhibition of genitals. The court of appeals wholly ignored this, and gave this provision a meaning that was far wider than it is written. Is it "substantially" overbroad? If four others will say that the state court's construction of this law reaches *National Geographic*, I would agree that it should be stricken down. If the law's overbreadth can be limited or abandoned, I would save it.

MARSHALL: I am closer to Byron and to Bill Brennan in affirming.

BLACKMUN: States may have broad regulatory statutes. But it is what the court of appeals did to this statute that creates the problem. Their construction requires affirmance, but if someone can find a way to reverse, I'll do it.

POWELL: Confirming the court of appeals opinion leaves us free to construe the statute. I could anyway go with Byron to say that the overbreadth doctrine is not served here by accepting the lower court's obviously erroneous reading of this statute. I can't say that a "compelling interest" analysis was followed. I would reverse.

REHNQUIST: I don't really know how the court of appeals construed the statute—that it couldn't reach anything other than what is obscene. On overbreadth, I would cut back on our use of the overbreadth doctrine in this kind of case. The people who distribute *National Geographic* would not be deterred by this law.

STEVENS: Everyone seemed to assume that the state could not require the identity of the publisher. I don't agree with that. The court of appeals opinion is not clear, but I read it to say that the statute applies to educational and other materials clearly protected by the 1st Amendment. In *Mini-Theatres*, the overbreadth doctrine was made doubtful, but that was civil case.[197] This is a criminal statute, and I am not ready to cut back here.

O'CONNOR: Didn't the court of appeals apply the wrong test in not requiring a compelling state interest analysis? I would scuttle overbreadth if there is a Court to do it.

197. *Young v. American Mini-Theatres*, 427 U.S. 50 (1976).

Result: The Court ruled 5–4–0 that the New York statute was neither underinclusive nor overbroad. The societal value of pornographic depictions of children, Byron White said, was "exceedingly modest, if not de minimis."[198] States were therefore entitled to more leeway to proscribe sexual depictions of children than would be permissible with other forms of pornography. Brennan, Marshall, Stevens, and Blackmun concurred in the result but did not join White's majority opinion. There were no dissents.

198. White's vote remained uncertain after the conference. After he initially passed at conference, Brennan marked White as voting to affirm, then erased it and marked him as voting to reverse, adding this note: "BRW gets opinion to try to write not 'substantially overbroad' because not really deterring of *National Geographic*." In his concurring opinion, Brennan was careful to maintain that the First Amendment protected depictions of naked children if the work had serious literary, artistic, scientific, or medical value.

CHAPTER 10

A FREE PRESS

PRIOR RESTRAINTS

New York Times v. United States, 403 U.S. 713 (1971)
(Douglas)

The New York Times *and* Washington Post *sought to publish* The Pentagon Papers, *a collection of classified material on American policy in Vietnam. The government tried to enjoin publication, claiming a threat to national security if the papers were made public. The Second Circuit Court of Appeals granted the injunction against the Times, but the Circuit Court of Appeals for the District of Columbia refused to enjoin the* Post. *The Supreme Court granted expedited review at what Burger termed a "feverish" pace, hearing oral arguments less than two days after the circuit courts entered their judgments.*[1]

Conference of June 26, 1971

—Motion for a limited in camera hearing: Yes: Harlan, Blackmun, Burger. No: Black, Douglas, Brennan, White, Marshall, Stewart.

—Motion to allow the solicitor general to submit his argument in writing under seal, in camera: Yes: Burger, Harlan, White, Blackmun, Stewart. No: Black, Douglas, Brennan, Marshall.[2]

—Grant the motion of amicus to argue today—all vote "no."

—Black insisted that no notes be taken in this conference as they would be bound to leak out somewhere![3]

BURGER: Gesell's standard was invalid.[4] No judge on any of the cases knows the whole facts. These cases should not have been tried on the panic basis in which they were tried.

---

1. Because this was a petition for expedited review, five Justices had to vote to grant certiorari, rather than the usual four. Black, Douglas, Brennan and Marshall quickly voted to grant, and after some hesitation Stewart and White joined them. The latter two, however, joined Burger, Harlan, and Blackmun to continue the temporary restraining orders barring the *Times* and the *Post* from publishing.

2. Solicitor General Erwin N. Griswold submitted a secret brief containing eleven items that he claimed would pose a grave threat to national security if made public.

3. After the case was argued, Griswold met privately with Warren Burger and told him that there was a leak on the Court. The Chief Justice called a conference to discuss the allegation the day after the Court's judgment was announced, but nothing came of it. Hugo and Elizabeth Black, *Mr. Justice and Mrs. Black*, 266.

4. Gerhard Gesell was a district court judge for the District of Columbia. In refusing the government's request for an injunction against the *Post*, Judge Gesell ruled that disclosure would not cause any harm, or

I am unable to vote on the merits. We have been rushed in this case. If the *Times* and *Post* win, I will write at once, and more fully during the summer.

BLACK: I disagree with the Chief Justice. There are no questions of fact. We should not destroy the First Amendment by providing a "loitering" ordinance that is vague and loose. It is not a question of fact. It would be the worst blow to the First Amendment to enjoin these publications. The president has deluded the public on Vietnam. This is an abridgment of freedom of the press. I affirm in the *Post* case and reverse in the *Times* case.[5]

DOUGLAS: That is also my view.

HARLAN: I agree with the Chief Justice that the judicial process has been made a travesty. It has been panicky and hurried. We are at the heart of the democratic process. It is not a question of standards of "public security." What is the real case is the scope of judicial review over the executive branch. The lower courts are wrong. I would affirm the Second Circuit in the *Times* case. I accept its premise that there was not an adequate hearing in the district court. In the *Post* case, I reverse. The court of appeals should give proper judicial review. There is a broader review of executive actions here than we permit under the A Proc Act.[6] Judicial review is very, very limited. It goes no further than to determine if there is a classification procedure and if that classification has been followed. If that is not right, then the judiciary is in the business of determining what our national security standards are. From the small exposure I have had to these documents, I am convinced that the judicial role is very limited. There are many imponderables in national security, and only the judgment of men in the field can be relied upon. I want to read those documents. I will need the help of my law clerks, otherwise I will have to disqualify myself.[7] To write out my views will take time, and so I will file later.

BRENNAN: This prior restraint case comes here with a heavy burden on the United States. I agree with the district court below that the government has not met that burden. Can any injunction be effective? Many papers are publishing the chronicles. That is another reason for the defeat of United States. What the *St. Louis Post-Dispatch* printed today is

that any harm done would not be enough to justify an injunction. He proposed using the government's own standard for classifying top secret material, saying that he would consider an injunction if the government demonstrated that allowing publication would cause: (1) a break in diplomatic relations; (2) an armed attack on the United States or on an ally; (3) a war; (4) a compromise of military or defense plans; or (5) a compromise of intelligence operations. Gesell's proposal infuriated the government, which attacked his proposal at length in its appellate brief. The Supreme Court never settled the issue. Glendon, "The Pentagon Papers—Victory for a Free Press."

5. Alexander Bickel, one of Felix Frankfurter's former law clerks, argued the case on behalf of the *Times*. He argued narrowly, conceding that there were times when national security outweighed the rights of speech and press. Hugo Black was unimpressed and told his law clerks, "Too bad that the *New York Times* couldn't find someone who believes in the First Amendment." Ball, *Hugo L. Black*, 197.

6. Presumably the Administrative Procedure Act, which requires administrative agencies to follow established procedures in promulgating public policies, such as providing for public hearings and comment periods.

7. One of the key questions was whether the Justices' clerks would be permitted to see the classified documents. Harlan by this time was virtually blind and depended on his clerks to read to him.

what the United States asks us to enjoin the *Post* and *Times* from doing. What sense is there in restraining the *Post* and *Times* if the stuff is coming out elsewhere?[8] I do not agree with Hugo and Bill Douglas. The solicitor general's submission of the ten points is written in terms of "might" or "could," not "will." And *Near* requires the last.[9]

STEWART: The executive branch has great powers in foreign affairs. Secrecy is of great importance in many affairs—it is essential to State, Defense, and the White House. These powers are unreviewable. Where is the responsibility to enforce that structure? I would give the executive full power of secrecy. But the president has failed here. These documents are now in the hands of the press. It is now immaterial whether the material was classified and how—that would arise in a later criminal case. Any judicial order to a paper not to publish is presumptively contrary to the Constitution. The First Amendment is not an absolute. If I am satisfied that publication would result in immediate, grave, and irreparable harm to the United States or would result in the sentencing to death of one hundred young men, this Court, as a court of equity, would have the power to enjoin that sort of publication. Is there any such threat here? This is a history that ended in 1968—the presumption is that a history of that kind does not relate to future events. I have not finished with the cases, and I pass.

WHITE: I will probably vote against the United States in this case. It is a prior restraint case. The United States abandoned its original position that there is a violation of a criminal act here. I think that there was, and that it would be a sound basis for a decision. Prior restraint cases are rare. Here, much of the damage has already been done. The material is already out. There is not much substance to the federal claim that it must have a prior restraint. An injunction will not help here, though, because the damage has greatly been done already. The *New York Times*'s possessions are unauthorized, and they are criminally liable under §793(e) of 18 U.S.C. Section 798 is aimed at cryptographers—it concerns publishing intelligence activities of the United States. Some of these things do. I would reverse in the *Times* case and affirm on the *Post* decision. I would prefer that these cases not be disposed of on the merits for a few days.

MARSHALL: The chief executive has broad powers. I would protects his right to secrecy except to Congress. His power to classify is clear. The First Amendment, when it says "no law," applies to all three branches of government. The executive can't do what Congress can't do. He has no inherent power to stop the *Times* from printing. There is no act of Congress here. The president's "inherent" power is limited by the First Amendment. I am close to Hugo and Douglas on that point. I affirm the *Post* case and reverse on the *Times*.

---

8. At 2:30 P.M., while the conference was under way, clerks from Black's and Brennan's chambers passed word to the conference that the government had just obtained a temporary restraining order against the *Post-Dispatch*. Solicitor General Griswold had claimed in oral argument that no further injunctions would be needed beyond those already obtained against the *Times* and the *Post*. At this point the Justices realized that copies of *The Pentagon Papers* had been widely distributed and issuing further injunctions would be pointless. Schwartz, *The Ascent of Pragmatism*, 160–161.

9. *Near v. Minnesota*, 283 U.S. 697 (1931).

BLACKMUN: These two cases are here on a preliminary injunction, not after full hearings. I do not join Hugo and Bill Douglas on their interpretation of the First Amendment. There is nothing in the material about breaking our code. But there is dangerous material that will harm this nation. Publication is reprehensible, and I have nothing but contempt for the *Times*. We should unite on the criminal aspects of the problem. I affirm on the *Times*, but am veering toward the position that it is too late to do anything. I reverse on the *Post*.

STEWART: I am close to the position of Bill Brennan and Byron, but I am not ready to vote.

Result: In a per curiam decision written by William Brennan, a majority of six Justices agreed that the government could not impose a prior restraint on either newspaper. Otherwise the Court was badly divided, with no opinion receiving more than three votes. Of the six Justices in the majority, two thought that prior restraints could never be imposed (Black and Douglas), while four thought that they could be imposed temporarily under exceptional circumstances not present here (Brennan, Stewart, White, and Marshall). The three dissenters (Burger, Harlan, and Blackmun) backed the government's position to varying degrees and objected to the haste with which the cases were decided. Widely praised by civil libertarians at the time, this case has subsequently drawn criticism as "the harbinger of a more deferential attitude toward national security claims . . . [because a] majority of the Justices were clearly willing to contemplate situations in which they would approve a prior restraint on publication of information."[10] Several years later, in an article in the Washington Post, *Solicitor General Erwin Griswold admitted that none of the material in* The Pentagon Papers *posed any threat to national security.*

This was Hugo Black's last major case. Already seriously ill when the Court's judgment was announced on June 30, 1971, Black retired from the Court on September 17 and died eight days later.

BROADCASTING

FCC v. Pacifica Foundation, 438 U.S. 726 (1978)
(Brennan)

A radio station owned by the Pacifica Foundation broadcast George Carlin's classic comedy sketch "Filthy Words," about the seven dirty words "you can never, ever say on the public airwaves." A father and his son listened to the broadcast one afternoon while driving around town and later complained to the FCC. The FCC found the sketch to be "patently offensive" in violation of 18 U.S.C. §1464, which prohibited the use of "obscene, indecent or profane language" in broadcasting. The federal court of appeals reversed the FCC's decision, with Judge Harold Leventhal dissenting.

---

10. Halperin, "The National Security State: Never Question the President," in *The Burger Years: Rights and Wrongs in the Supreme Court 1969–1986*, 50, 51. Halperin argued that Harlan's dissent, which urged deference to the executive branch in national security cases, subsequently became the de facto majority position on the Court.

Burger: I reverse on Judge Leventhal's opinion.[11]

Stewart: It comes down to §1464, and this Court has twice construed the cognate sections to require material to be "obscene" before suppression is tolerated by the First Amendment. I would construe §1464 similarly, and there is no claim that this broadcast was "obscene." I would affirm on that ground.

White: I agree with Brennan.

Marshall: This is censorship in violation of the First Amendment. I will follow Potter's CBS case.[12]

Blackmun: The FCC's order was not a very good one, and Leventhal tried to save it. I come out with him. "Indecent" is not equivalent to "obscene" in §1464.

Powell: The solicitor general took an extreme position in saying that the FCC ruling absolutely barred certain words for most of the day.[13] I think that Leventhal was on target in his conclusion as to narrow the FCC's order. So I agree with him and reverse.

Rehnquist: I agree with Leventhal.

Stevens: I have flip-flopped on this case and may do so again. This is TV and radio, and the government has greater latitude to regulate them than in newspapers. So even if this material would be protected in newspapers, even apart from protecting children anything that goes into my living room under TV and radio may be regulated in the public interest. So constitutionally, I would sanction this ban as Leventhal says. We should also accept the FCC representation that Leventhal correctly read its order. But is there statutory authority to prohibit this broadcast? BEW says that the "limited spectrum" ratio-

11. Judge Leventhal voted to sustain the FCC's order. He complained that the majority had distorted the FCC's order to make it look like it had prohibited the use of "the seven words you can't say on television" under any circumstances. Leventhal thought that the FCC had acted reasonably to limit the use of words that depicted sexual organs or activities and excretory activities in a patently offensive manner. The problem with the broadcast in question was that it had repeated these words over and over. More importantly, Leventhal noted, the FCC rightly emphasized the timing of the broadcast, which was in the early afternoon when children "were undoubtedly in the audience." Such a narrow order, based on the time of broadcast, would protect young children but "would not force on the general listening public ideas fit only for children." *Pacifica Foundation v. Federal Communications Commission*, 556 F.2d 9, 69 (CADC 1977).

12. *Columbia Broadcasting System v. Democratic National Committee*, 412 U.S. 94 (1973). The Democratic party and several other politically active groups asked the FCC to require broadcasters to accept paid political editorials by "responsible parties." The FCC, however, left private broadcasters free to accept such advertising as they saw fit. The court of appeals reversed, but the Supreme Court backed the FCC. Interestingly, Stewart's concurring opinion became better known—and more often cited—than Burger's majority. Stewart wrote, in part: "The First Amendment protects the press from governmental interference; it confers no analogous protection on the government. To hold that broadcaster action is governmental action would thus simply strip broadcasters of their own 1st Amendment rights. They would be obligated to grant the demands of all citizens to be heard over the air, subject only to reasonable regulations as to 'time, place and manner'.... To hold that broadcaster action is governmental action would thus produce a result wholly inimical to the broadcaster's own First Amendment rights, and wholly at odds with the broadcasting system established by Congress." 412 U.S. at 140.

13. Solicitor General Wade McCree.

374 CHAPTER 10: A FREE PRESS

nale of *Red Lion* supports only the fairness doctrine and that it does not extend to this preclusion.[14]

Result: In a 5–4 vote, the Court upheld the FCC order banning patently offensive broadcasts during the afternoon hours. John Paul Stevens, the most ambivalent member of the majority, wrote the lead opinion, to which he appended a complete transcript of Carlin's monologue.

Columbia Broadcasting System, Inc. v. FCC, 453 U.S. 367 (1981)
(Brennan)

Under the Communications Act of 1934 and the Federal Election Campaign Act of 1971, the FCC could revoke broadcast licenses "for willful or repeated failure" to allow qualified candidates for elected federal offices reasonable access to, or purchase of, broadcast air time. The Carter-Mondale for President Committee asked to buy thirty minutes of air time on the three major networks to coincide with Jimmy Carter's announcement that he would run for president. All three networks refused, citing the large number of potential candidates who might also demand air time. The FCC ruled 4–3 that the networks had denied the campaign committee reasonable access to the airwaves in violation of federal law. The court of appeals affirmed, ruling that Congress had created an affirmative right of access to broadcast media for individual candidates to federal elective office.

BURGER: The networks are not licensees, but that is irrelevant since they have licensed units. *DNC*[15] and *Red Lion*[16] held that TV has large discretion in editing—but not as great as the print media. On balance, I have a skeptical confidence in the FCC. I assume that both the networks and the FCC called the issues as they saw them. The networks had to plan in advance—they could permissibly take into account the advantages incumbents have over contenders. Could the networks' judgment as to when a campaign is in full swing be reviewed? I would be inclined to sustain the networks' judgment unless clearly wrong. Even if the networks make wrong decisions in my view, to avoid censorship I would give them benefit of doubt.

STEWART: This is a very close call. The basic controversy is whether §312(a)(7) changed existing law. I think that it did, and on that basis I am inclined to affirm.

WHITE: Congress intended to change the law. The old law never allowed candidates to do this. We have to decide this case on an applied basis, and I think that the FCC put too tight a grip on broadcasters—particularly on the threshold issue of when the campaign

---

14. *Red Lion Broadcasting Co. v. FCC*, 395 U.S. 367 (1969). This case upheld the FCC's fairness doctrine, developed in 1949, which required broadcasters to discuss public issues and to give both sides of these issues fair and balanced coverage. The main justification for permitting pervasive government regulation of broadcast media was that because there were only a limited number of broadcast frequencies available, this was not a "free marketplace of ideas." This meant that government had a special responsibility to manage this scarce resource and ensure that the broadcasters who were permitted to use the public airwaves acted in the public interest. This case was decided before the proliferation of cable channels and internet broadcasting.

15. *Columbia Broadcasting System, Inc. v. Democratic National Committee*, 412 U.S. 94 (1973).

16. *Red Lion Broadcasting Co. v. FCC*, 395 U.S. 367 (1969).

began. My standard would be something like: if reasonable men could differ, the networks' decision should be sustained.

MARSHALL: Networks are the biggest censors of all, and I don't mind the FCC censoring the censors.

BLACKMUN: I agree that the networks are before us under statute, though this came down to a right of access. Section 3127 changed the law, as §315(a) buttresses. I come out to affirm, on the ground that the solicitor general's standards in his brief are O.K.[17] I would let the commission decide when the campaign began.

POWELL: Section 317(a)(7) changed the law. It enlarged the established rules to give a legal right to legally qualified individual candidates to get access to the public airwaves. License revocation is the only sanction provided under the statute—a cease and desist power was not decided, so the statute is very odd. I agree largely with Byron and would reverse. The commission went beyond its authority in saying that it decided when campaign commenced, and particularly in ordering consideration of individual needs. I would focus on standards.

REHNQUIST: *Red Lion* and other cases entitle TV to the same protections as print media. Networks are responsible for wanting immediate decisions. Section 312(a)(7) changed the law in giving candidates a right of access, but I would read the statute as simply another condition that networks have to comply with to retain their licenses. I generally agree with Byron that the commission has gone too far.

STEVENS: I read §312(a)(7) as clearly creating a duty to accommodate individual candidates in a reasonable way. But any breach of this rule has to be serious enough to justify revocation of the station's license. We can't judge network behavior as unreasonable without judging their actions in the context of the total campaign. I agree with Byron.

Result: Both Burger and Powell changed their minds after the conference, and the Court voted 5–3 that Congress could require reasonable access to broadcast time for federal political candidates. Compare this decision with the Court's earlier ruling in Columbia Broadcasting System, Inc. v. Democratic National Committee *that, absent a congressional mandate to the contrary, networks could constitutionally refuse to sell air time for political advertisements and editorials.*

FCC v. League of Women Voters of California, 468 U.S. 364 (1984)
(Brennan)

The Public Broadcasting Act of 1967 created the Corporation for Public Broadcasting, which was intended to disburse federal funds to noncommercial broadcasters for station operations and programming. Section 399 of the act prohibited grant recipients from editorializing. The League of Women Voters challenged the constitutionality of this restriction, and a three-judge district court ruled summarily that §399 violated the First Amendment.

---

17. Solicitor General Wade McCree.

BURGER: The issue of the government's condition placed on the receipt of public grants is here on the merits. But jurisdiction also bothers me. It is like the question in *Griggs*, which dealt with the appealability of a case while something is still pending in the district court.[18] This is not a classic interlocutory appeal, either, since the motion sought a change in the lower court's judgment. Whether public broadcasting is as different as the solicitor general argues, and thus regulable in this way, is troublesome.[19] The government's strongest argument is the spending power.

BRENNAN:[20] On the jurisdictional question, I agree with the solicitor general that we have jurisdiction in this case. Because appeals pursuant to §1252 may be brought not only from final orders but also from interlocutory ones, and because it is clear, despite the Commission's Rule 59 motion, that the district court had said all it was going to say on the question of §399's constitutionality, I am satisfied that the district court's August 5 judgment is properly before us.

Turning to the merits, I am convinced that Congress carried its generally commendable efforts to control the character of public broadcasting too far when it imposed this absolute ban on editorializing by public stations. First, this ban seems clearly to be one based on the *content* of the speech, rather than its form. I fail to see how one can tell whether a particular speech by station management is proscribed by this statute without examining its content to determine if it amounts to "editorializing."

Second, the government's asserted interests in this prohibition—namely, to ensure that public stations not use the special privilege of federally-subsidized broadcasting to magnify their own views at the expense of others, and to prevent those stations from falling prey to political influence—are familiar ones. Indeed, we considered a very similar contention in the *Red Lion* case where the government argued that without some regulation, commercial station owners would have "unfettered power . . . to communicate only their own views on public issues, people and candidates, and to permit on the air only those with whom they agreed."[21] But the solution to this problem which we endorsed in

18. *Griggs v. Provident Consumer Discount Co.*, 459 U.S. 56 (1982). *Griggs* established a strict test for filing notices of appeal. After Robert and Jacqueline Griggs won their civil lawsuit against Provident Consumer Discount Company, the defendant company filed a motion with the district court to alter or amend the judgment. Rather than wait until that motion was decided, Provident also filed a notice of appeal—which it was not entitled to do while its prior motion was still pending. The court of appeals ruled that while the notice of appeal had been filed prematurely and was void, Provident's mistake was a harmless error and the company could file a second notice of appeal. The Supreme Court reversed, saying that the requirement of a timely notice of appeal was mandatory and jurisdictional. When a premature notice of appeal was filed, the majority said, it was as if no notice of appeal had ever been filed, meaning that the court of appeals had no jurisdiction even to consider the case.

The League of Women Voters, citing the *Griggs* case, claimed that the Supreme Court lacked jurisdiction because the FCC had filed its notice of appeal while the district court's final judgment was still pending. The Court ultimately rejected this argument and distinguished *Griggs* on the ground that it was governed by the Federal Rules of Appellate Procedure, while this case came directly to the Supreme Court from the district court under the more flexible Supreme Court Rules.

19. Solicitor General Rex Lee.
20. Adapted from Brennan's talking papers, Brennan Papers, OT 1983, box 649.
21. *Red Lion Broadcasting Co. v. FCC*, 395 U.S. 367, 392 (1969).

Red Lion was *more* speech rather than an outright silencing of all editorials by commercial licensees. In my view, the same medicine should be applied to alleviate the problems identified by the government in the public broadcasting context.

Third, the force of the government's asserted interest in §399 is considerably blunted for the simple reason that Congress has already put in place the statutory means of accomplishing these goals: for example, by forbidding any attempt by government to influence, supervise or control public stations, the Corporation for Public Broadcasting, or any of its grantees. Moreover, I don't see why the fact that some of these stations are owned by state and local governments should lend the government's interests any greater immediacy or weight. After all, if the heads of those governments wish to express their position on a public issue, they have the power to hold a press conference which will be covered by local news stations and reported in the press. There doesn't seem to me to be any great danger that these officials will resort to public stations to get their views across when there are so many other more effective means open to them.

Finally, I think our cases concerning the spending power do not support the broad position advanced by the solicitor general. It would be one thing if Congress had narrowly prohibited public stations from using federal funds for editorializing and had imposed some accounting requirements to monitor that restriction. But it is quite another matter to say that simply because a station receives 20 percent of its funding from federal sources, that it is then completely barred from engaging in debate on public issues. I affirm.

WHITE: This is a tough case. The government has imposed no programming limits and no restrictions on any news. So what really harms anything in this prohibition? I am also troubled that the prohibition against endorsing candidates is not before us. If constitutionally that is O.K., it is hard to differentiate this case. Can't the same result be obtained by appointments? Technically, I will reverse.

MARSHALL: Editorializing to support or oppose candidates is a tough problem, but I will see if I can affirm.

BLACKMUN: The jurisdiction issue is tough. *Griggs* is a trap, and I would like to find jurisdiction to avoid its result. On the merits, limitations on broadcast speech have been upheld on a frequency scarcity ground. But this prohibition is at the core of the First Amendment. The spending power is no real consideration, I think. The government must justify its actions and has not, so I will affirm.

POWELL: I can go either way on jurisdiction. On the merits, I think that I am to affirm. We could distinguish candidate support. This is a regulation of speech content with a negligible state interest at stake.

REHNQUIST: I would find jurisdiction for Bill Brennan's reasons. On the merits, this is an act of Congress specifically prohibiting what is at issue here, and it is entitled to deference. I would tell people that you get money on condition, and if you want it you must comply with the conditions. The government has control over broadcasting beyond that which it has over the press. There is very little restriction on speech here, anyway.

STEVENS: I am about where Byron is. I can't distinguish this from a candidate prohibition, and I also have trouble distinguishing this from commercial broadcasting. True, it is content regulation, but it is neutral—there is no bias at all. Also, a station's views can be broadcast over any but their own station. When they state the station's view, it also gives the impression that it is an official view because of public funding. There is also a broad justification for government regulation in television and radio. We could still dismiss on jurisdiction.

O'CONNOR: I could join a Court to dismiss for want of jurisdiction. On the merits, a complete ban goes to the heart of the First Amendment. I don't think that the government's interest is compelling. The spending power argument was not made below. You can't limit a station's use of private money.

Result: William Brennan, writing for a 5–4 majority, agreed with the district court that §399 violated the First Amendment. Brennan found a substantial government interest in ensuring adequate and balanced coverage of public issues but concluded that the blanket ban on editorials was not narrowly tailored. Prohibiting all editorials in noncommercial broadcasting was not necessary to protect the media against government interference, nor was it required to prevent the public from wrongly believing that the editorials represented the official views of government.

DEFAMATION

New York Times v. Sullivan, 376 U.S. 254 (1964)
Abernathy v. Sullivan
(Douglas) (Brennan)

L. B. Sullivan was one of three city commissioners in Montgomery, Alabama. He claimed that he was defamed by an advertisement in the New York Times *placed by several prominent civil rights leaders and signed by a long list of activists, entertainers, and celebrities, including Ralph Abernathy and Marlon Brando. The advertisement, entitled "Heed Their Rising Voices," solicited contributions for Martin Luther King's legal defense fund. The ad contained several false statements—nearly all of them innocuous—about alleged police misconduct during a recent civil rights demonstration at the state capitol and on the campus of Alabama State College.[22] While Sullivan was not named in the ad, he claimed that it defamed him because he was the commissioner in charge of supervising the police. Sullivan sought $500,000 in damages from the* Times *and from four local clergymen. A month later four other public officials, including Governor John Patterson and Mayor Earl James, joined Sullivan's suit. The trial judge instructed the jury that the statements were libelous per se, meaning that the plaintiffs did not have to prove actual damages to recover. The judge instructed the jury to presume malice and refused to instruct them that proof of actual intent to harm or recklessness was necessary to award punitive damages. He also refused to caution the jury to distinguish between ordinary damages and punitive damages in its verdict. The jury awarded the plaintiffs a total of $3 million, the full amount asked for, and the Alabama Supreme Court affirmed.*

---

22. The advertisement falsely claimed that the campus cafeteria was padlocked as part of a conspiracy to starve protesting students into submission, that "truckloads of police" were called in, and that police had surrounded the campus. Sullivan also complained that the ad falsely claimed that Dr. Martin Luther King had been jailed seven times when in truth he had been arrested only four times, and that it falsely claimed that the student protesters sang the national anthem when in fact they sang *My Country 'Tis of Thee.*

At the U.S. Supreme Court, Herbert Wechsler argued the case for the Times, *and M. Roland Nachman represented Sullivan. The Justices struggled in conference to find a serviceable standard for this case. They looked at obscenity cases, coerced confessions, expatriation cases, and a criminal case where the defendant was convicted for shuffling his feet.*

Conference of January 10, 1964

WARREN: I reverse. I would not go with the *Times* across the board and say there is no libel unless there is actual malice. But in this area of speech and press, where the article is a comment on government and official conduct, we must scrutinize it carefully to see if it is "fair comment." And we ought to require a high degree of certainty that it involved this official. Inaccuracies alone do not make it libelous. Here, the inaccuracies are so slight that it can't be called libel. Martin Luther King was put in jail four times, not seven, but that does not make it libelous. Similarly, the "padlocked cafeteria" is not attributable to Sullivan anyway, but probably to the school authorities on the scene. The claim that police "ringed the courthouse"[23] is not libelous—it was really synonymous with the police deployment which actually occurred. What is the test of "fair comment"? It is not an unlimited right to comment falsely. Yet what Alabama does is too strict for the First Amendment. I am inclined to take the totality of the situation discussed in the particular circular.[24]

BLACK: If libel laws are at all valid on the press when it talks about public affairs or criticizes official conduct, then I would find it hard to set this judgment aside. These kinds of cases provide a method to put newspapers out of business. The amount of the verdict reflects the local feeling that the *Times* belongs to a foreigner who is an enemy of Alabama. Punitive damages reflect their sense of outrage at the injury to a person's feelings. When you charge the police with something, you charge the commissioner at the top as well as the chief of police. This case is hard to reverse. The purpose of the First Amendment is to keep public affairs open to discussion and not to outlaw public discussions, even where they falsify. Damages as against public officials are largely speculative anyway.[25] It did reflect

---

23. The ad claimed that the police had ringed the *campus*, not the courthouse. It is not clear whether the error here was Warren's or Douglas's. Another error in the ad—and possibly the source of the confusion here—was that it falsely claimed that the students had been expelled for protesting at the capitol building, when in fact they were expelled after they demanded service at the segregated lunchcounter inside the county courthouse.

24. This is another instance where Warren's political views changed significantly after he became Chief Justice. As a young assistant district attorney, Warren prosecuted three criminal libel cases against a local newspaper publisher who criticized local politicians and public figures. He lost each time.

After Warren was elected attorney general of Alameda County, he twice shielded William Randolph Hearst and Hearst's mistress, Marion Davies, from allegedly defamatory books by sending his lead investigator, Oscar Jahnsen, to the printer's shop with a squad of police and firemen to seize the books and burn them. No arrests were ever made and no charges were ever filed. Warren just wanted to destroy the books before they could be distributed. Cray, *Chief Justice*, 438.

25. Hugo Black, who knew something about Alabama politics, thought that this case was an attempt to punish the press for its sympathetic coverage of the civil rights movement. Far from damaging Sullivan's reputation in the South, Black said, "Commissioner Sullivan's political, social, and financial prestige has likely been enhanced by the *Times'* publication." Cray, *Chief Justice*, 438. The *Times* was not widely read in Alabama. The newspaper had a paid circulation in Birmingham of just five newspapers and statewide sales of 394 papers a day. Clark, *Justice Brennan*, 207; Eisler, *A Justice for All*, 185.

on this officer—he says he is going all the way, but what the whole distance is he does not say. If there is anything clear to me, it is that in public affairs it was intended to foreclose any kind of proceedings which would deter free and open discussion. *At least in the field of public affairs*, a state cannot keep a person from talking.

DOUGLAS: In the area of public affairs, the doctrine of fair comment is available to protect the *Times* and other publications. I would reverse on the First Amendment.

CLARK: On damages, we can't reach that issue through the Constitution. On libel, I would separate private libels from those on groups or in public affairs or government. In private libels, I would allow a less onerous burden of proof. In proving libel of public officials or on public issues, I would create a much heavier burden of proof—it must be tied to the official. Here, the respondent is not tied to the ad. The only way to get a libel out of this would be for the chief of police to step up and sue. The only one who could sue on this would be a policeman. The *Times* case does not control #40 [*Abernathy*] because the former turns on the lack of identity of the respondent in the ad. I will go on due process—lack of proof.

HARLAN: I reverse. The First Amendment does not outlaw state libel laws, even in the field of public affairs. Look at *Edwards*.[26] This case presents a classic illustration of how the First Amendment's protection of the public interest in discussion must be accommodated against private rights—including the private right not to be defamed. We must lay down new constitutional rules for state libel laws. We should finally dispose of this case. The rule must not permit retrial of this case, but should not leave loopholes for other cases. Let's say that we would abide private libels for the purposes of this case. In a federal libel rule, I would establish a two-pronged test in the public affairs field: (1) a high standard of proof across the board on all elements of the action (like the burden of proof in denationalization cases); and (2) while punitive damages are not constitutionally outlawed, they cannot be imposed without proof of *actual* malice. These requirements would leave state libel laws untouched except in the public affairs area. I would analogize this situation to the standard of proof in obscenity cases and in coerced confessions. I may go so far as to say that criminal libel will have to take care of punitive damages in civil suits.

BRENNAN: I reverse. The First Amendment does not outlaw all libel laws, even in this field. But the press is entitled to broad freedom in criticizing public officials. I am not far from John in saying that there must be federal standards and *actual malice*. I would embrace "clear, convincing and unequivocal" evidence from our expatriation cases. It applies to each element. The issue of identification is the crucial one, and here Sullivan was not mentioned in the advertisement.

---

26. *Edwards v. South Carolina*, 372 U.S. 229 (1963).

STEWART: There is a federal question here under the First Amendment. This case should be decided along the lines set out by John and Bill Brennan. Obscenity cases are the closest analogy. I would reverse, but not for a new trial. I would require proof of actual malice for punitive damages *in this area*, for punitive damages are to deter.

WHITE: I agree with John, Bill Brennan, and Potter. I would reverse and would rely on obscenity cases and our approach in that area. At the outset is the formulation of words. General damages can be presumed from some things which are said. These words are not of that kind—these are not the kind of words that can destroy an official, and they do not get to him as a person. None of these charges amount to this, and I could reverse just on the ground that this was not defamation. At the worst, they show that Sullivan exercised poor judgment in the use of the police. A jury verdict can be set aside even at common law if it is against the weight of the evidence.

GOLDBERG: I reverse. I do not think that John's test will work. If another jury was so instructed in this case, they still would find for Sullivan. We should not make special rule for punitive damages in libel cases. I think that all punitive damages may be constitutionally infirm. This is not a case where a governor is charged with adultery—this is a "what kind of a commissioner are you?" case. In that realm, the speaker must be protected even if the accusations are false. That is different from charges of corruption. We should not go off on standards of proof. What is being talked about here is official misconduct. Public misconduct should be subject to complete criticism. Private libels can be resorted to by public officials, but here we are in the public domain.

WHITE: There is a difference where there is malice. Look at Emerson's article on the First Amendment.[27]

---

27. Emerson, "Toward a General Theory of the First Amendment," 922–23. Emerson said, in part:
"A member of a civilized society should have some measure of protection against unwarranted attack upon his honor, his dignity and his standing in the community.... [In purely private defamation cases] the harm caused ... tends to be direct and instantaneous.... In this sense, therefore, true private defamation tends toward the category of 'action,' and hence is subject to reasonable regulation....
More difficult issues arise when the public interest becomes more directly involved, as where the person who considers his reputation impaired is a public official, a candidate for public office, or someone functioning in the public arena.... If the damaging statement affects such a person purely in his private and personal capacity, the ordinary principles of libel and slander would obtain. On the other hand, if the alleged defamation relates essentially to the public performance of the person claimed to be injured, the issue is no different from the problem of criminal libel [Emerson later rejects the doctrine of criminal libel].... There remains, however, an intermediate category where the alleged defamation is mixed in character, pertaining to both private and public capacities. This occurs, for example, where the honesty of an official in connection with the discharge of his public duties is challenged. The best resolution of such a problem would appear to be through the development of a doctrine of fair comment. Under such a rule, the communication would be protected if it is based upon the facts, or what a reasonable man would accept as the facts, is fair, and is not malicious. This standard of fair comment, if rigorously pressed against unpopular defendants, could cut off much public discussion. Still it may be justified if employed only in private litigation and if the judiciary accepts its obligation to act as a firm defender of the First Amendment interest."

Conference of January 10, 1964

No. 40—Abernathy v. Sullivan

WARREN: There is no evidence against these people. They did not put it in the papers.[28] I would reverse on the *Shuffling Sam* case.[29]

BLACK: I agree. The letter from Randolph is pure hearsay.[30] There was a failure to deny the charges when called on to retract the advertisement—but that statute had for its purpose the reduction of damages.[31] The respondent tries to use it for a different purpose here.

DOUGLAS: I agree with the Chief.

CLARK: I would turn this case on the *Shuffling Sam* case, because there is a question of whether the *Times* case would control. Calling the Negro "Lawyer Gray" is not error—it represents an old custom of talking.[32] I agree with the Chief that there was no evidence here.

HARLAN: I reverse, and will go on the standard of proof requirement I set down for #39.

BRENNAN: I reverse, and agree with John.

STEWART: There is nothing on the racial issues in the case. I could go on lack of evidence, as the Chief suggests. The retraction statute has nothing to do with this.

GOLDBERG: I would reverse.

Result: The Court ruled that the First and Fourteenth Amendments prohibited any award for defamation of a public official for comments relating to their official duties absent proof of actual malice, where the false statements were made either with knowledge of their falsity or with a reckless disregard for the truth. While the judgment was unanimous, not everyone joined Brennan's majority opinion,

---

28. At least some of the people named in the advertisement, including Abernathy, neither signed nor endorsed the ad and were not even aware of its existence until they saw it in the morning paper.

29. *Thompson v. Louisville*, 362 U.S. 199 (1960). The Court ruled that state loitering and disorderly conduct charges brought against "Shuffling Sam" Thompson were so totally devoid of evidentiary support that his conviction violated the due process clause of the Fourteenth Amendment. For more details on this case, see chapter 9. This case provided a tempting precedent for the Court in race cases, because the Justices could reverse summarily without having to address the underlying racial issues.

30. A. Philip Randolph was the chairman of the committee that paid for the ad. He sent a letter to the *Times* certifying that everyone named in the ad had consented to have his or her name used. As it turned out, few, if any, of those named in the ad had given their consent. Randolph made several other claims in connection with the advertisement that also turned out to be exaggerated or false.

31. Under Alabama law, public officials were precluded from recovering damages unless they first demanded a retraction. Sullivan demanded a retraction in writing and received a letter in return asking him how he thought that the advertisement referred to him in any way. Without answering the letter, Sullivan filed his defamation suit the next day.

32. The trial judge referred to one of the defendants' lawyers as "Lawyer Gray" rather than "Mr. Gray," and this reference was repeated in the state Supreme Court's opinion. The defendants also objected at trial to the manner in which one of Sullivan's counsel pronounced the word "Negro."

and there was considerable disagreement over the proper test. Hugo Black, William O. Douglas, and Arthur Goldberg concurred in the result but favored giving the press greater protection than the majority was willing to allow.

Several of the Justices, notably John Marshall Harlan, initially argued that the Court should be more conciliatory and that the case should be remanded for a new trial. The majority, however, had learned its lesson about dealing with southern politicians from earlier race cases. On March 3, 1964, Warren wrote Brennan a short note saying that under no circumstances should the case be sent back: "Otherwise we will merely be going through a meaningless exercise. The case would be remanded, another improvisation would be devised and it would be back to us in a more difficult posture." In the end, Harlan assented and the Alabama Supreme Court's decision was reversed without a remand.

Curtis Publishing Co. v. Butts & Associated Press v. Walker, 388 U.S. 130 (1967)
(Douglas)

These two cases were published together but discussed separately in conference. In the first case, Wally Butts was the athletic director at the University of Georgia. He sued the Saturday Evening Post *for libel after the magazine falsely accused him of conspiring with University of Alabama football coach Paul "Bear" Bryant to fix a football game between the two schools.*[33] *A federal jury awarded Butts general and punitive damages, which were later reduced to $480,000. The trial judge refused to order a new trial after* New York Times Co. v. Sullivan *was decided, ruling that there had been ample evidence of reckless disregard for the truth on the part of the* Post.[34] *The Fifth Circuit Court of Appeals affirmed.*

Associated Press v. Walker involved an AP report concerning a white riot at the University of Mississippi protesting the court-ordered enrollment of the school's first black student, James Meredith. The report falsely claimed that Edwin Walker, a well-known southern political figure, took command of the hostile white crowd and confronted federal marshals who were attempting to enforce the court's order. The state trial judge instructed the jury that it could award general damages if the story was not substantially true and it could award punitive damages if the story was motivated by ill will or "complete want of care." Despite AP's claim that the story was responsibly investigated and reported, the jury awarded both general and punitive damages. The trial judge threw out the punitive damages but allowed the general damages award to stand. He ruled that the New York Times *standard was not applicable, but added that if it were then the jury verdict would have to be reversed, because there was no evidence of malice or reckless disregard for truth. The Texas Court of Civil Appeals affirmed, and the Texas Supreme Court denied review.*

---

33. George Burnett, an insurance agent from Atlanta, claimed to have overheard a Butts-Bryant telephone conversation when a malfunction accidentally cross-connected him to the line on which the two men were talking. Burnett eavesdropped and took notes as Butts allegedly told Bryant about Georgia personnel, team tendencies, and plays. A week later, Alabama beat Georgia 35–0. Burnett's co-workers encouraged him to remain silent, but word leaked out. Under pressure to recant, Burnett hired a lawyer who negotiated the deal with the *Post*. Neither Butts nor Bryant ever admitted that the phone conversation took place. Kirby, *Fumble*, 30–54. Kirby claims that the conversation almost certainly took place and that the circumstances were suspicious, but that the information Butts provided was unimportant and probably did not affect the outcome of the game.

34. *New York Times Co. v. Sullivan,* 376 U.S. 254 (1971).

Conference of February 24, 1967

Associated Press v. Walker

WARREN: I reverse. It is not necessary to decide if Walker was a public official. He put himself into a situation where he can't disassociate himself from the facts. He was in the thick of the demonstration, and he then can't complain if his conduct was subject to press comment. It is not liable, absent malice. He was a leader in the movement—there was no malice here.

BLACK: I would reverse on a broad ground. If there was ever a public subject matter, it was this one.

DOUGLAS: I reverse.

CLARK: I can go on either ground for reversal. This is either a "public affair" or Walker is a "public official." Or I would combine the two. He was a public character, having an image which he created. I would reverse for a new trial on "malice."

HARLAN: I am not at rest on this case, nor the next. We are at a turning point. Can the *Times* rule be contained in terms of public officials? In this case and in *Butts*, the real issue is whether we will retain the *Times* doctrine to embrace any issue of public interest, whether political or not. *Butts* is as of much public interest as *Walker*. Walker is not a public official.

BRENNAN: If we go to the subject matter, it is immaterial who the person is, and then it is wide open. How would you define a "public event"? We tried in *Rosenblatt* to restrict the public official category. "Public figure" is perhaps more manageable than "public event." *Butts* does not bother me, for in that context Butts is no less an official than Rosenblatt was. My doubts on *Butts* go to the horrible record, which strongly indicates malice. I agree that we are at the crossroads. There is an important state interest in libel. I would draw a circle around "public figures" and reverse on that ground.

STEWART: The destruction of a man's character is terrible. Money damages is a crude remedy, but society is entitled to preserve that value. Everything in a newspaper is newsworthy—if we adopt that standard, then all of the law of libel goes out. I would reverse on the fact that this was a self-created crisis into which Walker injected himself. I would go for reversal only in that narrow framework.

WHITE: I would reverse. I am not sure that the trial court handled the "malice" issue properly.

BRENNAN: We can't remand with directions to dismiss. This is a state case. We only reversed in the *New York Times* case.

WHITE: I am unwilling to say that the *New York Times* defense was waived. I reverse.

FORTAS: I reverse. This is a hot news context and the press needs latitude. I agree with Potter and his philosophy against libeling individuals—this is a hard core public event.

Curtis Publishing Co. v. Butts

WARREN: I affirm. I am close to Potter Stewart and Abe Fortas. The mere fact that a man is a public figure does not take away his right to have his character secure. Butts had not injected himself into any situation. The fact that a man is in the limelight as a star athlete does not make him different, so far as defamation is concerned, from anyone else. Butts was minding his own business. The petitioner tried to destroy him and did destroy him. If he had got into a row over the Amateur Athletic Union, he would be in a different situation. Butts is not a "public official" but probably that need not be decided. In any event, he has a case of "malice" if anyone ever did. I would affirm on "malice."

BLACK: Everyone should be treated alike by the Constitution and this Court. I am not willing to draw a line between Butts and Walker. I do not share the views of Potter Stewart and Abe Fortas, for that entails changing the Constitution. The press cannot survive these highly emotional judgments. We must retreat from *New York Times*, or draw myriad lines to save the press from huge judgments. I reverse.

DOUGLAS: I reverse.

CLARK: Butts was a "public figure" and football was a "public event": (1) sophisticated muckraking is evidence of "malice"; (2) the article was written to destroy Butts; and (3) they made no investigation in time to stop the story, even though they had leads indicating that the story was false. We can find that there was "malice." I would affirm.

HARLAN: I can't distinguish this from *Walker* on the Constitution. I would come out the same in each. *New York Times* must be confined or reversed, but the First Amendment is not an absolute. I pass.

BRENNAN: I am not sure if the case of "malice" is made out. Apart from that, I would reverse on *Rosenblatt*,[35] for Butts was a public official. It would have to go back on that, and if the jury found that Butts was a public official, there is strong evidence of "malice" and the jury would have to determine that.

STEWART: The petitioner acted in total disregard of the facts. Assuming that the petitioner is fully protected by *New York Times* rule, this is a clear case of "malice." Should we say so, or let the jury do that? I am not settled. This was a deliberately defamatory article. I will vote to affirm or remand.

WHITE: I would reverse. The trial judge's instructions on malice were not *New York Times* instructions. They must have a new trial on that issue.

FORTAS: I agree with Potter Stewart.

---

35. *Rosenblatt v. Baer*, 383 U.S. 75 (1966). Frank Baer, a former supervisor at a county-owned ski resort and recreation area, filed a defamation action against Alfred Rosenblatt, a New Hampshire newspaper columnist. Rosenblatt implied in a column that Baer had been incompetent and corrupt (without naming Baer, Rosenblatt asked, "What happened to all the money last year? And every other year?"). The trial judge instructed the jury that Baer was not a public official and that the *New York Times* standard did not apply. The jury awarded Baer damages. The Supreme Court reversed on the ground that any government employee who had or appeared to have substantial responsibility for or control over government affairs was a public official. In order to recover damages, Baer had to prove actual malice. William Brennan, writing for the majority, argued that the term "public official" should be defined broadly to preserve the compelling interest in full and vigorous discussion of public issues and the performance of government officials.

Conference of March 10, 1967

HARLAN: I reverse.

Result: John Marshall Harlan, the last Justice to make up his mind in conference, wrote for a unanimous Court in reversing the damage award in Walker *but allowing the jury award to stand in* Butts *on a close 5–4 vote. All nine Justices agreed that both men were public figures, but they were divided over which standard applied. Four Justices (Harlan, Clark, Stewart, and Fortas) favored allowing damages to public officials if the falsehood substantially endangered the person's reputation and if the defendant's conduct represented an extreme departure from the ordinary and reasonable standards of investigation and reporting. Warren, Brennan, and White favored using the "actual malice" rule for public figures as well as public officials, while Black and Douglas argued that the First Amendment gave publishers absolute protection from libel suits.*

In Walker, *all nine Justices agreed that the evidence did not even support a finding of negligence on the part of the Associated Press. In* Butts, *however, Harlan's plurality opinion upheld the jury's verdict because the magazine's investigative standards were grossly inadequate and unreasonable. The Chief Justice concurred in the result and provided the crucial fifth vote to uphold the damage award in* Butts. *He thought that the* Post's *conduct had been so reckless that it amounted to actual malice. Later cases have narrowed the category of public figures but have consistently applied the "actual malice" standard to both public officials and public figures.*

Time, Inc. v. Hill, 385 U.S. 374 (1967)
(Douglas) (Brennan)

In 1952, a group of escaped convicts broke into James Hill's home in Whitemarsh, Pennsylvania, and held Hill and his family hostage for more than nineteen hours. The incident ended without violence, but it attracted extensive media coverage. The Hill family sought to avoid publicity and moved to another town to escape attention. Several years later, author Joseph Hayes wrote a violent novel loosely based on the incident, which was turned into a play entitled The Desperate Hours. *The play was the subject of a* Life *magazine pictorial, complete with photographs staged in the Hills' former home. The article contained a number of factual errors, including the false claim that the play was a reenactment of "the desperate ordeal of the James Hill family," and contained pictures that falsely suggested that the kidnappers had physically abused two of Hill's five children. The family sued* Time, Inc., *the magazine's parent company, claiming that they had been portrayed in a false light. The Hills used a state privacy law that prohibited the use of names, portraits, or pictures for advertising or trade purposes without the written permission of the individuals involved.*

The trial judge instructed the jurors that they could find the magazine liable if the article was published not for its news content but to advertise the play or boost the magazine's circulation. He told the jury that punitive damages were permissible if the magazine failed to make a reasonable investigation to discover the facts. The first jury awarded both compensatory and punitive damages. The New York Court of Appeals affirmed the verdict but reversed and remanded on the issue of damages. The second jury awarded only compensatory damages, and the Court of Appeals affirmed.

Richard Nixon made his only appearance as an advocate before the Supreme Court in this case, arguing on behalf of the Hill family. By most accounts he did quite well, especially during the first

round of arguments. Nixon even won over Earl Warren, who otherwise hated his fellow Californian.[36]
The main issue at conference was whether the New York Times v. Sullivan *"actual malice" standard
for public officials would be extended to public figures in invasion of privacy suits.*

Conference of October 21, 1966

WARREN: I affirm. This is not a violation of the First Amendment. It is not a question of
news. This was an invasion of privacy by fictionalizing an account of this family's life
and experience. The New York law is not too clear, but the specific holding below was
correct. This case has gone on for eleven years and we should resolve any doubts about
the New York law. In this limited application, I see no threat to a free press.

BLACK: I reverse. They did not flee from the state, but only moved to another city as
they planned to do anyway. This law is unconstitutional as being too broad and vague.
The act also violates the First Amendment. Newspapers have the right to report on and
to criticize plays. This is nothing but a statute prohibiting the press from publishing certain things.

DOUGLAS: I reverse. The "trade and commerce" phrase doesn't mean anything.

CLARK: I reverse. The New York act is too broad. The judge's instructions were also bad.

HARLAN: Last term I affirmed on a non-circulated, concurring opinion. I have changed
my mind and will reverse and remand for a new trial. The act should be judged as applied, not on its face. There is room here for a constitutional application of this act, but
the judge's charge let the jury find that if there was fictionalization, that alone was sufficient to award damages. That is not a constitutional application.

BRENNAN: At least we should reverse for a new trial. If the act means what Rayborn [*sic*]
said, it is unconstitutional when the New York Court of Appeals merely affirms.[37] It means
that they do not agree with the opinion below. When they intend to adopt the lower
opinion they say so—and that's what they did here. Look at *Aquilino*.[38] I would (1) give

---

36. Nixon later explained that he had counted on Warren's vote all along because the Chief Justice
was an experienced politician who "knew firsthand how fierce and lacerating the press could be when it
fastened on a target." Leonard Garment, "Annals of Law," *New Yorker*, Apr. 17, 1989, 97.

37. Judge Samuel Rabin wrote a concurring opinion in the case below for the Supreme Court of New
York, Appellate Division. *Hill v. Hayes*, 18 A.D. 2d 485 (1963). Judge Rabin argued that if it could be clearly
demonstrated that a newsworthy item was presented "not for the purpose of disseminating news, but rather
for the sole purpose of increasing circulation . . . [then] the privilege to use one's name should not be granted
even though a true account of the event be given—let alone when the account is sensationalized and fictionalized."

38. *Aquilino v. United States*, 363 U.S. 509 (1960). In a three-way legal dispute, a group of subcontractors sued a delinquent general contractor to recover money owed on a construction project. The Internal
Revenue Service sought to claim priority over the subcontractors' liens because the defaulting general contractor was also a delinquent taxpayer.

The Supreme Court of New York held that the government's tax lien was invalid because it had not
been filed in the office designated under New York law for the filing of liens against real property. The
appellate division affirmed on other grounds—that there was no debt to which the government's tax lien

a new trial; (2) declare the act unconstitutional; or (3) remand to the New York Court of Appeals for clarification of its opinion. I would prefer option two.

STEWART: What Rayborn [*sic*] said was dictum in a concurring opinion. It had nothing to do with this case. Under the First Amendment, there can be state laws protecting privacy. They can't hold a newspaper liable for anything more than a deliberate falsification. The jury was not so instructed. [DOUGLAS: Stewart apparently argues for a more restricted liability here than in defamer case.]

WHITE: I would reverse for a new trial.

FORTAS: The jury found this statement to be knowingly, recklessly, and wilfully untrue. It was apropos of exemplary damages. The jury found exemplary damages. The New York Court of Appeals reversed only on question of damages. On compensatory damages, the trial judge's instructions were not too clear. Can deliberate fabrication or the deliberate use of the name of a living person without his consent be made actionable? Most New York decisions relied on here are from lower courts and they are fuzzy. None has assessed a penalty for news. I would not strike down the act, but would try to sanction it as construed. I affirm.

Result: Initially there were six votes in favor of the Hill family, and Earl Warren assigned the opinion to Abe Fortas. Fortas's draft opinion, however, established a fundamental right of privacy that was much broader than the Court had previously recognized. The Justices also began to bicker over the scope of the New York statute. Byron White argued that the state law was overbroad because it permitted liability for publishing truthful accounts of newsworthy events if the jury found that the publication was solely for purposes of trade. Fortas disagreed and thought that the statute required an intentional and pervasive fictionalization of events. To resolve the disagreement, the Justices ordered reargument on the issue of whether the state law was limited to fictionalized accounts.[39]

Conference of April 29, 1967

WARREN: I affirm. The article was fiction that was false in material respects. The play was also fiction. New York has so limited its act as not to interfere with freedom of speech.

BLACK: I reverse. A newspaper can report on plays. It can use fiction under the First Amendment. Privacy is no defense. This is really a libel action, and it is a flagrant violation of the First Amendment.

---

could attach, because any money that the property owner "owed" to the contractor really belonged to the subcontractors. The New York court of appeals reversed on the ground that the federal tax lien had priority because it took effect prior to the subcontractors' liens.

The U.S. Supreme Court vacated the court of appeals' judgment, ruling that the courts must first look to state law to determine the nature of the contractor's property interest. Once the courts determined that the contractor had a property interest, then federal law controlled whether the government tax lien attached and whether the government had priority over other creditors. The Court viewed this bifurcated process as a traditional state function and also thought it necessary for the uniform administration of federal revenue statutes. David, "Ignoring State Homestead Laws."

39. Laura Kalman, *Abe Fortas*, 262–265.

DOUGLAS: I reverse.

CLARK: I affirm. I agree with the Chief.

HARLAN: I affirm. I agree with the Chief Justice. This is not a mere comment on the play. This is not dredging up new facts about an old event. It is a fictionalized account invading privacy.

BRENNAN: The state act, as construed, authorized suits for commercial uses of fiction about a real person. *Times v. Sullivan* was different.[40] We did apply *Times* to *Lynn* [*sic*]. I can't find any First Amendment rationalization.[41] I affirm.

STEWART: I am in doubt. This was a false concoction. I would affirm.

WHITE: I will probably reverse. New York could not give a remedy for a truthful account of a past event. If so, then a negligent use of data can't be the basis of the suit. Deliberate falsehood was not charged. If so, no First Amendment rights. If the act is limited to knowing, conscious falsehoods, then I would affirm.

FORTAS: I affirm.

Result: Fortas lost his majority, and Hugo Black reassigned the case to William Brennan.[42] The new majority extended New York Times v. Sullivan *to cover public figures as well as public officials. Because the trial judge's instructions allowed the jury to find the magazine liable even when the falsehoods were innocent or merely negligent, a new trial was necessary. John Harlan dissented in part but joined Brennan's opinion to reverse and remand the case for a new trial.*

Fortas toned down his dissenting opinion significantly from earlier drafts. His sweeping claims for privacy rights disappeared, and his blistering attack on the press was blunted and rather dull. Ironically, Fortas's original drafts of his planned majority opinion read like an impassioned

---

40. *New York Times Co. v. Sullivan*, 376 U.S. 254 (1964).

41. *Linn v. United Plant Guard Workers of America*, 383 U.S. 53 (1966). William C. Linn, a corporate official, sued the union, union officials, and a company employee for defamation that allegedly took place during a union organizing campaign. The corporation also filed unfair labor practice charges with the National Labor Relations Board (NLRB). The NLRB rejected the company's grievance, and the courts dismissed Linn's defamation case on the ground that the NLRB had exclusive jurisdiction over unfair labor practice claims. The Supreme Court reversed on a 5–4 vote, ruling that the National Labor Relations Act did not deprive the courts of jurisdiction in defamation suits growing out of labor disputes. Jurisdiction was limited, however, to defamation cases that met the *Sullivan* test—where defamatory statements were made either with knowledge of their falsity or with reckless disregard for the truth.

42. Black was especially critical of Fortas's attempt to balance privacy and free press rights. For Black, there was no balancing to be done; the Constitution unequivocally protected freedom of the press. And no matter how hard he looked, Black still could not find a right of privacy mentioned anywhere in the Bill of Rights. In a memorandum to the conference, Black blasted Fortas for balancing imaginary rights against explicit constitutional protections and for substituting Fortas's "perceptions of fairness for the Founding Fathers' wisdom." Black said that instead of following John Marshall's advice that "we must remember that it is a Constitution that we are *expounding*," Fortas believed that "we must always remember it is a Constitution we are *rewriting*." Laura Kalman, *Abe Fortas*, 265.

and unrestrained dissent. His published dissent, however, had the subdued tone of a majority opinion.[43]

Gertz v. Welch, 418 U.S. 323 (1974)
(Brennan)

After Chicago policeman Richard Nuccio was convicted of murdering seventeen-year-old Ronald Nelson, the victim's family hired attorney Elmer Gertz to sue Nuccio for civil damages. An article in American Opinion, *a monthly published by the John Birch Society, falsely accused Gertz of framing Nuccio as part of a Communist conspiracy to discredit the Chicago police department.*[44] *Gertz filed a defamation suit. The court of appeals applied* New York Times v. Sullivan, *holding that Gertz could not recover damages for defamation absent a malicious or reckless disregard for the truth.*[45]

BURGER: The question is whether the *Times* standard applies; and if it does, did the petitioner here get a fair chance to prove malice? I reject the idea that a lawyer becomes a public figure because his client is a public figure. And Gertz seems to be just another lawyer. That is different from *Rosenbloom,* who was a target among the law breakers.[46] We must reverse.

STEWART: I did not accept *Rosenbloom.* Gertz for me is not a public figure in the *Times* sense, merely because he's a prominent and well-known lawyer. So I would let him have a state remedy limited only as to punitive damages. So I would reinstate the jury verdict.

---

43. Ibid., 266–67.

44. The article "*Frame-Up*: Richard Nuccio and the War on Police" alleged that the Communist party "railroaded" Nuccio as part of a conspiracy to undermine police authority. It falsely accused Gertz of being a Leninist and a "communist-fronter" and wrongly implied that he had a criminal record.

45. *New York Times v. Sullivan,* 376 U.S. 254 (1964).

46. *Rosenbloom v. Metromedia, Inc.,* 403 U.S. 29 (1971). George Rosenbloom distributed nudist magazines in Pennsylvania. He sued a Philadelphia radio station for defamation when, in reporting a police raid on Rosenbloom's place of business, the reporter initially described the magazines as "obscene." After the first two reports, the reporter revised his copy and subsequently said that the seized magazines were "*allegedly* obscene." Rosenbloom also charged that he had been defamed by an unrelated report by the same station, where local adult magazine distributors (without identifying Rosenbloom) were described as "smut distributors" and "girlie book peddlers."

The district court held that Rosenbloom did not have to meet the *New York Times v. Sullivan* standard because he was neither a public official nor a public figure. The court of appeals reversed, ruling that *Times* was the proper standard. A badly divided Supreme Court affirmed. A 5–3 majority agreed that whatever constitutional standard applied, there was not enough evidence in this case to support an award for damages. The Justices, however, could not agree on the proper standard. Brennan wrote for a plurality of three (joined by Burger and Blackmun) that the *Times* standard applied whenever the alleged defamation related to the plaintiff's involvement in a matter of public or general concern—regardless of whether the plaintiff was a government official, public figure, or private person. Hugo Black argued that the media were immune from all defamation suits, even in cases of actual malice. Byron White argued that absent a requisite showing of knowing or reckless falsity, the press and the broadcast media had a First Amendment privilege to report and comment on government actions in full detail, with no requirement to spare from public scrutiny the reputation or the privacy of any individual involved in or affected by the action. Harlan, Stewart, and Marshall dissented. William O. Douglas did not participate in the decision.

WHITE: I am not interested in extending federal restrictions on state libel laws. I would prefer to remand this case to the court of appeals to determine the "public figure" issue.

BLACKMUN: I joined *Rosenbloom v. Metromedia*, and so would reverse for new trial—with the refinement that any evidence of falsity could be imputed to the publisher.

POWELL: I can't accept the proposed "public interest" standard, because it leaves power to the press to determine what is in the "public interest." I have more trouble with the meaning of the phrase "public figure."

Result: By a 5–4 vote, the Court held that in defamation cases where the victim was neither a public official nor a public figure, New York Times v. Sullivan *was not applicable. The ruling made it considerably easier for Gertz to press his defamation suit against* American Opinion *and the John Birch Society. Lewis Powell wrote for the majority that there was no greater protection for the media when defamatory statements concerned an issue of public interest. Despite broad initial support for Powell's position in conference, there were significant defections afterward. Burger, Brennan, and White all changed their minds and dissented, and Powell saw his initially comfortable 8–1 majority shrink to the narrowest of margins.*

CHAPTER 11

RELIGION AND STATE

THE ESTABLISHMENT CLAUSE

In Civic and Commercial Life

Cantwell v. Connecticut, 310 U.S. 296 (1940)
(Douglas)

Russell Cantwell and two other Jehovah's Witnesses were arrested while selling religious publications and playing anti-Catholic phonograph records on public streets in a largely Catholic neighborhood. They were convicted of common law breach of the peace and of violating a state law prohibiting public solicitations for religious causes without a permit.

For oral argument on March 28, 1940, lawyers requested that a copy of the phonograph be played in Court. Chief Justice Hughes rejected the idea on the ground that it would unnecessarily sensationalize the case, saying, "If a man insults my wife it makes little difference if he were purring or shouting."[1]

Douglas's conference notes deal only with the third and fifth counts.

Conference of March 30, 1940

HUGHES: On the third count, I would interpret the statute so as to *require* the issuance of a permit on a showing that this group was a religious sect. There should be no standard other than that. This statute clearly is valid as respects charitable and philanthropic groups. As respects religious sects, is the statute bad on its face as construed? There are fake religious groups. The pith of the Connecticut court's decision on the statute was whether there was a solicitation. It held that it was solicitation, and we would not disturb that.

On the fifth count, the common law is what the Connecticut court said it was. If there was no question of privilege, there would be nothing here at all. The real point is: is there a constitutional privilege to do what they did? Suppose there had been a statute which had provided that the playing of a graphophone[2] on the streets announcing religious ideas was not allowed—would that be invalid? I would affirm.

McReynolds: I would reverse.

---

1. Frank Murphy, Memorandum of March 28, 1940, Case 632—*Cantwell (Jehova) v. State of Connecticut,* Frank Murphy Papers.

2. A phonograph that played records made of wax.

Result: Owen Roberts, writing for a unanimous Court, reversed all of the convictions as impermissible prior restraints on the free exercise of religion. The fact that the defendants' speech and actions were peaceful meant that their convictions for breach of the peace also violated the First and Fourteenth Amendments.

McGowan v. Maryland, 366 U.S. 420 (1961)
Two Guys from Harrison-Allentown v. McGinley, 366 U.S. 582 (1961)
Braunfeld v. Brown, 366 U.S. 599 (1961)
Gallagher v. Crown Kosher Market, 366 U.S. 617 (1961)
(Clark) (Brennan)

In 1961, the Court debated the constitutionality of Sunday closing laws (also called blue laws). The Court accepted four cases from three states: Maryland, Pennsylvania, and Massachusetts. In the first case, Margaret McGowan and other employees of a large department store in Maryland were convicted of selling proscribed products on Sunday. State law prohibited the Sunday sale of most merchandise, except "necessities" such as newspapers, bread, fruit, milk, gasoline, and tobacco products.

In the second case, Two Guys department store stayed open on Sundays, violating two Pennsylvania statutes prohibiting "all worldly employment or business" on Sundays. In the third case, Abraham Braunfeld and others also challenged the same Pennsylvania laws. The plaintiffs were a group of Orthodox Jewish merchants who closed their businesses on the Jewish Sabbath, from nightfall Friday through nightfall Saturday. To compensate, Braunfeld and the others remained open on Sundays, claiming that otherwise they would suffer undue economic hardship.

In the fourth case, a group of Orthodox shoppers, rabbis, and a kosher market sued Raymond Gallagher, the chief of police of Springfield, Massachusetts, challenging that state's blue laws. They argued that after observing the Jewish Sabbath they needed to be able to buy kosher food on Sundays, and the merchants claimed it was economically impractical for them to open on Saturday nights after sunset and close by 10:00 A.M. on Sunday, as the law allowed.

McGowan *and* Gallagher *were initially tried in state courts, while* Two Guys *and* Braunfeld *were tried in federal courts. All four courts upheld the constitutionality of state blue laws.*

WARREN: I would sustain all of these laws. It is O.K. to say that everyone must have one day of rest per week. Proper economic and social objectives support these laws. Do they have the right to select a particular day? Why is a particular day bad? Picking Sunday only conformed to the usages and habits of most people, and this does not mean an invasion of religious beliefs or a preference for one particular belief.

1. This is not an establishment of a church. There might be some interference with their practice of religion. The "Lord's Day" use is of no consequence.[3]
2. Economic losses do not matter, although equal protection might enter here somewhere. But somebody is always going to be "hurt." Orthodox Jews might lose two days.
3. "Two Guys" profess no religion. How do they have standing? This is not presently a religious law.

---

3. The Massachusetts law said in part: "Whoever on the *Lord's Day* keeps open his shop . . . or does any manner of labor . . . except works of necessity and charity, shall be punished by a fine of not more than fifty dollars."

4. The rabbis have the best point.

5. Maryland law is not a religious law (slots, etc.).

BLACK: There is no question of standing, I think. Everyone had standing to challenge these laws, since each was in a business that will be affected by these laws. I do not base my decision on religion. I believe that each state has the power to declare one day of seven a holiday or a day of rest, and I don't think that this is affected by the fact that some religious groups would prefer a different one. The Maryland (*McGowan*) and Pennsylvania (*Two Guys, Braunfeld*) laws are both O.K.—they have no garments of religion and I can see nothing unconstitutional about them. I can't say that it interferes with one's religion to declare a holiday on the same day that one celebrates his holy day. I feel differently about the Massachusetts law (*Gallagher*), which has those habiliments and on its face relates to a holy day. But the Supreme Judicial Court of Massachusetts has stripped off these habiliments in *Has*.[4] I would sustain all of these statutes, but with a caveat that we are accepting the Massachusetts court's construction. Otherwise, I agree with the Chief.

FRANKFURTER: The *Braunfeld* complaint in count three is different. Hence, it should be remanded for proof. I agree with the Chief as to all of the others.

DOUGLAS: None of these statutes comports with the First Amendment. I think that we are entitled to our religious scruples, but I don't see how we can make everyone else attune to them. I can't be required to goose step because eighty or ninety percent goose step. And if I go over that, I can't see an answer to Magruder's equal protection argument.[5] I would strike down all of these statutes.

CLARK: I would sustain all of the statutes.

HARLAN: I would sustain all of the statutes.

WHITTAKER: I agree with the Chief and sustain all of the laws.

STEWART: These laws impose the exercise of certain religions and put pressure on them to desert their own religions. At the very least we ought to exempt conventional Sabbatarians.[6]

Results: The Court upheld all of the Sunday closing laws. McGowan *and* Two Guys *were decided by an 8–1 vote. Both were treated solely as economic injury cases, and the free exercise clause was not*

---

4. *Commonwealth v. Has*, 122 Mass. 40 (1877). This case called the state's closing laws little more than a mere "civil regulation providing for a fixed period of rest."

5. *Crown Kosher Super Market v. Gallagher*, 176 F. Supp. 466 (1959). Writing for a 2–1 majority, Judge Calvert Magruder struck down the Massachusetts Sunday closing laws as an establishment of religion, a violation of due process, and a violation of equal protection. On the equal protection claim, Magruder noted that only some types of stores were forced to close on Sundays, while others were allowed to remain open— even though the exceptions were as destructive of the state's claimed interest in establishing a common day of public rest and relaxation as allowing kosher markets to remain open on Sundays. Magruder also dismissed *Has* as offering nothing more than an "ad hoc improvisation" to justify the state's blue laws.

6. Twenty-one states exempted Sabbatarians from Sunday closing laws. At the time, such exceptions were thought to be constitutionally permissible but not required.

considered. Nor did the majority see any problems with the establishment or free exercise clauses in Braunfeld *or* Gallagher, *although the vote was somewhat closer at 6–3. Whatever might have been the original purpose of state blue laws, Earl Warren wrote, they had lost their religious character over time. State legislatures could properly set aside a common day of rest, and Sunday was as good a day as any other—perhaps better, because it conformed to the habits of most residents. While the laws created some unfortunate economic and shopping problems for some people, they did not unduly interfere with the free exercise of religion and similar problems, and inconveniences would occur no matter which day of the week the state chose as the common day of rest.*

In Braunfeld *and* Gallagher, *Brennan and Stewart would have reversed on the free exercise claims. William O. Douglas, the only Justice to dissent in all four cases, argued that the blue laws all had their genesis in the Fourth Commandment and were all essentially religious in origin and intent. Two years later, in* Sherbert v. Verner, *the Court significantly modified the stance it took in* Braunfeld *and* Gallagher, *ruling that the government was required to demonstrate a compelling interest to justify such restrictions on religious liberty.*[7]

Marsh v. Chambers, 463 U.S. 783 (1983)
(Brennan)

The Nebraska legislature used public funds to maintain an official state chaplain. Robert E. Palmer, a Presbyterian, had been the state chaplain for more than fifteen years. Among his duties was the opening of each legislative session with a prayer. Several members of the legislature, including Ernest Chambers, challenged the practice on the ground that it violated the establishment clause. The district court ruled that opening the legislative session with a prayer was permissible but that the use of public funds to pay the chaplain was unconstitutional. The court of appeals ruled that the state office of the chaplaincy violated the establishment clause regardless of whether public funds were used. Frank Marsh was the state treasurer.

BURGER: This is a tempest in a saucer so far as I am concerned. Any legislator can say what a chaplain can say. The First Amendment was adopted by Congress, which opened with a prayer. The emphasis here was on a paid chaplain, but I don't think that makes a difference. I do not see any religious purpose, or effect, or entanglement, so I would reverse.

BRENNAN:[8] I would affirm the judgment of the Eighth Circuit, although on different grounds than those upon which it relied.

This is a hard and sensitive case, which I would have preferred not to have to confront. But it is here, and we should approach it in a principled manner consistent with

7. *Sherbert v. Verner,* 374 U.S. 398 (1963). When a South Carolina textile mill changed from a five-day to a six-day work week, Adell Sherbert, a Seventh-Day Adventist, was fired for refusing to work on Saturdays. The state denied her claim for unemployment benefits on the ground that her refusal to work on Saturdays meant that she would not accept "suitable work." The Supreme Court ruled that South Carolina's unemployment laws, as applied, violated Sherbert's First Amendment free exercise rights. There was no compelling state interest in South Carolina's eligibility requirements to justify the "substantial infringement" on Sherbert's religious freedoms, nor did accommodating her beliefs amount to an "establishment" of the Seventh-Day Adventist religion.

8. Adapted from Brennan's talking papers, Brennan Papers, OT 1983, box 652.

our long-held view that the establishment clause requires the government to be absolutely neutral in matters of religion. Legislative prayer is a classic example of the government imbuing a religious exercise with the authority of the state. It doesn't just hurt anti-religious "troublemakers" like Senator Chambers—it also offends the rights of a good many profoundly religious people who don't want to have their government transform the act of communion with God into a trite and perfunctory public ritual.[9] Although the government may, in general, "speak" on virtually any subject, the establishment clause requires that the particular subject of religion not be one of them, and that religion be left, as much as possible, to private choice and private action. Unlike the Eighth Circuit, I don't think that we can distinguish between some legislative prayer practices and others; they all suffer from the same infirmity, and I think that that infirmity is fundamental.

As a doctrinal matter, legislative prayer cannot be sustained under the "three-prong" *Lemon* test. (1) Such prayer clearly serves religious *purposes*; to claim that it serves the purely secular purpose of getting the legislators to shut up or inspiring them with a secular sense of duty and seriousness is not only silly, but insults the intelligence of the perfectly honorable people who instituted and continue the practice. (2) Legislative prayer also has the clear *effect* of promoting religion. It may not increase the number of enrolled churchgoers, but we've never thought that to be the touchstone of "effect": if it were, even the actual creation of a State Church might not be an establishment clause violation. As I see it, the "effect" here is obvious on its face and consists in the official and explicit identification of the government with a religious point of view. Moreover, legislative prayer cannot be upheld as an attempt to mediate the tensions between the free exercise and establishment clauses: Reverend Palmer's function is not to minister to the religious needs of individual legislators, but to imbue the legislative body as a whole with a collective sense of religious reverence. (3) Finally, legislative prayer is clearly an *entanglement* of church and state: it sows religious animosities, and it requires the legislature to undertake the unseemly task of deciding which religion or religions, and which representatives of those religions, should be given this very special public seal of approval.

I recognize that the first Congress approved the practice of legislative prayer. But that historical fact cannot be dispositive. It is entirely possible that the same men who wrote a broad and lasting mandate for religious neutrality into the Constitution would, under the pressures or passions of the moment, violate the very principle they had enacted. History can give us guidance in a broad sense; it cannot validate forever every piece of legislation passed by the first Congress, or prevent us from reading the Constitution in light of the realities of the day and the requirements of evolving legal principle. I affirm.

WHITE: I agree with the Chief Justice. History weighs heavily with me.

MARSHALL: Money has nothing to do with it—it's the prayers.

---

9. State senator Ernest Chambers of Omaha diplomatically described himself as a non-Christian (he was an atheist). A lifelong political maverick, he had another brush with fame when he introduced legislation in 1989 that would have required the state to pay University of Nebraska football players as professional athletes.

BLACKMUN: The Court can't win this case. We have a basic doctrinal choice to make. We can affirm on *Lemon*.[10] We can also write a persuasive opinion to reverse following the historical basis of Byron's. *Walz*[11] would help, and Brennan's *Schempp*[12] decision goes pretty far. It is a judgment call, and after my vote in the Minnesota case I have to reverse.[13]

POWELL: I agree with Harry.

REHNQUIST: The "page of history" theory requires reversal for me.[14]

STEVENS: It is significant for me that the same minister was used for sixteen years, meaning that he reflects the Protestant religion of the majority. That seems inconsistent with the principle of neutrality. I would not go so far as Brennan, however. On the facts here, I would affirm.

O'CONNOR: History is my basis.

Result: The Court ruled 6–3 that Nebraska's use of public funds to maintain a state chaplain did not violate the establishment clause. In his majority opinion, Warren Burger ignored his own Lemon *test and based his decision on historical practice. Unlike school prayer, Burger wrote, there was a long history of legislative prayer that began with the first Congress—the same Congress that passed the First Amendment. The Chief Justice offered no constitutional interpretation or theory to justify the practice beyond tradition.*

In dissent, William Brennan argued that the state chaplaincy clearly failed the Lemon *test and violated the establishment clause. For Brennan, the fact that the first Congress passed the Bill of Rights did not mean that the first generation of legislators was infallible or incapable of violating the First Amendment. Brennan noted that although James Madison was the primary author of the First Amendment, voted for the bill that created the office of congressional chaplain, and served on the committee*

10. *Lemon v. Kurtzman*, 403 U.S. 602 (1971).

11. *Walz v. Tax Commission*, 397 U.S. 664 (1970). Frederick Walz sued as a property owner to enjoin enforcement of New York's tax exemption for real property owned by religious organizations and used for religious purposes. Walz claimed that he and other taxpayers were compelled to subsidize religious activities in violation of the establishment clause. The Supreme Court rejected his claim on the ground that the intent of the state law was not to establish, sponsor, or support religion but to spare nonprofit organizations—including nonprofit religious organizations—from the burdens of taxation routinely placed on for-profit institutions. The majority argued that any entanglements between church and state under this law were far less than what taxation of church property would require. Granting religious organizations tax-exempt status also helped to separate and insulate government from religious authority—which was the main intent of the establishment clause. Finally, the Court noted, the grant of tax-exempt status to religious and other charitable organizations had been an established tradition for nearly two centuries, and far from establishing a religion it had served to strengthen the free exercise of all shades of religious beliefs.

12. *Abington School District v. Schempp*, 374 U.S. 203 (1963).

13. Blackmun was probably referring to *Larson v. Valente*, 456 U.S. 228 (1982). On a 5–4 vote, the Court struck down a Minnesota law that exempted religious organizations from state registration and reporting requirements if they received more than 50 percent of their contributions from members or affiliated organizations. Brennan wrote the majority opinion, with Burger, White, Rehnquist, and O'Connor in dissent.

14. Oliver Wendell Holmes wrote that "a page of history is worth a volume of logic." *New York Trust Co. v. Eisner*, 256 U.S. 345, 349 (1921).

that selected the Reverend William Linn as the first chaplain, he later changed his mind and decided that the practice was unconstitutional.

Lynch v. Donnelly, 465 U.S. 668 (1984)

(Brennan)

For more than forty years, the town of Pawtucket, Rhode Island, sponsored an annual Christmas diorama in Hodgson Park, near the town's central shopping district. The display included, among other things, a Christmas tree, a snowman, Santa Claus's house, a sign saying "Season's Greetings," a clown, an elephant, a teddy bear, and a nativity scene. With the support of the American Civil Liberties Union, Daniel Donnelly sued Mayor Dennis Lynch in federal court, claiming that the nativity scene violated the establishment clause.[15] The district court and court of appeals agreed that including the creche in the town's Christmas display violated the First Amendment.

BURGER: This has been a practice for over a century—decorations for Christmas that are a clear mix of religious and secular activity. Whether part of a larger scene or separate, I see no First Amendment violation. It is not a secular activity, but it is no different from chaplains for me.[16] This would pass my *Kurtzman* tests.[17]

BRENNAN:[18] The issue in this case is whether the public display by a municipality of a nativity scene as a part of its annual Christmas celebration violates the establishment clause of the First Amendment. After my dissent last Term in *Marsh*, it probably comes as no surprise to hear that I find that this display does run afoul of establishment clause principles.

In saying that, however, I do not mean to concede that the majority opinion in *Marsh* controls this case. In my view, the two situations are indeed very different. In their briefs and at oral argument, both the petitioners and the solicitor general were unable to come forward with any historical evidence concerning the publicly financed display of nativity scenes that is in any way equivalent to the "unique history" supporting the practice of legislative prayer that was relied upon in *Marsh*.[19] And I find it difficult to imagine that any equivalent historical evidence can be found to justify Pawtucket's creche.

In addition, the petitioners and the solicitor general both stated at oral argument that the creche retained a distinctly religious symbolic character. Therefore, unlike *McGowan v. Maryland*, we are faced not with the mere recognition of a particular day or holiday that has taken on a wholly secular meaning and purpose, but rather we are confronted

---

15. Mayor Lynch claimed that the ACLU filed the lawsuit out of jealousy, because "in the whole organization there aren't three wise men or a virgin." Strossen, "Religion and Politics," 450.

16. *Marsh v. Chambers*, 463 U.S. 783 (1983).

17. *Lemon v. Kurtzman*, 403 U.S. 602 (1971).

18. Adapted from Brennan's talking papers, Brennan Papers, OT 1983, box 652.

19. Solicitor General Rex Lee argued as amicus curiae in favor of allowing Pawtucket to sponsor the creche scene. The mayor and city were represented by William F. McMahon, a lawyer from Providence. He argued that the diorama was part of a secular folk festival that had religious roots and that the display merely acknowledged Christmas as an American tradition. Not directly represented in the case were Pawtucket's merchants, most of whom thought that the main purpose of the nativity scene was to draw shoppers downtown during the year's main buying season.

with governmental sponsorship of an unambiguously religious symbol that is closely associated with particular denominations.[20]

Because neither *Marsh* nor *McGowan* can be invoked to justify this display, we are left to consider the creche under the *Lemon* test. After all, in the school financing cases, the state financing schemes under review always involve a complex and otherwise secular statutory framework. But our principal focus in those cases has always been on the primary purpose, effect, and entanglement risks presented by that portion of the overall financing scheme that touches upon or sponsors religion.

If we are to remain faithful to our prior decisions in this area, then the creche must, as both the district court and the court of appeals concluded, be found to violate the establishment clause. For that reason I would affirm the judgment of the First Circuit.

WHITE: I agree with the Chief Justice.

MARSHALL: I agree with Bill Brennan. We ought to require them to get rid of the creche when there is a substantial objection. Christ is not like a Thanksgiving turkey.

BLACKMUN: This is another case we can do without. If affirmed, it should be done narrowly. The crass commercialization of Xmas[21] sickens me. Little is lost, I suppose, however we decide this. *Marsh* is not controlling—there is no similar history here. If we apply *Lemon*, affirmance is hard to avoid, yet the entanglement is difficult to see. Still, public support leads me to affirm.

POWELL: *Nyquist* makes the primary test whether the purpose here is to advance religion.[22] I can't see that here. The setting here has a creche in middle of a 4,000 square foot display. It is primarily associated not with the Christian religion, but with a national holiday. It can't have a primary effect of advancing religion, because viewers don't have their minds on that.

REHNQUIST: This case is much like a pee-wee. People are not really bothered by this in its Xmas context.

STEVENS: I feel much as Harry does. We relied on history in *Marsh*, but here we don't have that, so in effect the Court is allowing *Lemon*. The findings of fact by the trial judge can't be ignored as to the effects and religious significance.

O'CONNOR: This is not an easy case. *Marsh* doesn't help—there was no significant history at the time of the drafting of the First Amendment. The *Lemon* tests then come into play. But I would acknowledge that the purpose and effect of the display are not to be treated separately; rather, they should be treated in tandem. Looking at them that way, the district court did not view the whole setting and I would therefore reverse.

---

20. *McGowan v. Maryland*, 366 U.S. 420 (1961).

21. The commercial spelling of "Xmas" is Brennan's, and no doubt a little private joke at Blackmun's expense.

22. *Committee for Public Education and Religious Liberty v. Nyquist*, 413 U.S. 756 (1973).

Result: The Court ruled 5–4 that Pawtucket could include a creche in the context of its seasonal Christmas display. Warren Burger, writing for the Court, argued that the display met his Lemon *test. The city's motives for creating the display were secular—the diorama was intended to help local business and show the historical origins of Christmas. The scene did not impermissibly advance the cause of religion, as any benefit to religion was indirect, remote, and incidental. Finally, the display caused no excessive entanglements between church and state. Political divisiveness alone was not enough to block the town's inclusion of a creche in the midst of an essentially secular holiday diorama.*

In dissent, William Brennan argued that the primary effect of the nativity scene was "to place the government's imprimatur of approval on the particular religious beliefs exemplified by the creche." In his judgment, the display failed the Lemon *test and clearly violated the establishment clause.*

PUBLIC FINANCIAL SUPPORT FOR RELIGIOUS EDUCATION

Everson v. Board of Education, 330 U.S. 1 (1947)
(Burton) (Murphy)

Under New Jersey law, local school districts could reimburse parents for bus fares paid to transport children to public or nonprofit private schools. In Ewing Township, the law meant in practice that reimbursements were paid only for transportation to public and Catholic schools. The New Jersey Supreme Court struck down the state law but the state court of errors and appeals reversed, ruling that the law did not violate either the state or federal constitutions.

Conference of November 23, 1946

VINSON: There is no discrimination here. The statute and resolution were for the benefit of education and children, and included any school. Anyone could come in. This involved primary schools. There was a compulsory school law, and all taxpayers contributed to public schools. This case was as strong or stronger than the *Cochran* case.[23] I would affirm.

BLACK: I affirm.

REED: I affirm.

FRANKFURTER: My view is otherwise. I reverse, but with difficulty. We could have settled this with our *Cochran* ruling, but since then much has changed, with our ruling last term for freedom of speech for company towns representing a new trend. I voted with the majority for freedom of speech to company towns. Also, consider *Thomas v. Collins*.[24] This case shifted our latest views about our democracy. When legislation makes inroads here,

---

23. *Cochran v. Louisiana State Board of Education*, 281 U.S. 370 (1930). Cochran sought to enjoin the state from spending taxpayer money to provide free textbooks for children at both public and private schools. The Court held that the practice did not violate the Fourteenth Amendment by taking private property for private purposes. Charles Evans Hughes, writing for a unanimous Court, argued that the textbooks were not given to the schools but were intended exclusively for the use of the children. They were the same books as those purchased for public schoolchildren and were entirely secular in their subject matter and content.

24. *Thomas v. Collins*, 323 U.S. 516 (1945). This case is discussed in chapter 9.

the justification must be very compelling. If there is one thing beyond anything else that involves religious freedom, it is the insulation of church and state. The framers wanted *complete and absolute* separation of church and state. Secretary Root's instructions to Taft as governor general of the Philippines were imperative—and here the shredding of it can be discussed.[25]

These are contributions to parochial schools, and it makes no difference to me that it is Catholic or Jewish schools involved. It is a "little one"—but we have rejected that distinction. Here, it is unjust for education. It leaves out those schools that are run for profit.

VINSON: Do you think, Felix, that this establishes religion?

Frankfurter: No. I do think that due process protects me against the blending of ecclesiastical and state affairs. The establishment clause does not have the fixed meaning of the Episcopal Church, nor merely that of giving money to religious institutions. I went to school in Vienna, where there was an established church—Catholics, non-conformists, and others in three rooms. I reverse.

DOUGLAS: I affirm. I don't think that this is the same as an endowment of religious groups by the state.[26]

MURPHY: I pass.

JACKSON: I am inclined to affirm. The argument that it is for the children rather than for the schools is refuted. There is not a sufficient basis for this finding. But this Amendment does not stop the states from teaching some forms of activity that are in favor of religion and vice versa. A lot of this argument about "child benefit" is damned dishonest.

RUTLEDGE: I agree with Frankfurter. We must draw the line at public schools, or we would have to draw the line at *all* schools and not exclude private schools. If you did the latter, you would not discriminate against any private, public, or sectarian schools. But if you fall short of that, it is discrimination, and this law falls short. The mere fact that this is for profit does not make this the line. It is all education, and they must supply this support for all. If this resolution were a statute, it would be invalid *on its face*. Public and Catholic schools would have to *show* that they are the only schools in the area.

Once this is done, the field is wide open and there is no telling where this ends. First it was textbooks, now buses and transportation, and next it will be lunches and teachers. It all benefits the schools. You can't draw the line between a little and a lot of pregnancy. If you can justify this law, then you can go much further. Even if *all schools* were included,

---

25. In 1900, following the Spanish-American War, Secretary of War Elihu Root wrote the official instructions for the first American governor of the Philippines, William Howard Taft. Root instructed Taft to govern the Philippines in the interest of the Philippine people and to give them the full benefit of the American Bill of Rights—except for the right to jury trial and the right to bear arms. Root stressed the importance of imposing a separation of church and state in the Philippines, citing that country's long and often unhappy history of close association between secular and ecclesiastical authorities under Spanish rule. Henry F. Pringle, *The Life and Times of William Howard Taft* 182–84 (1939).

26. During oral argument, Douglas passed a note to Hugo Black that said, "If the Catholics get public money to finance their religious schools, we better insist on getting some good prayers in public schools or we Protestants are out of business." Ball, *Hugo L. Black*, 134.

I still might consider it bad. This will throw everything into the legislature. Every religious institution in the country will be reaching into the hopper for help if you sustain this. It forces people to pay for the religious education of others. We must stop this thing right at the threshold of the public schools.

BURTON: I affirm. We are not considering the wisdom of the law, but whether it is prohibited by the Constitution. I can't find that they went that far in the Constitution. This is not an established church. The Constitution has not prohibited this step here. I think that the door is open, but the Constitution did it.

JACKSON: I am doubtful. All that Wiley has said is true but his conclusion. If the state decided to support private schools, it could do so. I don't see how you can read it in. If the federal Constitution did stop the states from doing those things, I might have to reverse.[27]

RUTLEDGE: The Fourteenth Amendment carries it in.[28]

BLACK: I won't go in a whole hogically way to contribute to a church—only this far.

VINSON: I try to think of the case in front of me. I think that the church itself would probably resist state control.

Result: After agonizing about his decision at length, Frank Murphy made up his mind to give Hugo Black a 5–4 majority to uphold the New Jersey law. The Court approved the reimbursement of bus fares as a benefit to families, rather than directly benefiting religious schools or churches. Black ignored the issue of whether it was proper for Ewing Township to limit compensation to Catholic schools. He began with Jefferson's metaphor of a high and impregnable wall between church and state, but with his next breath countenanced a major breach in that wall: "The First Amendment has enacted a wall between church and state. That wall must be kept high and impregnable. We could not approve the slightest breach. New Jersey has not breached it here."

After intense lobbying by Frankfurter, Jackson, and Rutledge, Harold Burton changed his mind and joined the dissenters. In the lead dissent, Rutledge grimly noted that the wall between church and state was "neither so high nor so impregnable today as yesterday." He cited Madison's Memorial and Remonstrance, *saying that even "three pence" of state support for a church was too much. Robert Jackson compared Hugo Black to Byon's Julia, who "whispering 'I will ne'er consent,'—consented."[29] The dissenters (Frankfurter proudly called them "the anti-Everson lads") continued to fight a rear-*

---

27. The fate of incorporation—whether the Fourteenth Amendment extended the Bill of Rights to the states—was at stake during the 1946 Term. Two months after *Everson* was decided, the Court rejected the idea of total incorporation and refused to apply the privilege against self-incrimination to the states. *Adamson v. California,* 332 U.S. 46 (1947). Black, Douglas, Murphy, and Rutledge dissented. Black and Douglas argued in favor of total incorporation, while Murphy and Rutledge argued that the protections provided by the Fourteenth Amendment were not limited to the Bill of Rights, a hybrid approach often referred to as "incorporation plus."

28. Murphy's conference notes attributed this argument to Frankfurter. It is not clear who was right, but because Jackson was talking to Rutledge at the time, it seems likely that Douglas's version was correct.

29. In his diary, Felix Frankfurter observed that this case was a "beautiful illustration" of Black's tendency "to utter noble sentiments and then depart from them in practice." Lash, *Diaries of Felix Frankfurter,* 343 (Tuesday, Mar. 9, 1948).

guard action against further erosion of the wall separating church and state, such as student released-time for religious instruction at issue the next term in McCollum v. Board of Education.

McCollum v. Board of Education, 333 U.S. 203 (1948)
(Burton)

The Champaign, Illinois, school board adopted a proposal by the Council on Religious Education (representing local Protestant, Catholic, and Jewish congregations) to excuse students with parental permission from classes so that they could receive religious instruction on school grounds. Students not participating in the program could continue their regular studies. Vashti Cromwell McCollum, a Free-thinker, refused to let her son participate in the program. She sued when she found out that her son, James Terry McCollum, was forced to sit in the hallway while students made fun of him as they passed by on their way to religion classes.[30]

VINSON: I reverse.

BLACK: I reverse.

REED: I affirm. Although this is a First Amendment case, she has standing to object. This is much less advantageous to the school than *Everson.* They can pass this.

FRANKFURTER: I reverse. Do not make it turn on the school hours. It appears that *Everson* stands in conflict with reversal here, especially where it says that the state shall be neutral. It is not enough to say that the states should be neutral. [BURTON: Frankfurter quotes Jeremiah Black (secretary of state to Buchanan, 1856) and Elihu Root (secretary of state to Theodore Roosevelt)—both at great length—as to state and church.][31] The appellee's supplemental brief is *wrong* in saying that these schools are non-sectarian schools. They are un-sectarian. The impulse to this movement is the Protestant faith. Such a use may be involved even where instruction is elsewhere. The authority and machinery of the public schools can't be used for recruitment. I object to the settlement. In this country, the *church* is *subordinate* to the state. They must not interlock.

DOUGLAS: I reverse. The state has to be neutral as between denominations. The problem does not stop there. It is enough here that they are giving religious instruction in the schools.

---

30. Harassment of the McCollum family increased and intensified. The family received over six thousand hostile letters, and endured taunts, abuse, and ultimately ostracism from their community. James McCollum was beat up so often that he was sent to live with his grandparents in Rochester, New York. Epstein, "Rethinking the Constitutionality of Ceremonial Deism," 2170–71.

31. Jeremiah S. Black was secretary of state and attorney general under President Buchanan. He was also an unsuccessful Supreme Court nominee, whose confirmation was rejected by a margin of one vote in 1861. Elihu Root was secretary of state during President Theodore Roosevelt's administration. Both men vigorously opposed any breaches in the wall between church and state. In Frankfurter's concurring opinion in *McCollum,* he quoted Jeremiah Black as saying, "The manifest object of the men who framed the institutions of this country was to have a State without religion, and a Church without politics." *McCollum,* 333 U.S. at 220. Some forty years later, Root expressed a nearly identical sentiment in support of a New York constitutional amendment to prohibit the use of public money to support sectarian education.

MURPHY: Pass.

JACKSON: I reverse. This cuts the Protestants out of the schools at the same time that we are paying for Catholic schools' buses. Protestants don't have a good means of standing out.

RUTLEDGE: Reverse.

BURTON: Reverse.

Result: Although eight of nine Justices voted to strike down the Illinois released-time program, they disagreed among themselves in virtually every other respect. Jackson and the other anti-Everson lads initially led the charge to overturn Everson, arguing that if Everson were allowed to stand, Protestants would be precluded from government support while taxpayers were "paying for Catholic school buses." But the lads' coalition did not last. Harold Burton thought that released-time programs were constitutional if public buildings were not used.[32] Frankfurter thought that the majority opinion should not even mention Everson, while Hugo Black, who had been assigned the case, refused to write or join any opinion that did not confirm Everson. Frankfurter was furious when Black convinced Burton and Rutledge to join his opinion, breaking up the gang of four lads. In the end, Frankfurter wrote a lengthy concurring opinion—although he pointedly refused to call it a concurring opinion because he could not bear to be associated with Black's position, however remotely. The case caused considerable public controversy, with respected constitutional scholar Edward S. Corwin charging that the Court had set itself up as a national school board.[33] Stanley Reed was the only Justice who voted in favor of the released-time program.

Zorach v. Clausen, 343 U.S. 306 (1952)
(Douglas) (Clark)

A New York law allowed students with parental permission to leave campus during school hours to go to religious centers for religious instruction and devotional exercises. The programs were organized by private parties rather than the schools. Students were not compelled to attend, and those who did not participate remained—without receiving any additional instruction—in their regular classrooms. This case was factually similar to McCollum, except that the religious instruction did not take place on school grounds. Tessim Zorach was the parent of a child enrolled in a Brooklyn public school who did not participate in the released-time program (the Zorach children attended religious lessons outside of school hours). Andrew Clausen was a member of the New York Board of Education.

Conference of February 2, 1952

VINSON: Children give jurisdiction to maintain the suit. The people who raise these constitutional questions are parents and taxpayers. Can they use a shotgun attack, or do they have to show that they have been affected by the conduct? The question of discrimination is raised—the law is said not to give recognition to all duly constituted religious groups. No discrimination was shown as respects these people. Maybe a taxpayer could

---

32. Berry, *Stability, Security and Continuity,* 55–56.
33. Corwin, "The Supreme Court as National School Board."

use this broadside attack, but certainly not the parents. *McCollum* does not control this.[34] There, sectarian sects were aided by the use of the facilities of the schools, etc. School funds and school time are not used here. The only issue here is on the religious groups to which these parties belong. Hence we do not have to pass on all the horribles posed by the appellant—i.e., atheists, Jews, Jehovah's Witnesses, etc. I affirm.

BLACK: I vote tentatively to reverse.

REED: I affirm. I will start with the Constitution. There is no interference here with the free exercise of religion. The students are free to stay or go, and the state keeps records of truancy. All of the difficulties of *McCollum* are not here. Look at it as a matter of a privilege given to parents to withdraw pupils for a religious day. Our schools must be a place to teach the various problems of life—subject to all the pull and haul—in the schools, including religion. *I believe in keeping state and church separate, however.* These students don't have to go to any services, etc. See my dissent in *McCollum.* I affirm.

FRANKFURTER: The establishment of religion means more than establishing a church. *McCollum* decided more than that. *McCollum* decided just the opposite of what Reed says. The problem is here because we extended the Amendments to the states. McCarthyism is a filthy, dirty, smearing technique, but there is another group who feels that they alone are *God's anointed* who also smear others. Secularism in the schools is a fighting issue. I agree with Bryce, who says that sectarianism has ruined Europe and secularism has saved America from exclusions, etc.[35] The real issue in *McCollum* was whether the school was put behind sectarianism. Religious institutions of the country must be kept out of the schools if public schools are to be free of sectarianism. The public school system is being used to get children into schools of religion. That is a sectarian project. The public school system should not be used as a tail to the bite of religious schooling. These groups are using the whole machinery of the school system to get the children into religious places because otherwise they will not go there. This is more than a mere dismissal of children, this is a coercive instrument. I agree with Judge Fuld and his dissent.[36]

JACKSON: I reverse.

BURTON: There is no religious instruction in the public schools. This is not dismissal. It encroaches a bit, perhaps, but it does not infringe on the Constitution. I affirm.[37]

CLARK: Affirm.

MINTON: Affirm.

---

34. *McCollum v. Board of Education,* 333 U.S. 203 (1948).

35. James Bryce, *The American Commonwealth.*

36. Justice Stanley Fuld of the New York Court of Appeals was the sole dissenter in the decision below, 100 N.E.2d 463 (1951).

37. In his bench memorandum, Burton compared the program to "excusing a child for medical treatment." He did not accept his clerk's argument that the schools were "actively directing children to religious instruction." Berry, *Security, Stability, and Continuity,* 105.

Result: By a 6–3 vote, the Court upheld the New York statute. William O. Douglas, writing for the majority, distinguished and limited the scope of McCollum, *ruling that off-campus released-time programs were permissible where there was no evidence of religious favoritism, exclusion, or coercion. Douglas adopted a reasonableness standard, stating that an absolute separation between church and state was not required because "we are a religious people whose institutions presuppose a Supreme Being." Absolute separation between church and state was not only impossible, Douglas argued, it would lead to increased tensions between the two estates—which was not what the framers intended.*

Black and Jackson dissented because they could not see any significant difference between this case and McCollum. *In both cases, government authority was being used to promote religious training. The state was impermissibly helping religious sects through its power of compulsory school attendance, with the schools serving "as a temporary jail for [students] who will not go to church." Frankfurter dissented on the grounds that the record failed to show whether children had been coerced to participate and because while the schools remained open when most students were off-campus receiving religious instruction, the students left behind did no substantive work and were deprived of even the pretense of instruction. New York's released-time program remains in effect today.*

Epperson v. Arkansas, 393 U.S. 97 (1968)
(Douglas) (Brennan)

Arkansas law prohibited teaching the theory of human evolution in public schools and universities. Violating the statute was a misdemeanor, and anyone convicted could be fired. Susan Epperson, a high school biology teacher, sought a declaratory judgment that the "Arkansas monkey law" violated the First and Fourteenth Amendments. She asked for an injunction prohibiting the state from firing her for teaching lessons on evolution contained in a district-mandated biology textbook. Chancellor Murray O. Reed of the Arkansas Chancery Court struck down the law, ruling that the act established the Christian religion and violated Epperson's freedom of speech. The Arkansas Supreme Court reversed in a two-sentence opinion, saying that the law was a proper exercise of state power over school curriculum.

WARREN: This act is too vague to stand. The Supreme Court of Arkansas opinion says as much, for even it does not know how far the act goes. They can't say whether it goes to teaching, or explanation, or what. I reverse on vagueness. The state has shown no compelling need for an act of this kind.[38] The state has broad authority to fix curriculum, but a prohibition like this should have some reason related to police power—such as morals, safety, public order, welfare, and the like. Here, however, the state shows no special need for this law. I would not want to go too far, so I would rest on the vagueness of this law as the safest basis. I also think that the overbreadth approach of *Butler v. Michigan* could work here.[39] I reverse.

---

38. The Court ordinarily would not require a state to demonstrate a compelling interest to justify a law unless it infringed on a fundamental right or resorted to a suspect classification. Because Warren wanted to avoid a ruling based on the fundamental rights of speech or religion, his use of the strict scrutiny test seems inappropriate under the circumstances.

39. *Butler v. Michigan,* 352 U.S. 380 (1957). The Court, in a Felix Frankfurter opinion, struck down a state law prohibiting the sale of lewd material that might damage young people. Frankfurter wrote, "The state may not reduce the adult population of Michigan to reading only what is fit for children. . . . Surely this is to burn the house to roast the pig" (383).

BLACK: I will try to avoid the constitutional issues in this case. I would rest on vagueness, which would leave the basic issue undecided. This Court is going to change soon. I can't go on any ground that this statute is thought to be unreasonable or arbitrary, because that is not an acceptable constitutional standard. I object to McReynolds's philosophy that any unreasonable law is bad.[40] I utterly reject that. There is no case or controversy here between this lady and the state of Arkansas. There has been no effort to enforce this law in Arkansas. There is no law in Arkansas, in effect, that produces this effect. We have already gone a long way in regulating schools. I would leave everything else to local school boards. [DOUGLAS: He delivers a diatribe against centralized government interfering with local agencies, and sounds like Governor Wallace running for office.] This case is too minor for us to deal with. I want to pass for today.

DOUGLAS: Vagueness is here and that's enough for me. I would put this solely under the conventional rules of vagueness. I think that Butler v. Michigan would be a mistaken approach. I don't think that the establishment of religion is really in the case, but I might go on the establishment clause. I think that the brightest of us are the very young, and the danger is that we would try to make them like us. I reverse.

HARLAN: I would like to get this case back to the Arkansas courts and compel them to decide this, but I do not know how to do it. Underlying it all, I think that it is an establishment clause case, but Arkansas throws no light on that place. It would be hard to write that up here, although not impossible. If it can't be decided on establishment grounds and it can't be ducked—I would not rest on Poe v. Ullman—I am inclined to affirm.[41]

BRENNAN: Arkansas has tried to repeal this law, but the Faubus forces fought it. So did Johnson, who ran against Fulbright.[42] I do not know how to get this case back to

40. Black often criticized McReynolds's conception of substantive due process. In his dissenting opinion in Tinker v. Des Moines School District, he said: "We have previously rejected 'the old reasonableness-due process test, the doctrine that judges have the power to hold laws unconstitutional upon the belief of judges that they 'shock the conscience' or that they are 'unreasonable,' 'arbitrary,' 'irrational,' 'contrary to fundamental "decency,"' or some other such flexible term without precise boundaries. I have many times expressed my opposition to that concept on the ground that it gives judges power to strike down any law they do not like. . . . It will be a sad day for the country, I believe, when the present-day Court returns to the McReynolds due process concept." Tinker v. Des Moines School District, 393 U.S. 503, 520 (1969).

41. Poe v. Ullman, 367 U.S. 497 (1961). A badly divided Court—without any majority opinion—dismissed the Connecticut birth control case on the ground that it presented no justiciable controversy. In the lead opinion, Frankfurter and three other Justices argued that there was no live case or controversy, because the state law criminalizing contraceptives had been on the books more than seventy-five years with only one attempted prosecution and because contraceptives were sold openly throughout the state. Harlan, Douglas, and Stewart dissented, arguing that the case was properly before the Court and should be decided on the merits. Black also dissented and argued that there was a real case or controversy, although unlike the other dissenters he refused to say how he would have resolved the issues on the merits. In the Epperson conference, Harlan appears to be criticizing Black for failing to acknowledge that the risk of prosecution in this case was at least as high as it was in Poe.

42. Arkansas governor Orval Faubus vigorously opposed repeal of the statute, as did former Arkansas Supreme Court Justice Jim Johnson, an ardent segregationist who ran unsuccessfully against Senator William Fulbright in 1956 and in 1968.

Arkansas. The narrowest basis is vagueness. I would reverse on that ground. I could go for *Butler v. Michigan.*

STEWART: We should not put this case with *Butler v. Michigan,* because then we are prescribing the curriculum for Arkansas. I have trouble with vagueness. The Arkansas Supreme Court may have made the act vague, but if teaching evolution can be a crime or saying this is such a thing can be a crime, then the law is not vague. And if one of the alternative interpretations is not an unconstitutional prohibition, then we can't say that the statute is void for vagueness. So we have to go to the basic issue of what a teacher can teach in the classroom under the cloak of the First Amendment. This law is prohibiting a teacher from speaking out. This to me is simple violation of the teacher's First Amendment rights, because it prohibits freedom of speech. I reverse.

WHITE: I could go on vagueness if someone can articulate it, as I have not been able to. I am having trouble spelling it out. I thought that the case could be reversed on the First Amendment, but doesn't that get us into the whole school curriculum business? I reverse doubtfully on vagueness.

FORTAS: I would reverse on what to me is the narrowest ground—the establishment of religion. I don't have trouble getting to that issue. I don't like to strike down state laws on vagueness unless it is clear that it gives state officials a choice of options that suits a result. We should stay away as far as possible from getting into school cases and local educational systems. I would not say that this is a violation of teachers' First Amendment speech rights.

STEWART: I would go along on that ground, alternatively.

HARLAN: I agree.

MARSHALL: I would reverse. I agree with Abe.

Result: Earl Warren gave Abe Fortas the assignment, and the Court struck down the Arkansas statute as a violation of the establishment clause. Whether the law was vague was irrelevant, Fortas wrote, as was whether the law was intended to prohibit advocacy or explanatory teaching of Darwin's theories. Either way, the law was unconstitutional. Hugo Black, John Marshall Harlan, and Potter Stewart concurred in the result.

In 1981, Arkansas passed a new "creation-science law," requiring public schoolteachers to balance the teaching of evolution with an equal dose of biblical creationism. That law was struck down the following year.[43]

Tilton v. Richardson, 403 U.S. 672 (1971)
(Douglas)

Eleanor Taft Tilton and other Connecticut taxpayers and residents brought suit against various federal officials and church-affiliated colleges and universities in the state. Tilton alleged that the Higher

---

43. *McLean v. Arkansas Board of Education,* 529 F. Supp. 1255 (E.D. Ark. 1982), aff'd, 723 F.2d 45 (8th Cir. 1983).

Education Facilities Act of 1963 violated the free exercise and establishment clauses. The act provided federal aid for private and religious colleges to build facilities for secular educational purposes (the law prohibited any federal money from being used for sectarian instruction or worship or for divinity schools or departments) and provided government oversight through on-site inspections. The restriction that federally funded facilities be used exclusively for secular activities lasted for twenty years, after which time the facilities could be converted to religious purposes. A three-judge district court ruled that the act was constitutional, and Tilton appealed directly to the Supreme Court. Elliot Richardson was the secretary of health, education, and welfare.

<u>Conference of March 5, 1971</u>

BURGER: There is a difference between aid to higher education and elementary education. Congress intended to aid both. The potential for conflict is less in colleges than in elementary schools. The purpose of churches in running elementary schools is to inculcate the young. Secular character at college level is easier than at the elementary level. I am concerned about future involvement and entanglement. At the college level it is minimal—it is less than in the busing or text book cases.[44] This is not unlike grants to medical schools. I affirm.

BLACK: I reverse.

DOUGLAS: I reverse.

HARLAN: I affirm. If the First Amendment is an absolute, these cases are simple. But that has not been the course of our decisions. I approved *Everson*. There must be room for accommodation. Consider *Schempp*, and *Allen*, and *Walz*.[45] *Walz* gives government support if there is no discrimination. This is a very serious issue. It would be very disruptive to say that the federal government can't come to the aid of parochial schools. I affirm. The same basic principle covers all three cases.

BRENNAN: I pass. I have not made up my mind.

STEWART: The federal grant program is uniform and nationwide, and covers private and public schools. Churches are not preferred. I affirm.

WHITE: I affirm.

MARSHALL: I affirm. I agree with John Harlan. This is out of the realm of parochial schools. This is in the realm of private schools. When parents get welfare money and give it to the church, that is not aid to churches. There is no way out. This is not mixing up state and church—there is no difference between this and *Everson*.

BLACKMUN: This is a carefully drawn act. Urgent need does not make it constitutional. Divinity schools are excluded. There are no restrictions on books. There is no govern-

---

44. *Everson v. Board of Education*, 330 U.S. 1 (1947) (transportation); and *Board of Education v. Allen*, 392 U.S. 236 (1968) (textbooks).

45. *Abington School District v. Schempp*, 374 U.S. 203 (1963); *Board of Education v. Allen*, 392 U.S. 236 (1968); *Walz v. Tax Commission*, 397 U.S. 664 (1970).

ment support for religious activities. After twenty years, the building goes to the church, but depreciation takes care of that. If the test is purpose and effect, I am satisfied. I affirm. This is not a continuing arrangement—only a one-shot deal.

Result: A badly divided Court vacated the district court's judgment and remanded the case. There was no majority opinion. Five Justices agreed that federal aid to sectarian colleges for the construction of buildings and facilities to be used for secular educational purposes did not violate the Constitution. Eight Justices, however, agreed that allowing the schools to convert these facilities to religious purposes after twenty years amounted to an impermissible government contribution to religious institutions and violated the establishment clause.

Burger announced the judgment of the Court in a plurality opinion, joined by Harlan, Stewart, and Blackmun. White provided the crucial fifth vote upholding the first part of the act. In his concurring opinion, White argued that in assisting sectarian schools to perform their secular functions, the act had a secular purpose and only incidentally benefited religion.

Douglas, Black, and Marshall dissented in part. Douglas argued that the entire act should have been struck down as a violation of the First Amendment and academic freedom. He argued that religious institutions were directly and materially aided by the federal subsidies, because any money saved through federal funding could be used to support the religious missions of sectarian schools. In addition, Douglas thought that the act created excessive entanglements among the government, religion, and institutions of higher education through the program of mandatory government inspections. Brennan dissented separately, arguing that the entire act was unconstitutional as applied to sectarian colleges and universities. He favored remanding the case for the lower court to determine whether the schools named in the lawsuit were sectarian institutions.

Lemon v. Kurtzman, 403 U.S. 602 (1971)
Earley v. DiCenso
Robinson v. DiCenso
(Douglas) (Brennan)

Pennsylvania allowed its superintendent of public instruction to purchase "secular educational services" from private schools, which enabled the state to subsidize secular education at religious schools, including teachers' salaries and state-approved textbooks and materials. Alton Lemon sued David Kurtzman, the state superintendent, claiming that the law violated the free exercise and establishment clauses. A three-judge district court rejected Lemon's claims and ruled that the law was constitutional.

In the companion case, Rhode Island subsidized parochial schoolteacher salaries, paying up to 15 percent of a teacher's annual salary to teach secular subjects. To be eligible, teachers had to be certified by the state board of education and teach in schools where the average per-pupil expenditure on secular education was less that the state average for public schools. They had to teach the same secular subjects taught in public schools and had to agree in writing not to teach religion so long as they received state salary supplements. Participating schools had to submit extensive financial data to the State Commissioner of Education. In practice, the salary supplements went exclusively to teachers at Catholic schools. A three-judge federal court struck down the state law as a violation of the establishment clause on the ground that it created "excessive entanglements" between church and state.

Conference of March 5, 1971

BURGER: I have grave doubts about this aid. I don't see any difference between the Pennsylvania and Rhode Island plans; these are same as in *Earley v. DiCenso* and *Robinson v. DiCenso*. These are elementary schools where attendance is mandatory, and that fact pulls two ways. Crisis, distress, and emergency do not give force in favor of finding these laws constitutional. About 30 percent of the students involved are in Catholic schools. As a legislator, I would vote for this law. I would prefer to transfer to public schools the teaching of the same courses. Entanglement is the only problem I see here. The potential entanglement is large. There is already a great deal of supervision of the secular activities—it is the crux of accreditation.

In Minnesota, there is a state audit that covers courses taught and teacher qualifications for accreditation. That is not great surveillance, that is a service. Here there is more. Teachers are paid public salaries: (a) directly to the schools in Pennsylvania; and (b) to teachers in Rhode Island. And in the Rhode Island case there is state surveillance of the number of teachers. I am troubled by these cases. Here surveillance is over teachers, yet this is a question of degree. I am influenced by the financial crisis that exists. I pass.

BLACK: I reverse.

DOUGLAS: I reverse.

HARLAN: I would affirm, but I would reverse the district court decision knocking out the lone individual plaintiff for lack of standing. If it is permissible, as I think it is, for public funds to be used to support the lay part of religious schools, and if we can protect against the trespass of religion into the public part of education, then policing is not entanglement in the sense of inhibiting the recipients of public funds from using those funds for religion. Safeguards can be set up. This involves entanglements, but it is not fatal. The recipients asked for the money, and they can accept these safeguards.

BRENNAN: I pass.

STEWART: I reluctantly reverse. The elementary schools are different. Here, the grants are being aimed directly at helping the parochial schools, and that violates the establishment clause. I don't think that the inspection angle means much. The entanglement doctrine is relevant only to the free exercise of religion. But pouring in public funds enables these schools to continue, and they are religion.

BRENNAN: If public funds are not given, parochial schools will not perish. Two winds are blowing: (a) in the United States, education is no business of Catholics; and (b) it won't be many years until Notre Dame is like Harvard, etc.

WHITE: There is no difference in these cases. I affirm. A state can decide to give students a secular education wherever they go. The state can say, "Wherever you want your secular education, we'll pay for it." "Entanglement" is only another word for saying that a state should not muffle or interfere with the free exercise of religion. I might vacate on the standing issue, because the court should not have dismissed the individual litigant. On the constitutional issue, I affirm.

MARSHALL: Takes no part because the NAACP is a party.[46]

BLACKMUN: These are outright grants, which means that the schools are free to use their own funds any way that they want for other purposes. That is different from the partial grants in college cases under the federal act. These cases go further than *Allen*[47] and *Everson*,[48] as the grants are to the schools. The logical end of these cases is complete public support of parochial schools. I am inclined to reverse.

Result: The Court moved from a tie vote at conference to a 9–0 vote to strike down the Pennsylvania law and a 7–1 vote to overturn the Rhode Island statute. Despite his ambiguous vote in conference, Warren Burger assigned the opinion to himself and managed to build a near consensus. He wrote that the Pennsylvania statute provided impermissible cash subsidies to parochial schools and that the Rhode Island law created excessive entanglements between church and state by requiring extensive state supervision of religious schools. Burger established a three-pronged test for establishment clause cases. To be valid, state laws must (1) have a secular purpose; (2) neither advance nor inhibit religion nor promote one religion over another; and (3) avoid excessive entanglements between church and state. Ironically, soon after this case was announced, the Chief Justice began to distance himself from his own test, claiming that Lemon *was not really a test but a flexible set of guidelines.*

Thurgood Marshall joined Burger's opinion in the Rhode Island cases but did not participate in the Pennsylvania case. Byron White concurred with the majority's decision to strike down the Pennsylvania law, although he disagreed with Burger's finding that the law was facially invalid. White dissented alone in the Rhode Island cases, arguing that the state law was constitutional.

On remand, the Pennsylvania District Court enjoined state payments for services rendered after Lemon I. *The judge, however, allowed the state to pay for services performed prior to the Court's decision. Alton Lemon appealed, asking that parochial schools be required to reimburse the state treasury for subsidies received before* Lemon I *was decided.*

Lemon v. Kurtzman (Lemon II), 411 U.S. 192 (1973)
(Douglas) (Brennan)

Conference of November 10, 1972

BURGER: Appellants made no effort for a whole year to enjoin these payments. The three-judge court has exercised a broad equitable power. This case is not easy. The equities

---

46. Marshall participated in the two Rhode Island cases where the NAACP was not a party.

47. *Board of Education v. Allen*, 392 U.S. 236 (1968). A New York law required local school boards to loan textbooks free of charge to all children in grades seven through twelve, including students at private parochial schools. The state supreme court (i.e., the trial court) ruled that the law violated both the establishment and free exercise clauses. The appellate division reversed on the ground that the plaintiffs lacked standing. The state court of appeals reversed on standing but ruled that the statute was constitutional. The U.S. Supreme Court affirmed on a 6–3 vote. Byron White wrote that there was no First Amendment violation because (1) the law was neutral and universal—all children benefited equally from the state's universal program of free textbooks; (2) the books remained the property of the state, not the schools; (3) the books were technically furnished at the request of the parents and children, not the schools; (4) any financial benefits went to parents and children, not the schools; (5) all the textbooks were secular and used to further secular educational goals; and (6) there were no allegations that the plaintiffs were coerced in any way regarding their religious beliefs.

48. *Everson v. Board of Education*, 330 U.S. 1 (1947).

weigh considerably in favor of payments, and to let things remain as they are. It is a classic example of action taken to one's own detriment in actual reliance. Entanglement is all in the past. I affirm.

DOUGLAS: I would reverse. This is a constitutional violation whether the payment was in the past or future.

BRENNAN: This is a naked subsidy. We have ruled on it—retroactivity has nothing to do with it. I would reverse.

STEWART: It is a harsh and inequitable result, but whether draconian or not I would reverse.

WHITE: I affirm.

MARSHALL: Takes no part.

BLACKMUN: This is a spoiler's lawsuit. Prospective only ruling should be an exception. My initial reaction is to reverse. The court of appeals were trying to do equity, and respondents have a lot of equity. All entanglement angles are behind, not prospective. I tentatively affirm, but am not at rest yet.

POWELL: I would affirm. I agree with the Chief Justice and Harry—the entanglement aspects are behind, not ahead.

REHNQUIST: This is more like the *Chico Drainage* [*sic*] case—enough in it to affirm.[49]

Result: The Court affirmed the district court's decision on a 5–3 vote. Warren Burger, writing for the majority, found that the district court had acted within its discretion as a court of equity to allow the state to honor the obligations it incurred before Lemon I.

Committee for Public Education and Religious Liberty v. Nyquist, 413 U.S. 756 (1973)
(Douglas) (Brennan)

In the early 1970s, New York and Pennsylvania each created new programs designed to aid private elementary and secondary schools. First, New York gave state grants of up to thirty dollars per student annually to qualified schools for facility maintenance and repair. To qualify, schools had to be private, nonprofit, and serve largely poor students. In practice, these grants mostly benefited Catholic

---

49. *Chicot County Drainage District v. Baxter State Bank*, 308 US 371 (1940). This was a res judicata case. An Arkansas drainage district took advantage of a federal law to restructure its indebtedness to bondholders. A group of bondholders sued but during the trial did not challenge the federal law's constitutionality—although they had ample opportunity to do so—nor did they comply with the judge's decree to retire the original bonds within the time provided. After the case was decided, the Supreme Court ruled the law unconstitutional in another case, and the bondholders sought to use that decision to reopen the case. The Supreme Court ruled unanimously that the bondholders could not attack the judge's decree in a collateral proceeding. Res judicata, the Court said, may be pleaded to bar not only matters actually litigated previously but any matters that *might* have been raised during the original proceedings.

schools. Second, both New York and Pennsylvania provided partial tuition reimbursements to poor families with children in private schools. Third, New York offered special tax relief for middle-class parents who were not poor enough to qualify for tuition reimbursement. A three-judge district court unanimously struck down the facilities maintenance and tuition reimbursement programs, but over Circuit Judge Hays's dissent approved New York's tax credit program on a 2–1 vote. Ewald B. Nyquist was the commissioner of education in New York.

Conference of April 20, 1973

BURGER: Part 1 involves maintenance and repair of schools. Part 2 involves tuition reimbursement. Parts 3, 4, and 5 are tax benefits. Maintenance is unconstitutional under our previous decisions and must fall. Tuition reimbursement hangs in mid-air for me. Public money is given here to private persons. But reimbursement can be distinguished from tax credits. Tax credits to low income families would provide little benefit to people at the $5,000 annual income level. The state has a very high—perhaps compelling—interest in keeping private schools going. I see a parallel between tax credits and tax exemption or contributions credit under *Walz*.[50] People can make contributions to the schools and get tax deductions. Nothing here is violative under part 3 if *Walz* is sound. The district court found part 3 good, with Judge Hays dissenting.

DOUGLAS: I affirm on part 1 and part 2. I reverse on 3, 4, and 5. It is all the same no matter how thin you slice it.

BRENNAN: That's my vote, too. These are only devices to try a law which would get by. This is not like tax exemptions or contributions—it is just a device to avoid our prior decisions.

STEWART: This is a very difficult case. The doctrinaire approach is given by Douglas and Brennan. Part 1 is different for me. Our decisions in *Allen*[51] and *Everson*[52] point the other way. As presently advised, I agree with Judge Hays. But I find that the maintenance issue is almost more difficult in the face of *Allen* and *Everson*. *Bona fide* deductions would pass muster, but this is not that. It is more akin to a credit, and that is a direct subsidy.

WHITE: I will reverse on maintenance and tuition and affirm on the tax breaks. I would not strike this down on its face. This is a good way of transforming religious schools into secular schools.

MARSHALL: Part 1 is bad. *Everson* is wrong. I will not give money to them. I affirm. On part 2, I reverse. On part 3, the tax credit issue, I affirm.

BLACKMUN: These are hard cases. These schools are important in our structure and I want to sustain them. On part 1, I affirm. On part 2, I affirm. On parts 3–5, I will follow Judge Hays.

---

50. *Walz v. Tax Commission*, 397 U.S. 664 (1970).
51. *Board of Education v. Allen*, 392 U.S. 236 (1968), approving state-supplied textbooks for students in both public and private schools.
52. *Everson v. Board of Education*, 330 U.S. 1 (1947), approving state-supported bus transportation for students in both public and private schools.

POWELL: I agree with Harry. Tuition grants are different from exemptions. Tax laws across the board apply to all educational institutions, making deductions permissible. Tuition is bad. Once you start tuition grants or tax credits, the pressures would start in every legislature to increase the public grants. I will reverse parts 3–5.

REHNQUIST: I agree with Byron. This is not the use of public funds to support a state church—only a school run by the state.

Result: After the conference, William Rehnquist changed his mind and decided that the school maintenance grants were unconstitutional. Thurgood Marshall also changed his mind about the tuition reimbursements and tax credits and joined the majority to strike down all three programs. Burger eventually joined the dissenters in arguing that the tuition grants to poor families were constitutional. In the end, the Court voted 8–1 to strike down the maintenance grants and 6–3 to strike down the tuition grants and tax credits.

Mueller v. Allen, 463 U.S. 388 (1983)
(Brennan)

Minnesota allowed parents to deduct from their taxes the costs of tuition, textbooks, and transportation for children enrolled in elementary or secondary schools. Van Mueller and June Noyes sued the state and parents of children enrolled in parochial schools, claiming that the law violated the establishment clause by providing state support to religious schools. The district court upheld the state law, ruling that the statute was neutral on its face and as applied and did not have a primary effect of advancing or inhibiting religion. The court of appeals affirmed.

BURGER: This is a deduction. Our decisions in *Nyquist*[53] and *Walz*[54] are relevant here. But *Nyquist* was a direct subsidy and this isn't. Yet this comes close. *Walz* isn't quite so close for me. The state has a legitimate secular purpose here: (1) it lifts a substantial burden off public schools; (2) it fosters diversity; (3) private schools do a better job of education; and (4) the plan provides a method of measuring greater contribution to education goals. This is only a fraction of the total cost.

BRENNAN:[55] I vote to reverse the decision of the Eighth Circuit. In my view, the Minnesota statute violates the First Amendment. While I recognize that the statute at issue here is distinguishable from the one involved in *Nyquist* on the grounds that it applies to educational expenses incurred for both public and private education and involves a deduction for expenses actually incurred rather than a straight tax credit, I still believe that the principles of *Nyquist* and our other cases control. The state statute at issue here has the impermissible effect of advancing religion.

Although the record in this case is woefully incomplete, it is clear that the principal beneficiaries of the state statute are parents who send their children to private schools. Less than 10 percent of the children in Minnesota attend private schools. Of these, 96 percent

53. *Committee for Public Education v. Nyquist,* 413 U.S. 756 (1973).
54. *Walz v. Tax Commission,* 397 U.S. 664 (1970).
55. Adapted from Brennan's talking papers, Brennan Papers, OT 1982, box 630.

attend sectarian schools. We should not allow the facial neutrality of the statute blind us to the reality these figures reflect: the principal beneficiaries of the statute are parents who send their children to church-related private schools. Under our cases, the statute has the impermissible effect of advancing religion. There is no doubt that a deduction is, as a practical matter, a subsidy. As I stated in *Meek*, quoting from Justice Rutledge's dissent in *Everson*, the amount of the subsidy is irrelevant: "not even three-pence (can) be assessed."[56]

To me, it is equally irrelevant that the state may derive some benefit from supporting private schools. The state cannot pursue a legitimate end, the education of its children, through illegitimate means, the subsidization of religious education.

In addition to the tuition deduction, I also think the textbook deduction is unconstitutional. We already have upheld state textbook aid and Minnesota has such a program. The conclusion that the textbook deduction has the impermissible effect of advancing religion is therefore inescapable. The same analysis compels invalidation of the deduction for field trips.

As I have suggested, we should not allow the fine-tuned statute we have before us, with its apparent facial neutrality, to blind us to the reality that only seventy-nine students in the state paid public school tuition and that this statute was enacted with the apparent purpose, and clear effect, to subsidize religious education. I would reverse the judgment of the Eighth Circuit and invalidate the statute.

WHITE: I have been out of step with the Court for years. I would not extend *Nyquist*, and would affirm.

MARSHALL: I have misgivings even as to textbooks and transportation.

BLACKMUN: An affirmance here goes a long way toward killing off our public schools. I agree with the First Circuit. This fails the "primary effects" prong of our establishment clause decisions. I see no parallel to §170 of the Federal Code.[57] I don't agree that parochial schools produce a superior product to public schools.

POWELL: Public schools benefit from parochial school education. We can distinguish *Nyquist*, and the truth is that our cases are far from consistent. Can we say on this record that this twenty-five-year-old statute has fostered any of the evils that the establishment clause was designed to prevent? I don't think that I can say so. If we strike this statute down, I can't think of any aid to parochial schools that can survive.

---

56. *Meek v. Pittenger*, 421 U.S. 349 (1975). Two Pennsylvania laws authorized public schools to lend equipment and personnel free of charge to private and parochial schools, including: (1) textbooks, instructional materials, and other equipment, including charts, maps, films, projectors, periodicals, audio recordings, and laboratory equipment; and (2) professional staff to provide "secular" services, such as psychologists, remedial and accelerated instruction, counseling, testing, and speech and hearing therapy. Seventy-five percent of the private schools participating in the program were parochial schools.

The Supreme Court approved the textbook loans but struck down the rest of the program. Writing on behalf of a 6–3 majority, Potter Stewart ruled that the instructional material and equipment violated the establishment clause because these items were loaned directly to the schools, not to the students. The resulting support, which amounted to $12 million annually, was a direct and substantial advancement of religion.

57. Section 170 of the federal tax code allows deductions for contributions or gifts to qualified tax-exempt organizations. It does not distinguish between religious and nonreligious charitable organizations.

REHNQUIST: All of our cases are really only holdings on particular facts. This covered group is broader than that in *Nyquist*.

STEVENS: I would agree with Brennan on the basic problem. I can distinguish *Nyquist* all right. I question whether the diversity of educational facilities helps states. My views are much like Brennan's and Harry's.

O'CONNOR: It is hard to distinguish *Nyquist*, and the cases are difficult to reconcile. This is a true tax deduction, and while it is a form of subsidy it is indirect, and on that ground I would affirm.

Result: William Rehnquist wrote the majority opinion in a 5–4 decision upholding the Minnesota statute. The majority found that the state law met all three prongs of the Lemon[58] *test: it had a secular purpose, the primary effect of the law neither advanced nor inhibited religion, and it created no excessive entanglements between church and state.*

Bob Jones University v. United States, 461 U.S. 574 (1983)
(Brennan)

Under §501(c) of the Internal Revenue Code, Congress granted tax-exempt status to religious, educational, and charitable organizations. In 1970, the IRS took action to revoke the tax-exempt status of private schools that practiced racial discrimination. Among the first targets were Bob Jones University in South Carolina, and the Goldsboro Christian Schools in Goldsboro, North Carolina.

Under pressure from the IRS, which in a 1970 ruling threatened to revoke the school's tax-exempt status because of its segregationist admissions policies, Bob Jones University began to enroll a limited number of blacks in 1971, on the condition that they agreed not to advocate or practice interracial dating or marriage.[59]

The Goldsboro Christian Schools justified their racially exclusive admissions policies by claiming that Noah's three sons founded the different races: Ham (Asians and blacks), Shem (Jews), and Japheth (Caucasians), and any mixing of these three racial lines violated God's law. The Goldsboro schools were among the many "segregation academies" that sprouted everywhere in the South following Brown v. Board of Education. All together, these "seg academies" enrolled 400,000 students throughout the south in 1970.

In 1976, the IRS revoked the tax-exempt status of both schools, retroactive to 1970. Both schools paid their back taxes (Bob Jones University at the time owed approximately $500,000 in federal taxes alone) and then sued for a refund, claiming that the IRS policy violated their First Amendment rights. The district court ruled in the schools' favor, but the court of appeals reversed. The Reagan administration refused to support the government's position on appeal, and Solicitor General Rex Lee declined

---

58. *Lemon v. Kurtzman*, 403 U.S. 602 (1971).

59. In 1971, the school admitted five black students. At the time that the case was argued to the Supreme Court, the school had fewer than a dozen black students out of a student body of more than 6,300.

*to argue the case before the Supreme Court. In his place, the Court appointed William T. Coleman Jr.
to argue on behalf of the Internal Revenue Service.*[60]

BURGER: The question is whether the statutory authority to revoke these schools' tax
exemption was within the IRS's grant of discretion. In 1970, the exemption was withdrawn on a common law "charitable" basis. Does the statute embody this? I think that it
did. I would not reach the equal protection argument. The fact that the statute lists other
"charitable" organizations doesn't trouble me. The common law concept of charitables
embraces all. Congress has acquiesced in the exemption for at least twelve years. We can
distinguish race from age, sex, and other forms of discrimination. If we reach the Constitution, our decision in *Norwood* would mean that the government—.[61]

BRENNAN:[62] On the statutory issue, I am convinced that an otherwise "educational" institution that practices racial discrimination is not entitled to tax exempt status under
the Internal Revenue Code. When Congress first included exemptions for "religious, educational, or charitable" organizations in the code, it was obviously drawing upon a recognized common law tradition that gave certain non-profit entities special privileges in
recognition of the benefits they bestowed upon society. Each of the distinct exempt uses
listed in the statute must therefore be read in light of that common basic idea. Moreover, the history of the act's administration is entirely consistent with this reading of
§§501(c)(3) and 701.

The evidence of Congress's actions over the past decade only nails the coffin shut. We
affirmed *Green v. Connally* in 1971.[63] Not only did Congress not act to overrule that de-

---

60. William T. Coleman Jr. was Felix Frankfurter's law clerk during the 1948 term. He later became
secretary of transportation during the Ford administration and went on to become a prominent and powerful Washington lawyer.

61. *Norwood v. Harrison*, 413 U.S. 455 (1973). A group of parents from Tunica County, Mississippi,
sued in federal court to enjoin state officials from loaning state textbooks free of charge to children attending racially segregated private schools. A three-judge district court dismissed the complaint, but the Supreme
Court reversed and remanded, ruling that the state program was unconstitutional. Unlike earlier cases
involving free textbooks for children in parochial schools, Mississippi's textbook program provided tangible financial assistance to the schools themselves. This violated the state's constitutional obligation not
to provide tangible assistance to schools that practiced racial or other invidious forms of discrimination.
Burger wrote the majority opinion.

62. Adapted from Brennan's talking papers, Brennan Papers, OT 1982, box 612.

63. *Green v. Connally*, 330 F. Supp. 1150, 1162 (D.D.C. 1971), aff'd sub nom., *Coit v. Green*, 404 U.S. 997
(1971). William Green and other black parents sued John Connally, the secretary of the treasury, to enjoin
the federal government from granting tax-exempt status to racially discriminatory private schools in Mississippi. White parents of children who attended these schools intervened to defend the tax exemptions
and the deductibility of their contributions. After a three-judge district court granted a preliminary injunction against the government, the IRS announced that it would no longer recognize the schools' tax-
exempt status or allow deductions for contributions.

The district court then granted declaratory relief and a permanent injunction against the Treasury
Department not to grant such institutions tax-exempt status. Circuit Judge Leventhal ruled that under the
Internal Revenue Code, racially discriminatory private schools were not entitled to tax-exempt status, nor
were donors entitled to tax deductions for their contributions because the operation of these schools was
contrary to federal public policy. Moreover, the privileges that the common law ordinarily granted to charitable trusts did not apply when the organization's activities were contrary to public policy. The court based

cision, but it explicitly built upon it in passing §501(i). Even the Ashbrook amendment was careful to leave in place the original revenue ruling cutting off exemptions from schools that engaged in racially discriminatory practices.[64]

The solicitor general devotes a good deal of effort to attempting to show that the word "charitable," as used in the litany of exempt uses, should be read narrowly rather than in the broad common law sense.[65] As I see it, however, that observation, even if true, is essentially irrelevant. Congress may very well have decided to limit tax exemptions to certain subclasses of the broad universe of common law charitable uses. That does not mean that the subclasses it did choose to include should be read independent of their common character as types of common law charities. John Paul Stevens's questioning at oral argument was particularly incisive on this point: the word "charitable," when used to describe the whole litany of exempt uses, may mean something quite different than the word "charitable" when used to describe one of the particular exempt uses included in the litany.

I recognize that the IRS must not be allowed to be a roving policeman enforcing its particular view of what constitutes "public policy." But this case does not present that problem. However we limit the notion of "public policy," racial discrimination—especially in education—is clearly inconsistent with it. Indeed, I can think of few things more inconsistent with national public policy, however narrowly defined.

This same consideration should also settle Goldsboro's and Bob Jones's free exercise claim. I have long believed that the exercise of choices grounded on religious belief should not be penalized except in the face of the most powerful governmental interests. There are, however, virtually no governmental interests *more* compelling than the cause of racial justice. What Holmes said in another connection is also true of that goal—"Here," he said, "a national interest of very nearly the first magnitude is involved."[66] Bob Jones

---

its ruling primarily on the IRS code, because Judge Leventhal thought that it would provide a more enduring, permanent source of relief than a declaration of policy based on "shifting" common law principles. The Supreme Court affirmed summarily without comment.

64. In 1978, President Carter proposed new federal regulations to deny tax-exempt status to racially exclusive private schools. This set off a firestorm of opposition among congressional Republicans and southern Democrats. In 1979, Rep. John Ashbrook (R-OH) sponsored an amendment denying the IRS any funds to enforce the proposed regulations. Ashbrook blasted the Carter administration and criticized the IRS for "permitting itself to be used as an instrument to implement certain social policies." As a result of the Ashbrook amendment, the proposed regulations were never implemented. Presidential candidate Ronald Reagan used the controversy to appeal to fundamentalist Christian voters, accusing the Carter administration of mounting a "regulatory vendetta . . . against independent schools."

65. Acting Solicitor General Lawrence Wallace reluctantly signed the Reagan administration brief in support of Bob Jones University, although he personally disagreed with much of what the brief said. On the other hand, William Bradford Reynolds, the assistant attorney general for civil rights and head of the Civil Rights Division, wholeheartedly supported Bob Jones and the Goldsboro schools during oral arguments. Rex Lee, the solicitor general, had removed himself from the case, because as a private lawyer he had represented the Mormon church in similar litigation. After the case was decided, the Justice Department lost confidence in Wallace's loyalty to the administration and stripped him of his responsibilities in civil rights cases. Caplan, *The Tenth Justice*, 50–61.

66. *Missouri v. Holland*, 413 U.S. 416, 435 (1920). This case involved the power of the federal government to enforce a treaty to protect migratory birds against an uncooperative state government. Missouri claimed that under the Tenth Amendment it had exclusive, sovereign authority to regulate any wildlife within its jurisdiction. Holmes, writing for the Court, found that the federal government's treaty powers took precedence over any "quasi-sovereign" rights or police powers that the states might have otherwise retained.

and Goldsboro may be entirely sincere in their religious beliefs, but they cannot expect, in light of the governmental interest at stake here, to be spared the consequences of the racially discriminatory practices that have arisen out of those beliefs. I affirm.

WHITE: I agree with Bill Brennan. We have to reach the constitutional issue of free exercise. I would not reach the question of whether the Constitution forbids tax exemption for religious organizations.

MARSHALL: I think that the statute obligates the IRS to deny the exemptions in this case. Section 501(c)(3) embraces only those charitables in a common law sense. The admissions policies of both schools invalidate both national policy and §1981. The Constitution bars these practices, and furthermore, *Norwood* makes that clear.

BLACKMUN: *Bob Jones* should be the lead case on our opinion—it is the primary case. But Coleman was a disappointment.[67] In my practice, these schools certainly had an exemption—to put this on public policy is to put it to risk of the vagaries of change.

On the statutory issue, "or" is really "and."[68] The common law concept of public benefit permeates charitables.[69] These schools are not churches, which would be another case. Congress has ratified the 1970 interpretation—§501(i) is strong evidence of this. On the constitutional arguments, there was no establishment clause violation under our three-prong test. The free exercise burden is less than the question of overwhelming governmental interest.

POWELL: I would affirm along Harry's line of reasoning, rather than any other approach. I don't think that the IRS could construe the law as it did in 1970, because it can't create social policy. Only Congress can do that. Although Congress hasn't ratified the IRS po-

---

67. Several years later, Blackmun again singled Coleman out in conference for poor oral advocacy in *Garcia v. San Antonio Metropolitan Transportation Authority*, 469 U.S. 528 (1985).

68. Section 501(c) (3) of the code provided tax-exempt status to "corporations . . . organized and operated exclusively for religious, charitable . . . *or* educational purposes" (emphasis added). Both schools argued that the plain language of the statute guaranteed them tax-exempt status, because no language in the statute expressly required exempt organizations to be "charitable" in the common-law sense. They argued that the disjunctive "or" separating the categories in §501(c) (3) meant that if an institution fell within *any one* of the specified categories it was automatically entitled to exemption, without regard to whether it was "charitable." Blackmun's view ultimately prevailed; Burger's majority opinion in this case rejected the schools' statutory argument on the ground that it was "a well-established canon of statutory construction that a court should go beyond the literal language of a statute if reliance on that language would defeat the plain purpose of the statute."

69. The common law had long recognized the idea that charitable organizations were tax-exempt and that gifts to such organizations were tax deductible. An organization's tax-exempt status depended on established common law standards of charity, namely whether the institution served a public purpose and did not operate contrary to public policy.

Blackmun's view—ultimately adopted by the majority—was that Congress had been guided by the common law in enacting § 501(c)(3) and that Congress had explicitly incorporated the "public benefit" theory concerning charitable trusts. This is the theory that the government is compensated for any loss of tax revenue by: (1) being relieved of financial burdens that otherwise would be paid from public funds; and (2) using charitable organizations to help promote the general welfare. Galvin and Devins, "A Tax Policy Analysis of *Bob Jones University v. United States*," 1362.

sition explicitly, it certainly hasn't overruled the IRS for twelve years. The 1976 passage of §501(i) implicitly approved it. I have no difficulty with the constitutional issue. Bob Jones is primarily a secular institution.

REHNQUIST: You can't make a case at all until 1970. I can't agree that the doctrine of "common law charitables" covers them all. And I don't understand how you can conclude congressional ratification, although I agree that is your strongest argument. Therefore, I don't reach the First Amendment argument, although I would not find it meritorious if I did. Congress can allow or deny an exemption.

STEVENS: I agree with the Chief Justice's analysis. It is no problem for me to distinguish sex discrimination—I doubt whether the IRS could grant them exemptions. I thought that the IRS had authority to do what it did in 1970—being a charitable organization in the common law sense was a condition to exemption, it was not an automatic grant. *Tank Truck* settled that.[70] The IRS was clearly right in following settled policy. I would not reach *Norwood* as compelling a tax exemption.

O'CONNOR: I agree with the long ratification theory, although I am not sure what was ratified. Was it that the common law applied to all categories, or only to the schools' application in *Coit v. Green*.[71] On the constitutional issue, I agree that the public policy interest is compelling and overcomes the First Amendment.

Result: In a 7–1–1 decision, the Court upheld the IRS's decision to revoke both schools' tax-exempt status. Chief Justice Burger wrote that Congress intended to tie tax-exempt status to good public policy. Because taxpayers effectively were donors to tax-exempt entities, the schools' policies could not be "so at odds with the common community conscience as to undermine any public benefit that might otherwise be conferred."

The Court also rejected the claim that the schools' tax-exempt status was protected by the First Amendment's free exercise clause. Religious liberty could be limited if there was an "overriding governmental interest," and here the government's interest in ending racial discrimination easily outweighed the burden imposed on the two schools' free exercise rights by the loss of their tax-exempt status. Powell concurred in part and concurred in the judgment, while Rehnquist was alone in dissent.

---

70. *Tank Truck Rentals, Inc. v. Commissioner*, 356 U.S. 30 (1958). The Tank Truck Rentals company was assessed fines of nearly $38,000 in 1951 for repeatedly violating Pennsylvania's maximum truck weight law. The company sought to deduct the fines from its federal taxes as an "ordinary and necessary" business expense. The Court unanimously denied the deduction, saying that to allow it would undermine government policy. These fines were not like toll fees or other ordinary and necessary expenses—they were punitive measures designed to punish wrongdoers, to protect state roads from damage, and to promote highway safety. To allow the company to deduct such expenses would reduce the sting of the penalties and would amount to a public subsidy for illegal behavior. The Court was careful to point out that it made no difference whether the violations in this case were purposeful or unintentional—they were not deductible in either case.

71. *Green v. Connally*, 330 F. Supp. 1150, 1162 (D.D.C. 1971), aff'd sub nom., *Coit v. Green*, 404 U.S. 997 (1971).

Aguilar v. Felton, 473 U.S. 402 (1985)
(Brennan)

Under Title 1 of the Elementary and Secondary Education Act of 1965, local elementary and secondary schools received a total of $3 billion per year in federal funds, most of it going to poor urban schools. New York was the largest recipient of Title 1 money. In 1982, the state accepted $147 million in Title 1 funds, with $20 million (13.5 percent) going to private schools: 84 percent of them Catholic and 8 percent of them Jewish.

New York City used its share to pay public school employees to teach secular subjects at parochial schools. Most classes were remedial reading, math, and English as a second language (ESL). A complex supervisory scheme was created to insulate secular classes from religious influences, and classrooms were cleansed of all religious symbols each day before classes began.

Betty-Louise Felton and five other taxpayers sued Yolanda Aguilar, the secretary of the Department of Education, and the New York City Board of Education alleging that this public support of religious schools violated the establishment clause. The Justice Department sided with New York, arguing that Title 1 provided important remedial programs for all children, regardless of where they went to school. The district court sided with the government, but the court of appeals ruled that public subsidies for private religious schools were unconstitutional.

BURGER: Does this Title 1 program fail? Henry Friendly felt he that he had to strike it.[72] I can't agree with it so far, as it announces an absolute test. Can *Meek* be distinguished because there is nothing in the record about advancing religion?[73] But what of the surveillance element?

BRENNAN:[74] That children are forced to flee from the hell of urban schools is a tragedy. These children are the victims of the darkest side of our culture, and my sympathies go out to them. My sympathies also go out to those children who, in being left behind, face the daily horrors of urban public schools. We have been told—and I think it beyond challenge—that if all of the money involved in this case were redistributed to public schools, there would remain an abundance of children in those public schools who would still need assistance. If we were to balance the equities, I think that the scale would tip towards those children who have not been so fortunate as to escape the public schools. Surely theirs is the more hostile environment, theirs the more impoverished education.

---

72. Judge Henry J. Friendly of the Second Circuit Court of Appeals was one of Felix Frankfurter's protégés, part of a large and closely knit group known as "Felix Frankfurter's Happy Hot Dogs." On Frankfurter's recommendation, Friendly clerked for Justice Louis Brandeis after graduating from Harvard Law School. After Dwight Eisenhower was elected president, Frankfurter actively campaigned for more than fifty-six months to secure a judicial appointment for his former student. Eisenhower finally appointed Friendly to the federal bench in 1959, where he became one of the most highly regarded judges in the country. Judge Friendly later developed a close friendship with Thurgood Marshall when both men served together on the Second Circuit. Years later, Friendly also became one of Warren Burger's close friends and was one of the Chief Justice's favorite sources of law clerks. After Friendly committed suicide in March 1986, Burger spoke at his memorial service.

73. *Meek v. Pittenger,* 421 U.S. 349 (1975).

74. Adapted from Brennan's talking papers, Brennan Papers, OT 1984, box 685.

As to the legal argument, two points need be made. First, the assistance that is being provided is substantial, bot economically and symbolically. As was noted at oral argument, the classes taught by public school teachers take the place of school time that would otherwise be filled by the parochial schools. Slower students are siphoned off and taught by public teachers, while the religious school teachers are permitted the luxury of smaller and more efficient classes. The parochial school is also spared the considerable expense and manpower that would be needed to provide remedial assistance.

Second, because these programs are remedial in nature, they serve the principal purpose of integrating the child, both socially and educationally, into the parochial school. Such services foster in the child a profound dependence on the religious school and therefore should not be performed by the state. Few practices could be quite so antithetical to the concept of the separation of church and state.

In summary, I find Title 1 programs directly at odds with our opinion in *Meek* and more generally, with the secular effects and excessive entanglements prongs of the *Lemon* test. I would affirm.

BLACKMUN: It was a good panel of judges below.[75] This case is indistinguishable from *Meek*, and maybe we should overrule it. Until we do, I must affirm.

STEVENS: Friendly's opinion correctly lays out our prior cases. The fact that this was remedial makes the argument stronger.

O'CONNOR: I would reverse in this one. I would retreat.

Result: The Court ruled 5–4 that New York's program violated the establishment clause. The majority ruled that the permanent and pervasive supervision that the state must exercise to ensure that the money was not used to advance religion would result in excessive entanglements between church and state. Burger, White, Rehnquist, and O'Connor dissented.

In 1997, the Supreme Court reversed itself in Agostini v. Felton, 521 U.S. 203 (1997). This time, the Court ruled 5–4 that public schoolteachers could be sent to parochial schools during school hours to provide remedial education without violating the establishment clause. O'Connor wrote the majority opinion, with Souter, Stevens, Ginsburg, and Breyer in dissent.

PRAYER AND RELIGIOUS INSTRUCTION IN PUBLIC SCHOOLS

Engel v. Vitale, 370 U.S. 421 (1962)
(Douglas) (Brennan)

In 1951, the Board of Regents of New York composed an official state prayer called the "Regents' Prayer," which public schoolchildren recited at the beginning of each school day. The prayer went: "Almighty God, we acknowledge our dependence upon Thee and we beg Thy blessings upon us, our parents, our teachers, and our country." Any student who did not want to participate could remain silent or

---

75. The three judges were Chief Judge Wilfred Feinberg and Circuit Judges Henry Friendly and James L. Oakes.

leave the room. Steven Engel and four other parents sued William J. Vitale Jr. and other members of the New Hyde Park school board to stop the prayers.[76] The New York courts upheld the Regents' Prayer on the ground that it did not favor one religion over another and did not promote the teaching of religion.

Conference of April 3, 1962

WARREN: It is practically conceded that this is religious instruction, and is so intended. It is a violation of the church-state rule under the First Amendment. There is no question of standing. The fact that we speak of God with reverence does not mean that we can take the prayer into the school—it is the camel's head under the tent. Little children might refrain, but it is difficult for them as a practical matter to do it.[77]

BLACK: I reverse. This is, of course, religious. I will not go back on *McCollum*.[78] They can't spend the taxpayer's money for a religious object.

FRANKFURTER: I reverse. This was a religious exercise. A prayer is one thing, and merely articulating the name of the deity is another. This is a prayer, and the question is whether any kind of prayer having religious direction is saved merely because children may include themselves out. There is an inherent compulsion on children to take part and to force parents to acquiesce.[79] This is a disguised religious practice in public school. We ought not forget that public schools are secular, where the introduction of any kind of religion is prohibited. There is standing, even though the prayer fits the theology of the objector.

DOUGLAS: I reverse.

CLARK: I reverse. Compulsion on the children is present.

HARLAN: I reverse reluctantly. It is inescapable to reverse in light of the direction the cases have taken. If this were de novo, I would say that it was no violation. This is not a celebration of a patriotic ritual. It is not the flag salute or the last stanza of "America the Beautiful"—this is a prayer and nothing else.

BRENNAN: I reverse.

STEWART: I am still in doubt, and am not at rest.

Result: Before the decision could be announced, Felix Frankfurter suffered a cerebral stroke that forced him to retire, and Charles Whittaker resigned in March 1962. This left Potter Stewart as the sole dissenter in a 6–1 decision to strike down the Regents' Prayer.

---

76. The plaintiffs were a mixed religious group: two were Jewish, one Unitarian, one Protestant, and one agnostic.

77. In his memoirs, Earl Warren said that in deciding this case he was influenced by the bloody confrontations in nineteenth-century Philadelphia over whether to use the Protestant or Catholic Bible in public school devotions. Warren, *Memoirs*, 316.

78. *McCollum v. Board of Education*, 333 U.S. 203 (1948).

79. Frankfurter's comment about the inherent coercion of the situation was significant because the trial court had ruled that there had been no state coercion in this case. Unlike the flag salute cases, where students had been compelled to participate, students here had the choice to participate, remain silent, or leave the classroom. This made it more difficult for the Court to strike down the law as an infringement of free exercise rights.

The case caused more public controversy than any case since Brown, *and this time the hostility was not confined to one region of the country—although southerners were more angry than most. As Alabama congressman George Grant complained, "They put Negroes in our schools, and now they've driven God out."*[80] *Over the next few years there were 147 bills introduced in Congress to permit school prayer. Thirty-two state legislatures—only two fewer than the necessary two-thirds—called for a constitutional convention to reconsider the Court's school prayer and reapportionment decisions.*[81]

However, unlike the aftermath of Brown, *when President Eisenhower pointedly refused to support the Court, President Kennedy quickly and forcefully endorsed the Court's decision and told those who disagreed with the decision that their proper remedy was private prayer.*[82]

School District of Abington Township v. Schempp, 374 U.S. 203 (1963)
Murray v. Curlett
(Douglas)

Pennsylvania schools were required by law to begin each school day by reading at least ten Bible verses. In the Abington School District, verses were read over the school intercom, followed by the Lord's Prayer and the flag salute. Children could be excused from participating in the prayers only with written permission from a parent or guardian. Edward and Sidney Schempp, Unitarians from Germantown, Pennsylvania, sued the school district on behalf of their children, Roger and Donna. A federal appeals court agreed with the Schempps that the prayers were unconstitutional.

In the companion case, a different federal appellate court upheld a 1905 Baltimore ordinance requiring city schools to begin each day by reading a chapter from the Bible and/or the Lord's Prayer. Atheist Madalyn Murray sued to stop the practice on behalf of her son, William Murray III. The conference discussion is noteworthy because of Potter Stewart's interesting perspective on the establishment clause and Arthur Goldberg's response.

Conference of March 1, 1963

Murray v. Curlett

WARREN: Unless we reverse *Vitale* we must reverse here. This case is stronger than that case was. This is a violation of the establishment clause.

---

80. Weaver, *Warren: The Man, the Court, the Era,* at 258.

81. Community reaction against the plaintiffs and their families was hostile and at times violent. Angry neighbors placed rags soaked with gasoline in the shape of a cross and set them on fire in the middle of one of the families' driveways. All of the families were harassed and threatened for years after the Supreme Court's decision was announced.

82. Kennedy's position was the culmination of a pivotal campaign speech he made to a group of Baptist ministers in Houston, Texas, in 1960. After several leading Protestants claimed that Catholics would never accept a separation between church and state and implied that Kennedy might impose papal rule on the United States, Kennedy sought to reassure the assembled Baptist ministers that he considered religion to be a private matter and that his religious beliefs would be irrelevant to his performance as president. Going farther than the Supreme Court has ever gone, Kennedy told the conference, "I believe in an America where the separation of church and state is absolute," and he promised to resign if any conflict ever arose between his religious beliefs and his constitutional responsibilities as president.

BLACK: I reverse.

DOUGLAS: Reverse.

CLARK: Reverse.

HARLAN: I agree that this is a reversal on *Vitale*. I vote tentatively to reverse, but I am going to examine the whole subject de novo, and I may in the end come out differently.

STEWART: This is more of an establishment clause case than *Vitale*. This is sectarian. All of our establishment cases are wrong, historically. The establishment clause is obsolete today, like the right to bear arms. The free exercise clause is the important one. The 18th Century fear of establishment is no longer relevant. I am inclined to remand the cases so that the states can give every sect a chance to have religious exercises in schools—including atheists. The state has an affirmative duty to create a religious atmosphere in schools where anyone and everyone can pray and worship as he wishes.

CLARK: It would be O.K. to open up the schoolroom to all religious exercises by all religious groups.

WHITE: I would reverse.

GOLDBERG: I reverse.

Conference of March 1, 1963

Abington Township v. Schempp

WARREN: I affirm. This was a violation of the establishment clause of the 1st Amendment.

BLACK: Affirm.

DOUGLAS: Affirm.

CLARK: Affirm.

HARLAN: I affirm with doubts, and I will reexamine the vote. I would remand the case and await a decision in state court regarding the meaning of the state statute.

BRENNAN: Affirm.

STEWART: I would remand for the same reasons given in #119.[83]

WHITE: Affirm.

GOLDBERG: I affirm. We are dealing with statutes that are explicit and which would prevent doing what Potter wants to do. Affirmance here is necessary, following *Vitale*,[84] because this is a much more religious prayer than the one in *Vitale*. This issue is a heated one. People, however, should be reassured. I think that the establishment clause is not

---

83. *Murray v. Curlett*, the companion case.
84. *Engel v. Vitale*, 370 U.S. 421 (1962).

obsolete. Schools can't be opened to every sect—how about the Black Muslims? How about screwball groups? You can't draw a line that is a viable one. It would mean drawing lines that would interfere with free exercise. There is no better way to respect religion than to follow *Vitale*.

Result: By identical 8–1 votes, the Court struck down both laws on the ground that they violated the establishment clause. Tom Clark, writing for the majority, said that the mandated devotional exercises were clearly religious and were constitutionally objectionable because: (1) they were conducted by state employees (2) in public schools (3) where attendance was mandatory. This violated the strict state neutrality toward religion required by the establishment clause.

Public reaction was impassioned and mostly hostile. The Court narrowly avoided a constitutional crisis when Congress fell just a few votes short of passing legislation that would have stripped the federal courts of jurisdiction to hear establishment clause cases. Congress also came within a couple of votes of promulgating new constitutional amendments to overrule the Court's decision. Perhaps wisely, the Justices avoided deciding another school prayer case for more than twenty years.

Wallace v. Jaffree, 472 U.S. 38 (1985)
(Brennan)

An Alabama statute provided for a one-minute period of silence in state public schools for "meditation or voluntary prayer."[85] Ishmael and Mozelle Jaffree brought suit on behalf of their three children, claiming that the law violated the establishment clause. In upholding the statute, the district court judge found that the main purpose of the act was to encourage religious activity but ruled that the establishment clause only prohibited the federal government—not the state governments—from establishing a religion. The court of appeals reversed. Governor George C. Wallace, with the support of the Reagan administration, appealed to the Supreme Court.[86]

Conference of December 7, 1984

BURGER: Is there a case or controversy here? Aren't they just telling students that they may have a moment of silence? On the merits, a moment of silence is completely neutral. The reference to "prayer" in the statute does not change this for me. The statute serves a secular purpose, since each student can use the moment for anything he pleases.

BRENNAN:[87] If we are to decide the facial validity of the Alabama statute, I would hold that the moment of silence for meditation or voluntary prayer violates the establishment clause. On the record in this case, there can be no doubt that the legislative purpose in passing the statute was to endorse religious practice in public schools.

---

85. Ala. Stat. §16–1–20.1. At the time, twenty-three states had enacted "moment of silence" statutes.

86. In 1978, the Alabama legislature authorized a period of silence for meditation only. The district court judge upheld this provision along with the rest of the prayer statute, but Jaffree chose not to appeal this part of the district court's decision. In 1982, the statute was amended to allow teachers to lead "willing students" in a prescribed prayer to "Almighty God . . . the Creator and Supreme Judge of the world." The Supreme Court summarily affirmed the court of appeal's ruling that this section was unconstitutional, and so this amendment was not at issue here.

87. Adapted from Brennan's talking papers, Brennan Papers, OT 1984, box 675.

According to the legislative sponsors and the governor of Alabama, this statute was intended to bring back school prayer. As such, it was a clear effort to advance the practice of religion in the public sphere. Moreover, the mere act of amending the pre-existing moment of silence statute by adding the words "or voluntary prayer" was intended to make clear to students that they could pray during the moment of silence; the legislature showed no similar solicitude for any other type of thought or activity. In the context of the legislative purpose to thrust prayer back into the schools, this amendment must be read as state endorsement of religious practice. Certainly the young Jaffree children and others at their impressionable age, hearing each morning the authoritative voice of their teacher instruct them that they must observe a moment of silence for voluntary prayer, would receive the message of official endorsement of the religious practice.

Quite apart from the administrative entanglement that any conscientious effort to police the bounds of this statute would inevitably entail, the clear purpose and effect of advancing religion compel invalidation under the *Lemon v. Kurtzman* approach. As far as I am concerned, this statute cannot be squared with the crucial values of neutrality and separation that I have long thought the establishment clause embodies. Though not specifically sectarian, the statute is not neutral, because it endorses the religious as opposed to the nonreligious. And in purpose and effect, the statute thrusts religion into the school. In essence, the schoolhouse becomes each morning a house of worship for that moment.

I am somewhat troubled by reaching the issue of the facial validity of the statute. Because, as John Stevens's letter yesterday suggested, Jaffree alleged, and the district court found, that teachers led organized vocal Christian prayers, it may be that the proper course is to hold the statute unconstitutional as applied to the Jaffree children, as it surely is in light of these findings.[88] This resolution would, I suppose, require us to vacate the current injunction with respect to all schools in the state and to remand for fashioning of an appropriate decree.

I am also reluctant to reach the issue of facial validity because on the current record we do not have a clear idea what the statute means and what it authorizes. If the new statute was intended to mean nothing more than the old, and thus was not intended to authorize teachers to instruct students each morning that they may pray, the statute might pass muster. Because the district court held the establishment clause inapplicable to the states, it had no need to grapple with the precise meaning of the statute. Absent any authoritative state construction or any specific implementation of the statute from which

---

88. John Paul Stevens's December 6 memorandum to the conference discussed the fact that defendants Julia Green, Charlene Boyd, and Pixie Alexander led their classes in prayer activities. As early as September 1981, Boyd led her classes in singing:

God is great, God is Good
Let us thank him for our food
Bow our heads, we all are fed
Give us Lord our daily bread
Amen!

Stevens, Memorandum to the Conference, Dec. 6, 1984, in Brennan Papers, OT 1964, box 675.

we can infer statutory meaning, the proper course may be to hold that the issue is not ripe for review. This would entail vacating the current injunction with respect to this law, but it would not entail any decision on the constitutional merits.

WHITE: On the case or controversy issue: the vocal prayers, on whatever authority, we have disposed of. On the moment of silence: the statute poses a realistic threat to opponents, so there is a case. On the merits, I agree with the Chief Justice. The addition of "prayer" to the statute poses no problem.

MARSHALL: As a student, you are not absolutely free to think of what you will—you must do what the school tells you to do, and here the purpose was to get prayer back in school.

BLACKMUN: The appellees concede that the meditation statute is constitutional. So I am not sure how much case or controversy over the amended statute is here. The overall motive is so apparent that they can't possibly say that this is neutral. I think that our decided cases compel affirmance.

POWELL: This is a unique statute and is not controlled by our earlier decisions. This, of course, was purposed [sic] to advance religion, but I don't think it can ever do that—it is a meaningless enactment. As Paul Freund suggests, it promotes free exercise and that is enough to sustain it.[89]

REHNQUIST: On the case or controversy question, this is a facial attack on the Alabama statute, and that is here. If we had an "as applied" attack, as John Stevens may think, that is a different case. There was no invidious purpose to try to get something that will pass.

STEVENS: There was no facial attack ruling in either the district court or the court of appeals. The practice after the 1981 statute was passed was the object of this lawsuit— teachers leading their classes in prayer activity on no authority but this statute.[90] So this is an attack as applied, and it should be affirmed.

O'CONNOR: This case came to us as an applied one. If we had a bona fide moment of silence, I would have no problem. But whether the applied or facial history is here, this record requires me to affirm.

Result: On a 6–3 vote, the Court struck down the Alabama statute as a violation of the establishment clause. John Paul Stevens, writing for the majority, ruled that states had no more right than Congress to establish or promote a religion. Because the sole purpose of the state law was to endorse religion and promote prayer in public schools, there was no secular legislative purpose; the law violated the first prong of the Lemon *test.[91] Lewis Powell and Sandra Day O'Connor concurred in the judgment but claimed that a majority of the Justices was prepared to uphold a carefully written statute allowing an organized moment of silence during the school day.*

---

89. Paul Freund, "The Legal Issue," *Religion and The Public Schools,* 23.

90. The 1981 statute was the only law at issue here. The "pure meditation" provision was passed in 1978, and the prescribed prayer for "willing students" was added in 1982.

91. *Lemon v. Kurtzman,* 403 U.S. 602 (1971).

THE FREE EXERCISE CLAUSE

Minersville School District v. Gobitis, 310 U.S. 586 (1944)
(Murphy)

In 1936, twelve-year-old Lillian Gobitis and her ten-year-old brother William were expelled from school in Minersville, Pennsylvania, for refusing to participate in the daily flag-salute ceremony. The Gobitis family, Jehovah's Witnesses, refused to salute the flag because Exodus 20:4–5 prohibited the worship of graven images. Walter Gobitis placed his children in private schools, but this proved too expensive and too galling, so he sued for damages and sought an injunction to prohibit the school board from requiring his children to participate in the flag salute as a condition of attendance.

District Court Judge Albert B. Maris ruled in favor of the Gobitis children. He declared that the flag salute was "used as an instrument to impose a religious test as a condition of receiving the benefits of a public education. And this has been done without any compelling necessity of public safety or welfare." The Third Circuit Court of Appeals unanimously affirmed, and the school board appealed to the Supreme Court.

Compulsory flag-salute laws had previously been litigated in at least seven states, and the Supreme Court had never disapproved the practice. The Justices had recently rejected three similar cases in per curiam decisions on the ground that they did not present a substantial federal question. Most Court watchers were surprised when the Justices granted cert in this case.

HUGHES: It is the requirement of the salute that is objected to. We can't say this requirement is contrary to state law. We must look at it in the same way as if we did have a state decision. Under the Fourteenth Amendment, the state cannot establish a religion or church—the question here is one of the free exercise of religion.

Religious scruples or belief will not give a citizen immunity from payment of taxes or instruction in military science. As Justice Cardoza [*sic*] has said, "The right of private judgment has not been exalted over and above, etc."

Consider first the nature of the requirement. If the requirement is aimed at religion then it lies outside the sphere of regulation, because the Amendment prohibits such regulation. So we must first inquire—is it a reasonable regulation that the state asks? Under proper needs for the social order, the state could require not devotions, not family prayers or religious observances, because all that is in the prohibited field. But if the state acts in its proper sphere, then the scruple of the individual cannot avoid proper state power.

So let's look at it. The pledge is one of allegiance. The gesture is objected to as a token of loyalty to the flag.

As I see it, the state can insist on inculcation of loyalty. It would be extraordinary if in this country the state could not provide for respect for the flag of our land. It has nothing to do with religion—indeed it has to do with freedom of religion.

Who is entitled to a judgment on the general effect of what is required? Almost anything the state might do may be offensive to many people. If the legislature has judgment there is room for belief that the effect of that judgment would be good.

I come up to this case like a skittish horse to a brass band.

I am disturbed that we have this case before us. There is nothing that I have more profound belief in than religious freedom, so I must bring myself to view this case on the question of state power.

There is no legitimate impingement on religious belief here. What is required of those who salute the flag is a legitimate object.

We have no jurisdiction as to the wisdom of this. We have to deal with state power, and consider whether this is a proper exercise of it. I don't want to be dogmatic about this, but I simply cannot believe that the state has not the power to inculcate this social objective.

Result: As the Justices were deliberating, the war was entering its darkest days. The British had just been forced to flee from Dunkirk, as Denmark, Holland, and Belgium fell to the Nazis. Hughes assigned the case to Felix Frankfurter. This was going to be a patriotic decision, and no one on the Court was more patriotic than Frankfurter. A naturalized citizen, Frankfurter freely confessed that he had the zeal of a convert and that no native American could be more appreciative of the blessings of American citizenship. He liked to whistle Stars and Stripes Forever *and other patriotic songs while walking down the hallways of the Supreme Court building.[92]*

In analyzing the school board's decision, Frankfurter used a variation of the rational basis test, all but ignoring the religious freedom and free speech issues embedded in the case. The government, he said, had a legitimate reason for enforcing the practice (instilling patriotism and national loyalty in schoolchildren), and the means used were not unreasonable. Such policy judgments, he concluded, were best left to the democratic institutions of government.

Stone circulated his dissent at the last minute, and no one had the time to read it before the case was decided.[93] Hugo Black said that upon reading Stone's dissent, Douglas and Murphy and he immediately realized that they had made a serious mistake.[94] The three men met around the swimming pool at Murphy's hotel and agreed that Frankfurter's opinion had to be overruled as soon as possible.[95] Frankfurter's opinion also sparked an editorial backlash in the press, which might have influenced the three apostates. The next fall, Douglas told Frankfurter that if they had it to do over again, "Hugo would not go with you in the Flag Salute case." Frankfurter asked, "Why, has he reread the Constitution during the summer?" Douglas responded, "No, but he has read the papers."[96]

---

92. Simon, *The Antagonists*, 109.

93. According to Douglas, Stone's dissent grew out of his service during World War I as a member of a three-man board of inquiry charged with deciding claims for exemption from military duty. Stone traveled around the country interviewing conscientious objectors and judging their claims. He often talked about his experiences, which made him especially sensitive to the Witnesses' arguments. Douglas, *The Court Years*, 45–46.

94. Douglas claimed that he, Black, and Murphy were led astray by Frankfurter, whom they all held in high regard. Douglas wrote his mistake off to his naiveté and his reluctance as junior Justice to change his vote.

95. Newman, *Hugo Black*, 284.

96. Lash, *From the Diaries of Felix Frankfurter*, 209 (Friday. Mar. 12, 1943).

Jones v. City of Opelika, 316 U.S. 584 (1942) and 319 U.S. 103 (1943)[97]
Bowden and Sanders v. Fort Smith
Jobin v. Arizona
(Murphy)

Jehovah's Witnesses in Opelika, Alabama, Fort Smith, Arkansas, and Casa Grande, Arizona, were fined for violating local ordinances against selling books or pamphlets within the city limits without a bookseller's license. Licenses cost from $5 to $100 per year. Opelika exempted Bible sellers but included all other books; the other two ordinances made no exceptions. Rosco Jones, Lois Bowden, Zada Sanders, and Charles Jobin sold religious materials door to door while proselytizing. Note Harlan Fiske Stone's comment about the inevitable consequences of free speech.

Jones Conference (1941 Term)

STONE: This case is to me an unexplained mystery. There was a reversal in the circuit court of appeals, without more. We don't even know that there was a waiver. That court was bound to take it up, and that we must dismiss because of a lack of final judgment in the court below.

Bowden Conference (1941 Term)

STONE: Here there were several defendants. Several were ringing doorbells, others were on the street. They were all propagandizing their ideas. Here, the state tax is higher than in the other case. What do you do with a man in the street?

ROBERTS: I hold that you could not pick him out and tax him.

BLACK: I am for complete reversal. I think that the statute is bad. It is too broad, for as applied people in a bona fide exercise of religion are not peddling.

REED: *Cole* bothers me.[98] The city has a right to put a small license on it.

STONE: It was a religious meeting. Only the house to house business is involved here. One of the necessary consequences of free speech is *riots!*

Result: In a 5–4 decision, the Court ruled that cities had the right to impose reasonable taxes on booksellers as long as the ordinances were applied in a general and nondiscriminatory way. Licensing fees could be required of religious organizations selling sectarian "propaganda" without violating First Amendment protections of speech, press, or the free exercise of religion.

The dissenters—Stone, Murphy, Black, and Douglas—thought that the cities' licensing schemes were an unconstitutional infringement on the right to disseminate ideas. Stone noted that the licenses were revokable at will, at the sole discretion of city administrative officers. In the dissenters' judgment, this sort of absolute, uncontrolled administrative discretion violated the defendants' First Amendment speech, press, and religious rights.

---

97. *Jones v. City of Opelika,* 316 U.S. 584 (1942); rehearing granted, 318 U.S. 796 (1943); original decision reversed, 319 U.S. 103 (1943).

98. *Bowden and Sanders v. Fort Smith* was reported below as *Cole v. Fort Smith,* 151 S.W. 2d 1000 (1941).

Black, Murphy, and Douglas used this case to confess that they had been wrong in deciding Gobitis *and implied that they were prepared to reverse that decision given an appropriate case.*[99] *Frankfurter was furious and pointed out that the issue had not been raised in* Jones *or even mentioned at conference.*[100]

After the case was initially decided, Jimmy Byrnes resigned on October 3, 1942. President Roosevelt nominated Wiley Rutledge to take his place, and Rutledge was confirmed on February 15, 1943. On the same day, the Court voted to reconsider the Jones *case. The case was reargued on March 10 and 11, 1943, and the Justices reversed their original decision by a 5–4 vote on May 3, 1943. Outside of Rutledge, no other Justice changed his vote, making this case a good example of how the timely appointment of a single Justice can have a profound impact on judicial decisions.*[101]

United States v. Ballard, 322 U.S. 78 (1944)
(Murphy)

Guy W. Ballard, the leader of the I Am religious cult, claimed to be the prophet of St. Germaine, an "ascended master" of the universe. Ballard and other cult members were charged with using the mails to commit fraud and conspiracy to commit fraud. Authorities alleged that cult members sold goods by invoking religious doctrines and beliefs they knew to be false, including phonograph records that were said to hold the keys to salvation. Group members also falsely asserted that they were divine messengers who could cure serious diseases. The trial judge instructed the jury not to consider the truth or falsity of I Am doctrine but to decide only whether the defendants sincerely believed their representations to be true.

BLACK: Thus the First Amendment is destroyed. This was foreseen by the First Amendment. There is a degree of fakery in all of this. But I am not going to let some one determine this belief of another. They were beyond challenge of judge or jury under the First Amendment. But if you take money away from them, you take away that by which they exist under our economy. I don't believe in a one of them. But men like me will not send one to jail because the others are of other beliefs. This is exactly the same as Christ when he was on this earth. They found it out centuries ago that you couldn't trust one group's beliefs to another.

DOUGLAS: We have here, at bottom, a First Amendment case.

Result: In a 5–4 decision, William O. Douglas, writing for the majority, ruled that the prosecutions violated the First Amendment's freedom of religion. In dissent, Stone, Jackson, Roberts, and Frankfurter called the I Am scheme old-fashioned fraud in the guise of religion.

---

99. *Minersville School District v. Gobitis*, 310 U.S. 586 (1940).

100. Urofsky, "Conflict Among the Brethren," 88. The Court reversed *Gobitis* the following year in *West Virginia State Board of Education v. Barnette*, 319 U.S. 624 (1943).

101. See Levitan, "The Effect of the Appointment of a Supreme Court Justice."

United States v. Seeger, 380 U.S. 163 (1965)
(Douglas) (Brennan)

*In 1917, Congress created a narrow exception to the country's draft laws, exempting from military ser-
vice members of "well-recognized" religious sects and organizations that prohibited members from
participating in war in any form. Congress expanded this exemption in 1940 to include anyone who
"by reason of their religious training and belief" was opposed to war in any form. In 1948, Congress
defined "religious training and belief" as an individual's belief in a "Supreme Being" and specifically
excluded personal opposition to war based on "essentially political, sociological, or philosophical views,
or merely a moral code."*[102]

*During the Vietnam War, Daniel Seeger, Arno Sascha Jakobson, and Forest Britt Peter all claimed
to be conscientious objectors and sought exemptions from the draft under §6(j). None of them professed to believe in a Supreme Being as such. Seeger was an agnostic who believed in a sort of transcen-
dental goodness based on his reading of Plato, Spinoza, Gandhi, and others. Jakobson believed in what
he called a "supreme reality," and Peter believed in an unspecified universal power beyond mankind.
All three were convicted in district court for refusing induction. Seeger's and Jakobson's convictions
were overturned on appeal; Peter's was affirmed.*

*At conference the Justices struggled to find a statutory interpretation—however implausible—
that would allow the Court to avoid finding §6(j) unconstitutional. Chief Justice Earl Warren closed
the conference with a war story.* Seeger *was case no. 50,* Jakobson *no. 51, and* Peter *no. 29.*

Conference of November 20, 1964

WARREN: I have difficulty here. If we had only *Peter* and *Jakobson* I would have no trouble,
for both petitioners in those cases believe in a power higher than themselves. Peter and
Jakobson believe in a guiding spirit—one from within and one from without—and that
is enough to give them the exemption. Their good faith is conceded, and I am against
the United States in those cases. I am not so sure about *Seeger,* where petitioner Seeger
does not believe in any deity. He acts in good faith. But if we sustain the United States,
we run afoul of some of our other cases.

I don't know how to define "Supreme Being," and perhaps judges ought not do so.
The trouble with Seeger is whether *Torcaso* doesn't establish a principle that "religion"
encompasses all religions—and thus the "Supreme Being" requirement is discriminatory.[103] [DOUGLAS: Warren reads from the *Torcaso* opinion.] If "Supreme Being" includes
only some gods, the act establishes some religions. It is the same result if it excludes non-
conventional religions. Conscientious objection to all wars should be enough. It would

---

102. Section 6(j) of the Selective Training and Service Act. 50 U.S.C. §456 (1958).

103. *Torcaso v. Watkins,* 367 U.S. 488 (1961). The governor of Maryland nominated Roy Torcaso to
become a notary public, but he was denied a commission because he refused to declare his belief in God as
required by the state constitution. In unanimously striking down the oath as a violation of the free exercise
clause, the Court, through Hugo Black, said, "We repeat and again reaffirm that neither a State nor the
Federal Government can constitutionally force a person 'to profess a belief or disbelief in any religion.'
Neither can constitutionally pass laws or impose requirements which aid all religions as against non-
believers, and neither can aid those religions based on a belief in the existence of God as against those religions founded on different beliefs."

not be sufficient if he is opposed only to *this* war or he is against war only in certain circumstances; he must be against all war as a matter of conscience. The Constitution requires Congress to go this far. I will be willing to reverse here.

BLACK: Congress could require everyone to go to war and fight, even though they were opposed to all wars. But the United States can't deny equal protection to separate groups of conscientious objectors on the basis of morality. All conscientious objectors should be—must be—classified as such. If they are honest and conscientious, that is enough.

DOUGLAS: I disagree with Hugo on the point that the government could require everyone to bear arms. I don't think as a matter of power that the government could require a man to bear arms if it is against his religious scruples. But that issue is not here. This is a classification question, and Augustus Hand's *Kauten* opinion states the correct view.[104] As Hand best says it, they are not here discussing philosophical or political ideas—if their conscience is hooked to one or three or no gods, they all fall into the broad conception of religion.

CLARK: I think that we can get this under statutory interpretation. The phrase "Supreme Being" in the act does not mean a God, but includes all religious beliefs. I would affirm *Seeger* by construing the act to include this man. I would follow the procedures established in *Berman*.[105]

HARLAN: I am against the United States in all of these cases. I have difficulty in going on construction of the act, and find it a little difficult not to reach the constitutional question. I agree with Hugo that Congress could force everyone to fight and deny all exemptions. But having granted an exemption, they cannot discriminate between religions or pick and choose among religious beliefs. These people have a "religion" under the First Amendment. Certainly Seeger is religious under the *Kauten* test. Congress runs afoul of the establishment clause in making these classifications in conformity with the due process requirement of the Fifth Amendment. Congress can't classify under the First Amendment or this

---

104. *United States v. Kauten*, 133 F.2d 703 (2d Cir. 1943). Mathias Kauten was arrested and convicted of avoiding induction into the armed services during World War II. Kauten claimed that his conviction was erroneous because he qualified as a conscientious objector. He admitted that he was either an atheist or agnostic and admitted that his opposition to war was based on his artistic, philosophical, and political views and did not stem from any conventional "religious training or belief." The draft board and the Court found that Kauten's opposition to war was sincere but refused to grant him conscientious objector status because the ultimate source of his pacifism was not religious. Judge Augustus "Gus" Hand conceded that the original 1917 statute limited conscientious objector status to those with religious objections to war but argued that the 1940 amendments were meant to be read much more broadly. Hand concluded that Congress, in amending the 1917 statute, intended "to take into account the characteristics of a skeptical generation and make the existence of a conscientious scruple against war in any form, rather than allegiance to a definite religious group or creed, the basis of exemption."

105. *Berman v. United States*, 156 F. 2d 377 (CA 9th 1946). The federal court of appeals accepted Herman Berman's argument that his sincere and conscientious objection to war, based on his devotion to a philosophy of socialism and social welfare (even absent the concept of a deity), was "religious" in nature and met the "religious training and belief" requirement of the Selective Training and Service Act of 1940, 50 U.S.C. §301 et seq. Berman, the judges decided, sincerely believed that war was inherently wrong and futile, that it was invariably conducted solely to benefit capitalists, and that to participate would have meant betraying his deepest beliefs and his perceived duty to his fellow citizens.

becomes a Fifth Amendment (due process) discrimination under the First Amendment—maybe.

BRENNAN: I am against the United States in all of these cases. I favor Tom Clark's approach under the statute. We can stretch the statute to cover all religions. I would prefer not to reach the Constitution. The obstacle is the legislative history.

STEWART: I see a lot of constitutional problems. If this is an honest free exercise claim, then Congress must give a broad exemption to believers and non-believers alike. This would mean overruling *Hamilton*.[106] It comes down to exempting everyone who sincerely does not want to go into the army. Due process and equal protection would mean any belief, political or not, would require exemption. If they have that broad a right, so does anyone under the other clauses of the First Amendment who is politically opposed to *this* war. If this is an establishment claim, it has other difficulties. The establishment clause would proscribe exemptions limited to particular faiths. I doubt whether we can decide these cases on an equal protection basis. I think that I can vote against the United States only on Tom Clark's ground of construing this act. In *Jakobson*, there is a question of Jakobson's sincerity, but I would not change my view on that account. "Religion" in this act means what *Kauten* said, and that is what Congress must have intended.

WHITE: I agree with the Chief.

GOLDBERG: I think that we must go on the statute. Below, the federal government argued that Seeger was religious in the *Kauten* sense. The legislative history is not determinative for the government here. "Religion" in the act is broad enough to include this man. Seeger believed in a "Creative Being." I am strongly in favor of the Tom Clark approach. I would not impute to Congress an intention to repudiate a known religious view that was genuinely such. The only difference between Seeger and Buddhism is that Seeger isn't a Buddhist. The statute doesn't say "God"—it goes more broadly.

WARREN: Refers to his experience at Fort Lee, Virginia in World War I, where one-third of his company were hillbillies from Arkansas and West Virginia who believed "Thou shalt not kill" was a religious command. He said they turned them all loose. They were Baptists "and were not worth a damn."

Result: Tom Clark, writing for a unanimous Court, ruled that the proper test of religious belief was whether a person had a sincere and meaningful belief that occupied a place parallel to that filled by the god of persons admittedly qualified for the exemption. The Court avoided deciding the status of atheists but broadened the meaning of "Supreme Being" well beyond the plausible limits of congressional intent. The Justices wanted to avoid finding the statute unconstitutional because they worried

---

106. *Hamilton v. Regents of the University of California*, 293 U.S. 245 (1934). Albert Hamilton, a student at UC Berkeley, refused to participate in the university's compulsory military drills and was expelled. He challenged the school's mandatory exercises on the ground that his religious beliefs prohibited his participation in such exercises. The Court ruled that because Hamilton voluntarily enrolled at the university knowing that military drills were a condition of enrollment, he could not later claim an exemption from those requirements.

that Congress would simply refuse to enact any exemptions at all for conscientious objectors. The decision was announced on March 8, 1965, the same day that American combat troops landed at Da Nang to begin the Americanization of the war in Vietnam.

Congress reacted angrily to Seeger, *amending the Selective Training and Service Act to delete the phrase "Supreme Being" and restoring the older, narrower standard of "religious training and belief." In* Welsh v. United States, *however, the Court interpreted the newly amended statute even more broadly than in* Seeger—*ruling that all persons opposed to war on moral or ethical grounds were exempt.*[107] *This time John Marshall Harlan dissented, saying that the Court had performed "a lobotomy" on the federal statute.*

Wisconsin v. Yoder, 406 U.S. 205 (1972)
(Douglas) (Brennan)

Amish parents customarily withdrew their children from local public schools after the eighth grade, when they had reached thirteen to fourteen years of age. Wisconsin law required students to attend school until the age of sixteen. Jonas Yoder and several other Amish parents were convicted of violating the statute and fined five dollars each. The state conceded that the children continued to receive informal vocational training at home intended to prepare them for adult life in the Amish community. The state also stipulated to the parents' sincere belief that continuing their children's formal education beyond the eighth grade threatened their traditional Amish values and beliefs. The Wisconsin Supreme Court ruled that the state law, as applied, violated the free exercise clause.

Conference of December 10, 1971

BURGER: The First Amendment pulls against the state's response. This is an ancient religion, not a new cult. I agree with Jefferson that the issue of discipline and having these kids get training from their fathers is as good as anything they would get in Wisconsin schools. Being raised on an Amish farm is equal to or better than vocational school training. This is a very difficult case. I would affirm—I agree with the Supreme Court of Wisconsin.

DOUGLAS: I would affirm. *Pierce v. Society of Sisters* governs.[108]

BRENNAN: I affirm—*Pierce* governs.

STEWART: I affirm. It would be difficult to sustain if the group merely did not want its children to be able to read.

WHITE: I affirm. There has been little talk of the interest of the children. The rights of children have independent standing. They are not competent to make this decision.

---

107. *Welsh v. United States,* 398 U.S. 333 (1970).

108. *Pierce v. Society of Sisters,* 268 U.S. 510 (1925). A unanimous Court ruled that an Oregon law requiring children between the ages of eight and sixteen years to attend public schools violated the Fourteenth Amendment rights of parents and guardians to direct the upbringing and education of their children. The fundamental theory of liberty on which the country was founded, James McReynolds wrote, excluded any general power of government to force families to send their children only to state-run public schools.

MARSHALL: I affirm. The Black Muslims go back before Christ.

BLACKMUN: I would affirm on this full and devastating record. I would not paint broadly for all cases, however.

Result: Chief Justice Burger, writing for a unanimous but short-handed Court of just seven Justices, ruled that the state's interest in education had to be balanced against the defendants' fundamental right of free exercise of religion. The Yoders had clearly demonstrated the adequacy of their alternative vocational education to satisfy the state's interest in education, and Burger saw only minimal differences between what the state required and what the Amish community offered their children. Burger wrote narrowly, emphasizing that the Amish had a three-hundred-year history of responsibility and self-sufficiency. William O. Douglas affirmed as to the Yoder family but dissented in part on the ground that the Amish children involved had rights to be considered independently of their parents and the state.

CHAPTER 12

RIGHTS OF THE ACCUSED

INVESTIGATION, SEARCH, AND SEIZURE

Arrest and Search Warrants

Harris v. United States, 336 U.S. 145 (1947)
(Murphy)

The FBI suspected that Oklahoma residents George Harris and C. R. Mofgett mailed a forged check for $25,000, drawn on the Mudge Oil Company, to New York to be cashed by the Guaranty Trust Company. Agents obtained an arrest warrant for the two men for mail fraud but did not obtain a search warrant. Five FBI agents arrested Harris at his home in Oklahoma City and handcuffed him to his living room chair. Then they searched Harris's apartment for five hours, looking for two other checks allegedly stolen from Mudge. They did not find any checks but seized a small sealed envelope marked "George Harris Personal Papers." The agents opened the envelope and inside found military draft documents—draft registration certificates and notices of draft classification—which Harris had no legal right to possess. Harris was convicted of violating the Selective Training and Service Act and sentenced to five years in prison. The court of appeals affirmed. Harris claimed that the warrantless search violated the Fourth and Fifth Amendments.

VINSON: It is clear that when you have a proper arrest warrant and you take him into custody that you have the right to make a painstaking search. They have the right to take the envelope and to use what is in it for evidence.

REED: I am with you. I think it important.

FRANKFURTER: I am nuts about this, because there is no provision of the Constitution more important to be nuts about. There is nothing more important in the Bill of Rights than search and seizure. The cases go contrawise to what you have said. There are emotional attachment behind religion and a free press. But in search and seizure we are burdened with a counter-appeal—a fear of criminals. John Adams said that American liberty was born when Otis spoke about general warrants.[1]

---

1. James Otis spoke out against the use of general warrants by British authorities in Massachusetts in 1761. His articulate defense of privacy rights was later written into Article 14 of the Massachusetts Constitution of 1780, which in turn became the model for the Fourth Amendment. John Adams said later that it was with Otis's speech that "American independence was then and there born." Adams, 2 *Works*, 523–25; Adams, 10 *Works*, 247.

Learned Hand said it all in the *Kirschenblatt* case.[2] "This was rummage at will," as Hand says. It is indistinguishable as to a general warrant. The moral of this is: don't get a search warrant. Wigmore's book on evidence is the greatest in the English language. This Court has given the Fourth Amendment greater depth than anything.

A search without a warrant is a restriction upon the warrant. So what is the scope of the restriction? Look at *Dillon v. O'Brien* and the Irish cases.[3] The limit to the seizure there was what the eye could see at once. *Search and Seizure: It is a prohibition to be construed consistently.* You can't sustain this with the *Lefkowitz* case.[4]

DOUGLAS: I agree with the Chief Justice.

MURPHY: I disagree with the Chief Justice—this is an unreasonable search and seizure.

JACKSON: *The warrant of a person does not carry with it right to search the premises.* That is a strong view. My notion is for affirmance, but I am not strong on it.

RUTLEDGE: A man's home is his castle. To prevent breach of the peace was one reason for the prohibition on searches and seizures. To me it is important that it was his *home.* That should be more restricted than a business. I think that this is making new law. It means that you can trump up a charge, then ransack the whole place. I go so far as allowing the seizure of things that are open and visible. That is a device which could be used widely and generally to go far and search and seize.

---

2. *United States v. Kirschenblatt,* 16 F. 2d 202 (1926). In a Prohibition-era bootlegging case, police obtained a warrant and made a lawful arrest, but then conducted a general search of the premises looking for anything that might be incriminating. The court ruled that this sort of indiscriminate search and seizure exceeded the scope of the warrant and exceeded police authority to search incident to a lawful arrest. Learned Hand said: "After arresting a man in his house, to rummage at will among his papers in search of whatever will convict him, appears to us to be indistinguishable from what might be done under a general warrant; indeed, the warrant would give more protection, for presumably it must be issued by a magistrate. . . . Such constitutional limitations arise from grievances, real or fancied, which their makers have suffered, and should go pari passu with the supposed evil. They withstand the winds of logic by the depth and toughness of their roots in the past. Nor should we forget that what seems fair enough against a squalid huckster of bad liquor may take on a very different face, if used by a government determined to suppress political opposition under the guise of sedition." *United States v. Kirschenblatt,* 16 F.2d 202, 203 (1926).

3. *Dillon v. O'Brien and Davis,* 20 L.R. Ir. 300, 16 Cox C.C. 245 (Exch. Div. Ire. 1887). This case was the first judicial challenge to the ancient English tradition permitting general searches incident to arrest. The challenge failed and the traditional rule was affirmed. Frankfurter distinguished the case by arguing that the English rule was limited to "plain view" seizures.

4. *United States v. Lefkowitz,* 285 U.S. 452 (1932). Another Prohibition case. Dan Lefkowitz and others were charged with conspiracy to sell intoxicating liquors. After the suspects were arrested in their office, police searched all desks, cabinets, wastebaskets, and other areas looking for evidence. They found books, papers, and other evidence used in soliciting liquor sales. The Supreme Court reaffirmed that it was unconstitutional for police to conduct general searches to look for evidence and ruled that this search exceeded the scope permissible for a search incident to a lawful arrest. Nonetheless, the Court approved the search on the ground that it was not conducted merely to obtain evidence to convict someone of a crime. The Court ruled that such searches were permissible if conducted: (1) to find stolen goods for return to the owner; (2) to take property that has been forfeited to the government; (3) to discover property concealed to avoid payment of duties; or (4) to seize items such as counterfeit coins, burglars' tools, gambling paraphernalia, or illicit liquor in order to prevent the commission of crime.

Result: In a 5–4 decision, the Court ruled that this was a permissible search incident to a lawful ar-
rest. Chief Justice Vinson wrote for the majority that such searches may extend to the premises under
the immediate control of the suspect as long as it was reasonable. It was not relevant that the search
involved a home rather than a business, or that the evidence seized had no relation to the reason for
the arrest. The officers could search beyond the room in which the suspect was arrested as long as the
search was not more intensive than reasonably necessary under the circumstances. Vinson argued that
a protracted search was reasonable in this case because the agents were looking for two checks that
could have been hidden anywhere. The Chief Justice noted that the agents had not seized Harris's private
papers and that the search was not based on Harris's political or religious views.

In dissent, Frankfurter warned that the Fourth Amendment was the Constitution's most vulner-
able right because it usually worked to protect criminals who had few friends and deserved little sym-
pathy. Frankfurter thought that the search was illegal from its inception and that police should not be
permitted to cobble together retroactive rationalizations for their misbehavior just because they found
incriminating evidence. The search in this case was conducted under the same rules and conditions as
the hated English general warrants—with the FBI "rummaging through the place" without a search
warrant. It was an illegal search that the Fourth Amendment was specifically *designed to prevent.*
Frankfurter ended his opinion with a long quote from Learned Hand.[5] Frank Murphy also ended his
dissent with a pithy Hand quote.[6]

Aguilar v. Texas, 378 U.S. 108 (1964)
(Douglas)

Houston Police obtained a warrant from a local justice of the peace to search Nick Aguilar's home for
heroin. The supporting affidavit contained no information about the informant's trustworthiness or
any evidence to support the informant's assertion that heroin would be found on the premises. The
main issue at conference was whether the states would be held to the same Fourth Amendment stan-
dards as the federal government.

Conference of March 27, 1964

WARREN: I reverse on the inadequacy of the affidavit for the search. The affidavit says
that the affiant believes that because an informant believes there were narcotics there.
That does not satisfy the federal standard of *Giordenello* and should not therefore pass
muster here.[7] If affidavits can be so thin, they are not useful.

---

5. See note 2 above.

6. "If the prosecution of crime is to be conducted with so little regard for that protection which centuries of English law have given to the individual, we are indeed at the dawn of a new era; and much that
we have deemed vital to our liberties, is a delusion." *United States v. Di Re,* 159 F.2d 818, 820 (1947).

7. *Giordenello v. United States,* 357 U.S. 480 (1958). On his own complaint, Agent Finley of the Federal
Bureau of Narcotics obtained an arrest warrant for Veto Giordenello but did not seek a search warrant.
The arrest warrant was not based on the agent's personal knowledge, did not mention the source of his
belief that petitioner had committed a crime, and contained no other information to show probable cause.
Finley arrested Giordenello and seized narcotics in his possession. The Court reversed Giordenello's conviction and ordered the evidence suppressed because there was no probable cause to support the arrest
warrant or the warrantless search.

BLACK: I affirm. The state statute has nothing to do with it. It does not contain a constitutional standard. *Giordenello* is not germane—the Fourth Amendment does not give a separate trial on issues like this. Probable cause is one thing, evidence of guilt is another. They need not show a prima facie case of guilt to get a search warrant. There was plenty of probable cause here for the warrant.

DOUGLAS: I reverse. I would apply *Giordenello* to state as well as federal searches.

BLACK: *Giordenello* rests on a federal statute, not on the Fourth Amendment.

CLARK: I affirm. There is no supremacy power over state searches. *Giordenello* passes by the question of hearsay.

HARLAN: My first impulse is to affirm, but in light of *Ker* I think that it should be reversed. The Fourth Amendment standards now apply to the states.[8] In *Giordenello*, I held that so far as the federal constitution is concerned, the current affidavit would be bad. I cannot distinguish this from *Giordenello*. If *Ker* means anything, it means that an affidavit which is not good for a federal search would also not be good for state search.

BRENNAN: I reverse under *Wong Sun* and *Giordenello*. [DOUGLAS: Brennan reads from it.][9] There was no recital in this affidavit of the basis for the reliability of the informant.

STEWART: The federal rules are not applicable here. This conforms with *Wong Sun* and *Draper*.[10] The affidavit states that it was "reliable" information, and I assume that the local justice of the peace knew the officers and whether they were reliable officers. The Constitution is satisfied here. We should not put officers in the straitjacket of *Wong Sun*.

WHITE: I agree in part with Potter—the words in this affidavit meant as much as the words in *Wong Sun*. Is what you hear from this reliable person enough to establish probable cause? That is the question. I think that it would be bad if the agent alone had said this, and there is no difference when the informant is not declared or evaluated. I would reverse.

---

8. *Ker v. California*, 374 U.S. 23 (1963).

9. *Wong Sun v. United States*, 371 U.S. 471 (1963). A person in custody with no established record as a police informer told federal narcotics officers that he had purchased heroin from someone he knew only as "Blackie Toy," the proprietor of an unnamed laundry. Without seeking an arrest warrant, officers arrested James Wah Toy and Wong Sun on narcotics charges, and both men were convicted in a nonjury trial. In a 5–4 decision, the Supreme Court quashed their convictions and ordered a new trial. There was no probable cause for the arrest, because the informant had no previous track record to establish his reliability and his information was too vague. Brennan wrote the majority opinion.

10. *Draper v. United States*, 358 U.S. 307 (1959). A paid informant told an experienced federal narcotics agent that James Alonzo Draper was peddling narcotics in Denver and that Draper planned to return to Chicago with a supply of heroin on either September 8 or 9, 1956. The informant had a long track record as a reliable source of information and gave a detailed physical description of Draper. The agent arrested Draper without a warrant when he arrived in Chicago, and a pat-down search yielded heroin and a syringe. The Court held 6–3 that the arrest, search, and seizure were valid. The arresting officer had probable cause within the meaning of the Fourth Amendment and "reasonable grounds" within the meaning of §104(a) of the Narcotic Control Act of 1956, which authorized warrantless arrests if the arresting officer had reasonable grounds to believe that the person arrested had violated, or was in the process of violating, federal narcotics laws.

GOLDBERG: You can't distinguish this case from *Nathanson*.[11] I would reverse.

HARLAN: If an opinion affirms that gets away from *Ker*, I will join it.

WHITE: I will, too.

Conference of April 3, 1964

WHITE: [DOUGLAS: It was White who asked that this case go over.] I now adhere to my initial vote to reverse.

GOLDBERG: I think that this warrant is sufficient as indicating it was based on reliable information.

HARLAN: I change my vote to affirm.

Result: Arthur Goldberg wrote for the 6–3 majority that there was no probable cause to support the search warrant. He established a two-prong test to determine when an informant's tip amounts to probable cause: (1) the affidavit must establish the underlying reasons why the informant reasonably concluded that the suspect was involved in criminal activity (the "basis of knowledge" prong); and (2) the affidavit must establish that the informant was credible or that the information provided reliable (the "veracity" or "reliability" prong). Harlan and White reluctantly voted with the majority. Both felt constrained by Ker, *which held that the test for reasonableness under the Fourth and Fourteenth Amendments were identical and that states were subject to the same search and seizure standards as the federal government. But for* Ker, *both Justices said that they would have voted to affirm Aguilar's conviction.*

There was extraordinary fluidity in deciding this case. Harlan and Goldberg both changed their minds twice—initially voting to reverse, then to affirm, then to reverse again. Byron White also appeared ready to change his mind and dissent but ultimately voted with the majority to reverse Aguilar's conviction.

Davis v. Mississippi, 394 U.S. 721 (1969)
(Douglas)

Police investigating the alleged rape of an eighty-six-year-old white woman in Meridian, Mississippi, rounded up sixty-five young black men and took them to the police station for questioning and fingerprinting. Without warrants or probable cause, police kept John Davis and most of the other men in

---

11. *Nathanson v. United States,* 290 U.S. 41 (1933). In a customs case, a federal magistrate issued a search warrant supported only by a customs official's unsubstantiated belief that J. J. Nathanson had smuggled liquor hidden inside his home. The affidavit contained no supporting facts or evidence. The circuit court held that while the search warrant was inadequate for an "ordinary" search, the rules for customs searches were more relaxed because of the government's pecuniary interest in finding smuggled goods. The Supreme Court reversed on the ground that regardless of circumstances, *all* unreasonable searches and seizures were forbidden by the Fourth Amendment. James McReynolds, writing for the Court, ruled that magistrates could issue search warrants only on a showing of probable cause, gathered from the facts and circumstances and presented under oath or affirmation. Mere affirmance of an officer's belief or suspicion was not enough. Nathanson's conviction was overturned and all evidence seized from his home was suppressed.

jail overnight. The next day, they were questioned again. Davis signed a statement and was fingerprinted a second time. His prints—along with those of twenty-three others—were sent to the FBI for analysis. On this evidence, Davis was tried and convicted of rape. The Mississippi Supreme Court affirmed.

WARREN: There were no warrants for these detentions. They were all fingerprinted. It was a dragnet—there weren't any warrants. I reverse.

BLACK: I reverse, but not on the Chief Justice's ground. *Schmerber* was wrongly decided.[12] I would overrule *Schmerber*. This is a violation of the Fifth Amendment, not the Fourth Amendment.

DOUGLAS: I would reverse.

HARLAN: I reverse. The second lot of fingerprints was used. I would not authorize fingerprinting in an investigative arrest.

BRENNAN: This is not unlike a stop and frisk. It is hard to call this an arrest, yet it is hard to stomach. I reverse doubtfully.

STEWART: I affirm. The police can make some detentions for interrogation.

WHITE: I reverse doubtfully, like Brennan. It is harmless error, as they can now take his fingerprints and use them.

FORTAS: Did not participate.

MARSHALL: I reverse. They were arrested illegally, and what the police discovered was not admissible as evidence.

Result: The Supreme Court reversed Davis's conviction on a 5–1–2 vote, with Harlan concurring. Brennan, writing for the majority, ruled that because Davis's detention was unlawful, his fingerprints were obtained in violation of the Fourth and Fourteenth Amendments and were inadmissible as evidence. Black and Stewart dissented.

Chimel v. California, 395 U.S. 752 (1969)
(Douglas)

Armed with an arrest warrant but no search warrant, police went to Ted Chimel's house to arrest him in connection with the burglary of a coin shop. Chimel was not home when the police arrived, but Chimel's wife invited them inside to wait. When Chimel returned, the officers served the warrant and

---

12. *Schmerber v. California,* 384 U.S. 757 (1966). After an automobile accident, Schmerber was taken to the hospital and arrested on suspicion of drunk driving. Police then directed the attending physician to draw a blood sample, which was drawn without a search warrant and over Schmerber's repeated refusals, on advice of his lawyer, to consent to any blood tests. The blood test indicated that Schmerber was intoxicated at the time of the accident. Schmerber claimed that the involuntary extraction of his blood deprived him of his Fourth (unreasonable search and seizure), Fifth (self-incrimination), and Sixth (right to counsel) Amendment rights. Brennan wrote for a 5–4 Court that Schmerber's civil rights had not been violated. Black and Douglas dissented on the ground that the compelled extraction of blood violated Schmerber's Fifth Amendment right against self-incrimination.

asked whether they could look around. Chimel refused to consent, but the police searched the house anyway and seized several items later used as evidence against him. Chimel was convicted and the California Court of Appeal affirmed. The state court invalidated the arrest warrant because the supporting affidavit was conclusory, but ruled that the search was reasonable because there was probable cause to arrest Chimel even without the warrant (meaning that the search was incident to a valid arrest) and because police had acted in good faith.

Note William O. Douglas's concern about Abe Fortas's request to have the case reargued and Earl Warren's low opinion of the Los Angeles Police Department and Chief William H. Parker.

Conference of March 28, 1969

WARREN: This search was bad as a search incident to an arrest. The police went through everything. A warrantless search incident to arrest is limited. In thirty-seven years, 1,939 search warrants were issued in this county of five million—about 50 a year. This reflects the policy of Chief Parker, who cuts lots of corners. In L.A. County there were about 200 search warrants a year. I assume that it was a valid arrest here. I would reverse and would overrule *Harris*.[13]

BLACK: I affirm.

DOUGLAS: I reverse and will vote to overrule *Harris*.

HARLAN: I would have voted with the dissenters in *Rabinowitz*.[14] *Kremen* was too broad a search—I proposed overruling *Rabinowitz* at that time.[15] It has been the rule for over twenty years, and the rule is being followed everywhere and we have refused to touch it. Too much water has passed under the dam to turn back. Look at *Warden v. Hayden* and the mere evidence rule.[16] Any rule we make blankets the entire country because of *Mapp*[17] and *Ker*.[18] Problems of getting warrants varies from place to place. I affirm.

---

13. *Harris v. United States*, 331 U.S. 145 (1947).

14. *United States v. Rabinowitz*, 339 U.S. 56 (1950). Knowing that Rabinowitz had already sold four forged postage stamps to a government agent, federal officers obtained an arrest warrant but did not seek a search warrant. They arrested Rabinowitz in his place of business and carefully searched his office, including a desk, safe, and several file cabinets, and found 573 forged stamps. Rabinowitz was convicted of possessing, concealing, and selling forged postage stamps. The Supreme Court held that both the search and seizure were lawful. Sherman Minton stressed the facts of the particular case, ruling that the search was reasonable because it was: (1) incident to a lawful arrest; (2) the locus of the search was a place of business open to the public; (3) the room was small and under the immediate and complete control of the suspect; and (4) the search did not extend beyond the room.

Black, Frankfurter, and Jackson dissented (Douglas took no part), arguing that the police had ample opportunity to obtain a search warrant and should have done so. Frankfurter blasted the majority for ignoring the history of the Fourth Amendment in this "sordid little case" and observed that if it were true that hard cases made bad law, then petty cases were even more likely to make bad law.

15. *Kremen v. United States*, 353 U.S. 346 (1957). Police suspected Shirley Kremen and two others of harboring a fugitive. Although officers obtained an arrest warrant for only one of the suspects, all three were arrested. Police searched the entire home and seized its contents, which were taken two hundred miles away for inspection. In a brief per curiam opinion, the Court ruled 6–2 that the search and seizure were illegal and that the three would have to be retried. Burton and Clark dissented; Whittaker did not participate.

16. *Warden v. Hayden*, 387 U.S. 294 (1967).

17. *Mapp v. Ohio*, 367 U.S. 643 (1961).

18. *Ker v. California*, 374 U.S. 23 (1963).

BRENNAN: I would reverse and overrule *Harris.*

STEWART: We haven't had a case since I arrived involving a search as wide as this. I reverse and vote to overrule *Harris.*

WHITE: I will adhere to *Harris* and affirm. The real problem is the right to arrest without a warrant or probable cause. That is never questioned here.

FORTAS: I would like to have it reargued. If arrests may be had on probable cause and searches are also included, then warrants are read out of the Fourth Amendment. I have concluded that the Fourth Amendment was fundamental to the Bill of Rights. These are my views: (1) An arrest without a warrant is permissible only where an officer sees a crime committed or there are some exigent circumstances. (2) A search of the person is permissible incident to a lawful arrest. (3) A search beyond the person is not permissible if the time and place permit a warrant. I do not want to read the warrant clause out of the Fourth Amendment. Where it is impractical to obtain a search warrant, police may have latitude to search confined to what is "reasonable under the circumstances." I would reverse, although I want it reargued. Here, the arrest is unlawful, and therefore no search is lawful. [DOUGLAS: To reargue the case would put it over when Warren is not here, and that would mean losing the case, reaffirming *Harris,* and affirming the decision below.]

Marshall: I reverse and would overrule *Harris.* I do not reach the arrest warrant issue.

Result: Harlan and Fortas both changed their minds after the conference, yielding a 7–2 majority to reverse Chimel's conviction and limit the scope of warrantless searches. The Court, in an opinion by Potter Stewart, ruled that even assuming a lawful arrest, a warrantless search of a suspect's entire house was unreasonable. Police could search areas within the immediate control of the suspect to look for weapons or to prevent the destruction of evidence, but to search areas outside this zone required a search warrant. The decision was announced on the same day that Warren Burger was sworn in as the new Chief Justice, replacing Earl Warren. At the very next conference, Burger announced that Chimel "must be overruled."[19]

Coolidge v. New Hampshire, 403 U.S. 443 (1971)
(Brennan) (Douglas)

Police went to Edward Coolidge's home to question him about the brutal torture-murder of fourteen-year-old babysitter Pamela Jean Mason. Coolidge showed the officers three guns and agreed to take a lie detector test. Several days later, he voluntarily went to the local police station for questioning. While he was at the station, two plainclothes officers went to Coolidge's home to question his wife, Joanne. She allowed them to take four guns and some of her husband's clothing. Several days later, police returned with a search warrant, arrested Coolidge, and seized his car. The warrant was issued by New Hampshire attorney general William Maynard, who was legally authorized to issue search warrants in his dual capacity as a justice of the peace. Maynard was also in charge of the murder investigation and later served as the chief prosecutor at Coolidge's trial.

---

19. Douglas, *The Court Years,* 231.

Police impounded Coolidge's car for more than a year and searched it repeatedly, vacuuming it several times for microscopic evidence. On the basis of evidence found in his home and automobile, Coolidge was convicted of murder. The New Hampshire Supreme Court affirmed.

Conference of January 15, 1971

BURGER: This is an anomalous case. Every lawyer in the state is a justice of the peace. The prosecutor issued the warrant. As to the validity of the warrant and as to wife's delivery of the weapons, I would argue that the latter was not a search or seizure at all. If what the wife did was a search, then I would say that it was a reasonable one. Her husband had shown prior to that time that he was cooperating with police. If it was a search, it was reasonable. The action of the attorney general in issuing warrants is a more difficult problem. The attorney general had apparent authority to issue a warrant. If the same information on which he acted had been presented to a neutral magistrate, the warrant would have issued. The facts on which he relied would have justified anyone using the act and issuing the warrant. I affirm.

BLACK: I affirm.

DOUGLAS: I agree on the wife issue. I also see nothing constitutionally wrong with a system that makes the attorney general a justice of peace, but that issue wasn't in this case. I reverse solely on the fact that the attorney general was the prosecuting attorney and was also the justice of the peace who issued the warrant.

HARLAN: I reverse on that point. I don't see how we can sustain this decision on the basis of our decisions requiring an independent magistrate to issue warrants.

BRENNAN: I reverse on that ground, and on the package, and on the wife's ground, too.

STEWART: There is nothing shocking or raw about this case. It was only a technical violation. This man was not a detached magistrate, and a detached and neutral magistrate is required. I reverse. I agree with the Chief Justice on the wife point.

WHITE: This is an automobile case for me and I would affirm on *Chambers,* holding that there was probable cause to search the car.[20] I don't have a problem with the wife. There was no neutral magistrate, but *Chambers* governs here. A predicate of *Chambers* was not

---

20. *Chambers v. Maroney,* 399 U.S. 42 (1970). Shortly after a service station was robbed at gunpoint, police obtained a detailed eyewitness description of the getaway car and two of the thieves. Police stopped a car matching the description and a warrantless search uncovered revolvers, bullets, property stolen from the service station, as well as other evidence linking the men to an earlier robbery. The Court upheld the search on a 7–3 vote. The majority admitted that the search was too remote in time and place to be considered a search incident to a lawful arrest but ruled that as long as there was probable cause to arrest the occupants there was also probable cause to search the car for guns and stolen property. Because automobiles were mobile, the Court decided that they could be searched without a warrant under circumstances that would not justify a warrantless search of a home or office. So long as there was probable cause to arrest the occupants or to search the car, the majority saw no constitutional difference between obtaining a search warrant and conducting an immediate, warrantless search.

the "incidental to arrest" requirement as in *Preston*.[21] This is *Carroll*[22] and *Brinegar*.[23] There was probable cause to search, and probable cause for a warrant.

MARSHALL: The search warrant is bad.

BLACKMUN: There was no real challenge to the arrest. The events of January 28 are very important. Coolidge offered to turn over his guns and to show the cops the automobile. His consent is critical. His claims that what happened on February 2 was different seem specious—implied consent can be spelled out. So I agree that *Chambers* governs this case. So we get down to the significance of the invalidity of the search warrant. The warrant is of limited importance. I have no difficulty with the wife angle. His wife presented his clothes and guns to the police. The validity of the search warrant is not an issue. This suit is outrageous. See my *Roberts* opinion in the Eighth Circuit.[24] I affirm.

Result: A badly divided Court reversed Coolidge's conviction. Potter Stewart's majority opinion, fully joined by just three other Justices, held that the search warrant was invalid because it was not issued by a neutral and detached magistrate. The repeated automobile searches also violated the Fourth

---

21. *Preston v. United States*, 376 U.S. 364 (1964). Three men who sat in a parked car for several hours were arrested for vagrancy and searched. Police towed their car to a nearby garage and searched it, finding enough incriminating evidence to convict all three of conspiracy to rob a bank. A unanimous Court ruled that the warrantless search was unreasonable and the evidence inadmissible, because the search was too remote in time and place to be a search incident to a lawful arrest. This decision was six years prior to *Chambers*.

22. *Carroll v. United States*, 267 U.S. 132 (1925). This case first introduced the "moving vehicle exception" to the warrant requirement. George Carroll was convicted of violating the National Prohibition Act after a warrantless search of his car produced sixty-eight quarts of whiskey and gin. The Court ruled that the Fourth Amendment recognized an essential difference between what was required to search a store, dwelling, or other fixed structure from what was required to search a ship, wagon, automobile, or other moving vehicle. The crucial difference was that the latter may quickly be moved out of the locality or jurisdiction in which the warrant was originally sought. Warrantless searches of automobiles and other movable vehicles was permissible, the Court decided, if the officer had reasonable cause to believe that it contained contraband.

23. *Brinegar v. United States*, 338 U.S. 160 (1948). During Prohibition, two federal officers saw Brinegar driving a heavily loaded Ford coupe east of Quapaw, Oklahoma—a known source of illegal liquor. Officer Malsed had previously caught Brinegar transporting bootleg liquor and knew him to be a "hauler." After a brief chase Brinegar stopped; when questioned he admitted that he had twelve cases of liquor in his car. The officers searched the car and found more than twelve cases of illegal whiskey. The Court followed *Carroll*, ruling that even before Brinegar confessed there was probable cause to search the car. Malsed's knowledge of Brinegar's past behavior and other facts derived from the officers' observations were sufficient to justify the warrantless search and seizure.

24. *Roberts v. United States*, 332 F.2d 892 (8th Cir. 1964). Raymond Roberts was arrested for the murder of a doctor at a veterans' hospital. Police interrogated Roberts's wife, who provided incriminating information and consented to a search of the family home. Police found incriminating evidence, including a bullet that Roberts had previously fired into his ceiling, which ballistics tests matched to the murder weapon. Roberts maintained that his wife could not waive *his* Fourth Amendment right to be secure in his home and personal effects. The court ruled that Roberts's wife had full authority to give her voluntary consent to officers to search a premises she occupied jointly with her husband and over which they exercised joint control. Circuit Judge Vogel wrote the opinion.

Amendment because they did not fall into any of the accepted exceptions to the search warrant requirement. The exclusionary rule required the suppression of all illegally seized evidence.

John Marshall Harlan, the crucial fifth vote, reluctantly concurred in the result because he felt bound by Mapp[25] and Ker.[26] Harlan urged the Court to repudiate those two cases and to allow states greater flexibility in admitting such evidence at state trials. Hugo Black's dissent criticized the exclusionary rule but fell short of calling for Mapp to be overruled. Edward Coolidge eventually pleaded guilty to second-degree murder. After spending nearly twenty years in prison, he was released on March 16, 1991.

EXCEPTIONS TO THE WARRANT REQUIREMENTS
Search Incident to a Lawful Arrest

Ker v. California, 374 U.S. 23 (1963)
(Douglas)

Los Angeles police received information that George and Diane Ker had purchased a large quantity of marijuana that they intended to resell. Without a warrant, four officers obtained a passkey from the building manager and late at night entered the Kers' apartment unannounced to arrest the couple. Police searched the apartment and the family car, finding marijuana in both places. The officers claimed that they disregarded the state's "knock and announce" law because they wanted to take the Kers by surprise and avoid the possible destruction of evidence. The trial court rejected the Kers' motion to suppress the evidence as the fruits of an illegal search, and both defendants were convicted. The state court of appeal affirmed, ruling that there was probable cause for the arrest and that the searches were incident to a lawful arrest. In conference, Warren again criticized the Los Angeles Police Department. The key question was whether California was free to establish its own standards of "reasonableness" or whether states would be held to the same constitutional standards as the federal government in search and seizure cases.

Conference of December 14, 1962

WARREN: I would reverse. There was no basis for probable cause for the arrest. L.A. wipes out all formalities governing arrests. What the police did here does not satisfy the requirements established in *Miller*.[27] Police officers made an illegal entry when they got a key on threat of breaking down the door.

---

25. *Mapp v. Ohio*, 367 U.S. 643 (1961).

26. *Ker v. California*, 374 U.S. 23 (1963).

27. *Miller v. United States*, 357 U.S. 301 (1958). When William Miller answered a knock on the door and saw police waiting for him, he quickly slammed the door shut. Police kicked in the door and arrested Miller on suspicion of narcotics violations. Police did not have a warrant and did not announce their purpose for demanding entry. A search produced marked currency that was used in evidence against him. By a 6–3 vote, the Court held that the arrest was illegal and the evidence inadmissible. Under local law, police were authorized to break down a door to make an arrest only if denied admittance after first announcing their authority and purpose. The only exception to the rule was if an announcement would have been useless. The majority ruled that under the facts and circumstances known to the officers at the time, it was not "virtually certain" that Miller already knew the officers' purpose so that any announcement would have been useless.

BLACK: I am not inclined to upset the findings of the state courts. This case is close on its facts. I will affirm.

DOUGLAS: I reverse. I agree with the Chief.

CLARK: I affirm. *Mapp* makes each case turn on its facts.[28] Though the rule is federal, here there was probable cause by federal standards. *Miller* applied state law. The state law here is supportable by the facts. *Draper* is not nearly as strong as this case.[29] It was not necessary for police to get a search warrant even if there was time to do so, provided that the officers had probable cause.

HARLAN: I affirm. *Mapp*—as Tom Clark says—does not adopt federal standards across the board. If this were a federal case, I do not know how I would come out. By state standards, there is nothing wrong here.

BRENNAN: I have difficulty saying that there was not probable cause for the arrest. If they had arrested Ker on the street it would have been O.K., but they broke down the door—figuratively. Some basic fundamentals would reach the states under *Mapp*, and one of these is that you don't break down the doors of houses at night. I do not reach the question of whether a warrant need be obtained if there were time.

STEWART: Does *Mapp* apply federal Fourth Amendment standards to the states? *Cahan* is a state court decision where they refused precisely to follow federal rule—in other words, I did not think that *Mapp* made the Fourth Amendment applicable to the states.[30] California is free to develop its own ground rules so far as it is not an unreasonable search. I affirm.

WHITE: I affirm. I am not sure about the evidence found in the car.

GOLDBERG: I would reverse. I thought that *Mapp* incorporated the Fourth Amendment. This is a Fourth Amendment violation. They entered the house out of curiosity, not because they were sure of the facts. Breaking down the door or sneaking a key is a shocking invasion of privacy.

---

28. *Mapp v. Ohio*, 367 U.S. 643 (1961).

29. *Draper v. United States*, 358 U.S. 307 (1959).

30. *People v. Cahan*, 44 Cal. 2d 434 (1955). The California Supreme Court found that the Los Angeles police department had obtained evidence against George Cahan in a horse racing investigation "in flagrant violation of the United States Constitution." Police had surreptitiously broken into several houses to place illegal listening devices and had made numerous other forcible entries and seizures without warrants. Justice Roger Traynor noted that police had candidly admitted "their deliberate, flagrant acts in violation of both Constitutions and the laws enacted thereunder. It is clearly apparent from their testimony that they casually regard such acts as nothing more than the performance of their ordinary duties for which the city employs and pays them." Traynor presented a strong defense of the exclusionary rule. He complained, however, that federal application of the rule had at times been arbitrary and confused, and reserved the state's right to follow its own course: "In developing a rule of evidence applicable in the state courts, this court is not bound by the decisions that have applied the federal rule, and if it appears that those decisions have developed needless refinements and distinctions, this court need not follow them. Similarly, if the federal cases indicate needless limitations on the right to conduct reasonable searches and seizures or to secure warrants, this court is free to reject them."

BLACK: *Mapp* held that the Fourth and Fifth Amendments applied to the states. That did not make federal statutes or *McNabb* applicable to the states.[31] I won't upset the findings of two courts. If they have the right to enter a house, they have a right to make the arrest.

CLARK: My views are the same as Hugo's, except on the Fifth Amendment.

Result: The Court affirmed the Kers' convictions in a 4–1–4 decision by Tom Clark, ruling that the officers' entry into the Kers' home was reasonable and their warantless search and seizure was a valid search incident to a lawful arrest. Harlan concurred in the result, while Brennan, Warren, Douglas, and Goldberg dissented.

There was, however, broad agreement (8–1) that state and federal governments were subject to the same constitutional standards of reasonableness under the Fourth Amendment. Only Harlan dissented on this issue, calling the majority view an unwise and ill-conceived "constitutional adventure" and complaining that it would place states in a "constitutional strait jacket." Harlan preferred variable state standards of reasonableness and wanted state practices judged "by the more flexible concept of 'fundamental' fairness, of rights 'basic to a free society,' embraced in the due process clause of the Fourteenth Amendment."

The uniform national standard in search and seizure cases was more firmly established in Malloy v. Hogan, *which overruled both* Adamson v. California *and* Twining v. New Jersey.[32]

Exigent Circumstances

Warden v. Hayden, 387 U.S. 294 (1967)
(Douglas)

Police were informed that an armed robbery suspect had just entered Bennie Joe Hayden's house. Officers arrived on the scene a few minutes later and asked the woman who answered the door— Hayden's wife—for permission to search the house. She did not object, and police arrested Hayden when he proved to be the only man inside the house. A search produced weapons, ammunition, and clothing that fit eyewitness accounts of the crime and Hayden was convicted. The Ninth Circuit Court of Appeals granted Hayden's petition for a federal writ of habeas corpus. While the search was legal, the clothing seized was not an instrumentality of the crime but was "mere evidence" and therefore immune from seizure under the Supreme Court's decision in Gouled v. United States.[33] *At conference, Chief Justice Warren again expressed his concerns about the Los Angeles Police Department.*

---

31. *McNabb v. United States,* 318 U.S. 332 (1943).

32. *Malloy v. Hogan,* 378 U.S. 1 (1964); *Adamson v. California,* 332 U.S. 46 (1947); *Twining v. New Jersey,* 211 U.S. 78 (1908).

33. *Gouled v. United States,* 255 U.S. 298 (1921). The Court ruled that property rights were the foundation of the Fourth Amendment and limited the government's right to search and seize private property. Government could not seize property "simply for the purpose of proving crime"; only the instrumentalities or fruits of a crime could be seized. This became known as the "mere evidence" rule.

Conference of April 14, 1967

WARREN: The robbery was seen and the robber was followed. Police went into the house in hot pursuit. They picked up the clothes, and if they had not they should be censored. I would not reach *Gouled*, but would be willing to limit *Gouled*. I reverse.

BLACK: I reverse. *Gouled* is different. There, papers were stolen. I do not understand the "mere evidence" rule. *Entick* treated some things differently.[34] I would draw a difference between seizing political documents and others. But under the Fourth Amendment you can get "mere" evidence.

DOUGLAS: I affirm.

CLARK: I reverse. I would not disturb *Gouled*. This is close to our line-up cases. I agree with the Chief that these are instrumentalities of the crime.

HARLAN: I reverse. I agree with Hugo. Is it a "reasonable" search? I would not try to bring pants into the category of instruments of a crime. I would prefer to treat this as a search, in hot pursuit, for anything.

BRENNAN: *Gouled* holds that there are some things that can't be seized. I would draw the line between self-incriminating material (like a confession) and incriminatory materials. I would get rid of the idea of pants being instrumentalities of the crime. I would abolish the mere evidence rule. This was a complete house search, and went beyond *Harris*.[35] This is like *Gilbert*, except that no one was there when they went into the apartment in *Gilbert*.[36] I would rule on the "mere" evidence point only and reverse.

STEWART: A lawful search was the finding below and I do not question it. The distinction between types of evidence in *Gouled* should be eliminated. "Mere evidence" is not a valid line. Once there is a lawful search, then anything turned up is O.K. to use. I would reverse.

---

34. *Entick v. Carrington*, 19 How. St. Tr. 1029 (1765). In the King's name, the Earl of Halifax authorized a general warrant to search John Entick's house on suspicion of seditious libel. Entick sued Nathan Carrington and the other government agents who conducted the search for trespass. The Lord Chancellor, Lord Camden, argued that the king's power to conduct searches must derive either from the common law or from statute and that it was for the courts to determine the limits of the king's prerogative. Camden's decision rested largely on his views of privacy and the sanctity of home and private property. Borrowing freely from John Locke, Camden wrote that "the great end for which men entered into society was to secure their property. . . . Papers are the owner's goods and chattels; they are his dearest property; and so far from enduring a seizure, that they will hardly bear an inspection; and . . . where private papers are removed and carried away, the secret nature of those goods will be an aggravation of the trespass, and demand more considerable damages in that respect." Entick prevailed, and Lord Camden's opinion became a direct inspiration for the Framers of the Fourth Amendment.

35. *Harris v. United States*, 331 U.S. 145 (1947).

36. *Gilbert v. California*, 388 U.S. 263 (1967). Jesse James Gilbert was accused of armed robbery and murdering a police officer. While searching for Gilbert, police conducted a warrantless search of his locked, unoccupied apartment and seized photographs later used in evidence against him. Police claimed that the search fell under the "hot pursuit" or "exigent circumstances" exceptions to the Fourth Amendment's warrant requirement. The Court avoided the Fourth Amendment issue, dismissing certiorari as improvidently granted on that question and deciding the case on other grounds.

WHITE: I reverse.

FORTAS: Unless we are very careful, every search warrant will be general and you will turn back history. If there are no limits on hot pursuit, then there are none on search warrants. *Gouled* involved a warrant searching for papers. We must not commit mayhem on the Fourth Amendment. I would stay with *Gouled* rather than modify it. On a universal theory, you would hold police to a narrow ambit of searches, whether with a warrant or in hot pursuit. Clothing is not an instrumentality of a crime. I reverse, but narrowly. I would add to *Gouled* a fourth category of identification of the accused or suspect.

WARREN: We must put some limit on the police, for they are lawless in many areas—particularly in L.A.

FORTAS: I affirm.

Result: By a 5–3–1 vote, the Court decided that the warrantless search was reasonable because of exigent circumstances—the hot pursuit of a suspected armed felon. Brennan, writing for the majority, threw out the mere evidence rule and announced that federal courts would no longer distinguish between items of mere evidential value and the instruments or fruits of a crime. Brennan also rejected Gouled *because it connected the Fourth Amendment to property rights and established the modern rule that the Fourth Amendment protects people, not places. Warren, Black, and Fortas concurred in the result without joining Brennan's opinion. Douglas was alone in dissent.*

Stop and Frisk

Terry v. Ohio, 392 U.S. 1 (1968)
(Douglas) (Brennan)

Cleveland police detective Martin McFadden saw John Terry and two other men repeatedly walking past a jewelry store window, talking with each other and acting suspiciously. McFadden approached the men to investigate. Because he was afraid that they might have weapons, he patted down the outside of Terry's clothing and found a gun. Terry was convicted of carrying a concealed weapon, and his conviction was affirmed on appeal. Among the issues the Court had to face in conference was whether this "stop and frisk" tactic was a seizure or a search within the meaning of the Fourth Amendment and, if so, whether the detective's actions were reasonable.

Conference of December 13, 1967

WARREN: There was no stop and frisk law here. Did the police officer have "probable cause": (1) to talk to them; or (2) to believe that his life was in danger? An officer who sees what he saw has a duty to pursue it and to find out if there is a crime about to be committed. But people don't have to answer and they may walk away—at that point there would be no probable cause—but their actions may give him probable cause to think that he is in danger. I am having in mind how a trained policeman may react differently from ordinary citizens. He can protect himself by seeing if they are armed. I affirm. I rest solely on "probable cause." I would not downgrade probable cause to reasonable suspicion. There was probable cause here: (1) to talk to the men; and (2) to fear that he might be endangered. A stop and frisk law can't change these principles. I would use this case to lay down a good rule for stop and frisk. A statute can't enlarge a policeman's right here.

BLACK: I affirm. I agree with the Chief to stick by "probable cause" and not reasonable suspicion.[37] I would construe "reasonable suspicion" in the New York law to mean probable cause. He did not make an arrest by talking to them. [DOUGLAS: Marshall interrupts Black to say that the police did not go up to them to question them.] I don't think that they arrested these people until after he got their guns—he arrested them only when he stands them up. Does a police officer have the right to interrogate people doing peculiar things? I don't know that this is forbidden by anything in the Constitution. The right to stop and question people is part of the body of law; it does not stem from the Fourth Amendment. The Fourth Amendment does not get into it until there is an arrest. A policeman has the right to defend himself and to frisk people to save his life. Evidence taken would be admissible. I would say that the citizen can't just walk away and refuse to talk to the police when questioned—there is a right to investigate. The officer could delay him temporarily, though not arrest him. We need not decide that now, but that is how I would decide it. I don't want anything said that the police can't make a guy stay until he answers or stubbornly refuses.

DOUGLAS: I agree with the Chief and affirm.

HARLAN: I affirm. The frisking took place pretty early. A cop can't do that without probable cause that a crime is being committed. I do not look at this as a questioning case.

BRENNAN: I affirm. There is a Fourth Amendment issue here. It deals with the seizure of persons, and there must be probable cause. There is a seizure, not for the purpose of booking him for a crime, but for the purpose of frisking. Is there probable cause to stop him, question him, and frisk him? [DOUGLAS: He passes over the case where there is a frisk and nothing found, and yet police detain him.] Look at our decision in *Miranda*, and custodial detention outside a jail.[38]

STEWART: I agree with the Chief and affirm. I would not say that a citizen can refuse to answer a cop. States can establish stricter standards than required by the Fourth Amendment. We need not reach the case where the frisk turns up contraband.

WHITE: I affirm. Questioning is not included under the Fourth Amendment. It is involved in a frisk or search for those in detention.

---

37. Relying only on Brennan's conference notes, Bernard Schwartz claimed that Black advocated using *both* probable cause and reasonable suspicion standards during this conference. This would not have made sense, as the two standards are mutually exclusive. Schwartz apparently omitted the word "not" while transcribing Brennan's conference notes. As Brennan reported, what Black actually said was: "Agree that we should use 'probable cause' and *not* reasonable suspicion" (emphasis added). See Bernard Schwartz, *Super Chief*, 686; see also Barrett, "Stop and Frisk," 788.

38. *Miranda v. Arizona*, 384 US 435 (1966).

FORTAS: I affirm. With a precisely refined opinion—not a *Miranda* type—we are inventing a new kind of probable cause. I would be cautious and would go case by case. I would leave untouched the round-up type of frisk.

MARSHALL: I affirm.

Result: The Court ruled 8–1 that the stop and frisk was a search and seizure under the Fourth Amendment but that McFadden's actions were reasonable. The initial seizure was permissible because the officer had a reasonable suspicion that the men were involved in wrongdoing. Because McFadden reasonably believed that the men might pose a danger to himself or to a bystander, he could then search any legitimately detained persons to check for weapons, even absent probable cause to arrest. The search was reasonable, Warren emphasized, because it was confined to what was minimally necessary to find out whether any of the men were armed. William O. Douglas dissented.

Consent

Schneckloth v. Bustamonte, 412 U.S. 218 (1973)
(Douglas)

Robert Bustamonte was a passenger in a car stopped by police for a traffic violation. The officer asked for permission to search the car; all six passengers, including Bustamonte, consented. The officer found three forged checks and a check-writing machine stolen from a nearby car wash. Bustamonte's motion to suppress the checks was denied, and he was convicted of illegal possession of checks with intent to defraud. The state appellate courts affirmed. After filing for a federal writ of habeas corpus, the Ninth Circuit Court of Appeals ruled that Bustamonte had not validly consented to the automobile search. The court argued that in order to waive their rights, Bustamonte and the others first had to know that they could refuse to consent. Police did not advise Bustamonte or the others of their right to withhold their consent, and the state could not prove that the men already knew their rights.

Conference of October 13, 1972

BURGER: The court of appeals held that consent to search was valid only if one knew that consent could be withheld. But "reasonable" under the Fourth Amendment entails consideration of all the circumstances. Consent was voluntarily given. I reverse. I would not reach *Kaufman*.[39]

---

39. *Kaufman v. United States,* 394 U.S. 217 (1969). In a federal trial for armed robbery, Harold Kaufman's only defense was insanity. He was convicted and the appellate courts affirmed. Kaufman then sought to reopen his case and vacate the judgment, claiming that some of the evidence used against him had been illegally seized and should have been suppressed. The lower courts denied relief on the ground that search and seizure claims must be raised on direct appeal and could not be raised in a motion to vacate sentence or in any other collateral attack. The Supreme Court reversed in a 5–4 decision, ruling that Kaufman's failure to raise the issue on appeal did not deprive federal postconviction courts of jurisdiction to decide the merits of his constitutional claims (citing *Fay v. Noia,* 372 U.S. 391, 409 [1963]). *Kaufman* has often been criticized and its reach today is limited, but it has never been overruled. Brennan wrote the majority opinion.

DOUGLAS: I agree with the court of appeals on consent, and I would stand by *Kaufman*.

BRENNAN: On consent, the state has the burden of proof. I also affirm on *Kaufman*.

STEWART: *Kaufman* was based on §2255, not habeas corpus.[40] The state has the burden of proof. If there is consent, the Fourth Amendment does not apply at all. I think that the state proved consent. I also think that we should reach the *Kaufman* point. I reverse.

WHITE: I reverse. The search here was voluntary. The state carried the burden of proof.

MARSHALL: I affirm.

BLACKMUN: I reverse. *Ker v. California* was never overruled.[41] It drew a distinction between state and federal cases and left the states elbow room.

POWELL: I reverse on the consent issue. I do not agree with *Kaufman*. I agree with Hugo Black's dissent in *Kaufman*. Loss of public confidence in our judicial system is a consequence of the open-ended attack on judgments of conviction through collateral attack, where guilt or innocence is not in issue.

REHNQUIST: On the merits of the search and seizure issue, there was consent. On the statute, there has been a mangling. The exclusionary rule is not mandated by the Constitution—look at *Harris*. It follows that case to say that the exclusionary rule is not required by the Constitution. I would reverse *Kaufman* and overrule the constitutional aspect of *Kaufman*.

BRENNAN: *Kaufman* was a statutory case. The exclusionary rule permits a defendant to raise the issue on direct appeal. But in a collateral attack it has no constitutional basis.

WHITE: I will stand by *Kaufman*, but I would re-do and reformulate *Mapp*.

STEWART: I would not reach *Kaufman* here.

[DOUGLAS: To overrule *Kaufman*: Powell, Rehnquist, Berger (*sic*).]

BLACKMUN: I would have voted with the dissent in *Kaufman*. I could overrule it, but I do not think it necessary.

Result: The Court ruled 6–3 that automobile passengers were not in custody during a traffic stop and that the voluntariness of their consent to searches must be determined from the totality of circumstances. Whether Bustamonte actually knew that he could refuse his consent for the police to search the car was only one factor to consider, and the state was not required to prove that Bustamonte knew his rights.

---

40. 28 U.S.C. §2255 provides remedies for federal prisoners who attack their sentence on the ground that sentence was imposed in violation of the Constitution or laws of the United States. This statute was the primary basis for Brennan's decision in *Kaufman*.

41. *Ker v. California*, 374 U.S. 23 (1963).

United States v. Mendenhall, 446 U.S. 544 (1980)
(Brennan)

Twenty-two-year-old Sylvia Mendenhall fit a Drug Enforcement Agency (DEA) profile for drug couriers. Two DEA agents stopped Mendenhall in the Detroit airport concourse and briefly talked to her. Mendenhall agreed to accompany the agents to their office for further questioning. Once there, the agents asked to search her handbag, and Mendenhall told them to "go ahead." A female agent then asked Mendenhall to submit to a strip search, and after some hesitation she agreed. The female agent found two packages of heroin hidden in Mendenhall's undergarments and arrested her. The district court denied Mendenhall's motion to suppress the evidence, finding that the initial approach was a "minimum intrusion" investigative stop that did not require probable cause, and the subsequent searches were all conducted with Mendenhall's consent. The court of appeals reversed, saying that Mendenhall's consent had been coerced.

> BURGER: The DEA profile is really irrelevant. The problem is the use of addict couriers, and the profile is just a technique for the guidance of agents. We should look at it through the experienced eyes of agents. The stop for identification was not a seizure or arrest. She could have refused and walked away. The court of appeals wrongly said that the first question at the first stop was a seizure.

> STEWART: If there were consents back to go to the office and to allow the search of the handbag, that is the end of case, whatever may be case as to the original stop.

> WHITE: When they got her into the office, there may not have been an arrest but there was a temporary restraint, defended only on the ground of reasonable suspicion. I don't think that the government can win without proving consent.

> MARSHALL: Two agents and one woman. That is coercive, and she was never told that she was free to go.

> BLACKMUN: The consents are here, and so I agree with Potter—everything else drops out.

> POWELL: Stops may be made short of probable cause. Even if the stop here was not based on probable cause, there was at least reasonable suspicion. I could balance interests here in favor of the government operation, focused on drug couriers. But I could also reverse on consent grounds.

> REHNQUIST: No one has the right to refuse the police an answer to a question. There was no seizure or detention under the Fourth Amendment, and I would prefer to reverse on that ground.

> STEVENS: I agree with Byron. It is unusual for a young person to be up in the agents' office.

Result: The Court affirmed the decision below and ruled that there had been no violation of Mendenhall's Fourth Amendment rights. The majority, speaking through Potter Stewart, thought that while it was not irrelevant that Mendenhall was a young and uneducated black female initially confronted by two white, male DEA agents, these facts alone were not dispositive. Mendenhall was not subjected to any force or threats and was informed of her right to refuse her consent to any search. Moreover, according to Stewart, there was no objective reason for Mendenhall to believe that she was in custody or that she was not free to leave at any time. Under this "totality of the circumstances" test, the Court ruled that Mendenhall had voluntarily consented to the interrogations and searches.

Automobiles

United States v. Chadwick, 433 U.S. 1 (1977)
(Brennan)

Police received information that a group traveling by train from San Diego to Boston was transporting illegal drugs. Boston police officers observed the suspects carrying a double-locked footlocker from the train to Joseph Chadwick's car and watched as they stored it in the car's trunk. At that point, officers moved in to arrest the men and later impounded the car at Boston's Federal Building. An hour and a half later, police searched Chadwick's car and the footlocker without a warrant or consent, and inside the footlocker they found a large amount of marijuana. The district court suppressed the marijuana as the fruit of an illegal search, and the court of appeals affirmed.

BURGER: To hold them until police can reach a magistrate is a greater intrusion than what happened here.

STEWART: We would have to overturn too many precedents to reverse this.

WHITE: There is no question here whether police could have searched incident to a valid arrest. If there were, I would say that they could. But when they took this to the station house, that means that we would give the police open season to the search of personal effects without warrants. *Cooper* is a problem for me, unless we draw a line between cars and trunks.[42]

MARSHALL: I don't leave the Fourth Amendment at home when I leave my house.

BLACKMUN: I could not buy a broad argument that containers seized in public can be searched without a warrant. But I think that this is really a search incident to an arrest, and I would reverse.

POWELL: I don't think that this is a search incident to an arrest and I would affirm. I would prefer to leave open the question of whether the police, even incident to arrest, can seize and search a locked trunk.

---

42. *Cooper v. California*, 386 U.S. 58 (1967). After Joe Nathan Cooper was arrested on narcotics charges, his car was impounded and forfeiture proceedings began under state law. More than a week later, police searched the car twice without a warrant. They found one marijuana seed and a piece of paper that prosecutors alleged was used to wrap packages of heroin. The state supreme court held that the searches were unconstitutional but refused to order a new trial because the evidence found was incidental to conviction and amounted to "harmless error." The Supreme Court, in a 5–4 decision, affirmed on other grounds. The Justices ignored the "harmless error" issue and ruled that the car had been properly seized and the searches were reasonable because they were closely related to the reason Cooper was arrested.

REHNQUIST: We would have to strain some to say that this is a search incident to an arrest. The privacy intrusion by a search of a briefcase is greater than this bust. *Chimel*[43] plus *Robinson*[44] would sanction it. Anyway, the Fourth Amendment's warrant requirement does not distinguish seizure from search.

STEVENS: There is a substantial privacy interest in a footlocker. Seizure may be justified by exigent circumstances, but only temporarily pending getting a warrant. There was no safety threat or destruction of evidence justification here.

Result: The Court ruled 7–2 that the search violated the warrant clause of the Fourth Amendment. Burger's majority opinion incorporated Thurgood Marshall's conference argument that citizens had privacy interests outside of the home. The Chief Justice also recognized a higher expectation of privacy for locked luggage than for the car itself. This search did not fall under any recognized exception to the warrant requirement, including the automobile exception. Nor was the search incident to a lawful arrest, as it was too remote in time and place.

Robbins v. California, 453 U.S. 420 (1981)
(Brennan)

After observing Jeffrey Robbins driving his car erratically, highway patrol officers DePue and Stoltz pulled him over. As DePue approached the vehicle, Robbins opened the car door and DePue smelled marijuana. DePue searched the passenger compartment and found a small amount of marijuana and some drug paraphernalia. Robbins told the officers, "What you are looking for is in the back." They opened the car's luggage compartment and found a tote bag and two packages wrapped in opaque plastic. DePue unwrapped the packages and inside found two fifteen-pound bricks of marijuana. Robbins's motion to exclude the marijuana from evidence was denied and he was convicted. The state court of appeal affirmed, finding that a warrantless search was permissible because any experienced observer could have reasonably concluded that the two packages contained marijuana.

BURGER: Robbins's erratic driving led to the stop. There was probable cause to arrest. Robbins's statement that, "What you were looking for is in the back," is not relied on by the state as consent. Secured packages prevented the officer from seeing the marijuana contents inside. Could not the officer know the profile of marijuana bricks? The tote bag was not sealed. The cookie tin and the plastic bag were in the body of the car.

STEWART: The officer may have had probable cause to believe that there was marijuana, but I think that a warrant was required and that *Sanders* controlled. We can't affirm without overruling *Sanders* and other cases.[45]

---

43. *Chimel v. California,* 395 U.S. 752 (1969).
44. *United States v. Robinson,* 414 U.S. 218 (1973).
45. *Arkansas v. Sanders,* 442 U.S. 753 (1979). An informant told state police that Lonnie Sanders would arrive at the airport carrying a green suitcase full of marijuana. Officers observed Sanders as he retrieved a green suitcase matching the informant's description. Not long afterward, police stopped the taxi in which Sanders was riding. Without a warrant or consent, the officers retrieved the luggage from the car trunk, opened the locked suitcase, and found marijuana. The Arkansas Supreme Court reversed Sanders's conviction on the ground that it was the product of an unreasonable search.

WHITE: *Chadwick* rejected the application of the automobile exception. Police had to get a warrant however much probable cause you had.[46] *Sanders* held that just because luggage is in an auto, you still can't search it without a warrant. A package is luggage unless you can see it in plain view. There is no difference whether it is a grocery bag if you can't see in it. Maybe an exigent circumstances exception should be recognized.

MARSHALL: I agree with Byron.

BLACKMUN: My votes in *Chadwick* and *Sanders* compel me to affirm. I would overrule them.

POWELL: We crossed the stream when we departed from the automobile exception in *Chadwick*. *Sanders* emphasized "luggage," and we can distinguish this case on that ground. But I guess that I have to agree that I can't readily say how to distinguish paper bags and so forth. Exigent circumstances might be recognized as an exception in any opinion.

REHNQUIST: I would adopt the automobile exception as a bright line. If police have probable cause to search for an object in an automobile, they don't need a warrant.

STEVENS: I would not overrule *Chadwick* or *Sanders* on its facts. The opinion there was overbroad and pure dicta. Once police have probable cause to search a car, I don't see how they should distinguish packages. I would follow the Chief Justice's *Sanders* opinion, which focused only on the luggage, and not on the car.

Result: In a plurality decision, the Court ruled that opening the packages without a warrant violated the Fourth and Fourteenth Amendments. Stewart's lead opinion held that luggage and other opaque containers found in cars deserved the same protection as luggage found anywhere else. There was no other valid exception to the warrant requirement available to justify this search. Stewart specifically rejected the state's claim that the packages' contents could reasonably be inferred by their outward appearance ruling that containers discovered during a valid car search could not be searched without a warrant unless they clearly and obviously announced their contents by configuration, transparency, or otherwise. Burger and Powell concurred in the result but did not join Stewart's opinion. Blackmun, Rehnquist, and Stevens dissented. For more on Robbins, *see* United States v. Ross, *below.*

New York v. Belton, 453 U.S. 454 (1981)
(Brennan)

After stopping an automobile for speeding, state trooper Douglas Nicot smelled marijuana inside the car. Looking through the side window, he spotted an envelope on the floorboard labeled "Supergold." Suspecting that the envelope contained marijuana, he opened it, and when his suspicions

---

The U.S. Supreme Court affirmed in a close 5–4 vote. Powell wrote that the warrant requirement of the Fourth Amendment applied to luggage taken from an automobile to the same degree as it applied to luggage found in any other location. In the absence of exigent circumstances, police had to seek a warrant. *Sanders* was later overruled by *California v. Acevedo,* 500 U.S. 565 (1991).

46. *United States v. Chadwick,* 433 U.S. 1 (1977).

were confirmed he ordered everyone out of the car and arrested them for possession of a controlled substance. Nicot then searched each occupant and the passenger compartment. Inside the car he found a jacket belonging to Roger Belton. Nicot unzipped the pockets and inside found a small amount of cocaine.

Belton sought to suppress the cocaine as the product of an illegal search. State prosecutors claimed that the search was incident to a lawful arrest. The trial judge sided with prosecutors, and Belton pleaded guilty to a lesser charge of attempted possession of a criminal substance. Belton reserved his right to challenge the search and seizure ruling, and on appeal the New York Court of Appeals reversed, ruling that the search violated the Fourth Amendment.

STEWART: The issue here is the permissible geographic scope of a lawful custodial arrest. I would hold that when the occupants of a car are all lawfully arrested, the permissible geographic scope is the automobile. *Robbins* was not defended on that ground, but only on the ground that the sealed bricks were giveaways of their contents.[47]

WHITE: I don't agree with the theory of the court of appeals that once the car's occupants are subdued, a search requires a warrant. The respondent did not try to support that holding. I cannot see how this can be distinguished from *Robbins*. If a package is on the back seat with the jacket, how can you say that you have to get a warrant for one and not the other?

MARSHALL: I lean toward affirming, but I want to see the record. I could agree with Potter.

POWELL: I agree with Potter. This is clearly different from *Robbins*. It implicates *Robinson*[48] and *Chimel*.[49] The Fourth Amendment allows a search even though the object has been taken from the arrestee and is out of his control. So where you are dealing with a passenger car, the interior of car is a finite space, normally under the control of passengers in it.

REHNQUIST: One officer and four arrestees here has relevance, but I can go with Potter.

STEVENS: My *Robbins* rule would apply here. There was probable cause to arrest in both cases, but the search can't be justified here as incident to a lawful arrest. There was probable cause to believe that there were drugs in the jacket. Is there any difference between the back seat and the trunk? I don't think so. This has to be affirmed if *Robbins* is reversed.

Result: The Court extended Chimel, *holding that officers may search the entire passenger compartment as well as any luggage, boxes, or other containers found there as part of a search incident to a lawful arrest. The entire passenger compartment, Stewart reasoned, was within the arrestees' immediate control, including the glove compartment and other similar recesses. John Paul Stevens changed his mind after the conference and concurred in the result, but he did not join Stewart's majority opinion. Brennan, White, and Marshall dissented.*

47. *Robbins v. California*, 453 U.S. 420 (1981).
48. *United States v. Robinson*, 414 U.S. 218 (1973).
49. *Chimel v. California*, 395 U.S. 752 (1969).

United States v. Ross, 456 U.S. 798 (1982)
(Brennan)

An informant told District of Columbia police that a man was selling drugs out of the trunk of his car at a specified location. Police went to the spot and saw a man sitting in a car that matched the informant's description. After a brief stakeout, police approached the car and arrested and handcuffed the driver, Albert Ross, a.k.a. "The Bandit." Without a search warrant or consent, police opened the car trunk and found a paper bag, which the officers opened. Inside they found several small glassine bags, which later proved to contain heroin. After impounding the automobile at police headquarters, police conducted another warrantless search of the car and found a leather pouch, inside of which was a large amount of money. Over Ross's objection, the district court admitted the drugs and money into evidence and Ross was convicted of possession of heroin with intent to distribute. The court of appeals reversed, stating that while police had probable cause to stop and search the car without a warrant, they needed a warrant to open the paper bag and leather pouch.

BURGER: We need a bright line—a French Connection search—a complete exception from the warrant requirement. I can't see the passenger compartment versus trunk distinction as to any privacy element. "Unreasonable" is key word for me in the Fourth Amendment. I can't see how to distinguish different kinds of containers, either.

BRENNAN:[50] I agree with Mr. Frey's answer to my question at oral argument.[51] We cannot reverse the judgment of the court of appeals here unless we abandon the plurality opinion in *Robbins v. California.* Because I am not willing to do that, I vote to affirm the judgment of the Court of Appeals for the District of Columbia. I would affirm.

WHITE: *Chadwick* said don't apply the auto exception to luggage.[52] I think that we should stick to *Robbins*—I don't see how you have to have a warrant to open a suitcase in a hotel but not in a car.[53]

MARSHALL: This is a non-case. He was arrested and handcuffed. You just wanted to get a case to overrule *Robbins,* and I am going to write that.

BLACKMUN: All my past votes relying on reasonableness require reversal. I might go through *Carroll* and let them go whole hog.[54] I would even overrule *Evans, Chadwick,* and *Robbins.*

POWELL: I did not think our earlier *Sanders* or *Chadwick* decisions were auto cases.[55] We ought to have a bright line for the benefit of police. An automobile is very different from a residence.

REHNQUIST: Like Harry, I dissented in most of these cases. The best chance for a bright line is the government's second position—that the police can search for anything in the

---

50. Adapted from Brennan's talking papers, Brennan Papers, OT 1981, box 596.
51. Deputy Solicitor Andrew Frey argued the case for the government.
52. *United States v. Chadwick,* 433 U.S. 1 (1977).
53. *Robbins v. California,* 453 U.S. 420 (1981).
54. *Carroll v. United States,* 267 U.S. 132 (1925).
55. *Arkansas v. Sanders,* 442 U.S. 753 (1979).

car on probable cause to search the car, limited by the rule that they can't search for a waffle in a paper bag.[56]

STEVENS: I come out the same as Rehnquist. The government says first that there can be different rules for different kinds of containers—only Lewis has gone for that. The other possibility is that the auto exception contains everything in the car—that the police can make as much of a search as they could with a warrant.

O'CONNOR: I would not decide this case based on the worthiness of the container. I would allow the police to search anywhere in the car.

Result: On a 6–3 vote, the Court held that if police had probable cause to believe that there was contraband anywhere in a car, they did not need a search warrant. They could, in Harry Blackmun's words, "go whole hog" and conduct a full search of the entire car, including the trunk and any containers, as if a magistrate had issued a warrant. The scope of the search was defined only by the object of the search, not the nature or location of the container. This case greatly expanded the Carroll *automobile exception and effectively overruled both* Robbins *and* Sanders.

Michigan v. Long, 463 U.S. 1032 (1983)
(Brennan)

Deputies Howell and Lewis saw a speeding car swerve suddenly and veer into a ditch. They stopped to investigate, and when they looked into the car's passenger window they saw a hunting knife lying on the floorboard. They conducted a pat-down search of David Kerk Long, the driver. Howell used a flashlight to examine the passenger compartment and spotted "something leather" sticking out of the armrest. Upon closer inspection, it proved to be a pouch containing marijuana. After the deputies decided to impound the car, Howell jimmied open the trunk with his pocket knife and found seventy-five pounds of marijuana. Long was convicted for possession of marijuana but the state supreme court reversed, holding that Terry v. Ohio *could not justify the warrantless search of an automobile passenger compartment.*[57]

---

56. During oral arguments, Deputy Solicitor General Frey used a small paper bag to demonstrate the kind of container that he claimed should not be protected from warrantless searches, because such a small bag was not likely to contain personal effects. E. Barrett Prettyman reported this unusual exchange between Frey and the Justices:

Q: Is that bag stapled together?
A: No, it is not.
Q: Would it make any difference in your argument? . . .Suppose what they were hunting for was, say, a waffle iron, a stolen waffle iron or something else that couldn't go in the paper bag. You might have probable cause to search the car for the waffle iron, but if you got to the paper bag, you wouldn't be searching it, would you?

Prettyman, "The Supreme Court's Use of Hypothetical Questions at Oral Argument," 559.

57. The Michigan Supreme Court ruled that a *Terry*-style "pat-down" search was premised solely on the need to protect police officers and passersby and found that the search conducted in this case could not be justified on those grounds. *Terry v. Ohio,* 392 U.S. 1 (1968).

There were two key issues at conference: (1) whether the Court should dismiss the case without deciding the merits; or (2) whether to extend Terry-*style protective searches to cover automobile passenger compartments. The Justices also showed off a new verb, "to Krivda."*

BURGER: I am ready to tell the states that we are going to assume that their decisions rest on federal and not state grounds if they cite federal statutes and cases. I would not reach the issue of searching the car's trunk, but only the interior of car. I would extend *Terry*.

WHITE: I would not dissent from a decision to *Krivda* here, but I would not be adverse to spelling out a requirement that state courts must say whether they are deciding a case on an independent state ground.[58] I agree with the Chief Justice on the merits—the police had probable cause on these facts and that allowed them to go all though the car, including the trunk.

MARSHALL: I would *Krivda*.

BLACKMUN: I would not *Krivda*, and I agree with Byron to reverse.

POWELL: I would *Krivda*, otherwise I would agree on the merits.

REHNQUIST: This case meets our *Delaware v. Prouse* standard, and I would take the state court's opinion within its four corners and say that there is no adequate and independent state ground.[59] On the merits, I would decide this case on the *Terry* issue and say that *Terry* extends to protective searches of the inside of a car.

STEVENS: Arguably, *Prouse* held that the state court was following federal cases in interpreting the state constitution. The old view was that in a balanced case, the presumption was against federal jurisdiction when a state relied on both constitutions.

---

58. *California v. Krivda*, 409 U.S. 33 (1972). In a drug possession case, a California superior court judge suppressed evidence that police had obtained by searching the defendants' trash cans without a search warrant. The judge then dismissed the case, and the California State Supreme Court affirmed. The U.S. Supreme Court unanimously vacated and remanded the case when after briefing and argument the Justices were unable to determine whether the state supreme court had based its holding on the federal or state constitution, or both.

To *Krivda* a case means that when there is a possible adequate and independent state ground for a state court decision and the precise ground of the state court's ruling is unclear, the Court should vacate and remand the case to give the state courts an opportunity to clarify whether its decision rested on adequate and independent state grounds. This would mean that, in most cases, the state court decision would not be subject to further U.S. Supreme Court review.

59. *Delaware v. Prouse*, 440 U.S. 648 (1979). Police in New Castle County randomly stopped cars to check for drivers' licenses and vehicle registration cards. After stopping William J. Prouse for no reason other than to check his licence and registration, an officer smelled marijuana smoke and saw marijuana in plain view on the floorboard. The Court held 8–1 that random and arbitrary seizures of a motorists without specific, articulable reasons for believing that a violation of the law has occurred was unreasonable and violated the Fourth Amendment. The majority added, however, that states were free to develop other methods of conducting spot checks that were less intrusive or did not involve an unconstrained exercise of police discretion, such as briefly stopping and questioning *all* drivers at roadblocks.

O'CONNOR: State constitutions are trying to shift the blame for certain decisions to this Court. I would not *Krivda* here, but would reach the merits and reverse. This is a logical extension of *Terry*.

Result: On a 6–3 vote, the Court extended Terry v. Ohio *to permit police under certain circumstances to search passenger compartments as part of a protective search. In this instance, Sandra Day O'Connor wrote, the discovery of a knife in plain view justified a broad protective search of the automobile. The case was remanded to the state courts to determine whether the drugs found in the car trunk would be admissible in light of the Court's decision.*[60]

Plain View

United States v. Jacobsen, 466 U.S. 109 (1984)
(Brennan)

When two Federal Express employees examined the contents of a damaged package in their care, they found white residue and a clear plastic bag containing white powder stuffed inside a tube. They notified the DEA and then placed the bag back inside the tube. When the DEA agent arrived, he removed the bag from the tube and reopened it. After a field test indicated that the powder was cocaine, DEA agents obtained a search warrant and went to the address listed on the package, the home of Bradley and Donna Jacobsen. There agents found additional incriminating evidence and arrested the Jacobsens. The federal trial judge rejected a defense motion to suppress the evidence, and both defendants were convicted. The court of appeals reversed, holding that the warrantless search and testing of the package's contents were illegal. This meant that the search warrant was invalid and all of the evidence against the Jacobsens had to be excluded.

BURGER: Is there a violation by field testing? The respondent conceded that the bag could have been seized and a warrant obtained. Once it was seeable, I can't see any invasion of privacy. *Walter* is distinguishable, because there the writing on the outside of the package disclosed what was inside.[61]

---

60. On remand, the state court of appeals ruled that the marijuana found in the trunk was admissible, but the Michigan Supreme Court again reversed on the ground that under the federal constitution, the drugs found in the trunk were the fruits of an improper inventory search. The search was improper because the police department had no established procedures for inventory searches. The state high court vacated Long's sentence and excluded the marijuana found in the trunk from being introduced as evidence in any new trial. *Michigan v. Long*, 359 N.W.2d 194 (1984).

61. *Walter v. United States*, 447 U.S. 649 (1980). Twelve boxes shipped interstate by a private carrier were mistakenly delivered to "L'Eggs Products, Inc.," rather than to "Leggs, Inc.," the intended recipient. L'Eggs employees opened the boxes and found individually boxed 8mm movies with descriptions and drawings indicating that the films contained graphic homosexual sex. The employees called the FBI, which sent agents over to open the boxes and watch the films without obtaining a search warrant or seeking consent. Subsequently, William Walter and others were arrested and charged with interstate shipment of obscene materials. The Supreme Court reversed, but the Justices were deeply divided on the grounds. None of the three opinions written by members of the majority gathered more than two votes, although five Justices agreed that the FBI agents had violated the Fourth Amendment by viewing the films without first obtaining a warrant or seeking the consent of either the sender or rightful recipient of the films. Stevens wrote the lead opinion, joined by Stewart. Blackmun, Burger, Powell, and Rehnquist dissented.

WHITE: The magistrate found that the bags were visible when the agents arrived. The district court did not agree, but the court of appeals did. If that is the case, then there was probable cause to believe that it was drugs, and I don't see why they would need a warrant in those circumstances. It runs protection into the ground to say that they can't test on the spot.

MARSHALL: I can't believe that someone can put stuff in a glassine bag and then say that no one can look at it.

BLACKMUN: I agree with the Chief Justice.

POWELL: I agree with Thurgood that a clear plastic bag is not a container that can't be opened.

REHNQUIST: The commonsense position is that you can open what you can see and where you have probable cause to believe that it is contraband. I could even say that it is no search in these circumstances.

STEVENS: *Walter* is distinguishable—there is no privacy interest in powder as there is in pictures. Treating powder as visible makes it easy, but even if it was not visible the privacy concerns of packages is not same as for houses. Getting into the bag was an intrusion into a property interest, but it was supported by probable cause.

O'CONNOR: There was probable cause to seize the bags. There was a search to do field testing, but there was no privacy interest that was unreasonably infringed.

Result: By a 7–2 vote, the Court ruled that the search, seizure, and field testing were all reasonable. The independent actions by private citizens at Federal Express by definition did not violate the Fourth Amendment (which applies only to government searches), and the DEA field agent did nothing more than reopen the same package. At that point, the drugs were in plain view and could reasonably be tested to see whether the material was contraband. The test results, in turn, served as probable cause to justify a warrant to search the Jacobsens' home. John Paul Stevens wrote the majority opinion, while Thurgood Marshall changed his mind after the conference and joined Brennan in dissent.

Border Searches and Roadblocks

Almeida-Sanchez v. United States, 413 U.S. 266 (1973)
(Douglas)

As part of Congress's efforts to control illegal immigration, the Immigration and Nationality Act allowed warrantless searches of vehicles traveling within a "reasonable distance" of the border, which the attorney general defined as within one hundred air miles of the frontier. The INS employed roving patrols within this zone to conduct warrantless searches for illegal aliens and other contraband. This case involved a warrantless search executed twenty-five air miles north of the Mexican border. A roving INS patrol stopped and searched a car belonging to Condrado Almeida-Sanchez, a Mexican national with a valid permit to work in the United States. Inside the car, agents found 161 pounds of marijuana. The government conceded that there was no probable cause to stop or search the car. Almeida-Sanchez was convicted of knowingly transporting marijuana, and the court of appeals affirmed.

Conference of March 23, 1973

BURGER: The physical facts are decisive. The border area is largely unpopulated. Eighty percent plus of all narcotics come across the border, and some 400,000 aliens come across illegally every year. The United States is not powerless. An automobile search is easier than one of the person. This was a random stop. They can do this at the border, and they can they do it one hundred miles away, or fifty miles in this case. This is a hard case. I pass.

DOUGLAS: I reverse. Nothing in our Constitution permits a random search.

BRENNAN: This is twenty air miles from the border. The regulation is at issue here, and the zone is one hundred miles. The cert questions the validity of the regulation on its face. I can't sustain it on its face. I reverse.

STEWART: I reverse. This was a search without probable cause. I would uphold any search at or near the border, but not this one. The regulation cannot be justified under the Fourth Amendment. I reverse. Section (b) of the regulation is the only one that is deficient. The regulation is facially invalid.

WHITE: I affirm. This search is O.K., because while someone under different circumstances might have valid objections to the search, this person does not. Speech was not involved. This search was conducted without probable cause, but it was reasonable.

MARSHALL: This was an unreasonable search. They can stop anyone's car.

BLACKMUN: It is a matter of balancing under the standard of reasonableness. This regulation is O.K. This act is O.K. The act and regulation are both reasonable. I affirm.

STEWART: There is no authority under this act to search without a regulation.

POWELL: There were 393,000 illegal entries in 1972. There are only twenty-four legal checkpoints. Aliens merely walk across. The United States must have flexibility to control this problem. It is a balancing case. I would affirm on the facts in this case.

REHNQUIST: I affirm.

BURGER: I could strike down the regulation as excessive and sustain the search under the act. I pass.

Result: The Court held 5–4 that the Fourth Amendment prohibited the use of roving patrols to conduct warrantless searches, except at international borders. Potter Stewart, in his majority opinion, took pains to point out that this was not a border search and the special rules that governed those searches were not at issue. Powell changed his mind—apparently persuaded by a memorandum written by one of his clerks—and concurred in the judgment of the Court.

United States v. Ortiz, 422 U.S. 891 (1975)
(Brennan)

The Border Patrol operated a permanent traffic checkpoint on the freeway at San Onofre, California, near San Clemente and sixty-two air miles from the Mexican border. All cars were stopped briefly, and some drivers were either questioned in line or asked to pull off the road for a more extensive examination. Luis Ortiz was stopped and his car searched. Agents found three illegal aliens hiding in the trunk. Prior to the search, the agents had no reason to believe that illegal aliens were hiding in the car. Ortiz was convicted in federal court of knowingly transporting illegal aliens, but the court of appeals reversed in an unpublished decision on the ground that the Border Patrol needed probable cause or consent to search cars at immigration checkpoints.

BURGER: Lewis's idea sounds like a general warrant, or else that you can't set up any kind of roadblock without judicial authorization. A lot of *Boyd v. United States* is a lot of unmitigated nonsense.[62] We are getting to the point of becoming a wholly unregulable society, and it's the Court's fault.

---

62. *Boyd v. United States,* 116 U.S. 616 (1886). This was the first major American case dealing with government seizure of an individual's personal papers and effects and compelled testimony. The Boyd family contracted with the federal government to import glass for government buildings in Philadelphia. In exchange for a price discount, the government agreed to waive import duties on a limited amount of glass imported for the project. Later, the government suspected that the Boyds had imported far more duty-free glass than the contract permitted and filed charges. The trial judge ordered the Boyds to produce an invoice showing how much glass they had imported. Under protest, they complied with the order and were convicted.

The Supreme Court reversed and ordered a new trial on the grounds that the judge's subpoena had violated the Boyds' Fourth and Fifth Amendment rights. Justice Joseph Bradley referred to Lord Camden's decision in *Entick v. Carrington* as "the true doctrine on the subject of searches and seizures," setting forth "the true criteria of the reasonable and unreasonable character of such searches"—to protect the sanctity of home, person, and private property.

The principles laid down in this opinion . . . apply to all invasions, on the part of the Government and its employees, of the sanctity of a man's home and the privacies of life. It is not the breaking of his doors and the rummaging of his drawers that constitutes the essence of the offence; but it is the invasion of his indefeasible right of personal security, personal liberty and private property. . . . Any forcible and compulsory extortion of a man's own testimony or of his private papers to be used as evidence to convict him of crime or to forfeit his goods is within the condemnation of that judgment. In this regard the Fourth and Fifth Amendments almost run into each other. . . .

For the "unreasonable searches and seizures" condemned in the Fourth Amendment are almost always made for the purpose of compelling a man to give evidence against himself, which in criminal cases is condemned in the Fifth Amendment; and compelling a man "in a criminal case to be a witness against himself," which is condemned in the Fifth Amendment, throws light on the question as to what is an "unreasonable search and seizure. . . ." And we have been unable to perceive that the seizure of a man's private books and papers to be used in evidence against him is substantially different from compelling him to be a witness against himself. . . .

Any compulsory discovery by extorting the party's oath . . . is contrary to the principles of a free government. It is abhorrent . . . to the instincts of an American. It may suit the purposes of despotic power; but it cannot abide the pure atmosphere of political liberty and personal freedom.

It is difficult to say which parts of the opinion Burger considered to be unmitigated nonsense.

STEWART: There should be no retroactivity here. This was a search at a fixed checkpoint near San Clemente. There is no claim that this is a functional equivalent of a border inspection point. I see no constitutional distinction between this and the activation of roving patrols in *Almeida-Sanchez*.[63] Factually it is, of course, less obtrusive, less scary, and so forth.

WHITE: I think that there is a sufficient distinction between roving patrols and a fixed checkpoint. At least they imply an official administrative decision as to the checkpoint's location, and that bears on reasonableness. On balance, therefore, I would strike in favor of the government, although I might accommodate myself to a warrant requirement.

BLACKMUN: I agree with Byron that a fixed checkpoint is different. I could also reverse on the non-retroactivity of *Bowen*.[64]

POWELL: I am where I was in *Almeida-Sanchez*. I see a difference between checkpoints and roving patrols, but I think that the judge ought to determine in advance the reasonableness of checkpoint locations. I am doubtful of the location of this one at San Clemente. There is also a question of how stops are determined. We ought to require at least a founded suspicion and not allow federal officers to exercise a wholly unfettered discretion just because someone looks like a Mexican. Rule 41 has a too limited ten-day limit— we ought to allow renewal.[65] There must be a return on the warrant. I would allow a search as well as a stop.

REHNQUIST: I can't agree with Lewis. Only Congress should legislate such a procedure.

Result: The Court decided unanimously that the Fourth Amendment prohibited the Border Patrol from searching private vehicles at fixed traffic checkpoints away from the border, absent consent or probable cause. These checkpoints, Lewis Powell wrote, were the functional equivalents of the roving patrols in Almeida-Sanchez. *The search was impermissible in this case because, as the government admitted, there was neither probable cause nor consent to search. Rehnquist joined the majority opinion but also wrote a concurring opinion stating that the decision applied only to full searches and that fixed checkpoints*

---

63. *United States v. Almeida-Sanchez*, 413 U.S. 266 (1973).

64. *United States v. Bowen*, 422 U.S. 916 (1975). Border Patrol agents stopped John Lee Bowen at a fixed checkpoint thirty-six miles from the Mexican border. While searching Bowen's camper for illegal aliens, they found marijuana and other drugs. Bowen was arrested and convicted on drug charges. While his appeal was pending, the Supreme Court announced its decision in *Almeida-Sanchez v. United States*, barring the Border Patrol from using roving patrols to search vehicles away from the border. In light of that decision, Bowen's case was remanded. The Ninth Circuit reaffirmed his conviction on the ground that while *Almeida-Sanchez* applied both to roving patrols and fixed checkpoints, the decision was not retroactive. The Supreme Court affirmed Bowen's conviction on a 5–4 vote, on the ground that prior to *Almeida-Sanchez* Border Patrol agents had reasonably relied on appellate court decisions that such searches were permissible. The majority, however, reserved the question of whether *Almeida-Sanchez* applied to fixed traffic checkpoints and warned that the Ninth Circuit's ruling on the issue was not authoritative.

65. The Federal Rules of Criminal Procedure §41(c) provides a ten-day time limit between the issuance and execution of a warrant.

could still be used to stop traffic briefly to inquire about citizenship. Burger, White, and Blackmun concurred in the judgment only. The San Onofre checkpoint remains in operation today.[66]

United States v. Montoya de Hernandez, 473 U.S. 531 (1985)
(Brennan)

American customs agents detained Rosa Montoya as she deplaned from a flight originating in Bogota, Colombia. They suspected that she was a "balloon swallower"—someone who smuggled drugs into the country by ingesting small balloons full of heroin or cocaine. The agents gave Montoya three choices: return to Colombia on the next flight, submit to an x-ray, or remain in detention until she had a supervised bowel movement. When Montoya chose to return home, the agents claimed that they could not place her on an outbound flight. After holding her incommunicado for sixteen hours, the agents obtained a court order to do a rectal exam. Their search produced ninety-nine balloons filled with cocaine. The court of appeals overturned Montoya's conviction because at the time that she was first detained there had been no clear indication that she was smuggling drugs.

BURGER: Being a border case, that is enough to support all that was done here. This is not like a street arrest. Even citizens can be subjected to things at the border that are not permissible at other places.

WHITE: I agree with the Chief Justice.

MARSHALL: I agree with Brennan to affirm, but on the ground that she was held too long without getting a warrant.

BLACKMUN: This was a drug smuggler—enough said! Such desperate measures are justified by the drug traffic.

POWELL: I agree with the Chief Justice and Harry.

REHNQUIST: I agree with Harry.

STEVENS: The claimed distinction between criminal investigations and other border incidents is not acceptable. There are too many smuggling situations that ought not let them go back—the border is just different. Besides, one x-ray can't possibly be intrusive of privacy.

O'CONNOR: Whether you are talking about the length or the manner of detention, unreasonableness is the issue. But she had enough opportunities to avoid it.

Result: The Court ruled 6–1–2 that Montoya's sixteen-hour detention was acceptable. William Rehnquist, writing for the majority, explained that there were only two standards for searches under the Fourth Amendment: reasonable suspicion and probable cause. For border searches, reasonable suspicion was the proper standard. Montoya's detention was justified because customs agents, on all

---

66. Subsequent cases have allowed Border Patrol personnel who operate fixed checkpoints to question drivers briefly about citizenship and residency. After initial questioning, agents may direct selected drivers to a secondary inspection area for further questioning. While consent or probable cause are still required for a full search, some less intrusive searches have been employed without probable cause, such as the use of drug-sniffing dogs. See, for example, *United States v. Martinez-Fuerte*, 428 U.S. 543 (1976).

available facts, reasonably suspected that she was smuggling contraband. John Paul Stevens concurred in the judgment, while Brennan and Marshall dissented.

Surveillance and Eavesdropping

Massiah v. United States, 377 U.S. 201 (1964)
(Douglas)

Winston Massiah was freed on bail after being indicted for possession of three pounds of cocaine and conspiracy to smuggle cocaine into the United States. Unknown to Massiah, one of his confederates, Jesse Colson, allowed federal agents to install a radio transmitter in his car. Massiah was coaxed into Colson's car, where he made incriminating statements that were used against him at trial. Massiah argued that police tactics amounted to an unreasonable search and seizure under the Fourth Amendment and deprived him of effective right of counsel under the Fifth and Sixth Amendments by questioning him through a confederate rather than through his attorney. Massiah was convicted and sentenced to nine years in prison. The Second Circuit Court of Appeals affirmed.

Conference of March 6, 1964

WARREN: This case involved the taking of statements from a defendant after indictment and after a defense lawyer was appointed. I would prefer to follow the minority opinion in *Spano*.[67] The federal government can continue the investigation after indictment, but after that date it can't set a trap for him, lead him into it, and get him to talk about matters relevant to the indictment. I would reverse.

BLACK: I reverse on the concurring opinion in *Spano*. If he had been taken to a courtroom before a judge and prior to trial talking to him and trapping him, we would reverse. This is as bad. The federal government impaired the usefulness of the counsel the accused had by using this device. He loses a large part of the value of having counsel. I would go on constitutional grounds.

DOUGLAS: I reverse. I agree with the Chief and with Hugo.

CLARK: I possibly will join a reversal, but the petitioner here was not in custody—he was out on bail. He was not physically forced to [illegible]. There is a lot to be said against

---

67. *Spano v. New York*, 360 U.S. 315 (1959). After Vincent Spano was indicted for murder, he was taken to a police station in the Bronx for questioning. Police ignored his repeated requests to speak to his lawyer and interrogated him for more than eight hours. One of the interrogating officers, who was a close friend of Spano's, under orders from his superiors, falsely told Spano that because of their friendship his job was on the line and his family—including three children and a pregnant wife—faced financial disaster. Spano confessed and was convicted. The Supreme Court unanimously reversed. Writing for the Court, Earl Warren ruled that given the facts of this case: (1) Spano's will was undermined by official coercion, fatigue, and false sympathy; (2) his confession was involuntary and violated due process; and (3) there must be a new trial, even if there was sufficient untainted evidence to justify conviction. Douglas, Black, Brennan, and Stewart concurred but argued that denial of counsel to an indicted defendant was the more crucial constitutional violation and alone required reversal.

this practice, for here he was sort of trapped. This is a very close case. I would not over-rule *On Lee*.[68] I might reverse, or affirm with a "?"

HARLAN: I see no constitutional basis for objecting. I do not agree with the dissent in the court of appeals. I think that a man is more apt to spill his guts in talking with the U.S. attorney without knowing it, as happened here, than when he knows it. This is not a case where the government is trying to circumvent counsel. I would deal with this case under our supervisory power, not reaching the Constitution. I would say here that an investigation among accomplices is not barred, as there is no circumvention of counsel. I affirm. I would not overrule *On Lee*. As a practical matter, a defendant's lawyer does not know what is going on between conspiratorial group after indictment. As a U.S. prosecutor in New York, I put wiretaps on defendants and accomplices after indictment, but not on lawyers' wires.

BRENNAN: I reverse. I would either reverse *On Lee* or follow the concurring opinion in *Spano*.

STEWART: The officers had a duty to continue this investigation after indictment, but I would not allow this man's recorded words to be used against him at his trial. I would follow the rationale in *Spano* reverse.

WHITE: I affirm doubtfully.

GOLDBERG: I reverse. I think that it is an evasion of the right of counsel and of the right to be tried before a jury in the courthouse.

Result: The Court ruled 6–3 that police tactics deprived Massiah of his right to counsel under the Sixth Amendment. The Justices avoided the Fourth Amendment issue and did not overrule On Lee. *White, Clark, and Harlan dissented.*

United States v. U.S. District Court, 407 U.S. 297 (1972)
(Douglas)

After a CIA office was bombed in Ann Arbor, Michigan, three suspects were arrested and charged with conspiring to destroy government property. The White House issued an executive order authorizing warrantless surveillance to gather additional evidence against the alleged conspirators. President Nixon claimed that §2511(3) of the Omnibus Crime Control and Safe Streets Act of 1968 recognized the president's inherent authority to order warrantless phone taps and to conduct other forms of surveil-

---

68. *On Lee v. United States*, 343 U.S. 747 (1952). While On Lee was out on bail awaiting trial in a narcotics case, police wired one of his confederates with a concealed radio transmitter. The accomplice secured damaging admissions from Lee, which were broadcast to a nearby government agent. The Court ruled 5–4 that the use of a concealed radio transmitter was not a trespass, was not a search or seizure for Fourth Amendment purposes, and was not inconsistent with notions of "fair play" in federal law enforcement. *Katz v. United States*, 389 U.S. 347 (1967) implicitly overruled *On Lee* in part, ruling that the use of a concealed listening device was a trespass after all. Otherwise, however, *On Lee* has been much criticized and limited in scope, but has never been formally overruled.

lance in the interest of national security without prior judicial notification or approval.[69] *The district court held that the warrantless surveillance conducted here violated the Fourth Amendment, and the court of appeals affirmed.*

In conference, Douglas got in a dig at Burger's alleged habit of passing in order to control opinion assignments, and several Justices commented on the poor lawyering at oral argument.

BURGER: I am not ready to vote. The arguments were not good. There is some inherent power in the executive branch. I do not, however, go as far as the Justice Department. Congress in 1968 gave discretion to its use. The Department of Justice must meet those standards, and I do not think that it did. I lean toward saying that the statute has preempted the powers of the executive. The record does not show that they met it. I pass. [DOUGLAS: He usually passes, hoping to be in the majority and able to assign.]

DOUGLAS: I affirm on the constitutional ground. We need a constitutional amendment to do this.

BRENNAN: I affirm and agree with Douglas.

STEWART: The case was not tried on the basis of the congressional act. There was no compliance with the act. I would reach the constitutional question. If *Weeks* were overruled, this case would go away.[70] I could understand if electronic surveillance was held not to be a search, as Black believed. Nor was this case tendered on the basis that another exception to probable cause should be made. Congress has the power to protect the public in investigations and otherwise. The Foreign Relations Committee could tap the president's phone, if this can be done. I have never seen a worse job of lawyering than this case presents. I affirm.

WHITE: I affirm the judgment. I do not agree with the opinion below. It rests on the act of Congress, not on the Constitution. The department's approach to domestic subversion is much too broad. If they had tagged this as a foreign influence case, it would be different. The *Steel Seizure* case shows that congressional action clips the president's power. We would make a terrible mistake in saying that the president cannot have no-probable-cause surveillance in foreign subversion cases.[71] Neither the president nor Congress will pay any attention to what this Court decides. I will probably go on the statute.

MARSHALL: I am not going to rely on the act—it's not constitutional. If King George can't come into my house, neither can the president. I affirm.

BLACKMUN: Kinoy was the worst lawyer I have ever heard.[72] I definitely affirm. I agree with Byron.

---

69. Section 2511(3) stated that nothing in the act limited the president's constitutional power to guard against any clear and present danger to the government's structure or existence.

70. *Weeks v. United States,* 232 U.S. 383 (1914).

71. *Youngstown Co. v. Sawyer,* 343 U.S. 579 (1952).

72. In his autobiography, Rutgers law professor Arthur Kinoy claimed that he made a brilliant oral argument, holding the entire Court spellbound and single-handedly saving the country from a fascist conspiracy "wrapped in an American flag." Kinoy, *Rights on Trial: The Odyssey of a People's Lawyer,* 26–28, 31–32.

POWELL: The act does not fit this case. Every attorney general recognized that electronic surveillance is needed to meet crime-fighting needs. This act is not very helpful to resolve the problems in this area. We can bypass the foreign espionage problem, nor do we have an ordinary crime. Here we have a third category of domestic subversion. The federal government needs the power to make surveillance in that area. There are no standards. I hope that the Court will affirm and provide standards in a *Katz* type of opinion.[73] It seems feasible to say that a court order is required, and that the Court of Appeals in the District of Columbia be designated as the proper tribunal.

WHITE: The affidavits filed here do not satisfy §2511(3) of the act.

BURGER: I affirm on the act.

Result: Lewis Powell, writing for a 6–2–0 majority, found that §2511(3) amounted to nothing more than a congressional disclaimer of any intent to define the president's powers in national security cases.[74] *The act neither granted nor recognized executive authority to conduct unsupervised, warrantless surveillance.*

The warrant process, Powell wrote, was central to the Fourth Amendment's requirement of reasonableness, and the executive branch was required to obtain prior judicial approval for such surveillance. The Court refused to recognize yet another "exigency" exception to the warrant requirement based on national security. Powell dismissed the government's arguments that judges lacked the experience to make judgments involving national security and could not be trusted to protect the nation's confidences in sensitive cases. He implied, however, that Congress could establish a less stringent definition of probable cause to make it easier to obtain warrants in national security cases, given the nature and seriousness of the crimes and the difficulty of identifying "exact targets" in internal security investigations. Burger and White concurred in the judgment but did not join Powell's opinion. There were no dissents. Rehnquist did not participate.[75]

California v. Ciraolo, 476 U.S. 207 (1986)
(Brennan)

An anonymous tip led police to Dante Ciraolo's house to search for marijuana. When police found that they could not peek over the tall fences surrounding Ciraolo's property, they flew a private plane over the house at approximately one thousand feet. On the basis of naked-eye observations and photographic evidence, police obtained a search warrant, entered Ciraolo's property, and seized a large number of marijuana plants growing in the backyard. After the state trial judge admitted the evidence over the defendant's objection, Ciraolo pleaded guilty to possession of marijuana. On appeal,

---

73. *Katz v. United States,* 389 U.S. 347 (1967).

74. There was some controversy over the assignment of the opinion in this case. After conference, the Chief Justice assigned the case to Byron White. Douglas, however, argued that he was the senior justice among the majority of five Justices who voted for reversal on constitutional grounds (Burger, White, and Blackmun favored reversal on statutory grounds) and assigned the case to Powell. After an exchange of memoranda, the case went to Powell. Urofsky, *The Douglas Letters,* 140, 144.

75. Rehnquist recused himself because he had helped to draft the law in question as a member of President Nixon's Justice Department.

Ciraolo claimed that the aerial surveillance violated the Fourth Amendment. The state court of appeal reversed his conviction, and the California Supreme Court declined to review the case.

BURGER: Aerial observation by naked eye from an airplane is the issue here. Did the respondent have a reasonable expectation of privacy that society is prepared to accept? In 1787 and 1791, there were no airplanes and the Framers didn't anticipate them. I could assume a violation if these were deliberate photos of sunbathing. But flying is so routine that people can't say that they have an expectation of privacy.

BRENNAN:[76] Because I believe that the aerial surveillance of the respondent's backyard constituted a warrantless "search" of his property, I would affirm. In *Oliver*, we recognized that an individual may legitimately demand privacy for activities conducted out of doors in the area immediately surrounding the home.[77] In this case, the respondent was entitled to a reasonable expectation of privacy. This expectation was reinforced by the extensive measures he undertook to maintain his privacy. Respondent surrounded his property with a fence, and apart from covering it with an opaque dome, there was nothing more he could do to protect his privacy. The police circumvented the respondent's legitimate expectation of privacy by observing his property from the air. To allow the police to engage in this type of surveillance would effectively eliminate any privacy interests in the area surrounding the home. I cannot understand how the aerial surveillance that took place here can be considered anything but a search of the respondent's property.

The police would certainly have conducted a "search" of the respondent's property if they had set a ladder up next to his fence and looked over into his backyard. To my mind, the situation here is no different. In both cases, the surveillance is meant to circumvent the individual's reasonable expectation of privacy.

I do not believe that the government should never be allowed to engage in aerial surveillance of curtilage areas. I would merely hold that the use of aerial surveillance to observe what is otherwise hidden from view constitutes a "search" implicating Fourth Amendment concerns. This would subject the government's use of aerial surveillance to judicial scrutiny, and would protect both the individual's strong privacy interests and the government's interest in effective law enforcement.

WHITE: I agree with the Chief Justice.

MARSHALL: The respondent knew that he would be surveilled and he built fences to prevent this. I agree with the Chief Justice.

---

76. Adapted from Brennan's talking papers, Brennan Papers, OT 1985, box 708.

77. *Oliver v. United States*, 466 U.S. 170 (1984). The main question was whether police had the right under the "open fields" doctrine to conduct warrantless searches of remote farm property to search for marijuana. The district court held that Ray Oliver had a reasonable expectation that his gated, posted field would remain private and that it was not an "open field" inviting casual intrusion. The Supreme Court disagreed, ruling that the "special" Fourth Amendment protections for "persons, houses, papers, and effects" did not extend to open fields, except in areas immediately surrounding homes. (The field in question was more than a mile from Oliver's home.) The Court ruled that warrantless state intrusions into open fields were not searches under the Fourth Amendment, even though they might be considered trespasses under common law.

BLACKMUN: I would apply traditional warrant requirements here. I agree with Bill Brennan, since it involves the home. The plane was a surrogate for an entry. I would reserve the question of routine air patrols.

POWELL: If we start down the road of cutting back on the Fourth Amendment, we won't know where to stop. Here we admittedly have a curtilage where you have a reasonable expectation of privacy. If you can't get up on ladder to see, why permit this here? I would affirm—such a deliberate intrusion is not reasonable.

REHNQUIST: This is a tough case, but I would reverse on these facts.

STEVENS: I would reverse in this case. The mere fact that it is an airplane, which was not around in 1789, is not inconsistent with the basic principles of the Fourth Amendment. Given modern transportation, we don't have a reasonable expectation of privacy against people looking down—it is no different just because police do it to detect crime.

O'CONNOR: I agree with the Chief Justice.

Result: The Supreme Court reinstated Ciraolo's conviction on a 5–4 vote. Warren Burger, writing for the majority, held that no search had taken place under the "reasonable expectation of privacy" standard announced in Katz.[78] *Warrantless, naked-eye observations of private property made from aircraft operating in public airspace were permissible, even when the overflight was specifically intended to search for contraband on enclosed private property. The majority ignored the police department's use of a 35mm camera.*

Thurgood Marshall changed his mind after the conference and joined Brennan, Blackmun, and Powell in dissent. The dissenters argued that Ciraolo had an overriding privacy interest in outdoor activities carried on within his enclosed curtilage and that his privacy rights could not be defeated by police misuse of public airspace.

DUE PROCESS AND THE EXCLUSIONARY RULE

Wolf v. Colorado, 338 U.S. 25 (1949)
(Douglas)

In a criminal case for conspiracy to perform abortions, state police arrested a Colorado physician and, without obtaining a warrant, confiscated his office, medical equipment, and records. By interviewing patients named in Wolf's appointment book, state officials gathered enough evidence to convict him. Wolf argued that the seizures violated the Fourth Amendment and that the evidence should have been suppressed under the exclusionary rule. The only question for the Court was whether the exclusionary rule, announced in Weeks v. United States, *was applicable to the states through the Fourteenth Amendment or whether states were free to adopt or reject the rule at their discretion.[79]*

78. *Katz v. United States,* 389 U.S. 347 (1967).
79. *Weeks v. United States,* 232 U.S. 383 (1914).

Conference of October 23, 1948

VINSON: I affirm.

BLACK: On the constitutional scope of the Fourth Amendment, as construed by the Court, I would reverse. If it has the exclusionary evidence penalty then it should apply in state courts, whatever view of due process is taken. The Fourth Amendment in its full scope is the law of each state.

REED: I hope that we do not have to go that far. I would prefer to say that it was a valid arrest and that the search was a valid one. I would go no farther than *Harris*.[80]

FRANKFURTER: We need a more accurate analysis of the relationship of the Fourteenth Amendment and the first eight Amendments. This should be affirmed. I do not change my views regarding the lawless action of police officials. Since the *Weeks* case, all states but one have passed on this question. Most of the states have followed *Weeks*. On the other hand, England does not bar the illegally seized evidence, nor does Scotland, Canada, or New Zealand.

MURPHY: I reverse.

JACKSON: I affirm.

RUTLEDGE: I reverse, partly on Frankfurter's argument.

BURTON: I affirm and also agree with Frankfurter.

Result: Writing for a 6–3 majority, Felix Frankfurter extended the "core" of the Fourth Amendment to protect individuals from states as well as the federal government. States were not required, however, to adopt the exclusionary rule as long as police tactics were not so offensive that they shocked the conscience. Frankfurter argued that the exclusionary rule was not necessary to enforce the Fourth Amendment, because victims could file private lawsuits against offending police officers and because police would naturally maintain "internal discipline" to minimize any abuses.

Hugo Black concurred in the judgment, arguing that Frankfurter had reached the right result for the wrong reasons. Black thought that the Fourth Amendment was fully applicable to the states (not just in its "core functions") but agreed with Frankfurter that illegally seized evidence need not be excluded from state trials. Black argued explicitly what Frankfurter was content to imply—that the exclusionary rule was a judicially created rule of evidence rather than a constitutional requirement and that Congress and state legislatures were free to modify or even abandon the rule if they wished.[81]

---

80. *Harris v. United States*, 331 U.S. 145 (1947).

81. John Frank said that Hugo Black's position in *Wolf* was perhaps "the most restrictive interpretation of the Fourth Amendment by any Justice in the Court's history." Black certainly read the Fourth Amendment more narrowly than he read the rest of the Bill of Rights. Roger Newman traced this anomaly to the deep respect that Black developed for police officers while he served as a Birmingham prosecutor. Newman, *Hugo Black*, 370–72. Almost a decade later, while deliberating on *Mapp v. Ohio*, Black reluctantly abandoned his view that the exclusionary rule was merely a rule of convenience and grudgingly accepted that it was constitutionally required.

The three dissenters, William O. Douglas, Frank Murphy, and Wiley Rutledge, mocked Frankfurter's claim that there were effective alternative remedies for Fourth Amendment violations. They argued that suing police departments for damages and relying on police self-discipline were hopelessly unrealistic solutions. The exclusionary rule, they maintained, was constitutionally required because it was the only effective remedy for unconstitutional searches and seizures.

Rochin v. California, 342 U.S. 165 (1952)
(Douglas)

Police received information that Antonio Rochin was selling drugs out of his home. Without a warrant, three officers raided Rochin's house and forced their way into his bedroom, catching him and his common-law wife in bed. When police asked Rochin to explain the presence of two small capsules on his bedstand, Rochin grabbed the pills and swallowed them. Police choked Rochin and stuck their fingers down his throat in an attempt to extract the capsules. When that failed, they took him to a hospital where he was force-fed an emetic solution to pump his stomach until he vomited the capsules. Tests showed that the pills contained morphine, and Rochin was convicted of narcotics possession. The California Court of Appeal affirmed but sharply criticized the arresting officers for (1) unlawfully breaking into Rochin's home; (2) illegally assaulting Rochin twice, first in his bedroom and again at the hospital; and (3) engaging in what one concurring justice called a "shocking series" of constitutional violations. Like most states at the time, California did not recognize the exclusionary rule. Victims of police misbehavior were told to file civil lawsuits, even though everyone knew that such suits had little hope of success.

Conference of October 20, 1951

VINSON: The petitioner relies here on California cases. The police used coercion to get the admission. On the confession end of it, the reason for the rule is that a man under pain will tell a lie and the evidence is apt to be untrustworthy. That is not in issue here. The capsules were seen and known. It is a shocking case, but the confession rule does not control.

BLACK: I reverse.

REED: This case troubles me. The case makes me puke.[82] I affirm. It is only a search of the person. The police can use force to search a man's pockets and they can use force here.

FRANKFURTER: The case makes me puke. The confession rule does not rest on a test of trustworthiness alone, but on decency. This violates due process.

JACKSON: I reverse. This problem gives me difficulties. Involved are rights to take blood samples, lie detectors, physical examinations, and so forth.

BURTON: These are borderline questions. It boils down to the difference between the reasonable and unreasonable use of force; the former is good, the latter is bad. This is in the latter category.

CLARK: I reverse.

---

82. Oliver Wendell Holmes reportedly once said that his test for whether a law was constitutional was whether a case "made him want to puke." Urofsky, *Felix Frankfurter*, 206.

Result: Felix Frankfurter, writing for the majority, reversed Rochin's conviction as a violation of the Fourteenth Amendment's due process clause. Police behavior, he said, violated due process whenever it "shocked the conscience" of the Court or went against the "decencies of civilized conduct."

Hugo Black and William O. Douglas concurred in the judgment but were harshly critical of Frankfurter's analysis. They thought it foolish to ground a constitutional guarantee on whether an event shocked the consciences of five Supreme Court Justices and proposed what they thought was a more objective and enduring constitutional standard: Rochin's Fourth Amendment rights against unreasonable searches and seizures and his Fifth Amendment protection against self-incrimination.[83]

This case clearly illustrates the fundamental ideological differences between Frankfurter's and Black's competing theories of constitutional interpretation. Black believed that the primary purpose of the Fourteenth Amendment's due process clause was to incorporate the first eight amendments of the Bill of Rights and apply them to the states. Frankfurter thought that this view was historical non-sense and believed that the Fourteenth Amendment's due process clause called for a subjective but dispassionate judicial determination of what Frankfurter called the "English sporting sense of fair play."[84] For his part, Black thought that Frankfurter's approach threatened to undermine all of the specific protections in the Bill of Rights, reducing the rights of the accused to the subjective and capricious whims of unelected judges.

Irvine v. California, 347 U.S. 128 (1954)
(Douglas)

Police suspected that Patrick Irvine was involved in bookmaking and other gambling activities but lacked the evidence necessary to obtain a warrant. Instead, an officer secretly made a key to Irvine's door and used it on several occasions to enter his home surreptitiously and plant a microphone—at first in a hall-way and later in Irvine's bedroom. Irvine made incriminating statements that were used to convict him of bookmaking.

Conference of December 5, 1953

WARREN: I find no merit in the federal tax point, nor in the point of admission of the evidence over his objection.[85] The third point is serious—that the search was illegal under state law. Does that conduct rise to the infamy of *Rochin*?[86] I am not friendly to that kind of police action. But does the state encourage it, or is this merely an occasional instance?

---

83. In a later interview, Warren criticized Frankfurter's approach in *Rochin* as building a constitutional right on shifting sand. When the reporter asked him to explain, Warren groused, "What's so bad about a stomach pump? I've had my stomach pumped lots of times." Schwartz and Lesher, *Inside the Warren Court*, 130.

84. Mendelson, *Justices Black and Frankfurter*, 65.

85. Prosecutors used Irvine's federal wagering tax stamp, tax returns, and other IRS documents as evidence of gambling. Irvine claimed that these federal tax documents were private and confidential documents that had been illegally seized. He also claimed that federal requirements to pay wagering taxes and keep wagering records amounted to a federal license to operate a gambling business.

86. *Rochin v. California*, 342 U.S. 165 (1952).

The latter is true here. California has strong laws on wiretapping, and tries to discourage this kind of conduct. I would not alter *Wolf* or the *Texas* case.[87] I would affirm.

BLACK: I pass.

REED: I agree with the Chief.

FRANKFURTER: I take the other view, though adhering to *Wolf.* I think that *Rochin* governs. Each case must stand on its own. The conduct here was sanctioned by the state, although I feel strongly in sympathy with the Chief Justice.

DOUGLAS: I reverse.

JACKSON: If you take each case by itself, you cannot give the rule necessary for law enforcement. I do not like the practice, but will go along.

BURTON: I reverse. This is too shocking a practice.

CLARK: *Wolf* governs. We should stick by it as long as it is on the books. *Rochin* whittled *Wolf.* I do not like *Wolf,* but I will stand by it. This is a mere rule of evidence.

MINTON: I would adhere to *Wolf.* There is lots of difference between forcing a key into a lock and forcing a pump into a stomach. I affirm.

Result: The Court upheld Irvine's conviction and allowed California to use the illegally gathered evidence in trial. Robert Jackson, writing for a plurality of four Justices, said that police tactics did not violate Irvine's rights and did not break any federal laws. Following Wolf *and* Rochin, *Jackson said that the federal Constitution did not require states to exclude illegally obtained evidence unless it had been obtained in a way that shocked the conscience or violated universal norms of fundamental fairness. The majority found that police behavior was obnoxious and illegal, but it did not involve coercion, violence, brutality, or other physical assault. Evidence gathered "merely" by illegally trespassing and eavesdropping was admissible.*

Clark concurred, arguing that while he preferred to extend Weeks *and apply the federal exclusionary rule to the states,* Wolf *remained a valid precedent and he would reluctantly follow it for the time being. It was preferable, he thought, to the ad hoc approach to due process represented by* Rochin.

In dissent, Hugo Black argued that police had violated Irvine's Fifth Amendment right against compelled testimony. In a separate dissent, Douglas maintained that Irvine's Fourth and Fifth Amendment rights had been violated. Frankfurter and Burton also dissented, arguing that police behavior was shocking and violated the Rochin *due process test.*

---

87. *Wolf v. Colorado,* 338 U.S. 25 (1949); *Schwartz v. Texas,* 344 U.S. 199 (1952). *Schwartz* involved a warrantless wiretap on Thomas Schwartz, a pawnbroker suspected of directing a theft ring. Schwartz sought to exclude the contents of the wiretap from his trial. He cited the FCC Act, which explicitly provided that any evidence obtained from an illegal wiretap was inadmissible. In affirming his conviction, the Supreme Court narrowly read the act to require the exclusion of illegally obtained wiretap evidence in federal trials, but not in state criminal proceedings.

Breithaupt v. Abram, 352 U.S. 432 (1957)
(Douglas)

Paul H. Breithaupt smashed his pickup into another car on a New Mexico highway, killing three people and seriously injuring himself. While Breithaupt lay unconscious in a hospital, a state trooper claimed that he could smell alcohol on the injured man's breath and asked an attending physician to draw a blood sample. Using a hypodermic needle, the doctor extracted blood from Breithaupt's arm, which when tested indicated a blood alcohol level of .17 percent. The blood evidence was used against Breithaupt at trial over his objection, and he was convicted of involuntary manslaughter. The New Mexico Supreme Court affirmed.

Breithaupt sought a federal writ of habeas corpus, claiming that the state's extraction of blood without his consent violated his Fourth and Fifth Amendment rights against unreasonable searches and seizures and his privilege against self-incrimination. He urged the Supreme Court to incorporate these rights via the Fourteenth Amendment and apply them to state criminal trials. Breithaupt also argued that the state's actions violated his due process rights as established in Rochin v. California. *Morris Abram was the warden of the New Mexico State Penitentiary*

Conference of December 14, 1956

WARREN: I reverse. This is distinguishable from our identification cases. It might be distinguished from the drunkometer, but it is difficult to distinguish from *Rochin.*[88] The absence of a struggle is not material—if one protest is good, another is. Here, the petitioner was unconscious. There is no basic difference between a stomach pump and a blood test. If we sustain this, police will be doing it, not doctors. Promiscuous use of this device is very dangerous. The presence of a statute is not important.

BLACK: I reverse on my opinion in *Rochin.* If I had to apply the "shocking" test, it was still bad under *Rochin.* It is not as bad as pulling finger nails out, but it is in that category. It is the same as an extraction of a confession at the point of a gun. You can't force people to testify against themselves by a contract in advance or otherwise. If this is sustained, *Rochin* should be reversed.

REED: I affirm.

FRANKFURTER: [DOUGLAS: He talked for forty minutes trying to distinguish this case from *Rochin.*]

DOUGLAS: I reverse.

BURTON: I affirm. It is the public responsibility of each citizen to submit to a blood test.

CLARK: I affirm. This affects a use of state statutes. This was not forced self-incrimination. It is not different from fingerprinting, which is mandatory.

WARREN: It is the violating of his body that is bad. If they can break the skin, they can do anything.

---

88. *Rochin v. California,* 342 U.S. 165 (1952).

HARLAN: This is not *Rochin*. If the cops take the blood, it would be *Rochin*. Here, it was properly done by doctors. I affirm. If there was a struggle, it would be *Rochin*. If they put him to sleep it would be bad.

BRENNAN: I affirm. This must be circumscribed. It is not self-incrimination. [DOUGLAS: He talks at length about the drunkometer test and paternity cases in New Jersey.][89]

Result: In a 6–3 vote, the Court affirmed Breithaupt's conviction. Tom Clark, writing for the majority, distinguished Rochin *by arguing that there was nothing brutal, offensive, or shocking about taking blood with a hypodermic needle. Modern medical practices in most states made such procedures routine. Earl Warren, Hugo Black, and William O. Douglas dissented. The Chief Justice criticized the Court's reliance on the "shifting sands" of* Rochin, *while Douglas blasted the majority for sanctioning what he called a disturbing police assault on an unconscious man.*

Elkins v. United States, 364 U.S. 206 (1960)
(Douglas)

James Elkins and Raymond Clark were suspected of tapping and intercepting private telephone communications. State police searched Elkins's house and seized tape recordings, bugging devices, and other evidence. The Oregon Supreme Court ruled that the seizures were unlawful and suppressed the evidence, and the state charges were dropped for lack of additional evidence. Elkins and Clark were immediately charged with the same offense in federal court, and federal officials sought to use the same evidence that had been excluded from the state courts. Prosecutors claimed that this was permissible because there was no evidence of federal involvement in the illegal search and seizure. This practice, known as the silver-platter doctrine, was a widely accepted law enforcement tactic at the time. Elkins and Clark were convicted, and the Ninth Circuit Court of Appeals affirmed.

Conference of April 1, 1960

WARREN: Can the federal government use in its courts evidence that has been illegally obtained in state courts? I would abolish the "silver platter" rule. I would not reach the Constitution, but would rest on our own supervision over federal trials. I reverse. Otherwise people are whipsawed between state and federal prosecutions. *Elkins* shows an absolute clash between the two jurisdictions, with the state enjoining its own officers from testifying. There are twenty-one states that have the exclusionary rule.

BLACK: Where evidence is taken in a manner which, if taken by federal officers, would be unconstitutional, it should not be used in a federal prosecution. My opinion in *Feldman* reflects the same philosophy.[90] I reverse.

---

89. Brennan was born in New Jersey, practiced there as a corporate lawyer, and served from 1949 to 1956 as a judge on the state's superior and supreme courts.

90. *Feldman v. United States*, 322 U.S. 487 (1944). With Frankfurter writing for the majority, the Court ruled that the Fifth Amendment did not prohibit the federal use of compelled testimony given in a state proceeding. In his dissent, Black tweaked Frankfurter by using Frankfurter's own standard for evaluating due process cases (an approach that Black personally rejected), writing that the use of compelled testimony

FRANKFURTER: This problem is far-reaching. It is important that the truth come out in criminal prosecutions. This testimony was relevant. One could join any of these grounds for exclusion: (a) the Constitution; (b) the statute; (c) this Court's supervisory power; (d) comity between state and federal courts. This case does not involve (a). If it had been done by a federal official, it would be excluded. I would overrule *Harris* and *Rabinowitz in futuro*, but not to upset any convictions, for the lower courts are entitled to rely on them.[91] *Wolf* means that there was no constitutional violation here.[92] Option (b) is illustrated by *Benanti*, where the federal act was violated.[93] As to (d), if the state court had enjoined its officers from testifying, and if that order had preceded knowledge of federal trial, then the federal court should react. Not least, I would require the federal prosecutor to go to the state court and ask that the state injunction be lifted. The state judge issued the injunction because he interested himself improperly in the federal prosecution—he violated comity. As to (c), what rule of evidence should we shape? We should not exclude all that is dismissed under state law. I do not reject the "silver platter doctrine," although I am sorry that I ever used the phrase. The federal government properly says that *Weeks* is disciplinary in effect on officers.[94] I think that is nonsense and I would refer to Cardozo's opinion in the——case.[95] For a federal court to bar evidence because of the effect it will have on state courts is to proceed on a very speculative basis. The *Burdeau*

---

in federal trials was "shocking to the universal sense of justice" and "offensive to the common and fundamental ideas of fairness and right." Black argued that because Feldman's testimony could not have been used in federal court if it had been compelled by federal officials, there was no reason to permit its use simply because the state, rather than the federal government, had compelled Feldman to testify. Rejecting Frankfurter's attempt to restrict the scope of the Fifth Amendment "to the narrowest plausible limits," Black argued that the Fifth Amendment "must have a broad construction in favor of the right which it was intended to secure."

91. *Harris v. United States*, 331 U.S. 145 (1947). *United States v. Rabinowitz*, 339 U.S. 56 (1950).

92. *Wolf v. Colorado*, 338 U.S. 25 (1949).

93. *Benanti v. United States*, 355 U.S. 96 (1957). The Court ruled unanimously that evidence obtained from a state-authorized wiretap could not be used in a federal criminal prosecution, where the wiretap violated §605 of the Federal Communications Act and would have been inadmissible had it been executed by federal officials.

94. *Weeks v. United States*, 232 U.S. 383 (1914).

95. Douglas missed the case reference in conference; but in his dissenting opinion in *Elkins*, Frankfurter cited two Cardozo opinions, *Palko v. Connecticut*, 302 U.S. 319 (1937), and *People v. Defore*, 150 N. E. 585 (New York 1926). Potter Stewart's majority opinion preempted several of Cardozo's best quotes on the exclusionary rule, including his most famous: "The criminal is to go free because the constable has blundered." *People v. Defore*, at 587. Stewart also included a longer quote from the same case: "The Federal rule as it stands is either too strict or too lax. A Federal prosecutor may take no benefit from evidence collected through the trespass of a Federal officer. . . . He does not have to be so scrupulous about evidence brought to him by others. How finely the line is drawn is seen when we recall that marshals in the service of the nation are on one side of it, and police in the service of the States on the other. The nation may keep what the servants of the States supply. . . . We must go farther or not so far. The professed object of the trespass rather than the official character of the trespasser should test the rights of government. . . . A government would be disingenuous, if, in determining the use that should be made of evidence drawn from such a source, it drew a line between them. This would be true whether they had acted in concert or apart." *People v. Defore*, at 588.

dealt with a very special case that was unseemly and shoddy.[96] We should go on the facts of individual cases and not establish a general rule; I would rest on the notion of "decency." I would be violently opposed to a rule that prohibited the use of this evidence. I affirm.

DOUGLAS: I reverse.

CLARK: The rule should not be changed. Our main law enforcement is in the hands of local authorities, and most local officers take the evidence over to federal officers. That is the established practice and it should be followed. There is no real abuse in this field. There are very few cases. State officers are most useful in producing evidence for the federal men.

HARLAN: I will affirm both cases. It would be a step backward to abandon the "silver platter" rule. This is good example of what you get into if you abandon the rule. There is real force to the federal government's argument that the federal courts should not get mixed up in local squabbles between political factions. Bill Douglas's idea would deliver the federal courts to more state control, and that would be bad in my view. Federal participation in a state search would exclude the evidence. There is no violation of comity here.

CLARK: If an exclusionary rule is adopted, it should not include private people who often give evidence to us.

BRENNAN: I reverse. It is immaterial that there has been any state proceedings. This is a federal proceeding. Even if there had been no challenge in state courts, the evidence should not be admitted. Federal standards apply, not state standards. The *Weeks* rule is the one means of giving real effect to the Fourth Amendment. The same policy in federal courts would or should obtain even if state officers had seized in a way that federal officers could not lawfully do. Federal courts should apply the federal standard even if state officers had done it. I reverse for a new trial. The district court did not evaluate the evidence because it thought that the silver platter rule applied.

WHITTAKER: With the latter statement, I agree. Originally I would have thought that the exclusionary rule was not evidentiary but constitutional. I would not make wrongful state action insulation for federal crimes. If it is so shocking as to violate one's conscience,

---

96. *Burdeau v. McDowell*, 256 U.S. 465 (1921). The Court allowed federal officials to use evidence illegally seized by private individuals that had been gathered without the participation or knowledge of government officials. A private citizen ransacked J. C. McDowell's office and stole his personal papers. They were later handed over to federal investigators, who sought to use them in a grand jury investigation of possible mail fraud. McDowell sued Joseph Burdeau, a U.S. attorney, for the return of his property and sought to block the use of any incriminating evidence in any investigation or trial. In allowing this evidence to be used against McDowell, the majority ruled that the Fourth Amendment prohibited unreasonable searches and seizures through *state action* but did not reach private behavior. The Court was content to assume that McDowell would have other legal recourse against the person who stole his property. The Court also rejected McDowell's Fifth Amendment claim on the ground that the right against self-incrimination was meant only to protect citizens from coerced confessions. William Rufus Day wrote the majority opinion, while Brandeis and Holmes dissented.

as in *Rochin*, it should be excluded, even though taken by state officers.[97] That cannot be sensed in this case. I affirm. Any conduct of state officers which, if done by federal officers, would be "shocking" should be excluded.

STEWART: The district court did not determine if the search by state officers would have been invalid under the Fourth Amendment. He assumed that it was, and on his finding that there was no federal participation he allowed the evidence in. I agree with Bill Brennan. I do not look at all to see what a state court has done. Federal standards should apply. We have *McNabb* power, plus the power to shape the rules of evidence.[98] My exclusionary rule would exclude evidence seized by state officers if it would have been illegal if seized by federal officials. I reverse.

WARREN: I agree with Potter and Bill Brennan.

Result: The Court ruled 5–4 that it did not matter whether federal officials had been involved in the illegal search and seizure. Federal evidentiary standards—including the exclusionary rule—limited how the federal government could obtain and use evidence, regardless of whether it was seized by state or federal authorities. If a search and seizure by state authorities would have violated the Fourth Amendment had it been conducted by federal agents, then the evidence could not be used in a federal criminal prosecution. Potter Stewart wrote for the majority. Frankfurter, Clark, Harlan, and Whittaker dissented. The silver platter doctrine was no more, and perhaps more importantly the long-anticipated frontal assault on Wolf *was less than a year away.*

Mapp v. Ohio, 367 U.S. 643 (1961)
(Douglas) (Brennan)

Police asked Dollree Mapp for permission to search her house for evidence of a suspected bomb plot. When she refused to consent, the officers forced their way past her and into the house. When Mapp demanded to see a warrant, one officer flashed a piece of paper that he claimed was a warrant. Mapp grabbed the paper out of the officer's hand and stuffed it inside her bra. The officers forcibly retrieved it. Inside Mapp's house, police found "lewd and lascivious materials" but no evidence of bombmaking. Mapp was tried and convicted of violating state obscenity laws.[99] Neither the police nor the prosecutors ever produced a warrant.

On appeal to the Supreme Court, Mapp's lawyer, A. L. Kearns, stated that he was not prepared to challenge Wolf v. Colorado *and focused his arguments exclusively on the constitutionality of Ohio's obscenity laws.[100] Several of the Justices, however, were looking for a vehicle to overrule* Wolf *and extend the exclusionary rule to the states.[101]*

---

97. *Rochin v. California*, 342 U.S. 165 (1952).

98. *McNabb v. U.S.*, 318 U.S. 332 (1943).

99. Mapp's pornography collection was modest—a few dirty pictures and a risqué adult comic book (popularly known as a "Tijuana bible") illustrating the sexual exploits of Popeye the Sailor.

100. *Wolf v. Colorado*, 338 U.S. 25 (1949).

101. In its amicus brief, the American Civil Liberties Union only briefly raised the possibility of overruling *Wolf*.

Conference of March 31, 1961

WARREN: I reverse, although I have troubles. On the possession of contraband point, I see no difference between this and narcotics, except insofar as it cuts across First Amendment rights. First Amendment rights are involved here. The statute is too vague and too broad to accomplish its purpose, and on that basis I would reverse. The mere reading of the book is made an offense here.[102]

BLACK: I reverse.

FRANKFURTER: "Knowing possession" under this statute is a crime—that is unconstitutional. This is substantive due process for me. Libraries often have "erotic" collections. I would go on *Butler v. Michigan*, not on vagueness.[103] It is not vague to me—it's too clear.

DOUGLAS: I would reverse on (a) the First Amendment; (b) *Wolf* and the Fourth Amendment. This case is in the pattern of *Butler v. Michigan.*

CLARK: I reverse. This statute is too broad. *Roth* covers the sale of obscene materials.[104]

HARLAN: I reverse. There was no distribution here. This is a thought control statute. Lewd thoughts in one's own diary would be covered here.

BRENNAN: I agree with John Harlan and will vote to reverse. This is a candidate for overruling *Wolf.* The officers have no warrant—they go through her cellar and find this stuff in a box belonging to someone else. I would overrule *Wolf.*

WARREN: I will overrule *Wolf.*

CLARK: I will overrule *Wolf.*[105]

WHITTAKER: This is too broad a statute. I reverse.

STEWART: *Roth* says that this material is not covered by the First Amendment. If this stuff isn't covered by the First and Fourteenth Amendments, I would have trouble. I would re-examine *Alberts.*[106] I reverse—I think that these decisions were too broad.

---

102. Warren, Frankfurter, Harlan, and Brennan, and to a lesser degree Clark, Stewart, and perhaps Whittaker, all questioned the idea of whether states could criminalize the mere possession of obscene material in the privacy of one's home. Their views anticipated Thurgood Marshall's landmark opinion in *Stanley v. Georgia*, 394 U.S. 557 (1969).

103. *Butler v. Michigan*, 352 U.S. 380 (1957). Michigan law made it illegal to make available to the public books, magazines, movies, or other materials "tending to the corruption of the morals of youth." The Court struck down the law as a violation of due process. Frankfurter wrote for the majority that to reduce the adult population of Michigan to reading only what was fit for children was "to burn the house to roast the pig."

104. *Roth v. United States*, 354 U.S. 476 (1957).

105. Schwartz and Lesher argued that Clark did not decide to overrule *Wolf* until after this conference (*Inside the Warren Court*, 173–74). One of Earl Warren's biographers, Ed Cray, claimed that Clark's conversion took place during a postconference elevator ride with William Brennan (*Chief Justice*, 374). Douglas's notes, however, indicate that both Warren and Clark changed their minds during the conference.

106. *Alberts v. California*, 354 U.S. 476 (1957). This was one of the companion cases to *Roth v. United States.*

Result: At conference, all nine Justices agreed that Mapp's conviction should be reversed but disagreed as to why. Five Justices based their decision on the obscenity issue, while four wanted to use the case to revisit Wolf.

In the end, Hugo Black switched sides and a 5–4 majority coalesced to overrule Wolf *and extend the exclusionary rule to the states. Four Justices in the majority tied the exclusionary rule to the Fourth Amendment. Black, the crucial fifth vote, wrote a concurring opinion linking the exclusionary rule to* Mapp's *Fourth and Fifth Amendment rights. What mattered most was that for the first time five Justices accepted the principle that the exclusionary rule was the only effective means of enforcing suspects' constitutional rights and that it was not merely a procedural device that could be modified or abandoned at will.*[107]

The other four Justices voted to reverse Mapp's *conviction on obscenity grounds. Although Potter Stewart did not mention it in his concurring opinion, from his comments in conference it was clear that he was already dissatisfied with the* Roth/Alberts *obscenity test.*

Bivens v. Six Unknown Named Agents of the Federal Bureau of Narcotics, 403 U.S. 388 (1971)
(Brennan) (Douglas)

In 1965, without a warrant or probable cause, a team of Federal Bureau of Narcotics agents stormed Webster Bivens's home late at night with guns drawn, shoving his wife to the floor and forcibly dragging Bivens out of bed. In front of his wife and children, the agents roughly handcuffed Bivens, ransacked the house, and threatened everyone with arrest. The agents took Bivens to the courthouse, where he was strip-searched and interrogated. Because all charges against Bivens were eventually dropped, the exclusionary rule was not at issue. Bivens had no remedy except to file a federal civil suit for damages. It was, in John Marshall Harlan's words, "damages or nothing." The district court dismissed his suit on two alternate grounds: failure to state a federal cause of action and sovereign immunity. The court of appeals affirmed on the first ground. At conference, note Warren Burger's view that this case represented a significant step toward eliminating the exclusionary rule.

Conference of January 15, 1971

BURGER: Should the courts create a cause of action for constitutional violations? The district court said that federal agents are immune from damage suits. The petitioner is proposing more than I can accept. Congress could create a damage remedy or repeal one established by the courts, and has created one against state officials. It seems significant that Congress stopped short. So I would follow the court of appeals and affirm. I agree, however, that it is a good first step toward abolishing the exclusionary rule.

BLACK: I affirm.

---

107. Black struggled for years to make up his mind about the nature and scope of the exclusionary rule. Despite his vote in this case, he continued to criticize the exclusionary rule and in *Coolidge v. New Hampshire* restated his earlier view that the Fourth Amendment, "properly construed, contains no such exclusionary rule." 403 U.S. 443 (1971). While ambivalent about the rule's social costs, Black never advocated overruling *Mapp.*

DOUGLAS: We have created sanctions under *Weeks* and *Mapp*, and we should add this one until Congress goes one way or the other.[108]

HARLAN: I affirm.

BRENNAN: I reverse. I agree with Bill Douglas.

STEWART: I reverse, but am in doubt.

WHITE: In view of the existence of an injunction remedy, the fact is that any cases would be tried in federal courts and before federal judges, even if the cause of action is state. Even a state remedy would be governed by federal standards.

MARSHALL: I don't think that a narcotics agent can have the benefit of *Matteo* as a defense.[109] I would join four to reverse. I do not reach the immunity issue.

STEWART: We need not deal with immunity.

BLACKMUN: I would affirm. I am fascinated by *Bell v. Hood*.[110] I was impressed by Lombard's [*sic*] opinion.[111] I am inclined to leave these sorts of cases to state trespass laws until Congress acts.

Result: The Court ruled 5–1–3 that Fourth Amendment violations by federal officials acting under color of law were actionable under 28 U.S.C. §1331(a), even without explicit congressional authorization.[112] Writing for the majority, Brennan argued that a broad reading of §1331 was necessary "to make good the wrong done." The Court did not reach the issue of sovereign immunity, as the court of appeals had not ruled on the issue. Harlan concurred in the judgment. Burger, Black, and Blackmun dissented, arguing that Congress, not the Court, was responsible for creating new federal causes of action. Bivens eventually settled out of court with the federal agents for a nominal amount.

---

108. *Weeks v. United States*, 232 U.S. 383 (1914). *Mapp v. Ohio*, 367 U.S. 643 (1961).

109. *Barr v. Matteo*, 360 U.S. 564 (1959). In a press release, William Barr, the acting director of the Office of Rent Stabilization, blasted his subordinates' plan to spend $2.6 million in agency funds by firing most of the department's full-time employees, giving them severance pay, and then immediately hiring them back as "temporary" employees. Barr announced that he would suspend from active duty the two department employees responsible for the plan, Linda Matteo and John Madigan. Matteo and Madigan sued, claiming that Barr's remarks had defamed them. The Court ruled 4–1–4 that Barr, as a senior government policymaker, had acted within his authority and enjoyed absolute immunity, even if his statements were retaliatory, injurious, and intended only "to vent his spleen upon others."

110. *Bell v. Hood*, 327 U.S. 678 (1946), involved a private action against the FBI to recover damages allegedly sustained when agents violated the petitioners' Fourth and Fifth Amendment rights. The lower courts had dismissed the suit for failure to state a federal cause of action, but the Supreme Court reversed and ruled that the Court had jurisdiction to consider cases brought under the Constitution. The Court reserved the question of whether an action against federal agents for unconstitutional conduct was a cause of action for which relief could be granted but stated that "federal courts may use any available remedy to make good the wrong done." Hugo Black wrote the majority decision. Stone and Burton dissented, while Jackson took no part in the decision.

111. Judge J. Edward Lumbard wrote the opinion below in *Bivens v. Six Unknown Agents of the Federal Bureau of Narcotics*, 409 F.2d 718 (2nd Cir. 1969).

112. Section 1331(a) gives federal district courts original jurisdiction of all civil actions arising under the Constitution, laws, or treaties of the United States.

Stone v. Powell, 428 U.S. 465 (1976)
Wolff v. Rice
(Brennan)

When Lloyd Powell was arrested for vagrancy in Nevada, police searched him and found a revolver that was linked to a murder in California.[113] *Extradited to California and put on trial for murder, Powell sought to suppress the gun evidence, arguing that the Nevada vagrancy statute was unconstitutional and that his arrest, search, and seizure were unconstitutional. In the unrelated companion case, David Rice was accused of murder in Nebraska. He sought to suppress evidence seized by officers executing an allegedly invalid search warrant at his home.*

The state courts in California and Nebraska both held that any police error was harmless and that prosecutors were free to use the incriminating evidence. Powell and Rice were both convicted and their convictions were affirmed on appeal. Both defendants filed for writs of habeas corpus in federal court, and in both cases federal courts of appeals ruled that the seizures were unconstitutional and that the evidence should have been suppressed.

Two main issues were before the Supreme Court: (1) the scope and applicability of the exclusionary rule; and (2) what limits should be placed on federal habeas corpus and other collateral proceedings involving a defendant's Fourth Amendment rights when the defendant had already had the opportunity to litigate Fourth Amendment issues at trial and on direct review.

BURGER: The issues in *Wolff v. Rice* are like the next case, *Stone v. Powell.* I would (1) modify or eliminate the exclusionary rule, or (2) overrule *Kaufman.*[114] I prefer option one, but I can go along with option two.

STEWART: I would not alter the rule of *Weeks v. United States,* which I regard as a rule of evidence in federal courts.[115] The "imperative of judicial integrity" for me refers only to federal courts. So for me, *Mapp* was a thunderbolt. I will pass for the present.[116]

WHITE: The exclusionary rule should be modified but not discarded. It should be sort of an immunity rule, with a good faith, objective standard. But I joined *Kaufman,* and I think it would be a mistake to limit federal review to that by this Court. And the statute here hardly seems to support construction to exclude some kinds of Fourth Amendment claims. I am clear to reverse in *Stone,* but *Wolff v. Rice* is a closer case. I can't see how, if we modify the rule for states, we can fail to modify the federal rule.

MARSHALL: I am receptive to a limitation of the exclusionary rule, if some workable plan can be devised.

BLACKMUN: I would cut the exclusionary rule back and go along with states, unless there is a blatant disregard of the rules.

---

113. Powell and three other men attempted to steal a bottle of wine from a California liquor store. When confronted by the store manager, Powell shot and killed the manager's wife.

114. *Kaufman v. United States,* 394 U.S. 217 (1969).

115. *Weeks v. United States,* 232 U.S. 383 (1914).

116. *Mapp v. Ohio,* 367 U.S. 643 (1961).

POWELL: I see four possibilities: (1) there is no Fourth Amendment violation in either case; (2) we could modify the exclusionary rule to except good faith violations—I would gladly join this disposition; (3) we could view the exclusionary rule differently on collateral attack than from direct appeal, recognizing a good faith exception at least in habeas cases (habeas is basically an equitable doctrine, as *Fay* said);[117] or (4) we could recede from my *Bustamonte* opinion to the extent of a claim of innocence.[118] Judge Leventhal had the best discussion I have seen of this.[119]

REHNQUIST: I could modify the exclusionary rule to an objective test of reasonableness. *Calandra* and *Peltier* lay the groundwork for that.[120] I also could agree to go only to collateral attacks. I could also go on Lewis's *Bustamonte* approach.

STEVENS: I come out close to Powell's position on *Bustamonte*, except as to the innocence element. I can't say that the rationale is unfairness to the accused, because I can't find the non-retroactivity or standing cases defensible. If we rely on a deterrence rationale, we think of preventing our society from becoming a police state. I would be rigid on that score in applying the exclusionary rule in the federal area. But where you are talking about federal collateral attacks on judgments for state prisoners, deterrence simply doesn't happen. Moreover, the resulting overload of cases threatens quality of federal judicial work. Too, these cases are the devil on state judicial systems, and they pass the buck to federal courts.

So a good faith modification is not my idea of the best way to approach this. Rather, I would make a drastic distinction between direct and collateral review, where the exclusionary rule is constitutionally compelled, and leave the question of whether the state afforded a fair chance to litigate this.

---

117. *Fay v. Noia*, 372 U.S. 391 (1963).

118. *Schneckloth v. Bustamonte*, 412 U.S. 218 (1973). In a search and seizure case brought before the Court on a petition for habeas corpus, Powell argued in his concurring opinion that "federal collateral review of a state prisoner's Fourth Amendment claims—claims which rarely bear on innocence—should be confined solely to the question of whether the petitioner was provided a fair opportunity to raise and have adjudicated the question in state courts."

119. *Thornton v. United States*, 368 F. 2d 822 (1966). Judge Harold Leventhal wrote the majority opinion that Powell admired so much. Leventhal wrote, in part: "Whether collateral attack is permissible depends on the nature of the constitutional claim, the effectiveness of the direct remedies, and the need for choices among competing considerations in quest of the ultimate goal of achievement of justice. . . . The courts are called on to evolve and provide procedures and remedies that are effective to vindicate constitutional rights. However, where effective procedures are available in the direct proceeding, there is no imperative to provide an additional, collateral review, leaving no stone unturned, when exploration of all avenues of justice at the behest of individual petitioners may impair judicial administration of the federal courts, as by making criminal litigation interminable, and diverting resources of the federal judiciary."

120. *United States v. Calandra*, 414 U.S. 338 (1974). The majority ruled that the exclusionary rule was a judicially created remedy intended to deter unlawful police conduct, rather than a constitutionally mandated remedy intended to vindicate personal constitutional rights. Application of the rule, Powell argued, should be restricted to areas where its deterrent and remedial objectives were most efficaciously served. The second case, *United States v. Peltier*, 422 U.S. 531 (1975), was a Rehnquist opinion that indicated in dicta that the exclusionary rule was judicially created rather than constitutionally required. Rehnquist's conference argument was that these two cases could be combined as precedent to justify a case-by-case judicial balancing of the costs and benefits using "objective" factors.

Result: The Court ruled 6–3 that where states have already provided a full and fair hearing on defendants' Fourth Amendment claims, absent "unusual circumstances" defendants would not be allowed to relitigate the same claims in federal courts. Warren Burger's majority opinion emphasized that the deterrence benefits of the exclusionary rule in these two cases were minimal compared to the rule's high social costs, and he argued that state court judges were as vigilant and competent as federal judges in enforcing the Fourth Amendment.

Illinois v. Gates, 462 U.S. 213 (1983)
(Brennan)

Police in Bloomingdale, Illinois, received an anonymous letter alleging that Lance and Susan Gates were trafficking drugs. The letter included details about how the pair purchased drugs in Florida and transported the contraband to Illinois. In cooperation with the DEA, police put the couple under surveillance and independently confirmed much of what the letter said. Submitting the letter and a police affidavit to a magistrate, police obtained a search warrant for the Gates's car and home and found drugs in both places. The state trial court suppressed the evidence, because under established law an anonymous letter and police affidavit alone were not sufficient to show probable cause. The warrant application violated both prongs of the Aguilar-Spinelli *test: (1) providing sufficient specific evidence as to the informant's basis of knowledge (the knowledge prong); and (2) providing sufficient facts to establish either the informant's veracity or reliability (the veracity prong).[121] The Illinois Supreme Court affirmed.*

After the initial round of oral arguments, the Justices ordered reargument on the question of whether there should be a good faith exception to the exclusionary rule.

BURGER: My dissent from denial of cert lays out my position. The warrant-issuing process is not a trial. Anonymity is only one factor. The detail was extensive here, and while not everything was corroborated, *Draper* compels reversal here.[122] The case hasn't been tried yet. We should give more deference to the magistrate than we do. I would reverse definitely on the car search, and would, if pushed, send this case back to the trial court on the home search issue.

BRENNAN:[123] I vote to affirm the decision of the Illinois Supreme Court.

The state court properly applied the *Aguilar-Spinelli* test. The state court held that the detail in the anonymous letter, coupled with the corroborative evidence, was insufficient to establish probable cause under *Aguilar* and *Spinelli*. The state court found that the letter was insufficiently detailed to satisfy the "basis of knowledge" prong. In addition, as counsel for the respondent pointed out, the letter did not provide a precise address and erroneously stated that the wife would fly back after the husband flew to Florida to pick up the car. The state court also found that the corroboration of innocent activity

---

121. *Aguilar v. Texas*, 378 U.S. 108 (1964); *Spinelli v. United States*, 393 U.S. 410 (1969). The Illinois Supreme Court ruled that the anonymous letter and police affidavit failed the "knowledge" prong because there was too little detail and failed the "veracity" prong because the police had only corroborated some of the "innocent details" contained in the letter.

122. *Draper v. United States*, 358 U.S. 307 (1939).

123. Adapted from Brennan's talking papers, Brennan Papers, OT 1982, box 613.

was insufficient to satisfy the "veracity" prong. Even assuming that the corroborative evidence was sufficient to satisfy the "veracity" prong, we are still left with the failure to satisfy the "basis of knowledge" prong. Corroborative evidence is not sufficient to satisfy the "basis of knowledge" prong.

Draper is distinguishable. There was a reliable informant in *Draper*, and the information he provided was far more detailed and accurate. As such, the information was sufficient to satisfy the "basis of knowledge" prong.

I also agree with Justice Stevens that the state's case is even weaker with respect to the search of the apartment than it is with respect to the search of the car. The state's attorney very nearly conceded as much at oral argument. There is very little information in the anonymous letter about the apartment and there appears to have been nothing in the way of corroborative evidence.

I do not think *Aguilar* and *Spinelli* should be overruled. The test established by those cases insures that the information acted on by the police is reliable and is based on first-hand knowledge. Acting on an anonymous letter, which is inaccurate in certain respects, is treacherous business. On the facts of this case, it is clear that the *Aguilar-Spinelli* test was not satisfied.

WHITE: The state court may be wrong, but its findings are arguably defensible. I would prefer to say here that the good faith of the officers means that we ought not to apply the exclusionary rule. This *Aguilar-Spinelli* test is not satisfied—so what? The officers and the magistrate acted in good faith under the authorization of a warrant, so we ought not to apply the exclusionary rule.

MARSHALL: If Illinois wants to protect its citizens against itself, let them.

BLACKMUN: I am no fan of *Aguilar* and *Spinelli*. This case is stronger than in *Draper*. We don't have to get to the good faith exception issue, but I am willing to do so.

POWELL: I am interested in Byron's good faith exception proposal, and I prefer to do that. If we don't go that way, I think that the details are overwhelming as to the car, although weaker as to house.

REHNQUIST: Byron's good faith exception rule gets rid of *Aguilar* and *Spinelli*, and I can go along with that. If we don't, then I would say that there is a tension between *Aguilar-Spinelli* on the one hand and *Draper* on the other, and it should be resolved in favor of a *Draper* analysis.

STEVENS: The warrant should be analyzed in light of what the magistrate knew. He didn't know of the twenty-three-hour trip—he knew only that they lived in a condominium, that they would go to Florida, and that she would fly back.[124] For me, there is a great difference between the car and the house. So I would affirm as to the house but reverse as to car, although I have doubts.

---

124. The informant's letter alleged, and police confirmed, that the average drive time between West Palm Beach, Florida, and Bloomingdale, Illinois, was between twenty-one and twenty-three hours.

O'CONNOR: I can join in Byron's good faith exception to the exclusionary rule, although I could say *Draper* and not *Aguilar* and *Spinelli*.

Conference after Reargument

BURGER: I would not abandon the exclusionary rule entirely, but I certainly would modify it with a good faith exception if the officer has a warrant. I also would overrule *Spinelli* and *Aguilar*.

WHITE: We have jurisdiction to reach the good faith question, as subsumed in the 4th Amendment submission as the reason for exclusion of the evidence: *Dewey v. Des Moines*,[125] *Stanley v. Illinois*,[126] and *Mapp v. Ohio*.[127] On the state statute, I would say that it was no bar when the decision below was on a federal ground. I would address good faith, and say that

---

125. *Dewey v. Des Moines*, 173 U.S. 193 (1899). Dewey, a resident of Illinois, also owned property in Iowa. After the city of Des Moines assessed his property for tax purposes, Dewey failed to pay his property taxes and the city began forfeiture proceedings. Dewey sued, alleging that the city had assessed his property at far higher than fair market value in order to finance a local street-paving project. Dewey lost in state court, and on appeal to the U.S. Supreme Court he only raised one cognizable federal issue: because he was not a resident of Iowa and had no notice of the assessment proceedings, due process prohibited the city from holding him personally liable for tax assessments in excess of the property's fair market value. After the Supreme Court agreed to hear the case, Dewey attempted to raise a second issue: the assessment itself was an unconstitutional taking under the Fourteenth Amendment. The immediate question for the Court was whether Dewey could raise this second issue for the first time on appeal.

The Court decided that while the parties were not bound by the precise *arguments* they raised below, they were ordinarily bound by the *issues* raised below. Justice Rufus Peckham listed three main exceptions to this rule: (1) if the "new" question was an enlargement of the question properly raised on appeal (the "mere enlargement" doctrine); (2) if the "new" issue was very closely connected with the existing federal question in substance and form; or (3) if the state court could not possibly have issued its judgment without also deciding the "new" issue.

Because none of these conditions applied to Dewey's case, the Court confined its attention to the single federal question presented in the record. Nonetheless, the Court ruled that under the taking and due process clauses the Iowa law was unconstitutional, and that Dewey could not be compelled to pay taxes on the excessive assessments.

126. *Stanley v. Illinois*, 405 U.S. 645 (1972), was a paternal fitness case with no obvious relevance to this case. It is likely that White meant *Brown v. Illinois*, 422 U.S. 590 (1975). After police arrested Richard Brown without probable cause and without a valid warrant, Brown was read his *Miranda* rights and afterward made incriminating statements implicating himself in a murder. The state argued that even if the arrest was illegal, the *Miranda* warnings meant that Brown's statements were voluntary and admissible. The Supreme Court reversed and ordered the evidence excluded on the ground that giving a suspect Miranda warnings did not mean that any statements induced by an illegal arrest were necessarily voluntary or admissible.

It is also possible that White was referring to *Stanley v. Georgia*, 394 U.S. 557 (1969). In that case, Stewart, White, and Brennan argued in a concurring opinion that Stanley's conviction for possession of obscene films should have been reversed solely on Fourth Amendment grounds. They acknowledged that police had a valid search warrant and conducted their search in good faith but concluded that the search exceeded the scope of the warrant (which was limited to Stanley's alleged gambling activities) and that the seizure could not be justified on other grounds (e.g., plain sight, exigent circumstances, or a search incident to a valid arrest). It was a general, exploratory search that constituted a "bald violation" of Stanley's Fourth Amendment rights.

127. *Mapp v. Ohio*, 367 U.S. 643 (1961).

if an officer has a warrant and executes it in good faith, then the exclusionary rule should not apply. I would still reverse on *Aguilar* and *Spinelli*, but would not overrule them.

MARSHALL: I would affirm, as the good faith issue is not jurisdictionally here.

BLACKMUN: *Aguilar* and *Spinelli* are here, and I would reverse by "reversing" *Draper* without overruling it. On the good faith issue, I disagree with Byron. The issue was not raised in the state courts, and had it been Illinois could interpose its statute and provide an adequate and independent state ground.

POWELL: In *Brown v. Illinois*, I said that I would be for a good faith exception to the exclusionary rule, and if the issue is here I would reverse on that ground.[128] I am sorry that we requested reargument—not so much on the independent state ground basis, but because I would reverse on *Aguilar*. I don't see how we can go on to reach some other ground that assumes invalidity. So my bottom line is to reverse solely on the *Aguilar-Spinelli* point.

REHNQUIST: My tentative view is that we have no jurisdiction to decide the good faith issue, and we made a mistake in setting this case for reargument. Harry put his finger on it—the conjunction of the failure to raise the issue below and the existence of a passable adequate state ground, and either doctrine says that we don't review such grounds. Not thinking good faith is here, I would go with reversal for Harry's reasons.

STEVENS: We ought not decide the good faith issue, except in a case where the evidence is otherwise concluded. There is no deterrence of the police officer involved—it's of the magistrate, since the officer acts under the order of the court expressed in the warrant. *Nathanson v. United States* is directly on point in this case.[129] Aguilar and Spinelli created nit-picking, although I wouldn't abandon the basic theme of those decisions. But here, there were different considerations to get a warrant to search the car. The search of the house was not sufficiently supported, so there was no probable cause there. So I would reverse as to the car.

O'CONNOR: I agree with Harry and Bill Rehnquist that we should not have reargued. So I would reverse, relying on *Draper* and cutting back on *Aguilar* and *Spinelli*.

Result: After a wide-ranging debate on Byron White's proposed good faith exception to the exclusionary rule, the Court decided to leave the issue for another day. By a 5–1–3 majority, the Court replaced the Aguilar-Spinelli *test (without explicitly overruling either case) with a more flexible "totality of the circumstances" test. The new standard was whether the magistrate had a "substantial basis" to determine probable cause. The Court found that police corroboration of much of the information contained in the anonymous informant's tip was sufficient. White concurred with the judgment but criticized the majority for abandoning the Aguilar-Spinelli test, saying that the new test threatened to eviscerate the probable cause standard. John Paul Stevens changed his split vote in conference and joined*

---

128. *Brown v. Illinois*, 422 U.S. 590 (1975). Powell and Rehnquist concurred in part, arguing that to trigger the exclusionary rule police misbehavior had to be willful, or at least negligent. In their judgment, "technical" violations of the Fourth Amendment—such as where police arrested an individual in good faith in reliance on a warrant later invalidated—would not trigger the exclusionary rule.

129. *Nathanson v. United States*, 290 U.S. 41 (1933).

the dissenters, arguing that the search warrants were invalid even under the newly announced test. Brennan and Marshall also dissented.

United States v. Leon, 468 U.S. 897 (1984)
(Brennan)

Armed with a search warrant, police entered three private residences and found large amounts of methaqualone and other drugs. Alberto Leon, Patsy Stewart, and Ricardo del Castillo were arrested and charged with possession of drugs with intent to sell. The district court later ruled that the police affidavit used to obtain the warrant was flawed and that the warrant was invalid. The mistake was innocent—the police and the magistrate had acted in good faith, but the trial judge felt compelled to suppress the evidence because there was no established exception for good faith errors. The court of appeals affirmed. In conference, although Burger advocated the good faith exception, he seems to have made his peace with the exclusionary rule.

BURGER: I would adopt the good faith exception. It would be a disaster to write anything that might be read as wiping out the exclusionary rule. We must write tightly to avoid that.

BRENNAN:[130] In this case, I fail to see why the proper disposition is not simply to vacate and remand in light of *Gates*.[131] It seems to me quite reasonable to assume that the search warrant found to be defective in this case under the *Aguilar-Spinelli* test would, under the new "totality of the circumstances" test announced in *Gates*, be found valid.[132] The police clearly conducted an extensive surveillance of the respondents' activities—a surveillance which the lower court, if given the opportunity to consider the warrant application in light of *Gates*, might well find provides a sufficient showing of probable cause to support the issuance of the warrant.

As in *Sheppard*, however, if there are five to reach the good faith issue in this case, then I will be in dissent.[133]

WHITE: I would adopt the good faith exception.

BLACKMUN: I prefer to vacate on *Gates*.

REHNQUIST: I agree that under *Gates* there would be a different result, but again no issue was presented here. We must therefore reach the good faith issue.

STEVENS: It is unwise to reach good faith here. We only need say that there is no Fourth Amendment violation here. We ought not to have another *Miranda*. I agree with Potter

---

130. Adapted from Brennan's talking papers, Brennan Papers, OT 1983, box 656.

131. *Illinois v. Gates*, 462 U.S. 213 (1983).

132. *Aguilar v. Texas*, 378 U.S. 108 (1964); *Spinelli v. United States*, 393 U.S. 410 (1969).

133. *Massachusetts v. Sheppard*, 468 U.S. 981 (1984). On a 6–2–1 vote, the Court established an exception to the exclusionary rule where the seizure was based on a facially invalid warrant on which an officer had reasonably relied (the warrant was bad because it had failed to specify the items sought). Stevens's concurring opinion avoided the "good faith" issue, arguing that the warrant and search were both valid under the Fourth Amendment. Brennan and Marshall dissented.

that good faith should not be adopted. The reasonableness standard of the Fourth Amendment itself suffices. The need for good faith is perhaps greater in warrantless searches.[134]

O'CONNOR: It is time to restrict the scope of the exclusionary rule. The Founders relied on tort law to remedy search and seizure violations, as did the English. A good faith exception will require an adjustment of tort remedies to replace the exclusionary rule.

Result: The Court used this case to establish a good faith exception to the exclusionary rule. Byron White's majority opinion emphasized the high social costs of the exclusionary rule and the "marginal or nonexistent benefits" of applying the rule when the police had done all that they reasonably could to obtain a search warrant. Prosecutors would be allowed to use illegally seized evidence when police reasonably—but mistakenly—relied on facially valid warrants issued by neutral magistrates.

This was an instance when a strongly worded majority opinion pushed the minority (who at conference appeared willing to reverse on other grounds) to change their votes and write equally combative dissents. Brennan and Marshall blasted the majority for their "determined strangulation" of the exclusionary rule, while Stevens accused White of absurdly claiming that a search was both "unreasonable" and "reasonable" at the same time. Stevens warned that the new rule would encourage slipshod police work and tempt police to seek warrants on minimal evidence, just to see if magistrates "would take the bait."

INS v. Lopez-Mendoza, 468 U.S. 1032 (1984)

(Brennan)

The Immigration and Naturalization Service (INS) arrested Adan Lopez-Mendoza and Elias Sandoval-Sanchez as suspected illegal aliens. While in custody, both men admitted that they had entered the United States illegally. At his deportation hearing, Sanchez claimed that his arrest was illegal and that his confession should be suppressed. Mendoza, however, did not raise this issue until after his deportation hearing. An immigration judge ordered both men deported, and the Board of Immigration Appeals (BIA) affirmed. The court of appeals reversed as to Sanchez, holding that his detention violated the Fourth Amendment and that his confession was inadmissible. The court of appeals remanded Mendoza's case to the BIA to determine whether his arrest had also violated the Fourth Amendment.

BURGER: Should the exclusionary rule be extended to civil deportation proceedings? I reject the argument that this is more like a criminal case, despite the hardship incident to deportation. I would not extend the exclusionary rule and would reverse the decision below.

BRENNAN:[135] I think that we can all agree that the starting place for our analysis should be the principles set out in Harry's opinion in *United States v. Janis*.[136] I start with three basic propositions that, in my view, distinguish this case from *Janis*.

---

134. Brennan, Marshall, and Stevens all voted at conference to reverse and remand on the basis of *Gates*.

135. Adapted from Brennan's talking papers, Brennan Papers, OT 1983, box 660.

136. *U.S. v. Janis*, 428 U.S. 433 (1976). This case established a balancing test for the exclusionary rule: whether the benefits of excluding unlawfully obtained evidence outweighed the likely costs of applying the rule.

First, unlike *Janis*, there is a direct connection between the conduct of INS agents and the application of the exclusionary rule in deportation proceedings. The basic law-enforcement mission of the INS is to see to it that undocumented aliens are deported; criminal prosecutions against deportable aliens are very rare, and the deportation hearing is therefore the only forum in which the agency's efforts are tested. *Second*, the fact that the INS is a single, integrated federal agency actually weighs in favor of applying the rule here. Because of the integrated nature of the INS, the results of such challenges can be easily and quickly disseminated throughout the agency. We can be especially confident that applying the exclusionary rule will yield substantial benefits in terms of deterring unconstitutional law-enforcement activity. *Finally*, despite Andy Frey's protestations, the evidence that we have suggests that the exclusionary rule has been thought for many, many years to apply in deportation proceedings.[137] Indeed, the authoritative treatise on immigration procedure, authored by a former general counsel of the INS, had stated prior to the Board of Immigration's 1979 decision that the rule applied in deportation hearings.[138]

I simply can't believe the solicitor general's argument that a "special class" of permanently immunized, although illegal, aliens will be created by application of the exclusionary rule in this context. In the first place, it is very likely that the INS will have other untainted evidence of deportability that can be relied upon to support deportation. Secondly, even if the INS has no other evidence, the chances are good that the few undocumented aliens who are actually released will be picked up in future factory surveys or in other INS area control operations.

I would conclude that the balance of costs and benefits that we considered in *Janis* tips decisively in favor of applying the rule to deportation hearings. I would therefore affirm the judgment of the Ninth Circuit.

WHITE: I am no fan of the exclusionary rule, but as long as we have it and we regard deterrence as the only factor to be considered, I don't see how we can fail to apply it here. I might be persuaded if someone can come up with a persuasive argument to the contrary.

MARSHALL: This isn't a civil proceeding—this alien is in handcuffs and behind bars.

BLACKMUN: Although I wrote *Janis*, this for me is a civil proceeding and I won't extend a judge-made rule to cover it. The societal costs greatly exceed the benefits here.

POWELL: I can't see any burden or penalty on illegal aliens who have violated the laws of the United States. It can't be a criminal proceeding. Anyway, it wouldn't apply to a civil proceeding.

REHNQUIST: Don't let the exclusionary rule spread is my base belief. A *Janis* cost-benefit analysis comes out in favor of INS.

---

137. Deputy Solicitor General Andrew Frey argued the case on behalf of the INS. A few months after this case was decided, President Reagan nominated Frey to serve on the Circuit Court of Appeals for the District of Columbia. Reagan angrily withdrew Frey's name when he found out that Frey had contributed $25 to Planned Parenthood and had made small donations to the National Abortion Rights Action League and the National Coalition to Ban Handguns. Frey resigned from the solicitor general's office and went into private practice.

138. Gordon and Rosenfield, *Immigration Law and Procedure*, §5.2c, pp. 5–31.

STEVENS: What has the law been? I am persuaded that the exclusionary rule has been applied here over the years. The government's argument that this is now a flood is purely phony. A cost-benefit analysis tips in favor of applying the exclusionary rule.

O'CONNOR: Even though the BIA has applied the exclusionary rule, we should not mandate it—at least not in a non-egregious situation that does not amount to a due process violation.

Result: Sandra Day O'Connor, writing for a 5–4 majority, ruled that the costs of the exclusionary rule outweighed the benefits in civil deportation cases and that the two confessions were admissible. In dissent, White and Stevens agreed that a cost-benefit analysis was appropriate but thought that the benefits of the exclusionary rule outweighed the costs in deportation cases. Brennan and Marshall argued that the exclusionary rule was constitutionally required regardless of any cost-benefit analysis.

CUSTODY AND INTERROGATION

RIGHT TO COUNSEL

Betts v. Brady, 316 U.S. 455 (1942)
(Murphy)

Smith Betts, an unemployed farmhand, was arrested and charged with robbery. Unable to pay for a lawyer, he asked the trial judge to appoint one. The judge refused, because Maryland provided defense lawyers only in rape and murder cases. Betts waived his right to a jury trial and conducted his own defense. He was found guilty and sentenced to eight years in prison. Claiming that Maryland's refusal to appoint counsel violated his Fourteenth Amendment rights, Betts filed for a writ of habeas corpus from another local judge, who rejected his petition. He then applied to Chief Judge Carroll T. Bond of the Maryland Court of Appeals, who also denied relief and remanded Betts to the custody of Warden Patrick J. Brady of the Maryland Penitentiary. Betts appealed to the U.S. Supreme Court.[139] At conference, note Robert Jackson's thumbnail social history of the Fourteenth Amendment.

STONE: On jurisdiction, we should not waste time. The judge was at least as high as any court in the state that could be reached.

On the merits, the question is whether the states, by the adoption of the Fourteenth Amendment, made it compulsory on the state to provide counsel in every case. No one thought at the time that the Constitution was adopted that due process required the state to provide counsel. When we come to the Fourteenth Amendment, it is a pure due process question. Louis Brandeis, in the *Palko* case, wrote this wisely.[140] The practice of providing counsel is desirable, but the state should not be so compelled. I do not see any ground on which we can review this case. His only point was that upon application, he was denied counsel.

---

139. The state court of appeals was the highest state court from which Betts could seek a writ of habeas corpus and a decision on his federal due process claim.

140. *Palko v. Connecticut,* 302 U.S. 319 (1937). Brandeis wrote that due process included those procedures "implicit in the concept of ordered liberty" and "essential to the substance of a hearing."

This Court has jurisdiction, but does the federal Constitution require Judge Bond to determine this question? By saying that the Fourteenth Amendment forced on the states the necessity of counsel, we are going very far.

ROBERTS: I agree with the Chief Justice.

BLACK: This is the highest court—that is, there is no court higher than this—of the state for this kind of a question. There is no res adjudicata in habeas corpus proceedings. A decision in a habeas corpus matter is a federal decision. Usually we have said that that is enough. Part of due process is the right to be heard. He can't be heard unless he has counsel. This case means that Maryland can't say that we expect our courts to look after the right to counsel.[141]

How many times in your practice do you think that any man could plan his defense, summon witnesses, and otherwise conduct trial in face of organized competition? Does any layman do it capably? The question is: does he have to depend on the Constitution, or the judge's opinion?

I believe that he is entitled to a lawyer from the history of the Fourteenth Amendment. It was intended to make applicable to the states the entire Bill of Rights.

The Court has rested on due process in other cases. Due process cases are decided under prevailing doctrine. If you can find in history a practice that violates their instincts, then they hold that is a violation of due process. But in one case—Brandeis—that under new experiences we find that if the Constitution is offended, we are law makers. And if I am to pass on what is fair and right, I will say that it makes me vomit to think that men go to prison for a long time. No man should be tried against the constabulary of the government without a lawyer.

FRANKFURTER: If Judge Bond would say flatly, a decision could be had in the court of appeals in Maryland.[142] We would have a decision that could have been determined by the court of appeals of Maryland.

The Fourteenth Amendment did not incorporate the first ten amendments. If it did, you would uproot all the structures of the states.

"Unreasonable" must have meant that there were some standards of reason. We ought not to make due process something to shirk from. It has an ancient lineage. It is for the protection of individuals when in the contact forum. It is there to be appealed from. I would affirm on the merits.

DOUGLAS: I would reverse on merits. I think that this is an inappropriate ground to throw it out on—the ground that he could go up on appeal.

MURPHY: I would reverse on the merits.

JACKSON: I have no feeling of sanctity of the Fourteenth Amendment. It was passed in the most scandalous and lousy period in our history. For the time being, I would not upset Maryland's legal system.

---

141. It is not clear from Murphy's notes whether these remarks were made by Black, Stone, or Roberts. They seem to correspond most closely to Black's views, and so are attributed to him.

142. Judge Bond technically granted the writ of habeas corpus but then denied relief and immediately remanded Betts to prison.

Result: In a 6–3 decision, the Court asserted jurisdiction and affirmed Judge Bond's decision to deny Betts's petition. Owen Roberts argued that the Fourteenth Amendment did not specifically incorporate the Sixth Amendment unless the violations were so outrageous that they amounted to a denial of due process. The due process standard was flexible, Roberts acknowledged, prohibiting any denial of fundamental fairness that was shocking to the universal sense of justice. Denial of counsel did not necessarily violate this standard, and future claims would have to be evaluated on a case-by-case basis.

Black's dissent, joined by Douglas and Murphy, argued that the Fourteenth Amendment fully incorporated the Sixth Amendment. Moreover, Black argued, the right to counsel was a fundamental right, as Brandeis established in Palko v. Connecticut.

Glasser v. United States, 315 U.S. 60 (1942)
(Murphy)

Daniel "Red" Glasser and Norton Kretsky were assistant U.S. attorneys in charge of prosecuting Chicago bootleggers during Prohibition. Both men were convicted of conspiracy to defraud the United States by accepting bribes in exchange for not prosecuting certain defendants. On appeal, Glasser claimed that the trial judge, James H. Wilkerson, should not have appointed attorney William Scott Stewart— whom Glasser had previously retained as his own personal lawyer—to represent both himself and Kretsky at the same time. Kretsky's lawyers had bowed out just before the trial was to begin, and Judge Wilkerson assigned Stewart to represent both co-defendants. Glasser initially objected and Wilkerson temporarily dropped the idea, but then changed his mind and made the dual appointment. Glasser did not repeat his objection either before or during the trial. The key question was whether Glasser had waived his right to counsel by failing to object a second time.

The defendants raised several other issues that were discussed in conference, including whether the exclusion of women from jury duty violated their right to a fair trial. Although a new state law enacted in July 1939 allowed women to serve as jurors, women were still being excluded from federal jury panels in August, when Glasser and Kretsky were indicted. The defendants also complained about prejudicial judicial instructions and claimed that some of the evidence used against them was illegally seized and should have been excluded.

Conference of November 22, 1941

STONE: Let's explore the main points. There are a large number of technical objections. An exploration of the record shows that the verdict was returned in open court. I do not find the verdict fatally defective. You can't say that women were excluded, since they were not called on. The way women were selected on the empaneling of the jury—it might be granted, but on appeal I would pay no attention to it.[143]

A more serious question is that Glasser made a personal objection to the dual appointment of counsel and he never withdrew it. But I do not think there is anything to this. Dual counsel is not a right, but here was assented to.

There is also an objection to two of the exhibits. I think that they were properly introduced. The instructions were O.K. The trial judge participated more than he should have—it troubles me.

---

143. The only women included in the jury pool were taken from lists provided by the League of Women Voters.

There was no evidence that Glasser received any money. The final test was the examination of the large numbers—it shows a pattern explainable by the fact that he was acting corruptly. These were proved to the hilt. We should therefore scrutinize *unfairness when a case is as close as this.* But the cumulative effect of it is the point. And while the judge is subject to criticism, I do not think it enough to upset the case. I don't like this case; however, with doubt, I would let it stand.

ROBERTS: I think it ought to be reversed. All of these statements were introduced on the theory that it would all be connected up. They pick 18 cases out of 900. The judge had searing comments.

STONE: The performance of the judge bothers me the most.

BLACK: The record satisfies me that Glasser objected to the lawyer situation. I don't believe that the lawyer could properly represent both defendants. I would reverse, but I wouldn't go into the evidence because we don't know what it would be in a new trial.

REED: I don't think that there is enough to go to the jury.

FRANKFURTER: Regarding the judge's attitude, I think that he acted soundly. He was not a hanging judge. I went through the *English* practice on this subject. They are much stricter than we are in reversing, but they wouldn't here. On the basis of this record—it went to the jury—the circuit court of appeals affirmed, and I would, too—but I note that no exception was taken to the charge.

BYRNES: I would reverse—on the Constitution. If we rest this in part or wholly on counsel, Kretsky took no exception. But Roth did.[144] Would the acquittal of Glasser take the others out of the conspiracy? Would the conspiracy fail?

ROBERTS: If we take Glasser out, we can't do anything as to the others under the indictment.

FRANKFURTER: I don't see how you can do that—there are other cases in this court.

ROBERTS: This isn't from a state court—it is from federal court. We have the fullest authority here.

BLACK: Let Murphy get a memorandum.

Result: The Court overturned Glasser's conviction on a 6–2 vote (Robert Jackson did not participate) but affirmed Kretsky's conviction. Frank Murphy, writing for the majority, rejected the argument that the jury had improperly excluded women. He noted that the law allowing women to serve as jurors had been enacted in July but gave states until September 1939 to include women in the jury pool. The juries were drawn in August, well within the transition period. Moreover, at the time of trial, none of the other state or federal jurisdictions in the area had begun to use women as jurors. Murphy noted that there was no evidence that the flawed jury selection procedures had any effect on the trial. This

---

144. Alfred Roth was a prominent defense lawyer who was also allegedly involved in the conspiracy. Also charged were Louis Kaplan, a car dealer and bootlegger, and Anthony Horton, a bail bondsman.

case marked the first time that the Court referred to a "cross-section of the community" in discussing juries.

Murphy also ruled, however, that Judge Wilkerson had violated the fair trial requirements of the Sixth and Fourteenth Amendments by denying Glasser effective assistance of counsel. It was difficult for one lawyer to "serve two masters," especially where one of the joint defendants had objected to the arrangement. Glasser's initial objection was sufficient to put the trial judge on notice that the defendants' interests might be inconsistent.

Frankfurter and Stone dissented on the ground that Glasser never reiterated his constitutional claim at any point during the trial and that his belated attempt to resurrect the claim was "obviously a lawyer's afterthought" and could not be taken seriously.

Gideon v. Wainwright, 372 U.S. 335 (1963)
(Douglas) (Brennan)

Clarence Earl Gideon was charged with breaking and entering a poolroom with the intent to commit a misdemeanor, which was a felony under Florida law. He requested a state-appointed attorney, but the trial judge refused because Florida provided attorneys for indigents only in capital cases. Gideon conducted his own defense "about as well as could be expected from a layman" but was convicted and sentenced to five years in prison. He filed for a writ of habeas corpus, claiming that he had a constitutional right to a state-appointed lawyer.

Abe Fortas represented Gideon before the Supreme Court, giving what William O. Douglas called "the best single legal argument" he had ever heard.[145] But it probably did not matter much; the Justices had already agreed among themselves that Betts v. Brady had to go.

Conference of January 18, 1963

WARREN: There is no constitutional difference between capital cases and other cases so far as the right to counsel goes. I would reverse *Betts v. Brady.*[146] Where do we draw the line? At petty offenses? Do we abolish the distinction between capital and non-capital serious felonies, or what? We should not go all the way and say that a man is entitled to counsel in all criminal cases if we don't have to here. Maybe the thing to do is to stick to this case and fashion a uniform rule for all felony cases. We should not base our rule on that clan of cases in which only the well-to-do have counsel. I reverse. As to the retroactive phase of the problem, I do not think that we can make it prospective only. We can encourage a cut-off point, as Illinois did after we decided *Griffin.*[147]

---

145. Urofsky, *The Douglas Letters*, 135.

146. *Betts v. Brady*, 316 U.S. 455 (1942).

147. *Griffin v. Illinois*, 351 U.S. 12 (1956). The Court struck down an Illinois law providing indigents with free trial transcripts only in capital cases and required states to provide indigents with free trial transcripts in all noncapital cases for use on appeal. After the ruling, Illinois sought to limit the retroactive effect of the Court's decision by allowing indigents to apply for free trial transcripts only as of April 23, 1956. If no trial transcript had been made prior to that date, the state refused to go through the effort and expense of attempting to recreate a transcript from existing records. The Supreme Court approved this policy in *Norvell v. Illinois*, 373 U.S. 420 (1963), as long as the state was not to blame for the trial transcripts being unavailable. In Willie Norvell's case, the trial transcript was unavailable and could not be recreated because the court reporter had died.

BLACK: I reverse, based on my dissent in *Betts v. Brady*.[148] I would not try to limit the right. We need not limit it here any more than we did in *Johnson v. Zerbst*.[149] We should say that the states are bound by the same rule as the federal government. I would not make the rule prospective only.

DOUGLAS: I reverse. The Sixth Amendment is incorporated into the Fourteenth Amendment.

CLARK: I reverse. There is no distinction between capital and non-capital cases.

HARLAN: I reverse. *Powell v. Alabama* does not lay down a per se rule.[150] *Betts v. Brady* applies whenever a defendant was prejudiced. *Ferguson* and *Hamilton v. Alabama* were the first cases that presumed prejudice.[151] I am inclined to think that I would have been with the dissenters in *Betts v. Brady*. But now *Griffith* can't be distinguished. It leaves *Betts v. Brady* with no vitality. I can't say that *Betts v. Brady* is unworkable. It is a freak, and we should get done with it. I will not go on equal protection. I will go on straight due process, but I will not incorporate the Sixth Amendment into the Fourteenth.

BRENNAN: I reverse. The Sixth Amendment is absorbed into the Fourteenth. I would apply to the states the same distinctions that are applicable to the federal government.

STEWART: Due process requires that a man be represented by counsel if he is to have a fair trial. I would not "incorporate" or "absorb" the Sixth into the Fourteenth Amendment. There are no circumstances when the absence of counsel can produce a fair trial. I reverse.

WHITE: I reverse, even if it means applying the Sixth into the Fourteenth to the states.

---

148. *Betts* employed the *Rochin*-style due process analysis, which Black detested.

149. In *Johnson v. Zerbst*, 304 U.S. 458 (1938), the Court ruled that the Sixth Amendment guaranteed government-appointed counsel for all indigent *federal* defendants in felony cases. Black wrote the opinion.

150. *Powell v. Alabama*, 287 U.S. 45 (1932), was Justice Sutherland's landmark decision holding that indigent defendants in state capital cases had the right to appointed counsel under the due process clause of the Fourteenth Amendment. The case left several important questions open, such as whether the right to appointed counsel was available to all indigents or just those who were "friendless, ignorant and illiterate." It also was not clear at what point in the legal process the right attached, or whether there was any right to counsel in noncapital cases.

151. *Ferguson v. Georgia*, 365 U.S. 570 (1961). Georgia was the last common law jurisdiction in the world to prohibit criminal defendants from testifying under oath. The state permitted defendants to make an unsworn statement to the jury without a right of cross-examination. After Billy Ferguson took the stand during his murder trial, the trial judge refused to allow his own attorney to ask him any questions. The Supreme Court ruled that Georgia law, as applied, deprived Ferguson of effective assistance of counsel and violated the due process clause.

Hamilton v. Alabama, 368 U.S. 52 (1961). Charles Clarence Hamilton was arraigned without counsel for a capital offense. In Alabama, arraignment was a critical part of criminal proceedings because it was the only time that a defendant could plead insanity or challenge the composition of the grand jury. The Supreme Court held that depriving Hamilton of counsel at this crucial point in the legal process violated due process. Hamilton did not have to prove actual prejudice; the majority ruled that defendants in capital cases had an absolute right to counsel, regardless of whether the absence of legal representation caused any demonstrable prejudice, harm, or injury.

BRENNAN: I refer you to my article on the Sixth Amendment as applied to the states.

GOLDBERG: I reverse. The Constitution absorbs the right of counsel into the Fourteenth Amendment.

WHITE: Equal protection of the laws would apply in civil cases, and would require a lawyer where the state is a litigant—and only then.

Result: The Justices overruled Betts v. Brady *and established the modern rule that all indigent defendants in criminal cases have the right to be represented by a government-appointed attorney. This case was Hugo Black's revenge on Felix Frankfurter's approach to due process, which had been adopted in* Betts. *Black's victory was not complete, however; in order to hold his majority he had to abandon his total incorporation theory and settle for a more limited ruling that the Sixth Amendment's guarantee of counsel was a fundamental right and therefore applicable to the states. Douglas was left to carry the torch for total incorporation in his concurring opinion, which Black joined in spirit if not in fact. Afterward, Black and Douglas began to view selective incorporation as a practical means to achieve total incorporation piecemeal—in individual bites rather than in one mighty gulp.*

In his concurring opinion, John Marshall Harlan agreed that Betts *should be overruled but thought that it deserved "a more respectful burial." He argued that the Court should establish a more flexible rule, limited to cases where there was "the possibility of a substantial prison sentence." Harlan favored Frankfurter's approach of applying to the states only those procedural elements that were essential to fundamental fairness. In his view, the Fourteenth Amendment neither incorporated the Bill of Rights nor was limited by its terms. Different meanings and standards were applicable, depending on the rights and circumstances involved. Harlan believed that this approach would foster procedural diversity and flexibility, which would protect individual liberties within the context of American federalism. Douglas's concurrence attacked Harlan's argument as a "watered-down version of what the Bill of Rights guarantees." Tom Clark also concurred in the result.*

INTERROGATION AND SELF-INCRIMINATION

Chambers v. Florida, 309 U.S. 227 (1940)
(Douglas)

After a man was robbed and murdered in Dade County, Florida, forty black men were rounded up without warrants and held incommunicado while officers threatened and abused them. One by one the men were released, until five days later only four tenant farmers remained in custody, including Isiah Chambers. After a final, fifteen-hour interrogation session, all four men confessed shortly after dawn on their sixth day in custody. The incident became known as the "sunrise confessions" case. The trial judge left the question of whether the confessions were voluntary to the jury, and the jury convicted all four defendants. The men appealed, claiming that their confessions had been coerced in violation of the due process clause of the Fourteenth Amendment.

Conference of January 6, 1940

HUGHES: The fundamental issue is: were the confessions involuntary? Were they the sole basis of the conviction? I think that they were, although it is not clear from the record.

If the sole basis of the conviction was a confession unlawfully obtained, then there is not due process. Was this one unlawful or obtained by unlawful means? This involves action by the state, and this confession can be attributed to the state officials since they participated. There was a corrective process provided to reach this result. Is that due process here? This was no mere formality—it was a real trial. If it is just a question of the weight of the evidence, there is no federal question. To justify our intervention, it must be clear beyond question that the confessions were involuntary. That depends solely on the repeated questioning, and not on any force and violence. But the confessions were obtained by repeated questioning. Has the line been passed? It is one of degree. Does it clearly appear that that limit has been exceeded? Yes.

ROBERTS: First, the same result would follow even if there was other evidence of guilt. Second, these men were not entitled to be questioned. They had no lawyer; they were ignorant, and they did not know that they had constitutional rights. That is also a denial of due process.

Result: After initially voting not to hear the case, Hugo Black wrote the majority opinion in a unanimous decision. Stanley Reed and James McReynolds voted to affirm all four convictions in conference but were persuaded to remain silent. Chief Justice Hughes postponed announcing the decision for a week so that it could be handed down on Lincoln's Birthday. Viewed narrowly, Chambers *established that the question of whether confessions were voluntary would not necessarily be left to juries but could be determined by federal judges as a question of law. As a matter of law, Black wrote, these confessions were involuntary because they were obtained by repeated interrogations without access to counsel and because the interrogations had been conducted in a manner intended to inspire terror. More broadly,* Chambers *marked the beginning of Hugo Black's (unsuccessful) efforts to incorporate the first eight amendments of the Bill of Rights through the Fourteenth Amendment and apply these rights against the states.*[152]

---

152. Black thought that two wrongly decided cases led the Court into a grave historical misunderstanding of the intent and scope of the Fourteenth Amendment. The first case was *Twining v. New Jersey*, which failed to incorporate the right against self-incrimination under the Fifth Amendment and refused to concede that the Fourteenth Amendment incorporated *any* of the Bill of Rights. The second case was *Palko v. Connecticut*, in which the Court declined to incorporate the Fifth Amendment's double jeopardy clause. Benjamin Cardozo's *Palko* decision, however, contained a bit of dictum that established the process of selective incorporation of the Bill of Rights. Cardozo's majority opinion, which Black joined, argued that those rights that were *essential* or *fundamental* to ordered liberty, or rights whose violations would create an *acute* and *shocking* hardship, were applicable against the states. At that time, the list of fundamental rights was short: (1) the prohibition against the taking of private property without just compensation; and (2) free speech.

In 1942, Black first called for the full incorporation of the first eight amendments in his dissent in *Betts v. Brady*. Black developed his theory further in his 1947 dissent to *Adamson v. California*, 332 U.S. 46 (1947). In *Adamson*, the Court refused to apply the Fifth Amendment's protections against self-incrimination to the states. Black, joined by Douglas, said that if forced to choose, he preferred *Palko's* partial incorporation to *Twining's* nonincorporation theory—but that he really wanted "to extend to all of the people of the nation the complete protection of the Bill of Rights." Black based his argument on the stated intentions of the two main congressional sponsors of the legislation that launched the Fourteenth Amendment (John Bingham in the House and Jacob Howard in the Senate) to make the entire Bill of Rights applicable to the states.

McNabb v. United States, 318 U.S. 332 (1943)
(Murphy) (Douglas)

The McNabbs were a Tennessee mountain family who sold bootleg whiskey and neither collected nor paid taxes on sales. When federal revenue officers arrived at the family cemetery (where the whiskey was distilled and stored), shots were exchanged and an officer was killed. Four McNabb brothers—Freeman, Raymond, Emuil, and Barney—and a cousin, Benjamin McNabb, were arrested. They were held incommunicado and interrogated for three days without access to counsel or family and without being charged with a crime. After making several incriminating statements, Freeman, Raymond, and Benjamin were convicted of murder in a federal court and sentenced to forty-five years in prison. The federal court of appeals affirmed.

Conference of November 24, 1942

STONE: Three of them were convicted of second degree murder. An agent was shot. Police took five members of the family into custody. Instead of taking them to jail for arraignment, they kept them for three days and kept them for questioning. They made statements that were used against them at trial. They objected to the use of this evidence. The jury came in against them.

First, did the questioning violate the rule established in the *Chambers* case?[153] Three days of questioning while being held overnight without food in a room without bedding or an opportunity to sit down. One was undressed. You could hardly say it was carried to that point of exhaustion and oppression under the rule of the *Chambers* case.

Second, there is a duty on federal officials to take an arrested man before a proper officer and have him arraigned. There are several statutes on the books which require arraignment "forthwith," for example, §595.[154] It should be the duty of the marshal to take defendants before a committing magistrate. The officers disobeyed all of the applicable statutes, in particular §595. Did these statutes establish the policy of the United States, so that we could say that the arresting officer disobeyed it? And did it affect the admissibility of the evidence in violation of those statutes?

In cases of violence against the Fourth Amendment, we keep evidence out. The officers' breach of duty may cause evidence to be excluded, such as wire-tapping and search and seizure. In a case like this one, should we apply the rule? My instincts are outraged by conduct of this kind. Did they warn these men of their constitutional rights? There is a dispute here whether these men were warned of their constitutional rights. One officer said that they did warn them. There is no testimony that the defendants asked for counsel. If you adopt a rule of exclusion, it is difficult to apply here. It is difficult to draw the line. This business of extensive questioning of men under arrest is offensive and dangerous, because it always develops into this sort of thing.

There is also a question of entrapment. Where men are entrapped to crimes, their convictions are not sustained and evidence so obtained will be rejected. I would not put our decision on the Constitution, but on the following: (a) a statutory duty to arraign

---

153. *Chambers v. Florida,* 309 U.S. 227 (1940).

154. 18 U.S.C. §595 required police to take persons in federal custody before the nearest commissioner or other judicial officer "forthwith" for arraignment.

promptly; (b) the conduct here was oppressive; (c) the evidence is untrustworthy; and (d) it is competent for federal court to reject this kind of testimony.

The breach of duty on the part of the officers is serious. This was an extreme violation, and therefore the evidence collected under it should be excluded. Our difficulty is that we haven't a system to provide questioning, and that raises this question.

ROBERTS: There must be some other way of getting at it, rather than punishing the officers. [MURPHY: Roberts mentions Louis Brandeis.] There was a time when this Court was stern about the Fourth and Fifth Amendments. This is different from entrapment. The *Goldman* cases [*sic*] run counter to other cases mentioned by the Chief.[155] If we take the position that we will judge and right the effects of illegal acts, we will have to sit and appraise on a case-by-case basis. We will be sitting and appraising these cases all the time. In the *Lisenba* case, you had a problem involving a denial of constitutional rights.[156] There is no constitutional problem here. Shall we stop here and free thousands that zealous officers have captured? The basis of our excluding evidence is not the likelihood that the evidence is false, but that it is all so offensive we must stop it. It is serious for us to say that this sort of thing turns loose a man regardless of his guilt, because as a matter of practicality they are freed. We ought to sustain their convictions and point out to the Department of Justice to end this sort of practice.

BLACK: Assuming that the practice is bad, it won't be stopped by public sentiment or any man's lawyer. You can't depend on lawyers. If a man has sufficient means and prestige, this won't occur. If he is a man of privilege this doesn't happen. These are hillbilly mountaineers and they are ignorant. They wouldn't have access to legal counsel. The president of a coal mining company would be out in fifteen minutes. It is a potent instrument for convicting great numbers of people. That innocent people can be convicted in this

---

155. In *Goldman v. United States*, 316 U.S. 129 (1942), the Court held that electronic bugs and other listening devices were not regulated by the Communications Act. The Court narrowly interpreted the act to cover only wiretaps and other actual physical manipulations of telephone wires and lines. In *Goldstein v. United States*, 316 U.S. 114 (1942), the Court held that wiretap evidence could be used against third parties, not just against those whose conversations had been monitored.

156. *Lisenba v. California*, 314 U.S. 219 (1941). Major Raymond Lisenba (a.k.a. Robert James) sought to kill his pregnant wife in order to cash in her life insurance policy, which provided double indemnity in the event of accidental death. With the help of an accomplice, Lisenba unsuccessfully tried to kill Mary James with rattlesnakes (the poison was not strong enough) and a purposefully botched abortion operation, before drowning her in the bathtub and placing her body in a fish pond. Police arrested Lisenba and held him incommunicado for three days, interrogating him in shifts. He was deprived of sleep and rest and was physically abused.

Roberts, writing for the Court, noted that the police had committed numerous illegal acts, including failing to bring Lisenba promptly before an examining magistrate, holding him incommunicado for three days, and physically assaulting him. According to Roberts, the police department's lawless practices "took them close to the line" but did not violate due process. The test was whether there had been "a failure of that fundamental fairness essential to the very concept of justice." Roberts noted that Lisenba was intelligent and street-smart. "He exhibited a self-possession, a coolness, and an acumen throughout his questioning, and at his trial, which negatives the view that he had so lost his freedom of action that the statements made were not his but were the result of the deprivation of his free choice to admit, to deny, or to refuse to answer." Black and Douglas dissented.

way outweighs the freeing of a guilty one. It is the extraction of evidence against their will that is contrary to Constitution. *Brown* is the case that covers this.[157] These people were compelled to give evidence against themselves. I would reverse on that ground—that these men were compelled to give evidence against themselves.

ROBERTS: I would put it on due process, not on what you have said.

REED: It is a question of coercion. Disputed questions of fact I leave to the court below. Now in this case, we have undisputed facts. These undisputed facts indicate coercion. Here, there was enough to say that there was coercion here. I would vote to set this aside.

FRANKFURTER: What is relevant for me is that there is great variety of crimes of a criminal nature in all of these states. We are the guardians of the system. The duty and authority of this Court about the federal courts is different than for state courts.

The yardstick is not the Constitution of the United States. I put *Brown* and *Chambers* aside. These cases must not rest on due process and the Bill of Rights. And so far as this case is concerned, we won't affirm a conviction that raises serious doubts. I would rest it on the rules of evidence.

STONE: If you come within the *Chambers* case, you don't need to use a constitutional question to reverse.

JACKSON: I would hate to see constitutional grounds set forth. You have to question men. You have detention rooms in every prison.

STONE: For this case, I would not put this on constitutional grounds. I think that the statutes of the United States are controlling, and we should state that it is their duty to take this man before a magistrate forthwith. This particular case was oppressive.

ROBERTS: The statute about taking a man before magistrates means nothing.

FRANKFURTER: I would put this case on the ground that the prosecution did not put it on certain grounds that met its burden of proof.

REED: It must be on constitutional grounds.

BLACK: The Constitution prohibits a man from incriminating himself involuntarily. Look at the *Brown* case. That is what I think is here. I will never agree that when facts raise doubt, that therefore we set it aside. I go on the ground that these men were compelled to testify against themselves. I would not put it on due process. I believe that Frankfurter's doctrine makes this Court an overlord. While on the other hand, I believe that the Bill of Rights was violated. Contrary to the Fifth Amendment, these people were compelled to incriminate themselves.

---

157. *Brown v. Walker*, 161 U.S. 591 (1896). Justice Henry Brown explained how the right against self-incrimination had grown in the United States from a limited right against abject coercion to a far broader and more humane privilege: "So deeply did the inequities of the ancient system impress themselves upon the minds of the American colonists that the states, with one accord, made a denial of the right to question an accused person a part of their fundamental law, so that a maxim, which in England was a mere rule of evidence, became clothed in this country with the impregnability of a constitutional enactment."

Murphy: I affirm.

[Murphy: All others affirm. Douglas: Reverse. Black: Reverse. Stone: Reverse.]

Result: Felix Frankfurter, writing for a 7–1 Court (Wiley Rutledge did not participate), reversed all three convictions and ordered the exclusion of all incriminating statements made during the course of the three-day interrogation. Frankfurter criticized the federal officers' flagrant disregard for the defendants' statutory right to a prompt arraignment and ruled that the Supreme Court's supervisory powers over the administration of justice empowered to Court to act. Frankfurter's approach avoided the more controversial Fifth Amendment issue. For Frankfurter, however, police abuses of custody and interrogation were fundamentally questions of due process, and "the history of liberty has largely been the history of observance of procedural safeguards."[158] Only Stanley Reed dissented, arguing that the Court was "broadening the possibilities of defendants escaping punishment" by imposing "increasingly rigorous technical requirements" on police and prosecutors.[159]

Ashcraft and Ware v. Tennessee, 322 U.S. 143 (1944)
(Douglas)

Police arrested E. E. Ashcraft for the murder of his wife, Zelma. He was held incommunicado and interrogated for thirty-six consecutive hours until he confessed to hiring John Ware to do the killing. Ware was also arrested and interrogated at length before he confessed. Because Ware was illiterate, he signed his confession with a simple mark. Following a joint trial, both men were sentenced to ninety-nine years in the state penitentiary, and the Tennessee Supreme Court affirmed. On appeal to the Supreme Court, both men claimed that their confessions had been coerced and should have been excluded from evidence.

Conference of March 4, 1944

Stone: There was prolonged questioning of Ashcraft. It is difficult to say that Ware's confession would be inadmissible by itself. The trial court ruled on the voluntary character of his confession and said that it was not coerced. That testimony is not here, but some testimony, the parties say, is in the record on the issue of credibility. This is a somewhat undefined *Chambers* case.[160] The main difficulty is that if Ashcraft's confession goes out, Ware's stays in. I am doubtful if we could reverse both. On that I am not clear. I think that such a procedure as that used against Ashcraft violates due process. He was not allowed to go home. There is a question of how much is too much.

Roberts: I find it difficult to distinguish this case from *Lisenba*.[161] There was no brutality. These are men of intelligence. It is one question to say if his confinement was violative of due process, but it is quite another to say that the use of confession is a lack of due process. We have here a question of state practice. I cannot say that his trial was so utterly reprehensible as to violate due process. I affirm.

---

158. *McNabb v. United States,* 347.
159. Ibid., 349.
160. *Chambers v. Florida,* 309 U.S. 227 (1940).
161. *Lisenba v. California,* 314 U.S. 219 (1941).

BLACK: I reverse.

REED: I reverse and would distinguish *Lisenba*. I would also reverse on *Ware*.

Conference of February 9, 1946

STONE: On retrial the admissions were used. These admissions immediately preceded his confession. It was presented to the jury in such a way as to indicate that he had confessed. I cannot sustain this. It looks like an evasion of our judgment. It is not enough if Ware's confession stood alone to say that it was involuntary. The joint trial is not fatal; that is a matter of discretion. Under state law, they had to be tried together. But the state says that if Ashcraft's conviction is set aside, Ware's should be as well. I reverse.

BLACK: I agree.

REED: I agree.

FRANKFURTER: I dissented in the first case and will leave it to the majority here.

MURPHY: I reverse and think that separate trials should be had.

RUTLEDGE: I reverse.

BURTON: I reverse.

Result: In a 6–3 decision, the Court reversed Ashcraft's conviction outright and vacated Ware's conviction. Hugo Black, writing for the majority, ruled that Ashcraft's confession was coerced in violation of his Fourteenth Amendment due process rights. Ware's case was remanded on the ground that the Tennessee state courts had affirmed his conviction on the mistaken assumption that Ashcraft's confession was voluntary. In dissent, Jackson, Roberts, and Frankfurter argued that both confessions were presumptively valid and that the defendants had not met their burden of proving that their confessions were involuntary.

Mallory v. United States, 354 U.S. 449 (1957)
(Douglas)

Police arrested Andrew Mallory on suspicion of rape early in the afternoon and took him to the police station for questioning. He was not informed of his rights and was not taken before a committing magistrate for arraignment, even though several magistrates were readily available. After a long and intensive interrogation, Mallory confessed that evening at 9:30 P.M. The following morning, Mallory was taken before a magistrate and arraigned. After a brief trial, he was convicted and sentenced to death.

Conference of April 5, 1957

WARREN: I reverse. If we follow the federal government here, we must read "without unnecessary delay" to give the United States the time it wants to get the admissions. A man must be taken as reasonably as possible before a magistrate. In this city there are thirty judges in one building—they held him near this building.

BLACK: I reverse.

FRANKFURTER: I reverse. I query whether we should not pass on the charge.

Douglas: I reverse.

Burton: I affirm. *McNabb* does not require taking this man to a magistrate.[162]

Clark: I reverse. They were close to the courthouse.

Harlan: This is a close case. Three suspects were being held, and the police had discretion to hold them until they spotted the potential defendant. The physical problem of getting a man to a magistrate is not to deceive one. There was no delay here in order to get a confession. *McNabb* is not governing here. The jury charge is O.K. If you add the time of detention to the low intelligence of the petitioner, plus the admission of the confession—on that ground I could reverse.

Brennan: *McNabb* was aimed at the prompt arraignment of an arrested person so that he can have counsel, etc. Unnecessary delay is related simply and solely to that problem. I am opposed to reaching the judge's charge in this case.

Whittaker: I reverse. I would not reach the question of the judge's charge. Rule 5 is a good one.[163] "Unnecessary" relates to all of the circumstances of the case. I do not agree with Brennan that it is merely a question of physical nearness to a magistrate.

Frankfurter: It is not a lack of due process here. *McNabb* goes farther than due process. The place for a preliminary investigation is before the magistrate.

Result: A unanimous Court reversed Mallory's conviction, ruling that his confession could not be used against him in federal court because his detention violated Rule 5(a) of the Federal Rules of Criminal Procedure. The case touched a public nerve, because it reversed the conviction of a rapist on what appeared to be a legal technicality. It did not help that Mallory was black at a time of high white anxiety over interracial crime, or that after being released from prison he committed another series of violent rapes. Andrew Mallory was eventually killed by police in the aftermath of a brutal robbery and sexual assault.

Malloy v. Hogan, 378 U.S. 1 (1964)
(Douglas)

While on probation for a gambling conviction, William Malloy was ordered to testify during a state fact-finding investigation into gambling activities in Hartford County, Connecticut. He refused to testify, citing his right against self-incrimination, but did not explain his reasons for refusing to answer questions put to him. Malloy was held in contempt and imprisoned. The state courts denied Malloy's application for a writ of habeas corpus. Patrick Hogan was the sheriff of Hartford County.

---

162. *McNabb v. United States*, 318 U.S. 332 (1943).

163. Rule 5(a) of the Federal Rules of Criminal Procedure require that persons taken into federal custody must be taken before a committing magistrate or other authorized judicial officer "without unnecessary delay."

Conference of March 6, 1964

WARREN: The Fifth Amendment applies to the states. It is absorbed by the Fourteenth Amendment. We need not go to due process to so hold. This man had a privilege which he exercised—this was a one man grand jury investigating general crimes. The petitioner was already convicted. I reverse.

BLACK: I reverse.

DOUGLAS: Reverse.

CLARK: The petitioner had no ground for apprehending incrimination. It is governed by *Hoffman*, but I would not overrule *Twining* and the rest.[164] I affirm on all grounds.

HARLAN: I affirm. The Fifth Amendment does not apply to the states. This is a due process question. I would not overrule *Twining*. The *Hoffman* test is not met here. There is no indiscriminate use of the legal process in an abusive way.

BRENNAN: I would extend the Fifth Amendment to the states. The federal standard is laid down in *Hoffman*. The questions may be obviously incriminating, so that he need give no explanation, though as respects others I may go on *Pillo*.[165] It was apparent here that they were incriminating. I reverse.

STEWART: The Fifth Amendment comes in through the due process clause, if at all. I affirm.

WHITE: Affirm.

GOLDBERG: I reverse. I agree with the Chief and Bill Brennan.

---

164. *Hoffman v. United States*, 341 U.S. 479 (1951), established a broad definition of "incrimination," extending the Fifth Amendment privilege against self-incrimination beyond answers that would support a criminal conviction to include answers that would furnish a link in the chain of evidence needed to prosecute. Tom Clark, writing for the majority, was willing to acknowledge a broad federal privilege against self-incrimination but did not extend these protections to the states.

Much earlier, in *Twining v. New Jersey*, 211 U.S. 78 (1908), the Court refused to extend Fifth Amendment protections to state criminal trials. Justice William Moody, writing for the Court, allowed a state trial judge to comment on the defendant's failure to testify and to imply that the defendant's silence amounted to an admission of guilt.

165. *In re Pillo*, 11 N.J. 8 (1952). This was a Brennan opinion, written while he was on the New Jersey Supreme Court. After Patsy Pillo refused to answer forty-four questions put to him in a grand jury investigation of local gambling activities, the state sought to compel him to answer a reduced list of thirty-five questions. Brennan reasoned that because the Fifth Amendment had not been applied to the states and the state constitution did not contain a "no self-incrimination" clause, New Jersey's privilege against self-incrimination was statutory rather than constitutional. Under applicable state law, Brennan concluded, grand jury witnesses could remain silent only if there was a "real and appreciable apprehension of danger" of prosecution. Brennan threw out two of the questions because they posed a real and appreciable threat of prosecution but ordered Pillo to answer the remaining thirty-three questions because the questions referred to: (1) earlier events for which the statute of limitations had already passed; or (2) activities for which Pillo had already been convicted, so that any further prosecution was barred by the double jeopardy clause.

Result: In a 5–4 decision, the Court overruled both Twining *and* Adamson v. California, *holding that the Fifth Amendment was applicable to the states via the Fourteenth Amendment. William Brennan, writing for the majority, explained that because the United States had an accusatorial rather than an inquisitorial system, the privilege against self-incrimination was a fundamental and essential part of our legal system. The Court also ruled that all federal standards regarding the right against self-incrimination must also apply to the states. Brennan thought that the* Hoffman *standard was clearly met and that Malloy had no duty to explain his reasons for claiming his Fifth Amendment rights, because any response or explanation could have led to injurious disclosures.*

In dissent, Harlan, Stewart, and Clark warned that the doctrine of selective incorporation would have mischievous, if not dangerous, consequences for the federal system. They argued that the fundamental rights of the accused would be better protected through the due process clause. In a separate dissent, Byron White blasted the majority for turning the Fifth Amendment into a broad and virtually self-defined right. White thought it preferable to allow the trial judge to determine the scope of Malloy's right to remain silent, rather than allowing Malloy to determine the matter for himself and without explanation.

Escobedo v. Illinois, 378 U.S. 478 (1964)
(Douglas)

Danny Escobedo was arrested and interrogated for the fatal shooting of his brother-in-law, Manuel Valtierra. While in custody, Escobedo repeatedly ask to see his lawyer. Even though his lawyer was in the police station trying to reach him, police told Escobedo that his lawyer did not want to see him. After intense questioning, police arranged for Escobedo to meet his suspected accomplice "accidentally" in the hallway. When Escobedo saw Benedict DiGerlando, he shouted, "I didn't shoot Manuel— you did it!" Escobedo later made other incriminating statements, admitting that he had paid DiGerlando $500 to kill Valtierra because he had abused Escobedo's sister, Grace Valtierra.[166] *Escobedo was convicted of murder, and the Illinois Supreme court upheld his conviction.*

Conference of May 1, 1964

WARREN: I reverse. It is not necessary to overrule *Crooker*[167] and *Cicenia.*[168] We can say on the totality of the circumstances that this was a coerced confession. They had prob-

---

166. Grace Valtierra was charged with paying Escobedo and DiGerlando $500 to kill her husband, but was acquitted.

167. *Crooker v. California,* 357 U.S. 433 (1958). Police arrested John Crooker, a thirty-one-year-old college graduate who had attended one year of law school, on suspicion of murdering his estranged girlfriend. Crooker told police that he did not object to talking to them but wanted to talk to a lawyer first. Police refused his request. A police officer advised Crooker that he was not compelled to answer any questions. Questioning was intermittent, and Crooker was provided with food, milk, and cigarettes. He refused to take a lie detector test and refused to answer police questions on several occasions. After fourteen hours in custody, he confessed. Police claimed that his confession was voluntary. Crooker claimed (1) his confession was coerced; or (2) even if his confession was voluntary, the police refusal to honor his request to speak to counsel violated due process. The Court, in a 5–4 opinion by Tom Clark, ruled that Crooker's confession was voluntary and that he had failed to prove that the absence of counsel during interrogation was so prejudicial that it violated rules of fundamental fairness essential to liberty. Douglas, Warren, Black, and Brennan dissented, arguing that the refusal to honor Crooker's repeated requests for counsel violated due process.

168. *Cicenia v. Lagay,* 357 U.S. 504 (1958). Vincent Cicenia had already retained counsel prior to his arrest on a murder charge. After his arrest, police denied him access to counsel until he confessed. Cicenia

able cause to arrest him. His lawyer asked to see him, but they barred the lawyer. The man was deprived of counsel.

BLACK: I can reverse on the counsel point or on the totality.

DOUGLAS: I reverse.

CLARK: I reverse on the totality of the circumstances.

HARLAN: I affirm. We must accept fairly litigated facts. Here, the confession was properly introduced. I won't say that denial of counsel alone was fatal.

BRENNAN: This case requires *Cicenia* and *Crooker* to be overruled. I will not decide it on "totality." We took this case to decide the counsel point, and that's all.

STEWART: A man with a lawyer sitting outside is better off than a man without a lawyer. To reverse here on that ground would require appointment of counsel to everyone once he is arrested. This man had the "advice" of a lawyer—he wants a lawyer actually present. The consequences of that are staggering. I might go along on "totality," but it looks like *Cicenia* to me.

WHITE: I affirm. The principle on counsel is decided by *Massiah*.[169]

GOLDBERG: I reverse and will go along on "totality." On the counsel point, this is a counsel case. He hired a lawyer and the state knew of it—he was involved with the state at that time.

Result: The Court ruled 5–4 that Escobedo's interrogation was not part of a general inquiry into an unsolved case but that the legal process had begun to focus on a particular suspect who was in custody. This meant that the police refusal to allow Escobedo to consult with his lawyer and their failure to warn Escobedo of his right to remain silent violated Escobedo's Sixth and Fourteenth Amendment rights. While none of the Justices switched sides after conference, there was considerable movement within the majority, as the Justices sought a compromise between those who wanted to decide the case on the "totality of the circumstances" and those who wanted to focus solely on Escobedo's right to counsel.[170] Goldberg wrote the majority opinion, and Harlan, Clark, Stewart, and White dissented.

This was a narrow case in terms of precedent, because it applied only to defendants who already had lawyers and had asked to see them. But it set the stage for a broader ruling defining the rights of the accused. That day came two years later, after police in Phoenix, Arizona, found a stolen 1953 Packard parked in front of Ernesto Miranda's house.

---

argued that police violated his right to counsel and that his conviction violated due process. Harlan, writing for a 5–3 majority (Brennan did not participate), ruled that Cicenia's confession was voluntary and that he was not denied due process.

169. *Massiah v. United States*, 377 U.S. 201 (1964).

170. Subsequently, Escobedo was convicted numerous times on a variety of drug charges, weapons violations, violent assaults, and child molestation. His last conviction, for attempted murder, was in 1987.

Miranda v. Arizona, 384 U.S. 436 (1966)
Vignera v. New York
Westover v. Unites States
California v. Stewart
Johnson v. New Jersey, 384 U.S. 719 (1966)
(Douglas) (Brennan)

Eleven days after an eighteen-year-old Phoenix woman was kidnapped and raped, police found her 1953 Packard parked in front of Ernesto A. Miranda's house. The victim picked Miranda out of a lineup, and following a routine two-hour interrogation Miranda confessed.[171] Miranda's lawyer acknowledged that there had been no physical coercion during the interrogation but argued that Miranda had not been informed of his rights and had waived them without knowing the consequences of his decision.

By the time the case reached the Supreme Court, it included similar interrogation cases from California, Missouri, New Jersey, and New York. In each case the suspects had been questioned without being warned of their constitutional rights, and in each case the suspects made incriminating statements used against them at trial.

Conference of March 18, 1966

WARREN: [DOUGLAS: The Chief reads a printed statement he had prepared.] I do not accept New York's approach that this is a legislative problem only. I do not accept the Solicitor General's view that "totality" governs.[172] Basically, the issue is under the Fifth Amendment and "being a witness against himself." It also might be under the Sixth Amendment, in case there was a lawyer being sought. The right against interrogation involves the Fifth Amendment. Talking to the police is different from being interrogated by the police. The right to counsel commences at least when a man is taken into custody, or when police undertake to put him there. Our system is accusatory; there is no right to arrest for investigation, only on probable cause or with a warrant. His right to counsel commences at that moment—the case commences then. This does not mean that a lawyer must be appointed then, but later—interrogation is such a "later" time. He must be advised (1) of his right to remain silent; (2) that what he says may be used against him; (3) that in time the court may appoint a lawyer; (4) he must be given an opportunity to get a lawyer before he is interrogated, unless he waives that right; (5) the burden is on the government to show a waiver; and (6) no distinction should be made between one who has a lawyer and one who does not, or between one who can hire one and one who can-

---

171. There was ample evidence to prosecute Miranda without his confession, but police routinely sought confessions to encourage defendants to plead guilty and avoid the time and expense of jury trials.

172. Solicitor General Thurgood Marshall argued in favor of retaining the *Escobedo* standard of using the totality of the circumstances to determine whether incriminating statements were made voluntarily. Marshall also argued that the government had no duty to provide counsel to indigents during custodial interrogations.

not. *Gideon* controls this case. The routine of "booking" is not a violation of the Fifth Amendment. I would follow *Linkletter* and not make it retroactive.[173]

The solicitor general's letter on FBI practice states my views down to the point where the man does not have a lawyer. The FBI leaves it to the discretion of the agent whether there has been a "waiver," but I do not agree with that. I reverse in *Miranda*. There was no warning by police. I also reverse in *Vignera* on the same ground, plus the fact that the state barred the petitioner from proving at trial that no warnings were given. In *Westover*, I reverse because he was not advised of his right to counsel. In *Johnson*, I affirm. The rule is not retroactive, and also there was no involuntariness issue, as it was waived at trial. In *California v. Stewart*, I affirm on the failure to give adequate warnings.

BLACK: I agree with a large part of what the Chief says. But I think that the focus is on the privilege against being a witness against one's self. Look at the Magna Carta. The right to counsel comes in as to a confession as having a bearing on whether the confession was taken in defiance of this privilege. A man is entitled to all of the benefits of a defendant when the government moves against him. I said in *Ashcraft v. Tennessee* that this act was "inherently coercive," and that thereafter you can't make him be a witness against himself.[174] He has a constitutional right not to be witness against himself. There is no right of questioning while he is in custody. When a man is in custody, he is a witness against himself. I am not sure at that stage whether he can be put into a lineup or fingerprinted. When arrested, he cannot be asked questions—you can't get him a lawyer then. I think that it is coercion. I give no credence to "warning the accused." I would reverse all of these cases, except *California v. Stewart*.[175] I will probably go along in affirming *Johnson*, though at least for now I will vote to reverse.

DOUGLAS: I agree largely with the Chief, but I think that this is a critical stage and is largely, therefore, a right to counsel case.

CLARK: I am pretty close to the Chief. When does government "move" against a suspect? When you put it under the Fifth Amendment, you must put it under "interrogation." We do not have to pass on investigation, fingerprinting, lineup, or photography issues here. Once the police are thinking of interrogation, they must warn him on (1) his right to silence; (2) anything he says can be used against him; (3) he can have a lawyer; (4) he is entitled to court-appointed counsel if he can't afford one. But statements not

173. *Linkletter v. Walker*, 381 U.S. 618 (1965). This case established new guidelines concerning the retroactivity of Supreme Court decisions in criminal cases. Whether decisions would be applied retroactively depended on two factors: (1) reliance placed on the previous view of the law; and (2) the effect that retroactivity would have on the administration of justice.

Linkletter was later overruled by *Griffith v. Kentucky*, 479 U.S. 314 (1987). The Court eliminated the Linkletter test and said that Supreme Court decisions in criminal cases would be applied retroactively to all criminal cases pending on direct review at the time that the new rule was announced.

174. *Ashcraft v. Tennessee*, 322 U.S. 143 (1944).

175. In *California v. Stewart*, 400 P.2d 97 (Cal. 1965), the California Supreme Court reversed Roy Stewart's capital murder conviction on the ground that there was no evidence to indicate that he had been informed of his right to remain silent or his right to counsel and that the state had failed to meet its burden to prove that Stewart had voluntarily and knowingly waived his rights.

elicited by interrogation should not be barred. In *Stewart*, the record is silent. The burden is on the state to show a waiver.

HARLAN: What the Chief Justice, Hugo, and Bill Douglas have said repudiate all of our precedents and history and the American Bar Association proposals. I would leave law reforms to others who have more information and ability. Our conference room is in an abstract medium—I can't see why we should reverse the course of history and make these radical changes. All of the studies that are going on will become abortive. I am not prepared to slam the door on more deliberation and more empirical data being assembled. What we do, if the Chief's views obtain a majority, should be done by constitutional amendment. I would modify *Linkletter* to make this new rule applicable only to cases that start *after these decisions*.

BRENNAN: I agree substantially with the Chief. I would make the new rule applicable to all pending cases, not just to these five alone. As for the timing of the warning, if you wait until "interrogation," rather than arrest, you will get into difficulties. "Focus" on him is not enough. When he is arrested is the better test. As to retroactivity, we might make them apply back to the date of *Malloy*.[176] In *Tehan*,[177] we made it retroactive from the date of *Griffin*.[178] Perhaps it should be made retroactive to *Escobedo*.[179]

STEWART: I disagree with the Chief. The privilege against self-incrimination is only a testimonial privilege. "Compulsion" is not present here within the framework of our coerced confession cases. "Compelling" means only coerced statements. I would stick to the totality of facts on coercion. I more or less agree with John Harlan.

WHITE: I also disagree with the Chief Justice, and agree with John and Potter.

FORTAS: In general, I agree with the Chief.

Result: The Court ruled that incommunicado interrogations were inherently coercive and jeopardized suspects' Fifth Amendment rights. Writing for a 5–1–3 majority, Chief Justice Warren held that prosecutors could not use incriminating statements resulting from a police interrogation initiated while the person was in custody or otherwise deprived of liberty in any significant way, unless the state could demonstrate the use of effective procedural safeguards to secure the suspect's Fifth Amendment rights against self-incrimination. Absent other effective procedural safeguards, suspects must be clearly warned

---

176. *Malloy v. Hogan*, 378 U.S. 1 (1964), extended the Fifth Amendment to cover defendants in state trials.

177. *Tehan v. United States ex rel. Shott*, 382 U.S. 406 (1965). In a state criminal trial, Ohio prosecutors commented to the jury extensively about defendant Edgar Shott's decision not to testify at his own trial. Shott was convicted, and in 1963 his conviction was affirmed on appeal. After the Supreme Court subsequently prohibited state prosecutors from commenting on a defendant's failure to testify in *Griffin v. California* (1965), Shott applied for a writ of habeas corpus, claiming that his conviction should also be reversed. The Court ruled 5–4 that *Griffin* would not be applied retroactively to 1963 and that defendants who had exhausted their direct appeals prior to 1965 could not take advantage of the rule change. Black and Douglas dissented, arguing that *anyone* who had been imprisoned as the result of an unconstitutional conviction should have their convictions set aside. Dan Tehan was the sheriff of Hamilton County.

178. *Griffin v. California*, 380 U.S. 609 (1965).

179. *Escobedo v. Illinois*, 378 U.S. 478 (1964).

that (1) they have a right to remain silent; (2) anything they say can be used against them; (3) they have a right to consult a lawyer; (4) they have a right to have their lawyer present during questioning; and (5), if they are indigent, a lawyer will be appointed to represent them.

Warren's first draft opinion focused on racial aspects of police interrogations and police brutality. William Brennan convinced Warren that class, not race, was the real problem—that the rights of the rich and the privileged were generally respected, while the rights of the poor and uneducated were constantly at risk.[180]

Despite Tom Clark's significant contributions in conference to the formulation of the majority opinion, he ultimately refused to join Warren's opinion, claiming that it went "too far, too fast." Clark, however, was equally critical of the three dissenters for not going far enough, fast enough. A week after Miranda *was announced, the Court decided that it would not apply the new rule retroactively to challenge convictions obtained before June 13, 1966.*[181]

Ernesto Miranda was retried without any reference to his confession. He was convicted and sentenced to thirty years in prison. After he was paroled in 1972, he spent much of his time in local bars, selling autographed Miranda cards for a dollar or two apiece. Four years after being released from prison, he was stabbed to death in a bar fight. The suspect was dutifully read his rights in both English and Spanish and exercised his right to remain silent. When he was released from custody, he quickly disappeared, and no one was ever charged in the killing of Ernesto Miranda.

Michigan v. Mosley, 423 U.S. 96 (1975)
(Brennan)

Richard Mosley was arrested in connection with a robbery. Officer James Cowie of the Robbery Bureau read Mosley his rights and began to question him. When Mosley said that he did not want to talk, Cowie promptly ended the interrogation. Two hours later, in another part of the courthouse, Officer Hill of the Homicide Bureau again read Mosley his rights and questioned him about another robbery and murder. Mosley made some incriminating statements that were used against him at his subsequent murder trial. He was convicted, but the Michigan Court of Appeals reversed on the ground that Mosley's initial assertion of his right to remain silent tainted the second interrogation.

BURGER: This was all done in the same court house, on a different floor, with a second detective. They knew that Mosley had said that he would not talk about the robberies, yet they questioned him about a killing during the course of a robbery. *Santobello.*[182] The

---

180. When actress Hedy Lamarr was arrested later the same year for shoplifting, columnist Drew Pearson wrote a sympathetic column that excused her behavior as a symptom of "a disease with which some people are afflicted." Warren retorted, "When poor people are afflicted with the disease they are jailed. Richer people are given a chance to return the property." Cray, *Chief Justice,* 459.

181. *Johnson v. New Jersey,* 384 U.S. 719 (1966).

182. *Santobello v. New York,* 404 U.S. 257 (1971). After prosecutors broke several promises made in a plea bargain agreement with Rudolph Santobello, the trial judge sentenced Santobello to the maximum jail term allowed by law. Santobello immediately sought to withdraw his guilty plea, but the trial judge refused and his decision was affirmed on appeal. The Supreme Court unanimously reversed and remanded. Warren Burger wrote that the interests of justice demanded that the state courts would have to decide whether (1) the prosecutors' promises should be specifically enforced; or (2) Santobello should be allowed to withdraw his guilty plea and proceed to trial.

Michigan court adopted a per se rule. This is no occasion to overrule *Miranda*. I can go along with a narrow basis, like Lewis suggests.

STEWART: It is wholly consistent with *Miranda* to reverse this for consideration of other issues not decided by the state court of appeals. It could have been proper for the first detective to question Mosley about the murder after stopping questions about robberies.

WHITE: Mosley said that he did not want to talk about any robbery, and the second detective opened up a robbery during which a killing occurred. This was more than dictum. I am no fan of *Miranda*, and I am willing to say if the warnings were given, the question then becomes the totality of the circumstances to say whether his will was overborne. Otherwise, I would affirm. So would I overrule *Miranda*, at least to the extent of the issue of voluntariness after the first warnings were given.

MARSHALL: The FBI rules for interrogation should have been adopted in toto by *Miranda*.

BLACKMUN: The Michigan court's per se rule is wrong—indeed, it is way far out. This is no case, however, to overrule *Miranda*. I prefer deciding this case on its own facts, emphasizing that Officer Cowie honored Mosley's refusal to talk about robberies, but Officer Hill of Homicide asked about the murder even though it was related to another robbery. I would remand for a decision of other issues, including totality.

POWELL: I also disagree with the per se rule. *Miranda* says that even if an interrogation goes on (4 of 5) there is a heavy burden on the state to show the voluntariness of the waiver. So we can decide this case within the framework of *Miranda* without overruling or qualifying that decision.

REHNQUIST: I can go for Lewis's position that the question, after the first warnings were given, is whether there was a voluntary waiver of his *Miranda* rights.

Result: Without a majority to overrule Miranda, *Potter Stewart, writing for a 5–1–2 majority, tried to reconcile the two cases by claiming that police conduct in this case was consistent with* Miranda. *Stewart stressed three facts: (1) that the police had respected Mosley's wishes to stop the initial interrogation; (2) that there had been a significant lapse of time between the two interrogations; and (3) that fresh* Miranda *warnings were given before the second interrogation. White concurred in the judgment, while Brennan and Marshall dissented for a short-handed Court.*[183]

Brewer v. Williams, 430 U.S. 387 (1977)

(Brennan)

Robert Anthony Williams, an escapee from a Missouri state mental hospital, surrendered to police in Davenport, Iowa, and was charged in the disappearance of ten-year-old Pamela Powers. Powers had vanished without a trace from the Des Moines YWCA on Christmas Eve, 1968. Williams's lawyer, Henry McKnight, talked to Williams by telephone from Des Moines and advised Williams not to talk to police until he was transferred to Des Moines and could confer with McKnight in person.

---

183. Douglas had suffered a debilitating stroke several months earlier and was unable to participate. He resigned from the Court on November 12, 1975, a little more than a month after oral arguments in this case.

The two detectives who transported Williams to Des Moines promised not to question him en route, but drove well out of their way to take a remote road through the woods where they thought the girl's body might be. Detective Cletus Leaming knew that Williams was deeply religious. He called Williams "Reverend," and the two officers talked in his hearing about how badly everyone wanted to find Pamela's body. The poor little girl, Leaming said, had been abducted and murdered on Christmas Eve, her body abandoned somewhere in the cold and snowy woods. Pamela and her family were all good Christians, the detective continued, and the girl deserved a good Christian burial. Leaming also expressed concern that if the search teams did not locate her body that evening, they might never find it, because a big snowstorm was due that night. Williams broke down and told the detectives where to find Pamela's body. He was convicted of first-degree murder, and the Iowa Supreme Court affirmed.

Williams filed for a writ of habeas corpus in federal court, claiming that he had been denied assistance of counsel under the Sixth and Fourteenth Amendments. The district court agreed and ruled that any evidence found as a result of the detective's "Christian burial speech" could not be used against Williams at trial. The court of appeals affirmed.

BURGER: Despite the state supreme court's affirmance, and without the record, the habeas court arrived at different conclusions. That violated §2254(d), because it ignored the state court's findings. I would apply *Stone v. Powell.*[184] Also, I would either reverse or remand with directions. I would not overrule *Miranda* when the system has adjusted to it.[185]

STEWART: This is like the *Massiah* case, and I would affirm.[186] I thought that *Stone v. Powell* dealt only with the Fourth Amendment.

WHITE: The court of appeals did not reach the issue of voluntariness and neither would I. But as long as *Massiah* is law, this was tantamount to an interrogation.

MARSHALL: On *Massiah.*

BLACKMUN: The police used tactics that were subtle, but they gave three *Miranda* warnings. We don't have to overrule *Miranda*. I don't think that Williams waived his right to be free of interrogation, but I would accept the state court's finding that it was not interrogation. I would reverse and remand.

POWELL: *Stone v. Powell* did not reach the Fifth or Sixth Amendments, only the Fourth Amendment. I took the case because I thought that the Fifth Amendment laid down a per se rule that after warnings, you can't ever interrogate. This is not my reading now. If there ever was a case with lawyers at both ends, this was it. And there was an interrogation as I saw it, and I would affirm. *United States v. Pheaster* and *Inciso*, Aug. 19, 1976, Renfrew, J.[187]

184. *Stone v. Powell,* 428 U.S. 465 (1976).
185. *Miranda v. Arizona,* 384 U.S. 436 (1966).
186. *Massiah v. United States,* 377 U.S. 201 (1964).
187. *United States v. Pheaster* and *United States v. Inciso,* 544 F.2d 353 (CA 9th 1976). District Judge Charles Renfrew of the Northern District of California wrote the majority in this 3–1 decision. Hugh Macleod Pheaster was a suspect in a kidnapping and murder case. After his arrest, the FBI ignored his request to have his lawyer present during questioning. An agent interrogated Pheaster while transporting him by car by a long, circuitous route to the county jail. The interrogation consisted mostly of the agent talking about the evidence against him and asking him where the victim was. Pheaster made several incriminating statements and showed police where to find physical evidence of the crime.

REHNQUIST: This was neither a *Miranda* nor a right of counsel violation, nor any assur-
ances. But I could remand on the issue of voluntariness.

STEVENS: In view of their assurance not to interrogate him, he had a right to counsel
during the trip. I would be bothered at the notion that *Stone v. Powell* might be extended
here. On the interrogation finding, the two-court finding is that there was something
tantamount to an interrogation.

*Result: In a 5–4 decision, the Supreme Court agreed that Williams had been deprived of his Sixth Amend-
ment right to counsel. Writing for the majority, Potter Stewart ruled that police had deliberately elicited
incriminating information in a manner that was "tantamount to interrogation," despite Williams's
consistent assertions that he wanted to exercise his right to counsel. The constitutional violations in this
case, Stewart said, were simply too serious to ignore. But Williams was not out of the woods yet.*

Nix v. Williams, 467 U.S. 431 (1984)
(Brennan)

*In Brewer v. Williams, the Court ruled that while Robert Williams's statements could not be used
against him, other nontestimonial evidence—such as the condition and location of Pamela Powers's
body—might be admissible on a theory of "inevitable discovery."[188] Williams was retried and again
convicted of first-degree murder, and the state supreme court affirmed. On a federal writ of habeas
corpus the court of appeals reversed, ruling that even assuming the existence of an inevitable discovery
exception, the state had failed to prove that the police had not acted in bad faith.*

*Note in conference how the Justices struggled to define "inevitable" discovery. Chief Justice Burger
defined it as "a reasonable probability" of discovery, while John Paul Stevens and Sandra Day O'Connor
thought that it meant a "preponderance of the evidence" test.*

BURGER: Was evidence of the girl's body properly admitted? This raises the inevitable
discovery exception. If there was a reasonable probability of discovery, we should admit
the evidence. If good faith required, kill off. I could also extend *Stone v. Powell* to foreclose habeas on Sixth Amendment cases. *Rose v. Mitchell* refused to extend *Stone v. Powell*
on grand jury selection, but that's distinguishable.[189]

The government, Judge Renfrew said, had the heavy burden to demonstrate that Pheaster had knowingly and intelligently waived his right to remain silent and his right to counsel. Renfrew found that the government met its burden and that Pheaster had voluntarily waived his right to counsel, in spite of his earlier
request for a lawyer. Renfrew distinguished interrogation from merely "presenting the evidence available" to
a suspect in an objective and undistorted way. Renfrew also ruled that repeatedly asking Pheaster where the
victim was less an interrogation than a reflection of "the agent's justifiable concern for the [victim's] safety."

188. *Brewer v. Williams*, 430 U.S. 387 (1977).

189. *Rose v. Mitchell*, 443 U.S. 545 (1979). James Mitchell and James Nichols sought in a habeas corpus
proceeding to have their murder indictments dismissed on the ground that grand jury foremen in Tipton
County, Tennessee, were selected in a racially discriminatory manner. The Court ruled that allegations of
racial discrimination in grand jury selection procedures could be litigated in habeas proceedings even where
there were no constitutional problems with the petit jury and where the defendants were convicted following a fair trial. The majority, led by Harry Blackmun, ruled that the costs of permitting a federal court
to interfere in state criminal proceedings were outweighed by the need to combat racism in the administration of justice. Blackmun distinguished *Stone v. Powell*, saying that racial discrimination in grand jury

BRENNAN:[190] It seems clear to me that the language of the Sixth Amendment *compels* the exclusion of evidence acquired as a result of an interrogation at which a defendant's lawyer is not present. Therefore, our authority to refine the rule of exclusion is quite constrained, both as to an inevitable discovery rule and as to remedying Sixth Amendment violations in habeas corpus proceedings.

The Sixth Amendment provides that: "In all criminal prosecutions, the accused shall enjoy the right . . . to have the Assistance of Counsel for his defense." If an accused has been questioned without the assistance of counsel but he is never tried, or the evidence is never introduced at his trial, there has been no Sixth Amendment violation. *Massiah* and *Weatherford* support this view.[191] Instead, the violation of the Sixth Amendment occurs when the non-counsel-assisted questioning is used to promote the "prosecution." In this case, that would occur when the result of that questioning—the girl's body—is introduced at trial. At that point, the accused can no longer be said to have enjoyed the right to assistance of counsel for his defense in a criminal prosecution. That is, without the exclusion of evidence, there is a *direct constitutional violation*. Therefore, the exclusion of non-counsel-assisted evidence serves the purpose of *preventing a violation*, not of providing a remedy for a violation that has already occurred. As a result, an inevitable discovery rule could be adopted only under the rationale that the non-counsel-assisted interrogation did not really *cause* the discovery of evidence at issue. That was the rationale of the independent source rule applied in *Wade*.[192]

---

selection procedures violated a direct command of the equal protection clause, while *Stone v. Powell* involved the exclusionary rule. The Court, however, found that Mitchell and Nicols had not made out a prima facie case of discrimination and rejected their petitions for habeas corpus—in effect, affirming their convictions.

190. Adapted from Brennan's talking papers, Brennan Papers, OT 1983, box 655.

191. *Massiah v. United States*, 377 U.S. 201 (1964); *Weatherford v. Bursey*, 429 U.S. 545 (1977). *Weatherford* was a criminal case involving a vandalized selective service office. Bursey, one of the defendants, met several times to discuss trial strategies with his lawyer and a "co-defendant," who was actually a government undercover agent. Bursey claimed that the agent's attendance at these confidential meetings deprived him of effective assistance of counsel and violated due process. The Court ruled that even though the agent testified against Bursey at trial, there had been no constitutional violation because: (1) the agent attended the meetings only to protect his secret identity; (2) the agent communicated nothing to prosecutors about the defendant's trial strategy; (3) the agent's testimony related only to events prior to the meetings in question; and (4) none of the state's evidence was obtained through the agent's attendance at these meetings.

In dissent, Brennan and Marshall argued that it was essential to prohibit all intrusions into confidential lawyer-client communications and that providing relief only when defendants could prove bad intent or actual disclosure of damaging information was only a little better than having no rule at all.

192. *United States v. Wade*, 388 U.S. 218 (1967). In a federal bank robbery case, Billy Joe Wade was placed with others in a lineup and required to say the same words that witnesses said the robbers used. Wade's court-appointed lawyer was not permitted to attend the lineup. Several witnesses identified Wade at the lineup and again identified him in open court. The Supreme Court ruled that Wade had the right to counsel at the postindictment lineup. Because unconstitutional lineup procedures were used, the question remained of whether the subsequent in-court identifications were also tainted. The Court ruled that the in-court identifications had to be suppressed unless the government could show by clear and convincing evidence that: the in-court identifications had independent origins from the tainted lineup or that the government's use of the tainted evidence amounted to harmless error.

In the context of the independent source rule, there is no real problem of the police purposefully engaging in constitutional violations *in reliance* on the expectation that later developments will allow the admissibility of the fruits of their violations. That, however, is quite possible under an inevitable discovery rule.

Finally, because the exclusion of evidence is compelled by the Sixth Amendment, we cannot extend *Stone v. Powell* to this case.[193] *Stone v. Powell* was based on the view that the exclusionary rule in the Fourth Amendment context is a "judicially created" remedy designed to deter Fourth Amendment violations. Based on that view, the Court felt free to weigh the deterrent value of extending the rule to habeas corpus proceedings against the cost of extending the rule. None of that has any relevance where the purpose of the exclusion is to avoid a constitutional violation.

WHITE: I agree with the Chief Justice. I would reverse on inevitable discovery. I don't think that good faith is relevant.

MARSHALL: I agree with Bill Brennan.

BLACKMUN: I would adopt the inevitable discovery exception. We can protect defendants' Sixth Amendment rights by (a) putting clear and convincing burden on government; (b) imposing a good faith requirement to deter future violations; (c) *Harlow v Fitzgerald* points to objective standard that government proves no objective bad faith.[194] I would not extend *Stone v. Powell*, because exclusion is constitutionally required.[195]

POWELL: I agree that the inevitable discovery exception is appropriate where there is almost volition, as here. We don't need to get to *Stone v. Powell*.

REHNQUIST: Good faith is irrelevant in applying the inevitable discovery rule. I can reverse on that, but I could also extend *Stone v. Powell*.

STEVENS: *Brewer* approved the inevitable discovery rule and I joined it. I don't think that the officers' good faith is relevant to such an inquiry. We should remand the case to decide the inevitable discovery issue. What is the burden? I would not require clear and convincing proof. I would adopt a preponderance test that the body inevitably would be discovered—*not* "more probably than not."

O'CONNOR: I am willing to extend *Stone v. Powell*. I recognize the inevitability of *Brewer*. The lower courts found this as a fact. The preponderance standard suffices, and good faith is irrelevant.

Result: On a 6–1–2 vote, the Court affirmed the inevitable discovery exception to the exclusionary rule. Warren Burger, writing for the majority, emphasized that the state was not required to prove an absence of bad faith by the police. The state had to establish, by a preponderance of the evidence, that the incriminating information would inevitably have been discovered by lawful means. The Court found that the massive volunteers' search was sufficient proof that Pamela Powers's body eventually

---

193. *Stone v. Powell*, 428 U.S. 465 (1976).
194. *Harlow v. Fitzgerald*, 457 U.S. 800 (1982).
195. *Stone v. Powell*, 428 U.S. 465 (1976).

*would have been recovered. John Paul Stevens concurred in the result but did not join Burger's major-
ity opinion. Brennan and Marshall dissented.*

New York v. Quarles, 467 U.S. 649 (1984)
(Brennan)

*A woman approached several New York police officers in Queens and told them that she had just been
raped. She described her attacker, told them that he had a gun, and said that she had seen him walk
into a nearby supermarket. When Officer Frank Kraft spotted Benjamin Quarles inside the store,
Quarles ran. During the chase, Kraft temporarily lost sight of Quarles before capturing him. Kraft
frisked Quarles and found an empty holster. After handcuffing Quarles, Kraft asked where the gun
was. Quarles said, "It's over there," and pointed to some nearby cartons. Officer Kraft found and secured
the gun, then arrested Quarles and read him his rights. Quarles waived his rights and made several
incriminating statements.*

*During a preliminary hearing on weapon charges (rape and sodomy charges were dropped after
the woman refused to file charges), the trial judge, Nicholas Ferraro, suppressed Quarles's initial statement and the gun after ruling that both had been obtained in violation of Quarles's* Miranda *rights.
The later statements were also excluded because they were tainted by the initial* Miranda *violation.
Prosecutors suspended the case to appeal the trial judge's ruling. The New York Court of Appeals affirmed. In conference, a clear majority wanted to reverse but could not agree on how to proceed.*

BURGER: Can exigent circumstances excuse a failure to give *Miranda* warnings, and in
any event can physical evidence be excluded, as it was here? The respondent was in custody, but in that setting it was natural for the officer to ask where the gun was. He was
also interrogated within the rules we established in *Innis*.[196] I think that we should craft
an exception to *Miranda* for exigent circumstances, but I would not overrule *Miranda*. I
could reverse by extending the *Terry* principle or I could reverse on the ground that
nontestimonial fruits of a *Miranda* violation need not be suppressed.[197]

BRENNAN:[198] I do not find it necessary to think of this case as one in which *Miranda*
would serve a merely "prophylactic" purpose. The police had Quarles in handcuffs and
presumably had their guns drawn when they asked him: "Where is the gun?" When the
police ask a question like that while in essence putting a gun to your head, and later charge
you with gun possession, I think it is as plain as can be that they thereby compel you to
be a witness against yourself within the terms of the Fifth Amendment.

The solicitor general invites us to make an exception for this case because of "exigent
circumstances," or the fact that the question was asked "incident to arrest." It seems to
me that any such exception will only complicate the policeman's life and undermine one
of *Miranda*'s principal virtues: simple and clear application.

The New York Court of Appeals was, in my judgment, plainly right to exclude the
statement. There can be no serious argument that the gun was obtained as a result of

---

196. *Rhode Island v. Innis*, 446 U.S. 291 (1980).
197. *Terry v. Ohio*, 392 U.S. 1 (1968).
198. Adapted from Brennan's talking papers, Brennan Papers, OT 1983, box 652.

that statement, and I therefore believe the court of appeals was right to suppress that as well.

I should add that, if we decide to adopt an inevitable discovery rule in *Nix v Williams*, I would be willing to remand this case for application of that rule here. Under these facts, I think the state would have little trouble establishing that without regard to Quarles's sstatement, they would have found the gun hidden a few feet away.

WHITE: *Orozco* and another case took *Miranda* out of the station house and the focus came to whether information was obtained under coercive circumstances.[199] But the statement was admissible, and in any event the gun is admissible as a non-testimonial fruit and also under the doctrine of inevitable discovery.

MARSHALL: This is like a res gestae case, but I will find some way to affirm. He was under arrest.

BLACKMUN: The public safety interest is compelling here. This "custody" is not the *Miranda* type—this was a spontaneous question incident to an arrest. We would not have to reach either inevitable discovery or admissibility of the gun.

POWELL: I would have a per se rule that a cop learning that a weapon is in the vicinity should be *required* to ask this question. It would be gross negligence on his part not to ask this question in his own interest and for public safety. We don't have to cut back on *Miranda* to do that.

REHNQUIST: This is res gestae, and that is the key to reversal here—it is incident to arrest, as the solicitor general argues.[200]

STEVENS: The arrest was not a very pretty site [*sic*]. And if they know of a gun, they should go after it. Under the inevitable discovery suggestion, that is easy. But the answer here was a compelled answer. On inevitable discovery, that question is not before us, and at best we should remand.

O'CONNOR: I would affirm as to his answer to the gun question—that was compelled. However, that does not require the suppression of non-testimonial fruits.

Result: The Court ruled 5–1–3 that all of the evidence against Quarles was admissible. Concern for public safety, William Rehnquist wrote for the majority, must take precedence over the literal lan-

---

199. *Orozco v. Texas*, 394 U.S. 324 (1969). In a murder investigation, police went to Reyes Orozco's boardinghouse and rousted him from his bedroom at 4:00 A.M. Without giving any *Miranda* warnings, four police officers interrogated Orozco in his bedroom, and he gave incriminating answers that were used against him at trial. In a 6–2 decision (Fortas did not participate), the Court reversed Orozco's conviction and extended *Miranda* to cover all custodial interrogations, not just those conducted inside police stations. White and Stewart dissented, protesting the majority's "unwarranted" extension of *Miranda*.

The second case to which White referred in conference was probably *Mathis v. United States*, 391 U.S. 1 (1968). In that case, the Court extended *Miranda* to cover government interrogation of a person who was already confined in a state prison on another charge.

200. Solicitor General Rex Lee. David A. Strauss argued the case on behalf of the United States as amicus curiae.

guage of Miranda. *With this case the Court created the so-called public safety exception to* Miranda, *where questions asked to secure the safety of officers or the public are permitted, as long as they are not designed solely to elicit testimonial evidence. Sandra Day O'Connor concurred in part and dissented in part. She would have admitted the gun as nontestimonial evidence but felt compelled by precedent to suppress Quarles's initial statement because it violated* Miranda. *Brennan and Marshall dissented.*

Oregon v. Elstad, 470 U.S. 298 (1985)
(Brennan)

Eighteen-year-old Michael Elstad was suspected of burglarizing a neighbor's home and stealing $150,000 worth of art. A police officer went to the Elstad family home and, without giving Miranda *warnings, briefly questioned Elstad and told him that he believed that Elstad was involved in the burglary.*[201] *Elstad admitted, "Yes, I was there." Elstad was later read his* Miranda *rights, but he waived them and signed a written confession.*

At a pretrial suppression hearing, the trial court excluded Elstad's first statement because it had been obtained in violation of Miranda, *but allowed the written confession on the ground that Elstad had been Mirandized and had volunarily and knowingly waived his rights before signing the confession. The state court of appeals reversed, ruling that both statements should have been excluded. After the first inadmissible confession, the court said, "the cat was out of the bag," and police impermissibly used that knowledge to coerce Elstad into signing the second confession.*

BURGER: It was not an admission of guilt, but it was certainly more than an admission simply that he was there. His second confession was made after a proper warning. The Constitution forbids only "compelled" confessions. Anyway, there was no real "fruit" here. More broadly, fruits are admissible if the first statement was not exploited. I would not overrule *Miranda*, but I won't expand it.

BRENNAN:[202] First, as John Stevens noted during oral argument, the central question here is whether a *Miranda* violation is a *constitutional* violation to which fruit-of-the-poisonous-tree principles should apply, or rather whether it is a mere "procedural" failure to follow "prophylactic" guidelines. With all due respect to the Court's suggestions in *Michigan v. Tucker* and *New York v. Quarles*, the only principled conclusion is that a *Miranda* violation is a violation of the Fifth Amendment.[203] *Miranda* did not promulgate a code of judicially preferred interrogation procedures—a function this Court is powerless to perform. Rather, it set forth "*constitutional* standards for protection of the privilege" against self-incrimination.[204] We held there that custodial interrogations are *presumptively* coercive. We held that the Fifth Amendment not only requires that a boy like Michael Elstad be able to remain silent if he wishes, but that he *knows* that he has such a right. We held that a boy like Elstad not only has the right to consult with counsel, but that the Constitution requires that he must *know* that he has this right.

---

201. *Miranda v. Arizona*, 384 U.S. 436 (1966).
202. Adapted from Brennan's talking papers, Brennan Papers, OT 1984, box 675.
203. *Michigan v. Tucker*, 417 U.S. 433 (1974); *New York v. Quarles*, 467 U.S. 649 (1984).
204. *Miranda v. Arizona*, 384 U.S. 436, 491 (1966).

As the majority in *Tucker* and *Quarles* observed, we did state in *Miranda* that "the Constitution (does not) necessarily require . . . adherence to any *particular* solution for the inherent compulsions of the interrogation process." But this does not mean that *Miranda* was a mere prophylactic. We went on to emphasize that "unless we are shown other procedures which are at least as effective in *apprising accused persons of their right of silence and in assuring a continuous opportunity to exercise it*, the . . . safeguards [we set forth] must be observed." *That* is the *constitutional* requirement of *Miranda*—that an accused have *knowledge* of his rights. There is nothing "procedural" or "prophylactic" about this requirement, and I haven't heard any alternative suggestions in this case for how Michael Elstad's right to *know* his rights could have been safeguarded other than through *Miranda* warnings.

Second, having concluded that this violation was a "poisonous tree," the result in this case seems clear to me. The "cat out of the bag" analysis is fully applicable here. As Justice Harlan emphasized in his concurrence in *Darwin v. Connecticut*, a defendant who already has given an unconstitutional confession will likely "think he has little to lose by repetition," so that a second confession—even if it is perfectly voluntary—is presumptively unconstitutional as well.[205] As John noted there, the government must bear the burden of proving "not only that the later confession was not itself the product of . . . coercive conditions, but also that it was not directly produced by the existence of the earlier confession." The first confession in *Darwin* was coerced, but the "little to lose" rationale applies with equal force whether the confession was obtained through actual beatings or through the "inherent coercion" recognized in *Miranda*.

We have applied this logic to numerous other cases in numerous other contexts. In *Fahy v. Connecticut*, for example, we held that a defendant's admissions that are induced by confronting him with illegally seized evidence may not be admitted at trial—unless the taint is purged.[206] *Costello v. United States* applied the same reasoning to jury statements.[207] And Harry Blackmun's opinion in *Brown v. Illinois* recognized that Richard Brown's first inadmissible statement "bolstered the pressures for him to give the second, or at least vitiated any incentive on his part to avoid self-incrimination."[208]

Third, accordingly I apply *Wong Sun*'s attenuation analysis to the circumstances of this case. I must conclude that Elstad's second confession was not "attenuated" from the first. *Miranda* warnings alone did not of course cure the impression that the first confession would be admissible, and at no time did the police advise Elstad that the first confession could not be used against him. Moreover, only one hour had elapsed since the first confession, and there were no significant "intervening circumstances." Finally, as we recognized in *Brown*, the "purpose and flagrancy of the official misconduct" are relevant to attenuation analysis. Here the police misconduct was particularly flagrant. I believe the record clearly shows that the arresting officers, who arrived at the house with warrant in hand, delayed advising Elstad that he was under arrest precisely so that they

---

205. *Darwin v. Connecticut*, 391 U.S. 396 (1968).
206. *Fahy v. Connecticut*, 375 U.S. 85 (1963).
207. *Costello v. United States*, 365 U.S. 265 (1961).
208. *Brown v. Illinois*, 422 U.S. 590, 605 (1975).

could elicit incriminating statements from him before having to give him his *Miranda* warnings.

For these reasons, I would affirm the judgment of the Court of Appeals of Oregon.

WHITE: *Miranda* is a constitutional rule, but it is also prophylactic. The "cat out of bag" rationale does not automatically apply—it is not a per se rule that makes the second statement a fruit of the first—maybe when first admission was coerced, but not here. I wouldn't let "cat out of the bag" be the rationale otherwise.

MARSHALL: I am at dead center. If *Lyons* is good law, it requires reversal here.[209] I will try to affirm.

BLACKMUN: The second statement was voluntary, and that is enough.

POWELL: I agree with the Chief Justice—the trial court expressly found that the second statement was voluntary.

REHNQUIST: The "cat out of bag" rationale is useful only if there is some evidence of a connection. *Miranda* is constitutional, but the rule is flexible. The first statement is not covered.

STEVENS: *Miranda* is a mirage. *Wong Sun* is not controlling for me.[210] The real question is whether the second confession was voluntary. We must presume that the first was presumptively coerced; was the second confession voluntary if the first was not admissible? The burden was on the state, and it did not meet its burden here.

O'CONNOR: I adhere to my dissent from denial.

Result: The Court ruled 6–3 that what happened to Elstad was merely a "procedural" Miranda violation and that the second confession was admissible. The circumstances, Sandra Day O'Connor wrote for the majority, did not merit a broad application of the exclusionary rule. Miranda was based on the Fifth Amendment's right against compelled testimony, and failure to give a Miranda warning merely created a presumption of coercion. Miranda did not necessarily require the exclusion of later voluntary statements unless there was evidence of coercion or other circumstances calculated to undermine the suspect's free will. While Elstad's first statement had to be excluded, the intervening administration of Miranda warnings was enough to prove that Elstad knowingly and voluntarily waived his rights, whether or not the cat was out of the bag. Brennan, Marshall, and Stevens dissented.

---

209. *Lyons v. Oklahoma*, 322 U.S. 596 (1944). In a murder case, the Court ruled that if the defendant's first confession was coerced, subsequent voluntary admissions might still be admissible. Where the evidence as to coercion was conflicting, or where different inferences could be drawn from admitted facts, the question of whether a confession was voluntary was for the jury or other trier of fact. The 6–2 majority ruled that the evidence in this case supported the jury's judgment that the coercive nature of the first confession had dissipated prior to the second confession, and that the latter confession was voluntary and therefore admissible. Rutledge and Murphy dissented. Marshall argued the case for the petitioner on behalf of the NAACP.

210. *Wong Sun v. United States*, 371 U.S. 471 (1963).

TRIAL

The Right to a Fair Trial

Ex parte Quirin, 317 U.S. 1 (1942)
(Frankfurter) (Black)

On June 13, 1942, a Nazi U-boat landed four saboteurs on the East Coast of the United States, near Amagansett, Long Island. Several days later, the same submarine put ashore four more saboteurs at Ponte Vedra beach near Jacksonville, Florida. They had orders to fan out across the country in teams of two, attacking trains, bridges, and war production facilities. Team members were specially trained in demolition and sabotage. They had all spent considerable time in the United States as children and young adults, and were all perfectly fluent in English.

The first two teams, led by thirty-nine-year-old George Dasch, landed on Long Island in a thick fog and accidentally encountered John Cullen, a Coast Guard enlisted man on routine beach patrol. They threatened Cullen but released him unharmed. Cullen reported the incident to his superiors, but no one believed him until he found an empty pack of German cigarettes on the beach. Coast Guard authorities then notified the FBI, but the agents who interviewed Cullen did not believe his story.

On June 14, Dasch had second thoughts about the mission and called the FBI, but no one believed him. Dasch persisted, and five days later he finally convinced federal authorities to take him seriously. Dasch told his teammate, Ernest Burger, what he had done and Burger also cooperated with the FBI. The other six saboteurs were quickly located and placed under surveillance. After several days, they were all arrested without incident. J. Edgar Hoover then leaked the story to the press to make it look like the FBI had cracked the case single-handedly.

President Roosevelt told his aides that he wanted all of the saboteurs dead. He ordered that they be tried by a top-secret military commission composed of eight army generals.[211] There would be no appeal, except to Roosevelt himself. All eight saboteurs were secretly tried in the Department of Justice building and found guilty. Roosevelt sentenced all but Dasch and Burger to death. At the recommendation of the commission, Dasch received thirty years in prison and Burger was sentenced to life in prison. Appointed counsel for the saboteurs filed for a writ of habeas corpus with the Supreme Court.[212] The defendants argued that under Ex parte Milligan *they had the right to be tried in a civilian court with full constitutional protections, including grand jury indictments and trial by jury.[213]*

---

211. The commission was composed of four major generals—Frank McCoy, Walter Grant, Elanton Winship, and Lorenzo Gasser—and three brigadier generals, Guy Henry, John Lewis, and John Kennedy. The prosecutors were Attorney General Francis Biddle and Major General Myron Cramer. The defense team, assigned by the War Department, included Major Lauson Harvey Stone (the son of Harlan Fiske Stone), Colonel Cassius Dowell, and Colonel Kenneth Royal.

212. The convicted spies were prisoners of Brigadier General Albert Cox, the provost marshall of the Military District of Washington, D.C. Cox was the named party in the prisoners' habeas corpus petitions.

213. *Ex parte Milligan*, 71 U.S. (4 Wall.) 2 (1866). Lambdin P. Milligan, a civilian resident of Indiana, was arrested at his home in 1864 and charged with conspiracy. He was tried by a military commission, which found him guilty and sentenced him to be hanged. Milligan applied for a writ of habeas corpus on the ground that he had a constitutional right to trial by jury in a civilian court. The Court agreed and ordered Milligan discharged from federal custody on the ground that the military commission had no right to try or punish

The Justices returned early from their summer recess to meet in a rare Special Term. On July 30, 1942, they convened in conference to discuss this case. Hugo Black took notes on the argument and the conference. This is one of the few surviving examples of Black's conference notes. It was saved because Douglas missed most of the proceedings in this case and borrowed Black's notes for his own files. Frankfurter wrote a fascinating memorandum to the conference in a last-ditch effort to drive the Justices to a unanimous decision, and his "soliloquy" follows Black's conference notes.[214]

Oral Argument

The Court met in special session on this date. The Chief Justice announced the purpose of the session, and also announced that Douglas was unavoidably detained but was on his way and would participate in the case. Murphy was not participating because of things said in conference about it.[215] Attorney General Biddle and Colonel Royal agreed that the Chief Justice should not disqualify himself.

Royal began his argument. Frankfurter immediately began to ask questions. Royal argued jurisdiction under Act of 1891, and cited *Ex parte Yerger*,[216] and the *Bollman and Swartout* case.[217] He argued that this procedure was the only method possible. Counsel

---

him. David Davis's majority opinion noted that federal authority was maintained and the civilian courts remained open in Indiana throughout the war. All nine Justices agreed that the president could not unilaterally suspend the writ of habeas corpus and impose martial law under such circumstances. Five Justices agreed that not even Congress and the president together could have authorized such an action. Davis was also careful to point out, however, that Milligan was not a citizen of a rebellious state, a current or former member of the military, or a prisoner of war.

214. Frankfurter Papers, part 3, reel 43, pp. 485 et seq.

215. Anxious to participate in the war effort, Murphy convinced President Roosevelt and General George C. Marshall to commission him as a lieutenant colonel in the Army Reserve in June 1942. Murphy showed up at the special hearing in *Quirin* proudly wearing his uniform, which caused such a scandal among the other Justices that he felt obligated to recuse himself. Howard, *Mr. Justice Murphy*, 275, 300.

216. *Ex parte Yerger*, 75 U.S. (8 Wall.) 85 (1868), was decided a year after *Ex parte McCardle*, and the two cases were similar in many respects. Both involved criminal charges against a southerner brought by a military commission and challenged in a federal habeas corpus proceeding. One significant difference was that Yerger claimed that the Court had jurisdiction under the Judiciary Act of 1789 rather than the Habeas Corpus Act of 1867. Congress had previously amended the latter act to strip away the Supreme Court's appellate jurisdiction in anticipation of *McCardle*. The Court used *Yerger* to reassert its broad appellate jurisdiction in habeas cases, recovering from its tactical defeat in *McCardle*. In finding jurisdiction, the Court ruled that "the general spirit and genius of our institutions has tended to the widening and enlarging of the habeas corpus jurisdiction of the courts and judges of the United States; and this tendency, except in one recent instance, has been constant and uniform; and it is in the light of it that we must determine the true meaning of the Constitution and the law in respect to the appellate jurisdiction of this court . . . the case is one of those expressly declared not to be excepted from the general grant of jurisdiction." Yerger's case became moot, however, when he was turned over to civilian authorities. The Court never ruled on the merits of the case and avoided a definitive ruling on the constitutionality of Reconstruction.

217. *Ex parte Bollman and Swartout*, 8 U.S. (4 Cranch) 75 (1807). Erick Bollman and Samuel Swartout were arrested in New Orleans in 1806 and charged with treason in connection with the Aaron Burr conspiracy. They applied for a writ of habeas corpus with the Supreme Court. Chief Justice John Marshall, writing for a short-handed 3–1 Court, asserted jurisdiction to hear their cases. Marshall wrote that Congress was constitutionally obliged to make the writ of habeas corpus available to all federal prisoners and that the Court would consider habeas cases as an appellate court. On the merits, Marshall adopted the position most embarrassing to Thomas Jefferson, ruling summarily that no acts of treason had occurred and ordering the prisoners discharged. Jefferson's first appointment to the Court, William Johnson, was the sole dissenter.

do not consider it to be their duty to engage in dilatory procedure. Frankfurter asked why an appeal was not perfected to the circuit court of appeals. The Chief Justice said that would not have enlarged our jurisdiction. He asked the Court to hear the argument today and grant the opportunity to take any additional steps which might prove necessary. Frankfurter asks if there is any case since the 1891 act which has held that this Court has a right to shortcut the circuit court of appeal. The Court granted Francis Biddle the opportunity to discuss jurisdiction, and he read the "original" jurisdiction section of the Constitution. He says, therefore, that there is no original habeas corpus jurisdiction, as held in *Marbury v. Madison*.[218] He says that if there is an order of a lower federal court having denied the writ, the Court can order appellate jurisdiction "in aid of appellate jurisdiction." He reads from *Mooney v. Holohan* "as a method of recover" the legality of his detention under a commitment from a state court. He says that there an appeal had been taken, and therefore there was no gap.[219]

The Chief Justice refers to the *Siebold* case, and asks whether Congress, by the act of 1895, intended to cut off this Court's traditional right of appeal.[220] He quotes §262 of the Federal Code, 28 U.S.C. §377.[221] We have jurisdiction only if a statute gives it.

Frankfurter says that the acts of 1891 and 1925 must be considered together. He says that there is an open question as to whether there was an implied exception to the general scheme of appeal for habeas corpus cases. He says that appellate jurisdiction granted by the Constitution can be exercised in the absence of clear statutory language prohibiting jurisdiction. Frankfurter says that this is not just this case; it opens up a way for other cases to be presented in the same manner. He asks what cases come here directly from a district court. He asks about the legislative history of the acts. Frankfurter says that all of his difficulties will be obviated if Biddle will join with Royal in appealing to the circuit court of appeals. Royal resumes argument.

---

218. *Marbury v. Madison*, 5 U.S. (1 Cr.) 137 (1803).

219. *Mooney v. Holohan*, 294 U.S. 103 (1935). After California prosecutors knowingly used perjured testimony to convict Tom Mooney of murder, the Supreme Court ruled that the due process clause governed state action, including misbehavior of state prosecutors, and that states had a duty to provide corrective judicial procedures. The Court refused to grant Mooney relief, however, ruling that there was a presumption that each state would do its duty and that Mooney had to exhaust his state remedies before asking the Supreme Court to issue a writ of habeas corpus.

220. *Ex parte Siebold*, 100 U.S. 371 (1879). In an election fraud case, Siebold petitioned the Supreme Court for a writ habeas corpus. Because his case fell within the Court's *appellate* jurisdiction, the Court ruled that it could only consider a petition for habeas corpus under the Court's *original* jurisdiction if Siebold had been detained by a tribunal lacking jurisdiction to hear the case, or if the tribunal's decision was illegal or void. The Court could not consider Siebold's petition if the tribunal's decision had merely been erroneous. The Court accepted jurisdiction in Siebold's case because he had alleged that the federal laws on which his conviction was based (making it a crime to stuff ballot boxes in congressional elections) were unconstitutional and void. After accepting jurisdiction, the Court decided that the laws in question were constitutional and denied Siebold's petition on the merits.

221. 28 U.S.C. §377 (1940). The "All Writs Act" provided that the Supreme Court and all courts established by Act of Congress were authorized to issue all writs necessary or appropriate in aid of their respective jurisdictions and agreeable to the usages and principles of law. This provision was subsequently renumbered; for the current version of this law, see 28 U.S.C. §1651.

On the Merits

Time questions were presented, and were capable of many and varied refinements. In essence: (1) do they, as aliens have right to enter civil courts; and (2) if so, have they made out a case of illegal detention?

Six are citizens of Germany. One is of questionable citizenship.[222] All have been in Germany, and all landed from submarines. Some landed in Florida, some in New Jersey. All brought explosives. None yet used. He argues that each of charges involves conduct made criminal by federal statute. He says that the president has not declared martial law, and thinks that his proclamation is beyond his constitutional power. He refers to Article 38, and says that the president has acted "contrary to or inconsistent with these Articles." He says that any violation of Art. of War 43 requires unanimous vote for death, ¾ for life sentence. Now he refers to Article 70. Now he refers to Article 46, which refers to Commissions, and to Article 50, second paragraph. These require transmission of the record to the judge-advocate general (JAG), but instead the orders were that the record must be sent straight to the president.

Francis Biddle for the government insisted that we must consider all of the petitioners as enemies of the United States, and that citizenship is irrelevant. He says that the right of an alien to sue out habeas corpus in time of peace is distinguishable. Stone says that his right to defend himself is recognized. Stone asks whether habeas corpus is anything more than a mode of defense.

Conference of July 30, 1942

STONE: Francis Biddle's argument is that aliens cannot resort to habeas corpus. I am reluctant to say that an alien enemy cannot resort to habeas corpus. I think that we should avoid this issue, if possible.

Our jurisdiction, since they filed their petition in district court, I think that the appellate power means the constitutional right to punish, provided that Congress sees fit to grant an appeal, and I think that it could grant an appeal from a military tribunal. Look at the *Siebold* case and later at the *Hudgings* case.[223] No appeal had been taken. No appeal taken, but the Court held the habeas corpus act. Last question: did Congress intend to cut off this longstanding right by the act of 1925? It would be astound-

---

222. Herbert Haupt claimed that he was an American citizen because his parents became naturalized citizens while he was a minor. Ernest Burger claimed that he was "uncertain" whether he was a citizen of the Reich or the United States. The Justices eventually decided to ignore the issue of Haupt's citizenship, while Burger was treated as a German citizen.

223. *Ex parte Hudgings*, 249 U.S. 378. (1919). Hudgings filed a petition for habeas corpus after a federal judge summarily found him in contempt for perjury. The trial judge believed that Hudgings had failed to testify truthfully and ordered him confined until he gave testimony that the judge deemed truthful. Worried that this sort of summary punishment would allow judges to intimidate witnesses and coerce agreeable testimony, the Supreme Court ruled that perjury could be punished as contempt only if it obstructed the exercise of judicial duty. In this case, that test was not met. Because the trial judge had no power to hold Hudgings in contempt, his decision was illegal and void. The Supreme Court invoked its original jurisdiction to consider Hudgings's petition and ordered him discharged from federal custody.

ing to me to say that it cut off the right. Van Devanter drew up the act.[224] I think that we have jurisdiction.

On the Merits: One—is spying under the acts of Congress? I have some difficulty in saying specifications allow offenses under Articles 81 and 82. I think that many things could be done which are not within the Articles of War. If, however, there is a law of war under which the commander-in-chief can go, outside the Acts of Congress, and provide for punishment.

What are the facts? I am not disposed to do what the Court did in the *Milligan* case. Here we have men who associated with the armed forces of the enemy—they were trained by the enemy. To carry that into effect, they were brought within our country not in uniform.

The Constitution makes the president the supreme commander, and Congress can carry on war. For time out of mind it is within the power of the commander-in-chief to hang a spy. The Articles of War recognize that there is a law of war. I would say that the whole history of the army shows that there is a common law of war—waging war. By all usages, they were not prisoners of war. We are bound to give some play to the executive branch as to an administrative agency.

Felix Frankfurter's "Soliloquy" on Ex Parte Quirin

After listening as hard as I could to the views expressed by the Chief Justice and Jackson about the *Saboteur* case problems at the last Conference, and thinking over what they said as intelligently as I could, I could not for the life of me find enough space in the legal differences between them to insert a razor blade. And now comes Jackson's memorandum expressing what he believes to be views other than those contained in the Chief Justice's opinion.[225] I have now studied as hard as I could the printed formulations of their views and I still can't discover what divides them so far as legal significance is concerned. And so I say to myself that words must be poor and treacherous means of putting out what goes on inside our heads. Being puzzled by what seem to me to be merely verbal differences in expressing intrinsically identical views about the government's legal principles, I thought I would state in my own way what have been my views on the issues in the *Saboteur* cases ever since my mind came to rest upon them. And perhaps I can do it with least misunderstanding if I put it in the form of a dialogue—a dialogue between the saboteurs and myself as to what I, as a judge, should do in acting upon their claims:

---

224. While on the Supreme Court, Willis Van Devanter was appointed to the committee that drafted the legislation that eventually became the Judiciary Act of 1925. Van Devanter became the act's chief draftsman and took the lead in lobbying Congress to push for its passage into law. The act was arguably the most significant judicial reform of the twentieth century, greatly expanding the Court's discretionary certiorari jurisdiction and giving the Justices nearly complete control over the Court's docket.

225. Robert Jackson circulated a memorandum agreeing with Chief Justice Stone that the prisoners were properly in military custody and could lawfully be tried by a military commission established by the president. But he added that he would refuse to consider the question of whether President Roosevelt's orders violated the Articles of War. The prisoners, he said, had no standing to claim any rights at all, either from "the majestic generalities of the Bill of Rights" or under the Articles of War. These men were, Jackson argued, spies and invaders and deserved no further consideration. Jackson, Memorandum to the Conference, Oct. 23, 1942, Douglas Papers, OT 1941, box 77.

SABOTEURS: Your Honor, we are here to get a writ of habeas corpus from you.

F.F.   What entitles you to it?

S.   We are being tried by a military commission set up by the president although we were arrested in places where, and at a time when, the civil courts were open and functioning with full authority and before which, therefore, under the Constitution of the United States we were entitled to be tried with all the safeguards for criminal prosecutions in the federal courts.

F.F.   What is the answer of the provost marshal to your petition?

S.   The facts in the case are agreed to in a stipulation before Your Honor.

F.F.   (After reading the stipulation) You damned scoundrels have a helluvacheek to ask for a writ that would take you out of the hands of the military commission and give you the right to be tried, if at all, in a federal district court. You are just low-down, ordinary, enemy spies who, as enemy soldiers, have invaded our country and therefore could immediately have been shot by the military when caught in the act of invasion. Instead you were humanely ordered to be tried by a military tribunal convoked by the commander-in-chief himself, and the verdict of that tribunal is returnable to the commander-in-chief himself to be acted upon by himself. To utilize a military commission to establish your guilt or innocence was plainly within the authority of the commander-in-chief. I do not have to say more than that Congress specifically has authorized the president to establish such a commission in the circumstances of your case and the president himself has purported to act under this authority of Congress as expressed by the Articles of War. So I will deny your writ and leave you to your just desserts with the military.

S.   But, Your Honor, since as you say the president himself professed to act under the Articles of War, we appeal to those Articles of War as the governing procedure, even bowing to your ruling that we are not entitled to be tried by civil courts, and may have our lives declared forfeit by this military commission. Specifically, we say that since the president has set up this commission under the Articles of War, he must conform to them. He has certainly not done so in that the requirements of Articles 46–50 ½ have been and are being disregarded by the McCoy tribunal.

F.F.   There is nothing to that point either. The articles to which you appeal do not restrict the president in relation to a military commission set up for the purposes of and in the circumstances of this case. That amply disposes of your point. In lawyer's language, a proper construction of Articles 46–50 ½ does not cover this case, and therefore on the merits you have no rights under it. So I don't have to consider whether, assuming Congress had specifically required the president in establishing such a Commission to give you the procedural safeguards of Articles 46–50 ½, Congress would have gone beyond its job and taken over the business of the president as commander-in-chief in the actual conduct of a war. You've done enough mischief already without leaving the seeds of bitter conflict involving the president, the courts, and Congress after your bodies will be rotting in lime. It is a wise requirement of courts not to get into needless rows with the other branches of the government by talking about things that need not be talked about if a case can be disposed of with intellectual self-respect on grounds that do not raise such rows. I therefore do not propose to be seduced into inquiring what powers the president has or has not got, what limits the Congress may or may not put upon the commander-in-chief in time of war, when, as a matter of fact, the ground on which you claim to stand—namely, the proper construction of these Articles of War—exists only in your foolish fancy. That disposes of you scoundrels. Doubtless other judges may spell this out with appropriate documentation and learning. Some judges would certainly express their views much more politely and charmingly than I have done. Some would take a lot of words to say it, and some would take not so many, but it all comes down to what I have told you. In a nutshell, the president has the power, as he said had, to set up the tribunal which he has set up to try you as invading German belligerents for the offenses for which you are being tried. And for you there are no procedural rights such as you claim, because the statute to which you appeal—the Articles of War—don't apply to you. And you will remain in your present custody and be damned.

Some of the very best lawyers I know are now in the Solomon Islands battle, some are seeing service in Australia, some are sub-chasers in the Atlantic, and some are on the various air fronts. It requires no poet's imagination to think of their reflections if the unanimous result reached by us in these cases should be expressed in opinions which would black out the agreement in result and reveal internecine conflict about the manner of stating that result. I know some of these men very, very intimately. I think I know what they would deem to be the governing canons of constitutional adjudication in a case like this. And I almost hear their voices were they to read more than a single opinion in this case. They would say something like this, but in language hardly becoming a judge's tongue: "What in hell do you fellows think you are doing? Haven't we got enough of a job trying to lick the Japs and the Nazis without having you fellows on the Supreme Court dissipate the thoughts and feelings and energies of the folks at home by stirring up an nice row as to who has what power, when all of you are agreed that the president had the power to establish this commission and that the procedures under the Articles of War for courts-martial and military commissions don't apply to this case? Haven't you got any more sense than to get people by the ear on one of the favorite American pastimes—abstract constitutional discussions? Do we have to have another Lincoln-Taney row when everybody is agreed and in this particular case the constitutional questions aren't reached? Just relax and don't be too engrossed in your own interest in verbalistic conflicts, because the inroads on energy and national unity that such conflict inevitable produce, is a pastime we had better postpone until peacetime.

Result: The Court ruled unanimously that Ex parte Milligan *was not applicable and that the saboteurs had no rights that Americans were bound to respect. They had no right to be indicted by a grand jury and no right to be tried by a jury or in a civilian court. As combatants who waged war by stealth, they were "offenders against the law of war, subject to trial and punishment by military tribunals."*

On August 8, 1942, Hermann Neubauer, Henry Heinck, Werner Thiel, Robert Quirin, Herbert Haupt, and Edward Kerling were executed consecutively in the District of Columbia's sole electric chair, nicknamed "Old Sparky." They waited quietly in line as each was executed in turn, the whole process taking sixty-four minutes. The oldest saboteur was thirty-five and the youngest, Haupt, was twenty-two. They were buried in numbered graves in Blue Plains. In the 1960s, their bodies were exhumed and returned to their families in Germany.

Dasch and Burger were freed three years after the end of the war and returned to Germany in 1948. Burger became a sales engineer for a Bavarian manufacturing company in Augsberg. Dasch drifted through Germany and Switzerland before settling down in the Rhineland and opening a small café. He later became a commodities trader. Dasch hated Germany, where he was constantly hounded for having betrayed his fellow saboteurs. For the next twenty years, he repeatedly but unsuccessfully petitioned the United States government to allow him to return to the country that he considered home.

In re Yamashita, 327 U.S. 1 (1946)
(Burton)

During the early days of World War II, General Tomoyuki Yamashita ("The Tiger of Malaysia") led the Japanese conquest of Southeast Asia. During the last months of the war, General Yamashita commanded a Japanese Army unit in Luzon Province in the Philippines. When Japanese forces surrendered to the Allies, he was arrested and charged with allowing his troops to commit murder, rape, and other war crimes against POWs and Philippine civilians. American authorities did not allege that the general himself participated in or ordered any atrocities, but charged that he had failed to control his troops. General Yamashita was tried by a special military commission established by President Roosevelt. He was convicted by a 5–0 vote and sentenced to death on December 7, 1945, the fourth anniversary of the Japanese attack on Pearl Harbor.[226] The commission's report stated that the crimes committed by Japanese forces were so extensive and widespread that the general must have known about them and that he should have taken steps to prevent such crimes and punish offenders.

General Yamashita applied for relief to the supreme court of the Philippines, but that court declined jurisdiction. He then applied to the U.S. Supreme Court for a writ of certiorari and also petitioned for a writ of habeas corpus, claiming that he had been deprived of his constitutional rights. Although Yamashita had appointed counsel, he was denied most other constitutional rights, including indictment by a grand jury and trial by jury. He was also denied the basic protections afforded by

---

226. Before the commission announced its verdict, an American journalist polled the twelve journalists who witnessed Yamashita's trial. They voted 12–0 in favor of acquittal. British journalist Henry Keyes wrote that the proceeding "isn't a trial, I doubt that it is even a hearing. . . . I hold no brief for any Jap, but in no British court of law would an accused have received such rough justice as Yamashita." Geoffrey Wheatcroft, "Justice or Vengeance," *The Guardian (London)* April 3, 1996, T4.

American rules of evidence. Yamashita claimed that the commission was improperly established and that the charges against him were hopelessly vague and did not allege any specific violations of the laws of war.

Conference of January 12, 1946

STONE: Petitioner Yamashita argues: (1) That this was not a properly created court because hostilities are over, that there was no authority in either the Constitution or statute, and that these were only military orders.

In the *Quirin* case, the question was whether there was authority to try belligerents who came into the United States without uniforms could be tried without a special act of Congress. We examined history and found that, by a hand of international law, the Constitution gave Congress the power to punish violations of the laws of war. Congress had not passed an act, except in the Articles of War the document *refers* to it (Article 15) and recognizes law of war trials by military commissions, so that Congress recognized trials by military commissions and had adopted international law on the law of war. The creation of the court, and so forth, were all covered. The question was whether the limitations on courts-martial mentioned in the Articles of War extended to the military commission. (In preparing the opinion, we said that these limitations had *not* been extended to trials by military commission, but this rule was not agreed to and it was put on other grounds.)

The trial in this case was after hostilities ceased. The *Quirin* case recited the history of such trials from Major André down.[227] Congress had, in effect, authorized the creation of the commission by the executive branch, and the president had done so. There are many cases of field commanders doing so. Either MacArthur or Styer had that authority.[228]

1. Was it properly created?
2. Was this a law of war case? (Properly charged)?
3. Were there errors in the evidence from the United States?
4. Was there sufficient notice to petitioner—knowledge—affect jurisdiction?

(2) This case is here only on *habeas corpus and denial of Yamashita's petition of habeas corpus.*

Military commission (not a court-martial)—if objections. In both cases, there is a special trial and a special review. Congress has provided no mode of review in the courts except by habeas corpus. What is its scope? There is only one question: is he being held within the power of the court (or agency) presently holding him? We don't review the evidence or the validity of his conviction unless there is a want of power to hold him. Was there a want of power to try him, and to hold him, and to execute sentence?[229]

---

227. Citing the rules of war, General George Washington ordered that British general John André be hanged as a spy for his part in the Benedict Arnold conspiracy. André was summarily executed on October 2, 1780.

228. General Douglas MacArthur was Supreme Commander, Allied Powers (SCAP). Lt. General Wilhelm D. Styer was the Commanding General of American Forces in the Western Pacific.

229. The government claimed that allegations about the inadequacy of the charges, mistakes in pleading or procedure, and other claimed errors were not subject to review on habeas corpus. For the most part, Stone accepted the government's arguments.

The first claim is that there was no right to try him before the military commission after hostilities had ceased. No prior decision says whether a trial by a military commission can punish him for violations after hostilities had ceased. But the "*war*" is not ended. Grotius says that there is a power during war—if the trial had started. First, the war has not ended. And second, the object is punishment for violations of the law of war and should not be cut off.

Did this bill of particulars charge a violation of the laws of war? The government does not charge that he ordered any violations—or even *knew* that it was done. The claim is that obedience to the law of war presupposes that a *commander is in control of his troops*. The government's opening statement that the prosecution did not have to prove that Yamashita ordered, did, or even knew of any violations. It is enough if he was lax in preventing them. Did he take reasonable precautions to prevent what happened?[230] You can't put less obligation here than in other cases where a responsibility exists. Otherwise, it would be too easy to escape responsibility.

The government argued that this is all a "political act." I agree, in the sense that it is governed by political orders by the government. But none of that would foreclose Yamashita appealing to us, or our listening to him. Apparently the government wants a trial agreeable to the laws of war, and our review should be when a collateral attack is made on a trial and no review is provided. For example, in deportation cases, which involve administrative officers, the rules give no review, but it still gives the right to issue a writ of habeas corpus.

(3) The use of depositions. General MacArthur provided that any evidence probative to reasonable men might be received, and also provided for the use of affidavits. (As he could, if not contrary to Act of Congress. This is the same idea as in the *Quirin* case.) But this is said to be prohibited by Articles 25 and 38 of the Articles of War.[231] These two articles may be read as forbidding affidavits.

Article of War 37 provides for special review.[232] First, a general review for all tribunals (it should not affect the results unless prejudicial) and it also says that it is of no effect unless there is an error which affects substantial rights. (1) *We can't review on habeas corpus.* (2) *Certainly with life*, the examining authority has had an opportunity to say whether or not it is prejudicial. We can't say whether it was prejudicial or not,

---

230. The Bill of Particulars alleged 160 atrocities committed by Japanese soldiers under Yamashita's command, but did not claim that he had been directly involved or that he had any personal knowledge of any alleged war crimes committed by his troops. Yamashita was tried and convicted solely on the basis of his command responsibility.

231. Article 25 established certain rules of evidence and gave defendants some evidentiary protections. Most importantly, General Yamashita claimed that Article 25 limited the use of depositions in capital cases to those submitted by the defense. Article 38 provided that the modes of proof in courts-martial must conform as nearly as practicable to the rules of evidence applicable to criminal cases in federal district courts. Article 38 also gave the president power to prescribe procedures for courts-martial and other military tribunals, including modes of proof, provided that all such rules were presented annually to Congress.

232. Article 37 prohibited disturbing the judgments of courts-martial "on the ground of improper admission or rejection of evidence or for any error as to any matter of pleading or procedure unless in the opinion of the reviewing or confirming authority . . . it shall appear that the error complained of has injuriously affected the substantial rights of the accused."

but we have no more right to review the facts here than on a habeas corpus proceeding from a district court.

(4) Last—Failure to give notice. The government claims that the Geneva Convention says before the trial of a POW, notice shall be given to the protecting power. It is *assumed* that no notice was given. The government says: (1) There is no necessity for affirmative notice. The Japanese liaison officers were present and helped as needed. (2) Failure to give them notice is a basis for diplomatic representation. (3) Japan as a *nation* has surrendered. It has no treaty rights. Their government has not been permitted to have this yet.[233]

This Court should be extremely cautious and tentative to review government proceedings from draft and war and where no review is provided. This is largely an executive procedure. Executive action cannot cut off what Congress has presented, but Congress *does not* permit us to review courts martial in military trials. It leaves us only the *writ of habeas corpus*—to test whether it was done *with authority* only. So we should keep our hands off.

I hesitate to say that we could review a military court trial of this kind, as we could a district court case. Do not issue habeas corpus and petition for certiorari. Where the court has refused to review on habeas corpus—even though rights were denied in trial—that is for the reviewing authority and not for this Court. Review under Article 63 of Geneva—by same court.

P.48 of Respondent's Brief—that trial by the same court—this goes to the question of constitutionality—as apart from any commander. American soldiers could be tried by these commissions.

BLACK: I disagree with much in the government brief, yet I come out at the same place. I would not give up on our rights of review of military courts, and we should not limit our review as much as we will in a *habeas corpus*. [BURTON: Stone meant to make it a test of procedure to try and determine.]

Whether Article of War 25 prohibited use of affidavits is a question [STONE: I would say so, also], and if Congress had prohibited it, MacArthur's order to use them would be included. If Hague Convention rules were applicable, we should review it and not permit this execution.

(1) We must find no violation of the law of Congress. It is not enough to say that we are trying a belligerent. [STONE: I agree.] You can shoot enemies—there is no treaty that says you can't try a man for his treatment of occupied territory. They could and should try him if he was caught in the act or is a responsible party. So, also, after the hostilities are over. It is a question of policy whether to do it or not.

The Reconstruction period cases are not good precedents. As to civilians, I am not willing to say that a war is going on, but here belligerents were involved. I don't question MacArthur's first order authorizing military trials everywhere.

I go on the ground that they have not violated a law of Congress. In the *Quirin* case, we held that the Articles of War did not apply, and that looking at the Articles of War 1 and 2—which determine who is covered under the Articles of War—these Articles do

233. The government also argued that Article 60 of the Geneva Convention, which required that notice of an impending trial of POWs be delivered to the protecting national power, applied only to crimes allegedly committed *after* capture.

not cover belligerents and do not cover their trials by military commissions. Articles of War 81 and 82, which even apply to civilians, seem to further Articles of War 1 and 2, which are broad enough to include belligerents.[234] These proceedings do not violate any law of Congress. But we should maintain our right to test that. Any officer who violates the laws of this country—this would apply everywhere. (*Mitchell v Harmony*.[235])

STONE: This is a trial by an American commission. *The trial goes with the military*, and the question is what it carries with it. It carries a habeas corpus test. A stranger—a belligerent—is accused in our courts. I would give him a right to these rules. They don't need to give notice where you have contact with his nation. I want to be clear that we are not abdicating our job.

REED: If there is a difference between Stone and Black, I favor Stone. Japan and Yamashita have lost their rights of protection by the Geneva Convention and the Articles of War. [?][236] I think that, probably, notice should have been given and diplomats were sent to aid. There was power for the military commission to act, and no power in us to review on evidence and procedure. Section 63 of the Geneva Convention is O.K. Our soldiers could have been tried by a military commission.

FRANKFURTER: I agree with Stone. Habeas corpus. I don't think that Article of War 25 applies, and it certainly does not apply to this right of the court. Article 37 gives a limiting effect to it. Article 2 does not say a *military commission* or court martial. Really at the nut is that General Crowder wanted to legalize the results of this military commission.[237] Look at Field's opinion in *Neal Dow v. Johnson*, 100 U.S. 158, 169.[238]

---

234. Article 81 defined the offense of relieving, corresponding with, or giving intelligence to the enemy. Article 82 provided that any person in time of war who was caught spying in or about a military installation would be tried by a court-martial or military commission and authorized the death penalty for anyone convicted under this article.

235. *Mitchell v. Harmony*, 54 U.S. (13 How.) 115 (1851). Manuel Harmony, an American trader, sued David Mitchell, an American army colonel, for trespass after Mitchell seized his goods and other chattel property in Chihuahua, Mexico, during the Mexican-American War. Colonel Mitchell claimed that he was worried that the property would be used by the enemy and that his seizure was justified by necessity. The Court rejected the necessity defense and ruled that because the American government had authorized Harmony to sell his goods in Mexico, the seizure violated American law and that Harmony was entitled to compensation. It did not matter that the illegal seizure took place in Mexico, rather than in the United States.

This case also represented an early repudiation of what would later become known as the "Nuremberg defense." Colonel Mitchell claimed that he should not be held liable because he had only been following orders. In rejecting that defense, Chief Justice Taney wrote that "it can never be maintained that a military officer can justify himself for doing an unlawful act, by producing the order of his superior."

236. The question mark was Burton's parenthetical comment.

237. Major General Enoch H. Crowder, the Judge Advocate General.

238. *Dow v. Johnson*, 100 U.S. 158 (1879). Justice Field said, "The military should always be kept in subjection to the laws of the country to which it belongs, and that he is no friend to the Republic who advocates the contrary. The established principle of every free people is, that the law shall alone govern; and to it the military must always yield." But Field allowed the military to seize property in enemy territory without civil or criminal liability and distinguished *Mitchell v. Harmony* because in the earlier case the property owner had obtained explicit federal authorization to take his property into enemy territory.

DOUGLAS: The Articles of War do not apply to belligerents.

MURPHY: *I do not agree.* I shall not embarrass the Court. I am glad that I was not in the *Quirin* case. [BURTON: If we are to be more moral, rather than strengthened.] The Philippines is a dependency of United States, and we are sovereign. The government has the power to create these commissions. But he cannot be tried with *insufficient knowledge.* I think that the Geneva treaty was in existence and that notice could have been given.

RUTLEDGE: My views are at odds with everyone except with Murphy. I think that Article 25 does apply. Notice does apply. Originally I thought that the charge was sufficient, but now I think not—which surprises me—and I would argue that the charge was insufficient.

Conference of April 19, 1946

STONE: (1) Claims: that the military commission was *not* properly organized—no martial law, no army of occupation, no statutory authority. We held in *Quirin* that these are laws of war, and we recognized the government's right to create such a commission. In that case, the criminal code was involved. The mode of creating and the subjects are fixed by the common law of the military, and for over one hundred years it had been done that way. Therefore, we have under *Quirin* what is necessary (recognized prisoners of war and violations of the laws of war that prevented proper solution).

(2) Charge: the presentment of the case is sufficient. The charge is not very precise. But it shows that the Japanese troops under this general committed acts that are clearly in violation of laws of war under the Hague Convention. But as to *him,* the government does not charge that he did this, but that he unlawfully *permitted this.* Does the law of war make a general this responsible? The Hague convention and the law of war recognizes that he must be responsible, under the "whole responsibility" doctrine. No efforts to stop these actions appear on his part. We don't have to reach this issue.

Result: In a 6–2 opinion by Chief Justice Stone, the Court ruled that decisions made by military commissions established under the Articles of War were not ordinarily subject to review by civilian courts. The majority limited its review to the question of whether the tribunal had lawful authority to try General Yamashita. The commission, Stone concluded, was fully authorized by the president, the military command, and Congress (which had passed a law authorizing the creation and use of such military commissions). Its authority did not end with the cessation of hostilities and could continue to function even after peace was restored. The commission had jurisdiction to consider whether General Yamashita had exercised sufficient control over those under his command. The Court also ruled that the Articles of War, particularly Articles 25 and 37, governing the admissibility of evidence, were not applicable to Yamashita's trial.[239] The mode of trial was entirely up to the military authorities, who were not obliged to provide the same due process guarantees as civilian courts.

---

239. In ruling that the Articles of War did not apply to enemy combatants tried by military commissions, Stone cited Article 63 of the Geneva Convention of 1929, 47 Stat 2052, which provided that "sentence may be pronounced against a prisoner of war only by the same courts and according to the same procedure as in the case of persons belonging to the armed forces of the detaining power." The Court limited the scope of Article 63, however, to proceedings against prisoners of war for offenses committed *while they were prisoners of war.*

Frank Murphy and Wiley Rutledge wrote stinging dissents, arguing that Fifth Amendment due process guarantees applied to any person accused of a crime in any American court. There were no exceptions; the rules were immutable, invariable, and freely available to "citizens, aliens, alien enemies, or enemy belligerents." Murphy also worried that the case set an impossibly broad and arbitrary precedent, so that "no one in a position of command in an army, from sergeant to general, can escape the implications of the procedure sanctioned today." Robert Jackson did not participate in the decision. On February 23, 1946, nineteen days after the Supreme Court announced its decision, American military authorities hanged General Yamashita at Los Banos, in the Philippines.[240]

Duncan v. Kahanamoku, 327 U.S. 304 (1946)[241]
(Murphy) (Burton) (Douglas)

After Japan bombed Pearl Harbor on December 7, 1941, Hawaii's territorial governor, Joseph P. Poindexter, declared martial law and suspended the writ of habeas corpus. In a shocking simultaneous announcement, Lt. General Walter C. Short unilaterally declared himself to be the new "military governor." Despite Governor Poindexter's understanding that martial law was to last no longer than thirty days, in practice it remained in effect throughout the war—even after Hawaii ceased to be a plausible military target following the Battle of Midway in June 1942.

In early 1942, Lt. General Delos Emmons replaced Short as military governor, and Lt. General Robert R. Richardson in turn succeeded Emmons in 1943. In August 1942, Ingram M. Stainback, a former federal judge and a vocal critic of army rule in Hawaii, replaced Poindexter as the territorial governor. While martial law remained in effect, he was legally subordinate to the military governor. Stainback, however, often harshly criticized what he saw as the excesses of military authority.

Although civilian courts in Hawaii remained open throughout the war, the army transferred most criminal cases to the military's provost marshall's courts. Military leaders thought that nonjury trials in military courts would be quicker and avoid problems with allegedly suspect juror loyalties in multiethnic Hawaii. Civilian authorities, notably Governor Stainback and District Court Judge Delbert E. Metzger, fought throughout the war with military leaders over whether civilian or military courts should be responsible for the administration of justice. Martial law was finally lifted after V-J Day in 1944, following three years of military rule.

The army won the war but lost the peace. Most Hawaiians deeply resented army rule and believed that using military courts to try civilians for civilian offenses illegally and unjustifiably deprived Hawaiians of their constitutional rights, especially their right to jury trials. Military court sentences

---

240. Before his capture, Yamashita was rumored to have buried $200 billion in gold and jewelry somewhere in the Philippines. Since the end of the war, hundreds of people have died looking for the general's hoard, mostly treasure-hunters killed when their crude exploratory tunnels collapsed. Before he came to power in the Philippines, President Ferdinand Marcos claimed to have found the general's treasure, including more than a thousand tons of gold. For more than fifty years the Marcos family has used this story to defend themselves from charges that they embezzled hundreds of millions of dollars from the Philippine treasury to finance their ostentatious lifestyle. The family still maintains that, far from stealing public money for their own use, Marcos enriched the Philippine treasury by spending Yamashita's gold on public projects.

241. Duke Kahanamoku was a legendary surfer, swimmer, and Hawaiian cultural icon. As sheriff of Honolulu in 1944, he was formally in charge of prisoner Lloyd Duncan pending the outcome of Duncan's appeal. Scheiber and Scheiber, "Bayonets in Paradise," 481.

were on average more harsh than those handed out by civilian courts. Even light punishments could be bloody: one of the most common sentences for minor infractions was to offer defendants the choice of paying a large fine or donating a pint of blood to the Red Cross. The military courts proved so unpopular that Red Cross officials had to ask the army to stop coercing donations, for fear that Hawaiians would stop donating blood voluntarily.

Lloyd C. Duncan, a naval worker, was convicted and sentenced by a military court to six months in prison for assaulting two Marine sentries in 1944. Harry E. White was a Honolulu stockbroker convicted in a court martial of embezzlement and sentenced to four years in prison in 1942. Both men appealed to the Supreme Court, and their cases were argued on December 7, 1945, the fourth anniversary of the Japanese attack on Pearl Harbor. The conference is perhaps most memorable for a series of quick exchanges between Stone, Reed, and Frankfurter.

Conference of December 15, 1945[242]

STONE: There is no question about the suspension of the writ of habeas corpus—it has been restored. What is the scope of martial law in the contingencies of this case? It is an exercise of the war powers. It has all of the proper sanctions: Congress gave a broad grant, the military executed it, and the president approved it. The question is, can there be a constitutional exercise of martial law under the war power so as to suspend the operation of civil courts? Can the military create tribunals to try people, and deny them their constitutional right to a jury trial, and apply penalties not in the law? I assume that it can be done under certain circumstances, but the real question is whether this can be done under the circumstances here. It is like that Jap case, *Hirabayashi*, in some respects.[243]

You ultimately get to this end: White was tried for embezzlement by the military at a time when the civil courts were open. Military authorities were permitting public gatherings, and civilian courts had been permitted to try certain cases. There was no showing that the presence of judge and jury in the courthouse had any more effect on public safety than in other trials. Moreover, this man got a sentence beyond what the civil law allows. I have my doubts whether I can go that far. The *Duncan* case is different, because there was an assault on a soldier. This case raises different questions. I have not made up my mind on these cases.

BLACK: They did not have the power to do this. I will vote "no" on both cases.

STONE: I am leaning strongly in that direction in the embezzlement case.

Conference of December 18, 1945

STONE: One defendant [Duncan] was tried by the military for assaulting military personnel in the line of duty at an approach to military quarters. The other defendant [White] was charged with embezzlement and sentenced by the military to a term beyond what Hawaii law permitted. There was no indictment, no jury, and none of the usual protections of civil trial. It all turns upon the effects of the Organic Act and the proclamations

---

242. Douglas listed this conference as taking place on December 8, 1945, while Murphy and Burton listed the conference as taking place on December 15, 1945.

243. It is not clear whether the pejorative was Stone's or Burton's (who recorded Stone's comments).

of the president. The attack on Pearl Harbor was a surprise attack, and on that day the governor of Hawaii proclaimed martial law, suspended the writ of habeas corpus, and notified the president. On the 9th of December, the president approved it by cable. The governor acted under §67 of the Organic Act.[244] In order to suspend the writ, there must be an insurrection, rebellion, or imminent danger of invasion. The suspension of the writ is not a current issue, because the suspension has been lifted and we are free to consider whether habeas corpus will lie.

I do not reach the constitutional question. We come to the question not of the governor's power to declare martial law, but what is involved when it is declared. The governor turned his job over to the military commander. Nothing in the Organic Act allows him to do that. The military commander immediately announced that he was the military governor. On December 8, the military governor closed the territorial courts, and in various degrees they were kept shut. If the military had not closed the courts, there is nothing in record to show they could not have continued to function.[245]

On December 16, 1941, under General Order #29, the courts were reopened but were not permitted to have jury trials. On January 27, 1942, the military governor authorized the courts to function, except for habeas corpus and jury trials. On February 2, 1942, the sale of liquor in bars was allowed under a permit system. June 2–6, 1942 was the Battle of Midway, and the threat of invasion afterward is said to have ended. There may still have been a danger of invasion, but that is not material for me. On August 25, White was tried for embezzlement. In December 1942, Governor Stainback began negotiations for the termination of martial law. On February 8, 1943, the governor and the generals issued a proclamation restoring civil authority in Hawaii. Emmons declared the islands free.[246] In 1943, the island legislature was again in session. Before White's trial, the bars were still open. In 1944, Duncan was tried and convicted. Movie houses were open and people were allowed to congregate.

We do not need to consider the suspension of the writ of habeas corpus. The real question is: what is the effect of this proclamation of martial law, and what is the extent of martial law?

Martial law is not novel. It amounts to no more than the execution of executive power to preserve order and public safety when the other law-making and administrative agencies fail. If the courts can't function, or if it imperils security if they do, then the executive can act to maintain such security as it can. The executive has extraordinary power; the measure of it is the public necessity for safety. It pertains to the executive branch of states as well as the nation. In this case, it is backed by the president's war power, but

---

244. The act authorized the territorial governor to declare martial law and to suspend the writ of habeas corpus in case of actual or imminent rebellion or invasion.

245. General Order No.4, issued on December 7, 1941, established a system of military courts to try civilians for violations of the United States or the Territory and for violations of the rules, regulations, orders, or policies of the military authorities.

246. Stone might have been mistaken. In his speech during the summer of 1942, General Emmons criticized the *Interior Department's* claim that Hawaii was out of danger of attack following the Battle of Midway and claimed that the danger of attack was still imminent. Scheiber and Scheiber, "Bayonets in Paradise," 535.

that does not enlarge it beyond the necessities of the case. This exercise of the power denies traditional civil liberties, and may also deny constitutional rights.

Was there a danger to public safety in the continued functioning of the courts in civil trials so as to endanger our military position? Was there any reasonable or excusable basis for saying that courts could not function, or that if they did that public safety would be involved? Nothing in this record supports the view that there would be a danger if courts opened. I find that the courts were able to function and I see no danger. There was nothing here to indicate that the courts could not have functioned if the military had permitted them to do so. Was it so dangerous to have public meetings as to justify the military decision to close the courts? Unless there was a sufficient basis so that they could fairly say that their functioning was dangerous, then such a step was not justified and the military went beyond their jurisdiction. People who are in authority must say that the civil courts are a menace. We must give wide latitude to people charged with this responsibility under the president's and Congress's approval. It would be different if there had been an invasion, for then the courts could not have functioned. But there was no invasion, nor an imminent danger of it.

Before either of those men were tried, the courts were open in at least a limited sense—but not to juries. Was there any reasonable basis for saying that the courts could not function to full extent in civil cases—or if so, it would be dangerous?

The only suggestion of danger was that there was no right of assembly. But at the time of these trials, saloons and movies were open and normal life was going on. The Japs might have been prejudiced jurors, but there was no danger because they could have been challenged. The military says that civil trials are not so speedy, but I see no relationship between the problem and speed. I see a danger to fair trial in military speed and military procedures. Without bothering with constitutional questions, I only look at the extent of martial law.

It seems to me that apart from the Constitution, the main problem goes to the statute. This use of martial law was an exercise of unconstitutional power. We have said before that martial law did not extend to the limits used. Martial law cannot go beyond the necessities of the case, and I cannot find the necessity of barring civil courts unless the courts are unable to perform their ordinary functions or they would endanger military. I sees no basis for substituting military courts for civil courts on these facts.

Was the situation different in the *Duncan* case? He violated a military order. But the *Duncan* case comes down to the same question—can the civil courts safely function? The military has no right to try him, apart from martial law. The articles of war exclude that jurisdiction. There is no difference here from the other case. It, too, was a matter for the civil courts. The military could repel the assault, arrest the man, hold him, and turn him over to civilian courts—but they can't try him, unless the civilian courts couldn't deal with him or there would be danger in it.

I would reverse both cases. Congress has not made civilians subject to military law. *I would reverse not on martial law or constitutional ground, but on the ground that when declared, martial law has definite limits.*

BLACK: What about Duncan? The Articles of War do not provide for the trial of civilians.

STONE: The army could make offenses against the military offenses in the Articles of War—but here they had not done so. So his status is the same as White's.

BLACK: I agree, and would also classify Duncan with White. I am not sure about the constitutional ground. Armies must have the right to do something to prevent assaults on their troops in an area of invasion and try him up to execution. But here I see no difference between Duncan and White. I think that *Milligan* is an adequate basis for our decision, and I would not deviate from it.

STONE: They tried him by substituting the provost's court for civil courts.

BLACK: I am not willing to overrule *Milligan*. But I see no reason why we cannot go along your way. I would reverse.

REED: I reach the Chief Justice's conclusion by a different route. I start with the fact that we have conquered territory, and there can be a military government in conquered territory. There can be the same in the face of a threat of invasion of this country. But I don't think that there was any real military government in Hawaii. What we have here instead is martial law. No more aggravated conditions could exist than existed after December 7, 1941, in Hawaii. There was no abdication of civilian authority—the military was merely employed as the governor's agent. It was thought that martial law might last a few days or longer. Their authority extended as broadly as necessary—they determined that, and they are entitled to a great range of discretion. I would find this limitation: while martial law is in effect, it does not suspend the Constitution. I don't see how you can suspend the Constitution in our territory.

The military has the power only to police and detain—not to try. Martial law was valid. The orders issued were within the discretion of the military. But he went beyond his power when he tried the civilians.

I would not allow the White or Duncan trials beyond military necessity. I would hold both trials invalid. They were entitled to a different kind of trial. The military authorities can hold a man during the period of martial law for a violation of military rules, but they cannot inflict punishment after martial law is over. Since it is over, these men must be released.

BLACK: They can detain, but they cannot project their authority?

STONE: They could try him in a military court if there was a necessity for it. But I don't see it.

REED: I don't see why they can't hold him as long as they want to while martial law is on. When martial law is over, they can be taken to civil courts. I would not reach the problem of a disregard of the need for releasing them.

STONE: I see no time when these trials could not have been held in perfect safety.

REED: I only give them the right to a civil trial after the period of martial law is over. I would hold them in jail until then.

STONE: What about double jeopardy? It subjected him to detention.

REED: If these fellows were not tried, but held, it is O.K.

FRANKFURTER: I come close to agreeing with Reed, and not with Stone or Black. The war power is part of the Constitution, and it limits the Bill of Rights. The whole question is whether there has been a suspension of constitutional rights. We are now four years after the war. Our job is that of historians. We sit here on December 6th, 1945. We must inject ourselves into 1942. My venerable uncle was held in a camp, and my mother's only surviving sister was burned for lard. It is arrogant to say that the danger of invasion was over at the time of Midway. General George Marshall's September 1944 letter to Dewey shows the critical junction in the war was even then.

Would we have enjoined this trial in August 1942? I don't think so. We would have said that the measure of judgment should have been left to the military. The military judgment here is entitled to great weight. It is the president of the United States who authorized this, and he had responsibility for conducting the war.

It is a nice judgment to make, whether the military should not have closed all courts at all times. I can't say that it was not dangerous to keep juries from congregating. During the Civil War, we did the same thing in Maryland and Kentucky. I can't say that the military authorities were capricious in allowing trials without a jury and barring jury trials. I agree with Reed. Hawaii was a theater of war operation—it was a bastion of war. I would not have enjoined the trial at that time. There was power to detain those who were violating the civil code.

I part from Reed in this—if they can detain them, they can try them. But the jails must be cleared when the martial law is over. I agree with Chase's concurrence in *Milligan*. Martial law is a preventive process. There is a question of res judicata. If he has been detained for embezzlement, double jeopardy applies since he has already suffered a penalty. A person actually in jail for his full term, though punished by the military, can raise a double jeopardy claim in case of a civil trial. I would reverse both cases. With the military's right to detain them terminated, they should now be returned over to civilian authorities.

STONE: I simply say that there was no inability of civilian courts to function.

FRANKFURTER: I do not go by the proof in the record here. It was in an area of war.

STONE: They had the right to apply martial law, and that is only for safety and good order.

FRANKFURTER: I am not justified in saying, near 1946, that a military decision made in 1942 was capricious. Getting in a panel of jurors means a true investigation. If I can't say I would not have voted for enjoining the military in 1942 , I can't do it now. This was an exertion of the war power, and they had the power to detain. I part company with Reed because I believe that they can't hold military provost trials. I think *Milligan* covers this. I would reverse. I would say that he had a constitutional confinement, but not a proper trial. I would keep him until all is over. He is not entitled to constitutional process only in the sense that what the military did was an exercise of war power.

REED: That was what I said—they couldn't try him at law.

STONE: What about the military executing a man after the courts are open?

FRANKFURTER: Martial law means nothing but that there was a war going on in Hawaii.

STONE: I don't think a war *was* going on there, any more than in Massachusetts.

DOUGLAS: I agree with you. I wouldn't go so far that we could not inquire into the military's judgment.

MURPHY: I am with the right of the military to declare martial law, but I agree with the Chief Justice as to what was necessary as to the courts and the public.

RUTLEDGE: I agree with the Chief Justice.

BURTON: I am with Reed and Frankfurter. I think that this was an invasion. The whole community was under attack.

STONE: I agree—but what was the danger of having the civil courts try these cases?

BURTON: The military was like the captain of ship—they had to handle it. The military has to take command all the way down the line, and everything else has to wait. The military has to have a margin of safety, and they can't take a chance. From there on, it is a question of gradual relaxation. You have a great population to handle. The military courts were necessary to relieve congestion of the jails. I am not sure whether they can be released now. It is not orderly to release them on the day that the civil authorities are restored. I would leave it to the military to determine when they get out, and would affirm.

BLACK: I haven't said that they could not detain people. I don't reach that.

Result: With a triumphant Governor Stainback present in the courtroom, the Supreme Court announced in a 5–1–2 vote that the island's military authorities had been wrong to usurp the functions of civilian courts. For the majority, Hugo Black wrote that the suspension of the writ of habeas corpus in Hawaii had been unconstitutionally executed and that civilians could not be tried in military courts for ordinary crimes unrelated to the laws of war, even during wartime in a territory under martial law. Black called the American system of government "the antithesis of total military rule." The military's job was to maintain an orderly civil government and to defend the country against invasion. In the absence of absence of specific congressional authorization, military authorities had no right to supplant civilian courts and replace them with military tribunals. Frank Murphy joined Black's opinion and also wrote a separate concurring opinion. Harlan Fiske Stone concurred in the result.

Harold Burton and Felix Frankfurter dissented. Burton criticized the majority for establishing a precedent in peacetime that might handicap executive authority during a future emergency and trigger a constitutional crisis at the worst possible time. Alluding to the limits of Supreme Court authority during national emergencies, Burton noted that had the Supreme Court decided these two cases under wartime conditions, the Court "might well have found itself embarrassed had it ordered such relief." Jackson did not participate in the case.

United States ex rel. Toth v. Quarles, 350 U.S. 11 (1955)
(Douglas) (Clark)

Five months after Robert Toth was honorably discharged from the army and returned to civilian life, military police tracked him down and arrested him on charges of murder and conspiracy to commit murder while he had been on active duty in Korea. Toth was flown to Korea to be court-martialed under §3(a) of the Uniform Code of Military Justice.[247] *Toth's sister filed for a writ of habeas corpus in the District Court for the District of Columbia. The district court ruled that Toth should not have been taken to Korea without a hearing but did not rule on the constitutionality of §3(a). The district judge ordered Toth returned immediately to the United States and released. Soon after Toth was returned to the United States, the court of appeals reversed, upholding the constitutionality of §3(a) and ordering Toth to surrender to military authorities for removal to Korea.*

Conference of February 12, 1955

WARREN: I affirm. It would be impossible for the United States to maintain a prosecution of this kind unless this procedure is valid. The military hand remained on the soldier even after his discharge. Congress made the choice of making the soldier subject to court-martial or letting him go free. It limited the area—it is just an extension of the old fraud statute of 1863, which has been upheld for ninety years.[248]

BLACK: For the present, I would tentatively reverse. This is a very close case. I do not know how many people the fraud law applied to, and whether it applied to contractors or not.[249] But now, in total war, the whole economy is mixed up with the war effort. I do not want to extend court martial jurisdiction unless I have to. We could limit it to people in the army, or to those who *had* been in the army. I am disturbed about trying civilians who happened to be attached to the army. I do not hold court-martial in high regard. From the words, it could be interpreted either way—it seems to me "arising from" means the soldier is still there. I would not extend court-marital trial any further than necessary. I still believe in *Ex parte Milligan*.[250] We don't have to extend this. People should be tried before juries where at all possible, and Congress can so provide.

REED: I agree with the Chief Justice. This is within the exception to the Fifth Amendment. Toth was in the army. This case "*arose*" while he was in the service. I affirm.

FRANKFURTER: If this were a recent statute, I would declare it unconstitutional. "Arising under" is different from "arose under." Policy issues are controlling here. It goes against my grain to have a civilian tried by the military. History gives me pause. But the

---

247. Passed by Congress in 1950, §3(a) provided that "any person charged with having committed, while in a status in which he was subject to this code, an offense against this code . . . for which the person cannot be tried in the courts of the United States . . . shall not be relieved from amenability to trial by courts-martial by reason of the termination of said status."

248. In 1863, Congress authorized the military to court-martial civilian contractors who furnished arms, equipment, munitions, or other goods and services to the military for fraud and other crimes. This law was declared unconstitutional by a lower court in *Ex parte Henderson,* 11 Fed. Cas. 1067 (Circuit Court for the District of Kentucky, 1878).

249. At the time, the Supreme Court had not yet definitively ruled on the question of whether civilian contractors were covered under the 1863 act. Five years after *Toth* was decided, the Court ruled that civilian employees of the armed forces overseas were not subject to trial by courts-martial. *McElroy v. Guagliardo,* 361 U.S. 281 (1960).

250. *Ex parte Milligan,* 71 U.S. (4 Wall.) 2 (1866).

Court never expressed itself on the point. There is an English case in 1760 which is the other way.[251] Also, see *Neely v. Henkel*.[252]

DOUGLAS: I tentatively vote to reverse.

BURTON: The Constitution sets up a separate class for military trials. Congress can overlap. Congress should be trusted to handle this phase of our military. In *Milligan*, the man never was in the service—here he was in and the crime follows him. The congressional statute gives a limited discharge. I affirm.

CLARK: I affirm.

MINTON: I affirm.

Conference of October 14, 1955

WARREN: I reverse. At the time that the Constitution was adopted, the purpose of military courts was to provide discipline in the armed services. The "necessary and proper" clause does not come into play. Any other construction would deprive the accused of his right to a jury trial. Reversal would not leave a vacuum. Congress can act in order to provide for trial of the accused by civil courts. If no remedy, it would affect discipline in the army. Congress can provide for trial in a district court. This is a very important case from the point of view of civil liberties. Section 3(a) is not consistent with the Constitution's jury trial guarantee.

BLACK: I reverse and agree with the Chief Justice.

REED: I affirm. A jury trial is not proper for military officers.

FRANKFURTER: I reverse.

DOUGLAS: I reverse.

---

251. George II asked Lord Mansfield and twelve judges of the King's Bench, Common Pleas, and Exchequer to offer an advisory opinion as to whether Lord General Sackville—who previously had been dismissed from the armed services—could be court-martialed for disobeying orders while on active duty during the battle of Minden. Reserving the right to change their mind when the case officially came before them, the judges advised the king that the military courts could assert jurisdiction. *Lord Sackville's Case*, 28 Engl. Rep. 940, 2 Eden's Chancery Reports, App., 371 (1760).

252. *Neely v. Henkel*, 180 U.S. 109 (1901). Charles Neely, an American citizen, was arrested in New York and charged under Cuban law with embezzling Cuban public funds while he was a postal official in Havana. Neely allegedly embezzled $57,000 while the island was under American occupation following the Spanish-American War. Neely fought extradition to Cuba, claiming that his detention and trial by Cuban authorities would violate his constitutional rights. The Court ruled that even under American occupation, Cuba remained an independent country and that Neely's American citizenship did not entitle him to the same rights in other countries that he enjoyed in the United States. He had no right to a trial "in any other mode than that allowed to its own people by the country whose laws he has violated and from whose justice he has fled." This case established the "non-inquiry rule," which held that Americans arrested or prosecuted abroad were not legally entitled to the protections afforded by American law. American courts traditionally do not inquire into the judicial procedures of foreign jurisdictions, and Americans who commit crimes in a foreign country must submit to locally established laws and procedures.

BURTON: Congress has the power to do what it has done here. I affirm.

CLARK: I reverse. I have changed my view from last Term.

MINTON: I affirm.

HARLAN: The dividing line must be found in the Constitution between military authority and civilian authority. I agree with Black's circulated opinion. I reverse.

Result: The Court found that Congress had exceeded its powers in passing §3(a) and that no executive authority or military consideration could justify depriving Toth of his constitutional rights to a civilian trial by jury. There was considerable shifting of opinion in this case. After the initial conference, Reed was assigned the majority opinion and Black took the lead in dissent. After seeing Black's draft dissent, Tom Clark changed his mind and joined it. Black and Douglas then convinced Earl Warren that the case should be reargued so that newly appointed John Marshall Harlan could participate. The Chief and Harlan both ultimately joined Black's opinion, transforming it into a 6–3 majority. Black wrote a strong endorsement of civilian justice and trial by jury. Reed, now in dissent, argued that courts-martial were not inherently inferior to civilian justice and that Congress could use the necessary and proper clause to permit military trials in such cases.

Reid v. Covert & Kinsella v. Krueger, 351 U.S. 470 (1956)
(Douglas) (Burton)

Clarice Covert was accused of murdering her husband, Master Sergeant Edward Covert, at an American airbase in England. Dorothy Smith was accused of murdering her husband, Colonel Aubrey Smith, at an army base in Japan. Both women were tried in military courts and convicted. Covert appealed on her own behalf. Smith's father, Walter Krueger, filed for a writ of habeas corpus on her behalf in a West Virginia district court.[253] The two cases were consolidated on appeal, and around the Supreme Court it was known as "The Case of the Murdering Wives." There were two key conferences a year apart.

Conference of May 4, 1956

WARREN: I come out for the wives. The things that bother me are whether the wives and kids are part of the armed forces. I doubt it. An engineer working with seabees would be. But it is hard to believe that a housewife and youngsters living in Tokyo or London are members of the armed forces for military purposes. The fact that they use the PX means nothing. If they are, and the army may try them, that is not in keeping with our traditions. I am fearful of the expansion of military power. I am not too clear on this, and my votes are not firm. I affirm in *Reid* and reverse in *Kinsella*.

BLACK: The military has no authority here. There is no doubt about the right of the government to subject soldiers and those working for the military to military jurisdiction. As to the power of civilian courts to try these persons, the Constitution and statutes say otherwise. Then we have to meet *In re Ross*, which said that consular courts could try

---

253. General Walter Krueger was the commanding general of the Sixth Army during World War II.

civilian citizens. I think that the old *In re Ross* case no longer is sound.[254] I am not willing to treat this act as under any power but the power to make rules governing the armed forces. I affirm in *Reid* and reverse in *Kinsella*.

REED: There is no problem here of camp followers. The latter are not subject to court martial except in time of war. These offenses took place after the war ended. Congress could make wives subject to courts-martial, I think—I am not sure—but this is not that case. Does the Constitution follow the flag? There is a long history of American courts abroad. It may be a better choice than letting England or Japan try them, or sending them back here. I am not prepared to say that the power is lacking. I am inclined to support the wives, but I am not sure.

FRANKFURTER: The real problem is that we can't say that these women are members of the armed services. History is against this power vesting in the military. *Blackmer*[255] and *Bowman*[256] are the most relevant cases bearing on *In re Ross*. I think that the case turns on *Ross*. The *Ross* case has stuff in it that is not so. In the *Blackmer* case there was a fine of $60,000. The money was collected. Hughes did not talk about *Ross*, except in a footnote— for a unanimous Court that an American citizen has certain duties. But there must be due process. The crime in *Bowman* was against the United States—the crime here is not against the laws of England. In *Ross*, we extended the right to consular courts to protect American citizens from despotic regimes. The United States can say that a citizen who kills another citizen is guilty of an offense. I would require that due process which the Constitution requires. In so far as it authorizes a court martial, it is beyond the power of

---

254. *In re Ross*, 140 U.S. 453 (1891). John Ross, a British citizen serving in the United States Navy, killed an American naval officer while in Japan. He was court-martialed, convicted, and sentenced to hang. In affirming Ross's conviction and sentence, the Supreme Court in effect ruled that the Constitution had no force or effect in a foreign territory. *Ross* also endorsed the practice of allowing American consular officials to make laws, indict, arrest, try, and even execute American citizens accused of crimes in Japan, China, and other "non-Christian nations."

Black viewed this blending of executive, legislative, and judicial powers as government absolutism at its worst, and at least in spirit he had some notable company. In the *Federalist Papers (No. 47)*, James Madison defined tyranny as the concentration of all government powers into the same hands, whether of one, the few, or the many.

255. *Blackmer v. United States*, 284 U.S. 421 (1932). This case established that American citizens living abroad remained subject to American law. Harry M. Blackmer, an American citizen living in France, was subpoenaed to testify in an American district court regarding the Teapot Dome scandal. When he refused to obey the summons, the district court found him guilty of contempt and fined him $30,000, which was satisfied by a court-ordered seizure and sale of American property Blackmer owned. The Supreme Court ruled that Blackmer's refusal to honor a lawful subpoena could be punished by American courts and that Blackmer remained subject to the taxing power of the United States. This was not a matter of international law, Charles Evans Hughes wrote for the majority, "but solely of the purport of the municipal law."

256. *United States v. Bowman*, 260 U.S. 94 (1922). Bowman was an American citizen involved in an international conspiracy to defraud the Emergency Fleet Corporation, which was wholly owned by the United States government. After his arrest, Bowman protested that all of his alleged illegal activities took place outside the United States, either on the high seas or in Brazil. The Court ruled that American citizens on the high seas or in foreign countries remained subject to American criminal laws passed to protect the United States and its property. The Court avoided the question of whether another of the alleged conspirators, a British citizen, also was subject to the federal government's extraterritorial authority.

Congress to include this woman in regulations governing the armed forces. I affirm in *Reid* and reverse in *Kinsella*.

DOUGLAS: I affirm in *Reid* and reverse in *Kinsella*.

BURTON: We must find in the Constitution the power to deal with this situation. I am not shocked at including the wives under military jurisdiction. Congress has it within its broad power to set up this machinery. I believe in the *Ross* case. Congress can act through consular courts or through military courts. I reverse in *Reid* and affirm in *Kinsella*.

CLARK: I pass on both cases.

MINTON: *Ross* controls, and it is sound. The Constitution does not follow me *there*. The Constitution does not make a foreign country cede its power to try a man under its terms. All that is done here is a cession of power by the foreign countries, such as England. I will concede that these women are not part of the army. England concedes the matter to us. The consular courts are the way out. If you can use consular courts, you can use military courts. I will stick to *Ross*. I reverse in *Reid* and affirm in *Kinsella*.

HARLAN: I agree with Minton, although I am tentative. The *Ross* doctrine does control this.

Result: After several changes of mind following the conference, the Court voted 5–3 that military trials of civilian dependents abroad did not violate the Constitution, with Frankfurter reserving judgment on the question. Fortunately for the accused, they applied for a rehearing at an auspicious time. Sherman Minton and Stanley Reed retired, leaving two vacancies on the Court. More importantly, John Marshall Harlan was quietly changing his mind about the case, with encouragement from Earl Warren and Felix Frankfurter. Although there were two vacancies on the Court, only William Brennan was seated in time to hear reargument in these cases; Charles Whittaker was confirmed later. This time the Justices emphasized the fundamental importance of trial by jury and the limits of Article 1's necessary and proper clause. Tom Clark tried a last-ditch procedural maneuver in a lost cause.

Reid v. Covert & Kinsella v. Krueger (II), 354 U.S. 1 (1957)
(Douglas)

Conference of March 1, 1957

WARREN: I can't rely on *Ross*. The necessary and proper clause can't enlarge the jurisdiction. Dependents in peace time are not subject to military rule. Congress has no power to put them under military jurisdiction. I hold for the wives in each case.

BLACK: I agree with the Chief.

FRANKFURTER: *Ross* is not a permissible ground. The real problem is Article 1, and whether the law is a fair regulation of the armed forces. It is not enough to say that the wives were not in the land and naval forces. All grants of power to Congress involve collateral powers. Interstate rates may be regulated under the commerce clause. But the war power and regulation of the army are limited by Fifth and Sixth Amendments. A wife does not have a military status. To put her in that status and try her by the army is a violation of due process. Historical materials are too meager to say that it was settled that women with the army were part of the army.

DOUGLAS: I am against military jurisdiction.

BURTON: I think that Congress has the power to do this under Article 1. I would go so far as to say that the "cold war" means that this is not a peacetime case. Our armed forces must be around the world. Congress can determine that there should be civilians with the armed forces. If Congress has the power, it can modify and control it. Congress has broad power over the armed forces, both in war and in peace. Congress is a civilian-minded body. The safety of the nation is involved in peacetime as well as wartime.

CLARK: I propose reargument before a nine-judge court, allowing the women out on bail meanwhile. If these women were tried abroad, they would not be able to get a jury to try them. A general can evacuate the civilians—he has complete control and needs it out of necessity. There is nothing new about military trials of women—the British do it all the time. *Toth* turned on a lack of necessity for discipline, which is present here.[257]

HARLAN: Our first opinion was on a false ground. I would sustain the federal government's position on Congress's Article 1 power, and I rest on the necessary and proper clause. The alternate is to try the wives over here. The real restraint is in the common views of our people. I would distinguish enclaves here and a port abroad. Cases arising here would not be appropriate for military trial because our courts are open. I would agree that the U.S. Army in London would have jurisdiction over a wife living in an apartment—historically, dependents were subject to courts martial.

BRENNAN: I am against the jurisdiction of the military. The first ten amendments are a qualification of the other powers. What is the composition of America's land and naval forces? I can't say that they do not include civilian employees—they may not be in the same position as dependents. Paid civilian employees may perform military functions. It would be grave mistake to say civilian employees are excluded from the land and naval forces. But a dependent is not a member of land and naval forces. Also, military commanders must have power to maintain law and order. The power to arrest is different from the power to try. Perhaps Congress could work out a way to have a trial by jury overseas.

FRANKFURTER: We need not define what the armed forces are. The necessary and proper clause gives effectiveness to the content. I would not say whether we should bring them back here or try them over there.

Result: Although Hugo Black's lead opinion had the support of only four Justices, Frankfurter and Harlan concurred in the judgment to give Black a comfortable 6–2 majority to reverse both convictions. Black wrote that when the United States acted against its own citizens abroad, it must follow the Constitution, including Article 3 and the Fifth and Sixth Amendments. Trying civilian dependents in military courts in foreign countries was not necessary and proper within the meaning of Ar-

---

257. *U.S. ex rel. Toth v. Quarles,* 350 U.S. 11 (1955).

ticle 1, and Congress's responsibility for the armed services under Article 1 did not extend to civilian dependents living on foreign military bases. The Constitution, Black concluded, gave civilian courts the exclusive power to try civilians for offenses against the United States. Frankfurter voted to limit the right of civilian dependents to be tried by civilian courts to offenses committed during peacetime, while Harlan thought that the right should be limited to capital crimes committed during peacetime.

Jencks v. United States, 353 U.S. 657 (1957)
(Douglas)

Clinton E. Jencks, a New Mexico labor union president, filed a false affidavit claiming that he was not a member of the Communist party. He was charged in federal court with violating the National Labor Relations Act. To assist in his defense, Jencks sought to obtain copies of reports submitted to the government by two paid FBI informants, Harvey Matusow and J. W. Ford. Jencks wanted to use the reports to cross-examine both informants. The federal government objected, arguing that the reports contained secret and sensitive information. At a minimum, Jencks argued, the trial judge should examine the documents to determine whether they were relevant. The district court judge rejected Jencks's requests, and he was convicted on the weight of Matusow's and Ford's testimony. The court of appeals affirmed. Matusow later confessed to having lied at Jencks's trial and in testimony before a variety of congressional committees.

Conference of October 19, 1956

WARREN: The district court should have looked at the FBI reports to see if they are inconsistent with the testimony of Matusow. A remand would be the course to follow, but for the bias of the district court in sending him to jail for three years as a perjurer. On the charge, the jury was told what circumstantial evidence it might consider, but not what it must consider.[258] On affiliation, the charge was vague.[259] The charge was not adequate on either ground. This paid informer is testifying to everything he can think of to incriminate a man over a period of years. He made written reports regularly. I reverse.

BLACK: I reverse and agree with the Chief. When a man is on trial for his liberty and an informer is testifying, it is not enough that the judge alone see the reports that the informer made. You can't retain evidence and send a man to jail on it because it's too confidential. If the government wants to keep the evidence confidential, they should try the case without the evidence.

---

258. In his jury charge on circumstantial evidence of party membership, the trial judge said: "In considering whether or not the defendant was a member of the Communist Party, you may consider circumstantial evidence, as well as direct. You may consider whether or not he attended Communist Party meetings, whether or not he held an office in the Communist Party, whether or not he engaged in other conduct consistent only with membership in the Communist Party and all other evidence, either direct or circumstantial, which bears or may bear upon the question of whether or not he was a member of the Communist Party on April 28, 1950."

259. In his charge on affiliation, the judge instructed the jury that "affiliation means something less than membership but more than sympathy." This allowed the jury to convict Jencks on the basis of intermittent cooperation, rather than based on a continuing course of conduct carried out on a "fairly permanent basis." *Jencks v. United States,* 353 U.S. 657, 679 (1957) (Burton, J., concurring).

REED: I am inclined to the view that defendant should have the reports. But I am not sure what the safeguards should be. I pass.

FRANKFURTER: I think that the reports should be produced, but I do not think that production should depend on a showing of contradictions. I would not extend the rule to require the reports of every agent made if the agent testifies, for many prosecutions are based on agent testimony. Informers are a special class. There was unfairness under Pitt's rule in England, and also in France. I do not want the trial judge alone to have the power of examination of the reports. It goes against my grain that the reports should be sealed so as to go up to the court of appeals. There should be no ex parte rulings in a criminal case. The motion should have been granted. But it was not an ex parte matter but for the counsel too. If this is a capital case, then the question of a "public trial" is raised. Look at *Snyder v. Massachusetts*,[260] and the *Dreyfus* case, and the non-disclosure of documents there.[261] The error was in failing to produce. If the documents are produced and no inconsistency is shown, then there is no reason for a new trial. If the case goes back on that ground alone, there can be no reversal.

WARREN: I wonder if there would not be grounds for reversal, even though ultimately no conflict in the reports were shown to exist. A failure to include an incriminating fact in the reports would be fatal also.

FRANKFURTER: I agree that inconsistency is not the test. It is the issue of the untrustworthiness of the witness. The trial judge's charges on membership and affiliation are also bad. Normally, if a case is sent back for a new trial it is wise to rule on the instructions, so that the same error will not be repeated. The *Mazzei* case had errors in the charge that we did not reach—but all we did was to reverse on perjury—then the trial court may now repeat the former errors.[262] If we treat here the error—the charge—we will have to say why we did not touch those matters in *Mazzei*. He may come back after a new trial on the same erroneous charge that was here before.

DOUGLAS: I reverse.

BURTON: The charges were erroneous and we should clarify them. On the reports, they should be submitted to the judge. I reverse.

---

260. *Snyder v. Massachusetts*, 291 U.S. 97 (1934). In a state murder trial, the judge granted the prosecutor's motion to a view of the murder scene. The judge, both counsel, jurors, and a court stenographer all visited the scene of the crime, but the judge refused to allow the accused to attend. The Supreme Court held that the exclusion did not violate the defendant's due process rights. Benjamin Cardozo ruled that due process required the defendant's presence only to the extent that a fair and just hearing would have been thwarted by his absence. The trial judge's decision, Cardozo decided, was consistent with historical practice dating back hundreds of years, and this tradition had not been invalidated by the adoption of the Fourteenth Amendment.

261. Captain Alfred Dreyfus was convicted of treason in France in 1899 and imprisoned on Devil's Island. He was later cleared when his supporters demonstrated that his conviction had been tainted by official corruption and antisemitism.

262. *Mesarosh v. United States*, 352 U.S. 1 (1956). In this case, the federal government admitted that a key government witness, Joseph Mazzei, had committed perjury. The solicitor general confessed error and asked that the case be remanded on that basis.

CLARK:[263] It would be a big mistake to open up the FBI's records on the showing here. We would have to overrule our conscientious objector cases. If these FBI reports are disclaimed, the lawyer will use them to a fare-thee-well. It is O.K. to let the judge see them, but not the lawyers.

HARLAN: The district attorney would want these reports in—the FBI has created the problem.

CLARK: It is the Justice Department, not the FBI, that treats the reports as confidential. We can't allow lawyers to go fishing. The defense has avenues to discredit Matusow that they did not use. Matusow was the defendant's witness. We can't let lawyers start trying the FBI. We should not disturb the exercise of judicial discretion where two lower courts agree. I would go only so far as to let the court see the reports. On the instructions, you would have to strike down both to reverse, as there were two counts and the sentences ran concurrently. The charge on membership followed *Douds* and is O.K.[264]

HARLAN: I reverse. The charge was bad in both respects. The defendant is entitled to see the records. I am inclined to favor disclosure of the report to the judge alone.

BRENNAN: I can't see why discovery of this kind can't be had in a criminal case. There should be nothing sacrosanct about the prosecution end. Disclosure should be to the counsel. I do not like just having the judge alone look at the report. On the charges, I am bothered. It is difficult to define membership or affiliation.

Conference of November 2, 1956

BRENNAN: If a witness has made a report, it should be produced. A contemporary report is apt to be reliable. Matusow made reports over his signature. There is no possible basis for refusing production of those reports. That is one kind of report. Another is the report of the FBI man on the stand, concerning what Matusow said. That should be submitted. If the report is obtained and the party requesting it does not use it, then the other side may introduce it. That is the rule held by all lower federal courts. Where a man who made the report is not on the stand, it's a different question.

FRANKFURTER: The government is different from any other party or witness. Look at the debate in the House of Commons on October 26, 1956, on the government's privilege to withhold documents.

---

263. While he was attorney general during the Truman administration, Clark compiled the government's first official list of subversive organizations.

264. *American Communications Assn. v. Douds*, 339 U.S. 382 (1950). The Labor Management Relations Act required labor unions to register with the National Labor Relations Board (NLRB) and to file annual "non-Communist affidavits" on behalf of all union officials. Failure to register or file the required affidavits meant that the union (in the case, the CIO) would be deprived of some of the benefits of the act and would be subject to certain restrictions on its activities. In approving the act, the majority balanced the union members' free speech rights against Congress's right to prevent politically motivated strikes that harmed interstate commerce.

Conference of March 22, 1957

WARREN: I reverse. The court refused to examine Matusow's reports. That was error. The issue was raised in the defendant's motion for new trial. There is a direct conflict as to what was said. The court should have resolved it. I do not think that the case should go back to the district court on this point, as the district court judge was prejudiced. His instruction on membership was also erroneous.

BLACK: I reverse.

FRANKFURTER: The judge's charge is defective on membership. As to the disclosure of informer reports, there are many types of situations to deal with. We should lay down a rule of practice that it is not protective of the defendant to exclude his counsel from a debate on whether the reports are material.

DOUGLAS: I reverse.

BURTON: I reverse. The FBI reports should be examined by the judge. The trial judge's instructions were dubious on membership and on affiliation.

CLARK: The trial judge alone should look at the informer reports—counsel would distort them. I think that the instructions are O.K.

HARLAN: I reverse on both grounds.

BRENNAN: I reverse. On disclosure of reports, if a witness admits making a statement on the subject concerning his testimony, that is enough to let the defense see it. *Gordon* is a little inconsistent.[265] Inconsistency is not the test—counsel should see the reports as well as the judge. If the judge decides that national security is at issue, then the government should either let it be used or dismiss the indictment.

Result: In a 5–2–1 decision, the Supreme Court ruled that Jencks was entitled to see the FBI's written reports on Matusow and Ford. If the government refused to cooperate, Brennan wrote for the majority, then the government "can invoke its evidentiary privileges only at the price of letting the defendant go free." Jencks's conviction was overturned and his case remanded. Burton and Harlan concurred, and Whittaker did not participate. Tom Clark, in dissent, warned that the ruling would lead to "a Roman holiday for rummaging through confidential information as well as vital national secrets."

President Eisenhower, rarely at a loss for superlatives when discussing the Warren Court, said that he had "never been as mad in [his] life" as when he heard about this decision. Congress reacted

265. *Gordon v. United States*, 344 U.S. 414 (1953). Gordon and several others were convicted of possession and transportation of stolen goods in interstate commerce. During the trial, a key government witness admitted that he had made previous statements to prosecutors that conflicted with his trial testimony. He also admitted that he had pled guilty in another court to unlawful possession of the same stolen goods and that the judge had delayed sentencing pending the outcome of this case. The Supreme Court reversed Gordon's conviction, saying that under the circumstances the trial court (1) should have granted the defendants' request for prosecutors to turn over the witness's conflicting written statements; and (2) should have admitted into evidence a transcript of trial proceedings in the witness's earlier case showing that the judge deferred sentencing the witness and instructed the witness, "to tell the probation authorities the whole story, even though it might involve others."

quickly, taking less than three months to pass what became known as the Jencks Act, which placed new limits on the sorts of documents defendants could demand from the government.

Machibroda v. United States, 368 U.S. 487 (1962)
(Douglas)

John Machibroda pled guilty to federal bank robbery charges and was sentenced to forty years in Alcatraz prison. Three years later, he alleged that the U.S. attorney had induced him to plead guilty by falsely promising him that he would be sentenced to no more than twenty years in prison. He also claimed that the U.S. attorney warned him not to tell his own lawyer of the deal or the government would file additional charges against him. Finally, Machibroda claimed that the trial judge had not given him a chance to speak before he was sentenced. The trial judge ruled that Machibroda's story was patently unbelievable and summarily denied his request for a new hearing. This is a relatively minor case, but it contains an especially sharp exchange between Earl Warren and Felix Frankfurter.

Conference of December 8, 1961

WARREN: I reverse. Counsel was not furnished, and without counsel he can't be expected to act intelligently. Rule 11 requires the trial court to make sure that the plea was knowingly made—it was violated here.[266] He is entitled to a hearing on whether the prosecutor had got him to plead guilty on the use of coercive tactics.

BLACK: One thing about this that bothers me is that the man never says he is not guilty and wants to withdraw the plea—he wants his plea of guilty vacated. I doubt whether we should do that here and give him a trial. I reverse only on the sentence.

WARREN: A man is entitled to have the judge ask the man if he committed the offense. Many lesser crimes are often included.

FRANKFURTER: I affirm. Rule 35 not available for this purpose.[267]

CLARK: I affirm.

HARLAN: I affirm. A coerced plea is open under §2255, but the lower court had discretion to say that this was not a bona fide claim.

BRENNAN: I reverse.

WHITTAKER: Rule 35 does not cover mere error. The allocution point is just that. I affirm.

STEWART: On the coerced plea issue, I am inclined to grant a hearing—but not on the Rule 35 point. [DOUGLAS: While the Chief was answering Potter Stewart's question on Rule 35, Frankfurter was snickering and passing notes to John Harlan, as is his custom.

---

266. Rule 11 of the Federal Rules of Criminal Procedure required trial judges to determine whether guilty pleas were made voluntarily.

267. Rule 35 of the Federal Rules of Criminal Procedure and 28 U.S.C. §2255 allow defendants to file a motion to vacate an illegal sentence. While Rule 35 technically provides for collateral review, in practice these motions are treated as a continuation of the original trial. Defendants must show (1) cause for not raising the issue at trial or on direct appeal; and (2) that "actual prejudice" resulted from the error.

The Chief stopped and said, "I am goddamn tired of having you snicker while I am talking. You do it even in the courtroom and people notice it." Frankfurter denied that he was snickering. There followed a long harangue in which the Chief said that he had reached the limits of his tolerance for Frankfurter.]

Result: The Court vacated and remanded the case for new hearings on whether Machibroda's guilty plea was voluntary. Stewart wrote for the opinion of the Court in a schizophrenic opinion representing two different majorities. In the first part of his opinion, Stewart was joined by Frankfurter, Clark, Harlan, and Whittaker in ruling that the judge's failure to ask Machibroda whether he had anything to say on his own behalf before sentencing (the judge had asked Machibroda's lawyer, but not the defendant himself) was not reviewable under Rule 35 or §2255. Warren, Black, Douglas, and Brennan dissented.

On the second issue, Stewart joined Warren, Black, Douglas, and Whittaker to find that the trial judge had erred in assuming that Machibroda's guilty plea was voluntary and that a new hearing was necessary to determine whether the plea had been secured through government threats or intimidation. Writing for the four dissenters on this issue, Clark noted that Machibroda had been represented by counsel, had voluntarily confessed his guilt during the trial of a co-defendant, and had waited three years to fabricate Munchausen tales designed to get him off the Rock.

United States v. Barnett, 376 U.S. 681 (1964)
(Douglas)

In the early 1960s Governor Ross Barnett and Lieutenant Governor Paul Johnson openly defied repeated orders from the federal district court and court of appeals to permit James Meredith to enroll as the first black student at the University of Mississippi. The court of appeals appointed the attorney general to prosecute both officials for criminal contempt. Both men demanded jury trials.[268] The court of appeals was equally divided on the issue of whether they had the right to a jury trial and certified the question to the Supreme Court.

Conference of October 25, 1963

WARREN: Does Barnett have the right to a jury trial? I answer the question "yes." I follow the *Greene* [*sic*] dissent.[269] That view is stronger now because Congress has passed an

268. The two men cited 18 U.S.C. §§402 and 3691, which guaranteed the right to a jury trial in contempt proceedings arising out of disobedience to the orders of a district court or any court within the District of Columbia, provided that the conduct complained of also constituted a criminal offense under federal or state law. The two statutes, however, did not explicitly include a right to jury trial for criminal contempt proceedings stemming from disobedience of a federal *circuit court* order.

269. *Green v. United States*, 356 U.S. 165 (1958). Gilbert Green and others were convicted of conspiracy to violate the Smith Act. Allowed to remain free pending appeal, they failed to report to federal authorities as ordered to begin serving their sentences after their appeals were exhausted. More than four years later they surrendered voluntarily, claiming that they had been justified in refusing to report for prison. A district judge sitting without a jury summarily found all of the defendants guilty of criminal contempt for wilfully disobeying the surrender order and sentenced each of the defendants to three years in prison. On a 5–4 vote the Supreme Court held that criminal contempt cases did not constitutionally require either jury trials or grand jury indictments. The four dissenters (Warren, Black, Douglas, and Brennan) argued that regardless of established precedents, it was time to establish a new rule that anyone charged with contempt for violating a court decree outside of the courtroom was entitled a jury trial following indictment by a grand jury.

act in the field and that act limits punishment to one year. The United States should not be able to bypass that statute and get a longer term. The United States came in as amicus and then instituted this criminal proceeding. "Any other court" in the act means "any other court of comparable jurisdiction."

BLACK: I adhere to my *Greene* dissent. I might go on the statute.

DOUGLAS: I pass. (I did not hear the oral argument due to illness.)

CLARK: The statute does not apply. I answer the question "no."

HARLAN: He is not entitled to a jury trial. The statutory grounds are not tenable. On the Constitution, precedent is against Barnett. This would be an unfortunate case in which to act. The courts should have power to correct a disgraceful situation. If they do not have the power, there is none, for a jury would go with the government. I urge the non-committed members of the Court to take that view. *Greene* can't be distinguished. He should be treated like one who throws an inkwell at the judge.

BRENNAN: This was not a district court order under the statute. Section 1509 might contain a pro tanto repeal of §401, but that is too difficult. I come to the Constitution. I did not join Hugo in *Greene*, and I do not think that there is a constitutional guarantee of a jury trial in criminal contempt proceedings.

STEWART: I see nothing that has happened to indicate that the history reflected in *Greene* has changed or should change. If this were a civil case in a district court, there would be a jury trial. But this is not a district court and it is not a civil but a criminal prosecution. The case is in the court of appeals and the statute does not apply. There is no right to a jury trial here.

WHITE: No jury trial—I agree with Potter.

GOLDBERG: It is a complete denial of due process of the United States to have proceeded as it did here. I can't approve it. This is not a government action—it was only an amicus. The United States can come in only as parens patriae. Congress can ask the federal government to sue or authorize it under Taft Hartley, but nothing like that was done here. I do not reach the other grounds. On the merits, I think that Barnett was entitled to a jury trial. But I go on the ground that the whole procedure was wrong, and there was no case or controversy.

BRENNAN: I would not reach that question, although I would be glad to put it down for argument.

Result: *On a 5–4 vote, the Court decided that neither Barnett nor Johnson had a constitutional or statutory right to a jury trial. Tom Clark wrote for the majority that while 18 U.S.C. §§402 and 3691 allowed jury trials in criminal contempt proceedings stemming from disobedience of a federal district court order, these laws did not apply to criminal contempt prosecutions based on willful disobedience of orders by the court of appeals—even if a district court order had also been willfully violated. Clark thought that it would be illogical to allow the court of appeals to punish contempt against it without a jury, but not when it also included contempt of a district court order. The majority ruled that there was no general* constitutional right to trial by jury in criminal contempt proceedings, although Clark acknowledged that there might be exceptions to the general rule based on the severity of the penalty imposed. Warren, Black, Douglas, and Goldberg dissented on both statutory and constitutional grounds.

TRIAL BY JURY

Representation and Exclusion

Thiel v. Southern Pacific, 328 U.S. 217 (1946)
(Burton) (Douglas) (Murphy)

Gilbert Thiel leaped from a moving train and was badly injured. He sued the railroad company, arguing that its employees should have known that he was "not in his right mind" and prevented him from jumping. After the railroad removed the case to federal court, Thiel objected to the federal jury pool, claiming that it was composed of business executives and others with an "employer's perspective." His protests were ignored and he lost his case. On appeal, Thiel caught the Supreme Court's attention when he discovered that the jury commissioner had intentionally and systematically excluded from jury service all persons who worked for a daily wage.

In conference, note Harold Burton's reluctance to sully the Court's reputation by endorsing a distasteful government practice. He would adopt a similar position eight years later when faced with state-mandated school segregation.

Conference of March 30, 1946

STONE: Thiel went crazy and jumped out of the train window. He went to trial before a jury, but before summoned he made a motion about the jury. The jury commissioner put three hundred names in the box. No women were drawn. The petitioner objected to the array on the ground that laborers were excluded. The exclusions were justified on the ground that men working for a daily wage lost their pay, and therefore they were excluded. By excluding those on a day wage, Thiel claimed, the jury lost its representative character by excluding this group. He did not refer to any federal or state statute that this person's rights were violated. Thiel relies on the provision that "fair and impartial juries" must be drawn, and that excluding those on a day wage deprived the jury of its representative quality.

There is no rule that every class must be represented in a petty jury. If you look at the jury as actually drawn, you will see that it was fairly representative of the community, and was as diverse and representative as any group you would ever get. One merchant seaman, one housewife, one employee of firm, one retired RR party clerk, one retired steel erector, two insurance brokers, one department manager of exporting/importing, one housewife, one retired commerce merchant, one [illegible], one rice broker. The chances are against you getting a fairer jury. The case narrows down to the question of whether the exclusion of men on daily wages would be enough to upset the jury. Here the purpose of the exclusions was to avoid excuses. I never supposed that excluding one class on grounds of hardship vitiated the jury panel. I am reluctant to upset this case. The old common law rule that you got the first twelve you can get. Under the "bystander" rule, you could get any bystanders to serve as jurors. I hesitate to lay down a rule that this so violated the jury system's rules that it must be set aside. I can't say that the fundamental experience of a man who works on a day wage is different from the same man who has retired.

BLACK: I would reverse it.

REED: I affirm. The federal statutes relate to a selected jury. It is subject to the qualifications of the highest court of state. Intelligence is required by law. We would have to give some directions if we set this aside. It was intended that a jury be selected. If we are going to have others than selected jurors, we must draw them by lot. Until that is done, I would sustain what was done here.

STONE: There is a geographical provision in the act. Jurors need not be drawn from the whole district until the court so orders, which has never been done.

FRANKFURTER: I agree with you and I will affirm. I cannot say that this violates his right of jury trial. There is no suggestion that it violates the Seventh Amendment. It does not violate any statute. We have supervisory powers over federal courts as to the standards of fairness. The heart of the matter is the rejection of day labor. There is nothing to indicate any grounds for the rejection of working men except for the expectation of excuses— I can't see any discrimination in a purposeful sense.

DOUGLAS: I heard this case discussed in San Francisco. There was a difference of opinion in the Ninth Circuit. The don't have to take jurors from all parts of the district. A case here was made of restricting the jury unduly. They have set out a class here. I would not want to say that this was the proper way to do it. It is a real problem. Judges know what to do about it, especially in the northern district of California. I think that *they have cut out a class*. I would reverse this. There was a conscious exclusion of a class of men.

MURPHY: Jury service did not go as far as they should. I reverse.

RUTLEDGE: I would reverse, and decide it on the basis of *McNabb*.[270] I would have difficulty sustaining a statute which excludes or excuses day workers. This is not a statute, but is a state *practice* extending that far. It is not a question whether this is fair or unfair.

BURTON: I have difficulty in sustaining it. I agree with Bill Douglas. If we set it aside, then something will be done. If we don't do it, we endorse a situation which has a subtle and undermining effect on juries. We can't afford to put our stamp of approval on it. If we do reverse it, we don't have to prescribe rules—we merely say you can't go so far.

FRANKFURTER: We ought to say that the system ought to be worked upon.

Result: The Court ruled that whether a person worked for a daily wage was irrelevant to their eligibility or capacity to serve as a juror. While actual hardship cases might individually be excused, there was no federal or state law that could justify the jury commissioner's blanket exclusion of wage-earners. The Court avoided making a broad constitutional ruling, relying on its supervisory powers over the federal administration of justice.

---

270. *McNabb v. United States*, 318 U.S. 332 (1943).

Hernandez v. Texas, 347 U.S. 475 (1954)
(Douglas)

Hernandez was convicted of murder by an all-white jury in Jackson County, Texas. He claimed that the systematic exclusion of Hispanics from local juries violated his Fourteenth Amendment equal protection rights. While 14 percent of the county's population had Hispanic surnames, none had served as a jury commissioner, grand juror, or petty juror in more than twenty-five years. The Texas court of criminal appeals rejected Hernandez's claims and affirmed his conviction.

Conference of January 16, 1954

WARREN: The petitioner has made out a case. There is evidence of discrimination against Mexicans in many phases of community life. I reverse.

BLACK: I reverse.

REED: Reverse.

FRANKFURTER: Reverse.

DOUGLAS: Reverse.

JACKSON: I reverse. It is clear that they disqualified part of population because of their national origin. The standard, however, is different from proportional representation.

BURTON: I reverse.

CLARK: I guess that I will go along. I don't know how it can be worked out. It is hard to prove when a racial group is kept off. We have gone pretty far in making inferences. There is no evidence of discrimination here. The white race serves on juries—that is all that matters. That is the flimsiest proof I have ever seen—that no people of Mexican "names" were on the list. In West Texas there is segregation in the schools. I will not dissent, but we are causing a lot of trouble to the states. I do not see how jury commissioners can do their jobs.

MINTON: I agree with Clark. If Mexicans are required on juries, there is no proof here—the evidence shows data for only one year, and an estimate of those Mexicans who were qualified for jury service. I reverse.

JACKSON: I would affirm on weak proof.

Result: The Supreme Court unanimously quashed Hernandez's conviction, with Clark, Minton, and Jackson reluctantly on board. For the first time, the Supreme Court extended the equal protection clause beyond race to include classifications based on ancestry and national origin.

Whitus v. Georgia, 385 U.S. 545 (1967)
(Douglas)

Phil Whitus and other blacks convicted of murder in Mitchell County, Georgia, alleged that county officials systematically excluded blacks from grand and petty juries. The federal district court dismissed their habeas petitions and the court of appeals affirmed. The U.S. Supreme Court remanded the case for further hearings on the question of discrimination.[271] *The district court again dismissed their petitions on the ground that the defendants had waived their rights, but the court of appeals reversed after finding systematic discrimination against black jurors in Mitchell County. Although more than 45 percent of the county's population and 27 percent of the county's taxpayers were black, none had ever served on a grand or petty jury in living memory. The court ordered the county jury commissioners to revise the juror lists.*

Georgia law required jury commissioners to pick from county tax rolls "upright and intelligent" citizens for jury duty. Georgia's tax books were segregated prior to 1965, with black taxpayers clearly marked.[272] *Even after the court of appeals ordered the county to revise its jury list, local commissioners continued to use the old segregated tax books and the original jury list to compile their "new" list. Three of thirty-three prospective grand jurors on the new list were black (one had already served by the time that this case made it to the Supreme Court) and seven of ninety prospective petty jurors were black (none had served before this case made it to the Supreme Court).*

Conference of December 9, 1966

WARREN: There was systematic exclusion. Yellow and white cards were used in the past. We sent it back on this issue once.[273] Forty-five percent of the people are Negroes. There is a background of no Negroes serving. Georgia on remand said that the issue was not properly raised. White lawyers will not raise the question, for it will hurt their social standing.

BLACK: I affirm—there is no evidence of systematic exclusion.

DOUGLAS: I reverse—there was systematic exclusion.

CLARK: I reverse.

HARLAN: I affirm. There is evidence of systematic exclusion. What happened in the past is irrelevant here. I can't see how the use of tax lists has any relevancy here.

BRENNAN: I reverse.

STEWART: The only way to comply with the mandate of the court of appeals. They had to put Negroes on the array, so they put some on. Ancient history is irrelevant. Yet I would reverse, because they had 3 out of 90 on the grand jury in one case, and 7 out of 99 out of the other. When the petitioner showed that evidence, the burden was on state to go forward.

WHITE: I affirm.

FORTAS: I reverse. The only purpose of the tax digest is for jury use.

Result: A unanimous Court found that the evidence presented a prima facie case of purposeful discrimination and that the state of Georgia had completely failed to rebut the evidence (the state made

---

271. *Whitus v. Balkcom,* 370 U.S. 728 (1962).

272. A taxpayer's race could be identified in two ways: (1) Georgia used white tax return sheets for white people and yellow tax return sheets for nonwhites; and (2) the names of black taxpayers were marked with a "c" in the tax receiver's books.

273. *Avery v. Georgia,* 345 U.S. 559 (1952); *Williams v. Georgia,* 349 U.S. 375 (1955).

no attempt to explain or defend its actions). The Court set aside the petitioners' convictions and ruled that they could only be retried using constitutional procedures.

Hoyt v. Florida, 368 U.S. 57 (1961)
(Douglas) (Brennan)

Under Florida law, women were not summoned for jury service unless they volunteered. After Gwendolyn Hoyt was tried and convicted of second-degree murder by an all-male jury, she claimed that Florida's jury selection procedures discriminated against women and violated her equal protection rights under the Fourteenth Amendment.

Conference of October 20, 1961

WARREN: The issue is women jurors in a criminal case. I would reverse. I would do this on the narrow ground. We need not get at the section itself and knock it down, but in this case Florida limited women's service to 10 a year out of 223 eligibles—that is 1/10 of one percent. That is tantamount to taking them all out. This is a particularly flagrant case where a woman needs the help of a woman. The subject is dying—only three states still keep women off juries.

BLACK: This was a denial of equal protection—I reverse.

FRANKFURTER: I affirm. There was no systematic exclusion of any part of the base. *Ballard* was decided on a statutory ground.[274] There was no systematic exclusion of women here. This is not like the Mexican case.[275]

DOUGLAS: I reverse.

CLARK: I affirm; I agree with Felix.

HARLAN: I affirm and agree with Felix.

BRENNAN: I think that the Chief really goes on *Yick Wo* grounds.[276] I can't go on that ground. I affirm, tentatively.

WHITTAKER: Applying *Ballard* to this case, I affirm. If the clerk arbitrarily left women out, that would be bad. But this was not purposeful or systematic.

STEWART: I affirm. I agree with Whittaker.

---

274. *Ballard v. United States,* 329 U.S. 187 (1946).

275. *Hernandez v. Texas,* 347 U.S. 475 (1954).

276. *Yick Wo v. Hopkins,* 118 U.S. 356 (1886). A San Francisco ordinance requiring commercial laundries to be operated in brick or stone buildings was constitutional on its face but invalid as applied. In practice, the law was used to discriminate invidiously against Chinese laundry owners, virtually all of whom operated their businesses in wooden buildings. As Justice Stanley Mathews wrote, "Though the law itself be fair on its face, and impartial in appearance, yet, if it is applied and administered by public authority with an evil eye and an unequal hand, so as practically to make unjust and illegal discriminations between persons in similar circumstances, material to their rights, the denial of equal justice is still within the prohibition of the Constitution."

Result: The Court unanimously upheld the Florida statute. The Justices refused to extend Hernandez v. Texas to discrimination based on sex. Warren, Clark, and Douglas concurred in the result, saying that they could not say from the record that Florida had not made a good-faith effort to include women jurors on a nondiscriminatory basis.

Peters v. Kiff, 407 U.S. 493 (1972)
(Douglas) (Brennan)

Dean Rene Peters was convicted of burglary in Macon County, Georgia, and his conviction was affirmed on appeal. Peters petitioned for a federal writ of habeas corpus, claiming that the systematic exclusion of blacks from county grand and petit juries violated his due process and equal protection rights. The Fifth Circuit Court of Appeals rejected his petition on the ground that Peters, who was white, had not personally suffered any discrimination. Peters never raised any statutory objections at trial or on appeal; he concentrated exclusively on his constitutional arguments. In conference, however, the Justices also discussed possible statutory grounds for reversal. C. P. Kiff was the warden of Macon Prison.

Conference of February 25, 1972

BURGER: A white defendant says that blacks were excluded from his jury. May only Negroes raise this question? A jury should fairly reflect a cross-section—no class should be excluded.

DOUGLAS: I reverse. I agree with the dissent in *Fay v. New York,* which is the closest to this case.[277] Our constitutional conception of the jury means that no one can be purposefully excluded. Constitutionally, it must be a cross-section of the community.

BRENNAN: The Civil Rights Act says that no person shall be disqualified as a juror in federal or state trials—*Strauder* refers to it.[278] Also 18 U.S.C. §243.[279]

BURGER: But he never raised the point in his trial.

BRENNAN: On Douglas's ground or on §243.

---

277. *Fay v. New York,* 332 U.S. 261 (1947). On a 5–4 vote, the Court upheld the use of a "special" or "blue-ribbon" jury in an extortion case. Frank Murphy's dissent, joined by Black, Douglas, and Rutledge, argued that "the equal protection clause of the Fourteenth Amendment prohibits a state from convicting any person by use of a jury which is not impartially drawn from a cross-section of the community. That means that juries must be chosen without systematic and intentional exclusion of any otherwise qualified group of individuals. Only in that way can the democratic traditions of the jury system be preserved." Murphy mocked the selection procedures for the blue ribbon jury, because selection rested on the "degree of intelligence" as revealed by a questionnaire sent to prospective jurors, augmented by personal interviews. It was a process, Murphy argued, that was meant not to find intelligent jurors but to find jurors that suited local officials. *Fay* was largely overruled by *Taylor v. Louisiana,* 419 U.S. 522 (1975).

278. *Strauder v. West Virginia,* 100 U.S. 303 (1880). The Court ruled that West Virginia's exclusion of black jurors violated the equal protection clause of the Fourteenth Amendment.

279. Originally part of the Civil Rights Act of 1875, the statute provided that "no citizen possessing all other qualifications which are or may be prescribed by law shall be disqualified for service as a grand or petit juror in any court of the United States, or of any State on account of race, color, or previous condition of servitude; and whoever, being an officer or other person charged with any duty in the selection or summoning of jurors, excludes or fails to summon any citizen for such cause, shall be fined not more than $5,000."

STEWART: *Strauder* and §243 emphasized not only the right of defendants, but that the right of Negroes to serve on juries may be asserted by defendants. The system of jury selections can't be one that excludes people by reason of race. I agree with *Fay v. New York*, and would reverse on §243.

BURGER: I am troubled by retroactivity.

POWELL: If we give relief where, as here, the point was not raised, it is difficult to limit it.

WHITE: We are back to the old hassle of *Stovall* as far as retroactivity is concerned.[280] I reverse. The statutory ground is O.K., and the narrowest. The next argument is Potter's *Turner* ground extended to the whole area. Also under *Turner*, Negroes can't be excluded from juries, and anyone has standing to raise the point.[281] The third possibility is the representative cross section requirement of the Sixth Amendment. Old cases imply that proof of actual prejudice is necessary, but I do not go on that. *Barrows v. Jackson* is analogous.[282] Also, the *Alexander* case I am now writing, which can't turn on §243 but must go on the Constitution.[283] On none of these grounds would this be retroactive unless you say that it involved actual prejudice, as did old cases.

---

280. *Stovall v. Denno*, 388 U.S. 293 (1967). In determining retroactivity, the Court provided three criteria: (1) the purpose served by the new standards; (2) the extent of reliance by law enforcement authorities on the old standards; and (3) the effect on the administration of justice.

281. *Turner v. Fouche*, 396 U.S. 346 (1970). In Taliaferro County, Georgia, jury lists were selected by six county jury commissioners, who were appointed by the state superior court judge. While the county's population was 60 percent black, local juries had only token black representation, and evidence indicated that commissioners used their broad discretion to exclude blacks from service. The Court ruled that blacks as a class had a constitutional right under the Sixth and Fourteenth Amendments to challenge their exclusion from local juries and other public service and that any member of the excluded class had standing to sue. This was an unusually broad reading of standing requirements under the Sixth and Fourteenth Amendments; in most cases the Court has limited standing to challenge jury selection procedures to criminal defendants and has only rarely extended this right to *potential* jurors.

282. *Barrows v. Jackson*, 346 U.S. 249 (1953), involved a racially restrictive covenant in Los Angeles. Olive Barrows sued her neighbor, Leola Jackson, a white property owner, after she broke the neighborhood covenant and sold her property to the Smally family, who were non-Caucasians. No legal action was taken against the Smallys, because *Shelley v. Kraemer* had already decided that racially restrictive covenants could not be enforced against nonwhite purchasers. In *Barrows*, the California courts extended *Shelley* and refused to enforce the terms of such covenants against white signatories, and the Supreme Court affirmed by a 6–1 vote. Sherman Minton wrote that while parties did not ordinarily have standing to argue the constitutional rights of third parties, there was an exception in cases where third parties might be deprived of their constitutional rights and it was difficult or impossible for them to defend their own rights in court. Chief Justice Vinson dissented. Reed and Jackson did not participate, presumably because they owned property covered by restrictive covenants.

283. *Alexander v. Louisiana*, 405 U.S. 625 (1972). Claude Alexander sought to quash his indictment on the ground that Lafayette Parish unconstitutionally excluded blacks and women from the grand jury. As evidence, Alexander cited two facts: (1) jury commissioners knew the race of all prospective grand jurors; and (2) although 21 percent of the adult parish population was black, less than 7 percent of the prospective grand jurors selected by local jury commissioners were black, and none of the grand jurors on the panel that indicted Alexander were black. Byron White, writing for a unanimous Court, found that Alexander had established a prima facie case of invidious racial discrimination and that the state had not met its burden of proving that it used racially neutral selection criteria in empaneling an all-white grand jury. White avoided the constitutional issues involving the exclusion of women from Lafayette grand juries.

MARSHALL: The Sixth and Fourteenth Amendments mean an "impartial jury" in the sense that no discernible or distinctive group is deliberately excluded. I reverse.

BLACKMUN: I am not at rest, although I am inclined to affirm. This case was tried below on an equal protection basis, and because there was no showing of prejudice that requires affirmance here. I might go on §243.

POWELL: I would reverse on a constitutional basis if we can make this prospective only.

REHNQUIST: Equal protection requires a showing of prejudice. There was none here. I do not buy the cross-section argument.

BURGER: I am like Lewis. If our decision can be sealed and not made retroactive, I will go along.

[DOUGLAS: I told Thurgood that on my jury I wanted a Black Buddhist.]

Result: A badly divided Court reversed the decision below. Thurgood Marshall, writing for a three-Justice plurality that included only Douglas and Stewart, ruled that Peters had standing and that there was no rule that equal protection claims could be asserted only by defendants who were members of the group excluded from jury service. Nor did Peters have to prove actual bias or personal discrimination; any defendant had the right to challenge unconstitutional jury selection procedures. A second three-person faction of White, Brennan, and Powell concurred in the result but wanted to decide the case on the narrower statutory ground. Burger, Blackmun, and Rehnquist dissented.

Swain v. Alabama, 380 U.S. 202 (1965)
(Douglas)

Robert Swain, a nineteen-year-old black man, was convicted of raping a seventeen-year-old white woman and was sentenced to die. Swain moved to have his conviction quashed because Alabama's procedures for selecting grand and petty juries discriminated against blacks. Although the adult population of Talladega County was 26 percent black, only 10–15 percent of grand jury panels were black (two blacks served on the grand jury that indicted Swain). Because state prosecutors habitually used their peremptory challenges to remove blacks from petty jury panels, no black had served on a Talladega trial jury for more than fifteen years. Of the eight blacks originally on Swain's jury venire, two were exempt from service, and the prosecutor used his peremptory challenges to remove the remaining six.

Especially interesting in conference are Hugo Black's defense of Alabama and peremptory challenges and Tom Clark's explanation of why Alabama had so few black jurors.

Conference of December 11, 1964

WARREN: I reverse, but not on the alleged use of peremptory challenges to keep Negroes off the jury, because peremptories may be used for any purpose. But here the system is administered by commissioners who use corrupt procedures in the drawing and selection of jurors, including challenges.[284] There is a prima facie case that the state has not

---

284. Southern jury commissioners developed a number of techniques to limit the number of blacks selected for jury duty and to ensure that those who were selected were assigned to criminal jury panels where they could be removed by peremptory challenges.

disproved, particularly where, as a result of these procedures, no Negro has ever served as a juror in the memory of man. Here, it is up to the state to disprove discrimination. I would rely on the totality of the situation.

BLACK: I am not ready to reverse as of yet. There are cases, including one of mine, putting the burden on states where no colored people have served on the jury. Here, however, there were Negroes on the juries, both grand and petit. I can't rest on peremptory challenges, as they can be used for any purpose. There is no case here, as I see it, of excluding Negroes from juries. All we have is that no Negro has actually *served* on a jury, not that Negroes were excluded from the panel. There is no lack of a constitutional percentage of Negroes on the jury panels. There is more feeling in the South against Negroes on a grand jury than on a petit jury, because of the more intimate association. But here there were Negroes on the grand jury. There is no prima facie case of discrimination here. I pass at this time.

DOUGLAS: The combination of peremptories with other restrictive use of Negroes sets up the prima facie case. I reverse.

CLARK: To reverse, you are going to have to rest on peremptory challenges entirely, and I can't do that. The NAACP didn't even argue about grand jurors. I affirm, unless we can *Cassell* this on the failure to go to the same clerks there for names.[285] Negroes are kept off of juries for many reasons. For example, large numbers of them are ministers who are exempt.

HARLAN: I agree with Tom Clark. You can't escape peremptory challenges being at the core of this case.

BRENNAN: I have trouble with case. If we get down to the peremptory challenges, I would probably affirm. I pass.

STEWART: I can't go along on the peremptory challenge basis, and to reverse, you have to cast doubt on the use of peremptory challenges. There is the historic fact that no Negro ever sat on a trial jury, and perhaps a combination of circumstances, including peremptory challenges, would justify reversal. I affirm.

WHITE: I affirm. You have to get to peremptory challenges to reverse. Can you say that if no Negro has ever served it must be wrong, and that it is impossible that there has never been one who has escaped the exercise of peremptory challenges?

GOLDBERG: I reverse. We need not rest on peremptory challenges. I think that this case can be decided on *Cassell, Hill,*[286] and *Smith,*[287] without ever reaching the peremptory challenge question. The state did not fairly select its venire to issue a fair cross-section. The methods used here show that the state used selection techniques to assure the under-selection of Negroes, and that the system in fact resulted in the under-selection of Negroes.

---

285. *Cassell v. Texas,* 339 U.S. 282 (1950).
286. *Hill v. Texas,* 316 U.S. 400 (1942).
287. *Smith v. Texas,* 311 U.S. 128 (1940).

WARREN: I would not require the user of a peremptory challenge to say why he uses it. But if the way in which the panel is selected is unfair, and if the number of peremptory challenges enables all Negroes to be eliminated, then you have a bad, unconstitutional system. If they use the peremptory challenge system to eliminate Negroes in all cases, then this system is bad.

BLACK: I now affirm. Some counties in Alabama have two Negroes to one white. Here there are two whites to one Negro. The peremptory challenge system is a good one. The Alabama Supreme Court passed this rule to give defendants a fair trial by jury, by giving them two challenges to every one for the prosecutor. I would not impair the peremptory system to reverse here. If we reverse here, Alabama would change its peremptory challenge rule and give each side, say, five challenges only.

Result: Byron White, writing for the majority, held that the underrepresentation of blacks on Talladega juries was not sufficient to prove purposeful discrimination. Swain had to demonstrate intentional and systematic racial discrimination and had failed to meet his burden. Nor was there sufficient evidence to convince the majority that the prosecutor's use of peremptory challenges to eliminate blacks was improper. Harlan and Black concurred in the result without joining White's opinion.

The case was met with devastating critical commentary and ultimately was overruled by Batson v. Kentucky, 476 U.S. 79 (1986). The modern rule is that the burden rests with prosecutors to prove that their peremptory challenges were not used to remove potential jurors solely on account of race.

Batson v. Kentucky, 476 U.S. 79 (1986)
(Brennan)

Before the ink was dry on Swain v. Alabama, Thurgood Marshall set out to overrule it. When Marshall's initial efforts failed to convince a majority to reverse Swain outright, he tried to find a way to emasculate it. At first, Marshall conceded that Swain's equal protection argument was frivolous. Instead of revisiting the Fourteenth Amendment equal protection issue, Marshall argued that the Sixth Amendment required an impartial jury that reflected a fair cross-section of the community and prohibited the systematic exclusion of any racial group. Later, however, he began to criticize Swain on both Sixth and Fourteenth Amendment grounds. After twenty years of lobbying, Marshall finally convinced his brethren to reexamine the issue during the Court's 1985 Term.[288]

At James Batson's burglary trial, the prosecutor used his peremptory challenges to strike all four blacks on the jury venire. Batson asked the trial judge to dismiss the jury on the grounds that the prosecutor's exclusions violated the Sixth and Fourteenth Amendments. The judge denied Batson's

---

288. Tushnet, *Making Constitutional Law,* 64–66. Marshall was aided by John Paul Stevens's opinion denying cert in *McCray v. New York,* 461 U.S. 961 (1983). In *McCray,* New York trial judge Eugene Nickerson anticipated *Swain's* demise, ruling that using peremptory challenges to eliminate people on the basis of race was unconstitutional. Nickerson rested his decision on equal protection. The New York Court of Appeals affirmed but relied on the Sixth Amendment. In a rare explanation of a decision to deny cert, Stevens, joined by Blackmun and Powell, invited other state and federal courts to take the lead in reexamining *Swain.* With Marshall and Brennan already on record against *Swain,* this meant that a majority of Justices had publicly expressed doubts about *Swain's* continued soundness.

motion and accepted the jury. Batson was convicted and the Kentucky Supreme Court affirmed, citing Swain v. Alabama.

Conference of December 13, 1985

BURGER: I would not argue equal protection, but only the Sixth Amendment's cross-section requirement. Our Sixth Amendment decisions do not suggest a different result from *Swain*, which was an equal protection case. *Taylor v. Louisiana* disposes of the Sixth Amendment argument.[289]

BRENNAN:[290] I would reverse. I appreciate the fact that the petitioner has asked this Court to focus its attention on the Sixth Amendment issue. However, in light of the way argument went, particularly the state's insistence that the Court should consider the equal protection issue, I think that we can and should decide it.

I think that we should overrule *Swain*, and hold that a black defendant can establish an equal protection violation based on the prosecutor's racially motivated use of peremptory challenges to eliminate a significant number of blacks from the venire. We should treat racial equal protection claims in the petit jury context basically the same way we treat other kinds of racial discrimination claims, as cases subsequent to *Swain* have developed.

I think that equal protection grounds are far preferable here to a Sixth Amendment fair cross-section approach. Lower courts, such as the Second Circuit and the supreme courts of California and Massachusetts, have evolved their cross-section jurisprudence to respond to the persistent problem of the racially motivated use of peremptories. An equal protection approach would be narrower and more closely tailored to the problem. It would also avoid potentially serious difficulties in defining what groups should be cognizable under the fair cross-section requirement. Because an equal protection theory would be available only to the singularly disadvantaged and distinct groups that receive special scrutiny, that approach should limit the number and types of challenges to the prosecution's use of peremptories.

The question whether the prosecutor may challenge the defendant's racially motivated use of peremptories is not before us in this case. I believe that we should wait for another case to answer that question.

I also believe that our development in this case of a specific standard defining what a defendant must show to make out a prima facie case and what the prosecutor must do to rebut it would be premature. Caution dictates that we leave the development of such a standard in the first instance to the lower courts.

I must say that I would strongly prefer not to reach the Sixth Amendment issue in this case. If the Court believes that it can consider only the Sixth Amendment issue, I

---

289. *Taylor v. Louisiana*, 419 U.S. 522 (1975). In a kidnapping and rape case in St. Tammany Parish, Billy J. Taylor challenged his conviction on the ground that Louisiana systematically excluded women from jury service in violation of the Sixth and Fourteenth Amendments. Under state law, women were not called for jury duty unless they filed annual affidavits with the state declaring their desire to serve. The Court ruled 8–1 that women as a class could no longer be excluded from jury service or given automatic exemptions based solely on their sex. Rehnquist was the lone dissenter.

290. Adapted from Brennan's talking papers, Brennan Papers, OT 1985, box 718.

would like either to set this case for reargument on the equal protection issue, or delay resolution in this case and set argument in one of the cases held for it, such as *Nurse v. Illinois*, No. 85–5190, which clearly presents the equal protection issue. If the Court insists on resolving the Sixth Amendment question, my views are reflected in my join of Justice Marshall's dissent from denial of cert in *McCray v. New York*.

WHITE: Direct proof that the reason for the strikes was racial would be an equal protection violation, but *Swain* said that no inference would support that inference. I would revisit *Swain* on the equal protection ground, and say here that contrary to *Swain*, if a defendant can prove that there is a striking on account of race, you can require the prosecutor to justify his actions. I don't think that the Sixth Amendment rationale can possibly work. I would not make this retroactive.

MARSHALL: Like Byron and Bill Brennan, I would go on the equal protection ground. I will not go to the other side of the constitutional issue. I would take peremptories away from both sides. You can't ever decide whether a peremptory strike is racially motivated.

BLACKMUN: Peremptories have a place in the law. *Swain* was decided before *Duncan* extended the Sixth Amendment to the states. I would reject the Sixth Amendment issue outright and hit *Swain* head on under equal protection. I would cut back on *Swain*, and it is discriminatory to assume that blacks are acquittal prone. Peremptories have few state interests to support them. I'll cut back, and I like California's approach. I am inclined to make it two-way street, but not retroactive.

POWELL: We have to overrule *Swain's* holding that we won't permit inferences that striking causes an inference to arise of racial basis for peremptory strikes. I would reject the Sixth Amendment argument flat out and apply equal protection analysis. There would be a violation when a qualified person is stricken solely because of race. I would leave it to the trial judge to determine when to require prosecutors to justify their actions.

REHNQUIST: I agree with the Chief Justice—you must have a practice of strikes before a denial of equal protection can be asserted.

STEVENS: State action by a prosecutor is different from a private law suit. It is also different from a defendant's use of peremptories. We can address this on equal protection—it was passed on by the state courts and raised below. Courts that have assumed that *Swain* held that prosecutors could use peremptories on a racial basis are wrong. We should say that it is constitutionally impermissible, as *Swain* should have been read.

O'CONNOR: I agree with Byron. I reject the Sixth Amendment argument, and I am not sure that it is right here to reach the Fourteenth Amendment. But since there is a Court to do so, I won't dissent. I'll hold, too, that under equal protection, if disparate impact and intentional discrimination are shown, there is a prima facie case and it would require prosecutors to justify their actions.

Result: The Court ruled 7–2 that while James Batson had no constitutional right to a jury composed of members of his own race, the equal protection clause precluded the state from excluding members of the defendant's own race from the jury solely on account of their race. Lewis Powell, writing for the majority, found that racially motivated peremptory challenges also discriminated against the rights of excluded jurors and warned that if left unchecked, such race-based exclusions could undermine public confidence in the judicial system.

The Court effectively overruled Swain, *largely by shifting the burden of proof from defendants to prosecutors. Under* Swain, *defendants had to prove that prosecutors' systematic use of peremptory challenges were racially motivated. Under the new test, defendants merely had to show a racial pattern in the prosecutor's use of peremptory challenges. The burden of proof then shifted to prosecutors to demonstrate that their peremptory challenges were not based solely on racial considerations.*

Thurgood Marshall concurred but wanted to go farther than the majority. He advocated the outright elimination of peremptory challenges. None of the other Justices agreed with him. Warren Burger and William Rehnquist dissented, saying that Swain *had been rightly decided.*

Witherspoon v. Illinois, 391 U.S. 510 (1968)
Bumper v. North Carolina, 391 U.S. 543 (1968)
(Douglas) (Brennan)

These two cases were discussed together in conference, although ultimately they were published separately. In selecting a jury to try William Witherspoon for murder, the prosecutor challenged all prospective jurors who expressed any doubts about the death penalty. The prosecutor said that he wanted to "get these conscientious objectors out of the way, without wasting any time on them."[291] He successfully challenged forty-seven jurors—half of the venire. The resulting jury convicted Witherspoon and sentenced him to death. On appeal, Witherspoon's lawyers presented evidence to show how the prosecutor's exclusions had biased the jury in the state's favor.

In the second case, Wayne Darnell Bumper was a suspect in a rape case. Police went to his grandmother's house, where Bumper lived, and told the sixty-eight-year-old woman that they had a search warrant. She told police to "go ahead" and search. Inside the house, police found a rifle allegedly used during the rape. No warrant was ever presented, but the prosecutor claimed that the search was valid because the grandmother had consented. Bumper was tried for capital rape. Prosecutors sought the death penalty and excused all potential jurors who said that they had scruples against capital punishment. Bumper was convicted and the jury recommended life imprisonment. The Illinois and North Carolina supreme courts affirmed both convictions. Unlike Witherspoon, *Bumper's lawyers did not submit any evidence on appeal to show how the prosecutors' exclusions may have biased the jury.*

Conference of April 26, 1968

Witherspoon v. Illinois

WARREN: I reverse *Witherspoon.* This act disqualifies jurors who have mere consternation, scruple, or opposition against the death penalty. That is bad. Further, the way it was administered shows a system of excluding a juror merely on the ground of scruples. He nonetheless might be a good juror. If his scruples prevented him from bringing in a capital verdict, he should be disqualified. The trial judge handled it the same way, so I would say that where that is the system, it falls. There ought to be a determination whether, notwithstanding your scruples, you can follow the instructions on the law as given by the trial judge.

---

291. Tushnet, *Making Constitutional Law,* 147.

BLACK: I affirm.

DOUGLAS: I reverse. On choice of verdicts, a juror should not be disqualified because he has scruples against the death penalty. I would also reverse on search and seizure in *Bumper*.

HARLAN: The state has the right to say that scruples against capital punishment disqualify a juror.

BRENNAN: I reverse on the Chief's ground.

STEWART: To say that the exclusion of jurors with scruples against the death penalty is in error will upset thousands of trials. Yet in a nation where the majority are opposed to capital punishment, the exclusion of these jurors produces an unrepresentative jury in cases where death has been imposed, which is to deny a proper jury trial without due process of law. That would be retroactively true of all cases where death was imposed. I would not say that the North Carolina system is bad, because death was not imposed. In the future, however, North Carolina would have to discard the practice because a reduction of a death penalty would not be possible.

WHITE: I affirm, although I may change.

FORTAS: I reverse.

MARSHALL: I reverse.

Bumper v. North Carolina

WARREN: Here there was a full inquiry as to whether jurors could bring in a verdict according to the law, notwithstanding scruples against hanging in a capital offense. So on that issue, I would affirm. On the Fourth Amendment issue, the old lady was told that there was a search warrant, and now the government tries to say that she would have let them search even if they hadn't said it.

BLACK: I affirm.

Douglas: I am not so sure whether we reach the juror question here, but if we do I would come out differently. If a jury can find a number of different verdicts, I would say that the prosecution can't have a jury biased for the death penalty. The prejudice against capital punishment might not disqualify him in that case, since he could bring in other verdicts of guilt. I would reverse both on the juror point and on the Fourth Amendment.

HARLAN: I affirm. Scruples are a bar.

BRENNAN: I reverse on the Fourth Amendment. We need not say anything about the scruples point.

STEWART: He got life imprisonment, so he can't upset the verdict on the scruples point. But in future cases, I would not let a state qualify jurors as was done here, even if the result is life imprisonment. I would not insist on a bifurcated trial.

FORTAS: The penalty is death or life imprisonment, and it is up to the jury to determine the penalty.

STEWART: In future trials, those jurors of scruples could not be excluded.

WHITE: I affirm on the jury point.

FORTAS: I reverse on the Fourth Amendment. Any warrant was abandoned, and to say that they had one gives you no consent.

MARSHALL: I am not sure of the Fourth Amendment point.

WARREN: On the Fourth Amendment point, I reverse. The old lady let them search, but her consent was not to a search without a warrant. Her consent was irrelevant. I reverse.

DOUGLAS: I reverse on the Fourth Amendment.

HARLAN: I do not reverse on the Fourth Amendment. Consent was adequate.

BRENNAN: I reverse and agree with the Chief on the Fourth Amendment.

STEWART: Consent is a nullity if it was given on the basis of a non-existing warrant. But there was a warrant here. I probably reverse.

WHITE: I affirm doubtfully on the Fourth Amendment. If there is a misrepresentation, there is no consent.

FORTAS: I reverse on the Fourth Amendment. Since the warrant was not served, there was no warrant at trial to attack or scrutinize. There was no return on the warrant.

MARSHALL: No warrant was served, so no consent. I reverse.

Results: In Witherspoon, *the majority ruled that the jury fell "woefully" short of being impartial, in violation of the Sixth and Fourteenth Amendments. According to Potter Stewart, the selection procedures unacceptably "stacked the deck" against Witherspoon and seated a "hanging jury"—so unrepresentative that it could not serve as the conscience of the community. The Court reserved the question of whether states could exclude prospective jurors who said that they would not vote for the death penalty under any circumstances. Douglas concurred in the judgment but did not join Stewart's opinion. Hugo Black dissented, arguing that if the Court wanted to declare the death penalty unconstitutional, it should do so "forthrightly," rather than making it all but impossible for states to find jurors who would agree to impose the death penalty in appropriate cases. In* Bumper, *the Court reversed on the ground that the grandmother did not voluntarily consent to a warrantless search of her home.*

Lockhart v. McCree, 476 U.S. 162 (1986)
(Brennan)

In a capital case against Ardia McCree, the trial judge excused all eight prospective jurors who said that they would not under any circumstances impose the death penalty (so-called Witherspoon *excludables). The resulting jury convicted McCree of murdering giftshop owner Evelyn Boughton during a Valentine's Day robbery. After a separate sentencing hearing, the same jury recommended life imprisonment without possibility of parole. After the state supreme court affirmed McCree's conviction, he filed for a federal writ of habeas corpus, claiming that the use of a "death qualified" jury prior to the sentencing phase of his trial violated the fair cross-section and impartiality requirements of the*

Sixth Amendment. The district court agreed and reversed McCree's conviction. The court of appeals affirmed, but rested its decision solely upon the fair cross-section argument.

BURGER: There are Fifth and Sixth Amendment issues here, and affirmance would affect hundreds of cases and death penalty statutes. What is an impartial jury? One that will follow the law as instructed, and *Witherspoon* has operated as an anti- not a pro-capital punishment case.[292]

BRENNAN:[293] I think that McCree has succeeded in proving that death qualified juries are, as a general matter, conviction prone. Barring significant changes in empirical studies, I think that the Court should take judicial notice of McCree's proof and assume in the future that the exclusion of *Witherspoon* excludables from the determination of guilt violates a defendant's Sixth Amendment right to a fair cross section. I affirm.

WHITE: Is it unconstitutional to inquire into jurors' views on capital punishment? No. Excluding this group is his argument—that cross-section approach is his emphasis. I can't accept it—it is too far-fetched. We don't know how many persons opposed to the death penalty actually sit on guilt or innocence. The studies don't help me as to that, and I therefore reverse.

MARSHALL: They always try to pick a jury for you. We can't really pick a jury that is a cross-section, but we should try to get as close as possible.

BLACKMUN: This is a lot of Tony Amsterdam stuff—trying to outlaw the death penalty through the back door.[294] *Witherspoon* is not one of my favorite cases, but it keeps the cross-section principle pretty well intact, at least as to race and sex. But this evidence does not convince me, and I would reverse.

POWELL: Agreed this jury not impartial, but only that the *Witherspoon* excludables had testified that they could not and would not comply with state law on the death penalty—they would not impose death. On the fair cross-section argument, the only identifiable protected classes have been sex or racial minorities—never on whether they would refuse to follow state law. We don't have to balance anything here, because there is no "identifiable group." This is just another Amsterdam ploy, as Harry said.

REHNQUIST: The fair cross-section test was the court of appeals' basis, rather than going on the impartial jury requirement as the district court did. "Impartial" applies only to the trial jury, and this right was not denied here. "Cross-section" bars the exclusion of identifiables—race and sex—not *attitudes*, as urged here. In any event, the state has conceded the right to exclude these jurors from the penalty phase. The notion of alternates is not supported by anything in the Sixth Amendment.[295]

292. *Witherspoon v. Illinois*, 391 U.S. 510 (1968).

293. Adapted from Brennan's talking papers, Brennan Papers, OT 1985, box 712.

294. Professor Tony Amsterdam of the New York University School of Law worked extensively with death penalty cases. He was one of the architects of the NAACP's anti–death penalty campaign, which began in the late 1960s.

295. In some jurisdictions, "death-qualified" jurors may join the jury during the postconviction sentencing phase to replace trial jurors who are categorically opposed to capital punishment.

STEVENS: There is really no "identifiable" group here. The strongest rationale for affirmance is *Witherspoon* itself. There was no biased jury there, but forty-seven potential jurors were excluded. Studies are very persuasive that if you exclude all who say that they can't vote for the death penalty that is 20 percent, and the remaining 80 percent is likely to be conviction-prone. Of the 20 percent, only a few are nullifiers and the state can exclude them. But the 17 percent who would sit on guilt or innocence, if excluded, skews the jury and that is a violation of due process.

O'CONNOR: In light of *Witherspoon* and *Adams*, the Court spoke in terms of requirements beyond any particular jury bias.[296] I would assume that these empirical studies are valid and correct. On the cross-section argument, "identifiable groups" has never included groups of "attitudes." So the issue for me is whether the chance of skewing jury is a constitutional violation. Necessarily it would be a prophylactic rule. We have already approved unitary juries.[297]

Result: By a 5–1–3 vote, the Court ruled that the jury had been properly empaneled and that McCree had been fairly tried, convicted, and sentenced. There were no constitutional violations, William Rehnquist wrote for the Court, even if as an empirical matter so-called death qualified juries proved to be somewhat more conviction-prone than ordinary juries. Blackmun concurred in the result, while Marshall, Brennan, and Stevens dissented.

Prejudice

Ham v. South Carolina, 409 U.S. 524 (1973)
(Brennan) (Douglas)

Gene Ham was a bearded, black civil rights activist charged with drug possession in Florence, South Carolina. The trial judge refused Ham's request to question prospective jurors during voir dire about racial prejudice and prejudice against people with beards. Ham was convicted, and the Supreme Court of South Carolina affirmed.

---

296. *Adams v. Texas*, 448 U.S. 38 (1980). In a murder trial, the trial judge excused all prospective jurors who refused to swear that the state's mandatory death penalty law would not affect their deliberations as to any issue of fact. Texas had a bifurcated system, and after convicting Randall Dale Adams of murder, the jury met again to determine his sentence. By law, the jury had to answer three questions: (1) whether the killing was deliberate; (2) whether Adams might continue to be a threat to society; and (3) whether the killing was an unreasonable response to any provocation on the part of the victim. If the jury answered all three questions in the affirmative, the trial judge was required to sentence Adams to death. Otherwise, the judge was required to sentence him to life in prison. The jury answered all three questions in the affirmative, and the trial judge sentenced Adams to death.

The Supreme Court held that (1) it was unconstitutional to exclude prospective jurors who were unwilling or unable to swear that the state's mandatory death penalty would not affect their deliberations; and (2) Texas could not carry out a death sentence imposed by a jury where all such persons were excluded. *Witherspoon*, the Court ruled, offered the broadest permissible grounds for excluding prospective jurors based on their opposition to the death penalty. This was a per se rule, meaning that Adams was not required to prove that his jury was in fact prejudiced against him because of the state's improper jury selection procedures.

297. *McGautha v. California*, 402 U.S. 183 (1971).

Conference of November 10, 1972

BURGER: This is a marijuana case. These were custom-made questions about this accused. There is no record on newspaper clippings, so Question 4 washes out of the case.[298] Questions 1 and 2 can be treated together.[299] Question 3 as to prejudice against beards seems irrelevant, because many men wear beards.[300] On Questions 1 and 2, is there a constitutional requirement entitling a Negro defendant to an inquiry of the venire as to racial prejudice? The *Aldridge* decision doesn't seem to be constitutional decision, and must have been decided on the basis of the Court's supervisory powers.[301] The judge's questions came pretty close to what was asked of him. This case falls between *Aldridge* and the state cases cited. I can't find a constitutional deficiency and there is no sense of injustice here, although in a federal prosecution I might feel that we should reverse on *Aldridge*.

DOUGLAS: I think that it is a constitutional question of due process and fair trial rights. I think that *Aldridge* would do so.

BRENNAN: Reverse on *Aldridge*.

STEWART: This is a pee-wee case. I would DIG or otherwise reverse on *Aldridge* and due process.

WHITE: My vote to affirm is tentative until I read the transcript of the oral argument.

MARSHALL: A general charge does not meet the problem. Prejudice is deep, and specific questions are needed to inform it. Reversal and a due process determination here can have a prophylactic and therapeutic effect. I reverse. An impartial jury must be one without racial prejudice, and this is necessary for a fair trial.

BLACKMUN: The trial judge was stiff-necked not to ask these questions. A statute can't exclude questions that are pertinent. Are the issues truly here? Certainly not Question 4, and I would dismiss that one. As to the others, was the constitutional issue raised in the trial court or in the state supreme court? *Aldridge* does not deliver the constitutional case to me. If I can get over the question raised, I can reverse—but maybe we should DIG. I reverse with a question mark.

---

298. Question 4 asked whether potential jurors had seen newspaper clippings or a recent television program publicizing local drug problems.

299. Questions 1 and 2 dealt with racial prejudice.

300. Question 3 asked whether potential jurors would be prejudiced against people with beards.

301. *Aldridge v. United States*, 283 U.S. 308 (1931). The Court ruled that Alfred Aldridge, a black male on trial for the murder of a white District of Columbia police officer, had the right to ask prospective jurors whether they had any racial prejudices that might prevent them from returning a fair and impartial verdict. This right, the Court said, extended to all jurisdictions—even to those where blacks already had the same rights and privileges as whites. The majority based its decision on what Charles Evans Hughes called "essential fairness" and the common practice in other jurisdictions. James McReynolds dissented, arguing that the Court should have deferred to the trial judge.

POWELL: There is some therapeutic value in reversal. The questions fairly went to the partiality of the jury. The trial judge should be lenient in allowing these questions. Couldn't we dispose of this by a per curiam, reversing on *Aldridge*?

REHNQUIST: The question is whether the question was properly raised. The state supreme court passed on it. I am inclined to think that the question was not properly raised, and I would DIG. I would not dissent from an opinion that focused on race, the complexion of Florence, South Carolina, the context of the trial, and so forth.

BURGER: I have decided to reverse, and may do a per curiam myself.

Result: The Court unanimously agreed that the trial judge's refusal to allow Ham to ask questions on racial prejudice violated his Fourteenth Amendment due process rights. Rehnquist's majority opinion affirmed the trial judge's refusal to allow questions on prejudice against beards, over the objections of Douglas and Marshall. Rehnquist's suggestion that the conference focus on local conditions in Florence, South Carolina, came into play three years later, when the Court was asked to extend Ham *to a Massachusetts case where three black defendants were charged with a violent assault on a white security guard.*

Ristaino v. Ross, 424 U.S. 589 (1976)
(Brennan)

James Ross was one of three black men accused of armed robbery and aggravated assault on a white security guard. Ross wanted to ask prospective jurors whether they believed "that a white person is more likely to be telling the truth than a black person." The trial judge agreed to ask several general questions about juror impartiality but refused to ask any specific questions about racial prejudice. The state courts affirmed Ross's conviction, and he petitioned for a writ of habeas corpus in federal court. The local federal district court sided with Ross, and the circuit court of appeals affirmed, citing Ham v. South Carolina.[302]

BURGER: The Massachusetts Supreme Judicial Court limited *Ham*, and said that the case did not apply where there was no claim that the accused selected a special target on the basis of race. The court of appeal, on other hand, held that *Ham* applied when there was a black accused and a white victim. We have to be careful about introducing a racial element—a "them" versus "us." The questions actually asked were sufficient, since two veniremen answered that they did not like blacks.

STEWART: I am inclined to reverse.

WHITE: I would not apply *Ham* retroactively. The rule was to take precautions when asked to ask questions. But that is different from retroactive application. We don't have to get to the scope of *Ham* then. If we did, I would think *Ham* applied where there is a crime of violence by a black accused against a white victim.

302. *Ham v. South Carolina,* 409 U.S. 524 (1973).

MARSHALL: I think that *Aldridge*, back in Hughes's day, settles that it is retroactive. I will follow my opinion the last time the case was here.[303]

BLACKMUN: I don't like the "special target" rule of the Massachusetts Supreme court. But on balance, I think that I am where Byron is—but I may not stay there.

POWELL: It is a due process problem. I would not favor a rule that a court must allow this question under every circumstance. We ought to tell trial judges in the South to allow these questions.

REHNQUIST: *Ham* does not foreclose either result here. If *Ham* took over the *Aldridge* opinion, then *Ham* applies here. *Ham*, however, was written on due process, not on a Sixth Amendment basis—thus, the fairness of trial determination is the crux of our decision. When state courts come out as here, I would leave *Ham* alone on retroactivity. I'm not sure.

Result: The Court ruled 5–1–2 that there was no general constitutional right to ask prospective jurors specific questions about racial prejudice, absent circumstances comparable to Ham. In the final analysis, the crucial difference was that Gene Ham was tried in South Carolina and James Ross was tried in Massachusetts. White concurred in the result. Brennan and Marshall dissented, and Stevens did not participate.

Size and Unanimity

Johnson v. Louisiana, 406 U.S. 356 (1972)
(Douglas) (Brennan)

Louisiana allowed majority jury verdicts in criminal cases. A New Orleans jury convicted Frank Johnson of armed robbery on a 9–3 vote. Johnson claimed that the majority verdict violated his due process and equal protection rights under the Fourteenth Amendment and violated the reasonable doubt standard required for all criminal convictions. Duncan v. Louisiana, which incorporated the Sixth Amendment into the Fourteenth Amendment, was decided after this case began. Because Duncan was not retroactive, Johnson could not use the case as a precedent to bolster his Sixth Amendment argument.

Conference of March 5, 1971

BURGER: On the jury issue, it is a novel question. Once I thought that if a two-thirds vote was coupled with a two- or three-hour interval, it would be different.[304] But I have discarded that idea. Reasonable doubt is not a valid argument here. Unanimity was not required at common law—no one really knows its origins. Majority verdicts were common prior to the Constitution. Madison's failure to get a unanimous verdict is relevant,

303. *Aldridge v. United States*, 283 U.S. 308 (1931).
304. English law since 1967 has allowed super-majority verdicts after jurors have made a reasonable attempt to reach a unanimous verdict. In practice, English judges have generally required at least two hours of deliberations before accepting an 11–1 or a 10–2 verdict.

and suggests that the standard was to be left to the states. The British system uses majority verdicts. States can do this if they want to do so. I affirm.

BLACK: I affirm. Since unanimity was not required when the jury requirement was written into Constitution, it is not required now. A majority of one would be too few.

DOUGLAS: I reverse. Unanimous verdict plus reasonable doubt are my grounds.

BRENNAN: I reverse.

STEWART: Under the Sixth Amendment, I would reverse. Under the Fourteenth Amendment, I would affirm. If the Sixth Amendment is incorporated by the Fourteenth and applies across the board, I would have to reverse. And since *Duncan* is not retroactive, I am more confused than ever. I am inclined to reverse on the ground that the Sixth Amendment requires a unanimous jury.

WHITE: You won't get around the retroactivity issue. *Duncan* is not retroactive, so I say that the Sixth Amendment does not apply in this case. Therefore, I would affirm.

MARSHALL: I affirm. The only qualification of the Sixth Amendment's guarantee of jury trial is "impartial," not unanimous. The state can cut the number from twelve to nine, but not to one. There is no difference between twelve and five or six or nine.

BLACKMUN: This is not an easy case. I am not bothered by the "arrest" point.[305] On the jury point, if the Oregon act falls, this one does, too.[306] Louisiana grades offenses, requiring unanimous verdicts in death cases. I am inclined to affirm, with a question mark.

STEWART: The arrest was in violation of the Constitution. The line-up is not error—the petitioner is trying to extend *Wong Sung*.[307]

Conference of January 14, 1972[308]

BURGER: On the main issue it is close. This was not a well argued case.[309] The question of unanimity was not settled at the time of the Constitution. Madison failed to get a requirement for unanimous verdicts, and this leaves the question with the states. I affirm.

DOUGLAS: I reverse. The federal rule is unanimity, and the state rule is the same.

BRENNAN: I reverse.

---

305. Johnson was arrested without a warrant following his identification by a witness from a photograph. He was also later identified in a lineup. Johnson subsequently claimed that his arrest violated the Fourth Amendment and that the lineup identification should be suppressed as the fruit of an illegal arrest.

306. *Apodaca v. Oregon*, 406 U.S. 404 (1972), upholding an Oregon law that permitted non-unanimous verdicts as close as 9–3.

307. *Wong Sun v. United States*, 371 U.S. 471 (1963).

308. After the first conference there were two personnel changes on the Court: Lewis Powell replaced Hugo Black, and William Rehnquist replaced John Marshall Harlan. Because of these changes, the case was held over for a year and reargued.

309. Arguing the case before the Court were Richard A. Buckley for Johnson and Louise Korns for Louisiana. With her on the briefs were Jack P. F. Gremillion, the Louisiana attorney general, and Jim Garrison.

STEWART: Under our decisions, this is Fourteenth Amendment case. This is pre-*Duncan*, which is not retroactive. The Fourteenth Amendment required a representative jury for one hundred years. Those cases are academic if the majority of a jury can decide a case. I reverse.

WHITE: A non-unanimous verdict will not have an impact on "beyond reasonable doubt." These cases are more symbolic than actual. I affirm.

MARSHALL: On the first point, I would leave it alone—it is a can of worms.[310] On the jury issue, I go on reasonable doubt and the jury point. Here the jury was out twenty minutes. It must be a unanimous jury. I reverse.

BLACKMUN: Reasonable doubt does not equate with a unanimous verdict. I affirm.

POWELL: I would like to reserve my vote for a week. In Virginia, there is a unanimity rule in the Constitution. I did not think in Virginia that the Fourteenth Amendment would bar changing a unanimous verdict, though I am for states experimenting, but I was against Virginia changing its rule. The federal standard requires unanimity, but the Fourteenth Amendment does not. I have not been able to sort out all of my views. I am inclined to go with the Fortas opinion in *Duncan*, but I want it to go over.

REHNQUIST: I find nothing in the Fourteenth Amendment that requires unanimous verdicts. I would rely on *Maxwell*[311] and *Hurtado*.[312] I affirm.

Result: On a 5–4 vote, the Court permitted the use of super-majority verdicts down to 9–3 in state criminal trials. Byron White used the rational basis test to reject Johnson's equal protection claim, ruling that the state had a rational interest in reducing costs and increasing the efficiency of its judicial system. Majority verdicts, White said, did not create an invidious classification or violate a fundamental right and did not violate procedural due process or the reasonable doubt standard of proof required in criminal trials.

---

310. The "can of worms" was whether Johnson's lineup identification should have been suppressed as the fruit of an illegal arrest.

311. *Maxwell v. Dow*, 176 U.S. 581 (1900). Maxwell was charged with robbery in Utah by information presented to a magistrate rather than being indicted by a grand jury, and he was tried and convicted by a petit jury of only eight persons. In his habeas corpus petition, Maxwell claimed that the Fourteenth Amendment required a grand jury indictment and prohibited the use of petit juries of fewer than twelve persons. In rejecting his petition, the Court ruled that states could prosecute by information rather than by indictment and could use eight-person juries in noncapital, state criminal cases so long as the same rules applied equally to all. Justice Peckham said, "The Fourteenth Amendment was not designed to interfere with the power of a state to protect the lives, liberty, and property of its citizens, nor with the exercise of that power in the adjudications of the courts of a state in administering process provided by the law of the state."

312. *Hurtado v. California*, 110 U.S. 516 (1884). Under California law, defendants could be charged with crimes either by grand jury indictment or on information presented to a magistrate. Hurtado was committed to trial for murder by information, convicted, and sentenced to death. The Court ruled that Hurtado's trial did not violate due process and implied that states were free to abolish grand juries entirely if they wished. This case and *Maxwell v. Dow* proved to be useful precedents for William Rehnquist and others who favor allowing states more flexibility in establishing criminal procedures than the federal government has under the constraints imposed by the Sixth Amendment.

The decision was closer than it looked. With Powell and Rehnquist replacing Black and Harlan on the Court, and Thurgood Marshall switching sides, Powell found himself in the role of tiebreaker. After passing on the case in conference, Powell later joined White's opinion to decide the case.

This case broke the pattern established by the incorporationists, especially Black and Douglas, that state governments should be held to the same constitutional standards as the federal government in Sixth Amendment cases, and posthumously vindicated Harlan's "fundamental fairness" theory of due process. Harlan believed that federal and state due process standards should be independently established and that federal standards should be applied to state courts only to the extent that they were necessary for a fair trial. While nonunanimous juries might be unconstitutional in federal courts, the majority found that unanimous juries were not essential to fundamental fairness, and states remained free to allow 11–1, 10–2, or 9–3 verdicts.

The four dissenters attacked the ruling as a radical and unjustifiable departure from tradition. Douglas and Marshall argued that unanimous juries were as indispensable to justice as the presumption of innocence and the reasonable doubt standard. Brennan questioned the logic by which unanimous juries could be constitutionally required for federal criminal trials but not for state trials. He noted that unanimous juries promoted a healthy diversity of viewpoints and protected minorities from being steamrollered by the majority. Potter Stewart stressed that unanimous juries were essential to seating impartial juries and maintaining public confidence in jury verdicts. Stewart thought that majority verdicts were especially problematic in cases where members of particular groups were judged by jurors who voted along identifiable group lines.

Colgrove v. Battin, 413 U.S. 149 (1973)
(Brennan)

Federal district courts in Montana permitted six-person juries in civil cases. Miles City attorney Roland Colgrove sued District Court Judge James F. Battin, claiming that the local rule violated the Seventh Amendment, a federal law protecting jury trials in common law suits, and Rule 48 of the Federal Rules of Civil Procedure. Rule 48 assumed a standard jury size of twelve but allowed smaller juries if stipulated by both parties. The district court and the Ninth Circuit Court of Appeals upheld the Montana rule.

BURGER: I don't see any constitutional problems under the Seventh Amendment. "Common law" is simply a distinction from equity. Brandeis's *Peterson* decision is apropos.[313] So this case comes down to a construction of the Rules. Rule 48 is not a limitation on the district court's power as such. Nor do I think that the local rule is inconsistent with Rule 48.

STEWART: We don't need to get to the Constitution in light of §2072—the act of Congress which requires, as I read it, a twelve-man jury.[314]

---

313. *Ex parte Peterson,* 253 US 300 (1920). Brandeis wrote: "The command of the Seventh Amendment that 'the right of trial by jury shall be preserved' does not require that old forms of practice and procedure be retained. . . . New devices may be used to adapt the ancient institution to present needs and to make of it an efficient instrument in the administration of justice. Indeed, such changes are essential to the preservation of the right. The limitation imposed by the Amendment is merely that enjoyment of the right of trial by jury be not obstructed, and that the ultimate determination of issues of fact by the jury be not interfered with."

314. 28 U.S.C. §2072. The law provides that the Supreme Court has the power to prescribe general rules of practice, procedure, and evidence in federal courts but that it cannot abridge, enlarge, or modify any substantive right.

POWELL: The constitutional issue is difficult, and I would prefer a statutory approach construing §2072 to require a twelve-man jury.

REHNQUIST: The constitutional question isn't the same as *Williams*, but after that I think that this question comes out the same way.[315] The more difficult question is whether the statute or Rule 48 mandates a twelve-man jury.

Result: After passing in conference, the Chief Justice provided the fifth vote in a 5–4 decision to permit the use of six-person juries in federal civil trials. William Brennan wrote for the majority that the local rule did not conflict with the Seventh Amendment, federal law, or procedural norms. Of the four dissenters, Douglas and Powell argued that the local rule violated Rule 48, while Marshall and Stewart argued that six-person juries violated both Rule 48 and 28 U.S.C. §2072.

Ballew v. Georgia, 435 U.S. 223 (1978)
(Brennan)

After Williams v. Florida *permitted states to use six-person juries in criminal trials, the question remained of whether states could empanel juries with fewer than six persons.[316] A five-person Georgia jury convicted Claude Ballew on a misdemeanor obscenity charge.*

BURGER: The figure of five versus six doesn't bother me—I can't see how there is a constitutional issue.

STEWART: I reverse on each or any of four issues: (1) the use of a five man jury; (2) the use of a five man jury in obscenity cases; (3) the injunction; and (4) vel non obscenity to consenting adults.

WHITE: I reverse on the five-man jury—even across board, but at least in obscenity cases. We ought not go below six in criminal cases generally.

MARSHALL: I would reverse on the jury instructions.

BLACKMUN: I can't see why *Williams* wouldn't support five as well as six.

POWELL: I thought that *Williams* might be controlling—yet five is too small. Six should be the minimum where a jury is required. I also thought that the instructions were hard to defend, but we need not reach that.

REHNQUIST: I don't distinguish from obscenity cases. Juries below six and down to five seem O.K. to me, yet I might join an opinion saying that six is the minimum in any criminal case.

STEVENS: I would decide only the six-man jury question and say that six is the minimum.

BURGER: I change my vote to reverse on the five-man jury. Five is constitutionally inadequate.

---

315. *Williams v. Florida,* 399 U.S. 78 (1970), ruling that the Sixth Amendment's requirement of twelve-person juries did not apply to the states and that six-person juries were permissible in state criminal trials.
316. *Williams v. Florida,* 399 U.S. 78 (1970).

BLACKMUN: I change my vote to go along with six as the minimum.

Result: While the Justices unanimously agreed that a five-person jury was unconstitutional, they were deeply divided as to why. Harry Blackmun announced the judgment of the Court and ruled that a jury of fewer than six persons threatened the Sixth and Fourteenth Amendments. The law also failed because Georgia provided no persuasive justification for the use of five-person juries. Only John Paul Stevens joined Blackmun's plurality opinion. Byron White concurred, arguing that a five-person jury violated the fair cross-section requirement of the Sixth and Fourteenth Amendments. Lewis Powell, joined by Burger and Rehnquist, agreed that five-person juries were impermissible but offered no real explanation or justification. William Brennan, joined by Stewart and Marshall, also concurred but argued that Claude Ballew should not be subjected to another trial because the state obscenity statute was unconstitutional on its face.

The Right to a Jury Trial in Civil Cases

Dairy Queen, Inc. v. Wood, 369 U.S. 469 (1962)
(Douglas)

The McCullough Dairy Queen company ("MDQ") licensed their trademarked name, "Dairy Queen," to Dairy Queen, Inc. ("DQI") for use in Pennsylvania. MDQ later sued DQI in federal court, alleging that DQI had breached its licensing contract by not paying the required minimum yearly licensing fee. Among other relief, MDQ sought an injunction to prevent DQI from using the name "Dairy Queen," an accounting to determine the precise amount of damages, and $150,000 in damages. DQI demanded a jury trial, but District Judge Wood refused on two alternative grounds: (1) that the action was purely equitable (by tradition there is no right to trial by jury in equity cases); and (2) because he thought that the common law issues that were raised were "merely incidental" to the equitable issues in the case. The court of appeals affirmed.

Conference of February 23, 1962

WARREN: This is a suit for an accounting. It is a close case. The basic issue was whether there was a contract and whether it had been breached. That means a jury trial. I reverse.

BLACK: I reverse and agree with the Chief.

FRANKFURTER: *Beacon Theatres* decides that there was no equitable suit.[317] If he had pleaded in that case a breach of contract, he would not necessarily have had a jury trial.

---

317. *Beacon Theatres, Inc. v. Westover,* 359 U.S. 500 (1959). Fox West Coast Theaters suspected that Beacon Theatres was preparing to file an antitrust lawsuit against it over a movie distribution deal. To preempt Beacon, Fox brought an equitable suit in federal court for a declaratory judgment and an injunction against Beacon. Beacon filed a counterclaim, alleging that Fox had violated federal antitrust laws. Beacon claimed that it had a right to a jury trial, but District Judge Harry Westover refused on the ground that Fox had sued first in equity (common law actions seeking cash damages generally have the right to trial by jury, while actions in equity—including declaratory judgments and injunctions—are usually tried before a judge).

Beacon applied for a writ of mandamus ordering Judge Westover to conduct a jury trial. Hugo Black, writing for the majority, noted that any curtailment of the right to trial by jury must be scrutinized with the utmost care. Beacon, he wrote, was entitled to a jury trial on its antitrust claims and could not be deprived of this right merely because its adversary sued first in equity.

The difference between equity and law in these situations is the remedy sought. This seems like a suit in unfair trade practice.

DOUGLAS: I pass.

CLARK: I reverse and agree with the Chief Justice.

Harlan: I reverse. He is entitled to jury trial. He is suing to recover damages on this con- tract—not an accounting for profits. It's looking at the books, but it is really damages. This does not smell like a real ancillary equitable claim—it is a fortiori from *Beacon*. It does not do away with the equitable clean-up doctrine.

BRENNAN: Paragraphs 10, 12, 14 of the complaint are the guts of the case. There was an agreement to pay $150,000. This is an open and shut claim for refusal to pay a sum cer- tain. It is a classic jury case.

WHITTAKER: I reverse. This case is controlled by *Beacon*.

STEWART: The district court judge was wrong, in my analysis of the complaint, to deny a jury trial. I think that the complaint was one sounding in unfair competition.

Result: Hugo Black wrote the majority opinion reversing the decision below, joined by Warren, Clark, and Brennan. Stewart, Harlan, and Douglas concurred in the result, giving a 7–0 decision that DQI had the right to a jury trial. The Court was short-handed for this decision. While Felix Frankfurter participated in the conference and voted to affirm the decision below, he suffered a stroke and did not participate in the final stages of the case. Charles Whittaker also resigned after the conference and was replaced by Byron White, who did not take his seat in time to participate.

THE PRESS AND THE RIGHT TO A FAIR TRIAL

Nebraska Press Association v. Stuart, 427 U.S. 539 (1976)
(Brennan)

In the small town of Sutherland, Nebraska, Erwin Charles Simants was charged with the rape and murder of a young girl, the brutal murder of five other members of the Henry Kellie family, and the defilement of several of his victims' bodies. Anticipating a crush of media coverage for the trial, Judge Hugh Stuart issued a broad gag order restraining the media from reporting on most aspects of the case, including the evidence and courtroom proceedings. The Nebraska Supreme Court upheld the gag order to protect Simants's Sixth Amendment right to a fair trial.

BURGER: Assuming that prior restraints may in some cases be permissible, alternatives must first be explored. We decided this case when we decided the *Pentagon Papers* case.[318]

STEWART: I agree with Bill Brennan and would not object to an opinion that talked about the alternatives of venue changes and the like—but I would not speak of gag orders on lawyers.

---

318. *New York Times Co. v. United States*, 403 U.S. 713 (1971).

WHITE: I agree with Brennan.

MARSHALL: I agree with Brennan, but would think that a confession could be kept out of the press.

BLACKMUN: I make no apologies whatsoever for my two opinions.[319] They accomplished most of what I was after with the Nebraska Supreme Court. I could join no opinion that rated the First Amendment above the Sixth. But there should be no prior restraint on what has occurred in open court. The danger is that reversal here will result in closed hearings. But I don't want to close the door completely against some restraints.

POWELL: If we accept our precedents on prior restraint, this is an easy case. The courts can't impose prior restraints with respect to public hearings or information that press gets on its own, however shabbily it gets it.

REHNQUIST: You can't forbid the press to report what was said at an open preliminary hearing, and I would go no further in reversing. So I would affirm in part and reverse in part.

STEVENS: There is no clear and present danger proved here, so I would reverse outright.

Result: The more cautious wing of the Court prevailed, reversing Judge Stuart's gag order but leaving the door open for more carefully crafted restraints in some cases. Four Justices (Brennan, Stewart, Marshall, Stevens) concurred in the judgment but favored significantly broader protection of press rights than the majority was willing to recognize.

Simants was convicted, and Judge Stuart sentenced him to death by electrocution. His conviction was overturned when it was discovered that Lincoln County sheriff Gordon "Hop" Glister, a witness for the prosecution, had played cards with jurors during the trial. On retrial, Simants was found not guilty by reason of insanity and committed to a state mental hospital.

Nixon v. Warner Communications, Inc., 435 U.S. 589 (1978)
(Brennan)

During the Watergate trials, written transcripts of approximately twenty-two hours of President Nixon's White House tape recordings were made public. Several press organizations asked trial judge John Sirica to allow the media access to the original tapes. Judge Sirica referred the matter to District Judge Gerhard Gesell, who tentatively ruled that the tapes were part of the public record and that the press had the right to examine and reproduce them. Gesell, however, postponed his final judgment until after the Watergate trials were over. After four of the former White House officials were convicted, the press

---

319. After Stuart imposed his initial gag order, the affected media organizations sought to stay the judge's orders from going into effect. After the Nebraska Supreme Court announced that it would not consider the case for a month or more the media appealed to Harry Blackmun, sitting as a circuit judge, to stay Judge Stuart's order. Blackmun refused to act, saying that he had been assured that the state supreme court would promptly announce its decision. *Nebraska Press Assn. v. Stuart,* 423 U.S. 1319 (1975). After the state supreme court failed to act for another twelve days, the media again appealed to Blackmun, who granted the stay on the ground that the delay had "exceeded tolerable limits." *Nebraska Press Assn. v. Stuart,* 423 U.S. 1327 (1975).

again sought access to the tapes.[320] *Judge Sirica ruled that because of pending appeals, the Watergate trials were not yet over and media access to the tapes could still prejudice the defendants' rights to a fair trial. The court of appeals reversed, ruling that the mere possibility of prejudice could not override the common law right of public access to judicial records.*

BURGER: The common law right to see public records and the Sixth Amendment right to a public trial were Judge Gesell's grounds, and these were agreed to by the court of appeals. It seems to me that there is a difference between exhibits and a witness's recorded testimony. The former belong to their owners and there is no interest of justice served by their release to commercial disseminators. Will there be an inhibitory impact on witnesses by the release of depositions or otherwise? On the privacy aspect, I doubt whether Nixon can claim any now. I would try to shape a rule that protected third parties.

STEWART: When cert was here, I thought that this evidence was dedicated to the public and was public property akin to court records. I don't think so now. I don't think that it is correct that Nixon is without privacy interests. Subpoenaed exhibits are not part of the court records for me, and therefore are not within the *Cox* doctrine.[321] These were Nixon's confidential conversations brought into trial by a subpoena duces tecum, and their use fully satisfied any public trial rights. The press has no constitutional right to access, but once you give access to the press then First Amendment rights would arise. The whole thing boils down to the discretion of the trial court on whether or not to release the exhibits. This discretion is controlled by an inhibition against release when release is objected to by someone with standing to object. Abuse of discretion can be claimed whenever you think there is a final order.

WHITE: This is not a final, appealable order. Judge Sirica intended to come back after the appeals of the defendants' convictions were settled. So my first preference is to remand and to say so. On the merits, I agree with Potter, except as to Nixon and others involved with materials such as this is. His personal privacy claim is nothing with respect to matters pertaining to the conduct of public business. He has no residual privacy claim. Therefore, Sirica could have given them to the GSA and let it, under statute, treat it just like the others since Congress has spoken.

---

320. The four convicted defendants were John Ehrlichman, H. R. Haldeman, Robert Mardian, and John Mitchell.

321. *Cox Broadcasting Corp. v. Cohn*, 420 U.S. 469 (1975). During a televised report from the scene of a notorious Atlanta rape trial, Thomas Wassell, a local television reporter for Cox Broadcasting, referred to the seventeen-year-old deceased victim, Cynthia Cohn, by name. Wassell had obtained her name from official court records available for public inspection. The victim's father, Martin Cohn, sued for invasion of privacy under a Georgia law that made it a misdemeanor to publish the name of any rape victim.

The Court ruled that the First and Fourteenth Amendments protected Wassell and Cox from liability where the information was obtained from public records. Besides the constitutional and public interests in maintaining a free and vigorous press, the crime and subsequent trial were events of legitimate public concern. Cohn's privacy claims were further weakened by the fact that the information was part of the public record. Byron White confined his majority opinion to the "narrower interface between press and privacy" and avoided the broader question of whether truthful publications could ever be subjected to criminal or civil liability. William O. Douglas argued in his concurring opinion that the ruling should have been absolute and should have barred *any* government efforts to interfere with a free press.

MARSHALL: I doubt that we have jurisdiction. But on the merits, I don't see how any GSA thing can affect what this Court does. This is not a case where the documents were sealed—so I don't see why copies of exhibits shouldn't be available to anyone.

BLACKMUN: I am not sure whether we have no jurisdiction, and I might have to join a Court on that. On privacy, I initially thought Nixon had some, and I still think that he has some left. This case comes down to a crass commercial use of this material. I think that it may be that a sound reproduction is constitutionally different from a typed transcript—there is an aspect of privacy in the former. But I will stop short of that. I will assume jurisdiction and reverse.

POWELL: I would find that there is jurisdiction by resolving any doubtful questions that way. On the merits, I see no constitutional questions here. There is a common law rule of access, but that does not extend to subpoenaed materials. Or if there is a presumption, it should be against turning these materials over to anyone over the objections of someone with standing. I don't go so far as Potter, perhaps. I agree that the GSA statute would resolve the historical interest argument, so I could agree with Potter or Byron if they are not too far apart.

REHNQUIST: I am not persuaded that this is a non-appealable order, but I will reserve judgment. If this was an ancillary decree, the complete denial makes it a final order. On the merits, I thought that this case was a simple housekeeping sort of thing respecting what to do with exhibits after the trial was over. I was originally inclined to affirm on the theory that Nixon's privacy interests were exhausted in the subpoena for the tapes. I am inclined to leave liability for use of the tapes to other proceedings. I disagree with Potter that allowing access to the media gives them a First Amendment right to use. But if you need me to get Court, I could go Byron's way.

STEVENS: I am not sure about jurisdiction—I am dubious about it. And maybe we have to explore the whole question of whether we have any jurisdiction to entertain this application at all. I would not read the GSA statute as interposing a barrier. I would read this without the statute, and treat this as only Nixon objecting. I agree that Nixon has standing and I don't agree that his embarrassment is irrelevant. But I think that the trial judge's discretion can't require him to deny if Nixon objects. Here these judges thought that after the trials and appeals were over, they would turn these materials over. I would not distinguish between transcript and exhibits. I think that the right of public access survives the end of the trial to enable the public to be sure there was a fair trial. The district court's job was done by Gesell.

Result: The Court ruled 5–4 that the common law right of access to court materials was not absolute, and that such judgments were best left to the discretion of trial judges. Lewis Powell, writing for the majority, refused to recognize any special First Amendment press rights of access to the tapes. Nor did the Sixth Amendment's guarantee of public trials give the media special rights not enjoyed by the general public. Finally, Powell pointed out that Congress, in passing the Presidential Recordings and Materials Preservation Act , had already provided a reasonable alternative means for public access to the tapes.

Gannett v. DePasquale, 443 U.S. 368 (1979)
(Brennan)

Two defendants in a murder case asked the trial judge to bar the press and public from a pretrial suppression hearing where crucial evidence would be discussed. Prosecutors did not object to the closure. Over protests from the media, the judge granted the defendants' motion and sealed the transcripts, ruling that the defendants' right to a fair trial outweighed any public or press interest in access to the hearing or transcripts. The New York Court of Appeals affirmed. The defendants pled guilty to reduced charges, and transcripts of the suppression hearing were released immediately afterward.

BURGER: There is no Sixth Amendment public trial issue here, because a motion to suppress is not part of the trial. On the First Amendment argument, there isn't any for me.

STEWART: I don't think that Gannett's First Amendment claim is valid, since the press has no greater rights than the public. This case resolves to the Sixth Amendment issue. I can't agree that a motion to suppress is not part of trial, but I would limit our decision to this problem of suppression hearings. The right to a public trial is explicitly given to the accused. But there is a public interest, and who but the accused can trigger that? *Singer* indicates that the accused can't waive his right to a jury trial, but no one can force the defendant to take the stand.[322] I am inclined to hold that only the prosecutor can speak for the public where a motion for closure is made by the defendant. But there should be a transcript of the proceedings to be released when the trial is over—that protects the public interest.

WHITE: A suppression hearing is part of the trial, but I agree with Potter—we don't have to have the press in to vindicate the public interest. But the trial judge himself has some responsibility to make findings. You don't need a lawyer for the press or the public. At least some stricter standard than was applied here should govern.

MARSHALL: A suppression hearing is part of the trial. The public has a right here, because if the accused is done dirt, the public interest is hurt. The public is entitled to hear what happens when it happens.

BLACKMUN: There was very little factual basis for the judge's closure order. He seemed to rely primarily on the fact that defendant Greathouse was sixteen.[323] Any modification of the closure order here must be very carefully done. I agree that the concern of the Sixth Amendment is for the public character of trials. At common law, it was the duty of the public to attend trials.

---

322. *Singer v. United States,* 380 U.S. 24 (1965). In a federal mail fraud case, Mortimer Singer asked to waive his right to a jury trial. Although the trial judge agreed, prosecutors refused to give their consent. Federal Criminal Procedure Rule 23(a) required that the defendant, the government, and the trial judge all had to agree before Singer could waive his right to a jury trial. Singer was tried before a jury and convicted. In affirming his conviction, the Supreme Court ruled unanimously that Rule 23(a) was valid and that the Constitution provided no affirmative right to criminal defendants to have their cases tried before a judge alone.

323. Defendant Greathouse was sixteen years of age; the other defendant, Jones, was twenty-one.

The transcript of the proceeding here shows no open hearing by the trial judge, yet he just stopped when the prosecution agreed and made no findings. I think that the public directly and the press indirectly have an interest in preventing any abuse of public business. I would take the Sixth Amendment approach and open the motion to suppress, because it is presided over by the trial judge and is part of the trial. And I would bar closure, at least in the absence of findings—more like Byron.

POWELL: I agree with Byron and Harry—this is a Sixth Amendment case and not a First Amendment case. I also agree that the suppression hearing is part of the criminal trial, and that the accused hasn't a right to prevent judicial consideration of the public interest. I can't go as far as Bill Brennan to make it constitutionally required, although I would prevent a trial judge from allowing the press to be heard. Here, the trial judge did not do enough when he heard the accused and the prosecutor agree to the closure. I would not give the press or the public a right to access through lawyers.

REHNQUIST: This case is not moot, since there will be other proceedings or other cases. I am with the Chief Justice. All public interest reasons for access are meritorious, but the Sixth Amendment means to me only protection for the right of the accused. Whatever the common law is, the framers did not give a public right to access. I would not even require a transcript or that a transcript be published. For my view, I can assume that a pretrial suppression hearing is a part of the trial.

STEVENS: The question of mootness troubles me. There is a critical difference between seeing a live hearing and reading a transcript of it. If the public has a right of access to a live performance, we will be holding that the electronic media must be allowed. I think it is in the interest of the accused, and on the record before us this judge did not abuse his discretion.

Result: The majority ruled that the Sixth Amendment's right to a public trial was intended solely to benefit defendants and did not give the press or public any independent right of access to pretrial proceedings—at least not when all participants agreed to a closed hearing to protect the defendants' constitutional right to a fair trial. Lewis Powell's change of heart after the conference transformed a 5–4 conference vote to reverse to a 5–4 decision to affirm. Harry Blackmun, who received the original assignment, wrote an opinion recognizing a broad First Amendment right of public access to criminal proceedings. But when Powell changed his mind and decided that this was really a Sixth Amendment case, Blackmun lost his majority and Potter Stewart's planned dissent became the new majority opinion.

Richmond Newspapers, Inc. v. Virginia, 448 U.S. 555 (1980)
(Brennan)

John Stevenson's first murder trial ended in a mistrial. So did his second trial. And his third. At the beginning of the fourth trial, the judge granted a defense motion for a closed trial. Neither the prosecutor nor the media present in the courtroom objected. Later that same day, the Richmond Newspapers Corporation asked for a hearing on the closure. The judge held a brief hearing but did not change his mind. The next day, behind closed doors, the judge excused the jury, granted a defense motion to strike the prosecution's evidence, found Stevenson not guilty, and ordered him released. The Virginia Supreme Court subsequently denied the newspaper's appeal from the judge's closure order.

At conference, the Justices readily agreed that there was a constitutional interest in public trials, but they could not agree on the constitutional basis for a decision. The First, Sixth, Ninth, and Four- teenth Amendments were all floated as possibilities.

BURGER: We can treat this case as a cert if we must. *Gannett* did not decide this case.[324] There is a common thread for public trials, but what is the constitutional handle? The assumption all along has been that trials must be public. They were taken for granted from 1787 to 1791. I am not persuaded that it is in the First Amendment, either as an ac- cess right or an associational right. I would rely on the fact that it was part of judicial proceedings before the adoption of the Bill of Rights. The Ninth Amendment is as good a handle as any.[325]

STEWART: The Sixth Amendment was resolved against public trials in *Gannett.* The press has no right superior to the public in terms of access to institutions like prisons, etc., which are traditionally closed. But trials have been open traditionally, subject to time, place, and manner regulations. Tribe's Sixth Amendment argument is not ap- pealing, but I agree that there is a First Amendment right subject to an overriding in- terest in a fair trial.[326]

WHITE: I agree with Bill Brennan and Potter. We might, however, get some mileage out of the Sixth Amendment.

MARSHALL: I agree that the First Amendment will suffice.

BLACKMUN: The fourth trial cuts in favor of openness. I won't use Ninth Amendment trickiness as to this right, but we can get around it—no spokesman here.

POWELL: Out.[327]

REHNQUIST: There are tensions between *Gannett* and this case. What I said in *Gannett* I still say, whether it's the First or the Sixth Amendment.

STEVENS: The anti-corruption rationale is silly. *Gannett* decided that under the Sixth Amendment it is the right of the accused. I can't agree with Tribe's Sixth Amendment argument. On the First Amendment issue, I dissented in *Houchins* and said that the First Amendment protected some right of access.[328] I don't find the "traditionally open and

---

324. *Gannett Co. v. DePasquale,* 443 U.S. 368 (1979).

325. Had the other Justices followed Burger's lead on the Ninth Amendment, this case might have been remembered as a landmark opinion reviving "the forgotten Amendment." No one else picked up on the idea, however, and the Ninth Amendment was relegated to a brief mention in footnote 15 of Burger's majority opinion.

326. Laurence Tribe represented Richmond Newspapers, Inc. He argued that both the First and Sixth Amendments were involved. Stewart (along with the rest of the Court, save for White and Rehnquist) re- jected this argument because he wanted to distinguish this case from *Gannett.*

327. Although Powell did not participate in this case, his concurring opinion in *Gannett v. DePasquale* and his dissenting opinions in three similar cases suggest that he probably would have voted with the majority. See *Pell v. Procunier,* 417 U.S. 817 (1974); *Saxbe v. Washington Post Co.,* 417 U.S. 843 (1974); *Houchins v. KQED, Inc.,* 438 U.S. 1 (1978).

328. *Houchins v. KQED, Inc.,* 438 U.S. 1 (1978).

closed" analysis any help. The point is that there is no reason given for closure. I would be prepared to hold that in the absence of any rational basis for denying public access, the benefits of openness argue for it.

Result: While the Court reversed the decision below on a 7–1 vote, no opinion garnered more than three votes. Warren Burger wrote the lead opinion. Speaking for himself and two other Justices, Burger argued that the First and Fourteenth Amendments gave the public and press the right to attend most trials, and trial judges were constitutionally required to articulate adequate reasons before closing any trial to the public or press. Brennan, Marshall, Stewart, and Blackmun concurred in the judgment. William Rehnquist was alone in dissent. Lewis Powell did not participate in the decision.

Globe Newspaper Co. v. Superior Court of Norfolk, 457 U.S. 596 (1982)
(Brennan)

Massachusetts permitted closed trials in cases involving sexual attacks on minors. In a highly publicized rape trial involving three young victims, the state's supreme judicial court ruled that state law required the public and press to be excluded during the victims' testimony. The Globe Newspaper Company appealed, but the rape trial ended in an acquittal before the issue could be fully litigated.

BURGER: Justification for access has to lie in the public's interest in what is going on when a prosecution witness suffers trauma. The state needs to have crimes reported. The state needs to get testimony so that rapists may be brought to justice. The desires of the victim are not controlling, nor are the desires of the defendant. Should there be a hearing before closure? The state, in my view, may have this statute balancing the victims' ordeal along with the public interest in having open trials.

BRENNAN:[329] I am reluctant to uphold any per se rule barring the press and public from any part of a trial, and if this law were being attacked facially I would not hesitate to strike it down. But as construed by the supreme judicial court and applied in this case, I am inclined to find the provision constitutional.

(1) It is clear since our *Richmond Newspapers* decision that the press and public have a First Amendment right to a public trial, independent of the accused's Sixth Amendment right. But I think that the *Richmond Newspapers* principle is not offended by the present statute as construed and applied here. Since the law applies only to the minor prosecutrix's testimony at trial, it seems to me that the benefits of trial openness—namely, public supervision of the performance of the participants in the judicial system, deterrence of perjury, public education, and promotion of the retributive and deterrent purposes of criminal law— are not foreclosed. Further, every other form of testimony at the trial—the testimony of the police, scientific and medical experts, corroborative witnesses, the defendant himself and his corroborative witnesses—*will* be open to the press and public. A transcript of the testimony of the prosecutrix herself will eventually be available to the press, as well. These sources can easily be pieced together to form a coherent picture of the case sufficient to serve the informative function usually ensured by total trial openness.

---

329. Adapted from Brennan's talking papers, Brennan Papers, OT 1981, box 600.

Moreover, the provision as construed and applied seems to be as narrow as it could be without undercutting its purposes. I was persuaded from the oral argument that a case-by-case adjudication of the propriety of openness would probably unavoidably impair the privacy interests that the statute intends to protect.

(2) Appellants point out that the closure mandated here cannot be waived even by the prosecutrix, whose privacy interests are the nominal purpose of the provision. This point is troubling, but I am persuaded that the state acting as parens patriae is entitled to preempt the risks of a minor's choice of openness—for example, the risks that the prosecutrix would not give effective testimony, and that her credibility would thus be impaired before the jury.

My vote is to affirm the judgment of the supreme judicial court.

WHITE: I agree with Bill Brennan. The state's interest is too narrow when it is limited to a victim's testimony.

MARSHALL: Mandatory closure goes too far.

BLACKMUN: People hate to get involved in rape cases whether in an open or closed courtroom. So the trauma thing doesn't impress me. A Sixth Amendment approach would require reversal. Under the First Amendment, I agree with Bill Brennan and Byron.

POWELL: I would leave it to a case by case analysis, with discretion to the trial judge to hold an in camera hearing. Rape victims are the most reluctant of all to go to court. I could join to reverse if we made it very clear that the press had no First Amendment right to be present at such a hearing. I would eliminate the mandatory closure rule.

REHNQUIST: If you want to encourage the reporting of rapes, you ought to be able to encourage the victim by mandatory closure.

STEVENS: I am not at rest. I am very dubious about mandatory closure. But I am also concerned about the abstract way in which the case got here—isn't it moot? The order of the trial court has been set aside, and we are reviewing an advisory opinion. So I would *Rescue Army* this case and find it moot.[330] If I reach the merits, I would reverse. But I'll dismiss.

O'CONNOR: The First Amendment in *Richmond Newspapers* requires invalidation of this law.

Result: The Court ruled that the state law, as construed by the Supreme Judicial Court of Massachusetts, violated the First and Fourteenth Amendments. Writing for a 5–1–3 majority, William Brennan wrote that states could not impose a blanket prohibition of public and press attendance during trials, even during the testimony of minors. Sandra Day O'Connor concurred in the result, while Burger, Rehnquist, and Stevens dissented.

---

330. *Rescue Army v. Municipal Court of Los Angeles,* 331 U.S. 549 (1947). The Court held that federal courts should not consider the constitutionality of a state statute in the absence of a controlling interpretation of the law by state courts.

POSTCONVICTION PUNISHMENT AND REMEDIES

HABEAS CORPUS

Fay v. Noia, 372 U.S. 391 (1963)

(Douglas)

Charles Noia, Santo Caminito, and Frank Bonino were convicted of murder in New York. Noia did not appeal; the other two defendants appealed unsuccessfully and then filed for federal writs of habeas corpus. A federal court ruled that Caminito's and Bonino's confessions were coerced and quashed their convictions. At that point, the state admitted that all three confessions had been coerced. But when Noia applied to a state court for a coram nobis review of his conviction, it was denied because he had not filed a timely appeal.[331] Noia petitioned the federal courts for a writ of habeas corpus against Edwin Fay, the warden of New York's Greenhaven Prison. The district court rejected Noia's petition, ruling that he had not filed a timely appeal and had failed to exhaust his state remedies. The court of appeals reversed.

Conference of January 11, 1963

[DOUGLAS: Black presides, as the Chief, though present, has lost his voice.]

BLACK: District courts have habeas corpus jurisdiction when people are in prison in violation of the Constitution. This jurisdiction need not be exercised at all times. It depends on the facts. Exhaustion of state remedies has nothing to do with this case. State remedies have been exhausted. Look at *Mooney v. Holohan.*[332]

WARREN: I agree with Hugo, and I agree with Bill Brennan's analysis in his memo that was circulated. Here there is a stipulation that the respondent was unconstitutionally convicted.

DOUGLAS: I agree with the Chief and Hugo.

CLARK: I reverse. There was an adequate state ground at one time—appeal—that he did not use. I would rely on the *Daniels* case.[333] Also, habeas corpus is no substitute for an appeal.

HARLAN: I adhere to my views in the memo. Federalism, and respect for it, requires federal courts to keep our hands off. There is a great confusion in the cases between exhaus-

---

331. *Coram nobis* ("our court") is an archaic writ that asks the original trial court, rather than an appellate court, to correct errors of fact attributable to duress, fraud, or excusable mistake. Errors cannot, however, be the product of a defendant's calculated decisions or negligence.

332. *Mooney v. Holohan,* 294 U.S. 103 (1935).

333. *Daniels v. Allen,* decided *sub nom., Brown v. Allen,* 344 U.S. 443 (1953). Bennie and Lloyd Daniels were convicted of capital murder in North Carolina. The state supreme court refused to review their cases on direct appeal because they failed to perfect their appeals within the sixty-day limit provided by law (they did not perfect their appeals until the sixty-first day). Both men sought a federal writ of habeas corpus. The Supreme Court rejected their petitions on the ground that in missing the appeal deadline they had failed to use an available state remedy. There was a statutory requirement that all state remedies be exhausted before filing a federal habeas petition, and absent some interference or incapacity there could be no further review where the prisoners had not availed themselves of all available and effective state remedies.

tion (*Darr v. Burford*) and adequate state grounds.[334] The former involves a degree of discretion. Exhaustion is a red herring. There was exhaustion, for Noia sought a state coram nobis. Exhaustion means exhaustion at this time, not at an early time. But adequate state ground goes to state power. He failed to follow state procedures, and that is why he is being held. To overrule the state ground is to take a drastic step that opens up the federal constitutional right to require state procedures and to get review in the federal courts. Look at the *Sunal* case, of which I approve and would carry over to the state domain.[335]

BRENNAN: I affirm and agree with Hugo. Noia's failure to appeal is no good reason to deny him relief by federal habeas.

STEWART: I was wrong in *Irvin v. Dowd*.[336] *Edwards* is wrong.[337] There is exhaustion here of the state remedy. [DOUGLAS: At the point, the conference degenerates into a long harangue between Harlan, Brennan, and Stewart, with Goldberg taking a part. It's a waste

---

334. *Darr v. Burford*, 339 U.S. 200 (1950). On a 5–4 vote, the Court established that absent special circumstances, state prisoners on appeal must at least *apply* for certiorari to the U.S. Supreme Court as a prerequisite of applying for a federal writ of habeas corpus. This rule not only applied to direct appeals but also to any collateral proceedings. If the state prisoner did not apply for certiorari to the U.S. Supreme Court at every opportunity, then the federal district court could only inquire into the alleged special circumstances that might justify making an exception to this rule. Where the prisoner had applied for certiorari at each opportunity, then the district court had full authority to consider the petition on the merits.

335. *Sunal v. Large*, 332 U.S. 174 (1947). Theodore Sunal, a Jehovah's Witness, was prosecuted for avoiding the draft during World War II. The federal district court improperly refused to allow him to prove that the local draft board had wrongly classified him as "available for military service" when he should have been classified as a conscientious objector. Sunal was convicted and imprisoned but did not appeal. When he later applied for a writ of habeas corpus, the Supreme Court rejected his petition on the ground that he had failed to file a direct appeal. Habeas corpus was not intended to be a substitute for direct appeal, and Sunal's excuse—that any direct appeal would have been futile because of the state of federal law at that time—could not justify an exception to the rule.

336. *Irvin v. Dowd*, 366 U.S. 717 (1961). On trial for a notorious serial murder, defendant Leslie Irvin had several grounds for appeal after the trial judge denied his second request for a change of venue, and especially after two-thirds of Irvin's jury admitted that they had concluded that he was guilty even before the trial began. After Irvin's conviction he escaped from prison, leaving a note behind saying that if he got a new trial he would turn himself in. Irvin's lawyers appealed his conviction in his absence. The state supreme court rejected the appeal, although it was not clear whether it reached Irvin's constitutional claims or rested its decision on Irvin's escape. After Irvin was recaptured, he filed a petition for habeas corpus. The district court denied his petition on the ground that Irvin had failed to exhaust his state remedies.

The Supreme Court reversed. Brennan interpreted the Indiana Supreme Court's decision as having reached and rejected Irvin's constitutional claims, meaning that Irvin had exhausted his state remedies. Brennan worked hard behind the scenes to build a majority. The crucial vote was Potter Stewart, who was deeply ambivalent about the case. To appease Stewart, Brennan dropped his original plan to abolish the exhaustion requirement. Instead, Brennan artfully avoided the question of whether federal habeas corpus would have been available had the state supreme court explicitly rested its decision on Irvin's escape. Coltharp, "Writing in the Margins: Brennan, Marshall, and the Inherent Weaknesses of Liberal Judicial Decision-Making."

337. *Covington v. Edwards*, 264 F.2d 780 (4th Cir.), cert. denied, 361 U.S. 840 (1959). This case set a strict standard requiring exhaustion of state administrative remedies. The decision was subsequently widely criticized, but never overruled.

of time because everyone has made up his mind.] As of now, I think that if there was a reasonable, valid, constitutional rule or state law on which the prisoner has made a choice, he is barred from habeas corpus in federal court. I reverse here only for a hearing on why he failed to appeal. He probably did not waive a right. He was probably ignorant. Waiver must be deliberate and knowing, and he must be competent. I want findings on that score.

WHITE: I affirm. I can't think of this in terms of state power. Congress could give this power to the district court. I agree with the consensus on exhaustion. *Darr v. Burford* should be disposed of by this case. I would overrule it. As to the adequate state ground, I think that it is not sufficient to bar federal relief. If the case is individualized, it will not upset much law. The federal court has the power to remedy a constitutional right. I would put some limits on the power, and would not be inclined to release many—probably no more than John Harlan.

GOLDBERG: I affirm. I agree with Byron, Hugo, and Bill Brennan. The act settles the question except for matters of policy, which the courts must decide. Whether it is called adequate state ground or something else, it is not a constitutional barrier. It goes only to federal policy on the issuance of this writ in a given case. Two constitutional questions are here—the Tenth Amendment and the Fourteenth Amendment (due process).

WHITE: Congress could provide that a man convicted in a state court could go on appeal either to state court or to a federal court on federal questions.

GOLDBERG: I agree. Issuance of the writ is in the discretion of the federal court.

Result: William Brennan, writing for a 6–3 majority, ruled that coerced confessions were constitutionally intolerable and that issuing a writ of habeas corpus under such circumstances did not violate any principles of federalism. The Court overruled Darr v. Burford *and greatly expanded the federal courts' habeas corpus powers. Brennan's view was that Noia was in prison on a technicality and that it was just this sort of injustice that the "great writ" was intended to remedy. If Noia's incarceration did not conform with the fundamental requirements of law, he was entitled to immediate release. The requirement that prisoners must first exhaust their state remedies, Brennan wrote, was a matter of comity and was not required by any constitutional limits on federal judicial authority. Federal judges should exercise their broad habeas powers in appropriate cases, he concluded, unless the accused deliberately sought to bypass state procedures by intentionally forgoing an opportunity for state review.*

Brennan's opinion proved controversial and was restricted piecemeal by a series of congressional statutes and Supreme Court decisions during the Burger years. In two cases during the early 1990s, the Rehnquist Court overruled Fay *outright.*[338]

PRISONERS

Burrell v. McCray, 426 U.S. 471 (1976)
(Brennan)

Three state prisoners sued in federal court, alleging that they had been abused by Maryland State Penitentiary guards. The prisoners claimed that they were (1) placed naked in isolation cells for up to

---

338. *Coleman v. Thompson,* 501 U.S. 722 (1991); *Keeney v. Tamayo-Reyes,* 504 U.S. 1 (1992).

forty-eight hours; (2) denied access to certain reading material (including Gay Liberator *and the* Akwesasne News*); and (3) deprived of medical care. The threshold question was whether state prisoners had to exhaust available state administrative remedies before pursuing their cases in federal court. The court of appeals ruled that absent a definitive statement to the contrary by Congress or the Supreme Court, exhaustion was not required.*

BURGER: I don't want to close the §1983 door to prisoners, but things are getting out of hand. These new internal procedures are being helpful.

STEWART: The law is as Bill Brennan described it, but it is law we backed into. But after *Preiser*[339] and *Steffel*,[340] I don't see any principled way to carve out an exception for prisoners. I would think that if the majority feels this way, we ought to DIG and avoid reaching the merits.

WHITE: On the constitutional claim, if prisoners have any damages, this could not be decided in administrative proceedings. Yet I have to agree that many of these would disappear in such proceedings.

BLACKMUN: We will never say that solitary confinement is cruel and unusual per se. But the description of the one here is not that it is warm and clean. I am inclined, however, to think that the court of appeals was wrong on the Eighth Amendment.

POWELL: I would reverse on the merits. There is no Eighth Amendment violation here. On exhaustion, I am up a tree. *Monroe v. Pape* is a monstrosity and ought to be overruled on "color of law," "exhaustion," and every other ground.[341] "Color of law" should

---

339. *Preiser v. Rodriguez,* 411 U.S. 475 (1973). In a combined civil rights and habeas corpus suit, three New York state prisoners challenged disciplinary action taken by prison authorities to take away their good behavior credits. The district court ruled that because the prisoners' habeas corpus claims were adjuncts to their civil rights claims, the prisoners were not required to exhaust their state remedies. The Supreme Court reversed, holding that the sole federal remedy for state prisoners seeking accelerated release from prison was habeas corpus, which required the exhaustion of all effective state remedies. Stewart wrote the majority opinion, while Brennan, Douglas, and Marshall dissented.

340. *Steffel v. Thompson,* 415 U.S. 452 (1974), involved a threatened criminal prosecution for distributing anti-Vietnam war handbills at a Georgia shopping center. It is possible that Stewart meant to cite *Wolff v. McDonnell,* 418 U.S. 539 (1974). In that case, Robert McDonnell and other Nebraska state prisoners brought a civil rights action under §1983 against prison officials, claiming that prison disciplinary proceedings—including the forfeiture of good behavior credits and the use of solitary confinement—violated due process. McDonnell also complained that the inmate legal assistance program was inadequate and that the prison's policy of opening attorney-inmate mail was unconstitutional. The Court confirmed *Preiser v. Rodriguez,* holding that §1983 was not available to prisoners who wanted to complain about the loss of good behavior credits. The Court also ruled, however, that state prisoners were entitled to at least minimal due process protections and that the need for prison order and discipline had to be balanced against constitutional principles and values.

341. *Monroe v. Pape,* 365 U.S. 167 (1961). The Court held that under §1983, individual state law enforcement officials could be sued in federal court for depriving people of their civil rights under color of law. The Court broadly defined "color of law" to include complaints where officials did not have authority to act. On the question of exhaustion, the Court ruled that the federal remedy was *supplementary* to existing state remedies and that state remedies did not have to be exhausted before seeking the federal remedy. This case was widely criticized and was partly overruled in a string of later decisions, including *Adarand Constructors v. Pena,* 515 U.S. 200 (1995); *Canton v. Harris,* 489 U.S. 378 (1989); and *Monell v. Department of Social Services,* 436 U.S. 658 (1978) .

be limited to a custom, statute or regulation—and that's the only way that this problem can be effectively addressed. I would join four to require exhaustion in prisoner cases.

REHNQUIST: I would reverse on the Eighth Amendment. It applies only when something is imposed as a punishment. On exhaustion, I agree that you don't have to exhaust state judicial remedies. It shouldn't follow that *adequate* administrative remedies don't have to be exhausted. How do you know when a state has deprived you of something under "color of law"? So no exhaustion, but there is a "color of law" question.

STEVENS: A theft from a prisoner by a guard might be under "color of law," but until we know what remedy the state will give, one can't say, can one, that there is a denial of due process. But here, it is an Eighth Amendment claim of deplorable prison conditions, and the "punishment" requirement was satisfied by his sentence. I can't say that the Eighth Amendment issue was improperly decided by the court of appeals. I also can't say that exhaustion would be proper here.

Result: The Court avoided deciding the case on the merits and dismissed the writ of certiorari as improvidently granted. John Paul Stevens wrote an opinion concurring with the decision to DIG, arguing that dismissing the case after oral argument did not threaten the integrity of the rule of four, because at least one of the Justices who originally voted to grant certiorari also voted to DIG the case. Although Stevens chose not to be specific, in fact three of the four Justices who originally voted to hear the case changed their minds and voted to DIG: Burger, Powell, and Rehnquist. William Brennan's dissent argued that the spirit of the rule of four was violated by dismissing the case after oral argument. The three dissenters, Brennan, White, and Marshall, would have affirmed the decision below.

Bell v. Wolfish, 441 U.S. 520 (1979)

(Brennan)

New York City's Metropolitan Correctional Center (MCC) was a federally operated short-term custodial facility housing mostly pretrial federal detainees. Louis Wolfish claimed that conditions at the MCC were unconstitutional, because even though most detainees had not been convicted of any crimes: (1) they were double-bunked in rooms designed for only one person; (2) no hardcover books were permitted unless mailed directly from publishers, bookstores, or book clubs; (3) no food or personal items from outside the institution were allowed; (4) body cavity searches were conducted any time a detainee had contact with outside visitors; and (5) detainees' rooms were periodically searched while detainees were forced to wait outside.

The district court agreed with Wolfish and enjoined all of these practices. The court of appeals affirmed. Both courts ruled that the government had failed to demonstrate a "compelling administrative necessity" to justify these practices with respect to pretrial detainees—who were by law presumed to be innocent. There were two main issues on appeal: the source of the detainees' claimed rights and the proper judicial standard for reviewing MCC policies. Griffin Bell was the U.S. attorney general.

BURGER: The strip searches went too far, but I wouldn't say that prison authorities can't do anything. The prohibition of packages seems O.K. if there is not enough manpower to examine them. The books prohibition can be supportable. Roving inspections don't violate any constitutional guarantees. There is a protectable interest here that does not raise to an Eighth Amendment violation. They can deprive of some circumstances. I would reverse in part and modify.

BRENNAN: There is a protected interest, but these five things can be justified by a compelling administrative necessity, and the government has not had a hearing.

STEWART: So far as someone already convicted is concerned, the constitutional limitation is the Eighth Amendment. But here they are not convicted, but merely charged. He can't be punished at all because he is presumptively innocent. There is no claim here that the Eighth Amendment was violated as to anyone. But as to pretrial detainees, there can be no punishment at all. But here there is no punishment on any of these things. So I would reverse. The only doubt I have is as to hardcover books, since it implicates the First Amendment.

WHITE: There is no Eighth Amendment violation here. I agree with the government that there can be a violation of a constitutional right that falls short of punishment. There is a due process protection, but I don't see any violation here. I am not ready to second-guess prison authorities; they have a tough enough job as it is.

MARSHALL: This is just a temporary situation. I would affirm with modifications and give the government an opportunity to put its full case on. I would apply a middle tier standard, and not compelling administrative necessity.

BLACKMUN: The government says that the emphasis by the court of appeals was on the presumption of innocence. There is strict review where fundamental liberties are involved—in this case, the First Amendment—and no administrative convenience where privacy interests are involved. *Moore v. East Cleveland*, which established a middle standard of review, is relevant but not controlling.[342] For all other actions by prison officials, cost and feasibility are enough under the rationality standard. I would establish standards and send the case back for redetermination. I would reject the compelling necessity test. I would go along with the solicitor general on 1, 2, and 4, but remand on 5.[343]

POWELL: The critical decision is the standard to be applied. For me, "reasonableness" is derived from the Fifth Amendment. I would reverse as to everything except perhaps where the First Amendment is implicated, and that can only be the book restriction. On security matters, prison authorities, not judges, are the better authority. I would leave the body cavity issue for reexamination.

REHNQUIST: It is hard for me to spell out one abstract standard without some relation to specific practices. I would apply the standard here to these five policies. I would say that none of five amounts to punishment, but if they were unreasonable I would say that they might be. So I would reverse across the board.

STEVENS: The most important question is the difference between an Eighth Amendment punishment and mere punishment in a due process sense. What kind of treatment is per-

---

342. *Moore v. City of East Cleveland*, 431 U.S. 494 (1977).
343. Solicitor General Wade McCree. The case was argued by Deputy Solicitor General Andrew Frey.

missible of those who are presumed innocent? I would think that it was punishment to body search a girl picked up simply for speeding. If that is true, you can't measure the justification as a cost of making a change. I would remand to reexamine the case in light of what we say is punishment. Is the severity of the conditions of confinement related to two permissible state objectives in (1) making sure that they show up at trial; and (2) security?

Result: The Court deferred to the security concerns of MCC officials and approved all the contested practices employed at the center. Powell concurred in part and dissented in part, giving Rehnquist a 6–3 majority on all issues except the body cavity searches. On that issue, Powell joined the dissenters and narrowed Rehnquist's majority to 5–4.

Hudson v. Palmer, 468 U.S. 517 (1984)
(Brennan)

Russell Palmer, an inmate at the Bland Correctional Center in Virginia, alleged that prison officials violated the Fourth and Fourteenth Amendments by conducting an intentionally malicious shakedown search of his prison cell and locker and by destroying his private property solely to harass him. The district court entered summary judgment against Palmer, but the court of appeals ruled that prisoners had privacy rights and were constitutionally protected against searches conducted solely to harass or humiliate. Ted Hudson, one of the prison officials accused of misbehavior, appealed to the Supreme Court.

BURGER: Is an intentional tort different from *Parratt's* negligent tort?[344] A prisoner doesn't lose all of his constitutional rights, but there is a difference between homes and prisons for Fourth Amendment purposes.

BRENNAN:[345] There are two separate, but related, issues presented by this case. As to the inmate's Fourth Amendment claim, I believe that the allegations in this case rise to the level of a Fourth Amendment violation. The Court has previously recognized that the full protections of the Fourth Amendment do not apply in the prison context, but we have also insisted that all constitutional rights do not end at the prison entrance. Where the search of the inmate's locker and the seizure of his papers is assumed to be harassing and abusive, I would find the basis of a Fourth Amendment violation. If the Court were to do otherwise, we would be sanctioning abusive searches and seizures.

On the procedural due process issue, I would also agree with the court of appeals that *Parratt's* reasoning should be extended to some intentional deprivations of property—those which are random and unauthorized, and for which it would be impracticable to have a pre-deprivation hearing. I would not apply the rule where there are completely adequate post-deprivation remedies (i.e., internal grievance procedures with judicial review, or where there are state judicial remedies under tort or property law). It should be limited to the random and unauthorized deprivation alleged here. I affirm in both cases.

---

344. *Parratt v. Taylor,* 541 U.S. 527 (1981), held that negligent deprivation of a prisoner's property by state officials did not violate the Fourteenth Amendment, at least where adequate postdeprivation state remedies existed.

345. Adapted from Brennan's talking papers, Brennan Papers, OT 1983, box 655.

WHITE: I agree with the Chief. Prison officials can do a shakedown of cells like this without a plan or a procedure. *Parratt* covers destruction of property without payment, but here they have a fund to pay.

MARSHALL: I will vote to affirm, but I'll probably not stick to it.

BLACKMUN: The complaint alleged a shakedown and destruction of personal property to harass—that equates with a violation of the Fourth Amendment. On due process, I would affirm.

POWELL: The alleged invidious destruction of personal property is the only thing that troubles me.

REHNQUIST: I agree with the Chief Justice on both issues. There are no Fourth Amendment rights for a prisoner to me, except as to his person. That is not the case here.

STEVENS: This case is the same whether it was negligence or intentional. On the Fourth Amendment, the court of appeals opinion is in error. But I would recognize some Fourth Amendment interest against such things as personal mail or a diary in his locker. I would affirm the judgment only.

O'CONNOR: I agree with Bill Rehnquist. We should give the prisons some guidance and tell them that there is no Fourth Amendment interest in prisoners' *property*—only in one's person.

Result: Powell resolved his doubts to give Warren Burger a 5–4 decision that prisoners have no reasonable expectation of privacy and virtually no Fourth Amendment protections while in prison. Even if the destruction of Palmer's property was intentional and malicious, Burger wrote, there was no need for constitutional protection because there were adequate remedies available under state tort laws. Brennan, Marshall, Blackmun, and Stevens dissented.

CRUEL AND UNUSUAL PUNISHMENT

Status Crimes

Robinson v. California, 370 U.S. 660 (1962)
(Brennan) (Douglas)

California law made it a misdemeanor to be addicted to narcotics. Persons could be charged at any time before they reformed, even if they had never used drugs in California and had never committed any other crime.

In this case, a police officer casually observed needle marks and a scab on Lawrence Robinson's arm and arrested him on suspicion of being an addict. Robinson was not suspected of any other criminal behavior. He admitted to the "occasional" use of narcotics and was convicted of being an addict. On appeal, Robinson claimed that the state law inflicted a cruel and unusual punishment in violation of the Eighth and Fourteenth Amendments. He also claimed that his arrest violated the Fourth Amendment. The appellate division of the superior court affirmed his conviction, and the state supreme court declined review.

WARREN: Robinson was charged with barbiturate use and addiction, and we don't know which ingredient the jury went on. "Addict," in another statute, has a definition which was not the instruction given here by the trial judge. This makes this instruction a constitutional requisite.

BLACK: I have no complaint against the instructions, and I can't say that this statute is unconstitutional on vagueness grounds. And there are no search and seizure grounds for reversing.

DOUGLAS: The verdict does not say what ingredient of use or what ingredient of addiction entered into the jury's verdict. To the extent that one is a sick person, just being one can't be made a crime.

HARLAN: It is hard to say that status can't be reached criminally. Conventionally, it has been dealt with that way.

Conference of May 11, 1962

HARLAN: There is no element of "use" here—merely being an "addict" is enough. I would not strike the act down on face, but would strike the statute down as applied.

DOUGLAS: I reverse.

WARREN: If there is a reversal on the statute being bad as applied, I will reverse.

STEWART: The statute as construed is a bad statute on its face. "Use" would not be a good statute.

HARLAN: The trial court did not charge the jury on "use." The evidence of "use" was extremely weak.

Result: On a 5–1–2 vote, the Court ruled that as construed and applied, the California statute amounted to cruel and unusual punishment. Stewart's majority opinion did not reach Robinson's Fourth Amendment claim. This case was a landmark in the battle to incorporate the Bill of Rights and helped set the stage for Gideon v. Wainwright. Harlan concurred in the result but did not join the majority opinion. He thought that the law punished mere status and a "bare desire" to commit a criminal act, making it an intolerably arbitrary exercise of state power. Clark and White dissented, while Frankfurter did not participate.

The Death Penalty

Louisiana ex rel. Francis v. Resweber, 329 U.S. 459 (1947)
(Douglas) (Burton)

On May 3, 1946, seventeen-year-old Willie Francis was strapped into the Louisiana electric chair, nicknamed "Gruesome Gerty."[346] *The executioner threw the switch and said, "Goodbye, Willie." Francis groaned as the charge went through his body. His lips puffed out and he jumped so hard that the chair's*

---

346. Gerty was the state's only electric chair. Built in 1941, it was portable and was carried from parish to parish as needed. For Francis's execution, it was brought to the St. Martinville courthouse from Louisiana's Angola Prison.

legs came off the floor. He screamed, "Take it off! Let me breathe!" But he did not die. After it was clear that the attempt to execute Francis had failed, guards unstrapped him and took him back to his cell. Prison authorities rescheduled Francis to be executed again the following week. Warden Harold Resweber vowed to kill Francis the next time if he had to do it with a rock.[347]

Conference of November 23, 1946

VINSON: The question is whether this is double jeopardy. It is clear to me that it should be affirmed.

BLACK: I affirm.

REED: I affirm.

FRANKFURTER: This is not an easy case. It is a good example of the function of the due process clause. It is not necessary to go into the technicalities of double jeopardy. Cruel and unusual punishment is a progressive notion, shocking the feelings of the time. Here, though it is hardly a defensible thing for a state to do, it is not so offensive as to make me puke—it does not shock my conscience. We need to say something—it is hardly a defensible thing to do. I affirm.

DOUGLAS: I affirm.[348]

MURPHY: I reverse.

JACKSON: I affirm.

RUTLEDGE: I reverse.

BURTON: I affirm. I was impressed with the peculiarity of this instance. It seems to me that there may be due process for executive relief. We should not let them go through it again. They should go to executive clemency. I reverse.[349]

Result: Writing for a 4–1–4 Court, Stanley Reed cleared the way for Louisiana to electrocute Francis a second time. A second attempt, he wrote, would not violate the double jeopardy clause or amount to cruel and unusual punishment and would not violate due process. The malfunction was unintentional, Reed concluded, and it would be no more cruel to execute Francis a second time than it was the first time. Frankfurter provided the crucial fifth vote to give Reed a court, and he also wrote a concurring opinion.

Harold Burton, writing for the minority, condemned Louisiana's actions as a violation of due process and the Eighth Amendment. How many tries, he wondered, would the state of Louisiana get before Francis's treatment could be considered cruel and unusual? This was "death by installments," and whether

---

347. Francis killed the brother of St. Martinville's police chief.

348. In his autobiography, Douglas claimed to have voted to reverse in conference (see Douglas, *The Court Years*, 123), but his own records indicated that he initially voted to deny certiorari and later voted to affirm on the merits. Harold Burton's conference notes also record Douglas as voting to affirm.

349. Douglas's records seem to indicate that Burton initially voted to affirm and then quickly changed his mind and voted to reverse. This seems unlikely, and Burton's own records more plausibly indicate that he wanted to reverse from the beginning.

unintentional or not it amounted to torture. It was precisely this sort of barbarism, Burton noted, that the Eighth Amendment was meant to prevent. Douglas, Murphy, and Rutledge also dissented.

Gruesome Gerty succeeded in killing Willie Francis on the second attempt in 1947, one year and six days after the botched first attempt. In 1956, Gerty ceased her travels and was permanently installed in Angola Prison. She stayed in business until 1991, when Louisiana switched to lethal injection.

Rosenberg v. United States, 346 U.S. 273 (1953)
(Clark)

Ethel and Julius Rosenberg were convicted under the Espionage Act of 1917 of passing atomic secrets and other classified information to the Soviet Union. The court of appeals affirmed and the Supreme Court denied certiorari. The Rosenbergs' attorneys tried six times without success to convince the Supreme Court to hear the case.[350] On June 13, 1953, the Court denied yet another petition for habeas corpus and a request for a stay of execution on a 5–4 vote. The Justices announced their decision on June 15, 1953, the last day of the term before the Court's summer recess. Later that same day, two lawyers previously unconnected to the case, Fyke Farmer and Daniel Marshall, approached Justice Douglas and asked for a stay of execution. Douglas denied their petition because it failed to raise any new issues, but he gave them until the next morning to come up with something new before he left for his summer home in Washington state.

At 10:00 A.M. the following day, Farmer and Marshall returned and asked to intervene in the case on behalf of Irwin Edelman—a West Coast political activist with no prior connection to the case—as a "next friend" of the Rosenbergs.[351]

They asked Douglas for a stay of execution and a writ of habeas corpus on the basis of a novel argument, first proposed by Edelman and never raised by the Rosenbergs' own lawyers: that the couple had been convicted under the wrong federal statute. Instead of being prosecuted under the Espionage Act of 1917, Edelman argued, the Rosenbergs should have been tried under the Atomic Energy Act of 1946 (AEA), which superseded the Espionage Act.[352] The crucial difference between the two statutes

---

350. Only the two old antagonists, Black and Frankfurter, voted to hear the Rosenbergs' appeals all six times. William O. Douglas was the most inscrutable actor, voting against the Rosenbergs in five of the Court's six votes. He represented the crucial fourth vote needed to hear the case on at least two of those occasions. Simon, *Independent Journey,* 300–305. Frankfurter and Jackson thought that Douglas enjoyed grandstanding in public to promote his image as a great civil libertarian, while doing nothing at all behind the scenes to help the Rosenbergs. Jackson called Douglas's behavior "the most shameful, most cynical performance that I have ever heard of in matters pertaining to law." Simon, *Independent Journey,* 303. Douglas's defenders argued that he honestly believed that there were no credible issues in the Rosenbergs' earlier appeals to merit Supreme Court review. Cohen, "Justice Douglas and the Rosenberg Case," 217.

351. Irwin Edelman, who had been expelled from the Communist party, published a pamphlet criticizing the Rosenbergs' defense team and outlining his own legal strategy for reversing the Rosenbergs' convictions. Farmer and Marshall, representing a loose coalition of civil liberties and religious groups, were intrigued by Edelman's theory and saw it as their last hope. None of the men had any direct connection to the Rosenbergs or their defense team, which was a plus in Douglas's eyes. Douglas believed that the Rosenbergs' closest advisers wanted the pair to become Communist martyrs, and he was not surprised that it took three outsiders to raise the first new and substantive issues worthy of review. Douglas, *The Court Years,* 79–80.

352. While the Rosenbergs' overt acts regarding atomic espionage ended before the passage of the Atomic Energy Act in 1946, they remained active Soviet agents as late as 1950, and Edelman argued that that brought them under the new law.

was that under the later act the district court judge would have been precluded from imposing the death penalty.[353] *Douglas sought Frankfurter's and Black's advice. Both told Douglas that they thought that the matter should be looked into. Douglas then talked to Fred Vinson, who rejected the idea but suggested that the matter could be discussed at conference. After Douglas left Vinson's office, the Chief Justice and Robert Jackson secretly contacted Attorney General Herbert Brownell and met privately with him on June 16 to discuss the case. Vinson promised Brownell that he would convene a special session of the Court if Douglas issued a stay of execution. On June 17, Douglas granted a stay of execution to allow the lower courts to decide whether the AEA precluded the Rosenbergs' execution. Douglas then left town by car, headed for Yakima.*[354]

When news of the stay reached the Chief Justice, Vinson immediately called the other Justices to meet in a Special Term. Douglas, who had reached Uniontown, Pennsylvania, by that time, heard the news on the radio and returned to the capital. Although Douglas was angry that Vinson had not contacted him directly, he did not challenge the Chief Justice's decision.[355] *Hugo Black, who had just checked into the hospital for a hernia operation, angrily checked himself out and returned to work.*[356] *All of the Justices consented to the special session except for Black, who was furious.*[357] *The Court convened in special session at 2:00 P.M. on June 18 to hear oral arguments for several hours before meeting in conference.*

Conference of June 18, 1953

VINSON: The petitioners raised points all of which could have been raised before. (1) On habeas, they cannot raise new questions that were apparent, i.e., the bill of particulars motion was dropped out on appeal. On the AEA, they had it or not—they raised it on sentencing (cruel and unusual punishment). (2) I worry how Edelman can break into the trial of this case. It might be serious to the defendants to let just anyone break into a case. (3) On the legal point regarding the AEA, I have no serious doubt that their overt acts preceded the passage of the AEA. On this crime claimed to be subsequent to the AEA, it turns out that it was not fissionable material—they were working on sonar devices (anti-submarine fire control) and servo mechanisms. I do not think that they presented, in light of the history of the case, anything of merit. On the time element, that is another question. (4) The power of Bill Douglas to grant the stay is admitted.

---

353. Section 10 of the Atomic Energy Act provided that the death penalty could be imposed only (1) upon a showing of intent to injure the United States; and (2) upon recommendation of the jury. Neither condition was met here.

354. Before he left town, Douglas received a telegram from Yakima, Washington, promising that if he granted a stay of execution, "there will be a lynching party waiting for you here." Douglas wired back: "If there is to be a Yakima lynching party, you'll have to furnish your own whiskey." Douglas, *The Court Years*, 81.

355. Douglas was traveling west with his mistress (and soon-to-be second wife) Mercedes Davidson. Vinson hesitated to ask state troopers to find Douglas because he was afraid that the officers might find the pair in a compromising situation. Simon, *Independent Journey*, 308.

356. Both Black and Douglas were under FBI surveillance at the time, possibly with the knowledge and consent of President Eisenhower and/or Vinson. Roger Newman, *Hugo Black*, 422–25.

357. Black fumed that the Chief Justice thought that he was the manager of a baseball team who could simply summon the Court whenever he wished. Black insisted that the Court could be convened in special session only by a vote of the conference. None of the other Justices objected, however, and in the end Black participated, although he recorded his objection in the case report.

BLACK: It is terrible to take this matter up without more information. None of us know enough about it, and *even if we did* I would oppose any action today. This is a race for death. I know of no case that has been so handled. This will be a black day for the Court. I *plead* that it not be decided today.

My inclination is to hold that the statute applies which provides for the lesser penalty. Anything I say is wholly useless. I never would vote on a picked up session like this to vote to overrule a Justice during vacation time.

This was a conspiracy to do something over a number of years, 1944–50. Where there is a conspiracy that continues before and after the enactment of a statute, then we must apply the lighter punishment. We should not pass on the merits at this time, but we should have arguments and decide the case after we have shown that the Court is not swayed by the winds of the time.

REED: Regarding the propriety of the stay order—§1651—writs in aid to jurisdiction. We have on several occasions overruled Justices. *Johnson v. Stevenson* (mentioned in the government brief), was an expansion of an order by Black, J.[358]

Is the death penalty permissible in light of the AEA? The issue was never raised, but it was in the case from the beginning. If a constitutional question in the case on jury and was known at the time and no objections were raised—although they had bad attorneys— we would not consider the case by habeas. *Brown* and *Daniels* were either raised or raisable.[359] Regarding a delay of execution, or a delay in the announcement of our judgment, I see no occasion to delay if the majority are satisfied that it is clear.

FRANKFURTER: The only power we have is, *what could we do on appeal?* In two cases we have said on a writ issued in chambers there is no power to review. While this is not habeas corpus, it is in aid of such power of habeas corpus. I doubt whether we can invoke the aid of appellate jurisdiction when we don't have it. But Douglas conceded that the Court *could* set aside his order.

First, I should like to part company with Black on his opening sentence as to the futility of talking. Second, the chief problem is *waiver*. It comes into play only where waiver can be effected, but where the statute says "only life—" then it cannot be *waived*. It is never too late to allow a sentence to be carried out when there is no warrant in law for it.

---

358. *Johnson v. Stevenson*, 335 U.S. 801 (1948). Former Texas governor Coke Stevenson sued in federal district court to block the certification of Lyndon Johnson as the state's Democratic candidate for the Senate and to have himself declared the nominee. Stevenson, a hard-line, segregationist Dixiecrat, alleged that widespread voting fraud permitted Johnson to steal the primary election. Johnson won by eighty-seven votes (out of more than a million votes cast), in an election where it was widely assumed that Johnson's supporters had proved themselves to be marginally better at stuffing ballot boxes than Stevenson's supporters. On his own authority, Hugo Black issued an order on September 29, 1948, stopping a federal hearing that would have examined the ballots in one crucial precinct and declared that the matter was a state rather than a federal issue. Black's ruling effectively ended Stevenson's chances of overturning Johnson's tainted primary victory.

Reed was mistaken in one respect. When the full Court met to reconsider Black's order, the other Justices *denied* Stevenson's motion to modify the order. The majority opinion in *Rosenberg* corrected Reed's mistake, admitting that "it is true that the full Court has made no practice of vacating stays issued by single Justices, although it has entertained motions for such relief."

359. *Daniels v. Allen*, decided *sub nom., Brown v. Allen*, 344 U.S. 443 (1953).

If I were clear that there was *no doubt* that the 1946 act qualified the Espionage Act, then I would not be bothered by the waiver, etc. I cannot say that *I am not clear*—I did not know the existence of this point until Monday. No overt acts are required. I can write only that I can't write.

DOUGLAS: If the Court thinks I acted for insubstantial or frivolous reasons, my stay should be set aside. There is no reason for delay. *There could be an indictment under the Espionage Act.*[360] The only question that goes to the death penalty is respecting crimes committed wholly or in part involving atomic secrets before and after the AEA. Did the penalty of the Atomic Energy Act take the place of the penalty in the Espionage Act?

JACKSON: There is no substantial question. You can't apply the AEA to a crime beginning before and continuing after the act. Did the AEA supersede? How could it?

BURTON: I should go along with Bill Douglas—perhaps we should—but I believe that the government is right.

MINTON: There is no conflict. The Espionage Act may be enforced alone. The indictment was drawn under the Espionage Act, and the penalty goes under it. Bloch and Finesky [*sic*] did not think of it as being substantial.[361]

Result: In conference, Harold Burton initially voted with Black, Frankfurter, and Douglas to uphold the stay. When no fifth vote materialized, Burton switched sides and voted with the majority to vacate the stay. The Justices decided to postpone announcing their decision for a day, mostly for the sake of appearances. At noon on Friday, June 19, the Court announced that it had lifted the stay of execution on a vote of six to three. Afterward, events moved with breathtaking speed. Within hours of the Court's announcement, President Eisenhower rejected the Rosenbergs' last-ditch appeal for clemency, noting that millions of innocent people might die because of what the two spies had done. The Rosenbergs were scheduled to be executed at 11:00 P.M. that evening, but because of the Jewish Sabbath the time of execution was moved up. At 8:00 P.M. on June 19, just before sunset, the Rosenbergs were electrocuted together in Sing Sing prison, becoming the only two people in American history to be executed for espionage during peacetime.[362] The case also triggered the first of several congressional attempts to impeach William O. Douglas.

---

360. From the context, the italics probably do not reflect Douglas's own vocal emphasis but are Clark's attempt to highlight Douglas's apparent concession that the Atomic Energy Act might not have superseded the Espionage Act after all.

361. Imanuel (Manny) Bloch was the lead attorney for the Rosenbergs. John H. Finerty, a noted civil rights attorney, was another key member of the Rosenberg defense team. They argued before the Court on June 18, as did Farmer and Marshall. Acting Solicitor General Robert Stern appeared for the government.

362. Douglas claims that a month before Fred Vinson's death in 1953, the Chief Justice talked about the case at length with Douglas's brother, Arthur, over drinks of bourbon and branch water. Vinson allegedly said that he was very sorry about the Rosenbergs and that Douglas had been right. Douglas, *The Court Years*, 85. It is a plausible claim. In Vinson's published opinion in the *Rosenberg* case—his last opinion as a Supreme Court Justice—the Chief Justice went out of his way to defend Douglas and to compliment his handling of the case.

Maxwell v. Bishop, 398 U.S. 262 (1970)
(Douglas) (Brennan)

William L. Maxwell, a twenty-one-year-old black male, was sentenced to death in Garland County, Arkansas, for raping Stella Spoon, a thirty-five-year-old white woman. This case marked the beginning of a new NAACP strategy to attack alleged racial bias in capital cases. With the help of anti-death penalty activists such as Tony Amsterdam, the NAACP's Legal Defense Fund gathered extensive data that they claimed proved racial bias in capital cases involving black defendants and white victims. Maxwell sought a writ of habeas corpus in federal court. In an opinion by Harry Blackmun, the Eighth Circuit Court of Appeals rejected the LDF's arguments. The Supreme Court granted limited review on two issues: (1) whether two separate proceedings were necessary to determine guilt and to impose sentence; and (2) whether standards were necessary to guide juries in sentencing.

In Arkansas, juries determined guilt and imposed the sentence in a single proceeding. This meant that defendants could not present mitigating evidence on their own behalf during the trial without subjecting themselves to cross-examination and effectively waiving their Fifth Amendment right against self-incrimination. Maxwell also complained that state juries were not given any standards to guide their sentencing deliberations. O. E. Bishop was the superintendent of the Arkansas State Penitentiary.

Conference of March 6, 1969

WARREN: The jury cannot be given the absolute right to give life or death without standards to guide their choice. On the term of years problem, I think that it is different. The rehabilitation factor is involved there, for example.

Death seems to be reserved usually for the poor and underprivileged. No person of any affluence is ever executed. Death falls unequally on the poor and the unpopular. The jury should have ground rules. Now they have absolute discretion to send him to death. I reverse. We should follow the *Witherspoon* formula and not send everyone back for a new trial.[363] The only issue attacked here is the death penalty. I would not reverse the conviction, but simply convert it to a life sentence.

BLACK: I disagree with the Chief. The Court is usurping the power of the legislature. The only issue here is whether the death penalty is valid. We can't formulate standards. They are too vague. The policy question is not for us. The Constitution gave states the power and we can't overrule them.

---

363. During jury selection, several prospective jurors were removed from the panel when they voiced "general objections to the death penalty or expressed conscientious or religious scruples against its infliction." The Court ruled that such exclusions were impermissible in *Witherspoon v. Illinois,* 391 U.S. 510 (1968). However, because *Witherspoon* was decided after Maxwell's trial and because his lawyers had not raised the issue at trial, Warren's preference was to remand the case to allow the lower courts to consider the issue. This disposition would have allowed the Court to avoid deciding the difficult issues of standards and bifurcation in capital cases.

DOUGLAS: I reverse. I agree with the Chief and with Tobriner's dissent on the California Supreme Court.[364]

HARLAN: I can't go along on the standards point. Some acts provide the death penalty unless the jury recommends mercy or votes for a life sentence. This introduces the compassion of the jury, and seems to me to put the case against standards in its most striking form. Basically there is no difference in the present act. Do juries need standards to exercise their "mercy" power? What should the standards be? I can't see either why standards wouldn't reach the Executive's commutation power. Why not standards here, too? And then where do we stop as to standards? Won't we be in the business of second-guessing? That is a legislative problem. The Constitution is satisfied when the jury is given the last say. I would reserve the question of whether death is a cruel and unusual punishment. I have trouble with the split trial issue. If he takes the stand on guilt, he is subject to cross-examination on that issue when it might be desirable to have the jury know that. I reverse on the issue of punishment.

BRENNAN: I reverse. I agree with the Chief.

STEWART: The *Witherspoon* issue is here, and I would dispose of case on that basis. It seems to me that if you have standards you must have a bifurcated trial, because in a unitary trial they can't know anything about him. If a jury is prejudiced, no instructions will curb it. I would reverse on the *Witherspoon* point. There is no problem of reaching it, because this is a federal habeas—the record is here.

WHITE: I would reverse on *Witherspoon* and go no further.

STEWART: I am willing either to do that or to remand to the district court.

FORTAS: I have doubts on whether the lack of jury standards is a valid point. A unitary trial violates due process in a rudimentary sense, because the jury is kept from relevant facts it should know on the life or death punishment issue. I would not reach the issue of standards. I reverse on the unitary trial point. I agree with John Harlan, who also reverses on that ground. I do not rest on *Witherspoon*. I would agree on a remand to tell the lower court to give him life only.

MARSHALL. I would go on *Witherspoon*. I go with John Harlan on the unitary trial question. That places too great a burden on the defendant's Fifth Amendment rights. I reverse.

364. *In re Anderson*, 447 P.2d 117 (Cal. 1968). Justice Matthew Tobriner, in a concurring opinion (Douglas mistakenly called it a dissent), argued that the Fourteenth Amendment required the state to provide judges and juries with standards to help them decide why one defendant should die while another should live. Otherwise, he said, the fate of each defendant would be left to whim and caprice, which was not only irrational but was the antithesis of due process.

WARREN: A unitary trial is fortified by our decision in *Spencer*.[365]

[DOUGLAS: Those who would go on the unitary trial—reversal: Chief Justice, Harlan, Brennan, Fortas, Marshall. Those who would go on *Witherspoon*: Black, Douglas, Harlan, White, Chief Justice.]

Result: Black assigned the majority opinion to Douglas, who quickly went to work to create workable standards and establish a legal rationale for requiring bifurcated trials. But he lost his majority on the standards issue when Harlan, Fortas, and Marshall all changed their minds.

Douglas's opinion was too sweeping for Harlan, who was having trouble making up his mind on the bifurcation and standards questions. Fortas and Marshall decided that legislated standards were not workable and would inevitably favor prosecutors. This put Douglas in a difficult spot. It would be hard to justify a bifurcated trial unless the second phase of the trial focused on standards.

Things briefly looked up for Douglas when Harlan decided that defendants should have the right to present personal testimony to the jury to explain why they should not be put to death. But Harlan needed more time to work out his position and asked that the case be reargued. In the meantime, Earl Warren and Abe Fortas left the Court and were replaced by Nixon appointees Warren Burger and Harry Blackmun. Douglas's once-solid 6–3 majority evaporated. Because of Blackmun's participation in this case as a circuit judge, he did not participate in the case at the Supreme Court. This left open the prospect of an evenly divided Court.

Conference of May 6, 1970

BURGER: There are three problems presented here: (1) standards; (2) bifurcated trial; (3) *Witherspoon*.

On standards: I see no way of shaping standards. I wish that there were some. The search is too elusive. The jury is the agency for mitigating the harshness of judges. The American Law Institute (ALI) has useful appeal, but on analysis it does not hold up. It is impossible to articulate all that is relevant. The sum total of the life experiences of the jurors is the best that you can do. The jury is the "conscience" of the community, and that is it. You can't read standards into the due process clause or any other clause of the Constitution.

On bifurcation: In Washington, D.C., the court of appeals let a district court bifurcate a trial in a warranty case. It was only a one-judge court. That is not satisfactory. I am not sure it is a useful device, and I am not sure whether it helps a defendant—it is not a blessing to the accused. It is also not a component of due process.

On Witherspoon: I do not see it as a *Witherspoon* case. I see no merit in that argument, as yet.

BLACK: For me, it is nothing but a jury trial problem, and if one wants a jury trial he must want the variety of views that it gives. Anyway, this is only a fight to abolish capital

---

365. *Spencer v. Texas*, 385 U.S. 554 (1967), also involved a unitary trial in a capital case. Jurors were informed of Spencer's prior convictions but were instructed not to consider the information in deciding his guilt or innocence. Spencer argued that he had a right to a bifurcated trial so that he could keep out evidence of his prior convictions until the sentencing phase of his trial. In a 5–4 decision, the Supreme Court upheld Texas's unitary trial procedure. Harlan admitted that a two-stage trial might be preferable but ruled that the practice of a unitary trial with limiting instructions to the jury was not unconstitutional. Warren, Douglas, Brennan, and Fortas dissented.

punishment, and it is not unconstitutional. It is a matter for the legislature and not the courts.

BURGER: I would vote in Congress to abolish capital punishment.

DOUGLAS: I reverse on standards and bifurcation.

HARLAN: I think that there is a *Witherspoon* issue here, but we ought to dispose of this case on either of the other two grounds. Standards are not needed under the Constitution. Is it unconstitutional to delegate an unstandardized judgment to a jury to be reached as they see fit, laying aside only their personal biases? I don't think so. I can't say that it is unconstitutional to delegate discretionary power to juries. The jury can fix the sentences. If standards are necessary for juries, then they are for judges. If they are necessary in capital cases, then they are necessary in other criminal cases. [DOUGLAS: On the latter, I agree.] On bifurcation, I have gone both ways. At the end of last term, I thought that bifurcation was not necessary. Now I think that it is. If the sentence is committed to the unrestricted judgment of the jury, then you can't restrict what the defendant wants the jury to consider in sentencing. It violates basic due process to disallow a defendant from getting into the hopper all of the elements bearing on punishment and the exercise of the jury's discretion. It is an element of fundamental fairness. This is one of the clearest cases of denial of fundamental fairness that I have seen. I reverse on that.

BURGER: The same result could be obtained by restricting the scope of examination of the defendant to matters put to him on direct examination.

HARLAN: This case is different from *Spencer*, as the jury sentencing question was not involved there. Warren Burger's suggestion is a possible one.

BRENNAN: I reverse on standards and on bifurcation. I have trouble with Warren Burger's suggestion. We should not fix the standards.

STEWART: I don't think that the Constitution requires either bifurcation or standards. But unlike John, I think that if you have bifurcation then you must have standards.[366] There is a clear violation of *Witherspoon*, which is retroactive. I am inclined to vacate and remand on *Witherspoon*.

WHITE: Standards and bifurcation are all presented in a very abstract way. There is no ruling excluding evidence on penalty. If there were, then the issue would be here and John Harlan's point is inescapable. If state rules of evidence prohibited the admission of relevant evidence bearing on the state's theory of punishment (rehabilitation or other), then there would be a due process problem. If the defendant wanted to put in evidence bearing on penalty, but was barred by state law on guilt, the case would be different. Or if the evidence was not offered because of prejudice, the case would be different. But to say so if you can get it in is something else. I affirm on standards and bifurcation.

HARLAN: There was no tender of evidence, but the state of the law precluded it. He should have a bifurcated trial if he wants it.

366. Douglas quotes Stewart as saying, "If there were standards, there must be a bifurcated trial."

MARSHALL: On the bifurcated trial issue, I think that it is required by the Constitution. The man has a right of allocution. Courts-martial are bifurcated—if it is good enough there, it is good enough for civilian trials. On standards, I think that there should be. I agree with Bill Brennan's view in his opinion last term.

BLACK: Anyone who opens up allocution opens up the state to smear the defendant. It won't help a defendant.

BURGER: There is an Arkansas statute giving the Arkansas trial judge the power to revise the jury's verdict.

BLACK: I dissented in *Witherspoon*.

Result: After reargument, the Court deadlocked 4–4 on whether a bifurcated trial was required. Harlan now favored bifurcated trials, but Burger did not. By a 5–3 conference vote, the Justices appeared ready to reject mandatory jury standards. Stewart opposed both standards and bifurcated trials but said in conference that if a majority of the Court favored bifurcated trials, he would vote in favor of standards. It was a hopeless muddle, and the Court finally agreed 7–1 to vacate and remand the case for further hearings on the Witherspoon *issue. Black dissented. The Justices then went looking for a new capital case to decide the issues of jury standards and bifurcation where Blackmun could vote. Their next opportunity came the following year with McGautha v. California.*

On December 29, 1970, Arkansas governor Winthrop Rockefeller commuted Maxwell's death sentence, along with the sentences of fourteen other felons on the state's death row.

McGautha v. California, 402 U.S. 183 (1971)
Crampton v. Ohio
(Douglas)

The year after their standoff in Maxwell v. Bishop, *the Justices revisited the issues of bifurcation and jury standards in death penalty cases from California and Ohio. A California jury convicted Dennis McGautha of murder and robbery, and after the sentencing phase of the trial sentenced him to death. State law provided for a bifurcated trial but gave juries absolute discretion in deciding whether or not to impose the death penalty. In Ohio, James E. Crampton was sentenced to die for the cold-blooded murder of his wife (after repeatedly threatening her, he shot her with a .45-caliber pistol while she was sitting in the bathroom). Ohio provided for a single trial to determine both guilt and punishment and gave jurors absolute discretion in imposing the death penalty. There were two due process questions facing the Court: (1) were defendants' rights infringed by allowing juries to impose the death penalty without state standards and guidelines; and (2) was it permissible to have a single trial in a capital case, or were bifurcated trials required? Note the Chief Justice's views on changing constitutional values and Harlan's latest change of heart regarding bifurcation.*

Conference of November 13, 1970

BURGER: The argument did not give us a set of standards. This is an oblique attack on capital punishment. Bifurcated trials are a dubious thing. Some states have abandoned them, one has adopted them. That is enough for me to refuse to put bifurcation into a constitutional mould. Someday we may come to it, but not now. This is a developing area, and we should allow experiments. Capital punishment has distorted the whole criminal process. Abolition of capital punishment is what this case is really all about. In *Crampton*, he would have three trials. In California, there are at least 100 who have been found guilty in three trials on this issue. Bifurcation is not a due process issue under our standards. I affirm.

BLACK: I agree with the Chief Justice. A bifurcated trial is not required under the Constitution, and I doubt its wisdom from the defendant's viewpoint. I affirm.

DOUGLAS: I reverse in each case.

HARLAN: Is there a constitutional right of allocution? That is all the bifurcated trial means. The United States's brief has convinced me that I should affirm both cases.

BRENNAN: I reverse in each case.

STEWART: I affirm in each case. In Ohio, if there is a doubt as to guilt no jury will impose death. You can get anything in that you want to get in where guilt is clear.

WHITE: I affirm.

MARSHALL: I'll go with Bill Douglas to reverse in both cases. I have my doubts about a man taking the stand. *Jackson v. Denno*—once he takes the stand, he leaves himself open.[367] States have a choice to let the judge do it or the jury. Sentencing should be a separate hearing. *Jackson v. Denno* gives a separate hearing in coerced confessions. I would do this in all cases.

BLACKMUN: *McGautha* is less difficult than I thought. Many protective devices are used in California's procedure. I affirm. *Crampton* is harder. It comes down to whether allocution is of constitutional dimensions. I think not. *Spencer v. Texas* is of aid to Ohio.[368] I will affirm.

Result: The Court ruled 6–3 that states could conduct either single or bifurcated trials without violating the due process clause. It was left to the states to determine whether juries could be trusted with unfettered discretion in imposing capital punishment. Harlan again changed his mind on the single

---

367. *Jackson v. Denno*, 378 U.S. 368 (1964). Nathan Jackson confessed to the murder of a police officer but later claimed that his confession had been coerced. Under New York law, the trial judge first had to determine whether there was a fair question of fact as to whether the confession was voluntary. If so, then the judge submitted the issue to the jury to decide. The judge in this case instructed the jury to disregard the confession if they found that Jackson's confession had been coerced, but if they determined that his confession was voluntary then they were free to consider it during their deliberations. The jury convicted Jackson after he took the stand in his own defense and his testimony differed significantly from his confession.

On certiorari, the Supreme Court reversed and remanded the case to the district court. Byron White, writing for a 5–4 majority, ruled that the state procedures in this case violated due process and that Jackson was constitutionally entitled to a separate hearing to determine whether his confession was voluntary. The jury, White wrote, could not be assumed to have reliably found Jackson's confession voluntary and only then determined whether his confession was truthful.

368. *Spencer v. Texas*, 385 U.S. 554 (1967). The difference between *Spencer* and *Crampton* was that Spencer wanted a bifurcated trial so that he could keep out evidence of his prior convictions until the sentencing phase. Crampton, however, simply wanted to preserve his right to testify on his own behalf during the sentencing phase without sacrificing his right to remain silent during the trial-in-chief.

verdict system and wrote the majority opinion. The Court's original 6–3 vote to strike down the Arkansas death penalty in Maxwell *was now a 6–3 vote to relax constitutional controls over state procedures in capital cases. But the Court's vacillations on the death penalty would continue for another five years.*

Dennis McGautha escaped the gas chamber in 1972 when the California Supreme Court struck down the state's death penalty statute as a violation of the state constitution.[369] *Crampton was spared several months later when the U.S. Supreme Court struck down all existing state death statutes in* Furman v. Georgia.

Furman v. Georgia, 408 U.S. 238 (1972)
(Douglas) (Brennan)

This case combined a capital murder case from Georgia and two capital rape cases from Georgia and Texas.[370] *A fourth case from California was dismissed after the California Supreme Court struck down that state's death penalty on state constitutional grounds.*[371] *The issue in all the cases was the same: whether state death penalty statutes violated the Eighth and Fourteenth Amendments.*[372] *The conference discussion presents a fascinating dialogue about murder, rape, and capital punishment.*

Conference of January 21, 1972

BURGER: States have the power to impose the death penalty. I affirm. There is no equal protection issue here, only the Eighth Amendment. The Constitution contemplated the death penalty and affirmatively recognized its existence. It is not compromised by the infrequency of the use of capital punishment. The infrequency of capital punishment is not synonymous with "unusual," and that argument does not impress me. All of us have reservations about the death penalty. Even Jim Bennett wants to use it in case of murder by a lifer in prison.[373] I affirm in the homicide cases. As to rape, I would set aside the death penalty for some types of crime. The Texas case gives me some trouble. Rape is a closer question. As a legislator, I would vote against capital punishment for rape. Where there is rape without bodily harm, it is difficult. A woman who surrenders to fear may have serious traumatic experiences. There are cruel rapes and mild rapes. I affirm in all cases.

---

369. *People v. Anderson,* 493 P.2d 880 (Cal. 1972).

370. *Furman v. Georgia* (murder), *Jackson v. Georgia* (rape), and *Branch v. Texas* (rape).

371. *Aikens v. California,* 406 U.S. 813 (1972) (murder); *People v. Anderson,* 493 P.2d 880 (Cal. 1972).

372. This is a good example of an instance where the conference privately agreed to decide an issue and then went looking for cases to serve as the instruments of judicial policy. According to William Brennan, in the wake of *McGautha* (which was a due process case rather than an Eighth Amendment case), Hugo Black convinced a majority of the conference that it was time to decide the Eighth Amendment question "once and for all." Brennan and Potter Stewart were delegated the job of finding "clean" cases for the Court to decide. This committee of two selected *Furman, Jackson, Branch,* and *Aikins.* The Court granted cert in all four cases on June 28, 1971, at the end of the 1970 Term and then adjourned for the summer. Brennan, "Constitutional Adjudication and the Death Penalty," 322.

373. James V. Bennett was a former director of the United States Bureau of Prisons. Bennett submitted an amicus brief sharply critical of the death penalty. Bennett was a maverick reformer who strongly believed in rehabilitating prisoners. Among his innovations as director of the Bureau of Prisons were prisoner job training programs and halfway houses.

DOUGLAS: We are locked in where reversal is almost mandatory. *McGautha* was a wild card—there was complete jury discretion without any standards whatever.[374] Statistics show that the death penalty is used primarily against minority groups. The lack of standards makes the system discriminatory. If it is discriminatory in practice, it is "unusual" under the Eighth Amendment. I reverse.

BRENNAN: The Eighth Amendment reflects a gradually changing concept. The mode of death is not here, only the penalty itself. The objective facts must show the contemporary standards that reject the death penalty. Before the Civil War, the movement for abolition of the death penalty was great. Since the beginning of this century, the feeling has increased. The death penalty is the ultimate word. There are no standards of decision making. Imposition of the penalty is susceptible to infrequent, selective use. The aggregate of those receiving the penalty shows the selectivity of this sentence. The death penalty is a highly suspect penalty. Suspect classifications must be shown by "compelling" reasons. Standards of decency require "compelling" reasons for imposing the death penalty. Goldberg and Dershowitz wrote an article on this last year (1970).[375] Its parent was a memo Goldberg circulated in the *Rudolph* case.[376] If a state enacted a law making the death penalty mandatory, the case might be different. But legislatures would never do that.[377] Even if the death penalty were restricted to a select form of murder, it would fall. I reverse.

STEWART: As of now, I cannot uphold the constitutionality of the death sentence. Someday the Court will hold that the death sentence is unconstitutional. If we hold it constitutional in 1972, it would only delay its abolition. It is unfortunate that these cases are here. On the merits, I reverse. Each argument made may show that it cannot be condemned as a non-deterrent. The petitioners say that vengeance is improper, but I cannot agree with that. I can't distinguish between murder and rape.

WHITE: The way that the death penalty now operates in this country is impermissible. But we must give further meaning to the Eighth Amendment than the former cases have done. The nut of the case is that only a small proportion are put to death, and I can't believe that they are picked out on the basis of killing those who should be killed. I can't believe that it is meted out fairly. The community participates on the penalty—one jury will put a person to death while on the same facts another person is not put to death. The

---

374. *McGautha v. California*, 402 U.S. 183 (1971), holding that neither legislative standards nor bifurcated trials were required for state death penalty statutes. The majority opinion indicated that granting the jury or judge virtually unlimited discretion to determine whether or not to impose capital punishment was not only permissible, it was desirable.

375. Goldberg and Dershowitz, "Declaring the Death Penalty Unconstitutional."

376. *Rudolph v. Alabama*, 375 U.S. 889 (1963). Goldberg dissented along with Douglas and Brennan, calling on the Court to decide whether the death penalty violated the Eighth and Fourteenth Amendments as applied to rape cases. Goldberg's activism in such cases led Sherman Minton to call Goldberg "a walking Constitutional Convention." Letter from Sherman Minton to Frankfurter, Oct. 22, 1964, Felix Frankfurter Papers.

377. Brennan was wrong. Soon after *Furman* was announced, several states enacted mandatory death penalty laws, including Louisiana and North Carolina. These laws were among the five state death statutes tested in *Gregg v. Georgia*, discussed below.

community has made its judgment on the use of the death penalty. Steadily, the jury has rejected the death penalty. The fact that it remains on the books doesn't answer it. If the trend goes on, the community wouldn't impose it. A few laws make it mandatory—then you seldom get a conviction, or if so, it is not affirmed. Judges and juries fight it. Can you say that retribution and vengeance are valid bases for capital punishment? To uphold the death penalty, retribution must be exalted. Retribution is a valid issue, and so is deterrence. Can you deter Joe by killing John? We should not give sanction to the idea of a man getting his desserts. We should not legalize the death penalty at this time in our history. I reverse in all of these cases.

MARSHALL: I am not impressed with the effort to show an overwhelming state interest. The death penalty is available to any one who is low man on the totem pole.[378] This has given way in American jurisprudence to the idea of rehabilitation. The Eighth Amendment was intended to be considered in light of contemporary history. I reverse.

BLACKMUN: Minnesota abolished capital punishment in 1911. It got along as well as other states. I believe in evolving standards, as I said in *Jackson v Bishop*.[379] On the other hand, in *Maxwell* I said while I was personally against death penalty, it was a legislative decision.[380] We have repeatedly said that the death penalty is permissible. If you knock it out, it is knocked out for assassinators of presidents, for treasonable acts, and so forth. I am disturbed that not a word was said in argument about the victims and their families. I am inclined to affirm shakily. I am not at rest. I might join a reversal opinion, but not now. Rape cases are harder to uphold than murder. In Minnesota there are few rapes— they are prosecuted for carnal knowledge.

POWELL: The Eighth Amendment has been discussed in only ten cases, and in only one did we indicate that this Court had power over state decisions. We cannot say that the Eighth Amendment covers death sentences. While the Constitution covers general principles, it would be improper to hold the death penalty unconstitutional. Eight of our earlier cases contain dicta that the death penalty is constitutional. The Constitution itself contemplates the death sentence. The contemporary meaning in 1791 never thought that the death penalty was cruel and unusual. Constitutional interpretation has given a wide sweep to the terms of the Constitution, but this has gone *too* far. The fact that our legislative guardians have abdicated their responsibilities, hoping that this Court would take the problem off of their backs, can't justify our doing the job for them. Standards of decency have not reached the point where we can say that they ban the death penalty. In

---

378. Marshall's views were influenced by his experiences as an NAACP lawyer defending southern blacks in capital cases before all-white juries. He claimed that he knew for certain that his clients were innocent if they only received life sentences.

379. *Jackson v. Bishop*, 404 F.2d 571 (8th Cir. 1968). Blackmun declared that the disciplinary whipping of Arkansas state prisoners was per se cruel and unusual punishment, in spite of the longstanding historical view that such practices were not necessarily unconstitutional.

380. *Maxwell v. Bishop*, 398 F.2d 138 (8th Cir. 1969), vacated and remanded, 398 U.S. 262 (1970).

their own way, juries have begun to move ahead of the legislatures. I reject seeing this Court freeze the Eighth Amendment into banning the death penalty. I affirm.

REHNQUIST: To hold that the death penalty is bad, we would have to go beyond forty-one legislatures. I can't do that. We crossed the bridge in *McGautha*.[381] If it is good law, I will follow it. As a legislator, I would keep it. I am not torn by the problem and I affirm.

BURGER: I withdraw my vote.

Result: On a 5–4 vote, the Court, in a per curiam decision, struck down the Georgia and Texas death penalty statutes. Behind the scenes, the majority struggled unsuccessfully to find common ground for deciding that capital punishment itself was unconstitutional. Douglas focused on discrimination in the imposition of the death penalty, while Brennan and Marshall argued that it categorically violated the Eighth Amendment. Potter Stewart, however, wrote the key concurring opinion by avoiding the question of whether death penalty violated the Eighth Amendment and focusing on the infrequent and arbitrary way that capital punishment was imposed. Stewart concluded that the death penalty statutes in Georgia and Texas were "cruel and unusual in the same way that being struck by lightning is cruel and unusual." The Court, he said, could not tolerate laws that permitted "this unique penalty to be so wantonly and freakishly imposed." While Stewart personally thought that the death penalty in America was finished, he left the door open for states to rewrite their death statutes and try again.

Byron White was also on the bubble. He thought it obvious that the death penalty was cruel and unusual in the dictionary sense, but it was a much closer question whether it was cruel and unusual in the constitutional sense because at the time that the Constitution was written, "it was thought justified by the social ends it was deemed to serve." It was only when the death penalty ceased to further these important societal goals, White argued, that capital punishment would violate the Eighth Amendment as a "pointless and needless extinction of life with only marginal contributions to any discernible social or public purposes."

The four dissenters agreed that as legislators they would have voted to abolish the death penalty, or limited it to a small category of heinous crimes. But they argued that the issue was for Congress and the state legislatures to decide, not the courts. Warren Burger's dissent argued that states remained free to reform their death penalty statutes to define capital offenses more narrowly or to adopt mandatory death sentences. William Rehnquist's opinion summed up the mood of the dissenters by observing that the Court had not been "granted a roving commission, either by the Founding Fathers or by the framers of the Fourteenth Amendment, to strike down laws that are based upon notions of policy or morality suddenly found unacceptable by a majority of this Court."

After this case was decided, Warren Burger publicly stated that he doubted whether anyone would ever again be executed in the United States. State legislators, however, took heart from his dissent, which promised that a majority of Justices would uphold more carefully and narrowly drawn death statutes.

---

381. *McGautha v. California*, 402 U.S. 183 (1971).

Gregg v. Georgia, 428 U.S. 153 (1976)
Proffitt v. Florida
Jurek v. Texas
Woodson v. North Carolina, 428 U.S. 280 (1976)
Roberts v. Louisiana, 428 U.S. 325 (1976)
(Brennan)

After Furman, *thirty-five states drafted new death statutes, most using Burger's dissent as their template. Five such laws made it back to the Supreme Court during the 1976 term. Two were mandatory death penalty statutes, in North Carolina (premeditated murder)*[382] *and Louisiana (first degree murder).*[383] *The other statutes from Florida, Georgia, and Texas gave juries discretion in deciding whether to impose the death penalty. In the lead case, Troy Leon Gregg was convicted of armed robbery and murder, and a Georgia jury sentenced him to death.*

The new statutes were more narrowly drawn than those struck down in Furman, *and they gave juries at least some guidance in weighing aggravating and mitigating factors in recommending punishment. The states claimed that "guided discretion" allowed juries to give more particularized treatment to individual cases. Critics of the new laws countered that the reforms only increased the possibility of jury confusion and arbitrary sentencing.*

Mandatory death statutes were specifically designed to meet Stewart's and White's concerns about the freakish and arbitrary way death sentences had been imposed under the old laws. These laws, however, struck some of the other Justices as being overly rigid and draconian, if not bloodthirsty.[384]

Death penalty opponents were concerned that soon after Furman *was decided there had been an important personnel change on the Court. John Paul Stevens replaced William O. Douglas, and no one knew for sure which way Stevens was going to vote. Note below how the "evolving standards" theory of the Eighth Amendment, which favored death penalty opponents in 1972, suddenly cut the other way in 1976.*

BURGER: On the basic question, my view remains that this is primarily a legislative prerogative. Since I could have sustained in *Furman,* I would a fortiori sustain here.

STEWART: There was more to say for Bill Brennan's views at the time of *Furman* than there is now. Death statutes then were dead letters—but what 35 state legislatures have done since 1972 was focused on why there should be death penalty for specific, serious offenses. This establishes what evolving standards of decency are in 1976. The imposition and execution of death sentences is not a violation of the Eighth and Fourteenth Amendments. Byron and I didn't say the same thing in *Furman.* My view was (1) this penalty is different from any other, and is unusual in that sense; (2) the death penalty was imposed with no rhyme or reason by juries uninstructed as to standards and uniformed as to relevant considerations, and whose will and uncontrolled discretion was unreviewable. I thought that Byron's view was that this was a particular defect. Georgia

---

382. *Woodson v. North Carolina,* 428 U.S. 280 (1976).

383. *Roberts v. Louisiana,* 428 U.S. 325 (1976).

384. In North Carolina, the number of death sentences jumped 500 percent after the mandatory sentencing law went into effect. Tushnet, *Making Constitutional Law,* 154.

and Florida have devised constitutionally tolerable systems (discretion in prosecutor and judge is not unrestrained, and reject Black's theses).[385] Louisiana and North Carolina retain jury irrationality. Texas is marginal.

WHITE: My emphasis in *Furman* was upon the infrequency of imposition. That was an aspect of disproportionality. So I did not emphasize, as Potter did, the standardlessness, freakishness, and the lack of instructions. I think that North Carolina and Louisiana have met the test I had in mind in *Furman*. I thought in *McGautha* that once you provide juries with standards the number of death sentences would increase, and that is what is happening. We did not take a rape case, and it must make a difference what the offense is. Any opinion must note that we don't address the death penalty in rape cases.

BLACKMUN: I am disturbed by the use of capital penalty for rape.

POWELL: States have provided safeguards against systems that operated like bolts of lightening, so *Furman* served a salutary role. Looking at statutes individually, in light of Potter's and Byron's opinions in *Furman*, only North Carolina raises doubts in my mind. It touches a wide sweep of crimes.

STEVENS: *Furman* is the law for me. That is my starting point, and therefore I think that the death penalty is permissible in some circumstances under an evolving standards concept. I think that Thurgood's and Bill Brennan's views will eventually become law, but not yet. Also, when the Eighth Amendment is the only issue, one must make a procedural analysis study of the total picture. That is *Furman's* teaching for me. I haven't yet figured out the significance of the breadth of crimes reached here. This problem dramatically changes, as Bill Douglas's opinion in *Furman* shows, when rape is involved, because that is where the racial element enters into it. Look at the North Carolina and Louisiana statistics, as of now, on this disproportionate theory. Death is impermissible for rape. Only five or six states have it and they are deep South, with the potential of racial bias behind it. Among the held cases, we should perhaps take a rape sentence. The North Carolina statute has produced more penalties than it should, rather than cutting down on the numbers of executions. To have created a monster like North Carolina, which increases the incidence of the penalty, is abhorrent. Moreover, neither North Carolina nor Louisiana had a separate sentencing hearing, and there is an escape hatch in each—lesser included offenses are out. That is a lawless use of the legal system. I originally felt the same way about the Texas statute, but I can't object to a separate jury determination, even if it is essentially standardless.

Result: Warren Burger initially assigned all five cases to Byron White. But White could not command a Court, because he now thought that all the laws were constitutional (as did Burger and Rehnquist). A majority of Justices voted in conference to strike down North Carolina's mandatory death statute, and there was little more support for Louisiana's mandatory death statute. At a brief conference on May 5, the cases were reassigned to Potter Stewart. Burger then asked Stewart to write a joint opinion for the Court explaining why capital punishment did not violate the Eighth Amend-

---

385. Charles Black, *Capital Punishment: The Inevitability of Caprice and Mistake* (1974).

ment, but Stewart refused.[386] *In the end, Stewart announced the judgment of the Court in* Gregg, Proffitt, *and* Jurek, *although only Powell and Stevens joined his opinion. Stewart wrote that the guided discretion provided to juries under these statutes sufficiently reduced the likelihood of capricious or arbitrary sentencing. White, Burger, and Rehnquist concurred in the judgment. Blackmun published a separate concurrence. Brennan and Marshall dissented, arguing that the death penalty was dehumanizing and uncivilized, and that it was a cruel and unusual punishment prohibited by the modern meaning of the Eighth and Fourteenth Amendments. On the same day, the Court struck down the two mandatory death penalty statutes.*[387]

In 1980, Gregg escaped from death row from the Georgia State Prison in Reidesville. A day later, swimmers discovered his body in Mountain Island Lake, North Carolina. From the blunt force trauma on his head and neck, authorities concluded he had been stomped to death by one of his fellow escapees.

Ford v. Wainwright, 477 U.S. 399 (1986)
(Brennan)

Alvin Ford was convicted of capital murder for killing a Florida police officer. While incarcerated, he became mentally disturbed and delusional. Following established state procedures, the governor appointed a panel of three psychologists who interviewed Ford for thirty minutes in a semi-public setting. The panel declared him to be sane. Ford's lawyers sought to submit additional evidence regarding Ford's mental health, but the governor refused to consider any further evidence and signed Ford's death certificate, clearing the way for his execution. A federal district court refused the lawyer's request for an evidentiary hearing on Ford's mental condition, and the court of appeals affirmed.

BURGER: The power to reprieve, like the power to give clemency, is the same here and is not subject to judicial review.

WHITE: The Eighth Amendment does not include such a right. But the state has created a liberty and a procedure, and under *Solesbee*[388] and *Caritativo*[389] that is enough.

MARSHALL: I agree with Brennan.

---

386. Tushnet, *Making Constitutional Law,* 154.
387. *Woodson v. North Carolina,* 428 U.S. 280 (1976); *Roberts v. Louisiana,* 428 U.S. 325 (1976). Both decisions were 3–2–4, with Stewart, Powell, and Stevens in the majority; Brennan and Marshall concurring; and Burger, Blackmun, White, and Rehnquist in dissent. The majority ruled that mandatory death penalty statutes were unduly rigid and harsh and merely "papered over" the problems of unguided and unchecked jury discretion without allowing for proper consideration of the individual circumstances of either the defendant or the crime.
388. *Solesbee v. Balkcom,* 339 U.S. 9 (1950). Georgia state law prohibited the execution of insane prisoners. The determination of sanity was made by the governor on the advice of a panel of doctors. Solesbee claimed that this situation violated due process and that he had a right to a judicial determination of sanity. There was no Eighth Amendment claim, as the Eighth Amendment had not yet been applied to the states. The Court determined that the state procedures satisfied due process.
389. *Caritativo v. California,* 357 U.S. 549 (1958). California law prohibited the execution of insane prisoners but gave the supervising prison warden the exclusive right to initiate postconviction competency hearings. If the warden initiated proceedings, then a jury made the ultimate determination of sanity. But if the warden declined to act, there was no alternative means to initiate postconviction competency hearings. Again, the Court found that state procedures did not violate due process.

BLACKMUN: *Solesbee* is a relevant precedent, but it was decided before *Robinson v. California* applied the Eighth Amendment to the states.[390] I think that the Eighth Amendment bars the execution of incompetent persons. If the Eighth Amendment bars executions for rape, I don't see why it doesn't apply here. Due process requires an adversarial hearing, and that's not given here.

POWELL: There is centuries-old common law here. *Solesbee* was before the Eighth Amendment was applied to the states. I agree with Bill Brennan that a preliminary finding of incompetency to trigger a hearing would help.

REHNQUIST: If you give this to one sentenced to death, how do you avoid giving this to one sentenced to a prison term?

STEVENS: Should we introduce another layer in death cases? But shouldn't one have the opportunity to make peace with his maker? It is a religious consideration, of course, but for us it is an Eighth Amendment right. I would impose a stiff threshold requirement and a strong presumption of the finality of state findings.

O'CONNOR: Most states say that no incompetent person shall be executed, and provide for a determination by the judicial branch. We can recognize here that the state has created a liberty interest. We need not rest on the Eighth Amendment. Procedural due process may be satisfied by other than the courts. But Florida says that there is no obligation on the part of the governor even to look at submissions.

Result: A 5–2–2 Court, in an opinion by Thurgood Marshall, found that the Eighth Amendment prohibited the execution of insane persons. Four Justices—Marshall, Brennan, Blackmun, and Stevens— thought that Ford was entitled to a de novo evidentiary hearing in a district court because of inadequate state procedures, chief among them the fact that the executive branch had complete control over the process of determining whether prisoners were sane. Lewis Powell, the crucial fifth vote, agreed that Ford's claims had not been fairly adjudicated and that Florida's procedures violated Ford's Eighth Amendment and due process rights. Powell's concurring opinion defined Ford's Eighth Amendment protections more narrowly than the rest of the majority, and he wanted to leave more discretion to the states than Marshall had been willing to recognize. Sandra Day O'Connor and Byron White concurred in part and dissented in part, rejecting the majority's reading of the Eighth Amendment but agreeing that Florida's minimalist procedures violated Ford's due process rights. Warren Burger and William Rehnquist dissented outright.

JUVENILE JUSTICE

In re Gault, 387 U.S. 1 (1967)
(Douglas) (Brennan)

Fifteen-year-old Gerald Gault and a friend were accused of making lewd phone calls to a neighbor. In a streamlined juvenile court proceeding, Judge McGhee found Gault responsible and ordered him

---

390. *Robinson v. California*, 370 U.S. 660 (1962), holding that the cruel and unusual punishments clause of the Eighth Amendment was fully applicable to the states.

confined to a juvenile custodial facility for six years, until Gault reached twenty-one years of age. For an adult, the maximum punishment for the same crime would have been a $50 fine or sixty days in jail.

Gault's parents challenged the Arizona Juvenile Code procedures, citing, among other things: inadequate notice of charges, no right to counsel, no right to confront witnesses, no right to cross examine witnesses, no right against self-incrimination, no right to a transcript of the proceedings, and no right to appellate review.

Conference of December 9, 1966

WARREN: I reverse. I start with the premise that this is not a criminal proceeding. The purpose of these acts is to get away from strict criminal proceedings. But even if it is a non-criminal proceeding, the same due process is required. It varies according to the nature and character of the proceeding. It is one thing in a property foreclosure case, and another matter in a criminal case. We can set out minimal standards. There is no right to a jury trial. There is no Fifth Amendment right. But due process requires minimum standards and they were not met here. Minimally, I would require (1) a lawyer; (2) proper notice of proceedings to the family; (3) a fair hearing; and (4) a right of confrontation. I would not require a privilege against self-incrimination.

BLACK: It is not our prerogative to lay out constitutional limitations on the states. I reverse for a denial of constitutional rights. I would allow all constitutional guarantees. You can't draw a line between adult and juvenile proceedings, nor between civil and criminal. When a person is restrained of his liberty, then the Constitution applies the standards, and he is thus entitled to all of the guarantees. I would overrule *Maxwell v. Doud* [*sic*].[391]

DOUGLAS: I pass.

CLARK: I reverse. There was no notice and no counsel here. Perhaps *Miranda* should be extended here, as well.[392] I agree with Hugo that this is a criminal case.

HARLAN: I agree with the Chief. This is a due process case. I appreciate states' efforts to avoid criminal law and to take the sociological route in dealing with juvenile problems. Though a conventional lawyer reacts against these procedures, we can't put these cases in that mould. The Fifth Amendment can't apply—this is not a criminal procedure. I do not know whether lawyers should be appointed. I am hesitant to require it. I am incapable of making an intelligent judgment as to what should be done in this type of case. There is nothing in this case that is worthy, except notice. I would go slow and permit experimentation. I affirm.

BRENNAN: Restraint of liberty is not involved here. It is a specialized problem that should not be confined to traditional criminal procedure. I start with the premise that a child is different from an adult. *Gallegos* shows that if the state treats a child in the adult fashion,

---

391. *Maxwell v. Dow*, 176 U.S. 581 (1900).
392. *Miranda v. Arizona*, 384 U.S. 436 (1966).

he is entitled to all of the benefits.[393] There are universal protections. They do not include the Fifth Amendment—they can't start on the problem unless they get the kid talking. There must be safeguards on a hearing. If they allow lawyers to be retained, they should be appointed. I reverse, at least on notice.

STEWART: I am not at rest. This is not a criminal prosecution. That does not mean that there can be no due process. Notice is required. Confrontation is needed, but it need not be in open court and may be by affidavit. The Fifth Amendment is not applicable. A record is not required. I reverse. I am not sure on the lawyer point.

WHITE: The Fifth Amendment applies even in a civil proceeding. This act reaches conduct that would never be treated as criminal conduct. Juveniles are getting shortchanged. But this is not a criminal proceeding. I would require procedural due process. It won't hurt the juvenile court to get a lawyer. The juvenile court does not require a kid to testify. I wonder about *Miranda*. The fact-finding process should have integrity. It is hard through the constitutional provisions to work out the procedures that are needed. We can't say that no one can have custody of a child.

FORTAS: We should proceed cautiously. *Kent* has had a good effect.[394] The Fifth Amendment issue is raised in a different way. Juvenile courts do not or should not put pressure on the juvenile. It is not a question of either giving juveniles rights or detracting from the courts. They can function with counsel. We must start with the requirements of a hearing. Where what was done by juvenile would be a crime if done by adult, then there must be a hearing. I reverse.

Result: Writing for a 7–1–1 Court, Abe Fortas used a piecemeal approach to establish which due process rights attached to juvenile proceedings and which did not. Where there was a possibility of detention, procedural safeguards must provide, at a minimum: (a) access to counsel; (b) appointed counsel for indigents; (c) adequate notification of charges; (d) the right to confront witnesses; and (e) rights against self-incrimination. These rights were necessary, Fortas argued, to preserve juveniles' due pro-

---

393. *Gallegos v. Colorado*, 370 U.S. 49 (1962). Robert Gallegos, a fourteen-year-old boy, robbed and injured an elderly man in an ambush attack that yielded $13. When arrested, Gallegos immediately confessed. The boy was then held incognito for more than five days and was not allowed to see a judge, lawyer, his family, or any other friendly adult. After five days he signed a formal confession. Two weeks later, Gallegos was taken to a juvenile court where he was convicted of assault and given an indeterminate sentence. The victim subsequently died, and prosecutors immediately filed murder charges. Gallegos was tried in a state court and convicted in a jury trial. On a 4–3 vote, the Supreme Court reversed his conviction on the ground that police had coerced the boy's confession in violation of due process. Clark, Harlan, and Stewart dissented, while Frankfurter and White did not participate.

394. *Kent v. United States*, 383 U.S. 541 (1966). This was one of Abe Fortas's first opinions. Sixteen-year-old Morris Kent, who was on probation, was charged in the District of Columbia's juvenile court with housebreaking and rape. The trial judge refused Kent's request for a hearing and refused to allow Kent's lawyer to see the boy's probation file. After a "full investigation," the juvenile court judge removed the case to an adult criminal court. Fortas ruled that the transfer was invalid because there had not been an adequate investigation of the case before the juvenile court surrendered jurisdiction. Although the case was decided on statutory grounds, Fortas hinted that juvenile offenders might have at least some of the same due process rights as adults in criminal prosecutions.

cess rights in the name of "fairness, impartiality, and orderliness." Fortas failed to answer some other obvious questions, such as why some rights attached to juvenile proceedings while others did not, and whether these rights meant something different when applied to juvenile justice. Perhaps the simplest and most pragmatic answer is that he did as much as he could while preserving his majority.

Fortas emphasized the facts of the case and the close parallels in Gault's case to adult criminal proceedings.[395] The crucial difference between the two proceedings as far as Fortas was concerned was that Arizona's juvenile procedures lacked even the most basic procedural safeguards and was nothing more than a "kangaroo court." Earl Warren praised Fortas's opinion as the "Magna Carta for juveniles."

Harlan changed his mind after the conference and voted with the majority. Harlan could not agree with Fortas on which rights applied, however, and in the end concurred in part and dissented in part. Hugo Black concurred but tied his vote to his own theory of incorporation rather than to due process. Potter Stewart voted tentatively to reverse in conference but changed his mind afterward and ended up alone in dissent. Stewart focused on what he saw as the essential differences between juvenile proceedings and adult adversarial trials. He argued that emphasizing the similarities between adult and juvenile proceedings would force juvenile justice to take "a long step backwards into the nineteenth century."

In re Samuel Winship, 397 U.S. 358 (1970)
(Douglas)

A New York Family Court judge used the preponderance of the evidence standard to find that Samuel Winship, a twelve-year-old boy who stole $112 from a woman's pocketbook, had committed the juvenile equivalent of larceny. On appeal, Winship claimed that the federal Constitution required the judge to use the same beyond a reasonable doubt standard used in adult criminal cases. The New York Court of Appeals rejected Winship's argument and affirmed the juvenile court's ruling.

Conference of January 23, 1970

BURGER: The only issue is the weight of the evidence. We could have all criminal trials by preponderance of the evidence. I do not see the constitutional question. Every step the Court has taken in juvenile field has been toward the abolition of juvenile courts. I affirm.

BLACK: This is a hard case. *Gault* finished the juvenile court system.[396] "Reasonable doubt" is another question. It is not constitutionally guaranteed, although my opinion may support it. The state can use the preponderance of evidence test. This case should be dismissed for want of a federal question. Congress could pass a law saying that juveniles could be treated differently.

---

395. As Laura Kalman noted, Fortas wrote the facts of the case more as an advocate than as a judge. He wanted to emphasize the injustice that he believed Gerald Gault had suffered. For example, Gault had previously participated in a purse snatching—an incident that Judge McGhee relied on in finding that Gault was a delinquent who was "habitually involved in immoral matters." Fortas minimized Gault's involvement in the crime by saying that Gault had merely "been in the company of another boy who had stolen a wallet from a lady's purse." Kalmen, *Abe Fortas,* 252.

396. *In re Gault,* 387 U.S. 1 (1967).

DOUGLAS: I reverse. This is a criminal case, and "beyond reasonable doubt" is a constitutional question. *Davis v. United States* held that it is the required standard, and the decision was not put on a supervisory basis.[397]

HARLAN: I want briefs on mootness from each side, because we noted jurisdiction after the boy had been released. First, there is constitutional mootness when there are collateral circumstances. Second, mootness cannot result from operation of the judicial process by delay and so forth. On the merits, I reverse. If this act had been committed by an adult, he would have protection of reasonable doubt. Juveniles should likewise have that protection. This would cover only "crimes" for which an adult could be tried.

BRENNAN: I reverse. After *Gault*, we can't retreat. *Davis is not explicit*, but it suggests that the Constitution protects the reasonable doubt standard. Earlier than that was presumption of innocence, which was also a constitutional decision. On mootness, we hurdled it in *Korackes* [sic].[398] Juvenile records are made freely available to the military.

STEWART: This is a difficult case. If I follow my earlier view, I would affirm. If I follow *Gault*, then there must be proof "beyond a reasonable doubt." If the state makes a specific offense that is a crime the basis of delinquency, then full criminal procedures should be followed. I pass.

WHITE: I reverse. It follows from *Gault*. In future prosecutions and for the military, these records are available. I do not need more information on mootness.

MARSHALL: I reverse. He was charged with a crime, or at least a form of a crime. "Person" in the Bill of Rights includes juveniles.

---

397. *Davis v. United States*, 160 U.S. 469 (1895). *Davis* involved an insanity defense in a murder case. The first John Marshall Harlan, writing for a unanimous Court, wrote, "Strictly speaking, the burden of proof . . . is never upon the accused to establish his innocence or to disprove the facts necessary to establish the crime for which he is indicted. It is on the prosecution from the beginning to the end of the trial and applies to every element necessary to constitute the crime."

398. *Carafas v. LaVallee*, 391 U.S. 234 (1968). James Carafas was convicted in a New York state court of burglary and larceny, and his conviction was affirmed on appeal. He applied for a federal writ of habeas corpus based on the same claim he made on appeal—that prosecutors used illegally seized evidence against him at trial. After the circuit court of appeals rejected his petition, Carafas's prison term expired and he was unconditionally released from custody two weeks before he filed his petition for certiorari with the U.S. Supreme Court. Edwin LaVallee, the warden of Auburn State Prison, argued that Carafas's release mooted the case. Fortas, writing for a unanimous Court, rejected this argument and held that the court of appeals had erred in dismissing Carafas's appeal in the face of the district court's certificate of probable cause. Although the habeas statute required that Carafas be "in custody" when the original application was filed, his case was not moot because relief was not limited to discharging the applicant from physical custody but could include other remedies "as law and justice require." Fortas concluded: "It is clear that petitioner's cause is not moot. In consequence of his conviction, he cannot engage in certain businesses; he cannot serve as an official of a labor union for a specified period of time; he cannot vote in any election held in New York State; he cannot serve as a juror. Because of these 'disabilities or burdens [which] may flow from' petitioner's conviction, he has 'a substantial stake in the judgment of conviction which survives the satisfaction of the sentence imposed on him.' On account of these 'collateral consequences,' the case is not moot."

Result: The Court found that the use of the reasonable doubt standard was essential to due process and procedural fairness whenever a juvenile was charged with an act that would be considered a crime if committed by an adult. Brennan wrote the majority opinion. Harlan joined the majority opinion but wrote a brief concurring opinion echoing many of the same doubts that he had expressed in Gault. *Burger, Black, and Stewart dissented.*

Ingraham v. Wright, 430 U.S. 651 (1977)
(Brennan)

James Ingraham and other junior high students filed a federal lawsuit seeking damages and an injunction to stop corporal punishment in public schools. They claimed that being swatted with a wooden paddle violated their Eighth and Fourteenth Amendment rights against cruel and unusual punishment and their due process rights. The district court dismissed the case and the court of appeals affirmed.

BURGER: The constitutional right against cruel and unusual punishment is limited to the criminal context. On due process, it is hard to see how we can say "yes" if the punishment is severe but not otherwise.

STEWART: There are two discrete questions: (1) whether corporal punishment in the school system is cognizable under the Eighth Amendment; and (2) even if not, whether there is a right to procedural due process. There is no cognizable Eighth Amendment guarantee here. It has to be a prosecutorial criminal system. On procedural due process, I see no life, liberty, or property deprivation, but yet I am just not at rest on that question.

WHITE: I tentatively agree with Bill Brennan on the Eighth Amendment. On the second question, *Goss v. Lopez* didn't answer it.[399] I would not say that the mere fact that corporal punishment was to be imposed automatically triggers the same due process requirements. Maybe so if a "severe" punishment is planned—then "liberty" would be invaded. So I reverse only in part, for the time being.

MARSHALL: The authority of the teacher to inflict punishment is always a defense to tort action. I can't say that punishment is automatically cruel and inhuman. The clause for me is limited to cases of people subject to bail or fine—that is, criminals. I could reverse perhaps on the facts of this case.

BLACKMUN: It is conceded that there is a state constitutional action. The Eighth Amendment is confined to a criminal context. I see no basis for procedural due process.

---

399. *Goss v. Lopez,* 419 U.S. 565 (1975). Under Ohio law, school principals were authorized to suspend students summarily for up to ten days or to expel them for misconduct. Principals were only required to notify parents of their decision within twenty-four hours and to state the reasons for their decision. Eileen Lopez complained that her due process rights were violated when she was suspended from school without a hearing. White, writing for a 5–4 majority, held that the state statute violated the due process clause. There were important property and liberty interests at stake that could not be taken away without observing minimum due process requirements. For suspensions of ten days or less, due process required that students be given notice of the charges against them, an explanation of the evidence, and an opportunity to present their side of the story. Absent exigent circumstances, notice and a hearing should precede a student's removal from school and otherwise should follow as soon as possible.

POWELL: The courts are too deep already into the schools. "Punishment" under the Eighth Amendment does not embrace discipline in schools. Maybe if there were "confinement," as in mental institutions, it might be more troublesome. As to procedural due process, I see nothing.

REHNQUIST: The Eighth Amendment is confined to criminal punishment. There is no deprivation of liberty here, so there is no due process issue.

STEVENS: If you have to have criminal process preceding punishment, then "confinement" can't make the difference. There is a restriction of liberty while you inflict punishment. Therefore, if it is sufficiently severe, it is cruel and unusual. On the record here, it is not open and shut that this was cruel and unusual—I would define a high threshold. It is a question of law, both as to degree and for what offenses involve a "grievous loss" to trigger due process.

Result: In a 5–4 decision, the Court held that the Eighth Amendment did not apply to disciplinary corporal punishment in public schools. Similarly, there was no Fourteenth Amendment deprivation of liberty or a right to procedural formalities such as prior notice or a formal hearing. The proper limits of corporal punishment in schools, Powell wrote, were established by state and common law, not the Constitution. Florida, he said, provided adequate procedural safeguards and remedies to protect students from abusive treatment.

New Jersey v. TLO, 469 U.S. 325 (1985)[400]
(Brennan)

A high school teacher caught fourteen-year-old Terry Lee Owens and a friend smoking in a school restroom and marched them down the hall to Assistant Vice Principal Theodore Choplick. When Owens denied that she smoked, Choplick asked to see her purse. Inside he found a pack of cigarettes and some rolling papers. A more thorough search of Owens's purse produced marijuana, forty dollars (mostly in one-dollar bills), an index card with the names people who owed Owens money, and other evidence indicating that she was dealing drugs. At her delinquency hearing, Owens sought to suppress the evidence on the ground that Choplick's search violated her Fourth Amendment rights. The juvenile court ruled that while the Fourth Amendment was applicable to school searches, the vice principal's search was reasonable. The state supreme court reversed and ordered the evidence suppressed.

The Justices were faced with two main issues: (a) did the Fourth Amendment apply to school searches; and if so (b) did the same requirements and procedures limiting police searches apply to school searches, or was there a lesser standard of reasonableness?

First Conference

BURGER: The state court held that the Fourth Amendment applied, but imposed a lower hurdle to get over to justify searches by school officials. I want the exclusionary rule held inapplicable here. But can we reach that without addressing whether there was a Fourth Amendment violation? Is the teacher an officer of the state? Or a parent?

---

400. Because Owens was a minor, only her initials were used.

WHITE: I don't think that applying the exclusionary rule as a deterrent would stop teachers from doing this.

MARSHALL: I can't differentiate teachers from officers in use in criminal cases. I could DIG.

BLACKMUN: Is there an adequate state ground? I agree with Byron and would reverse.

POWELL: I agree with Byron.

REHNQUIST: I am not certain that good faith should apply only to law enforcement officers.

STEVENS: I had hoped that we could DIG this case. If a teacher acts for the state and yet does not violate the Fourth Amendment in these circumstances, that's appalling. So I would DIG or affirm.

O'CONNOR: We should not have taken this case. I would not agree with a holding of violation, but we can't reach that. I would DIG or affirm.

Second Conference

BURGER: If we reach the application of the Fourth Amendment, drugs and the like conditions are prevalent in schools and I would say that the Fourth Amendment does not apply in most circumstances. If it does apply, something substantially less than probable cause should be the standard. Here, much more than mere suspicion was present, and I would sustain this search. If we treat teachers as surrogate parents, that is basic for holding the Fourth Amendment inapplicable. On the exclusionary rule, I would not extend it here even if the Fourth Amendment is applicable.

BRENNAN:[401] I find no indication in the text or history of the Fourth Amendment, or in our prior cases, that school teachers—unlike all other state actors—are immune from the Constitution's dictates. I therefore agree with all parties but the State of New Jersey, and would hold that the Fourth Amendment's proscriptions do apply to the schools.

I can see some justification for eliminating the warrant requirement within the schools. Teachers are to some extent responsible for the safety and well-being of students, and students themselves are less able than adults to conform their conduct to social norms. In order to have the needed flexibility, I would hold warrantless probable cause searches like this one reasonable.

However, I would go no farther at this time in limiting the Fourth Amendment's protections. The justifications given for adopting a "reasonable suspicion" standard are that school authorities need this flexibility to deal with the real dangers of weapons or drugs. But ordinary constitutional standards have great flexibility already. For instance, in *Terry* we recognized that some searches are reasonable even if based on less than probable cause. *Terry's* rationale would justify similar searches within the schools. Moreover, the very structure of the school—the fact that students and teachers are confined in close quar-

---

401. Adapted from Brennan's talking papers, Brennan Papers, OT 1984, box 674.

ters and get to know each other well—mean that the probable cause standard will be an easy one for school authorities to meet when they conduct a search.[402]

We should not depart from our ordinary Fourth Amendment standards unless and until we are certain, at the very least, that that departure will actually advance some significant purpose. Permitting school authorities to rummage around in pocketbooks—or to conduct strip searches, for that matter, without probable cause when they suspect violation of any minor school regulation, will hardly give those authorities an effective way to fight the serious problems of crime or drugs in the schools. *This* case is certainly not one to depart from ordinary probable cause standards. TLO violated a minor administrative regulation. The vice principal had probable cause to open her pocketbook and find the cigarette package. But there was no need to go farther. The mere possession of cigarette papers did not provide probable cause to continue the search. It serves no serious purpose to give him authority to tear apart her purse when he suspects her of smoking cigarettes and has already found the evidence of this violation of minor school regulations.

In short, nothing in this case convinces me that ordinary Fourth Amendment standards unduly constrain the authority of school officials when they must search for weapons or drugs. When the case arises in which ordinary Fourth Amendment standards unduly constrain school authorities, we can assess the need for and the scope of any exceptions to those standards. Because I believe that such a need has not been shown here, and because I believe that the exclusionary rule clearly applies in this case, I would affirm.

WHITE: I could hold, however applicable, that reasonable suspicion sufficed, and I would not apply the exclusionary rule in juvenile court proceeding.

MARSHALL: This kills a gnat with a sledge hammer. This child was guilty of something and the vice-principal didn't have to search her purse to discipline her for that.

BLACKMUN: The Fourth Amendment applies in a school setting. The Constitution does not stop at the school house door, and the Fourth Amendment is not limited to law enforcement officials. So for me what is the standard? No warrant is necessary, and I could go for reasonable suspicion. That was satisfied, I think, and on that ground I would reverse.

POWELL: The Fourth Amendment has some application, but there was no violation here. The standard is one of reasonable suspicion, not probable cause. I would reverse.

REHNQUIST: I agree with Bill Brennan that the Fourth Amendment applies, and would not say that the exclusionary rule does not apply. I would rather not say reasonable suspicion, but simply that this search was "reasonable," as the Fourth Amendment says. No warrant is needed.

STEVENS: We should decide the exclusionary rule issue, because if we say that it is not applicable we don't have to reach the other issues. I think that it does apply to this juvenile proceeding. I agree with Bill Rehnquist that the concept of reasonableness should be our

---

402. *Terry v. Ohio*, 392 U.S. 1 (1968).

inquiry. The most minimum kind of suspicion is enough to make a search for drugs and such, whereas a violation of this smoking regulation makes this search unreasonable.

O'CONNOR: This is a juvenile delinquency proceeding, and I think that we must reach the exclusionary rule. I think that the Fourth Amendment applies and the exclusionary rule applies. The reasonable suspicion standard is proper. Bill Rehnquist's reasonableness standard is more workable, however. Applying that test, I would reverse.

Result: The Court held 5–1–3 that the Fourth Amendment applied to school searches but that school officials were not held to the same strict standards that other state agents had to meet for off-campus searches. The key, White wrote for the majority, was to balance students' legitimate expectations of privacy against the state's interest in maintaining a proper school learning environment. School officials did not need probable cause to search, nor were they required to obtain a warrant. The test was whether school officials had reasonable grounds for suspecting the search would produce evidence that a student violated either the law or school rules. The trial judge had to determine whether the search was reasonable from its inception and whether the scope of the search was reasonably related to objective of the search without being excessively intrusive. In this case, the Court ruled that the search had been reasonable from its inception and that the evidence was admissible. Blackmun concurred in the judgment but did not join White's majority opinion. Brennan, Marshall, and Stevens agreed that the Fourth Amendment applied to school searches but otherwise dissented.

Terry Owens was declared a delinquent and placed on probation for a year. Two years later, Assistant Vice Principal Choplick lost his job due to budget cutbacks and went to work in a family-run ladies' handbag shop in Flemington, New Jersey.

Parham v. JL and JR, 442 U.S. 584 (1979)
(Brennan)

JL and JR were minor children who were committed by their parents to a Georgia mental hospital. Lawyers representing the children alleged that state procedures for the voluntary commitment of minors violated the due process clause of the Fourteenth Amendment. Under Georgia law, two steps were required to commit a minor "voluntarily" to a state mental hospital: (1) a parent or guardian applied on behalf of the child for voluntary commitment; and (2) the hospital admitted the child temporarily for "observation and diagnosis." If the hospital found evidence of a treatable mental illness, the child could be admitted for an indefinite period. Periodic medical reviews were required, and the child could be released either on application of a parent or on the order of a qualified doctor.

The district court held that the Georgia law failed to protect the minors' due process rights. At a minimum, the judge said, Georgia must give adequate notice and provide at least one adversarial hearing before an impartial tribunal. Among the issues discussed in conference were the limits of parental authority and the problems of state governments acting in loco parentis on behalf of orphans and other wards of the state.

First Conference

BURGER: There is state action here, but the opinion below deals too broadly and should be reversed. Parental authority can't be brushed under the rug. The appellants have gone too far in claiming that there is an inherent conflict between children and their parents or state psychiatrists.

STEWART: Society has regarded children as incapable of deciding their own interests, and lets parent decide for children unless they are unfit. I think that the Georgia statute does this.

WHITE: They should not have said "give them 46 different treatments or release them," and I reverse to that extent. I don't think that you should take the parents' word without more. There should be some medical corroboration, at least, provided that there are enough providers. I reverse on both, although I might join an opinion that says that these procedures are inadequate.

MARSHALL: Even if only admissions are involved here, I would encourage the use of New Jersey's procedures and to have someone outside the institution to protect the child's interest. I would modify the order.

BLACKMUN: Out.

POWELL: There is state action, and there is a liberty interest implicated. Present Georgia procedures are constitutionally inadequate. I agree with Thurgood that the New Jersey plan is desirable in creating a special tribunal and requiring that the interest of the child, parents, and the state have all been considered. I affirm as to this deficiency, but reverse on the use of involuntary procedures and I also reverse on substantive due process issues.

REHNQUIST: There is state action and a liberty interest. Can parents surrender the child's liberty interest? I don't feel competent to say anything more than what Georgia provides is necessary.

STEVENS: I agree with Lewis. Parents must speak for their children about many things, but institutionalization requires giving the child some protections. Georgia's committal procedure is simply inadequate.

Second Conference

BURGER: Finding a liberty interest for the child doesn't get us far. The question is whether the parent exercises it for the child. I would not give the stigma aspect any weight. I think that Georgia has given ample protection here. I see no facial invalidity or any invalidity as applied. Commitment to a state-run institution constitutes state action, but not to licensed, regulated, private institutions. So long as the personnel are medically qualified, that is enough for me and no more due process is required.

STEWART: The parties equate this improperly with involuntary commitment, and if it was, there is no question that due process protections would be required. But isn't this simply a voluntary commitment by a parent and thus to be equated with an adult's voluntary commitment? The common law right of parents may be adopted by a state without violating the Constitution. The state can't be required to stay out, but can conform to a centuries-old rule at least so long as there are procedures to determine fitness of parent and the state has the checks it provides in this case.

WHITE: The Constitution imposes some limits on parental authority, and the real question is whether Georgia has provided adequate protections. I think that there are enough protections here, although I am really shaky on both the procedural and substantive due process issues. I am particularly bothered as to children who are wards of the state.

MARSHALL: Parents don't have an absolute authority. There should be someone to chaperone the child—a social worker rather than judges or lawyers would satisfy me.

BLACKMUN: We are on the threshold of a very important development, and we must decide these cases as narrowly as possible. Georgia concerns only state commitment, and the Pennsylvania cases concern both state and private commitment. But I would assume state action in Pennsylvania. A child has a liberty interest, but that would not foreclose emergency confinement. I would reverse in principle here. It is a shaky vote, not unlike Byron's. I would say that some protection is necessary, but Georgia's procedures are O.K.

POWELL: There is state action as to state but not private institutions. There is a liberty interest implicated, but that doesn't answer these cases. I could, however, sustain the Georgia and Pennsylvania statutes if the protections were a bit better. For example, the Georgia provider reviews may be deficient. Shouldn't the system provide for some threshold decision whether the parent is qualified and fit to speak for child? An administrative provision for that decision by a social worker, for example? If so, the only other check I would require would be a medical judgment.

REHNQUIST: Some check on the unfettered discretion of parents should be in place, but that is provided here, so I reverse.

STEVENS: The adverse consequences in some cases argue against an automatic hearing. Perhaps limiting the hearing to the qualifications and fitness of the parents would be O.K. But the chance of railroading children is too real to give parents an unfettered right of control. If you can't require a child to get parental consent to obtain an abortion, this is a fortiori that we can't give a parent the right to confine a child. I am suspicious, too, of the objectiveness of state-employed psychiatrists and social workers. We need some third party to look at the situation, and if he thinks everything is kosher then he can waive any hearings, as in Pennsylvania. I would modify the Georgia case to follow Pennsylvania.

Result: After the first conference the Court was evenly divided, and a tie vote would have automatically affirmed the decision below. At the second conference, Powell and Blackmun switched sides to give Warren Burger a 5–1–3 majority to reverse. Burger wrote a paean to the Georgia law and to parental authority. Parents, he declared, must retain a substantial, if not dominant, role in making decisions on behalf of their children. Parental power to commit their children to mental hospitals was not absolute; it was limited by law and by the independent judgment of the medical establishment. Georgia's commitment procedures were sufficient to protect juveniles' liberty interests and to satisfy the Constitution's due process requirements. Stewart concurred in the result but did not join Burger's opinion. Dissenters Brennan, Marshall, and Stevens would have found the Georgia statute unconstitutional as applied to juvenile wards of the state. They also would have required that all juveniles be entitled to at least one postadmission adversarial hearing.

CHAPTER 13

EQUAL PROTECTION

RACIAL DISCRIMINATION

School Desegregation

Sipuel v. Board of Regents, University of Oklahoma, 332 U.S. 631 (1948)
(Douglas) (Burton)

At age nineteen, Ada Lois Sipuel applied to the University of Oklahoma Law School. An honors student at Langston University, she easily would have qualified for admission but for her race and perhaps her gender.[1] *In 1940, there were 3,243 lawyers in the state, but among them only 25 black men and 50 white women.*[2] *Sipuel met with Oklahoma president George Lynn Cross, who told her that she would not be admitted because of her race. State law required segregated education, and schools or individuals who violated the law were subject to state sanctions. Senior NAACP counsel Thurgood Marshall fought unsuccessfully to delay Sipuel's case and bring* Sweatt v. Painter *to the Supreme Court instead, because he thought the record in that case was stronger.*[3]

Conference of January 10, 1948

VINSON: I reverse.

BLACK: I reverse.

REED: This case is not that easy. I am not in sympathy with what the Court has been doing in this field. I pass.

FRANKFURTER: The petitioner asks for the rejection of *Gaines*. It makes a difference whether you start with the *Gaines* case or with the principle of no segregation.[4] If *Gaines*

---

1. Langston University was Oklahoma's segregated public university for blacks. It was intended for general undergraduate education and did not have a law school. As a public university, Langston was administered by the all-white state board of regents.

2. Hill, "Tribute to Thurgood Marshall," 131.

3. Sipuel's trial lawyers initially indicated that she was willing to attend a segregated law school, but they failed to demand that the state create one for her. The lower courts used this technical omission to reject Sipuel's lawsuit, and Marshall worried that this and other flaws in the record might lead the Supreme Court to establish a damaging precedent. In the end, however, Marshall felt obliged to appeal Sipuel's case because the NAACP had committed itself to her defense. Tushnet, *Making Civil Rights Law,* 129.

4. *Missouri ex rel. Gaines v. Canada,* 305 U.S. 337 (1938). This was the first major step in the NAACP's strategic war against *Plessy.* The University of Missouri Law School refused to admit Lloyd Gaines solely

governs, then the Board of Higher Education could have done one of four things if she had applied: (a) provide a new law school; (b) permit her to attend regular classes at the Oklahoma Law School provisionally until a segregated school could be constructed; (c) establish separate instruction in a temporary school; (d) permanently admit her. We must decide which one of these four we take. There is a fuss about notice. It is notorious. I prefer to ride no harder on this issue than is necessary. This case must be treated as if notice or a request had been given and received. This Board of Regents had the powers they are said to have.

VINSON: It starts with the right of this Negro girl to have a legal education. The *Gaines* case is the view of the Court. The talk about demand and the "no notice" question is shadow boxing.

FRANKFURTER: I would give the state the same chance now as it originally had. Oklahoma should not be penalized for not following *Gaines* two years ago. Oklahoma must satisfy her in one of the four ways. She is entitled to a decision at once.

DOUGLAS: I reverse. Admit her to the Oklahoma Law School.

MURPHY: I reverse and would hold to admit her to the Oklahoma Law School. I am opposed to the equal but separate doctrine.

JACKSON: I thought it very simple, and every discussion of the race problem makes it worse. I hope that we can dispose of it in a per curiam on Monday. I reverse.

RUTLEDGE: I reverse.

BURTON: I reverse on *Gaines.*

RUTLEDGE: I would not do it per curiam.

[BURTON: The rest agreed to do it per curiam.]

Result: The Court issued a per curiam decision only four days after oral argument, ordering Oklahoma to provide Sipuel with a legal education "in conformity with the equal protection clause." The Justices avoided revisiting Plessy *and relied on* Gaines *to allow Oklahoma the option of providing separate but equal facilities. The Oklahoma Board of Regents responded by establishing the new Langston University School of Law. It was created almost overnight by roping off three rooms of the state capitol and assigning three local white lawyers to instruct Sipuel and other "similarly situated"*

---

because of his race, but the state offered to pay his tuition at any law school in any adjacent state that would accept him. At the time, Illinois, Iowa, Kansas, and Nebraska accepted blacks into their state law schools. Gaines refused the offer and said that he wanted to go to law school in Missouri. The Supreme Court voted 6–2 that Missouri had violated Gaines's equal protection rights and that it must admit him to the University of Missouri. The state's promise to establish a black law school "as soon as practicable" was not sufficient, nor was the out-of-state scholarship offer. Chief Justice Charles Evans Hughes said that Missouri had a duty to provide the same professional training to all qualified residents based on an equality of right. The state could not furnish a privilege for some citizens but deny it to others on the basis of race. *Gaines,* at 349–50.

students. The NAACP appealed, but the Supreme Court refused to consider whether the new school provided Sipuel with an equal education.[5]

With only one student, Oklahoma closed the Jim Crow law school after only eighteen months and admitted Sipuel to the University of Oklahoma. She was required to sit alone in the back of the room, seated behind a chain in a chair marked "Colored." She also had to eat separately at the school cafeteria. Sipuel graduated in 1951, the only black and the only woman out of five hundred students. Another ten years passed before the school admitted its second black student.[6] *Sipuel practiced law and later taught at Langston University. In 1992, she was appointed to the Board of Regents of the University of Oklahoma.*

Sweatt v. Painter, 339 U.S. 629 (1950)
McLaurin v. Oklahoma State Regents, 339 U.S. 637 (1950)
(Douglas) (Burton)

Although the Court published these two cases separately, they were discussed together in conference. In the first case, George McLaurin was a sixty-eight-year-old black professor at Langston University who had sued and earned the right to enter the University of Oklahoma's graduate program in education. Although the university regents had decided not to offer separate graduate programs for blacks within the state university system, state law still required segregated instruction. Initially, all of McLaurin's classes were scheduled to meet in the same room, which had a small anteroom where McLaurin sat by himself. Later he was allowed to sit in the same classroom as white students, but had to sit in a separate row behind a wooden rail in a chair marked "Colored." He was also assigned a separate table in the library and cafeteria.[7] *A three-judge district court approved these arrangements.*

In 1946, Heman Marion "Bill" Sweatt applied to law school at the University of Texas and was rejected because of his race.[8] *By law, the University of Texas excluded blacks from its law school. University president Theophilus Painter sought the advice of the state attorney general, who issued an advisory opinion reaffirming the "wise and long-continued policy of segregation." President Painter offered to enroll Sweatt in a new, segregated law school being built at Prairie View University in Houston.*[9] *The new school, to be called the Texas State University for Negroes, was temporarily housed in a basement near the state capitol building in Austin until permanent facilities could be completed.*

---

5. *Fisher v. Hurst,* 333 U.S. 147 (1948). In the interim, Sipuel married and changed her last name to Fisher. In rejecting her plea, the Court noted that in her initial lawsuit she had not questioned the state's right to satisfy the equal protection clause by establishing a separate law school for blacks. Murphy and Rutledge dissented.

6. Ifill, "Thurgood Marshall."

7. Ibid.

8. Sweatt was a World War II veteran, a Houston postal worker, a member of the Houston NAACP, and an activist in the local postal workers' union. In exchange for filing this lawsuit, the local NAACP agreed to pay all costs and gave Sweatt a stipend of $3,500 per year while the case was being litigated. The agreement was both legally and ethically improper and later caused significant trouble for the NAACP and its Legal Defense Fund. Tushnet, *Making Civil Rights Law,* 126–28.

9. Texas also offered black students scholarships if they went to law school in another state. Sweatt originally wanted to go to law school in Michigan but chose to remain in Texas after his father suffered a heart attack. Tushnet, *Making Civil Rights Law,* 342.

The trial court ruled that the two law schools were substantially equal, and the state appellate courts affirmed. The University of Texas had 19 faculty, 850 students, a library with 65,000 volumes, a law review, and a reputation as an established law school. Texas State University for Negroes had 5 professors (all on loan from the University of Texas), 23 students, a library with 16,500 books, no law review, one alumnus admitted to the state bar, and no accreditation.[10]

These two cases were the first planned tests of the NAACP's new offensive on segregated education.[11]

Conference of April 8, 1950

McLaurin v. Oklahoma State Regents

VINSON: In *Sipuel,* segregation was not in issue per se, but it has been with us all the way.[12] The Fourteenth Amendment was considered. In *Sipuel,* we told Oklahoma that under the Constitution she was entitled to an education at state expense. Oklahoma was called upon to admit her, and if they did not then they could not admit any whites. [BURTON: We did not mention restrictions.] If Oklahoma had provided separate but equal facilities, we would have said that segregation was not involved. But Oklahoma did not do that.

Here, they admitted McLaurin to the state's white college. The single row of chairs and the separate tables were used as a formal "out" to meet their constitutional and statutory promises. There is color discrimination in their treatment of Negroes. I reverse. McLaurin and the other twenty-three are entitled to no discrimination. Negroes are entitled to enter the university without restriction if they are admitted at all.

BLACK: Two roads are open. First, on a separate but equal theory. As in *Gaines,* I would think that they did not have it equal here, or in *Sweatt.* I would put the burden—a heavy one—on the state—as heavy, or heavier, than has been done in the jury cases involving discrimination against Negroes. It is not *equal* to isolate. There is a custom in elementary and high schools going way back to the Civil War days. The debates referred to that type of education. But you can't set up a separate law school overnight that is equal to the old one. The diplomas have a different value. I would hold on the record here that the state has *not* met its burden in the legal field by showing in *Sweatt* that the school for

---

10. By the time the case made it to the Supreme Court, Texas State University's law school had moved to its permanent home in Houston. Under Dean Ozie Johnson, it was accredited by the American Bar Association, but the Association of American Law Schools refused to accredit the school while Sweatt's lawsuit was pending. Tushnet, *Making Civil Rights Law,* 135.

11. The NAACP's legal staff was divided over this strategy. Thurgood Marshall favored attacking segregated transportation first because he thought that these cases would be less likely to introduce sensitive questions of social equality that might "confuse the Court's thinking." His colleagues Robert Carter and William Hastie favored attacking segregated education first, because they thought that the "gross inequities" of segregation were more obvious.

There were also disagreements over how quickly to push for change. Hastie and Marshall favored moving slowly, because they feared that if pushed too quickly the Supreme Court would dig in its heels and reaffirm *Plessy.* After considerable debate, they decided to (1) seek to desegregate universities and professional schools more or less immediately; and (2) attack gross inequalities in elementary and secondary education more cautiously, without demanding an immediate end to segregation. *Sweatt* and *McLaurin* were the first crucial tests of this compromise strategy, and the results would determine the subsequent course of litigation. Tushnet, *Making Civil Rights Law,* 126–27.

12. *Sipuel v. Board of Regents of University of Oklahoma,* 332 U.S. 631 (1948).

Negroes was equal. It can't be done quickly. Up to now, Negroes have not been admitted at all. There has been *no custom* here in the Southern law schools or graduate schools comparable to that in high schools and preparatory schools. That fact adds some strength to Tom Clark's memo, in favor of reversal in *Sweatt.* There is a deep-seated antagonism to racial commingling. At this time, it might make trouble in the South in the lower schools. Schools would close rather than mix races at the grade and high school levels. I would not send it back for evidence. It is self-evident. I reverse both *McLaurin* and *Sweatt.*

The second road is whether we can make a decision for graduate schools. I can't say that the Fourteenth Amendment was not intended and designed to prevent a caste system—and that is what this is. It is a hangover from the days when the Negro was a slave, and the racial humiliation of sitting together. Brown's premise in *Plessy* is not sound—it has been refuted by the facts and by history. I can't subscribe to any one of his principles. We could find some people who would say that prevention of violence was the ground for segregation. If I have to meet the issue, there is nothing to make me subscribe to *Plessy.* It can reach people other than Negroes. It was Hitler's creed—he preached what the South believed. The South may never accept that view until the races amalgamate, as they do when they live side by side. The caste system, throughout the country, is the negation of the idea of the Fourteenth Amendment—which is that we will try out the experiment of no caste system, and leave it to them to choose how they will associate. It may be that the Fourteenth Amendment policy can not work anywhere. It is basic, and is the opposite of Hitler's idea and of the Indian untouchables.

Is it necessary here to reach these questions beyond separate and equal? The advantage of the first path is that it is a gradual approach. The Fourteenth Amendment gave Congress the power to outlaw any practice or statute of a state. This Court was not wrong when it decided that due process permitted this Court to strike down all conduct that Congress could strike down and could bar. The Court reached up and held that confiscation was a violation of due process.

The Court struck down an act of Congress in the *Civil Rights Cases,* and said that it was not true that the purpose of the Fourteenth Amendment was to give *Congress* the right to *outlaw* segregation in theaters, and so forth. The *Civil Rights Cases* were not true to the purposes of Fourteenth Amendment, and therefore we could reverse on separate but equal. On grounds of reasonableness [BURTON: This is the *Plessy* test], the Oklahoma segregation is unreasonable. I can't subscribe to *Plessy.* The door of "reasonable segregation" was left open in public schools. *This,* however, involves *graduate schools* and is wholly unreasonable. It would strike at a basic idea in the South—that the races can't mix. [BURTON: Black would reverse all three cases, but he does not state that he would go *now* beyond separate and equal.][13] It may bring clashes, but these are clashes that will disaffect many people either way.

REED: When you admit a person to school, should he have full freedom? You must admit him on an equal basis. I reverse.

---

13. The "third case" was *Henderson v. United States,* 339 U.S. 816 (1950), which is reported separately below.

FRANKFURTER: I would not put it on Reed's grounds. That kind of a division is [BURTON: Should be] insalubrious. That is a circumstance that makes it so. I would rest on the proposition that that kind of segregation is bad. It produces self-consciousness and introduces an irrelevance that it is bad. I reverse.

DOUGLAS: We should overrule *Plessy*. We are faced with the segregation issue in *McLaurin*.

JACKSON: These cases are fraught with great harm to the Court and the country.[14] These cases can do this Court more harm than any other case. I don't know the answer. I have not made up my mind. I never had any segregation personally until I came here. Whites as well as blacks are victims of this system. I find no basis for the idea that the Fourteenth Amendment reached schools.[15] Historically, the Fourteenth Amendment was not aimed at schools. There is no basis for saying that Congress has decided the issue. They have not done it in housing, or the Army, or in atomic energy. We must amend the Fourteenth Amendment if we are to ban segregation. Is it a wise course? It is easier to get segregation banned by statutory interpretation than by constitutional interpretation. The only solution, ultimately, is amalgamation. It would be unfortunate if we have to proceed on the theory that this is a badge of "inferiority" and is bad on that ground. It is not a badge of inferiority today. It is a historical hysteria.

We can't show a constitutional line between segregation in graduate schools and in elementary schools. We owe the South candor. It is building regional schools for Negroes and is spending lots of money. I don't see how, in candor, you can draw a line between different types of education. Segregation is too expensive to whites. It is breaking down at the top levels. Maybe we will do the subject more harm than good. I don't know what it takes to make an equal law school. We probably must reverse these three cases. I would reverse all on *Henderson*.[16]

BURTON: He is admitted. He can't be in and not the same. You can't segregate where they are not separated. Graduate work is professional work.

CLARK: I reverse. [BURTON: See Clark's comments in *Sweatt*.]

MINTON: There may be a reasonable regulation. Both of these cases involve the same issue—equal protection. In the Oklahoma case, if you admit him, it must be on an equal footing. This is not a reasonable classification. I reverse.

---

14. Jackson's comments, as recorded by Douglas, indicate that he was talking not only about *McLaurin v. Regents of the University of Oklahoma* and *Sweatt v. Painter*, but also about *Henderson v. United States*, 339 U.S. 816 (1950). Jackson's comments here are taken from Burton's notes in the two school cases and from Douglas's notes on *Henderson*.

15. Jackson was impressed by the Texas brief, which proved to his satisfaction that most of the Fourteenth Amendment's original supporters did not intend to interfere with state-imposed segregation in education, and that even those who opposed segregated schools at that time conceded the point. For Jackson, this meant that the question for the Court was not whether to "fill gaps or construe the Amendment to include matters which were unconsidered," but "whether we will construe it to include what was deliberately and intentionally excluded." Letter from Jackson to Charles Fairman, April 5, 1950, cited in Tushnet, *Making Civil Rights Law*, 143. Jackson was unusually straightforward in admitting that the Court would have to decide these cases based on political rather than legal considerations. He was even more blunt about this in the later *Brown* conferences.

16. *Henderson v. United States*, 339 U.S. 816 (1950).

Conference of April 8, 1950

Sweatt v. Painter

VINSON: Here they attempted to exercise the separate but equal doctrine. There is separate treatment. The petitioner said that he would not enter the separate but equal school and argued that there can be no separate and equal facility in the professional field. The issue has been ever present, and I would rely on the legislative history surrounding the adoption of the Fourteenth Amendment and the Act of 1866. [BURTON: History said that it does not cover schools.][17] I can't conceive that Congress did not have the problem in front of them. The public school problem was preeminent in the Fourteenth Amendment problem. Also, later language was deleted as to public schools. After this, the District of Columbia had segregated schools. States of the North as well as states of the South had separate schools. Separate schools were deemed perfectly constitutional then, under *Plessy.* (Harlan's dissent in *Plessy* does not mention schools. The majority's opinion does illustrate with schools, and the opinion O.K.'s it.) Segregation in public schools was always considered an a fortiori case.[18]

All of our cases assume that schools are different. In *Cumming*—Harlan wrote for the Court—we said that states could have separate schools.[19] *Gong Lum*, the Mississippi case, recognizes separate schools.[20] In *Gaines v. Canada*, the equal facility language is strong.[21] In *Sipuel* we cite it. Also in *Fisher, Hurd, Shelley v. Kraemer*, and so forth.[22] In *Shelley v. Kraemer*, we reviewed old cases that recognized separate schools. *Shelley v. Kraemer* re-

---

17. Solicitor General Philip Perlman filed an amicus brief supporting the NAACP's position and indicating that *Plessy* should be overruled. Perlman later opposed filing a similar brief in *Brown v. Board of Education* because he and other leading Democrats thought that it would hurt Adlai Stevenson's election chances. Rowan, *Dream Makers, Dream Breakers*, 191.

18. *Plessy v. Ferguson*, 163 U.S. 537 (1896).

19. *Cumming v. Richmond County Board of Education*, 175 U.S. 528 (1899). The school board in Richmond County, Georgia, closed the only black high school in the district while the white high schools remained open. Black taxpayers sought to enjoin the school board from spending any more public funds on white schools until equal black facilities were restored. The trial judge found that the school board's actions violated the separate but equal doctrine, but the Georgia Supreme Court reversed. The first John Marshall Harlan, writing for a unanimous Court, affirmed on the ground that restoring the injunction would only harm white students without helping blacks. He concluded that public schools were a state responsibility and that federal courts could get involved only if a state had clearly and unmistakably violated the Constitution. In *Sweatt*, both Vinson and Frankfurter believed that this case proved that Harlan had no constitutional objections to racially segregated schools. Otherwise, there was nothing to prevent him from siding with the trial judge and finding that the Richmond school board had violated the separate but equal doctrine. Nor would he have left black high school students without a school to attend when several white high schools were available nearby. See, for example, Yarbrough, *John Marshall Harlan*, 121–23.

20. *Gong Lum v. Rice*, 275 U.S. 78 (1927). Martha Lum, an American of Chinese descent, sued to reverse a decision by local Mississippi school administrators requiring her to attend segregated black schools. In rejecting her arguments, Chief Justice William Howard Taft reaffirmed the separate but equal doctrine, ruling that it did not matter whether Mississippi officials chose to place Lum with whites or blacks, as long as the schools were substantially equal. None of the parties in this case directly challenged the separate but equal doctrine.

21. *Missouri ex rel. Gaines v. Canada*, 305 U.S. 337 (1938).

22. *Fisher v. Hurst*, 333 U.S. 147 (1948); *Hurd v. Hodge*, 334 U.S. 24 (1948); *Shelley v. Kraemer*, 334 U.S. 1 (1948).

affirmed the state action doctrine. Some words there are bothersome. *Corrigan v. Buckley* did not present the question, but we said some words in that case.[23]

It may be that *now* we should expand the Constitution. But when the problem is so sensitive, and in view of those who wrote the early legislation and the Fourteenth Amendment, I can't say that the Civil War decided that the schools shan't be separate. It is difficult to say that *that* was decided—that there was to be no segregation under that Amendment. As to professional schools, nothing I have seen in the history of the Fourteenth Amendment applies specifically to professional schools. I have found nothing that discusses that level of education. As a matter of policy, no great harm would result from the mingling of races in professional schools. But I don't see how we can draw the line there. I can't distinguish professional and elementary schools.[24]

The next question is whether the facilities were equal. If the issue is here in *Sweatt* [BURTON: Technically, it is not] then (1) what has been presented in the record is equal; or (2) we should insist on a much more complete record. I am inclined to think that I would affirm and not remand.

BLACK: I reverse. See *McLaurin.*

REED: I would prefer to put it on the question of equality. Every appeal raises this issue. Are the facilities equal? If we have to decide, I would say that the facilities were equal. I accept the finding on equality, but I would be willing to remand for further findings. [BURTON: That means that we meet and uphold the separate but equal test.] I affirm.

---

23. *Corrigan v. Buckley,* 271 U.S. 323 (1926). The NAACP's first attempt to attack private racially restrictive covenants failed when a unanimous Court decided that the case did not present a substantial federal question. Irene Corrigan sold her house in Washington, D.C., to a black family, even though the property was subject to a racially restrictive covenant. A white neighbor, John Buckley, sued to block the sale. Corrigan sought to have the suit dismissed, arguing that racial covenants were unconstitutional and against public policy. Courts in the District of Columbia refused to dismiss the case and issued an injunction against the sale, and the U.S. Supreme Court affirmed. Edward Sanford wrote that the Constitution applied only to state action, not to private individuals concerning the control and disposition of their own property. Sanford noted, however, that the issue of whether states could constitutionally *enforce* racially restrictive covenants was a separate question not before the Court. He could not resist adding, however, that any such claim would be "lacking in substance." Twenty-two years later, the Court proved Sanford wrong in *Shelley v. Kraemer,* 334 U.S. 1 (1948).

24. Vinson was probably responding to Tom Clark, who wrote a lengthy memorandum to the conference saying that while he supported ending segregation in graduate and professional education, he was not prepared to desegregate elementary or high schools.

Segregated graduate schools were constitutionally untenable, Clark argued, because blacks would not have the equal opportunities necessary to build specific professional skills and because intangible factors such as reputation made truly equal education impossible. Segregated grammar schools might regrettably encourage racial prejudice among young children, but this was a problem of social equality rather than educational equality. Clark claimed that he had not made up his mind about the constitutionality of segregated grammar schools but stated that he would strongly prefer to avoid the issue. Clark, Memorandum to the Conference (Apr. 7, 1950), discussed in Hutchinson, "Unanimity and Desegregation," 21–23; and Tushnet, *Making Civil Rights Law,* 144.

FRANKFURTER: We should not go beyond what is necessary here. We should not go out and meet problems. I was for ten years counsel for the NAACP.[25] The *Sweatt* case is the easier of the two. In *McLaurin*, it would not work to put the South on the same basis. It is absurd to say that this is a *Dred Scott* case.[26] To me, it is clear that the two schools are not equal, and that there cannot be equality at the graduate level. The strength of a law school is in its student body. [DOUGLAS: Frankfurter reads from Holmes's address at the Harvard Law School on the education of lawyers as "specialists."] There never was discrimination at Harvard Law School—students or faculty. Law schools are limited in the number of good teachers. There is great competition to get them. Intercourse among the students is the life of the place. At Texas University, there are twenty-three men on the faculty—eight of whom are men of distinction, and there may be others. The Texas University law library has 65,000 volumes, compared to 20,000 volumes for the other school. This is not equality. I reverse on a separate and equal basis.

We do not need to go beyond the needs of graduate education. We should abstain from saying anything about segregation as such. This is before us on a writ of mandamus, and here we have a right to judge as of the time of the mandamus, and we can judge on the facts before us.

DOUGLAS: The schools are not equal. You can't do it at the graduate level. But if the statutes stand, they warned us that they would act to send it back. (That would approve the idea of separate and equal, and we should not do this.)[27] I might go along on the ground that this is not equal.

JACKSON: I reverse on *Henderson*.

BURTON: A law school is at the professional level, and cannot be segregated. I would be willing to say that it was not equal here, saving the broader question. I would like to overthrow the *Plessy* doctrine at the graduate level.

CLARK: I can't say that the Constitution applies to graduate school but not to elementary school. I also can't say that there is equality between schools here. It is ridiculous to

---

25. Frankfurter was actively involved with the NAACP during the 1920s while he was a young Harvard professor. He also served as an adviser for some of Harvard's black law students, including Charles Hamilton Houston. As the school's only Jewish professor, Frankfurter knew something about being a minority in a largely homogeneous professional environment. As a Justice, however, whenever Frankfurter mentioned his NAACP credentials during conference discussions, it usually meant that he was about to disagree with the NAACP's position.

26. In *Dred Scott v. Sandford*, 19 How. 393 (1857), the majority initially intended to decide the case narrowly and avoid the broader issue of whether the Missouri Compromise Act was constitutional. The case was certainly capable of being decided on narrow grounds, because the Missouri Compromise had already effectively been repealed by the Kansas-Nebraska Act of 1854. However, after John McLean and Benjamin Curtis announced their intent to argue in dissent that the Missouri Act was constitutional, the majority decided to reach the constitutional issue, with disastrous results for Court and country.

In *Sweatt* and *McLaurin*, Frankfurter wanted to avoid the larger constitutional issues and used *Dred Scott* as a cautionary example. He argued that there was no need to revisit the separate but equal doctrine because the two schools were clearly not equal.

27. It is difficult to say from Burton's conference notes whether this parenthetical comment was Douglas's or one of Burton's asides.

say that it is equal. I don't think that they could build a school equal to the University of Texas.[28] Their standing is wide apart. You can't have this graduate school separate and equal under the Constitution. While I feel that there can't be a separate and equal doctrine under the Fourteenth Amendment—and perhaps we should overrule *Plessy*—I don't want to affect elementary schools. It is important to have as many of us as possible in this opinion. I am willing to subscribe to the doctrine that in the Texas case the two schools were not equal. We should do as Robert Jackson says. We should say that there can't be equal schools at the graduate level, or otherwise Texas will try to build one. I would say that separate and equal is O.K., but you can't have it now at the graduate level. I reverse in *McLaurin* and *Sweatt*.

MINTON: Here, he can't get into the law school. It is an unreasonable classification to refuse admission to graduate schools on racial grounds. I reverse.

FRANKFURTER: Equality cannot be obtained in segregated graduate schools. That is different from saying that segregation is *not reasonable* when applied to graduate schools.

Result: In McLaurin, *the Court ruled that Oklahoma violated the Fourteenth Amendment because segregating black students from their classmates precluded them from the free discussions and interactions with other students and faculty necessary to learn their profession. The key was that the state had imposed conditions which by law precluded any possibility of free association.*

In Sweatt, *the Justices found that the two law schools were not substantially equal. The Justices carefully avoided the question of whether separate schools could be made equal under different circumstances but expanded their working definition of equality to include intangible factors such as reputation. Largely because of harassment by students and faculty, including cross burnings, destruction of his personal property, and verbal abuse, Bill Sweatt dropped out after his first year at the University of Texas. He later earned a master's degree in social work at Atlanta University in Georgia and served for twenty-three years as assistant director of the Urban League's southern regional office in Atlanta. In 1987, the University of Texas renamed a portion of its property the Heman Sweatt Campus.*

Brown v. Board of Education, 347 U.S. 483 (1954)
Bolling v. Sharpe, 347 U.S. 497 (1954)
(Burton) (Douglas) (Jackson) (Clark)

The most famous Supreme Court case in American history was made necessary by a self-inflicted wound—Plessy v. Ferguson, *which established the "separate but equal" doctrine and became the legal foundation for Jim Crow laws and state-sanctioned segregation throughout the south.[29]* Brown *com-*

---

28. Clark graduated from the University of Texas law school. As Thurgood Marshall hoped, Clark thought highly of his alma mater and was susceptible to the argument that no segregated facility could ever be its equal.

29. *Plessy v. Ferguson,* 163 U.S. 537 (1896).

bined five school desegregation cases from Kansas,[30] South Carolina,[31] Virginia,[32] Delaware,[33] and the District of Columbia.[34] Among the five cases, only the Delaware state courts struck down laws re-

---

30. *Brown v. Board of Education.* Oliver Brown was an assistant pastor and a welder for the Santa Fe Railroad. He sought to enroll his eight-year-old daughter Linda at Sumner Elementary School near their home. Although the neighborhood was integrated and the local school had a mix of white and Hispanic students, blacks were not permitted to attend. Linda had to walk six blocks through a train yard to catch a bus that took her several miles across town to an all-black school. A unanimous three-judge district court, in an opinion by former governor and Circuit Judge Walter Huxman, conceded that segregated education harmed black children but ruled that the black and white schools in Topeka were substantially equal and refused to order desegregation.

Before the case could be argued before the Supreme Court, the Topeka Board of Education voted to desegregate its schools voluntarily, and district officials subsequently refused to argue the case in favor of segregation. Kansas attorney general Harold R. Fatzer also initially refused to submit a brief. It took a threat from the Supreme Court to convince him to defend the state's segregation law. Ten days before oral argument, Fatzer assigned the case to his thirty-six-year-old assistant, Paul Wilson. Wilson, who was dubious about the legality of the state's segregation statute, had to prepare his case without assistance. He had never argued an appellate case at any level and had never been to Washington, D.C. By all accounts, he wrote an effective brief and presented a competent oral argument. Kluger, *Simple Justice,* 547–49, 568.

31. *Briggs v. Elliott.* Harry Briggs and other black parents challenged the segregated school system in Clarendon County, South Carolina. Although several plaintiffs were fired from their jobs in retaliation for their lawsuit (Briggs, an auto mechanic, among them), they continued to press their case. A three-judge district court found that the black schools were inferior and ordered the state to equalize facilities, but refused to order desegregation. The court was ideologically divided: J. Waties Waring was openly sympathetic with the NAACP, George Timmerman was a committed segregationist, and John Parker was a moderate but a great believer in precedent. Judge Parker wrote the opinion, which emphasized that segregation was a legislative rather than a judicial problem. Waring dissented, dismissing *Plessy* as nothing more than an outdated railroad case. He concluded that "segregation is per se inequality," and afterward he privately pressed Thurgood Marshall to quote the phrase in his Supreme Court brief. Tushnet, *Making Civil Rights Law,* 161.

32. *Davis v. School Board.* The move to desegregate schools in Prince Edward County, Virginia, began when fifteen-year-old Joan Johns and her sister Barbara led a student boycott at all-black Moton High School, a decrepit school with tarpaper buildings. A three-judge district court ruled that the black schools' buildings, curricula, and transportation were unequal and ordered an equalization program, but upheld the doctrine of separate but equal on the ground that segregation benefited both whites and blacks.

33. *Gebhart v. Belton.* Vice Chancellor Collins Seitz of the Delaware state chancery court enjoined enforcement of the state's segregation laws and ordered the immediate desegregation of the state's public schools. Seitz blasted the separate but equal doctrine and predicted that it would soon be overturned, but noted that he had no authority to overrule *Plessy.* Seitz ruled that the plaintiffs deserved an effective and immediate remedy. He ordered Delaware schools to integrate immediately, at least until substantially equal facilities could be established. The Delaware Supreme Court affirmed.

In an earlier case, Seitz had ruled that an unaccredited undergraduate college, the Delaware State College for Negroes, was not and could never be substantially equal to the University of Delaware. This was one of the few NAACP-sponsored lawsuits involving *undergraduate* college education. *Parker v. University of Delaware,* 75 A.2d 225 (Del. Ch. 1950).

34. *Bolling v. Sharpe.* Spottswood T. Bolling sued District of Columbia school officials, including C. Melvin Sharpe, arguing that segregated schools in the nation's capital violated the due process clause of the Fifth Amendment. The District Court for the District of Columbia dismissed the complaint and the Supreme Court immediately granted certiorari, taking the unusual step of bypassing the Court of Appeals. The NAACP knew that this case was potentially more difficult than the state cases. While states were required by the Fourteenth Amendment to provide equal protection of the laws, Congress and the federal

quiring segregated schools.[35] Bolling v. Sharpe, *the District of Columbia case, was discussed at conference at the same time as the four state cases, although it was eventually published separately.*

*These notes offer an extraordinary behind-the-scenes look at Supreme Court decision-making.
Among the highlights are the initial ambivalence of Vinson, Reed, Frankfurter, Jackson, and Clark
toward ending state segregation in public education, Frankfurter's later efforts to portray himself as
the Court's mastermind in these cases, and a professor's false charge that Hugo Black had considered
reaffirming* Plessy v. Ferguson. *There are a number of surprises here, including unexpected leadership roles played by two of the "forgotten Justices," Harold Burton and Sherman Minton. Both men
proved to be articulate, pragmatic, and passionate opponents of segregation. Burton, in particular,
was a seasoned politician who brought his personal experience as a big city mayor to bear on this most
political of decisions.*[36] *The key to the Court's decision, however, was the addition of another career
politician to the Court in 1953—Governor Earl Warren of California.*

Conference of December 13, 1952

VINSON: I am not sure what we should do today. It is 3:30 P.M.

#413 Bolling v. Sharpe (District of Columbia): There is a body of law in back of us on
separate but equal. The District of Columbia statutes—1862 and later—were enacted close
to the dates of the Civil War Amendments. The same men were in Congress then who
passed the Civil War Amendments. However you construe it, Congress did not pass a
statute determining the issue and ordering *no* segregation. It is hard to get away from
that contemporary interpretation of the Civil War Amendments. Congress evidently did
not want to pass this. Sumner's bill against segregation failed, and therefore the District
of Columbia has had segregated schools for ninety years.[37] Harlan's dissent in *Plessy* is
careful *not* to refer to schools. That has significance, because Harlan was strong on other
items and later wrote the *Cumming* case for this Court.[38] I don't see in the District of

---

government were not bound by the Fourteenth Amendment, and the Fifth Amendment has no equal protection clause. The NAACP used precedents won in the earlier restrictive covenant cases to argue that the
due process clause of the Fifth Amendment contained an implicit "equal protection component."

Ironically, this case threatened to undermine the NAACP's Fourteenth Amendment argument in the
state cases, because the same Congress that passed the Fourteenth Amendment had also established segregated public schools in Washington, D.C. Vinson and Frankfurter used this fact to argue that the Fourteenth Amendment could not have been intended to desegregate state schools.

35. In 1954, seventeen states required segregation in public schools: Alabama, Arkansas, Delaware, Florida,
Georgia, Kentucky, Louisiana, Maryland, Mississippi, Missouri, North Carolina, Oklahoma, South Carolina,
Tennessee, Texas, Virginia, and West Virginia. Four states permitted local school districts to establish segre-
gated schools at their discretion: Kansas, New Mexico, Arizona, and Wyoming. Cray, *Chief Justice,* 277.

36. Burton was mayor of Cleveland from 1934 to 1940. A reform-minded Republican, Burton was extraordinarily down to earth and accessible for a big-city mayor. He even listed his home telephone number in the Cleveland phone book. Berry, *Stability, Security and Continuity,* 9–11.

37. Between 1867 and 1874, Senator Charles Sumner (R-MA) tried and failed to pass legislation to prohibit racial segregation in public schools, including the District of Columbia. He included a desegregation
provision in legislation that eventually became the Civil Rights Act of 1875. After Sumner died in 1874, his
provision was eliminated before the bill became law. As a result, the District of Columbia maintained a
segregated school system even at the height of Reconstruction. Klarman, "An Interpretive History of Equal
Protection," 252–53; McConnell, "Originalism and the Desegregation Decisions," 986–89.

38. *Cumming v. Richmond County Board of Education,* 175 U.S. 528 (1899).

Columbia case how we can get away from this Court's long and continued acceptance of these patterns of Congress ever since the Civil War Amendments.

As to having mixed school classes, I think that Congress has the power to act for the District of Columbia and for the states. It may act in the District either directly through the Board of Education, or by passing a few statutes. I don't think much of the idea that it is for *Congress* and not for us to act.[39] If they *do not act*, this leaves us with it. It would be better if Congress would act. Congress may act for the District of Columbia, but probably will *not* act for the states. (They will probably be content in the District of Columbia to leave it to the board of education.) In the absence of congressional action, we have the commerce clause cases and these cases.

#101 Briggs v. Elliott (South Carolina): The facilities are equal here. It took some time to make them equal. Thurgood Marshall says that it will be necessary to state a *time* for it to be made effective. The abolition of the separate school system in the South raises serious practical problems. In *Sipuel* and *McLaurin* we said that the right was personal and that they should get in right now, but it is difficult when there are large numbers.[40] The situation is very serious and very emotional. We can't close our eyes to the seriousness of the problem in various parts of the country, although the problems are hotter in some parts of the country than in others. We face the complete abolition of the public school system in the South. It may be easy to say that the result is of no consequence to us, but I think that it is. It is said that we should not consider this, but I can't throw it *all* off. We can't avoid taking it into consideration. Boldness is essential, but wisdom is indispensable.[41]

#448 Gebhart v. Belton (Delaware) and *#191 Davis v. School Board* (Virginia): The schools here are not equal at the moment, but they are moving toward it. I am inclined toward giving these states the time to make their facilities equal.

#101 Briggs v. Elliott (South Carolina) and *#8 Brown v. Board of Education* (Kansas): The history of the South Carolina case shows what time can do. Where you have a large percentage of colored people, it is hard to say that they cannot be equal. The Kansas judge said that it is detrimental to Negroes to be segregated.[42] Virginia was to the contrary. In Virginia, the finding was that the court could not say that the proof on that side was preponderant, and that commingling would bring on humiliation and so forth. Affirm?

---

39. This comment might have been aimed at Robert Jackson, who suggested this course of inaction during oral argument.

40. *Sipuel* and *McLaurin* each involved a single person who sought admission to a graduate school. In contrast, the *Brown* cases potentially involved millions of schoolchildren nationwide. At this point, the Justices had not decided whether to limit these cases to the named litigants or to treat them as class-action suits. The issue became a matter of discussion at subsequent conferences.

41. This quote is from Clark's notes. Burton records Vinson as saying, "Courage is needed, but also wisdom." While Vinson was clearly ambivalent about desegregation, this passage is perhaps the strongest hint that he would ultimately have joined a decision to desegregate public schools, as he had done in earlier cases involving graduate and professional schools.

42. The tangible inequalities were less noticeable in Kansas than in the other school districts. This made the psychological and other intangible effects of discrimination crucial. Tushnet, *Making Civil Rights Law*, 161.

BLACK: To start off, I am not at all sure that Congress is barred by the same limitations as the states. Congress can legislate where the states cannot, for states are bound by the Fourteenth Amendment. I see an anomalous result of permitting segregation in the District of Columbia and not elsewhere under the equal protection clause. (All parties seem to have felt that they were all the same.)

First, we must decide: is segregation a per se violation of the Fourteenth Amendment? Marshall understates and the others overstate the effects of such a ruling.[43] It would be serious and drastic. There will be serious incidents and some violence if the Court holds segregation unlawful. States would probably take evasive measures while purporting to obey. South Carolina might abolish its public school system. One of the worst features is that the courts will be on the battle front. It will be law by injunction and contempt, and I don't believe in law by injunction.

If we had decided this case right after passage of the Civil War Amendments, I believe that we would have held originally that the way to enforce this was through Congress. Now, however, the courts have taken jurisdiction. I can't draw a rational distinction between this case and other cases under the Fourteenth Amendment as respects a self-executing agreement. If we can declare confiscation or other laws unconstitutional, then we can do the same with segregation.

I am driven to the segregation issue with the knowledge that it will mean trouble. I am compelled to say for myself that I can't escape the view that the reason for segregation is the belief that Negroes are inferior. I do not need books to say that.[44]

I am also compelled to say for myself that the Civil War Amendments have as their basic purpose the abolition of such castes, and to protect the Negro against discrimination on account of color. And that is what is behind the opposition now. Southerners always say that segregation is meant to prevent the mixture of the races. This is the idea behind the southern view that the mixture of races is thought to be very dangerous and weakens the white race.

If I have to meet it, I can't go contrary to the truth that the purpose of these laws is to discriminate on account of color. The Civil War Amendments were intended to stop that. I have to say that segregation *of itself* violates the Constitution, unless the long line of decisions and stare decisis prevents such a ruling. I don't think that Congress went as far as they thought the Civil War Amendments went. They didn't go all the way that was intended in the old cases. *I have to vote that way*, to end segregation. And if a majority votes the other way—to segregate and to preserve equal and separate—then there should be leeway for change.[45] If equal and separate is going to be the rule, then wide latitude should be given to findings in the state courts. I reverse.

---

43. Jackson's conference notes state: "Marshall overestimates ease, other side evils."

44. Black appears to be saying that he did not need books like Gunnar Myrdal's *An American Dilemma* or other sociological studies introduced into evidence by the NAACP to make up his mind about the causes and effects of segregation.

45. Political scientist Sidney Ulmer claimed that during this conference Black was willing to consider reaffirming *Plessy* if the majority voted that way. Ulmer's charge was based on his reading of Justice Burton's conference notes. In 1970, Ulmer sent Black a draft of his article on the *Brown* decision. When Black read Ulmer's account of the conference, he vehemently denied that his vote had ever been in doubt. In an ex-

REED: I approach this problem from a different view than Black. There are some who want to hold Negroes down and deprive them of educational equipment. I know that some desire to keep the Negro as a laborer. The race came out of slavery a short time ago. The state legislatures have informed views on this matter. Negroes have not thoroughly assimilated. There has been some amalgamation of the races, as shown by the counsel who appeared here. States are authorized to make up their own minds on this question. We must try our best to give Negroes benefits. We must start with the idea that there is a large and reasonable body of opinion in various states that separation of the races is for the benefit of both. Then there is the determination of when the changes are to be made. There has been great, steady progress in the South in the advancement of the interests of the Negroes. States should be left to work out the problem for themselves. It is the right of the states to improve Negroes' status. *Think of the advancements: transportation, voting, FEPC,* and so forth.[46] Segregation is gradually disappearing. This applies to both North and South. It is optional in Kansas, Kentucky, and other states. We don't have the same problems in Kentucky as in the South. The facilities are not equal in Kentucky, but they are better than they are in the South.

I agree that the meaning of the Constitution is *not* fixed. What was due process in 1860 may not be due process today—and that is going forward. To say that today, we would have to reverse what we have said before, and say that segregation is *no longer* permissible. Why not let it go on?

When will there be changes? If the body of people think that it is unconstitutional. I cannot say that the time has come when we can say that seventeen states are denying equal protection or due process. We must allow time. Segregation in the border states will disappear in fifteen or twenty years. Ten years in Virginia, perhaps. Ten years would make it really equal. Every year helps. In the Deep South, separate but equal schools must be allowed. I uphold segregation as constitutional.[47]

FRANKFURTER: I am very glad that Vinson started with the District of Columbia case. The District of Columbia raises very different questions than the state cases. It just shows

---

change of letters, Ulmer continued to press his view. Black was furious, and even though Ulmer eventually struck the accusation from the published version of his paper the damage had been done. The incident precipitated Black's decision to destroy his conference notes. It was, Black said, "the final nail in the coffin."

The crucial paragraph of Burton's notes reads: "Have to say segregation of itself violates Constitution (unless long line of decisions prevents). Didn't go all the way that was intended in old cases. Will vote that way, and if majority other way—to segregate—then there should be leeway for change. Reverse." It is difficult to see how Ulmer drew his inference from this passage, and when Burton's conference notes are combined with those of other Justices, it is clear that Ulmer was wrong. Black was more profoundly wrong, however, to claim "that history will not lose too much" because of his decision to burn his conference papers. Yarbrough, *Mr. Justice Black and His Critics*, 237–39; Newman, *Hugo Black*, 610; Ulmer, "Earl Warren and the *Brown* Decision."

46. The Fair Employment Practices Commission (FEPC) was created during World War II to enforce civil rights laws and federal antidiscrimination policies in war-related industries.

47. Reed was the only Justice to vote unambiguously at this conference to uphold segregation in both the state and federal cases. He agreed that the Constitution prohibited racial discrimination, but was not convinced that segregation was inherently discriminatory. Reed also told his clerk that he worried about the country slipping toward krytocracy, or rule by judges. Fassett, *New Deal Justice*, 566–67.

the different effects on people. I do not agree with Hugo Black that the states are *more* limited than Congress.[48]

We need an effective way to deal with this, and we should set all of these cases down for reargument on specific issues. This is *not* a delaying tactic—this is not an *unjustifiable* delay. It is important *when* we decide. Brandeis said that the most important thing of this Court is what we do *not* do.[49]

The District of Columbia is the nation's capital. I am prepared to vote today that segregation in the District of Columbia violates the *due process clause*. I have never had close living relation to Negroes, but I have had much to do with their problems. I was once assistant counsel to the NAACP. I also belong to the Jewish minority. I am familiar with the experiences of colored people here, especially Coleman, one of my old law clerks.[50] It is *intolerable* that this government should permit *segregation in D.C. life*. But I deprecate the use of needless *force* in changing this—it is important for the government that will be responsible to enforce it.[51] It is very important that the District of Columbia case be set down for reargument after the new administration comes in.[52] It is a gain in law administration if it comes not as a pronouncement of coercive law, but with the help of the new administration that has promised to change the law here in the District. The *due process clause* brings in special points, and I would set the case down for special consideration, for shaping decrees and for the District of Columbia to address themselves to

---

48. Black and Frankfurter engaged in a running debate about the meaning and scope of the Fifth and Fourteenth Amendments. Black interpreted the Fifth Amendment narrowly, but thought that the Fourteenth Amendment fully incorporated the Bill of Rights and created a broad grant of federal judicial and political authority to regulate state action, especially in race discrimination cases.

Frankfurter spent almost twenty years preparing an academic treatise on the passage and original intent of the Fourteenth Amendment and considered himself an expert on the topic. He was convinced that the amendment was never intended to provide a general federal authority over state governments, not even to end state-imposed segregation. Segregation might have bothered Frankfurter's conscience, but it did not shock him as *Rochin* had. Frankfurter, however, thought that the due process clause of the Fifth Amendment gave federal courts considerable authority to regulate federally mandated segregation. This made *Bolling v. Sharpe* an easy case for him.

On this occasion, Black accepted Frankfurter's argument in *Bolling v. Sharpe* and temporarily abandoned any pretense of following what he had always understood to be the meaning of the Fifth Amendment. Black admitted to his clerks that this was just one of those cases where legal principles had to yield to political and moral considerations.

49. Louis Brandeis's famous dictum was that what the Court did *not* do was often more important than what it did. See, for example, William O. Douglas, *We, The Judges*, 53; Alexander Bickel, *The Least Dangerous Branch*, 71.

50. William T. Coleman Jr. became the first black law clerk in Supreme Court history when Frankfurter selected him for the 1948 Term. When the selection committee at Harvard asked whether Coleman's appointment would cause Frankfurter any problems, Frankfurter responded that he did not care about his clerks' skin color any more than he cared about their religion. Urofsky, *Felix Frankfurter*, 129. Coleman went on to a distinguished career in government and as a Washington, D.C., lawyer and lobbyist. He also argued a number of cases before the Court, although in this capacity he is mentioned elsewhere in this book in a less favorable light.

51. Clark's conference notes quote Frankfurter as saying, "I deprecate any activities by force of law *that might be used.*"

52. The incoming Eisenhower administration would be responsible for enforcing any decree.

the decree. Set down very specific questions, such as the manner in which it would be carried out and so forth. We should hold all of the cases. The social gains of having them accomplished with executive sanction would be enormous.

As to the states, these are equity suits. They involve imagination in shaping decrees. I would ask counsel on reargument to address themselves to the problems of enforcement. I favor reargument in the state as well as the District cases. We can't treat these cases as sociological questions.

Few things are more dangerous than the familiar. How does Black know what the framers of the Civil War Amendments meant? I have read all of its history, and I can't say that it meant to abolish segregation. You cannot say from the legislative history that they meant to abolish segregation; there are many views. You cannot fairly say, "*Yes,* these fellows meant to abolish segregation," or vice versa. The proponents used evasive words so as not to stir the issue. I don't see anything in the United States Code or in the equal protection clause on the basis on which such a decision could be made. That leads me to say that must look only on *physical things.* It is arbitrary to say that "equal rights" means physical things. If Kansas were here alone, I would just reverse on the findings of the trial court and say that they applied the wrong legal principle. I would ask counsel that, assuming this wording of law, can they say that this Court has long misread the Constitution? What justifies us in saying that what *was* equal in 1868 is not equal *now*? Equal protection does not mean what *was* equal, but what *is* equal. I would ask counsel to demonstrate what it is that justifies their saying that what has gone on before is all wrong.

I conclude nothing going to the merits. I can't say that it is unconstitutional to treat a Negro differently than a white, but I would put all of these cases down for reargument. The further maturing process would be highly desirable. The cases should be set down for reargument, say, *1st March.*[53]

---

53. The conventional view of Frankfurter's role in *Brown* is that Vinson abdicated his leadership role in the desegregation cases, and Frankfurter stepped into the breach to become the de facto leader of the Court until Earl Warren arrived to forge a final consensus. A crucial part of this story is that Frankfurter maneuvered brilliantly at this conference to have the case postponed in the hope that a solid majority to strike down segregation would have time to coalesce. How Frankfurter anticipated Vinson's death is not clear. See, for example, Bernard Schwartz, *Super Chief,* 72–79; Kluger, *Simple Justice,* 596–602, 614; Kurland, "Earl Warren, the 'Warren Court,' and the Warren Myths."

This heroic representation of Frankfurter is at best exaggerated. As Frankfurter's conference remarks indicate, he was openly skeptical about the Court overruling *Plessy* and ending segregation in state schools by judicial decree. Frankfurter's defenders have been forced to argue that he did not really mean what he said at conference, while condemning Fred Vinson, Robert Jackson, and Tom Clark for expressing similar ideas. See, for example, Schwartz, *A History of the Supreme Court,* 288. Frankfurter clearly favored stalling, but he was hardly alone. Avoiding final decisions in segregation cases was a longstanding Court tradition, and it was neither a difficult proposition nor a brilliant stratagem to convince the other Justices to postpone their decision (the vote was unanimous).

That Frankfurter was not the hero of *Brown* is hardly surprising, given his consistent advocacy of judicial restraint in dealing with social and political problems. Although Frankfurter personally opposed mandatory segregation, at this conference he sided with the group of five Justices (along with Vinson, Reed, Jackson, and Clark) who hesitated to use judicial power to end racial segregation in state schools. Even after Earl Warren became Chief Justice, Frankfurter did not abandon his view that, as a matter of constitutional history, *Plessy* had been correctly decided. Frankfurter's ambivalence about judicial involvement in

DOUGLAS: Segregation is a very simple constitutional question for me. No classification on the basis of race can be made. I can't avoid the same conclusion that Hugo has reached in the state cases, that *states* can't classify by color for education. The Fourteenth Amendment prohibits racial classifications, and so does the due process clause of the Fifth Amendment. Segregation is unconstitutional, whether by the states or Congress. A Negro can't be put by the state in one room because he's black and another student put in the other room because he's white. The answer is simple, though the application of it may present great difficulties. Can't play the factor of time.[54] It will take a long time to work it out. I would not mind setting down the D.C. case for reargument in March, but not the others. Not rush pronouncements.

JACKSON: If we are going to take turns, it is better *not to take a vote now.* I would start with these cases as a lawyer would. I find nothing in the *text* that says this is *unconstitutional.* Nothing in the opinions of the courts say that it is unconstitutional. Nothing in the history of the Fourteenth Amendment says that it is unconstitutional. There is nothing in the acts of Congress either way. On the basis of precedents, I would have to say that it *is* constitutional. Marshall's brief starts and ends with sociology, not legal issues. I don't know *the effect* of *segregation, or the reason* for it. You can't *cure* this situation by putting children together.

I was never really conscious of racial problems until I came to the District of Columbia. We had segregation in Jamestown, New York in the 1860s and 1890s. White lawyers (Catholics and Jews) would not let Negroes use books in the library (ordered library out of the courthouse).

I won't be a party to immediate unconstitutionality—to say that it is unconstitutional to practice segregation tomorrow. It will be bad for the Negroes to be put into white schools. But segregation is nearing an end. (If two or three deaths on the Court—this will come—it is no way out.) We should perhaps give them time to get rid of it, and I would go along on that basis. I would not object to such a holding with a reasonable time element. These are equitable remedies that can be shaped to the needs. If we can work it out so we can say segregation "bad"—under approval of the Constitution and with the support of Congress—*and that it must* be done in a certain period. I would suggest that

---

race issues comes into sharper focus when his conference comments here are read in conjunction with his remarks in other race cases, such as *Sweatt, McLaurin, Naim,* and *NAACP v. Button.*

After *Brown* was decided, Frankfurter led a personal army of ex-clerks and academic protégés to rebuild his reputation as the intellectual leader of the Court and the strategic mastermind behind the desegregation cases. As the conference notes reveal, however, Frankfurter was more of a camp follower than a leader in these cases. For a critique of the Frankfurter myth, see Tushnet and Lezin, "What Really Happened in *Brown v. Board of Education?*" 1867–85.

54. This sentence is from Jackson's notes, and it varies significantly from what other Justices, including Douglas himself, report Douglas as having said in conference. All of the other Justices' notes indicate that Douglas said that time *was* a relevant factor—that the constitutional question was simple, but putting the principle into practice would be complicated. It is likely that Jackson misunderstood Douglas, although it is possible that Douglas tried to have it both ways and said something to the effect that the Court should not delay in ordering the public schools to desegregate (the Court "can't play the factor of time") even though putting the decision into effect would likely take some time ("It will take a long time to work it out").

the District of Columbia case can be reargued, and that the Senate and House Judiciary Committees be asked to file briefs and argue. If stirred up to a point, they may abolish it.

BURTON: They have the right to come to us. We have the Constitution. I agree that this should be done in as easy a way as possible. *Sipuel* and *Sweatt* crossed the threshold of these cases, and we must be guided by them. We must not depart from these cases. Education is more than buildings and faculties. It is a habit of mind. With the Fourteenth Amendment, states do not have the choice—segregation violates equal protection. The total effect is that separate education is not sufficient for today's problems. It is not reasonable to educate people separately for a joint life. [DOUGLAS: He refers to his policies as mayor of Cleveland in putting colored nurses in white hospitals, coloreds having respect, and so forth.] The Fifth Amendment also bars segregation. But we can use time— I would give plenty of time in this decree. I would go the full length to upset segregation. I reverse. I will support reargument in the District of Columbia case.

CLARK: I favor reargument in the D.C. case. The result must be the same in all of these cases. I will probably affirm in Delaware. In Texas, the problem is as acute as anywhere. The Mexican problem is more serious. Far more retarded.[55] A Mexican boy of fifteen is in a class with a Negro girl of twelve. Some Negro girls get in trouble. If we delay action (is Bob's idea) it will help. Our opinion should give the lower courts the opportunity to withhold relief in light of troubles. I would be inclined to go along with that. Otherwise, I would say that we have led states on to believe that separate but equal is O.K., and we should let them work it out.[56]

MINTON: The hour is late. We are confronted with a body of law that lays down separate and equal. We have chipped and chiseled it away with *Sweatt* and *McLaurin*. Classification by race does not add up. It is *not reasonable. It is invidious* and it can't be maintained. Congress, in the District of Columbia, has authorized segregation—but it's not legal. Confrontation with the states is not final. There will be trouble, but this race grew up in trouble. The Negro is oppressed and has been in bondage for years after slavery was abolished. *Segregation is per se unconstitutional. I am ready to vote now.*

Result: The Justices unanimously ordered all five cases to be reargued, asking the parties to focus on two specific historical questions: the meaning and intent of the Fourteenth Amendment, and whether the courts had the authority to end segregation under the Fourteenth Amendment or the courts' equitable powers.[57]

Then Chief Justice Fred Vinson died of a heart attack on September 8, and President Eisenhower appointed Earl Warren to take his place. A recess appointment, Warren had not yet been confirmed by the Senate when the case came back before the Supreme Court during the 1953 Term. Reargument

---

55. Clark presumably was referring to the slow pace of integration in Texas and elsewhere, although from the context this is not entirely clear.

56. Burton's conference notes add a final, cryptic sentence: "Can see anything in Constitution that we can segregate." It is likely that Clark actually said that he could *not* see anything in the Constitution that justified segregation.

57. The most perceptive Court-watchers were not fooled and saw the delaying tactics for what they were. See, for example, Pritchett, *Civil Liberties and the Vinson Court*, 137–38.

took three days. While the oral arguments were considered high drama at the time, Philip Elman from the solicitor general's office was probably right when he said that "nothing that the lawyers said made a difference. Thurgood Marshall could have stood up there and recited 'Mary Had A Little Lamb' and the result would have been exactly the same."[58]

Conference of December 12, 1953
(Burton) (Douglas)

WARREN:[59] The previous plan was to discuss these cases informally in view of their importance, and that no vote be taken at this time. I favor that idea of delay—there is great value in unanimity and uniformity, even if we have some differences.

We are now down to the point of deciding the issues. Ben Franklin at the constitutional convention. I do not yet know what we should do. I am for pooling all of the humble wisdom of the Court and having, perhaps, many discussions. We should decide it this Term. I have read as much as time allows, and I was much interested in the oral arguments. The case was well argued, and the federal government was very frank in its brief and orally. I can't escape the feeling that the Court has finally arrived at the place where we *must* determine whether segregation is allowable in public schools.

The thing that concerns me is whether we are called upon to overrule our older cases and lines of reasoning. The more I read and hear and think, the more I come to conclude that the basis of the principle of segregation and separate but equal rests upon the basic premise that the Negro race is inferior. That is the only way to sustain *Plessy*—I don't see how it can be sustained on any other theory. If we are to sustain segregation, we must do it on that basis. If oral argument proved anything, the arguments of Negro counsel proved that they are not inferior.

I don't see how we can continue in this day and age to set one group apart from the rest and say that they are not entitled to *exactly the same* treatment as all others. To do so is contrary to Thirteenth, Fourteenth, and Fifteenth Amendments. Those amendments were intended to make those who were once slaves equal with all others. That view will perhaps cause trouble, but personally I can't see how today we can justify segregation based solely on race and so forth.

I recognize that the time element is important in the Deep South. We must act, but we should do it in a tolerant way. It would be unfortunate if we had to take precipitous action that could inflame the issue more than necessary. The conditions in the extreme South should be carefully considered by the Court. Kansas and Delaware are not much different from California—500,000 Negroes, 100,000 Japs, 100,000 Chinese. But not so in the Deep South. It will take all the wisdom of the Court to do this with a minimum of commotion and strife. How we do it is important. At present, my instincts and tentative

---

58. Elman and Norman, "The Solicitor General's Office."

59. Earl Warren was a recess appointment. After some delay caused by Senator William Langer of North Dakota (who was concerned about the tendency of presidents to overlook North Dakotans when it came to federal judicial appointments), the Senate confirmed Warren without dissent on March 1, 1954, five months after he first took his seat on the Court.

feelings would lead me to say that in these cases we should abolish, in a tolerant way, the practice of segregation in public schools.[60]

BLACK: Out.[61]

REED: I can understand Warren's attitudes. I am trying to approach this question without past prejudices. I want to work this out in the best way. I am not sure whether I will sit in the South Carolina or Virginia cases, but I may. If writing on clean slate, I probably would say that they should have segregation. It is an unfortunate thing. Each of us *can* accept it personally, but this is not the problem. I also recognize that this is a dynamic Constitution, and what was current in *Plessy* might not be current now.

The power of the states is an issue. I would leave states with complete power in the *Briggs* case, etc. Some states have put it into law and some have abolished it in their own way.[62] But *here*, it is an issue of the Fourteenth Amendment. Equal protection has not been satisfactory. The result has been less facilities, etc. for Negroes. Equal opportunity has not been enforced. I can't say that there has been a denial of equal protection as it looks, although in fact it has not been equal. (District of Columbia—not under that.)

---

60. While the *Brown* decision was pending, President Eisenhower invited Earl Warren to a White House dinner. The president seated the Chief Justice next to John W. Davis, who led the southern legal team defending segregation. Eisenhower repeatedly referred to Davis as "a great man" and took Warren aside to tell him privately that southerners were not bad people. "All they are concerned about," Eisenhower reportedly said, "is to see that their sweet little girls are not required to sit in school alongside some big, black bucks." Bernard Schwartz and Stephan Lesher, *Inside the Warren Court*, 87. In his memoirs, Warren quoted Eisenhower as saying, "These are not bad people. All they are concerned about is to see that their sweet little girls are not required to sit in school alongside some big overgrown Negroes." Warren, *Memoirs*, 291.

Apart from his involvement in the segregationist cause, Davis had a long and often distinguished career in New York and Washington. He served in Congress and as solicitor general, and he later became one of the country's most famous private attorneys, arguing 140 cases before the U.S. Supreme Court. Not all of his cases were for reactionary causes; Davis served as defense counsel for Robert J. Oppenheimer during the scientist's loyalty hearings before the Atomic Energy Commission.

61. Black was in Alabama visiting his sister-in-law, who was seriously ill. He sent word to the conference that his vote was to end segregation. This was the last public trip Black made home for more than a decade after *Brown* was decided. Local reaction to the case was so hostile that it became impossible for Black to make official visits. Black paid the highest price on the Court for his votes to end segregation. He lost most of his Alabama friends, his son was driven out of his Montgomery law practice and had to leave the state, and Black's alma mater, the University of Alabama, refused to send him an invitation to attend his fiftieth law school class reunion. Dunne, *Hugo Black and the Judicial Revolution*, 384.

62. The year before the case was filed, Clarendon County claimed to have spent $180 per white student and $43 for each black student. Carl Rowan calculated that, including all expenses, Clarendon County spent $1,432 per white student and $350 per black student annually. For the most part, white schools were brick-and-mortar buildings, while black schools were decrepit wood and tarpaper structures. In one Clarendon County school district, the student/teacher ratio was 23:1 in the white schools and 67:1 in the black schools. To head off an anticipated finding by the federal district court that South Carolina's white and black schools were grossly unequal, Governor (and former Supreme Court Justice) James F. Byrnes implemented the state's first sales tax to support nearly $80 million in state bonds, which were earmarked to bring funding for black schools closer into line with state expenditures for white schools. Tushnet, *Making Civil Rights Law*, 158; Rowan, *Dream Makers, Dream Breakers*, 13.

Children may be forced to separate without a violation of the equal protection clause. It is not a denial of liberty to say that people must separate to go to school.

Segregation is not done on a theory of racial inferiority, but on racial differences. It protects people against the mixing of races. The argument was not made here that the Negro is an inferior race. Of course there is no "inferior race," although they may be handicapped by a lack of opportunity. But on equal protection, they demonstrably have equal protection. It is a police power that has been exercised. Its purpose has been to maintain a policy status. Growth is toward the ending of segregation. [BURTON: Reed refers to an editorial in the *Atlanta Journal Constitution.*]

If segregation is bad, it is because of a denial of due process. You have to go to due process. There is not much difference. It is a question of reasonable classification. That brings forth the historical question. There has been a contemporary interpretation of the problem since the Fourteenth Amendment. Look at the administrative construction at the time of the adoption of the Fourteenth Amendment, and at the contemporaneous approval of segregation. People were familiar with it at first hand. The practice has been constantly the other way, and has long sanctioned segregation. The existence of early school segregation statutes was contemporaneous with the Fourteenth Amendment. Congress never could pass the integrated schools laws. Integration was never written in, and separated schools existed—and equal services. *Long Gum* [*sic*] said that it was valid to have separate schooling.[63] Congress has had the power to end segregation in the District of Columbia. The President has had the power to end segregation in the armed forces. Those efforts failed, so they come to the courts and ask this Court to say it was or has become *un*constitutional. They left aside the intermediate aspects, and so wait to see what this Court does. This is not a political question, but we should not move to change the law. If there is to be a change, Congress should do it.

FRANKFURTER: One has to curb one's tongue when dealing with such problems. I would put no time limit on when the decision should come down. The awful thing about the *Insular Cases* was not too many opinions (two hundred pages), it is that they looked in too many directions.[64] This is among my chief concerns. These cases raise this question because the "due process" clause puts on this Court a burden that no court should have. Other nations have *not* put a due process clause into their constitutions, including Aus-

---

63. *Gong Lum v. Rice*, 275 U.S. 78 (1927).

64. *The Insular Cases* were a group of cases argued together, including *Dooley v. United States*, 183 U.S. 151 (1901); *Downes v. Bidwell*, 182 U.S. 244 (1901); *Armstrong v. United States*, 182 U.S. 243 (1901); *Dooley v. United States*, 182 U.S. 222 (1901); and *De Lima v. Bidwell*, 182 U.S. 1 (1901). *Downes* alone contained seven opinions and ran a total of 147 pages. In a 1953 article, Frankfurter quoted "that great philosopher, Mr. Dooley," who said that what he was able to gather from these cases was that "the Supreme Court decided that the Constitution follows the flag on Mondays, Wednesdays, and Fridays." Mr. Dooley also said, "no matther whether th' Constitution follows th' flag or not, th' Supreme Coort follows th' iliction returns." The estimable Mr. Dooley was a fictional character created by Finley P. Dunne, a humorist and political commentator. Frankfurter, "Chief Justices I Have Known"; Dunne, *Mr. Dooley's Opinions*, 26.

tria, Ireland, or India. We cannot escape the statesmanship issue, but this is not our job. We are kind of a trustee "of due process."[65]

As a pure matter of history, in 1867 the Fourteenth Amendment *did not* have as its purpose to abolish segregation. The due process and equal protection clauses certainly did not abolish segregation when the Fourteenth Amendment was adopted. The most that the history shows is that the matter was inconclusive. A host of legislation passed by Congress presupposes that segregation is valid. A host of legislation and history in Congress and in this Court indicates that *Plessy* is right.[66]

What did the leaders intend? You can't imprint all views on it. District of Columbia legislation and also *federal legislation* was based on the *assumption* of segregated schools, as in the national school lunch acts, and so forth, as late as 1950.

We must not be self-righteous and "Gold Almighty" when writing this. (Goldberg says that the question "is settled"—we should not say that.)[67]

History speaks clearly, and the question arises—does history determine this question? In 1922, the Court said that free speech was not protected by the Fourteenth Amendment, and last Term we said the opposite. Holmes said that the Fourteenth Amendment did not make all states alike. Joseph McKenna said well, "time works changes." Principles must be capable of another application than this version, and that gives it best. Psychological changes, and that is what this is about.

---

65. If Frankfurter thought that the due process clause was a burden, it was one that he enjoyed. The due process clause was Frankfurter's preferred instrument of judicial authority when government decisions "shocked the universal sense of justice" and grossly violated Frankfurter's sense of fair play. The due process clause fit Frankfurter's sense of the judicial role, because in his view it required judges to exercise a subjective but dispassionate judgment in evaluating claims. See, for example, *Rochin v California*, 342 U.S. 165 (1952). Frankfurter also thought that the due process clause helped to limit the ability of activist judges to insert themselves into matters best left to the legislative and executive branches. Frankfurter, however, was among those who advised India not to include a due process clause in their new constitution following that country's independence from Great Britain in 1947.

66. This was an extraordinary thing for Frankfurter to say at this point in the Court's deliberations. Some scholars doubt that Frankfurter said what Douglas recorded. Tushnet, *Making Civil Rights Law*, 211. Tushnet, however, offers no evidence that Douglas was mistaken. Douglas's conference notes are generally not prone to exaggeration—even regarding Frankfurter. This was a historical argument that Frankfurter had long believed, so it is hardly inconceivable that he would have clung to his views even at this late date. Burton's notes are more ambiguous but do not contradict Douglas.

67. Arthur J. Goldberg and Thomas E. Harris wrote an amicus brief on behalf of the Congress of Industrial Organizations. Goldberg eventually succeeded Frankfurter on the Court in 1962. Frankfurter's reaction in this case provoked an ironic echo six years later. According to Douglas, during a conference discussion in *United States v. Thomas* (1960), Frankfurter scolded Douglas for having pushed the Court to decide the segregation issue "prematurely." Frankfurter claimed that Douglas had advocated deciding the issue as early as 1946 and told the conference that had the issue of desegregation been brought to a vote then, Frankfurter "would have voted that segregation in the schools was constitutional, because 'public opinion had not then crystallized against it.'" Frankfurter allegedly claimed that the Eisenhower Court had heralded a change in public opinion on the subject that enabled him to vote against segregation. William Brennan's response was, "God Almighty!" Urofsky, *The Douglas Letters*, 169.

DOUGLAS: On the four state cases, I would join Earl Warren's conclusion and his reasons. History does shed a mixed light on it.[68] In *this* day and age, race and color can't *now* be salient. Don't try to anticipate too much. We should recognize that adjustments will have to arise. The Court this Term is deciding its principles. It is a simple problem. Race and color cannot be a constitutional standard for segregating the schools. In the District of Columbia case there is a different problem (and Hugo Black is probably of the same view.) That complaint is for a declaratory judgment on the basis that segregation in the District of Columbia is *mandatory*. But I have doubts that it is *mandatory*. I would send the District of Columbia case back to the court of appeals to determine whether the statutory system in the District of Columbia is mandatory or permissive. I would let them have further time on that.

JACKSON: Cardozo said that much of constitutional interpretation is partly statutory construction and partly politics. This is a political question. To me personally, this is not a problem. But it is difficult to make this other than a political decision. Lincoln was not quoted in the NAACP's argument—he was extremely limited in his objectives. It is pure hypocrisy to say that there was strong feeling on this issue at that time. There is not much legislative history. We don't have custom or precedents against segregation in education. Education at the time of the Fourteenth Amendment was not an issue. The precedents and custom are for segregation. I don't know how to justify the abolition of segregation as a judicial act.

If we have to decide this question, then representative government has failed. We would have to give advice to the lower courts. Some would put all boards of education in jail, and others would not give Negroes any relief.

The problem is to make a judicial basis for a congenial political conclusion. I don't think it wise to just throw the abolition of segregation into the hopper, and leave the rest to another fight.[69] We must go way beyond what the government has wanted. The resistance will be immeasurably increased by a flat and immediate doctrine. As a political decision, I can go along with it—but with a protest that it is politics.

BURTON: We have no choice in this matter but to act. I hope that we act this Term. We can work it out on a judicial basis. The problem is a judicial one. On the four state cases, I go on equal protection. Prior to the Fourteenth Amendment, states could do what they liked. Now they cannot. The Fourteenth Amendment problems have been a gradual development. There is a trend away from separation of the races in restaurants, the armed

---

68. Over the summer of 1953, Frankfurter had one of his clerks, Alexander Bickel, prepare a memorandum on the legislative history of the Fourteenth Amendment. Four days before oral argument, Frankfurter circulated Bickel's sixty-three–page report. In Bickel's (and Frankfurter's) judgment, the historical record was inconclusive and it was impossible to say whether Congress had intended to outlaw segregation or sanction it. At Frankfurter's urging, Bickel later rewrote his memorandum and published it. Bickel, "The Original Understanding and the Segregation Decision."

69. Several of the Justices, led by Douglas, leaned toward holding that segregation in public schools was unconstitutional but postponing any decision as to a remedy. Jackson, however, was adamant that the Court must also issue a decree and not leave the job half-done. Hutchinson, "Unanimity and Desegregation," 40–41.

forces, and so forth. The Fourteenth Amendment is nationwide, and calls for uniform practices. You can't draw a line between types of schools—the same principle that is applicable to graduate school is equally applicable to primary school. At the time of the Fourteenth Amendment life was separate; now it is inadequate preparation for life today.

As to the District of Columbia, we must rest on due process. And due process is equal protection, for that is what the rest of the country requires. On the congressional statutes, the District of Columbia never made segregation mandatory, but only permissive. I would go a long way to agree to put off enforcement for awhile, and to give the district courts discretion.

CLARK: I am closer to this than anyone except for Hugo. I have lived with it. We can't handle this by a brief policy statement. There is a danger of violence if this is not well handled. In some counties, it runs up to 60 percent colored in Mississippi, and Alabama is much the same. They can get their temper from Byrnes. He made a strong statement that he would just abolish the public schools.[70] Violence will follow in the South. This is a very serious problem. If segregation is unconstitutional, it must be handled very carefully, or we will cause more harm than good. I think that colored students in Texas get as good an education as the whites. Much progress has been made in voting there, in school boards, and so forth.

On relief, various conditions will require different handling. The opinion must indicate that clearly. There must be no fiat, or look like a fiat that has to be done promptly. It should not only have something in it, but it should be done in such a way that will permit different handling in different places.

On the merits, I was surprised at the legislative history. I had always thought it obvious that one of the purposes of Fourteenth Amendment was to abolish segregation. But the history shows differently, and we can't use that. It is also almost unanswerable that the same Congress and the same legislators that passed the Fourteenth Amendment also recognized separate schools. I can't well say that Congress has ignored it. They did not do it because southern congressmen could not do anything in the District of Columbia that would integrate the District of Columbia. People couldn't vote to integrate here and then return home to the South. There was no disclosure of the vote.

JACKSON: There is no great loyalty to *public* schools in the South. There will be trouble when you send white children to colored schools and locations.

MINTON: Segregation is on its way out in Indiana. You can have a choice of schools. We did have segregated schools, but not now. The population now is 10 percent Negroes.

---

70. South Carolina governor James F. Byrnes served on the Supreme Court for less than a year, 1941–42. After he resigned, he became a vocal critic of the Court and a leader of southern segregationist movement. He vowed repeatedly to close down South Carolina's public school system if the Court overturned the separate but equal doctrine. It was Byrnes who hired John W. Davis to lead the southern legal team in *Brown*. In 1956, Governor Byrnes wrote an article for *U.S. News and World Report*, claiming that in its indulgent treatment of blacks and Communists, the Warren Court gave great comfort to "Communists and their fellow travelers." He urged Congress to restrict the Court's appellate jurisdiction "before it is too late." Byrnes, "The Supreme Court Must Be Curbed," *U.S. News and World Report* (May 18, 1956).

CLARK: In Texas, several counties are predominantly Mexican. There is trouble with Mexicans and whites, and in the last few years they have been segregated in San Antonio and along the border. I don't like the system of segregation and will vote to abolish it, as I said before, even though we can't rely on the legislative history. But the remedy must be carefully worked out, and some variations permitted to fit the trial courts.

MINTON: I don't discount the seriousness of this decision. There may be trouble in the offing, but I doubt it. Look at developments in the army with respect to segregation.[71] The only justification for segregation is the inferiority of the Negro. So many things have broken down these barriers. Slavery went out with the Civil War. Then came the Fourteenth Amendment, which was intended to wipe out the badges of slavery and inferiority. The *Slaughterhouse* and *Strauder* cases say so—they establish a bundle of *equal* rights. The Fourteenth Amendment says *equal rights*, not *separate but equal. Separate* is a lawyer's addition to the language that came in by this Court. Our early cases indicated that these badges should be wiped out. *Plessy v. Ferguson* henceforth said *separate and equal*, and that laid down the new view. But *Henderson* and *McLaurin* greatly weakened *Plessy*. In those cases, we struck down segregation. *Plessy v. Ferguson* is a weak reed today.

In the state cases, I would go on equal protection. I can't imagine a valid distinction based on *color*. I would go further in the District of Columbia and would apply due process. You can't classify on the basis of color. It is also a freedom of choice, or liberty. On segregation today, it is a different world today than in the 1860s when they were just out of slavery. In the District of Columbia, the law amounts to a mandatory practice, whether or not it is mandatory in form. As to possible remedies, I am inclined to let the district courts have their heads in this matter, and not merely see our opinion.

Memorandum for the File
(William O. Douglas)

May 17, 1954

The above cases which were decided today were twice argued—once in December 1952 and once in December 1953. At the original conference in December 1952 it was decided that there should be no recorded vote in the cases because of the likelihood that there might be some leaks.

In the original conference there were only four who voted that segregation in the public schools was unconstitutional. Those four were Black, Burton, Minton and myself. Vinson was of the opinion that the *Plessy* case was right and that segregation was constitutional. Reed followed the view of Vinson and Clark was inclined that way. In the 1952 conference, Frankfurter and Jackson viewed the problem with great alarm and thought that the Court should not decide the question if it was possible to avoid it. Both of them expressed the view that segregation in the public schools was probably constitutional. Frankfurter drew a distinction between segregation in the public schools in the states. He thought that segregation in the public schools of the District of Columbia violated due

---

71. President Truman ordered the American armed forces to desegregate in 1948.

process, but he thought that history was against the claim of unconstitutionality as applied to the public schools of the States.

So as a result of the informal vote at the 1952 conference, it seemed that if the case were to be then decided the vote would be five to four in favor of the constitutionality of segregation in the public schools in the States, with Frankfurter indicating he would join the four of us when it came to the District of Columbia case.

The matter dragged on during the 1952 Term until as a result of further discussions it was decided to put the case down for reargument. But it is apparent that if the cases had been decided during the 1952 Term there would probably have been many opinions and a wide divergence of views and a result that would have sustained, so far as the states were concerned, segregation of students.

By the time the cases were reached for reargument, Vinson had died and Warren had taken his place. At the conference following that argument in December 1953 Black was absent but he sent in his vote indicating that he thought that segregation in the public schools was unconstitutional. His vote, together with Burton's, Minton's and my own made four. Chief Justice Warren was very clearly of the view that segregation in public schools was unconstitutional. That made a bare majority for the reversal of the judgments below. Reed voted the other way. He thought that segregation was constitutional. Clark was inclined that way although doubtful. So was Frankfurter and so was Jackson. The latter two expressed the hope that the Court would not have to decide these cases but somehow avoid these decisions.

It was once more decided to treat the matter informally, not to take a vote and to have the Chief Justice prepare a memorandum.

The matter was brought back to conference for further discussion. During the Term I mentioned it to the Chief Justice and I think Harold Burton did also and each time he said he was working on the matter. He circulated proposed opinions in the two sets of cases on May 7, bringing them around to our offices by hand. These were in typewritten form. After they were read and suggestions made, the opinions were typed up and they went through revision between May 7 and May 15, the date of our conference. Everyone thought that at least Justice Reed was going to write in dissent but he finally agreed to leave his doubts unsaid and to go along. Frankfurter, Jackson (who was in the hospital recovering from a mild heart attack), and Clark agreed to do the same. It was then decided to get the cases down either May 17 or May 24. Someone suggested that they be delayed until May 24 because there were still some primaries in the South that the decision might adversely affect. But at the end of the conference on Saturday, May 15 it was decided, if possible, to get them down on May 17 to prevent any leaks or advance information or tip-offs or rumors about the opinion.

It was decided by a few of us (Black, Burton, and myself) who worked closely with Chief Justice Warren on the matter that these opinions should be short and concise and easily understood by everyone in the country, that they should be written for laymen and not for lawyers, that they should be brief, succinct and to the point.

Result: Led by Earl Warren, the Justices continued to discuss the case informally among themselves, without voting. They talked about the case together in chambers, at meals, and during conferences on other cases.[72] *A formal vote was finally taken in February or March, with all the Justices agreeing that the doctrine of separate but equal had no place in public schools.*[73]

On May 17, 1954, a unanimous Court ruled that Plessy v. Ferguson *had no place in public education. The Chief Justice, writing for the Court, rejected the doctrine of separate but equal and held that state action to segregate public schools on the basis of race was inherently unconstitutional. While the case was limited in scope to the public schools, it tolled the death of Jim Crow in public facilities, accommodations, and transportation.*[74]

The Court ordered a third round of arguments to discuss the nature and speed of judicial remedies. This seemed routine, but it marked the beginning of the Court's long, arduous, and often unsuccessful attempt to enforce Brown.

Brown v. Board of Education (Brown II), 349 U.S. 294 (1955)
(Burton) (Douglas) (Frankfurter) (Warren)

Because of the anticipated complexities in implementing Brown, *the Court invited all parties to reargue three key issues. First, the original* Brown *decision had not specifically ordered anyone to do anything. The Court still had to decide whether to issue detailed decrees, to appoint a special master to take additional evidence and make recommendations, or to remand the cases to local district courts with instructions to write their own decrees at the local level.*

The second issue concerned the pace of desegregation. Thurgood Marshall argued for immediate desegregation,[75] *while southern governments sought an open decree with no deadline at all.*[76] *On behalf*

---

72. One of Stanley Reed's clerks, George Mickum, claimed to have witnessed Earl Warren pressuring Reed to secure a unanimous vote. According to Mickum, Warren cornered Reed and told him, "Stan, you're all by yourself in this now. . . . You've got to decide whether it's really the best thing for the country." Mickum reported that Warren was "quite low key and very sensitive" but was "quite firm on the Court's need for unanimity." Kluger, *Simple Justice,* 698.

73. Warren, *Memoirs,* 285.

74. This piecemeal dismantling of *Plessy* led to a long transitional period in many southern states where some public activities remained segregated while others integrated fairly rapidly. Buses and sit-down restaurants remained segregated for many years, while elevators and stand-up snack bars quickly became integrated. Southern writer Henry Golden used these incongruencies to develop a satiric "vertical integration plan" for southern schools. Looking at the list of integrated and segregated activities in the late 1950's, Golden saw a pattern: where people sat down the facilities tended to be segregated, but where people had to stand up accommodations were often integrated. The obvious answer to integrate southern education, he concluded, was to remove all of the desks and chairs from the schools and make the students stand up. Schwartz and Lesher, *Inside the Warren Court,* 221–22 (1983).

75. The NAACP did not expect the Court to take at face value its request for an "immediate" or "forthwith" decree. Marshall was a realist; he expected that even a "forthwith" decree would take several years to implement. Tushnet, *Making Civil Rights Law,* 218.

76. In Kansas, Delaware, and the District of Columbia, desegregation efforts were already under way by the time the cases were reargued. Compliance was less certain in the Deep South, as oral arguments clearly indicated. Some of the arguments presented to the Court had nothing to do with education policy and were crudely racist. Lawyers representing southern states used miscegenation, racial mongrelization, sexual promiscuity, and sexually transmitted diseases as stalking horses to attack school desegregation. Archibald Robertson, representing the state of Virginia, emphasized what he called "health and morals" issues. Robertson noted that tuberculosis rates among blacks were double that among whites and that illegitimacy rates were one in fifty white births, but one in five black births. Although blacks made up only

of the federal government, Solicitor General Simon Sobeloff asked that primary responsibility for implementing Brown be left to the district courts and that a ninety-day grace period be included to allow local school boards to draft individualized desegregation plans. Sobeloff also requested that a special master be appointed to oversee the process of desegregation.

The third question was to determine the scope of relief, especially whether these cases would be limited to the specific individuals named in the lawsuits or whether the named plaintiffs represented a class that potentially included millions of schoolchildren in racially segregated districts throughout the country.

The Justices wanted to postpone the case until after what Warren called the "sound and fury" of the 1954 election abated. Robert Jackson's unexpected death on October 8, 1954, made the decision easy to justify publicly. By the beginning of the next term, John Marshall Harlan had replaced Jackson on the Court.

Over the summer of 1954, the Justices pooled six law clerks from different chambers to prepare a memorandum on how to frame a remedy to desegregate southern schools.[77] Most of the clerks favored issuing a simple decree and remanding the cases to the local district courts. This would allow local judges to decide most of the important issues themselves (such as whether to appoint special masters) according to local circumstances. The clerks recommended providing guidelines to help local judges determine whether school districts were making good faith efforts to desegregate, to help them distinguish real efforts from subterfuge, and to help insulate them from public criticism for making what inevitably would be difficult and unpopular decisions.

The clerks also addressed the issue of how quickly southern schools should be desegregated. Only one of the six clerks favored requiring immediate compliance. One wanted to allow local courts to set their own timetables, while another endorsed a twelve-year time frame. The remaining three clerks favored any reasonable time limit, as long as there were good faith efforts to comply. All agreed, however, that any appearance of indecisiveness would only give extremists "more time to operate" and that "the mere passage of time without any guidance and requirements by the courts produces rather than reduces friction."[78]

Conference of April 16, 1955

WARREN: I have not formed a fixed or definite opinion at this time, and we might want to talk this over as we did in the main cases. I think that there are some things that we should not do. We should *not*:

---

22 percent of Virginia's population, he noted, they accounted for "78 percent of all cases of syphilis and 83 percent of all cases of gonorrhea. . . . Of course the incidence of disease and illegitimacy is just a drop in the bucket compared to the promiscuity." These arguments had little to do with public education and seemed intended to shock the Justices. Virginia attorney general J. Lindsay Arnold followed with a long discussion of problems caused by allowing blacks and whites to use the same public drinking fountains and toilets. Arnold also repeated Jimmy Byrne's threat that southern states would simply close down their public schools if ordered to desegregate. Urofsky, *Felix Frankfurter*, 140; Rowan, *Dream Makers, Dream Breakers*, 229–32.

77. On November 17, 1954, the clerks produced their first memorandum, the *Segregation Research Report*, which focused largely on the reaction to *Brown I* in southern and border states. In April 1955, the same group presented to the Chief Justice the memorandum discussed here, entitled *Law Clerks' Recommendations for Segregation Decree*. Hutchinson, "Unanimity and Desegregation," 52–53.

78. Berry, *Stability, Security, and Continuity*, 159–60; Kluger, *Simple Justice*, 737–38.

a. follow the government's suggestion and appoint a master.[79]

b. indicate to the district courts that they should appoint a master. But of course each district court has that power and *could* appoint a master.

c. fix a date for completion of the program of desegregation, or suggest to the lower courts that they fix such a date. That should be left to the district courts to do what they think best.

d. require the district courts to call for a plan for the school districts. The district courts might well do so—but *we* should not require it.

e. make any procedural requirement for the lower courts—this is an equity proceeding.[80]

What appeals to me: Should we give guidance to the lower courts in an opinion or in a formal decree? I think that we are better off writing an opinion which would set forth the factors and conditions which the lower courts should take into consideration, rather than issuing a formal decree. It is better done this way, and it would circumscribe the district courts as such. The lower courts would get more comfort that way than with a formal decree. I would not make the decree a mere bare-bones decree.[81] We should say something that will help the district courts. We ought to give them guidance—it would make it much easier. It would be rather cruel to shift these back and let them flounder. I would put into our opinion the principles and limits, and then decree a base line. Our decree will be to act in accordance with that opinion and brief. Here are some ground rules for what the opinion *should* say:

a. these are class actions, which involve not only the named plaintiffs but all of the students in the education districts that they sued.

b. these rights are personal rights for the named defendants and the class they represent.

c. *every judge* is entitled to take into consideration administrative problems, fiscal problems, or physical facts essential for completion of our decree. I would not say or intimate that the lower courts could take into consideration psychological or sociological attitudes. If that were allowed, it would defeat the decree.

---

79. Frankfurter initially pushed the idea of a national master, but dropped the idea in favor of allowing district court judges discretion to appoint local masters if they wished. Kluger, *Simple Justice*, 738.

80. Warren wanted to avoid having the Supreme Court become a national school board and favored leaving the procedural details to the discretion of local district courts judges.

81. In a memorandum circulated on April 14, 1955, Frankfurter outlined two alternative decrees. The first was a "bare bones" decree, permanently enjoining the exclusion of children on the basis of race in the school districts involved in the litigation. The cases would then be returned to the lower courts to execute the Court's broad mandate. This approach, Frankfurter noted, "Would maximize flexibility with. . . due regard for relevant local circumstances." The potential disadvantage was that "local conflicts would be left on the doorsteps of local judges. . . without any guidance for them."
Frankfurter's preferred alternative was to issue a relatively detailed decree containing a list of physical, financial, and administrative conditions that would trigger the courts' equitable powers, and a second list of considerations relevant to fashioning equitable decrees—what Frankfurter called "attitudes." Frankfurter favored this approach but staunchly opposed establishing any specific deadlines. Hutchinson, "Unanimity and Desegregation," 53–54.

d. the lower courts should consider whether the plans submitted represent progress, and whether there has been a real initiation of a program.[82]

We should give the district courts as much latitude as we can, and also as much support as we can.

BLACK: I have no fixed views. I am not sure that I have any definitive views worth submitting. I think that it is important to have unanimous action. If humanly possible, I will do anything to achieve a unanimous result. My tentative ideas vary from the Chief Justice's.

At present, I would write a decree and quit. The less we say, the better off we are.

Certain things may be, and probably are, true. In the South, I was brought up in an atmosphere against federal officials. They are just now beginning to feel some respect for federal officials. The root of the problem was the race question. Some counties won't have Negroes and whites in the same school this generation.[83] My law clerk does not think that Negroes and whites could go to school together in Lowndes County in his lifetime.[84] I agree that attitudes should not be mentioned in the decree, but we cannot ignore them.

Clarendon County in South Carolina is typical of much of the South. It has some resemblance to Alabama counties. They would never be a party to allowing whites and Negroes to go to school together. We have no more chance to enforce this in the Deep South than to enforce Prohibition in New York City.

I would start with the thought that nothing could injure this Court more than to issue orders that cannot be enforced. It is futile to think that in these cases we can settle the question of segregation in the South.

We need a careful statement that segregation is *unconstitutional*. I would remand the Kansas, Delaware, and District of Columbia cases for further proceedings in accordance with our prior decision of May 17.

The South Carolina and Virginia cases are decrees for setting a pattern. These cases are not going to settle the issue or control the destiny of the South. There is a great deal of stubbornness. People there are going to fight this. There will be a deliberate effort to circumvent the decree. We can't undertake to settle the problem.

It becomes desirable to write as narrowly as possible. I do not believe that an enumeration of principles would be helpful. We can't dispose of it merely by establishing principles for action. Not one federal judge in the South is in favor of this. I think I know *them all.*[85]

---

82. Frankfurter's conference notes record Warren as saying that the lower courts "must consider whether initiation of movement toward progress of desegregation."

83. During oral arguments, Attorney General Thomas Gentry of Arkansas told the Court that to desegregate Arkansas schools would require 422 separate lawsuits, one for each of the state's school districts. Tushnet, *Making Civil Rights Law,* 227.

84. Daniel J. Meador was a Birmingham, Alabama, native. He later served for nearly forty years as a distinguished law professor at the University of Virginia.

85. Black seems to imply that he had little faith in the commitment of the forty-eight district court judges and ten circuit judges who would be expected to enforce *Brown*. In retrospect, however, these judges struggled to enforce the Court's desegregation decisions, often at great personal cost. Peltason, *Fifty-Eight Lonely Men: Southern Federal Judges and School Desegregation.*

My idea may be unworkable. I am not fond of class law suits. I am not sure how many Negro students would want their names included in this litigation. Many don't want to be included. Therefore, I would treat these as *individual* cases. If the named plaintiffs are all we deal with, the administrative difficulty would not be great.

Second go: There is alternative prayer for an injunction against school boards refusing admissions. If we granted that, it would protect all students, but I am not sure that the students would want to go.

My present, tentative suggestions for a decree: First, write an opinion in decree form saying that it is unconstitutional, and that these students must be admitted. Then send it back and issue a decree that these seven children should not be excluded by reason of their color. Enjoin the school board not to refuse—avoid contempt. The same in Virginia. There are forty-three students named in South Carolina, and one hundred fifty in Virginia. We should move gradually—like a glacier—for states on the outside. I am by no means sure, if they are to abolish public schools, whether it is better to do it now. Georgia is sure to do so. One of the most eloquent men I have heard at the bar was the man from South Carolina.[86]

REED: I don't know the *Deep* South. I have a firm belief that there is a considerable group wanting to give this decision sympathetic consideration. When *some* schools are opened, it will have a further effect.

These are class suits, and those who might come in and be parties would be beneficiaries of any court order. I think that all students who are not plaintiffs who want to intervene can do so up to the time of final judgment. It might be better, however, *not* to mention that these are class suits. We can think of them as class suits, but not state it in the decree. We should either say nothing about this class, or we should specifically authorize the lower courts to admit the class. It is essential to say, or at least to look at, what must be done. I am agreeable either way, to say that these are class suits or not.

I would remand these cases, directing that these schools are to be opened to the named plaintiffs with all convenient speed. We should put it in the form of an opinion and a short decree. I favor a short opinion, asserting the constitutional principles and some guidelines and then sending these cases back with limited ground rules in there. I favor an opinion as well as a decree, as it would be more flexible. I question whether we should call for the submission of a plan. We should not require it. I question whether we should mention it at all. I would suggest that the lower courts could call for a plan if they want one, and it might be well to authorize the lower courts who want a plan to ask for one. They might classify on grounds of sex, or they might integrate class by class.

I would not set a time limit or fix definite terms, but would follow the language of the *Jaybird* decree.[87] The direction in the *Jaybird* case [*Terry v. Adams*] is enough. That will

---

86. The two advocates representing South Carolina were S. E. Rogers and Robert McCormick Figg. Black was probably referring to Figg, who by most accounts was articulate, candid, and reasonable in discussing the prospects for desegregation in Clarendon County. Soon after arguing this case, Figg left private practice to become dean of the University of South Carolina's law school.

87. *Terry v. Adams*, 345 U.S. 461 (1953). After *Smith v. Allwright* outlawed white primaries, Texas Democrats tried yet again to exclude blacks from effective participation in the primary process. The Jaybirds were an all-white organization within the Democratic party that held a whites-only election *prior* to the Democratic primary. Winners of the Jaybird primary then ran against other candidates in the regular Demo-

result in doing more with the public schools in these areas. Our order may result in public schools being abolished. We can't *require* public school systems. *The border states will be examples.*

FRANKFURTER: I welcome greatly that we can talk in a candid, relaxed way of general direction. The Kansas, Delaware, and District of Columbia cases are easy. But we must conceive of the environment of the decree in South Carolina, Virginia, and so forth. The attitude of the South is a fact to be taken into consideration as much as administrative difficulty and so forth. [DOUGLAS: *He now says he filibustered this problem under Vinson for fear that the case would be decided the other way under Vinson!!*]

The right here vindicated was a right created only last year. The important thing is not the decree, but an opinion. By all means there should be an opinion. This is a slow process and something should be said about it. What we do is largely educational. [DOUGLAS: *He refers to Holmes as the greatest judge who ever sat on this Court.*] This is a *law suit.* Concrete procedures, but a different kind of a law suit. This is an unreal problem as to class suits, because no matter how you restrict the decree to names, the same demand will be made for others. The multitude will spring up and others will be joined. But the whole school system is geared on this basis.

In the South Carolina and Virginia cases, the matter is before three judges. It is fortuitous that these cases are in courts of three, and we should require three judges to sit on the remand. They can share the burden, and there is more wisdom with three than with one judge. We should be specific that it be three-judge court, and §2106 gives us the power to require that.[88] I don't know whether the local court—to order a decree—whether it is important that there be three judges.

What we say and the kind of feeling we impart is important. The United States Supreme Court is for all of the country, including the South. I do not agree with Thurgood Marshall that southern attitudes are to be left out of consideration. I do not agree with the Texas polls.[89] By gradual infiltration of border states, the process of desegregation can spread to the Deep South.

DOUGLAS: We should have an opinion. Don't add much opinion. We should say that we have benefited from their argument. Statistics. Include the items that the Chief Justice mentioned. *We should give a push.* We should suggest as fast as circumstances permit. I would not suggest a date, but use language like *Jaybird,* and words to show that we must get along with this matter. Like Hugo, I have doubts about treating these cases as class action suits. I am inclined to make a decree restricting relief to the named individuals. I am inclined to a cut-off for named plaintiffs.[90]

---

cratic primary election, which was open to both whites and blacks. The Jaybird candidate almost invariably won the party primary and the general election. The Court ruled 8–1 that the Jaybird scheme was unconstitutional.

88. 28 U.S.C. §2106 says, in part, that the Supreme Court may affirm, modify, vacate, set aside, or reverse any judgment and that it may require any further proceedings as may be just under the circumstances.

89. Several southern states commissioned polls that indicated deep local opposition to *Brown* among government leaders, social elites, and ordinary citizens. One poll indicated that 75 percent of public officials disagreed with *Brown,* including 30 percent who "disagreed violently." Kluger, *Simple Justice,* 724.

90. Warren's conference notes say "only named *defendants.*"

BURTON: I favor an objective declaration of unconstitutionality, and I would enjoin such segregation as rapidly as possible. I would not restrict relief. In its nature, we are dealing with a class. The problem is the *race* line, not just putting in a few colored children. Neither this Court nor the district courts should act as a school board or formulate the programs. There should be no masters. We must order nothing that will be futile. It is vital that it be unanimous—this is the *demonstrating factor*. I believe in a short opinion followed by a decree. The decree would declare segregation and all laws supporting it to be unconstitutional. I would remand for the purpose of making it effective: (a) good faith efforts in eliminating segregation; (b) parties defending shall present plans; and (c) pending completion, there should be reports and the courts should retain jurisdiction.

CLARK: I am closer to Felix than to anyone else. Texas is not going to present many acute problems; there will not be too much trouble there. But there are some Clarendons there. The disparity between white and colored schools is great. The administrative problem is great. Lots of new school buildings would have to be erected. We can't simply relocate between colored schools and white schools, putting five hundred students in shacks and five hundred students in good schools. Whites will go to school with colored children, but they never will allow white students under colored teachers.[91] Many will still go to wholly colored schools. We can't restrict these suits to named plaintiffs.

They are going to try to do what this Court says. We could not have a "forthwith" order as Hugo suggests. [DOUGLAS: Clark speaks of need for slow speed.] We need to be careful what we say. Three judge courts are good. A *Jaybird* decree is desirable.

MINTON: I agree with Hugo and Harold, and will go along with the majority. Unanimous action by the Court is of primary importance. I doubt the advisability of writing much, and I have doubts about writing many opinions. We should not make big talk in the opinion and little words in the decree. The main thing is to get to work in the area. Democracy should never reveal its own impotence. We should be careful not to issue a futile decree that we cannot enforce. But we must do something in the area. The decree should look like this:

a. a declaration of unconstitutionality;

b. we should enjoin school authorities from admitting or excluding on the basis of a person's color;

c. we should direct them to file with the district court on or by 9/1/55 a plan of admissions with equal treatment; and

d. rites are to be given in the district courts.

HARLAN: All of my ideas have been expressed by others. I would emphasize that whatever our conclusion, it is of the essence that our opinion be unanimous. This is political statesmanship. I am deeply impressed by what Hugo Black said about the Deep South,

---

91. Black teachers were concerned that integration would lead to massive layoffs of black teachers. The NAACP tried to assuage these fears and prepared new legal strategies to thwart the anticipated racial cleansing of faculty rooms. Tushnet, *Making Civil Rights Law*, 152.

and the importance of taking those factors into account. I am surprised at the degree of unanimity on the basic issues.

We might be mistaken in thinking that writing might not help—it might have just the opposite effect. A properly written opinion reflecting our basic approach might be helpful. Issuing only a decree might be too cold and heavy-handed. I am disposed to have an opinion and a decree, with the decree in the simplest possible form. Outside of May 17, there should be no time limits. The injunction should carry out by the 17th.

I agree with the Chief Justice as to the scope of our opinion. We should:

a. reiterate our holding of May 17.

b. make some reference to the steps that have been taken for advice as to implementation.

c. make some reference to the broad positions taken by the plaintiffs and the states.

d. make it clear that we have proceeded under equity powers, and that we have the power and duty to mold exigencies and to liquidate history.

e. recognize that the school problem is local, and that is not changed by the views expressed here, and that we are remanding these cases to the local courts.

As to whether or not these are class suits, I originally felt that these were not true class suits—and they probably are not. But as a practical matter, the class suit may be a helpful device. It is a guide—a coming in of people. It would be worthwhile to make clear what we are holding. We should include only those who joined before a certain date. We should embrace the idea of a class suit, and so phrase it as to limit it as a precedent.

Result: Just as they had done in Brown I, *the Justices agreed to deliver a unanimous opinion written by the Chief Justice. After a brief conference on May 27 to discuss Warren's proposed draft, Frankfurter changed his mind and insisted on an unsigned per curiam decision. Under pressure from the other Justices, however, he eventually relented. The Justices also agreed that relief would be limited to the parties, rather than providing a class remedy.*

Warren's opinion was very short, just seven paragraphs. It gave local authorities primary responsibility for desegregating public schools under federal court supervision. The opinion contained no formal decree. Instead, the Court dismissed the decisions below and ordered local district courts to enter new orders and decrees consistent with the Court's opinion. District court judges were ordered to put public schools "on a racially nondiscriminatory basis with all deliberate speed." This famous and unfortunate phrase came from Frankfurter, who in turn borrowed it from Oliver Wendell Holmes.[92]

---

92. *Virginia v. West Virginia,* 222 U.S. 17, 20 (1911). It is less clear where Holmes found the phrase. He claimed that it was a customary saying of English chancery, but Richard Kluger more plausibly claims that it came from Francis Thompson's 1893 poem *The Hound of Heaven*:

I fled Him, down the nights and down the days;
I fled Him, down the arches of the years. . . .
From those strong Feet that followed, followed after.
But with unhurrying chase,
And unperturbed pace,
Deliberate speed, majestic instancy. . . .

There was massive southern resistance to Brown, *and there was not much the federal courts could do about it without the support of the executive and legislative branches of government.*[93] *President Eisenhower let it be known that he personally opposed the* Brown *decision, and Congress offered no real support for nearly a decade.*[94] *The few southern school districts that tried to desegregate in good faith were often intimidated and forced to back away from their initial efforts to comply with* Brown.

While some school districts made progress toward desegregation, in most places the pace of change was painfully slow until Presidents John F. Kennedy and Lyndon Johnson were in the White House and convinced Congress to become involved in federal desegregation efforts. After Kennedy's assassi-

---

The phrase was useful because it simultaneously promoted two equally plausible but opposite meanings. As Kluger noted, the tortoise raced the hare with all deliberate speed. *Simple Justice,* 744. Frankfurter knew, of course, that both Thompson and Holmes used the phrase to emphasize delay rather than dispatch. Other Justices, among them Black and Douglas, later claimed that they did not understand the true meaning of the phrase. This is nonsense; the phrase was consistent with Black's own suggestion that the Court "move like a glacier," and captured perfectly the mood of the Court. Even Frankfurter later tried to distance himself from the controversy, claiming that Warren had used the phrase without his consent. Letter to Mark DeWolfe Howe, May 5, 1958, Frankfurter Papers. This simply was not true, as several contemporary memoranda from Frankfurter to Warren make clear. Memoranda from Felix Frankfurter to Earl Warren, May 24 and 27, 1955, Earl Warren Papers, box 574.

While interesting, the eternal debate over the Court's use of the phrase "all deliberate speed" probably exaggerates the significance of these unfortunate words. The phrase did not cause southern noncompliance with *Brown,* nor were there any alternative magic words that the Supreme Court could have uttered to make the south comply. Southern defiance of *Brown* was due to a lack of federal will, not words. All three branches of government, including the Supreme Court, signaled the south in a number of ways that it lacked the resolve to enforce the Court's desegregation order. The "all deliberate speed" standard was not the real problem; it was the institutional body language that accompanied the phrase that encouraged the south to hold fast. But see Black's comments in *Alexander v. Holmes County,* below.

93. Senator Henry F. Byrd of Virginia coined the battle cry of "massive resistance" to *Brown.* The idea of massive resistance galvanized the Deep South. The struggle against desegregation took many forms, including reanimating the long-ago discarded doctrine of interposition. "Massive resistance" also meant closing down public schools, white riots, and white harassment of black schoolchildren and parents. The white resistance movement culminated in the Southern Manifesto of 1956. Formally called the "Declaration of Constitutional Principles," the manifesto was a frontal attack on the Court and a pledge to fight integration at all costs. It was signed by 101 of 128 southern members of Congress, including all but three southern senators. The lone holdouts were Albert Gore and Estes Kefauver of Tennessee, and Lyndon Johnson of Texas.

In addition to overt defiance, southern governments resisted *Brown* in hundreds of more subtle ways, such as by enacting facially neutral laws implicitly designed to maintain segregation. "Free choice" legislation, for example, gave parents the right to send their children to any public school they wanted. Though seemingly neutral, these laws ensured that white parents could continue to send their children to all-white schools with the understanding that few—if any—black parents would dare to force their own children to break the color barrier at these schools.

94. Harry Truman blamed Eisenhower for most of the problems of desegregation. He told author Merle Miller, "If the fella that succeeded me had just given people a little leadership, there wouldn't have been all that difficulty over desegregating the schools, but he didn't do it. He didn't use the powers of the office of the President to uphold a ruling of the Supreme Court of the United States, and I never did understand that. If he'd got out in front and told people that they had to uphold the law of the land, it's my opinion that they'd have done it. But he didn't; he shillyshallied around, and that's the reason we're in the fix we're in now." Miller, *Plain Speaking* 259–60.

nation, President Johnson's determined lobbying efforts convinced Congress to pass the Civil Rights Act of 1964, the most significant civil rights legislation of the century.

In 1964, ten years after Brown, *only 1.2 percent of southern black children went to school with white children. While southern governments actively resisted segregation, northern efforts to desegregate public schools often triggered white flight from urban school districts, resulting in increased levels of social segregation. Even with Congress on board, the pace of desegregation remained slow in many parts of the country.*

Among the original school districts involved in the Brown *litigation, the Kansas and Delaware schools were largely desegregated by the mid-1960s. In Virginia, Prince Edward County closed its public schools from 1959 until 1964. As late as 1969, only two dozen white schoolchildren attended public schools alongside 1,800 black children in Prince Edward County. Things moved even more slowly in South Carolina's Clarendon County. In 1974, twenty years after* Brown *was decided, one Clarendon school district had an enrollment of 3,000 black students and one white student.*

Alexander v. Holmes County Board of Education, 396 U.S. 19 (1969)
(Douglas)

Beatrice Alexander and other Mississippi parents filed a lawsuit in federal court to compel thirty-three state school districts to abandon their dual systems of racially segregated schools. After years of litigation, in July 1969 the Fifth Circuit Court of Appeals ordered the federal Department of Health, Education, and Welfare (HEW) to submit a desegregation plan to help the court enact a comprehensive desegregation order scheduled to go into effect at the beginning of the school year in September. On August 11, HEW submitted its plan. On August 28, however, the Nixon administration—through Attorney General John Mitchell and HEW Secretary Robert Finch—asked the circuit court to postpone implementing any desegregation order. The appellate court agreed to the delay, and Alexander immediately appealed to the Supreme Court.

The main issue at both the certiorari and argued cases conferences was the status of the "all deliberate speed" standard fourteen years after Brown II.

Certiorari Conference of October 9, 1969

BURGER: The school term has already started, so we can't put the plan into effect for this term. I would hate to put off the plan until September 1970. I have a lot of respect for the Fifth Circuit—they are entitled to great deference on that court. I will defer my vote until others talk.

BLACK: I also have a great respect for the Fifth Circuit. I do not think what they did now was a Fifth Circuit action. This is the result of what the Attorney General did. Our decision in 1954 meant that the practice was unconstitutional, and that it could not be relitigated every time. "All deliberate speed" meant that to me, and I was opposed to it. It should not be made a current political issue. [DOUGLAS: He refers to his early recollections of colored people in the South, the carpetbaggers, and the efforts to purchase Negro votes.] I think that there is no chance of getting the colored people into integrated schools unless we eliminate "all deliberate speed." The issue can't be litigated every time the problem is presented. It has been made into a political football by Nixon, and others will do the same. I would set the case down for argument, and after argument I would provide for instant integration.

BURGER: I agreed with what Hugo wrote in this case this summer. The only question to me is whether we can make them do something between now and the next term. I would not re-examine the basic premise of *Brown*.

BLACK: Unless we eliminate "all deliberate speed," the whites in the South will win the battle.

DOUGLAS: I challenged Hugo's history of "all deliberative speed." It never was meant to invite relitigation of the basic constitutional issue—it related only to the problem of the five school districts before us as respects buildings, teachers, and so forth. I would reverse summarily.

HARLAN: I would grant and put the case down for argument. I was here for *Brown II*. The problem will be solved in the rubric of the law. "All deliberate speed" was put in for the physical readjustments necessary to produce a unitary system in education. In the decree, there is an explanation of "all deliberate speed" as not including temporizing. There is nothing in any of our opinions that supports the political implications of "all deliberate speed." I would not grant the cross petition.

BRENNAN: This is a crucial case. It would be fatal to the Court if we did not take the case. I would put this case down promptly.

STEWART: I agree that the "all deliberate speed" standard does not permit relitigation of the basic issue. If we put it down, we may in fact slow up the process. I would prefer to deal with it summarily and remand it to the Fifth Circuit Court of Appeals.

WHITE: I would grant the petition, deny the cross petition, and put the case down for argument.

MARSHALL: I don't need the record. They applied the wrong standard. I would reverse per curiam—an argument is useless.

HARLAN: It would be a mistake to act summarily, as the Department of Justice and the court of appeals are involved.

BRENNAN: In view of the political nature of the problem, we should not act summarily.

BURGER: I vote to grant and have oral argument.

Conference of October 24, 1969

BURGER: I hope that we all speak with one voice. I support remanding it to the court of appeals with directions to remand to the district court for a hearing on the HEW plan, to be submitted by November fifteenth and with a shortened time for reply, with a view of terminating segregation no later than December 31, 1969. "All deliberate speed" means to get it done, not get it started. It means "right now."

BLACK: I reject the use of "all deliberate speed." I disagree with the Chief Justice. I will say that the dual system is dead. Integration should be "right now."

DOUGLAS: We should declare (1) integration right now; (2) the end of the dual system; and (3) remand the case to the court of appeals to do those two things.

HARLAN: I would remand to the court of appeals to go over the HEW plan, have hearings, and put them into effect as is, or as modified. They would be interim plans to become effective by December 30. The order should be followed by an opinion.

BRENNAN: Now means *now*. The real question is a delay on litigating the plan. I had that problem in the Denver case. There I made the plan effective by letting litigation follow if the plaintiffs have no objection as to the plans. Put them in effect now, and litigate later. I would not let a school district object when the HEW approves a plan.

HARLAN: I agree with that. We should not direct a plan to be put into effect that we have not seen.

BRENNAN: There is a presumptive validity to HEW plans.

STEWART: I agree that no time is available. This district court is not a good tribunal to send this to. I agree with Bill Douglas to remand this case to the court of appeals. Due process may require adversarial hearings. At least the court of appeals should know what is in the plans. I would give the court of appeals a tight schedule. I would put the HEW plans into effect in ten days or two weeks.

WHITE: The judge could order any plan in effect as an interim plan. That would satisfy due process. I would not remand to the district court. I would tell the court of appeals to put the HEW plan into effect. I would give them eight days—hearings on the plans can go on later than that. I would not leave the time table to the discretion of the court of appeals.

MARSHALL: I have read the plans and understand them. On October 1, they made a report to the court of appeals. These cases must go to the court of appeals. We should give them a time schedule. Two of the HEW plans must go back. HEW is doing a fine job.

BURGER: The order should come first, our opinion later.

BLACK: I would do away with the dual system, and I would not fool around with interim plans.

DOUGLAS: I would suggest that the Chief Justice, Hugo, and Bill Brennan form a drafting committee to write the order.

Result: In a per curiam decision, a unanimous Court ruled that the continued operation of dual school systems was no longer permissible and that the time for desegregating public schools with "all deliberate speed" was over. The Court ordered Mississippi to desegregate its schools immediately and empowered the court of appeals to compel the state's school districts to implement at once any or all of the HEW recommendations. District court judges would be permitted to consider proposed amendments to the HEW guidelines at a later date, although the court of appeals would have to approve any proposed changes. This case marked the end of the "all deliberate speed" standard as an open-ended excuse for southern inaction and delay in school desegregation.

Swann v. Charlotte-Mecklenburg Board of Education, 402 U.S. 1 (1971)
(Brennan)

James Swann and other black students claimed that the city of Charlotte, North Carolina maintained a dual system of education in violation of Brown v. Board of Education.[95] Of 24,000 black students in the Charlotte schools, 14,000 went to one-race schools, and only a handful of white students attended black-majority schools. District Court Judge James B. McMillan ordered the local school board to submit a proposal for creating a unitary educational system. Judge McMillan decided that the school board's initial plan was too timid and asked both the board and a court-appointed expert, Dr. John A. Finger of Rhode Island College, to submit new proposals. The school board's new plan remained modest. Dr. Finger's proposal was more ambitious and included the pairing of black and white schools, attendance zones that crossed racially distinct neighborhoods, and busing.

With a few modifications, Judge McMillan adopted the board's desegregation plan for the district's secondary schools and accepted Dr. Finger's plan to desegregate the city's elementary schools. McMillan wrote that his aim was to obtain a racial balance in each school that roughly approximated the racial composition of the entire district—71 percent white and 29 percent black.

The court of appeals vacated the second part McMillan's order (adopting the expert's plan for Charlotte's elementary schools) on the ground that busing such young students was unreasonable and excessively burdensome. While the case was pending before the U.S. Supreme Court, Judge McMillan strengthened his position by persuading the school board to endorse Dr. Finger's plan for desegregating the elementary schools.

BURGER: I query whether any particular demographics are either required or forbidden by the Constitution. *Brown I* said that the right is a right to be free from discrimination—separation solely because of race was outlawed. Racial composition of a unit is to look at the facts to see if there is evidence of discrimination. The rigidity of the 71/29 ratio set by McMillan disturbs me. There must be some play in the joints—perhaps a 15 percent leeway? I think that the Fifth Circuit has swerved away from its original basis.

BLACK: This boils down to a very simple proposition. It is foolish to think that this question will be solved in our or our children's lifetimes. We fought a Civil War over our treatment of the Negro. What was clear was that there was to be no legal discrimination on account of race by any government. I have always had the idea that people arrange themselves often to be close to schools. I never thought that it was for the courts to change the hearts of the people in choosing where to live. The slavery amendments allow us only to enforce a prohibition against denial of equal protection and permit Congress to enforce it. Policies in preventing discrimination are therefore not for us, but for Congress. If a state wants to get rid of buses and the federal government disagrees, let Congress provide the buses.[96] The Constitution doesn't require a particular proportion.

DOUGLAS: I don't think that the issue is too involved. Is there a prohibited discrimination in busing? The problem is what is the power of the courts without the help of Con-

---

95. *Brown v. Board of Education,* 347 U.S. 483 (1954).

96. Poking fun at Black's constitutional literalism, Brennan claimed after the conference that Black opposed mandatory busing programs because he could not find the word "bus" in the Constitution. Urofsky, *The Douglas Letters,* 178.

gress to correct a violation of the Constitution? If there is an antitrust violation, we give a broad discretion. What can be done in this area? To be a denial of equal protection rights, there must be invidious discrimination where some classification may be. Is it invidious to take certain steps to remedy discrimination? We ought to let the district court decide how best to disestablish segregation. They can force this through within narrow limits.

HARLAN: The problem is to sort out these cases. What are the basic principles? Busing is only one facet of a much more complicated problem. This stage is almost as important as the stage that the Court was in at the time of *Brown I*. *Brown I* settled that state-enforced racial discrimination was a denial of equal protection. *Brown II*, on implementation, was used as a bridge to give the federal *courts* the job of enforcement—not the Congress under §5 of the Fourteenth Amendment.[97] We have largely left the matter to the lower courts, stepping in only where we became concerned with delay. Now we must pronounce standards to guide the implementation process. On the state action question, these are conventional state action cases involving state-enforced segregation. I therefore would lay aside whether there is state action involved in housing patterns. It is relevant to whether the school board is proceeding in good faith. *Secondly*, given the duty to disestablish dual school systems created by *Brown II*, that duty includes a duty to mix races.[98] *Third*, there is no constitutional requirement of racial balancing, and I don't think that McMillan proceeded on that theory. It was simply a legitimate point of departure, like that approved by Hugo Black in *Montgomery*.[99] *Fourth*, busing is not an impermissible tool. *Fifth*, the neighborhood school is not a constitutional requirement if departure from it is necessary to disestablish a segregated system.

---

97. *Brown v. Board of Education* (*Brown II*), 349 U.S. 294 (1955).

98. Harlan believed that there was no general constitutional right to be educated in racially balanced schools or to have "integration or race-mixing." But in a memorandum to the Chief Justice, he wrote that government had a duty to act when segregation was "the outgrowth of the political process in which the majority race, having entirely disenfranchised the minority race, forcibly confined the children of the black community to schools designated for their own race." Under those conditions, government had the duty to eliminate racially identifiable schools and to create a unitary school system. Harlan thought that federal judges could use a wide variety of means to remedy de jure segregation, including busing and racial quotas. In his view, any dual school system that maintained even one predominantly one-race school would have a heavy burden to justify the status quo. Harlan looked forward to the day, however, when judges could "label a system 'unitary' and depart from the education business. . . ." Harlan memorandum to Warren Burger, February 16, 1971, Harlan Papers, box 490, cited in Yarbrough, *John Marshall Harlan*, 265–67.

99. *United States v. Montgomery Board of Education*, 395 U.S. 225 (1969). In 1964, District Court Judge Frank Johnson of Alabama ordered schools in Montgomery County to integrate. Judge Johnson conducted annual hearings to gauge the county's progress, and when it failed to integrate school faculty and staff as promised, Johnson ordered the school board to move toward a target where "the ratio of white to Negro faculty members is substantially the same as it is throughout the system." He ordered each public school with fewer than twelve full-time teachers to hire at least one teacher whose race was different from the race of the majority of the faculty at that school, and required schools with twelve or more full-time teachers to hire at least one minority teacher for every six faculty/staff members. The overall ratio of white to black full-time teachers in the entire school system at the time was 3:2. Judge Johnson reserved the right to modify these targets in the future. The court of appeals modified his order by eliminating the use of specific ratios, but the Supreme Court reversed and in a unanimous opinion by Hugo Black approved Judge Johnson's original order.

We won't help this problem if we're fussy about it. I start from *Green's* implicit principle that segregated schools must be disestablished.[100] I would reflect the court of appeals "reasonableness" standard. There is also a power in it to require some mixing in order to avoid segregation.

STEWART: What is it that must be done now? How are we to convert a dual system into a unitary school system? Not only desegregation, but affirmative integration is required. Certainly as to faculty, non-faculty employees, extracurricular official activities, equal facilities, and quality of education. These cases are concerned with what is the composition of individual schools that a unitary system requires? I can't say that predominately black or white schools are intolerable. In these de jure situations we must say what a court (a) must do; and (b) may do to dismantle historically segregated systems. We should lay down a rule whether the school board may require a precise proportion in every school. Courts must do the same thing in the *non-student* segment of the school population that *Green* requires for the student body. The Constitution certainly permits, and may require (a) benevolent gerrymandering, taking race into account; and (b) an absolute majority to minority transfer right for Negro children; but (c) no quota can be required—McMillan's 71/29 ratio was wrong.

MARSHALL: You don't need a unitary system. If you disestablish all schools, necessarily you end up with a unitary system. There is no such thing as freedom of choice for the Negro child in the South.

BLACKMUN: I am prejudiced toward neighborhood schools. People buy homes to be near schools. *Green* seems to be the starting point. Also *Kemp v. Beasley*.[101] We should not

---

100. *Green v. County School Board*, 391 U.S. 430 (1968). The New Kent County school board in Virginia adopted a freedom-of-choice plan that allowed parents to choose the public school in which to enroll their children. The New Kent school system had just two schools, one white and one black. The implicit assumption was that all of the white parents would choose the traditionally white school and that few black parents would dare to send their children there. The district court approved the plan on the ground that it met *Brown's* mandate to establish nonracial admissions policies in public schools. The court of appeals agreed, although it remanded the case on other grounds. The Supreme Court unanimously ruled that the freedom of choice plan did not meet the state's duty to create a unitary school system. Brennan stressed that not one white child had enrolled in "the Negro school" and that while a few blacks had enrolled in the white school, 85 percent of the county's black children still attended one-race schools.

101. *Kemp v. Beasley*, 423 F.2d 851 (8th Cir. 1970). Dossie Wayne Kemp and other black schoolchildren, parents, and teachers claimed that the El Dorado school district in Arkansas maintained a dual school system in violation of *Brown v. Board of Education*. After considerable delay, the school district adopted a controversial "freedom of choice" plan. The third time the case came back before the court of appeals, Circuit Judge Harry Blackmun wrote the opinion for the court. He approved the district's freedom of choice plan and commended the school board's progress in desegregating local high schools and junior high schools. Noting that segregation remained a problem in the district's elementary schools, Blackmun ordered immediate corrective action and rejected the district's plea for more time, saying that the time for "all deliberate speed" had passed. He noted, however, that the court had not yet ruled on several issues, including the issue of neighborhood schools, the problem of residential segregation, the use of busing programs, or the need for precise racial balancing of students or faculty. Blackmun added that the district court would retain jurisdiction until the school district complied with *Brown* and established a unitary school district.

emphasize the facts in these cases so much as the principle involved. Do we want to lay down standards? We must. I was much taken with Bill Douglas's spring memo, but we must take another look. I feel much as I did when I wrote *Kemp*. Busing is only a consequence of some other decision. I like the neighborhood school idea, at least at the elementary school level. I am worried about continuing judicial surveillance. Racial balancing is at least a tool. *Mobile* is the toughest case for me.[102]

Result: Writing for a unanimous Court, Warren Burger affirmed Judge McMillan's plan for desegregating Charlotte's public schools.[103] Because the school board had failed to establish a unitary system of education or eliminate the vestiges of state-imposed segregation, the district court had broad powers as a court of equity to remedy the situation.

Burger added some additional advice regarding four of the main problems in desegregation: (1) racial quotas *(there was no requirement that each school must look like the system as a whole, and any proposed ratios should be flexible); (2)* one-race schools *(not necessarily per se evidence of state discrimination, but should be closely scrutinized); (3)* attendance zones *(adjustable on an interim basis to reform past discrimination, and techniques such as pairing schools were acceptable); and (4)* transportation *(busing could be used to dismantle dual school systems.) The Court also found that there was no perpetual need to rebalance racial percentages once a unitary system had been established and the taint of state discrimination overcome.*

In September 1999, District Judge Robert D. Potter, a Reagan appointee, ruled that the city's dual school system had been eliminated.[104] Judge Potter ordered Charlotte to end its race-based desegrega-

---

102. *Davis v. Board of School Commissioners of Mobile County*, 402 U.S. 33 (1971). After a district court judge approved a school desegregation plan for Mobile, Alabama, the court of appeals found the plan deficient and ordered three major modifications: (1) that faculty and staff be reassigned so that the racial balance in each school would be substantially the same as for the district as a whole; (2) that the eastern metropolitan area be excluded from any desegregation plan (94 percent of the city's black students resided on the east side); and (3) that busing could not be used in any desegregation plan. Warren Burger, writing for a unanimous Court, approved the integration plan for faculty and staff but reversed on the other two points. The Justices ruled that (1) the exclusion of the eastern part of the metropolitan area from the desegregation plan would have perpetuated Mobile's dual school system; and (2) the circuit court had given inadequate consideration to the busing issue before prohibiting its use as a tool to establish a unitary school system.

103. This was another case where Douglas claimed that Burger cast no vote in conference, which should have left it to Douglas to assign the majority opinion. Immediately after the conference Douglas assigned the case to Stewart, only to find that Burger had already assigned the case to himself. Brennan's conference notes, however, list Burger as voting to affirm, and Burger's conference remarks clearly indicate that he was leaning to affirm from the beginning.

Douglas claimed that Burger wanted to write the majority opinion to promote Richard Nixon's preference for "freedom of choice" plans into law. See Urofsky, *The Douglas Letters*, 178–79. Regardless of his motives, Burger's decision to take the case himself created considerable problems for the conference. The other Justices were appalled by Burger's initial drafts, which were openly hostile to Judge McMillan's approach and seemed to signal a retreat from *Brown*. It took considerable work by the other Justices to bring Burger around. Tushnet, *Making Constitutional Law*, 77–82.

104. In 1969, long before Robert Potter became a federal judge, he participated in the fight against the original 1969 desegregation suit as a private citizen. Fullwood, "Rear-View Look at Busing Ruling: Trailblazer Goes Back to South in Wake of Judge's Order to End Race-Based Integration," *Los Angeles Times* (November 6, 1999).

tion programs and return to its traditional neighborhood school system. School officials immediately appealed the ruling, arguing that if the school system ended its desegregation programs almost all of the district's 151 schools would quickly revert to being predominantly one-race schools.

Keyes v. School District No. 1, Denver, Colorado, 413 U.S. 189 (1973)
(Douglas) (Brennan)

This was the first major school desegregation case in a northern state. When the number of students in the predominantly black Park Hill area of northeast Denver began to outgrow existing facilities, the local school board put students into mobile classrooms rather than placing them in nearby white schools. Wilfred Keyes and other black parents sued, alleging that while the school board had never explicitly adopted a policy of racial segregation, its policies were intended to keep the Park Hill schools black and adjoining schools predominately white. The plaintiffs noted that in some parts of Denver parents were allowed to enroll their children in the school of their choice, but this option had never been permitted in Park Hill.

District Court Judge William Doyle ruled that racial segregation in Park Hill was the result of state action. He ordered Park Hill's eight schools desegregated and adopted a remedy whereby 4,000 Denver students would be bused. The plaintiffs then sought to expand their suit to include the entire city, including 119 schools and 90,000 students. Judge Doyle refused on the ground that the petitioners had not proved the existence of district-wide, de jure segregation necessary to impose a district-wide remedy.[105] Outside of Park Hill, he said, "racially identifiable" schools were the result of voluntary, private residential segregation rather than government policies. Doyle also found, however, that Denver's inner-city schools were inferior to schools elsewhere in the district and he ordered the school board to equalize school facilities, citing Plessy v. Ferguson.[106] *Under this part of Doyle's ruling, another 7,000 students were to be bused. The court of appeals affirmed Judge Doyle's orders regarding Park Hill but reversed his plan to equalize inner city schools. The circuit court ruled that while there had been de jure segregation in Park Hill, segregation elsewhere in the city was the result of private residential patterns. As this was de facto rather than de jure segregation, it could not be used to justify a district-wide remedy.*

Conference of October 13, 1972

BURGER: This is not the typical *Brown* case. In the Denver school district there are 66 percent whites, 14 percent Negro, and 20 percent Chicano. The district court judge found as fact that no school has refused admission of a student on racial or ethnic grounds. The

---

105. *De jure* segregation results when racial separation is the product of state law or policy. *De facto* segregation is when racial separation occurs without state sanction or intent, merely as a consequence of individuals making private choices about where to live and where to send their children to school. *Keyes* was a crucial test of whether the traditional distinction between de jure segregation (justiciable) and de facto segregation (nonjusticiable) was still in effect.

106. Denver's response to Judge Doyle's desegregation order was not dissimilar to southern reaction to similar judicial orders. White families began to move out of the city in large numbers and into new suburban school districts. There was also scattered violence. Forty-six school buses were allegedly damaged by explosives, and Judge Doyle's and Wilfred Keyes's homes were vandalized. Delgado and Stefancic, "Home-Grown Racism," 778.

petitioners have the burden to show discrimination, and of showing in the court of appeals that the district court judge's findings were clearly erroneous. The factor of age or experience of teachers is not of itself conclusive of discrimination. The assignment of all Negro teachers to Negro schools would be in error, as indicated by Hugo Black's opinion. The drop-out rate is not relevant, nor is the condition of the school buildings. *Senior* teachers are under union contracts, which give them broad power to select their own schools. Usually teachers are bad for schools [*sic*]. Judge Doyle waffled a lot on the issues.[107] There are few clear-cut issues or findings. This is not a classical dual school system. I would affirm the court of appeals' decision.

DOUGLAS: What has been called de facto discrimination is in most cases de jure. Housing programs and restrictive covenants involve lots of state and federal action. I would just apply *Swann* and reverse.[108] If this is not de jure, then how do we remedy inequality among schools? These schools are separate and unequal, and how to deal with that may be a much bigger problem. Federal judges have many tools, though—such as busing to make them share the second- and third-rate schools. Or financial remedies, such as in *Rodriguez*, maybe. Equality is the problem. Also, this is de jure and not de facto discrimination. I reverse.

BRENNAN: This is not de jure, except for the northeast section. That is challenged in the case we are holding. The burden is on the plaintiffs to prove de jure discrimination, and they did it in the northeast section of the district. I doubt whether Judge Doyle was right on the rest of the city. The record gives a prima facie case for the school board to rebut. The record shows de jure discrimination—at least, I would remand on that. I reverse.

STEWART: I come out not far from Bill Brennan. I am not willing to say as a matter of law that the facts here add up to de jure segregation. But I would remand on that phase. Moreover, in the core area they kept taking action favoring whites. All Negro teachers were assigned to Manual High School. The fact that a dual school system happened before *Brown v. Board of Education* does not make it immune to judicial remedy.[109] I would remand because there was a prima facie case of de jure segregation. I do not face the issue of de facto segregation, nor whether public housing, restrictive covenants, and so forth constitute de jure segregation. But it is not far for me in thinking that the impact of funding as to the northeast, and other added facts, created a prima facie case of de jure discrimination for the school board to meet. I would remand for further hearings.

WHITE: Takes no part.

MARSHALL: I agree with Potter and Bill Brennan pretty much. I have trouble seeing how the school board can be good for one section and not for other, though like Brennan and Douglas I could say that it was de jure. You cannot bifurcate the school board and say

---

107. Judge Doyle published four separate opinions in connection with this case: 303 F. Supp. 279 (1969) (issuing a preliminary injunction); 303 F. Supp. 289 (1969) (issuing supplementary findings and conditions); 313 F. Supp. 91 (1970) (ruling on the merits); and 313 F. Supp. 90 (1970) (ordering relief).

108. *Swann v. Charlotte-Mecklenburg Board of Education*, 402 U.S. 1 (1971).

109. *Brown v. Board of Education*, 347 U.S. 483 (1954).

what they did in the northeast section they did not do elsewhere. I reverse. I could reverse on *Swann*.

BLACKMUN: Judge Doyle concluded that there was no intentional discrimination in the core area. I think that there was segregation in the core area. I would not agree that this adds up to de jure segregation. At the elementary school level there is great value in neighborhood schools. There is less value in neighborhood schools at the junior high level, and none at all at the high school level. My inclination after argument was to reverse and remand and go with Judge Doyle. I would like to squelch the idea that blacks do better with black teachers. I would probably go along with a remand. I am not inclined to affirm. I am still crawfishing a bit, but am not inclined to affirm across the board.

POWELL: The distinction between de jure and de facto can't be defended constitutionally or logically. The Court has worked itself into a position which ignores that population trends have been the product of state action of all sorts. I so stated my views in my brief in *Swann*. Separation has resulted from varied forces. It is unreal to say that some are state action and others are not. But if the Court won't take that step, the distinction between Park Hill and the core area strikes me as artificial. The district court found that there was no de jure segregation, and the court of appeals affirmed this. I am not willing to upset it. So I affirm. I am also unwilling to say that the inferior education that resulted is a *Plessy v. Ferguson* violation.[110] If it were, I would correct it. Socioeconomic conditions determine the quality of the schools. The low quality of education for low income whites is the same as the low quality of education for blacks. I affirm.

REHNQUIST: It never occurred to me to reject the distinction between de jure and de facto segregation. If a school board draws a line along racial lines, the remedy is to change the line. So I agree with the two courts below.

Result: In a narrow, 5–2–1 compromise opinion, the Court ruled that Judge Doyle had applied the wrong legal standard and remanded the case for further consideration. Brennan's opinion, however, held that the school board's actions could amount to de jure segregation of the entire system. He advanced two main arguments for Judge Doyle to consider on remand. First, proof of intentional segregation in a "substantial portion" of a school district could support a finding of a dual system. Second, where intentional segregation was maintained in a "significant portion" of the school district, the school district had the burden of proof to demonstrate a lack of segregative intent elsewhere in the district. Judge Doyle was asked on remand to determine whether de jure segregation in the Park Hill area should be considered in isolation from the rest of the district, or whether it meant that the Denver school district as a whole was a dual system of education. Burger concurred in the judgment. Powell concurred in part but mostly dissented, and Rehnquist dissented. White did not participate.

There was significant fluidity and negotiation among the Justices behind the scenes. One of the more fascinating aspects of this case was that five justices—Douglas, Brennan, Stewart, Blackmun, and Powell—agreed in a fascinating exchange of private memoranda that the distinction between de jure and de facto segregation should be abandoned.[111] Instead, they proposed that the mere existence

---

110. *Plessy v. Ferguson*, 163 U.S. 537 (1896).

111. Blackmun was the most ambivalent of the group, saying later that he thought the distinction between de jure and de facto discrimination would "eventually" have to give way.

of segregated public schools would be prima facie evidence of a constitutional violation. This group remained divided by other issues, however, and never coalesced into a working majority. In the end, only Douglas and Powell held to the position that there was no constitutional distinction between de jure and de facto segregation.[112]

School Board of the City of Richmond v. Bradley, 412 U.S. 92 (1973)
(Douglas) (Brennan)

Carolyn Bradley and other black parents sued the Richmond school board in 1961, claiming that the city maintained a dual school system in violation of Brown v. Board of Education. *In a long-delayed attempt to comply with* Brown, *the local federal district court ordered the largely black Richmond city school district to merge with two adjoining white districts in order to achieve a better racial balance.*[113] *District Judge Robert Merhige posted a target of between 20 and 40 percent black students in each school but made it clear that he was not imposing a quota. The court of appeals reversed on the grounds that: (1) the Richmond school district was already a unitary school system; (2) the district court's order violated the Tenth Amendment; and (3) Judge Merhige's order exceeded his equitable powers established in* Swann.

Conference of April 1973

BURGER: This looks like a racial balance case. I pass.

DOUGLAS: There is no constitutional question. It is a matter of administration and an equitable remedy. I agree with Judge Winter below.[114] I reverse, although I hope that the Court can be unanimous in what it does.

---

112. Powell, a native Virginian, served as the chair of the Richmond school board from 1952 to 1961. As a board member, he rejected segregationist pressure to close Richmond's public schools in the wake of *Brown v. Board of Education.* Powell's position in this case was unique and revealing. He thought that the de facto/de jure distinction was the product of northern hypocrisy in the Court's desegregation cases. Powell's dissent in *Keyes* noted that little progress had been made to desegregate northern cities with large minority populations, compared to what had been achieved in many southern cities. This was, he maintained, because the de jure/de facto distinction allowed northern cities to escape judicial review of their discriminatory racial practices, while federal courts routinely condemned and punished southern segregation. The Supreme Court, Powell said, must abandon this untenable distinction "and formulate constitutional principles of national rather than merely regional application" (*Keyes*, at 218–19). At the same time, Powell sought to limit the scope of available remedies in order to protect neighborhood schools and insulate local school boards from overly intrusive judges.

113. The Richmond city school district was 64 percent black, the Henrico school district was 92 percent white, and the Chesterfield school district was 91 percent white. Combined, the three districts would have been 67 percent white and 33 percent black.

114. Circuit Judge Harrison L. Winter rejected the majority's ruling that Richmond had established a unitary school system and said that the city had long maintained a de jure, dual system of education. He pointed to "the sordid history of Virginia's, and Richmond's, attempts to circumvent, defeat, and nullify the holding of *Brown I*" and argued that combining the Richmond, Henrico and Chesterfield school districts was a reasonable way to bring the city at last into compliance with *Brown.* Judge Merhige's proposed targets did not establish a rigid racial quota or permanent racial balancing but merely served as a starting point for reform. The district judge, Winter concluded, had acted within his equitable powers under *Swann* to establish a unitary school system.

BRENNAN: The majority position in the court of appeals is false. Winter's approach is correct. This is not a racial balance case. Is this remedy proper? If the state had consolidated the three cases, this would have been proper. I am loathe to interfere with a district court decree. I reverse.

STEWART: Correctly analyzed, this is a matter of remedy. Since there was no manipulation of lines here, and no cooperation among the districts to exchange students to maintain a segregated system, I would affirm. This is simply a Richmond school district lawsuit, and it ought to stay within Richmond lines. There was no defiance, or manipulation, or anything of that kind. It's not that there is no power in the district court—it is just that the judge exceeded his discretion.

WHITE: It is a matter of remedy. I don't think that the district court was disempowered to disregard school district lines in fashioning a remedy. I think that is what the court of appeals did, and that is wrong. The court of appeals never considered the case of fashioning a remedy crossing district lines. I would want them to be given the correct standard and then have them fashion a remedy based on crossing county lines. I would reverse and remand to the court of appeals to have them reconsider that issue.

MARSHALL: I would reverse outright. There is no dispute on either side on state law. If the local school board and local district court agree as we said in *Brown*, we should buy it.

WHITE: The court of appeals opinion states that it is a racial quota case, but the court of appeals never reached the question of an equitable remedy.

MARSHALL: I agree with Winter.

BLACKMUN: I am not at rest. Byron's suggestion is O.K. with me, I think. Started out with opposition to forcing the disregard of district lines. We should stop arguing about whose fault it is. There is a great deal to be said on the metropolitan aspect.

WHITE: Perhaps the court of appeals is wrong in calling this a quota. If school district lines are not a barrier, the alternative to the district court is not a three-district decree. We have constantly disregarded state-drawn lines in reapportionment cases.

REHNQUIST: There is no joint wrong, so no joint remedy. The district court has the power to adjudicate the rights of anyone. The court of appeals does not mean that kind of power. The substantive issue disappears if there is a manipulative purpose. I affirm.

Result: With Powell out of the case, the Court deadlocked 4–4, meaning that the decision of the circuit court of appeals was affirmed by default, though without setting a precedent.[115] The Court's decision was announced without any opinion or explanation.

---

115. Powell recused himself because he had previously served as the chair of the Richmond school board.

Milliken v. Bradley, 418 U.S. 717 (1974)
Allen Park Public Schools v. Bradley
Grosse Pointe Public School System v. Bradley
(Douglas)

Among 289 Detroit city schools in 1970, 69 were at least 90 percent white and 133 were at least 90 percent black.[116] By 1973, white flight left virtually all Detroit city schools predominantly black—an urban bull's-eye surrounded by a ring of white suburban school districts. Ronald Bradley and other black families sued Michigan governor William G. Milliken, demanding that the city's school system be integrated.

The trial court found that the Detroit school board had been partly responsible for intensifying segregation in city schools and promoting one-race schools. District Judge Stephen J. Roth ruled that there was sufficient state action to justify a finding of de jure segregation. This triggered the court's equitable powers to craft an effective remedy. Judge Roth also found that Detroit city schools could not be integrated without including fifty-three suburban school districts (503,000 students, most of them white) with Detroit's 276,000 urban students (70 percent of whom were black.) Treating the greater metropolitan area as a single community, Judge Roth created a comprehensive, multidistrict plan to integrate Detroit public schools that encompassed a variety of remedies, including redistricting and busing.

The court of appeals affirmed the district court's finding of de jure segregation in Detroit city schools and endorsed the need for an multidistrict remedy, but vacated the lower court's judgment and remanded the case so that the suburban school districts could be joined as parties and participate directly in the ongoing litigation.

Conference of March 1, 1974

BURGER: This is a highly factual case. Each district is a separate entity. Outlying districts keep a unitary system. They are here to implement a decree merging them with Detroit. The district court found that desegregation could not be achieved in the Detroit School District alone. I could find that only on a "racial balance" theory. The outlying schools, never having been part of a dual system, are urged to merge with other outside schools. The district court judge went way beyond what he could do, and the court of appeals erred in affirming. I reverse. It's like *Richmond.*[117]

DOUGLAS: I affirm. There are no due process questions. The state has several districts, and they are homogeneous. The district court can deal with them as a unit.

BRENNAN: I affirm. Suburban school districts still have a hearing to decide their fates. I voted to reverse in the *Richmond* case. If I am wrong on it, I am not wrong in the New Jersey case.

---

116. *Bradley v. Milliken,* 484 F.2d 215, 245 (6th Cir. 1973). In 1960, of 251 city schools, 100 were at least 90 percent white and 71 were at least 90 percent black.

117. *Bradley v. School Board of the City of Richmond,* 462 F.2d 1058 (4th Cir. 1972), aff'd by an equally divided Court, 412 U.S. 92 (1973).

STEWART: I agree with the solicitor general, and vote to vacate and remand.[118]

WHITE: I affirm. I have not changed my mind since *Richmond*. The state here is guilty of de jure segregation. If it was restricted to Detroit, nonetheless, as a matter of remedy, you are not barred from going into other districts. Perhaps the district court has overtones. I am not in favor of an overall "racial balance."

MARSHALL: I affirm. There are white schools in Detroit a half mile from black schools—Deerfield, for example.

BLACKMUN: Some question that this is not a final order. The case is weaker than in *Richmond*, where only three counties were involved and each was pro-segregationist. I am inclined to go along with the solicitor general. I reverse.

POWELL: This is open-ended jurisdiction, with as many as eighty-four districts. No remedy has been as far reaching as this one. It is a monstrosity on its face. The plan would in operation be chaotic. It would destroy local government and the power to issue bonds and raise revenues. I agreed initially with the solicitor general's memo, although I think that there may be an inter-district remedy.

REHNQUIST: I follow the Chief Justice, Potter, and Lewis. I reverse.

Result: After sustaining a tradition of consensus in school desegregation cases for more than twenty years, the Court's cohesiveness first wobbled in Keyes v. School District No. 1 *and then fell apart here. Warren Burger wrote for the 5–4 majority that the trial court improperly sought to establish a racial balance in Detroit schools at any cost and that the multidistrict remedy proposed here far exceeded the constitutional wrong done by the Detroit school board. Because there was no evidence of de jure segregation on the part of suburban schools—they were the result of de facto social segregation—Judge Roth had no right to include them in his desegregation plan for Detroit schools. The proposed interdistrict remedy, Burger said, overwhelmed our "deeply rooted" attachment to local control of schools and would wrongly transform the constitutional right established in* Brown—*to be free from government-sponsored racial discrimination—into a "right" to attend racially balanced schools. This was unsound constitutional law and unwise public policy. Regrettably, Burger concluded, only the few remaining white students in Detroit schools could be reshuffled to help balance the city's one-race schools.*

Byron White's dissent blasted Burger for being "talismanic" about local control of education and exaggerating the sanctity of district lines. He accused the majority of failing to address the real constitutional problems posed by the case. Douglas's dissent claimed that the majority condemned black Detroit schoolchildren to a separate and inherently inferior education. More ominously, he said, when combined with the Court's previous decision in San Antonio v. Rodriguez, *the Court was condemning urban schools to a separate and unequal existence, in worse shape than they would have been in under* Plessy v. Ferguson.

Thurgood Marshall, in a lengthy dissent, charged that the Court's rulings in this case and in San Antonio v. Rodriguez *were "making a solemn mockery of* Brown."[119] *After twenty years of small,*

---

118. Solicitor General Robert Bork argued in favor of reversal.

119. *San Antonio v. Rodriguez*, 411 U.S. 1 (1973). This case is discussed below in the section on wealth and poverty.

often difficult steps toward equal justice under law, Marshall wrote, the Court was taking "a giant step backwards." The majority had "emasculated" the equal protection clause and denied American children of all races an equal start in life and an equal opportunity to reach their "full potential as citizens." In Marshall's opinion, local district lines were artificial and flexible borders, and district judges had discretion to change these boundaries in order to shape an effective remedy to desegregate city schools. The Supreme Court, Marshall concluded, should be courageous in requiring integration, even if it involved disruptions: "In the short run, it may seem to be the easier course to allow our great metropolitan areas to be divided up each into two cities—one white, one black—but it is a course, I predict, our people will ultimately regret."

Milliken v. Bradley (Milliken II), 433 U.S. 267 (1977)
(Brennan)

In Milliken I, *the Supreme Court ruled that even if Detroit's inner-city schools were segregated due to state action, suburban school districts could not be included to create a unitary school district without evidence that the outlying districts had contributed to de jure segregation.[120] On remand, the Detroit school board submitted a new plan to the district court, asking permission to begin new compensatory and remedial programs. The district court approved the plan and ordered new programs in reading, teacher training, testing and counseling. Judge Roth ordered that the costs for these new programs be shared by the Detroit school district and the state of Michigan. The court of appeals affirmed. Michigan claimed that it was immune from having to pay retrospective damages under the Eleventh Amendment and* Edelman v. Jordan.[121]

BURGER: The private plan here focused on pupil reassignment. The school board plan added educational components. Did the district court exceed its powers? This type of remedy has been familiar in other plans. I think that the district court was empowered to do this, and the real problem for me is the Eleventh Amendment. There is no real problem about the scope of remedy, since the city affirmed the plan.

STEWART: I don't have problems with the Eleventh Amendment, but on the scope of the remedy. To let the state, even if guilty, be subject to a court order to share costs—I'm going to pass. The order of action in the future takes this out of the Eleventh Amendment and places it within *Edelman.*

WHITE: I see no problem on the scope of the remedy. The things ordered have a direct relation to the violation. And there can be no Eleventh Amendment bar or we could never order a state to do anything.

MARSHALL: I affirm on the arguments of counsel for the school board.

---

120. *Milliken v. Bradley,* 418 U.S. 717 (1974).

121. *Edelman v. Jordan,* 415 U.S. 651 (1974). The Court overturned a lower federal court injunction ordering state officials to reimburse plaintiffs for welfare benefits lost before the date of judgment. The Court interpreted the Eleventh Amendment to bar such retroactive relief, including the payment of cash damages from the state treasury, when the federal law invoked (in this case, the Social Security Act) did not authorize such suits. One of the main questions facing the Court in *Milliken II* was whether the remedies were retrospective and barred by *Edelman* or prospective and therefore constitutionally permissible.

BLACKMUN: The state was a violator, and so I have no trouble with the scope of the remedy here. If we allowed only busing and knock out the other components of the remedy, nothing would be done actually to desegregate. I see no problems with the Eleventh Amendment.

POWELL: This is more of a watershed case beyond *Swann*.[122] I have sat on a school board and the rest of you have not. It is not the Eleventh Amendment that bothers me, but the idea of putting courts into the seats of the school board—that's all wrong. This is the most far-reaching intrusion I have seen yet. There was no testimony of discrimination with respect to these components, so for me there is no constitutional violation proved.

REHNQUIST: I approach this case somewhat differently from Lewis. I see a serious Eleventh Amendment problem. The school board and the district court made a sweetheart arrangement, since the district court did what the board asked. But the state was put under a judicial order to pay money—an order that of course required a preceding finding of constitutional violation. So it is a cash award for past action, which *Edelman* held that the Eleventh Amendment prohibits. *Fitzpatrick v. Bitzer* is not relevant, since that turned on a statute enacted under §5 of the Fourteenth Amendment.[123] And even if the Eleventh Amendment was no bar here, I would agree with Lewis on the scope of the remedy.[124]

STEVENS: I agree with Harry. I don't regard the absence of findings as to components as even relevant. Like an anti-trust decree, you add remedial measures to correct a finding of wrongdoing. This is a rip-off against the state. You have got two joint wrongdoers, which is what calms the case as against the state. You couldn't really correct this without doing what was done. On the Eleventh Amendment *Edelman* may be enough, but this is really an *Ex parte Young* situation. Strike a balance there as to *future* relief.[125]

---

122. *Swann v. Charlotte-Mecklenburg Board of Education*, 402 U.S. 1 (1971).

123. *Fitzpatrick v. Bitzer*, 427 U.S. 445 (1976). This was a class-action suit alleging that the Connecticut state retirement plan discriminated against men, in violation of Title 7 of the Civil Rights Act of 1964. The trial court granted injunctive relief but refused to award retroactive retirement benefits or attorney's fees on the ground that such relief was barred by the Eleventh Amendment and *Edelman*. The Supreme Court upheld the injunction but reversed the trial court's refusal to order compensatory damages or attorney's fees. Rehnquist's majority opinion ruled that under §5 of the Fourteenth Amendment (which empowered Congress to enforce the terms of the Amendment by appropriate legislation), Congress could make states liable for cash damages and attorney's fees in employment discrimination cases. Brennan concurred on the ground that states did not have a general grant of sovereign immunity, and the Eleventh Amendment only barred suits by citizens of other states. Stevens concurred on the ground that the commerce clause provided sufficient authority for Congress to authorize such suits.

124. Rehnquist's broad interpretation of the Eleventh Amendment was a distinctly minority view in 1977. By 1999, however, his views dominated the Court. In a series of 5–4 decisions, the Rehnquist Court used the Eleventh Amendment to bar a broad range of lawsuits against states. See, for example, *Alden v. Maine*, 527 U.S. 706 (1999); *College Savings Bank v. Florida Prepaidpostsecondary Ed. Expense Bd.*, 119 S. Ct. 2219 (1999); *Florida Prepaidpostsecondary Ed. Expense Bd. v. College Savings Bank*, 119 S. Ct. 2199 (1999).

125. *Ex parte Young*, 209 U.S. 123 (1908). The Court ruled that state officials who enforced an unconstitutional statute could be sued in their individual capacities. The state had no power to grant immunity to such persons against the supreme authority of the United States. Federal courts could enjoin state officials from enforcing unconstitutional statutes and could grant other equitable relief.

Result: The Court unanimously affirmed the district court's order that the state and the city school district must share the costs of remedying de jure segregation in the Detroit school district. Lewis Powell and Thurgood Marshall wrote separate concurrences, mostly aimed at each other.[126] *After more than five years of litigation, Ronald Bradley's position had not noticeably improved. When this case was filed in August 1970, Bradley was assigned to attend kindergarten in a Detroit school that was 97 percent black. In September 1976, he was ready to enter the sixth grade of the Clinton School, which was— and remains—99 percent black.*

RACIAL CLASSIFICATIONS

Korematsu v. United States, 323 U.S. 214 (1944)
(Douglas) (Jackson) (Murphy)

With World War II raging and the West Coast bracing for an anticipated Japanese attack, Franklin Roosevelt appointed Lt. General J. L. De Witt commanding general of the Western Defense Command. In March 1942, De Witt declared the West Coast a military zone and imposed a curfew and travel restrictions on German, Italian, and Japanese nationals. He also imposed a curfew on American citizens of Japanese descent and prohibited them from leaving the coastal zone. On May 2, De Witt issued Civilian Exclusion Order No. 34, directing all persons of Japanese ancestry to be removed from the West Coast military zone. Because of the war, military authorities claimed that there was no time to determine individual loyalties.[127] *All ethnic Japanese were ordered to report to local assembly centers, where they stayed until they could be sent to relocation centers inland. Within two months, more than 120,000 ethnic Japanese, including 70,000 American citizens, were relocated to isolated camps scattered across the western United States and Arkansas. Many lost their homes and property, and many more lost their businesses and way of life.*[128]

Fred Toyosaburo Korematsu, an American citizen, was arrested and convicted of violating the exclusion order after he failed to report to his assigned assembly center.[129] *The Ninth Circuit Court of*

---

126. Powell thought that this case was a "sport," a friendly suit between the plaintiffs and the Detroit school board to extort more money from the state treasury. Thurgood Marshall responded that the Detroit school board was simply acknowledging its "responsibility for the injuries that Negroes have suffered." Tushnet, *Making Constitutional Law,* 89.

127. General De Witt's order was authorized by President Roosevelt's Executive Order 9066, issued in February 1942 and ratified by Congress. There was no effort to determine individual wrongdoing or loyalty. In part, this was because of the unprecedented severity of the emergency. After Pearl Harbor, there was no effective American military presence in the Pacific, and military experts believed that a Japanese invasion of the West Coast was imminent. It is also fair to say that racism clouded American policymaking. As General De Witt later told a congressional committee, "A Jap's a Jap. . . . It makes no difference whether he's an American citizen or not. There is no way to determine their loyalty." Newman, *Hugo Black,* 313.

128. In 1948, Congress passed a law that provided compensation for those who lost real or personal property. The act did not provide compensation for damages caused by death, injury, inconvenience, hardship, suffering, or business losses. In all, 26,000 claims were filed and approximately $37 million was distributed, about 10 percent of total estimated losses of $400 million. American-Japanese Evacuation Claims Act, 50 U.S.C. §§1981–1987 (1948).

129. One of the relatively few *Nisei* (American-born, second-generation ethnic Japanese) who did not report as ordered, Korematsu had plastic surgery to hide his racial identity because he did not want to leave his girlfriend, who was of Italian ancestry.

Appeals affirmed his conviction. While waiting for his case to be heard, Korematsu spent two years at the Tanforan Assembly Center, a converted horse racetrack in San Bruno, California.

Conference of October 16, 1944

STONE: There is no indication of disloyalty—we cannot know. The question is the government's power to exclude and to hold in an assembly center. Are we confined to the exclusion order, or was it so tied in with the relocation orders that it must be considered with them?

(1) Assuming that it was merely the exclusion order: The circuit court of appeals, if right in that premise, is right in its conclusion. The status of the exclusion order is precisely the same as the curfew order. If the curfew order was authorized, then plainly the exclusion order would also be covered by the same statute.

(2) A change of situation is said to undercut the authorization and its justification. As to that, I have two things to say. First, since the order was valid when made, anyone challenging it must show that the danger was ended. Second, we can hardly say that under the *Chastleton* case.[130] We cannot say that there is no longer danger of sabotage or that the military might not think so.

(3) Can the exclusion order be treated separate and apart from detention? Paragraph 88 of the order sets off a certain area and directs exclusion. It also provides an exception in paragraph 4 of the assembly centers. Could they obey this order by doing anything but go into the assembly zone? Other orders forbade them from going elsewhere without permission. I assume at this point that the exclusion order could not be obeyed without going to the assembly center. I do not rely much on the fact that he might escape from the assembly center. I cannot say, as a matter of law, that one who goes to an assembly center will go into a relocation center. We cannot say whether such an order ever would be made. It probably would, but we cannot say that it certainly would. We must read the order as if it said that he should go to assembly center and stay there, subject to further orders. We must treat this indictment as disobedience of the order to go to the assembly center. If I am right, that ends the case.

---

130. *Chastleton Corp. v. Sinclair*, 264 U.S. 543 (1924). In 1919, Congress passed emergency wartime rent-control legislation for the District of Columbia and repeatedly reenacted the law, each time declaring that the emergency still existed. After Congress renewed the law a third time in 1922, the District of Columbia Rent Commission imposed retroactive rent cuts on an apartment building owned by the Chastleton Corporation. The company sued Sinclair and other rent commissioners to enjoin the rent cut, claiming that the state of emergency no longer existed and that the rent control law was no longer supportable.

Oliver Wendell Holmes, writing for the Court, admitted that a law which depended on a state of emergency may cease to operate once the emergency is over, and he recognized that it was a proper subject for judicial inquiry whether the exigency on which the law depended still existed. He noted that the federal government's wartime demand for federal employees had considerably diminished, as had the influx of new people into Washington, which ameliorated the housing squeeze that had justified the original act. If the question before the Court was whether the statute presently remained in force, Holmes continued, the Court might be compelled to reply in the negative. In this instance, however, it was essential to establish the conditions existing in Washington at various different dates in the past. Such complex fact-finding, he concluded, was more easily done at the trial court level, and so the case was remanded for additional fact-finding.

(4) If you take the other view—that the order was confinement in a relocation center—you come to a larger question. If the president should order zones to be made for exclusion and order machinery for moving them out, it would be constitutional. Once you concede the point of danger and sabotage, and the power of Congress to take proper means to make exclusion effective, the real question is: did Congress and the president intend it? You can make an ingenious argument that confinement was not included in authorization. There was no suggestion of enforcement in the materials before Congress. But almost immediately before the act, a proclamation established the relocation centers. Congress appropriated funds for these relocation centers. It was dealt with in an off-hand manner. But it was a large order to say that Congress and the president never intended to confine people. I think that Congress ratified this by appropriation, and that the act does authorize relocation centers as a place of confinement.

I would find the authority. I think that this order was within the government's power. I would decide this case on *Hirabayashi*.[131] In case of a citizen whose loyalty was not established and who was ordered to report, it was too early to attack the confinement phase of the same on constitutional grounds. If Congress authorized it, its power to do so was clear on constitutional grounds. If Congress did not, it is doubtful if the president would have the power to do so alone. I think that we cannot consider the relocation provision; I would confine the issue to the presence there and not question detention. I would follow the court of appeals and treat this merely as an exclusion order. I think that the order is valid, anyway. If they can keep them out of one area, they may keep them in another. I affirm.

ROBERTS: There was no martial law on the Pacific Coast. I would start with the *Hirabayashi* case. The action of the commander-in-chief was endorsed by Congress. I think that they might also have excluded them. But they did not have option of leaving the zone—he would have been arrested. He also did not have the option of staying. His only choice was to go to prison. It ends my consideration when he could not stay, and could not go, and he must go into the arms of authority. That is so violative of the constitutional rights of citizens that I think that he was wrongfully convicted. I reverse.

BLACK:[132] I agree with the Chief. He was given a chance to leave voluntarily. If so, *Hirabayashi* supports exclusion. It would take too long to classify individuals. If we hold Endo to be freed, it would go a long way to hold that this case involved the same principle.[133] I affirm.

---

131. *Hirabayashi v. United States,* 320 U.S. 81 (1943).

132. Black and De Witt had been close friends for more than a decade before *Korematsu* was decided. No one else on the Court knew of their friendship except for Douglas. Both Black and Douglas had been guests at De Witt's West Coast home before the war began. Ball, *Hugo L. Black,* 175–76.

133. Mitsuye Endo was an American citizen of Japanese descent. After she was removed from the West Coast and imprisoned in a relocation center, she petitioned the federal courts for a writ of habeas corpus. On the same day that *Korematsu* was decided, the Court ruled that Endo could not be detained in a relocation camp without evidence of having committed a crime. There were two crucial differences between Endo and Korematsu. First, the American government had admitted that Endo was a loyal American citizen. Second, unlike Fred Korematsu, she had obeyed the expulsion order and so had not been charged with any crime. *Ex parte Endo,* 323 U.S. 283 (1944).

REED: These acts were authorized. I agree with the Chief Justice and Black. What was done was within valid orders and acts. I would look at it narrowly. I would say that there was a violation of the order not to remain in the area, and stop there. He was not indicted for his refusal to go to the assembly center. I affirm.

FRANKFURTER: On the merits, I agree in substance with the Chief Justice. I cannot say that there was an absence of security reasons here. I take it as though Congress had spelled out the whole thing. See *Tiaco v. Forbes* on ratification.[134] I affirm.

DOUGLAS: I reverse. There was no constitutional authority to arrest without probable cause.

MURPHY: I am troubled. I dissented in *Hirabayashi* and then changed my mind.[135] I think that we were wrong in *Hirabayashi*. [DOUGLAS: Murphy pays tribute to DeWitt—he compares him to Freemont [*sic*] and Lincoln.][136]

JACKSON: I would not limit this to sabotage—it was a state of war. I don't think that he could be excluded because of his Japanese ancestry. I stop with *Hirabayashi* last year, and no further. They say that the courts have got to become a part of it. I don't accept military orders as something that we have to accept without any inquiry into their reasonableness. I reverse.

STONE: You are saying that the Congress's and president's actions together are unable to make zones to protect us against military espionage and sabotage? If you can do it for a curfew, you can do it for exclusion.

RUTLEDGE: I had to swallow *Hirabayashi*. I didn't like it. At that time, I knew that if I went along with that order then I had to go along with detention for a reasonably necessary time. Nothing but necessity would justify it because of *Hirabayashi*, and so I vote to affirm tentatively. I think that the authorities could hold him to determine loyalty.

STONE: I affirm on this record.

---

134. *Tiaco v. Forbes*, 228 U.S. 549 (1913). This case involved the deportation of a Chinese national from the Philippines on the order of the governor general. Some time later, Congress passed legislation authorizing such deportations. The Court upheld the deportation order on the ground that it was a valid exercise of executive authority that had been confirmed, at least in retrospect, by subsequent congressional ratification.

135. *Hirabayashi v. United States*, 320 U.S. 81 (1943). Murphy originally wrote a sharp dissent in Hirabayashi but did not publish it. Under pressure from the majority, he relented and concurred in the result to make the vote unanimous. Fine, *Frank Murphy: The Washington Years*, 443. In *Hirabayashi*, the Court decided only the narrow issue of whether General De Witt's curfew order was valid, and refused to consider the thornier questions of detention in assembly centers and relocation to internment camps.

136. It is not entirely clear to what Murphy was referring. Lincoln's relationship with John C. Frémont was ambivalent, at best. Frémont was an unsuccessful Republican candidate for president in 1856 and a Civil War general in charge of Missouri during the early part of the war. In 1861, General Frémont issued an order on his own authority freeing all slaves in Missouri. Abraham Lincoln quickly rescinded the order, stating that neither the military nor the president could promulgate permanent rules of property by proclamation. Lincoln held this belief until 1863, when he issued the Emancipation Proclamation. Neely, "Emancipation Proclamation." Lincoln eventually relieved Frémont of his Missouri command on the ground that Frémont was "too isolated from the situation around him."

Result: On a 6–3 vote, the Court upheld the government's exclusion order and ruled that Fred Korematsu had unlawfully violated the order. Black's opinion focused solely on the constitutionality of Korematsu's detention and did not address the more difficult and divisive questions involving the constitutionality of the assembly centers and internment camps. Douglas changed his mind after the conference to give Black a relatively comfortable majority in support of the government's position.

While Black's opinion has been subjected to withering criticism by civil libertarians, Korematsu *established the modern principle that laws which create categories based on race are inherently suspect and subject to strict judicial scrutiny.*[137] *Black reasoned, however, that the exclusion order was not a group punishment based on race but a temporary exclusion based on a reasonable military determination during a world war: that in the middle of a most grave national emergency it was impossible to separate immediately the disloyal from the loyal, and it was better to be safe than sorry.*

The three dissenting Justices—Roberts, Murphy, and Jackson—assailed Black's position. Owen Roberts bluntly called the relocation centers concentration camps, while Frank Murphy decried what he called the "legalization of racism" and condemned the government's punishment of persons based solely on their ancestry. With its wartime policy of forced relocation and internment, Murphy said, America stood on the edge of "the ugly abyss of racism." The third dissenter, Robert Jackson, warned against undermining the principle of individual guilt and worried about the virtually unlimited discretion that the majority allowed the government and the military during claimed emergencies. For Jackson, that sort of unquestioned, absolute power was more consistent with a Leninist model of absolute dictatorship than with American democratic government. This sort of racial discrimination and wholesale imprisonment of American citizens, he wrote, "lies about like a loaded weapon ready for the hand of any authority that can bring forward a plausible claim of an urgent need."

Immediately after the October 16 conference, Douglas wrote—but did not publish—a dissenting opinion in which he sought to distinguish between the forced evacuations, which he thought constitutional, from imprisonment in internment camps (Douglas euphemistically referred to them as "havens"), which he thought unconstitutional. Douglas also believed that Americans detained under such circumstances must be provided with the opportunity to be heard and reclassified as loyal citizens.[138] *Black, Frankfurter, and Stone lobbied hard behind the scenes to persuade Douglas that the constitutionality of the assembly centers and relocation camps as not at issue and should be left for another day. On December 6, the eve of the third anniversary of Pearl Harbor, Douglas withdrew his dissent and joined the majority, to his later regret. In his autobiography, Douglas acknowledged that for the rest of his life the case of Fred Korematsu rested heavily on his conscience.*[139]

---

137. The NAACP later relied heavily on *Korematsu* in its arguments before the Supreme Court in *Brown v. Board of Education*, arguing that the case raised the bar for racial classifications from a reasonableness test (*Plessy*) to requiring strict judicial scrutiny.

138. In *Hirabayashi v. United States*, Douglas explained in several memoranda circulated to the conference in May and June of 1943 that he thought that these extraordinary precautions were justified because the exigencies of war did not "permit enough time to sort out the sheep from the goats." He said that he would go along with the Court on two conditions: (1) that the group treatment was temporary; and (2) that individuals would have the opportunity to be reclassified as loyal citizens. Urofsky, *The Douglas Letters*, 103.

139. Douglas, *The Court Years*, 280.

Ex parte Endo, 323 U.S. 283 (1944)
(Murphy) (Douglas)

As part of the wartime exclusion and internment program, Mitsuye Endo, an American citizen from Sacramento, reported as ordered in May 1942 to the assembly center at a converted racetrack near the state capital. Conditions at the camp were crude; many families lived in whitewashed horse stalls. In June 1942, Endo was transferred to the Tule Lake War Relocation Center at Newell, California, and later to an internment camp in Topaz, Utah. In July 1942, she sought a writ of habeas corpus, which the district court in northern California rejected a year later, in July 1943. Endo then received official clearance from the War Relocation Authority to apply for a permit to leave the Topaz camp. Camp officials refused to release her, however, citing local resettlement problems in Utah. Because the government admitted that Endo was a loyal American citizen and because she had broken no laws, the question was whether the government had any right to detain her.

Conference of October 16, 1944

STONE: She was an American of Japanese descent. Her loyalty was not contended. She went through the mill and went to a relocation center and got leave, but insisted on her right to a discharge. The district court had jurisdiction over her place of confinement. Someone for the government appeared in opposition to her petition. But below and here, the government concedes that leave clearance implied that she was not disloyal and would not be a danger.

The question is: can a loyal citizen be held in a relocation center under restraint, for the purpose of containing her there, unless she applied for release on condition? The whole basis of these orders was the presence of disloyal people among the mass of Jap citizens. All orders were based on the possibility of danger from those who might be disloyal. Once loyalty is shown, the basis for the military decision disappears. On the merits, this woman is entitled to summary release.

So the question comes down to this: are we in a position to release her? What is the authority of the Court in a case like this? She is no longer subject to the orders of the district court. The writ has not yet issued. The prayer is that the writ be issued against those who are in charge. Assuming that the respondents have control of her (which we do not know), does this Court have jurisdiction? Does her removal from the area deprive this Court of jurisdiction? No. Orders run against the person in whose custody the applicant is. If that person is under the jurisdiction of this Court, this Court has jurisdiction of the case. The solicitor general has filed a letter with the Court saying that the Interior Department will deliver the petitioner if any officer of the Department is served. That shows that the case is not moot if any officer is before the district court. If not, this might require an amendment of her petition. We could issue our own writ. This Court has reversed convictions of military authority on the theory that habeas corpus—.[140] It is within our appellate power to do so, although perhaps it would not be wise to reach that question. I would give reasons why a writ should issue, so that the district court could act on it. This is an appeal that is properly before us.

---

140. *Ex parte Milligan,* 71 U.S. (4 Wall.) 2 (1866).

REED: An admittedly loyal citizen cannot be constitutionally restricted from the general freedom of other loyal citizens, even in wartime. Classes of citizens can be barred from certain areas for fear of espionage, sabotage, and so forth, but all admittedly loyal citizens must have the same privileges of movement.[141]

FRANKFURTER: The case is not moot. We ought to spell it out. Rule 45(1) ought to bring it out on the merits.[142] To me, the problem is the same as if all citizens of California were in it.

Result: A unanimous Court ordered Endo's unconditional release but conspicuously avoided ruling on the constitutionality of the relocation order itself. Endo was released on a technicality—that the orders establishing the evacuation and relocation program had not specifically included the detention of loyal citizens.

Endo's case was helped by the fact that West Coast fears of Japanese invasion and sabotage had largely subsided by 1944. As early as March 1943, the director of the War Relocation Authority had suggested repealing the exclusion and relocation orders.

The Court's decision was announced on the same day as Korematsu, *December 18, 1944. The decision was ready more than a month earlier, on November 4, but Chief Justice Stone delayed the case until after Roosevelt officially rescinded the wartime internment order on December 17, 1944. Roosevelt did not want to end the relocation program until after the November elections, and Stone collaborated with the Roosevelt administration to spare the president any possible embarrassment.[143]*

McLaughlin v. Florida, 379 U.S. 184 (1964)
(Douglas)

Dewey McLaughlin and Connie Hoffman were an unmarried interracial couple prosecuted under a Florida law that made it a crime for a black person and a white person to "habitually live in and occupy in the nighttime the same room." They were jailed for thirty days and fined $150 apiece. Florida also had an antimiscegenation law that criminalized interracial marriage; but to be prosecuted under that law the couple would have had to meet Florida's requirements for a common law marriage. Alternatively, couples of any race could be prosecuted under the state's adultery and fornication statutes, but those laws required proof that sexual intercourse had taken place. The interracial cohabitation statute had no such requirements.

---

141. Reed's comments are from his talking papers prepared for the conference. Fassett, *New Deal Justice,* 342.

142. Supreme Court Rule 45(1) provided that: "Pending review of a decision refusing a writ of habeas corpus, the custody of the prisoner shall not be disturbed." At the time the suit began, Endo was within the territorial jurisdiction of the district court that considered her habeas corpus petition. The government subsequently removed her to another jurisdiction and then claimed that Rule 45(1) barred the Supreme Court from ordering her released. The Court ultimately decided that the policy behind the rule meant that the government could not defeat the Court's jurisdiction merely by moving Endo to another jurisdiction, even if her removal was for a legitimate reason. This case established the rule that the Court had jurisdiction to review a habeas corpus petition so long as it had jurisdiction over the person holding the petitioner in custody.

143. Howard Ball, "Loyalty, Treason, and the State: An Examination of Justice William O. Douglas's Style, Substance, and Anguish," in Wasby, *"He Shall Not Pass This Way Again,"* 14.

Conference of October 16, 1964

WARREN: I reverse on equal protection or on *Dorsey*.[144] I can't see any justification for denying common law marriage to those of different races and granting it to others.

BLACK: I do not see how the question can be decided without deciding the marriage question. If we reverse here, state marriage laws would have to go also. This is a bad case to reach the issue. The record indicates that both of these people are married. If we do not dismiss—

CLARK: I would dismiss.

DOUGLAS: I would dismiss as improvidently granted, because no marriage is involved and I thought there was when I voted to grant certiorari.

HARLAN: If a state can base a miscegenation act on race, they can have a cohabitation act based on race. Both would be unconstitutional, I think, but I have to go through the history of the Fourteenth Amendment first. I pass.

BRENNAN: I reverse. I voted to take the case on the crime now presented. This act is unconstitutional. The history of the Fourteenth Amendment may show that miscegenation laws were not outlawed, but this is different. The proof on Negro blood was not adequate by our vagueness test.

STEWART: The cohabitation act is unconstitutional. I would not reach the miscegenation act. Our decisions over the last ten years require us to reverse both this and the miscegenation act.

WHITE: I reverse and agree with Potter.

GOLDBERG: I reverse and agree with Potter. There was a lewdness statute under the theory that where any couple, no matter their color, could be convicted. No miscegenation issue is here.

Result: The Court unanimously struck down Florida's cohabitation statute on equal protection grounds, but left the state's antimiscegenation statute intact. Byron White's majority opinion noted that Florida had to prove fornication before it could punish same-race unmarried couples but that there was no such requirement for interracial relationships. Florida also imposed higher penalties for interracial cohabitation than for same-race adultery or fornication. Using strict scrutiny, White concluded that the interracial cohabitation statute was not necessary to protect the state's interest in protecting the morals of its citizens. White ignored Warren's and Brennan's inspired idea to link boxing and dating, and did not mention Dorsey in his majority opinion. Harlan, Stewart, and Douglas concurred, with the latter two pushing the Court to go further and strike down all race-based legislation as invidious discrimination.

---

144. The suggestion to decide this case based on *Dorsey* was originally Brennan's. *Dorsey* involved a Louisiana statute that prohibited interracial boxing matches. Joseph Dorsey, a black prizefighter, asked a three-judge district court to enjoin the Louisiana Athletic Commission from enforcing the statute. The district court agreed and issued the injunction. The Supreme Court summarily affirmed in a one-sentence per curiam "opinion." *State Athletic Commission v. Dorsey*, 359 U.S. 533 (1959).

Loving v. Virginia, 388 U.S. 1 (1967)
(Douglas)

On June 2, 1958, Virginia residents Mildred Jeter and Richard Loving went to Washington, D.C., to be married and then returned to Virginia to live. Because Mr. Loving was white and Mrs. Loving was part black and part American Indian, their marriage violated Virginia's 267-year-old antimiscegenation law. Five weeks after the Lovings were married, police went to their house in the middle of the night and arrested them. The couple pled guilty to avoid a jail sentence; they received a suspended sentence of one year in jail on the condition that they left the state for twenty-five years. In announcing his judgment, the trial judge said that

> *Almighty God created the races white, yellow, malay and red, and He placed them on separate continents. And but for the interference with His arrangement there would be no cause for such marriages. The fact that He separated the races shows that He did not intend for the races to mix.*

The Lovings moved to Washington, D.C., but were unhappy there and secretly returned to Virginia, where they lived with family and friends for five years. In 1963, Richard Loving wrote a letter to Attorney General Robert Kennedy asking for help. Kennedy forwarded the letter to the American Civil Liberties Union, which agreed to represent the couple in court.

At the time, sixteen states still had antimiscegenation laws on the books, and fourteen other states had recently repealed similar laws. Miscegenation cases had come to the Supreme Court as early as 1954, but at that time the Court was under fire for its school desegregation decisions,[145] and the Justices chose to duck the issue for more than a decade.[146] Emboldened by the Civil Rights Act of 1964, the Justices decided in 1966 that the time had finally come to face the issue squarely. Because the Justices had long ago agreed privately that these laws were unconstitutional, the conference discussion was disappointing, except as a showcase of Abe Fortas's flair for bawdy rhyme.

Conference of April 14, 1967

WARREN: This is a single equal protection case. The Fourteenth Amendment was intended to wipe out discrimination on the basis of race. Miscegenation statutes maintain white supremacy. They should all go down the drain. I reverse.

---

145. Segregationists saw school desegregation and miscegenation as two sides of the same coin. Southern legal arguments against school desegregation had in part been based on the view that racial mixing in schools would inevitably lead to miscegenation and mongrelization of the white race.

146. One particularly troubling miscegenation case was *Jackson v. State,* 72 So. 2d 114 (Ala. Ct. App.), cert. denied, 72 So. 2d 116 (Ala.), cert. denied, 348 US 888 (1954). Linnie Jackson, a black woman, was sentenced to five years in the state penitentiary for marrying a white man. The U.S. Supreme Court, fearing that a decision striking down the Alabama statute would cause irreparable harm to its efforts to enforce *Brown,* dismissed Jackson's handwritten petition for certiorari without comment, leaving her to serve out her term. The following year, in *Naim v. Naim,* 350 US 891 (1955), Frankfurter convinced the other Justices to use a dubious technicality to avoid deciding another miscegenation case that came to the Court on mandatory appeal—meaning that the Court was legally obligated to decide the case.

BLACK: I reverse. It violates equal protection then (1868) and now.[147]

DOUGLAS: I reverse.

CLARK: I reverse. Its purpose was to promote white supremacy.

HARLAN: I reverse. If the history of the Fourteenth Amendment showed exclusion of this matter, I would affirm. The Fourteenth Amendment is not ambulatory, so legislative history is relevant. The subject matter here is within the Fourteenth Amendment. The 1866 Act measures the scope of the Fourteenth Amendment.

BRENNAN: Reverse.

STEWART: Reverse.

WHITE: Reverse.

FORTAS: Reverse.

Three Poems to William O. Douglas from Abe Fortas regarding Loving v. Virginia:

The argument sociologically
Is overwhelming anthropologically
But the legal principle
Is not so non-sensible.

*   *   *

A number of spouses
Is not like grouses
Many spouses add up to spice
Many grouses mean lots of grice
A grouse in hand is worth a lot
A spouse in hand may be or not
But grice in the bush are wasted
While spice in the bush may be tasted.

*   *   *

Loving may marry a Jap
A gal from anywhere on the map
But not a black, even one-third
With two-thirds blood of the Byrd.[148]

---

147. As a young southern politician, Black favored antimiscegenation laws and apparently believed that northern states would eventually adopt them as well. In 1929, he wrote that "the intelligent Northern and Eastern people will in all probability come to realize the merit in our Southern legislation along this line." Newman, *Hugo Black: A Biography,* 129.

148. The Byrd family has been a dominant force in Virginia politics for many years. At the time that *Loving* was decided, Senator Harry F. Byrd (D-VA) was the state's leading segregationist and supporter of the state's antimiscegenation law. Note from Abe Fortas to William O. Douglas (April 10, 1967), Douglas Papers, Box 1378.

Laura Kalman found a fourth *Loving v. Virginia* poem that Fortas penned for his own files:

> If the Lovings lie asleep all night
> Fearful of the copper's light
> Instead of tasting true love's might
> Why the hell did they get married in the first place?[149]

Result: The Court unanimously struck down Virginia's antimiscegenation statute. Earl Warren's first draft opinion tied the decision to Meyer v. Nebraska, *holding that some freedoms fundamental to family life were protected by the Fourteenth Amendment. Hugo Black protested that this approach would reanimate the discredited doctrine of substantive due process. Black maintained that marriage was not a constitutionally protected right and insisted that the* Meyer *citation be struck or he would not join the opinion. Warren deleted all references to* Meyer, *and Black joined the second draft to make the decision unanimous.*

STATE ACTION AND PRIVATE DISCRIMINATION

Shelley v. Kraemer, 334 U.S. 1 (1948)
McGhee v. Sipes
Hurd v. Hodge, 334 U.S. 24 (1948)[150]
Urciolo v. Hodge
(Burton) (Douglas)

J. D. and Ethel Lee Shelley, a black couple, bought a house in an all-white neighborhood from Robert Bishop, a local church pastor who sold real estate. Bishop did not tell the Shelleys that the property was covered by a racially restrictive covenant. Fern and Louis Kraemer, a white couple who lived in the neighborhood, sued to prevent the Shelleys from taking possession of the property. The trial judge ruled in favor of the Shelleys on the ground that the covenant was not intended to go into effect unless everyone in the neighborhood agreed—and nine households had not signed on. The Missouri Supreme Court reversed.

While the Supreme Court had little problem striking down state laws mandating segregated housing, in this case there were no state laws requiring segregation—only private agreements among individual homeowners. The key question was whether state court enforcement of these private covenants amounted to state action by involving the state in racist policies and practices.

The NAACP initially did not want this case appealed to the Supreme Court. It fell well outside the organization's carefully constructed strategy to attack private racial discrimination, and the organization feared that this case might set a bad precedent and set back their plans by a decade or

---

149. Kalman, *Abe Fortas*, 320.

150. *Hurd v. Hodge* involved two restrictive covenant cases from the District of Columbia. Because the District is not a state, the Fourteenth Amendment's equal protection clause did not apply. Instead, it was argued that judicial enforcement of the covenants was prohibited by the due process clause of the Fifth Amendment.

more.[151] *At the last minute, the organization found some unexpected support when the federal government intervened in the case and for the first time filed a brief arguing against racially restrictive covenants. This unprecedented step was due to the personal interest taken in the case by President Harry Truman, Attorney General Tom Clark, and Solicitor General Philip Perlman. Only six Justices participated in this case. Justices Reed, Jackson, and Rutledge all recused themselves because they owned property covered by restrictive covenants.*

Conference of February 2, 1948

VINSON: This should be reversed on the letter of the Fourteenth Amendment, as interpreted many times by this Court. There is state action. They have been deprived of their constitutional rights. I reverse.

BLACK: I can't see a difference between an act by a legislature and the actions of courts on a constitutional level. Courts can't enforce this. I am not sure whether the covenant in the District of Columbia case is violated. I reverse.

FRANKFURTER:[152] That is my view, as well. I reverse. Once again I will state that it is *Buchanan v Warley* to which I adhere.[153] I counted the number of times Bradley, J. [BURTON: One of "F's heroes"] referred to the government's procedures—eighteen times. The *state*, through its laws or *other agencies*, including judicial or executive action. If you get a judicial decree and it is disobeyed, the executive power comes in to enforce it. It also was held the same way in a number of other cases. I don't need to rely on society data.[154]

---

151. The guiding organization in this case was the St. Louis Real Estate Brokers' Association. George Vaughn, a lawyer for the brokers' association and a member of the local chapter of the NAACP, appealed to the Supreme Court against the wishes of Thurgood Marshall and the national leadership of the NAACP. After Vaughn filed the appeal, Marshall reluctantly committed himself to what he considered a factually suspect and poorly timed case. To make matters worse for Marshall, Vaughn was often stubborn and uncooperative. To make sure that the NAACP's views were fully represented, Marshall applied for a writ of certiorari in a Michigan covenant case, *Sipes v. McGhee*, 25 N.W.2d 638 (Mich.), cert. granted, 331 U.S. 804 (1947). Fortunately for Marshall, the Supreme Court consolidated the two cases when they accepted certiorari. The Court later added two other cases from the District of Columbia, *Hurd v. Hodge*, 332 U.S. 789 (1947), and *Urciolo v. Hodge*, 332 U.S. 789 (1947), both of which were being litigated by Marshall's mentor, Charles Hamilton Houston. Rubenstein, "Divided We Litigate: Addressing Disputes Among Group Members and Lawyers in Civil Rights Campaigns," 1627–29.

152. Burton's entry for Frankfurter was nearly illegible and should be read with particular caution.

153. *Buchanan v. Warley*, 245 US 60 (1917). In one of the first NAACP attacks on segregated housing, a unanimous Court, led by William Day, struck down a Louisville ordinance requiring segregated housing as a violation the Fourteenth Amendment. The state's interest in preserving racial harmony, Day wrote, could not be sustained by depriving citizens of their constitutional right to dispose of private property as they saw fit. Day suggested, however, that private racial covenants might be constitutional. Private racial covenants subsequently became common, although some segregation ordinances remained on the books.

154. The NAACP had been compiling sociological data to demonstrate the social and economic impact of racially restrictive covenants. Their study had not yet been completed when George Vaughn appealed *Shelley* to the Supreme Court. The federal government conducted its own study of the impact of these covenants on ten federal agencies, including the Department of the Interior. During oral arguments, Frankfurter closely questioned Thurgood Marshall as to whether such data was relevant. Frankfurter apparently believed that it would be relevant only regarding nonconstitutional, equitable arguments against racial covenants. Tushnet, *Making Civil Rights Law*, 91–92.

In the *Corrigan* case, the covenant *as such* was "violated."[155] The *Corrigan* case should be candidly discarded in so far as it differs.

DOUGLAS: I reverse.

MINTON: I reverse.

BURTON: I reverse. There was state action through the court's decree.

BLACK: I am not sure that the $2,000 penalty is invalidated in D.C. (equity disposed.)

FRANKFURTER and VINSON: Vacate the district court on this issue.

FRANKFURTER: The district court can go in equity.[156]

Result: The Court ruled in a 6–0 opinion by Chief Justice Vinson that while the Fourteenth Amendment did not prevent private parties from entering into racially restrictive covenants, the equal protection clause prohibited state courts from enforcing the terms of such covenants. This was a revolutionary interpretation of the state action doctrine, and it initially caused a flood of commotion and commentary. It soon became clear, however, that the broad definition of state action established here would not be expanded or extended. While Shelley *deservedly remains a famous case, its practical importance has diminished over the years. Anthony Lewis called it "a piece of lawyer's law, a sort of crooked case, that had no lasting impact on its time."[157]*

Henderson v. United States, 339 U.S. 816 (1950)
(Douglas) (Burton)

In 1942, Elmer W. Henderson traveled overnight by train from Washington, D.C., to Birmingham, Alabama. Henderson worked for President Roosevelt's Committee on Fair Employment Practices and was on government business. Three times he asked for dinner in the train's segregated dining car, and each time he was refused service. The two end tables nearest the kitchen were conditionally reserved for black passengers and could be separated from the rest of the car with a retractable curtain.[158] That evening, however, several whites were eating at both tables, and Henderson, who was black, was not permitted to join them. The dining car was detached from the train at 9:00 P.M., and Henderson went hungry.

---

155. *Corrigan v. Buckley*, 271 U.S. 323 (1926).

156. In *Hurd v. Hodge*, Frankfurter encouraged the Court to use its equitable powers to decline to enforce racial covenants in federal courts. The majority, however, based its decision on §1 of the Civil Rights Act of 1866, which guaranteed to all citizens the same property rights as white citizens had. The Court also suggested that judicial enforcement of these covenants would be contrary to public policy. This gave the Supreme Court authority to act in its supervisory capacity over the federal courts in the District of Columbia to prohibit judicial enforcement of racially restrictive covenants. Frankfurter concurred in the judgment.

157. Quoted in Richard Kluger, *Simple Justice*, 588.

158. Prior to the war and the corresponding increase in rail traffic, black and white passengers were customarily fed at different times. The railroad served black and white soldiers together; the company's segregation policies applied only to civilian passengers.

After he returned to Washington, Henderson filed a complaint with the Interstate Commerce Commission (ICC.) The ICC found that Henderson had suffered "undue and unreasonable prejudice and disadvantage," but concluded that what occurred was an isolated incident and required no further action. A three-judge federal district court in Maryland rejected the ICC's dismissal of Henderson's complaint and remanded the case for further proceedings.[159]

In the meantime, the railroad changed its regulations. Under the new regulations, ten tables in the dining car were reserved exclusively for whites and one table at the end of the car, separated from the rest of the tables by a wooden partition or a curtain, would be reserved exclusively for blacks. The ICC approved the new rules.

Henderson asked for a court order to provide equal dining facilities and to remove the signs, curtains, and partitions. He apparently dropped his original claim for damages. The same three-judge district court that heard his first appeal rejected his request and approved the new regulations.[160] *Henderson appealed to the Supreme Court, claiming that his treatment violated the Interstate Commerce Act and the Constitution.*[161] *The railroad defended its rules as necessary to preserve peace and order.*

Henderson's due process claim was problematic because the railroad was a private company. He argued that ICC inaction amounted to state action endorsing racial discrimination. The ICC submitted a brief claiming that its decision was obviously correct under Plessy v. Ferguson. *At that point the federal government, led by Solicitor General Philip Perlman and Attorney General Howard McGrath, renounced the ICC's argument, admitted error to the Supreme Court, and filed a brief supporting Henderson's claims and asking the Court to overturn* Plessy v. Ferguson.[162]

Conference of April 8, 1950

VINSON: *Mitchell* gives him standing to sue.[163] The statute says that there shall be no discrimination—it was violated. I reverse.

BLACK: The statute covers it. It is an act of Congress to prevent discrimination. I reverse.

REED: It is difficult for those of us who have felt the impact of segregation *personally* to pass on this issue.[164] It is a question of power. We have the power to declare something

---

159. *Henderson v. United States*, 63 F. Supp. 906 (D.C. Md. 1945).

160. *Henderson v. United States*, 80 F. Supp. 32 (D.C. Md. 1948).

161. Section 3(1) of the Interstate Commerce Act made it illegal to "subject any particular person. . . . to any undue or unreasonable prejudice or disadvantage in any respect whatsoever."

162. Elman, "The Solicitor General's Office," 820–21.

163. *Mitchell v. United States*, 313 U.S. 80 (1941). Black congressman Arthur W. Mitchell (D-IL) purchased a first-class ticket between Chicago and Hot Springs, Arkansas. When the train reached the Arkansas border, Mitchell was required by state law to move to an all-black car. Because the railroad had assigned a limited number of Pullman compartments to black passengers and they were already full, Mitchell had to settle for a second-class coach. He sued, claiming that the law violated the Interstate Commerce Act. A unanimous Court, in an opinion by Charles Evans Hughes, held that this was an unreasonable disadvantage under §3(1) of the act. The Court, however, did not question the right of states to require segregated cars.

164. Two years after this case was decided, the Court unanimously struck down a District of Columbia law requiring segregated restaurants. *District of Columbia v. John R. Thompson Co., Inc.*, 346 U.S. 100 (1953). This ruling affected Reed personally, as he and his wife ate virtually all of their meals at their segregated residential hotel. After the conference discussion in that case, Reed had second thoughts about his vote and reportedly complained, "Why—why, this means that a nigra can walk into the restaurant at the Mayflower Hotel and sit down to eat at the table right next to Mrs. Reed!" Richard Kluger, *Simple Justice*, 595.

unconstitutional—but to extend it to segregation? It is impossible to say that segregation per se is prohibited by the Constitution. It is like child labor or capital punishment and other great movements.

The historical approach is the most important. It is impossible for me to say that what has been accepted in our history is bad under the Constitution. When the Fourteenth Amendment came into effect, it was *not* intended to be legislation against segregation. It has not yet *grown into* that type of legislation, because the policy has been to go slowly. There have been no statements by Congress or the president that segregation is *unconstitutional*. Yet we have made progress (housing, *Bob-Lo*, voting, juries.)[165] It would be an unfortunate move, when one quarter have lived under it, to say that it is unconstitutional. I am prepared to follow Vinson and Black.

Under the statute, words almost reach into the races. The *Mitchell* case distinguishes segregation and discrimination.[166] I might rely on §1(4) even more than on §3(1.) I will reverse.

FRANKFURTER: It is futile to talk about what the Fourteenth Amendment "intended." [DOUGLAS: Frankfurter cites the non-discriminatory tradition at Harvard.] This is the difficult case. Does the *statute* prohibit this? Did Congress write segregation into this statute? In 1887, you cannot draw this distinction that segregation is out. "Discrimination" was written into the act in 1887. It does not carry overtones against segregation. It was a provision in the absence of service—*not segregation*. The solicitor general said that in fact there were not enough facilities for blacks. In fact, there was *no* provision for colored. That is *Mitchell*, and I could go for that.

On the procedural ground, I have difficulty with Henderson's standing to sue to get an injunction against future abuse, although *Mitchell* probably decides it. There is even a difficulty in the *Mitchell* case, where there was a damages suit pending. It is hard to distinguish *Mitchell* from the *McCabe* case, where the Court threw out the suit.[167] Reverse (?)

---

165. *Bob-Lo Excursion Co. v. Michigan*, 333 U.S. 28 (1948), upholding a Michigan state civil rights law prohibiting segregated public transportation. An amusement park offering steamboat rides to an island on the Canadian side of the Detroit River refused to transport a black girl who was with a group of forty white girls. The Court stretched to save the state statute from running afoul of the commerce clause, ruling that this international commercial enterprise was "highly local" and that the island was "economically and socially, though not politically, an amusement adjunct of the city of Detroit." Jackson and Vinson dissented, arguing that the decision gave states too much power to control foreign commerce and that the majority had abandoned sound legal reasoning and principle out of sympathy with Michigan's progressive civil rights policies.

166. Douglas's notes put a slightly different spin on Reed's discussion of *Henderson* and *Mitchell*. While Burton was careful to note that Reed drew a distinction between racial discrimination and segregation, Douglas quotes Reed as saying: "Segregation is bad under statute in *Henderson*—same problem under *Mitchell*."

167. *McCabe v. Atchison, T & S. F. R. Co.*, 235 U.S. 151 (1914). Oklahoma law required segregated train coaches and accommodations. The law also allowed public carriers to provide coaches, sleeping cars, dining cars, and other amenities reserved exclusively for whites. Before the law went into effect, McCabe and four others sought to enjoin enforcement of statute. For its part, the railroad company claimed that due to low demand it would be unreasonable to provide equal facilities for blacks. A unanimous Court, led by Charles Evans Hughes (with four Justices concurring in the result), threw out the case on the ground that the plaintiffs had failed to show sufficient personal need for an injunction and had not proven the inadequacy of their remedies at law. Hughes noted that there was no indication that the plaintiffs had actually

DOUGLAS: I have difficulty as to the statute. With logic, you can read it to include segregation—but not as to dining. I also have difficulty with the solicitor general's analysis.[168] We are faced with a question of whether a statute would be constitutional that permitted segregation. Such a statute *would not* be constitutional. I think that the *Mitchell* case does not cover it. Suppose that there were *no statute*—we probably could not reach this if the railroad alone was doing it. They never intended in 1887 to overrule *Plessy*.[169] I reverse.

JACKSON: For Justice Jackson's comments on this case, see *McLaurin v. Regents of the University of Oklahoma*, and *Sweatt v. Painter*—both reported above.

BURTON: The ICC early on applied this statute to racial questions and discrimination. The present regulation discriminates, for when there are no seats left in the colored section, he is out. That is bad. Putting up signs and rope is also bad. I would narrowly decide the case, but I would not approve segregation by implication.

CLARK: I reverse.

MINTON: It is a waste of time to say that the question is not here. *Henderson* is different from *Mitchell*. He got what he wanted, for the trip he made, in the ICC. He had a cease and desist order that had been applied to him. The regulation was set aside and never applied to him. That is *McCabe*.

Henderson is *not* here with a *right* to object. If we reach the merits, then there is no constitutional question—merely a question of statutory interpretation. It is not reasonable to segregate on the basis of race. This law was passed in 1887. If no such act, this railroad could have made this regulation and no one could stop it (contra to ICC authority). I reverse.

---

ridden or attempted to ride the railroads or that they had sought and been refused the use any accommodations offered by the company.

In a famous dictum, however, Hughes said that equal protection was a personal right, and if certain facilities were provided for some passengers, there must be substantial equality of treatment for others. He found that the Oklahoma Separate Coach Law impermissibly discriminated against blacks by allowing carriers to provide certain accommodations to whites only and that this provision offended the Fourteenth Amendment even if there were limited demand for such accommodations among blacks and even if the railroad lost money in the bargain. While Hughes's opinion indicated for the first time that the Court might begin to take the "equal" part of the separate and equal doctrine seriously, he did not question Oklahoma's right to require segregated accommodations and reaffirmed *Plessy v. Ferguson*.

168. Solicitor General Philip Perlman "confessed error," admitting that the government's previous arguments in support of the ICC were mistaken, that the doctrine of separate but equal was wrong, and that *Plessy v. Ferguson* should be overruled. Perlman argued that America's international standing and its foreign policy objectives were weakened by segregation. The practice, he said, was a national embarrassment. It not only provided material for hostile propaganda by America's enemies but raised doubts about the country's sincerity among friendly nations. Perlman concluded, "Our position and standing before the critical bar of world opinion are weakened if segregation not only is practiced in this country but also is condoned by federal law." *Brief of the United States*, at 60.

169. Congress could not have intended to overrule *Plessy v. Ferguson* in 1887 because that case was not decided until 1896. *Plessy v. Ferguson*, 163 U.S. 537 (1896).

Result: Writing for a unanimous Court, Harold Burton wrote that racial segregation in the railroad's interstate dining cars violated §3(1) of the Interstate Commerce Act. The railroad had offered no evidence to justify its discriminatory practices, Burton noted, and the use of curtains and other symbolic partitions only underlined the rules' artificiality. The Court avoided the constitutional and state action issues. Tom Clark decided not to participate in the case (the published claim that he took no part in consideration of case was not entirely true, as he spoke during the conference.) Douglas concurred in the result but did not publish a separate opinion. Henderson *was announced the same day as* Sweatt v. Painter *and* McLaurin v. Oklahoma State Regents.

Rice v. Sioux City Memorial Park Cemetery, Inc., 348 U.S. 880 (1954)
Rice v. Sioux City Memorial Park Cemetery, Inc., 349 U.S. 70 (1955)
(Douglas) (Burton) (Clark)[170]

The Sioux City Memorial Park Cemetery in Iowa was reserved exclusively for Caucasians. At graveside funeral services for Sergeant John Rice, who had been killed in action in Korea, cemetery officials grew suspicious when they noticed that most of the mourners were Indians. After a quick check revealed that Sergeant Rice was eleven-sixteenths Winnebago Indian, park officials refused to allow the casket to be lowered into the ground. When Rice's widow, Evelyn, sued for emotional distress, cemetery officials countered with the purchase contract for the burial plot, which clearly stated that the cemetery was reserved for whites only. The Iowa Supreme Court ruled that although the racial covenant was unenforceable under the state and federal constitutions, it did not void the entire contract and cemetery officials could use it to defend themselves against Rice's lawsuit.

President Harry Truman was so incensed by the incident that he ordered Sergeant Rice buried with full military honors at Arlington National Cemetery and had an Air Force plane fly the Rice family to Washington, D.C., to witness the ceremony.

Conference of November 13, 1954

WARREN: I am not entirely clear. This woman who made the contract for burial does not have to give up the entire contract if a clause is illegal. If the cemetery solicits for three additional persons, it is their trouble. Even if that theory is not sustained, she may be entitled for damages for the manner in which the contract was broken. The broad implications may be troublesome, but I would start off that way, at least. I reverse.

BLACK: I would have felt differently if Iowa had said that the contract was wholly void and could not be sued upon—I would have agreed to affirm. If the cemetery had brought suit, it would fail. Here, Iowa has allowed the petitioner's suit and has given as a defense the discriminatory clause. The Iowa court held that it had to look to the discriminatory clause to protect the cemetery. *This cannot be a disguise.* This judgment gives them affirmative relief for a contract restriction, like *Shelley v. Kraemer.*[171] I reverse.

REED: I differ. In the *Barrows v. Jackson* case, we said that you cannot use state courts to enforce unlawful contracts. But this is not an unlawful contract. The state could declare

---

170. In his case files, Clark mistakenly labeled this case *Rice v. Sioux Indians.*
171. *Shelley v. Kraemer,* 334 U.S. 1 (1948).

such a policy (for example, the *Corsi* case in New York).[172] We have never said that there is an affirmative duty to take in private persons. Hotels can refuse to take colored people, and so can apartment houses. This contract is legal and has nothing to do with racial discrimination. I, too, have been worried about the circumstances here—the body refused after the grave was dug, etc. I am bothered by the way in which this was done. But the suit here is not for damages for mortification and sorrow—it is merely a suit on a contract. A private cemetery may select who can be buried in their grounds, *until the state* adopts a different policy. This is not a denial of due process in light of history. I affirm.

FRANKFURTER: I agree. We can't decide this case without deciding a lot of other cases. If you reverse this, you must overrule the *Civil Rights Cases*.[173] I would not for the life of me reverse here and not overrule *Civil Rights Cases*. I won't do this. A hotel need not take everyone. The old inns had to take everybody, and yet you can make a separate rule for barber shops and so forth. Does the Fourteenth Amendment amount to an FEPC?[174] This whole fight in the FEPC would be unnecessary if the Fourteenth Amendment requires it. It is not a question of whether it is affirmative. There is much difference where a person comes in to enforce an illegal agreement. *Corsi* was the reverse of this case. The Fourteenth Amendment does not say that you can't make this contract, and we should not make Iowa enforce a contract that the parties themselves did not make. I affirm.

WARREN: Suppose another person who owns a lot in the cemetery came in and sought to restrain the burial of the Indian—we would not grant the injunction.

FRANKFURTER: I would not grant the injunction, as between equally meritorious parties you leave the loss where it falls.

WARREN: Suppose that the body was already buried, and the cemetery later dug him up?

FRANKFURTER: If I were on the Iowa Supreme Court, I would not tolerate it. But if I was here, I would say that it is not under the Fourteenth Amendment and it is up to Iowa. Congress could take away from us our appellate jurisdiction in state cases—they did it once before.[175]

DOUGLAS: This case has its problems. This is a contract, and if the cemetery sues to prohibit the petitioner from burial, we would not enjoin her and put the force of law behind this. To affirm is to put our weight behind a discriminatory clause based on race. This is the same thing as *Barrows*. It puts the sanction of the state behind a contract based on race. I reverse.

---

172. *Railway Mail Ass'n. v. Corsi*, 326 U.S. 88 (1945). When a New York law prohibited unions from discriminating on the basis of race, the union claimed that its right of free association permitted it to maintain racially exclusionary policies. The Supreme Court ruled that the union could not legally exclude nonwhite postal clerks. Reed wrote the majority opinion.

173. *Civil Rights Cases*, 109 U.S. 3 (1883).

174. The Fair Employment Practices Commission was created during World War II to enforce civil rights and government antidiscrimination policies in war-related industries.

175. *Ex parte McCardle*, 74 U.S. (7 Wall.) 506 (1869).

BURTON: The parties did not contract for this. She is trying to collect damages on a contract that the parties never made. What right did they have to get damages? What breaks down is when you knock out this discriminatory clause, the cemetery company could still decide not to bury him. I affirm.

CLARK: Here, people took the law in their own hands and refused burial. This is the same as *Barrows*.[176] I can't see a distinction between a suit in equity and a suit for damages—in each case the state is asked to put its weight behind a discriminatory clause. They can't go into court to keep him out. I reverse.

MINTON: I affirm. I can't see how, when suing on a contract that the parties did not make, Iowa violates the Constitution. Iowa can withhold a remedy for a contract the parties did not make.

Result: In a brief per curiam opinion, the Justices summarily affirmed the judgment below by an evenly divided Court. Within days, however, the Court unexpectedly granted Evelyn Rice's petition for a rehearing. The case was again briefed and argued. Felix Frankfurter lobbied hard behind the scenes to DIG the case, which the Court abruptly did on a 5–3 vote.[177] Writing for the majority, Frankfurter tried to justify the sudden dismissal by claiming that the Court had granted certiorari without knowing that Iowa had recently passed new legislation prohibiting cemeteries from refusing burial on account of race.[178] The intervening state law, Frankfurter said, meant that the problem was unlikely to be repeated, making it an "improper subject" for discretionary review. The Court, he sniffed, "does not sit to satisfy a scholarly interest in such issues . . . [and] does not sit for the benefit of the particular litigants."

Frankfurter's position was disingenuous in several respects. Most obviously, the "new" statute had been clearly cited in the Iowa Supreme Court's published decision. Frankfurter also conveniently ignored the fact that the Supreme Court often decides cases affecting only a small number of persons or cases where intervening statutes have made the Court's decisions academic.[179]

In truth, the Justices were worried about the political implications of race cases like this one, especially in view of the problems the Court was having enforcing Brown v. Board of Education. *The Court's decision to duck this case fit a consistent pattern of Warren Court behavior during the mid-1950s. The Justices sought to avoid most controversial race cases during this period, in the hope of appeasing the south and preserving its landmark school desegregation decisions. The Court did not refuse to decide* Rice *because the Justices thought that the case would have too little impact, but because they were afraid that it might have too much of an impact.[180]*

---

176. *Barrows v. Jackson*, 346 U.S. 249 (1953). Three neighbors sued a California property owner for failing to live up to the terms of a racially restrictive covenant, claiming that their property values plummeted when several black families moved into the neighborhood. Sherman Minton, speaking for the Court, ruled that California could not compel a property owner to pay damages for breaking a covenant that neither the state nor federal governments could legally enforce. Vinson, who wrote the majority in *Shelley v. Kraemer*, dissented.

177. *Rice v. Sioux City Memorial Park Cemetery, Inc.*, 349 U.S. 70 (1955).

178. The new law expressly did not cover cases "already in litigation." The sole effect of this qualification was to prevent Evelyn Rice from benefiting from the new law.

179. Wasby, *Desegregation from* Brown *to* Alexander.

180. Dickson, "State Court Defiance and the Limits of Supreme Court Authority," 1472–81.

Burton v. Wilmington Parking Authority, 365 U.S. 715 (1961)
(Douglas) (Brennan) (Clark)

The Eagle Coffee Shop leased space from the city of Wilmington, Delaware, in a publicly owned and operated car park. The restaurant refused to serve William Burton because he was black. Burton sued, claiming that the restaurant's actions violated the equal protection clause of the Fourteenth Amendment. He argued that because the city owned and operated the car park and was the restaurant's landlord, there was enough state action to trigger the Fourteenth Amendment. The Delaware Supreme Court denied relief, ruling that there was no state or federal law that required restaurants to serve all comers. This was private discrimination, the court concluded, and the owner was free to refuse service to anyone he wished.

Conference of February 24, 1961

WARREN: This project was built by public funds, including tax money. People who occupy it get a tax exemption. Eminent domain took this property, and it must have been for a public purpose. They designed the project as a single enterprise. The very people who are paying for it through tax monies can't be discriminated against in its use, whether the property is operated directly by a public agency or by a lease. There is an exercise here of state power. I reverse.

BLACK: This was a unitary project, with the government supplying the money and the taxpayers taking the losses. Though the property is leased, the lessor does not become separated from it. This was created and financed by the public. I would not make a distinction in any kind of lease—I would find it difficult to distinguish a shoe store or a jewelry store. The common law right of a private owner to pick his own customers is not in this case, and should not be injected into it.

FRANKFURTER: We should not go beyond the necessities of this case. I do not want to decide whether discrimination is proved merely because of eminent domain and tax support. Look at the *Stuyvesant Village* case.[181] I do not want to say that the covenant not to discriminate runs with the land. I reverse.

DOUGLAS: The federal government leases property out on the same kind of a contract. Concessions are all over in national parks. A lease is one way of a government to do business, and to see that a state policy is performed. A lease of government land is—at least presumptively—a governmental instrumentality for this area. I reverse.

---

181. *Dorsey v. Stuyvesant Town Corp.,* 299 NY 512, 87 NE 2d 541, cert. denied, 339 U.S. 981 (1950). The Stuyvesant Town Corporation received a tax exemption and other government assistance to redevelop and rehabilitate substandard residential housing. When the company refused to rent apartments to blacks, Joseph Dorsey sued, claiming that the company's policies violated both the federal and state constitutions' equal protection clauses, as well as state antidiscrimination laws. Dorsey claimed that the close relationship between the company and the government in redevelopment and public housing projects amounted to state action to trigger the Fourteenth Amendment. The New York Court of Appeals dismissed Dorsey's complaint, ruling that while the corporation received significant state assistance, it remained a private corporation and there was no state action to trigger either the federal or state constitution's equal protection clauses. The court also ruled that the corporation's discriminatory policies did not violate state antidiscrimination laws.

CLARK: This state statute starts county funding of this project. Public bonds were issued for this facility for a public purpose. It all adds up to the fact that this is a public project which is a single, interrelated unit. I reverse.

HARLAN: I can see no state action whatever. There is not a bit of effort on the part of the state to mask a discriminatory practice or purpose. There is nothing here to show that the state was asserting a putative power. The state's interest in divesting itself was not in furtherance of a public purpose. The nature of the business itself was unimportant to the state. The only purpose was to raise money. The lease itself does not require this to be a public restaurant. It could be run for one group, not another. The ultimate question is whether or not a state is fettered in exercising the rights it has to exercise eminent domain and to dispose of surplus property. The state is not fettered by reasons that do not fetter the individual. The state could have sold the land and not been liable. This is a disposal of surplus land for revenue purposes for twenty years. The state has only a reversionary interest, and as long as the lease stands it has no control of or relationship to the enterprises being conducted there. A possible power of state action is §1501 of Delaware Code.[182] Perhaps the Delaware court meant either that it was only an incorporation of common law, or that it restricts the common law. If the latter, by granting summary judgment the Delaware court would have assumed that Negroes were offensive to a majority of people. On that reading of the Delaware opinion, I could remand for findings and for an interpretation of the statute. Is it declaratory of the common law, or does it impose a lesser duty? If the latter, to say that as a matter of law Negroes as a group are offensive to the majority population—that is state action. If the proof showed there was prejudice, then there would be no state action. If judges, however, acted merely on the basis of judicial notice, then there is state action.

BRENNAN: *Derrington* was a lease incidental to a courthouse.[183] This lease was indispensable to the existence of the public parking authority. I would put aside the lease of surplus property or its sale. This kind of facility can't be built without incidental provisions for its commercial use. I would say that the lease is a necessity for the financing of the project. I reverse.

---

182. 24 Del. Code §1501 provided, in part, that "no keeper of an inn, tavern, hotel, or restaurant, or other place of public entertainment or refreshment of travelers, guests, or customers shall be obliged, by law, to furnish entertainment or refreshment to persons. . . [who] would be offensive to the major part of his customers, and would injure his business."

183. *Derrington v. Plummer*, 240 F.2d 922 (C.A. 5th Cir. 1956). When Harris County, Texas, built a new courthouse, it leased basement space, furnishings, and equipment to W. F. (Dee) Derrington to operate the courthouse cafeteria. Derrington refused to serve blacks, and M. W. Plummer and others sued. Derrington and Harris County claimed that there was no state action and that Derrington, as a private businessman, had the right to choose his own customers. The county claimed that its lease was analogous to disposing of surplus government property for private use. The circuit court decided that even assuming that the county government was not an active partner in racial discrimination, and even apart from the fact that the government provided water and other utilities to Derrington's business, there was still sufficient state action. The courthouse was built with public funds and was intended for the use of all citizens. The county planned, equipped, and furnished the basement for use as a cafeteria, and the lease was specifically intended to provide public food services. This was not, the court concluded, the diversion of government property to a purely private use; Derrington's conduct was "as much state action as would be the conduct of the county itself."

WHITTAKER: If we reverse, it is to hold that a state cannot lease any property without Fourteenth Amendment restrictions. If the text is the "concurrence of state and private action," all lessees are included. That means that public property can't be profitably used. This is no different from where the state sells its property. A state can convey its interest in land. I affirm.

STEWART: I share having trouble regarding a finding of state action with Harlan and Whittaker. I don't get to the facility argument. But I find state action in §1501, and would review on that ground. The Delaware legislature has passed a statute, which is adopted by the Delaware court as meaning that Negroes are offensive to a majority of people and can be kicked out. A statute that permits a Negro to be turned out on that ground is violative of the Fourteenth Amendment. So I would treat the case as here on appeal.[184]

FRANKFURTER: I can't act here except on very narrow grounds. I suggest that we creep along rather than be general.

Result: The Court ruled on a 5–1–3 vote that state involvement in this case was "nonobvious" but significant and that there was enough state action to trigger the Fourteenth Amendment's equal protection clause. Tom Clark, writing for the majority, emphasized that the land and garage were publicly owned and developed and that the rents went directly into municipal coffers. Such interdependence between private and public enterprise amounted to joint participation in racial discrimination. This meant that the restaurant owner was bound by the Fourteenth Amendment just as the state would have been had it owned and operated the restaurant directly. Stewart concurred in the judgment, while Frankfurter, Harlan, and Whittaker dissented.

Garner v. Louisiana, 368 U.S. 157 (1961)
Briscoe v. Louisiana
Hoston v. Louisiana
(Douglas)

These three cases involved student sit-ins at segregated lunch counters in Baton Rouge, Louisiana. In Garner, *two black students from Southern University went into Sitman's drugstore, which welcomed blacks as "good customers," except at the store's segregated lunch counter. The students took seats at the counter and ordered coffee, but were refused service. A police officer observed the incident and called his superior. When the supervising officer arrived he asked group to leave, and when the students refused to move they were arrested.*

In Briscoe, *seven blacks sat down and requested service at a Greyhound Bus Station lunch counter reserved for whites. They were asked sit at the counter reserved for blacks, and when they refused to move the manager called police, who came and arrested them.*

184. Technically, this case came to the Court on appeal. Eight Justices, with Stewart dissenting, voted to dismiss the appeal on the ground that the state court's judgment did not depend on a finding that a state statute was constitutional. After dismissing the appeal, the Justices treated the case as a discretionary petition for certiorari and voted to grant cert.

In Hoston, *Jannette Hoston and six other Southern University students sat down at an S. H. Kress lunch counter reserved exclusively for whites. The waitress asked them to move to the other side of the counter, but they refused. The manager, who was eating his lunch at the counter, finished his meal and then called police, who came and arrested the students.*

All of the protesters were charged under the same state law, which prohibited people from disturbing the peace by acting "in such a manner as to unreasonably disturb or alarm the public." The defendants did nothing more than sit at the lunch counter after they were asked to leave. There were no demonstrations, speeches, violence, threats, boisterous acts, hostile crowds, or public disturbances. All of the students were convicted and sentenced to four months in jail, with three months suspended upon payment of a $100 fine.

Certiorari Conference of March 17, 1961

WARREN: I vote to grant cert in *Garner* and hold the other two. *Garner* is like *Thompson v. Louisiana* in my view.[185] There was no disturbing of the peace except by sitting at a lunch counter. There was no argument or altercation. No customers complained. The proprietor did not complain or summon the police. The other two cases are in keeping with this, except that they are not quite as clear.

BLACK: If the ordinance is valid, I cannot say that they did not prove it. I have doubts about the standard in the statute—whether it is vague or clear. Many people in the South would be alarmed at the mere presence of black people sitting there. The owner of a store has the right (absent an act of Congress or state statute) to say who can and cannot come into his store or stay there. Louisiana could not pass a valid law that requires segregation in commercial places.

First, is the statute too vague? *Second*, is this state action? A merchant can make his stores segregated or desegregated. If it was a trespass after a warning by the owner, the case would be different. I am not prepared to say that the evidence is inadequate.

FRANKFURTER: I vote to deny all three cases. If a merchant wants to serve only one race, he can follow it. If Louisiana required segregation, it would be different. A state can go beyond the Constitution and say that as matter of policy merchants should not discriminate. There, the owner wanted a segregated service. This is not too vague an ordinance. There is enough evidence here. The *Thompson* case does not govern. The owner need not call in police, and the police need not wait until there is a fracas.

DOUGLAS: I vote to grant all three—these cases are like *Shelley v. Kraemer*.[186]

CLARK: I vote to deny all three. This ordinance is not void for vagueness. The evidence is sufficient—"menacing public peace" was also the standard in *Cantwell*.[187] The proprietor in each case expressed his decision not to serve them.

185. *Thompson v. Louisville*, 362 U.S. 199 (1960). The Court reversed "Shuffling Sam" Thompson's conviction for disturbing the peace on the ground that there was not enough evidence to support the conviction. For a more detailed discussion of this case, see chapter 9.

186. *Shelley v. Kraemer*, 334 U.S. 1 (1948).

187. *Cantwell v. Connecticut*, 310 U.S. 296 (1940).

HARLAN: I vote to deny all three. I agree with Felix and Tom Clark.

BRENNAN: I agree with Bill Douglas and grant all three. *Shelley v. Kraemer* controls these cases.

WHITTAKER: As a citizen, I can invite a Negro into my house—the state has no right to prevent him. Until I have revoked the invitation, the Negro is not a trespasser. In *Garner*, the drug store gave an unlimited invitation, and there was no direction to leave the store on the part of the proprietor. The police are saying that the invitation is not in accord with state policy. The state can't say that. I vote to grant all three.

STEWART: I vote to grant cert in *Garner* and hold *Briscoe* and *Hoston*.

BLACK: They did not try them under the owner's statute. The convictions are based upon state policy, not employer policy. This is not a trespass ordinance—this is a public alarm statute. They can sit there whether the state wants them there or not.

FRANKFURTER: The state need not pass a trespass law—the owner here made clear his desire.

BLACK: The law in this field has to be drawn precisely and narrowly as a trespassing statute to be constitutional.

FRANKFURTER: The statute is applied to enforce the owner's desire.

BLACK: The statute is not aimed at protecting the owner's privacy.

FRANKFURTER: You can't say that the owner offered the Negro and drink and the cops said, "No."

WHITTAKER: The owner said, "Come in," and he was in and until ordered out he was entitled to service. I would hold *Briscoe* and *Hoston*.

FRANKFURTER: If *Garner* goes off on *Thompson*, it does not help *Briscoe* and *Hoston*.

WARREN: I originally suggested taking only *Garner* and remanding *Briscoe* and *Hoston*. Now I have decided to take all three.

Conference of October 20, 1961

WARREN: I do not reach the constitutional issue. I reverse on lack of evidence as in the *Louisville* case.[188]

BLACK: I reverse. I agree with the Chief Justice. I would also say that the language is too vague to meet due process. I do not want to reach the question of whether the ordinance is invalid in segregating the races in stores and restaurants.

---

188. *Thompson v. Louisville,* 362 U.S. 199 (1960).

FRANKFURTER: I am being asked to take judicial notice and either reverse or affirm. The respondent says that what was done here was inherently riotous. The petitioner says that this is state action against Negroes all over the state. I take judicial notice of neither. The writ runs to the Supreme Court—it should have run to the lower court, as the writ of certiorari is discretionary. All they ruled was that on the face of the statute it is not unconstitutional. It is not unconstitutional on its face. So I am remitted to the opinion of the lower court. In a *Thompson* situation, you consider the statute as applied. But I prefer to rest on the record as not showing the quantum of proof needed for a criminal conviction. I do not reach the indefiniteness of the standard.

DOUGLAS: I reverse. A state cannot restrict either by statute or by judicial decision the use of any public place to one race. I doubt the validity of the *Thompson* ground or the ground of vagueness.

CLARK: I reverse. I could not agree with Bill Douglas. I reverse on *Thompson*.

HARLAN: I can't reverse on *Thompson*, and I can't reverse on Bill Douglas's ground. I reverse on vagueness. I can't say that there is no evidence: (1) there were other people in the restaurants; (2) the forseeability issue is close, but I am not prepared to say that the first aspect of judicial notice is inadequate. I would strike the act down for being vague as applied. Look at *Cantwell* on disorderly conduct. Liberty of demonstration is an issue here—the state cannot, in a general statute, condemn this protected Fourteenth Amendment right—for they were there with the owner's consent. To reach this conduct, the statute would have to be explicit and narrowly drawn.

BRENNAN: I agree with Bill Douglas, but I believe that the case can go on *Thompson*.

WHITTAKER: I reverse on *Thompson*.

STEWART: I reverse on *Thompson*.

HARLAN: These people were there "with the consent of the owners."

FRANKFURTER: I disagree with that.

Result: The Court unanimously reversed all of the convictions. Six Justices reversed on the basis of Louisville v. Thompson, *ruling that the convictions were so totally devoid of evidentiary support that they violated the due process clause of the Fourteenth Amendment. Warren wrote the majority opinion. Douglas concurred on the ground that restaurants were public facilities in which states could not enforce policies of racial segregation. Frankfurter concurred on the ground that the record showed no evidence of actual disturbance or public alarm. Harlan concurred on three grounds: that the petitioners' conduct had occurred with the implied consent of the management and was a protected form of expression under the Fourteenth Amendment; that the petitioners' conduct was not punishable under a general breach of peace statutes; and that the state law was unconstitutionally vague and uncertain as applied.*

The Sit-In Cases (1962 Term):
Peterson v. City of Greenville, 373 U.S. 244 (1963)
Avent v. North Carolina, 373 U.S. 375 (1963)
Lombard v. Louisiana, 373 U.S. 267 (1963)
Gober v. Birmingham, 373 U.S. 374 (1963)
Shuttlesworth v. Birmingham, 373 U.S. 262 (1963)
Wright v. Georgia, 373 U.S. 284 (1963)
(Douglas) (Warren)

During the 1962 and 1963 Terms, the Court decided a controversial series of race cases, collectively known as the "Sit-in Cases." In Peterson, the lead case, ten black students sat down at a whites-only lunch counter at an S. H. Kress department store in Greenville, South Carolina. The manager called for police, turned off the store lights, announced that the counter was closed, and asked everyone to leave. The protesters remained quietly seated until police arrived and arrested them for trespassing. At trial, the manager said that he had asked the group to leave because of local custom and because a city ordinance required segregated restaurants. The protesters were convicted, and each was sentenced to a choice of thirty days in jail or a $100 fine. The state supreme court affirmed.

The Court's conference discussion in this case focused primarily on the nature of property rights and whether merchants had the legal right to choose their own customers.

Conference of November 9, 1962

WARREN: I will discuss *Peterson* first. A federal question is raised—an ordinance prohibits the serving of Negroes and whites. I reverse.

BLACK: I am ready to meet these cases on their merits, if it is necessary. The Court would have to assume or pass on the constitutionality of a store owner choosing his own customers. We have a system of private ownership of property—we should not turn down these rights by constitutional construction. I believe that a store owner, the same as a home owner, has a right to say who can come on his premises and how long they can stay. A store owner, like a house owner, can tell a customer to leave. If he has that right, he cannot be helpless to call the police and get help to throw the customer out. One man on another man's property can be thrown off with force, if necessary. That rule is necessary if private property is to be protected. I would rank stores along with homes, although there is, of course, a difference in history and sentiment. I would have no difficulty in sustaining a state law or a federal law under the Fourteenth Amendment (despite the *Civil Rights Cases*) that would prevent racial discrimination and require a retailer to serve all people.[189] But it cannot make a constitutional difference.[190]

---

189. *Civil Rights Cases,* 109 U.S. 3 (1883). The Civil Rights Act of 1875 prohibited private racial discrimination in offering public accommodations and conveyances. The law provided that "all persons within the jurisdiction of the United States shall be entitled to the full and equal enjoyment of the accommodations, advantages, facilities, and privileges of inns, public conveyances on land or water, theaters, and other places of public amusement; subject only to the conditions and limitations established by law, and applicable alike to citizens of every race and color, regardless of any previous condition of servitude."

The *Civil Rights Cases* combined five cases involving (1) two property managers who refused to allow nonwhites to stay in their hotels (Stanley and Nichols); (2) two theater managers who refused to allow blacks

If the merchant orders a Negro out and he does not leave, there is trouble in the South. I am willing to meet that issue. In these cases, however, it was not shown that it was the owner's choice, not the state's, that they leave. On the other hand, when the state attempts to prosecute for such conduct, it is the burden of state prosecutors to show that the owner exercised free choice. And if the state has a law that makes it illegal for the races to eat together, it is unconstitutional. I would not get the Court in the morass of deciding what the motives were in *Peterson, Shuttlesworth,* and *Gober.*[191]

---

to purchase theater tickets (Ryan and Singleton); and (3) one case against a railroad company for refusing to allow a black woman to ride in the "ladies' car" (the Memphis & Charleston R.R. Company).

The Supreme Court ruled 8–1 that the law exceeded Congress's authority under the Thirteenth and Fourteenth Amendments. Joseph Bradley, writing for the majority, limited the applicability of the Fourteenth Amendment's equal protection clause to instances where the *state* was a party to racial discrimination. This created the state action requirement, which has characterized all subsequent Fourteenth Amendment litigation. As Bradley saw it, the Fourteenth Amendment did not grant to Congress unlimited power to regulate or prohibit private discrimination or to protect citizens from other citizens. It was intended only to empower Congress to regulate racially discriminatory state action.

Bradley acknowledged that the Thirteenth Amendment allowed Congress to reach private action, but only in a limited way. Congress could use that amendment to end slavery and involuntary servitude and to eliminate the "badges or incidents" of slavery. In Bradley's estimation, the Thirteenth Amendment could not be used to justify this particular statute, because private racial discrimination was not a badge or incident of slavery. Otherwise, private discrimination could be regulated by the states using their police powers, but such laws were generally beyond the reach of Congress.

The first John Marshall Harlan was the lone dissenter. He argued that the Thirteenth Amendment was sufficient to justify this law. In his judgment, discrimination in public accommodations and conveyances was one of the badges of slavery that the Thirteenth Amendment was designed to eradicate.

190. A few of the sit-in cases, including *Peterson,* involved clear state action where racial segregation was mandated by state or local law. In most of these cases, however, there was little if any state involvement in the racial discrimination complained of by the petitioners. In much of the south—and the north, for that matter—there was often little need for laws to maintain segregation because it was enforced informally out of local habit and custom, including the asserted right of shop owners to choose their own customers. Here, the Justices had to decide whether to (1) overrule the *Civil Rights Cases* and eliminate the state action requirement; (2) find state action somewhere—anywhere—to reverse under the equal protection clause; (3) find some alternative means to reverse these convictions (such as the due process clause); (4) avoid deciding the cases on the merits; or (5) acknowledge that private racial discrimination was beyond the reach of the federal courts.

191. *Peterson* was the lead case. The other cases included:

No. 11 *Avent v. North Carolina,* 373 U.S. 375 (1963). Following a sit-in by five black and two white students at a lunch counter in Durham, North Carolina, all seven students were convicted of criminal trespass.

No. 58 *Lombard v. Louisiana,* 373 U.S. 267 (1963). Three black students and one white student refused to vacate at a segregated refreshment counter in New Orleans and were charged with criminal mischief.

No. 66 *Gober v. Birmingham,* 373 U.S. 374 (1963). Ten black students were convicted of criminal trespass after refusing to vacate white lunch counters in Birmingham, Alabama.

No. 67 *Shuttlesworth v. Birmingham,* 373 U.S. 262 (1963). Two black ministers, F. L. Shuttlesworth and Charles Billups, were convicted of aiding and abetting in a criminal trespass case for their support of the students charged in *Gober v. Birmingham.* The two men were originally sentenced to six months at hard labor.

In *Shuttlesworth*, they charged that he "incited," but they have no evidence of it. He was in his own home. The fact that he said he would get them out of jail is no evidence. In the *Echo Park* case, the state was acting through its chosen agent, the deputy sheriff, to impose a denial of constitutional rights.

I would try to work out an opinion to reverse on all of these cases. In the Louisiana case (*Lombard*): (1) petitioners offered to prove what the arrangement between the owner and the police was; and (2) the mayor's statement is state action. There is a clear state holding here that is constitutional. These states have laws that we should assume are obeyed.

DOUGLAS: I would reverse in all these cases. My views are in diametric opposition to Hugo's—that retail stores cannot segregate constitutionally. My preference would be to decide these cases in a manner that would solve the whole problem. I could not join Black's views. I would go farther than we did in *Garner*.[192]

CLARK: I agree with Hugo as to the fundamental issue of the owner's right to be selective. I would reverse in all of these cases, but on different grounds than those of the Chief Justice. I would say that the owner has the right to choose his customers. He can turn them out for food, even though he lets them in for other purposes. The owner can put in separate toilet facilities and elevators. On the burden of proof, I differ from Hugo and would follow the state rule. If an ordinance is present, there is state policy on segregation.

1. *Avent*: They did not introduce the ordinance. I would vacate to see if the Negro exercised free choice. North Carolina has been doing well on the racial issue.
2. I think that in *Peterson*, I would reverse on custom as state law and on the statement of the policeman.
3. *Gober*: I would vacate.
4. *Shuttlesworth*: reverse on the *Shufflin' Sam* case.[193]
5. *Wright*: I would reverse on the statement of police.
6. *Griffin*: I would vacate.
7. *Lombard*: I would reverse on the statement of the Mayor.

HARLAN: On the broad view, I agree entirely with Hugo on private property. There can be private discrimination if it is not induced by state policy. I disagree with Hugo on the

No. 68   *Wright v. Georgia*, 373 U.S. 284 (1963). Six young blacks were arrested and convicted of violating the state breach of the peace statute when they continued to play basketball in a city park after Savannah police warned them to leave, as the park was customarily used only by white people. The defendants claimed that the statute violated the due process clause of the Fourteenth Amendment because it did not give adequate warning that their conduct was punishable.

No. 26   *Griffin v. Maryland*, 378 U.S. 130 (1964), was initially among the cases discussed at this conference, but it was later severed from the other cases and discussed separately. *Griffin* was eventually held over a year and renumbered the following term as No.6.

192. *Garner v. Louisiana*, 368 U.S. 157 (1961).
193. *Thompson v. Louisville*, 362 U.S. 199 (1960). See chapter 2.

burden of proof. On state action, I think that the burden is on the one who claims that the action is unconstitutional.

The existence of an unrepealed ordinance should not deprive the store owner of his choice. We must pay attention to state ground hurdles. I would not accept the per se state action doctrine on account of the segregation ordinance. I agree with the solicitor general that the existence of an ordinance is a highly relevant fact.[194] If the defendant introduces the ordinance, the burden of moving forward is on the state.

1. In *Peterson*, where the ordinance was the operative force—this is the easiest case, and I would reverse.[195]

2. In *Gober*, the record is muddy. Failure to pursue was the action of the trial court in refusing to admit the ordinance. I would vacate and remand in light of *Peterson*.

3. *Avent*: I would vacate.

4. *Lombard*: Reverse for a new trial, but not on the mayor's statement.

5. *Griffin*: I affirm.

6. *Shuttlesworth*: I would affirm, except for *Gober*. I would send it back in light of *Gober*.

7. *Wright*: There is an adequate state ground on the equal protection issue. The state court has said that playing basketball peacefully constituted a violation. I would reverse on vagueness.

BRENNAN: We need not deal with the broad problem discussed by Hugo and Bill Douglas. For the ordinance cases, *Peterson* should be the key case. The existence of ordinances forecloses any defense that the owner had an individual choice. This would get us over the hurdle in *Avent* and *Gober*. Alternatively, if there were a court for the proposition that the ordinance was in the record and that the state did not come forward to show an individual choice, I would agree to go along. I would be willing to remand if necessary for a new trial. I would reverse all of these cases across the board; also the non-ordinance cases:

4. *Griffin*: Reverse on the deputy sheriff.

5. *Wright*: Reverse because Negro—

6. *Shuttlesworth*: Reverse on *Shufflin' Sam*.

STEWART: I will cooperate, but the one thing I cannot agree to is Bill Douglas's theory. There is state action, but there is not necessarily a denial of equal protection. On this subject, I agree with Hugo on the right of owners to choose their customers. If the individual wants to practice segregation, he can do so. I favor *Peterson v. Greenville* for our

---

194. Solicitor General Archibald Cox. After this case, Phyllis Cox told Elizabeth Black that her husband had three recurring nightmares: that he would be late to court, forget his argument, and look down during his argument and discover that he was dressed only in his BVDs. Hugo Black and Elizabeth Black, *Mr. Justice and Mrs. Black*, 108.

195. Warren's notes quote Harlan as saying that he would "perhaps reverse."

basic opinion. Here, there is an ordinance and evidence of a custom that amounts to a denial by the state of equal protection. It is not necessary to get fouled up in the adequate state ground question. If I have to get involved in such things, *Avent* would bother me. In *Lombard*, I probably could be persuaded to reverse on the mayor's statement. In *Gober*, Alabama courts take juridical notice, and so do we. *For the non-ordinance cases: Wright*— with some difficulty, I accept the government's argument and reverse. A motive in the arrest was that they were *Negroes. Shuttlesworth*—reverse on a combination of *Shufflin' Sam* and free speech.

WHITE: I stand with Bill Brennan, except that I have some trouble with *Gober*. If we state that an owner has a choice of customers, it means nothing if we except *Gober*. I probably could go along with reversal in *Gober*. I might go on a per se ordinance, but am doubtful about it. I would prefer to say that where there is an ordinance, the state must disentangle itself from it. In the Alabama cases I reverse. In Louisiana, I reverse. In the South Carolina case, I reverse. In *Avent*, I reverse. In *Shuttlesworth*, I reverse on free speech.

WARREN: No one would ever admit that he was acting under an ordinance, but he would say that it was his choice.

WHITE: That position would probably result in the repeal of the ordinance, and I would be willing to go for that. I think that the narrower ground is better than the broad ground suggested by Bill Douglas.

STEWART: I do not prefer the per se rule, because the individual should have the choice of selecting his own customers.

GOLDBERG: I think that there is a lot to what Bill Douglas says, especially in light of *Shelley v. Kraemer*.[196] However, it is not necessary to face the broad issues. I would like to have unanimity. Potter's suggestion has merit, but is not practical because there will be more and more cases here. I would like to go on a little broader ground.

1. *Peterson*: I would reverse, because the ordinance was relied on.
2. *Gober*: Alabama must take judicial notice. So must we.
3. *Lombard*: This is clear cut. Reverse on the mayor's statement.
4. *Wright*: Reverse on the statute as applied. Perhaps also on the *Shufflin' Sam* case.
5. *Avent*: Remand under *Peterson*.
6. *Griffin*: Reverse on the deputy sheriff, who also swore out the warrant.

WARREN: We should announce a per se rule on ordinances.

Result: A unanimous Court reversed the convictions in Peterson, *ruling that the department store's actions violated the defendants' equal protection rights. Warren wrote on behalf of eight Justices that while the restaurant manager might have been able to exclude Peterson and the others in the absence of a city ordinance requiring segregation, the ordinance removed the matter from the sphere of private choice and amounted to state action.*

---

196. *Shelley v. Kraemer*, 334 U.S. 1 (1948).

John Marshall Harlan concurred in the result on the ground that the store manager had excluded blacks because of the ordinance mandating segregated restaurants. He dissented in the other Sit-in Cases where the connections between state and private action were less clear.

The Sit-In Cases (1963 Term):
Bell v. Maryland, 378 U.S. 226 (1964)
Griffin v. Maryland, 378 U.S. 130 (1964)
Barr v. City of Columbia, 378 U.S. 146 (1964)
Bouie v. City of Columbia, 378 U.S. 347 (1964)
Robinson v. Florida, 378 U.S. 153 (1964)
(Douglas) (Warren) (Brennan)

The third wave of sit-in cases was decided during the 1963 Term, as protesters seeking to integrate various public accommodations were arrested and charged with criminal trespass or breach of the peace.[197] In the lead case, Robert Mack Bell and eleven other black students were arrested following a sit-in at a segregated Baltimore restaurant and convicted of trespassing in a Maryland state court. This was the most difficult of the sit-in cases, because Maryland had no state or local laws that mandated segregation and there was no "easy" way to reverse. The owner sought to use racially neutral state trespass laws to enforce a private policy of racial segregation. The key question was whether the Supreme Court would use this case to extend Shelley v. Kraemer and declare that using the courts to enforce facially neutral laws in a discriminatory manner violated the Fourteenth Amendment.

The crucial division in conference was over Hugo Black's view that restaurant and amusement park owners, as well as shopkeepers and homeowners, had the right to determine who would be allowed to enter their property. Clark, Harlan, Stewart, White, and Goldberg were inclined to agree with Black's analysis and sympathized with his defense of private property rights.

This provoked Douglas to complain that if Black had his way, the Court would create a modern version of Plessy v. Ferguson, where private businesses replaced state governments in promoting and enforcing segregation. Douglas wanted to overrule the Civil Rights Cases and extend the Fourteenth Amendment to prohibit racial discrimination in all public accommodations, including restaurants, lodging, and amusement parks.[198] Warren, Brennan, and Goldberg initially sided with Douglas. In the end, there was considerable shifting of opinion, with Stewart and a clearly conflicted Tom Clark slowly falling away from Black, while Brennan, Warren, and Goldberg began to distance themselves from Douglas.

---

197. Although black civil disobedience "officially" began with Rosa Parks and the Montgomery bus boycott of 1955–56, the sit-in cases of the early 1960s marked a fundamental change in the nature of race litigation. During the 1940s and 1950s, NAACP lawyers carefully planned and initiated selected lawsuits in a systematic attack on racist laws and practices. By the early 1960s, however, community protests, demonstrations, and civil disobedience began to dominate the civil rights movement. These were usually led by ministers and community activists rather than by lawyers, who were brought in only later to defend protesters against criminal prosecutions. Thurgood Marshall said that the sit-in cases showed him that he had "kind of outlived [his] usefulness" as a strategic litigator. Tushnet, *Making Civil Rights Law*, 301.

198. *Civil Rights Cases*, 109 U.S. 3 (1883).

Conference of October 23, 1963

WARREN: I had hoped that we could take these cases step by step, not reaching the final question until much experience had been had. That course seems to me to be impracticable. I don't go for the solicitor general's suggestion to avoid the main issue and go off on grounds of vagueness.[199] The constitutional issue can't be avoided in some of these cases, and therefore it should be decided in all of them.[200] We should ask the solicitor general for his views on the fundamental merits of these cases.[201] The solicitor general says that he is willing to express himself. I think that the government should be on record here. I could dispose of *Griffin*, as I wrote last year, because of the deputy sheriff. That is state action, and it is not pressing too far.[202] I could reverse *Barr* on the same ground, because of police action.[203] The police notified the owner—they sent two deputies and participated in the order to remove. The state was working with the owner, who said "We were working as a group," and that is unconstitutional state action. In *Bouie*, the police also established the policy.[204] The police participated in establishing the offence by themselves directing the petitioners to leave and, apparently without an express request to arrest them, did arrest them. They arrested on their own, not at the insistence of the owner. The owner or manager did not request it—the police are supplying material elements of the arrest. Also in *Barr* and *Bouie*, it was a department store to which all were invited and welcomed, with the exception of the lunch counter.

I believe that in *Barr* and *Bouie*, the actions of the police make the convictions particularly vulnerable because of the plethora of segregation statutes of South Carolina. The action of police in the environment of the South Carolina segregation statutes makes this state action in support of a state policy of segregation.

In *Robinson*, we again have a department store. The police were called and instructed the owner on what to do to make petitioners commit a crime. Also there were two whites who were arrested solely because they were with Negroes.[205] The statute, construed to mean that the owner can eject people for other than offensive conduct, does not give

---

199. Solicitor General Archibald Cox originally argued for the United States. On reargument, Ralph S. Spritzer represented the United States as amicus curiae.

200. Earl Warren's notes on his own comments indicate that he said, "If we must reach the basic question in any, we should probably reach it in all."

201. Douglas's notes attribute this statement to Warren, but Warren's notes attribute the comment to Brennan. If the comment was Brennan's, it is not clear whether Brennan interrupted Warren or made the comment later and Warren simply noted the remark in the margin next to his own comments.

202. *Griffin v. Maryland*, 378 U.S. 130 (1964), involved a protest at a segregated amusement park near Washington, D.C. William Griffin and four other young blacks were ordered to leave the park by a park employee, who also worked as a deputy sheriff. When the group refused to leave, the park employee/deputy sheriff arrested then and charged them with criminal trespass.

203. *Barr v. City of Columbia*, 378 U.S. 146 (1964). This case involved a sit-in at a segregated drugstore lunch counter in South Carolina, where the defendants were convicted of breach of the peace and criminal trespass.

204. *Bouie v. City of Columbia*, 378 U.S. 347 (1964), involved several convictions for criminal trespass following a sit-in at a drugstore restaurant in South Carolina.

205. *Robinson v. Florida*, 378 U.S. 153 (1964). Another prosecution for criminal trespass following a sit-in at a segregated Miami restaurant.

warning, because it says "intoxicating, brawling, etc.," or those who, in the opinion of the manager, it would be detrimental to such a restaurant to entertain. That means that the statute is construed to support ejection for something other than offensive conduct of the kind put into the act. This is not sui generis, and conflicts with the particularity required of criminal acts. This is not of the same species as drunkenness, and so forth. If the legislature wanted to give unlimited discretion to the owner, they would have drawn a different statute.

In the *Bell* case I hit hard bottom.[206] Here we get to the raw of the problem, except for the probable case of prior notice that no Negroes were allowed. No matter, however, that this owner served only a segment of the public. In the field of public accommodations, the owner of such facilities abandons his private choice and his right of privacy to own or control his own property as he sees fit. If you have a private property for private use, you can call on the state to throw people off. A person can keep anyone out of his home, or hog pasture, or warehouse, provided that it is strictly private. A church can limit its membership any way it wants and no one could crash the gates, although if the church allows all it could not shut out Negroes. In the field of public accommodations, the owner is advertising to the world for customers without restriction. He gives up some rights of privacy. As long as customers are orderly and behave themselves, they have the same right as all other people to be in that place, and the owner can't have police help to throw them out. The state would then unconstitutionally enforce discrimination. *Shelley v. Kraemer* is also violated, for there we held that private grievances and arrangements having races excluded will not be enforced.[207] Here it is worse, because we are putting people in jail. We could even do that on the principle of *Marsh v. Alabama*.[208] It is not quite the same here—they did invite the public to come indiscriminately and to buy in all the departments except this one. An owner can't so legislate in light of *Marsh v. Alabama*. This certainly meets the principle of *Shelley v. Kraemer*.

If we are to say that the owner of public accommodations has the right to keep a person out, we endanger the public accommodation laws of some thirty states. If one state can toss them out on racial grounds, so can another.

BLACK: I do not object to the solicitor general submitting a new brief on the merits. If we affirm, a state or federal government could change the result by legislation. For us to say that this Court can enforce a policy of non-segregation here would be to overrule the *Civil Rights Cases*.[209] To adopt the Chief Justice's views would overrule the *Civil Rights Cases*. I would be willing to overrule those cases if that was all that was involved.

---

206. *Bell v. Maryland*, 378 U.S. 226 (1964). Warren "hit hard bottom" here because there appeared to be no way to reverse the twelve convictions involved in this case without reaching the state action issue.

207. *Shelley v. Kraemer*, 334 U.S. 1 (1948).

208. *Marsh v. Alabama*, 326 U.S. 501 (1946).

209. *Civil Rights Cases*, 109 U.S. 3 (1883). Black and the conservative wing of the Court were determined to defend private property rights and uphold state prosecutions under racially neutral laws. When Earl Warren signaled that the liberal bloc was ready to reverse all of these convictions while avoiding the crucial state action question, Black was prepared to fight. He thought that Warren's approach would implicitly—and dishonestly—overrule the *Civil Rights Cases*. Klarman, "An Interpretive History of Modern Equal Protection," 274.

The Constitution, without more, does not bar segregation in public places. Florida was making an honest effort to protect a property owner. We have a system of private ownership. The Constitution does not distinguish between a home and a store. We cannot sit here and redesign the Constitution when we think it is just. When a man owns property, he owns it. *Shelley v. Kraemer* and *Marsh v. Alabama* do not control this. I would rather overrule these cases than hold that these trespass statutes are void. Bradley was right in the *Civil Rights Cases*, when he said once the barrier of privacy is broken down then there is no stopping. If these businesses can be regulated by the Court in this way, so can private homes. I have no objection to regulation by a proper body of rights of policy, but we are not the proper agency to do it.[210]

I would not hold that Florida failed to give proper notice. Nor would I do that in *Bell v. Maryland. Kraemer* is too broad in its language. I will go the whole way to protect discrimination by government, but not discrimination by private people. I think that the right of association is vital to American life, and reversal here would endanger it. Colored people want to be treated socially like the rest of us. Perhaps Hitler could make that come to pass, but I will not foist it on people. Congress can pass a law making it a duty for a storekeeper to sell to all comers.

DOUGLAS: I reverse in all of these cases.

CLARK: I agree with Hugo and all that he says. On *Barr* and *Bouie*, I could reverse on lack of notice. In *Griffin* I am inclined to affirm. Although I do not like the delegation of authority in *Bell* and *Robinson*, I would face the constitutional issues and affirm both. There is no state action here under the *Civil Rights Cases*—I see none. I would think that the only alternative would be "self-help."

HARLAN: I cannot subscribe more than I do to Hugo's views. I do not reach the *Civil Rights* issues. I am not ready to overrule them. [DOUGLAS: Though Hugo says that he would.] I cannot say that all this current debate in Congress is beside the point.[211] A man has a right to exclude from his property any man that he wishes. The vagueness argument is not valid in any of the five cases here. When it comes to "fair notice," it is not realistic to say that the parties were not aware of the facts of the law and the consequences. I affirm all these cases except for *Barr*. As to that case, I would vacate and send it back for a new trial on the ground that the petitioners made out a prima facie case of state action. *Griffin* is not state action—it was a private policeman.

BRENNAN: I reverse on all of these cases. I agree generally with Earl Warren and with Bill Douglas. Criminal laws cannot enforce the owner's choice in this field. If we do so

---

210. This was a crucial point for Black. Unlike the other dissenters in the sit-in cases, Black agreed with Douglas that the *Civil Rights Cases* had been wrongly decided. However, while Black believed that *Congress* could pass legislation prohibiting both public and private racial discrimination under the Fourteenth Amendment, he thought that the Court could not *on its own authority* punish private racial discrimination in the absence of state action.

211. Harlan was not the only Justice who was worried about pending congressional civil rights legislation. The issue subsequently became the determining factor for William Brennan. See Douglas's memorandum on *Bell v. Maryland*, below.

hold, then neither Congress nor the states can legislate otherwise. Under §5 of the Fourteenth Amendment, Congress could not override that private choice. As respects state statutes, how can a state deprive a person of his private choice to seek the aid of criminal law to support his right to a private choice? I reverse all of these cases on *Shelley v. Kraemer* or on more limited grounds.

STEWART: In *Griffin* I could reverse, agreeing with what the Chief Justice wrote last year. In *Barr* and *Bouie*, I could find sufficient state participation and reverse. In *Bell* and *Robinson*, I would reach the basic issue. I agree with Hugo that the result has nothing to do with what a state may do under its police powers, and what Congress could do under the commerce clause. The question is whether to say that this is "state action." It is not a "state denial of equal protection."

WHITE: I agree with Hugo. I would reverse in *Barr* and *Bouie*. I would affirm *Bell* and *Robinson*. I am not sure about *Griffin*, but will probably affirm.

GOLDBERG: I agree with the Chief and Douglas and HLB.[212] I could reverse on narrow grounds in *Griffin* and in *Barr* and *Bouie*. I would reverse broadly in *Robinson* and *Bell*.

BLACK: I can go on the solicitor general's grounds in a few cases.

[DOUGLAS: In summary on the basic issue of right to deny service, the Court is 5–4 in favor of the restaurant owner's right to serve only the ones he wants to serve.][213]

Conference of October 26, 1963

GOLDBERG: I would like to elaborate my views on this case [*Griffin*], and in *Barr, Bouie, Bell*, and *Robinson*. This is the most serious problem before the Court in recent years. This will be the first time in the history of the country where if we say that the petitioners are not entitled to their rights, we legitimize racial discrimination. If we say that these stores have a right to discriminate, we will have to overrule *Shelley v. Kraemer*, and repudiate the basis of the majority in *Civil Rights Cases*, and embrace the majority in *Plessy v. Ferguson*.[214] I agree with the first John Marshall Harlan's dissent in the *Civil Rights Cases*.

We have progressively implemented the policy of desegregation. Now we are receding—why? Bradley's opinion assumes that Congress was dealing with individual action, not state action. He says that the Fourteenth Amendment is aimed at state action "of every kind."

The majority opinion must say that *Shelley v. Kraemer* was wrong and that Bradley was wrong in the *Civil Rights Cases*, for he assumed that the state had a duty to protect Negroes in their access to public accommodations. It is also a "privilege and immunity" to live in a society where public areas are free of discrimination.

---

212. It is difficult to see how Goldberg could agree with Warren and Douglas on the one hand and with Black on the other. It is possible that he was casting about for some sort of compromise that would satisfy both camps. Or Douglas might have mistakenly written "HLB" when he meant to write "WJB" (i.e., Brennan).

213. The five Justices voting in favor of the private right to refuse service were Black, Clark, Harlan, Stewart, and White. The four Justices against: Warren, Douglas, Brennan, and Goldberg.

214. *Plessy v. Ferguson*, 163 U.S. 537 (1896).

I would suggest that it is impossible to write this except by overruling *Shelley v. Kraemer* and repudiating Bradley.

I think that the *Slaughterhouse Cases* were wrong. The Thirteenth, Fourteenth, and Fifteenth Amendments, if they did nothing else, provided that people shall live in an open and free society where there is no public discrimination.[215] Racial discrimination is a badge of slavery.

I agree with *Adamson*.[216] I think that the Fourteenth Amendment incorporates the Bill of Rights. Whether they intended to incorporate all of the Bill of Rights is not important here, but certainly the Fourteenth Amendment decided to get rid of racial discrimination.

Slavery was followed by the Black Codes, and they were followed by segregation. Police are now used to enforce state policy of segregation. There was no segregation in slave days, for when a slave traveled with his master, he was taken in.

There is no equality here, for a Negro eating has to stand up while a white man sits down. No "equal facilities" are furnished to these Negroes.

I fear the results of an affirmance in these cases. *Shelley v. Kraemer* does not cover all private rights. Constitutional rights must be "accommodated." We have to reconcile conflicts.

The Fourteenth Amendment does not give a right to discriminate in the public area. Yet the majority must rely on that. It is shocking to me beyond words to predicate the decision on that ground. A majority vote to that effect will take the Court very far back.

I believe that Hugo Black's views are colored by Alabama's background of slavery. My family also had a store in Elgin, but they served all comers because Illinois never knew slavery.[217]

If we decide these cases as we must, and if we allow public discrimination in public places, I am convinced that we will set back legislation indefinitely. Our society will then have an evil virus inside it that will keep it frozen on racial lines. [DOUGLAS: He refers to last paragraph of Harlan's dissent in the *Civil Rights Cases*.][218] It would be a great disservice to the nation to decide this issue 5–4. There is legislation pending. The federal

---

215. *Slaughterhouse Cases,* 83 U.S. (16 Wall.) 36 (1872).

216. *Adamson v. California,* 332 U.S. 46 (1947).

217. Goldberg's father was originally a Chicago pushcart peddler; he later opened a small shop in the suburb of Elgin, Illinois.

218. Harlan wrote, in part:

It is, I submit, scarcely just to say that the colored race has been the special favorite of the laws. The [Civil Rights Act] of 1875, now adjudged to be unconstitutional, is for the benefit of citizens of every race and color. What the nation, through Congress, has sought to accomplish in reference to that race, is—what had already been done in every State of the Union for the white race—to secure and protect rights belonging to them as freemen and citizens; nothing more. . . . The one underlying purpose of congressional legislation has been to enable the black race to take the rank of mere citizens. The difficulty has been to compel a recognition of the legal right of the black race to take the rank of citizens, and to secure the enjoyment of privileges belonging, under the law, to them as a component part of the people for whose welfare and happiness government is ordained. At every step, in this direction, the nation has been confronted with class tyranny, which a contemporary English historian says is, of all tyrannies, the most intolerable, "for it is ubiquitous in its operation, and weighs, perhaps, most heavily on those whose obscurity or distance would withdraw them from the notice of

government's argument is not implausible. Rather than handing down a 5–4 decision Black's way, I think that it is better to put these cases off on the ground urged by the United States, reversing them narrowly and not reaching the broad ground. I am prepared to vote to reverse on the narrow government grounds.

DOUGLAS: I would suggest that we put the matter over until we can look at the cases we are holding for these.

HARLAN: I urge that the matter be tabled until the next conference, so that we can consider the question.

WARREN: I suggest that we have these cases put down for November 7.

Results: The vote at conference was 5–4 to sustain the convictions in Bell *on the ground that there was no state action. That vote remained intact until just a few days before the decisions were scheduled to be announced in May 1964. At the last second, Tom Clark changed his mind—apparently because he did not want to be the decisive fifth vote to uphold these racially motivated convictions.[219] He wrote a draft opinion implausibly finding state action in* Bell *and said that he would now vote to reverse the convictions in all the sit-in cases. This threw the Court into a storm of last-minute negotiations and recriminations. The new majority appeared poised to revolutionize the state action doctrine and greatly expand the reach of* Shelley v. Kraemer. *Among this new majority, however, Brennan was determined to avoid a controversial decision that might jeopardize passage of pending civil rights legislation (which eventually became the landmark Civil Rights Act of 1964). Brennan went looking for another way to reverse the convictions without addressing the state action question. Douglas's memorandum to the file offers an interesting peek behind the scenes as the conference maneuvered to reach the desired outcome without creating unnecessary public controversy.*

Bell v. Maryland
Memorandum for the Files
(Douglas)

June 20, 1964

Brennan's opinion, which will be filed on Monday, June 22, 1964, was the product of his plan to keep the Court from deciding the basic constitutional issue of the Fourteenth Amendment.[220]

---

single despot." To-day, it is the colored race which is denied, by corporations and individuals wielding public authority, rights fundamental in their freedom and citizenship. At some future time, it may be that some other race will fall under the ban of race discrimination. If the constitutional amendments be enforced, according to the intent with which, as I conceive, they were adopted, there cannot be, in this republic, any class of human beings in practical subjection to another class, with power in the latter to dole out to the former just such privileges as they may choose to grant.

219. For a lucid explanation and analysis of the postconference maneuvering in these cases, see Klarman, "An Interpretive History of Modern Equal Protection," 274–76. See also Douglas's memorandum, reproduced below.

220. In deciding these cases, Brennan was acutely aware of the comprehensive civil rights legislation that was making its way through Congress. He feared that indiscrete handling of the sit-in cases might cause

He wrote it only after the Court had voted, and the majority agreed to Black's opinion. He said at the time that he would not think of filing it if the Court had held that the sit-ins were constitutional. Later he changed his mind and decided to file it anyway, not as a matter of principle, but because he had been somewhat shamed into sticking to the position he had taken, which came about this way.

Clark for some reason finally left Black just before the opinions were to be announced, and joined Brennan's opinion that would vacate and remand. Goldberg also joined Brennan's opinion, even though he also filed an opinion on the merits. The Chief Justice joined my opinion, and he also joined Goldberg's opinion, so there were three to reverse outright. Then there were three for Brennan's opinion, which Brennan maintained was a reversal but which in fact was only a vacating and remanding for reconsideration. He dressed it up, however, with the word "reversing."

Black then amended his opinion, saying that there were only three who avoided the merits, the majority of the Court reached the merits, the three who avoided the merits did not really reverse but only vacated, and therefore if the vote had been taken of those who reached the merits the decision would be one of affirmance, since there were four to affirm and only three, myself, Goldberg, and the Chief Justice, voting to reverse.

This position greatly disturbed Clark, and at the noon Conference he said he wanted the cases to go over, as he might write something. It turned out that what he wrote was an opinion to reverse on the merits. This opinion was conceived in my office in a talk I had with Clark. After he finished it, he came back; I read it and approved it with a few minor changes. Then he went on and cleared it with the Chief, with Brennan and with Goldberg. At that point there was a majority of the Court to reach the basic constitutional issue and to reverse on the merits. At that point also, Stewart in Conference said something that apparently hit Brennan pretty deep, because he implied that Brennan's opinion merely to vacate was an opinion not of principle, but of expediency; and if it was good principle to be applied on the judgments below which ought to be affirmed, it was good principle to apply on the judgments below which were about to be reversed. The exchange between them was brief, but Brennan said he would talk to Stewart. Several days passed and Potter Stewart got hold of Tom Clark and told Clark that if he would return to Brennan's opinion to vacate he, Potter Stewart, would join. That would leave Brennan with himself, Potter Stewart, and Clark, because in the meantime Goldberg had talked with me and decided he would not go along with Brennan's opinion to vacate.

The Chief had gone to Stanford to get an honorary degree and was out of the city that weekend. I saw him Monday, June 15. The issue on the sit-ins was still in doubt.

---

a public controversy and kill this crucial legislation—no matter how defensible or well intentioned the Court's actions might be. Brennan knew that in the long run a strong congressional commitment to civil rights would accomplish far more than anything the Court could do on its own. Black and Douglas both failed to appreciate Brennan's thinking and lashed out at him from both sides. Ball, *Hugo L. Black*, 230–31.

What had transpired between Brennan and Stewart I do not know, but Brennan at that point had Tom Clark and Potter Stewart only. At the same time, Clark had not withdrawn his opinion to reverse on the merits, although he expressed a preference to go the way of Brennan's opinion rather than to reach the merits.

I saw the Chief and told him what the situation was. I suggested that if he indicated to Clark he would not join Brennan's opinion, Brennan then would still lack a majority for vacating and remanding, and Clark's basic worry on that concern would still remain. The Chief said he did not think he should talk to Clark.

Between that conversation and the next day, which was June 16, Clark had talked with the Chief, and the Chief, instead of staying put, not only joined Brennan, but also got Goldberg to join. That, together with Brennan, Clark, and Stewart, made up a majority of the court to vacate and remand.

The Chief came in to see me about it after it was all over, and said he thought that was probably the best thing to do under the circumstances.

On thinking it over, he had decided not only to join Brennan, but also to join Goldberg and me on the merits.

Then I recirculated, adding Part I of my opinion, to be filed June 22, 1964, criticizing the Court for not meeting the issue on the merits.

The Chief decided to join only Goldberg and not me, although there was nothing in the other parts of my opinion with which he disagreed.

Result: The majority, led by Brennan, ignored the constitutional issues and Shelley v. Kraemer, *and artfully decided* Bell v. Maryland *on the basis of intervening changes in state law. While Bell's case was being appealed, Maryland enacted new state and local laws prohibiting discrimination in public accommodations. The majority vacated all twelve convictions and remanded the case to the state courts for further consideration in light of these new laws. Douglas, Warren, and Goldberg concurred but favored reversing the convictions outright on equal protection grounds. Black, Harlan, and White dissented. Douglas and Black used their opinions mostly to snipe at each other, and both criticized the majority for not deciding the constitutional issues embedded in these cases.*

In Griffin, the Court reversed the criminal trespass convictions on a 6–3 vote. Warren wrote for the Court, while Black, Harlan, and White dissented.

In Barr, Black wrote the majority opinion holding that there was no evidence to support the breach of peace convictions. In a brief per curiam, the Court also struck down the criminal trespass convictions. Black then wrote a dissent from the per curiam. This meant that Black wrote both the majority and dissenting opinions. Harlan and White also dissented.

In Bouie, the Court reversed the criminal trespass convictions on a 6–3 vote, ruling that the statute was too vague and that the convictions violated due process. Brennan's majority opinion also criticized the state supreme court for waiting to construe the statute until after the alleged offense had taken place, and then expanding the scope of the law significantly to cover these defendants and applying its decision retroactively. This, Brennan wrote, amounted to an impermissible ex post facto law. Black, Harlan, and White dissented.

Finally, the Justices unanimously reversed the criminal trespass convictions in Robinson. Writing for the Court, Black found state action in several state regulations that required separate facilities in restaurants.

Heart of Atlanta Motel v. United States, 379 U.S. 241 (1964)
Katzenbach v. McClung, 379 U.S. 294 (1964)
(Douglas)

The Civil Rights Act of 1964 was the most significant civil rights act of the twentieth century. It barred discrimination in a broad range of American life, including education, voting, and employment. In Title 2 of the act, Congress used its commerce clause powers (and possibly its Fourteenth Amendment powers) to prohibit racial discrimination in public accommodations (a) if discrimination were supported by state action; or (b) if the facilities were provided to interstate travelers; or (c) if a substantial portion of the goods or services provided moved through interstate commerce.

Almost a century earlier, the Supreme Court struck down a similar act, the Civil Rights Act of 1875, on the ground that it exceeded Congress's constitutional authority.[221] The key question this time around was whether the Warren Court would interpret either the commerce clause or the Fourteenth Amendment more broadly to allow Congress to attack private racial discrimination.

Just six months after President Lyndon Johnson signed the Civil Rights Act of 1964 into law, two cases challenging its constitutionality reached the Court. In the first case, the Heart of Atlanta Motel, located in downtown Atlanta, refused to accept black guests. Owner Moreton Rolleston, Jr. argued that (a) Congress had exceeded its constitutional authority in passing the law; (b) the statute wrongfully deprived Rolleston of his Fifth Amendment property rights without due process or compensation; and (c) in one of the more ironic moments in Supreme Court history, Rolleston argued that the act violated his Thirteenth Amendment right against involuntary servitude by forcing him to serve black customers against his will.

In the second case, Ollie McClung Sr. and Ollie McClung Jr. co-owned Ollie's Barbecue restaurant in Birmingham, Alabama. The McClungs refused to serve black customers inside the restaurant, although they allowed them to order at the take-out window. The McClungs claimed that their restaurant was a local business and did not seek interstate business. Although 46 percent of the food they served had moved through interstate commerce, they argued that their small restaurant had no discernible impact on interstate commerce.[222]

Conference of October 5, 1964

WARREN: The case is here, and I would decide both *Heart of Atlanta* and *McClung* on the merits. I would protect us by what we write against the other judges denying this. On the merits, both sides admit that the motel and restaurant are under the act, and the question of constitutionality is here. We should not concern ourselves with the Fourteenth Amendment. Congress need make no findings. The commerce power is adequate.[223] The precedents are all in line. I would not rely on any effect of demonstrations on commerce. I affirm in *Heart of Atlanta* and reverse in *McClung.*

---

221. *Civil Rights Cases,* 109 U.S. 3 (1883).

222. See, e.g., *Wickard v. Filburn,* 317 U.S. 111 (1942).

223. There were two likely reasons why Warren advocated using the commerce clause rather than the Fourteenth Amendment. First, the legislative history was not clear about whether Congress claimed authority under the Fourteenth Amendment to pass Title 2. Perhaps more important, if the Court decided the case on the basis of the Fourteenth Amendment, they would likely have to overrule the *Civil Rights Cases.* Deciding the case on the basis of the commerce clause, however, would allow the Court to sidestep these troublesome issues.

BLACK: I share that view. I would prefer to go on the Fourteenth Amendment, but I think that Congress limited the act to the commerce clause. Otherwise, I would be for overruling the *Civil Rights Cases*. The temporary injunction in *McClung* was not based on harassment, but only on one law suit. But since that has been stayed, the case is in the posture of a declaratory judgment. Both cases are under the act. In *McClung*, the goods have moved into state in commerce. Section 201(c) uses "substantial," otherwise I would be bothered. The "affecting" commerce test, as defined in our cases, is satisfied here. I affirm in *Heart of Atlanta* and reverse in *McClung*. The necessary and proper clause supports the power of Congress to pass this act. Hughes used it in "affecting" commerce cases, and that hurt him when he was up for confirmation as Chief Justice.[224]

DOUGLAS: I would rest on the Fourteenth Amendment and follow my concurring opinion in *Edwards*.[225]

CLARK: I would not rest on the Fourteenth Amendment. I will go on the commerce power. I affirm *Heart of Atlanta* and reverse *McClung*. I have doubts about the equity point in *McClung*. In *Heart of Atlanta*, 75 percent of his clients are interstate. In *McClung*, it is no objection that the test is "have moved" in commerce—that was also the basis in the Sullivan Act cases.

HARLAN: I agree with what has been said on the procedural point. I would treat it as an appeal from one judge in a declaratory judgment case. On the merits, I share Bill Douglas's view that this is really *the* Fourteenth Amendment question, not a commerce clause question. The real object is not commerce, but civil rights. That, of course, does not defeat the commerce clause. On the Fourteenth Amendment, I would stand by the *Civil Rights Cases* and hold this act unconstitutional. In this act, Congress, by the use of "state action," has adopted the *Civil Rights Cases* and has used it in the judicial sense of the term. In *Heart of Atlanta*, I have no problem under the commerce clause. In judging congressional action under the commerce clause, we have not followed a presumption of validity as we have in the case of state laws. Congressional findings are not necessary, but a record showing the relationship of the actions to commerce is required. Otherwise, the courts will not be able to know if it in fact "affects" commerce. In *Heart of Atlanta*, the legislative record made sustains the application of the act. I reserve the question whether non-interstate travelers are also protected by the act.

In *McClung*, I am not ready to vote. Is "affecting commerce" here the effect on the sale of food, or on other aspects of interstate trade, e.g., department store sales? I am not sure of the government's position on it, and I want to read the supplemental briefs. If

---

224. As a senator, Black voted against Hughes's confirmation as Chief Justice in 1930. Black was convinced that Hughes had sold out to corporate interests after he resigned from the Court for the first time in 1916 and entered private practice. Black feared that Hughes accepted the doctrine of substantive due process and would use a restrictive view of the commerce clause to strike down progressive social legislation in favor of big business. After a bitter Senate debate, Hughes was confirmed by a vote of 52–26.

225. *Edwards v. California*, 314 U.S. 160 (1941). Douglas argued that the California law prohibiting the importation of indigents into the state was primarily a right to travel case under the privileges and immunities clause of the Fourteenth Amendment. The majority, however, decided the case on commerce clause grounds.

the solicitor general is dependent on "affecting" food in commerce, he is in trouble. There is no substantial effect on interstate food movement, as distinguished from other movements in commerce. He would not be in trouble on the broader impact of segregation on commerce. If there is a basis for that, the act is O.K. I would tentatively reverse in *McClung.*

BRENNAN: I affirm *Heart of Atlanta* and reverse *McClung.* The district courts should be cautious against entertaining this kind of suit. The act has procedural devices that normally should be followed. I think that the "state action" definition followed the *Civil Rights Cases,* and that these cases must go on the commerce clause. I think that we are not precluded either by congressional findings or lack of findings. We can and should review here the adequacy of the legislative record. In *Heart of Atlanta,* it is irrelevant that 75 percent of the motel's customers were interstate. If the Court wants to go narrowly, I will go along. In *McClung,* this is clearly within our cases. On this record, there is food served by this restaurant that has moved in commerce.

STEWART: Resting on the commerce clause, I affirm *Heart of Atlanta* and reverse *McClung.*

WHITE: I agree with Potter. The fact that Congress in *McClung* relied on "food" sales does not preclude us from finding other grounds for upholding the act as applied under the commerce clause.

GOLDBERG: I share some of the troubles of Bill Douglas. It's a race statute. Both the commerce power and the Fourteenth Amendment power were used. I would sustain it under either or both. If we go on the commerce clause, we will get a lot of little messy cases. The legislative history shows confusion on the Fourteenth Amendment issue. It utilized §5 as they thought §5 might be read, no matter how broadly. I would join a commerce clause opinion if it were written broadly. Congress exercised its full power as to "motels" but not on "restaurants." As to the latter, the movement of food is not the only basis for the assertion of Congress's commerce power. The effect of desegregation on business generally is relevant. All restaurants could have been included.

Result: In Heart of Atlanta, *the Court upheld Title 2 as a valid exercise of Congress's commerce clause powers. Justice Clark, writing for a unanimous Court, tied the result to three main facts: (1) the motel advertised nationally for interstate travelers; (2) the motel was easily accessible to several interstate highways; and (3) 75 percent of motel patrons were interstate travelers. Clark also cited a congressional finding that black interstate travelers often had difficulty finding proper accommodations. The Court brusquely rejected Rolleston's Fifth and Thirteenth Amendment claims and distinguished the* Civil Rights Cases, *noting that the new Civil Rights Act of 1964, unlike the Civil Rights Act of 1875, was limited to businesses affecting interstate commerce. As for Ollie's Barbecue, Clark found that while the restaurant's use of interstate foodstuffs was insignificant considered alone, its cumulative impact with other similar businesses was enough to trigger the commerce clause.[226] In both cases, Black, Douglas, and Goldberg joined Clark's majority opinions but also wrote separate concurring opinions.*

---

226. Citing *Wickard v. Filburn,* 317 U.S. 111 (1942).

Moreton Rolleston refused to integrate his motel and soon went out of business. Ollie's Barbecue integrated and remains a popular Birmingham landmark.

Jones v. Alfred H. Mayer Co., 392 U.S. 409 (1968)
(Douglas) (Brennan)

An act of Congress, 42 U.S.C. §1982, guaranteed all citizens the same property rights as whites. Joseph Lee Jones alleged that the Alfred H. Mayer Company refused to sell him a house because he was black. The district court dismissed Jones's complaint, ruling that §1982 was passed pursuant to Congress's Fourteenth Amendment powers and applied only to cases involving state action. Accordingly, the law did not cover a private company's refusal to sell property on the basis of race. The court of appeals affirmed in an opinion by future Supreme Court Justice Harry Blackmun.

In conference, the Justices knew they wanted to reverse but could not agree on a rationale. They debated three alternatives: (a) to find state action somewhere and decide the case under the Fourteenth Amendment and Marsh v. Alabama;[227] (b) to rule that §1982 covered private discrimination under the Thirteenth Amendment (this was problematic because the statute, which was more than one hundred years old, had never been interpreted this way); or (c) to ignore §1982 entirely and decide the case using Title 8 of the recently enacted Civil Rights Act of 1968.[228] The conference took place on the day after Martin Luther King Jr.'s assassination. As the Justices deliberated, much of Washington, D.C., was beset by violent race riots.[229]

Conference of April 5, 1968

WARREN: I would not decide this case on the 1866 statute. I would not apply the 1968 act.[230] I would not make this a state action case under the Fourteenth Amendment. I would put this on *Marsh v. Alabama.* There are 250 homes in the subdivision—it is large enough to be a city fourth class. They have assessment power. It uses water, sewage, and the light system of the city. Trustees run the park. The streets are dedicated. *I reverse.* Doing it that way, Congress can take care of it under pending legislation. If we put it on state action, Congress will retreat.

BLACK: I would reverse on §1982, and not on *Marsh.* The statute was passed by Congress and covers this.

DOUGLAS: I would reverse on any of four or five different grounds, preferably §1982. I could reverse on both the Chief's and Hugo's grounds, and at least two others. I could go with Potter, too.

HARLAN: I am not at rest. I would like to see Congress deal with this problem and moot this case. It should be treated by Congress. As presently advised, I could perhaps join a *Marsh* ground, *but no other.* This is, in effect, a delegation of municipal power—a local

---

227. *Marsh v. Alabama,* 326 U.S. 501 (1946).
228. A broadly applicable fair housing act. It was passed after oral argument in this case and was not due to take effect until the end of 1968.
229. Klarman, "An Interpretive History of Modern Equal Protection," 278.
230. 42 U.S.C. §1982.

taxing power—to this development group. Once you do this §1982 comes into play, but not otherwise for me. I don't think that §1982 is a valid statute apart from state action. I reverse.

BRENNAN: I reverse on *Marsh*.

STEWART: I go much broader than *Marsh*. Section 1982 was enacted prior to Fourteenth Amendment, and under §2 of the Thirteenth Amendment. It is valid even without state action. Therefore, I think that this is a valid law operating against private people. I reverse. Even language in the *Civil Rights Cases* supports this analysis. You can't refuse to sell land because the man is a Negro any more than one can refuse to sell bread. I rest on §1982.

WHITE: I reverse on *Marsh*.

FORTAS: I reverse on *Marsh*.

MARSHALL: I reverse on *Marsh*. Although I am willing to go on §1982, I hope that it can be decided on narrow grounds or not decided at all if a new law passes.

HARLAN: Section 1982 is not valid legislation unless there is state action.

MARSHALL: I am more doubtful about going on §1982, as I am afraid that Congress would repeal it.

Conference of April 19, 1968

[DOUGLAS: Potter Stewart, who was assigned the case for an opinion, asked if anyone wanted the case to be disposed of under new act passed after case was argued, and not on the law as argued.][231]

DOUGLAS: I opposed the delay or any disposition under the new act.

WHITE: I suggest that a new response be obtained as to the impact of the new act.

[DOUGLAS: Warren, Douglas, and Stewart do not want to pass this case by for the new act. They believe that §1982 is valid under the Thirteenth Amendment.]

MARSHALL: Section 1982 is not clearly applicable. I want to pass this case, discuss it, and let the new act apply.

BLACK: The new act does not control this case. Section 1982 is a valid act.

FORTAS: As a matter of general policy, it is not our duty to relieve Congress of responsibility. I am inclined to let this case pass and go under the new act. But I am willing to decide it under §1982, and I suggest that there be a request for a response, as Byron suggested. Perhaps the builder has given up. I hope that a response will get the respondent to say that he will sell the house so that we can avoid any decision under §1982.

MARSHALL: I am anxious for us not to decide the case and am anxious to get a response. *Reverse under §1982:*

---

231. The Civil Rights Act of 1968.

Yes: Marshall (doubtful), Fortas (but he wants new response), Douglas, Black, Warren, Stewart.

No: White, Harlan.

Get New Response: White, Brennan, Harlan, Fortas, Marshall.

Result: In a dramatic reinterpretation of §1982, the Court ruled 6–1–2 that the law rested on Congress's authority under the Thirteenth Amendment and covered both private and public racial discrimination. The majority held that Title 8 of the Civil Rights Act of 1968 was not applicable because it was passed after the events which led to this lawsuit took place. Douglas concurred in the result.

Harlan and White dissented on the ground that the legislative history of the Civil Rights Act of 1866 demonstrated that the statute was passed under Congress's Fourteenth Amendment powers and was never intended to apply to private discrimination. The dissenters also argued that the case should have been dismissed because the Fair Housing Act of 1968 limited the significance of any Court decision.

The Court later extended Jones *to cover suits for monetary damages as well as claims for injunctive relief.*[232] *Harlan and White again dissented, along with newly appointed Chief Justice Warren Burger.*

Griggs v. Duke Power Co., 401 U.S. 424 (1971)

(Douglas)

The Duke Power Company required either a high school diploma or a satisfactory score on a general intelligence test as a condition of being hired or transferring to a new job within the company. Willie Griggs and other black employees sued under Title 7 of the Civil Rights Act of 1964, claiming that the tests had nothing to do with job performance and were racially discriminatory. The act specifically allowed the use of ability tests, as long as they were not designed, intended, or used to discriminate. The district court ruled that because the power company no longer discriminated against blacks and because Title 7 provided only prospective relief, the petitioners were not entitled to a remedy. The Fourth Circuit Court of Appeals held that residual discrimination caused by prior company practices could still be remedied but affirmed the lower court's finding that there was no proof of discriminatory purpose in the company's use of intelligence tests as a condition of hiring and promotion.

---

232. *Sullivan v. Little Hunting Park,* 396 U.S. 229 (1969). Little Hunting Park was a nonstock corporation organized to manage a neighborhood park in Fairfax County, Virginia. Each area homeowner was entitled to purchase a membership share, which entitled the family to use the park. If homeowners rented their homes, they could assign their share to their tenants subject to approval by the board of directors. Sullivan leased his house to the Freeman family and tried to assign his membership share, but the board refused to approve the assignment when they found out that the Freemans were black. The board expelled Sullivan from the corporation after he protested the board's action, and he sued for injunctive and compensatory damages. The trial court dismissed the complaints on the ground that the corporation was a private social organization. The Supreme Court reversed, ruling 5–3 (it was a short-handed Court) that the board's actions violated 42 U.S.C §1982, which guaranteed to all citizens the same property rights enjoyed by whites. Harlan, Burger, and White dissented, arguing that the case should have been DIGGED because the Fair Housing Title of the Civil Rights Act of 1968 provided a comprehensive scheme for dealing with such problems and because "it was very unwise. . . to use §1982 as a broad delegation of power to develop a common law of forbidden racial discriminations."

Conference of December 18, 1970

BURGER: This case involves the use of intelligence tests for transfers from one department to another. The impact is severe on Negroes. This case is difficult and close. I hesitate to affirm, but it is a small plant with little turnover. Tests and standards must be related to the job. If there was no history of past discrimination, I would have no problems. The arbitrary requirement of a high school diploma has a severe impact. I can affirm if Sobeloff's standards were accepted.[233]

BLACK: It is a new act. There are difficulties in complying with it. This company was doing its best to comply with it. I am inclined to affirm. Sobeloff's standards do not suit me, as that is a legislative function.

DOUGLAS: I would reverse and remand. The employer has the burden of showing that these tests were job related.

HARLAN: I agree with Bill Douglas. These tests must be job related. Administrative practice points that up. It is very difficult to affirm. Reversal is not on the Constitution, but on the act. Sobeloff's view of the act is right. I would reverse and remand—the tests must be job related.

STEWART: I agree with Bill Douglas and John Harlan. I would reverse—I cannot affirm.

WHITE: I reverse. Does job relatedness refer to a particular job or a future job? The tests were not job related in either sense. Promotion was from inside the company—they can screen out people who never would get beyond one job.

MARSHALL: Not everyone employed need not be qualified for higher jobs. I stay with the U.S. position, not with Sobeloff—I reverse.

BLACKMUN: I am inclined to reverse. The legislative history favors Duke. I agree with Byron on the difficulties of the case. An employer has the right to hire only those promotable employees—people like to work up through the ranks. I would not restrict the employer to only a present job.

BURGER: An employer has a right to test for more than a particular job. I am flexible, and can do the job by reversal or affirmance.

Result: Warren Burger wrote for a unanimous Court reversing the Fourth Circuit in part. Hugo Black changed his mind after the conference and joined Burger's opinion, which closely tracked Sobeloff's opinion below.

---

233. Chief Judge Simon E. Sobeloff concurred in part and dissented in part in the circuit court's decision in this case. 420 F.2d 1225 (4th Cir. 1970). For Sobeloff, the key issue was that jobs were denied to blacks who could not meet educational requirements or pass standardized tests but who might otherwise have been qualified for the jobs in question. He noted that racial discrimination in employment paralleled discrimination in other areas, where overt bias was often "supplanted by more cunning devices designed to impart the appearance of neutrality, but to operate with the same invidious effect as before." In Sobeloff's judgment, allegedly objective or neutral standards that favored whites but did not serve legitimate business needs were unlawful.

This case helped to define the scope of Title 7. The law, Burger wrote, did not require companies to hire or promote anyone merely because they were members of a minority group; it simply required companies to remove "artificial, arbitrary, and unnecessary barriers to employment when the barriers operate invidiously to discriminate on the basis of race or other impermissible classification."[234] Any test that disproportionately impacted racial minorities, however, even one that appeared neutral on its face, must have a significant relation to job performance. While the Court found no evidence of intent to discriminate, there was no clear relationship between the tests and job performance. This meant that under Title 7 the consequences of the tests—and not just the company's intent—could be considered.

The "disparate impact" test established here proved to be exceptionally important to subsequent discrimination lawsuits and affirmative action programs. Plaintiffs no longer had to prove that employers were motivated by prejudice or ill will; they only had to demonstrate that performance exams had a disparate impact on minority groups. This shifted the burden to employers to prove that performance tests were job related or a business necessity. This proved difficult and costly to do, and many companies adopted affirmative action plans as a cheaper alternative to litigation. As the Court grew more conservative after the late 1980s, it began to back away from Griggs. In 1989, the Rehnquist Court revisited Title 7 in Wards Cove Packing Co. v. Atonio *and made it more difficult to establish a prima facie case of discrimination.[235] Congress reacted by passing the Civil Rights Act of 1991, which reversed significant aspects of* Wards Cove *and restored most of the* Griggs *standards.*

Moose Lodge No. 107 v. Irvis, 407 U.S. 163 (1972)
(Brennan) (Douglas)

When K. Leroy Irvis visited the Moose Lodge as the guest of a member, he was refused service in the dining room and bar because he was black. Irvis claimed that the club's actions violated the equal protection clause of the Fourteenth Amendment. Although the lodge was a private organization and ordinarily would not be subject to the Fourteenth Amendment, Irvis argued that state action existed in the form of the club's state liquor license.

The Moose Lodge maintained that it was strictly a private organization and that the Fourteenth Amendment did not reach private discrimination. Lodge members also claimed that the right of free association meant that they could exclude whomever they wished. The three-judge district court ruled that the club's liquor license amounted to state action and ordered the license revoked for as long as the lodge continued to discriminate on the basis of race.

Conference of February 28, 1972

BURGER: I can't agree with Freedman and the Third Circuit.[236] This is not state action. I see no state action here any more than with city water and so forth. I am not sure that it is crystal clear that we have a case or controversy here.

---

234. *Griggs v. Duke Power Co.,* 401 U.S. 424, 431 (1971).

235. *Wards Cove Packing Co. v. Atonio,* 490 U.S. 642 (1989).

236. The decision was not by a circuit court but by a three-judge district court for the Middle District of Pennsylvania. Circuit Judge Freedman wrote the majority opinion, *Irvis v. Moose Lodge #107,* 318 F. Supp. 1246.

DOUGLAS: State permits and licenses usually lead me to find state action. But here, the 1964 act shows a legislative history for excepting private clubs, and Congress can set up guidelines to which I am inclined to give deference. That is a *Katzenbach v. Morgan* approach.[237] I reverse.

BRENNAN: My dissent in *Adickes* indicates affirmance.[238]

STEWART: There is state action here, but is there state discrimination in violation of the Fourteenth Amendment? I would modify this judgment as to that part of the liquor license which requires that its by-laws be enforced, insofar as they require racial discrimination. Otherwise, I basically agree with Bill Douglas.

WHITE: I am not sure whether there is a case or controversy here. Not all members of the class have a case or controversy, and there is no continuing controversy with the club. This case has become moot because, like *Sierra*, it's only a right of every citizen.[239] On the merits, I prefer to go Bill Douglas's route that in this arguable area, Congress's excluding of private clubs in the 1964 act controls this case.

STEWART: Congress can legislate on §5 of the Fourteenth Amendment if there is this much state involvement.

MARSHALL: I agree with Byron on the jurisdictional point. When he said that any Negro can come in and have a drink, the case became moot. When he requested a motion to amend the judgment to allow him in as a guest, the lawsuit ended. I agree with Bill Douglas on the 1964 act. His approach appeals to me. If Congress limits state action, we can disagree. The 1964 act does not do that. I reverse.

BLACKMUN: Jurisdiction has two aspects: (1) whether there was enough for a three-judge court; and (2) whether there was a case or controversy. It was a proper three-judge court, but the case or controversy requirement bothers me. Irvis did not claim membership, but once he rejected it I think his lawsuit went out the window. On the merits, I can't deny the association and privacy rights claimed here. On the merits, I reverse. I don't think that there was any state action here. I am not sure about Bill Douglas's 1964 act approach, but his suggestion is interesting and I can be persuaded.

POWELL: I have not studied the jurisdictional issues. I hope that we can resolve this case on the merits rather than on jurisdictional grounds. On the merits I would reverse, whether on Bill Douglas's ground or on a constitutional basis. We should not deny this right of privacy.

---

237. *Katzenbach v. Morgan*, 384 U.S. 641 (1966). The Court upheld §4 of the Voting Rights Act of 1965, which banned New York's use of English literacy tests as a condition of voting. The tests had been used to deny the franchise to large numbers of otherwise eligible voters who had been schooled in Puerto Rico and spoke only Spanish. The Court ruled that §4 was a proper exercise of Congress's power to enforce the Fourteenth Amendment.

238. *Adickes v. Kress & Co.*, 398 U.S. 144 (1970).

239. *Sierra Club v. Morton*, 405 U.S. 727 (1972).

REHNQUIST: On the merits, I am inclined to Potter's view that *Shelley v. Kraemer* requires striking down that portion of the law requiring conformation to by-laws and tying the license to racial discrimination.[240] I have trouble tying it to the 1964 act. I would not be sure about Bill Douglas's approach, but would prefer to say outright that there was no state action.

Result: Despite a great deal of initial interest in Douglas's creative approach to reverse, even Douglas quickly lost interest in his idea after the conference. Douglas and Marshall both switched sides and joined William Brennan in dissent. The majority ruled that while Irvis did not have standing to contest the Lodge's membership practices (because he had never applied for membership), he could sue over his treatment as a guest. The Court then decided 6–3 that the mere fact that the lodge held a state liquor license was not sufficient to constitute state action and trigger the Fourteenth Amendment.

Runyon v. McCrary, 427 U.S. 160 (1976)
(Brennan)

Michael McCrary and Colin Gonzalez were denied admission to several all-white private schools in Virginia solely on account of their race. They sued through their parents, claiming that their rejection violated §1981, guaranteeing all persons in the United States the same right to make and enforce contracts as whites. They also argued that §1981 was passed under Congress's Thirteenth Amendment powers which, unlike the Fourteenth Amendment, could reach private discrimination. The district court agreed that the schools' actions violated §1981. The trial judge enjoined the named schools and a local association of private schools from discriminating on the basis of race. The court awarded a variety of remedies, including cash damages and attorneys' fees. The court of appeals affirmed, but reversed on the issue of attorneys' fees.

BURGER: Section 1981 has been held over three dissents to reach private school discrimination. Our cases support that, although there is a question of how far private contracts that discriminate are reached by §1981. On the issue of counsel fees, I don't see bad faith on a statutory basis. Statutory interpretation is usually not reconsidered, and I don't see much difference, if any, between §1981 and §1982.

STEWART: Section 1981 applies only to racial discrimination, not to religion, sex, and query ethnic discrimination. I would set aside the Fourteenth Amendment argument—there has been too much water under the bridge. If you had a bona fide religious tenet of "whites only," it might be tough.

WHITE: It is difficult not to affirm if §1981 applies to private parties, and I have grave doubts about that. Section 16 of the 1870 statute is what's before us, and that's a Fourteenth Amendment statute.

MARSHALL: I would limit §1981 to this case.

---

240. *Shelley v. Kraemer,* 334 U.S. 1 (1948).

BLACKMUN: I don't think that §1981 was intended for this kind of thing, but I wrote *Tillman*[241] and *REA*,[242] following *Sullivan*[243] and *Jones*.[244] But I could be had by Byron if he can prove a case. I had assumed that the cases settled that §1981 applied to private discrimination. If there was a majority to reconsider the question (and Byron may enlighten me) I would join it. The opinion must limit §1981 to private racial discrimination to hold me to affirmance. Mutuality is a vital tenet of contract, but you can't make an offer to the whole world except Negroes.

REHNQUIST: On the basic §1981 issues, I am satisfied that there is a prima facie case that part of §1981 pushed up in the 1875 revision was not intended to apply to private action. But I joined Harry in *Tillman* and *REA*.

STEVENS: The §1981 argument of Byron's is not too persuasive. I think that both the Thirteenth and Fourteenth Amendments support this statute. I can't distinguish between §1981 and §1982, but I think that *Jones v. Mayer* was wrongly decided. All they did was to give freed slaves equality in a legal capacity in certain ways. But our cases are against me, and thus my problem is stare decisis. Certainly in the modern social context we ought affirm, and I will probably end up that way.

Result: The Court ruled 7–2 that §1981 prohibited private, commercially operated, nonsectarian schools from denying admission to students on account of race. Stevens joined Stewart's majority opinion, but in a brief concurring opinion he said that he did so only because of stare decisis. White and Rehnquist dissented.

---

241. *Tillman v. Wheaton-Haven Recreation Assn.*, 410 U.S. 431 (1973). A homeowners' association in Silver Springs, Maryland, operated a community swimming pool for the use of association members. When a black couple moved into the neighborhood, the association rejected a resolution that would have allowed them to become members, and the family was actively discouraged from applying for membership. The board also changed its rules to prevent white members from bringing nonwhite guests to the pool. Murray Tillman and a racially mixed group of homeowners and guests sued. The Court unanimously held that the association was not a private club (since membership was open to every white person within a defined geographic area and there was no selective element other than race) and that it violated 42 U.S.C. §1982, which granted all citizens the same property rights as white citizens. Blackmun wrote the majority opinion. The case, he concluded, was indistinguishable from *Sullivan v. Little Hunting Park, Inc.*, 396 U.S. 229 (1969).

242. *Johnson v. Railway Express Agency, Inc.*, 421 U.S. 454 (1975). Willie Johnson filed an employment discrimination charge with the EEOC under Title 7 of the Civil Rights Act of 1964. Because of bureaucratic delays and problems with finding a lawyer, Johnson delayed several years before filing a second discrimination action under 42 U.S.C. §1981. By that time, the state statute of limitations had expired. On a 6–3 vote, the Supreme Court rejected Johnson's argument that the statute of limitations on his §1981 action should have been tolled while his Title 7 claim was pending. Blackmun wrote the majority opinion. Marshall, Douglas, and Brennan dissented in part. They argued that the federal policy favoring EEOC conciliation procedures to settle discrimination claims would be frustrated if employees were required to file a second lawsuit under §1981 while EEOC conciliation efforts were still underway.

243. *Sullivan v. Little Hunting Park, Inc.*, 396 U.S. 229 (1969).

244. *Jones v. Alfred H. Mayer Co.*, 392 U.S. 409 (1968).

AFFIRMATIVE ACTION IN SCHOOLS

DeFunis v. Odegaard, 416 U.S. 312 (1974)
(Douglas) (Brennan)

Marco DeFunis Jr. was denied admission to the University of Washington law school in 1971. That year, the University of Washington accepted 275 students out of 1,601 applicants.[245] *Of this number, 37 nonwhite students were admitted on the basis of their race or ethnicity. DeFunis, who was white, sued in state court claiming that he had been denied admission to the law school on the basis of his race, in violation of the Fourteenth Amendment's equal protection clause. The trial judge agreed and ordered DeFunis admitted to the state law school. After DeFunis enrolled and began his studies, the Washington State Supreme Court reversed. DeFunis appealed to the U.S. Supreme Court. Justice Douglas stayed the state supreme court's judgment pending Supreme Court review, and by the time the case was briefed and argued, DeFunis had already registered for his final quarter of classes. The law school stipulated that he would be allowed to graduate regardless of the outcome of the case.*

Conference of March 1, 1974

BURGER: The question is the extent to which race may be taken into account to exclude DeFunis from a public law school. In all of our school cases race was a factor, but only to consider what room he was in. So far, we have never allowed a person to be excluded because of his race. The premise here seems to be that because blacks suffered oppression, it is the state's duty to redress the harm. The use of our *Swann* statement falls flat in face of the fact that he is not excluded.[246] The case may become moot. Where a finding of discrimination is shown, the existence of a long-standing wrong is a predicate of present action. Minority groups need minority lawyers. This is a state institution, but any schools receiving federal aid are bound by federal standards. There is no "compelling" need for this regulation. No one was ever kept out by reason of race until now. Minority groups were separately evaluated. Is race the basis of classification? This case may formally be moot by June.

DOUGLAS: I was never sure that the decision not allowing pro rata in the grand juries was right. Some things transcend race. I can't believe that where an aristocracy of talent is a problem that you can force a state university to take blacks in some jobs. I am suspicious of tests, and maybe we ought to say that all at the bottom of the class must be taken in. I pass.

BRENNAN: On mootness, the case is probably not moot even if he graduates in June. What has the law school done? This is a business of excluding people, but not for color. Can the school as an educational policy have a law class selected in light of a racial component? Harvard took high school graduates, not only prep schools. What is done here is done to right a wrong done to blacks. If that is it, whites could not be excluded. The proper approach is: is this an educational policy or racial? I think that it is educational. They

---

245. One hundred fifty students matriculated.
246. *Swann v. Charlotte-Mecklenburg Board of Education,* 402 U.S. 1 (1971).

could prefer a New Yorker over a Washington state resident. If the Fourteenth Amendment does not bar this, the act does not. I affirm.

STEWART: The case is moot. This is not a class action suit, and is not remotely akin to *Roe* or *Doe*.[247] This is a third-year student in his final quarter. He will finish. He is in the middle of his class. If he was first-year man, the case would not be moot. I do not express any views on the merits.

WHITE: The case is not moot. On the merits, I agree with Bill Brennan. The state may do what it does here. I affirm.

MARSHALL: I affirm. I agree with Brennan.

BLACKMUN: The case is moot. I am not sure whether I should sit on this case. For twenty years I interviewed Harvard admissions and I may be biased. There is a lot to be said for what Bickel and Kurland say in their briefs.[248] I may not sit. There are good arguments on both sides on the merits.

POWELL: I am on the Board of Washington and Lee, a private school. It has no graduate work except law. As to mootness, I assumed that we crossed this bridge when we took the case. But the case probably is moot. If I reach the merits, I strongly believe in what Bill Brennan said, that the courts have no business in limiting admissions policies so long as there is no clear racial discrimination. Race per se is not an impermissible consideration in such a policy. The courts have no business limiting in any significant way admissions policies of graduate schools. The University of Washington fouled its nest. I am doubtful if any educational policy was obtained here. Race, however, is a factor that can lawfully be considered. I tentatively affirm.

REHNQUIST: The case is moot, and a decision on the merits is not required. If a student is denied admission, he can keep it alive. His only claim was to get in, and he got in. On the merits, I pass.

Result: Douglas changed his mind after the conference and decided that the case was not moot. Powell, however, changed his mind the other way and in a 5–4 per curiam decision the Court mooted the case. Brennan, Douglas, White, and Marshall dissented. Marco DeFunis graduated from the University of Washington Law School in 1974 and practices law in Seattle.

Regents of the University of California v. Bakke, 438 U.S. 265 (1978)
(Brennan)

Allan Bakke applied twice for admission to medical school at the University of California, Davis, and was rejected both times. The university had a two-track admissions procedure: out of an entering class of 100, 84 seats were open to all applicants on a competitive basis; the remaining 16 seats were reserved

---

247. *Roe v. Wade,* 410 U.S. 113 (1973), and *Doe v. Bolton,* 410 U.S. 179 (1973).

248. Alexander Bickel, Philip Kurland, Larry Lavinsky, and Arnold Forster submitted an amicus brief urging reversal on behalf of the Anti-Defamation League of B'nai B'rith.

exclusively for racial and ethnic minorities. Applicants on the special admissions track did not have to meet the minimum academic standards required of other applicants.[249] *Bakke sued, claiming that he had been denied admission on the basis of his race in violation of Title 6 of the Civil Rights Act of 1964 and the equal protection clause of the Fourteenth Amendment.*[250]

The California Supreme Court ruled that all racial classifications, even those used for "benign" purposes, required strict scrutiny.[251] *The state court found that California had a compelling interest to increase the number of minority physicians, but struck down Davis's affirmative action program on the ground that it was not the least intrusive means to achieve that goal. Because school officials admitted that Bakke was qualified and would have been admitted but for the special admissions program, the state supreme court ordered Bakke admitted to Davis's medical school. University officials appealed directly to the U.S. Supreme Court.*

BURGER: I could affirm on Title 6. I have considered what Davis could do constitutionally. Diversity is a desideratum, but it ought be sought at lower levels than graduate school. Davis could have make-up courses and so forth.

STEWART: There is nothing in the equal protection clause that forbids a state from barring admission to other than applicants based on geography, alumni, athletics and so forth. I would decide this case on the Fourteenth Amendment, since that was (1) the basis of the California Supreme Court's decision; (2) Title 6 would be broader than the Fourteenth Amendment; and (3) Congress could not have meant to forbid what the equal protection clause permitted. If the equal protection clause does nothing else, it forbids discrimination based alone on a person's race. That is precisely what Davis's program does, and an injurious action based on race is unconstitutional. No state agency can take race into account. My view on the Fifth Amendment might be different.

WHITE: On Title 6, I think that there is no private cause of action. But if it is congruent with the Fourteenth Amendment, then we must reach the Fourteenth Amendment. If Congress thought that the Constitution *required* color blindness when Title 6 was written, that would cement its meaning even if that reflected a wrong understanding of the Fourteenth Amendment. On the constitutional issue, Davis may set this quota and fill it with qualified Negroes. I will rely on the legislative and executive view of what is permissible under the Fourteenth Amendment.

MARSHALL: I agree substantially with Byron and Bill Brennan, although I am not sure that there is no private cause of action under Title 6. On the constitutional question, this is not a quota to keep someone out—it's a quota to get someone in.[252]

---

249. While white applicants with less than a 2.5 grade point average were automatically rejected, there was no equivalent Mendoza line for "special track" applicants. Minority applicants also received personal interviews with a special student-faculty admissions committee.

250. Title 6 provided that "no person shall on the ground of race or color be excluded from participating in any program receiving federal financial assistance."

251. *Bakke v. Regents of the University of California,* 18 Cal. 3d 34, 553 P. 2d 1152 (1976). Stanley Mosk wrote the majority opinion in a 6–1 decision, with Matthew Tobriner as the sole dissenter.

252. When Brennan asked Marshall whether it would be proper for school administrators to accord Marshall's son special consideration because of his race, Marshall replied, "Damn right, they owe us." Tushnet, *Making Constitutional Law,* 219.

POWELL: Title 6 is congruent with the Fourteenth Amendment. Most schools seem to operate along Harvard program lines. I can't join Thurgood, Byron, and Bill in thinking that 16, or 84, or any quota was O.K. The symbolic effect of the Fourteenth Amendment would be completely lost. Rather, while the admission policy should be left to university, the colossal blunder here was to pick a number. Diversity is a necessary goal to assure a broad spectrum of Americans an opportunity for graduate school. But not one of other three justifications has any merit. Each applicant should be able to compete with others, and taking race into account is proper, but never by setting aside a fixed number of places. I agree that the judgment must be reversed insofar as it enjoins Davis from taking race into account.

REHNQUIST: I basically agree with Potter. I don't agree with Lewis that race can be taken into account. Title 6 is more difficult for me—I am not sure that there isn't a private cause of action. I am not sure, either, that Title 6 and the Fourteenth Amendment are congruent.

STEVENS: I would decide this case on Title 6. If Bill Brennan, Byron, and Thurgood prevailed, we would have a permanent conclusion that blacks can never reach the point when they would not be discriminated against. Affirmative action programs have performed a fine service, but they ought to be *temporary*. I can't ever believe that the day won't come when two track systems will be unnecessary. If we can duck a constitutional holding, we should. The Davis program is not the product of careful thought. I think that Title 6 gives a private cause of action, and that less than Fourteenth Amendment proof is required. No intent needs to be proved, for example. I would hold that Title 6 is violated by a two-track quota system.[253]

Result: Two very different coalitions decided the main questions presented in this case. Lewis Powell wrote the lead opinion and was the only Justice to vote with the majority on all major issues.

First, backed by the conservative wing of the Court, Powell ruled that Davis's affirmative action program amounted to a quota system that impermissibly discriminated on the basis of race. On a 5–4 vote, the Court ordered Bakke to be admitted to the university's medical school. Powell wrote that strict scrutiny must be used to evaluate all racial classifications, even when they were allegedly used for benign purposes. While governments could remedy past state discrimination, there were no find-

---

253. According to John Jeffries, when Stevens intimated that he did not think that blacks would need affirmative action for very long, Marshall interrupted him to say that it would be needed for another hundred years. Jeffries, *Justice Powell*, 487–88.

One of Powell's clerks said later that Powell might have been persuaded to join the liberal position across the board had Marshall conceded that affirmative action programs would have to be temporary, perhaps limited to a period of ten years. But Marshall thought that parts of Powell's draft opinion were racist and Marshall was in no mood to reach out. Powell had sharply criticized the idea that some racial groups might be entitled to be treated as "special wards entitled to a degree of protection greater than that accorded others." To Marshall, this echoed the language of the *Civil Rights Cases*, where Justice Bradley wrote, in striking down the Civil Rights Act of 1875, that it was past time for blacks to become "mere citizen[s], and cease to be. . . special favorite[s] of the law." Tushnet, *Making Constitutional Law*, 127–28. Powell's opinion in *Bakke* caused Marshall to become noticeably more cynical and outspoken about the Court's treatment of blacks. For years afterward, when well-meaning visitors asked Marshall how he would solve America's racial problems, he often responded, "Kill all the white people." Everyone assumed that he was kidding.

ings of past discrimination in this case, and general societal discrimination was not sufficient to justify preferential treatment on the basis of race. Powell also rejected the state court's finding that the government's desire to produce more minority physicians was a compelling state interest.

Second, joined by the liberal wing of the Court, Powell established that state universities could take race into account as one factor in building a diverse student body. The goal of educational diversity was a compelling state interest and could be considered when designing affirmative action programs.

For Powell, the fatal flaw in Davis's affirmative action plan was that the school's special admissions policy established a quota based solely on race. Nonminority students were excluded from consideration under the special admissions program, and this was neither necessary nor narrowly tailored to achieve the state's compelling goal of creating a diversity of "experiences, outlooks and ideas" among the student body. Race could be considered as one factor in graduate school admissions, but it could not be the sole criterion.

In dissent, the four liberal Justices, led by Brennan, argued that Title 6 and the equal protection clause were identical. In Brennan's view, neither Title 6 nor the Fourteenth Amendment prohibited voluntary preferential treatment of racial minorities to remedy past societal discrimination. Such affirmative action, he maintained, should be subject to intermediate scrutiny rather than strict scrutiny. Benign racial classifications—those designed to meet remedial purposes—must serve important governmental objectives and must be substantially related to achieving those objectives. State action could not stigmatize any racial group or single out those least well represented in the political process and force them to bear the brunt of an affirmative action program. Brennan argued that Bakke was neither demeaned nor stigmatized with a badge of inferiority because of his race. Powell agreed that the scope of Title 6 and the equal protection clause were identical, although his overall approach was quite different from Brennan's.

Four conservative Justices, led by Stevens, argued that the entire case should be decided on statutory grounds, without reaching the constitutional arguments. Title 6, Stevens wrote, explicitly prohibited the exclusion of any individual from any federally funded program on the basis of race—regardless of whether the exclusion carried with it a racial stigma or resulted from an allegedly "benign" affirmative action program. Davis's special admissions program clearly violated Title 6 because it excluded Allan Bakke from medical school on account of his race.

Affirmative Action in the Workplace

Fullilove v. Klutznick, 448 U.S. 448 (1980)
(Brennan)

In 1977, Congress required that at least 10 percent of federal funds for public works projects had to be used to purchase services or supplies from businesses owned by American citizens who belonged to any of six specified minority groups: Negroes, Spanish-speaking, Orientals, Indians, Eskimos, and Aleuts.[254] H. Earl Fullilove and other contractors sued Secretary of Commerce Philip Klutznick, claiming that the set-asides violated the equal protection clause of the Fourteenth Amendment and the equal pro-

---

254. The language was part of the Minority Business Enterprise (MBE) provisions of the Public Works Employment Act of 1977. The statute allowed contractors to seek an administrative waiver of this requirement under some circumstances.

tection component of the Fifth Amendment's due process clause. The district court ruled that the set-asides were constitutional, and the court of appeals affirmed.

BURGER: May Congress condition grants to state and local entities on a 10 percent set-aside? The inclusion of Orientals and others makes this tough. What discrimination can be shown against them? Indians and blacks are clear. There is no explicit finding required for me as to them. Strict scrutiny applies, since past discrimination is known. This is a temporary, experimental program. Also, we should give more latitude to Congress than to administrative or state action. It is also important to cleanse the construction industry, with its history of exclusion of Negroes. *Bakke*[255] and *Weber*[256] are pertinent, as are *Katzenbach v. Morgan*[257] and *Lau v Nichols*.[258] Deference to Congress's hearings and means, only in racial area.

STEWART: The Constitution I understand is being replaced by a new Constitution. The Fifth and Fourteenth Amendments must mean that you can't predicate exclusions based on race—it is per se invidious, however loftily motivated.

BLACKMUN: The findings here are that less restrictive alternatives are ineffective. I have no problem about the congressional findings. This is not as stigmatizing as *Bakke*.

---

255. *University of California Regents v. Bakke,* 438 U.S. 265 (1978).

256. *United Steelworkers v. Weber,* 443 U.S. 193 (1979). Kaiser Aluminum and Chemical Corporation and the steelworkers' union entered into a voluntary collective bargaining agreement that contained an affirmative action plan. The plan was designed to eliminate longstanding racial imbalances in the company's skilled workforce. It established hiring targets and provided preferences for blacks who wished to attend on-the-job training programs. Brian Webber and other white workers sued, claiming that the racial preferences violated Title 7 of the Civil Rights Act of 1964.

The Court ruled 5–2 that the company's voluntary affirmative action plan did not violate Title 7. Brennan, writing for the majority, said that the spirit of the law was to eliminate the effects of past racial discrimination. Kaiser's voluntary, private affirmative action program was consistent with that spirit, because the racial preferences built into the collective bargaining agreement: (1) ameliorated longstanding racial imbalances; (2) did not cause white workers to be fired, demoted, or permanently barred from promotion; and (3) created only a temporary and modest preference for black workers. Burger and Rehnquist dissented on the ground that the program discriminated on the basis of race, which was prohibited by the plain language of Title 7. Such discrimination, they argued, could not be justified by metaphysical references to the act's "spirit." Powell and Stevens did not participate.

257. *Katzenbach v. Morgan,* 384 U.S. 641 (1966).

258. *Lau v. Nichols,* 414 U.S. 563 (1974). Kinney Kinmon Lau and 1,800 other non–English-speaking Asian students sued the San Francisco Unified School District, alleging that the district's failure to provide them with adequate English language instruction violated §601 of the Civil Rights Act of 1964, which banned discrimination based on race, color, or national origin in "any program or activity receiving federal financial assistance." They also alleged that the school district violated Department of Health, Education, and Welfare regulations. Douglas, writing for five members of the Court, ruled that in failing to provide non–English-speaking students with adequate English-language instruction, the school district had violated §601 and the implementing HEW regulations. Stewart, Burger, White, and Blackmun concurred in the result but would have decided the case based only upon the district's violation of HEW guidelines.

POWELL: I would have agreed with Potter twenty years ago, but the Court in *Brown*,[259] and *Green*,[260] and Congress in Title 7 and in the Voting Rights Act all have led me to assume that under strict scrutiny a substantive or compelling state interest permits some classifications based on race. The government interest here is very substantial. I would not accept that historic discrimination is enough. I would want definitive findings—and there is an adequate record here—and I would not second-guess Congress's choice of means.

REHNQUIST: I feel much as Potter does. How much review is there of Congress's decision to spend money? Anyway, it stands the Constitution on its head to say that Congress has more power here than the states. I can't see how can we give more deference to Congress than to state legislatures.

STEVENS: I am not really at rest. I don't agree with either the Chief Justice or with Potter. Racial groups may in some instances be made beneficiaries of special legislation. I would show greater deference to Congress than to state action. I disagree with *Wiesenfeld*.[261] I wish that this were concrete rather than a palliative. There are two justifications: (1) to remedy past discrimination; and (2) the country, in the long run, does better to spread this business around. The "fit" on the first ground is really very poor— the benefits go to only a few Negroes. So I am reluctant to approve this on past discrimination. I also have problems with the second justification—but maybe it can be defended on that ground.

---

259. *Brown v. Board of Education*, 347 U.S. 483 (1954).

260. *Green v. County School Board of New Kent County*, 391 U.S. 430 (1968). Faced with massive southern resistance to *Brown*, the Court lost patience with the slow pace of desegregation and the lack of good faith efforts on the part of local school boards. Brennan, writing for a unanimous Court, signaled that extraordinary remedial measures might be necessary to eliminate dual schools systems and that district court judges were to "take whatever steps might be necessary" to establish unitary school systems "in which racial discrimination would be eliminated root and branch." The Justices made it clear that they were prepared to tolerate a wide range of race-conscious remedies, including racial balancing of student bodies, faculty, and staff, and that remedial plans would be judged primarily by their results.

261. *Weinberger v. Wiesenfeld*, 420 U.S. 636 (1975). The Social Security Act provided different survivors' benefits for men and women. If the deceased was male, his widow and minor children received survivors' benefits. If the deceased was female, only her minor children received survivors' benefits; her surviving spouse received nothing. Upon the death of his wife, Stephen Wiesenfeld applied for Social Security benefits for himself and his infant son. While the boy received benefits, Mr. Wiesenfeld was declared ineligible because of his sex.

Writing for seven members of the Court, Brennan wrote that the law violated *women's* equal protection rights because female taxpayers were less able to provide for their families after death than male taxpayers. Such different treatment could not be justified by the archaic generalization that women's earnings did not contribute significantly to their families' well-being. Moreover, widow's benefits were not based on any special disadvantage suffered by women, nor were they intended to provide income to women who, because of economic discrimination, were unable to provide for their families. Widow's benefits were intended to allow the mother—but not the father—to choose not to work and to stay home to care for the children. Powell and Burger concurred on the ground that there was no legitimate government interest in discriminating against female wage earners by providing their families with less protection than male wage earners. Rehnquist also concurred with the result. Douglas did not participate.

Result: Although the Court was badly divided and there was no majority opinion, six Justices agreed that Congress had significant—though not unlimited—constitutional authority to pass affirmative action legislation. Warren Burger, in a plurality opinion joined only by White and Powell, upheld the federal set-asides as a valid exercise of Congress's powers under the spending and commerce clauses and the Fourteenth Amendment. The Chief Justice's opinion was unusually vague and failed to adopt any specific standard of review. Any program using racial or ethnic categories would be subject to "a most searching examination," although Congress's judgment in such matters would receive "appropriate deference." Burger found sufficient evidence to justify Congress's actions in this case: (1) there had been past racial discrimination in public construction contracts; (2) this discrimination had adversely affected interstate commerce; and (3) the problem was national in scope. Burger also thought that the means adopted were narrowly tailored to remedy past discrimination, and while innocent parties were burdened by the set-aside programs, their injuries were incidental and "relatively light."

Thurgood Marshall, in a concurring opinion joined by Brennan and Blackmun, argued that intermediate scrutiny should be used whenever Congress sought to use racial categories to remedy past discrimination. This meant that there had to be an important government objective and Congress had to use narrowly tailored means to achieve its objective. In this case, the government's objective of remedying past discrimination in the construction business sufficed.

Stewart, Rehnquist, and Stevens dissented. Stewart and Rehnquist argued that racial distinctions were inherently invidious. "Under our Constitution," Stewart wrote, "government may never act to the detriment of a person solely because of that person's race." Stewart implied that only the courts, using their equitable powers, could impose racially conscious remedies to correct past discrimination, because Congress had "neither the dispassionate objectivity nor the flexibility that are needed to mold a race-conscious remedy . . . [to eliminate] the effects of past or present discrimination."

Stevens criticized the set-aside program as creating monopoly privileges "for a class of investors defined solely by racial characteristics." The real beneficiaries of such programs, he said, were inevitably a privileged elite—members of a small, entrepreneurial subclass who had or could borrow working capital. Stevens acknowledged the need to remedy prior discrimination against blacks, but attacked the inclusion of other favored racial and ethnic groups in the program. While blacks had originally been "dragged to this country in chains to be sold into slavery," Stevens observed:

> *the "Spanish-speaking" subclass came voluntarily, frequently without invitation, and the Indians, the Eskimos and the Aleuts had an opportunity to exploit American's resources before the ancestors of most American citizens arrived. . . . Nothing in the legislative history suggests, much less demonstrates, that each of the subclasses is equally entitled to reparations from the United States Government.*

Several years later, in Richmond v. Croson Co., *the Rehnquist Court used strict scrutiny to strike down a state-mandated construction set-aside program modeled on the federal statute upheld here.[262] This seemed to indicate that state and local governments would be held to a higher standard than the federal government. This assumption was dealt a fatal blow when Fullilove was overruled by* Adarand Constructors, Inc. v. Pena. *This case established the modern rule that fed-*

---

262. *Richmond v. Croson Co.,* 488 U.S. 469 (1989).

eral and state governments are subject to the same standard—strict scrutiny—in passing any law categorizing people by race.[263]

Boston Firefighters Union Local 718 v. Boston Chapter, NAACP,
461 U.S. 477 (1983)
Boston Police Patrolmen's Association v. Castro
Beecher v. Boston Chapter, NAACP
(Brennan)

Under Massachusetts law, state civil service employees were protected by a last-hired, first-fired seniority system. When the Boston police and fire departments announced layoffs, minority groups sued in federal court claiming that layoffs based on seniority would undermine the state's new affirmative action program and disproportionately harm minorities. The district court enjoined both departments from laying off employees in any way that would reduce the overall percentage of minority officers below levels attained immediately prior to the commencement of layoffs. The court of appeals affirmed. The state legislature subsequently found new revenues and reinstated everyone who had been laid off, so the threshold issue at conference was whether the case was moot.

BURGER: The case is not moot. Neither *Weber* nor *Fullilove* controls here. The wrongs of third parties hit innocent whites. We now have a dozen minorities, and we can't remedy all of the wrongs that they suffered.

BRENNAN:[264] I believe that this case is moot. All officers laid off have been rehired, with lifetime statutory protection against being laid off again for economic reasons. Petitioners assert that two consequences turn on our decision: the rehired officers' entitlement to back pay, and the continuing effect of the district court's order. As to the first, the back pay proceedings are governed entirely by state administrative law; they are state administrative proceedings, and *none* of the parties to those proceedings—individual officers on the one hand, and the city of Boston on the other—is a party before this Court. No one has explained how state law would make Boston liable for back pay because it complied with a federal court injunction that was valid when issued but reversed on appeal. State law might make Boston liable whether the order was reversed or not, or it could make the officers bear the cost of a valid injunction, but it would raise serious supremacy clause problems if state entitlements turned on the legal correctness of a federal court's order. That would encourage cities to refuse to comply promptly with federal court orders that were valid on their face. No one has shown how our decision is relevant to back pay proceedings, and I do not believe that it could be.

---

263. *Adarand Constructors, Inc. v. Pena,* 515 U.S. 200 (1995). This case set off another debate among the new majority faction—whether any affirmative action program could pass strict scrutiny analysis under any circumstances. Justice O'Connor maintained that some affirmative action programs could still be approved, while Antonin Scalia and Clarence Thomas argued that racial discrimination was never benign and that the strict scrutiny test was "strict in theory, but fatal in fact."

264. Adapted from Brennan's talking papers, Brennan Papers, OT 1982, box 630.

As to the continuing effect of the injunction: by its terms, the injunction refers to a specific set of layoffs that are no longer taking place, and no layoffs are foreseeable in the near future. Even if layoffs did occur in the near future all officers hired since July 1981 could be laid off on a pure seniority basis. (The injunction preserves the level of minority representation at the July 1981 level—about 15 percent—and does not protect minority officers hired since then, all of whom will have increased the minority level above 15 percent.) The more senior officers have statutory protection against layoffs. Therefore, there is no reasonable prospect that the order at issue here will have any effect in the foreseeable future, and a *Munsingwear* order would take care of any speculative effects.[265]

The case as a whole does not have to be moot for one set of disputes within it to be moot. The fact that two parties have one ongoing dispute between them does not give them the right to ask a federal court for an opinion on some hypothetical question.

If we reached the merits, I would vote to affirm. Most remedies for constitutional violations in race discrimination cases benefit many people besides identifiable victims of specific discriminatory acts, usually at the cost of some comparative disadvantage to others. Seniority rights are not qualitatively different from other rights—say the right to be hired first if one scores highest on a civil service exam. A reversal in this case would cause havoc in a number of cases with ongoing remedial programs. Furthermore, the original order in this case was set by consent decree—the parties agreed not to adopt a procedure that would require proof on a person-by-person basis of who had been deterred from applying for a job because of the pervasive discrimination found. Such proof is costly, and we should not give litigants an incentive to demand it in every case, rather than settling on less costly methods. Finally, the harm from discrimination in public employment reaches beyond those who are not hired. Everyone in the community is harmed, and the remedy should reach their harm as well as that of unsuccessful job applicants. I would vacate as moot or affirm.

WHITE: The case is not moot; the order has an ongoing effect. On the merits, the police case had no Title 7 claims, and the firemen had both Title 7 and constitutional claims. If we go on Title 7, the statute on seniority, §703(h), would prevent the judgment below. To that extent, I would reverse. Absent any proof of intentional discrimination, we can't deal with it as constitutional case.

MARSHALL: Out.

BLACKMUN: The city escapes here without a penalty. I agree with Bill Brennan—the case is moot. On the merits, I would affirm. There is a consent decree here that is the law of the case.

---

265. *United States v. Munsingwear*, 340 U.S. 36 (1950). This case established the basic guidelines for dealing with cases that become moot on appeal. The Court tried to avoid the destruction of litigants' rights when cases were mooted by circumstances beyond the parties' control: "The established practice of the Court in dealing with a civil case from a court in the federal system which has become moot while on its way here or pending our decision on the merits is to reverse or vacate the judgment below and remand with a direction to dismiss. . . . That procedure clears the path for future relitigation of the issues between the parties and eliminates a judgment, review of which was prevented through happenstance. When that procedure is followed, the rights of all parties are preserved." (Munsingwear, at 39).

POWELL: I agree with Byron, although mootness is a close question. The original decree was based on racial effect, not intent, so the constitutional issue isn't here. The consent decree did not cover this situation and is not binding here. To the extent that this is a Title 7 case, seniority prevails.

REHNQUIST: The case is not moot. Modification of the decree is not over, despite re-hires. On the merits, if the 1971 decree were fully litigated now, it could not prevail. A consent decree is reopened at the peril of the applicants, and §703(h) applies anyway.

STEVENS: All litigants before us want to have the case declared moot. We ought to vacate and send this back in light of the new statute. I don't think that the case is moot. On the merits, innocent people always get hurt in situations like this. Since a violation was established, the judge's remedial powers are very broad.

O'CONNOR: We ought to vacate and remand or say that the case is moot. On the merits, I would reverse.

Result: In a per curiam decision, the Justices voted 8–0 to vacate the lower court's decision and remand the case to determine whether it was moot. Sandra Day O'Connor's vote was crucial, because she represented the potential fifth vote to reverse had the Justices reached the merits.

Firefighters Local Union No. 1784 v. Stotts, 467 U.S. 561 (1984)
(Brennan)

Carl Stotts, a captain in the Memphis Fire Department, filed a federal class-action suit claiming that the city fire department's hiring and promotion practices were racially discriminatory in violation of Title 7 of the Civil Rights Act of 1964. The parties signed a consent decree settling the case, but afterward city budget deficits forced layoffs. The district court issued a temporary injunction barring the city from laying off firefighters on the basis of seniority, which would have resulted in a disproportionate number of recently hired black firefighters losing their jobs. The court approved an alternate plan whereby more senior white firefighters would be laid off or demoted before less senior blacks. The court of appeals affirmed, ruling that the new layoff plan was a permissible judicial modification of the original consent decree. Within a month, the city found the money to rehire all the laid-off firefighters. Accordingly, the Supreme Court first had to decide whether the case was moot.

BURGER: Did the district court exceed its authority? The case not moot, since all lost seniority and back pay was not given to reinstated whites. The memo is unenforceable under state law, but that is irrelevant. It is still a bona fide seniority system under Title 7.[266] This was a modification, not a construction of the consent decree. The district court was just wrong in modifying the decree.

BRENNAN:[267] I've gone back and forth on this question several times, but I'm finally satisfied that respondents, as the proponents of mootness, have failed to meet their burden

---

266. Title 7 specifically protected bona fide seniority systems. Section 703(h) provides that it is not an unlawful for employers to apply different standards of compensation or different terms, conditions, or privileges of employment pursuant to a bona fide seniority system, provided that the differences are not the result of an intention to discriminate because of race.

267. Adapted from Brennan's talking papers, Brennan Papers, OT 1983, box 646.

of establishing that there is no longer a justiciable case or controversy between the parties in this case. As far as I can make out, the only continuing controversy concerns the one month's back pay and seniority credit for the laid-off white firefighters. Now, in my view, that dispute is essentially one between the city of Memphis and the Firefighters Union which represents those white firemen, rather than a dispute between the union and respondents. Nevertheless, our disposition of the merits will have considerable bearing on the resolution of the union's claim for backpay and seniority credit. Therefore, I would hold that the case is not moot.

In addressing the merits, I think our most difficult task is to try to understand with some care the precise nature of the complaint that was brought before the district court by the respondents back in May 1981. Such an understanding will help to shed light on the basis for the district court's order.

If we look at the respondent's initial application for a temporary restraining order, it is crystal clear that the black firefighter plaintiffs were not seeking new, additional relief under Title 7. Instead, their claim rested solely on the contractual terms of the consent decree. In their words, the city's proposed "layoff or reduction-in-rank will effectively destroy the affirmative relief granted by this Court in the consent decree entered on April 25, 1980."

It is important at the outset to recognize that the consent decree itself is valid. The decree was approved in April 1980 as adequate and fair with respect to all parties and as to affected non-parties. Significantly, the Firefighters Union was given ample notice of the decree, but never filed any objection.

Now, paragraph 6 of that 1980 consent decree made it very clear that the parties had agreed that "the long term goal established in this decree shall be . . . to raise the black representation in each job classification on the fire department to levels approximating the black proportion of the civilian labor force in Shelby County." At the time of the decree, of course, blacks constituted approximately 35 percent of the Shelby County labor force, but only around 10 percent of the fire department. Progress had been made since the decree was entered. But the respondents felt that the city's proposed layoffs would substantially undo that hard-won progress.

As everyone agrees, the terms of this decree did not deal with the impact of possible future layoffs on the agreed-upon purposes and goals of the decree, which is perfectly understandable since there had not been any municipal layoffs in the city's history. But the parties did expressly provide a mechanism in the decree for dealing with unanticipated contingencies, such as the proposed layoffs, and this fact is of critical importance to this case.

Paragraph 17 of the decree states that "the court retains jurisdiction of this action for such further orders as may be necessary or appropriate *to effectuate the purposes of this decree.*" In my view, this case can best be understood as an exercise by the district court of the power conferred on him by the parties' agreement embodied in paragraph 17 to enter further orders "to effectuate the purposes of the decree."

The clear purpose of the decree was to achieve a particular percentage of black employment within the fire department. As the district court recognized, the city's proposed layoffs threatened that purpose. In such circumstances, the district court plainly had the power, pursuant to paragraph 17, to enter an order mandating that the city "not apply [its] seniority policy insofar as it will decrease the percentage of black lieutenants, drivers, inspectors and privates that are presently employed in the Memphis Fire Department." The district court's order did not bar all layoffs of blacks, nor did it compel the layoffs of whites; instead, it was a limited, preliminary injunction designed to protect the essential purposes of the decree.

Of course, the district court itself and the court of appeals when it affirmed the district court's order did not follow the analysis I have sketched here. In my view, both the district court and court of appeals erred in analyzing this case explicitly under Title 7, and to that extent we should correct the court's reasoning. But when a court simply acts pursuant to equitable powers derived from a valid consent decree to protect the purposes of that decree, the court's action is permissible.

Indeed, if we are to honor the policy favoring the resolution of disputes through consent decrees, then courts must retain this limited power. The facts of this case illustrate perfectly the need for such flexibility. Here the city contracted to work in good faith toward the achievement and maintenance of certain hiring and promotional goals. None of the parties expected that these goals might be frustrated by layoffs, but the parties did recognize through their adoption of paragraph 17 that unexpected problems might arise, and by consent they gave the district court power to interpret the purposes of the decree and to effectuate those purposes by further order. Just as in commercial contracting, no consent decree will ever be perfect or will anticipate every problem that may arise. Therefore, in order for the parties' essential agreement to be preserved over time as these contingencies come up, courts must be able to use the power the parties have given them to enter further orders. I affirm.

WHITE: A modification that the district court had no power to impose on those who did not agree to it. The case is not moot.

MARSHALL: It's moot, and if not I affirm.

BLACKMUN: The case is moot. There is no controversy between the petitioners and respondents. If we get to the merits, I affirm.

POWELL: Mootness is close, but seniority and back pay questions are not wholly settled. If the case is not moot, I would reverse. This is a modification.

REHNQUIST: The case is not moot. It is not much, but there are enough unsettled issues. On the merits, I reverse.

STEVENS: On mootness, three employees can get back pay but there are problems that can arise affecting others under it. The case is not moot. On the merits, it is a fair reading is there was a modification and not a construction of the consent decree. Without regard to Title 7, you can't do that—it is an elemental principle of consent decree law. We ought to DIG.

O'CONNOR: The case is not moot because the situation is capable of repetition, yet evading review. On the merits, the district court incorrectly granted relief beyond his authority under the decree.

Result: The Justices voted 5–1–3 to reach the merits of the case and to strike down the district court's modified layoff plan. The Court ruled that the judge's plan was not a valid modification of the origi-

nal consent decree. John Paul Stevens concurred in the judgment but did not join Byron White's majority opinion. Brennan, Marshall, and Blackmun dissented.

Wygant v. Jackson Board of Education, 476 U.S. 267 (1986)
(Brennan)

Under a collective bargaining agreement, in the event of teacher layoffs the Jackson school district was required to release faculty according to seniority. In order to protect recent minority hires, Article 12 of the agreement prohibited the district from laying off a greater percentage of minority faculty than the overall percentage of minority teachers employed by the district at the time that the layoffs occurred.

When the district began laying off teachers during a budget crisis, senior white teachers were laid off ahead of more junior minority faculty. Wendy Wygant and other white teachers sued in federal court, claiming that they had been discriminated against because of their race in violation of the Fourteenth Amendment, the Civil Rights Act of 1964, and other federal and state laws.

The district court rejected Wygant's arguments, ruling that Article 12 of the collective bargaining agreement was a permissible attempt to remedy past societal discrimination by ensuring that proper role models would remain available for minority schoolchildren. The court of appeals affirmed. The Justices here continued their struggle to establish an appropriate standard of review in affirmative action cases.

BURGER: Societal discrimination has never commanded a court here. Close scrutiny, searching examination is the test—a compelling state interest must be shown, and the court of appeals said "reasonableness." Without a finding of actual discrimination, you cannot sustain the contract. A school board is not like Congress or a state legislature to decide these questions.

BRENNAN:[268] In *Steelworkers v. Weber,* an affirmative action plan that was the product of a collectively bargained agreement was upheld by a majority of this Court.[269] While there are some differences between the factual circumstances in *Weber* and those involved here, these are not "differences that make a difference." A comparison of the cases makes clear, I believe, that *Weber* controls this case.

First, the affirmative action program in *Weber* was adopted voluntarily. The contract here challenged was, of course, also voluntarily entered into.

Second, in *Weber* there were no judicial findings in the context of that litigation that either Kaiser or the Steelworkers Union had discriminated—Kaiser, in fact, denied that it had discriminated—but we took judicial notice of discrimination against minorities in the craft unions. In *Wygant:* (a) the school board is of course aware of its own course of conduct over the years, and it engaged in numerous inquiries through the years, which confirmed the fact that its poor record regarding minorities required redress; (b) we have been presented with the figures indicating that black teachers had never been hired until relatively recently; and (c) the fact of segregation and discrimination in American school is thoroughly documented. In *Weber,* despite the lack of "case specific" judicial findings, we accepted that the plan was remedial in nature.

---

268. Adapted from Brennan's talking papers, Brennan Papers, OT 1985, box 707.
269. *United Steelworkers v. Weber,* 443 U.S. 193 (1979).

It is true that the challenge in *Weber* was based on Title 7, rather than the Constitution, which is invoked here. But I find no evidence to even suggest that Title 7 was not intended to reach as far as the Fourteenth Amendment. On the contrary, it seems that the intent of Congress was to apply equal protection principles as fully and forcefully to the private sector as were applicable to the state. It seems to me evident that Title 7 does not provide whites or blacks with more rights than they have from the Fourteenth Amendment.

Because I believe *Weber* applies, and that the state has compelling interests in remedying past discrimination and creating a diverse faculty, the remaining question is whether the means chosen here are acceptable. I think they are. Although petitioners rely extensively on *Hazelwood School District v. United States* for the proposition that it was impermissible for the Jackson school board to compare the percentage of faculty to the percentage of students—and that the proper comparison is between the percentage of minority teachers in the school and the percentage of minority teachers in the relevant geographical area—petitioner fails to appreciate that our holding in *Hazelwood* addressed the kind of showing necessary to prove past discrimination.[270] It did not involve whether, in designing a remedy and seeking to obtain racial diversity, a school board could define the desirable or optimal level of diversity with reference to the racial composition of the student body. The concepts are entirely distinguishable and obviously so. It is really no different from saying that evidence which is inadmissible at a trial to prove guilt may be considered by a judge in sentencing. We should affirm.

WHITE: The desire to have a diverse faculty does not, without more, justify what is done here. I don't find any conclusion of discrimination, societal or otherwise. At least we should remand for a trial on what really went on here.

---

270. *Hazelwood School District v. United States*, 433 U.S. 299 (1977). The federal government sued Missouri's Hazelwood school district for systematic race discrimination in faculty hiring, in violation of Title 7 of the Civil Rights Act of 1964. This act was first applied to the school district in March 1972. The district court rejected the complaint on the ground that the government's hiring statistics did not prove a pattern or practice of discrimination. The Eighth Circuit Court of Appeals reversed, holding: (1) that the trial court relied on an irrelevant comparison between the percentage of black teachers and the percentage of black students in the district; (2) that the proper statistical comparison was the percentage of black teachers employed by the district compared to the percentage of qualified black teachers in the relevant area labor market; (3) that the city of St. Louis should be included as part of the relevant labor market (the school district opposed this on the ground that it would distort the area's labor market, because St. Louis had made an extraordinary effort to maintain a 50–50 white/black faculty ratio); (4) that government statistics showing a 15 percent black teacher ratio in the relevant labor market versus a 1 percent to 2 percent black teacher ratio in the Hazlewood school district established a prima facie case of discrimination; and (5) that because the school district had failed to rebut the prima facie case, the government deserved summary judgment.

The Supreme Court voted 8–1 to vacate the judgment and remand the case to the district court. Stewart, writing for the majority, agreed with the court of appeals as to the proper statistical comparison and the relevant labor market but vacated the summary judgment to allow the school district an opportunity to rebut the government's statistical evidence, or to prove that the apparent dearth of black teachers was due to hiring practices *before* Title 7 took effect in 1972, rather than due to discriminatory hiring *after* that date.

Brennan's concurring opinion sharply criticized the district court and urged the trial court to use greater caution in the use of statistical evidence. Stevens dissented, arguing that the court of appeals' judgment should have been affirmed.

MARSHALL: It is not clear whether this was done solely on race. There were segregated schools when this contract was made.

BLACKMUN: I stand with my *Bauke* [*sic*][271] and *Weber*[272] decisions and affirm. This was part of a plan to desegregate.

POWELL: The classification is based solely on race. It must be justified on compelling state interest grounds and the means adopted must be the least restrictive. There is no showing here that meets even the intermediate level of scrutiny.

REHNQUIST: The redress of societal discrimination requires far more evidence of actual discrimination than we have here.

STEVENS: I disagree with everyone. I don't rely on societal discrimination to justify this racial classification. I don't like having separate levels of equal protection. This was just an effort to integrate its faculty and student body. The idea was educational—to teach kids that whether you are black or white, everyone has chance to be a teacher. So there is a legitimate governmental interest, and if they need Article 12 to do that, it is also legitimate.

O'CONNOR: This Court has fashioned a standard of scrutiny for racial discrimination—strict scrutiny. The Sixth Circuit is wrong in applying a standard of reasonableness. Remedying this has been held not to be compelling. The school board is competent to make findings—does that require precise findings? I doubt whether we can require that much. So here we get to the means—is what happens here O.K.? I would prefer to vacate and remand.

Result: A deeply divided Court ruled 4–1–4 that Article 12 violated the equal protection clause of the Fourteenth Amendment. Powell's plurality opinion was joined in full by Burger and Rehnquist and joined in part by O'Connor. Powell stressed that all racial classifications required strict scrutiny. A general claim of societal discrimination was not enough to justify the school board's actions, because such a course of action had "no logical stopping point." At a minimum, Powell said, there must be a finding of prior discrimination by the governmental entity involved. In this case, there was no factual basis for any such finding. The "role model" justification was not compelling, nor was there a close relationship between the goal of providing racial role models and the means used to achieve it. Powell noted that the school board's "role model" argument could just as easily be used to limit the number of minority teachers. Byron White provided the decisive fifth vote that the plan violated the equal protection clause, but he merely concurred in the judgment and refused to join Powell's opinion. Marshall, Brennan, Blackmun, and Stevens dissented.

---

271. *Regents v. Bakke,* 438 U.S. 265 (1978).
272. *United Steelworkers v. Weber,* 443 U.S. 193 (1979).

NATIONALITY AND ALIENS

Oyama v. California, 332 U.S. 633 (1948)
(Burton) (Douglas) (Jackson)

California's Alien Land Law prohibited Japanese nationals from acquiring, owning, occupying, leasing, or transferring real property.[273] It provided that any property acquired in violation of the statute or transferred with "intent to prevent, evade, or avoid" the law would escheat to the state. The statute presumed that there was intent to evade the law whenever an ineligible alien paid for property transferred to a person who was legally entitled to own the property.

Kajiro Oyama, a Japanese national who was ineligible for naturalization, purchased two small parcels of agricultural property in Chula Vista, totaling eight acres. Oyama recorded title to the property in the name of his young son, Fred Oyama, who was an American citizen by birth and legally entitled to own property in California. One parcel was purchased in 1934, when Fred was six years old, and the second purchase was in 1937. Mr. Oyama went to the local superior court, disclosed the purchases, and was appointed Fred's guardian so that he could manage the property. In 1936 and 1937, Mr. Oyama sought judicial permission to mortgage the property. Both times the judge agreed, ruling that Oyama was acting in his son's best interests.

Oyama managed the property until 1943, when the family was sent to an internment camp in Utah. In 1944, while the Oyamas were still imprisoned in Utah, the district attorney sought to seize the property on the ground that Mr. Oyama had purchased the land with intent to evade the Alien Land Law. The state trial judge ruled in the state's favor, and the state supreme court affirmed.

Conference of October 25, 1947

VINSON: The state can take a federal statute as a basis for determining who can hold land. Then there is the question of the classification of Jap parents.[274] The classification here is reasonable. The argument that the law was aimed at Japs fades out of the picture—Hindus and others were also included. The state would have a right to protect its statute against ineligibles, and the gift of the father to the son, by saying that the infant son should not be used to circumvent the statute.

On the gift from the father to the son, it is hard to get at, as the dividing point is the vesting of the title. If the title vests in the son, it vests. After it vests in the citizen—and he is the guardian and because he did not make reports—the state says that shows a

---

273. The law prohibited aliens who were not eligible to become naturalized citizens from owning property in the state. Under federal law in effect when the law was first enacted, only free white persons and persons of African descent were eligible to be naturalized. Later, Congress liberalized naturalization rules to include all groups indigenous to the western hemisphere, Chinese, Filipinos, most people from India, and others. By the 1940s, the Japanese were among the few ethnic groups and nationalities who were still ineligible to become naturalized citizens. California argued that because the federal government created this special class of aliens who were not eligible for citizenship, the state could use the same classification in its property laws.

274. It is not clear whether the use of the pejorative "Jap" was Vinson's or simply a convenient abbreviation for the note-takers (both Burton and Douglas used the term in their conference notes).

scheme.[275] Their failure to make reports is not relevant here. There are other ways to protect the child without canceling the deed.

You finally end up on the presumption.[276] The *presumption* is the thing. But the act itself (the deed) to the son vested title in the son—and I think that the son can hold the title. It takes the title before he got it. If the father had taken the stand, as he did in two other cases, then California would overrule its presumption.[277] But the deed *itself* vests ownership in the citizen—and I come out saying that Fred can hold the title. I would reverse.

BLACK: I reverse.

REED: I affirm. So far as the main part of the statute is concerned, that is valid—it is a good classification. The statute is valid, that is clear. I think that aliens can be banned from owning land. I had great difficulty with the presumption—illegality is the intent to evade the act. California has a right to protect its valid act, and did so not by the presumption but by a secondary act—that anyone who sought to transfer their interest will forfeit their interest. The father was paying the money. His intent is to evade the act. This attempt to evade the law is an illegal act.

The statute is valid. The act regarding "intent to evade" is valid. The presumption is relevant to the intent and is valid. I affirm.

FRANKFURTER: I substantially agree with the Chief. We do not have to consider the challenge to our *Terrace* case.[278] They do not have a connection to the underlying cases. Here the question is the right of this American citizen to receive land from his alien father. Suppose California had said that it was crime for the father to make a gift to his son— that would be unconstitutional.

---

275. The state alleged that Kajiro Oyama did not file the annual reports that the Alien Land Law required of all guardians of agricultural land belonging to the minor children of ineligible aliens. The Oyamas, however, claimed that the law did not require such reports until 1943, and that it was impossible to file the reports in 1943 and 1944 because the family was excluded from the state from 1942 until late 1944, long after the state began forfeiture proceedings.

276. Most state laws presumed that whenever a parent paid for a property conveyance to a child, a gift was intended. Under the Alien Land Law, however, the statutory presumption was that any conveyance paid for by an ineligible alien and recorded in a minor's name was not a gift but was solely for the alien's benefit.

277. Oyama did not testify at the escheat hearing, and the trial judge inferred from his absence that his testimony would have supported the state's claim that he had intended to evade the Alien Land Law. Oyama had testified about the property twice previously, when he sought to mortgage the property in 1936 and 1937.

278. *Terrace v. Thompson*, 263 U.S. 197 (1923). This case involved a challenge to a Washington state law prohibiting aliens who had not declared their intent to become American citizens from having an interest in property. An American landowner and a Japanese national who wanted to lease the land sued to enjoin the state attorney general from beginning threatened forfeiture proceedings, on the ground that the state law violated both federal and state constitutions and a treaty with Japan. The Court claimed equity jurisdiction and ruled 6–2 that the state law did not violate the federal Constitution or conflict with the United States–Japan Treaty of 1911. The Washington state courts had earlier ruled that the law did not conflict with the state constitution. Butler wrote the majority opinion. Brandeis and McReynolds dissented on the ground that there was no justiciable question involved and that the case should have been dismissed for want of equity. Sutherland did not participate in the decision.

If a citizen son has the right to receive a gift, then it is O.K. to give it. On the general question, that was by a narrow margin and Brandeis and McReynolds dissented.[279] *Cockrill v. California* and the whole Court (including Brandeis and McReynolds.)[280] I reverse.

REED: The *Cockrill* case also passed on this principle.

FRANKFURTER: Not if it was a gift to the son.

DOUGLAS: I am for reversal on several grounds. I think that the state cannot prohibit property ownership as they have done here. The alien class is treated as an inferior class. States could not have the power to put this ineligible alien into a different class as to land ownership any more than in any employment. Perhaps it could do so in periods of danger—except under legally protected class. But it is enough to go on the Chief's ground.

MURPHY: I reverse.

MINTON: I reverse.

JACKSON: Any state that has power over real property can exclude any or all aliens from owning it. This type of law is generally used in most countries. They can lift that exclusion for some classes. They could lift it, for example, as to all those eligible to become U.S. citizens. But this is a normal classification that follows the naturalization law.

If title came to the father, it could be escheated. We are dealing with the *power* of the state. The state's presumption amounts to this: a conveyance will not pass title to the son if the money came from the father as the putative general manager. That is not always a reasonable inference. The infant son is not going to manage the farm. The newer inference is that it is the father's property. But if the state has any power at all, this would be a normal and not an invalid presumption. The presumption is reasonable. If the boy wanted the land, and so forth, it could be overcome. I would like to reverse, but it is hard to do it. I have difficulty in rationalizing a reversal. I can't go on Bill Douglas's ground. The only plausible way would be on Dean Acheson's ground—I could go that way.[281] I am tentative to affirm.

RUTLEDGE: I reverse.

BURTON: The statute is O.K. and should be upheld. As to the presumption, it depends on how you approach it. The statute approaches it from the viewpoint of evasion. You can't have an alien put money into the land and then give title to his infant son. I affirm.

---

279. *Terrace v. Thompson*, 263 U.S. 197 (1923).

280. *Cockrill v. California*, 268 U.S. 258 (1925). The Supreme Court upheld the Alien Land Law where a Japanese citizen had paid for property that was recorded in the name of an unrelated, white American citizen. Butler wrote the opinion for a unanimous Court.

Oyama argued that *Cockrill* could be distinguished because it would be natural for a father to make a gift of this sort to a son. Such a gift, Oyama argued, would inherently be bona fide and could not be presumed to have been intended to evade the statute.

281. Dean Acheson represented the Oyamas before the Court. He argued that in other California cases, the actions of parents making such gifts to citizen children were presumptively legal and the motives for the gifts were irrelevant. Burton Papers, box 174.

Result: *In a 6–3 decision, the Supreme Court ruled that the Alien Land Law was unconstitutional as applied because it denied Fred Oyama equal protection of the laws. Vinson wrote that the state impermissibly discriminated against Fred Oyama solely on the basis of his parents' country of origin without any compelling justification. It made no sense to Vinson that the state sought to punish the child because of his father's actions, especially when the sole basis for the punishment appeared to be the mere fact that the father was Japanese. Black and Douglas concurred and also joined Vinson's opinion. Murphy and Rutledge also concurred.*

Murphy's concurring opinion condemned the California law as "racism in one of its most malignant forms." Black unsuccessfully urged Murphy to soften his rhetoric because he feared that Murphy's strongly worded opinion would be used in foreign propaganda. Frankfurter contemptuously dismissed Murphy's concurrence as "a long-winded, soap-boxy attack against racism."[282] Reed, Burton, and Jackson dissented. After the war, Kojiro Oyama and his wife Kohide became naturalized citizens, and Fred Oyama became a junior high school mathematics teacher.

In re Griffiths, 413 U.S. 717 (1973)
(Douglas) (Brennan)

Fre le Poole Griffiths was a Dutch citizen. She was married to an American citizen and was a legal resident of Connecticut. Upon graduating from law school, Griffiths applied to the state bar but was rejected because Connecticut limited bar membership to American citizens. Griffiths, though eligible to become an American citizen, refused to renounce her Dutch citizenship and sued, claiming that her exclusion violated her equal protection and due process rights. The Connecticut courts upheld the state's citizenship requirement.

BURGER: State control of professionals is involved here. The petitioner wants the best of both worlds. A lawyer is in a different category than anyone else. In Connecticut, a lawyer is a special person, since he is a commissioner.[283] I affirm. This is well over the line.

DOUGLAS: I reverse. The fact of alienage may give the bar a wider scope of inquiry. Alienage might go to her ability to take a required oath, but the bare fact of alienage is not enough.

BRENNAN: I agree with Bill Douglas.

STEWART: Connecticut has a weaker case than New York in our public employment cases.[284] This is not state employment—it is basically private employment. I reverse, and agree with Bill Douglas.

---

282. Lash, *From the Diaries of Felix Frankfurter,* 341.

283. The Connecticut bar argued that its lawyers were not purely in private practice but had public duties and powers that justified limiting bar membership to state citizens. Under state law, all lawyers were also commissioners of the superior court with statutory power to "'command' actions by county sheriffs and town constables." Connecticut lawyers, the bar maintained, were officers of the court in a literal, not symbolic, sense. *In re Griffiths,* 294 A. 2d 281, 284 (Conn. 1974). Burger accepted this argument and thought that Connecticut lawyers should be treated as public officials rather than as private practitioners.

284. *Sugarman v. Dougall,* 413 U.S. 634 (1973). New York law provided that only American citizens could hold permanent positions in competitive positions within the state civil service. Under this law, four legal resident aliens were fired from their competitive civil service positions in New York City. For an 8–1

WHITE: This case is weaker for Connecticut than the New York case. I reverse. This is a common profession.

MARSHALL: I reverse.

BLACKMUN: I affirm. I always thought that attorneys were fiduciaries in a strict sense. They influence legislation and are part of the judicial process. I do not like this kind of statute, but I can't say that it is unconstitutional. I would go back to the Lumbard reservation in the New York case.[285]

POWELL: We admit Communists to the practice of law. The interests of the state are met if they have permanent residence by reason of federal laws. One who passes the bar is under the disciplinary regime of the bar. I reverse.

REHNQUIST: Connecticut could say that it would not want this woman as a commissioner, which she is. I affirm.

Result: In a 7–2 decision, Lewis Powell, a former president of the American Bar Association, ruled that restricting state bar membership to American citizens violated Griffiths's equal protection rights. State laws that discriminated against legal aliens created a suspect classification, he said, would be subjected to close judicial scrutiny. In this case, there was no necessary or compelling reason for a categorical exclusion of resident aliens from the legal profession. Connecticut lawyers might be considered officers of the court, but they were not government officials. Moreover, while states could require applicants to meet certain professional standards, Connecticut had failed to demonstrate why the blanket exclusion of aliens was necessary to maintain proper standards. Burger and Rehnquist dissented.

Hampton v. Mow Sun Wong, 426 U.S. 88 (1976)
(Brennan)

The Civil Service Commission enacted regulations barring noncitizens from virtually all competitive civil service positions, from janitors to senior policymakers. Mow Sun Wong and four other legal resident aliens sued, claiming that such exclusions violated their due process rights under the Fifth Amendment. The district court sided with the commission, but the court of appeals reversed on the ground that the regulations were overbroad.

---

majority, Blackmun ruled that the categorical exclusion of resident aliens in the state civil service was indiscriminate and overbroad and violated the equal protection clause. The majority avoided the issue of whether the state law also violated the supremacy clause. Rehnquist dissented, arguing that the Fourteenth Amendment did not protect any minorities other than racial minorities.

285. *Dougall v. Sugarman,* 339 F. Supp. 906, 911 (SDNY 1971). In his concurring opinion, Judge J. Edward Lumbard argued that states could, in an appropriately defined class of positions, limit certain public offices to citizens where citizenship "bears some rational relationship to the special demands of the particular position." Blackmun agreed, and in his opinion in *Sugarman v. Dougall* implied that when states sought to place citizenship restrictions on offices that executed broad public policy or dealt with "matters resting firmly within a state's constitutional prerogatives," a lesser level of judicial scrutiny—the rational basis test—might be employed.

STEWART: Since Congress can be as discriminatory as it pleases in admitting immigrants, *Johnson* isn't a departure.[286] Yet I can't say that the Fifth Amendment is wholly inapplicable. Congress can't say, for example, that no resident alien shall have a right of appeal. Congress could condition admission to the country, but this civil service regulation isn't that kind of a statute.

WHITE: Congress could condition entry into this country, and this is tantamount to that.

MARSHALL: This has nothing to do with immigration, and once they are here without conditions, you can't deny them equal protection.

BLACKMUN: *Sugarman* reserved the federal questions and therefore does not dictate the result here.[287]

POWELL: This regulation is so sweepingly broad that analysis on a rational basis is difficult. We have admitted these people without condition, and I don't see any legitimate governmental interest that sustains this broad regulation.

After Reargument[288]
(Brennan)

BURGER: Surviving parties still remain, despite the fact that some are now citizens. We have ninety years' worth of history of executive orders, although Congress has not barred aliens. I can't say that aliens are discrete and insular classes for all purposes, even though they may be for some. There has been a long period of legislative acquiescence in this regulation. These people may have lots of rights—religion, etc., but they have no constitutional right to a job. If an opinion made clear that Congress had the power to do this, I might go along.

STEWART: Is this regulation equivalent to an act of Congress? I think that it is, in light of the legislative history. On the merits, *Graham*, etc., bear on this case, and they gave sus-

---

286. *Kelley v. Johnson*, 425 U.S. 238 (1976). The police union in Suffolk County, New York, sought to invalidate local regulations prohibiting male officers from having long hair, sideburns, or beards. The union claimed that these regulations arbitrarily violated officers' Fourteenth Amendment liberties. The circuit court of appeals held that personal appearance was a liberty protected by the fourteenth Amendment and said that the police department had failed to show any relationship between the regulations and any legitimate state interest. The regulations simply mandated uniformity for uniformity's sake.

The Supreme Court reversed, ruling 6–3 that while government could not act in a patently arbitrary or discriminatory manner, government regulations affecting Fourteenth Amendment liberty interests were valid if they had a rational connection to a legitimate government end. In this case, it was enough that the government desired police officers to be similar in appearance, whether to make them readily recognizable to the public or to build esprit de corps. Rehnquist wrote the majority opinion.

287. *Sugarman v. Dougall*, 413 U.S. 634 (1973).

288. With Douglas out, the Court was deadlocked at 4–4. On February 14, 1975, all eight Justices agreed to have the case reargued the following term. Douglas officially retired on November 12, just after the beginning of the 1975 Term. His replacement, John Paul Stevens, took his judicial oath on December 19 and immediately found himself in the hot seat as the potential tie-breaker.

pect classification status to aliens.[289] It seems odd, but there it is as to *states*, and it can't be explained away on that ground. But the federal government has broad and important interests in the regulation of aliens. But each "person" is protected by the Fifth and Fourteenth Amendments, not each "citizen." So I pass.

BRENNAN: This is a regulation and not a statute, and I don't see any legitimate governmental interest. I could apply suspect classification.

WHITE: This is a federal issue, and the government can constitutionally exclude aliens from its employment.

MARSHALL: I can't see how you can have First Amendment and due process rights but no equal protection rights. So I affirm.

BLACKMUN: The *Sugarman* and *Graham* opinions that I wrote don't wholly answer this for me. This regulation does equate with an act of Congress. But I would reverse, largely for Byron's reasons. Yet it is true that aliens are employed in sensitive jobs, in the post office, and so forth. But Congress has immigration and naturalization power, and that should be enough.

POWELL: I don't think that *Sugarman*, *Graham*, and *Griffiths* are irrelevant. But it doesn't follow that aliens are a suspect class when federal government employment is concerned. But "person" in the Fifth Amendment includes aliens, and if this is an act of Congress, does it serve a legitimate interest of government? That's where I have trouble—it sweeps so broadly. If we let them in, how can we not treat them as "persons?" Congress ought to write a narrow statute limiting the exclusion to sensitive jobs. The only interest I can identify is an economic one, and I can't see how you can discriminate if you admit them unconditionally.

REHNQUIST: It seems to me that this regulation is notice that they are admitted conditionally and that they can't have federal jobs. This is a fortiori after my dissents in *Sugarman* and the rest.

STEVENS: There is a difference in equal protection between the Fifth and Fourteenth Amendments. The government has the power to exclude or condition entry, provided

---

289. *Graham v. Richardson*, 403 U.S. 365 (1971), combined two welfare cases from Arizona and Pennsylvania. Arizona limited welfare benefits to American citizens and resident aliens who had legally resided in the United States for at least fifteen years. Pennsylvania limited state welfare payments to American citizens. Carmen Richardson and other indigent and disabled aliens sued, claiming that these restrictions violated the equal protection clause of the Fourteenth Amendment. In the first part of the decision, on an 8–1 vote (Harlan dissenting), the Court struck down both laws on equal protection grounds. Harlan then joined the rest of Blackmun's opinion, as the Court unanimously struck down both laws because they impermissibly interfered with national immigration and naturalization policies. The Court found that indigent and disabled aliens who were lawfully within the United States had an equal right to enter and reside in any state and that states could not exclude them by denying them necessary public assistance. The Court also unanimously rejected Arizona's argument that the Social Security Act of 1935 authorized states to impose residency requirements.

the decision to do so is made by arm of government that has an interest in doing so. Both Congress and president could do that. Maybe the secretary of state, too. But that is not the case here. Congress did not decide to do this, nor did the president, nor did any other official having an interest in doing it. The standard specified was only efficiency of service. Even the president did not exclude these aliens. The regulation only says what jobs are reserved for citizens. I would not decide this case on a lack of government power, but on the ground that the decision was not made by an appropriate arm of government.

Result: In a 5–4 decision, the Court ruled that the regulations violated the Fifth Amendment's due process clause by denying legal resident aliens a significant liberty interest—the opportunity to look for work in a major sector of the economy. Writing the majority opinion in the first case he heard as a Justice, John Paul Stevens wrote that because Congress and the president had already granted these persons legal status in the United States,

> *due process requires that the decision to impose that deprivation of an important liberty be made either at a comparable level of government, or if it is permitted to be made by the Civil Service Commission, it must be justified by reasons which are properly the concern of that agency.*

Administrative convenience and efficiency were not sufficient justifications for such arbitrary and injurious rules. Three months after the decision was announced, however, President Gerald Ford issued an executive order authorizing the Civil Service Commission to continue to exclude noncitizens from competitive civil service positions.[290]

Plyler v. Doe, 457 U.S. 202 (1982)
In re Alien Children Litigation
(Brennan)

Texas law authorized local school districts to refuse to enroll undocumented aliens and withheld public funds from schools that chose to admit them. Two groups of illegal aliens sued in federal court, arguing that the law violated their equal protection rights. They asked the courts to apply strict scrutiny in evaluating the challenged law, claiming that education was a fundamental right and that aliens were a suspect class.

BURGER: Illegal aliens are not entitled to welfare, Medicare, and so forth. They are not a suspect class. Equal protection applies, but it has limits. As to one continuing to be illegal, if public policy suggests educating them, Texas employers don't cooperate with the IRS and have prevailed with Congress not to handle the problem in a way that would deny them the labor. The level of scrutiny, whatever it is, gives no constitutional right to welfare or education. Although the Fourteenth Amendment applies, it does not compel states to give these kids an education.

---

290. Witt, *The Supreme Court and Individual Rights,* 273.

BRENNAN:[291] I think that Texas Education Code §21.031 violates the equal protection clause of the Fourteenth Amendment. There is no doubt that the undocumented children are persons within the jurisdiction of the state for the purposes of the equal protection clause of the Fourteenth Amendment.

I think strict scrutiny could be applied. The statute makes a suspect classification based on alienage and therefore must be justified by a compelling state interest under the *In re Griffiths* line of cases.[292] Alternatively, we might follow the line we have taken in the illegitimate children cases, such as *Lalli v. Lalli*, where we have refused to employ strict scrutiny but have said that classifications are invalid under the Fourteenth Amendment if they are not substantially related to permissible state interests.[293]

Under either of these approaches, and perhaps under a rational basis test as well, the state interests are insufficient to sustain this statute. The state interest in controlling illegal immigration is simply not a permissible *state* interest—that is a federal matter. The state's other purported interest is in expending funds for education in an efficient manner. The state's theory is that children of illegal immigrants are more expensive to educate and less likely to remain in the state than other children. The state acknowledges that illegal immigrants help to contribute financially to the school by property taxes and sales taxes, etc. Assuming that it is ever permissible to deny benefits to a class of people in order to save money, the evidence did not suggest that the state's interest was "substantially related" to the classification they have drawn here.

I could consider affirming on the basis of preemption, but I do think that we might have to cut back substantially on *DeCanas v. Bica* to do so. I don't think we really have to decide in this case what the result would be if there were an affirmative national policy directing the states to deny education to children of illegal immigrants. In this case the federal policy, as far as it has been evidenced by the Elementary and Secondary Education Act (ESEA), is to educate all immigrants. As *Matthews v. Diaz* made clear, Congress

---

291. Adapted from Brennan's talking papers, Brennan Papers, OT 1981, box 590.

292. *In re Griffiths*, 413 U.S. 717 (1973).

293. *Lalli v. Lalli*, 439 U.S. 259 (1978). Robert Lalli alleged that he was the illegitimate son of Mario Lalli. When Mario died without leaving a will, Robert claimed that he was entitled to a share of the estate. Under state law, illegitimate children could only inherit from intestate fathers if, during the father's lifetime, there was a formal judicial declaration of paternity. Although Mario had acknowledged that Robert was his son, there had never been a formal judicial proceeding to establish paternity. Robert claimed that the state requirement violated the equal protection clause of the Fourteenth Amendment because it discriminated against him on the basis of his illegitimate birth.

The Supreme Court rejected his claims. The Justices were badly divided, however; while five Justices agreed that the state law did not violate the equal protection clause, they agreed about little else. A majority agreed that the proper test was whether statutory classifications based on illegitimacy were substantially related to permissible state interests, but the Justices disagreed on how to apply the test. Powell, Burger, and Stewart argued that the state law was substantially related to the goal of providing for the just and orderly disposition of estate property, in view of difficulties as to proof of paternity and the risk of spurious claims. Brennan, White, Marshall, and Stevens claimed that the state's interest could have been served by less restrictive means, such as by requiring clear evidence of the father's formal acknowledgment of paternity.

has a great deal of leeway in decisions of immigration and naturalization.[294] We need only note that the problem of a denial of benefits to undocumented aliens by the federal government is not before us. I would *affirm* the opinions of the Fifth Circuit.

WHITE: I agree with the Chief Justice. It's a national and not a state problem. The state has no obligation to do anything for illegals. Make Congress do it under §5 of the Fourteenth Amendment. There is a line beyond which states have no obligation to serve aliens, even legal ones.

MARSHALL: I agree with Bill Brennan. These kids are not involved in anything illegal—they are victims of being born. It is the kids we must focus on, and I can't treat them as "illegals."

BLACKMUN: These children are likely to remain. The statute is founded on alienage, not domicile. I can affirm on preemption rather than equal protection. But I can go on either. I could hold *De Canas* to employment cases.[295] The Texas statute is invalid so long as it applies to non-deportables. The equal protection justifications are irrational here.

POWELL: I would affirm, but it's hard. On equal protection, I would recognize that the classification is children and that they have no responsibility for being there. It is hard to think of a category more helpless than the children of illegal aliens. I don't think that education is a fundamental right, but if some children get it I can't see how they can deny it to others. So a narrowly drawn classification applicable to a real resident, as an equal of a citizen.[296]

---

294. *Mathews v. Diaz*, 426 U.S. 67 (1976). The Supreme Court unanimously held that Congress could withhold federal Medicare benefits from aliens unless they (1) had been admitted for permanent residence and (2) had resided in the United States continuously for at least five years. Because immigration law concerned foreign policy and fell within the province of the legislative and executive branches, the Court deferred to the other two branches of government and adopted a narrow standard of review. Stewart, writing for the Court, noted that the law had a possible effect on foreign relations, since the aliens involved were noncitizens and presumably retained citizenship benefits from other countries. The proper standard was a "reasonableness" test, and Congress had no constitutional duty to provide aliens with the same support provided to American citizens. Santiago Diaz, a Cuban refugee residing in Florida, was the lead plaintiff in this class-action suit. David Mathews was the secretary of Health, Education, and Welfare.

295. *De Canas v. Bica*, 424 U.S. 351 (1976). Leonor Alberti De Canas and other immigrant farmworkers claimed that they were fired from their jobs because Anthony Bica and other farm labor contractors knowingly decided to hire illegal aliens rather than qualified legal residents of the United States. De Canas cited a California law prohibiting the knowing employment of illegal aliens if such employment would have an adverse effect on lawful resident workers. Brennan, writing for a unanimous 8–0 Court (Stevens did not participate), ruled that the state law (1) was not an unconstitutional infringement on the exclusive federal power to regulate immigration; (2) was not preempted under the supremacy clause by the federal Immigration and Nationality Act, which was not intended to preempt state authority to regulate employment consistent with federal law; and (3) was within the state's police powers to regulate employment. The Court remanded the case so that the state courts could interpret the statute and decide whether the statute conflicted with any federal laws or regulations.

296. Richard Fallon, one of Powell's clerks, reported that on the morning of the conference, Powell arrived at the Court looking as if he had not slept and admitted that he had been awake much of the night. Powell told Fallon that he was deeply disturbed by the prospect of denying an education to innocent children. While he thought it legally difficult to uphold the children's claims, he knew that it was in no one's interest "to create a perpetual underclass of uneducated permanent residents." Fallon, "A Tribute to Justice Lewis F. Powell," 403.

REHNQUIST: There are intractable problems in the Southwest. Wetbacks or not, the question is the validity of Texas's policy choice, however unwise. We are not talking only about five- or six-year-olds. Federal funding can be denied Texas to the extent that it won't educate these children. I can't agree that the classification is irrational, and I would reverse.

STEVENS: I can't find preemption here. On equal protection, Texas has two interests: (1) keeping illegals out. But the impact of this statute is slight to that extent, so no there is no substantial result. Maybe the merest rationality standard is satisfied. (2) Cost. We seem to assume some, but it is not great. There are the countervailing costs to society in not educating children. So this argument fails.

These kids are not being deported, but will remain.[297] So what is the treatment for these innocents? Judges as a whole would not attribute the fault of their parents to them. I could apply *Royster* or Lewis's substantiality standard.[298]

O'CONNOR: I would go on equal protection and not preemption. But what level of scrutiny? The state can restrict its public services in its drug education program for the benefit of citizens or domiciliaries. I have trouble with this statute in its application to people who illegally entered but have been allowed to stay. The law may not survive the rationality test in that aspect. But tentatively I would reverse.

Result: William Brennan, writing on behalf of a 5–4 majority, struck down the state law. The majority declined to apply the strict scrutiny test on the grounds that illegal aliens were not a suspect classification and education was not a fundamental right. Brennan acknowledged, however, that the case required "special" constitutional sensitivity because (a) education, though not a fundamental right, played a pivotal role in society; (b) the children involved were not responsible for their disabling status; and (c) the hardships suffered by these children under this statute could last a lifetime.

The majority used a modified rational basis test, requiring the law to further effectively a substantial state goal. Brennan concluded that the mere fact that these children were not legal residents was not sufficient reason to deny them the same education that other children received. While Texas had a substantial interest in preserving its limited resources for lawful residents, the state law in question was not an effective means for achieving that goal.

All three Justices from the southwest dissented (Rehnquist and O'Connor from Arizona, White from Colorado), as did the Chief Justice. They argued that the rational basis test was the proper standard and that the law in question was rationally related to the government's legitimate interest in ensuring that the state's limited state educational resources were used to educate legal residents.

---

297. The last paragraph of Stevens's conference comments was printed on the back of Brennan's talking papers. Brennan Papers, OT 1981, box 590.

298. *F. S. Royster Guano Co. v. Virginia*, 253 U.S. 412, 415 (1920). On equal protection grounds, the Court struck down a Virginia law that exempted from state taxation the out-of-state profits of a select few domestic corporations. This case is often cited as authority for the Aristotelian view of the equal protection clause: that all persons similarly situated must be treated alike. Stevens believed that in terms of education, the children of illegal aliens were similarly situated with the children of legal residents.

GENDER

MOSTLY WOMEN

Frontiero v. Richardson, 411 U.S. 677 (1973)
(Douglas) (Brennan)

Under federal law, spouses of military men were automatically considered dependents and were eligible for increased quarters allowances, medical and dental care, and other benefits. Spouses of female military personnel, however, were not considered dependents unless the husband received at least half of his financial support from his wife. The different treatment was justified solely on the grounds of administrative convenience.

When the air force denied Lieutenant Sharron Frontiero's claim for increased spousal benefits for her civilian husband, she sued, claiming that the law violated her Fifth Amendment due process and equal protection rights. The district court ruled that the different treatment of male and female military dependents was constitutional.

BURGER: *Reed* has nothing to do with this.[299] There are differences between men and women. This is a tempest in a teapot. The implications beyond this case are enormous. The military has the right to draw lines. *I affirm.*

DOUGLAS: I reverse. 1 U.S.C. §1 defines "his" as including "hers." This is a violation of equal protection.

BRENNAN: I reverse. I can't distinguish *Reed* from this case.

STEWART: This provision on its face is grossly discriminatory against a readily identifiable class in a in basic area of life—it is constitutionally invalid.

WHITE: This law discriminates against men married to women in the military, and I reverse.

MARSHALL: I tentatively reverse.

BLACKMUN: I am doubtful. Logically it should be struck down, yet the argument on the other side is powerful. I reverse with questions.

POWELL: I reverse. This law discriminates against men.

REHNQUIST: The government is entitled to treat different classes differently. More married women are dependent than married men. I affirm.

---

299. *Reed v. Reed,* 404 U.S. 71 (1971). When their minor son Richard died, both Sally and Cecil Reed, who were legally separated at the time, sought to be appointed administrator of the boy's estate. The probate judge appointed Cecil Reed administrator because Idaho law required that whenever a man and a woman were equally entitled to serve, the man had to be selected. The state justified this preference on the basis of administrative convenience. The Supreme Court unanimously agreed that the law was arbitrary and violated the equal protection clause. Warren Burger was vague about what test would be used for evaluating gender-based classifications, although he clearly used a stricter standard than the conventional "rational basis" test, which would have been satisfied by the state's claim of administrative convenience.

Result: Warren Burger changed his mind after the conference and joined an 8–1 majority to reverse the decision below and uphold Frontiero's claim. The apparently overwhelming majority hid some major doctrinal differences. There was no majority opinion. Four Justices (Brennan, Douglas, White, and Marshall) argued that gender was an inherently suspect classification that deserved the highest level of scrutiny. The other four Justices in the majority (Stewart, Burger, Blackmun, and Powell) thought that the district court's decision should be reversed without deciding whether gender was a suspect classification. William Rehnquist was alone in dissent. This case was the closest that the Court has ever come to applying strict scrutiny to gender classifications.

Kahn v. Shevin, 416 U.S. 351 (1974)
(Brennan) (Douglas)

Under Florida law, widows—but not widowers—received an annual $500 property tax exemption. Mel Kahn, a widower, claimed that the law discriminated against him on the basis of sex in violation of the equal protection clause of the Fourteenth Amendment. The Florida Supreme Court upheld the state law. Robert Shevin was the state attorney general.

BURGER: If this is not sex, if women have been discriminated against for so long, Florida can give them economic benefit. There is a compelling state interest, no doubt. There are all kinds of reasons why women should receive favorable treatment. The state has a compelling interest.

DOUGLAS: Without retreating from *Frontiero,* I think that the state can do this.[300] Women, as widows, are largely destitute. I am inclined to affirm.

BRENNAN: I reverse on *Reed.* It would be an overinclusive class. Some widows are rich. The law is not rationally constructed to save the exemption.

STEWART: Any state law that impinges on a basic liberty is invalid. This law does not do that. In the "pure" equal protection area, any state law that makes a classification based on race is presumptively invalid. But this is a tax statute, and we rarely strike down classifications in tax area. Take our decision in *Lehnhausen* last term, for example.[301] I affirm.

WHITE: I reverse.

MARSHALL: I reverse tentatively.

BLACKMUN: I have some discomfort about "compelling" and "rationality," and am ending up at a middle tier approach. Logically that would lead to reversal. This statute is

---

300. *Frontiero v. Richardson,* 411 U.S. 677 (1973).

301. *Lehnhausen v. Lake Shore Auto Parts Co.,* 410 U.S. 356 (1973). Under Illinois law, corporations and other business entities were required to pay state taxes on personal property. Individuals were exempt from the tax. The Lake Shore Auto Parts Company sued, claiming that the law violated the company's equal protection rights. The Supreme Court unanimously rejected the company's arguments, noting that states had broad discretion to create tax classifications and to draw lines in order to produce reasonable taxation systems.

theoretically based on need, but is really based on widowhood. I am inclined to reverse, but if we do it has a wide application on tax laws. In tax situations I would be very careful, and so would affirm tentatively.

POWELL: I agree with Potter. This is a tax statute, and if we try to make tax classifications logical we risk tearing up federal tax laws and the tax laws of most of the fifty states. Tax acts are presumptively valid. This Florida act is one hundred years old. Before Social Security, widows would starve.

REHNQUIST: I affirm.

BURGER: The state here shows a compelling interest. I affirm.

Result: The Court upheld the Florida statute in a 6–3 decision. William O. Douglas wrote for the majority, while Brennan, White, and Marshall dissented.

Califano v. Goldfarb, 430 U.S. 199 (1977)
(Brennan)

Under the Social Security Act, survivors' benefits were paid to a widow regardless of her dependence on her husband's income. Survivors' benefits to widowers were paid only if they had received at least half of their support from their wives. When Hannah Goldfarb died, the federal government refused to pay survivors' benefits to her husband, Leon. He sued, claiming gender discrimination. A three-judge district court ruled that the Social Security Act invidiously discriminated against female wage earners by making them less able than men to provide for surviving spouses. Joseph Califano was the secretary of Health, Education, and Welfare.

BURGER: I see a tension between *Kahn v. Shevin*[302] and *Wiesenfeld*[303] —less as to *Frontiero.*[304]

STEWART: Our invalidation of provisions of the Social Security Act is beginning to bother me. That whole act is filled with all sorts of discrimination. I would slow up on this trend. But it is almost impossible to do in light of *Frontiero. Wiesenfeld* and Harry's *Mathews v. Lucas* distinguish sex discriminations.[305]

---

302. *Kahn v. Shevin,* 416 U.S. 351 (1974).
303. *Weinberger v. Wiesenfeld,* 420 U.S. 636 (1975).
304. *Frontiero v. Richardson,* 411 U.S. 677 (1973).
305. *Mathews v. Lucas,* 427 U.S. 495 (1976). Robert Cuffee was survived by two illegitimate children, Ruby and Darin Lucas. Their mother, Belmira Lucas, applied on the children's behalf for survivors' benefits under the Social Security Act. The secretary of Health, Education, and Welfare declined their application on the ground that the children had not demonstrated their dependency on Cuffee. A three-judge district court reversed on the ground that the Social Security Act unconstitutionally discriminated against illegitimate children by requiring them to prove dependency while presuming that legitimate children were dependent. The Supreme Court reversed on a 6–3 vote, holding that the federal act did not unreasonably discriminate against illegitimate children. The law was reasonably related to the goal of ensuring that only dependent children received benefits. Treating legitimate and illegitimate children differently was a reasonable reflection of reality and allowed Congress to avoid the burden and expense of case-by-case determinations of dependency in most cases, while providing illegitimate children an opportunity to prove actual dependency. Stevens, Brennan, and Marshall dissented on the ground that discrimination against illegitimate children could not be justified by mere administrative convenience.

WHITE: This distributive principle is honored for men but assumed for women. We don't have to decide that the man gets paid—we ought to let the government decide if it wants to cut off non-dependent women.

BLACKMUN: We ought to balance *Kahn v. Shevin* against *Wiesenfeld*. If the focus is on what has been purchased, we must affirm. If we decide this case on welfare policy and need, we should reverse. I don't think that *Wiesenfeld* or *Frontiero* necessarily control, nor does *Shevin*, nor *Ballard*.[306]

POWELL: If I were writing a law school exam, I would have to affirm on *Frontiero* and *Wiesenfeld*. But I think that they can be distinguished—*Wiesenfeld* because of the child, and *Frontiero* because it was question of equal compensation for military personnel of equal rank.

REHNQUIST: I agree with Harry. When we are dealing with a complex actuarial schedule, we can't be put into the position of tearing it down provision by provision.

STEVENS: The main difficulty was for me was the adoption of equal protection in the Fifth Amendment. I don't see how we can retreat at this late date. *Frontiero* and *Wiesenfeld* seem to require affirmance. *Mathews v. Lucas* seems to me to support reversal.

Result: In a plurality opinion, the Court ruled that the spousal benefits provisions of the Social Security Act unconstitutionally discriminated against female wage earners. William Brennan announced the decision of the Court. John Paul Stevens provided the deciding vote in a 4–1–4 decision, but in his concurring opinion he argued that requiring widowers to prove financial dependence on their spouses violated the widowers' *rights, not the rights of female wage earners.*

Personnel Administrator of Massachusetts v. Feeney, 442 U.S. 256 (1979)
(Brennan)

Massachusetts gave a permanent, absolute preference to war veterans in the hiring and promotion of state civil servants. The preference applied to both male and female veterans, including military nurses.

---

306. *Schlesinger v. Ballard,* 419 U.S. 498 (1975). Under navy rules, after Lieutenant Robert C. Ballard was passed over for promotion two consecutive times in nine years of active service, he was involuntarily discharged. He sued for reinstatement, arguing that female officers were entitled to thirteen years of service before they were subject to mandatory discharge for want of promotion. Ballard claimed that the different treatment violated the equal protection component of the Fifth Amendment's due process clause.

In a 5–4 decision, the Court ruled that it was constitutionally permissible to use different standards for male and female officers. Although the government did not submit any evidence to justify different treatment, the majority concluded that Congress *might* reasonably have decided to treat male and female officers differently because women were restricted in available combat and sea duty assignments and did not have the same opportunities for promotion as men. Congress *might* reasonably have concluded that women needed a longer period of tenure in order to have fair and equitable opportunities for advancement.

Brennan, Douglas, White, and Marshall dissented on the ground that gender classifications should receive "close judicial scrutiny." Under this test, the government had the burden to prove a compelling justification for gender classifications. Brennan noted that the government had not even tried to meet its burden, and that the majority had simply "conjured up" its own rationalization out of thin air.

Helen Feeney consistently scored near the top on civil service exams when she applied for a promotion, but she invariably lost out to less qualified veterans. Feeney sued in federal court. A three-judge district court ruled that the state's absolute preference for veterans violated the equal protection clause of the Fourteenth Amendment. While the goals of the law were legitimate, the court found that the grossly disproportionate impact on women was inevitable and could not have been entirely unintentional.

BURGER: The statute discriminates for a purpose, but that is a legitimate purpose.

STEWART: I can't distinguish this from any other statutes that favor veterans. There is no intent here to discriminate against women.

WHITE: I think that Massachusetts may discriminate in favor of veterans, and can go even further than the feds.

MARSHALL: I agree with Bill Brennan.

BLACKMUN: The intent was to benefit veterans and not to discriminate against women. That's about the end of case for me.

POWELL: This statute discriminates against all non-veterans, not just women. We would wash *Davis*[307] and *Arlington Heights*[308] out of the books if we acted on the law's impact, in the face of its conceded purpose to favor veterans.

REHNQUIST: I agree with the Chief Justice.

STEVENS: I agree with the Chief Justice.

---

307. *Washington v. Davis*, 426 U.S. 229 (1976). The Washington, D.C., police department used a standardized communications skills test ("Test 21") to measure whether police recruits had a minimum level of verbal and writing skills. Alfred Davis, an officer who had been passed over for promotion, and two black police recruits whose job applications were rejected claimed that the test was discriminatory and violated the Fifth Amendment and Title 7 of the Civil Rights Act of 1964. They argued that a disproportionate percentage of blacks failed the test and that it bore no relationship to their job performance as police officers. Walter Washington was the police commissioner (and later mayor) of Washington, D.C.

In approving the use of Test 21, the Supreme Court ruled 7–2 that a racially disproportionate effect was not sufficient to prove invidious discrimination, absent evidence of intentional discrimination. The majority found that the test had a rational relationship to employment in that police officers needed to communicate orally and in writing with other officers and the public. Brennan and Marshall dissented on the ground that the government had not met its burden to justify the test.

308. *Arlington Heights v. Metropolitan Housing Development Corp.*, 429 U.S. 252 (1977). A nonprofit corporation (MHDC) sought to purchase fifteen acres of land in Illinois to build a racially integrated model housing project. The village of Arlington Heights refused to re-zone the land from single-family to multiple-family use. MHDC and local black families sued, claiming that the government's refusal to re-zone the land violated the Fourteenth Amendment and the Fair Housing Act. The federal court of appeals ruled that the "ultimate effect" of the government's refusal to re-zone was racially discriminatory and violated the Fourteenth Amendment.

The Supreme Court reversed and remanded. Powell's majority opinion held that (1) the government's actions were not unconstitutional merely because they had a racially disproportionate impact; (2) proof of racially discriminatory intent was required to demonstrate that race was a motivating factor in the government's decision; (3) there was no evidence to indicate that the refusal to re-zone was racially motivated; and (4) because the court of appeals had not yet considered the plaintiffs' statutory claim, it should do so on remand.

Result: By a 7–2 vote, the Justices agreed that the absolute preference for war veterans was constitutional. The law was gender neutral on its face, Potter Stewart wrote for the majority, and the adverse effects on women were not invidious. There was no evidence that the legislature intended to discriminate against women, as the law discriminated equally against all nonveterans, whether female or male. Marshall and Brennan dissented.

Grove City College v. Bell, 465 U.S. 555 (1984)
(Brennan)

Title 9 prohibited sex discrimination in any educational "program or activity" receiving federal financial assistance. Grove City College was a private institution that received no direct federal assistance, although many of its students received federal assistance, including Basic Educational Opportunity Grants (BEOGs).

The college refused to fill out required Department of Education (DOE) forms certifying that the school was in compliance with Title 9. The DOE ruled that because students received federal aid, the school was a recipient of federal financial assistance and was required to comply with Title 9. The government began proceedings to cut off federal aid to Grove City College students until the school certified that it was in compliance. Grove City College sued Secretary of Education Griffin Bell in federal court.

The district court found that the student grants amounted to federal financial assistance for the college but ruled that the government could not terminate this aid—which went directly to students—to punish the college. The court of appeals reversed, ruling that the government could terminate all federal aid if Grove City College refused to comply with Title 9.

The conference discussion centered on two key questions. First, who was the recipient of federal funds in this case—the students or the college? The second question involved the scope of Title 9. The phrase "program or activity" could be construed narrowly to apply only to the specific departments of the university that practiced discrimination (for example, cutting off federal support for the school's athletics program if that department discriminated on the basis of sex) or could be read broadly to affect federal funding for the entire institution if any of its departments failed to comply with Title 9.

BURGER: (1) Are BEOGs federal financial assistance? (2) Does Grove City College receive such assistance? (3) May the government terminate BEOGs? The solicitor general concedes the difficulty of construing what the term "program" means. The problem for me is Bator's argument that food stamps and so forth are not covered as a "program."[309] Must Grove City College take these minorities? The statute thus entraps the school.

BRENNAN:[310] The first question in this case is the recipient issue. In my view, Grove City is clearly "receiving federal financial assistance" through the indirect receipt of BEOG monies granted to students. In fact, Title 9 was enacted in the same public law as the BEOG program, and the legislative intent is clearly focused on such financial aid programs. Moreover, such coverage has always been contemplated by the HEW regulations. That students rather than the college are the payees of the government checks is a result

309. Acting Solicitor General Paul M. Bator.
310. Adapted from Brennan's talking papers, Brennan Papers, OT 1983, box 648.

of the accounting method chosen by Grove City, and does not control the impact of that financial aid.

Grove City now concedes that if it is a recipient, then at least its "BEOG program" (whatever that may mean) is subject to Title 9. Therefore, the college should be required to sign the assurance of compliance form, which clearly states that it is only effective "to the extent that Title 9 is applicable."

This could end the case for the Court. We could stop at this point, and not reach the program-specificity issue. At this stage of the controversy between Grove City and the government, nothing really turns on whether a narrow (e.g., the "program" is the BEOG program), broad (e.g., the "program" is whole institution), or some compromise (e.g., the "program" is the financial aid program) approach is taken. The eventual remedy for refusing to sign the assurance form would be the same—the total cutoff of all BEOG funds. Indeed, since the only violation of Title 9 that has yet been proven, or even alleged, is the failure to sign the form, there is no reason to go beyond that question. Moreover, facts concerning the administrative and organizational setup of Grove City are not in the record before us, and thus it would be difficult to decide the program-specificity issue without this information. Finally, I am convinced that, given the recent change in position by the solicitor general, a broader reading of "program or activity" has not been adequately represented before the Court.

If the Court were to reach the program-specificity issue, I believe that, under the facts and circumstances of this case—where the federal assistance received is general tuition monies that *directly* benefit all aspects of Grove City—the entire undergraduate college at Grove City is subject to Title 9. The undergraduate college is an entity comprised of all the programs and activities that receive federal money. A different case would be presented on different facts—for example, if the federal financial assistance was a research grant to a chemistry professor, then the chemistry department would properly be the affected program; if school lunch money was at issue, then the school cafeteria would be the problem. And a different case might be presented if a college drew a Chinese Wall around any general financial assistance it received from the federal government. But there has been no such limitation in this case, and the clear intent of BEOG money is to provide general financial aid, not only to students but to the college, as well. This is also fully consistent with the program-specificity limitation we recognized in *North Haven*, which requires that only program or activities receiving federal financial assistance be covered by Title 9.[311] When general financial assistance is at issue, as in this case, then all of the various programs of the college are covered, because all the programs receive federal financial assistance.

---

311. *North Haven Bd. of Educ. v. Bell*, 456 U.S. 512 (1982). In a Title 9 action brought against a Connecticut school district, the Supreme Court ruled that the law's directive that "no person" may be discriminated against on the basis of gender included both students and employees, and applied broadly to employment discrimination claims. Blackmun's majority opinion also ruled that Title 9's terms were program-specific and that the government's authority to terminate funds was limited to the particular programs found to have violated Title 9. Powell, Burger, and Rehnquist dissented, arguing that Title 9 prohibited discrimination only against beneficiaries of federally funded programs and activities and did not apply to employment discrimination by organizations receiving federal funds.

Such a reading of the statute fully comports with the contemporaneous legislative history. Moreover, it is clear that subsequent amendments to both Title 9 and the BEOG program have been made since 1972 by a Congress fully aware of the broader scope of HEW's regulation. This "post-enactment" history, which really is full-fledged legislative history of subsequent amendments, is a powerful source of legislative intent in this case. Indeed, the regulations which Congress has relied on in recent years are all couched in terms of programs or activities covered by Title 9, thereby satisfying the program-specificity requirements. At the same time, these regulations contemplate that, depending on the facts of a given case, a full undergraduate college could be subjected to Title 9. As in the examples I mentioned, the scope of coverage depends on the scope of the financial assistance provided. And, to the extent that it may be possible to read these or other regulations more broadly (e.g., to cover the institution when only one program in a college receives federal money), I would interpret them narrowly, as we did in *North Haven.*

Finally, I find the solicitor general's position completely untenable, because it is based on assumptions that are at best unknown and at worst false.[312] For example, we don't know whether Grove City even has a "financial aid program." For all we know, BEOG monies could be paid to the bursar's office, or to the registrar's office, wholly separate from where the college dispenses its own financial scholarships. Or the college may have only one administrative office that handles all of these functions, along with admissions and academic advising. The solicitor general's position, therefore, rests on a legal fiction that ignores the realities of the general financial aid provided to the college through the BEOG grants.

In conclusion, although I do not think it necessary to reach the program-specificity issue, the words of the statute and our decision in *North Haven* direct that Title 9 is program specific. In this case, because BEOG monies are intended as general aid for tuition and fees, a program-specific application requires that all of the programs in the undergraduate college be covered by Title 9. I affirm.

WHITE: Some programs receive aid, although I would like to say that the college is not recipient. But I disagree with Bill Brennan that it is a college-wide recipient. The solicitor general makes more sense—don't follow the money through the students to all school activities. The regulation here is giving federal money to students, not the college. I would go all the way with the solicitor general and so affirm in part.

MARSHALL: Bill Brennan lost me. The solicitor general's supplemental brief persuades me, and I would affirm in part, like Byron.

BLACKMUN: The original plan was to give money directly, and the HEW regulation only allows grants to students.[313] We have to define the program. Congress intended Title 9 to apply to colleges getting student aid. I would hold that the college is the recipient. Is it covered as a whole? I would go along with the solicitor general and say that the financial aid program is sufficient and satisfies program specificity.

312. The solicitor general was Rex Lee.
313. The Department of Health, Education, and Welfare originally had responsibility to administer the BEOG program, but transferred its responsibilities to the Department of Education.

POWELL: I would like to go all the way with the college. This is Big Brother at his worst. Grove City is a recipient all right. But "program specific" precludes application to the entire college, and as the solicitor general argues, it is limited to the primary funding purpose. There is no grant here to allow the college to spend money any way it wants. I would reverse the contrary holding of the court of appeals and send the form issue back.

REHNQUIST: I agree with Byron and Lewis.

STEVENS: I agree that the college is the recipient. The statute applies only to programs supported by financial aid. But what do we know of Grove City's operation? How does it spend the money? Maybe it goes further than the solicitor general argues. Since we agree unanimously that some program is supported, we ought go no further. I would affirm without defining "program."

O'CONNOR: The college is a recipient. I would decide the program specificity question. I would agree with the solicitor general on that. Look at the federal grant program—it is a student aid program, and with that what the college gets is irrelevant.

Result: The Court unanimously ruled that student receipt of federal education grants was sufficient to trigger Title 9 and that the DOE could cut off federal student aid if Grove City College refused to comply. While agreement on the bottom line was unanimous, the Justices were badly divided on the details. Byron White's majority opinion limited the scope of Title 9, ruling that it did not apply to Grove City College as a whole but only to the specific programs for which federal funding was received—in this case, the financial aid program.

Three Justices—Brennan, Marshall, and Stevens—refused to join this part of White's opinion. They argued that as long as Grove City College accepted federal funds, it should be required to comply with Title 9 on an institution-wide basis. Brennan, in particular, thought that White's program-specific limits were absurd and ignored clear congressional intent by permitting gender discrimination in any college program or department not administered by the school's financial aid office.

In 1987, Congress overruled the Court's decision when it passed the Civil Rights Restoration Act of 1987 (20 U.S.C. §1687) over President Reagan's veto. The act provided that any college receiving federal funds must comply with Title 9 on an institution-wide basis. The law strengthened Title 9 and allowed for more aggressive enforcement of its provisions. The most noticeable change has been to bring university support for women's athletic programs up to par with men's sports.

Grove City College remains a private Christian school and refuses to accept any federal financial aid. It no longer allows students to apply for federal financial assistance, although they may apply for state aid.

MOSTLY MEN

Craig v. Boren, 429 U.S. 190 (1976)
(Brennan)

Oklahoma law prohibited the sale of low-alcohol, 3.2 percent "baby beer" to males under the age of twenty-one and females under the age of eighteen. The state categorized this beverage as "non-intoxicating."

Curtis Craig, who was under twenty-one years of age when the case was filed, sued Governor David Boren, claiming that the state law invidiously discriminated against males in violation of the equal protection clause of the Fouteenth Amendment. Carolyn Whitener, a licensed saloon keeper, claimed separate standing to raise the same issues.[314] *Oklahoma argued that the law was substantially related to traffic safety and presented data showing relatively high drunk driving arrests and traffic accidents involving young men compared to young women. The state also argued that the Twenty-first Amendment granted states ultimate authority to regulate the sale of alcohol. A three-judge district court agreed and upheld the state law.*

BURGER: The saloon keeper, it seems to me, has no standing. This is not a case of minors unable to assert their own claims. This is an isolated case and I would dismiss it on standing. If we reach the merits, I would reverse.

STEWART: The saloon keeper has standing. The case then comes down to whether or not the state have extraordinary powers under the amendment and can do what otherwise would violate equal protection.[315] I have concluded that the Twenty-first Amendment does not have that effect. The state has a wholly deficient justification for this discrimination.

WHITE: *Murgia* was talking about the very lowest level of scrutiny.[316] But this is another level. Even if the legislature need not show purpose, but currently it appears that a purpose is served, here the means are not rationally related to any end.

MARSHALL: I can use my first tier.

BLACKMUN: I don't think that this is an *Eisendstadt*[317] or a *Singleton* case.[318] I have concluded, maybe, that there is no standing here. If we got to merits, I don't see an applica-

---

314. During oral argument, Widener was in the courtroom when Burger referred to her from the bench as a "mere saloon keeper." Darcy and Sanbrano, "Oklahoma in the Development of Equal Rights," 1042.

315. The Twenty-first Amendment repealed Prohibition and provided, in part, that "the transportation or importation into any State, Territory, or possession of the United States for delivery or use therein of intoxicating liquors, in violation of the laws thereof, is hereby prohibited."

316. *Massachusetts Board of Retirement v. Murgia*, 427 U.S. 307 (1976). In a 7–1 per curiam decision, the Court upheld a mandatory retirement age of fifty for police officers. Robert Murgia argued that the law violated the equal protection clause by discriminating against him on the basis of age. All eight participating Justices agreed that because there was no suspect classification or a fundamental right at stake, the proper standard was the rational basis test—the most deferential level of analysis. The Justices briefly considered scrapping the traditional equal protection standards but ultimately decided not to. Thurgood Marshall, alone in dissent, argued that the age limit was arbitrary and irrational. Stevens did not participate.

317. *Eisenstadt v. Baird*, 405 U.S. 438 (1972).

318. *Singleton v. Wulff*, 428 U.S. 106 (1976). Two doctors, George Wulff and Michael Freiman, challenged the constitutionality of a Missouri law excluding abortions from Medicaid coverage for poor women unless "medically indicated." They claimed that Thomas Singleton, the responsible state official, had wrongly refused to authorize Medicaid payments for abortions they had performed for poor women. The doctors also alleged that they planned to perform such abortions in the future and would personally benefit if the law were struck down. Finally, they claimed that the law threatened their right to practice medicine. The district court dismissed the suit on the ground that the doctors lacked standing. The court of appeals found that the doctors had standing and summarily invalidated the state law.

The Supreme Court unanimously ruled that the doctors had standing, because they had a financial stake in the outcome of the case and because their personal rights were at stake. The Court also reversed

tion of the Twenty-first Amendment, and would think that *Reed*[319] and *Stanton*[320] would require reversal.

POWELL: On standing, I don't think there should be standing to promote an economic interest by asserting the rights of third parties. So I would dismiss on standing. Otherwise, I would reverse on the merits.

REHNQUIST: She has no constitutional claim of her own. On the merits, I would affirm.

STEVENS: On standing, it seems to me that a male isn't going to fight to get the right to drink. I think that there is standing under Bill Brennan's cases, particularly where a male has been in. On the merits, we must reverse on the basis that some level of scrutiny above mere rationality has to be applied.

Result: The Court ruled that the case was moot as far as Curtis Craig was concerned because he had turned twenty-one before the case was decided. However, a majority decided that saloon owner Carolyn Whitener had standing to raise the same issues. On the merits, the Justices voted 6–1–2 that the Oklahoma law violated the equal protection clause. Brennan, writing for the majority, ruled that the Twenty-first Amendment limited Congress's commerce clause power but did not limit any individual constitutional rights, including equal protection. This case established a middle-tier analysis for equal protection cases involving sex discrimination. Blackmun and Powell joined most of Brennan's majority opinion and concurred in the judgment. Potter Stewart also concurred in the judgment but criticized the majority's treatment of the equal protection claim. Burger and Rehnquist dissented, arguing that the rational basis test was the proper level of scrutiny and that the state law was constitutional.

---

the court of appeals's summary decision striking down the state law, allowing both sides to argue the merits of an issue never before decided by the U.S. Supreme Court.

The Court divided on the issue of whether the two doctors also had standing to argue their patients' constitutional rights. Four Justices—Blackmun, Brennan, White, and Marshall—argued that they did, while Powell, Burger, Stewart, and Rehnquist argued that they did not. Stevens was somewhere in between, although he leaned toward the latter group.

319. *Reed v. Reed*, 404 U.S. 71 (1971).

320. *Stanton v. Stanton*, 421 U.S. 7 (1975). Following a divorce decree and stipulation, James Stanton agreed to pay his ex-wife Thelma child support for a daughter and son. The decree did not define the age at which child support payments would stop. James Stanton stopped his daughter's support payments when she turned eighteen, the age of majority for girls under state law. State law set the age of majority for boys at twenty-one. Thelma Stanton sued to continue her daughter's support payments, claiming that the Utah law violated the due process and equal protection clauses of the Fourteenth Amendment. The Supreme Court ruled 8–1 that as applied to a parent's obligation to pay child support, the state law violated the equal protection clause. Writing for the majority, Blackmun could find no rational reason to establish different ages of majority for boys and girls, apart from stereotypical notions of expecting females to marry young, while boys were expected to receive additional education and training before assuming adult responsibilities. Blackmun's decision left it to the state courts to determine whether to set the age of majority for both sexes at eighteen or twenty-one. Rehnquist dissented, arguing that the Court should have avoided the constitutional question.

Orr v. Orr, 440 U.S. 268 (1979)
(Brennan)

Lillian Orr sought to have her ex-husband, William Orr, held in contempt after he stopped making alimony payments that he had agreed to pay as part of his divorce settlement. Mr. Orr claimed that Alabama's alimony law was unconstitutional because only men could be required to pay.[321] The trial court upheld the statute, and the state court of civil appeals affirmed.

BURGER: Can we avoid the merits? Is the case here, and from what court? Wasn't there a waiver by the agreement? Isn't it out for want of a properly presented federal question?[322]

STEWART: The case would be clear if the husband sought and was refused alimony. But the appellant conceded from the outset that his wife was entitled to alimony. He argues that state law made it impossible for him to get alimony—yet he never argued that he should not have had to pay his wife. If I had to meet the merits, I would hold this statute unconstitutional. I see this as due process—a *Boddie*[323] and a *Groppi* kind of case.[324]

WHITE: I think that the merits are here. The appellate court thought that it could decide it. Reaching the merits, I would reverse.

MARSHALL: If he had raised this issue without entering into an agreement, I would hear him. I don't think that he can be heard now, and I would dismiss.

BLACKMUN: I originally voted to dismiss for want of standing, and I think maybe that is within the scope of "want of a properly presented federal question." But I think that the case is here, and on the merits I would reverse.

POWELL: I agree that we ought to dismiss the appeal. He has contradicted himself out of court. I am as puzzled as Bill Brennan on how to phrase the ground of dismissal. Alabama

---

321. Under the terms of their divorce agreement, William Orr promised to pay his wife $1,250 per month for her support.

322. Arguably, William Orr's contractual agreement to pay alimony meant that the state court's decision rested on an adequate and independent state ground and that there was no federal question for the Court to decide.

323. *Boddie v. Connecticut,* 401 U.S. 371 (1971). Gladys Boddie brought a class-action lawsuit on behalf of female welfare recipients in Connecticut who wanted divorces but could not afford to pay court fees and costs. Harlan, joined by five other Justices, held that the social importance of marriage and the state's monopoly of divorce procedures meant that Connecticut had a duty under the due process clause to allow indigents to file for divorce without paying required fees or costs. Douglas concurred but argued that the equal protection clause was the proper foundation for the decision. Brennan concurred on two grounds: (1) that both the due process and equal protection clauses were involved; and (2) that states must make the same exception for all types of legal action. Black dissented, arguing that requiring everyone to pay nominal court costs did not violate due process or equal protection rights.

324. *Groppi v. Leslie,* 404 U.S. 496 (1972). After James Groppi led a public protest in the Wisconsin state assembly chamber, he was arrested and jailed for disturbing the peace. Two days later, the state assembly cited Groppi for contempt and ordered that he be kept in jail. The Supreme Court ruled unanimously that the resolution violated the due process clause of the Fourteenth Amendment because the state legislature did not give Groppi adequate notice or an opportunity to respond to the charges against him. Powell and Rehnquist did not participate in the decision.

courts can't foist jurisdiction on this Court. If we invalidate this statute in this context, we would wreak havoc with every alimony decree in Alabama. I would reverse on the merits.

REHNQUIST: We should not reach questions we do not have to decide—if there was waiver here. *Rescue Army*,[325] *Doremus*,[326] *Black v. Cutter*[327] suggest that if an injury was actually the result of the contract, it can't be heard.

STEVENS: I basically agree with Byron and Harry. This statute imposes a burden on the appellant and that should give him standing. Does the underlying agreement preclude relief? That is a state law question and is still open on remand.

Result: The Court voted 6–3 that the Alabama statute violated the equal protection clause. The state law, Brennan wrote for the majority, improperly used a sexual classification as a proxy for economic

---

325. *Rescue Army v. Municipal Court of Los Angeles*, 331 U.S. 549 (1947). Rescue Army, a religious charitable organization, was charged with violating the Los Angeles municipal code, which regulated the solicitation of charitable donations. Rescue Army claimed that these ordinance violated its First Amendment free exercise rights. The Supreme Court declined to decide the constitutional issues on the ground that the issues presented were in an abstract and speculative form and because the state courts had not yet clearly interpreted the relevant code provisions. Wiley Rutledge cited the Court's longstanding practice to resolve constitutional issues only when they were presented in clear-cut and concrete form, unclouded by serious problems of construction or interpretation on the part of state courts. The Court remanded the case to the state courts for further proceedings.

326. *Doremus v. Board of Education*, 342 U.S. 429 (1952). A New Jersey law required the reading of five Bible verses at the beginning of each school day. Donald Doremus challenged the law as a taxpayer, and Anna Klein challenged the law as a parent (her child graduated before the case could be resolved). The state supreme court accepted jurisdiction and upheld the statute. The U.S. Supreme Court dismissed the case on appeal, arguing that neither Doremus nor the Kleins had standing. Robert Jackson, writing for the majority, ruled that Doremus did not have a sufficient personal stake in the outcome of the case and that the case was moot as far as the Kleins were concerned.

Douglas, Reed, and Burton dissented on the ground that both the Doremus and the Kleins had sufficient interest in the operation and management of public schools to allow standing and that the case presented a real case or controversy under Article 3. Douglas observed that the New Jersey courts had already recognized that both parties had standing to sue, and he saw no constitutional reason to overrule the state courts' judgment.

327. *Black v. Cutter Laboratories*, 351 U.S. 292 (1956). Cutter Laboratories fired Mabel Black, ostensibly because she was a member of the Communist party. Under the company's collective bargaining agreement, Black could only be fired for "just cause." An arbitration board ordered her reinstated on the ground that the company had known about her communist political affiliations for years and by keeping her on the job the company had waived its right to fire her because of her party membership. The board further ruled that Black had really been fired because of her union activities. The trial court agreed, but the state supreme court reversed on the ground that Black's reinstatement would violate public policy.

The Supreme Court initially accepted the case on certiorari then changed its mind and dismissed the writ. Clark, writing for the Court in a 5–1–3 decision, claimed that the Court had originally believed that the state supreme court's ruling had rendered unenforceable virtually all contracts entered into by Communist party members. Upon closer examination of the record, however, the majority concluded that the state court's decision was much narrower than they had initially thought. The state court's decision involved only a routine judicial interpretation of a local contract under local law and presented no substantial federal question. Reed would have affirmed the judgment below. Douglas, Warren, and Black dissented, arguing that there was a vital constitutional question at stake: whether state courts could deny relief to employees wrongfully discharged solely because of their political beliefs.

need.[328] *This sort of gender distinction was arbitrary, if not perverse, because it protected wealthy women while it handicapped needy men. Powell, Rehnquist, and Burger dissented.*

Rostker v. Goldberg, 453 U.S. 57 (1981)
(Brennan)

The Selective Service Act authorized the president to require young males to register for the draft. In 1980, President Carter reactivated the draft registration process and recommended that the act be amended to include women. When Congress failed to act, Robert L. Goldberg and other men sued Bernard Rostker, director of Selective Service, claiming that the act amounted to sex discrimination in violation of the equal protection component of the Fifth Amendment's due process clause. A three-judge district court agreed.

Five of the nine Justices deciding this case were war veterans.[329]

BURGER: This action, right or wrong, satisfies the test established in *Boren v. Craig* [*sic*].[330] I am ready to hold, however, that this is the business of Congress. Congress could draft women.

STEWART: This is a gender-based classification. The exercise of an explicit power gets us nowhere—all powers are alike in being subject to limitations. The question is, whether the equal protection limitation invalidates this classification. I don't agree with our tier tests in equal protection cases—whether discrimination is invidious is the only test. Congress can differentiate between women and men only if they are not similarly situated. They are not similarly situated here. We must consider this only as to registration, not for the draft—and women and men are not freely interchangeable in combat. So I would reverse.[331]

WHITE: I don't think that the question is whether all of the military can be filled with men. Women can fill some jobs without interfering with combat readiness. Military men concede that. But those jobs can be filled without registering or drafting women. Neither Rostker nor the military witnesses said that women could not be obtained without registration or a draft.[332]

---

328. Brennan acknowledged that there were "some indications" in the record that William Orr's alimony obligations were part of a stipulation entered into by both parties, and there was a "possibility" that the state courts below had decided the case on an independent and adequate state ground. Brennan quickly brushed aside any such concerns, however, and turned to the merits of the case.

329. Bill Brennan, for example, was an army colonel during World War II. He spent most of the war in Washington, D.C., working on war production issues, including labor disputes and procurement. Cushman, *The Supreme Court Justices,* 447. The other Justices are discussed below.

330. *Craig v. Boren,* 429 U.S. 190 (1976).

331. Stewart served in the navy during World War II on a fuel transport ship in the Atlantic and Mediterranean. His service record included several combat awards.

332. After White was rejected by the marines (he was color-blind), he enlisted in the navy and became an intelligence officer in the Pacific. He was the officer in charge of the report on the sinking of John Kennedy's PT-109. The incident allowed White to renew his friendship with Kennedy, whom he had met in England in 1939 when White was a Rhodes scholar and Kennedy's father was the ambassador to Great Britain. For his wartime service, White earned two bronze stars and left the navy as a lieutenant commander. Cushman, *The Supreme Court Justices,* 462.

MARSHALL: I agree with Bill Brennan.

BLACKMUN: There are no problems of standing or ripeness. Congress can take one step at a time—it may legislate the registration of women. There is a danger of stereotyping, but I would reach reversal under *Craig v. Boren*.

POWELL: The president did not assert a military need to induct women—it was equity that required women and men to serve. I would apply *Boren* and come out to reverse. Registration and induction are part of the same cloth. Men will litigate numbers at every stage if we affirm this case. The defense of our country should, of all cases, require deference to congressional findings.[333]

REHNQUIST: Equal protection says that the government can't treat similarly situated people differently. Since the prohibition against women in combat is not challenged here, they are not similarly situated. We must treat registration as the draft to decide this case. This case does not meet either our heightened scrutiny test or any other test.

STEVENS: On the proper level of scrutiny, Powell and I wrote separately in *Craig v. Boren*. Lewis analogized "substantial" to the *Royster* standard.[334] I read *Boren* as describing our holding in *Reed v. Reed*.[335] Our cases invoke (1) a strong presumption of invalidity in race cases; or (2) the idea that gender cases are not all the same—some are like race, while others are like statutory rape. These are differences that make sense.[336] Are they fungible for this classification? No one agreed to that here. Rather, it is accepted that combat distinctions may be made. If a quota system can be made like that, then this distinction is permissible. Congress can therefore make this distinction.[337]

Result: On a 6–3 vote, the Court ruled that Article 1—which entrusted to Congress the responsibility to raise and regulate the armed services—permitted the legislature to exempt women from registering for the draft. William Rehnquist reasoned that Congress's judgment in such matters was entitled to great deference and that Congress could make its decision on the basis of military need rather than equity. Rehnquist questioned the utility of conventional equal protection tests, which he claimed were "facile abstractions used to justify a result." But the majority agreed that women and men were not similarly situated when it came to the armed services, in part because women were by law barred from assuming combat roles. As a result, there was no invidious discrimination and no supportable equal protection claim.

In dissent, Byron White saw no reason to exempt women from registration when they could be drafted to fill any number of noncombat and support roles. Thurgood Marshall, in a lengthy and

---

333. Powell served as an intelligence officer in the air corps during World War II (he originally sought to enlist in the navy, but his eyesight was too poor). Powell was chief of operational intelligence for General Carl Spaatz, the commander of American bomber forces in Europe, and was involved in project ULTRA, which broke the German military codes. Cushman, *The Supreme Court Justices* 492.

334. *Royster Guano Co. v. Virginia*, 253 U.S. 412 (1920).

335. *Reed v. Reed*, 404 U.S. 71 (1971).

336. The statutory rape reference was almost certainly to *Michael M. v. Superior Court*, 450 U.S. 464 (1981), discussed below.

337. Stevens was a naval officer during World War II and earned a bronze star for his work as part of a code-breaking operation. Cushman, *The Supreme Court Justices*, 501.

impassioned dissent, criticized the exclusion of women from this "fundamental civic obligation." Instead of asking whether treating women and men alike was necessary for military preparedness, for Marshall the real question was precisely the reverse—whether treating women and men differently was necessary for military preparedness.[338] *The only reason offered here was administrative cost, which in Marshall's judgment was not a substantially important government interest and was not sufficient to justify such blatant discrimination. Marshall concluded that congressional testimony about the large number of noncombat positions that would have to be filled in case of war clearly justified the joint registration of women and men.*

   No one questioned the underlying assumption that women were unfit for combat roles and incapable of performing as soldiers on an equal footing with men.

Michael M. v. Superior Court of Sonoma County, 450 U.S. 464 (1981)
(Brennan)

Michael McMillan was a seventeen-year-old boy charged with the statutory rape of a sixteen-year-old girl. The girl, identified only as Sharon, initially refused McMillan's demand for sex, but submitted after McMillan hit her in the face. After the two had sex on a park bench, the boy rode off on his bicycle and left Sharon alone and crying. Citing insufficient evidence of forcible rape, the district attorney's office charged McMillan with statutory rape. McMillan claimed that California's statutory rape law violated the equal protection clause of the Fourteenth Amendment because only males could be prosecuted. The California Supreme Court ruled that the statute was constitutional even under the strict scrutiny test, because the state had a compelling interest in avoiding the costs of teenage pregnancies, abortions, and childbearing out of wedlock.

BURGER: None of our equal protection cases give much help. The state does not have to treat boys and girls alike for all purposes, at least in a sexual context. Protection against teen-aged pregnancy is a state interest, even if protection against teenage chastity is not. Rationality analysis suffices. The case really presents the question of what values the judicial system should support—and female chastity has always been regarded as a higher value than male chastity.

STEWART: Intellectually this is a very puzzling case. Males and females are not similarly situated, and therefore no equal protection violation is involved here. The statute is based on biological differences, contrary to all other equal protection cases.

WHITE: I agree with Bill Brennan that a gender-neutral statute can better achieve the state's interests. We ought to do this as applied. I could not reach the same result if the man were fifty and the girl eleven.

BLACKMUN: I come down to affirm even under *Craig v. Boren*, accepting the California Supreme Court's holding as to the purpose of the statute.[339]

POWELL: I agree with Harry that even under *Craig v. Boren* we can come out to affirm.

338. Tushnet, *Making Constitutional Law*, 107.
339. *Craig v. Boren*, 429 U.S. 190 (1976).

Rehnquist: This is not a sexual stereotype case at all. There is a difference between men and women that provides a perfectly acceptable basis for the difference in treatment.

Stevens: If the pregnancy basis is accepted, why say no punishment for a woman but punishment for a man? That is irrational under whatever standard you use. I think that this law is bad on its face, and not only as applied.

Result: The Court upheld California's statutory rape law on a close 4–1–4 vote. William Rehnquist's plurality opinion appeared to backpedal from the intermediate scrutiny test announced for gender cases in Craig v. Boren *and hinted that laws placing a heavier burden on males than females may no longer receive heightened scrutiny. Citing* Reed v. Reed, *Rehnquist argued that laws establishing categories based on sex were permissible if they bore a fair and substantial relationship to legitimate state ends. While Blackmun provided the fifth vote to uphold the statute, he pointedly did not join Rehnquist's majority opinion and argued that* Craig v. Boren's *intermediate scrutiny test provided the proper standard for gender-based classifications. Brennan, White, Marshall, and Stevens dissented.*

The district attorney's office eventually dropped all charges against Michael McMillan after Sharon and her family moved out of the jurisdiction and could not be located.

Mississippi University for Women v. Hogan, 458 U.S. 718 (1982)
(Brennan)

The Mississippi University for Women (MUW) was a state-supported university with enrollment limited to women. While men were allowed to audit courses in the school's nursing program, they could not receive academic credit or earn a degree or certificate. Joe Hogan was a qualified applicant to the nursing school who was denied admission solely because he was male. He sued, claiming that MUW's policy violated the equal protection clause of the Fourteenth Amendment.

Burger: I don't think that the all-woman college must go down the drain.

Brennan:[340] The issue is whether MUW violated the Fourteenth Amendment in refusing to admit Joe Hogan to the school of nursing. Under *Craig v. Boren* the answer depends upon whether MUW's exclusion of males from academic credit for participation in the nursing program is substantially related to achieving important governmental objectives.[341] I thus view the issue as quite a bit narrower than whether single-sex schools are ever constitutional.

We can assume without deciding that a state could show a substantial relationship between its important interest in meeting educational needs of its residents and single sex schools, which provided men and women with equal educational opportunities. But this case is different.

First, this is not a case of separate but equal educational opportunity for men and women. Mississippi offered no all-male nursing school, or even an all-male university. Joe Hogan did not have the same number of options for nursing programs as did female nursing students. Moreover, Joe Hogan was at a disadvantage in comparison to a simi-

---

340. Adapted from Brennan's talking papers, Brennan Papers, OT 1981, box 599.
341. *Craig v. Boren,* 429 U.S. 190 (1976).

larly (geographically) situated woman, since he would be seriously inconvenienced by having to travel a great distance to attend nursing school.

In addition to the fact that this is not a case of separate but *equal*, petitioners have made no showing of a substantial relationship to an important government interest. I am not willing to presume that a single-sex school automatically has a substantial relationship to an educational need, or that because a single-sex college is all-female it necessarily serves a governmental interest in affirmative action for women. Petitioners made no showing of a substantial relationship between MUW's admission policy and any important governmental interest below. Instead, they asserted that a rational relationship was all that was required. Now they contend that MUW's admission policy provides educational affirmative action for women. However, the record will not support this assertion.

The district court explicitly found *only* a rational relationship to a legitimate interest. The school's statutory statement of purpose and aim is the perpetuation of sexual stereotypes rather than any affirmative action. Moreover, it is difficult to believe that any affirmative action is needed in nursing programs—a traditionally female career. Finally, the state's assertion of interest is to some extent undermined by the university's policy of allowing males to participate fully in classes, and to pay tuition but not to receive a degree.

The declaratory judgment entered by the district court was that the policy of MUW, which excludes plaintiff because of his sex, violated the Fourteenth Amendment. It may be that this declaration is broader than necessary. If the declaration were limited to the invalidity of the policy of excluding men from the *nursing* school, this would avoid a conflict with Title 9, because the nursing school, which became operative in 1971, is not a traditional single-sex school. Moreover, at least in regards to the nursing school, it is impossible to accept the state's argument of a need for affirmative action for women.

I would affirm the judgment of the Court of Appeals for the Fifth Circuit.

WHITE: I would only decide the one professional school—nursing—problem. And discrimination is limited to males, not females.

MARSHALL: I would decide this case narrowly, as Bill Brennan suggests.

BLACKMUN: The statutory purpose should have been repealed long ago. I would like to limit our decision to the nursing school—I don't think that everything has to be co-ed. For the present, I would reverse.

POWELL: There are perfectly justifiable educational reasons for one-sex schools. So this guy could go to one of the co-ed nursing schools. They don't have to provide an all-male nursing school. I don't think that he was a victim of sex discrimination.

REHNQUIST: I agree with Lewis. We can't limit our decision to the nursing school. Strike it down there, and soon it's the end of the women's university. This discrimination is against men, and they weren't victims in the past.

STEVENS: I agree with Bill Brennan that there is a difference between a male in a nursing school—I agree with him.

O'CONNOR: I go with Bill Brennan's approach. On the broader question, I can't say that there can be no single-sex school, but they should provide more than they have here.

Result: Using intermediate scrutiny, Sandra Day O'Connor, writing for a 5–4 majority, found no important government objectives for excluding men from MUW's nursing program. Nor were the means adopted substantially related to any claimed state objectives. The MUW program was not designed to compensate for past discrimination; if anything, the practice only perpetuated the invidious stereotype that nursing was women's work. Allowing men to audit nursing classes undermined the state's claim that women were adversely affected by the presence of men, which left the school without any "exceedingly persuasive justification" necessary to sustain the gender-based classification. Burger, Blackmun, Powell, and Rehnquist dissented. After the Court's decision, the school's Board of Visitors voted to make the school fully co-educational. Joe Hogan was not among the 131 men who enrolled at MUW that fall.

WEALTH AND POVERTY

Edwards v. California, 314 U.S. 160 (1941)
(Douglas) (Murphy)

In December 1939, Fred Edwards drove from Marysville, California, to Spur, Texas, to pick up his brother-in-law, Frank Duncan, and take him back to California. Edwards knew that Duncan was unemployed and broke. After the two men arrived in California, Duncan filed for financial assistance from the Farm Security Administration. Edwards was subsequently charged with violating a state law making it a misdemeanor to bring into the state any nonresident known to be indigent.

Conference of May 3, 1941[342]

HUGHES: The statute does not define "indigent." I would refer to the *Miln* case as to paupers.[343] Story dissented. While there is a state statute, only the California attorney appears and he does not argue.[344] Unless we have it reargued with the attorney general of California present, we have no clue as to the meaning of "indigent."[345] All we have is that the statute is construed and applied to this case. On these facts, is the act constitutional?

---

342. The Court was short-handed because James McReynolds retired on January 31, 1941.

343. *New York v. Miln*, 36 U.S. (11 Pet.) 102 (1837). The Court implied here that it was within the state's police powers to bar nonresident paupers from entering the state. A New York law required the master of each ship docking from a foreign port to report information about each passenger to state authorities. The law was intended to prevent foreign paupers from slipping into New York. The state sued William Thompson (the master of the ship *Emily*) and George Miln (one of the ship's co-owners) for failing to report the passenger information as required. Miln and Thompson argued that the law was unconstitutional because it regulated trade and commerce between New York and foreign ports in violation of the Constitution's prohibition against states imposing duties on imported goods.

The Court ruled that the state law was not a regulation of commerce but a valid exercise of the state's police powers. It was not a regulation of commerce because people were not "goods" and could not be subjects of commerce. The Court thought it elementary that New York had the right to protect itself from an influx of foreign paupers. So long as the state was acting within the scope of its legitimate powers applied to an allowable end, it could use whatever appropriate means it thought fit, subject to limitations imposed by the Constitution or federal law. Otherwise, New York had the right and the duty to advance the safety, happiness, prosperity, and general welfare of its citizens as it saw fit.

344. Charles A. Wetmore Jr.

345. The attorney general at the time was Earl Warren. On reargument, Assistant Attorney General W. T. Sweigert argued the case for California.

There is nothing to show that this man is a pauper. A pauper is one who is on poor relief. It is also sometimes defined as a person who is likely to go on relief. The stipulation says that the man is an indigent person. There is nothing to show he was unemployable or impaired in body or mind. The man who brings him in is a relative. It all comes down to the fact that this man has no money. As applied, the state act is unconstitutional. We should either hold that or have it reargued by the attorney general. I think the right here is a privilege and immunity of a citizen, one of the few protected by the Constitution.

STONE: I would set the case down for reargument.

ROBERTS: I would set it down for reargument, although I think that the act is bad on these facts.

Result: When the Court could not agree on a constitutional basis for striking down the California law, the Justices set the case for reargument the following term. In the interim, Chief Justice Charles Evans Hughes retired, Harlan Fiske Stone was promoted to Chief Justice, Jimmy Byrnes replaced McReynolds, and Robert Jackson took Stone's old seat.

Conference of October 25, 1941

STONE: It is troublesome because of the way in which the case comes here. The stipulation reveals that the person brought in was indigent. He was convicted on a stipulation which was upheld without any exposition of the statute. It is claimed that one object of the statute was to prevent the promotional bringing in of people. There are no facts as to whether the petitioner would be supported by relatives. I would not say that states could not control promoters in these cases. Contract labor law might well be valid. But it is interstate commerce, as our cases stand, for a person to pass from state to state.

It is arguable that it is a right of a citizen to move from state to state as a citizen of the United States. In a case before the Fourteenth Amendment was enacted, the *Colgate* case shows that it is arguable that it is a right of the citizen.[346] But it is clearly a violation of this clause to say that a person can be prevented from crossing into another state. If he may not be knowingly brought in, he could be prevented from coming in. The commerce clause does not admit the right of any state to say that he could not cross state lines. A state can regulate activities within the state, but not here. I think that this ought to be reversed and narrowly construed.

ROBERTS: I would affirm on the ground that the state is regulating the conduct of its citizens. I think that the state had the right to exclude paupers, and I would write it carefully and narrowly.

BLACK: I am for reversal, but the path is not so clear on the commerce clause. I start off on the assumption that we are a nation, and that people can travel from place to place.

Due process is out as due process. I would place this decision under the privileges and immunities clause—and this would come under privileges. Just because a man is poor, a state can't keep a citizen from moving from one state to another. We have a different situation when aliens are involved.

---

346. *Colgate v. Harvey*, 296 U.S. 404 (1935), allowing Vermont to tax corporate dividends earned outside the state but paid to Vermont residents.

REED: I would put this on the commerce clause.

FRANKFURTER: I agree with you, and I would most emphatically [not] put it on privileges and immunities.[347]

DOUGLAS: I would reverse on privileges and immunities.

MURPHY: The same.

BYRNES: I would put it under privileges and immunities.

JACKSON: I think it violates both.

STONE: I would regard with great anxiety any expansion of privileges and immunities clause. Privileges and immunities have been abandoned for seventy years—it is borrowing trouble to open it up again.

BLACK: There are limits under the Bill of Rights—there are no limits under the *Twining* case.[348]

[MURPHY: Those deciding the case under the privileges and immunities clause: Jackson (willing to go on commerce clause also), Byrnes, Murphy, Douglas, Black. Those deciding the case under the commerce clause: Frankfurter, Reed, Stone. Roberts affirms.]

Result: Writing for a unanimous Court, Jimmy Byrnes ruled that California's attempt to block an influx of indigents from other states placed an unconstitutional burden on interstate commerce. Miln notwithstanding, California's law was not a valid exercise of the state's police power, because the mere status of being unemployed was not a "moral pestilence."

Initially, five Justices were willing to decide this case based on the privileges and immunities clause. This would have resurrected a constitutional provision that the Supreme Court presumably assigned to oblivion in the Slaughter-House Cases.[349] *Frankfurter and Stone worked hard behind the scenes to dissuade Byrnes from taking this course, arguing that it might revive the discredited practice of substantive due process. In the end, Byrnes agreed to use the commerce clause to strike down California's*

347. Frank Murphy's conference notes quote Frankfurter as saying that he "would most emphatically put it on privileges and immunities." Given the context of Frankfurter's comments and his subsequent vote, however, it seems likely that Murphy was mistaken and Frankfurter actually said that he would *not* decide the case on the privileges and immunities clause.

348. *Twining v. New Jersey,* 211 U.S. 78 (1908), refused to extend the Fifth Amendment's protections against self-incrimination to the states. Black wanted to overturn *Twining* and extend Fifth Amendment protections to the states.

349. In *Saenz v. Roe,* 119 S. Ct. 1518 (1999), the Supreme Court struck down a California law limiting new residents' welfare benefits to the amount that they would have received in their previous home state. The law applied to families who had resided in California for less than a year and was expressly authorized by a federal statute. On a 7–2 vote, the Court ruled that the law violated the right to travel and the privileges and immunities clause. Stevens's opinion seemed to breathe new life into the privileges and immunities clause in establishing that new state residents enjoyed the same rights as all other residents. Rehnquist and Thomas dissented, and were sharply critical of the majority's "revisionist" interpretation of the privileges and immunities clause, which they claimed was at odds with the original meaning of the clause and contrary to all established precedents.

"anti-Okie" law.[350] *The four concurring Justices, Douglas, Black, Murphy, and Jackson, all favored striking down the law as a violation of an implied constitutional right of travel, based on the privileges and immunities clause. Only Owen Roberts voted to affirm. This case was Byrnes's only significant opinion in his brief, one-year tenure on the Court.*

Wyman v. James, 400 U.S. 309 (1971)
(Douglas) (Brennan)

Barbara James received monthly AFDC (Aid to Families with Dependent Children) payments from the government. New York required AFDC recipients to submit to home visits by a caseworker every three months as a condition of receiving benefits.[351] James was given two days' notice of the caseworker's visit, but she refused to allow the caseworker to enter her home without a search warrant. The state summarily terminated James's welfare benefits. James sued, claiming that the state caseworkers were bound by the warrant requirement of the Fourth Amendment. New York claimed that welfare was a privilege, not a right, and argued that when James accepted welfare she consented to certain conditions, including home visits. A three-judge district court ruled 2–1 that the visits violated the Fourth Amendment and enjoined the state from cutting off James's benefits. George K. Wyman was commissioner of New York's Department of Social Services.

BURGER: The welfare recipient refused admission to her caseworker. Is a search warrant needed? I don't see this as a search. It is a grant from the government on condition, and it is no different than a provision in a shipbuilding contract giving a right of inspection of work being done. I reverse.

BLACK: I agree with the Chief Justice. This is a reasonable search. It would be unreasonable for New York not to look into problems of this kind. I reverse.

DOUGLAS: I affirm.

HARLAN: This is both reasonable and constitutional. I reverse.

BRENNAN: I affirm. This is close in some respects to *Camara.*[352] [DOUGLAS: He reads from the opinion.] This involves an "official intrusion" into a private house. There is a "search." There must be some kind of surveillance. A search warrant can be used in *See* and *Camara.*[353]

---

350. Klarman, "An Interpretive History of Modern Equal Protection," 223.

351. Home visits were announced several days in advance and could only be conducted during normal business hours. Forced entry and general snooping were prohibited. New York claimed that the visits were intended to restore beneficiaries to self-sufficiency, to ensure that only those needing support received it, and to confirm that dependent children were benefitting from state aid.

352. *Camara v. Municipal Court,* 387 U.S. 523 (1967). Roland Camara refused to allow a San Francisco housing inspector to examine his apartment without a warrant. The Court held that such administrative searches were subject to Fourth Amendment protections, whether or not the search was conducted by police and whether or not it was based on suspected criminal activity.

353. *See v. City of Seattle,* 387 U.S. 541 (1967). Decided on the same day as *Camara,* this case established that government agents must seek warrants for administrative searches of nonpublic portions of commercial property. Norman E. See was the owner of a commercial warehouse.

STEWART: I pass to Byron on *Camara*.

WHITE: I reverse. *Camara* and *See* held that the Fourth Amendment went beyond criminal proceedings. There is no right in New York to go into the house against the occupants' will. If there is a refusal, the aid is cut off where it is difficult to get information without getting into the house. I can't say that consent given under this system is coerced. It is reasonable for New York to say that it does not have to take the recipient's word for it. It is like licensed businesses where injunctions are needed. This case is more like that than *Camara*. I don't think, therefore, that there is any Fourth Amendment question here at all.

STEWART: I reverse.

MARSHALL: I affirm. You can't contract away constitutional rights. The burden is on the recipient to show that she is spending the money on the child, and that can be shown by affidavit. Your house is a private zone, different from any business.

BLACKMUN: I reverse. What Thurgood says has force. This is an aid plan. The situation is fully protective of individual rights. It is routine for case workers to do this. It is the same as an IRS review disallowing deductions where confirmation is not given.

Result: In a 6–3 decision, the Court ruled that home visits by welfare workers were not subject to Fourth Amendment warrant requirements. While caseworker visits were in part investigative, Blackmun wrote, they were not searches "in the traditional criminal law context" of the Fourth Amendment. Home visits were not coercive, and unlike Camara *or* See, *there were no criminal penalties for refusing to allow the visits. The only consequence of refusing to allow the caseworker to inspect one's home was the loss of welfare benefits. The majority concluded that these visits were a reasonable administrative tool to make sure that state money was being put to intended uses. This was Blackmun's first opinion as a Justice. It was intended to be an easy case, but it did not turn out that way.*

In dissent, William O. Douglas wondered whether a prominent and affluent farmer receiving federal subsidies would have been judged as harshly had his cash subsidies been tied to allowing his home to be searched periodically. Thurgood Marshall, joined by William Brennan, blasted Blackmun and the majority for establishing one standard of privacy for the rich and middle class, and another for the poor. Marshall noted that fire and housing inspectors had to have search warrants to search businesses, and that after this case commercial warehouse owners would enjoy greater constitutional protections against government searches of their businesses than poor people had against government searches of their private homes.

San Antonio School District v. Rodriguez, 411 U.S. 1 (1973)
(Douglas) (Brennan)

Primary and secondary education in Texas was funded by a combination of state and local taxes. Approximately half of most school districts' budgets came from the state treasury. This money was intended to ensure that all districts could meet students' minimum educational needs. Each district could supplement these funds with additional money raised through local property taxes.

This system led to huge disparities in educational spending throughout the state. Annual per-pupil spending ranged from as little as $356 in poor school districts to as high as $594 in wealthier *districts.*[354] *Demetrio Rodriguez and other parents from poor school districts sued, claiming that the large disparities in student spending violated their equal protection rights.*

A three-judge district court held that wealth was a suspect classification and education was a fundamental right. This meant that Texas had to prove that (1) it had a compelling interest in maintaining such an unequal system of public school spending; and (2) it had adopted narrowly tailored means to achieve those compelling goals. The district court found that Texas not only failed meet its burden under the strict scrutiny test but it could not even pass the rational basis test—because there was no reasonable justification for the state's blatantly discriminatory system of school financing.

Conference of October 17, 1972

BURGER: Statewide school funding is supplemented by local taxation. Local property taxes vary from district to district, which results in disparate treatment. The three-judge court held that the Texas system violates equal protection. No explanation was offered as to why that is true. They follow Koon's [*sic*] theory that the amount of dollars available determines the quality of education, and that education cannot be a function of wealth.[355] I don't see any thoughtful analyses here. They confuse equal advantages with equal protection. Whatever the status of education may be, it does not outrank other duties. This three-judge court would overhaul the school systems and the fiscal and taxation structures across the land. I could support a constitutional amendment to reach this result. I can't see this as a violation of equal protection. I reverse.

DOUGLAS: Fiscal considerations aren't the whole story, but they are integral part of equal education. Money alone doesn't answer this. I affirm.

BRENNAN: Money is not the whole thing. Money, however, plays an important part. There is disparate treatment, so there is unequal treatment. There is state action here. I affirm.

STEWART: I am not at rest, although I am inclined to reverse. I would assume that money spent on schools provides some index of the quality of education. But I think that this approach exceeds the limits of the coverage of the equal protection clause. Equal protection does not require this. Moreover, I cannot find a discrete, identifiable class here. Until we can find a discrete class of people invidiously discriminated against, "poor," and "pauper" are too general. *Valtierra* seems to me to be an example of setting such limits.[356]

WHITE: I would probably agree with the district court insofar as it reaches the situation as here, and for the reason that it is a locked-in district. I wouldn't think that inequality of input of dollars would alone make a case. But in school districts that don't offer any opportunity to increase incomes spent on their schools, there would be a case made out.

---

354. Edgewood, one of the poorest school districts in San Antonio, was 90 percent Hispanic, 6 percent black, and 4 percent white. Each year, Edgewood schools received $108 per pupil in federal funds and $222 in state funds, but local taxes added only $26 per student for a total annual expenditure of $356 per student. In contrast, the Alamo Heights area of San Antonio was 81 percent white, 18 percent Hispanic, and 1 percent black. Each year, Alamo Heights received $36 per student in federal funds and $225 annually in state funds, but local taxes added an additional $333 per student for a total annual expenditure of $594 per pupil—60 percent higher than in Edgewood.

355. Coons et al., *Private Wealth and Public Education.*

356. *James v. Valtierra,* 402 U.S. 137 (1971).

People in each school district who would like to spend more money in their schools can claim equal protection. The Texas system does not allow any means for getting extra funds. I would affirm, but with a narrower opinion than the district court.

MARSHALL: You never will have an equal system, but you can equalize the money. I affirm. Their scheme does not shape up to the Fourteenth Amendment. Having picked out this scheme that operates discriminatorily against certain areas, that is a denial of equal protection. This is geographic discrimination.

BLACKMUN: I would much prefer to let the states struggle with this. I am sorry that this is a three-judge court. I wonder if our decree should be made prospective only in order to save district bonds. I definitely reverse on the assumption that the Texas system provides a basic minimum education for all children. This is almost a non-justiciable question—I don't think that we can effectively legislate equality in education. If we affirm, federal courts will destroy the state systems. This would be another step toward big government. Districts that are interested in education will taper off, and there will be a general lowering of educational standards.

POWELL: I reverse. The district court opinion would postulate a complete restructuring of local and state government, particularly taxation and the entire financial system of the states. The result will be regression, especially in urbanized areas. Education is not a fundamental interest in the constitutional sense—those rights are in the Constitution itself. Education does not require the application of the "compelling interest" test. We have never held that wealth is a badge of discrimination. Is there a rational basis for this kind of property tax? If not, there must be full state funding of education. The state would take over most local functions. Richmond has the largest black population, and they get a larger tax income than most parts of Virginia.[357] If there were state-wide funding, Richmond would drop from $800 to $600 in expenditures per student annually. Arlington County spends $1,300 per pupil—it, too, would drop. Those who would be hurt the most are those who can afford to be hurt the least. Only the legislative branch of government can solve this problem. I reverse.

REHNQUIST: I reverse. This kind of financing of school districts existed at the time of the adoption of the Fourteenth Amendment. There is no invidious gerrymandering; hence, there is no lack of equal protection. There is a rational basis for this system.

Result: In reversing the district court, Lewis Powell, on behalf of a 5–4 majority, reaffirmed that wealth was not a suspect classification and that education was not a fundamental right.[358] Powell

---

357. Powell was the chair of the Richmond school district from 1952 to 1961.

358. Powell argued that poverty was not a suspect classification because poor persons as a class had not suffered purposeful persecution or unequal treatment. Moreover, their status was not inherently an involuntary or immutable condition, and they were not a politically powerless or insular class.

While Powell recognized that education was important to the health of a democracy and supported the intelligent exercise of constitutional rights (among them free speech, press, and voting), this was not enough to justify classifying education as a fundamental right. Powell pointed out that education was no more important than food or shelter, neither of which have ever been categorized as fundamental rights.

claimed that he could not even find a definable class of poor people in this case, because many wealthy people lived in poor school districts and many poor people lived in wealthy school districts. Principles of federalism and comity, he said, dictated the use of less exacting scrutiny here. Using the rational basis test, Powell found a reasonable relationship between Texas's system of school financing and two legitimate state purposes: (1) to make sure that all students have their basic educational needs met; and (2) to permit flexibility, public participation, and local control over school financing.

The four dissenters, Douglas, Brennan, White, and Marshall, unsuccessfully sought to apply strict scrutiny to school funding on the grounds that education was a fundamental right and wealth was a suspect classification. They would have imposed a heavy burden on state governments to justify such grossly unequal treatment. Texas would have had to demonstrate that their system of school financing was necessary to achieve a compelling state interest and that there were no less restrictive alternatives.

A month after the Court's decision was announced, the New Jersey Supreme Court found that the use of property taxes imposed an intolerable burden on poor districts and ordered New Jersey officials to find a more equitable way to finance public education. By 1975, courts in California and Connecticut also ordered state officials to equalize public school financing. In short order, eleven other states passed new laws intended to reduce spending disparities between rich and poor school districts. Where the U.S. Supreme Court had been a progressive force in combating racial discrimination with Brown *and* Swann, *in this instance state courts and legislatures have led the way.*[359]

FAMILIES AND HOUSING

Village of Belle Terre v. Boraas, 416 U.S. 1 (1974)
(Brennan) (Douglas)

The Long Island village of Belle Terre sought to limit local housing to single-family dwellings. In defining "family," the town prohibited more than two unrelated persons from living together and banned all boardinghouses, fraternities, and multiple-dwelling houses. Edwin and Judith Dickman rented their home to six unrelated college students, including Bruce Boraas. All eight were cited for violating the town's housing ordinance. They claimed that the law violated their rights of equal protection, association, travel, and privacy. The district court upheld the ordinance, but the Second Circuit Court of Appeals reversed. Circuit Judge Mansfield ruled that it was irrational to exclude nonrelated groups in favor of conventional nuclear families.

BURGER: The non-family line is drawn at not more than two unrelated persons. Two is not logical, but neither is thirty-one. A line is O.K. if any state of facts can be imagined to justify it. In *Dandridge,* where basic human needs were at stake, we applied the rational-

---

359. This case marked a retreat from the Court's progressivism in American education. In a symbolic changing of the guard, Virginia school board patriarch Lewis Powell wrote the majority, while *Brown* veteran Thurgood Marshall brooded in dissent. Powell's opinion rekindled in Marshall his deep antipathy toward the white southern gentry, who covered up their racial preferences in the polite language of "local control" and "states' rights." Cooper, *Battles on the Bench,* 11–13; Kluger, *Simple Justice,* 770.

ity test in sustaining line drawing as to family units.[360] I can't distinguish this zoning from one that bars rooming houses or fraternity houses. There is no right to travel here. The same rights are denied to long-time residents as well as transients. Permanent residents are entitled to preserving the kind of community that they want. I reverse.

DOUGLAS: I reverse. I agree with the Chief Justice.

BRENNAN: Land use restriction is behind these zoning laws. That was *Euclid.*[361] Density control has involved acreage limitations, and square foot requirements for the ground floor. This act chooses a limitation turning on the number of people and their relationship. *Euclid* was prior to our right of association cases. That is the question raised here. The test is whether there is a compelling state interest. There are other ways of taking care of traffic, car parking, noise, and so forth. It can't be on a moral basis, because there is an exception for two people who are unmarried. The village has not met the test of showing a "compelling interest." I affirm.

STEWART: I am unable to discern a protected constitutional liberty asserted by the respondents. I don't see any right of association here. Therefore, it's an equal protection claim and a rational basis case. No right to travel is involved. If rights of association were involved, what of a Moose Lodge or a fraternity? A fraternity of fifty students could move in. To upset this zoning ordinance would upset hundreds of similar ordinances across the land. I reverse.

WHITE: I reverse.

MARSHALL: I affirm on one ground only—the right of association.

WHITE: I reverse. The *Younger* point is here.[362] It applies if a state proceeding came along during the federal case.

---

360. *Dandridge v. Williams,* 397 U.S. 471 (1970). *Dandridge* involved the federal Aid to Families with Dependent Children (AFDC) program. Maryland sought to cap AFDC benefits at $250 per month, regardless of a family's size or actual needs. Welfare recipients with large families sued, claiming that the state law violated the intent of the federal Social Security Act and also violated large families' equal protection rights. On a 5–4 vote, the Court applied the rational basis test and upheld the state law. The majority found that the law furthered the state's legitimate interests to allocate scarce resources to encourage employment and to ensure that welfare recipients did not enjoy a higher standard of living than the working poor.

361. This case recognized the use of zoning laws as an instrument of state police powers and established that local zoning decisions were constitutionally permissible unless they were "clearly arbitrary and unreasonable, having no substantial relation to the public health, safety, morals, or general welfare." *Euclid v. Ambler Realty Co.,* 272 U.S. 365, 395 (1926).

362. *Younger v. Harris,* 401 U.S. 37 (1971), held that federal courts should intervene in ongoing state criminal prosecutions only under extraordinary circumstances. Hugo Black, writing for the Court, expressed a strong preference for permitting state courts to try cases free from interference by federal courts, at least where the parties have an adequate remedy at law and will not suffer irreparable harm without federal relief. This doctrine was reinforced by federal notions of comity, accommodation, and respect for state governments. Under most circumstances, Black wrote, it was better to let states function in their own way, with minimal interference from the federal government. Federal sensitivity and restraint reinforces the essential federal nature of our government, reducing the potential for conflict and avoiding unnecessary duplication of effort.

BLACKMUN: No mootness, no right to travel, no concepts of morality.[363] The preservation of family enclaves is a legislative zoning objective. I am troubled about the standards that we apply in equal protection cases, since the selection of a standard too often determines the result of the case. I am offended by the "rationality" test. I would articulate a middle-tier approach. My test for equal protection is (1) whether it is reasonably and rationally related to the achievement of legitimate ends; and (2) that the classification contributes substantially to the achievement of the state's purpose. On that, I would reverse.

POWELL: I do not agree with the "compelling" state interest test. Personally, I would not go back to *McGowan* on equal protection—I would dream up any reason.[364] I can't go even with Thurgood's sliding scale—it has no bearings or moorings. I would reverse. I would stick with precedents, but I question bringing things under a compelling state interest. But for me, residential zoning is the guts of zoning, and the family is the single most important unit. I won't denigrate it as the Second Circuit did. Affirmance would kill efforts to preserve family neighborhoods. The board can plan a neighborhood that prevents intrusion on children of fraternity houses, and so forth.

REHNQUIST: I reverse. *McGowan* is satisfied.

Result: In a 7–2 decision, the Court applied the rational basis test and upheld the ordinance as a valid local land-use regulation. The ordinance, Douglas wrote, was not aimed at transients or other discrete and cognizable classes, and there was no selective disparity or deprivation of a fundamental constitutional right. The law was a reasonable means to achieve a permissible government objective—preserving the town's traditional, family-oriented character. Brennan and Marshall dissented.

Moore v. City of East Cleveland, 431 U.S. 494 (1977)
(Brennan)

Inez Moore lived in East Cleveland with her two sons, John and Dale, and their two sons, John Jr. and Dale Jr. A city ordinance limited houses to single-family occupancy, which was defined in such a way that the Moores were not considered a single family.[365] Mrs. Moore ignored repeated warnings that she was violating the ordinance, and eventually she was cited. Violating the ordinance was a criminal offense, and Mrs. Moore was convicted and sentenced to five days in jail and a $125 fine. She appealed,

---

363. Because the students who were parties to the suit had all moved away, the village of Belle Terre argued that the case was moot.

364. *McGowan v. Maryland,* 366 U.S. 420 (1961), included Earl Warren's commonly cited definition of the "minimal scrutiny" test, also called the "old equal protection" test. The equal protection clause, Warren wrote, permitted states broad discretion to enact laws affecting some groups of citizens differently than others: "The constitutional safeguard is offended only if the classification rests on grounds wholly irrelevant to the achievement of the State's objective. . . . A statutory discrimination will not be set aside if any state of facts reasonably may be conceived to justify it."

365. The Moores violated the ordinance in two ways. First, the law allowed only one adult child to live in a parent's home. Second, while the ordinance would have allowed both grandchildren to stay if they were siblings, the two boys were cousins and under the terms of the ordinance only one would be permitted to stay.

claiming that the ordinance deprived her and her family of their constitutional rights of association, privacy, and equal protection. The city argued that its zoning regulations were rationally related to state interests in population density, traffic congestion, and school overcrowding. Ohio state courts all sided with the city.

BURGER: This case involves a grandmother, and two adult sons—now divorced—and two grandchildren. Association, privacy, and equal protection are constitutional premises. I can see no rational state purpose in this limitation, so we don't have to bother about anything other than that this is a family unit. There is a density ordinance that takes care of overcrowding.

STEWART: This ordinance followed the growth of the middle class. This was an all-white satellite of Cleveland when blacks took over. The purpose of this ordinance was to preserve the city's middle class status and prevent ghettoizing.[366] Since there is a constitutional power to zone for single-family homes, they must also be able to define "family." And that's all this is. There is no constitutional merit to the association or privacy claims. There is only an equal protection possibility, and I don't see this definition of family as denying equal protection.

WHITE: This ordinance requires only our "rationality" scrutiny, and this definition passes muster.

MARSHALL: I don't accept Potter's emphasis on Negroes or emigrants from the ghetto. The purpose of this was to avoid slum areas, and that has been done by the density ordinance. I can't see any state interest in forcing the grandchildren out. The family unit is protected by the Constitution against being broken up.

BLACKMUN: *Belle Terre* and *Euclid* are distinguishable.[367] I start with the proposition that government has to have broad authority in passing density ordinances, etc. But this definition of family oversteps the line. *Boddie*, *Meyer*, and other cases show the significance of family.[368] Privacy is the best handle, I think, and it also fails on rationality.

---

366. This was not a conventional racial discrimination case. While the Moores were black, the government of East Cleveland was also predominantly black. The city had a black city manager and city commission. There was no explicit allegation of racial bias in the writing, enactment, or enforcement of the ordinance. Except for Brennan's concurring opinion (which Marshall joined), the other Justices either downplayed or ignored race as a factor in this case.

367. *Village of Belle Terre v. Boraas,* 416 U.S. 1 (1974); *Euclid v. Ambler Realty Co.,* 272 U.S. 365 (1926). These were—and arguably remain—the most important Supreme Court zoning cases. *Euclid* established that zoning ordinances deserved judicial deference and should be upheld so long as they have a rational relationship to a permissible state objective. *Belle Terre* reaffirmed and updated this doctrine of deference to local zoning decisions.

368. *Boddie v. Connecticut,* 401 U.S. 371 (1971), required the state to waive the $60 court fee for indigent couples who sought a divorce. John Marshall Harlan, writing for the majority, did not see a sufficient justification for the requirement and struck it down as a violation of due process. Justice Douglas concurred, but argued that the statute was a denial of equal protection, not due process.

In Meyer v. Nebraska, 262 U.S. 390 (1923), the Court essentially used a privacy argument when it struck down a state law prohibiting private schools from providing instruction in German and ruled that parents had a right to have their children instructed in a foreign language.

POWELL: I see no rational relationship between the asserted purpose and this unusual ordinance. The asserted traffic concerns and tax bases don't add up.

REHNQUIST: This ordinance shows that its purpose is to limit the city to single-family dwellings, and so it must define "family." There is nothing in the Constitution which bars their definition.

STEVENS: A zoning ordinance like this with a variance procedure strikes me as being O.K. Something smells about this case, but the legal question is only whether the city can have a single-family zoning ordinance. If so, they have to define it. I can't find any constitutional handle here except for substantive due process, and I won't go for that.

Result: In a plurality decision, Lewis Powell (joined by Brennan, Marshall, and Blackmun) struck down the city ordinance as a violation of liberty, privacy, and due process. Powell distinguished Belle Terre, *noting that the ordinance in that case specifically exempted relatives who were related by blood, marriage, or adoption. Powell also distinguished* Euclid. *When the government intrudes on family relationships, he wrote, the courts will not necessarily defer to local zoning decisions but will hold the government to a heightened standard of scrutiny. East Cleveland's ordinance impermissibly decided that some blood relatives would be allowed to live together while others would not. In this instance, the city sought to prevent a grandmother from living with her two grandsons—a result that at best had a tenuous relationship with the city's claimed objectives of avoiding crowding, traffic congestion, and easing the burden on local schools.*

John Paul Stevens changed his mind after the conference and concurred in the judgment. This gave Powell a court, if not a clear majority. Stevens argued that Euclid *was the proper standard but that the ordinance failed even that deferential test. In Stevens's judgment, the law was clearly arbitrary and unreasonable, and had no substantial relationship to public health, safety, morals, or the general welfare. There was no way to justify a rule that would allow grandsons who were brothers to live with their grandmother, but not two grandsons who were cousins.*

Brennan and Marshall were the only Justices to focus on racial issues, arguing in Brennan's concurring opinion that the Constitution did not allow "white suburbia" to impose its preference for nuclear families on black families, which often lived in extended family groups.

In dissent, Chief Justice Burger argued that Inez Moore had knowingly failed to exhaust her administrative remedies by refusing to ask for a zoning variance and that she should be barred from raising any constitutional issues in court. Stewart and Rehnquist argued that Belle Terre *governed the case and that there was no fundamental right of association at stake. Byron White, channeling the spirit of Hugo Black, warned that the majority advocated a slipshod and open-ended use of "liberty" which, he said, threatened to resurrect the discredited notion of substantive due process.*

CHAPTER 14

PRIVACY

Skinner v. Oklahoma, 316 U.S. 535 (1942)
(Murphy) (Douglas)

The Oklahoma Habitual Criminal Sterilization Act of 1935 permitted the involuntary sterilization of anyone who had been convicted of two or more felonies involving "moral turpitude." Before the law was passed, Jack T. Skinner had been convicted once in 1926 for stealing chickens and twice for armed robbery in 1929 and 1934. The state attorney general selected Skinner to test the new law, and in 1936 a jury was convened to determine whether Skinner's crimes justified sterilization. The jury thought that they did, and the state supreme court affirmed.

Certiorari Conference of April 11, 1942

STONE: The technical difficulty with this case is that there is a presumption of constitutionality. If we indulge in that, we have nothing to upset this. There is a *Harvard Law Review* article on this.[1] Whether there are any scientific authorities in support is not clear. Moronic minds are different. There is nothing to show that this man is not of normal mind. There are no statistics as to criminals. If they do not reproduce their criminal kind, and his civil rights are involved, then we have a serious question and he is entitled to hearing. Civil rights are involved, and if this man has a right to the protection of these civil rights then he has a right to be heard. The state should have to defend its statute. I would set this down for argument and issue a stay. This is not cruel and inhuman punishment. This is eugenic legislation.

ROBERTS: This is a eugenic law, and we are bound to give credence to what the legislature did. He comes up here and says that it is a penal statute and we deal.

FRANKFURTER: I would invalidate this law on §24. It does offend equal protection.

Conference of May 7, 1942

STONE: I will not apply the ordinary presumption in a field where I know that the legislature knows nothing. I do not like the equal protection point, although I will go along with it.

ROBERTS: I would go on the equal protection clause.

---

1. Thayer, "The Origin and Scope of the American Doctrine of Constitutional Law." Thayer's article helped to discredit the doctrine of substantive due process and advocated judicial deference to legislative judgments. Louis Brandeis and others later used Thayer's arguments to shift the burden of proof from the government to those who challenged the constitutionality of state or federal legislation.

Result: A unanimous Court struck down the state law on equal protection grounds. Skinner was aided by the fact that the Nazis had made eugenics less popular than it was at the time of the Court's first sterilization case in Buck v. Bell.[2] *The law violated equal protection, Douglas wrote for the majority, because there were too many inequities involved. Habitual larcenists were subject to sterilization, for example, but habitual embezzlers were not. Douglas tied his decision to the idea that the law would deprive individuals of "one of the basic civil rights of man"—to marry and procreate. This case was the first to hold that strict judicial scrutiny would be applied in equal protection cases dealing with fundamental rights and invidious discrimination. The case revived the equal protection clause (which Holmes once contemptuously called "the usual last resort of constitutional arguments"), which became a touchstone for the Court's landmark privacy decisions in the 1960s and 1970s.*

In an opinion that occasionally reads more like an argument against capital punishment, Douglas criticized the subtle, far-reaching, and devastating effects of the law: "There is no redemption for the individual whom the law touches. . . . He is forever deprived of a basic liberty." Douglas emphasized the need for strict judicial scrutiny, "lest unwittingly or otherwise, invidious discriminations are made against groups or types of individuals in violation of the constitutional guaranty of just and equal laws."

Harlan Fiske Stone, in his concurring opinion, advocated resting the decision on the due process clause. He wanted a narrower decision, because he thought that sterilization could legitimately be used in some cases to prevent the transmission of "socially injurious tendencies."

Robert Jackson also concurred, but from the opposite direction. Jackson, who later prosecuted Nazi war criminals at Nuremberg, thought that Douglas did not go far enough to stop all eugenic experiments, which invariably were conducted "at the expense of the dignity and personality and natural powers of a minority—even those who have been guilty of what the majority defines as a crime."

Tileston v. Ullman, 318 U.S. 44 (1943)
(Murphy) (Douglas)

Connecticut law proscribed the use of contraceptives and prohibited anyone from providing advice or counseling about contraceptives. The law was originally part of an 1879 obscenity statute, which was revised and reenacted as two separate statutes in 1930. Subsequent bills to revoke the laws failed to pass the state legislature. Wilder Tileston, a licensed physician, sought a declaratory judgment that the laws could not be used to prosecute doctors. Dr. Tileston claimed that married women had the right to consult with their doctors and to obtain advice and contraceptives when their health was at risk. He represented three patients, all married women whose health would be at risk if they became pregnant. One had high blood pressure, another had severe tuberculosis, and the third had carried to term three pregnancies in twenty-seven months and allegedly ran a serious health risk if she conceived again too quickly. The Connecticut Supreme Court of Errors ruled that the state ban on contraceptives was constitutional and that there was no exception for medical doctors. Abraham S. Ullman was the Connecticut state attorney.

---

2. *Buck v. Bell,* 274 U.S. 200 (1927), involved the forced sterilization of eighteen-year-old Carrie Buck under a Virginia law intended to prevent the transmission of insanity, idiocy, imbecility, epilepsy, or crime. Carrie and her mother were both state mental patients, and Carrie had just given birth to an illegitimate child. J. H. Bell was the superintendent of the Colony for Epileptics and Feeble Minded. In a brief three-page opinion upholding the law, Oliver Wendell Holmes came to the notorious conclusion that "three generations of imbeciles are enough."

Conference of January 16, 1943

STONE: The state of Connecticut has two statutes to prohibit contraception. The courts in the other case declined to say what they would do when a life was involved, and that explains this case.[3] The petitioner omitted to set up any injury to his own property or his practice or his equitable right to practice his profession. Only the right to "life" under the Fourteenth Amendment was alleged. He need not have limited his constitutional claim in this way, but he did. So the case comes here limited to the claim that this statute is an infringement on the Constitution in that it prevents him from saving life. His own life is not in danger.

This is an action for a declaratory judgment. To satisfy us, it must show a case or controversy under the federal Constitution. There has been close collaboration between the petitioner and defendant. We have nothing more in the way of facts than appear in the complaint. Everything is stipulated. It was alleged that the defendant "claims or may claim" that the plaintiff violates the act. I find a difficulty in saying there is a case in controversy, constitutionally speaking.

Can a doctor claim the protection of the Constitution over the life of his patient? On those grounds it seems to me that we have no case here. Not jurisdiction in a technical sense, but a lack of interest of the plaintiff to maintain the suit. This case ought to be dismissed per curiam. In *Wallace v. Louisville R.R. Co.*[*sic*] aspects of this case were dismissed.[4] We take cases only where there is a case or controversy, as defined in Constitution, though a state may hold differently under their declaratory judgment procedures.

Do we have a cause of action in equity, the court below having held that no question of his own life was involved? The physician could not prosecute a case of equity on behalf of his patients. They could not issue an injunction on those grounds.

ROBERTS: He has not raised a constitutional question.

BLACK: I am inclined to go along on the proposition that he didn't have a case for relief.

REED: The thing here is that he hasn't any standing in any controversy. And there isn't any case or controversy here.

---

3. *State of Connecticut v. Nelson*, 11 A. 2d 856 (1940). This was the only recorded prosecution under Connecticut's anticontraception laws. Two doctors and a nurse (Roger Nelson, William Goodrich, and Clara McTernan) were charged with dispensing contraceptives. The state supreme court refused to invalidate the laws, but charges against all three defendants were eventually dropped. It remained unanswered whether the statute could be used to punish women who needed contraceptives for health reasons or health care professionals who provided patients with contraceptive information and devices.

4. *Nashville, C. and St. L. Ry. Co. v. Wallace*, 288 U.S. 249 (1933). The plaintiff railroad company brought gasoline into Tennessee from out of state and stored it for later use on its interstate trains. Tennessee sought to impose an excise tax on the gasoline, and the railroad sought a declaratory judgment that the tax was an invalid interference with interstate commerce. The Court ruled that its ability to issue a declaratory judgment depended on the nature and substance of the plaintiff's claims as well as the likely effects of a judgment on the plaintiff's claimed rights. All cases must meet Article 3's "case or controversy" requirement and maintain the essential qualities of adversarial proceedings involving a real—not a hypothetical—controversy. In this case, the Court accepted jurisdiction and ruled that when the company unloaded the gasoline from the interstate conveyance and stored it for later use, the gasoline ceased to be a subject of interstate commerce and lost its immunity from state taxation.

FRANKFURTER: My views are the other way around. As matter of equity, I could find it adequate. As to the constitutional questions, I think that it is our duty to side-step or not raise such issues when there is no controversy before us.

Result: In a per curiam decision, the Court ruled that Tileston did not have standing to assert the constitutional claims or rights of his patients, absent any claim that his own constitutional liberty or property rights were at stake. The Justices avoided deciding whether the suit otherwise would have met Article 3's case or controversy requirement.

Poe v. Ullman, 367 U.S. 497 (1961)
(Douglas) (Brennan)

Two married couples and Dr. Charles Lee Buxton of the Yale Medical School asked the courts to declare unconstitutional the same Connecticut birth control law challenged in Tileston v. Ullman. *The plaintiffs claimed that the law violated the due process clause of the Fourteenth Amendment. The statute had been on the books since 1879, but there had been only one known prosecution and the charges in that case were dropped.[5]*

The threshold issue for the conference was whether to dismiss the case on procedural grounds or decide the case on the merits. John Marshall Harlan briefly articulated his theory of privacy, and Felix Frankfurter made another reference to Louis Brandeis.

Conference of March 3, 1961

WARREN: I don't see how we could declare this law unconstitutional on its face. If we did, it would be a return to substantive due process. As applied, however, it seemed to me that they had or could have pleaded a cause of action. But it seems to me now that they have made us guinea pigs for an abstract principle. The 1879 law was never enforced. There is no indication that it is going to be enforced. It looks like a contrived case, and I don't want to decide a contrived litigation. You can buy contraceptives in any drug store and make them for a doctor. There is no case or controversy. Could a doctor be convicted when he actively participated in a violation? I think perhaps not. In *Ullman,* the woman had used the contraceptive. If we are going to decide this case, we should have a record. Nothing is here by demurrer. Medical opinion was not sifted by any court below. I am not impressed by the unanimity of medical opinion. Moreover, the Connecticut court has not decided a number of questions: (1) Can a doctor be convicted without any proof of use by a patient? (2) Is the sale of contraceptives permissible? We don't have a proper record here on which to decide the constitutional questions. Whether this act is unconstitutional as applied can be determined only after a trial and findings. I would therefore send it back.

BLACK: I voted earlier to affirm on the basis of the record. I would still vote to affirm in the two cases of the patients. The *Ullman* case was right on the facts found there. It is not our province to inquire and vote on which is the better method. On the doctor's case, however, I feel differently. They argued that we must accept the meaning of the Con-

---

5. *State v. Nelson,* 11 A. 2d 856 (1940).

necticut law to be that mere advice violates the statute. Yet a doctor is entitled to talk to his patients under the First Amendment.

Personally I don't think that it makes any difference whether the devices were used or not. Do courts have the right under the due process clause to hear evidence to determine how good or bad this legislation was? I never thought so, and don't think so now. Courts have no business taking evidence on whether a law is wise or reasonable. There is no expressed barrier to this law so far as patients are concerned. And I don't think that you can get the doctor as an aider and abetter, for he is protected by the First Amendment. There is not much controversy between the state and the patients. I would affirm as far as the ladies are concerned, although I would not object to a remand as to them.

FRANKFURTER: I agree with the Chief Justice. To Hugo Black, due process in the Fourteenth Amendment excludes everything not in the first eight amendments. Even if it is justiciable, there is room for a determination because of what is involved in constitutional interpretation, and whether there is sufficient cause on the record before it to make a constitutional decision. The existence of jurisdiction does not necessarily imply a duty or requirement to exercise it. This is a raw, naked, declaratory suit, and equitable discretion exists to take it or not. We should exercise our discretion not to hear a case on the pleadings. Look at *McAdory*.[6] Brandeis was opposed to declaratory judgments because he thought that it would be used to get advisory opinions. There is always a danger of advisory constitutional judgments.

You can't prove the Connecticut offense, for the husband and wife can't testify against each other. You can't be an aider or abettor if there is no crime. I can't imagine a doctor not giving advice for fear of going to jail. They want hygienic stations. They should take the risk of going to jail and then bring the case of actual prosecution up here. We have no Connecticut law that says a doctor can't do this. My idea of due process is that a legislative act purportedly adopted for health reasons can be challenged on ground of no rational relation to heath. How can we decide that the "rhythm" method is no good? I would dismiss all three cases.

DOUGLAS: The case and controversy are here, and I would not dismiss. I think that this is a legitimate use of declaratory judgment. It has been used enough to get rid of issues. But on the merits, I would hold this act unconstitutional on its face.

CLARK: There is no case or controversy, and I would dismiss.

HARLAN: I think that we have no business dismissing these cases. This is an appeal, not a cert. This is not a fictitious suit. We can't say that this is a feigned business. There is a case or controversy and there is a final adjudication, as I see it, in Connecticut. They found the act constitutional on its face, and the court also interpreted the act as to the doctor.

I assume that people want to obey the law and not violate it. There is no room for fuzziness or debate as to the women—they act on the doctor's advice. I think that this act is unconstitutional on its face—it is the most egregiously unconstitutional act that I have seen since being on the Court.

---

6. *Alabama State Federation of Labor v. McAdory*, 325 U.S. 450 (1945).

I could not strike this law down under the First Amendment as applied to states. The argument submerged the real constitutional question. The due process clause has substantive content for me, apart from incorporation of the first eight Amendments. Due process protects the right to be let alone.

Despite having broad powers to legislate in the area of health, there are limits to the states' police powers. A state may not use any means for regulating marriage relations. This is a "use" statute—it is unique in that respect. Other statutes are sale or prescription laws, which would raise a different question. How to look at a statute as a "use" statute, as distinguished from advice statutes in this field? Nothing is more offensive to the concept of our right to be let alone than putting the criminal law into the privacy of the marriage relation. This is more offensive to the right to be let alone than anything else possible could be. A police officer can't get a search warrant to see if contraceptives can be found. All other searches pale in comparison to those permissible under this act. No matter what kind of a record we might have, this law is bad. If they have the constitutional power to regulate the "use" of contraceptives, then they have broad leeway and I could not say that it was harsh to apply. But since I feel that this act is unconstitutional on its face, I would not dismiss but turn to the merits.

BRENNAN: There is no case or controversy.

WHITTAKER: There is no case or controversy.

STEWART: It is cynical for us to dismiss a case on the ground that a law will not be enforced. A law is a law. It is not a dead letter when as a practical matter there is no clinic in Connecticut. On the merits, I agree with John Harlan.

Result: A badly divided Court dismissed the case without reaching the merits. Felix Frankfurter, writing for a plurality of four Justices, maintained that the case was not ripe because there was no immediate threat of prosecution or other adverse government action.[7] William Brennan concurred in the result, providing the fifth vote to dismiss.

Hugo Black voted to decide the case on the merits, but except for his privately expressed remarks in conference he did not publicly reveal his views on the substantive issues. Douglas, Harlan, and Stewart voted to reach the merits and strike down the Connecticut law. They noted that there had already been one prosecution under the law and there was a clear and present danger of additional prosecutions. They saw no need to require people to risk prosecution and punishment merely to test the constitutionality of the law—this was precisely what declaratory judgments were for. The dissenters criticized Frankfurter's opinion as cynical and disturbing, noting that it was unprecedented for a Supreme Court Justice to encourage Americans to flout the law.

---

7. Before the conference met, Frankfurter called Waterbury, Connecticut, prosecutor Bill Fitzgerald to discuss his affidavit that any person who violated the law "must expect to be prosecuted and punished." Their conversation confirmed Frankfurter's view that Fitzgerald was bluffing and that there was no real threat of prosecution. Devins, "Law and Equality," 1439.

Griswold v. Connecticut, 381 U.S. 479 (1965)
(Douglas) (Brennan)

Three years after the Court ducked the merits of Connecticut's contraception statute in Poe v. Ullman, *Estelle Griswold, the executive director of the Planned Parenthood League of Connecticut, and Dr. Charles Lee Buxton, now the organization's medical director, opened a birth control clinic in New Haven. In a planned test case, Griswold and Buxton invited arrest and were charged with giving married couples information on birth control and prescribing contraceptives. Both were convicted, and the Connecticut Supreme Court of Errors affirmed. This time, all nine Justices voted to grant certiorari and agreed to decide the case on the merits.*

Conference of April 2, 1965

WARREN: I am bothered with this case. The Connecticut legislature may repeal the law. The petitioners have standing as aiders and abettors. I can't say that this affects the First Amendment rights of doctors, and I can't say that the state has no legitimate interest in the field (can't apply to abortion laws). I can't balance, use equal protection, or use a "shocking" due process standard.[8] I can't accept a privacy argument. I might rest on *Yick Wo*, on the theory that there is no prohibition on sales and they don't go after doctors as such, but only clinics.[9] I prefer to hold that since the act affects rights of association, it must be carefully and narrowly drawn. Basic rights are involved here—we are dealing with a most confidential association, the most intimate in our life. This act is too loosely drawn—it has to be clear-cut and it isn't. I am inclined to reverse.

BLACK: I can't reverse on any ground. Only one of two possible grounds are conceivable for me—the doctors' First Amendment rights. The right of association is for me the right of assembly, and the right of a husband and wife to assemble in bed is a new right of assembly to me. I have a hard time saying that it is ambiguous enough to apply our overbreadth doctrine, which for me is only applicable where the First Amendment is involved. I would not extend *Cantwell* beyond the First Amendment.[10] The act is pretty clear and carefully drawn—it is not ambiguous. So I can't find why it isn't within the state's power to enact. If I can be shown that it is too vague on due process grounds, I can join it.[11] I might be seduced by a *Cantwell* approach, although I am not at rest on it. I am against the policy of the act.

---

8. This is a reference to Felix Frankfurter's use of the due process clause to exclude evidence gathered by means that shocked the collective conscience of the Court. Warren's reference might have been said partly in jest, because he was not a fan of Frankfurter's due process test. Ironically, Warren eventually joined Golberg's opinion using the Ninth Amendment to strike down the Connecticut birth control law on the ground that the "forgotten Amendment" allowed judges to look at the traditions and "collective conscience of the people" to determine fundamental rights—and marriage was one such right. In effect, Goldberg adapted Frankfurter's due process test and read it into the Ninth Amendment.

9. *Yick Wo v. Hopkins,* 118 U.S. 356 (1886). In *Yick Wo*, a facially neutral law was applied in a selective and discriminatory way. Warren thought that Connecticut's anticontraceptives law was also being selectively enforced.

10. *Cantwell v. Connecticut,* 310 U.S. 296 (1940).

11. Black believed that the due process clause incorporated the first eight amendments of the Bill of Rights. He thought that the alternative approaches being floated here threatened to create an open-ended

DOUGLAS: The right of association is more than the right of assembly. It is a right to join with and associate with—the right to send a child to a religious school is on the periphery. *Pierce* is such a case. We have said that the right to travel is in the radiation of the 1st Amendment, and so is the right of association. Nothing is more personal than this relationship, and if on the periphery it is still within First Amendment protection. I reverse.

CLARK: I reverse. I agree with Bill Douglas. There is a right to marry, to have a home, and to have children.

BLACK: A state can abolish marriage.

CLARK: This is an area where I have the right to be left alone. I prefer that ground for reversal.

HARLAN: [DOUGLAS: He restates his position in *Poe v. Ullman*—he relies on due process and reverses.] I would have difficulty if this were not a "use" act and if not applied to married couples.

BRENNAN: I reverse. [DOUGLAS: He continues the Chief Justice's, Clark's, and Douglas's views.] I would bring the realm of privacy in. I do not reach the act that applies only to unmarried people.

STEWART: There is nothing in the Bill of Rights that touches this. I can't find anything in the First, Second, Fourth, Fifth, Ninth, or other amendments, so I would have to affirm. The key to the petitioners' relief is in the Connecticut legislature. I affirm.

WHITE: I reverse.

GOLDBERG: I reverse. You may regulate this relationship and the state cannot. There is no *compelling* state reason in that circumstance to justify the statute. I rely on *Meyer v. Nebraska*,[12] *Schware v. Board*,[13] and *Pierce v. Sisters*.[14] These are all related to First Amend-

---

mandate for judges to create—or restrict—other rights. As Black complained in his dissent in *Griswold*, this course of action would allow judges to define or create new rights at will, transforming the Justices into "a bevy of Platonic Guardians"—a prospect that Black, like Learned Hand before him, found "irksome."

12. *Meyer v. Nebraska*, 262 U.S. 390 (1923). A Nebraska state law made it a crime to teach any modern language other than English to a child who had not completed the eighth grade. Robert T. Meyer, an instructor at Zion Parochial School in Nebraska, was tried and convicted of unlawfully teaching German to Raymond Parpart, a ten-year-old boy. Meyer was fined $25, which he refused to pay. The Supreme Court, in a James McReynolds opinion, struck down the law as a violation of liberty rights guaranteed by the Fourteenth Amendment.

13. *Schware v. Board of Bar Examiners of New Mexico*, 353 U.S. 232 (1957). In 1953, the New Mexico bar refused to allow Rudolph Schware to take the state bar examination on the ground that he was not of sound moral character. The Board of Bar Examiners cited Schware's former Communist party membership from 1933 to 1937, several previous arrests prior to 1940, and Schware's use of several aliases between 1933 and 1937. The Supreme Court ruled 5–3 that the state's actions were unreasonable and violated Schware's due process rights. Hugo Black, writing for the majority, ruled that there was no rational basis for finding that Schware had failed to meet the state's character requirements and that the state's actions amounted to invidious discrimination. Frankfurter, Clark, and Harlan concurred in part, agreeing that Schware's communist affiliations—which ended sixteen years before he applied to take the bar examination—were not sufficient to make him a person of questionable character. Whittaker did not participate in the decision.

14. *Pierce v. Society of Sisters*, 268 U.S. 510 (1925). Discussed in chapter 11.

ment rights—assembly—as we said in *Aptheker*.[15] If one can form a club, he can join his wife and live with her as he likes.

Memorandum from Byron White to Bill Douglas

Bill—

Re: *Griswold v. Connecticut*

Any one of the following dispositions would be wholly justified, wouldn't you [agree]?

(1) The Fourth Amendment—because the Connecticut law would authorize a search for the intra-uterine coil.

(2) *Escobedo* and the right to counsel—from a doctor.[16]

(3) *Robinson v. California*—since there is an obvious addiction to sex involved and it is cruel and unusual punishment to deprive one of it or to permit it only at the cost of having children. A grizzly [*sic*] choice.[17]

(4) *Reynolds v. Sims*—one man, one child.[18]

—Byron

Result: The Court ruled 3–4–2 that the state law violated the constitutional right of marital privacy. The majority could not agree, however, on the precise source and nature of this right. Earl Warren assigned the opinion to Douglas, who initially sought to tie the case to the First Amendment. Brennan suggested the Ninth Amendment instead, and Douglas went even further to include the First, Third, Fourth, Fifth, and Ninth Amendments, along with the "penumbras formed by emanations from those guarantees."[19] In concurring opinions, Goldberg and Warren advocated a broad interpretation of the Ninth Amendment to strike down the state law, while White and Harlan relied on natural law principles and substantive due process to reach the same result.

In dissent, Black and Stewart rejected all of the proposed privacy theories as constitutional nonsense. Douglas's majority opinion created a fanciful new constitutional right out of thin air, and Goldberg's, White's, and Harlan's alternatives were no better. As a constitutional doctrine, Black argued, the "right" of privacy was so vague and standardless that it could be infinitely expanded or restricted at will. He warned that Douglas's opinion would inevitably imperil rather than strengthen

---

15. *Aptheker v. Secretary of State*, 378 U.S. 500 (1964).

16. *Escobedo v. Illinois*, 387 U.S. 478 (1964).

17. *Robinson v. California*, 370 U.S. 660 (1962).

18. *Reynolds v. Sims*, 377 U.S. 533 (1964). This was a landmark reapportionment case. Modeling its bicameral legislature on Congress, Alabama sought to reapportion its house of representatives according to population, while the state senate was intended to represent counties. The Supreme Court emphatically rejected the plan on the ground that the equal protection clause required *both* houses to be apportioned substantially on a one-person-one-vote basis. Congress, Earl Warren wrote, was an inappropriate model for state governments because it represented unique historical circumstances and reflected a necessary compromise among thirteen formerly sovereign states.

19. Douglas published an early version of his theory of privacy in *The Right of the People* (1958). Douglas relied both on constitutional and natural law theories to advance his argument, finding a constitutional right to privacy in the First, Fourth and Fifth Amendments, as well as in "the penumbra of the Bill of Rights." These defined and protected basic human rights were not necessarily explicit but were "implied from the very nature of man as a child of God."

the explicit individual liberties enumerated in the Bill of Rights. Black called his dissent the most difficult opinion he ever wrote. The law was "viciously evil," but no matter how hard he tried he could not read a right of privacy into the Constitution. "I like my privacy as well as the next one," he wrote, "but I am nevertheless compelled to admit that government has a right to invade it unless prohibited by some specific constitutional provision."

Douglas did not use any of Byron White's mock "dispositions" in his opinion. More than twenty years later, however, Justice Powell earnestly resurrected White's whimsical Robinson *theory during the Court's 1986 conference discussion of homosexual behavior in* Bowers v. Hardwick, *which is reported below.*

Eisenstadt v. Baird, 405 U.S. 438 (1972)
(Douglas)

William Baird gave a lecture on contraceptives at Boston University, at which he invited students and faculty to take free samples of contraceptives. One woman took some contraceptive foam, which violated a Massachusetts law that prohibited dispensing contraceptives to unmarried persons and required that contraceptives for married persons be dispensed by a licensed physician or pharmacist. Baird, who was not a doctor or a pharmacist, was convicted of a felony and the Massachusetts Supreme Judicial Council affirmed. Baird filed for a writ of habeas corpus in federal court. The district court refused to issue a writ, but the court of appeals reversed, citing Griswold v. Connecticut.[20]

The state appealed to a short-handed, seven-person Court. After suffering a severe stroke, Hugo Black resigned on September 17, 1971, and died just eight days later. John Marshall Harlan was disabled by spinal cancer during the summer of 1971. He resigned on September 23, 1971, and died on December 29. Their replacements, Lewis Powell and William Rehnquist, were not confirmed in time to participate. Thomas Eisenstadt was the sheriff of Suffolk County.

Conference of November 19, 1971

BURGER: The matter is in the medicinal field, and the state can select the person to dispense the matter. I would sustain a statute that would say that you can't sell contraceptives except in a licensed store. The defendant is not a doctor.

DOUGLAS: I affirm on the First Amendment. This was not covered by *Roth.*[21]

BRENNAN: I can't go on that ground. The man did more than talk—he handed out a device—and *O'Brien* permits prosecution for that.[22] The court of appeals said that the act was unconstitutional. I affirm and follow the court of appeals—this is in the penumbra of *Griswold.*

STEWART: It looks like substantive due process. This is completely irrational—the health issue is phony, for it is as injurious to marrieds as to unmarrieds. The moral issue is phony—you are punishing the wrong person—any unborn children. Moreover, you are punishing fornication but not adultery. The defendant was convicted because he was not

---

20. *Griswold v. Connecticut,* 381 U.S. 479 (1965).
21. *Roth v. United States,* 354 U.S. 476 (1957).
22. *United States v. O'Brien,* 391 U.S. 367 (1968).

a doctor. Massachusetts has not persuaded me that this can only be prescribed by a doctor. I will go on *Griswold*.

WHITE: I would reverse, citing *Ferguson v. Scrupa* [*sic*].[23] The state can decide that bread can be sold only by a licensee—that is all there is to this case. Contraceptive devices are broadly related. There might be something to Tydings's argument on preemption.[24]

MARSHALL: I affirm.

BLACKMUN: I would like to affirm. There is no problem of standing—I stay clear of any standing issues. This is not a public health statute. I am bothered by the fact that a contraceptive device may be prescribed only by doctors.

WHITE: The state can sell this stuff or have it sold only through doctors. They can require a license to dispense, although they cannot distinguish between married and unmarried users.

BURGER: This is like cigarettes—a vendor's license is needed.

DOUGLAS: The state could control commercial operation—this was only free speech.

BURGER: I pass. I can't decide what the issue is.

Result: William Brennan, writing for a 4–2–1 majority, extended the right of privacy to apply to individuals rather than just to married couples. Brennan wrote, "If the right of privacy means anything, it is the right of the individual, married or single, to be free from unwarranted governmental intrusion into matters so fundamentally affecting a person as the decision whether to bear or beget a child." Douglas joined Brennan's opinion but claimed in a brief concurring opinion that the law also violated Baird's First Amendment rights. Byron White changed his mind after the conference and both he and Harry Blackmun concurred in the result without joining Brennan's opinion. The Chief Justice was the lone dissenter.

Roe v. Wade, 410 U.S. 113 (1973)
Doe v. Bolton, 410 U.S. 179 (1973)
(Douglas) (Brennan)

Jane Roe was pregnant, single, indigent, and wanted an abortion.[25] Because Texas prohibited all abortions except to save the mother's life, she could not obtain a legal abortion anywhere in the state. She

---

23. *Ferguson v. Skrupa,* 372 U.S. 726 (1963). Frank Skrupa was a Kansas "debt adjustor" who organized debtors' payments to specified creditors according to a negotiated plan. Under Kansas law, it was a misdemeanor for anyone but a practicing lawyer to be a debt adjustor. Skrupa, who was not a lawyer, sued Attorney General William Ferguson to enjoin enforcement of the statute on the ground that it violated the due process and equal protection clauses. The Supreme Court unanimously upheld the law. Hugo Black ruled that states had the power to protect its citizens from injurious commercial and business practices. Harlan concurred on the ground that the law was rationally related to a constitutionally permissible objective.

24. Former Senator Joseph D. Tydings (D-MD) argued the case for William Baird.

25. Jane Roe's real name was Norma McCorvey. McCorvey initially claimed that she had been raped. Many years later, she confessed that she had become pregnant as the result of a consensual affair she had in Florida while working as a ticket-seller for a circus freak show. She claimed that she had been raped because she thought that it would help her to get attention. Carl Rowan, *Dream Makers, Dream Breakers,* 323.

filed a lawsuit to challenge the state law along with three other parties: Dr. James H. Hallford, who had two state prosecutions pending against him for providing abortions, and a childless married couple who claimed that they would be injured if the wife became pregnant and could not obtain a legal abortion. Henry Wade was the Dallas County district attorney responsible for enforcing the state's abortion law.

A three-judge district court declared that the Texas statute was vague, overbroad, and violated the Ninth and Fourteenth Amendments, but refused to enjoin enforcement of the statute. The trial court dismissed the unmarried couple from the suit on the ground that their claim was remote and nonjusticiable.

In the Georgia case, under state law a woman could only obtain an abortion if in her doctor's judgment there was a danger to the life or health of the mother, if the fetus was likely to be born with a serious defect, or if the pregnancy resulted from rape. Georgia imposed four major procedural requirements before a woman could obtain a legal abortion: (1) she must be a Georgia resident; (2) the abortion must be performed in a hospital accredited by the Joint Commission on Accreditation of Hospitals (JCAH); (3) the abortion must be approved by the hospital staff abortion committee; and (4) the judgment of the attending physician must be independently confirmed by two other licensed physicians.

Mary Doe was pregnant woman who had been denied permission to seek a legal abortion.[26] Just twenty-two years old, Doe was pregnant for the fourth time by her estranged husband, a drifter with four prior convictions for various sex offenses. Doe told the hospital board that she would be unable to take care of another baby, but the board rejected her excuse. The district court struck down part of the Georgia law but left the procedural requirements intact.

Before the Supreme Court could hear the cases, Jane Roe gave birth to a baby boy and Mary Doe to a girl. Both children were placed for adoption.

At conference, the Justices first had to decide whether the live births made the cases moot and whether the doctor and the married couple in the Texas case had standing. Those attacking the statutes considered two possible grounds for reversal: vagueness and privacy. The vagueness argument was problematic because the Supreme Court had just upheld a broad anti-abortion statute the year before in United States v. Vuitch.[27] *As in* Eisenstadt v. Baird, *this was initially a short-handed Court of seven Justices. But some behind-the-scenes maneuvering changed all of that.*

---

26. Mary Doe's real name was Sandra Bensing Cano.

27. *United States v. Vuitch*, 402 U.S. 62 (1971), upheld Washington, D.C.'s abortion law, which outlawed all abortions except those necessary to preserve the mother's life or health. Milan Vuitch (a doctor) and Shirley Boyd (a nurse's aide) were prosecuted in two unrelated cases. District Court Judge Gerhardt Gesell invalidated the law on due process grounds, saying that the statute's "health" standard was impermissibly vague. The Supreme Court reversed. Hugo Black's majority opinion broadly defined the term "health" to include a woman's psychological condition as well as her physical well-being and placed the burden on the prosecution to prove that the abortion was not necessary to preserve the mother's life or health. Neither party raised any other constitutional issues. Black's opinion—at John Harlan's insistence—was silent on the question of whether there might be a constitutional right to an abortion. The day after the Court's decision was announced, the Justices quietly granted certiorari in *Roe v. Wade* and *Doe v. Bolton*.

Conference of December 16, 1971

Roe v. Wade

BURGER: Jane Roe is unmarried and pregnant. She does not claim health problems—she just doesn't want the baby. This is a class action. Another petitioner, the doctor, is under indictment. The married couple have no children, but might suffer if she had any. The district court dismissed the marrieds for lack of standing, but gave Jane Roe standing and a declaratory judgment holding the act unconstitutional. The doctor also got standing and declaratory relief. Injunctive relief was denied. As to the doctor, the act was held too vague. As to the doctor, the district court should have restrained itself. *Vuitch* disposes of his due process claim.[28] *Younger* forecloses the doctor's relief, and he has no standing on behalf of the women. As to the married couple, their interests are too speculative for standing. The unmarried girl, Jane Roe, has standing. She can't be prosecuted if the state gives her no remedy. Texas has no declaratory relief. Abstention would be dubious. On mootness, Jane Roe still has standing, although she gave birth. She still represents a class. There is no *Younger* problem as to Roe.[29] The declaratory judgment without an injunction is tantamount to a mere advisory opinion. So she is entitled to an injunction if the statute is unconstitutional. The balance here is between the state's interest in protecting fetal life and a woman's interest in not having children. Does an unmarried woman also represent married women? If so, what of a husband's interest where he won't consent? But I can't find the Texas statute unconstitutional, although it is certainly archaic and obsolete. There is nothing vague about it. Doctors in Texas perform abortions to protect the health of the mother. The law is not enforced as to rape and incest. Rule 23 and class are not treated by district court.[30]

DOUGLAS: The Texas abortion statute is unconstitutional. This is basically a medical and psychiatric problem. The law is vague and unclear. It gives a licensed physician no immunity for good faith abortions. There is no standard for doctors—the law is too vague at that level. This statute goes only part way. All parties have standing to get a declaration of rights, irrespective of injunctions. A declaratory judgment does not collide with *Younger*. I reverse.

BRENNAN: The Texas act does not allow an abortion ever for a twelve-year-old. Jane Roe has standing. The act is infirm. Perhaps she was raped. I am willing to say that the law is "vague." Declaratory relief is O.K. The doctor has standing. *Samuels* does not govern the case if the doctor's rights are derivative from Jane Roe's.[31] I would go beyond what the

---

28. *United States v. Vuitch*, 402 U.S. 62 (1971).

29. *Younger v. Harris*, 401 U.S. 37 (1971). The *Younger* abstention doctrine holds that federal courts will not enjoin pending state court prosecutions out of a sense of comity and respect for "Our Federalism."

30. Rule 23 of the Federal Rules of Civil Procedure established guidelines for class action suits.

31. *Samuels v. Mackell*, 401 U.S. 66 (1971). Queen's County District Attorney Thomas Mackell charged George Samuels with violating New York's criminal anarchy laws. Samuels filed a collateral suit in federal court seeking declaratory and injunctive relief. A three-judge district court upheld the state laws and dismissed Samuels's request for an injunction. The Supreme Court affirmed the lower court's refusal to issue an injunction on the ground that it was impermissible for a federal court to enjoin a pending state crimi-

district court did. I reverse. All parties have standing. I would reverse on standing and affirm in other aspects.

STEWART: Standing is not important. Issues of standing ought not confuse this if we agree that the unmarried girl has standing to get a judgment on the merits. She clearly has standing. The doctor has standing, but *Samuels* precludes this suit. The married couple probably has standing. The district court did not have to issue an injunction on the merits—it was not an error in not entering an injunction. I agree with Bill Douglas on the merits. I reverse.

WHITE: I agree with Potter on all of the preliminaries, but I take the other side on the merits. They want the right to get rid of a child apart from health reasons. They want us to say that women have this choice under the Ninth Amendment—a privacy argument. Does the state have the police power to protect a fetus that has life in it, as opposed to the desire of the mother? I am not at rest on the merits.

STEWART: The state can legislate in this field. They can require that only doctors can do this, they can decide that after a certain period of pregnancy that women can't have abortions, and so forth.

MARSHALL: I'll go along with Douglas and Brennan, but the time problem concerns me. I do not see what interest the state has in abortion in the early stages after conception, but why can't a state prohibit abortions after a certain stage? If a fetus comes out breathing and you kill it, it is murder. "Liberty" covers almost any right to have things done to your body. I would turn this on "liberty" under the Fourteenth Amendment as a constitutional base. I affirm.

BLACKMUN: On standing, Roe has it. It is then irrelevant whether the married couple or the doctor have it. *Samuels* bars the doctor. On the merits, can a state outlaw all abortions? If you accept fetal life, there is a strong argument that it can. If there is life from conception on, the state could ban all abortions unless the right of mother to life and health are opposed to the fetus. There are opposing interests—the right of the mother to life and mental and physical health, the right of parents in case of rape, by the state in case of incest. There is no absolute right to do what you will with your body. Jane Roe has Fourteenth Amendment rights here. This statute is a poor statute. It does not go as far as it should in some respects, and at the same time it also impinges too far on her Ninth Amendment rights. It is over-narrow. The Texas act does not go far enough to protect doctors. It impinges on Jane Roe's constitutional rights. I would affirm on the declaratory judgment. I could go so far as to grant an injunction. The Texas and Georgia laws are in good contrast. Georgia has a fine statute. The district court ruined the statute in Georgia.

---

nal proceeding, absent proof of great, immediate, and irreparable injury as a result of being prosecuted in the state courts (this would presumably have included bad-faith harassment or other similar injury). Hugo Black then ruled that the district court should *not* have decided the constitutional issue on the merits. The same principles that mandated restraint in issuing federal injunctions against state criminal proceedings also applied to federal declaratory judgments.

In *Roe v. Wade*, the Court eventually ruled that in Dr. Hallford's case, the district court had correctly refused injunctive relief but had erred in granting declaratory relief.

Conference of December 16, 1971

Doe v. Bolton

BURGER: We don't have to worry about standing if any one of the plaintiffs has standing. The district court said that only Mary Doe had standing. If she has standing, then relief can be granted to all. I think that there was standing as to the pregnant girl. She was twenty-seven weeks pregnant. I do not agree with this carving up of the statute by the three-judge court. The district court should have abstained. The state has a duty to protect fetal life at some stage, but we are not confronted with that question here.[32] No reasons were given for striking parts of the act. The district court made a poor statute out of a good statute. I would hold this act constitutional. It has more limitations than the Texas one.

DOUGLAS: This is a much better statute than Texas's. I don't know how this statute operates. Is it weighted on the side of only those who can afford this? What about the poor? I am inclined to remand to the district court for a hearing on whether in operation the system is discriminatory.

MARSHALL: In urban centers the scheme may work, but in rural areas there are no Negro doctors. I agree with Bill Douglas.

BRENNAN: The act may not cover all the situations where a doctor might order an abortion. The district court did not deal with Bill Douglas' problem or with the veto power that two doctors have over one. I would not reach the point that the Ninth Amendment right is absolute. The district court is right on (a) and (b), but I think that the rest is bad. I will affirm as far as it goes, and would go further to strike down the three-doctor thing as too restrictive.

STEWART: I agree with Bill Brennan.

WHITE: It is a hard case. The state can protect the unborn child.[33] This plaintiff had no problem getting the case reviewed. There is no burdensome procedure. The state has the power to declare abortions illegal. I think that the state has struck the right balance here, and I reverse.

MARSHALL: I affirm. I am in between Bill Douglas and Bill Brennan.

BLACKMUN: Medically, this statute is perfectly workable. The doctor has standing here, too. On procedure, the residence requirement does not bother me. The right to cross-examine the doctor is a spurious one. I see this kind of act operating well in a rural area of Minnesota. Some cases are borderline, and doctors like the security of a joint board. I would like to see an opinion that recognizes the opposing interest of fetal life and the mother's interest in health and happiness. This act strikes a balance that is good. Some of these boards operate without cost to the patient. I would be perfectly willing to paint some standards and remand for findings on Bill Douglas's points—does it operate to deny equal protection by discriminating against the poor? I am sympathetic to psychiatric people. We should try to provide standards.

---

32. Douglas's conference notes quote Burger as saying, "State has *right* to protect life at some stage" (emphasis added).

33. Douglas's notes quote White as saying "fetus" rather than "unborn child."

WHITE: Equal protection for those on medicare is a real issue, and I am willing to have a hearing. I am not sure, however, that equal protection is here.

[DOUGLAS: *In summary:* Douglas, Brennan, Stewart, and Marshall agreed that a state abortion law could require all abortions to be performed by a licensed physician, that a woman's psychological problems, as well as her health problems, must be considered and that some period must be prescribed protecting fetal life.][34]

Result: Blackmun's first draft opinion was a complete failure among the majority. Rather than striking down the Texas law on privacy grounds, Blackmun argued narrowly that the statute was too vague. A week later, he circulated his first draft in the Georgia case. While he did not go far enough to please Douglas, Brennan, Stewart, or Marshall, they were encouraged that Blackmun had at least faced the constitutional issues this time and had concluded that women had a limited constitutional right to decide for themselves whether or not to bear children.

---

34. Burger's vote at the first conference was ambiguous. Douglas assumed that Burger had voted to uphold both statutes, and that as the senior Justice voting with the majority, Douglas controlled the assignment. But when the next week's assignment list was circulated, Douglas found that Burger had assigned both abortion cases to Blackmun. Douglas was livid and wrote a memorandum on December 18, with copies to the other Justices: "Dear Chief: As respects your assignment in this case, my notes show there were four votes to hold parts of the Georgia Act unconstitutional. . . on equal protection. Those four were Bill Brennan, Potter Stewart, Thurgood Marshall, and me. There were three to sustain the law as written— you, Byron White, and Harry Blackmun. I would think, therefore, that to save future time and trouble, one of the four, rather than one of the three, should write the opinion."

Burger responded on December 20, saying that, "There were, literally, not enough columns to mark up an accurate reflection of the voting. . . . I therefore marked down no votes and said this was a case that would have to stand or fall on the writing, when it was done." Urofsky, *The Douglas Letters*, 181.

Douglas's own conference notes were ambiguous as to how Burger voted on the abortion cases. Brennan's notes, however, clearly indicated that Burger voted to uphold the Texas law, which should have left it to Douglas to assign the majority opinion. Harry Blackmun said that this sort of confusion "was unfortunately symptomatic of pervasive problems during the Burger Court era." Lazarus, *Closed Chambers*, 350.

Despite Douglas's protests, Blackmun kept the assignment. Douglas suspected that Burger was maneuvering to delay the case for a year until Lewis Powell and William Rehnquist could join the Court. Douglas threatened to publish a memorandum dissenting from any vote to delay. The memorandum charged the Chief Justice with deliberately violating the Court's policies on assigning opinions:

Russia once gave its Chief Justice two votes, but that was too strong even for the Russians. . . .

The Chief Justice represented the minority view in the Conference and forcefully urged his viewpoint on the issues. It was a seven-man Court that heard the cases and voted on them. Out of that seven there were four who took the opposed view. Hence, traditionally, the senior Justice in the majority would make the assignment. The cases were, however, assigned by the Chief Justice, an action no *Chief Justice* in my time would ever have taken. . . .

The main function of the Conference is to find what the consensus is. When that is known, it is only logical that the majority decide who their spokesman should be. . . .

When, however, the minority seeks to control the assignment, there is a destructive force at work in the Court. When a *Chief Justice* tries to bend the Court to his will by manipulating assignments, the integrity of the institution is imperiled. . . .

Urofsky, *The Douglas Letters*, 184–85. Brennan and Blackmun convinced Douglas not to publish, but a copy of the memorandum was leaked to the *Washington Post*. Douglas quickly wrote Burger to deny that he was the one who had leaked.

At that point, Chief Justice Warren Burger convinced Blackmun that the case should be reargued the following term, when the two new Nixon appointees would be able to participate. This maneuvering enraged several members of the majority—particularly Douglas, Brennan, and Stewart.[35] *In the end, however, neither the delay nor the addition of two new conservative Justices changed the outcome.*

Conference of October 13, 1972

Roe v. Wade & Doe v. Bolton

BURGER: The statute is bad in Texas. It is too restrictive, but I am not sure on whether it fails for vagueness. But a state cannot by criminal statute restrict abortions to save a life. I reverse. On the Georgia case, the act is much more complex. The state has a right to legislate in this area. Many operations are more serious than abortions. Is there a fetal life that is entitled to protection? In *Vuitch* we gave some standards. Fetal life is entitled to protection at some point.

DOUGLAS: I reverse on Texas. I agree with the Chief Justice. I also agree with Harry in his memo, modifying the three-judge court judgments.

BRENNAN: I am with Harry on his memo.

STEWART: I am in the same position as last term, but I think that a fetus should not be declared a person. The Connecticut and New York cases both dealt with it. A fetus is not a person, although that does not mean that a fetus has no right or can't be given them by the state. I cannot say that the Texas law is vague in light of *Vuitch*. I like John Newman's reasoning in his opinion for the three-judge court in the Connecticut case.[36] I cannot rest

---

35. Brennan sent Douglas the following note in June 1972:

Bill: I will be God-damned! At lunch today, Potter expressed his outrage at the high-handed way things are going, particularly the assumption that a single justice, if CJ, can order things his own way, and that he can hold up for months anything he chooses, even if the rest of us are ready to bring down 4–3, for example. He also told me he will not vote to overrule *Wade*, *Miranda*, etc. and resents CJ's confidence that he has Powell and Rehnquist in his pocket. Potter wants to make an issue of these things. Maybe fur will fly this afternoon.

—Bill [Brennan]

Douglas's response:

Bill: Potter just asked me as we came in if he could talk with me about the abortion cases—specifically he suggested that perhaps you, Thurgood, Harry, he and I ought to sit down and talk about them. I told him I was talking with you after the session—do you think we should ask him to join us?

—Bill [Douglas]

36. *Abele v. Markle*, 351 F. Supp. 224 (D.C. Conn. 1972), vacated as moot, 410 U.S. 951 (1973). District Judge John Newman wrote the opinion that Stewart admired. A 1972 Connecticut law banned all abortions except to save the mother's life. Janice Abele and others sued state Attorney General Arnold Markle for declaratory and injunctive relief. In striking down the law, Judge Newman noted that a woman's constitutional right to reproductive privacy had already been established by *Griswold v. Connecticut* and *Eisenstadt v. Baird* and that the state law in question did not merely regulate that right—it directly abridged it.

While tempted by Douglas's opinion in *Griswold*, which held that marital privacy was an absolute right, Newman felt bound to follow the majority of votes in *Griswold*, which seemed to adopt a more moderate position that states could abridge the right to privacy given a sufficiently compelling state interest. This test usually required a difficult balancing of interests. In abortion cases, however, asymmetrical interests

on the Ninth Amendment at all. This is a Fourteenth Amendment right, as John Harlan said in *Griswold*. Defining "person" is a constitutional question, not a theological one.

WHITE: What is a woman's right? It is in the Fourteenth Amendment. In Georgia, a woman has rights—life, liberty, and health are included. We should not hold that a fetus is a "person" for purposes of the Fourteenth Amendment. But this does not end the case. We have to weigh state interests against constitutional rights. Some state interests, whether constitutional or not, can override federal rights. Some federal rights are overridden by state laws—e.g., some First Amendment rights. I am not going to second guess state legislatures in striking the balance in favor of abortion laws.

On weighing the rights of the mother versus the fetus, there is an overbreadth problem in these cases. Would personal convenience of the mother be sufficient? I think not. Unless you can say that there is no conceivable reason that the state can refute, I don't see how we can strike these statutes down on their face. So these acts are not void on their faces. Why can't a state at least require, after a certain period of gestation, no abortion but only a caesarian operation for women who rest solely on convenience? No women in these cases assert an injury to life or health. I affirm in the Georgia case. On Texas, I pass. I would not go on vagueness in Texas.

MARSHALL: In Texas, a woman who aborts herself is in the clear. No doctor would perform an abortion when the case is an advanced one. I agree on the fetus point. I would reverse in Texas. I affirm in part in Georgia.

BLACKMUN: I stand by what I wrote last term. I have not changed from where I was last Spring. [DOUGLAS: He recites a Minneapolis paper saying our vote was 5–2 later term, with Burger putting the measure in for reargument.] I would prefer to make the Georgia case the lead case. I have revised both the Texas and Georgia opinions of last term. I stand by jurisdiction. The direct appeal is here, and there is standing both by the wife and by the doctors. The case is not moot. I want to put in the history of abortion. I rest on the Fourteenth, not the Ninth Amendment. There is a point where other interests are at stake, where the state can regulate.[37]

---

strongly favored women's constitutional rights. Based on his reading of the Constitution and precedent, Newman found that a fetus was not a person within the meaning of the Fourteenth Amendment. While the government could confer *statutory* rights upon a fetus, it did not have constitutional rights. This limited the state's ability to abridge the mother's *constitutional* rights in order to protect the fetus.

Newman acknowledged that there were widely divergent views over the essential nature of a fetus, from those who believed that it was a human being from the moment of conception to those who believed that a fetus became human only after live birth. To uphold a state law banning most abortions, he said, would impose one official view of life on those who had a constitutional right to base their private decisions upon a different philosophical view. The Bill of Rights and American law, Newman concluded, stood for the proposition that in the long run, patriotism, religion, and family life flourished better in an environment of individual liberty, free of state-imposed orthodoxy and regimentation of thought.

37. Powell asked Blackmun to change the starting point of state interest in regulating abortions from the end of the first trimester (Blackmun's original choice) to the point of viability. Blackmun then asked other members of the majority what they thought. Douglas favored the first trimester because he thought it was a more precise and enduring point of reference. Viability was less clear-cut, and Douglas was concerned that medical advances would eventually push back the point of viability, perhaps to the point of conception. Marshall supported viability. He thought that, as a practical matter, many women needed

I would hold invalid the requirement of JCAH approval. I would do away with the licensed hospital requirement, although states can have abortions performed in a licensed facility. The residence requirement goes too far. Requiring the approval of many doctors is bad. The Texas act is vague. Vagueness is not involved in Georgia. *Vuitch* can be reconciled. Texas, since last spring, has upheld the Texas act. I will demolish the Texas act, but I will make Georgia the leading opinion. If the Texas act falls, abortion laws in a majority of our states will fall. We might hold the mandate for awhile—I want to avoid complete disorganization.

POWELL: I am basically in accord with Harry's position, except that I am concerned about allowing doctors to rely on economic or other factors except as related to health. I think that Texas should be the lead case, and I would not go on vagueness grounds but on basic grounds.

BLACKMUN: I would be willing to bypass the vagueness issue and put the Texas and Georgia cases in that order.

REHNQUIST: I agree with Byron.

Result: In separate opinions by the same 7–2 vote, the Court struck down both the Texas and Georgia abortion laws. In Roe v. Wade, *the Justices ruled that only Jane Roe had standing to challenge the Texas abortion law. Notions of federalism and comity required Dr. Hallford to face pending state prosecutions before he could bring his case to the federal courts, while the damages claimed by the unmarried couple were too speculative to constitute a real case or controversy. On the merits, seven Justices found that the Texas law violated the due process clause of the Fourteenth Amendment and violated the mother's constitutional right of privacy. In* Doe v. Bolton, *the same majority ruled that the Georgia statute, including all of the procedural requirements, violated the Fourteenth Amendment. Georgia's attempt to limit access to abortion to Georgia residents also violated the privileges and immunities clause.*

In his majority opinion, Harry Blackmun presented a brief history of abortion laws and practices since antiquity and concluded that the criminalization of abortion came relatively late in history, during the mid-nineteenth century Victorian period. The Constitution, he said, protected fundamental rights implicit in the concept of ordered liberty, and the Court had already included the rights of marriage, procreation, contraception, and child rearing in that list of privacy rights. For Blackmun, these rights were rooted in the Fourteenth Amendment and possibly in the Ninth Amendment as well.

---

the extra time to confirm that they were pregnant and to decide what to do. Marshall also suggested that between the end of the first trimester and viability, Blackmun should limit the state's ability to restrict access to abortions to those regulations intended to protect women's health and safety. Blackmun adopted Marshall's suggestions and made them central tenets of his opinion. Tushnet, *Making Constitutional Law*, 7.

Despite all expectations to the contrary, medical technology has not yet pushed the point of viability back significantly since *Roe* was decided. In 1973, the point of viability was generally accepted to be twenty-eight weeks but as early as twenty-four weeks in some cases. Twenty-four weeks is now the rule rather than the exception, but it has proved to be a stubborn barrier and remains the effective limit of viability today.

The trick was to balance three competing interests: (1) the woman's (and her doctor's) right of privacy; (2) the state's interest in the health of the mother; and (3) the state's interest in the health of the fetus. Blackmun began by arguing that in the Anglo-American legal tradition, a fetus was not generally considered a "person." The same rule applied to the Fourteenth Amendment: for constitutional purposes, a fetus was not a person and did not have full constitutional protection. This did not mean, however, that the state had no interest in preserving and protecting the fetus as "the potentiality of human life."

At three points in a woman's pregnancy, the balance of these three competing interests shifted decisively: (1) From conception to end of the first trimester: Here, the right of the woman was nearly absolute, subject only to the unfettered medical judgment of her doctor. The state had no interest in the health of the woman or the fetus that could justify interfering with a woman's decision whether or not to abort her pregnancy. (2) The end of the first trimester to the point of fetus viability: During this stage of pregnancy, the health risks of abortion approached and perhaps surpassed the health risks posed by live birth. The state's interest in the health of the mother at this stage could justify reasonable regulations on abortion in the interest of maternal health. (3) The point of viability to natural live birth: *Here, the state had a compelling interest in both the life and health of both mother and fetus, and could regulate or perhaps even proscribe abortions, except when necessary to preserve the life or health of the mother.*[38]

The cases were announced on January 22, 1973, the same day that former President Lyndon Johnson died. As a result, Blackmun's opinion did not receive the full or immediate attention of the press. It took several days for the country to become aware of what the Court had done. While the initial reaction was slow in coming, the case has become the most controversial decision since Brown v. Board of Education.[39]

Not least among the surprises in this case was that three of the four Nixon appointees, Burger, Blackmun, and Powell, joined the majority to strike down the state abortion laws. Another unexpected result was that both Norma McCorvey and Sandra Cano later became pro-birth activists and joined Operation Rescue (a radical anti-abortion group), while the daughter Cano sought to abort and ultimately gave up for adoption became a pro-choice activist.[40]

Planned Parenthood of Central Missouri v. Danforth, 428 U.S. 52 (1976)
Danforth v. Planned Parenthood of Central Missouri
(Brennan)

Planned Parenthood challenged eight provisions of Missouri's abortion law, which (1) defined viability as "that stage of fetal development when the life of the unborn child may be continued indefinitely outside the womb by natural or artificial life-supportive systems" and required attending physicians

---

38. After *Vuitch*, "health" was generally accepted to include both the mother's physical and psychological well-being. This meant that even after viability there remained a relatively broad constitutional right to have an abortion to protect the mother's physical or mental health.

39. The Justices received thousands of angry letters protesting their decision. Southern Baptists organized a letter-writing campaign that resulted in over a thousand protest letters being sent to Hugo Black, who had been dead for sixteen months. Woodward and Armstrong, *The Brethren*, 283.

40. For an interesting and provocative account of the litigation from McCorvey's and Cano's perspectives, see McMunigal, "Of Causes and Clients: Two Tales of *Roe v. Wade*."

to certify that a fetus was not viable before performing any abortion not necessary to protect the life or health of the mother; (2) required women to sign consent forms for all abortions; (3) required the husband's written consent for abortions during the first twelve weeks of pregnancy; (4) required the consent of a parent or guardian if the female was unmarried and younger than eighteen years old; (5) imposed a duty of care on doctors to preserve the fetus's life and healthand subjected doctors to possible manslaughter charges and civil damages if they failed to meet that standard; (6) required that any aborted fetus that survived would become a ward of the state; (7) imposed record-keeping and reporting requirements on doctors and medical facilities; and (8) prohibited the most common abortion procedure—saline amniocentesis—after the first twelve weeks of pregnancy.

A three-judge district court upheld all of the law's provisions except the physician's duty of care. Planned Parenthood appealed directly to the Supreme Court.

STEWART: I would uphold the pregnant woman's consent provision, record keeping and viability, but otherwise reverse.

MARSHALL: Statistics are necessary.

BLACKMUN: The written consents to surgery are meaningless, and as a policy I would not recommend them. State codes, however, require consultations with a doctor. (1) I would affirm viability. (2) Requiring the written consent of the patient is O.K., although I would prefer saying that it is no good. (3) Requiring the written consent of the spouse bad. (4) Requiring the written consent of a parent is no good (even the Massachusetts provision).[41] (5) I would reverse the "ward of the state" provision. (6) I would reverse the saline prohibition. (7) As for the record-keeping requirements, I could either affirm or reverse. (8) I would affirm the preservation of life requirement in #1419.[42]

POWELL: A viability statute should have a specific date, so I would reverse as to that. I would uphold the *patients'* consent requirement. Spousal and parental consent under this statute is bad. Regarding the duty of the doctor to keep a viable child alive, I would sustain it if the statute is clear enough—and I doubt that it is. Termination of parental rights gives me problems too. If the parents don't want it, the state should keep custody. I would not sustain the saline prohibition, but would sustain the record-keeping requirements.

STEVENS: Viability is O.K. Patient consent is O.K. Spousal consent is *bad*. Parental consent is O.K. The "ward of the state" provision is *bad*. The saline ban is O.K. The record-keeping requirements are O.K.

Result: The Court unanimously approved the state's definition of viability, the consent requirement, and the state's record-keeping requirements. A 6–3 majority, led by Harry Blackmun, reversed the spousal consent requirement on the ground that the state could not delegate to another party a power that it did not have to begin with. The same majority also struck down the physician's statutory duty of care. A narrow 5–4 majority struck down the parental consent requirement on the ground that no blanket parental consent requirement could be imposed on minors during the first twelve weeks of pregnancy. The same 5–4 majority struck down the ban on saline abortions on the ground that the

---

41. The Massachusetts case is *Bellotti v. Baird*, discussed below.
42. Number 1419 was the companion case, *Danforth v. Planned Parenthood of Central Missouri.*

state prohibition was arbitrary and obviously designed to prevent the vast majority of abortions after twelve weeks. John Paul Stevens joined the majority on spousal consent and the doctor's duty of care, but voted to uphold the parental consent provisions and the restrictions on saline abortions. Burger, White, and Rehnquist argued in dissent that the spousal and parental consent provisions were both permissible, as were the physician's duty of care and the partial ban on saline abortions.

Bellotti v. Baird, 428 U.S. 132 (1976)
(Brennan)

Massachusetts required both parents to give their consent before an unmarried minor could obtain an abortion. If one or both parents refused, the minor could seek a judge's permission upon a showing of good cause. A three-judge district court ruled that the judicial bypass provision was inadequate and that the parental veto requirements were unconstitutional as applied to minors capable of giving informed consent. This case made it before the Supreme Court twice, the first time in 1976 and again in 1979.

STEWART: I would prefer abstention here. This suit began a month before the statute became effective.

BLACKMUN: This law is stricter than in Missouri, because two parents and not one must consent. Missouri only required one parent to consent.[43]

POWELL: The incapacity of minors has been a fact of life and law for thousands of years, and we ought not strike down those requirements for a discovery of a structured consent. The attending physician has the problem of a suit for battery.

Result: The Court unanimously held that the district court should have certified questions to the Massachusetts Supreme Judicial Court to allow the state to interpret key provisions of the statute concerning parental notification and consent. Lewis Powell wrote the plurality opinion announcing the judgment of the Court, joined by Burger, Stewart, and Rehnquist. Brennan, Marshall, Blackmun, and Stevens concurred in the result.

On remand, the three-judge district court certified specific questions to the state supreme court, asking whether state law permitted a judicial bypass of the statute's parental consent requirements. The state court ruled that under state law, parental consent had to be obtained for every nonemergency abortion unless both parents were unavailable. The state court also certified that parents had to be notified of any judicial proceedings brought by a minor to obtain an abortion and that trial judges were free to deny a minor's request for an abortion upon a finding that a parent's or the judge's own judgment was preferable. The district court again ruled that the state law was unconstitutional and enjoined its enforcement.

Bellotti v. Baird, 443 U.S. 622 (1979)
(Brennan)

BURGER: I don't agree that a girl who is old enough to become pregnant is old enough to make all of the decisions of life. Yet parents are not likely to consent if their religious

---

43. *Planned Parenthood of Central Missouri v. Danforth,* 428 U.S. 52 (1976).

beliefs are paramount. But Massachusetts gives judges a veto over parents. Haven't we decided this already?

STEWART: I would affirm in part and reverse in part. Under this law, no matter how mature or emancipated a pregnant girl is, she must try first to get parental consent. This is so before she can go to court, and the judge can still forbid it. I know that under *Roe* and *Doe* that is unconstitutional to that extent. But I would say that a pregnant girl's assertion that she is mature who gets a court to agree can get an abortion without parental consent.

WHITE: This is an extension of *Danforth*, and I would not agree to that.

MARSHALL: I agree with the Chief Justice.

BLACKMUN: The Massachusetts court's approach that this is what it means, but if you don't say what it does. There is no longer a controversy between the parents and the girl. *Danforth* invalidated only some aspects of parental participation. The Massachusetts court has held that there can be no parental bypass, and that creates a conflict with the minor's rights. On judicial override, the principle of informed consent goes to capacity—the best interest goes to quality.

POWELL: I joined Potter in *Danforth* and I'm still there. My problem is how to fit those views into this Massachusetts statute. It is clear that I would reverse as to some and affirm as to others. I am probably closest to Potter.

REHNQUIST: I agree with Byron and prefer to go that way. But if necessary, I could affirm in part and reverse in part—if there is a Court majority for that.

STEVENS: It is still my view that a parental consultation requirement limited to one parent is valid. But to require both parents violates *Danforth*. Is it saved by judicial review? In some applications it is clearly unconstitutional as to mature minors. You can't require both parents to consent. It is most improper for the Massachusetts court to tender this problem to us. So maybe we should affirm outright, although I can probably go along with an opinion affirming in part and reversing in part.

Result: The Court struck down the parental consent requirement on the ground that it did not provide minors with an adequate judicial bypass procedure. A pregnant minor had to be given the option to forego parental consent entirely and ask a judge or other competent state official to assess whether she had the maturity and judgment to make the decision for herself (or whether, even lacking capacity, an abortion would be in her best interests). Powell presented the judgment of the Court and wrote a plurality opinion joined by Burger, Stewart, and Rehnquist. Stevens, Brennan, Marshall, and Blackmun concurred in the judgment, and White dissented. After this case was announced, virtually all states with parental consent laws had to revise their judicial bypass procedures.

Maher v. Roe, 432 U.S. 464 (1977)
(Brennan)

Connecticut funded abortions for indigent women only with a doctor's certificate of medical necessity. Two indigent women claimed that the state's refusal to allocate Medicaid money for nontherapeutic, first-trimester abortions violated the equal protection clause. A three-judge district court ruled that where the state subsidized pregnancy and childbirth costs for indigent women, it could not refuse similar support for women seeking legal abortions.

BURGER: Abortion is singled out here to require a doctor's certificate of necessity, and also the consent requirement was struck down. The solicitor general[44] supports this state policy on *Dandridge*,[45] and says that *Roe*[46] and *Doe*[47] are inapplicable.

STEWART: I see nothing to the "burden on a constitutional right" argument, for however fundamental the right, the state has no duty to subsidize it. It is the equal protection clause that troubles me. I am not very hospitable to claims advanced to programs for distributing largess—the government has a great deal of discretion in that area. But those considerations are not relevant here. The state does finance pregnancies to term, so they can't rely on a fiscal argument here. But a state can have a policy to favor births over abortion.

WHITE: I could not put this on a "burden" argument, and I don't make out an equal protection case. There is a rational basis if it is not necessary. So the same reasoning in *Beal* on "necessary medical services" requires reversal here.[48]

BLACKMUN: On written consent I would reverse; on the requirement for prior state approval I would affirm.

POWELL: *Roe* dealt with an absolute deprivation. Although the state's refusal to fund abortions for indigent women burdens *Roe's* fundamental right, what is the end of the road to require funding? Although the state funds pregnancies to term, that is not a denial of

44. Solicitor General Robert Bork.

45. *Dandridge v. Williams*, 397 U.S. 471 (1970). Maryland imposed a $250 limit on the aid a family could receive under the Aid to Families with Dependent Children (AFDC) program, which was jointly funded by the federal and state governments. The limit applied to all families, regardless of size or actual need. Linda Williams and other parents with large families sued, alleging that the limit conflicted with federal law and violated the equal protection clause. Potter Stewart, writing for the Court, upheld the state law. States, he said, had great latitude in dispensing funds; the test was whether the regulation was rationally supportable and free from invidious discrimination. In this case, the law furthered the state's legitimate interests in encouraging employment and in maintaining an equitable balance between welfare recipients and the working poor. Douglas, Brennan, and Marshall dissented.

46. *Roe v. Wade*, 410 U.S. 113 (1973).

47. *Doe v. Bolton*, 410 U.S. 179 (1973).

48. *Beal v. Doe*, 432 U.S. 438 (1977). Pennsylvania limited Medicaid assistance for abortions to those certified as medically necessary by three doctors, where (1) continuance of the pregnancy may threaten the mother's health; (2) the infant may be born with an incapacitating physical deformity or mental deficiency; or (3) the pregnancy resulted from rape or incest. All abortions had to be performed in an accredited hospital. Ann Doe and other women sued Frank Beal, state secretary of the Department of Public Welfare, for declaratory and injunctive relief. Doe claimed that the restrictions violated the equal protection clause and the federal Medicaid program of the Social Security Act (Title 19). The Supreme Court ruled 6–3 that the state law was a valid exercise of state police power and that Pennsylvania was free to decide whether or not to fund nontherapeutic abortions. The issue of whether three doctors could be required to certify that an abortion was medically necessary was remanded to determine whether this requirement violated Title 19. Brennan, Marshall, and Blackmun dissented.

equal protection to exclude the funding of abortions. The state has a benign purpose to aid citizens, and does not have to include everything. The source of denial of funding is not state action. The state has a substantial interest in supporting life. Let the Congress and legislatures do this.

REHNQUIST: *Ross v. Moffitt* means that the state does not have to fund a lawyer, even though he can't be prohibited.[49]

STEVENS: There is a substantive due process and an equal protection argument. I don't think that the state's failure to subsidize abortions for poor women is a deprivation. In *Meyer*, the state can't forbid the teaching of German, but need not subsidize it.[50] The equal protection issue is more difficult, but *Roe* acknowledged an important state interest in life and that interest is sufficient to justify a difference in treatment between those who elect to abort and those who elect to go to term.

Result: Reaffirming the Court's traditional view that financial need alone did not create a suspect classification, the Court voted 6–3 that Connecticut's refusal to fund non-therapeutic abortions did not violate Roe's *equal protection or privacy rights. Lewis Powell wrote the majority opinion, with Brennan, Marshall, and Blackmun in dissent.*

Carey v. Population Services International, 431 U.S. 678 (1977)
(Brennan)

New York made it a crime to distribute contraceptives to minors under the age of sixteen, prohibited anyone but licensed pharmacists from dispensing contraceptives to adults, and banned all advertising and displays of contraceptives. A three-judge district court struck down the statute on First and Fourteenth Amendment grounds.

BURGER: I doubt without a minor as a party that there is either standing or a case or controversy here. On the merits, I would say that only the rational basis test applies and there is an abundance of them here. *Virginia Pharmacy* bears on the advertising question.[51]

STEWART: There are four issues here: (1) standing; (2) the prohibition against advertising; (3) the prohibition of sales of contraceptives to minors under the age of sixteen; and (4) the prohibition of sales except by a pharmacist.

On standing, *Craig,*[52] and *Eisenstadt*[53] seem to allow standing.

On advertising, unless Harry Blackmun can show me otherwise, *Bigelow*[54] and *Virginia Pharmacy* both seem to knock it down.

49. *Ross v. Moffitt,* 417 U.S. 600 (1974). The Court held that there was no equal protection or due process mandate requiring states to pay for defense lawyers for discretionary appeals or appeals to the U.S. Supreme Court.
50. *Meyer v. Nebraska,* 262 U.S. 390 (1923).
51. *Virginia Pharmacy Board v. Virginia Citizens Consumer Council,* 425 U.S. 748 (1976).
52. *Craig v. Boren,* 429 U.S. 190 (1976).
53. *Eisenstadt v. Baird,* 405 U.S. 438 (1972).
54. *Bigelow v. Virginia,* 421 U.S. 809 (1973).

On sales to minors, *Danforth* seems to invalidate the prohibition of the sale of contraceptives to minors—abortion is more severe than contraceptives.[55]

On prohibiting the sale of contraceptives except by a licensed pharmacist, if the prohibition on sales to minors were valid then this restriction might be also be valid, but not if I am right on *Danforth*. On statutory rape, we have said that in earlier cases.

WHITE: I pretty well agree with Bill Brennan and Potter about the effect on statutory rape, fornication, and so forth. *Eisenstadt* indicated that they were valid, but you can't deny contraception to unmarried people if married people can have them.

MARSHALL: I agree with Bill Brennan and Potter.

BLACKMUN: I can't add much to what Bill Brennan and Potter said. We crossed the bridge as to consent in *Bellotti*.[56] Contraception is safer than abortion. On advertising, the state did not separate these. I hope that this can be a narrow opinion.

POWELL: I am closer to the Chief Justice. The standing issue was resolved by *Boren v. Craig*. I think that this is a fraudulent device—the respondent is a non-profit corporation getting federal funds. The regulation of contraception sales to adults and limited to pharmacists may be defective as to adults. As to minors, the state has a far greater interest in regulating the morals of minors. I don't see how the Constitution goes into that area. As to advertising, if it is valid to restrict advertising by radio and TV of tobacco and liquor, I can't see why the state can't prohibit the same media from advertising here. I would say that the law was overbroad and leave the state free to regulate these.

REHNQUIST: I agree with the Chief Justice. We can distinguish our decided cases. If this case is affirmed, I can't see how we can save a statutory rape statute.

STEVENS: I am more to affirm than reverse. I don't have any doubt that the state can prohibit sexual intercourse by minors. But this statute is too broad—it reaches even parents and married children. So if it is conditioned on parental consent, I might sustain it. The pharmacy requirement may be O.K., however.

Result: The Court ruled that New York could not prohibit the sale of contraceptives to minors, could not require that nonhazardous contraceptives be dispensed exclusively by pharmacists, and could not ban all public advertisements and displays. William Brennan, writing for a 7–2 majority, declared that the decision to bear or beget children was a fundamental right that triggered strict scrutiny of any governmental restrictions. White, Powell, and Stevens joined most of Brennan's opinion, but concurred in the judgment that New York could not ban the sale of nonprescription contraceptives to minors without joining Brennan's opinion on that issue. Burger and Rehnquist dissented.

---

55. *Planned Parenthood of Central Missouri v. Danforth*, 428 U.S. 52 (1976).
56. *Bellotti v. Baird*, 443 U.S. 622 (1979).

Harris v. McRae, 448 U.S. 297 (1980)
(Brennan)

The Hyde Amendment limited federal Medicaid funding for indigent women who wanted abortions. Under the 1976 version of the amendment challenged here, a woman seeking an abortion was not eligible for Medicaid funds unless her life would be endangered if the fetus were carried to full term, or if the pregnancy resulted from rape or incest and the crime had been promptly reported to a law enforcement or public health agency.

Cora McRae sued Patricia Harris, the secretary of Health, Education, and Welfare, claiming that the Hyde Amendment (1) violated the liberty or equal protection component of the Fifth Amendment's due process clause; and (2) violated the religion clauses of the First Amendment. McRae also claimed that poor, pregnant women had a statutory right under Title 19 of the Social Security Act to obtain medically necessary abortions. A three-judge district court ruled that the Hyde Amendment violated the due process clause of the Fifth Amendment and the free exercise clause of the First Amendment.

BURGER: "Where life is endangered" is not covered by the Hyde Amendment. The lower court held that there was no rational basis between medically necessary abortions and medically necessary services elsewhere. I never regarded the *Does* as creating a new constitutional right, but only placing a limitation on the states.[57] I have no doubt that an indigent pregnant woman has greater risks. Congress's real motives are not open to judicial examination.

STEWART: There is no violation of equal protection. *Maher* on principle controls this case.[58] The First Amendment arguments are frivolous.

WHITE: This is different from *Maher*. The health of the mother makes it harder on the rational basis test. The Hyde Amendment distinguishes between medical procedures. But if we identify other interests, this is not *Moreno*.[59]

MARSHALL: Equal protection only—*Maher* normal childbirth is not possible here.

BLACKMUN: Repeal by implication by appropriation acts are not favored. But getting over that, there was no finding of any encouragement of normal childbirth. I don't agree with the First Amendment arguments. I agree with Bill Brennan on equal protection.

POWELL: This is a different issue than *Maher*, since therapeutic abortions are arguably involved here. There is no constitutional right to any medical care. But since some was provided, equal protection is implicated. So we get to rational bases. Is there a legitimate state interest here? *Maher* said that the state's interest in birth suffices, and it does here, also. Then the weighing of competing interests here must be with the federal government.

---

57. *Roe v. Wade,* 410 U.S. 113 (1973); *Doe v. Bolton,* 410 U.S. 179 (1973); and possibly *Maher v. Roe,* 432 U.S. 464 (1977).

58. *Maher v. Roe,* 432 U.S. 464 (1977).

59. *U.S. Dept. of Agriculture v. Moreno,* 413 U.S. 528 (1973). Federal food stamps were distributed to households rather than to individuals, and the term "household" was limited to people who were related. Jacinta Moreno and other plaintiffs were denied food stamps, even though they were poor, because they lived in groups where the members were not all related. The Supreme Court ruled that the federal law created an irrational and unjustifiable classification that violated the equal protection component of the Fifth Amendment's due process clause. Rehnquist and Burger dissented.

REHNQUIST: The right of privacy under *Stanley v. Georgia* did not prevent government restrictions on getting access to stuff.[60] So if this right is founded on privacy, that does not prevent government regulation of the right.

STEVENS: Originally I thought that *Maher* controlled this case. But I don't now. Here, the government interest at stake is the federal interest in fetal life. This is unlike the state, which ordinarily is the moral authority. But the denial of funds for abortion here is a conscious congressional decision to spend more on babies coming to term in order to prevent abortion. There is no constitutional right to get a constitutional right furthered, but there is no justification here in saving money, or encouraging normal child birth, or in increasing the population. The federal government has decided to harm certain people, and *Roe* said that you can't do that.

Result: In a 5–4 decision, the Supreme Court upheld the Hyde Amendment. Potter Stewart, writing for the majority, held that while women had a constitutional right to seek an abortion within the framework of Roe v. Wade, *there was no corollary entitlement to federal funding to pay for the procedure. The Hyde Amendment was permissible because it did not place any new obstacles for women seeking abortions. While it meant that it would be difficult—even impossible—for some poor women to obtain abortions, the government was not responsible for their financial condition and had no legal obligation to subsidize their abortions.*

The fact that the federal government paid special benefits to poor women who chose to bear children made no difference. The decision to subsidize childbirth while refusing to fund abortions were rationally related to legitimate government objectives of promoting childbirth and protecting potential life.

William Brennan's dissent characterized the Hyde Amendment as a transparent attempt to impose a political majority's judgment on a woman's constitutional right to make a private choice. The law's sole purpose, he said, was to coerce poor women into making a choice they would not otherwise have made. Thurgood Marshall's dissent advocated the use of his sliding scale approach to equal protection cases. Marshall accused the majority (both on the Court and in Congress) of being blind to the real world impact of the legislation on poor women. The Hyde Amendment imposed a "crushing burden" on indigent women who needed medically necessary abortions. It forced them to make a "grotesque" choice to seek an illegal abortion or attempt childbirth at significant risk to her own life and health and at the cost of her right to control her own life. Marshall could see no rational reason for Congress to conclude that a governmental interest in fetal life outweighed the brutal effects the law had on indigent women.

Bowers v. Hardwick, 478 U.S. 186 (1986)

(Brennan)

Michael Hardwick was charged with sodomy after Georgia police caught him in bed with another man inside a private home.[61] Georgia law defined sodomy as oral or anal sex and did not distinguish be-

---

60. *Stanley v. Georgia*, 394 U.S. 557 (1969).

61. Police went to the house to arrest Hardwick for failing to appear in court on a traffic charge of driving while drinking a beer, a violation of the state's open-container law. Hardwick later claimed, apparently correctly, that he was not required to appear because he had already paid the fine. After his arrest he

tween homosexual and heterosexual conduct. Hardwick claimed that the statute unconstitutionally criminalized consensual adult sex. John and Mary Doe joined the lawsuit as a married couple who wanted to engage in proscribed sexual conduct in the privacy of their own home. Because Georgia declined to prosecute Hardwick, the district court dismissed Hardwick's complaint for failure to state a valid cause of action. The court of appeals reversed, ruling that the Georgia law violated Hardwick's fundamental rights. Both the district court and court of appeals ruled that the Does lacked standing, and the Supreme Court refused to consider their claims on appeal. Michael Bowers was attorney general of Georgia.

> BURGER: Only homosexual activities are involved here—no marital privacy interests are at issue. Georgia agrees that an expansion to marital conduct would get them in trouble. Our society has values that should be protected. The teachings of history and custom frown on this, and sanction its prohibition. Unlike *Stanley*, this does not infringe on privacy rights.[62]

> BRENNAN:[63] We should affirm. This case is about conduct that is consensual, between adults, undertaken in the privacy of the home, intimate, and private. Accordingly, the case implicates two firmly established lines of our cases, namely, the right to privacy, as articulated in *Griswold v. Connecticut* and developed in such cases as *Eisenstadt v. Baird*,[64] and secondly, those cases which recognize that the home remains a sort of castle within our legal system. *Stanley v. Georgia, Payton v. New York.*[65]
>
> The question before us is limited to whether on remand this statute must be assessed under a rational basis test or under a heightened scrutiny standard. Because of the two interests implicated in this action—the privacy right and the sanctity of the home—I am convinced that heightened scrutiny is required. On remand, the state would be permitted to show that a substantial state interest is significantly advanced or furthered by the statute.
>
> This is a complicated case, and at least two points need to be addressed. The first involves limiting principles. I agree with what I thought Lewis implied at argument, that this case should be restricted to a consideration of conduct that takes place within the home, and that is: (1) non-commercial; (2) consensual; and (3) that involves the most private forms of sexual intimacy.

---

was charged with two crimes: sodomy and possession of marijuana. After the state dropped the sodomy charges, Hardwick pleaded guilty to possession of marijuana and paid a $50 fine. He then filed a federal civil suit asking for a declaratory judgment that the state's sodomy law was unconstitutional. Dripps, "*Bowers v. Hardwick*," 1423–25.

62. *Stanley v. Georgia*, 394 U.S. 557 (1969).

63. Adapted from Brennan's talking papers, Brennan Papers, OT 1985, box 714.

64. *Griswold v. Connecticut*, 381 U.S. 479 (1965); *Eisenstadt v. Baird*, 405 U.S. 438 (1972).

65. *Stanley v. Georgia*, 394 U.S. 557 (1969); *Payton v. New York*, 445 U.S. 573 (1980). In *Payton*, police had probable cause to arrest Theodore Payton for murder. Without a warrant, officers went to Payton's apartment to arrest him. When no one answered, they kicked in the door and entered the apartment. The apartment was unoccupied, but one of the officers found a shell casing in plain view and seized it as evidence. The trial judge denied Payton's motion to suppress the evidence, holding that the officers' actions were permissible under state law. The Supreme Court reversed on a 5–1–3 vote. John Paul Stevens, writing for the majority, ruled that the Fourth Amendment prohibited the police from making a warrantless, nonconsensual entry into a suspect's home to make a routine felony arrest. Blackmun concurred in the result, while White, Burger, and Rehnquist dissented.

Secondly, it is critical to remember that on remand, the state can show in this case—and in all others which Georgia now claims this case will also "decide"—that there is a legitimate state interest which the act advances significantly. In other words, a decision sustaining Frank Johnson's opinion will not mean the end of adultery and incest laws. I have no doubt but that a state would be able to show sufficient interest to defend these statutes. The point is only that the state must be made to articulate its reasons, beyond saying merely that they do not like oral sex, or sodomy, or homosexuals. As Byron said just last term in *City of Cleburne*, a state—even under a rational basis test—must advance reasons beyond naked preferences to support legislation.[66]

Incidentally, I thought that John Stevens made an interesting point with respect to Georgia's alleged compelling interest in the morality that this statute seeks to codify. He noted the failure of the state to prosecute this respondent, on whom they clearly had plenty of evidence.

Finally, I want to emphasize that to me, this is a case involving certain sexual conduct engaged in between consenting adults, regardless of their marital status, regardless of their gender. It is not about homosexuality, it is not about single persons. It is about sexual privacy in the home between consenting adults. The statute purports to make none of these distinctions, and it would be inappropriate for us to graft those classifications onto the act. This was, of course, Byron's point in his concurrence in *Eisenstadt*.

Thus, I would hold that an act such as this, which seeks to criminalize certain sexually intimate conduct between consenting adults, regardless of the marital status or gender of the adults, within the privacy of the home, must be defended by the state under a heightened standard of review. I simply cannot believe that this would be a controversial result.

WHITE: I agree with the Chief Justice.

MARSHALL: I agree with Bill Brennan.

---

66. *City of Cleburne v. Cleburne Living Center,* 473 U.S. 432, 435 (1985). The Cleburne Living Center (CLC) sought to lease a building in Cleburne, Texas, to operate as a group home for the mentally retarded. A city ordinance required the CLC to obtain a special use permit as a "hospital for the feebleminded." The city council rejected the CLC's application for a permit and the corporation sued in federal court, arguing that the permit requirement discriminated against the mentally retarded and violated the equal protection clause.

The court of appeals ruled that mental retardation was a quasi-suspect classification and that the law required more exacting judicial scrutiny than would have been accorded to ordinary social and economic legislation. Using a "heightened-scrutiny" equal protection test, the circuit court ruled that the ordinance was facially invalid, because it did not substantially further an important governmental purpose. The court also ruled that the ordinance was invalid as applied.

On appeal, the Supreme Court ruled that the mentally retarded were *not* a quasi-suspect classification and that laws distinguishing persons on the basis of mental capacity were subject to ordinary judicial scrutiny—the rational basis test. The majority nonetheless struck down the law on the ground that it was unconstitutional as applied. Byron White, writing for the majority, ruled that the record did not show any rational basis for believing that the proposed home posed any threat to the city's legitimate interests, which led the majority to conclude that the law reflected an irrational prejudice against the mentally retarded. Marshall, Brennan, and Blackmun concurred in part and dissented in part.

BLACKMUN: Johnson's opinion is very good.[67] This is not public conduct. It is limited to the home and reaches a marital situation. Much of the state's argument reminds me of *Loving*, and efforts to deregulate prostitution.[68] Hardwick, but not the Does, have standing. The privacy and association rights implied in *Stanley* are present here. The thought control aspects and the religious underpinnings of the state's sodomy statute are evident here.

POWELL: We ought to decriminalize this conduct. This statute has not been enforced for fifty years. *Robinson v. California*, invalidating criminal status of drug addiction, may be relevant. That case rested on the Eighth Amendment.[69] If we accept the allegation that only acts of sodomy can satisfy this fellow, isn't that pertinent? I would treat it as such, and hold that in the context of the home this conduct is not criminally punishable.

REHNQUIST: I agree with the Chief Justice and with Byron. The Fourth Amendment regulates home problems. I can't say that substantive due process supports an attack on a statute as limited to one's home.

STEVENS: Is this conduct that the state can proscribe? Nothing in the statute proscribes only homosexual conduct. This is a liberty interest case. It is not enough that a moral condemnation is made by the majority. If it were, the state could enforce this against married people. Isn't it part of liberty for everyone? I don't think the fact that it is in the home makes any difference, and I am not happy with the privacy analysis either. But this is a matter of choice. I would strike it down on that basis.

O'CONNOR: The right of privacy's source is the Fourteenth Amendment's guarantee of personal liberty. But this right is not absolute and does not extend to private, consensual homosexuality. The state's legislative power to enact this law is not unconstitutional as exercised.

Result: Lewis Powell's attempt to decriminalize homosexual conduct without bringing it within the right of privacy did not last long. Powell abandoned his novel Robinson *theory soon after the conference. After flirting with the idea of writing a concurring opinion that would have left the Court evenly divided at 4–1–4, Powell impulsively changed his mind and gave Byron White the crucial fifth vote necessary to uphold Georgia's sodomy statute. White's majority opinion focused almost exclusively on the homosexual aspects of the case, declaring that homosexual conduct was not a protected constitutional right.*

Powell wrote a brief concurring opinion that criticized the law's harsh sentencing guidelines (violations were punishable by up to twenty years in prison) and hinted that such draconian punishment

---

67. *Hardwick v. Bowers*, 760 F.2d 1202 (1985).

68. *Loving v. Virginia*, 388 U.S. 1 (1967), striking down Virginia's miscegenation law and stating that the liberty to marry a person of another race rests with the individual, not the state.

69. *Robinson v. California*, 370 U.S. 660 (1962). The Court invalidated a ninety-day prison sentence for the crime of being addicted to the use of narcotics. William O. Douglas held that a person could not be convicted solely on the defendant's status of being an addict. Powell's conference argument was that Hardwick was, in effect, addicted to sodomy and that the Georgia law impermissibly criminalized his status as a homosexual.

might violate the Eighth Amendment. Powell later admitted that he "probably made a mistake" in siding with the majority. On another occasion, he said that if he had it to do over again he would have voted to deny certiorari and avoided the matter entirely.

In dissent, Blackmun criticized White's approach and argued that the case was not about the right to engage in homosexual sodomy, as the majority claimed. For Blackmun, the case was about "the right most valued by civilized men"—the right to be let alone. The most crucial issues of the case were rights of privacy and "intimate association," and neither issue depended on Hardwick's sexual orientation.

Michael Hardwick died of AIDS in 1991. Michael Bowers resigned as attorney general in 1997 to run for governor. His campaign self-destructed when it was revealed that he had carried on a fifteen-year extramarital affair with a former aide and Playboy bunny. The Georgia Supreme Court struck down the state's sodomy law in 1997 on the ground that it violated the state constitution's right of privacy.[70]

---

70. As of 1999, thirteen states ban consensual oral and anal sex, regardless of sexual orientation. Five other states—Arkansas, Kansas, Oklahoma, Missouri, and Texas—prohibit only homosexual sodomy.

CHAPTER 15

THE RIGHT TO VOTE

OBSTACLES TO VOTING

Lassiter v. Northampton County Board of Elections, 360 U.S. 45 (1959)
(Brennan) (Douglas)

Article 6 of North Carolina's constitution required those wishing to vote to demonstrate that they could read and write. A grandfather clause exempted male residents of North Carolina as of 1867 and their lineal descendants from the state's literacy requirements.[1] *Louise Lassiter was a female, black resident of North Carolina. She refused to take a literacy test, alleging that it violated the Fourteenth, Fifteenth, and Seventeenth Amendments. The North Carolina Supreme Court rejected her claims and upheld the state's literacy requirements.*

Conference of May 22, 1959

WARREN: We should make it clear that the North Carolina constitution's grandfather clause is unconstitutional and void. I can't say that there is any evidence that the 1957 act is unconstitutional. If we made it plain that it isn't, then let them show us a new action based on *Yick Wo.*

BLACK: I am satisfied that the 1957 law on its face does not rest on the invalid grandfather clause, and unless as applied the grandfather clause is brought back in, the literacy test is valid and the judgment below should be affirmed.

FRANKFURTER: I affirm.

DOUGLAS: It is far from clear what the state court has done, and its opinion can be read as urged by appellant. This case shows the futility, sometimes, of sending these cases to state courts. We have to say that he can go back to the district court and prove his case, either that the grandfather clause is still operative or that the law is being applied unconstitutionally, as in *Yick Wo.*

CLARK: The grandfather clause is out absolutely, and I would so hold. If there is discrimination under the act, it would have to be proved in a federal case—but he must amend his complaint.

---

1. All parties agreed that the grandfather clause violateed the Fifteenth Amendment. A three-judge district court had previously ruled that the state legislature had implicitly repealed the grandfather clause when it revised the state's literacy test in 1957. This finding was not challenged on appeal; but because the grandfather clause technically remained on the books, the issue was not entirely resolved.

HARLAN: I affirm, taking the grandfather clause out.

BRENNAN: We must decide the constitutional question here.

WHITTAKER: I affirm.

STEWART: The opinion of the North Carolina court is vague, but it must be construed to mean that the grandfather clause is out.[2] We should say that the grandfather clause is out as to both pre- and post-1908 registrants.[3] The literacy test is constitutional on its face.

Result: William O. Douglas, writing for a unanimous Court, held that literacy tests were permissible so long as they were fairly applied to all voters irrespective of race, color, and sex. Just to be safe, the Court reaffirmed that the grandfather clause was no longer valid.

Katzenbach v. Morgan, 384 U.S. 641 (1966)
(Douglas) (Brennan)

Section 4(e) of the Voting Rights Act of 1965 provided that no one who had completed the sixth grade in Puerto Rico (or any other American-flag school where English was not the primary language of instruction) could be disenfranchised because they could not speak or write English. One of the act's main effects was to preclude New York from enforcing its English literacy voting law against its large Puerto Rican community. John and Christine Morgan of New York sued U.S. Attorney General Nicholas Katzenbach, claiming that their votes were diluted and impaired by ballots cast by nonEnglish speakers, who under New York law were not legally entitled to vote. A three-judge district court for the District of Columbia struck down §4(e) of the Voting Rights Act on the ground that it exceeded Congress's constitutional powers to regulate state voting requirements.

In conference, the Justices debated two ways to make sure that the Morgans lost: (1) finding that the Voting Rights Act was a valid exercise of Congress' Fourteenth, or Fifteenth Amendment powers; or (2) ruling that New York's literacy requirement was unconstitutional.

Conference of April 22, 1966

WARREN: I would reverse on the equal protection clause and not on the territorial clause, which refers to governments of the territories themselves.[4] Congress may legislate against discrimination against voting under §5 of the Fourteenth Amendment. Congress need not make findings or justify its actions if we can justify its conduct on any rational basis. Section 4(e) is constitutional.

---

2. The state high court had ruled that Article 6 was divisible and that the literacy test could remain in effect even if the grandfather clause was unenforceable.

3. The grandfather clause had a cutoff date of December 1, 1908. Lassiter argued that the law's sunset provision did not save the clause because a significant number of persons exempted from the literacy requirements in 1908 were still alive and voting in the 1950s.

4. In oral argument, the federal government claimed that Congress was empowered to make special rules for Puerto Ricans under the Territorial Clause, Article 4 §3, which authorized Congress to "dispose of and make all needful rules and regulations respecting the Territory or other property belonging to the United States." District Judge McGowan rejected this argument at the trial court level, *Morgan v. Katzenbach*, 247 F. Supp. 196, 204 (1965).

BLACK: I would not say that the New York statute is void on is face under the Fourteenth and Fifteenth Amendments themselves, but Congress has the power to do something like this under both §5 of the Fourteenth Amendment, and particularly under §2 of the Fifteenth Amendment. I go on Congress's enforcement powers of equal protection. I reverse.

DOUGLAS: I agree with the Chief Justice. The act of Congress makes it easier, but apart from the act I would still reverse here.

CLARK: I agree.

HARLAN: I affirm. The only possible ground for reversal is on a constitutional basis. But there is no racial element here. This is Congress saying that it is a denial of equal protection to have an English literacy test for Spaniards. But Congress can't define the equal protection clause—that is for us to say. Congress could not restore state poll taxes, for example, now that we have struck it down.[5]

BRENNAN: I reverse.

STEWART: The territorial clause is not relevant. The Fifteenth Amendment is not involved, as this is not racial. The law can be sustained under §5 of the Fourteenth Amendment, which gives Congress power to enforce the Amendment by explicit legislation. So our question is whether this legislation is appropriate and whether it violates any other provision of Constitution. But is it "appropriate," since the New York test is not discriminatorily applied as far as race is concerned? I have difficulty finding that it is "appropriate" here, but I might be persuaded. I have trouble with this case, but will try to reverse.

WHITE: I reverse. This is Congress's definition of "equal protection," and it is valid. A Ph.D might not be able to speak English. In light of this act of Congress, I would uphold the act. That means that we would allow Congress to declare what is a denial of equal protection. Without the statute, I would have trouble. But if it is not too far out of line in is O.K.

FORTAS: I agree with the Chief Justice and would reverse. We should avoid referring to race or color, as Puerto Ricans are extremely sensitive.[6]

Result: Writing for a 7–2 majority, William Brennan wrote that because there was a rational basis to conclude that state literacy tests might be used to deny voters' rights, the Voting Rights Act was a permissible exercise of congressional power under §5 of the Fourteenth Amendment. The supremacy clause meant that New York's literacy test could not stand, at least as applied to voters educated in the United States or Puerto Rico. Brennan distinguished Lassiter, *saying that there had been no challenge in that case to literacy requirements under the equal protection clause.*

---

5. *Harper v. Virginia State Board of Elections*, 383 U.S. 663 (1966), overruling *Breedlove v. Suttles*, 302 U.S. 277 (1937).

6. Fortas had many close personal and professional ties in Puerto Rico. Years later, after resigning from the Supreme Court, Fortas represented Puerto Rico in oral argument before the Court in *Rodriguez v. Popular Democratic Party*, 457 U.S. 1 (1982). It was Fortas's last case. He died two weeks later of heart failure, not knowing that he had won his last argument. Kalman, *Abe Fortas*, 398–401.

Harlan and Stewart dissented, arguing that §4(e) of the Voting Rights Act sought to overturn by congressional fiat the Court's ruling in Lassiter—*that fairly administered literacy tests were constitutional.*[7] *Congress was not free to determine for itself the meaning of the Fourteenth Amendment; it was up to the Court to define equal protection and to determine whether state literacy tests violated the federal Constitution. Because there was no legislative record to support a congressional finding of state discrimination in violation of the Fourteenth Amendment, Harlan and Stewart concluded that Congress's power to enforce the Fourteenth Amendment had not been triggered and could not be used to justify the Voting Rights Act.*

South Carolina v. Katzenbach, 383 U.S. 301 (1966)
United States v. Alabama
United States v. Mississippi
United States v. Louisiana
Louisiana v. Katzenbach
(Douglas)

The Voting Rights Act of 1965 suspended the use of literacy tests and other voting tests and devices in certain states and counties.[8] *The law authorized the U.S. attorney general to appoint voting examiners and registration supervisors to help blacks register and vote in these areas.*[9]

Section 5 was the act's most controversial provision. It provided that in any jurisdictions covered by the act, any planned changes in voting rules had to be submitted either to the U.S. attorney general or the District Court for the District of Columbia for prior approval. The attorney general had sixty days to review the proposed changes and could block the proposed changes from taking effect if they tended to deny or abridge the right to vote on account of race or color. The alternative approval route was through a special three-judge district court, that could issue declaratory judgments approving proposed changes on the same grounds. Either way, it was extraordinary for a federal law to require states to obtain prior federal approval before they could modify existing election laws or enact new ones.

South Carolina sought an injunction against Attorney General Nicholas Katzenbach to prevent him from enforcing the terms of the Voting Rights Act. The state claimed that the law (1) exceeded Congress's powers under the Fifteenth Amendment; (2) infringed on states' rights; (3) impermissibly treated states unequally; (4) was an unconstitutional a bill of attainder (because it allegedly inflicted legislative punishments on individual states and counties); (5) violated due process; and (6) violated separation of powers by giving unchecked judicial power to the attorney general and by allowing the district courts to issue advisory opinions.

---

7. *Lassiter v. Northampton Election Board,* 360 U.S. 45 (1959).

8. Section 4 of the act provided that the law applied to any state or county (1) which maintained a voting test or device on November 1, 1964; and (2) where, according to census figures, fewer than 50 percent of voting-age residents were either registered to vote as of November 1, 1964, or had actually voted in the 1964 presidential election. Among the states covered by the act were Alabama, Alaska, Georgia, Louisiana, Mississippi, South Carolina, Virginia, twenty-six counties in North Carolina, three counties in Arizona, one county in Hawaii, and one county in Idaho.

9. Section 6 authorized the attorney general to appoint federal examiners to enforce the terms of the Fifteenth Amendment.

Originally there were five separate lawsuits asking the Court to assert its original jurisdiction. At the first conference, the Justices discussed which of these cases, if any, to accept.

Certiorari Conference of November 5, 1965

WARREN: I propose that we take only the South Carolina case and remit the others back to the local district courts.

BLACK: I agree, although I have doubts if the declaratory judgment route is proper, as it comes close to an advisory opinion.[10]

DOUGLAS: I agree with the Chief Justice. I have no doubts that the declaratory judgment route is appropriate—the issues here are not feigned.

CLARK: I agree.

HARLAN: I prefer to send all of the states back to the district courts.

BRENNAN: I agree with the Chief Justice.

STEWART: I will go along with the Chief Justice, but I would prefer to remit all states to the district courts.

WHITE: I agree with the Chief Justice. These will be in one-judge courts after *Swift* comes down.[11]

FORTAS: I agree with the Chief Justice. I would like to treat no. 22 as the case of South Carolina versus the United States, and not against the attorney general.[12]

BRENNAN: There must be the consent of United States to do that, and there can be no consent here without an act of Congress (*Minnesota v. Hitchcock*).[13]

BLACK: Now I have doubts about even the South Carolina case. The act delegates to the attorney general selection of the states to which the law applies. If that issue is here, then evidence must be offered. The *Southern Pacific* case took three weeks of hearing evidence.[14]

---

10. In 1965, Texas congressman John Dowdy alleged that five Supreme Court Justices had "looked over and approved" the Voting Rights Act before Congress voted on the bill. The resulting scandal caused some public relations problems for the Court, although Senator Everett Dirksen helped to minimize the damage by telling everyone that Dowdy's accusation was a lie "as big as Texas." Hugo and Elizabeth Black, *Mr. Justice and Mrs. Black,* 108–9.

11. *Swift and Co. v. Wickham,* 382 U.S. 111 (1965). The Court overruled an earlier interpretation of the Three-Judge Court Act, holding that three-judge courts were not required for federal-state statutory conflicts brought under the supremacy clause.

12. The Court initially claimed original jurisdiction in this case on the ground that it was a suit between a state and a citizen of another state (Katzenbach was a New Jersey resident). In practice, everyone treated the case as *South Carolina v. United States,* with the federal government represented by its chief law official. McKusick, "Discretionary Gatekeeping," 203.

13. *Minnesota v. Hitchcock,* 185 U.S. 373 (1902), held that the United States could not be sued by a state without the federal government's consent.

14. It is not clear to which case Hugo Black is referring. The two leading candidates are *Southern Pacific Co. v. Arizona,* 325 U.S. 761 (1945) and *California Southern Pacific Co.,* 157 U.S. 229 (1895). In *South-*

HARLAN: I would like to put a motion for leave to file down for argument next week.

WARREN: I am opposed to that. There is no question as to our jurisdiction.

[DOUGLAS: On the final vote on *South Carolina v. Katzenbach*: Black, Harlan, and Stewart vote to deny leave to file.]

Result: As Earl Warren suggested, the Court accepted only the South Carolina case and remitted the others to their respective district courts. This was done, in part, because all of the cases raised the same issues and there were no significant issues of fact to be resolved. Instead, the Justices invited Alabama, Mississippi, Louisiana, Georgia, and Virginia to submit friend of the court briefs in support of South Carolina, while twenty-one other states supported the federal government and Attorney General Katzenbach. This helped to streamline the litigation, which was argued and decided quickly, at least by Supreme Court standards.[15]

Conference of January 21, 1966

WARREN: The attorney general made the case more complicated than it needed to be.[16] Section 2 of the Fifteenth Amendment gives Congress power by "appropriate" means to eliminate §1 discrimination. As long as the act is aimed at that, Congress can legislate any way it chooses. Congress knows what the problem is. It knows that the case by case method was ineffectual, so it changed its tactics and used drastic means. What it did was rational. I would limit the opinion narrowly and not try to answer all of the questions that may in time arise. We need to reach §4.[17] The attorney general acts on the basis of census figures—there was no unlawful delegation of power in that regard. The naming of examiners is reasonable. I would decided in favor of the federal government.

BLACK: I agree with the Chief Justice. Congress has the right to ban literacy tests under the Fifteenth Amendment. Congress decided that these old laws stood in way and it had the power to enforce the Fifteenth Amendment that way. Congress could legislate as to only one or two states. This is more like a tariff law. The formula for putting the law in effect is provided. I would not give the Attorney General power to make all kinds of decisions, but that is not here because there is judicial review. I would be willing to say that you can't make a court review the validity of new state constitutions—that involves §5.

BRENNAN: The federal government wants §5 adjudicated to avoid evasive state devices.

---

ern *Pacific Co. v. Arizona*, the trial before the Arizona County Court took about five and a half months, and oral arguments before the Supreme Court took two days. In *California v. Southern Pacific Co.*, the Supreme Court heard three days of argument before declining to assert original jurisdiction.

15. The Justices announced their decision in this case seven months and one day after President Johnson signed the Voting Rights Act into law. McKusick, "Discretionary Gatekeeping," 203.

16. Attorney General Nicholas Katzenbach argued the case on his own behalf, with Solicitor General Thurgood Marshall assisting him on the brief.

17. Section 4 defined which jurisdictions were covered by the Voting Rights Act, suspended literacy tests and other tests or devices for five years, and excused all persons who had attended American-flag schools (including Puerto Rico) from being required to take English literacy tests in order to vote.

BLACK: The United States does not need that. Congress can provide any other remedy. It is bad to have the attorney general deciding what new constitutional provisions are O.K.—I will not approve it here.

DOUGLAS: I am for the federal government's position.

CLARK: We must pass on §5, as well as §4. Section 5 is not invalid; neither are the other portions at issue here. We should approve the machinery for reviewing the changes that the states will make.

HARLAN: The act is constitutional. The 50 percent provision is O.K. The review power by the attorney general is rational. As to §5, I would pass on it. I have no difficulty with it on the merits—Congress can suspend all literacy tests.

BRENNAN: I agree with Tom. We must reach §5. Section 4 is appropriate and so is §5.

STEWART: The only issue is not whether the act is "appropriate." It might be "appropriate" and still invalid, for it might violate another provision of the Constitution. This act is grim and heavy-handed, and does not go to the evil of literacy tests. The act should have had federal officers enforce state laws. The problem is solved by putting illiterates on the ballot. Section 5 shocks me, because a state must go for approval to the Attorney General. If §4 is good, §5 is good. Bills of attainder do not apply to states, only to people. We must reach §5. On the whole, I can't say that the act is unconstitutional.

WHITE: We should decide as many issues as we can, and take all those that were decently argued. I would decide §5 as well as §4. Also §§11 and 12.[18] There is no evidence on Virginia that is recent—only historic evidence. We need not say that the act is constitutional as applied to Virginia, only to South Carolina.

STEWART: The escape hatch in the act would cover Virginia.[19]

FORTAS: We should decide the merits of South Carolina and only it. We should deny her prayers and declare §§4, 5, 6(b), 11, and 12 valid.[20] We should pass on §5—provisions in §5 are not necessarily binding on the courts.

Result: On an 8–1 vote, the Court upheld all of the challenged provisions of the Voting Rights Act. Earl Warren's majority opinion gave Congress broad discretion to enforce the Fifteenth Amendment by any appropriate means. He noted that Congress had previously tried other, more limited means to establish and protect equal voting rights without success, leaving the legislature little choice but to adopt broader and more invasive remedies. Hugo Black dissented in part. He joined most of Warren's majority opinion but argued that §5 was unconstitutional.

---

18. Sections 11 and 12 established civil and criminal sanctions for interfering with any person's rights under the act.

19. Virginia remains one of seven southern states still subject to the Voting Rights Act.

20. Section 6(b) empowered the attorney general to assign federal examiners to register qualified applicants in jurisdictions covered by the act and to take other steps to ensure that all eligible persons would be allowed to register and vote.

Oregon v. Mitchell, 400 U.S. 112 (1970)
(Brennan)

In 1970 Congress amended the Voting Rights Act to (1) lower the voting age to eighteen years in all federal and state elections; (2) extend the limited ban on literacy tests to prohibit the use of all such tests nationwide; (3) abolish state residency requirements for presidential elections; and (4) set a national standard for absentee voting. Four states, including Oregon, challenged these amendments. The Supreme Court exercised its original jurisdiction to hear these cases, so there were no lower court decisions.

BURGER: Regarding the *literacy test*: Congress has no power here except as relates to discrimination as an instrument of it, and maybe they have made a case. About the *procedural requirements*: that is closer to being a Fourteenth Amendment subject. On the *eighteen-year-old vote*: fixing the voting age is the business of the states under the old learning. And §2 has imposed a sanction only as to twenty-one years and older. I don't think that the "perceive a basis" test of *Morgan* is applicable until you can find a discrimination against eighteen to twenty-one-year-olds.[21] The legislative history does not help.

BLACK: I agree with the Chief Justice. If there is a discrimination on account of *race*, Congress has broad powers under §5. But I see nothing except *age* here, and where we are looking for invidiousness we have to consider the powers of both the states and the federal government. The federal government can control residence requirements for federal offices. Under Article I §4, Congress can prescribe who may vote in federal elections but not in state elections—I think similarly as to the literacy tests.

DOUGLAS: Literacy, residence, and age. Under equal protection I would sustain all of these provisions as valid.

HARLAN: I would knock down all three statutes for both federal and state elections. If we judge them solely against the sweep of this Court's decisions starting with *Baker v. Carr*, powerful arguments can be marshaled to sustain all three.[22] *Katzenbach v. Morgan* would have to be extended to reach the eighteen-year-old vote.

STEWART: I am not even tentatively at rest. I don't think that these questions are decided by our cases. I still agree with the reasoning of the dissent in *Katzenbach v. Morgan* that Congress doesn't have the "Grand Power" to find that something is invidious discrimination. Legislation with respect to the eighteen-year-old voting age is unconstitutional. Perhaps Congress has that power for congressional elections, but this legislation was drafted to reach all elections. I think that the issue of the literacy tests is tougher—I am inclined to agree that this may be all right. Residency might be O.K., too, under the enforcement clause of the Fourteenth Amendment, because there is discrimination between voters solely on length of residence.

WHITE: I would uphold all of them.

---

21. *Katzenbach v. Morgan,* 384 U.S. 641 (1966).
22. *Baker v. Carr,* 369 U.S. 186 (1962).

MARSHALL: I would uphold all of them.

BLACKMUN: *Literacy tests*: I would have been against *Katzenbach v. Morgan* if I had been here, even though it makes a good case against discrimination in practice. This means I sustain the literacy test. *Residency:* this is different. Its limitation to the president and vice-president seems odd. But I am inclined to uphold it. *The eighteen-year-old vote*: necessarily, fixing a minimum age for voting is arbitrary. But that has always been regarded as matter for states. I am inclined to regard this as unconstitutional in its application to the states.

Result: The Court struck down the provision permitting eighteen-year-olds to vote in state and local elections but upheld the other amendments. The ban on literacy tests was approved unanimously. The new residency requirements were approved 8–1, with Harlan dissenting. Lowering the voting age to eighteen for national elections was approved by a narrow 5–4 vote, with Black, Douglas, Brennan, Marshall, and White in the majority. Black switched sides on the issue of lowering the voting age in state and local elections, joining Burger, Harlan, Stewart, and Blackmun to strike down that part of the law. The Twenty-sixth Amendment, ratified in 1971, gave eighteen-year-olds the right to vote in state as well as national elections.

PRIMARY ELECTIONS

United States v. Classic, 313 U.S. 299 (1941)
(Murphy)

Patrick B. Classic, a Louisiana primary election official, was accused of altering ninety-seven ballots in a congressional primary and falsely certifying the election results. Classic and several other state election officials were charged under §§19 and 20 of the federal Criminal Code.[23] Louisiana primary elections were conducted at public expense and were regulated by state law. Classic claimed that the federal law was unconstitutional as applied. He argued that primary elections were not real elections and were not subject to Congress's power to regulate congressional elections under Article 1.

HUGHES: As I was counsel in the *Newberry* case, I prefer to have it started by Justice Stone.[24]

---

23. Section 19 made it a crime to conspire to injure or oppress any citizen in the free exercise of any right or privilege secured by the Constitution. Section 20 provided for the punishment of anyone who, under color of law, willfully deprived any person of their rights, privileges or immunities under the Constitution and laws of the United States or who inflicted unequal punishments on the basis of alienage, color, or race.

24. *Newberry v. United States,* 256 U.S. 232 (1921). As a private lawyer, Charles Evans Hughes represented Truman H. Newberry, who was charged with violating the Federal Corrupt Practices Act. The act limited the amount of money that individuals could contribute to or spend on behalf of congressional candidates at primary elections, party conventions, and in general elections. Newman, a candidate for the U.S. Senate from Michigan, was convicted for exceeding the spending limits for his primary election. Hughes argued that party primaries were an independent, private nominating process and were not subject to congressional regulation or oversight. The Supreme Court agreed, ruling that primaries were not elections in a constitutional sense but merely the method by which private political groups agreed upon the candidates that their party would support at the general election. Accordingly, the Court decided, Congress's constitutional powers to regulate federal elections under Article 1 §4 did not extend to primary elections or party conventions.

STONE: This case comes to us only on the questions of the validity and construction of the statutes. The government finds constitutional support for the section involved (Article I, §2 and §4). "Secured under the Constitution" means rights under the protection of the Constitution. Having in mind that this is a constitution we are interpreting, and the Constitution itself relates to the manner or method of election, it strikes me that the primary election is a manner or method of election. On the whole case, I would reverse it.

ROBERTS: My mind goes that way, but I have difficulty with *Herndon*[25] and *Grovey.*[26]

BLACK: I think that the Constitution permits each step to be regulated. I have grave doubts about extending the conspiracy statute.

ROBERTS: I think that §5510 is not applicable here.[27] You have to get them under §5508.[28]

BLACK: The power of federal government is supreme.

STONE: Both §19 and §20 applied.

---

25. *Nixon v. Herndon,* 273 U.S. 536 (1927). Nixon, a resident of El Paso, brought a civil action against the Texas Judges of Elections for refusing to allow him to vote in the Democratic primary solely because he was black. A state law provided that "in no event shall a Negro be eligible to participate in a Democratic party primary election held in the state of Texas. . . ." Nixon claimed that the law violated the Fourteenth and Fifteenth Amendments. Oliver Wendell Holmes, writing for a unanimous Court, found it hard to imagine a more direct or obvious infringement of the Fourteenth Amendment. Because the law clearly violated the Fourteenth Amendment, Holmes thought it unnecessary to consider the Fifteenth Amendment issue.

26. In *Grovey v. Townsend,* 295 U.S. 45 (1935), a unanimous Court held that voting in primaries was not a constitutional right but a privilege of party membership. Roberts wrote the opinion for a unanimous Court, agreeing that the county clerk in Harris County, Texas, could refuse to give a ballot to a black voter who, except for the color of his skin, would have been eligible to vote in the state Democratic primary. In Roberts's view, the state party convention had acted on its own and without state help to restrict party membership to whites. The Court ruled that the county clerk was not a state official, and that there was no state action to trigger the Fourteenth or Fifteenth Amendments. This was, Roberts concluded, private racial discrimination and beyond the reach of Congress and the Constitution.

27. This was §19 of the Criminal Code: "If two or more persons conspire to injure, oppress, threaten, or intimidate any citizen in the free exercise or enjoyment of any right or privilege secured to him by the Constitution or laws of the United States, or because of his having so exercised the same, or if two or more persons go in disguise on the highway, or on the premises of another, with intent to prevent or hinder his free exercise or enjoyment of any right or privilege so secured, they shall be fined not more than $5,000 and imprisoned not more than ten years, and shall, moreover, be thereafter ineligible to any office, or place of honor, profit, or trust created by the Constitution or laws of the United States." Revised Statutes §5510; Mar. 4, 1909, c.321, §19, 35 Stat. 1092.

28. This was §20 of the Criminal Code, which provided: "Whoever, under color of any law, statute, ordinance, regulation, or custom, willfully subjects, or causes to be subjected, any inhabitant of any State, Territory, or District to the deprivation of any rights, privileges, or immunities secured or protected by the Constitution and laws of the United States, or to different punishments, pains, or penalties, on account of such inhabitant being an alien, or by reason of his color, or race, than are prescribed for the punishment of citizens, shall be fined not more than $1,000, or imprisoned not more than one year, or both." Revised Statutes §5510; Mar. 4, 1909, c. 321, §20, 35 Stat. 1092.

Result: With Harlan Fiske Stone writing for the majority, the Court ruled 5–3 that where state law made primary elections an integral part of electing congressional representatives, or where the primary election effectively controlled the choices available in the general election, the right of qualified citizens to vote in the primary election and to have their ballots counted were constitutionally protected under Article 1 §2. Such elections were also subject to congressional regulation under Article 1 §4. This meant that §§19 and 20 of the Criminal Code could be used to punish Classic and other election officials. The Court backed away from Grovey, recognizing that Louisiana primary elections were conducted at public expense and that election officials had acted "under color of state law" in miscounting ballots and falsifying election returns.

Black, Douglas, and Murphy dissented, arguing that §§19 and 20 were not specifically meant to cover primary elections and could not fairly be interpreted to apply to this case. Their votes were a reflection of their sympathy for criminal defendants and did not reflect any antipathy for expanding the right to vote in party primaries. The dissenters all agreed that Congress had the authority to regulate state primary elections. Chief Justice Hughes did not participate in the decision, although he apparently participated in the conference discussion.

Smith v. Allwright, 321 U.S. 649 (1944)
(Murphy) (Douglas)

Dr. Lonnie E. Smith was a Houston dentist and an officer of the local chapter of the NAACP. He attempted to vote in the 1940 Texas primary but was refused a ballot on account of his race. He sued in federal court, seeking $5,000 in damages and a judicial declaration of his right to vote.

White primaries were a tricky constitutional issue for the Court. The Justices had difficulty deciding whether primaries were part of the public electoral process or a private nominating process. The Court initially leaned toward the latter position, ruling in 1921 that primary elections were not part of the public election process and that Congress had no constitutional power to regulate them.[29]

Hoping to convince the Court to change its mind, the NAACP sent Thurgood Marshall to Texas to investigate Smith's complaint. State officials refused to cooperate when they found out that Marshall was an NAACP lawyer, and Marshall posed as a newspaper reporter to obtain the names of the state's election officials so that he could name them individually in the lawsuit.[30]

Conference of November 13, 1943

STONE: State election officials registered voters. They rejected black voters because the Democratic convention enacted a decision that Negroes were not members of its party. The Democratic party excluded Negroes, and maintains that they have the right to exclude them. The election officials' actions were simply sanctioning what the party had done. Those election officials are officials of the state. There is no difference on that score between this case and the *Classic* case.[31] Under Texas law the state, through state officers,

---

29. *Newberry v. United States,* 256 U.S. 232 (1921).

30. Marshall was under considerable pressure to win this case. He admitted that had he lost, he would have been forced to move to Germany to live with "Adolf Hitler or some other peace loving individual who would be less difficult than the Negroes in Texas who had put up the money for the case." Letter from Thurgood Marshall to his office, Nov. 17, 1941, quoted in Tushnet, *Making Civil Rights Law,* 31.

31. *United States v. Classic,* 313 U.S. 299 (1941).

regulate who controls who should vote in the primary. The impression is that the primary was not an election. But we came to the view in *Classic* that the primary was the real place of choice—hence it is a constitutional problem, since it was an election. So far, *Classic* and this one are the same.

Can we say that since state officials followed the Democratic party's proposal that only those who the party wants will vote, they ceased to act as state officials? That will not do. They ran counter to the Constitution and a statute, and gave rise to this civil action.

Under the proration law of California, questions were raised about whether the state gave its sanction to proration because it worked through private parties.[32] It still was state action, and the same is true here. This was state action which resulted in control of an election. When it did that, they ran counter to federal statutes and gave rise to cause of action under §43 of the Civil Rights Act.[33] Now it appears that the Democratic party, for the purpose of primary elections, has no membership restrictions except to exclude the colored man. That did not appear in the *Grovey* case.[34] I would face the broader issue. It does not cease to be state action because of the Democratic party and so forth. The colored man is denied a vote. It is an exclusion from the election. It violates the Constitution of the United States. We have reached the conclusion that the primary is an election, this being state action. I cannot reconcile this case with the *Classic* case. We have more facts here on the nature of the primary than we had in the earlier case. We must overrule *Townsend*.

ROBERTS: I am for affirming here. It is not a state matter at all. I am not going to overturn *Grovey*.

BLACK: I agree with the Chief Justice.

DOUGLAS: I reverse.

MURPHY: I agree with the Chief Justice.

JACKSON: You are faced with *Grovey*, and then people may be liable for damages when they acted on our opinion.

Second Conference

STONE: Texas was interesting, but places nothing new. I still can't reconcile it with the *Classic* case.

ROBERTS: I affirm.

---

32. In 1940, California launched a scheme to stabilize raisin prices by authorizing raisin producers to adopt production quotas and price controls. The Supreme Court held that while such actions would violate the Sherman Antitrust Act if done by private parties, state involvement in the scheme clothed the growers' private actions as state action and exempted them from the Sherman Act, absent congressional intent to the contrary. *Parker v. Brown*, 317 U.S. 341 (1943).

33. Smith sued under 8 U.S.C. §43, which was part of the Civil Rights Act of 1871. The act was based on Congress's Fourteenth and Fifteenth Amendment powers, and there was a state action requirement. A long line of Supreme Court cases had established that ending private social discrimination was not within the intent or scope of these amendments. In 1952, this section was reclassified as 42 U.S.C. §1983.

34. *Grovey v. Townsend*, 295 U.S. 45 (1935).

REED: We must overrule *Townsend*. *Classic* did it, now we should do it clearly.

FRANKFURTER: I agree, but I would do it in a roundabout way.

JACKSON: I am not sure that this primary is an election. If it is not election, then you can't have control over it. You have here the rights of people to form groups. I don't see how you are going to work it out.

STONE: But I am not talking about all primaries, but their primary.

RUTLEDGE: This primary was an election.

FRANKFURTER: The primary system is the opportunity of bypassing political will. These institutions, like the Ku Klux Klan, are un-American but not unconstitutional.

REED: I start with Article 15. I would say that they were abridged in the majority as well as the minority party.

Result: Harlan Fiske Stone originally assigned the opinion to Felix Frankfurter but changed his mind after Robert Jackson warned that it would be a mistake to have Frankfurter serve as the voice of the Court in this case, because he was "Jewish, a New Englander, and not a Democrat."[35] *Jackson urged Stone to assign the opinion to a southern Democrat. Stone agreed, and after explaining the matter to Frankfurter reassigned the case to Stanley Reed.*

Because the Court was already under attack for overturning its own precedents, Reed wanted to be delicate about overruling Grovey, *a unanimous precedent that was less than nine years old.*[36] *He sought to deflect any criticism by noting that* Grovey *had already implicitly been overruled by* United States v. Classic. *It was a clever bit of creative writing. Unlike* Smith v. Allwright, Classic *was easily distinguishable from* Grovey; *neither the majority nor the dissent in* Classic *had even mentioned the case.*

Citing Classic, *Reed declared that primary elections were part of a unitary electoral process. Primaries involved the delegation of state functions, which transformed the party's actions into state action. Because Texas authorized the Democratic party to determine the qualifications of primary participants, the state had effectively endorsed, adopted, and enforced racial discrimination.*

Frankfurter, not unreasonably, thought that Reed had misused Classic *and dismissed Reed's opinion as disingenuous "pussy-footing and petty-fogging."*[37] *In a memo to Stone, Frankfurter complained that he had "tried hard to make Reed give the opinion the form and atmosphere of aggressive*

---

35. Jackson, who was on friendly terms with Frankfurter, did not make the recommendation out of personal prejudice but as a practical political matter based on "some of the ugly factors of our national life." Dunne, *Hugo Black and the Judicial Revolution*, 218–9.

36. Press criticism of Supreme Court activism was widespread, with accusations that the Court was acting "a third legislative house" and that the Constitution had become "a mere thing of wax in the hands of the judiciary." The Court's growing tendency to ignore precedent was attacked as "The New Guesspotism." Mason, *Harlan Fiske Stone*, 624. Most of the criticism came from newspapers that had earlier opposed the New Deal and applauded the reactionary activism of the Four Horsemen—Pierce Butler, James McReynolds, George Sutherland, and Willis Van Devanter.

37. Tushnet, *Making Civil Rights Law*, 106.

candor . . . but Reed has his own notions of appeasement which are bound to fail."[38] *In the end, Frank-furter concurred in the result.*

Owen Roberts, who wrote the majority opinion in Grovey, *dissented and assailed the majority for blithely overturning established precedents. This sort of judicial capriciousness, he warned, would damage the Court's reputation and destroy public confidence in the law by bringing Supreme Court adjudications "into the same class as a restricted railroad ticket, good for this day and train only."*

Terry v. Adams, 345 U.S. 461 (1953)
(Burton)

After Smith v. Allwright, *Texas and other southern states continued their efforts to prevent blacks from gaining political influence. The Jaybird Democratic Association was an all-white political organization founded in 1888 in Fort Bend County, southwest of Houston. All registered white voters in the county automatically became members of the association, while blacks were excluded. The organization held its own primary elections in May, six to eight weeks before the state Democratic primaries. The Jaybird elections were not governed by state laws and did not use any state funds or elective machinery. Winners were not certified by the association and had to file on their own to qualify for the Democratic primary. In practice, however, the Jaybird winners were usually the only candidates on the ballot in the Democratic primaries and they almost invariably won the general election. John Terry initiated a class action suit against A. J. Adams and other Jaybird officers, seeking $5,000 in damages and a declaration that blacks were entitled to vote in the Jaybird primaries.*

This case was especially difficult for the Court because the Jaybird organization was more like a private club than a traditional political party. Thurgood Marshall, the NAACP's senior litigator, argued against taking the case because he did not think that the NAACP would win.[39] *In his conference notes, Burton recorded his own vote to reverse quite emphatically.*

VINSON: I can't see that it is state action, using the mechanisms that they do. (*Rice v. Elmore.*)[40] I would affirm.

BLACK: If either the Republican or Democratic party had done what is done here, it would violate the Constitution. It would be a strange thing if we can be imprisoned by any words that prevent us from prohibiting this. There can be no denial of equal protection of the laws, on the basis of race and color particularly. It is clear what it does, and they can't do that. It means a violation of the Constitution. If this is approved, it will be seized upon. It is designed to deprive Negroes of the vote. I reverse.

REED: Hugo is right in his views, and logic is with Vinson. Either argument is unanswerable. The future of *Smith* depends on the ability of Negroes to vote. Something like this

---

38. Jackson to Stone, Jan. 17, 1944, quoted in Urofsky, *Division and Discord*, 101.
39. Tushnet, *Making Civil Rights Law*, 110.
40. *Rice v. Elmore*, 165 F.2d 387 (4th Cir. 1947), cert. denied, 333 U.S. 875 (1948). This circuit court decision invalidated South Carolina's attempt to remove all traces of state control over the state's Democratic primaries. Like Texas, South Carolina claimed that these partisan "clubs" were private groups and could exclude whomever they wanted. The court of appeals rejected the state's arguments and held that no election machinery could, in purpose or effect, deny citizens an effective voice in government on the basis of race or color.

is the right to jury trial. They don't have to *prove* discrimination. What South Carolina did in *Rice v. Elmore* was treated as no state action. The seriousness of this is overwhelming. I pass.

FRANKFURTER: I wish that Hugo would help us to see some things as he does. We are dealing here with an accepted *right* by all of us on this Court.[41] The Negro is entitled to the right to vote. Hugo says that he wants to enforce the Constitution, but Hugo says also no "state." I can't see where the state comes in. If it was the state's duty to disband them? I pass.

DOUGLAS: I reverse.

JACKSON: The Fourteenth Amendment prevents a state from setting up any form or device. But having set up a primary that is open does not prevent this. I don't think that its success makes it unconstitutional. People have some rights. I affirm.

BURTON. *Reverse.* [Said emphatically.]

CLARK: They have created here the only entrance to the Democratic primary. They do dilute the vote. They have warped, then, the primary process. They have already committed people to voting for certain candidates. Texas admitted that the implications are bad, but said that this was an 1889 organization and not a Johnny-come-lately. But I don't see how we could prohibit other organizations and not this one. I would give no weight to the organization's age. This is a very difficult case for me. To do otherwise would practically overturn the previous cases. Our decree should be reserved for state action in a technical sense. This is the entrance to the primary. I think that it comes down to effective state action. I reverse.

MINTON: I affirm.

Result: A lopsided 8–1 vote to open the Jaybird primaries to black voters only partly camouflaged the fact that the Justices were deeply divided. Black's plurality decision was joined only by Douglas and Burton, while Clark's concurring opinion was joined by Vinson, Reed, and Jackson. Frankfurter concurred separately. The Justices sought to paper over their disagreements by issuing a vague and equivocal decree to the district court "to enter such orders and decrees as are necessary and proper." The decree passed the burden of working out the details to the local district court. This tactic proved useful and was later resurrected during the Court's conference discussions in Brown v. Board of Education.

Shay Minton was the sole dissenter. Minton said that he was not at all concerned about the Jaybirds or their "unworthy scheme" but that he did not see "one iota" of state action necessary to justify the Court's decision. The Jaybirds were not associated in any way with the state or the Democratic party. To Minton, they were a purely private political group for political advocacy and lobbying, no different from any other special interest group—including the NAACP. As a private association, their choice to exclude blacks was beyond the reach of the Fourteenth and Fifteenth Amendments. Whether

---

41. Frankfurter worried that if the Court found state action in the Jaybird primary, the Jaybird Association would be compelled to admit blacks into their organization. For a number of reasons, Frankfurter wanted to avoid this result. Tushnet, *Making Civil Rights Law,* 111.

their goals were noble or venal, Minton concluded that the Court had no business telling the Jaybirds who to accept as members.

REAPPORTIONMENT AND REDISTRICTING

Colegrove v. Green, 328 U.S. 549 (1946)
(Burton)

Illinois congressional districts had not been reapportioned since 1901, despite four consecutive federal censuses that showed a significant population shift to urban areas. The ratio of population inequality among districts was approximately 9:1, ranging from 914,000 persons in the largest district to 112,000 persons in the smallest. Professor Kenneth W. Colegrove and two other voters sued Governor Dwight H. Green to block the 1946 elections, claiming that the state's congressional districts were illegal because they lacked population equality and territorial compactness (many of the state's districts were grossly gerrymandered). To support his claims, Colegrove cited the federal Reapportionment Act of 1911 and three provisions of the federal constitution: Article 1's apportionment requirements, Article 4's guarantee of a republican form of government, and the Fourteenth Amendment's voting rights guarantees.

STONE: Shall we reaffirm this on the *Broom* case, or dismiss the case on grounds that not this is not a proper case of equity?[42] In this case, the petitioners appeal to the Fourteenth Amendment, which was not in the *Broom* case. The clause does operate here, and if you get into it that is a nice question. In the *Broom* case, the parties cited and argued the Fourteenth Amendment, but nothing was said on it by the Court. I would say here that declaratory judgments are not necessarily equity (they asked for a declaratory judgment just to get equity jurisdiction). I have a serious objection to this Court deciding declaratory judgments on issues that Congress need not follow.

BLACK: It is difficult to think that this is the kind of case or controversy that the Constitution contemplates. If it is, this Court has power to act. But there is no cause of action, at least there is none of which we should take cognizance. [BURTON: Stone and Black and Reed do not want to put it on laches.][43]

---

42. *Wood v. Broom,* 287 U.S. 1 (1932). Mississippi voters sued to enjoin enforcement of the state's 1932 redistricting plan on the ground that it violated the federal Reapportionment Act of 1911. That act required congressional districts to have contiguous and compact territory and, as nearly as practicable, to have equal populations. The Supreme Court considered only the compactness issue, ruling that the Reapportionment Act applied only to districting plans enacted between 1911 and 1929—at which time Congress passed a new Reapportionment Act that did not include a compactness provision. Charles Evans Hughes's majority opinion explicitly left open the issue of unequal populations and Fourteenth Amendment issues and avoided the questions of whether the underlying issues were justiciable or whether an injunction or other equitable remedy would have been available. The four dissenters—Brandeis, Stone, Roberts, and Cardozo—thought that the case should have been dismissed for want of equity, without ruling on the merits.

43. Estoppel by laches is a term used in equity cases and is roughly equivalent to a statute of limitations. The argument was that the plaintiffs had waited too long to complain, and in the interim such a change of conditions had taken place that, even assuming that the plaintiffs prevailed on the merits, it would not be fair to permit them to enforce their claimed rights.

REED: I would not go on the ground that equity could enforce its decree. This type of case is for Congress to decide. This is a political question.

FRANKFURTER: Deal with this—*Kiernan v. Portland* and republican form of government.[44] That would take care of the Fourteenth Amendment.

DOUGLAS: I would reverse. This is not a political question—it is equitable.[45]

MURPHY: I reverse.

RUTLEDGE: This is not justiciable—it is a political question.

BURTON: This is a political cause of action. We have the power to order them not to certify the election, but the cause of action is political. Just rules to create a chaotic condition—that would indirectly lead to—

Result: This case was decided by a seven-person Court. Harlan Fiske Stone died a month after oral argument, and Robert Jackson was still in Europe serving as the chief American prosecutor at the Nuremberg trials. The Court ruled on a 3–1–3 vote that reapportionment decisions were nonjusticiable political questions. Felix Frankfurter's plurality opinion stressed that reapportionment questions posed considerable dangers for the Court. Frankfurter warned against entering the "political thicket" and argued that such matters were best left to the democratic branches of government. Only Reed and Burton joined Frankfurter's opinion. Wiley Rutledge concurred in the result but thought that reapportionment issues might be justiciable under different circumstances. In this instance, however, Rutledge thought that the case should be dismissed "for want of equity," because the elections were being held too soon to give the courts enough time to provide an adequate remedy.

Black, Douglas, and Murphy dissented. They argued that even if Illinois had to elect congressional representatives at large, it would be preferable to the current system because at least every voter would have an equal voice.

Gomillion v. Lightfoot, 364 U.S. 339 (1960)
(Douglas) (Brennan)

Charles Goode Gomillion, dean of the Tuskegee Institute, and other black residents of Tuskegee, Alabama, charged that the state legislature redrew the city's boundaries to exclude blacks from voting in municipal elections in violation of the Fourteenth and Fifteenth Amendments. The district court dismissed the suit, ruling that the federal courts had no authority over municipal boundaries. Phil M. Lightfoot was the mayor of Tuskegee.

---

44. *Kiernan v. Portland* 223 U.S. 151 (1912); see also *Pacific States Telephone Co. v. Oregon,* 223 U.S. 118 (1912). Both cases involved claims that Oregon's initiative and referendum system violated Article 4, §4, which required states to maintain a republican form of government. The plaintiffs argued that Oregon's initiative and referendum system was unconstitutional because it changed the state from a republican to a democratic form of government. Chief Justice Edward White, writing for a unanimous Court, dismissed both cases for want of jurisdiction because they raised nonjusticiable political questions.

45. Elsewhere in his conference notes, Burton noted that William O. Douglas was absent from this conference. It is not clear how Douglas's views were transmitted to the rest of the Court.

Among the issues discussed in conference were the likelihood of political opposition to the Court's decision, what to do about Colegrove, *whether this was a Fourteenth or a Fifteenth Amendment case, and which party had the burden of proof.*

Conference of October 21, 1960

WARREN: I reverse. We do not have to deal with the *Colegrove* problem.[46] The complaint states that petitioners have been deprived of voting rights by reason of color. The allegations are sufficient.

BLACK: I reverse. The distinction between this case and *Colegrove* is not sound. We should argue that this is a new field. Nothing up to date has been like this. [DOUGLAS: Black refers to the three-judge court opinion that knocked out the Boswell Amendment.][47] Cities move boundaries around to meet various problems. States can abolish counties, or increase or decrease their size, unless barred by an express provision of the Constitution. This was done for the express and exclusive purpose of preventing these Negro citizens from voting in Tuskegee. I would say that this could come under the Fourteenth Amendment's equal protection clause as well as the Fifteenth Amendment. Our opinion will be received with as much hostility as *Brown v. Board of Education*.[48] If political considerations are to keep us from adjudicating a case, this should be the one. All cities in the South do this.

FRANKFURTER: This is a simple case. The state here passed a single act nominally dealing with redistricting, but doing it in such a way as to show that it had nothing to do with geography, but only separating black from white. The state seeks cover under our *Colegrove* line of cases, but *Colegrove* is not even remotely relevant here. *Colegrove* is irrelevant because the Constitution gives Congress express power under Article I §4 to redistrict. But this is political in a constitutionally illegal way. Here Negroes are fenced out because they are Negroes. The state also relies on the series of cases as to fixing municipal lines, *Hunter v. Pittsburgh*, etc.[49] Any state can abolish municipal organizations. Our recognition of their "plenary" power was correct in that context, but not in this one.

DOUGLAS: This should be narrowly written. There are parts of this complaint which don't state a cause of action. The mere deprivation of votes by means of redrawing the lines is

---

46. *Colegrove v. Green*, 328 U.S. 549 (1946).

47. The Boswell Amendment to the Alabama constitution required prospective voters to explain a section of the state constitution to the satisfaction of a registrar of voters. *Davis v. Schnell*, 81 F. Supp. 872 (DCSD Ala. 1949), affirmed, *Schnell v. Davis*, 336 U.S. 933 (1949).

48. *Brown v. Board of Education*, 347 U.S. 483 (1954).

49. *Hunter v. Pittsburgh*, 207 U.S. 161 (1907). Citizens of Allegheny, Pennsylvania, sued to prevent the assembly from consolidating their town into the municipality of Pittsburgh without their consent. Allegheny residents claimed that they had already paid for civic improvements that Pittsburgh was just getting around to planning, meaning that Allegheny residents would be hit with an unreasonable tax increase and be forced to pay for the same civic improvements a second time without any benefit to themselves. The Court refused to stop the annexation, finding no constitutional right to any particular level of taxation nor any civic contract to use tax money only in the location where the money was raised. In *Gomillion*, Alabama claimed—unsuccessfully—that this case stood for the proposition that states had an constitutionally unrestricted authority to establish, change, or destroy its political subdivisions at will.

not enough. It is only on the allegation of the state's purpose to deprive Negroes of the right to vote that I think we can reverse. I reverse.

CLARK: I reverse.

HARLAN: I reverse.

BRENNAN: I would rely on the Fifteenth Amendment. I think that it is undesirable to go on the Fourteenth Amendment.

WHITTAKER: I reverse. The petitioners must show "motive," and not mere "effect," as Bill Douglas says. I would rest on the Fifteenth Amendment. I have difficulty in finding evidence to support legislative motive.

STEWART: I reverse. I would put it narrowly. We must confine this to the relevant allegations of the complaint under the Fifteenth Amendment. The plaintiff has the burden of proof. The federal government is wrong in saying that once an allegation is made the city has the burden of proof.

Result: A unanimous Court ruled that Alabama's power to fix its own municipal boundaries was limited by the Fifteenth Amendment. Frankfurter distinguished his earlier opinion in Colegrove, *ruling that the state could not redraw city boundary lines in order to deprive people of the vote on account of race. Frankfurter's job was made easier by the fact that the state had changed the shape of Tuskegee "from a square to an uncouth twenty-eight-sided figure" in a transparent attempt to disenfranchise virtually every black voter. Whittaker concurred in the judgment.*

For Frankfurter, this case was logically unrelated to Colegrove. *For Black and Douglas, however, it was the break they needed to launch a new frontal attack on Frankfurter's political question doctrine.*

Baker v. Carr, 369 U.S. 186 (1962)

(Douglas) (Brennan)

In 1901, the Tennessee legislature apportioned its general assembly seats among the state's ninety-five counties. Despite significant population growth and urbanization over the next six decades, the legislature never reapportioned the assembly districts.[50] *Charles Baker of Memphis sued secretary of state Joe Carr claiming that gross population imbalances among the state's assembly districts violated voters' equal protection rights under the Fourteenth Amendment. A three-judge district court dismissed*

---

50. Malapportionment resulting from legislative inaction is often called the "silent gerrymander." By 1960, it had become a chronic problem in many states. In Tennessee, the smallest state legislative district had a population of 25,000, while the largest had a population of 132,000. A mere 40 percent of the population elected 75 percent of the state legislature. In Vermont, which had not redistricted since 1793, one state legislative district had just 36 people in it, while another had more than 133,000 residents. In Florida, 19 percent of the population elected more than 50 percent of the state legislature. In California, more than half of the state senate was elected by less than 11 percent of the population. In Los Angeles County 6 million people elected one state senator, while a senate district in northern California had a population of just 14,000. There were similar imbalances among congressional districts. In more than half of the states, the largest congressional district had more than twice as many voters as the smallest district.

the case for want of jurisdiction, citing Colegrove v. Green.[51] *The solicitor general who aggressively—Frankfurter and Harlan thought recklessly—pushed the case to the Supreme Court was Archibald Cox.*

Conference of April 20, 1961

WARREN: I agree with the case as presented by the United States, and I reverse on that argument. But I think that we should say that the complaint states a cause of action. The district court has jurisdiction. I would reverse.[52]

BLACK: I reverse. My dissent in *Colegrove v. Green* covers this. I also still agree with my *Peters* dissent. There should be a trial on this complaint.[53]

FRANKFURTER: I affirm. Unless we affirm, we will get into great difficulty and this Court will rue the results. I think that the solicitor general was irresponsible in stating that there is a permissible remedy. In *Colegrove*, Stone and Jackson supported my view.[54] The costs will be very serious. The Tennessee constitution has nothing to do with the case—this must be a violation of the federal Constitution for the petitioner to get in federal court.[55] Every machinery of every state puts everyone on a par with everyone else. The solicitor general said that he was not arguing for "equality" in voting, but that history, the congregation of populations, and the like could be considered. All of these factors are not capable of being determined by the courts. Not one state is free of gerrymandering—how can courts determine what is fair in this area? The subject matter is not proper for

---

51. *Colegrove v. Green*, 328 U.S. 549 (1946). In *Colegrove*, the population variation was even worse than in *Baker v. Carr*. One rural Illinois congressional district had a population of 100,000 people, while an urban Chicago district had a population of over 900,000.

52. As governor of California, Earl Warren favored modeling the state's bicameral legislature along federal lines, with the Assembly apportioned according to population and the state Senate representing counties. This ensured that Warren's main constituencies in northern California and in rural districts (Warren's political support came largely from agriculture, forestry, and mining interests) would control the Senate. As Chief Justice, however, Warren saw the problems of apportionment and representation quite differently and concluded that the federal model was inappropriate for state legislatures. He publicly announced his change of heart in *Wesberry v. Sanders* and *Reynolds v. Sims*. See Cray, *Chief Justice*, 379–86, 432.

53. *South v. Peters*, 339 U.S. 276 (1950). Under Georgia law, state primary elections were run on a county-based electoral system. The most populous counties received six electoral votes, while the least populous counties received a minimum of two votes. Residents of Fulton County, the most populous county in the state, sued on the ground that a vote in Fulton County was worth less than one-tenth of a vote in more rural counties. The Supreme Court, in a brief per curiam opinion, dismissed the case as a nonjusticiable political question, citing *Colegrove v. Green*. Douglas and Black dissented.

54. Frankfurter tried to inflate the precedential value of *Colegrove* by claiming that a majority of five Justices supported his opinion in that case. In fact, only Reed and Burton joined Frankfurter's plurality opinion in *Colegrove*. Neither Stone nor Jackson participated in the case; Stone died before the case could be decided, and Jackson was in Nuremberg. To make matters worse for Frankfurter, on one of the most important questions decided in *Colegrove* Frankfurter was in the minority. Of the seven Justices who decided the case, a majority voted that the Court had subject matter jurisdiction: Black, Douglas, Murphy, and Rutledge.

55. The Tennessee constitution required a decennial census and reapportionment and provided specific regulations to ensure equitable reapportionments. The state legislature ignored its constitutional mandate and made no attempt to reapportion the state's legislative districts between 1901 and 1961.

judicial inquiry—look at *Luther v. Borden*.[56] Also look at our initiative and referenda cases. Also look at our decision in *Massachusetts v. Mellon*.[57]

DOUGLAS: I reverse.

CLARK: The precedents are against us. If we upset the Tennessee system, it would have no legislature. Equality is not the basis of voting in the electoral college. Equality is not a basic principle in American political voting.

HARLAN: I agree wholly with Felix's views. I think that the solicitor general was reckless in his desire to inject the judiciary into this field. There is no federally protected right in an individual based on equality of voting. Moreover, this is not a justiciable issue. This Court is not competent to solve this type of problem. I affirm.

BRENNAN: Our decisions have not yet held that this is not a federally protected right. The purpose of the Fourteenth Amendment was to give equality. Much of its history pertained to voting rights. I would rely on the equal protection clause. I do not believe that the remedies are insoluble—I have worked it out with a judicial remedy. I reverse.

WHITTAKER: If we wrote on a clean slate, I would say that petitioners have standing to sue and that they are being denied equal protection of the laws—then no relief in the state courts. If there is a constitutional right involved, the chancellor should not with-

---

56. *Luther v. Borden*, 48 U.S. (7 How.) 1 (1849). Unlike other states, Rhode Island refused to enact a new constitution after the Revolution and kept its original royal charter. The charter placed severe restrictions on the right to vote. The situation led Thomas Dorr and other disaffected citizens to call a constitutional convention to adopt a more democratic constitution. Statewide elections were held under the new constitution and a new government was installed, with Dorr as governor, in competition with the established charter government. This became known as Dorr's Rebellion (1841–42).

Martin Luther was a supporter of the Dorr government, while Luther Borden was a member of the charter government's militia. Luther brought an action in trespass against Borden and others for illegally breaking into and entering his home. Borden claimed that he was authorized to arrest Luther for aiding and abetting a rebellion against the lawful state government. Borden, who belonged to a company of infantry that controlled Luther's hometown of Warren, claimed that he had acted under lawful orders to arrest Luther and that he was authorized to break and enter Luther's home if necessary to take him into custody.

Borden won at the trial level. On appeal to the Supreme Court, Luther sought to challenge the charter government on the ground that it violated Article 4's "guarantee to every state in the union a republican form of government." The Court ruled 8–1 that this issue was a nonjusticiable political question. Roger Brooke Taney also noted that the president, as authorized by Congress, had recognized the charter government as the legitimate government of Rhode Island. Only Levi Woodbury dissented.

57. *Massachusetts v. Mellon*, 262 U.S. 447 (1922). The Maternity Act apportioned federal money to participating states to promote maternal and infant health. Funds could be withheld if a state did not comply with federal guidelines. Massachusetts sued to enjoin enforcement of the act on the grounds that (1) it impermissibly induced states to surrender their sovereign rights in violation of the Tenth Amendment; and (2) the burdens fell unequally on states, with most appropriations coming from industrial states such as Massachusetts. Andrew Mellon was secretary of the treasury.

The Supreme Court declined to decide the case on the merits. The federal program was strictly voluntary and Massachusetts was not required to do, pay, or surrender anything. The only tax burden fell on individual citizens, not the states. Because Massachusetts had not suffered any injury, the case presented only an abstract question of political power and was not justiciable.

hold relief. Precedents, however, say that this is a "political" issue. I am reluctant to over-rule those cases. So I affirm, but I would do so only on an equity ground.

STEWART: I am not at rest on the issue. I have trouble seeing that disproportionate voting is a violation of equal protection. A state can divide up its jurisdiction into unequal political units. I would uphold the Michigan system that is here in another case we are holding. Tennessee is different, because it has a law that requires equality, and the state's failure to apply it may raise an equal protection point. I have sufficient doubt that I pass.

Conference of April 28, 1961

STEWART: [DOUGLAS: This case was passed for him.] I think that this is as important a case as our school segregation cases. Under our precedents, we can go either way. It will establish a big precedent if we go in and let the federal courts supervise these affairs. I would suggest putting the case down for rehearing. [DOUGLAS: Since Potter has the critical vote, everyone agreed to put case down for reargument in October.][58]

After Reargument: Conference of October 13, 1961

WARREN: There is a violation of equal protection shown here. I don't think that we have to decide the merits on the question of republican form of government. All we have to decide is that there is jurisdiction. We have jurisdiction—no case says we do not. We don't have to say that the state must give precise equality. Here we have a classification that denies some classes the right to cast their ballots with the strength that others cast theirs.

We can't say that we must stay out of state election problems, since Congress has put us in it as the defense procedure for inquiring into the denial of the vote on racial grounds. Congress in the Civil Rights Acts has put watchers on the polls in state elections. We come in only where the line of arbitrariness has been crossed. All we need to do here is to say that this shows an arbitrary and capricious practice. The Court has jurisdiction. I would reverse solely on jurisdiction, and leave the rest of the case and the form of decree to the district court. I would not at this time say what decree should be entered, although I would suggest certain guidelines.

BLACK: I adhere to my views in *Colegrove v. Green*. Felix's memo in this case is a good brief for a weak cause. *Colegrove v. Green* is a weak reed on which to hang any notion of an established rule. That opinion was only agreed to by Frankfurter, Reed, and Burton. It did not rest on *Luther v. Borden*. I agree with *Luther v. Borden*, with each party having claimed to represent the state. It wasn't a dispute over a law passed by state, but an argument about which group *was* the state. Congress has the power to resolve that issue. Felix cited an Oregon case which said that Congress must decide "all" questions of whether

---

58. Stewart was the only Justice who had not made up his mind before the first oral argument. He was under tremendous pressure from Warren and Brennan on one side, and Frankfurter and Harlan on the other.

states have a republican form of government.[59] But as Wilson said, it is different when you attack a law that is not an attack on the state's form of government and whether it denies a republican form of government.[60] Here, no interlopers have tried to seize the government.

Here, it is simply a question whether the law passed bears so unequally—capriciously— as to deny equal protection. Does this act bear so unequally and arbitrarily as to deny equal protection? I think that it does, and I reverse. In *Luther v. Borden*, Congress could give relief. Here, Congress has no power to give relief to these people, whatever their power may be to pass legislation under the Fourteenth Amendment.

FRANKFURTER: [DOUGLAS: He refers to his long memo that has been circulated.][61] To reverse this, we will have to reverse the *Kidd* case, where we dismissed the appeal.[62] Asserting jurisdiction in this case is fraught with such consequences that to me are so dangerous to our whole system that I would stay out. Principles fundamental to society may sometimes be unenforceable by the Courts, as witness Part IV of the Indian Constitution.[63] What are the standards by which a remedy is to be fashioned?

DOUGLAS: *Gomillion* is a precedent leading to reversal here.[64] The equal protection clause is not designed just for Negroes—even he has to show an arbitrary discrimination. Negroes have no greater right under equal protection than whites. The difficulties of the judiciary doing anything about it, great as they are, can't deter us from doing our job.

CLARK: I would dismiss. The petitioners failed to show that they had exhausted other avenues to relief: (1) in Congress; and (2) there was no campaign in Tennessee to include

---

59. *Pacific Tel. & Tel. Co. v. Oregon,* 223 U.S. 118 (1912). The Court decided that it lacked jurisdiction to determine whether the Oregon Supreme Court had erred when it ruled that direct lawmaking by voters through state referenda and initiatives was consistent with a republican form of government. Pacific Telephone and Telegraph Company had argued that the referenda and initiative system were *democratic* rather than *republican* forms of government and that they would undermine the established representative institutions of government, particularly the state legislature.

60. Jack Wilson, the assistant attorney general of Tennessee, argued the state's case at oral argument.

61. Before this conference, Felix Frankfurter circulated a sixty-five-page memorandum warning the brethren of the "dire consequences" of entering the political thicket of reapportionment. With everyone else's mind already made up, the memorandum was probably written entirely for Stewart's benefit. Yarbrough, *John Marshall Harlan,* 275.

62. *Kidd v. McCanless,* 352 U.S. 920 (1956). Gates Kidd and other Tennessee voters sued George F. McCanless, the state attorney general, seeking a declaratory judgment that the state legislative Apportionment Act of 1901 was unconstitutional. Kidd also sought an injunction to stop any future elections under the act. The state supreme court dismissed the suit on the ground that courts had no power to compel either the legislative or the executive departments to perform duties committed exclusively to them by the constitution. In a one sentence per curiam opinion, the Supreme Court dismissed Kidd's appeal.

63. Part 4 of the Indian Constitution lists the Directive Principles of State Policy. Under Article 37, these principles are not judicially enforceable but enumerate the fundamental socioeconomic principles for governing the country. These principles include: minimizing inequalities of income, status, and opportunity; establishing equal pay for equal work for men and women; the right to a living wage and humane working conditions; free and compulsory elementary education; and free legal services for indigents.

64. *Gomillion v. Lightfoot,* 364 U.S. 339 (1960).

in its case this problem. Even if there was jurisdiction, I would not exercise it. Congress could act to end discrimination in the twenty-odd states where this discrimination exists. There are a dozen cases since 1932 when the Court has stayed out of this problem. Look at *MacDougall* and all of the cases that came to us after *Colegrove*. I think that we should adhere to *Colegrove*.[65]

HARLAN: My earlier views have been reinforced by reargument. If Tennessee had enacted this scheme in its constitution or by statute, an attack would assert no claim of violation of the Constitution. If a state can distribute its organs of government as it wishes without subjecting itself to federal judicial supervision or interference, then I can't see why a state may not—free of judicial federal restraint—chose the means whereby these organs are to be created and the rules enforced. I would not deal with this on an equal protection basis—there is no federally protected right involved here. But even if you got over this and say that there is an equal protection claim, I still can't see under our standards any disparity between urban and rural voters that offends equal protection. It is the fact that it is a violation of the state constitution that brings this case about. There is no jurisdiction here, because no federal cause of action is stated. It makes no difference whether the votes are loaded one way or the other. The *Tuskegee* case, on the other hand, was a denial of the right to vote, and that can't be denied because of race under the Fifteenth Amendment.[66] I would plead, for the protection of this Court, against getting into these political contests. The protection of this Court has been in refraining from getting involved in these problems. [DOUGLAS: My God—what does he think the *Segregation Cases* were—or the *Tuskegee* case?]

BRENNAN: There is an equal protection problem presented here. By historic tradition, one house in the states is always elected by the people. Here, there is a capricious and arbitrary denial of equal protection. I would assert jurisdiction, but not direct a specific decree. I think that an assertion of power will cause the Tennessee legislature to act. Look at Senate Bill No.2579 of September 19, 1961, which would amend the Constitution to provide for equitable representation, plus a bill which provides a standard. This was introduced by Senator Joseph Clark of Pennsylvania. I do not think that *Kidd* should be taken too seriously. We passed over quite a few Sunday Law cases before last term, when we took the cases and decided them.[67] I would reverse for a hearing on the merits of the complaint.

---

65. *MacDougall v. Greene*, 335 U.S. 281 (1948). An Illinois law required third parties to gather 25,000 voters' signatures in order to nominate candidates for political office, including at least 200 signatures from fifty of the state's 102 counties. Curtis MacDougall, a journalist and the Progressive party's candidate for U.S. Senate, sued Governor Dwight Green to require the state to place other Progressive party candidates on the ballot regardless of whether they met the state's signature requirements. The Supreme Court refused to intervene, ruling that Illinois had considerable discretion to regulate its own electoral process and that the law did not violate the federal Constitution. Rutledge concurred in the result, solely on the ground that there was too little time to fashion an adequate equitable remedy before the next election. Douglas, Black, and Murphy dissented.

66. *Gomillion v. Lightfoot*, 364 U.S. 339 (1960).

67. *McGowan v. Maryland*, 366 U.S. 420 (1961); *Two Guys from Harrison-Allentown v. McGinley*, 366 U.S. 582 (1961); *Braunfeld v. Brown*, 366 U.S. 599 (1961); and *Gallagher v. Crown Kosher Market*, 366 U.S. 617 (1961).

WHITTAKER: I affirmed last term but was very shaky on it. I have written two memos diametrically opposed to each other—one for asserting jurisdiction and one for affirmance. I now affirm, but not for lack of judicial power or jurisdiction. The district court dismissed this case on that ground, but it was wrong. That court also dismissed on the ground that the complaint failed to state a cause of action on which relief might be granted. We do not enforce state law, but equal protection of rights granted by state law. In *Kidd*, it was alleged that apportionment was not made in accord with the Tennessee constitution. It refused to pass on the de facto issue for Tennessee, because they would be without a government.

But the Tennessee constitution and statute have been read by the Tennessee Supreme Court. The Tennessee court held that the 1901 apportionment act is not judicially cognizable or enforceable, and the effect of that decision was to amend the state constitution and statute to say that neither shall be justiciable in the courts. If that is so, then the claim here that the petitioners have been deprived of a right granted by state law fails, for no right granted them by state law has been denied. The federal court has jurisdiction to entertain this type of claim, but there is no right to enforce.

STEWART: The district court had jurisdiction. This is not a so-called political question. A "political" question is a problem the determination of which the Constitution has precluded from the courts and placed in another branch of government. There is standing on the part of these petitioners. This is not a "republican form of government" case that involves the other branches of government. Given jurisdiction and standing, I can't say whether the district court can or cannot afford appropriate relief. Some of the suggestions of the solicitor general seem to me to be impractical. I can't follow here Rutledge's abstention in *Colegrove*, as the election is a year away. On the merits, there is an assumption that equal protection requires the legislature to apportion votes so that there is no discrimination. I would reject that view. Our entire American history presumes the contrary, and on that history I follow Frankfurter's memo.

I couldn't say that equal protection requires representation approximately commensurate with voting strength. States could give towns only one vote, whatever their size. States could allocate voting rights by taxes paid, education, and so forth. The only equality demanded is that of the Fifteenth Amendment. Every presumption here is in favor of every state action, like with the cases last term involving the Sunday Laws. So the state does not have to justify every departure from a one man one vote basis, and the greatest burden of proof is on the plaintiff to show an arbitrary and capricious system.

Basically, this is the same as if Tennessee had by its constitution ordained the present system. What is done by inaction is the same as what is done by direct action. Conceivably, there can be a denial of equal protection in an apportionment case—so there is a cause of action stated here. There was one in the Sunday Laws cases. If this was discrimination against red-haired people or those over fifty years of age, then we would have a case for action. It would then be wholly capricious. The giving of greater weight of votes to rural blocs is O.K. There may be difficulty here in justifying discrimination in contiguous counties. The fact that the state court says that the issue is not justiciable is not binding on the federal courts. On that score, I disagree with Whittaker—a state can't take away one's right to enforce a constitutional right. This is like the *Shelley* case, in that there is much being held for this case. I think that decision has unusual wisdom. On the merits, I agree more or less with Bill Brennan.

Result: When Earl Warren assigned the opinion to William Brennan after conference, both men expected to produce a sweeping decision that states were constitutionally required to reapportion periodically in order to maintain a fair population balance among state legislative districts. Brennan, however, had only four firm votes. Potter Stewart, the potential fifth vote, wanted a narrow decision. No one was more aware of the need to keep Stewart on board than Brennan, who often reminded his clerks that the most important skill a Supreme Court Justice could learn was the ability to count to five. "Five votes can do anything around here," he said, but with four votes you were dead in the water.

Determining who would have the burden of proof was also problematic. Stewart insisted that the plaintiffs must bear the burden in any equal protection challenge, a position that Douglas vehemently rejected.[68] In order to save his majority, Brennan limited his opinion to the question of justiciability and left the more contentious issues for another day. At that point Tom Clark unexpectedly changed his mind and concurred in the judgment, and the Court ruled 6–2 that reapportionment of state electoral districts was justiciable.[69]

If Gomillion cracked the door for the Court to decide apportionment cases, Baker v. Carr kicked it wide open. Brennan radically redefined the political questions doctrine, limiting it to a relatively narrow range of issues involving separation of powers and the co-equal branches of government. Disputes involving state governments or conflicts between the states and the federal government were no longer covered by the new political questions doctrine.[70] While Brennan's opinion was narrower than he or Warren might have wished, both agreed that the case was the most important decision of their careers.

For Felix Frankfurter, the case represented everything he despised about the Warren Court. It was also Frankfurter's last great judicial battle. He suffered a debilitating stroke and heart attack on April 6, 1962, and resigned in August.[71] This case also was the last straw for Charles Whittaker. He refused to participate in the decision after conference, then suddenly quit the Court the following week and went to work for General Motors.

---

68. Stewart believed that plaintiffs should have to prove both impermissible voting inequalities and improper motives or intent on the part of state lawmakers. Douglas argued that only discriminatory effects were required. Questions about the burden of proof were not crucial in this case, because the population disparities were huge and the legislature's motives were fairly clear. Both Stewart and Douglas knew, however, that the Court would inevitably receive closer and more difficult cases.

69. Tom Clark privately complained that *Baker v. Carr* handed state governments over to "control by the 'city slickers.'" Schwartz and Lesher, *Inside the Warren Court,* 194. Clark originally planned to dissent, but at the last minute he changed his mind and concurred in the result. Despite Brennan's best lobbying efforts, Clark refused to join Brennan's majority opinion and simply "acquiesce[d] in the decision to remand." The substantive issues left undecided in *Baker v. Carr* were ultimately resolved in *Wesberry v. Sanders,* 376 U.S. 1 (1964), and *Reynolds v. Sims,* 377 U.S. 533 (1964).

70. *Baker v. Carr* was widely credited with establishing the "one person, one vote" principle of apportionment. That famous standard, however, first appeared the following year in Douglas's opinion in *Gray v. Sanders,* 372 U.S. 368 (1963): "The conception of political equality from the Declaration of Independence, to Lincoln's Gettysburg Address, to the Fifteenth, Seventeenth, and Nineteenth Amendments can mean only one thing—one person, one vote."

71. Less than a month before he collapsed in his chambers, Frankfurter sent a sad and bitter note to John Harlan, complaining that the majority in *Baker v. Carr* had failed "to appreciate the intrinsic and

Wesberry v. Sanders, 376 U.S. 1 (1964)
(Douglas)

The population of Georgia's fifth congressional district was between two and three times larger than in the state's other congressional districts. District populations ranged from 272,000 persons in the small-est district to 823,000 in the fifth district. James Wesberry and a group of qualified Atlanta voters from the fifth district claimed that their votes were being diluted in violation of Baker v. Carr.[72] *A three-judge district court took judicial notice of the gross population imbalances among the state's congres-sional districts but ruled that the issue was a nonjusticiable political question and dismissed the com-plaint "for want of equity," citing* Colegrove v. Green.[73] *Carl E. Sanders was the governor of Georgia.*

Conference of November 22, 1963

WARREN: This is a congressional election case. The Constitution compels the apportion-ment of Congress by population. This one is grossly out of proportion. *Colegrove* should not defeat *Baker v. Carr.* I would follow Judge Tuttle's views and reverse, giving the leg-islature an opportunity to remedy it by next year in time for the 1964 elections, or alter-natively, to have the court reapportion.[74]

BLACK: I reverse. I would remand the case generally to the district court for action it deems best without referring to Tuttle's views.

DOUGLAS: I reverse.

CLARK: I reverse, and would say that the case stated a cause of action under *Baker v. Carr* and that the district court may hold it for one legislative term.

HARLAN: This case does not state a claim. I agree with *Colegrove*, as written by Frank-furter. There is no constitutionally protected right here. If there is any remedy, it is political. I would affirm or dismiss.

BRENNAN: I reverse. The justiciability issue must be faced. It was decided in *Colegrove*, and I would repeat what was said in *Baker*. On the remedy, I think that we would be wise only to reverse and let the district court fashion a remedy without giving any hints as to what it should do. There must be substantial equality. This one is way out of line.

STEWART: This is different than state apportionment. Here we have explicit constitu-tional history that members of House should represent equal constituencies—so it is different from the others. On the other hand, Congress is given an explicit power to act. If Congress acted to set up this lopsided districting, that act would be unconstitutional.

---

acquired majesty of the Court's significance in the affairs of the country." Frankfurter concluded: "Why do I bother you with this? I suppose to prove the truth of a German saying that when the heart is full it spills over. And so it spills over on you—who alone gives me comfort." Felix Frankfurter to John Marshall Harlan, March 5, 1962, Harlan Papers, box 534, quoted in Yarbrough, *John Marshall Harlan,* 276.

72. *Baker v. Carr,* 369 U.S. 186 (1962).

73. *Colegrove v. Green,* 328 U.S. 549 (1946).

74. District Judge Tuttle dissented in the decision below, relying on *Baker v. Carr* rather than *Colegrove. Wesberry v. Vandiver,* 206 F. Supp. 276 (1962). S. Ernest Vandiver was the governor of Georgia at the time; he was later succeeded by Carl Sanders.

This issue is justiciable. There should be abstention to allow Congress and the states to act. I would reverse and direct the district court to retain jurisdiction.

WHITE: I reverse. I would remand without giving explicit directions to the district court. If the district court decided to wait awhile, I would not reverse it.

STEWART: We are hitting Congress where it lives. Their jobs are involved. We should go slow and not act too fast, and certainly not tell the district court to do so. I would plead not for abstention, but for delay.

GOLDBERG: I reverse. This is biting off a big chew. I would let the district court have great leeway in fashioning remedy. Time should be a factor.

Result: In reversing, Hugo Black emphatically rejected Colegrove v. Green *and reaffirmed that apportionment cases were justiciable. The majority interpreted Article 1, §2 (requiring that representatives be chosen "by the People of the several States") to mean that congressional districts must have populations as nearly equal as practicable. Tom Clark concurred in part and dissented in part, voting to vacate the judgment and remand the case.*

With Frankfurter gone, John Marshall Harlan was the lone dissenter left to defend Frankfurter's conception of the political questions doctrine. Potter Stewart agreed with Harlan that the Court had no constitutional mandate to require that congressional districts maintain equal populations but conceded that the case was justiciable.[75]

---

75. The same year, the Court decided another landmark reapportionment case, *Reynolds v. Sims,* 377 U.S. 533 (1964). M. O. Sims and a group of Alabama taxpayers and registered voters sued Probate Judge George Reynolds (state probate judges in Alabama had certain duties and powers regarding the nomination and election of state legislators) and other state officials seeking to invalidate the apportionment of the state's bicameral legislature. The plaintiffs challenged three different state apportionment plans: (1) the existing plan; (2) the proposed new plan; and (3) the state's standby plan. Under the existing plan, state senate districts ranged from 15,000 to 635,000 persons, while house districts ranged from 7,000 to 105,000 persons. Under the proposed new apportionment plan, senate districts ranged from 11,000 to 635,000 persons, and house districts ranged from 11,000 to 42,000 persons. Under the standby plan, senate districts ranged from 31,000 to 635,000 persons, and house districts from 20,000 to 52,000 persons. A three-judge district court invalidated all three plans and ordered an interim apportionment for the upcoming 1962 elections that combined the proposed new apportionment plan (for the house) and the standby plan (for the senate). Alabama appealed, arguing that the federal courts lacked the authority to reapportion state legislatures and that the proposed new plan, which was modeled after the federal Congress (senators represented counties, while representatives were apportioned by population), was constitutionally permissible.

The Supreme Court affirmed on a 6–2–1 vote. In a majority opinion by Earl Warren, the Court ruled that (1) the equal protection clause required that *both* houses be substantially apportioned on a one-person-one-vote basis; (2) as nearly as practicable, all districts must have equal populations (although mechanical exactness was not required); and (3) any deviations must be based on legitimate considerations related to a rational state policy and must maintain the equal population principle. Warren rejected the argument that states could adopt the federal congressional model and apportion one house by population while the other house represented counties or some other political subdivision. Congress, Warren said, was an inappropriate model for state governments because it represented unique historical circumstances and reflected a necessary compromise among sovereign states required to form a nation. Clark and Stewart concurred in the judgment. Harlan dissented on the ground that the only constitutional limitation on state apportionment was the guaranty of a republican form of government, which in his view was inherently a political question and not justiciable.

White v. Regester, 412 U.S. 755 (1973)
(Brennan)

In 1970, Texas reapportioned its state legislative districts. Under the new plan there were seventy-nine single-member districts and eleven multimember districts for the 150-seat house. Diana Regester and other voters sued Secretary of State Mark White and other Texas officials, claiming that the state's redistricting scheme degraded their votes and discriminated against black and Hispanic voters in the multimember districts. Regarding the first claim, the range of district populations varied by 9.9 percent—from 5.8 percent overrepresentation to 4.1 percent underrepresentation. The standard deviation from the ideal population, however, was a modest 1.8 percent. The allegations of racial and ethnic discrimination involved two Texas counties, Bexar and Dallas.

A three-judge district court ruled that there was an unconstitutional disparity among district populations and found that the multimember districts in Bexar and Dallas Counties invidiously discriminated against black and Hispanic voters.

BURGER: Jurisdiction is here from the lower court's injunction, and the whole statute has a statewide impact.

STEWART: I would affirm on Dallas and Bexar Counties, but on the statewide impact, maybe we should remand in light of *Mahan.*[76]

---

76. *Mahan v. Howell,* 410 U.S. 315 (1973). In 1971, the Virginia legislature reapportioned election districts for both houses of the state legislature. Joan Mahan and other voters sued Henry Howell of the State Board of Elections to stop the plan from going into effect. Mahan alleged (1) that redistricting for the House of Delegates allowed impermissible population differences (districts varied in population by as much as 16 percent); (2) that the use of multimember districts diluted voter strength; and (3) that the redistricting plan for the state senate impermissibly allocated all 37,000 navy personnel stationed at the Norfolk Naval Station to the fifth senate district, even though only about 8,000 navy employees actually lived in the district.

A federal district court invalidated the house reapportionment statute because it violated the one person, one vote principle. The court substituted its own plan, which reduced the percentage variation to 10 percent. Unlike the original state plan, the judicially imposed district boundaries often ignored established city and county lines. The court also ruled that the fifth senate district discriminated against military personnel. Given the short time remaining before the next election, the court created an interim remedy whereby three adjacent single-member senate districts (where most of the navy personnel actually lived) were combined into one multimember district.

The Supreme Court affirmed in part and reversed in part. The Court affirmed that the assignment of all navy personnel to the fifth senate district was unconstitutional and that, given the severe time constraints, the district court did not abuse its discretion in creating an interim remedy. The Court reversed the rest of the lower court's decision, holding that (1) state redistricting plans were not subject to the same stringent standards applied to congressional reapportionment; (2) states only had to make an honest and good faith effort to fashion state legislative districts that were as nearly equal in population as practicable; (3) some divergences from the goal of population equality were permitted so long as they were reasonably based on rational state policy—including the use of existing city and county boundaries—and so long as these considerations did not undermine the goal of equal representation; and (4) while population disparities in Virginia approached tolerable constitutional limits, they did not exceed those limits. Rehnquist wrote the majority opinion. Brennan, Douglas, and Marshall concurred in part and dissented in part. They would have held state legislatures to the same strict standards that applied to congressional districts. Lewis Powell did not participate.

WHITE: Here, *Chavis* is satisfied.[77] Since there is a majority of Mexicans plus Negroes, they must have been shut out.

BLACKMUN: On the legislature's plan, taking *Mahan's* standard, the record is not good to show that Texas carried its burden of proof.

REHNQUIST: I am not sure that the statewide case is here, just because the court-ordered injunction was only against Dallas and San Antonio. On the merits, the state has compromised as Virginia didn't in *Mahan*. I would say either that a lesser duration than in *Mahan* needs no justification or a lesser one. A remand is not desirable, because *Mahan* does not offer any guidelines. So I would reverse. On multimember districts, I think that Dallas is egregious and I would affirm, but I would reverse on Bexar County.

Result: The Court reversed in part and affirmed in part. A 6–3 majority ruled that the district court erred in finding statewide discrimination where the standard deviation was only 1.8 percent. All of the Justices agreed, however, that the district court had been right to order the disestablishment of multimember districts in Bexar and Dallas Counties, because both counties had long-established histories of racial and ethnic discrimination.

White v. Regester (II), 422 U.S. 935 (1975)
(Brennan)

On remand in White v. Regester (I), *the district court looked at nine of the state's eleven multimember districts and ordered the state to change seven of them into single-member districts by the 1974 elections. Texas again appealed. While the case was pending before the Supreme Court, the state conducted the 1974 elections under the old rules. Meanwhile, the Texas legislature adopted a new redistricting plan that eliminated all multimember districts statewide. The legislation was not scheduled to take effect until 1976, and Texas wanted to conduct any intervening elections under the old rules.*

---

77. *Whitcomb v. Chavis*, 403 U.S. 124 (1971). Indiana created one multimember legislative district for Marion County, with fifteen state assembly seats and eight state senate seats. Patrick Chavis and other registered voters sued Governor Edgar Whitcomb, alleging that the use of multimember districts discriminated against racial minorities and that district populations statewide were grossly unequal. The plaintiffs' main statistical evidence of racial discrimination was that minority neighborhoods in Marion County had fewer resident legislators than expected, given their proportion of the county's population. On that evidence, the district court ordered the state to (1) redistrict multimember districts into single-member districts and (2) to equalize district populations statewide. After the state failed to act, the federal court redistricted the entire state on its own authority.

The Supreme Court reversed. Byron White, writing for a 5–4 majority, held that the statistical evidence did not prove invidious discrimination and that the district court should have considered more modest alternative remedies. Seven Justices agreed with White's second conclusion that the district court had acted properly in ordering statewide reapportionment to equalize district populations. Harlan dissented because in his view the problem was nonjusticiable and the federal courts did not have the authority to intervene. Douglas, Brennan, and Marshall dissented in part, on the ground that the plaintiffs had met the burden of proof regarding the invidious effects of multimember districting in Marion County. Stewart also dissented in part.

BURGER: A four-prong test: (1) access; (2) racist campaigning; and (4) [*sic*] consistent lack of success. I thought that the first prong was the question to be decided. On the second prong, I thought that the First Amendment allowed this—how can this be a factor in this case? The third prong includes indifference or apathy of elected representative toward their constituents. On the fourth prong, a "lack of success" standard is needed.

STEWART: There is no jurisdiction of this appeal under *Moody v. Flowers*[78] and *New Left.*[79]

WHITE: If we got to the merits, I would affirm except as to Lubbock, Nueces, El Paso and Travis. I am not at rest.

BLACKMUN: I thought that we had jurisdiction here. On that premise, *White v. Regester* (I) approached these cases somewhat as Goldberg did here.[80] That led me to affirm across the board.

POWELL: I don't think that we have jurisdiction. On the merits, I am about where Byron is. In counties where the deprived are 60 percent or 50 percent, I can't see a conclusion, and I would not apply to small counties with only a 2 percent or 3 percent deviation.

REHNQUIST: I am inclined to think that we have jurisdiction. I would treat these as specialized calls. Where there is only a 2 percent or 3 percent deviation in a county, I don't think we should invalidate it. But if it has a policy for large counties, special circumstances may apply.

Result: In a unanimous per curiam decision, the Court vacated the district court's judgment and remanded the case to determine whether the question of eliminating the multimember districts was moot. In effect, the Court's decision allowed Texas to conduct its intervening elections under the old rules, rather than forcing the state to redistrict immediately as the district court had ordered. Douglas did not participate.

---

78. *Moody v. Flowers*, 387 U.S. 97 (1967). This was a combined case dealing with county reapportionment plans in Houston County, Alabama, and Suffolk County, New York. Three-judge courts were convened in both cases. In Alabama, the district court threw out a suit by Earl Moody against state Attorney General Richmond Flowers. In New York, the district court invalidated part of the Suffolk County charter. On direct appeal, the Supreme Court unanimously vacated both judgments. The Court ruled that because the statutes in question were of limited application and involved only local officials, the three-judge courts were improperly convened and the Supreme Court lacked jurisdiction to hear the cases on direct appeal. Instead, the cases would have to be reconsidered at the district court level and then appealed to the circuit courts of appeals.

79. *Board of Regents of University of Texas System v. New Left Education Project*, 404 U.S. 541 (1972). New Left sought to enjoin enforcement of new rules governing distribution of literature and the solicitation of membership dues by political organizations at the University of Texas. A three-judge district court decided that the rules were unconstitutional and granted a permanent injunction. On direct appeal, the Supreme Court ruled 6–1 that the three-judge court had been improperly convened and the Supreme Court lacked jurisdiction to consider the case. The issues involved here concerned only a small fraction of the Texas system of higher education and did not reflect general statewide policy. This meant that the case should have been heard by an ordinary district court and appealed to the circuit court of appeals. Douglas dissented, while Powell and Rehnquist did not participate.

80. Circuit Judge Irving L. Goldberg wrote the majority decision for the district court. *Graves v. Barnes*, 378 F. Supp. 640 (1974).

Beer v. United States, 425 U.S. 130 (1976)
(Brennan)

New Orleans had a seven-member city council. Five councilors were elected from single-member districts, and two were elected at large. After redistricting in 1961, blacks constituted a majority of the population in one of the districts, but due to low voter registration blacks accounted for just half of the registered voters. In the other four districts, whites outnumbered blacks both in overall population and among registered voters. No black councilors were elected in New Orleans between 1960 and 1970.

Another reapportionment in 1970 yielded black population majorities in two districts, with a majority of black registered voters in one district. The U.S. attorney general sought to block the 1970 reapportionment plan under §5 of the Voting Rights Act of 1965 on the ground that it did not go far enough toward providing blacks with proportional representation on the city council. The lower courts agreed with the federal government and enjoined enforcement of the city's proposed reapportionment plan.

BURGER: The lower court gave a very expansive reading of §5. I would remand for re-examination on a proper standard of proof. I think that the court below set up a standard that is impossible to meet.

STEWART: We may have been wrong in holding in the *Georgia* case that reapportionment made a §5 change, but I would not overrule that.[81] The state has the basic burden of proof. If that means proof that a particular plan is the best possible, that is impossible. What then is the standard? I think that it is a Fifteenth Amendment standard, except that we have had no Fifteenth Amendment cases except for *Gomillion v. Lightfoot*.[82] Should we equate it with the Fourteenth Amendment equal protection standard of *Whitcomb v. Chavis*[83] or *White v. Regester?*[84]

WHITE: If this were a pure reapportionment case, I would have trouble finding a Fourteenth Amendment violation on this record. But Congress imposed this statute to re-

---

81. *Georgia v. United States*, 411 U.S. 526 (1973). Under the Voting Rights Act of 1965, Georgia was required to obtain prior federal approval for any changes in its voting laws. In 1971, Georgia submitted to the U.S. attorney general a reapportionment plan for the state legislature involving multimember districts. The attorney general objected to the plan, because the state failed to convince him that the proposed changes would not have a racially discriminatory effect on voting. Georgia enacted a second plan in 1972, which the attorney general rejected on the same ground. When the state vowed to ignore the federal government and conduct its upcoming state elections using the 1972 plan, the attorney general sued in federal court. The district court issued an injunction prohibiting the state from conducting any elections under the disapproved plan. The U.S. Supreme Court, however, stayed enforcement of the injunction, and Georgia conducted its general election as scheduled.

On the merits, the Supreme Court affirmed the district court's judgment. A 5–1–3 majority ruled that the burden of proof rested with the state and that the attorney general could properly withhold his consent unless satisfied that the proposed changes would not have a racially discriminatory purpose or effect. The Court enjoined any future elections using a disapproved reapportionment plan until Georgia complied fully with the Voting Rights Act. Burger concurred in the judgment; White, Powell, and Rehnquist dissented.

82. *Gomillion v. Lightfoot*, 364 U.S. 339 (1960).

83. *Whitcomb v. Chavis* 403 U.S. 124 (1971).

84. *White v. Regester*, 412 U.S. 755 (1973)

dress past discrimination. Therefore, the state has to prove that the proposed change has neither the purpose nor effect of discriminating. I would rather not tie the standard to the Constitution. The government won't say flat-out that lines must be drawn to prevent a minority from being shut out as a remedy for past discrimination. That means drawing lines on a racial basis.

MARSHALL: Negro or labor bloc voting are utter myths.

BLACKMUN: I disagree with *Richmond* on the use of compelling state interest analysis and on the "best possible plan" analysis.[85] But given the statute's "purpose and effect" language and our decision in *Allen*, I must affirm.[86]

POWELL: The concept of bloc voting is a myth. I think that the district court rule approved here is a segregationist rule, and I will have no part of it. I may say no more than that the statute is manifestly unconstitutional.

---

85. *Richmond v. United States*, 422 U.S. 358 (1975). The city of Richmond, Virginia sought to annex new territory that would have reduced the percentage of the city's black population from 52 percent to 42 percent. Because Virginia was subject to the Voting Rights Act of 1965, it sought a declaratory judgment from the District Court for the District of Columbia that the annexation did not have the purpose or effect of abridging the right to vote on the basis of race. The city proposed to change its council elections from an at-large system to nine single-member wards. Five wards would have substantial white majorities and four would have substantial black majorities. The district court ruled that the city had not proved that the proposed annexation was not intended to dilute the black vote and ruled that the ward plan did not cure the annexation's racially discriminatory purpose. On direct appeal, the Supreme Court ruled 5–3 that the proposed annexation did *not* have a discriminatory effect on black voting strength, because the proposed election reform plan would neutralize any adverse racial effects and essentially leave the black community in the same political position as before. The Court remanded the case for additional hearings on whether there were sound, nondiscriminatory reasons for the annexation. Brennan, Douglas, and Marshall dissented, while Powell did not participate.

86. *Allen v. State Board of Elections*, 393 U.S. 544 (1969). Mississippi and Virginia sought to change their voting laws and procedures. Without seeking prior federal permission as required under §5 of the Voting Rights Act, the Mississippi legislature: (1) changed county supervisor elections from district voting to at-large voting; (2) changed most county superintendents from elective to appointive positions; and (3) made it more difficult for independent candidates to be named on general election ballots. A three-judge district court ruled that these amendments did not fall under the terms of §5 of the Voting Rights Act and did not require prior federal approval. In Virginia, a three-judge district court dismissed a Voting Rights Act challenge to the state's new procedures for casting write-in votes.

The Supreme Court reversed the Mississippi decision, vacated the judgment of the Virginia district court, and remanded both cases. Seven Justices, led by Earl Warren, ruled that §5 of the Voting Rights Act meant that both states were required to seek prior federal approval before changing *any* state voting laws. The Court examined the legislative history of the Voting Rights Act and concluded that Congress intended the courts to give the act "the broadest possible scope." The majority concluded that the act applied to virtually any state law or regulation that affected voting, including rules regarding candidate qualifications and whether state officers were to be elected or appointed. A narrower majority of five Justices agreed that the Court's decision was prospective only. No new elections would be ordered, but both cases were remanded with orders to enjoin enforcement of the new rules until the states fully complied with the requirements of §5. Harlan, Marshall, and Douglas concurred in most of Warren's opinion but thought that more extensive relief should have been granted. Harlan also thought that the majority had construed §5 too broadly. Black dissented on the ground that §5 was unconstitutional because it impermissibly required states to obtain federal permission to change state voting laws.

REHNQUIST: Congress has laid down a statutory test that may be more rigorous than the constitutional test. It is fairly draconian and ought not to be construed too broadly. To expand it to reapportionment was unfortunate, and I would read it narrowly by applying a test that judges the situation against what was true before. This plan puts Negroes in no worse way than they were before. I can't say that the lower court's "effect" holding was correct, therefore, and I would let the district court address "purpose," which it did not reach.

Result: The Court upheld New Orleans's 1970 reapportionment plan on a 5–3 vote. Stewart, writing for the majority, ruled that the requirements of §5 of the Voting Rights Act was satisfied so long as reapportionment did not reduce minority voting strength below previously established levels (the "no retrogression" principle). In this case, since the two at-large council seats had existed since 1954, well before passage of the Voting Rights Act, the reapportionment plan could not be rejected solely because it failed to eliminate these two seats. The new plan did not violate the "no retrogression" test. None of the other five council districts under the old plan had a clear black majority, while the new plan ensured that blacks would be the majority population in two of the five districts and that one district would have a clear majority of black registered voters. White, Marshall, and Brennan dissented; Stevens did not participate.

Mobile v. Bolden, 446 U.S. 55 (1980)
(Brennan)

The city of Mobile, Alabama, was governed by a powerful three-member commission elected by the city at large. Wiley Bolden brought a class-action suit on behalf of black city residents, alleging that at-large elections diluted black voting strength. The district court found that black residents registered and voted without interference but agreed that the at-large system diluted black voting strength in violation of the Fourteenth and Fifteenth Amendments. The court of appeals affirmed. Among the main issues at conference was whether Bolden had to prove that the at-large system was instituted purposefully to discriminate against blacks or whether proof of discriminatory effect was sufficient.

BURGER: No case was made out here by the Negroes. They have not shown black voting discrimination. They don't make a case by showing that the commission form was in effect for so many years. They had to show some manipulation of this voting to shut them out, and they didn't. The dilution of vote theory does not persuade me.

STEWART: There was no violation of either the Fourteenth or Fifteenth Amendment for alternative reasons: (1) Intent is required, and inaction of the state legislature is insufficient evidence of intent; or (2) even if intent is not required, the criteria of *White v. Regester* is not translatable to the executive and legislative government of a city.[87]

WHITE: I agree with Brennan.

MARSHALL: The findings require affirmance.

---

87. *White v. Regester,* 412 U.S. 755 (1973).

BLACKMUN: *Washington v. Davis.*[88] We have dilution in fact, but there is slight evidence of purpose. A meld of intent and effect may be sufficient justification. The purpose then becomes crucial. The state has never wavered from this form.

REHNQUIST: I have little to add to what the Chief Justice, Harry, and Potter have said. I have a question about whether there is a concurring finding.

STEVENS: I would affirm only on the theory that the extreme facts here are bad enough that if it was Republicans—a total exclusion.

After Reargument

BURGER: This is a draconian remedy totally to rearrange the government of Mobile. This goes farther beyond the authority of the courts than anything I have seen. You can't infer anything from the failure of blacks to get themselves elected. Proportional representation is inconsistent with one man-one vote.

STEWART: I don't reach the issue of a remedy. The lower court was wrong on the merits. There is no violation of one man-one vote, since there are only at large elections. Assuming the applicability of *White v. Regester* to municipal election, there was proof here sufficient to meet that standard. The Fifteenth Amendment adds nothing to Fourteenth, and if there is an implied right of action under §2, it adds nothing to the Fifteenth Amendment.[89]

WHITE: I don't think that §2 goes any further than the Fifteenth Amendment, but this judgment can't rest on the statute. I would affirm on grounds used by the court of appeals.

BLACKMUN: I agree with Potter and the Chief Justice.

POWELL: I agree with Potter and would not reach the remedy.

STEVENS: I have a lot of trouble with "purpose." Once we have a case of free access to the ballot box, every group is fair game for tricks—and the use of an element to maintain the status quo does not make out a case of intent to subjugate a minority race. The mere inability of blacks to get elected isn't enough. The *Zimmer* factors are really irrelevant.[90]

---

88. *Washington v. Davis,* 426 U.S. 229 (1976).

89. Bolden also claimed that at-large elections violated §2 of the Voting Rights Act of 1965. Neither the district court nor the court of appeals ruled on this issue.

90. *Zimmer v. McKeithen,* 485 F. 2d 1297 (C.A. 5th Cir. 1973), aff'd on other grounds sub nom., *East Carroll Parish School Board v. Marshall,* 424 U.S. 636 (1975). Charles Zimmer sued John McKeithen in East Carroll Parish, Louisiana, a parish with a long history of racial discrimination in education and voting. Between 1922 and 1962, not a single black resident was allowed to register to vote. By 1970, 60 percent of the parish population was black, although the percentage of black registered voters was less than 50 percent. As the number of black voters increased and blacks began to be elected to county offices, white officials changed parish elections from single-member districts to at-large elections. Black voters challenged the reform under the Fourteenth and Fifteenth Amendments.

The district court held that it was impossible for an at-large election scheme to dilute black voting strength where blacks constituted a majority of the population, even if blacks remained a minority among registered voters. The circuit court of appeals reversed on the ground "that access to the political process

Result: In a plurality decision, the Court held that Mobile's at-large elections did not violate the Four-teenth or Fifteenth Amendments. On behalf of four Justices, Potter Stewart argued that both amend-ments required proof of purposeful discrimination; disproportionate effects alone were not sufficient. There was no Fourteenth Amendment right to proportional representation, and the district court's finding that blacks were allowed to register and vote without hindrance nullified Bolden's Fifteenth Amendment claim. Blackmun and Stevens concurred in the judgment but did not join Stewart's opin-ion. Brennan, White, and Marshall dissented.

Rogers v. Lodge, 458 U.S. 613 (1982)
(Brennan)

Burke County, Georgia, was governed by a board of five county commissioners elected at large. Although blacks outnumbered whites in the county, there were far fewer blacks than whites registered to vote and no black had ever served as a county commissioner. A group of black residents led by Herman Lodge sued in federal court, alleging that the county's at-large system diluted black voting strength in violation of the Fourteenth and Fifteenth Amendments. The district court found that past racial dis-crimination had prevented effective black political participation in the county and found evidence of voting in racial blocs. District Judge Anthony A. Alaimo ruled that while the at-large electoral system was racially neutral in origin, it had been maintained for invidious purposes in violation of the Four-teenth and Fifteenth Amendments. He ordered the county divided into five single-member commis-sion districts. The court of appeals affirmed, ruling that black residents met their burden of proof that the county's at-large electoral system was maintained for discriminatory purposes.

BURGER: The analysis of both courts was heavily laden with *Zimmer* criteria.[91] Accessi-bility of registration locales is the real flaw here. Were they used as a means of discrimi-nation? I am not sure that the lower courts treated this issue adequately. Maybe we should remand for that purpose.

BRENNAN:[92] We may begin with the premise that the decision whether to employ a dis-trict, or an at-large system of elections, is a question for the state to determine through its own political machinery. *But,* when that machinery has been purposefully, intention-ally, and effectively maintained to wholly exclude blacks from the political process, a district court would be derelict in its constitutional responsibilities if it failed to provide a meaningful remedy. So far as I can determine, Judge Alaimo correctly anticipated all our recent decisions, jumped through all the hoops and made all the findings that we

---

and not population was the barometer" of vote dilution. The circuit court ruled that if minorities had less opportunity than other groups to elect candidates of their choice, then the districting scheme was uncon-stitutional. The court developed a laundry list of factors to establish vote dilution, which became known as "Zimmer factors." They included: (1) a lack of minority access to nominating candidates for office; (2) leg-islative unresponsiveness to minority groups; (3) a "tenuous" state policy to justify multimember or at-large districts; (4) a history of de jure discrimination. Vote dilution claims could be proved by an "aggre-gate" of these factors. See, Kosterlitz, "*Thornburg v. Gingles:* The Supreme Court's New Test for Analyzing Minority Vote Dilution."

91. *Zimmer v. McKeithen,* 485 F. 2d 1297 (CA 5th Cir. 1973), aff'd on other grounds sub nom., *East Carroll Parish School Board v. Marshall,* 424 U.S. 636 (1975).

92. Adapted from Brennan's talking papers, Brennan Papers, OT 1981, box 599.

could reasonably require. There comes a time when we must simply trust the judgment of the district court judges who are far closer to the problem than we are.

As we are clearly holding in *Swint*, a finding of discriminatory intent is a factual determination subject to the "clearly erroneous" standard.[93] Indeed, the rule has special application to us where, not only did the district court make the proper findings, but where they were affirmed by the court of appeals.

There is nothing in this record that militates against the remedy chosen by the district court. When confronted with such a pervasive pattern of discrimination by a recalcitrant government body, the district court cannot go out and make sure that when blacks show up at the registration places they do not confront an out-to-lunch sign; the district judge cannot order people bused to register or to the polls; no number of prohibitory injunctions will suffice. In short, the only way to put an end to the system of intentional discrimination is to go to the heart of the problem. The at-large system of election is the lynch-pin of a seemingly unbreakable pattern of intentional discrimination; so long as it is in place, blacks in Burke County cannot even get a "foot-in-the-door."

WHITE: The argument of improper standards was repeated by the court of appeals. The finding of discriminatory intent was supported by the court of appeals. Whether single-member districts are a proper remedy—I would leave that issue to the district court's discretion.

MARSHALL: The district judge anticipated *Mobile*.[94]

BLACKMUN: I agree with Byron. The totality of the circumstances here support affirmance. But I don't agree with responsiveness as sine qua non.

POWELL: *Mobile* repudiated *Zimmer*, and it seems to me that the court of appeals tried to revive it. So I think that the standard was incorrectly applied. There are probably more at-large cities and counties than not—this is facially neutral. In any event, this is a matter for local folks. So a showing of discriminatory intent is not enough. If we are going to change voting structures, we ought to rely on the Voting Rights Act.

REHNQUIST: Clearly there was a finding of "neutral in origin but now discriminatorily maintained." But the lower courts also relied heavily on *Zimmer* factors. I vote tentatively to affirm.

STEVENS: My views on vote dilution cases are mine alone. Subjective intent would invalidate everything, and I think that is wrong and dangerous. I would apply a principle that differentiates vote dilution cases from one vote-one person cases. I would give a strong presumption to state government structures as valid and not set them aside merely because the majority hangs on and discriminates against a minority. It has to be as bad as *Tuskegee*.[95]

---

93. *Pullman-Standard v. Swint*, 456 U.S. 273 (1982).
94. *Mobile v. Bolden*, 446 U.S. 55 (1980).
95. *Gomillion v. Lightfoot*, 364 U.S. 339 (1960).

O'CONNOR: I would affirm the finding of intentional discrimination there. The real problem is the remedy. Maybe we should go with the Chief Justice to remand this to the lower court to explore further. I agree with Harry on the responsiveness error.

Result: The Court voted 6–3 that proof of discriminatory purpose or intent was required in vote dilution cases. In affirming the decision below, Byron White ruled that Lodge had met his burden of proof and that the findings of the lower courts were not clearly erroneous. Powell, Rehnquist, and Stevens dissented. The decision seemed to be inconsistent with the Court's earlier decision in Mobile v. Bolden. *One explanation is that Congress amended the Voting Rights Act in 1982 to codify the "effects" test employed in* Whitcomb v. Chavis *and* White v. Regester *and explicitly rejected the "intent" test proposed in* Mobile v. Bolden.[96] *While these amendments were not directly relevant to the Court's decision in this case, they may have had an effect on the Justices' deliberations.*

Davis v. Bandemer, 478 U.S. 109 (1986)
(Brennan)

Members of the Indiana state assembly were elected to two-year terms, with all one hundred representatives standing at each election. Some assembly districts were single-member and others were multimember districts. Indiana also had a fifty-member senate elected to four-year terms, with half of the body elected every two years. All senate districts were single-member districts.

In 1981, with Republicans in control of both houses, the state legislature reapportioned all of the state's legislative districts. The new assembly districts included sixty-one single-member districts, nine double-member districts, and seven triple-member districts. All the multimember districts were concentrated in metropolitan areas. The state senate remained composed entirely of single-member districts.

In the 1982 assembly elections Democrats won 51.9 percent of the vote but took only 43 percent of the seats. State Democrats argued that the Republican redistricting plan violated the equal protection clause of the Fourteenth Amendment. A three-judge district court agreed and struck down the 1981 reapportionment plan, ordering the state legislature to establish an acceptable reapportionment scheme before the next election.

Ironically, on appeal to the Supreme Court the Republican National Committee submitted an amicus brief arguing against Indiana's Republican-sponsored reapportionment plan. The RNC wanted to use this case to attack Democratic gerrymandering schemes in other states.

BURGER: The justifications offered for these oddball shapes are startling, and I have a problem seeing how we can apply a rational basis standard.

BRENNAN:[97] Although little time was spent on the issue at oral argument, the briefs focus mainly on whether the controversy is "justiciable." A number of different concerns are

---

96. Guinn and Sewell, "*Miller v. Johnson*," 912. Section 2 required that "no voting qualification... shall be imposed by any state... to deny or abridge the right of any citizen... to vote on account of race." The original test was that no state could change their voting practices or procedures with discriminatory *intent*—as inferred from the totality of the circumstances. Under the 1982 amendments, the test became whether the new practices or procedures had a discriminatory *effect*. Congress also expanded the scope of §2 so that it applied to all states, not just those jurisdictions covered by §5 of the Voting Rights Act.

97. Adapted from Brennan's talking papers, Brennan Papers, OT 1985, box 705.

subsumed under the heading "justiciability." Some relate to defining a right, others relate to whether there are judicially manageable standards for adjudicating that right once it has been defined, still other concerns focus on the appropriateness of judicial intrusion in light of the nature of the issue being adjudicated and the possibility of error, and finally, some concerns focus on the ability—or inability—of courts to fashion workable remedies.

Baker v. Carr recognized this, requiring a "discriminating inquiry into the precise facts and posture of the particular case" to determine justiciability. *Baker* recognized that, before we can determine whether a case is "justiciable," we must define with some precision the right asserted and the standards by which it is to be adjudicated.

The parties have loosely spoken of "justiciability" only in terms of our power to hear this case. Although, in my view, the concerns they identify are insufficient to compel the conclusion that we are divested of power, they do alter the way in which the case should be adjudicated. Properly examined, I think the court below should have applied a deferential rational basis scrutiny under which this apportionment plan should not have been struck down.

It is far too late in the day to find that we do not have the *power* to hear cases alleging discriminatory gerrymandering. Such claims were made in *Whitcomb v. Chavis, White v. Regester, Gaffney v. Cummings, Mobile v. Bolden,* and *Rogers v. Lodge.* Indeed, in two of these cases (*White* and *Rogers*), we affirmed the invalidation of state apportionment plans.

Each of these cases was based on allegations of intentional exclusion, not deviation from the one man-one vote principle. And, while most of these cases involved claims by racial minorities, *Gaffney* at least involved a claim of partisan rather than racial gerrymandering. Indeed, we have consistently recognized that claims of exclusion of racial "or political" groups in the districting process are judicially cognizable.

I am unwilling to overrule the race cases. Yet appellants have not provided any basis to distinguish racial from partisan gerrymandering in terms of judicial *power*; I do not think a distinction exists.

As discussed below, I think that it is apparent that there are "judicially manageable standards" for adjudicating this claim and that, consequently, the controversy is "justiciable."

The *right* asserted by the Democrats is the right not to be discriminated against solely because they are Democrats. This right is clearly established in our equal protection cases. Every individual has the right not to be treated differently solely because he is a member of a group, whether that group is blacks, Democrats or bakers, unless there is some legitimate public purpose for differential treatment. The crucial question in this case is how should the court have gone about determining whether there had been unjustified differential treatment here?

The court below did not simply ask whether this plan tended to further some legitimate state interest. Rather, the district court (1) scrutinized the legislative process for evidence of improper purpose; and (2) required the state in effect to show why it could not have achieved the goals it asserted in justification of its plan with other plans that did not have the same effect on Democrats. Such inquiries are the stuff of heightened scrutiny.

There is no justification for heightened scrutiny under this Court's equal protection cases. Obviously, Democrats are not the sort of "discrete and insular" minority to whom we have afforded special judicial protection. Historically, Democrats have not been discriminated against; certainly they are not a politically powerless group. This, of course, distinguishes the cases involving blacks and other racial minorities, all of which are based on suspect class analysis.

Similarly, no "fundamental interest" has been unequally distributed by this legislation: at least none that we have so far recognized. Every vote is equally weighted, and every eligible voter is allowed to vote. The only claim under this strand of equal protection analysis is that this apportionment plan results in unequal distribution of an "effective" vote. Such a claim would raise many of the "justiciability" concerns discussed by the parties: we cannot ensure the equal distribution of a thing we cannot define, and there is no way we can define what an "effective" vote is, because we have no norm upon which to make a judgment.

The lower court should have applied rational basis scrutiny to this apportionment plan. Our cases have long recognized a strong presumption in favor of the constitutionality of legislative action. Legislation that treats individuals differently—whether on its face or as a result of disparate impact—is upheld if the state can furnish any conceivable legitimate purpose that the statute tends to further.

Once such a legitimate objective has been established, the court's inquiry is ended. It is improper under rational basis scrutiny to examine statements in the legislative history in order to second guess the "real" motive of the legislators. It is improper to require the state to show why it did not use another plan that could have achieved the asserted goals without the challenged discriminatory effect. It is, in other words, improper to do what the district court did in this case. Such inquiries into "actual" legislative motivation are reserved for cases in which experience has justified more intrusive judicial scrutiny; as indicated above, this case is not one of these.

In partisan gerrymandering cases, it seems clear to me that anything greater than very deferential scrutiny of the legislature's purpose would be a mistake: (1) the likelihood of our wrongly striking down legitimate plans is quite high; (2) the costs to the states—political as well as economic—are great; (3) the problems for courts resulting from the inevitable flood of litigation are equally great; and (4) the need for judicial protection is minuscule. This is politics at its simplest level. Let the parties continue to fight it out between themselves without converting the courts into another tool in their battles.

Properly applying rational basis scrutiny in this case: (1) the controversy is justiciable; and (2) the court below should have upheld the plan. Judicially manageable standards exist to determine whether the apportionment plan attacked is rationally related to some legitimate state purpose. In this case, the state advanced several legitimate interests which its plan furthered. Nothing more was required of it to prevail.

WHITE: On justiciability we have gone a long way, but not far outside of racial and multi-member districts where, as here, the issue is "fair representation." I am not so sure. My vote is that the claim on the senate multi-member districts is justiciable. On the merits,

I would vacate and remand on multi-member of senate, and except for the multi-member districts in the assembly I would reverse.

MARSHALL: This is justiciable and I would reverse as Byron does.

BLACKMUN: One man-one vote is observed here. Justiciability is a hard question for me. There is no easy way to draw lines any more. I could say that partisan gerrymandering is not justiciable. If this doesn't carry, I would go Bill Brennan's route.

POWELL: This is justiciable. I would accept the rational basis test, but it is not met as to the assembly. I am not sure as to the senate, either. Compactness seems to be an independent value—and the district court found outrageous discrimination here. There was no satisfactory explanation from the state, and so I affirm at least as to the state assembly.

REHNQUIST: I would not get in as deeply as Lewis. I would fence this off as far as one can. If it is a purely partisan gerrymander, I would hold that it is not justiciable.

STEVENS: This is justiciable. We have already decided it really, even if not specifically. On the issue of judicially challengeable standards, we have developed some in our one man-one vote cases, and they are serviceable here. I would affirm as to the multi-member portions of this case, but I am not at rest on the rest of the case. We can't have a rational basis test that is so loose as to amount to non-justiciability.

O'CONNOR: Any legislator who does not do what this party did ought to be impeached. I would reverse outright, as Bill Brennan does.

Result: A 6–3 majority ruled that gerrymandering issues were justiciable, even if the electoral districts involved met the one person, one vote requirement. On the merits, a plurality of Justices approved the state's 1981 reapportionment plan. Byron White wrote on behalf of four Justices that it was "unsatisfactory" to rely on a single election to prove unconstitutional discrimination. Discrimination was actionable only when the electoral system was so arranged that it would "consistently degrade a voter's or a group of voters' influence on the political process as a whole." There also must be evidence of "continued frustration of the will of a majority of the voters, or effective denial to a minority of voters of a fair chance to influence the political process." In other words, both discriminatory intent and effect had to be proved. Burger, Rehnquist, and O'Connor concurred in the result, while Powell and Stevens concurred in part and dissented in larger part. O'Connor softened her strong conference views; her concurring opinion said only that in her view the case presented a nonjusticiable political question.

ELECTION FINANCING

Buckley v. Valeo, 424 U.S. 1 (1976)
(Brennan)

In 1974, Congress reacted to the Watergate scandal by radically revising the Federal Election Campaign Act of 1971. The new amendments (1) provided for federal funding of presidential elections; (2) imposed new limits on campaign expenditures and contributions; and (3) created the Federal Elec-

tion Commission (FEC) to serve as a federal election watchdog.[98] Senator James Buckley and other political candidates and contributors sued, claiming that the contribution and spending limits imposed by the new act violated their First Amendment rights.

BURGER: 1) The law limits contributions and expenditures. First, the individual limits for contributions to candidates are $1,000 to each candidate and a $25,000 overall limit. I have serious doubts about whether these limits are constitutional. The court of appeals was right in that conclusion.

2) Regarding §608(e), the court of appeals said that this provision was necessary and applicable to any clearly identified candidate. This has no limitation on the Andersons, Restons, Krafts, etc., who are much more influential than those who are precluded by this law from writing or distributing pamphlets.[99] I find this section even more troublesome than the contribution limits. This is pure speech.

3) Third are the limitations on personal and family contributions under §608(c). I have less trouble with this, and lean to think that it is all right.

4) Expenditures limits on candidates.

5) Public funding issues. Minor and independent parties are really shut out of this. I lean to reverse here

6) The $500 limits on volunteer service are probably O.K. It is a partial restriction on individual speech and conduct, and is an effort to limit a loophole.

---

98. Key provisions of the Federal Election Campaign Act of 1971:

1. (18 U.S.C. §591 et seq.):

§608(a): limited federal candidate expenditures for each calendar year. Limits varied by office.

§608(b)(1): contributions by individuals or groups to any federal candidate limited to $1,000.

§608(b)(2): contributions by political action committees limited to $5,000.

§608(b)(3): total annual contributions by any contributor limited to $25,000.

§608(c): limited overall campaign expenditures by candidates. Limits varied by office.

§608(e)(1): limited independent expenditures advocating the election or defeat of a clearly identified candidate to $1,000 per year.

2. (2 U.S.C. §431 et seq.):

§431: required political committees to report names of persons contributing more than $10, and making public the names of those who contributed more than $100 per calendar year.

§434: required every person making independent contributions or expenditures exceeding $100 per calendar year file a statement with the Federal Election Commission.

§437: provided that the six members of the Federal Election Commission would be appointed as follows: (a) two appointed by the President pro tempore of the Senate; (b) two appointed by the Speaker of the House of Representatives; and (c) two appointed by the President. All six members were subject to confirmation by the majority of both houses of Congress.

3. (26 U.S.C. §9001 et seq.): Provided for public financing of presidential election campaigns.

99. Jack Anderson, James Reston, and Joseph Kraft were three of the most influential political columnists of the late twentieth century. Anderson has written a nationally syndicated column for the past fifty years, Reston wrote a syndicated column for the *New York Times*, and Kraft wrote a syndicated column for the *Washington Post*.

7) Regarding the question of political committees being in existence for six months, the court of appeal sustained these as a limited intrusion to the right of association, and I agree.

8) The disclosure provisions are the heart of the whole thing for me. I think that these provisions are constitutional and highly desirable. It is a separate question as to the level at which disclosure is made. Lists of contributions over $10 must be retained, and another list kept for contributions over $100. These burdens bear more heavily on non-incumbents.

9) Regarding the appointment of the Federal Election Commission, Congress can delegate what it itself may do but some of things that the Commission can do, Congress can't. That goes too far, and I would have to reverse.

10) This power to strike people from the ballot is dubious certainly, and I would say that it is unconstitutional.

11) On presidential financing, the new party provision bothers me.

BRENNAN: 1) I would sustain the contribution limits.

2) I would sustain §608(e), unless vagueness, the First Amendment, and §608(i) (providing for criminal sanctions) require invalidation.

3) I would sustain the family and personal limits.

4) I won't vote on expenditure limitations today.

5) I would sustain public funding across the board.

6) The volunteer services limitation is O.K.

7) I agree on the six-month life for political committees.

8) I agree on disclosure, but not the $10 and $100 limits as applied to small and new parties.

9) Regarding the appointment of the FEC, I presently would affirm as to its composition.

10) The provision allowing names to be struck from the ballot is unconstitutional.

11) On the presidential financing scheme, I would affirm across the board:

    a) Congress has the power.

    b) For minor parties it is O.K. It gives a guy a chance to govern.

    c) The limits of public financing are O.K.

    d) The power to allocate funds rests in the FEC.

STEWART: 1) On contributions, I was predisposed to say that the statute is constitutional at first, but the more I get into this the more doubtful I became. If we can limit the discussion to $1,000–$25,000 limits, I am not at rest.

2) Section 608(e) is patently unconstitutional under the First Amendment.

3) Section 608(c) is unconstitutional in limiting the *candidate*, but contribution limits on the family are O.K.

4) The expenditures limitations are wholly unconstitutional under the 1st Amendment.

5) I have no trouble with basic public funding. It is the equal protection argument that may have substance, but I think that they pass muster.

6) Insofar as Congress may limit contributions, Congress can say that volunteer services are not contributions, and the $500 limit on travel is probably O.K.—but not if it impinges on §608(e).

7) I see no First Amendment problems in political committees.

8) I have no problems with the disclosure provisions constitutionally. It is for Congress to fix these limits and not for us to second guess them.

9) On the appointment of commission members, the question is separable in the sense that there is no First Amendment problem, but one of separation of powers. I pass for now.

10) On the power to strike people from the ballot, we should not reach it as court of appeal did not—I would affirm the court of appeals decision.

11) Congress has the power to authorize the public financing of federal elections. But matching funds and major party post-convention funding and minor party provisions all are O.K. This can be analogized to our ballot position cases in *Storer*, etc.[100] Unlike the expenditure limitations for those not getting public funding, Congress can condition limits as it has here.

WHITE: 1) On contributions, I am as firm as can be to affirm. Giving money is an act, and acts are regulable. Congress has said that the dangers of money to fuel corruption require regulation. Neither content of speech nor censorship are involved here.

2) Section 608(e) is troublesome, but I think that I can sustain it. Maybe we ought to duck vagueness for now.

3) Section 608(c) is O.K.

4) The expenditure limitations are constitutional because otherwise, despite the contribution limitations, you can get and spend all the money you want.

5) The public funding provisions are O.K. across the board.

6) I agree with the court of appeals on volunteer services and the $500 limitation.

7) I affirm as to political committees.

8) I affirm the disclosure requirement on their face, and note that we have nothing before us as to these requirements as applied, with the $10 and $100 limits.

9) On the appointment of the commission, this is troublesome but I think that I would sustain composition. There is no question for me but that Congress can authorize regulatory power, and that is not an executive function (the president, after all, signed the

---

100. *Storer v. Brown*, 415 U.S. 724 (1974). California law prohibited any person from running for office as an independent candidate if during the previous year he or she had a registered affiliation with an established party. In 1972, Thomas Storer sought to be an independent candidate for Congress in the Sixth District. Because he had recently been a registered member of an established party, Storer was disqualified from running as an independent under state law. He sued Secretary of State Jerry Brown, seeking a court order to place his name on the ballot.

The Supreme Court ruled that California was entitled to substantial discretion in regulating its own elections and had the power to keep newly declared "independent" candidates off the general election ballot. The test was one of reasonableness. The Court weighed (1) the facts and circumstances behind the law; (2) the interests the state claimed to be protecting; and (3) the interests of those who were disadvantaged by the classification. Six Justices, led by Byron White, thought that California had demonstrated a compelling interest in protecting the primary process and in maintaining the stability of its political system. The law, White noted, did not unduly discriminate against bona fide independent candidates. Brennan, Douglas, and Marshall dissented, arguing that the requirement imposed an impermissible burden on Storer's First and Fourteenth Amendment rights and that California had failed to demonstrate that there were no less restrictive alternatives.

bill). They don't have the power to prosecute criminally, and if they did it would be invalid. The commission can bring a civil enforcement proceeding, but the commission eschews that and we ought to wait until they try it. I am bothered about the final authority to cut up the presidential campaign fund and that power may be invalid. But that wouldn't put the FEC out of business.

10) On the power to strike names from the ballot I would affirm here, not reaching that issue.

11) Regarding presidential election funding, I would affirm across the board.

MARSHALL: 1) On contributions, I agree with Bill Brennan and Byron.

2) I think that §608(e) is constitutional.

3) Section 608(a) is unconstitutional in limiting the candidate, but is O.K. as to family limits.

4) The expenditures limitations are constitutional.

5) Public financing of elections is O.K.

6) I agree with the court of appeals on volunteer contributions and the $500 limit.

7) I would affirm as to political committees

8) I am against the $10 and $100 limits as unconstitutional. Otherwise, I like to sustain these provisions, but I doubt whether I can.

9) On the appointment of the commission I can affirm most of it, although I am bothered about the commission's civil enforcement powers.

10) The power to strike names from the ballot is unconstitutional.

11) On presidential election funding, I affirm across the Board.

REHNQUIST: 1) I don't agree with Bill Brennan's view of the First Amendment. For me, the core of the First Amendment is its proscription against *Congress*, and this act does not further First Amendment values. We may be a representative democracy, but this law abridges, rather than furthers, First Amendment values. Contributions to a candidate for him to spend I can uphold—that is action, not speech.

2) Section 608(e) is unconstitutional under the First Amendment.

3) Section 608 (c) is constitutional as to the family, but unconstitutional as to candidates.

4) The expenditures limits violate the First Amendment.

5) Public financing is within Congress's general power to spend money. I am tentatively inclined to affirm.

6) I am inclined to affirm on volunteer services.

7) I affirm as to political committees.

8) I affirm as to disclosures, but stay open as to small parties.

9) As far as commission appointments are concerned, I would not strike the composition down in toto, but I have a dimmer view of their functions than Byron and Bill Brennan. The issuance of regulations, even if it is a legislative function, has been a power of *independent* agencies. But is this an independent agency? There is simply no law on this, and I am not sure what the answer should be. So I would generally reverse.

10) On the power to strike names from the ballot, I pass. I am not sure.

11) On presidential election funding, I would like to reverse on the minor party provisions on equal protection grounds with First Amendment overtones. *Jenness* is a state case, and the state interest in ballot preparation is a different question from congressional

power to make minor parties await a 5 percent vote—and this even though the Constitution gives Congress specific powers in federal elections.[101] But if money is going to be paid out to people running for office, I don't see where only Republicans and Democrats can get it. On the rest, I would affirm.

POWELL: 1) This statute is a revolutionary change in the system under which we have lived for two hundred years. The entire act, in purpose and effect, perpetrates the grossest infringement upon First Amendment rights. This act, in effect, will advantage incumbents and disadvantage challengers. Instead of a system that is neutral on face, where all scramble for all money they can get, this law rigs the structure for incumbents. Moreover, exemptions for media, corporations, and labor unions only guarantee a greater concentration of power to keep the "ins" in office, or at least determine who shall be the representatives.

So I am not at rest on the contribution limits, but if any part of the act can be sustained I guess this is it. Section 608(e) is the most drastic abridgment of political speech since the Alien and Sedition Acts.

2) Section 608(e) is facially unconstitutional.

3) Section 608(c) constitutional as to family, but not as to candidates.

4) Expenditures limitations are unconstitutional.

5) Public financing is O.K. across the board.

6) I am inclined to affirm volunteer contribution limits.

7) I affirm as to political committees.

8) I affirm the disclosure requirements, including the established limits.

9) On commission appointments, I am closer to affirming than otherwise. I see this much like Byron, since many of the things authorized Congress can constitutionally authorize, including regulations, and ought to be all right. But the veto of regulations is troublesome. In short, I would not strike the commission down per se.

10) The power to strike names from the ballot is unconstitutional.

11) I affirm the presidential election funding, except that I am not sure whether accepting public funding limits might validate private expenditure limits that I think are unconstitutional.

BLACKMUN: 1) On contributions, as with other issues, the First Amendment is the core of our problem. We must balance interests. The effect is to equalize the interested with disinterested person. Nevertheless, there is serious First Amendment infringement that is simply indefensible in the expenditures provisions. Even in the disclosure provisions I can't go for much, except for a case by case approach. But I lean to reverse on contributions.

2) I agree that §608(e) is unconstitutional.

---

101. *Jenness v. Fortson*, 403 U.S. 431 (1971). Georgia law provided that candidates for public office who did not win a party primary could be listed on the general election ballot only if they filed a nominating petition signed by at least 5 percent of registered voters. Linda Jenness of the Socialist Workers party and other prospective candidates and registered voters sued state Attorney General Ben Fortson. A three-judge district court held that the petition requirement was constitutional and the Supreme Court affirmed. On a 7–2–0 vote, Potter Stewart ruled that the law did not violate the First or Fourteenth Amendments and did not amount to invidious discrimination against third parties. Black and Harlan concurred in the judgment. There were no dissents.

3) Section 608(c) is unconstitutional as to the candidate, but constitutional as to the family.

4) Expenditures limitations are unconstitutional.

5) Public financing is O.K. across the board.

6) I am inclined to reverse on volunteer services limitations.

7) I affirm as to political committees.

8) I am inclined to affirm on disclosure, but want to keep open the questions of the $10 and $100 limits.

9) On commission appointments, I generally feel negatively about the constitutionality of this. Maybe Senate confirmation is as much authority as Congress constitutionally can have.

10) The power to strike names from the ballot is unconstitutional.

11) On presidential election funding, I affirm across the board.

Result: In a per curiam opinion, the Court upheld most of the law but struck down three key provisions. The Court approved (1) the $1,000 limit on individual and group contributions to candidates and authorized campaign committees; (2) the $5,000 political action committee contribution limits; (3) the $25,000 total annual contribution limit; (4) disclosure requirements for contributions in excess of $10; and (5) the optional public financing of presidential campaigns. The Court struck down (1) expenditure limits on candidates, campaign organizations, and political parties; (2) limits on candidate expenditures from personal and family resources; and (3) the original appointment scheme for the FEC.

Congress quickly reconstituted the FEC but otherwise made little new headway in reforming campaign financing. Despite numerous election scandals, Congress has not passed any significant campaign finance reform legislation since 1974.

FEC v. National Conservative Political Action Committee,
470 U.S. 480 (1985)
(Brennan)

The Presidential Election Campaign Fund Act offered presidential candidates the option to conduct publicly financed campaigns. If a candidate accepted public funds, the law imposed certain conditions on the campaign, including prohibiting independent political action committees (PACs) from spending more than $1,000 apiece to further the candidate's election. Hoping to limit Ronald Reagan's legendary fundraising abilities, the Democratic party asked for a declaratory judgment that the statutory limitations on PAC donations were constitutional. The Federal Election Commission (FEC) intervened and claimed that it had exclusive standing to litigate the case. The FEC asked that the Democratic party be dismissed from the suit and that the FEC be allowed to pursue the same issues that the Democrats had raised. This meant that judges first had to decide whether the Democrats had standing or whether the FEC had exclusive standing. A three-judge district court ruled that both parties had standing and then ruled on the merits that the PAC limits were facially unconstitutional. Note Blackmun's blunt assessment of Buckley v. Valeo.[102]

---

102. *Buckley v. Valeo*, 421 U.S. 1 (1976).

BURGER: The holding below was that the First Amendment was violated and the Democrats could sue. This was wrong, but we don't have to reach it. *Buckley* drew a constitutional distinction between contributions and expenditures, and I would hold this legislation unconstitutional.

WHITE: This is different enough from *Buckley*, and I would sustain this prohibition.

MARSHALL: I agree with Byron.

BLACKMUN: *Buckley* is a disaster. I was to reverse in *Common Cause*, and I would also reverse here.[103]

POWELL: If this isn't unconstitutional, individual and small groups would be powerless to participate meaningfully in political campaigns.

Rehnquist: It would be a far worse disaster to reverse this decision. Spending money to say your piece in a presidential election must be at the core of First Amendment protections.

STEVENS: Without *Buckley*, I would have trouble with a distinction between contributions and expenditures. But I can't distinguish this committee from a wealthy individual.

O'CONNOR: Congress could regulate this to control corruption or to assure fair elections—but that is not this case. I would address the standing of the Democratic party and say that there was none.

Result: William Rehnquist wrote for the majority in a two-part opinion. In the first part, a close 5–4 majority ruled that the FEC had exclusive standing. White, Brennan, Marshall, and Stevens dissented. In the second part, the Court ruled 6–3 that the PAC spending limits violated the First Amendment. According to Rehnquist, PACs were different from other types of corporations whose campaign contributions were limited under the act. Because PACs are nonprofit organizations expressly created to participate in political debate, their expenditures are entitled to full First Amendment protection. Commercial corporations, however, are created primarily for economic gain, and their campaign contributions may be regulated, limited, or even prohibited. With respect to PACs, there was no compelling

---

103. *Common Cause v. Schmitt,* 455 U.S. 129 (1982). The lower court ruling (512 F.Supp. 489 [DC DC 1980]) was affirmed without comment by an equally divided Court, with Justice O'Connor not participating. In the original case, Common Cause and the Federal Election Commission sued Harrison Schmitt and five PACs who planned to spend millions of dollars promoting Ronald Reagan's 1980 presidential campaign. The plaintiffs claimed that the planned expenditures violated the Presidential Campaign Fund Act, which prohibited PACs from spending more than $1,000 to support publicly subsidized presidential campaigns. Because Reagan had accepted $30 million in federal funds, his campaign was subject to the provisions of the act. Schmitt and the PACs claimed the right to spend however much they wanted as independent supporters. All of the PACs, however, had extensive contacts with the Reagan campaign, including shared campaign officials, political consultants, and staff.

A three-judge district court struck down the $1,000 limit on independent expenditures as facially unconstitutional, arguing that *Buckley v. Valeo* had established that there was little risk of corruption from such expenditures. Despite considerable criticism, the decision has never been overruled.

state interest to justify any restrictions on their free speech and association rights. The majority saw little risk of corruption in permitting unlimited PAC expenditures, given the small individual donations on which PACs rely and given the absence of reliable evidence of corruption. Even if there were evidence of corruption caused by PACs, Rehnquist warned, the law was still fatally overbroad and not narrowly tailored to justify the restrictions challenged here. White, Brennan, and Marshall also dissented from the second part of Rehnquist's opinion.

CHAPTER 16

THE CONFERENCE IN CONTEXT

UNDER THE FIRST THREE CHIEF JUSTICES—JOHN JAY, JOHN RUTLEDGE, AND Oliver Ellsworth—the Court did not meet in conference. The Justices issued seriatim opinions, meaning that each judge announced his own judgment and reasoning independently of the others. No formal consultations were needed because there were no common opinions.

Everything changed in 1801, when John Marshall became the fourth Chief Justice of the United States. Marshall inherited a Supreme Court that was weak, dysfunctional, and adrift in a hostile political environment. The rest of the government was dominated by Thomas Jefferson's Democratic-Republicans, while the Supreme Court was the last outpost of the dying Federalist party. Marshall knew that the Court's best chance for survival was to present a united front. Cases had to be decided unanimously, or at least have the *appearance* of unanimity, if the Justices were to have any hope of being taken seriously. Marshall quickly ended the practice of issuing seriatim opinions and the Court began to speak with one voice—his.

Marshall's new, collective decision-making style encouraged compromise and consensus. The Justices began to meet in conference almost daily to deliberate and negotiate judgments acceptable to all. The results were announced as decisions of the Court, usually without any indication of who had written the opinion and without revealing whether there had been any concurring or dissenting votes. With some modifications, the habit of deciding most cases by common agreement remained in place for the next 140 years.

There have been three major phases in the history of the conference. From 1801 to 1863, group identity and cohesion were maintained primarily by *interpersonal loyalties* among the Justices. During the second phase, from 1864 to 1941, personal loyalties gave way to *institutional loyalties*. The final phase, from 1941 to the present, is characterized by *judicial individualism* and the breakdown of group cohesion.

Under John Marshall and Roger Brooke Taney, the life of the conference was shaped largely by personal loyalties among the Justices. During this period, the Justices lived together in common boardinghouses when the Court was in session. By eating, sleeping, working, and socializing together, the Justices developed such an intimacy in their personal and professional lives that they came to consider themselves a family and began to refer to themselves as "brethren." These strong personal attachments, guided by Marshall and Taney, proved unusually effective in persuading the Justices to subordinate individual interests to the good of the group.

Conference discussions, often fueled by the Court's private stock of madeira, allowed the Justices to reach consensus in most cases, or at least to work out compromises to avoid open dissent. The Justices did not necessarily disagree with each other then any less than they do today, but they made a concerted effort to find common ground and to avoid public disagreements. If consensus could not be reached, the dissenters were usually persuaded to remain silent. This sense of group identity and camaraderie helped the Justices to maintain an extraordinary level of outward cooperation and harmony during the Court's formative years.

The cohesion of the Marshall and Taney Courts is striking by modern standards. Between 1800 and 1807, the Court decided sixty-seven cases with only one dissenting opinion—a case dissent rate of just 1.5 percent. During the last five years of Marshall's tenure, all of Marshall's fellow Federalists were either dead or retired and the Court was controlled by Democratic-Republicans. While the dissent rate jumped significantly, Marshall held the Court together to a remarkable degree considering the profound political transformation taking place around him. Between 1830 and 1835 there were 26 dissenting opinions scattered among 276 cases, for a case dissent rate of 9.4 percent—high compared to Marshall's earliest years on the Court but quite modest by modern standards. For Marshall's career, 1800–1835, the Court was unanimous in 1,011 out of 1,081 cases, for an overall case dissent rate of 6.5 percent.[1] There was similar unity for most of Taney's tenure as Chief Justice, although serious internal divisions developed among the Justices during the years immediately prior to the Civil War. Between 1836 and 1863, the Taney Court decided 1,657 cases, with 194 cases containing at least one dissent, for an overall case dissent rate of 11.7 percent.[2]

The second phase in the history of the conference occurred between the Civil War and World War II. As the Court's authority became more secure and institutionalized, for various reasons the personal relationships among the Justices grew more detached and distant. After 1845, the Justices stopped living together and scattered to private homes and residential hotels throughout Washington. To make matters worse, because the Justices did not have chambers or office space in the Capitol building (where the Court met from 1801 until 1935), they were forced to work separately in their own homes. The Justices rarely saw each other outside of oral arguments and the now-weekly conference sessions. As they gradually lost their close personal attachments, the Justices came to identify with the Court rather than with each other.

---

1. Data compiled from Epstein, *The Supreme Court Compendium*, 195.
2. Ibid., 195–96.

Such institutional loyalties are comparable to students who identify with their university or sports fans who root for their favorite team. These loyalties often remain strong after personal bonds are broken, such as when individual students or professors leave or popular athletes are traded or retire. Because institutional loyalties transcend personal relationships, these bonds tend to be relatively stable and enduring, at least as long as the institution itself is not perceived to have changed significantly.

By the beginning of the Civil War, the Justices thought of themselves less as a family and more like a company board or a law firm, with the Chief Justice serving as the senior partner. Conferences were still used to build consensus, but the process depended less on personal relationships than perceived institutional needs. The personal equation remained important, but it was the good of the Court that mattered most.

Corporatist loyalties continued to inspire the Justices until well into the 1930s. Even free thinkers such as Holmes, Brandeis, and Stone regularly suppressed dissents in the name of unity. When Taft was Chief Justice (1921–30), Pierce Butler wrote on the back of a Harlan Fiske Stone slip opinion:

> I voted to reverse. While this sustains your conclusion to affirm, I still think reversal would be better. But I shall in silence acquiesce. Dissents seldom aid in the right development or statement of the law. They often do harm. For myself I say: "Lead us not into temptation."[3]

During this period in the Court's development, which ran roughly from Salmon Chase (1864–73) through Charles Evans Hughes (1930–1941), the Justices still strove to speak with one voice. If they did not always succeed, they put considerable effort into the attempt. The Justices met in conference not merely to tally votes but to establish the general will. Dissents were thought to weaken the Court's authority and were to be avoided whenever possible. Justices were encouraged to compromise and were expected either to negotiate an acceptable settlement or remain silent.

When Harlan Fiske Stone became Chief Justice in 1941, the nature of the conference was again transformed by the rise of judicial individualism. In contrast with the first two periods of the Court's development, which were based on different forms of group identity, judicial individualism emphasized the independence of each Justice to think, vote, and write as their consciences dictated, regardless of any claimed group needs or appeals to the greater good.

Under Stone, the nature of the conference changed from communal decision making, with a preference for collective responsibility and consensus, to a liberal model of decision making that stressed individualism and majority rule. The Justices, in effect, swapped Rousseau for Locke.

---

3. David Danelski, "The Influence of the Chief Justice in the Decisional Process," in Goldman and Sarat, *American Court Systems*, 496.

New Deal judges like Hugo Black and William Douglas, as well as some of the older progressives like Stone, began to decide cases based on their own idiosyncratic readings of the law. The practice of having the Court speak with one voice was no longer thought necessary, and the stigma of dissent quickly disappeared. The Court no longer functioned like a family, or even like a partnership. Instead, as the second John Marshall Harlan put it, the Supreme Court began to function like nine independent law firms, often working against one another.

The beginnings of this transformation can be traced to 1916, when Louis Brandeis was appointed to the Court. When Brandeis, the progressive outsider, teamed with Holmes to oppose the established conservative majority on the Hughes Court, dissent suddenly became respectable. Although Holmes had been on the Court for fourteen years before Brandeis joined him, Holmes had been well socialized in the Court's traditions. He hated to dissent alone, and even when he disagreed with a decision he generally "sat on [his] hands, mute and sorrowful." Before Brandeis came to the Court, Holmes was isolated and relatively ineffectual in conference. Together, however, these two great dissenters, became the role models for the next generation of New Deal Justices.[4] Dissent came to be seen as an heroic act, a howl of defiance against perceived injustice. Brandeis and Holmes proved that, far from harming themselves or the Court, great legal and political reputations could be made by dissenting magnificently.

After Stone became Chief Justice in 1941, the Supreme Court's case dissent rates skyrocketed. The Stone Court decided a total of 709 cases, including 357 cases with at least one dissent, for an overall case dissent rate of 50 percent.[5] As can be seen in Figures 1 and 2, the impact on the Court's decision making was extraordinary, if not revolutionary.

By the Warren era, the transformation of the conference was complete. As the second John Marshall Harlan observed, decisions on the Warren Court were

> not the product of an institutional approach, as with a professional decision of a law firm or policy determination of a business enterprise. They are the result merely of a tally of individual votes. . . . The rule of ultimate individual responsibility is a respected and jealously guarded tradition of the Court.[6]

Warren Burger tried to restore a measure of unity and teamwork to the conference, but failed. William O. Douglas complained that in contrast to Earl Warren, where "there

---

4. Brandeis was among the first to realize that Supreme Court decisions were no longer going to be the product of consensus but of majority rule. In a letter to Stone in February 1934, Brandeis wrote, "Who in hell cares what anybody says about [constitutional questions] but the Final Five of the August Nine?" Mason, *Harlan Fiske Stone*, 384.

5. Data complied from Epstein, *Supreme Court Compendium*, 198.

6. Harlan, "A Glimpse of the Supreme Court," 7; Frank, *If Men Were Angels*, 78.

Case Dissent Rate
Percent

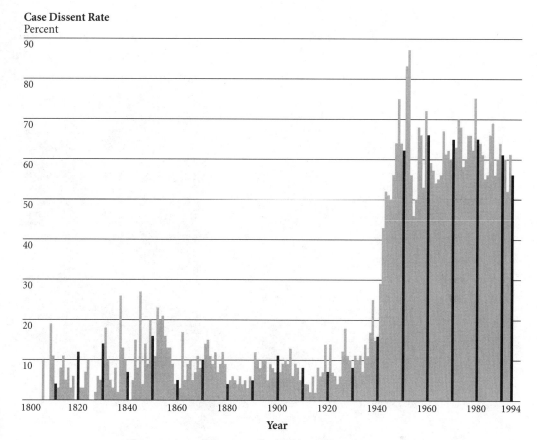

Figure 1. Annual Supreme Court Dissent Rate (1800–1994).

was an openness of ideas in judicial conference," under Burger there "was pressure to join ranks."[7] This seems to be a strange grievance, given the unprecedented dissent rates that characterized the Burger Court. Douglas's remarks show that the norms of the Court had changed so much by the 1970s that the very idea that a Chief Justice might try to encourage consensus in the conference was not only unfashionable, it was prima facie evidence of tyranny.

Professor David O'Brien argues that the modern conference "serves only to discover consensus."[8] In fact, this is precisely what has been lost. The conference no longer tries to find the consensus in difficult cases. The rules of the game have changed from working toward a consensus of nine to settling for a simple majority. William Brennan often reminded his clerks that with five votes the majority could do anything it wanted.

---

7. Yarbrough, *John Marshall Harlan*, 14.
8. O'Brien, *Storm Center*, 230.

Case Dissent Rate

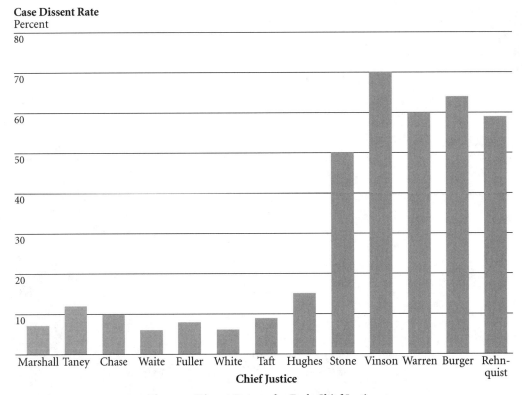

Figure 2. Dissent Rate under Each Chief Justice.

Today, dissent is viewed as both inevitable and unremarkable. The extra effort required to reach consensus is considered to be inefficient, impractical, and unnecessary. The chief exceptions to this rule include cases where the Justices feel politically isolated and vulnerable. In the school desegregation cases during the 1950s, the Justices were painfully aware that they stood virtually alone against a large number of recalcitrant state governments and could not rely on support from the other two branches of the federal government. Twenty years later, in *United States v. Nixon* (1974), the Court squared off against an openly hostile co-equal branch of government.[9] In both instances, the Justices went to extraordinary lengths to deliver unanimous verdicts. They did so because they feared that the losing parties might not comply with the Court's orders, particularly if there were any internal divisions among the Justices that could be exploited. Theodore Roosevelt once boasted, "I may not know much about the law, but I do know one can put the fear of God into judges."[10] Such fear can concentrate the judicial mind and cause the Justices to huddle more closely together.

---

9. *Brown v. Board of Education*, 347 U.S. 483 (1954); *Brown v. Board of Education*, 349 U.S. 294 (1955); *United States v. Nixon,* 418 U.S. 683 (1974).

10. Bickel and Schmidt, *The Judiciary and Responsible Government*, 24.

There is no reason to expect that the Court will ever return to a consensual model of decision making. First, the Justices no longer live together, and the boardinghouse mentality that resulted from these arrangements has been irretrievably lost. Second, there is no longer any sense among the Justices that their authority is threatened by dissent. Third, the Court has grown more diverse in terms of class, gender, ethnicity, race, education, and geography, and these differences tend to foster greater disagreement. Fourth, the Court's heavy caseload means that there is little time to work out a consensus in difficult cases.[11] Finally, new technologies, such as copy machines and personal computers, allow—even encourage—the Justices to work alone in chambers.[12] Just as the Court's institutional and technological structures originally encouraged cooperation and consensus, modern procedures, structures, and technologies tend to reinforce isolation and individual effort.

Several countertrends persist. First, some new technologies, such as e-mail, might encourage closer and more frequent communications among the Justices. Second, the clerks' network remains an active back-channel source of interchambers communication. Some recent changes in how clerks are used—notably the creation of the cert pool during the 1972 term—have encouraged modest new levels of interaction and cooperation among participating chambers.

Moreover, personal and institutional loyalties, and even an abstract preference for consensus, have never entirely disappeared. There remains a great deal of agreement among Justices in many routine cases, and the Justices still retain something of a group identity. In spite of the personal infighting and ill will that can occur inside the conference room, the public rarely hears about such matters from the Justices, who tend to join ranks in public in order to protect each other and the Court. Even bitter adversaries such as Douglas and Frankfurter routinely claimed to be friends in public because they worried that the Court's reputation would suffer should their personal enmity become front-page news. The same code of silence remains in place on the Rehnquist Court. Although personal antagonisms among the Justices are often open secrets and are periodically leaked to the press by clerks and other Court employees, Justices rarely speak ill of each other in public.[13] On occasion,

---

11. There have been some exceptions to this trend. In the *Buckley v. Valeo* campaign finance case, the Justices managed an impressive showing of cooperation and coordinated effort to resolve an especially difficult case. *Buckley v. Valeo,* 424 U.S. 1 (1976).

12. Another "new technology" that emerged during the twentieth century was the law clerk. By the time that Stone became Chief Justice, the Justices had grown to depend on their law clerks more than they depended on each other for support and information.

13. One exception has been Antonin Scalia, who has on several occasions blurred the line between doctrinal disagreements and personal attacks in his published opinions. His sarcasm is often aimed at two Justices who tend to be the swing votes in close cases, Sandra Day O'Connor and Anthony Kennedy. See *Webster v. Reproductive Health Services,* 492 U.S. 490 (1989) (attacking O'Connor); *Planned Parenthood v. Casey,* 505 U.S. 833, 979-980 (1992) (attacking O'Connor); *Lee v. Weisman,* 505 U.S. 577 (1992) (attacking Kennedy); *Romer v. Evans,* 517 U.S. 620 (1996) (attacking Kennedy). Scalia, who is known for his aggressive automobile driving, apparently believes that people who stand in the middle of the road deserve to be run over.

Justices are still willing to withhold dissents in controversial cases for the good of the Court. Murphy squelched a dissent in *Gobitis*, Douglas swallowed a dissent in *Korematsu*, and several Justices spiked dissenting or concurring opinions in *Brown v. Board of Education* and later school desegregation cases. But after the 1940s, such behavior became the exception rather than the rule.

These profound changes in the nature of the conference were a byproduct of the Court's workload and the imperative for greater efficiency. As Byron White and Lewis Powell observed, the nondeliberative and impersonal decision-making style of the modern Court was an inevitable consequence of the Court's growing workload.[14]

When Louis Brandeis was asked the difference between the Supreme Court and the other branches of government, he replied, "Here we do our own work."[15] If that was true in Brandeis's day, it is no longer the case. Over the last hundred years the Court has grown steadily larger and more bureaucratic. Each chambers now averages seven people: the Justice, three to five clerks, two secretaries, and a messenger. The Chief Justice's chambers are even more crowded, with several administrative assistants, up to five clerks, four secretaries, a messenger, and a driver.[16] The Court has become, in Chief Justice Rehnquist's words, a collection of nine autonomous opinion-writing bureaus.[17]

If the trend toward ever-increasing dissent rates continues, the Court's authority might eventually suffer. As Alexander Hamilton observed in *The Federalist*, the Supreme Court has neither sword nor purse to enforce its decisions; it has only the strength of words. The Court's persuasive powers could begin to erode if it consistently speaks in competing—and often contradictory—voices in deciding important and controversial cases. With Hamilton's warning fresh in their minds, Marshall and Taney nurtured a strong group identity and encouraged the Justices to sing as one. The tendency today is for the Justices to sing as nine competing soloists, each reading from a separate score. The resulting dissonance might weaken public confidence in the Supreme Court, although the Court is perhaps not as vulnerable on this count as it once was.

CONFERENCE LEADERSHIP AND TACTICS

With nine members for most of its history, the Supreme Court is relatively large for what social scientists generally consider to be a small group. Compared to smaller appellate courts of three to seven judges, the Supreme Court requires more formality and greater discipline to be effective.[18] This means that compared to smaller courts, the Supreme

---

14. Ibid., 123.

15. Stewart, "Reflections on the Supreme Court," 9.

16. While the Chief Justice's chambers is budgeted for five clerks, Chief Justice Rehnquist has only three.

17. O'Brien, *Storm Center*, 123.

18. Rehnquist, *The Supreme Court*, 293.

Court is less likely to operate according to consensus and more likely to break down into smaller, competing factions.

THE CHIEF JUSTICE: MANAGING THE CONFERENCE

The idea of forging a more collegial, unified Supreme Court lives on mostly in the imaginations of Chief Justices. Because of their unique responsibilities and perspectives, Chief Justices tend to value the Court's traditions of collegiality, unity, and consensus more highly than Associate Justices. Even modern Chief Justices, including Warren Burger and William Rehnquist, have continued to encourage cooperative decision making, usually with modest success. "To do our task," Warren Burger once said, "we must consult on each step and stage, and almost daily, as the decisions evolve."[19]

While Chief Justices may still dream of being able to herd cats, they have never been able to dominate the conference in a literal sense, not even in the golden days of Marshall, Taney, Taft, or Hughes. The Chief Justice cannot lead the Court in the same way that the president commands the military or a CEO runs a large corporation. They have surprisingly little leverage over Associate Justices beyond their powers of persuasion.

The tangible powers that Chief Justices possess are the right to speak first and preside at conference, the right to assign cases on the side with which they vote, and primary administrative responsibility for the Court's calendar and operations. Otherwise, Chief Justices have no real power beyond what the other Justices willingly cede them. They must earn their authority; they are in no position to demand it.

While the Chief Justice's powers are limited, they are not insignificant. The Chief Justice helps to shape the life of the conference. It is a truism of politics that the person who writes the questions can control the answers, and the Chief Justice performs this task for the conference. He sets the conference agenda, speaks first, frames the issues, moderates discussions, speaks last, sums up the sense of the Court, tallies the votes, and assigns cases.

The power to assign cases is especially useful. As David Danelski noted, judicious use of the assignment power can have a significant impact on case outcomes. Assuming that the Chief votes with the majority, he may decide to keep the case for himself or assign it to any other Justice. This power can be used to reward, or punish, or to pass the case to a Justice who will write an opinion that best fits the Chief's needs. It often depends on whether the Chief Justice wants a narrow or broad opinion, one that is written quickly or slowly, one that will appeal to the most Justices, one that will hold a majority in a tight case, one that is most likely to win public support or minimize an adverse reaction, or one that will be decided on a particular ground that the Chief desires.[20]

---

19. O'Brien, *Storm Center*, 123.
20. Danelski, "The Influence of the Chief Justice in the Decisional Process," 494.

The Chief Justice also has important responsibilities in administrative matters. The other Justices are generally content to allow the Chief Justice to make routine administrative decisions, and the Chief Justice has considerable discretion over the conference's administrative agenda. William Howard Taft refused to bring the idea of building a new Supreme Court building before the conference until he was certain that he had five supporting votes. Once the vote was taken, he declared the 5–4 vote a mandate and never raised the matter in conference again. More recently, Warren Burger steadfastly refused to discuss at conference the issue of videotaping oral arguments, despite considerable pressure to debate the matter from several of the Associate Justices. Burger also unilaterally lobbied Congress to create a new appellate court to relieve the Supreme Court's workload, even though he knew that a majority of the conference opposed his efforts.[21]

Although the Chief Justice is the leader of the conference, the nature of his power is easily misunderstood and often exaggerated. The Chief Justice's modest authority is hardly sufficient to bludgeon a group of intelligent, educated, and willful judges into submission. He often must yield to the will of the conference when faced with determined opposition. Burger's attempt to transform the conference room into his own ceremonial chambers was partly thwarted when the other Justices objected. The Chief often must defer to the wishes of a minority or even an individual Justice in some important internal decisions, such as the rule of four, or the longstanding tradition that a case will not be announced until every Justice is ready.

To be successful the Chief Justice must be an unconventional leader. Rather than seeking to dominate the conference like a CEO, the Chief Justice must be a combination of facilitator, mediator, and family therapist. The best Chief Justices are invariably a moderating force in conference—conciliatory and even deferential, rather than bullying or oppressive.

As a first among equals, the Chief Justice is a prototype of democratic leadership in small groups. The most effective leaders of such groups typically gain respect and authority by listening to, deferring to, and accommodating the wishes of the members, rather than by openly seeking to impose their own agendas on the group. There is a Zen quality to Supreme Court leadership—the most successful Chief Justices lead by following. They solicit, process, prioritize, patronize, and accommodate the needs of the other Justices, which in turn makes their own leadership more effective—at least as long as the Chief's ultimate goals are artfully designed and executed.

Harlan Fiske Stone was a failure as a Chief Justice largely because he continued to act as he had acted as an Associate Justice—arguing, fighting, and confronting other Justices rather than seeking to arbitrate among the Court's competing factions. Associate Justices might spar and strut in conference like roosters, but Chief Justices can rarely afford such reckless behavior. Similarly, Warren Burger's pomposity and exaggerated sense of

---

21. O'Brien, *Storm Center*, 119.

deportment interfered with his best intentions to lead the Court. Burger was partly for-given because of his unquestioned concern for the Court and the Justices' personal wel-fare. His efforts in these areas mitigated some of the antagonisms he caused with his un-bearable pretensions, his intellectual limitations, and his bumbling conference behavior.

David Danelski divided conference leadership into two distinct roles: task leader-ship and social leadership.[22] Task leadership involves getting the Court's work done in an effective and efficient manner. Task leaders initiate, shape, and control conference discussions by articulating and defending their ideas more successfully than others. They have intellectual abilities that the other group members admire and respect.

Social leaders, on the other hand, deal with the emotional needs of the group and work to maintain group cohesion. They tend to be amiable and accommodating and relieve group frictions by appealing to group sensibilities. Social leaders attend to the Justices' emotional needs by promoting their well-being, soliciting their opinions and suggestions, and appealing to their interests and egos.[23]

Although Chief Justices have certain advantages in exercising both types of leader-ship roles, they are usually more effective in one capacity than the other. Because task-oriented leaders tend to focus on the business of the Court, they often disregard the emo-tional well-being of the other members. Social leaders typically want to be liked and shy away from the more contentious duties of task leadership. While the ability to perform both roles well is rare, the two categories are not mutually exclusive. Danelski points to Charles Evans Hughes as one who was effective as both a task and social leader.

To the extent that the Chief Justice does not fulfill both leadership roles in confer-ence, other Justices will ordinarily step up to perform these functions. William Howard Taft, who was an excellent social leader, depended on Willis Van Devanter to be the Court's task leader. Taft often called Van Devanter his "Lord Chancellor." He was a shrewd and experienced judge, and Taft depended on him to arrange the conference's substantive agenda.

Earl Warren was perhaps more successful at social leadership than task leadership, although he was certainly capable of wearing both hats. During most of Warren's years in the center chair, Black, Frankfurter, and William Brennan all vied to be the Court's task leader. Brennan ultimately became Warren's de facto assistant, though in this role he was clearly subordinate to the Chief.

Warren Burger made an adequate social leader but a poor task leader. On a badly divided Court, Brennan often challenged Burger as both social and task leader. After Wil-

---

22. Danelski, "The Influence of the Chief Justice in the Decisional Process of the Supreme Court," 489–94. Danelski credits the small group studies of Bales, Slater, and Berkowitz for providing the empiri-cal foundation for his own pioneering work in Supreme Court leadership.

23. Ibid., 489–90.

liam Rehnquist was promoted to Chief Justice, however, he asserted himself and in short order became both an effective task leader and a good social leader.

In some cases, a Chief Justice may not perform either role well. When neither Stone nor Fred Vinson proved to be especially effective at either social or task leadership, Hugo Black assumed the task leadership of the conference. Unfortunately, no one stood out as social leader during Stone's tenure, which helps to explain why this was not an especially pleasant time to sit on the Court. Vinson was more effective as a social leader during his short time on the bench, and the atmosphere inside the conference—while still often tense—was noticeably less unpleasant than it was under Stone.

Task and social leaders help to organize, execute, and lubricate the functioning of the conference. Beyond the role of the Chief Justice, several important questions remain, including: what are the main purposes of the conference, and what are the main tactics employed to achieve those goals?

Conference Goals and Tactics

Justices use the conference to communicate their views, to persuade, and to negotiate. They also vote to decide the cases and tentatively establish rationales for their decisions. Broadly speaking, the factors that shape conference discussions include the law and the facts (as the Justices see them) and the Justices' own personal values, experiences, and preferences.

The Justices routinely go beyond the established facts as determined by the trial court and deal with external factual and policy considerations. As Justice Miller said, "In my experience in the conference room . . . I have been surprised to find how readily those judges came to an agreement upon questions of law, and how often they disagreed in regard to questions of facts."[24] While an appellate court like the Supreme Court is ordinarily expected to take the facts of the case as the trial court found them (unless the trial court's findings are completely unsupported by the evidence), in practice the Justices are free to reinterpret the facts and to consider the larger social consequences of their decisions.

The conference notes published here demonstrate that Justices routinely apply their own values, experiences, and policy preferences in deciding cases. These factors are usually only implicit in the Court's written opinions, but they are explicitly discussed during conference. Justices often stand the classic model of judicial decision making on its head, by first settling on the desired outcome and then searching inductively for a rationale to support their decision. Perhaps the clearest example of this sort of "backward" decision making is *Brown v. Board of Education*, where the Justices settled on the result well before reaching a consensus on a rationale or a plan of action.

---

24. Frank, *If Men Were Angels*, 78.

The Justices employ five main conference techniques to move cases toward resolution. These techniques are not mutually exclusive—the same communications might perform several different functions simultaneously—but they are all theoretically distinct and are helpful in charting the course of conference discussions.

Sharing Information

Justices frequently use conference discussions to share new information with the group and to help clarify their thinking about a case. Perhaps the best examples of this sort of informative discourse are the Chief Justice's case summaries, which are intended to provide an objective review and commentary of the facts and main issues of each case. During conference discussions the Justices routinely ask each other questions and solicit news or clarifications when they are in doubt. While informative communications are often (and perhaps inherently) also meant to persuade, their primary purpose is to educate and impart information to conference members.

A good example of this category are the professorial lectures that Frankfurter loved to give in conference—always, he said, to enlighten rather than persuade. Frankfurter claimed that he wanted only to promote a free discussion and interchange of ideas and thought that such exchanges were the primary means of attaining reason, although his lessons often bordered on hectoring.[25] Frankfurter's drive to be a teacher rather than a peer meant that he was rarely effective either as a consensus builder or as a conference leader. Even William Brennan, one of Frankfurter's ex-students, found Frankfurter's lectures boring and quickly stopped looking to Frankfurter as a source of useful information.

Advocacy

Advocacy can range from subtle persuasion to overt proselytizing. In its more vigorous and virulent forms, it can degenerate into bickering, browbeating, and infighting. The difference between sharing information and advocacy is often a matter of degree, and the line is perhaps inevitably arbitrary. But the Justices themselves recognize the difference, even if they do not always honor the distinction in practice. The Chief Justice's case summaries are supposed to educate and inform, and while they are no doubt also meant to persuade, a Chief Justice who is too heavy handed in using case summaries risks alienating the other Justices and undermining his own authority.

Some Justices live to persuade others to their point of view. This was essentially Douglas's view of Frankfurter's behavior in conference. Douglas said, "Most of us thought the function of the conference was to discover the consensus. [Frankfurter's] idea was different; he was there to proselytize and to gain converts."[26] Douglas's observation was

25. Ball, *Hugo L. Black,* 140.
26. Ibid., 140–41.

ironic, in that Douglas prided himself on his maverick status within the conference and rarely contributed much in the way of consensus-building. For his part, Frankfurter often complained that while Douglas "ought to act like a collaborator" in conference, he behaved as though he were engaged "in a rival grocery business."[27] Similarly, Tom Clark thought that Douglas was by nature a contrarian and inveterate dissenter and was on balance a destructive force in conference.[28]

One victim of the intense advocacy in conference was Charles Whittaker. According to Douglas:

> Whittaker would take one position when the Chief or Black spoke, change his mind when Frankfurter spoke, and change back again when some other Justice spoke. This eventually led to his "nervous breakdown" and his retirement for being permanently disabled in 1962. No one can change his mind so often and not have a breakdown.[29]

On the modern Court, William Brennan was arguably the most effective conference advocate, often speaking at length in an attempt to persuade the persuadable. He also politicked endlessly in hallways, in chambers, and anywhere that he could take a Justice by the elbow and speak quietly for a few minutes in private.

Negotiation

Negotiation is the process of conferring with opposing parties to arrive at a mutually agreeable decision, usually through discussion and compromise. There are often elements of both information sharing and persuasion present, but negotiation is less about persuading others to join your side than it is about offering to meet an opponent somewhere in the middle. Negotiating is a common conference behavior. The clearest examples of bargaining in conference are the frequent claims by Justices during conference discussions that their votes remain flexible and tentative and that they are willing to compromise in order to make a Court.

This sort of behavior was the primary task of the conference for more than 140 years, from John Marshall through Charles Evans Hughes. In those days, the Court was driven to seek consensus, and the Justices were encouraged to compromise with and accommodate each other in order, in Taft's words, "to mass the Court." Negotiating tactics can range from simple, benign compromises to more coercive behaviors bordering on blackmail. Justices have on occasion threatened to write a particularly harsh dissent or to publish sensitive or confidential information unless their views were accommodated.

---

27. Ball, "Loyalty, Treason, and the State: An Examination of Justice William O. Douglas' Style, Substance and Anguish," in Wasby, *He Shall Not Pass This Way Again*, 10.

28. Simon, *Independent Journey*, 353. Douglas eventually gave up and decided that trying to persuade others in conference was futile, if not counterproductive. Woodward and Armstrong, *The Brethren*, 46.

29. Urofsky, *The Douglas Letters*, 128.

Douglas was a master of playing conference hardball. He regularly wrote memoranda threatening to take extreme action in a case, only to let himself be talked out of it for a price.

Counting Votes

Routine cases are often disposed of in conference with little more than brief summary comments followed by a vote. Conference discussions in such instances are not really meant to inform, persuade, or even negotiate. The Justices simply want to record their votes and move on to other business. This is the most blatantly result-driven technique employed in conference. In such cases, the Justices are interested only in the final outcome and make little or no effort to find the consensus. Either they have already made up their minds individually or a sufficient number have coalesced to decide the case. Either way, further discussion is considered pointless. Several of his contemporaries reported that Douglas often approached the conference with this sort of attitude. According to Potter Stewart, Douglas rarely tried to inform, persuade, or negotiate in conference. When it was his turn to speak, Douglas would say, "'I take the other view.' There was no advocacy at all."[30] On the Rehnquist court, Harry Blackmun's ex-clerk, Edward Lazarus, alleges that conferences under William Rehnquist have lost their former importance and have degenerated into mere vote counting.

Avoidance

The last conference technique is decision avoidance. This can be accomplished in various ways. It is most commonly done by (1) voting to dismiss the case; (2) remanding the case for further consideration by a lower court; or (3) temporarily postponing a final decision without removing the case from the docket. Avoidance tactics are often initiated by a minority faction in an attempt to avoid losing a case on the merits, or by a majority who wish to postpone or avoid deciding a case for legal, political, technical, or other reasons—whether motivated by principle or expedience. Conference suggestions to DIG a case most often come from Justices who suspect that they will end up on the losing side if the case is decided on the merits.

The conference might also vote to postpone a decision temporarily, without surrendering jurisdiction. In *Brown v. Board of Education*, the conference delayed taking a formal vote on the case for more than a year in order to give the Justices additional time to build a clear consensus. Temporary avoidance is usually employed to give the Court more time to reconsider and refine its thinking, to avoid deciding a controversial case at an awkward or inauspicious time, or to secure some other tactical advantage. In 1973, the

---

30. Simon, *Independent Journey*, 352–53.

Court postponed its decision in *Roe v. Wade* for a year for three reasons: because the author of the decision, Harry Blackmun, needed more time to finish his opinion; because Warren Burger wanted two new Nixon appointees (Rehnquist and Powell) to take their seats and vote in the case; and because the Justices wanted to avoid issuing such a controversial decision during an election year. The Justices privately call the ducking of politically volatile cases "judicial statesmanship."[31]

EPILOGUE

On December 12, 2000, the Supreme Court issued its decision in *Bush v. Gore,* one of the most controversial decisions in modern Court history.[32] The next day, Justice Clarence Thomas sought to reassure a group of students that politics has "zero" influence in shaping Supreme Court decisions.[33] "The last political act we engage in is confirmation," he said, "that is the last act. And I have yet to hear any discussion, in nine years, of partisan politics . . . among members of the Court."

Thomas then turned his thoughts to the conference. "You know, I wish sometimes . . . that there was a way for the people who are citizens of this country to see the seriousness and the angst of the members of the Court when we sit in the conference room. When we go into conference, there is no staff in there. There are no recording devices. There are just the nine members of the Court. And I wish they could just see, just the concern and the people grappling for the answers, and being respectful of each other's opinions, and being humble enough. This is a humbling job. . . . It's a humbling process."

The Supreme Court, he continued, has nothing in common with the other two branches of goverment. "We may as well be on entirely different planets. . . .That's why I plead with you that, whatever you do, don't try to apply the rules of the political world to this institution." When reporters later asked Chief Justice Rehnquist whether he agreed that politics never entered into the Court's decisions, Rehnquist replied, "Absolutely, absolutely."

Justice Thomas's views reflect the ambivalence that most Justices have about the conference. If the public could just see what goes on in conference, he promises, we would understand that the Court is truly different from the political branches of goverment.

---

31. Douglas, *The Court Years,* 38.

32. *Bush v. Gore,* 531 U.S.— (2000).

33. Justice Thomas's comments were reported by the Federal News Service, "Remarks by U.S. Supreme Court Justice Clarence Thomas at C-Span Forum for High School Students" (Dec. 13, 2000). Compare Justice Thomas's comments with those of Justice Robert Jackson, who admitted to having mental reservations about the "teaching of Santa Claus or Uncle Sam or Easter bunnies or dispassionate judges." *United States v. Ballard,* 322 U.S. 78, 94 (1944) (Jackson, J., dissenting).

Yet he makes it clear that the Justices will continue to guard the secrets of the conference from public scrutiny.

Will disclosure of what happens inside the conference room reassure the public that the Supreme Court is apolitical? Or will it reveal that the Justices are politicians in black robes? Is the law just politics by other means? Or does the rule of law have meaning beyond providing cover for the personal preferences of judges?

For most of its history, the Supreme Court decided cases through collective negotiation and compromise. The conference was a crucial element of this process. On the modern Court, collaborative decision-making is on the wane and the significance of the conference is in decline. The Court today is less a collegial body than a collection of nine autonomous judges, and the conference appears to be in danger of being reduced to a vote-counting exercise. Fortunately, the conference notes published in this volume provide a unique glimpse into Supreme Court decision-making during an era when the conference still mattered.

It is difficult to say whether contemporary conferences notes will reveal anything as interesting as the notes reported here. Even so, it will be fascinating one day to read a firsthand account of the conference discussion in *Bush v. Gore,* provided that at least one Justice took Clarence Thomas's wish to heart and took notes, so that we might continue to learn about the Supreme Court in conference.

BIBLIOGRAPHY

PRIMARY SOURCES

Hugo L. Black Papers, Library of Congress, Manuscript Reading Room

William J. Brennnan Papers, Library of Congress, Manuscript Reading Room

Harold H. Burton Papers, Library of Congress, Manuscript Reading Room

Tom C. Clark Papers, Tarlton Law Library, University of Texas at Austin

William O. Douglas Papers, Library of Congress, Manuscript Reading Room

Felix Frankfurter Papers, Harvard University and Library of Congress, Manuscript Reading Room

Robert H. Jackson Papers, Library of Congress, Manuscript Reading Room

Thurgood Marshall Papers, Library of Congress, Manuscript Reading Room

Frank Murphy Papers, Bentley Historical Library, University of Michigan

Earl Warren Papers, Library of Congress, Manuscript Reading Room

BOOKS

Adams, Charles Francis. *The Works of John Adams.* Boston: Little, Brown, 1850.

Allen, Robert, and William Shannon. *The Truman Merry-Go-Round.* New York: Vanguard Press, 1950.

Ball, Howard. *Hugo Black: Cold Steel Warrior.* New York: Oxford University Press, 1996.

Berry, Mary Francis. *Stability, Security, and Continuity: Mr. Justice Burton and Decision-Making on the Supreme Court 1945–1985.* Westport, Conn.: Greenwood Press, 1978.

Beveridge, Albert J. *The Life of John Marshall.* Boston: Houghton Mifflin, 1919.

Bickel, Alexander. *The Least Dangerous Branch: The Supreme Court at the Bar of Politics.* New Haven: Yale University Press, 1962.

———. *The Unpublished Opinions of Mr. Justice Brandeis.* Chicago: University of Chicago Press, 1957.

Bickel, Alexander M., and Benno C. Schmidt, Jr. *The Judiciary and Responsible Government 1910–1921.* New York: Macmillan, 1984.

Black, Hugo L., and Elizabeth Black. *Mr. Justice and Mrs. Black.* New York: Random House, 1986.

Black, Hugo L., Jr. *My Father: A Remembrance.* New York: Random House, 1975.

Byrnes, James. *All in One Lifetime.* New York: Harper and Brothers, 1958.

Cannon, Mark, and David O'Brien. *Views from the Bench.* Chatham, N. J.: Chatham House, 1985.

Caplan, Lincoln. *The Tenth Justice.* New York: Vintage, 1987.

Clark, Hunter R. *Justice Brennan: The Great Conciliator.* New York: Birch Lane Press, 1995.

Clayton, Cornell, and Howard Gillman. *Supreme Court Decision-Making: New Institutionalist Approaches.* Chicago: University of Chicago Press, 1999.

Coons, John, William Clune, and Stephen Sugarman. *Private Wealth and Public Education.* Cambridge, Mass.: Belknap Press of Harvard University Press, 1970.

Cooper, Philip J. *Battles on the Bench: Conflict Inside the Supreme Court.* Lawrence: University Press of Kansas, 1995.

Cray, Ed. *Chief Justice.* New York: Simon & Schuster, 1997.

Cushman, Clare. *The Supreme Court Justices.* Washington, D.C.: Congressional Quarterly, 1995.

Danelski, David J. *A Supreme Court Justice Is Appointed.* New York: Random House, 1964.

Donovan, Robert J. *The Tumultuous Years.* New York: W.W. Norton, 1982.

Douglas, William O. *The Court Years: 1939–1975.* New York: Random House, 1980.

———. *The Right of the People.* Garden City, N.Y.: Doubleday, 1958.

———. *We the Judges: Studies in American and Indian Constitutional Law from Marshall to Mukherjea.* Garden City, N.Y.: Doubleday, 1956.

Dunne, Gerald T. *Hugo Black and the Judicial Revolution.* New York: Simon & Schuster, 1977.

———. *Justice Joseph Story and the Rise of the Supreme Court.* New York: Simon & Schuster, 1970.

Eisler, Kim. *A Justice for All.* New York: Simon & Schuster, 1993.

Ely, James W., Jr. *The Chief Justiceship of Melville W. Fuller, 1888–1910.* Columbia: University of South Carolina Press, 1995.

Epstein, Lee, Jeffrey A. Segal, Harold J. Spaeth, and Thomas G. Walker. *The Supreme Court Compendium: Data, Decisions, and Developments.* Washington, D.C.: Congressional Quarterly, 1996.

Epstein, Lee, and Jack Knight, *The Choices Justices Make.* Washington, D.C.: Congressional Quarterly, 1998.

Fairman, Charles. *Mr. Justice Miller and the Supreme Court.* Cambridge, Mass.: Harvard University Press, 1939.

———. *Reconstruction and Reunion 1864–1888.* 2 vols. New York: Macmillan, 1987.

Fallon, Richard. *The Federal Courts and the Federal System.* 4th ed. Westbury, N.Y.: Foundation Press, 1996.

Fassett, John. *New Deal Justice: The Life of Stanley Reed of Kentucky.* New York: Vantage Press, 1994.

Fine, Sidney. *Frank Murphy: The Washington Years.* Chicago: University of Chicago Press, 1979.

Fisher, Louis. *American Constitutional Law.* New York: McGraw-Hill, 1995.

Fiss, Owen. *Troubled Beginnings of the Modern State, 1888–1910.* New York: Macmillan, 1993.

Ford, Paul Leicester. *The Works of Thomas Jefferson.* New York: G.P. Putnam's Sons, 1904-05.

Frank, Jerome. *If Men Were Angels: Some Aspects of Government in a Democracy.* New York: Harper, 1942.

———. *Courts on Trial: Myth and Reality in American Justice.* Princeton: Princeton University Press, 1949.

Frank, John P. *Mr. Justice Black: The Man and His Opinions.* New York: Knopf, 1949.

Frankfurter, Felix. *The Commerce Clause under Marshall, Taney, and Waite*. Chapel Hill: University of North Carolina Press, 1937.

Friedelbaum, Stanley H. *The Rehnquist Court: In Pursuit of Judicial Conservatism*. Westport, Conn.: Greenwood Press, 1994.

Freund, Paul, and Robert Ulrich. *Religion and the Public Schools*. Cambridge, Mass.: Harvard University Press 1965.

Gerber, Scott Douglas. *Seriatim*. New York: New York University Press, 1998.

Goebel, Julius, Jr. *History of the Supreme Court of the United States: Antecedents and Beginnings to 1801*. New York: Macmillan, 1971.

Goldberg, Dorothy. *A Private View of a Public Life*. New York: Charterhouse, 1975.

Goldman, Roger, and David Gallen. *Thurgood Marshall: Justice for All*. New York: Carroll and Graf, 1992.

Goldman, Sheldon, and Austin Sarat. *American Court Systems*. 2d ed. New York: Longman, 1989.

Goodwin, Richard. *Remembering America*. Boston: Little, Brown, 1988.

Gugin, Linda, and James St. Clair. *Sherman Minton: New Deal Senator, Cold Warrior Justice*. Indianapolis: Indianapolis Historical Society, 1997.

Haines, Charles Grove. *The Role of the Supreme Court in American Government and Politics*. Berkeley: University of California Press, 1944.

Harper, Fowler. *Justice Rutledge and the Bright Constellation*. Indianapolis: Bobbs-Merrill, 1965.

Haskins, George, and Herbert Johnson. *Foundations of Power: John Marshall 1801–1805*. New York: Macmillan, 1981.

Highsaw, Robert B. *Edward Douglass White: Defender of the Conservative Faith*. Baton Rouge: Louisiana State University Press, 1981.

Hirsch, H. N. *The Enigma of Felix Frankfurter*. New York: Basic Books, 1981.

Hobson, Charles. *The Papers of John Marshall*. Chapel Hill: University of North Carolina Press, 1995.

Howard, J. Woodford. *Mr. Justice Murphy: A Political Biography*. New Jersey: Princeton University Press, 1968.

Hughes, Charles Evans. *The Supreme Court of the United States*. New York: Columbia University Press, 1928.

Jefferies, John C. *Justice Lewis F. Powell, Jr*. New York: Charles Scribner's Sons, 1994.

Johnson, Herbert. *The Papers of John Marshall*. Chapel Hill: University of North Carolina Press, 1974.

Kalman, Laura. *Abe Fortas: A Biography*. New Haven, Conn.: Yale University Press, 1990.

Kassin, Saul, and Lawrence Wrightsman. *The American Jury on Trial: Psychological Perspectives*. New York: Hemisphere, 1988.

Kinoy, Arthur. *Rights on Trial: The Odyssey of a People's Lawyer*. Cambridge, Mass.: Harvard University Press, 1983.

Kirby, James. *Fumble: Bear Bryant, Wally Butts, and the Great College Football Scandal*. New York: Harcourt Brace Jovanovich, 1986.

Kluger, Richard. *Simple Justice: The History of* Brown v. Board of Education *and Black America's Struggle for Equality.* New York: Knopf, 1976.

Kurland, Philip. *Mr. Justice Frankfurter and the Constitution.* Chicago: University of Chicago Press, 1971.

Lamb, Charles, and Stephen Halpern. *The Burger Court: Political and Judicial Profiles.* Urbana: University of Illinois Press, 1991.

Larrowe, Charles. *Harry Bridges: The Rise and Fall of Radical Labor in the United States.* Westport, Conn.: Lawrence Hill and Co., 1972.

Lash, Joseph. *From the Diaries of Felix Frankfurter.* New York: W.W. Norton, 1975.

Lazarus, Edward P. *Closed Chambers.* New York: Random House, 1998.

Lewis, Anthony. *Make No Law: The* Sullivan *Case and the First Amendment.* New York: Random House, 1991.

Mason, Alpheus. *Harlan Fiske Stone: Pillar of the Law.* New York: Viking Press, 1956.

———. *The Supreme Court from Taft to Warren.* New York: W.W. Norton, 1958.

———. *William Howard Taft: Chief Justice.* New York: Simon & Schuster, 1964.

Mendelson, Wallace. *Justice Black and Frankfurter: Conflict in the Court.* Chicago: University of Chicago Press, 1966.

Miller, Merle. *Plain Speaking: An Oral Biography of Harry S. Truman.* New York: Berkeley, 1974.

Murphy, Walter. *Elements of Judicial Strategy.* Chicago: University of Chicago Press, 1964.

Murphy, Walter, and C. Herman Pritchett. *Courts, Judges and Politics.* 4th ed. New York: Random House, 1986.

Newman, Roger K. *Hugo Black: A Biography.* New York: Pantheon, 1994.

Newmeyer, R. Kent. *Supreme Court Justice Joseph Story: Statesman of the Old Republic.* Chapel Hill: University of North Carolina Press, 1985.

O'Brien, David. *Storm Center: The Supreme Court in American Politics.* New York: W.W. Norton, 1986.

Pearson, Drew, and Robert Allen. *The Nine Old Men.* Garden City, N.Y.: Doubleday, Doran and Co., 1937.

Peltason, Jack. *Fifty-Eight Lonely Men: Southern Federal Judges and School Desegregation.* New York: Harcourt, Brace, and World, 1961.

Pringle, Henry. *The Life and Times of William Howard Taft.* New York: Farrar & Rinehart, 1939.

Pritchett, C. Herman. *Civil Liberties and the Vinson Court.* Chicago: University of Chicago Press, 1954.

Pusey, Merlo. *Charles Evans Hughes.* New York: Macmillan 1951.

Rehnquist, William H. *The Supreme Court: How It Was, How It Is.* New York: William Morrow, 1987.

Robertson, David. *Reports of the Trials of Colonel Aaron Burr.* New York: Da Capo, 1969.

Rowan, Carl. *Dream Makers, Dream Breakers.* Boston: Little, Brown, 1993.

Savage, David G. *Turning Right: The Making of the Rehnquist Supreme Court.* New York: Wiley, 1992.

Schmidhauser, John. *Constitutional Law in American Politics.* Monterey, Calif.: Brooks/Cole, 1984.

———. *Judges and Justices: The Federal Appellate Judiciary.* Boston: Little, Brown, 1979.

———. *The Supreme Court: Its Politics, Personalities, and Procedures.* New York: Holt, Rinehart and Winston, 1967.

Schuckers, J. W. *The Life and Public Services of Salmon Portland Chase.* New York: Da Capo, 1970.

Schwartz, Bernard. *The Ascent of Pragmatism.* Reading, Mass.: Addison-Wesley, 1990.

———. *A History of the Supreme Court.* New York: Oxford University Press, 1993.

———. *Super Chief: Earl Warren and His Supreme Court—A Judicial Biography.* New York: New York University Press, 1983.

Schwartz, Bernard, and Stephan Lesher. *Inside the Warren Court.* New York: Doubleday, 1983.

Schwartz, Herman. *The Burger Years: Rights and Wrongs in the Supreme Court 1969–1986.* New York: Viking, 1987.

Sharlitt, Joseph H. *Fatal Error: The Miscarriage of Justice that Sealed the Rosenbergs' Fate.* New York: Charles Scribner's Sons, 1989.

Simon, James F. *The Antagonists: Hugo Black, Felix Frankfurter and Civil Liberties in Modern America.* New York: Simon & Schuster, 1989.

———. *The Center Holds: The Power Struggle Inside the Rehnquist Court.* New York: Simon & Schuster, 1995.

———. *Independent Journey: The Life of William O. Douglas.* New York: Harper and Row, 1980.

Smith, Jean Edward. *John Marshall: Definer of a Nation.* New York: Henry Holt, 1996.

Swisher, Carl. *Roger B. Taney.* New York: Macmillan, 1935.

———. *The Taney Period 1836–64.* New York: Macmillan, 1974.

Tucker, D. F. B. *The Rehnquist Court and Civil Rights.* Aldershot, United Kingdom: Dartmouth Publishing Co., 1995.

Tushnet, Mark. *Making Civil Rights Law.* New York: Oxford University Press, 1994.

———. *Making Constitutional Law.* New York: Oxford University Press, 1997.

Urofsky, Melvin I. *Division and Discord: The Supreme Court Under Stone and Vinson 1941–1953.* Columbia: University of South Carolina Press, 1997.

———. *The Douglas Letters.* Bethesda, Md.: Adler and Adler, 1987.

———. *Felix Frankfurter: Judicial Restraint and Individual Liberties.* Boston: Twayne, 1991.

Warren, Charles. *The Supreme Court in United States History.* Boston: Little, Brown, 1922.

Warren, Earl. *The Memoirs of Earl Warren.* Garden City, N.Y.: Doubleday, 1977.

Wasby, Stephen L. *"He Shall Not Pass This Way Again": The Legacy of Justice William O. Douglas.* Pittsburgh: University of Pittsburgh Press, 1990.

Wasby, Stephen, et al. *Desegregation from* Brown *to* Alexander: *An Exploration of Supreme Court Strategies.* Carbondale: Southern Illinois University Press, 1977.

Weaver, John. *Warren: The Man, the Court, the Era.* Boston: Little, Brown, 1967.

Westin, Alan F. *An Autobiography of the Supreme Court.* New York: Macmillan, 1963.

———. *The Supreme Court: Views From Inside.* New York: W.W. Norton, 1961.

White, Edward. *The Marshall Court and Cultural Change 1815–1835.* New York: Macmillan, 1988.

———. *Thoughts and Lives: Justice Oliver Wendell Holmes: Law and the Inner Self.* New York: Oxford University Press, 1993.

White Burkett Miller Center of Public Affairs. *The Office of Chief Justice.* Charlottesville: University of Virginia, 1984.

Woodward, Bob and Scott Armstrong. *The Brethren: Inside the Supreme Court.* New York: Simon & Schuster, 1979.

Yarbrough, Tinsley. *John Marshall Harlan: Great Dissenter of the Warren Court.* New York: Oxford University Press, 1992.

———. *Mr. Justice Black and His Critics.* Durham, North Carolina: Duke University Press, 1988.

ARTICLES

Adams, Arlin. "Justice Brennan and the Religion Clauses: The Concept of a Living Constitution.'" 139 *U. Pa. L. Rev.* 1319 (1991).

Balcerzak, Stephanie. "Qualified Immunity for Government Officials: The Problem of Unconstitutional Purpose in Civil Rights Litigation." 95 *Yale L.J.* 126 (1985).

Bandes, Susan. "Reinventing *Bivens*: The Self-Executing Constitution." 68 *S. Cal. L. Rev.* 289 (1995).

Barist, Jeffrey, et al. "Who May Leave: A Review of Soviet Practice Restricting Emigration on Grounds of Knowledge of 'State Secrets' in Comparison with Standards of International Law and the Policies of Other States." 15 *Hofstra L. Rev.* 381 (1987).

Barnett, Randy. "Necessary and Proper." 44 *UCLA L. Rev.* 745 (1997).

Barrett, John. "'Stop and Frisk' in 1968: Deciding the Stop and Frisk Cases: A Look Inside the Supreme Court's Conference." 72 *St. John's L. Rev.* 749 (1998).

Baugh, Robert. "Applying the Bill of Rights to the States: A Response to William P. Gray, Jr." 49 *Ala. L. Rev.* 551 (1998).

Baumann, Edward, and John O'Brien. "The Enemy Within: In 1942, Nazi Saboteurs Came Ashore With a Plan to Cripple America." *Chicago Tribune Sunday Magazine*, 32 (Sept. 22, 1985).

Belknap, Michal. "The Warren Court and the Vietnam War: The Limits of Legal Liberalism." 33 *Ga. L. Rev.* 65 (1998).

Berger, Curtis. "*Pruneyard* Revisited: Political Activity on Private Lands." 66 *N.Y.U.L. Rev.* 633 (1991).

Bickel, Alexander. "The Original Understanding and the Segregation Decision." 69 *Harv. L. Rev.* 1 (1955).

Bittker, Boris. "The World War II German Saboteurs' Case and Writs of Certiorari Before Judgment by the Court of Appeals: A Tale of *Nunc Pro Tunc* Jurisdiction." 14 *Const. Commentary* 431 (1997).

Boardman, Dorothy Lowe. "*National League of Cities* Overruled—Supreme Court Rejects Tenth Amendment as an Affirmative Limitation on Congress' Power Under the Commerce Clause." 13 *Fla. St. U.L. Rev.* 277 (1997).

Boland, Tara. "Single-Sex Public Education: Equality Versus Choice." 1 *U. Pa. J. Const. L.* 154 (1998).

Brennan, William. "Constitutional Adjudication and the Death Penalty: A View from the Court." 100 *Harv. L. Rev.* 313 (1986).

———. "A Tribute to Justice Thurgood Marshall." 105 *Harv. L. Rev.* 23 (1991).

Bright, Stephen, and Patrick Keenan. "Judges and the Politics of Death: Deciding Between the Bill of Rights and the Next Election in Capital Cases." 75 *B.U.L. Rev.* 760 (1995).

Burley, Anne-Marie. "Law Among Liberal States: Liberal Internationalism and the Act of State Doctrine." 92 *Colum. L. Rev.* 1907 (1992).

Cady, James. "Bouncing 'Checkbook Journalism': A Balance Between the First and Sixth Amendments in High Profile Criminal Cases." 4 *Wm. & Mary Bill of Rts. J.* 671 (1995).

Calsyn, Jeremy, et al. "Investigation and Police Practice: Warrantless Searches and Seizures." 86 *Geo. L.J.* 1214 (1998).

Campbell, John A. "Benjamin Robbins Curtis: Address to the Bar of the Supreme Court of the United States." 87 U.S. (20 Wall.) viii (1875).

Caplan, Gerald. "Questioning *Miranda*." 38 *Vand. L. Rev.* 1417 (1985).

Carter, Dan. "'Let Justice be Done': Public Passion and Judicial Courage in Modern Alabama." 28 *Cumb. L. Rev.* 553 (1997).

Chow, Daniel. "Rethinking the Act of State Doctrine: An Analysis in Terms of Jurisdiction to Prescribe." 62 *Wash. L. Rev.* 397 (1987).

Clarke, Alan. "Habeas Corpus: The Historical Debate." 14 *N.Y.L. Sch. J. Hum. Rts.* 375 (1998).

Cohen, William. "Justice Douglas and the Rosenberg Case: Setting the Record Straight." 70 *Cornell L. Rev.* 211 (1985).

Coltharp, Donna. "Writing in the Margins: Brennan, Marshall, and the Inherent Weaknesses of Liberal Judicial Decision-Making." 29 *St. Mary's L. J.* 1, 36 (1997).

Corwin, Edward. "The Steel Seizure Case: A Judicial Brick Without Straw." 53 *Colum. L. Rev.* 53 (1953).

———. "The Supreme Court as National School Board." 14 *Law & Contemp. Probs.* 3, (1949).

Coyne, Randall. "Marking the Progress of a Humane Justice: Harry Blackmun's Death Penalty Epiphany." 43 *Kan. L. Rev.* 367 (1995).

Currie, David. "The Constitution in the Supreme Court: The Preferred-Position Debate 1941–1946." 37 *Cath. U.L. Rev.* 39 (1987).

Cushman, Barry. "A Stream of Legal Consciousness: The Current of Commerce Doctrine from *Swift* to *Jones & Laughlin*." 61 *Fordham L. Rev.* 105 (1992).

Daniels, Troy. "An Analysis of the United States' Foreign Sovereign Immunities Act." 4 *D.C.L. J. Int'l L. & Prac.* 175 (1995).

Danzig, Richard. "Justice Frankfurter's Opinions in the Flag Salute Cases: Blending Logic and Psychologic in Constitutional Decisionmaking." 36 *Stan. L. Rev.* 675 (1984).

Darcy, R., and Jenny Sanbrano. "Oklahoma in the Development of Equal Rights: The ERA, 3.2% Beer, Juvenile Justice, and *Craig v. Boren*." 22 *Okla. City U.L. Rev.* 1009 (1997).

David, Edward. "Ignoring State Homestead Laws: Satisfying Federal Tax Liens Through the Sales of Homestead Property." 60 *Chi.-Kent L. Rev.* 683 (1984).

Delgado, Richard, and Jean Stefancic. "Home-Grown Racism: Colorado's Historic Embrace—and Denial—of Equal Opportunity in Higher Education." 70 *U. Colo. L. Rev.* 703 (1999).

Devins, Neal. "Law and Equality: The Countermajoritarian Paradox." 93 *Mich. L. Rev.* 1433 (1995).

Dickson, Del. "State Court Defiance and the Limits of Supreme Court Authority: *Williams v. Georgia Revisited*." 103 *Yale L. J.* 1423 (1994).

DiPrima, Stephen. "Selecting a Jury in Federal Criminal Trials after *Batson* and *McCollum*." 95 *Colum. L. Rev.* 888 (1995).

Dripps, Donald. "*Bowers v. Hardwick* and the Law of Standing: Noncases Make Bad Law." 44 *Emory L.J.* 1417 (1995).

———. "Living with *Leon*." 95 *Yale L.J.* 906 (1986).

Duncan, Deidre. "Gender Equity in Women's Athletics." 64 *U. Cin. L. Rev.* 1027 (1996).

DuVal, Benjamin. "The Occasions of Secrecy." 47 *U. Pitt. L. Rev.* 579 (1986).

Eckhardt, Robert C. "The Adam Clayton Powell Case." 45 *Tex. L. Rev.* 1205 (1967).

Elman, Philip, and Norman Silber. "The Solicitor General's Office, Justice Frankfurter, and Civil Rights Litigation, 1946–1960: An Oral History." 100 *Harvard L. Rev.* 817 (1987).

Emerson, Thomas. "Toward a General Theory of the First Amendment." 72 *Yale L. J.* 877 (1963).

Epstein, Steven. "Rethinking the Constitutionality of Ceremonial Deism." 96 *Colum. L. Rev.* 2083 (1996).

Everett, Robinson, and Scott Silliman. "Forums for Punishing Offenses Against the Law of Nations." 29 *Wake Forest L. Rev.* 509 (1994).

Falcone, Rosemarie. "*California v. Ciraolo*: The Demise of Private Property." 47 *La. L. Rev.* 1365 (1987).

Fallon, Richard. "A Tribute to Justice Lewis F. Powell, Jr." 101 *Harv. L. Rev.* 399 (1987).

Ferguson, Karen. "Indian Fishing Rights: Aftermath of the *Fox* Decision and the Year 2000." 23 *Am. Indian L. Rev.* 97 (1998/99).

Fisher, Louis. "Constitutional Interpretation by Member of Congress." 63 *N.C.L. Rev.* 707 (1985).

———. "The Legislative Veto: Invalidated, It Survives." 56 *Law & Contemp. Prob.* 273 (Autumn 1993).

Fishkin, James. "*Nix v. Williams*: An Analysis of the Preponderance Standard for the Inevitable Discovery Exception." 70 *Iowa L. Rev.* 1369 (1985).

Fitzgerald, Edward A. "The Tidelands Controversy Revisited." 19 *Envtl. L.* 209 (1988).

Fram, David. "The False Alarm of *Firefighters Local Union No. 1784 v. Stotts*." 70 *Cornell L. Rev.* 991 (1985).

Frank, John P. "Fred Vinson and the Chief Justiceship." 21 *U. Chi. L. Rev.* 212 (1953).

Frankfurter, Felix. "Chief Justices I Have Known." 39 *Va. L. Rev.* 883 (1953).

French, Rebecca. "From *Yoder* to Yoda: Models of Traditional, Modern, and Postmodern Religion in U.S. Constitutional Law." 41 *Ariz. L. Rev.* 49 (1999).

Galvin, Charles, and Neal Devins. "A Tax Policy Analysis of *Bob Jones University v. United States*." 36 *Vand. L. Rev.* 1353 (1983).

Gardner, James. "Consent, Legitimacy and Elections: Implementing Popular Sovereignty Under the Lockean Constitution." 52 *U. Pitt. L. Rev.* 189 (1990).

Garrow, David. "'The Lowest Form of Animal Life'? Supreme Court Clerks and Supreme Court History." 84 *Cornell L. Rev.* 855 (1999).

Ginsburg, Ruth Bader. "Constitutional Adjudication in the United States as a Means of Advancing the Equal Stature of Men and Women Under the Law." 26 *Hofstra L. Rev.* 263 (1997).

———. "Informing the Public About the U.S. Supreme Court's Work." 29 *Loy. U. Chi. L.J.* 275 (1998).

Glendon, William R. "The Pentagon Papers—Victory for a Free Press." 19 *Cardozo L. Rev.* 1295 (1998).

Glicksman, Robert. "Severability and the Realignment of the Balance of Power over the Public Lands: The Federal Land Policy and Management Act of 1976 after the Legislative Veto Decisions." 36 *Hastings L.J.* 3 (1984).

Goldberg, Arthur, and Alan Dershowitz. "Declaring the Death Penalty Unconstitutional." 83 *Harv. L. Rev.* 1773 (1970).

Gressman, Eugene. "Irreverent Questions About Piercing the Red Velour Curtain." 22 *Buff. L. Rev.* 825 (1973).

Grossman, Joel. "Comments on 'Secrecy and the Supreme Court.'" 22 *Buff. L. Rev.* 831 (1973).

Guinn, David, and Paul Sewell. "*Miller v. Johnson*: Redistricting and the Elusive Search for a Safe Harbor." 47 *Baylor L. Rev.* 895 (1995).

Harlan, John Marshall. "A Glimpse of the Supreme Court at Work." 11 *Univ. of Chi. L. School Record* 1 (1963).

Hentoff, Nat. "The Constitutionalist." *New Yorker*, Mar. 12, 1990.

Herschman, Gary. "Interpreting *Harlow* and Its Progeny." 56 *Geo. Wash. L. Rev.* 1047 (1988).

Hill, Anita. "A Tribute to Thurgood Marshall: A Man Who Broke With Tradition on Issues of Race and Gender." 47 *Okla. L. Rev.* 127 (1994).

Howard, J. Woodford. "Comment on Secrecy and the Supreme Court." 22 *Buff. L. Rev.* 837 (1973).

Hutchinson, Dennis. "The Black-Jackson Feud." *The Sup. Ct. Rev.* 203 (1988).

———. "Frankfurter and the Business of the Supreme Court, O.T. 1946–O.T. 1961." *Sup. Ct. Rev.* (1980).

———. "Unanimity and Desegregation: Decisionmaking in the Supreme Court, 1948–1958." 69 *Geo. L. J.* 1 (1979).

Ifill, Sherrilyn A. "Thurgood Marshall." 68 *N.Y.U.L. Rev.* 220 (1993).

Johnson, Jill. "Title IX and Intercollegiate Athletics: Current Judicial Interpretation of the Standards for Compliance." 74 *B.U.L. Rev.* 553 (1994).

Johnson, Phillip. "The Return of the 'Christian Burial Speech' Case." 32 *Emory L.J.* 349 (1983).

Joondeph, Bradley. "The Good, the Bad, and the Ugly: An Empirical Analysis of Litigation-Prompted School Finance Reform." 35 *Santa Clara L. Rev.* 763 (1995).

Kamisar, Yale. "Confessions, Search and Seizure and the Rehnquist Court." 34 *Tulsa L.J.* 465 (1999).

———. "*Gates*, 'Probable Cause,' 'Good Faith,' and Beyond." 69 *Iowa L. Rev.* 551 (1984).

Kauper, Paul. "The Steel Seizure Case: Congress, the President and the Supreme Court." 51 *Mich. L. Rev.* 141 (1952).

Kerber, Linda. "'A Constitutional Right to Be Treated Like Ladies': Women, Civic Obligation, and Military Service." 1993 *U. Chi. L. Sch. Roundtable* 95 (1993).

Kindall, James. "Night of the Nazis: 50 Years ago, Long Islander Stumbled Upon German Saboteurs on the Beach." *Newsday*, June 14, 1992, 4.

Klarman, Michael. "*Brown*, Racial Change, and the Civil Rights Movement. "80 *Va. L. Rev.* 7 (1994).

———."An Interpretive History of Modern Equal Protection." 90 *Mich. L. Rev.* 213 (1991).

———. "The *Plessy* Era." 1998 *Sup. Ct. Rev.* 303.

———. "Rethinking the Civil Rights and Civil Liberties Revolutions." 82 *Va. L. Rev.* 1 (1996).

———. "What's So Great About Constitutionalism?" 93 *Nw. U. L. Rev.* 145 (1998).

Koh, Harold. "Why the President (Almost) Always Wins in Foreign Affairs: Lessons of the Iran-Contra Affair." 97 *Yale L.J.* 1255 (1988).

Kosterlitz, Mary. "*Thornburg v. Gingles*: The Supreme Court's New Test for Analyzing Minority Vote Dilution." 36 *Cath. U.L. Rev.* 531 (1987).

Kurland, Philip. "Earl Warren, the 'Warren Court,' and the Warren Court Myths." 67 *Mich. L. Rev.* 353 (1968).

Lacovara, Philip. "*United States v. Nixon*: Presidential Power and Executive Privilege Twenty-Five Years Later." 83 *Minn. L. Rev.* 1061 (1999).

Landis, John. "Constitutional Limitations on the Congressional Power of Investigation." 40 *Harv. L. Rev.* 153 (1926).

Landrum, Bruce D. "The Yamashita War Crimes Trial: Command Responsibility Then and Now." 149 *Mil. L. Rev.* 293 (1995).

Levinson, L. Howard. "Balancing Acts: *Bowsher v. Synar*, Gramm-Rudman-Hollings, and Beyond." 72 *Cornell L. Rev.* 527 (1987).

Levitan, David. "The Effect of the Appointment of a Supreme Court Justice." 28 *U. Tol. L. Rev.* 37 (1996).

Lewis, Anthony. "In Memoriam: William J. Brennan, Jr." 111 *Harv. L. Rev.* 29 (1997).

Mabry, Cynthia. "The Supreme Court Opens a Pandora's Box in the Law of Warrantless Automobile Searches and Seizures—*United States v. Ross*." 26 *How. L.J.* 1231 (1983).

Maddigan, Michael. "The Establishment Clause, Civil Religion, and the Public Church." 81 *Calif. L. Rev.* 293 (1993).

Maltzman, Forrest, and Paul Wahlbeck. "Strategic Policy Considerations and Voting Fluidity on the Burger Court." 90 *Am. Pol. Sci. Rev.* 581 (1996).

Maring, Mary. "'Children Should Be Seen and Not Heard': Do Children Shed Their Right to Free Speech at the Schoolhouse Gate?" 74 *N. Dak. L. Rev.* 679 (1998).

Marshall, William. "The Case Against the Constitutionally Compelled Free Exercise Exemption." 40 *Case W. Res.* 357 (1990).

Mazur, Diane. "A Call to Arms." 22 *Harv. Women's L.J.* 39 (1999).

McConnell, Michael. "The Crisis in Legal Theory and the Revival of Classical Jurisprudence: On Reading the Constitution." 73 *Cornell L. Rev.* 359 (1988).

———. "Originalism and the Desegregation Decisions." 81 *Va. L. Rev.* 947 (1995).

McGowan, Carl. "Presidents and Their Papers." 68 *Minn. L. Rev.* 409 (1983).

McKusick, Vincent. "Discretionary Gatekeeping: The Supreme Court's Management of Its Original Jurisdiction Docket Since 1961." 45 *Me. L. Rev.* 185 (1993).

McMunigal, Kevin. "Of Causes and Clients: Two Tales of *Roe v. Wade*." 47 *Hastings L.J.* 779 (1996).

Mease-White, Alexandra. "*Hopwood v. Texas*: Challenging the Use of Race as a Proxy for Diversity in America's Public Universities." 29 *Conn. L. Rev.* 1293 (1997).

Meiklejohn, Donald. "Speech and the First Amendment: Public Speech and Libel Litigation: Are They Compatible?" 14 *Hofstra L. Rev.* 547 (1986).

Miller, Arthur, and D. S. Sastri. "Secrecy and the Supreme Court: On the Need for Piercing the Red Velour Curtain." 22 *Buff. L. Rev.* 799 (1973).

Miller, Binny. "Who Shall Rule and Govern? Local Legislative Delegations, Racial Politics, and the Voting Rights Act." 102 *Yale L.J.* 105 (1992).

Mozer, Gary. "The Crumbling Wall Between Church and State: *Agostini v. Felton*, Aid to Parochial Schools, and the Establishment Clause in the Twenty-First Century." 31 *Conn. L. Rev.* 337 (1998).

Noonan, John. "How Sincere Do You Have to Be to Be Religious?" 1988 *U. Ill. L. Rev.* 713 (1988).

Note. "Government Control of Richard Nixon's Presidential Material." 87 *Yale L.J.* 1601–35 (1978).

Oppenheimer, David. "Martin Luther King, *Walker v. City of Birmingham*, and the Letter from Birmingham Jail." 26 *U.C. Davis L. Rev.* 791 (1993).

Paulsen, Michael. "Nixon Now: The Courts and the Presidency After Twenty-five Years." 83 *Minn. L. Rev.* 1337 (1999).

Penalver, Eduardo. "The Concept of Religion." 107 *Yale L.J.* 791 (1997).

Pendley, William. "*Adarand Constructors, Inc. v. Pena*: Reflections on an Appearance Before the United States Supreme Court." 31 *Land & Water L. Rev.* 561 (1996).

Post, Robert. "The Social Foundations of Defamation Law: Reputation and the Constitution." 74 *Calif. L. Rev.* 691 (1986).

Powell, Lewis. "What Really Goes on at the Supreme Court." 66 *ABA J.* 721 (1980).

Prettyman, E. Barrett Jr. "The Supreme Court's Use of Hypothetical Questions at Oral Argument." 33 *Cath. U.L. Rev.* 555 (1984).

Prevost, Ann Marie. "Race and War Crimes: The 1945 War Crimes Trial of General Tomoyuki Yamashita." 14 *Hum. Rts. Q.* 303 (1992).

Pringle, Katherine. "Silencing the Speech of Strangers: Constitutional Values and the First Amendment Rights of Resident Aliens." 81 *Geo. L.J.* 2073 (1993).

Rauh, Joseph. "Historical Perspectives: An Unabashed Liberal Looks at a Half-Century of the Supreme Court." 69 *N.C.L. Rev.* 213 (1990).

Regis-Civetta, Jennifer. "The Effect of the Endangered Species Act on Tribal Economic Development in Indian Country." 50 *Wash. U. J. Urb. & Contemp. L.* 303 (1996).

Reiner, Marc. "The Public Safety Exception to *Miranda*: Analyzing Subjective Motivation." 93 *Mich. L. Rev.* 2377 (1995).

Reynolds, Laurie. "Indian Hunting and Fishing Rights: The Role of Tribal Sovereignty and Preemption." 62 *N.C.L. Rev.* 743 (1984).

Richetti, Sandra. "Congressional Power vis-à-vis the President and Presidential Papers." 32 *Duq. L. Rev.* 773 (1994).

Roper, Donald. "Judicial Unanimity and the Marshall Court—A Road to Reappraisal." 9 *Am. J. of Legal Hist.* 118 (1965).

Rosen, Perry. "The *Bivens* Constitutional Tort: An Unfulfilled Promise." 67 *N.C.L. Rev.* 337 (1989).

Rosenkranz, E. Joshua. "Remembering and Advancing the Constitutional Vision of Justice William J. Brennan, Jr." 43 *N.Y.L. Sch. L. Rev.* 1 (1999).

Rosse, Dick. "'Old Sparky' And the Day Six Nazis Died; the Grim Anniversary of D.C.'s Electric Chair." *Washington Post*, F1 (Aug. 8, 1992).

Rubenstein, William. "Divided We Litigate: Addressing Disputes Among Group Members and Lawyers in Civil Rights Campaigns." 106 *Yale L.J.* 1623 (1997).

Salken, Barbara. "The General Warrant of the Twentieth Century? A Fourth Amendment Solution to Unchecked Discretion to Arrest for Traffic Offenses." 62 *Temp. L. Rev.* 221 (1989).

Saunders, Kevin. "Media Violence and the Obscenity Exception to the First Amendment." 3 *Wm. & Mary Bill of Rts. J.* 107 (1994).

Scheiber, Harry, and Jane Scheiber. "Bayonets in Paradise: A Half-Century Retrospect on Martial Law in Hawai'i, 1941–1946." 19 *Hawaii L. Rev.* 477 (1997).

Schmidhauser, John. "The Justices of the Supreme Court: A Collective Portrait." *Midwest J. Pol. Sci.* 1 (1959).

Schmitz, Amy. "Providing an Escape for Inner-City Children: Creating a Federal Remedy for Educational Ills of Poor Urban Schools." 78 *Minn. L. Rev.* 1639 (1994).

Schubert, Glendon. "One Touch of Adonis: On Ripping the Lid off Pandora's Box." 22 *Buff. L. Rev.* 849 (1973).

Shane, Peter. "School Desegregation Remedies and the Fair Governance of Schools." 132 *U. Pa. L. Rev.* 1041 (1984).

Silk, David. "When Bright Lines Break Down: Limiting *New York v. Belton*." 136 *U. Pa. L. Rev.* 281 (1987).

Sims, John. "Triangulating the Boundaries of the Pentagon Papers." 2 *Wm. & Mary Bill of Rts. J.* 341 (1993).

Sowle, Kathryn. "The Derivative and Discretionary-Function Immunities of Presidential and Congressional Aides in Constitutional Tort Actions." 44 *Ohio St. L.J.* 943 (1983).

Spoo, Robert. "Copyright Protectionism and Its Discontents: The Case of James Joyce's *Ulysses* in America." 108 *Yale L.J.* 633 (1998).

Stadtmauer, Marc. "Remember the Sabbath? The New York Blue Laws and the Future of the Establishment Clause." 12 *Cardozo Arts & Ent. L.J.* 213 (1994).

Stein, Theodore. "*Nixon v. Fitzgerald*: Presidential Immunity as a Constitutional Imperative." 32 *Cath. U.L. Rev.* 759 (1983).

Steinberg, David. "Religious Exemptions as Affirmative Action." 40 *Emory L.J.* 77 (1991).

Stewart, David. "And in Her Purse the Principal Found Marijuana." 71 *ABA J.* 50 (Feb. 1985).

Stewart, Potter. "Reflections on the Supreme Court." 8 *Litigation* 8 (Spring, 1982).

———. "The Road to *Mapp v. Ohio* and Beyond: The Origins, Development, and Future of the Exclusionary Rule in Search-and-Seizure Cases." 83 *Colum. L. Rev.* 1365 (1983).

Stone, Harlan F. "Chief Justice." 27 *A.B.A. J.* 407 (July 1941).

Strauss, Peter. "Was There a Baby in the Bathwater? A Comment on the Supreme Court's Legislative Veto Decision." 1983 *Duke L.J.* 789.

Strossen, Nadine. "Religion and Politics: A Reply to Antonin Scalia." 24 *Fordham Urb. L.J.* 427 (1997).

Thayer, James Bradley. "The Origin and Scope of the American Doctrine of Constitutional Law." 7 *Harv. L. Rev.* 129 (1893).

Thomson, James. "Inside the Supreme Court: A Sanctum Sanctorum?" 66 *Miss. L.J.* 177 (1996).

Torricella, Roberto. "Babalu Aye Is Not Pleased: Majoritarianism and the Erosion of Free Exercise." 45 *U. Miami L. Rev.* 1061 (1996).

Troutt, David. "Screws, Koon, and Routine Aberrations: The Use of Fictional Narratives in Federal Police Brutality Prosecutions." 74 *N.Y.U.L. Rev.* 18 (1999).

Tuchman, Claudia. "Does Privacy Have Four Walls? Salvaging *Stanley v. Georgia.*" 94 *Colum. L. Rev.* 2267 (1994).

Tushnet, Mark, and Katya Lezin. "What Really Happened in *Brown v. Board of Education*?" 91 *Colum. L. Rev.* 1867 (1991).

Ulmer, S. Sidney. "Earl Warren and the *Brown* Decision." 33 *J. Pol.* 689 (1971).

Urofsky, Melvin. "Conflict Among the Brethren: Felix Frankfurter, William O. Douglas and the Clash of Personalities and Philosophies on the United States Supreme Court." 1988 *Duke L.J.* 71 (1988).

Vacca, Richard, and H. C. Hudgins. "Student Speech and the First Amendment: The Courts Operationalize the Notion of Assaultive Speech." 89 *Ed. Law Rep.* 1 (1994).

Van Alstyne, William. "Trends in the Supreme Court: Mr. Jefferson's Crumbling Wall—A Comment on *Lynch v. Donnelly.*" 1984 *Duke L.J.* 770 (1984).

Wardle, Lynn. "*Loving v. Virginia* and The Constitutional Right to Marry, 1790–1990." 41 *How. L.J.* 289 (1998).

Weisselberg, Charles. "Saving *Miranda.*" 84 *Cornell L. Rev.* 109 (1998).

White, Byron. "The Work of the Supreme Court: A Nuts and Bolts Description." *New York State Bar Journal* 346 (Oct. 1982).

White, G. Edward. "Holmes and American Jurisprudence: Revisiting Substantive Due Process and Holmes's *Lochner* Dissent." 63 *Brooklyn L. Rev.* 87, 112 (1997).

———. "The Working Life of the Marshall Court, 1815–1835." 70 *Va. L. Rev.* 1 (1984).

White, Phillip. "The Tribal Exhaustion Doctrine: 'Just Stay on the Good Roads, and You've Got Nothing to Worry About.'" 22 *Am. Indian L. Rev.* 65 (1997).

Wilson, James. "Chaining the Leviathan: The Unconstitutionality of Executing Those Convicted of Treason." 45 *U. Pitt. L. Rev.* 99 (1983).

Woollcott, Alexander. "Abandonment of the Two-Pronged *Aguilar-Spinelli* Test: *Illinois v. Gates.*" 70 *Cornell L. Rev.* 316 (1985).

Worthen, Kevin. "Shirt-Tales: Clerking for Byron White." 1994 *B.Y.U. L. Rev.* 349 (1994).

Zane, Dale Edward. "School Searches Under the Fourth Amendment: *New Jersey v. T.L.O.*" 72 *Cornell L. Rev.* 368 (1987).

INDEX OF CASES

Note: Page numbers in **boldface** indicated extended discussion of case.

GENERAL INDEX

of public school exclusion of illegal aliens, 760,
  761, 763
of racial classifications, 125, 691, 694, 739, 740–
  41, 742, 744–45, 752
rational basis test vs., 116
Scalia's argument against, 125
of statutory rape, 779–80
wealth and poverty excluded from, 788, 789
See also heightened scrutiny; intermediate
  scrutiny
strikes
  Fuller Court and, 65
  presidential intervention, 168–82
  Vinson Court and, 102, 168–82
strip searches, 600, 601, 602
Stuart, Hugh, 587, 588
Stuyvesant Town Corporation, 706n.181
Styer, Wilhelm D., 537
Submerged Lands Act of 1953, 253, 254
substantive due process, 486, 727n.224, 803
  fears of return to, 696, 697, 793
  as Fuller Court's credo, 64–65, 66
  McReynolds's conception of, 407n.40
  Stone Court's abandonment of, 89, 93, 784
  Thayer article as discrediting, 794n.1
  Warren Court and, 111n.222
Subversive Activities Control Act. *See* Internal
  Security Act of 1950
Subversive Activities Control Board, 287–94
subversive movements
  alien deportation and, 200
  attorney general's list of, 103, 557n.263
  citizenship revocation and, 196–99
  curtailments of, 72, 102–4, 276–94
  fair trial issues, 276–77
  false informant testimony case, 555–59
  loyalty checks, 276n.6
  See also Communist party
suffrage. *See* voting rights
sugar trust, 66
Sullivan, L. B., 378, 379, 379n.25, 381, 382n.31
Sumner, Charles, 41, 47, 55, 237, 646n.37
Sunday closing laws, 393–95
super-majority verdict, 581n.304
supremacy clause, 828
Supreme Being, meaning of, 435–37
Supreme Court
  annual number of new cases filed, 63
  annual term duration, 44
  as apolitical institution, 13, 18–19
  appellate jurisdiction, 530nn.216, 217, 531n.220
  Article 3 jurisdiction, 29
  Barnette case's long-lasting effects, 95–96

Brown as most famous case, 644
bureaucratization of, 117, 882
Capitol basement courtroom description, 45
characterized as "nine independent law firms,"
  117, 878
communal lifestyle of Justices, 31–32, 34
conference. *See* conference
conservative trend, 57
criticized as ignoring precedents, 838n.36, 839
diversity jurisdiction of, 43
divisiveness over *Dred Scott* decision, 51–52
divisiveness over school desegregation plans, 684
efficiency moves, 74–75, 78
expansion to court of first resort, 29
first years of, 22–28, 875
Fuller's promotion of prestige of, 60–61
generational change in, 59
growth and complexity in new quarters, 79
John Marshall's remaking of, 28–34, 39, 875
persuasive power of, 882
postbellum rehabilitation, 50–56
precedent overturning by, 838
press coverage approach to, xxiv, 18, 19, 20
press critiques of, 838n.36
procedural reforms, 63
reputation decline in Fuller's later years, 67
rooms in Capitol building, 33, 33–34n.38, 45, 53
Rule 34, 177, 179
size changes and attempted changes, 24, 30n.26,
  47, 82, 87, 170–71n.8
sources for inside information on, xxii
unanimity advocacy, 39–40, 875
videotaping of oral arguments issue, 884
workload increases and management, 63, 78
See also Chief Justice; Justices; *specific Chief
  Justices and Justices*
Supreme Court building
  Justices' slow acceptance of, 80
  opening of, 33, 79–80
  as Taft project, 72–73, 884
surveillance and eavesdropping, 471–76, 479–80
  aerial, 114, 474–76
  as evidence against third party, 507n.155
  exclusionary rule, 482–85
  by executive branch, 189–90
  executive order for, 472–74
  by FBI of Black and Douglas, 607n.356
  Justices' conference room precautions against,
    xxv, 13–14
  Nixon's presidential authority claims, 472–73
  Nixon's taped White House conversations, 184–86
  silver-platter doctrine, 482–85
  wiretapping, 195n.62, 472, 480n.87